*A
Reference
Publication
in
Science Fiction*

L. W. Currey
David G. Hartwell
Advisory Editors

Donald B. Day
Photograph courtesy of Mrs. Donald B. Day.

■ INDEX TO THE
Science Fiction Magazines
1926–1950
REVISED EDITION

COMPILED AND ARRANGED BY
Donald B. Day

G. K. Hall & Co., 70 Lincoln Street, Boston, Massachusetts

TO MY WIFE
without whose patience, understanding and help the Index
could not have been prepared, this book is affectionately
dedicated.

CONTENTS

Announcement from the Original Edition vi

The Author vii

Preface vii

Introduction ix

Magazines Indexed in this Volume xi

How to Use the Index xii

Abbreviations Used in the Index xiv

Index by Authors 1

Index by Titles 125

Checklist of Magazines Indexed 272

Back Cover Pictures 287

ANNOUNCEMENT

From the Original Edition

The *Index to the Science Fiction Magazines* is a key. Its purpose is to unlock the doors leading to new worlds of the imagination. It is not a book to be *read,* but to be *used*! Used to obtain more enjoyment from the field of science fiction.

The Index contains the information you need to find whatever interests you the most in the science fiction magazines. The entire field is covered: all the science fiction and most of the fantasy magazines, from the first 1926 *Amazing Stories* thru 1950; over 1275 issues under 58 titles, all cross-indexed by author and title. Many verified pseudonyms are given. Length, magazine, date and page number are shown for every story and article.

The Index consists of 3 principal parts: the Index by Authors, the Index by Titles and the Checklist of Magazines Indexed, together with certain supplemental material.

Collectors, whether of one or many titles, will find this volume indispensable, as will those seeking the stories of certain authors.

The *Index to the Science Fiction Magazines* is the readers' handbook. Use it to get the most out of your magazines.

THE AUTHOR

Donald B(ryne) Day (1909-1978) was a noted science fiction editor, and publisher, and fan. Active since 1946 in the Science Fiction movement, Day participated in both local and national organizational work. For three years he edited the *Fanscient,* which was repeatedly voted "best fanzine," and in 1950 he served as the chairman of Norwescon, the eighth World Science Fiction convention. Day founded the Perri Press in Portland, Oregon, which first published *Index to the Science Fiction Magazines* in 1952. Today the index remains the primary bibliographic source for the science fiction collector.

PREFACE

Donald B. Day's *Index to the Science Fiction Magazines* is the pioneer work of periodical indexing in the science fiction field.

The enormous bulk of science fiction was first published in specialty magazines; only a tiny minority of SF published between 1926 and 1950 originated outside these magazines. Day's index provides access to almost all science fiction published during this period.

The contents of each issue of each magazine is indexed by author and title, with information on pseudonyms, stories in series, and sequels provided. A checklist of magazines indexed, by issue, with date, volume and issue number, page size, number of pages, and cover artist is included.

This edition incorporates several hundred corrections to the text. These were collated from Day's own annotated copy of the original edition, from published errata sheets from the early 1950s, and from certain issues of ephemeral fanzines of the period, to produce a thorough and complete new edition.

L. W. Currey
David G. Hartwell

INTRODUCTION

As an ever increasing number of readers seek to go further into the field, they come again and again to the source of most of the presently available material, the science-fiction magazines.

Not only are an overwhelming majority of the hardcover books reprints from the magazines, but numerous current magazines offer stories from the same source.

Even in the case of new stories, either in books or magazines, an attempt to find more material by the same authors usually leads right back to the pages of the magazines.

It is to make this material more readily available that this book is presented.

Ironically, it is only because until recently science fiction had a small following, that this book was compiled. It is but brief years since the day when the reader of science fiction was considered no less strange than the tales he read.

In 1935, there were some 278 magazines on my shelves. I did not consider them a "collection". They were bought to read and kept for re-reading. They happened to include all that had been published since the beginning of science-fiction magazines as such, but that was because I wanted to read everything available in the field. With that many magazines, it was becoming difficult to locate specific stories for re-reading.

Had there been a sufficiently wide public for science-fiction at the time, someone would doubtless have issued one. As it was, such a professional publication would have been financially disastrous, so if anyone wanted an index, they had to compile it themselves. I did!

This original index was a modest thing, filling a mere drawer and a half with its approximately 1400 cards.

With only three publications at the time, two on a bi-monthly basis, keeping it up was no problem until the early '40s brought the deluge. By that time the magazines were a "collection" and the index was so impressive that it called, or rather demanded to be kept up.

The war years with the paper shortage cut down the indexing to where it could be handled, even to catching up on my return from the service.

Soon, however, the interrupted boom resumed and shortly the number of magazines surpassed even the 1941 total of 104 magazines under 20 titles.

Following attendance at the PACIFICON, the 4th World Science Fiction Convention in 1946, I had become involved as an active science-fiction fan. This led to organizational work, publication of an amateur *fanzine*, The FANSCIENT and in 1950, to the chairmanship of the 8th World Science Fiction Convention, the NORWESCON.

All this activity somewhat complicated the task of indexing, though it taught me to get along without sleep, an ability which has proved invaluable in preparing this index.

It was the FANSCIENT that led directly to this work. Seeking to make available some of the material in the card-index, a department called AUTHOR, AUTHOR was made a regular feature. This included for a different outstanding author each time, an autobiographical sketch, a photo and a complete bibliography of his published works. So popular was this feature, that investigations were made to find if it would be possible to bring the entire index to the public.

It may be of interest to briefly describe the method of compiling the index. The first step was, of course, to assemble complete files of the magazines. The principal difficulty here was in time lost in seeking non-existent issues. Many of the magazines were published erratically. There were also such difficulties as when a publisher's error caused AMAZING STORIES QUARTERLY to jump from Volume 5, Number 3 to Volume 6, Number 4. Those "missing issues" were on the want list for nearly three years before the error was discovered.

The next step was to list the stories and articles on file cards. It was early discovered that stories were sometimes missing from the Table of Contents, or on occasion the title or author's name might be shown differently than on the story. To insure accuracy, the magazines were gone through page by page and the cards taken from the stories themselves. As soon as an issue was completed, the cards were rechecked against the table of contents.

Two cards were made for each story or article: one headed by the author's name, the other by the story title. Both cards contained such data as the length, magazine, date and, if a serial, the number of parts. These were alphabetically filed under author and title.

The files contained hundreds of entries concerning pseudonyms, compiled from various sources. In addition to the data itself, each card carried a notation as to the source of the information.

Nothing was taken for granted. The whole author file was gone through and inquiries made about all entries that had not been furnished by the authors concerned. All authors who could be reached were likewise asked about additional pen-names. In all, over 300 letters were sent just seeking or verifying pseudonyms.

In response to these letters many additional pseudonyms turned up. For each story under a pen-name entries had to be made on both title and author cards. In addition, cards had to be made cross-indexing the author's real name and the pen-name.

There is in my files a considerable mass of data on pseudonyms which does not appear in this volume. Doubtless much of it is correct, but unless it could be verified beyond question, it was omitted. There are also a few entries which do not appear at the author's request, or because they are in dispute.

The question has been raised as to why WEIRD TALES was not included in this index. The answer is simple. WEIRD TALES is not included in my collection. While admitting the desirability of including it and other fantasy magazines on the fringe of the science-fiction field, to do so would mean a delay of at least two years and a considerable outlay of money to accumulate a complete set of the back issues. I felt it was better to have an index to the science-fiction magazines now, than one including the weird field at some vague later date.

The final job was transcribing all this data from the approximately 20,000 file cards making up the index, while taking suitable precautions against mistakes.

In a work of this scope, it is inevitable that some errors will creep in. The publisher would appreciate hearing of any such as may be found as well as any additional information on pseudonyms for possible later release.

If you have gathered the impression that this Index represents a lot of work, you are so right. So much work, in fact, that no conceivable demand could have brought it about as a strictly commercial proposition.

This Index is primarily a labor of love and is presented in the hope that it will bring more enjoyment in the field of science fiction to an ever-widening circle of readers.

Portland, Oregon
August Fourteenth, 1952.

DONALD B. DAY

Magazines Indexed
in this Volume

AIR WONDER STORIES
AMAZING DETECTIVE TALES
AMAZING STORIES
AMAZING STORIES QUARTERLY
AMAZING STORIES ANNUAL
ASTONISHING STORIES
ASTOUNDING SCIENCE FICTION
ASTOUNDING STORIES
AVON FANTASY READER
CAPTAIN FUTURE
COMET STORIES
COSMIC STORIES
DYNAMIC STORIES
FAMOUS FANTASTIC MYSTERIES
FANTASTIC ADVENTURES
FANTASTIC NOVELS
FANTASTIC STORY QUARTERLY
FANTASY (British)
FANTASY BOOK
FANTASY FICTION
FANTASY STORIES
FUTURE combined with SCIENCE FICTION
FUTURE FANTASY and SCIENCE FICTION
FUTURE FICTION
GALAXY SCIENCE FICTION
GALAXY SCIENCE FICTION NOVELS
IMAGINATION
MAGAZINE OF FANTASY
MAGAZINE OF FANTASY and SCIENCE FICTION

MARVEL SCIENCE STORIES
MARVEL STORIES
MARVEL TALES
A. MERRITT FANTASY
MIRACLE STORIES
NEW WORLDS (British)
OTHER WORLDS
OUT OF THIS WORLD ADVENTURES
PLANET STORIES
SCIENCE FICTION
SCIENCE FICTION STORIES
SCIENCE FICTION QUARTERLY
SCIENCE WONDER QUARTERLY
SCIENCE WONDER STORIES
SCIENTIFIC DETECTIVE MONTHLY
STARTLING STORIES
STIRRING SCIENCE STORIES
SUPER SCIENCE NOVELS
SUPER SCIENCE STORIES
TALES OF WONDER (British)
THRILLING WONDER STORIES
TWO COMPLETE SCIENCE ADVENTURE NOVELS
UNCANNY STORIES
UNKNOWN
UNKNOWN WORLDS
WONDER STORIES
WONDER STORIES QUARTERLY
WONDER STORY ANNUAL
WORLDS BEYOND

All magazines complete
from First Issues thru 1950

How to Use the Index

ALPHABETIC ARRANGEMENT

Alphabetic arrangement is by one of the many variations of standard Library indexing. "A"s, "an"s and "the"s occurring at the beginning of a sentence are ignored. The balance of the title is considered in strict alphabetical order, except that all entries containing the same word are completed before passing to longer words containing the same letters.

Hyphenated words are considered as two words.

All abbreviations are treated as if spelled out ("Mr." as "mister", "St." as "saint", etc.).

Authors' names with the prefixes "de", "Mac", "van", etc. are treated as one word. "Mac", "Mc", and "M" are all indexed as if spelled "Mac".

The INDEX BY AUTHORS

The Authors are listed alphabetically by last names, with a list of each ones' stories following his name. The by-line as it appeared on the stories is all in capitals. In cases where it appeared differently on various stories, the occasionally used portions also appear in capitals, but in parentheses. Example:

LONG, A. (MELIA) R.(EYNOLDS)

Indicates that the name sometimes appear as A. R. Long and sometimes as Amelia Reynolds Long.

Where a portion of the name appears in parentheses and in lower case letters, it shows the author's full name, the uncapitalized portion not having appeared on stories. Example:

WELLS, H.(erbert) G.(eorge)

shows that while his full name was Herbert George Wells, it always appeared on his stories as H. G. Wells.

Pseudonyms, if any, used by an author are listed following his name. Example:

AYCOCK, ROGER D. See pseuds ROGER DEE (5), JOHN STARR (0)

shows that Roger D. Aycock has used the pseudonyms "Roger Dee" and "John Starr". The number (5) following "Roger Dee" is the number of stories here indexed under this name. The number (0) following "John Starr" indicates no stories under that name are listed herein, the

by-line having been used in a publication or at a date outside the scope of this Index. If the letter (h) also appears after a pseudonym, it indicates the name is a "house name", used by more than one person. In that case the (h) may be followed by either a number or a question mark, the latter showing that while the author has used the name, the number of stories is uncertain.

Pseudonyms are listed the same as real names, except that they are followed by the real name of the author, where known. Example.

AYRE, THORNTON *pseud of JOHN RUSSELL FEARN*

Under each by-line is an alphabetical listing of stories. Each entry includes the story title, length or classification, magazine, date and page number. A typical entry:

Perfect Weapon, The. .s. . . . . .ASF Feb 50 46

shows that "The Perfect Weapon", a short story, appears in Astounding Science Fiction for February 1950 on page 46.

Under "house names", the stories by each known author are listed separately, followed by a listing of stories of unknown authorship.

Collaborations are listed separately and following the stories which each author wrote alone.

The INDEX BY TITLES

Story titles are indexed alphabetically (ignoring initial articles). Each entry gives the title, author, length or classification, magazine, date and page number. Example:

WITCHES OF KARRES, THE by James H. Schmitz . . .
. .nt . . . . ASF Dec 49 7

shows that "The Witches of Karres" by James H. Schmitz, a novelette, appears in Astounding Science Fiction for December 1949 on page 7.

Stories appearing under pseudonyms are listed in the same manner, except that the author's real name (where known) follows the pseudonym. In the case of house names, the designation "h ps" follows the pseudonym and again the real author's name is given where known. Example:

WINKING LIGHTS OF MARS, THE by Gordon A.
Giles *ps (Otto Binder)*. .s. . . . . Amz Feb 41 120

shows that the story is by Otto Binder but appeared under the by-line, "Gordon A. Giles".

Where a story appears under the author's first and middle names, the last name is entered in parentheses. Example:

ZERO AS A LIMIT by Robert Moore *(Williams)*. .s . . . .
· . ASF Jul 37 34

shows that this story by Robert Moore Williams appeared under the by-line, "Robert Moore".

The CHECKLIST OF MAGAZINES INDEXED

The Checklist is a complete listing of all the issues of the magazines covered in this index. The magazines are arranged alphabetically, except where name changes would break the continuity, in which case they are run together in sequence and cross-indexed. For example: Air Wonder Stories, Science Wonder Stories and Thrilling Wonder Stores are all listed with Wonder Stories.

Under each title is a listing of its issues, giving the date, volume number, page size, number of pages and the name of the cover artist, where known.

In some cases, publications have been dated inconspicuously or not at all. In the first case, any dates shown are listed. In the latter, the year may be shown in parentheses, or the symbol "n/d" may indicate the lack.

If numbered by volume and number, both are shown; if by number only, that is given. Un-numbered issues are indicated by the symbol "n/#".

In some cases, particularly at the end of a year on quarterly magazines, there may be some confusion due to varying dates being given in different parts of the magazine. Except where no year is shown inside, the dates used are the ones taken from the Table of Contents page.

On the following pages is a list of the abbreviations used in the Index. Familiarize yourself with it thoroughly and refer to it when in doubt.

Abbreviations Used in the Index to the Science Fiction Magazines

a	article
a 2 pt	article in 2 parts (etc.)
AA	Amazing Stories Annual
AD	Amazing Detective Tales
AFR	Avon Fantasy Reader
AMF	A. Merritt Fantasy
Amz	Amazing Stories
Apr	April
AQ	Amazing Stories Quarterly
Ash	Astonishing Stories
ASF	Astounding Stories
	Astounding Science Fiction
Aug	August
Aut	Autumn
AW	Air Wonder Stories
bac	Back Cover Picture
bacover	Back Cover Picture
bacover pic	Back Cover Picture
biog	Biographical Sketch
biog sketch	Biographical Sketch
CF	Captain Future
Com	Comet Stories
Cos	Cosmic Stories
Dec	December
dept	department
DS	Dynamic Science Stories
ed	editorial
FA	Fantastic Adventures
Fal	Fall
FanF	Fantasy Fiction
FanS	Fantasy Stories
Fant	Fantasy (British)
FB	Fantasy Book
Feb	February
FFM	Famous Fantastic Mysteries
FN	Fantastic Novels
fr	from
F&SF	Magazine of Fantasy
	Magazine of Fantasy and Science Fiction
FSQ	Fantastic Story Quarterly
Fut	Future Fiction
	Future combined with Science Fiction
	Future Fantasy and Science Fiction
GSF	Galaxy Science Fiction
GSFN	Galaxy Science Fiction Novels
guest ed	guest editorial
(h)	house pseudonym
house ps	house pseudonym

house pseud	house pseudonym
h ps	house pseudonym
Im	Imagination
Jan	January
Jul	July
Jun	June
Mar	March
May	May
Mir	Miracle Stories
MSS	Marvel Science Stories
	Marvel Tales
	Marvel Stories
n	novel
n 2 pt	novel in 2 parts (etc.)
N	Number
nt	novelette
nt 2 pt	novelette in 2 parts (etc.)
Nov	November
NW	New Worlds (British)
Oct	October
OTWA	Out of This World Adventures
OW	Other Worlds
p	poem
pic	pictorial feature
pic feat	pictorial feature
PS	Planet Stories
ps	pseudonym (of)
pseud	pseudonym
r	review
rev	review
s	short story
SD	Scientific Detective Monthly
Sep	September
SF	Science Fiction
	Science Fiction Stories
SFQ	Science Fiction Quarterly
Spr	Spring
ss	short-short story
SS	Startling Stories
SSS	Super Science Stories
	Super Science Novels
STI	Stirring Science Stories
Sum	Summer
SW	Science Wonder Stories
2CSAB	Two Complete Science Adventure Novels
ToC	Table of Contents
ToW	Tales of Wonder (British)
tr fr	translated from
TW	Thrilling Wonder Stories

Uc	Uncanny Stories	WB	Worlds Beyond
UK	Unknown	Win	Winter
	Unknown Worlds	WQ	Science Wonder Quarterly
	From Unknown Worlds		Wonder Stories Quarterly
V	Volume	WS	Wonder Stories
w/	with	WSA	Wonder Story Annual

Alphabetical Index by Authors

A

AUTHOR
  Title. .Length . . . . Magazine, Date, Page

ABERNATHY, ROBERT
  Biog sketch, photo. . . . .
  . . . . Amz Mar 50 57
  Canal Builders, The. .s . . . .
  . . . . .ASF Jan 45 33
  Dead-Star Rover, The. .nt . . . . . .
  . . . . PS Win 49 2
  Failure on Titan. .s . . .PS Win 47 56
  Giants Return, The. .s . . PS Fal 49 43
  Heritage. .nt . . . . . .ASF Jun 42 114
  Hostage of Tomorrow. .nt. . . . . .
  . . . . PS Spr 49 86
  Mission from Arcturus. .s . . . . . .
  . . . . .SFQ Spr 43 130
  Peril of the Blue World. .s . . . . . .
  . . . . PS Nov 42 70
  Saboteur of Space. .s . . . .
  . . . . .PS Spr 44 48
  Strange Exodus. .s . . . . PS Fal 50 85
  Tower of Babble, The. .s . . . .
  . . . . Amz Jun 50 136
  Ultimate Peril, The. .n . . . .
  . . . . Amz Mar 50 8
  When the Rockets Come. .s . . . . .
  . . . . ASF Mar 45 158
ABRAMS, JOHN W.
  White Dwarf Stars. .a . . . .
  . . . . ASF Dec 47 83
ACHESON, MILES M.
  Apprentice, The. .s . . . .
  . . . . .ASF May 50 30
ACKERMAN, FORREST J. *See also
  pseuds NICK BEAL (0), JACQUES
  DeFOREST ERMAN (1), ALDEN
  LORRAINE (1), HUBERT
  GEORGE WELLS (1), WEAVER
  WRIGHT (1)*
  College of Scientifictional
  Knowledge. .quiz dept . . . . . .
  . . . . FS Nov 50 80
  Atomic Error. .ss. . . . .
  . . . . OW Jul 50 18
  Behind the Ate Ball. .ss. . . . .
  . . . . MSS Nov 50 128
  Destination Moon. .a . . . .
  . . . . .OW May 50 147
  Dwellers in the Dust. .s. . . . .
  . . . . FB #4 31

AUTHOR
  Title. .Length . . . . Magazine, Date, Page

  Hollywood on the Moon. .a . . . . .
  . . . . Amz Jun 50 186
  Mars Is—Hell!. .a . . . . . PS Nov 50 3
  Mute Question, The. .ss . . . .
  . . . . OW Sep 50 53
  No Time Like the Future. .ss. . . .
  . . . . MSS Nov 50 71
  Race to the Moon, The. .a . . . . . .
  . . . . MSS Nov 50 60
  Scientifilm Cycle, The. .a . . . . . .
  . . . . .OW Jul 50 153
  with BARBARA BOVARD
  Fantasy Circle. .dept . . . .
  . . . . .Ash Feb 43 85
  *with FRANCIS FLAGG (George
  Henry Weiss)*
  Earth's Lucky Day. .s . . . .
  . . . . WS Mar 36 926
  *with NEIL AUSTIN (artist) Text for
  MASTERS OF FANTASY, which see.*
  Ackerman (N), Henry Andrew
  Dreadnaughts of Doom. .s. . . . . . .
  . . . . .SSS May 42 124
  Europa Enchantment. .ss . . . . . .
  . . . . SSS Jul 40 112
  Fanatics of Mercury. .s . . . .
  . . . . .Fut Dec 42 86
  Martian Fantasy. .s . . .Sti Jun 41 16
  Phantom from Neptune. .ss . . . . .
  . . . . SSS Sep 40 121
  South to Propontis. .s. . . . .
  . . . . PS Fal 41 89
  . . . . PS Fal 11 89
ADAMS, GERALD H.
  Futility. .ss. . . . .
  . . . . WS Mar 36 964
ADAMS, JAMES R.
  Crisis on Titan. .s . . . . .PS Spr 46 79
  Formula for Conquest. .s . . . . . .
  . . . . PS Fal 45 110
  Joe Carson's Weapon. .s . . . .
  . . . . PS Spr 45 108
  Quest on Phoebe. .s . . PS Sum 47 87
  Steel Giants of Chaos. .s . . . .
  . . . . .PS Win 45 36
AFFORD, MALCOLM (R.)
  Gland Men of the Island, The. .s. .
  . . . . .WS Jan 31 828

AUTHOR
  Title. .Length . . . . Magazine, Date, Page

  Ho-Ming Gland, The. .s . . . .
  . . . . Amz Feb 33 1006
AIKEN, JOHN K.
  Cassandra. .n . . . . NW #5 49 2
  Edge of Night. .s . . . .
  . . . . .NW #4 49 43
  Dragon's Teeth. .nt . . . . . .NW #3 2
  Phoenix Nest. .nt. . . . . NW Spr 50 2
  PROBABILITY ZERO
  Camouflage. .ss . . . ASF Apr 43 88
AINSWORTH, LILLIAN M.
  with ROBERT WILBUR LULL
  Astral Gentleman, An. .s. . . . . . .
  . . . . FFM Jan 40 80
ALDEN, THAEDRA
  Biog sketch . . . . . . TW Jun 43 88
  Two-Timing Man. .s . . TW Jun 43 88
ALDEN, W. L.
  Volcanic Valve, The. .s . . . .
  . . . . .F&SF Win-Spr 50 115
ALDINGER, HARLEY S.
  Green Intelligence, The. .s . . . . . .
  . . . . SW Nov 29 550
  Heritage of the Earth, The. .s . . . .
  . . . . Amz Feb 32 1036
  Way of a Dinosaur, The. .ss . . . . . .
  . . . . Amz Apr 28 35
ALEJANDRO *Artist*
  *Covers for ASTOUNDING SCIENCE
  FICTION*
  Dec 1946
  Sep, Dec 1947
  Feb, May, Sep 1948
  Mar, Oct 1949
ALEXANDER, DANIEL A.
  Biog sketch, photo. . . . .
  . . . . TW Apr 42 83
  Twisted Dimensions. .s. . . . .
  . . . . TW Apr 42 81
ALEXANDER, W.
  Ananias Gland, The. .s . . . .
  . . . . Amz Nov 28 707
  Dog's Sixth Sense, The. .s . . . . . .
  . . . . Amz Sep 29 540
  Fighting Heart, The. .s . . . .
  . . . . Amz Feb 28 1099
  Million Dollar Gland, The. .s . . . .
  . . . . Amz Dec 34 129

AUTHOR
    Title. .Length . . . . Magazine, Date, Page

    New Stomachs for Old. .s . . . . . .
    . . . . Amz Feb 27 1039
    One Leg Too Many. .s . . . .
    . . . . Amz Oct 29 612
ALLERTON, J. J.
    Call of Duty. .s . . . . FA Apr 50 122
    Dr. Zauger's Cats. .nt . . . .
    . . . . .FA Jul 45 86
    Moon of Battle. .n . . . .
    . . . . Amz Dec 49 40
    Once Upon a Planet. .s . . . .
    . . . . Amz Dec 48 54
    Trumpet, The. .s . . . FA May 50 124
ALLPORT, ARTHUR pseud of
    RAYMOND Z. GALLUN.
    Gentle Brain, The. .s . . . .
    . . . . SFQ Sum 40 130
ALVAREZ, JOHN
    Fifth Freedom. .s . . . .
    . . . . ASF May 43 109
AMES, CLINTON
    Victims of the Vortex. .nt . . . . . .
    . . . . .Amz Jul 50 8
AMHERST, WES pseud of RICHARD
    S. SHAVER.
    Sons of the Serpent. .n . . . .
    . . . . OW Jan 50 6
ANDERSON, DAVID
    Utility. .nt . . . . . . ASF Jul 44 156
ANDERSON, (MURPHY) Artist
    Biog sketch . . . . .PS Win 44 35
    Covers for PLANET STORIES
    Win 1942
    Spr, Sum, Fal, Win 1947
    Spr, Sum, Fal, Win 1948
    Spr, Sum, Fal, Win 1949
    Spr, Sum, Fal 1950
    Cover for 2 COMPLETE SCIENCE
    ADVENTURE BOOKS
    Win 1950
ANDERSON, P.
    PROBABILITY ZERO
    Matter of Relativity, A. .ss . . . .
    . . . . ASF Sep 44 89
ANDERSON, POUL (See also
    A. A. CRAIG pseud (0))
    Double-Dyed Villains, The. .nt . . .
    . . . . ASF Sep 49 6
    Flight to Forever. .nt . . . .
    . . . . .SSS Nov 50 12
    Genius. .nt . . . .
    . . . . ASF Dec 48 6
    Gypsy. .s . . . . .ASF Jan 50 66
    Helping Hand, The. .nt . . . .
    . . . . .ASF May 50 6
    Logic. .nt . . . . . . .ASF Jul 47 51

AUTHOR
    Title. .Length . . . . Magazine, Date, Page

    Long Return, The. .nt . . . .
    . . . . Fut Sep-Oct 50 64
    Perfect Weapon, The. .s . . . .
    . . . . ASF Feb 50 46
    Prophecy. .s . . . . . ASF May 49 52
    Quixote and the Windmill. .s . . . .
    . . . . ASF Nov 50 95
    Star Beast, The. .nt . . SSS Sep 50 10
    Star Ship. .s . . . . . . PS Fal 50 66
    Time Heals. .s . . . . . ASF Oct 49 58
with GORDON DICKSON
    Trespass. .s . . . . . .FSQ Spr 50 131
with PAUL GERGEN
    Entity. .s . . . . ASF Jun 49 58
with F. N. Waldrop
    Tomorrow's Children. .nt . . . . . .
    . . . . ASF Mar 47 56
ANDERTON, DAVID A.
    Can V–2 Be Improved?. .a . . . . .
    . . . . .ASF Sep 47 106
ANDERTON, SEVEN
    King and the Pawn, The. .nt . . . .
    . . . . .AQ Fal-Win 32 354
ANDREWS, ELTON V. pseud of
    FREDERIK POHL
    (Used on one poem in Amazing
    Stories)
ANDREWS, THOMAS pseud of
    SEWELL PEASLEE WRIGHT
ANGEL, ROGER
    Just a Matter of Time. .s . . . .
    . . . . .F&SF Fal 50 73
NANNAS, HAL
    Ultimate Quest, The. .s . . . .
    . . . . Im Dec 50 60
ANTHOS
    Malignant Flower, The. .s . . . . . .
    . . . . Amz Sep 27 526
ANTON, LUDWIG
    Interplanetary Bridges. .n . . . . . .
    . . . . WQ Win 33 102
    (Tr fr the German by KONRAD
    SCHMIDT)
ARCHETTE, GUY pseud of
    CHESTER S. GEIER
    Bottle, The. .s . . . . . FA Dec 19 98
    Dynamite Planet. .nt . .Amz Oct 19 68?
    Fire Globe, The. .nt . Amz Oct 49 90
    (Author given as GUY ARCHETTE on
    story TOC list author as CHESTER
    S. GEIER)
    Haunted House. .s . . . FA Jun 49 90
    Justice Satellite. .nt . .Amz May 48 120
    Lost Power, The. .s . Amz Mar 19 42
    Meet Me In Tomorrow. .s . . . . . .
    . . . . Im Dec 50 6
    Miner Crisis on Io. .s . . . .
    . . . . Amz Oct 47 122

AUTHOR
    Title. .Length . . . . Magazine, Date, Page

    Not as Plotted. .s . . . FA Mar 47 108
    Omega. .nt . . . . . . .Amz Jan 50 108
    Rendezvous in Space. .nt . . . . . .
    . . . . .Amz Jul 49 104
    Return of Lan-ning, The. .s . . . . .
    . . . . FA Mar 49 40
    Secret of the Robot. .s . . . .
    . . . . Amz Apr 48 76
    (Author given as GUY ARCHETTE on
    story; ToC lists author as CHESTER
    S. GEIER)
    Secret of the Yellow Crystal. .nt . .
    . . . . Amz Apr 48 42
    Seed of Empire. .nt . . . .
    . . . . FA Aug 49 84
    Treasure Derelict. .s . . . .
    . . . . .Amz Jul 47 62
    Twin Satellite. .s . . . .FA Jul 49 70
    Twisted House. .s . . . .
    . . . . Amz Jun 49 54
    World Beyond, The. .s . . . .
    . . . . Amz Dec 47 86
ARCHIBALD, JOE
    Heaven Only Knows. .s . . . .
    . . . . FFM Sep 45 112
ARMSTRONG, GEOFFREY pseud of
    JOHN RUSSELL FEARN
    Superhuman. .s . . . . . .ToW #1 37 4
ARNO, ELROY
    Jenny—The Flying Ford. .s . . . . .
    . . . . Amz Nov 43 162
    Jones Buys War Blondes. .s . . . . .
    . . . . FA Dec 43 98
    Jones Gets the Willies. .s . . . .
    . . . . FA Mar 43 160
    Meet My Mummy. .nt . . . .
    . . . . .FA May 47 46
    Mistress of the Dark. .nt . . . .
    . . . . FA May 43 184
    Perfume for a Princess. .nt . . . . .
    . . . . FA Dec 47 122
    Secret of the Yomar. .nt . . . .
    . . . . .FA Jul 47 134
    Trick With a Brick. .s . . . .
    . . . . FA Oct 43 182
    Two Worlds to Conquer. .nt . . . .
    . . . . Amz Sep 45 130
    You Bet Your Life. .s . . . .
    . . . . FA May 48 150
ARNOLD, EDWIN LESTER
    Phra the Phoenician. .n . . . .
    . . . . FFM Sep 45 8
ARNOLD, FRANK EDWARD
    City of Machines. .nt . . . .
    . . . . .ToW Sum 39 54
    Mecanica. .nt . . . . . . .Cos Mar 41 6

AUTHOR
Title. .Length . . . . Magazine, Date, Page

Twilight People, The. .s . . . .
. . . . s . . . Com Jan 41 45
Wings Across Time. .nt . . . .
. . . . SFQ Win 42 82
ARNOLD, GUY
Sea Things, The. .s . . . SF Mar 39 82
Silent World, The. .s . . . .
. . . . SF Aug 39 102
ARNOLD, H. F.
Night Wire, The. .s . . . . .AFR #9 12
When Atlantis Was. .n 2 pt . . . . .
. . . . Amz Oct 37 12
ARNOLD, R. CROSSLEY
Secret of the Tomb, The. .nt . . . .
. . . . WQ Fal 30 106
ARNOLD, WESLEY
Struggle for Venus, The. .s . . . . .
. . . . WS Dec 30 716
Waves of Death. .s . . . WS Jun 30 58
Within the Planet. .s . . . .
. . . . WQ Spr 30 360
ARONIN, BEN
Doubt, The. .s . . . Amz May 32 180
ARTHUR, ROBERT
Cinerobot, Inc. . .s . . . .
. . . . TW Feb 43 105
Cosmic Stage. .s . . . . .SS Sep 39 90
                          FSQ Spr 50 125
Eternal Moment. .s . . SS Mar 41 103
Evolution's End. .s . . . TW Apr 41 75
Flying Eye, The. .s . . . .
. . . . FanF May 50 51
Footsteps Invisible. .s . . . .
. . . . AMF Dec 49 118
Gateway. .s . . . . . . UK Mar 40 104
Indestructible, The. .s . . . .
. . . . TW Mar 41 48
Indulgence of Negu Mah. .s . . . . .
. . . . .Com Jul 41 75
Meteoric Mr. Myrtle. .s . . . .
. . . . TW Aug 42 56
Mr. Jinx. .s . . . . . . UK Aug 41 107
Operation Successful. .s . . . .
. . . . ASF Dec 41 86
Postpaid to Paradise. .s . . . .
. . . . F&SF Win–Spr 50 61
Professor's Hobby, The. .s . . . . . .
. . . . UK Feb 41 140
Rabbit and the Rat, The. .s . . . . .
. . . . UK Jun 43 102
Song at Twilight. .nt . . . .
. . . . TW Jan 40 42
Space Command. .s . . . .
. . . . TW Win 44 97
Terror from the Sea, The. .s . . . .
. . . . WS Dec 31 890

AUTHOR
Title. .Length . . . . Magazine, Date, Page

Theft of the Washington Monu-
ment. .s . . . . Amz Oct 33 507
Time Dredge. .s . . . . ASF Jun 42 81
Tomb of Time, The. .s . . . .
. . . . .TW Nov 40 16
Tomorrow. .s . . . . . UK Jun 42 73
Tracks Across the Darkness. .s . . .
. . . . .Ash Mar 42 25
Vengeful Pearls of Madame
Podaire. .s . . . . . . .FanS Nov 50 89
Wall, The. .s . . . . UK Dec 42 90
Wheel of Time, The. .s . . . .
. . . . SSS Mar 50 75
ASHBY, RICHARD
Joke for Harry. .s . . . .
. . . . Amz Sep 49 116
Merchant of Venus, The. .nt . . . .
. . . . .OW Nov 50 36
ASHKANAZY, IRVIN
Headless Miller of Kobold's Keep,
The. .s . . . . AFR #14 95
ASHTON, FRANCIS (L.)
Jet Landing. .s . . . . . NW Spr 50 77
Long Way, The. .s . . . .
. . . . SSS May 50 42
ASHTON-WOLFE, H.
Message from the Ultra-Violet, A.
. .s . . . . .SD Jan 30 46
ASIMOV, ISAAC (See also GEORGE
E. DALE pseud (1))
Biog sketch . . . . . Amz Mar 39 126
. . .And Now You Don't. .n 3 pt. .
. . . . ASF Nov 49 5
Big and the Little, The. .nt . . . . .
. . . . ASF Aug 44 7
Black Friar of the Flame. .nt . . . .
. . . . .PS Spr 42 2
Blind Alley. .s . . . .
. . . . ASF Mar 45 139
Bridle and Saddle. .nt . . . .
. . . . ASF Jun 42 9
Callistan Menace, The. .s . . . . . .
. . . . .Ash Apr 40 66
Catch That Rabbit. .s . . . .
. . . . ASF Feb 44 159
Christmas on Ganymede. .s . . . .
. . . . .SS Jan 42 83
Darwinian Pool Room. .s . . . . . .
. . . . .GSF Oct 50 152
Day of the Hunters. .s . . . .
. . . . .Fut Nov 50 74
Dead Hand. .n . . . . . ASF Apr 45 6
Death Sentence. .s . . ASF Nov 43 32
Endochronic Properties of Resubli-
mated Thiotimoline, The. .a . . . .
. . . . ASF Mar 48 120

AUTHOR
Title. .Length . . . . Magazine, Date, Page

Evidence. .nt . . . . .ASF Sep 46 121
Evitable Conflict, The. .nt . . . . .
. . . . ASF Jun 50 48
Foundation. .nt . . . .
. . . . ASF May 42 38
"FOUNDATION" series includes:
FOUNDATION, BRIDLE AND
SADDLE, THE BIG AND THE LITTLE,
THE WEDGE, DEAD HAND, THE
MULE, NOW YOU SEE IT . . .AND
NOW YOU DON'T.
Half-Breed. .s . . . . . .Ash Feb 40 38
Half-Breeds on Venus. .s . . . .
. . . . .Ash Dec 40 6
Hazing, The. .s . . . . . TW Oct 42 89
Heredity. .s . . . . . . .Ash Apr 41 8
History. .s . . . . . . .SSS Mar 41 86
Homo Sol. .s . . . .
. . . . .ASF Sep 40 117
Imaginary, The. .s . . . .
. . . . .SSS Nov 42 74
Liar!. .s . . . . . . ASF May 41 43
Little Lost Robot. .nt . . . .
. . . . ASF Mar 47 111
Magnificent Possession, The. .s . . .
. . . . Fut Jul 40 71
Marooned Off Vesta. .s . . . .
. . . . Amz Mar 39 66
Misbegotten Missionary. .s . . . . .
. . . . GSF Nov 50 34
Mother Earth. .nt . . ASF May 49 59
Mule, The. .n 2 pt . . . ASF Nov 45 7
Nightfall. .nt . . . . . . ASF Sep 41 9
No Connection. .s . . ASF Jun 48 72
Not Final. .s . . . . . . ASF Oct 41 49
Now You See It. .s . . . ASF Jan 48 7
Paradoxical Escape. .s . . . .
. . . . ASF Aug 45 79
Pebble In the Sky. .n . . . .
. . . . 2CSAB Win 50 2
Reason. .s . . . . ASF Apr 41 33
Red Queen's Race, The. .nt . . . . .
. . . . .ASF Jan 49 65
Ring Around the Sun. .s . . . .
. . . . Fut Mar 40 89
Robot AL 76 Goes Astray. .s. . . .
. . . . Amz Feb 42 218
Runaround. .s . . . .
. . . . ASF Mar 42 91
Secret Sense, The. .s . . . .
. . . . .Cos Mar 41 87
Strange Playfellow. .s . . . .
. . . . SSS Sep 40 67
Super-Neutron. .s . . . Ash Sep 41 36
Trends. .s . . . . .ASF Jul 39 33
Victory Unintentional. .s . . . . . .
. . . . .SSS Aug 42 86

AUTHOR
Title. .Length . . . . Magazine, Date, Page

Weapon Too Dreadful to Use,
The. .s . . . . Amz May 39 110
Wedge, The. .s . . . .
. . . . ASF Oct 44 64
with JAMES MacCREIGH (Frederik Pohl)
Little Man on the Subway, The
. . . . FB #6 4
ATHANAS, W. V.
Madcap Metalloids, The. .s . . . . .
. . . . PS Sum 49 37
ATOMCRACKER, BUZZ-BOLT pseud of DON WILCOX
Confessions of a Mechanical Man
. .nt . . . . Amz May 47 36
AUCKLAND, ROI
Blind Reasoning. .s . . . .
. . . . ASF Feb 34 127
AUSTIN, FRANK *pseud of FREDERICK FAUST*
AUSTIN, NEIL *artist*
Cover for FANTASY BOOK #4
MASTERS OF FANTASY *(Pictorial feature about leading fantasy authors. With text by FORREST J. ACKERMAN.)*
Howard Phillips Lovecraft. . . . . .
. . . . FFM Aug 47 113
A. Merritt . . . . . . FFM Oct 47 97
Robert William Chambers . . . . . .
. . . . FFM Dec 47 103
Sydney Fowler Wright . . . .
. . . . FFM Feb 48 113
Algernon Blackwood . . . .
. . . . FFM Apr 48 121
Herbert George Wells . . . .
. . . . FFM Jun 48 101
Stephen Vincent Benet. . . . . . .
. . . . FFM Aug 48 113
Edgar Rice Burroughs. . . . .
. . . . FFM Oct 48 117
Arthur Machen . . . . FFM Dec 48 12
M. P. Shiel . . . . . . FFM Feb 49 91
John Taine. . . . . . . FFM Apr 49 87
Lord Dunsany. . . . .
. . . . FFM Jun 49 113
Clark Ashton Smith . . . .
. . . . FFM Aug 49 109
Ray Bradbury. . . . FFM Oct 49 119
Edgar Allan Poe . . . .
. . . . FFM Dec 49 113
Olaf Stapledon . . . FFM Feb 50 121
M. R. James . . . . . FFM Apr 50 113
AUSTEN, SIDNEY
Frightened Planet, The. .s . . . . . .
. . . . Amz Oct 48 28

AUTHOR
Title. .Length . . . . Magazine, Date, Page

AYCOCK, ROGER D. *(See pseuds ROGER DEE (5) and JOHN STARR (0))*
AYRE, THORNTON *pseud of JOHN RUSSELL FEARN*
Biog sketch . . . . . Amz Oct 38 141
Biog sketch, photo. . . . .
. . . . Amz Sep 39 143
Biog sketch, photo. . .FA Jan 41 132
Amazon Fights Again, The. .nt. . .
. . . . FA Jun 40 112
Case of the Mesozoic Monsters, The
. .nt . . . . Amz May 42 210
Case of the Murdered Savants, The.
. .nt . . . . Amz Apr 40 6
Children of the Golden Amazon. .
. .nt . . . . FA Apr 43 8
Domain of Zero. .s. . . . PS Fal 40 57
Face in the Sky. .nt . . . .
. . . . Amz Sep 39 90
Golden Amazon, The. .s . . . .
. . . . .FA Jul 39 32
Golden Amazon Returns, The . . .
. .nt . . . . FA Jan 41 78
Island in the Marsh. .s. . . . .
. . . . SS Nov 40 96
Locked City. .nt . . . Amz Oct 38 58
Lunar Concession. .nt. . . . .
. . . . .SF Sep 41 10
NW #2 46 34
Lunar Intrigue. .s. . . . FA Nov 39 56
Lunar Vengeance. .nt . . . .
. . . . Amz Sep 43 88
Man Who Saw Two Worlds, The. .
. .nt . . . . Amz Jan 40 76
Man Who Sold the Earth, The . . .
. .s . . . . .SF Oct 40 84
Mental Gangster, The. .s . . . . . .
. . . . FA Aug 42 64
Microbes from Space. .s . . . .
. . . . Amz Jun 39 86
Mystery of the White Raider. .s . .
. . . . FA Feb 40 58
Penal World. .s . . . .ASF Oct 37 110
Secret of the Moon Treasure . . . .
. .nt . . . . .Amz Jul 40 98
Secret of the Ring. .nt . . . .
. . . . Amz Nov 38 100
Amz Oct 42 64
Silver Coil, The. .s . . . .
. . . . Amz Nov 42 214
Special Agent to Venus. .nt . . . . .
. . . . FA Oct 40 78
Twilight of the Tenth World . . . .
. .nt . . . . .PS Win 40 104
Vampire Queen. .s. . . . PS Fal 42 52

AUTHOR
Title. .Length . . . . Magazine, Date, Page

Whispering Satellite. .s . . . .
. . . . .ASF Jan 38 97
White Mouse. .s . . . . .NW #1 46 59
World in Wilderness, The. .nt . . . .
. . . . .SF Jun 41 82
World Reborn. .nt . . . .SSS Mar 40 6
World Without Women. .nt . . . . .
. . . . Amz Apr 39 6
with A. R. STEBER (Raymond A. Palmer)
Mystery of the Martian Pendu-
lum. .s . . . . Amz Oct 41 116

B

BADE, WILLIAM (L.)
Advent. .s . . . . .ASF Jan 48 76
King of the Stars. .s . . . .
. . . . SSS Jul 50 48
Lost Ulysses. .nt . . . .
. . . . ASF May 49 109
New Lives for Old. .nt . . . .
. . . . ASF Feb 48 46
BAHL, FRANKLIN
Face Beyond the Veil. .nt . . . . . .
. . . . .FA Apr 50 8
BAIN, ARTHUR L.
Author's Adventure. .ss . . . .
. . . . Amz Apr 33 75
BAIRD, WESLEY P.
Moon Doom, The (Part 3). .n 4 pt
(each part by a different author) . .
. . . . WS May 33 978
BAKER, CHARLES A.
Treasure of Triton. .ss . . . .
. . . . .PS Spr 41 52
BALDWIN, C. A.
Peter Backs a Punch. .nt . . . .
. . . . .FA Jul 47 86
War Criminals of Renault Island . .
. .nt . . . . . Amz Dec 44 30
BALDWIN, ROBERT
Retribution. .ss. . . . Amz Nov 33 78
BALL, CLELLAND J.
Gravity King, The. .s . . . .
. . . . AQ Oct 28 564
BALMER, EDWIN
with WILLIAM B. MacHARG
Duel in the dark, The. .s . . . .
. . . . AD Sep 30 790
Eleventh Hour, The. .s . . . .
. . . . Amz Feb 27 1042
SD May 30 428
Fast Watch, The. .s . . . .SD Jan 30 21

AUTHOR
   Title. .Length . . . . Magazine, Date, Page

Hammering Man, The. .s . . . .
     . . . . Amz Mar 27 1118
                  SD Apr 30 314
Man Higher Up, The. .s . . . .
     . . . . Amz Dec 26 792
                  SD Feb 30 122
Man in the Room, The. .s . . . . . .
     . . . . Amz Apr 27 43
                  SD Mar 30 224
Matter of Mind Reading, A. .s . . .
     . . . . AD Jun 30 496
Private Bank Puzzle, The. .s . . . . .
     . . . . .AD Jul 30 608
Vapors of Death. .s . . . .
     . . . . AD Aug 30 712
BALTER, E. *(See ARTHUR*
   COOKE pseud (1))
BANAT, D. R. *pseud used by RAY*
   BRADBURY
BANKS, PENDLETON
   Turning Point. .s . . . .
     . . . . ASF Mar 47 80
BARCLAY, FRED M.
   Troglodites, The. .nt . . . .
     . . . . Amz Sep 30 486
BARCLAY, GABRIEL *house pseud*
by MANLY WADE WELLMAN
   Elephant Earth. .s . . .Ash Feb 40 54
real author unknown
   Hollow of the Moon. .s. . . . . . .
     . . . . SSS May 40 6
BARCLAY, LESTER
   Birds of a Feather. .s . . . .
     . . . . .FA May 50 134
   Charming Mr. Grant, The. .s . . . .
     . . . . FA Nov 48 134
   Column of Life, The. .s. . . . . . .
     . . . . FA Dec 49 120
   Handyman, The. .s. . . FA Oct 50 90
   I'll Be Seeing You. .s . . . .
     . . . . FA Oct 44 118
   Life Machine, The. .nt . . . .
     . . . . Amz Dec 44 84
   Man in the Moon, The. .s . . . . . .
     . . . . Amz Apr 48 90
   Siren Song. .nt . . . . . FA Feb 46 82
   Tiger Has a Soul, The. .s . . . .
     . . . . .FA Jul 45 70
   Venomous Girdle, The. .s . . . . . .
     . . . . Amz Feb 49 72
   Wee Men of Weehen, The. .s . . . .
     . . . . FA Aug 49 104
BARNES, ARTHUR K.(elvin) *See also*
   pseuds DAVE BARNES (1),
   KELVIN KENT (8).
   Biog sketch, photo. . . TW Oct 39 23

AUTHOR
   Title. .Length . . . . Magazine, Date, Page

Challenge of the Comet. .s . . . . .
     . . . . WS Feb 32 1036
Day of the Titans. .s. . . . .
     . . . . TW Feb 40 46
Dual World, The. .nt . . . .
     . . . . TW Jun 38 54
Emotion Solution. .s . . . .
     . . . . WS Mar 36 954
Fog Over Venus. .nt. . . . .
     . . . . TW Win 45 11
Forgotten Future. .s. . .SF Jan 41 47
"Gerry Carlisle" series includes:
   GREEN HELL
   THE HOTHOUSE PLANET
   THE DUAL WORLD
   SATELLITE FIVE
   THE ENERGY EATERS*
   THE SEVEN SLEEPERS*
   TROUBLE ON TITAN
   SIREN SATELLITE
with HENRY KUTTNER. Combined
   with the HOLLYWOOD ON
   THE MOON series.
Green Hell. .s . . . . . . TW Jun 37 91
Guardians of the Void. .s . . . . . .
     . . . . WQ Sep 32 72
Guinea Pig. .s . . . . . . .CF Spr 42 87
Hothouse Planet, The. .s . . . . . .
     . . . . TW Oct 37 12
                 SS Sep 49 84
Little Man Who Wasn't There,
   The. .s. . . . . TW Mar 41 59
Lord of the Lightning. .s. . . . . .
     . . . . WS Dec 31 868
Mole Men of Mercury, The. .s . . .
     . . . . WS Dec 33 476
Prometheus. .s . . . . Amz Feb 37 58
Satellite Five. .nt. . . . TW Oct 38 14
Siren Satellite. .s . . . . TW Win 46 64
Trouble on Titan. .nt . . . .
     . . . . TW Feb 41 14
Waters of Wrath. .nt. . . . .
     . . . . TW Oct 40 14
with HENRY KUTTNER
Energy Eaters, The. .s. . . . .
     . . . . TW Oct 39 16
                SS Sep 50 124
Seven Sleepers, The. .nt . . . .
     . . . . .TW May 40 93
BARNES, DAVE *pseud of ARTHUR*
   K. BARNES
House That Walked, The. .s . . . . .
     . . . . ASF Sep 36 37
BARNETTE, JACK
   Power Ray, The. .s. . . . .
     . . . . SD Mar 30 208
   Purple Death, The. .s . . . .
     . . . . .Amz Jul 29 370

AUTHOR
   Title. .Length . . . . Magazine, Date, Page

Vapor Intelligence. .s . . . .
     . . . . .SW Jan 30 702
BARNEY, B. H.
   Beyond the Veil of Time. .nt . . . .
     . . . . AQ Fal–Win 32 394
BARRETT, H. I.
   Mechanical Heart, The. .s . . . . . .
     . . . . .AQ Fal 31 564
BARRETT, JOHN
   Crash Beam. .s . . . . . . PS Fal 47 37
   Long Way Back. .s . . . TW Feb 48 84
   Stellar Snowball. .s . . . .
     . . . . .SS Mar 47 88
BARRISTER, ALAN
   His Aunt Thiamin. .s . . . .
     . . . . .SSS Nov 42 94
BARRY, B. X.
   Pirates of Space. .nt . . . .
     . . . . Amz Dec 31 798
BARSHOFSKY, PHILIP *pseud See*
   also PHILIP JAQUES BARTEL
   pseud (6)
   Imperfect Guess, The. .s . . . .
     . . . . WS Mar 36 942
   One Prehistoric Night. .s . . . . . .
     . . . . WS Nov 34 692
BARTEL, PHILIP J(ACQUES)
   pseud. See also PHILIP
   BARSHOFSKY (2)
   Elixir of Progress, The. .s . . . . . .
     . . . . WS Apr 35 1286
   Infinite Eye, The. .s. . . . .
     . . . . .Fut Nov 39 94
   One Hundred Generations. .s . . . .
     . . . . WS Sep 35 430
   Time Control, The. .s. . . . .
     . . . . Amz Dec 36 51
   Twenty Five Centuries Late. .s. . .
     . . . . WS Nov 34 704
   When Time Stood Still. .s . . . . . .
     . . . . Amz Feb 35 123
BARTON, FRED T.
with HUBERT KELLEY
   Raiders of the Air. .ss. . . . .
     . . . . .FFM May–Jun 40 75
BATES, HARRY *See also pseuds*
   ANTHONY GILMORE (8),
   A. R. HOLMES (1), H. G.
   WINTER (4)
   Editor ASTOUNDING STORIES
   from January 1930 (first issue) thru
   March 1933.
   Biog sketch, photo. . . . .
     . . . . .Amz Jan 42 235
   Alas, All Thinking. .nt . . . .
     . . . . ASF Jun 35 6

AUTHOR
  Title. .Length . . . . Magazine, Date, Page

Experiment of Dr. Sarconi, The . .
  ..nt . . . . .TW Jul 40 93
Farewell to the Master. .nt . . . . .
  . . . . ASF Oct 40 58
Matter of Size, A. .nt . . . .
  . . . . ASF Apr 34 38
Matter of Speed, A. .nt . . . .
  . . . . .ASF Jun 41 128
Mystery of the Blue God. .n . . . .
  . . . . Amz Jan 42 54
BAUER, E.
  Forgotten World, The. .s . . . . . .
  . . . . Amz Aug 31 436
BAUER, GEORGE PAUL
  Below the Infra Red. .nt . . . . . .
  . . . . Amz Dec 27 882
  Subterranian Adventure, A. .n 3 pt
  . . . . WS Jun 30 6
BAXTER, GEORGE OWEN pseud
  of FREDERICK FAUST
BEAL, NICK pseud of FORREST
  J. ACKERMAN
BEAN, NORMAN pseud of EDGAR
  RICE BURROUGHS
BEARD, JAMES H.
  Five Fathoms of Pearls. .s . . . . . .
  . . . . UK Dec 39 88
  with THEODORE STURGEON
  Bones, The. .s . . . . . UK Aug 43 107
  Hag Seleen, The. .s . . . .
  . . . . UK Dec 42 96
BEARDEN, JACK O.
  Notorious C39, The. .ss . . . .
  . . . . Amz Nov 33 50
BEATTIE, GEORGE B.
  Man Who Shrank, The. .s . . . . . .
  . . . . WS Apr 32 1256
  Martian Nemesis, The. .s . . . . . .
  . . . . WQ Win 31 238
  Murders on the Moon Ship, The . .
  ..s . . . . WS Feb 31 958
  "Platinum Planets", The. .s . . . . .
  . . . . WS Aug 32 246
BEAUMONT, DAVID H.
  When the Cycle Met. .s . . . .
  . . . . ASF Nov 35 71
BECK, ALLEN pseud of HUGH B.
  CAVE
BECK, CLYDE (F.)
  Anastomosis. .s . . . . . SS Nov 47 86
  Collision Orbit. .s . . . PS Sum 50 48
  When the Moons Met. .s . . . . . .
  . . . . WS Aug 30 236
BECKETT, WILLIAM C.
  Duel in the Space Lanes. .s . . . . .
  . . . . ASF Mar 38 56

BECKWITH, O. (L.)
  Heat Ray, The. .s . . . .
  . . . . AW Apr 30 890
  Robot Master, The. .s . . . .
  . . . . AW Oct 29 360
  Winged Death. .s . . . .
  . . . . AD Sep 30 786
BELARSKI, RUDOLPH artist
  Covers for CAPTAIN FUTURE
  (some doubt)
  Sum, Fal 1942
  Covers for STARTLING STORIES
  May, Jul, Sep, Nov 1941
  Jan, Sep 1942
  Jan 1943
  Mar 1947
  Covers for THRILLING WONDER
  STORIES
  Aug, Oct 1941
  Feb, Aug, Dec 1942
BELL, ERIC TEMPLE See JOHN
  TAINE pseud
BELL, EARL L.
  Moon of Doom, The. .n . . . .
  . . . . AQ Jan 28 4
  Young Old Man, The. .s . . . .
  . . . . Amz Sep 29 504
BELL, STANLEY D.
  Martian Guns. .nt . . .WS Jan 32 920
  Fut Apr 41 50
BELLEM, ROBERT LESLIE
  Biog sketch . . . . . . .FA Jul 41 136
  Robots Can't Lie. .s . . . .
  . . . . .FA Jul 41 116
  Short-Wave Superman. .s . . . . . .
  . . . . Amz Nov 41 98
BELLIN, EDWARD J. house pseud
  by HENRY KUTTNER
  Touching Point, The. .s . . . .
  . . . . Sti Apr 41 96
  Author's real name unknown
  No Place to Go. .ss . . . .
  . . . . .Cos May 41 64
  with A. H. JOHNSTON (artist)
  Dead Man's Tale. .comic . . . .
  . . . . .OTWA Dec 50 59
  with J. KUBERT (artist)
  Man-Eating Lizards, The. .comic. .
  . . . . OTWA Jul 50 61
BENEDICT, JERRY
  Bronze Door, The. .s . . . .
  . . . . Amz May 33 164
BENET, STEPHEN VINCENT
  Biog sketch in MASTERS OF
  FANTASY. . . . FFM Aug 48 113
  Gold Dress, The. .s . . . .AFR #5 62

BENET, WILLIAM ROSE
  with NEIL AUSTIN & (Forrest J.
  Ackerman) MASTERS OF
  FANTASY
  Stephen Vincent Benet. . . . . . .
  . . . . .FFM Aug 48 113
BENNETT, ALFRED GORDON,
  F.R.S.A.
  Ego of the Ant, The. .s . . . .
  . . . . ToW Win 38 96
  Insect Threat, The. .a . . . .
  . . . . ToW Win 39 64
BENNETT, KEITH
  Rocketeers Have Shaggy Ears, The
  ..nt . . . . .PS Spr 50 2
BENSON, ALLAN INGVALD See
  also VICTOR VALDING pseud
  (1)
  Psychopathic Martians, The. .ss . .
  . . . . .SSS Aug 41 105
BENSON, E. F.
  At the Farmhouse. .s . . . .
  . . . . FFM Dec 46 102
  Caterpillars. .s . . . . FFM Jun 47 116
  Mrs. Amworth. .s . . . .
  . . . . FFM Jun 50 106
  Outcast, The. .s . . . .
  . . . . .FFM Aug 42 130
  Roderick's Story. .s . . . .
  . . . . .FFM Apr 46 116
BENSON, EDWIN Name of a real per-
  son used in error as a "house name"
  on one story.
  by EDWIN BENSON
  Biog sketch, photo. . . . .
  . . . . Amz May 43 234
  Invasion of the Raindrops. .nt . . .
  . . . . FA Jan 45 26
  Lunar Loot. .s . . . . . FA Mar 40 64
  Priestess of the Floating Skull . . .
  ..n 2 pt . . . . Amz May 43 182
  by RICHARD S. SHAVER
  Marai's Wife. .s . . . .
  . . . . .OW Mar 50 152
BENTLEY, GARTH
  Beyond the Star Curtain. .s . . . . .
  . . . . WS Oct 31 640
  FSQ Fal 50 116
  Rebelion—5000 A.D. . .s . . . .
  . . . . .WS Jul 31 224
BERGEY, EARL K. artist
  Covers for CAPTAIN FUTURE
  Sum(?), Fal 1940
  Win, Spr(?), Sum 1941
  Win(?), Sum 1943
  Win, Spr 1944

AUTHOR
   Title. .Length . . . . Magazine, Date, Page

*Covers for FANTASTIC STORY
   QUARTERLY*
   Spr, Sum, Fal 1950
*Covers for FUTURE SCIENCE
   FICTION*
   May-Jun, Jul-Aug 1950
Covers for STARTLING STORIES
   Jul, Sep, Nov 1940
   Jan, Mar 1941
   Mar, May, Jul, Nov 1942
   Mar, Jun, Fal 1943
   Win, Spr, Sum, Fal 1944
   Win, Spr, Sum, Fal 1945
   Win, Mar, Spr, Sum, Fal 1946
   Jan, May, Jul, Sep, Nov 1947
   Jan, Mar, May, Jul, Sep, Nov
     1948
   Jan, Mar, Jul, Sep, Nov(?) 1949
   Jan(?), Mar (?), May (?), Jul,
     Sep, Nov 1950
*Covers for THRILLING WONDER
   STORIES*
   Sep, Oct, Nov, Dec 1940
   Feb, Mar, Apr, Dec 1941
   Apr, Jun, Oct 1942
   Feb, Apr, Jun, Aug, Fal 1943
   Spr, Sum 1944
   Win, Spr, Sum, Fal 1945
   Win, Spr, Sum, Fal, Dec 1946
   Feb, Apr, Jun, Aug, Oct, Dec
     1947
   Feb, Apr, Jun, Aug, Oct, Dec
     1948
   Feb, Apr, Oct 1949
   Jun, Aug, Oct, Dec 1950
BERLOW, SIDNEY D.
   Crystal Empire, The. .s . . . .
   · . . . . .WS Jan 32 962
BERN, DONALD
   Biog sketch, photo. . . . .
   · . . . . Amz Dec 40 133
   Man Who Knew All the Answers,
     The. .ss . . . . . . Amz Aug 40 124
   Map of Fate, The. .s . . . .
   · . . . . Amz Dec 44 72
   Mystery of the Amazing Battery. .
   · .s . . . . Amz Mar 41 124
   Ray That Failed, The. .s . . . .
   · . . . . FA Aug 40 84
   Somerset, the Scientific Monkey .
   · .s . . . . Amz Jan 42 44
   Three Wise Men of Space. .s. . . . .
   · . . . . AMZ Dec 40 102
   Wilbury's Incredible Gadget. .s. . .
   · . . . . FA Sep 41 104

BERNAL, A. W.
   Cosmic Menace. .s . . . .
   · . . . . .AQ Sum 31 408
   Draught of Immortality. .s . . . . .
   · . . . . Amz Dec 35 74
   King Arthur's Knight in a Yankee
     Court. .nt . . . . . . Amz Apr 41 48
   Paul Revere and the Time Machine.
   · . .s . . . . Amz Mar 40 50
BERNFELD, S. K.
   Solar Menace, The. .s . . . .
   · . . . . TW Aug 37 111
BERNSON, ALBERT
   Author Unknown. .ss. . . . .
   · . . . . FA Jul 50 126
BERRYMAN, JOHN
   Gentle Pirates, The. .s. . . . .
   · . . . . ASF Nov 42 93
   Rendezvous. .s . . . . ASF Aug 40 37
   Space Rating. .s. . . . ASF Oct 39 55
   Special Flight. .nt . . . .
   · . . . . ASF May 39 51
BERTIN, JOHN
   Brood of Helios. .n 3 pt . . . .
   · . . . . WS May 32 1302
   with EDWARD MORRIS
   Rebellion on Venus. .s . . . .
   · . . . . .WQ Sum 32 494
BEST, HERBERT
   Twenty-Fifth Hour, The. .n . . . . .
   · . . . . FFM Aug 46 11
BESTER, ALFRED
   Biog sketch, photo. . . . .
   · . . . . TW Apr 39 64
   Adam and No Eve. .s . . . .
   · . . . . ASF Sep 41 35
   Biped, Reegan, The. .s . . . .
   · . . . . .SSS Nov 41 66
   Broken Axiom, The. .s . . . .
   · . . . . TW Apr 39 64
   Devil's Invention, The. .s. . . . . . .
   · . . . . ASF Aug 50 133
   Guinea Pig, Ph.D. . .s . . . .
   · . . . . .SS Mar 40 116
   Hell is Forever. .n . . . .UK Aug 42 8
   Life For Sale. .nt . . .Amz Jan 42 166
   Mad Molecule, The. .s . . . .
   · . . . . TW Jan 41 29
   No Help Wanted. .ss . . . .
   · . . . . TW Dec 39 89
   Pet Nebula, The. .s. . . . .
   · . . . . .Ash Feb 41 33
   Probable Man, The. .nt . . . .
   · . . . . .ASF Jul 41 75
   Push of a Finger, The. .nt . . . . . .
   · . . . . ASF May 42 108

   Slaves of the Life Ray. .s. . . . . . .
   · . . . . .TW Feb 41 62
   Unseen Blushers, The. .s . . . . . .
   · . . . . .Ash Jun 42 84
   Voyage to Nowhere. .nt . . . .
   · . . . . .TW Jul 40 12
BEYNON, JOHN *pseud of JOHN
   BEYNON HARRIS*
   Biog sketch . . . . .ToW Sum 39 124
   Biog sketch . . . . . .Fant #1 38 128
   Biog sketch . . . . . . .Fant #2 39 92
   Adaptation. .s. . . . . ASF Jul 49 144
   Beyond the Screen. .nt . . . .
   · . . . . .Fant #1 38 92
   Derelict of Space. .s. . . . .
   · . . . . .Fant #3 39 2
   Invisible Monster. .s . . . .
   · . . . . .ToW Sum 40 6
   Judson's Annihilator. .nt . . . .
   · . . . . Amz Oct 39 104
   Living Lies, The. .nt. . . . .
   · . . . . NW #2 46 2
                OW Nov 50 96
   Perfect Creature, The. .s . . . .
   · . . . . ToW #1 37 116
   Phoney Meteor. .s . . . .
   · . . . . Amz Mar 41 96
   Puff-Ball Menace, The. .s. . . . . . .
   · . . . . .ToW Sum 38 51
   Secret People, The. .n. . . . .
   · . . . . FFM Apr 50 10
   Sleepers of Mars. .nt. . . . .
   · . . . . .ToW #2 38 4
   Technical Slip. .s. . . . Im Dec 50 24
   Time to Rest. .s. . . . . .NW #5 49 82
   Trojan Beam, The. .s . . . .
   · . . . . .Fant #2 39 60
   Venus Adventure, The. .nt . . . . . .
   · . . . . .ToW Sum 39 4
   Wanderers of Time. .nt . . . .
   · . . . . ToW Win 41 6
   Worlds to Barter. .s . . . .
   · . . . . ToW Spr 40 74
BIERCE, AMBROSE
   Inhabitant of Carcosa. .s . . . .
   · . . . . AFR #8 123
BINDER, EANDO *pseud Originally
   used for collaborations between
   brothers EARL ANDREW
   BINDER and OTTO OSCAR
   BINDER. Later used by OTTO
   alone.*
*by EARL BINDER and OTTO
   BINDER*
   Biog sketch of both . . . .
   · . . . . Amz Jun 38 7

AUTHOR
Title. .Length . . . . Magazine, Date, Page

Biog sketch of both, photos. . . . .
. . . . TW Jun 39 55
Blue Beam of Pestilence. .s . . . . .
. . . . Amz Dec 37 114
Chemical Murder, The. .s . . . . . .
. . . . Amz Apr 37 91
Dawn to Dusk. .n 3 pt . . . .
. . . . WS Nov 34 646
Eighty-Five and Eighty-Seven. .s. .
. . . . Amz Oct 34 84
Enslaved Brains. .n 3 pt . . . .
. . . . WS Jul 34 134
First Martian, The. .s . . . .
. . . . Amz Oct 32 651
Green Cloud of Space, The. .s . . .
. . . . WS May 34 1140
Moon Mines, The. .s. . . . .
. . . . WS Apr 33 858
Murder on the Asteroid. .s. . . . .
. . . . WS Jun 33 70
Robot Aliens, The. .nt . . . .
. . . . WS Feb 35 1032
                          WSA 50 160
Space Pirate, The. .s. . . . .
. . . . Amz Jun 38 108
Spore Doom, The. .s . . . .
. . . . WS Feb 34 678
                          FSQ Fal 50 98
Thieves from Isot. .nt . . . .
. . . . WS Oct 34 520
by OTTO BINDER
Biog sketch, photo of Otto . . . . .
. . . . .Amz Jan 39 129
"ADAM LINK" series includes:
   I, ROBOT
   THE TRIAL OF ADAM LINK, ROBOT
   ADAM LINK IN BUSINESS
   ADAM LINK'S VENGEANCE
   ADAM LINK, ROBOT DETECTIVE
   ADAM LINK, CHAMPION ATHLETE
   ADAM LINK FIGHTS A WAR
   ADAM LINK IN THE PAST
   ADAM LINK FACES A REVOLT
   ADAM LINK SAVES THE WORLD
Adam Link, Champion Athlete. .nt
. . . . .Amz Jul 40 28
Adam Link Faces a Revolt. .nt. . .
. . . . .Amz May 41 70
Adam Link Fights a War. .nt . . . .
. . . . Amz Dec 40 10
Adam Link in Business. .s . . . . . .
. . . . Amz Jan 40 44
Adam Link in the Past. .nt . . . . .
. . . . Amz Feb 41 62
Adam Link, Robot Detective. .nt .
. . . . .Amz May 40 42
Adam Link Saves the World. .nt . .
. . . . Amz Apr 42 10

AUTHOR
Title. .Length . . . . Magazine, Date, Page

Adam Link's Vengeance. .nt . . . .
. . . . .Amz Feb 40 8
After an Age. .n . . . .Amz Nov 42 8
And Return. .s . . . .Com Jan 41 100
Anti-Weapon, The. .s . . . .
. . . . ASF Feb 38 127
Chessboard of Mars, The. .nt . . . .
. . . . TW Jun 37 72
Comet Passes, A. .s . . . .
. . . . TW Oct 37 102
Conquest of Life. .s . . . .
. . . . .TW Aug 37 28
                          SS May 49 80
Double or Nothing. .s. . . . .
. . . . TW Oct 42 104
Eye of the Past. .s . . . .
. . . . ASF Mar 38 142
Five Steps to Tomorrow. .n . . . . .
. . . . SS Jul 40 12
Flame from Nowhere, The. .s. . . .
. . . . Amz Apr 39 88
Gems of Life. .s. . . . .
. . . . .TW May 40 30
Hormone Menace, The. .nt . . . . .
. . . . .TW Aug 36 34
I, Robot. .s. . . . . . Amz Jan 39 8
Ice, F. O. B., Mars. .s . . . .
. . . . .CF Spr 41 100
Impossible World, The. .n . . . . . .
. . . . .SS Mar 39 16
Invisible Robinhood, The. .s . . . .
. . . . .FA May 39 16
Judgement Sun, The. .nt. . . . . .
. . . . TW Apr 37 14
Jules Verne Express, The. .s. . . .
. . . . TW Apr 39 13
Land of the Shadow Dragons. . . .
. .nt . . . . .FA May 41 8
Life Battery, The. .s. . . . .
. . . . SS Jul 39 113
Life Disinherited. .nt . . . .
. . . . ASF Mar 37 58
Life Eternal. .s . . . . TW Feb 38 70
Little People, The. .nt . . . .
. . . . FA Mar 40 8
Man Who Saw Too Late, The. . . .
. .s . . . . FA Sep 39 70
Master of Telepathy. .s . . . .
. . . . Amz Dec 38 38
Memos on Mercury. .s . . . .
. . . . .CF Sum 41 94
Metal Ocean, The. .s. . . . .
. . . . TW Dec 38 100
Missing Year, The. .s . . . .
. . . . Amz Oct 39 54
Momus' Moon. .s. . . Com Dec 40 75

AUTHOR
Title. .Length . . . . Magazine, Date, Page

Moon of Intoxication. .s . . . . . .
. . . . TW Jun 39 53
Mystery World. .s . . . TW Apr 41 85
One Thousand Miles Below. .nt . .
. . . . PS Win 40 2
Orestes Revolts. .s. . ASF Oct 38 44
Prison of Time. .n . . . .
. . . . DS Apr-May 39 12
Queen of the Skies. .nt . . . .
. . . . ASF Nov 37 76
Rope Trick. .s. . . . . ASF Apr 39 73
Science Island. .s . . . . SS Jan 39 112
Secret of Anton York, The. .nt . .
. . . . .TW Aug 40 89
Set Your Course by the Stars. . . .
. .s . . . . ASF May 35 109
Ships That Come Back. .nt . . . . .
. . . . ASF Nov 35 54
Son of the Stars. .s. . . . .
. . . . .FFM Feb 40 70
SOS in Space. .s . . . .ASF Jan 37 68
Space Hitch-Hiker. .s . . . .
. . . . SSS May 42 64
Spawn of Eternal Thought . . . . .
. .n 2 pt . . . . ASF Apr 36 66
Static. .s . . . . TW Dec 36 37
Strange Vision. .s. . . . .
. . . . ASF May 37 46
Teacher from Mars, The. .s . . . .
. . . . .TW Feb 41 52
Three Eternals, The. .nt . . . .
. . . . .TW Dec 39 95
Time Cheaters, The. .nt . . . .
. . . . .TW Mar 40 14
Time Contractor, The. .s. . . . . .
. . . . ASF Dec 37 142
Time Entity, The. .s. . . . .
. . . . ASF Oct 36 73
Trapped by Telepathy. .s . . . . . .
. . . . Amz Mar 39 100
Trial of Adam Link, Robot,
   The. .s. . . . . .Amz Jul 39 30
Valley of Lost Souls. .nt. . . . . . .
. . . . Amz Feb 39 52
Vassals of the Master World. .n. . .
. . . . .PS Fal 41 2
Via Jupiter. .nt . . . . .TW Feb 42 44
(Final story of the "Via" series,
the rest of which appeared under
the GORDON A. GILES by-line.)
Wanderer of Little Land. .nt . . . .
. . . . FA Jun 41 40
Waters of Death. .ss . . . .
. . . . TW Jan 40 84
We Are One. .nt . . . Com May 41 34

AUTHOR
  Title. .Length . . . . Magazine, Date, Page

When the Sun Went Out. .s . . . .
. . . . ASF Sep 37 38
Where Eternity Ends. .nt. . . . . . .
. . . . .SF Jun 39 10
BINDER, EARL ANDREW *Collab-
  orator with brother OTTO
  BINDER under pseuds EANDO
  BINDER (15), JOHN COLE-
  RIDGE (15), DEAN D. O'BRIEN
  (1)*
BINDER, JACK *artist*
  Biog sketch, photo. . . TW Jun 39 90
  Cover for ASTONISHING STORIES
    Feb 1940
  Cover for SCIENCE FICTION
    QUARTERLY
    Sum 1940
  IF pictorial feature. 25 appearances
    in THRILLING WONDER
    STORIES between Jun 37 and
    Sep 40. For full listing see Title
    Index.
  THEY CHANGED THE WORLD
    pictorial feat. 12 appearances in
    STARTLING STORIES between
    Mar 39 and Nov 40. For full list-
    ing see Title Index.
BINDER, OTTO O.(SCAR) *See also*
  pseuds EANDO BINDER (86),
  JOHN COLERIDGE (11),
  WILL GARTH (h) (1),
  GORDON A. GILES (15),
  DEAN D. O'BRIEN.
  Ring Bonanza, The. .s. . . . .
  . . . . SS Jul 47 57
BIRD, ROGER
  Universal Merry-Go-Round. .s . . .
  . . . . Amz Apr 33 76
BISHOP, CAPT. H. G., U.S.A.
  On the Martian Way. .s . . . .
  . . . . Amz Feb 27 1008
BISHOP, ZEALIA BROWN
  Curse of Yig, The. .s. . . . .
  . . . . AFR #14 66
BISSIRI, AUGUSTO
  Lord of the Winds, The. .s. . . . . .
  . . . . Amz Dec 26 820
BIVINS, JACK
  PROBABILITY ZERO
  Valadusia. .ss . . . ASF Dec 42 105
BIVONA, FRANCESCO
  Final Struggle, The. .s. . . . .
  . . . . WS Oct 34 550
BIXBY, (Drexel) JEROME *See also*
  pseuds JAY B. DREXEL (2),
  THORNECLIFF HERRICK (h)

AUTHOR
  Title. .Length . . . . Magazine, Date, Page

  (0), D. B. LEWIS (0), HARRY
  NEAL (0)
Editor PLANET STORIES Sum 50
  thru Jul 51
Editor TWO COMPLETE SCIENCE
  ADVENTURE NOVELS. . . . . .
  . . . . Win 50 thru Sum 51
—and All for One. .s. . . . .
  . . . . .OW May 50 68
Tubemonkey. .s . . . .
  . . . . .PS Win 49 29
BLACKBURN, CLINTON
  Biog sketch . . . . PS Fal 44 55
BLACKWOOD, ALGERNON
  MASTERS OF FANTASY biog . .
  . . . . FFM Apr 48 121
Other Wing, The. .s . . . . AFR #8 74
Wendigo, The. .nt . . FFM Jun 44 90
Willows, The. .nt . . . FFM Apr 46 90
BLADE, ALEXANDER *pseud Orig-
  inally a personal pseud of DAVID
  VERN; later a house name.
  Among those whose work has
  appeared under it are: HOWARD
  BROWNE, MILLEN COOKE,
  CHESTER S. GEIER, HEINRICH
  HAUSER, BERKELEY LIVINGS-
  TON, WILLIAM P.MCGIVERN,
  DAVID WRIGHT O'BRIEN,
  LOUIS H. SAMPLINER,
  RICHARD S. SHAVER, DAVID
  VERN, DON WILCOX and
  LEROY YERXA.*
by HOWARD BROWNE
  Carbon-Copy Killer. .nt . . . .
  . . . . .Amz Jul 43 12
by HEINRICH HAUSER
  Brain, The. .n . . . . . Amz Oct 48 64
by LOUIS H. SAMPLINER
  Dr. Loudon's Armageddon. .s . . .
  . . . . Amz Sep 41 134
by RICHARD S. SHAVER
  Flesh Against Spirit. .s . . . .
  . . . . Amz Mar 48 140
by DON WILCOX
  Bye of the World, The. .n 2 pt . . .
  . . . . FA Jun 49 8
by LEROY YERXA
  Is This the Night?. .ss . . . .
  . . . . Amz Mar 45 102
Authors' real names unknown
  Beyond the Veil of Science. .a . . .
  . . . . .Amz Jan 49 134
  Brainstorm. .nt . . . . . FA Dec 48 74
  Death Seems So Final. .s. . . . . . .
  . . . . .Amz Jan 47 136

AUTHOR
  Title. .Length . . . . Magazine, Date, Page

  Death Wears a Rose. .s . . . .
  . . . . FA Jan 47 78
  Diamond of Doom. .n . . . .
  . . . . .FA Jul 45 10
  Dynasty of the Devil. .nt. . . . . . .
  . . . . Amz Jun 49 6
  Insane Planet, The. .nt . . . .
  . . . . Amz Feb 49 86
  Jinx, The. .s . . . .
  . . . . .Amz May 49 54
  Lamp of No Light. .s . . . .
  . . . . .FA May 49 70
  Laughing Death, The. .s . . . .
  . . . . .Amz Jul 50 152
  Man Who Laughed at Time. .nt . .
  . . . . FA Aug 49 6
  Man Who Wasn't Himself, The . . .
  . .s . . . . AMZ Dec 41 130
  Mermaid of Maracot Deep, The . .
  . .nt . . . . FA Mar 49 8
  Mr. Lahr Says His Prayers. .s . . . .
  . . . . Amz Oct 50 56
  Monster from Mars, The. .nt . . . .
  . . . . Amz Apr 48 8
  Octopus of Space, The. .nt . . . . .
  . . . . FA Oct 49 8
  Plotters, The. .s. . . . Amz Dec 48 30
  Professor Cyclone. .nt . . . .
  . . . . FA Dec 43 72
  Prometheus' Daughter. .nt. . . . . .
  . . . . .Amz Nov 49 8
  Return of a Demon. .s . . . .
  . . . . .FA May 43 88
  Scientist of the Air. .a . . . .
  . . . . Amz May 43 224
  Silver Medusa, The. .s. . . . .
  . . . . FA Feb 48 56
  Strange Adventure of Victor
    MacLeigh, The. .nt. . . . .
  . . . . Amz May 41 208
  Valley of Madness, The. .s . . . . .
  . . . . Amz Jun 48 84
  Vanishing Spaceman. .s. . . . . . .
  . . . . .Amz Jul 47 94
  VIGNETTES OF FAMOUS
    SCIENTISTS Dept. in AMAZING
    STORIES and FANTASTIC
    ADVENTURES. 54 appearances
    between Dec 42 and Aug 48.
    For full listing see Title Index.
  War of the Giant Apes. .nt. . . . . .
  . . . . FA Apr 49 8
  Warrior Queen of Mars. .nt . . . . .
  . . . . FA Sep 50 6
  World Is Dead, The. .nt. . . . .
  . . . . Amz Aug 49 96

AUTHOR
Title. .Length . . . . Magazine, Date, Page

BLADES, LESLIE BURTON
Fruit of the Forbidden Tree. .s. . .
. . . . FFM Nov 39 109
BLAIKLOCK, RUSSELL
Invisible Continent. .nt. . . . . . .
. . . . Fut Jun 42 10
BLANDFORD, CHARLES G.
Link to the Past, A. .a . . . .
. . . . Amz Sep 27 598
BLISH, JAMES *See also pseuds*
DONALD LAVERTY (1),
MARCUS LYONS (0),
JOHN MacDOUGAL (1),
ARTHUR MERLIN (1),
LUKE TORLEY (0)
Against the Stone Beasts. .s. . . . .
. . . . PS Fal 48 74
Airwhale, The. .s. . . .Fut Aug 42 95
Battle of the Unborn. .s . . . .
. . . . .Fut May-Jun 50 65
Bequest of the Angel. .s . . . .
. . . . SSS May 40 46
Bindlestiff. .nt . . . . . ASF Dec 50 6
Bore, The. .s. . . . . FSQ Sum 50 124
Bounding Crown, The. .s. . . . . .
. . . . SSS Jan 49 60
Box, The. .s . . . . . TWS Apr 49 130
Callistan Cabal. .s . . . Sti Apr 41 42
Citadel of Thought. .s. . . . .
. . . . Sti Feb 41 38
Emergency-Refueling. .ss . . . .
. . . . SSS Mar 40 101
Homesteader, The. .s . . . .
. . . . TWS Jun 49 135
Let the Finder Beware. .n . . . . . .
. . . . TWS Dec 49 11
Mistake Inside. .s. . . . .SS Mar 48 90
Okie. .nt . . . . ASF Apr 50 69
Phoenix Planet. .nt . . . .
. . . . Cos May 41 6
Real Thrill, The. .s. . . . .
. . . . Cos Jul 41 67
Solar Comedy, The. .s . . . .
. . . . Fut Jun 42 52
Solar Plexus. .s . . . . .Ash Sep 41 84
There Shall Be No Darkness. .nt. .
. . . . TWS Apr 50 72
Topaz Gate, The. .s . . . .
. . . . .Fut Aug 41 50
Weapon Out of Time. .s . . . .
. . . . .SFQ Spr 41 135
When Anteros Came. .ss . . . . . .
. . . . SFQ Win 41–42 143
with DAMON KNIGHT
Secret People, The. .s. . . . .
. . . . .Fut Nov 50 46

AUTHOR
Title. .Length . . . . Magazine, Date, Page

Tiger Ride. .s . . . .
. . . . .ASF Oct 48 142
Weakness of Rvog, The. .s. . . . . .
. . . . TWS Feb 49 77
BLOCH, ROBERT *See also pseud*
TARLETON FISKE (6)
Biog sketch . . . . Amz Aug 38 146
Biog sketch . . . . Amz Mar 39 126
Biog sketch, gag photo . . . .
. . . . Amz Aug 39 124
Biog sketch, gag photo . . . .
. . . . FA Apr 40 89
Black Lotus. .s . . . .
. . . . FB #1 18
Chance of a Ghost, The. .s. . . . .
. . . . FA Mar 43 142
Cloak, The. .s . . . . .UK May 39 75
                       FrUK 48 48
Devil With You!", "The. .n . . . . .
. . . . .FA Aug 50 8
End of Your Rope. .s. . . . .
. . . . FA Jul 50 110
Fane of the Black Pharoah. .s. . . .
. . . . .AFR #5 37
Fear Planet, The. .s . . . .
. . . . .SSS Feb 43 116
Gather Round the Flowing
Bowler. .s. . . . . . FA May 42 130
Genie With the Light Brown Hair .
. .s . . . . FA May 43 148
Girl from Mars. .s . . FA Mar 50 28
Golden Opportunity of Lefty Feep,
The. .s. . . . . FA Nov 42 106
Good Knight's Work, A. .s. . . . . .
. . . . UK Oct 41 66
Goon From Rangoon, The. .s. . . .
. . . . FA Jul 43 160
Horse On Lefty Feep, A. .s . . . . .
. . . . FA Oct 43 86
It Happened Tomorrow. .nt. . . . .
. . . . .Ash Feb 43 46
It's a Small World. .nt. . . . .
. . . . Amz Mar 44 16
Jerk the Giant Killer. .s. . . . .
. . . . FA Oct 42 148
Last Laugh. .s . . . . . SS Nov 41 91
"LEFTY FEEP" series includes:
TIME WOUNDS ALL HEELS
GATHER ROUND THE FLOWING
BOWLER
THE PIED PIPER FIGHTS THE
GESTAPO
THE WEIRD DOOM OF FLOYD
SCRILCH
THE LITTLE MAN WHO WASN'T ALL
THERE
SON OF A WITCH
JERK THE GIANT KILLER

AUTHOR
Title. .Length . . . . Magazine, Date, Page

THE GOLDEN OPPORTUNITY OF
LEFTY FEEP
LEFTY FEEP AND THE SLEEPY-TIME
GAL
LEFTY FEEP CATCHES HELL
NOTHING HAPPENS TO LEFTY FEEP
THE CHANCE OF A GHOST
LEFTY FEEP AND THE RACING
ROBOT
GENIE WITH THE LIGHT BROWN
HAIR
STUPORMAN
THE GOON FROM RANGOON
YOU CAN'T KID LEFTY FEEP
A HORSE ON LEFTY FEEP
LEFTY FEEP'S ARABIAN
NIGHTMARE
LEFT FEEP DOES TIME
LEFTY FEEP GETS HENPECKED
TREE'S A CROWD
Lefty Feep and the Racing Robot.
. .s . . . . FA Apr 43 70
Lefty Feep and the Sleepy-Time
Gal. .s . . . . FA Dec 42 146
Lefty Feep Catches Hell. .s . . . . .
. . . . .FA Jan 43 192
Lefty Feep Does Time. .nt . . . . .
. . . . FA Apr 44 156
Lefty Feep Gets Henpecked. .s. . .
. . . . FA Apr 45 116
Lefty Feep's Arabian Nightmare. .
. .s . . . . FA Feb 44 178
Little Man Who Wasn't All There,
The. .s. . . . . . . FA Aug 42 188
Machine That Changed History,
The. .s. . . . . . . SF Jul 43 88
Mad Scientist, The. .s . . . .
. . . . FA Sep 47 108
Man Who Walked Through Mirrors,
The. .s. . . . . . . Amz Aug 39 52
Murder from the Moon. .s. . . . . .
. . . . Amz Nov 42 154
Never Trust a Demon. .s . . . .
. . . . Amz Apr 43 164
Nothing Happens to Lefty Feep. .
. .s . . . . FA Feb 43 132
Pied Piper Fights the Gestapo,
The. .s. . . . . FA Jun 42 108
Queen of the Metal Men. .s . . . . .
. . . . FA Apr 40 62
Secret of the Observatory. .s . . . .
. . . . .Amz Aug 38 6
Seven Ages of Fan, The. .a . . . . .
. . . . TW Jun 49 160
Shoes, The. .s . . . . . . UK Feb 42 78
Son of a Witch. .s . . . FA Sep 42 32
Strange Flight of Richard Clayton,
The. .s. . . . . Amz Mar 39 78
Strictly from Mars. .nt . . . .
. . . . Amz Feb 48 106
Stuporman. .s. . . . . . FA Jun 43 22

AUTHOR
Title. .Length . . . . Magazine, Date, Page

Time Wounds All Heels. .s . . . . .
. . . . FA Apr 42 192
Tooth or Consequences. .s . . . . .
. . . . Amz May 50 118
Tree's a Crowd. .s . . . .
. . . . .FA Jul 46 74
Unspeakable Betrothal, The. .s . . .
. . . . AFR #9 75
Weird Doom of Floyd Scrilch,
The. .s . . . . .FA Jul 42 86
You Can't Kid Lefty Feep. .s . . . .
. . . . FA Aug 43 148
BLODGETT, WALTON
Other Worlds. .nt . . . . FA Jul 43 182
BLUMENFELD, H. J. artist
Cover for FANTASTIC
ADVENTURES . . . . . . .May 50
BLUMMER, JON L. artist
True—No Doubt! . . pic feat . . . .
. . . . .Ash Feb 40 87
BOCH, OSCAR A.
Spacewreck. .s . . . . ASF Nov 39 79
BOGART, WILLIAM G.
You Thought Me Dead. .s . . . . . .
. . . . UK Apr 39 63
BOGG, PETE
Specter of Shintoism, The. .a . . . .
. . . . Amz Dec 44 189
BOK, HANNES artist and author
Cover for COSMIC STORIES
May 1941
Covers for FUTURE comb w
SCIENCE FICTION
Oct, Dec 1941
Feb, Oct 1942
Cover for IMAGINATION
Oct 1950
Cover for OTHER WORLDS
Nov 1950
Cover for PLANET STORIES
Win 1942
Cover for SCIENCE FICTION
QUARTERLY
Win 1941–42
Spr, Fal 1942
Covers for STIRRING SCIENCE
STORIES
Apr, Jun 1941
Mar 1942
Alien Vibration, The. .s . . . . . .
. . . . .Fut Feb 42 74
Blue Flamingo, The. .n . . . .
. . . . SS Jan 48 13
Beauty. .s . . . . Fut Oct 42 49
Dusk on the Moon. .nt . . . .
. . . . .Fut Feb 43 20

AUTHOR
Title. .Length . . . . Magazine, Date, Page

Letter to an Invisible Woman. . . .
. .ss . . . . UK Oct 42 79
Sorcerer's Ship, The. .n . . . .
. . . . UK Dec 42 9
Starstone World. .n . . . .
. . . . SFQ Sum 42 88
Stranger from Space. .s . . . .
. . . . PS May 43 71
Web of Moons. .ss . . . .
. . . . Fut Apr 42 86
BOLKHOVITINOV, VIKTOR
with JASSILIJ ZAKHARTCHENKO
World of Nightmare Fantasies,
The. .a . . . . . (tr fr Russian) . . . .
. . . . .ASF Jun 49 158
BOLT, LEE pseud of FREDERICK
FAUST
BOLTON, PAUL
Chicago 2042 A.D. . .s . . . .
. . . . WS Oct 32 416
Time Hoaxers, The. .s . . . .
. . . . Amz Aug 31 428
BOND, NELSON See also pseuds
GEORGE DANZEL (1), HUBERT
MAVITY (1)
Biog sketch, photo. . . .FA Jul 39 88
Biog sketch . . . . .Amz Jan 40 131
Biog sketch . . . . . . PS Fal 41 105
Al Haddon's Lamp. .nt . . . .
. . . . UK Jun 42 110
Amazing Adventure of Wilberforce
Weems, The. .s . . . . FA Sep 39 48
Ballad of Blaster Bill, The. .(story
in verse). . . . . PS Sum 41 27
Ballad of Venus Nell, The. .(story
in verse). . . . . .PS Spr 42 56
Beyond Light. .s . . . . .PS Win 40 53
Brother Michel. .s . . FA May 42 202
Captain Chaos. .s . . . . PS May 42 70
Cartwright's Camera. .s . . . .
. . . . UK Nov 40 104
Castaways of Eros. .nt . . . .
. . . . .PS Win 43 62
Colossus of Chaos. .nt . . . .
. . . . PS Nov 42 2
Conquerors' Isle. .s . . . . AFR #4 48
Day We Celebrate, The. .s . . . . .
. . . . .ASF Jan 41 42
Dictator of Time. .nt . . . .
. . . . .PS Spr 40 98
Down the Dimensions. .s. . . . . . .
. . . . ASF Apr 37 102
Einstein Inshoot, The. .s . . . . . .
. . . . ASF Nov 38 103
F.O.B. Venus. .s . . . . FA Nov 39 34

AUTHOR
Title. .Length . . . . Magazine, Date, Page

Fertility of Dalrymple Todd,
The. .s . . . . FA Aug 40 48
Fountain, The. .n . . . . UK Jun 41 9
Fugitives from Earth. .s . . . . . .
. . . . Amz Dec 39 8
Genius of Lancelot Biggs,
The. .s . . . . FA Jun 40 92
Geometrics of Johnny Day,
The. .s . . . . ASF Jul 41 114
Gods of the Jungle. .n 2 pt . . . . .
. . . . Jun 42 194
"HORSESENSE HANK" series
includes:
THE SCIENTIFIC PIONEER
THE SCIENTIFIC PIONEER RETURNS
HORSESENSE HANK DOES HIS BIT
HORSESENSE HANK IN THE
PARALLEL WORLDS
Horsesense Hank Does His Bit . . .
. .s . . . . Amz May 42 178
Horsesense Hank in the Parallel
Worlds. .nt . . . . . Amz Aug 42 212
Jessifer Rides Again. .s . . . .
. . . . TW Oct 42 56
Judging of the Priestess, The . . . .
. .nt . . . . FA Apr 40 42
"LANCELOT BIGGS" series
includes:
F.O.B. VENUS
LANCELOT BIGGS COOKS A PIRATE
THE MADNESS OF LANCELOT
BIGGS
LANCELOT BIGGS: MASTER
NAVIGATOR
THE GENIUS OF LANCELOT BIGGS
THE SCIENTIFIC PIONEER
RETURNS
THE RETURN OF LANCELOT BIGGS
THE LOVE SONG OF LANCELOT
BIGGS
MR. BIGGS GOES TO TOWN
THE ORDEAL OF LANCELOT BIGGS
Lancelot Biggs Cooks a Pirate . . .
. .s . . . . FA Feb 40 40
Lancelot Biggs: Master
Navigator. .s . . . . . FA May 40 30
Land of No Return. .nt . . . .
. . . . .Ash Apr 43 10
Legacy. .s . . . . ASF Dec 40 33
Lightship, Ho! . .s . . . ASF Jul 39 67
Lorelei Death, The. .nt . . . .
. . . . PS Win 41 2
Love Song of Lancelot Biggs,
The. .s . . . . Amz Sep 42 46
Luxury Liner. .nt . . . .
. . . . .TW Feb 42 15
Madness of Lancelot Biggs. .s . . . .
. . . . FA Apr 40 70
Magic City. .nt . . . .
. . . . ASF Feb 41 9

AUTHOR
Title. .Length . . . . Magazine, Date, Page

Man Who Weighed Minus 12,
The. .s. . . . . FA Mar 40 48
"MEG, THE PRIESTESS" series
includes:
THE PRIESTESS WHO REBELLED
THE JUDGING OF THE PRIESTESS
MAGIC CITY
Mercurian Menace, The. .s. . . . .
. . . . DS Feb 39 59
Mr. Biggs Goes To Town. .s. . . . .
. . . . Amz Oct 42 126
Monster from Nowhere, The . . . .
. .s . . . . .FA Jul 39 46
Occupation: Demigod. .s. . . . . .
. . . . UK Dec 41 60
Ordeal of Lancelot Biggs,
The. .s. . . . . Amz May 43 72
Parallel in Time. .s. . . TW Jun 40 72
Pawns of Chaos. .nt . . . .
. . . . TW Apr 43 15
Peril on Phoebus. .s . . . .
. . . . TW Fal 43 74
Peter Pettigrew's Prisoner. .s . . . .
. . . . .Amz Jul 42 76
Phantom Out of Time. .nt . . . . . .
. . . . PS Fal 43 90
Prescience. .s . . . . . UK Oct 41 76
Priestess Who Rebelled, The . . . .
. .s . . . . Amz Oct 39 88
Prisoner's Base. .s . . . .
. . . . .TW May 40 14
PROBABILITY ZERO
Double, Double, Toil and
Trouble. . . . . . ASF Apr 43 90
Problem in Diatonics, A . . . .
. .s . . . . TW Aug 40 30
Proxies on Venus. .s. . . . .
. . . . .SF Jun 40 41
Return of Lancelot Biggs,
The. .s. . . . . Amz May 42 52
Revolt on Io. .nt . . . .
. . . . PS Spr 41 106
Saint Mulligan. .s. . . . FA May 43 74
Scientific Pioneer, The. .s . . . . . .
. . . . Amz Mar 40 88
Scientific Pioneer Returns,
The. .nt . . . . . . Amz Nov 40 88
Secret of Lucky Logan, The . . . .
. .s . . . . Amz Apr 42 96
Shadrach. .s . . . . . . PS Fal 41 106
"Shall Stay These Couriers" . . . .
. .s . . . . .TW Nov 40 80
Sons of the Deluge. .n 2 pt . . . . .
. . . . Amz Jan 40 8
Stowaway. .s . . . . ASF Aug 39 101
Take My Drum To England. . . . .
. .s . . . . UK Aug 41 124

AUTHOR
Title. .Length . . . . Magazine, Date, Page

That Worlds May Live. .n . . . . . .
. . . . Amz Apr 43 8
Trouble on Tycho. .s . . . .
. . . . .PS Mar 43 91
Ultimate Salient, The. .nt . . . . . .
. . . . .PS Fal 40 2
Uncommon Castaway. .s. . . . . . .
. . . . AFR #11 27
Union in Gehenna. .nt . . . .
. . . . FA Oct 42 98
Wanderers of the Wolf Moon . . . .
. .nt . . . . .PS Spr 44 72
When Freemen Shall Stand . . . .
. .n . . . . .FA Nov 42 8
World Within, The. .s . . . .
. . . . SSS May 42 90
BONESTELL, CHESLEY *artist*
Covers for ASTOUNDING SCIENCE
FICTION
Oct 1947
Apr, Jul 1948
Jun 1949
Jan 1950
Cover for MAGAZINE OF
FANTASY AND SCIENCE
FICTION
Dec 1950
BONNEY, NORMAN J.
Man Who Laughs, The. .s . . . . . .
. . . . WS Oct 30 438
BORR, T.
Family Tree of the Animal Kingdom,
The. .a. . . . . FA May 43 226
BOSWORTH, ALLAN R.
Jesus Shoes. .s. . . . . UK Apr 42 65
                          UK 48 128
BOTT, HENRY
High Vacua. .a . . . . ASF Nov 41 97
BOUCHER, ANTHONY *pseud of*
WILLIAM ANTHONY PARKER
WHITE
Co-editor (with J. Francis McComas)
of MAGAZINE OF FANTASY
AND SCIENCE FICTION
Fall 49 — *(all issues)*
Barrier, The. .nt . . . . ASF Sep 42 9
"Chronokinesis of Jonathan Hull,"
The. .s. . . . . . . .ASF Jun 46 118
Compleat Werewolf, The. .nt . . . .
. . . . UK Apr 42 68
                          UK 48 77
Elsewhen. .nt . . . . .ASF Jan 43 112
Expedition. .s . . . . . TW Aug 43 49
Ghost of Me, The. .s. . . . .
. . . . UK Jun 42 82
On a Limb. .a . . . . . UK Oct 41 92

AUTHOR
Title. .Length . . . . Magazine, Date, Page

One-Way Trip. .nt . . . .
. . . . ASF Aug 43 79
Pelagic Spark. .s . . . .
. . . . ASF Jun 43 32
Snulbug. .s. . . . . . . UK Dec 41 78
Sriberdegibit. .nt . . . .
. . . . UK Jun 43 81
They Bite. .s . . . . . UK Aug 43 127
Transfer Point. .s . . . GSF Nov 50 56
We Print the Truth. .n . . . .
. . . . ASF Dec 43 125
BOUNDS, SYDNEY J.
Spirit of Earth, The. .s . . . .
. . . . .NW Win 50 74
Too Efficient. .s . . . .
. . . . .NW #5 49 66
BOUR, LAURENCE, JR.
Call of Duty. .s . . . . . UK Feb 40 56
BOVARD, BARBARA
With FORREST J. ACKERMAN
FANTASY CIRCLE. .dept . . . . .
. . . . .Ash Feb 43 85
BOWERS, CHARLES GARDNER
Black Hand, The. .s . . . .
. . . . .Amz Jan 31 909
BOWMAN, B. L.
Laboratory Co-operator—3 . . . . .
. .s . . . . .ASF Jan 36 76
BOWMAN, GERALD
Kingdom of the ants. .s. . . . .
. . . . .SS Sep 40 113
BRACKETT, LEIGH *(Mrs. Edmond*
Hamilton)
Biog sketch . . . . . . .PS Win 42 39
Biog sketch, photo. . . . .
. . . . SS Fal 44 112
Beast-Jewel of Mars, The. . . . . .
. .nt . . . . PS Win 48 4
Blue Behemoth, The. .s. . . . .
. . . . PS May 43 54
Child of the Green Light. . . . . . .
. .s . . . . .SSS Feb 42 44
Child of the Sun. .s . . . .
. . . . .PS Feb 42 102
Citadel of Lost Ages, The . . . . . .
. .nt . . . . .TW Dec 50 9
Citadel of Lost Ships. .nt . . . . . .
. . . . .PS Mar 43 44
Cube from Space. .nt . . . .
. . . . .SSS Aug 42 11
Dancing Girl of Ganymede,
The. .s. . . . . .TW Feb 50 62
Demons of Darkside, The . . . . . .
. .s . . . . SS Jan 41 107
Dragon-Queen of Jupiter,
The. .s. . . . . PS Sum 41 34

AUTHOR
   Title. .Length . . . . Magazine, Date, Page

   Enchantress of Venus. .nt . . . . . .
   . . . . .PS Fal 49 4
   Halfling, The. .s . . . .Ash Feb 43 11
   Interplanetary Reporter. .s . . . . .
   . . . . SS May 41 100
   Jewel of Bas. .nt . . . . . .PS Spr 44 3
   Lake of the Gone Forever,
   The. .nt . . . . TW Oct 49 63
   Lord of the Earthquake. .nt. . . . .
   . . . . .SF Jun 41 60
   Martian Quest. .s . . . ASF Feb 40 78
   Moon That Vanished, The. . . . . .
   . .nt . . . . TW Oct 48 13
   No Man's Land in Space. .nt . . . .
   . . . . .Amz Jul 41 70
   Out of the Sea. .s. . . . .
   . . . . .Ash Jun 42 11
   Outpost on Io. .s . . . . PS Nov 42 58
   Queen of the Martian
   Catacombs. .nt . . . . .PS Sum 49 4
   Quest of the Starhope. .s. . . . . .
   . . . . TW Apr 49 45
   Retreat to the Stars. .s . . . .
   . . . . .Ash Nov 41 36
   Sea-Kings of Mars. .n . . . .
   . . . . TW Jun 49 9
   Shadow Over Mars. .n. . . . .
   . . . . SS Fal 44 11
   Sorcerer of Rhiannon, The . . . . .
   . .nt . . . . ASF Feb 42 36
   Stellar Legion, The. .s. . . . .
   . . . . .PS Win 40 95
   Terror Out of Space. .s. . . . . . .
   . . . . PS Sum 44 33
   Thralls of the Endless Night. . . .
   . .s . . . . PS Fal 43 54
   Treasure of Ptakuth, The . . . . . .
   . .s . . . . ASF Apr 40 72
   Truants, The. .s. . . . . . SS Jul 50 96
   Vanishing Venusians, The. .s . . . .
   . . . . .PS Spr 45 24
   Veil of Astellar, The. .s. . . . . . .
   . . . . TW Spr 44 50
   Water Pirate. .s . . . . . SSS Jan 41 35
   World Is Born, A. .s. . . . .
   . . . . .Com Jul 41 56
with RAY BRADBURY
   Lorelei of the Red Mist. .nt . . . . .
   . . . . .PS Sum 46 2
BRADBURY, RAY See also pseuds
   D. R. BANAT (0), WILLIAM
   ELLIOTT (0), LEONARD
   SPAULDING (0), BRETT
   STERLING (h) (1)
Biog sketch . . . . PS Spr 47 100
Photo . . . . .PS Win 49 110

AUTHOR
   Title. .Length . . . . Magazine, Date, Page

MASTERS OF FANTASY
   biog . . . . FFM Oct 49 119
   . . and the Moon Be Still As Bright . .
   . .s . . . . TW Jun 48 78
   Asleep in Armageddon. .s . . . . .
   . . . . .PS Win 48 58
                              AFR #11 79
   Blade of Grass, A. .s . . . .
   . . . . TW Dec 49 59
   Carnival of Madness. .s . . . . . .
   . . . . TW Apr 50 95
   Changeling. .s . . . . . . SSS Jul 49 98
   Chrysalis. .s . . . . . . .Amz Jul 46 70
   Concrete Mixer, The. .s. . . . . . .
   . . . . TW Apr 49 94
   Creatures That Time Forgot,
   The. .nt . . . . PS Fal 46 94
   Death-By-Rain. .s . . . PS Sum 50 35
   Death-Wish. .s. . . . . . PS Fal 50 29
   Defense Mech. .s . . . . .PS Spr 46 42
   Doodad. .s . . . . ASF Sep 43 49
   Dwellers in Silence. .s. . . . .
   . . . . .PS Spr 49 51
   Earth Men, The. .s . . . .
   . . . . TW Aug 48 69
PROBABILITY ZERO
   Eat, Drink and Be Wary . . . . . .
   . .ss. . . . . ASF Jul 42 113
   And Watch the Fountains
   Play. .ss. . . . . . .ASF Sep 43 105
   Exiles, The. .s. . . . .
   . . . . .F&SF Win-Spr 50 74
   Forever and the Earth. .s. . . . . .
   . . . . .PS Spr 50 26
   Homecoming. .s . . . . . AFR #3 117
   I, Mars. .s. . . . . . . .SSS Apr 49 35
   I, Rocket. .s . . . . . Amz May 44 108
   Impossible. .s . . . . . .SSS Nov 49 72
   Irritated People, The. .s . . . . . .
   . . . . TW Dec 47 90
   Jonah of the Jove-Run. .s . . . . . .
   . . . . .PS Spr 48 50
   Kaleidoscope. .s . . . TW Oct 49 129
   King of the Gray Spaces. .s . . . . .
   . . . . FFM Dec 43 120
   Lazarus Come Forth. .s. . . . . . .
   . . . . .PS Win 44 105
   Lonely Ones, The. .s . . . .
   . . . . SS Jul 49 135
   Man, The. .s . . . . . . TW Feb 49 69
   Man Upstairs, The. .s . . .AFR #4 90
   Marionettes, Inc. . .s . . . .
   . . . . .SS Mar 49 125
   Mars Is Heaven. .s . . . PS Fal 48 56
   Million Year Picnic, The. .s . . . . .
   . . . . PS Sum 46 95

AUTHOR
   Title. .Length . . . . Magazine, Date, Page

   Monster Maker, The. .s . . . .
   . . . . .PS Spr 44 39
   Morgue Ship. .s . . . . . PS Sum 44 51
   Naming of Names, The. .s . . . . .
   . . . . TW Aug 49 137
   Off Season, The. .s. . . . .
   . . . . TW Dec 48 99
   Outcast of the Stars. .s . . . .
   . . . . .SSS Mar 50 41
   Payment In Full. .s . . . .
   . . . . TW Feb 50 135
   Pillar of Fire. .s . . . .
   . . . . PS Sum 48 38
   Piper, The. .s . . . . . . TW Feb 43 89
   Promotion to Satellite. .s . . . . . .
   . . . . TW Fal 43 68
   Punishment Without Crime . . . . .
   . .s . . . . .OW Mar 50 6
   Purpose. .s . . . . SS Jul 50 91
   Rocket Skin. .s . . . . . TW Spr 46 85
   Rocket Summer. .s . . . .
   . . . . .PS Spr 47 44
   Shape of Things, The. .s . . . .
   . . . . TW Feb 48 47
   Silence, The. .ss. . . . .
   . . . . SSS Jan 49 30
   Square Pegs, The. .s . . . .
   . . . . TW Oct 48 101
   Subterfuge. .s . . . . . .Ash Apr 43 68
   Tomorrow and Tomorrow. .s. . . .
   . . . . FA May 47 102
   Undersea Guardians. .s . . . .
   . . . . Amz Dec 44 12
   Visitor, The. .s . . . . .SS Nov 48 131
   Way In the Middle of the Air . . . .
   . .s . . . . .OW Jul 50 142
   Women, The. .s . . . FFM Oct 48 104
   Ylla. .s. . . . . AFR #14 20
   Zero Hour. .s . . . . . . .PS Fal 47 40
                              AFR #8 65
with LEIGH BRACKETT
   Lorelei of the Red Mist. .nt . . . . .
   . . . . PS Sum 46 2
with HENRY HASSE
   Final Victim. .s . . . .
   . . . . Amz Feb 46 114
   Gabriel's Horn. .s. . . .CF Spr 43 105
   Pendulum. .s. . . . . .SSS Nov 41 102
BRADFORD, J.S.
   Even a Worm. .nt. . . FFM Jun 45 78
BRAGG, SIR WILLIAM
   Nature of Things, The. .a . . . . . .
   . . . . TW Aug 38 30
BRANCH, RUSSELL
   Invaders from the Void. .nt . . . . .
   . . . . Amz Aug 50 80

AUTHOR
Title. .Length . . . .Magazine. .Date. .Page

BRAND, MAX *pseud of FREDERICK FAUST*
Devil Ritter. .nt. . . . . FN May 49 90
John Ovington Returns. .s. . . . .
. . . . FFM Jun 41 106
Lost Garden, The. .s. . . . .
. . . . FFM Dec 41 96
Strange Loves of Beatrice Jervan,
The *(John Ovington
Returns)*. .s . . . . FanF May 50 36
That Receeding Brow. .nt . . . . . .
. . . . FN Mar 50 96
BRANHAM, BOLLING
Biog sketch . . . . . . TW Aug 43 128
Lotos Eaters, The. .s . . . . .
. . . . .TW Aug 43 58
Traffic. .s. . . . . TW Oct 50 59
BRAYMER, LAWRENCE
Wanted: A Tube. .a . . . .
. . . . ASF Nov 45 101
BRENGLE, WILLIAM *house
pseud*
Biog sketch, "photo". . . . .
. . . . FA May 43 234
by HOWARD BROWNE
Return to Lilliput. .n . . . .
. . . . .FA May 43 8
Star Shepherd, The. .nt. . . . . . .
. . . . FA Aug 43 12
Author's Real name unknown
"Your Rope Is Waiting". .s . . . . .
. . . . FA Aug 50 138
BRETNOR, R.(eginald)
Gnurrs Come from the Voodvork
Out, The. .s . . . .
. . . . F&SF Win-Spr 50 3
BREUER, MILES J., M.D.
Biog sketch . . . . Amz Mar 39 125
Appendix and the Spectacles,
The. .s. . . . . . . Amz Dec 28 774
Book of Worlds, The. .s . . . .
. . . . .Amz Jul 29 294
ToW Win 41 36
Breath of Utopia. .s . . . .
. . . . ToW Spr 42 31
Buried Treasure. .s. . . . .
. . . . Amz Apr 29 38
Captured Cross-Section, The . . . .
. .s . . . .; Amz Feb 29 968
AFR #12 67
Chemistry Murder Case, The . . . .
. .s . . . . Amz Oct 35 73
Company or the Weather,
The. .ss . . . . Amz Jun 37 51
Demons of Rhadi-Mu, The. .s . . . .
. . . . AQ Fal 31 506

AUTHOR
Title. .Length . . . .Magazine. .Date. .Page

Disappearing Papers, The. .ss . . . .
. . . . .Fut Nov 39 74
Driving Power, The. .s . . . .
. . . . Amz Jul 30 306
Einstein See-Saw, The. .s. . . . . .
. . . . ASF Apr 32 74
Finger of the Past, The. .s . . . . .
. . . . Amz Nov 32 703
Fitzgerald Contraction, The. . . .
. .s . . . . .SW Jan 30 678
SS Jan 42 94
Gostak and the Doshes, The . . . .
. .s . . . . Amz Mar 30 1142
AFR #10 92
Hungry Guinea-Pig. .s . . . .
. . . . .Amz Jan 30 926
Inferiority Complex. .s . . . .
. . . . Amz Sep 30 535
Lady of the Atoms. .s. . . . .
. . . . ToW Aut 41 47
Man With the Strange Head,
The. .s. . . . . . . .Amz Jan 27 940
Mechanocracy. .s. . . . .
. . . . Amz Apr 32 6
Millions for Defense. .s. . . . . . .
. . . . Amz Mar 35 77
Mr. Bowen's Wife Reduces . . . .
. .s . . . . Amz Feb 38 118
Mr. Dimmitt Seeks Redress . . . .
. .s . . . . Amz Aug 36 91
On Board the Martian Liner. . . . .
. .s . . . . Amz Mar 31 1080
Oversight, The. .s. . . . .
. . . . Com Dec 40 40
Paradise and Iron. .n . . . .
. . . . .AQ Sum 30 292
Perfect Planet, The. .s. . . . .
. . . . Amz May 32 136
Problem in Communication,
A. .s . . . . .ASF Sep 30 293
Puzzle Duel, The. .s . . . .
. . . . AQ Win 28 133
Raid from Mars, The. .s . . . .
. . . . Amz Mar 39 8
Rays and Men. .nt . . . .
. . . . .AQ Sum 29 360
Riot at Sanderac, The. .s. . . . . .
. . . . Amz Dec 27 878
Sheriff of Thorium Gulch,
The. .nt . . . . Amz Aug 42 44
Stone Cat, The. .s . . . .
. . . . Amz Sep 27 553
Strength of the Weak, The. . . . . .
. .s . . . . Amz Dec 33 33
Time Flight, The. .s . . . .
. . . . Amz Jun 31 274

AUTHOR
Title. .Length . . . .Magazine. .Date. .Page

Time Valve, The. .s . . . .
. . . . .WS Jul 30 102
with CLARE WINGER HARRIS
Baby on Neptune, A. .s. . . . . . .
. . . . Amz Dec 29 790
Child of Neptune *(A Baby on
Neptune)*. .s . . . . ToW Spr 41 54
with JACK WILLIAMSON
Birth of a New Republic, The . . .
. .n . . . . .AQ Win 30 4
BREWSTER, EUGENE V.
Saxe Murder Case, The. .s . . . . .
. . . . AD Aug 30 718
BRICKER, D. M.
Death Time. .s . . . . UK Apr 39 101
BRIDGE, FRANK J. *pseud of
FRANCIS J. BRUECKEL*
Mechanical Bloodhound, The. . . .
. .s . . . . WQ Spr 30 384
Via the Time Accelerator. .s . . . .
. . . . .Amz Jan 31 912
War Lord of Venus, The . . . .
. .n 3 pt. . . . . . WS Sep 30 294
BRIDGER, JOHN *pseud of JOE
GIBSON*
"I'm a Stranger Here Myself". . . .
. .nt . . . . Amz Aug 50 148
BRISBANE, COUTS
Biog sketch . . . . . ToW Win 39 93
Big Cloud, The. .s . . . .
. . . . .ToW Sum 39 42
Law of the Universe, The. .s . . . .
. . . . ToW Win 41 54
Lunar Missile, The. .s . . . .
. . . . ToW Spr 40 32
Planet Wrecker, The. .s. . . . . . .
. . . . ToW Win 39 39
BRITTAIN, WILLIAM (J.)
Burnt Planet, The. .s . . . .
. . . . .PS Win 48 80
Murderer's Base. .s . . PS Sum 48 60
Return of the Hun, The. .s . . . . .
. . . . .FA Jul 42 74
BRODY, JOHN
Dawn Breaks Red, The. .s . . . . . .
. . . . NW Sum 50 4
Foreign Body. .s . . . . .NW #2 46 48
Inexorable Laws, The. .s . . . .
. . . . .NW #3 58
World in Shadow. .nt . . . .
. . . . NW #4 49 3
BROOKE, JAMES
Stroheim. .s . . . . . . Amz Feb 38 55
BROOME, JOHN
Biog sketch, photo. . . . .
. . . . FA Sep 41 141

AUTHOR
Title. .Length . . . . Magazine, Date, Page

Appointment in Space. .s . . . . . .
. . . . TW Aug 41 85
Cosmic Derelict, The. .s . . . . . .
. . . . PS Sum 42 20
Land of Wooden Men. .nt . . . . . .
. . . . FA Apr 40 24
Mr. Pym Makes a Deal. .s . . . . . .
. . . . FA May 42 116
Pulsating Planet, The. .nt . . . . . .
. . . . FA Sep 41 114
Trail's End. .s . . . . . .SS Nov 41 109
BROTMAN, MORTON
Missing Hours, The. .s . . . .
. . . . WS Apr 35 1320
Phantom Killer, The. .s . . . .
. . . . AD Aug 30 724
BROUGH, PETER
Fingers of the Mist. .s . . . .
. . . . Amz Jun 29 264
BROWN, BERNARD (B. Sc.)
Photo Control. .s . . . .
. . . . Amz Aug 34 121
Prima Donna 1980. .s . . . .
. . . . Amz Oct 31 614
BROWN, BILL
Star Ducks, The. .s . . . .
. . . . .F&SF Fal 50 121
BROWN, FREDRIC *See also pseud*
FELIX GRAHAM (1)
Biog sketch . . . . . . .PS Spr 42 41
All Good BEMs. .s . . . .
. . . . TW Apr 49 124
And the Gods Laughed. .s . . . . . .
. . . . PS Spr 44 105
Angelic Angleworm, The. .nt . . . .
. . . . UK Feb 43 49
Arena. .nt . . . . ASF Jun 44 70
Armageddon. .s . . . UK Aug 41 119
Daymare. .nt . . . . . . TW Fal 43 15
Etaoin Shrdlu. .s . . . . UK Feb 42 67
From These Ashes. .s . . . .
. . . . Amz Aug 50 46
Frownzly Florgels, The. .s . . . . . .
. . . . OW Oct 50 30
Gateway to Darkness. .nt . . . . . .
. . . . .SSS Nov 49 10
Gateway to Glory. .nt . . . .
. . . . Amz Oct 50 120
Honeymoon In Hell. .nt . . . .
. . . . .GSF Nov 50 4
Knock. .s . . . . TW Dec 48 138
Last Martian, The. .s . . . .
. . . . .GSF Oct 50 145
Letter to a Phoenix. .s . . . .
. . . . ASF Aug 49 146

Mitkey Rides Again. .s . . . .
. . . . PS Nov 50 61
Mouse. .s . . . . TW Jun 49 89
New One, The. .s . . . . UK Oct 42 86
Not Yet the End. .ss . . . .
. . . . CF Win 41 96
Nothing Sirius. .s. . . . .
. . . . .CF Spr 44 106
Paradox Lost. .s . . . ASF Oct 43 83
Pi in the Sky. .s . . . . TW Win 45 46
Placet is a Crazy Place. .s . . . . . .
. . . . ASF May 46 118
Star Mouse, The. .s . . . .
. . . . .PS Feb 42 28
Starvation. .s . . . .ASF Sep 42 100
Undying Ones, The. .s . . . .
. . . . SSS Sep 50 60
Vengeance, Unlimited. .ss . . . . . .
. . . . SSS Jul 50 66
Waveries, The. .s . . .ASF Jan 45 126
What Mad Universe. .n . . . .
. . . . .SS Sep 48 11
Yehudi Principle, The. .s. . . . . . .
. . . . ASF May 44 68
with MACK REYNOLDS
Six-Legged Svengali. .s . . . .
. . . . WB Dec 50 2
BROWN, HOWARD V. *artist*
Biog sketch, photo. . . . .
. . . . TW Jun 39 89
Covers for ASTOUNDING STORIES
and ASTOUNDING SCIENCE
FICTION
Jan, Feb, Mar, Apr, May, Jun, Jul,
Aug, Sep, Oct, Nov, Dec 1934
Jan, Feb, Mar, Apr, May, Jun, Jul,
Aug, Sep, Oct, Nov, Dec 1935
Jan, Feb, Mar, Apr, May, Jun, Jul,
Aug, Sep, Oct, Nov, Dec 1936
Jan, Feb, Mar, Apr, May, Jul, Aug,
Oct, Dec 1937
Feb, Apr, Jul, Oct, Nov 1938
Covers for STARTLING STORIES
Jan(?), May, Jul 1939
Jan(?), May 1940
Covers for THRILLING WONDER
STORIES
(Most issues from August 1936
until cover credits began in 1939)
Apr, Jun(?), Aug, Oct, Dec 1939
Jan, Feb, Mar, Apr, May, Jun, Jul,
Aug 1940
BROWNE HOWARD *See also pseuds*
ALEXANDER BLADE (h) (1),
WILLIAM BRENGLE (h) (2),

H. B. CARLETON (h) (1),
LAWRENCE CHANDLER (h) (1),
JOHN EVANS (0), LEE FRANCIS
(h) (1), JOHN X. POLLARD
(h) (1)
Associate Editor AMAZING
STORIES
Jan 43 to Oct 47 issues
Editor AMAZING STORIES from
Jan 50 issue
Associate Editor FANTASTIC
ADVENTURES from Dec 42 to
Oct 47 issues
Editor FANTASTIC ADVENTURES
from Jan 50
Biog sketch, photo. . . . .
. . . . Amz Dec 42 239
Biog sketch, drawing . . . .
. . . . Amz Jan 50 6
Return of Tharn, The. .n 3 pt . . .
. . . . Amz Oct 48 40
Warrior of the Dawn. .n 2 pt . . . .
. . . . .Amz Dec 42 8
BROWNING, CRAIG *pseud of*
of ROGER P. GRAHAM
Armageddon. .n . . . .Amz May 48 8
Bubastis of Egupt. .nt. . . . .
. . . . .OW Nov 50 6
Exteroceptor Deceptor, The . . . .
. .s . . . . FA Jan 50 74
Form of Hunger, The. .s . . . .
. . . . FA Oct 49 70
Friendly Wolf, The. .s . . . .
. . . . FA Feb 50 138
Goddess of the Volcano. .nt . . . .
. . . . Amz Jun 50 8
Immortal Menace, The. .s . . . . . .
. . . . Amz Feb 49 112
Insane Robot, The. .s . . . .
. . . . FA Nov 49 34
Live in an Orbit and Love It!. .s . .
(Cover lists it as "Live in an Orbit
and Like It!") . . . . OW Mar 50 108
Lorelei Street. .s . . FA Sep 50 112
Rescue Beacon. .s. .(ROG PHILLIPS
given as author in ToC). . . . . . .
. . . . .OW Nov 50 86
Runaround, The. .s . . . .
. . . . FA Dec 49 108
Seven Come A-Loving. .s . . . . . .
. . . . .OW Nov 49 72
Spawn of Darkness. .s . . . .
. . . . FA May 50 106
Squeeze Play. .s. . . . .
. . . . Amz Nov 47 50

AUTHOR
Title. .Length . . . . Magazine, Date, Page

AUTHOR
Title. .Length . . . . Magazine, Date, Page

AUTHOR
Title. .Length . . . . Magazine, Date, Page

Tillie. .s . . . . Amz Dec 48 42
Two Against Venus. .nt . . . .
. . . . Amz Mar 50 144
Venusian, The. .n . . . .
. . . . Amz Aug 48 18
Vial of Immortality. .nt . . . .
. . . . Amz Jan 50 82
BROWNING, JOHN S. *Pseud of*
ROBERT MOORE WILLIAMS
Burning Bright. .s . . . ASF Jul 48 45
BROWNING, ROBERT
PROBABILITY ZERO
Secret Weapon. .ss . . . .
. . . . .ASF Jun 44 132
BRUDY, BILL
Biog sketch, photo. . . . .
. . . . .TW May 40 85
Dosage. .s . . . . .TW May 40 84
Hot Cargo. .s . . . . . TW Oct 41 99
BRUECKEL, FRANCIS J. *See*
FRANK J. BRIDGE (3), FRANK J.
BRUECKEL, Jr. (3)
BRUECKEL, FRANK (J.), (JR.)
pseud of FRANCIS J. BRUECKEL
Manuscript Found in the Desert,
The. .ss . . . . SW Mar 30 895
Moon Men, The. .s . . . .
. . . . Amz Nov 28 718
Professor Diel's Ray. .s . . . .
. . . . SW Mar 30 926
BRUELL, EDWIN
Men Without Sleep. .s . . . .
. . . . WS May 33 982
BRUHL, LEO AM
Garfield's Invention. .s . . . .*(tr fr the*
German by Francis M. Currier). .
. . . . .WS Jan 34 642
BRUSH *artist*
Cover for ASTOUNDING SCIENCE
FICTION
May 1950
BUCHAN, JOHN
No-Man's-Land. .nt . . . .
. . . . FFM Dec 49 82
BUCHANAN, CARL
with Dr. ARCH CARR
Discus Men of Ekta. .nt . . . .
. . . . ASF Feb 35 10
Warriors of Eternity. .nt . . . . . .
. . . . ASF Aug 34 74
BUCK, R. CREIGHTON
Joshua. .ss . . . . . . UK Jun 41 126
PROBABILITY ZERO
The Qwerty of Hrothgar. .ss . . .
. . . . ASF Jul 42 112

BUCKNER, BRADNER
Biog sketch . . . . . Amz Apr 39 125
City of Oblivion, The. .s . . . .
. . . . .Amz May 39 56
Day Time Stopped Moving,
The. .s . . . . Amz Oct 40 70
Masters of Madness. .s . . . .
. . . . .SF Jan 41 92
Revolution on Venus. .nt . . . . .
. . . . Amz Apr 39 100
BUDDHUE, JOHN DAVIS
"When Dead Frogs Kick—" . . . . .
. .a . . . . ASF Nov 38 93
BUDWIG, MARGE SANDERS
Associate Editor OTHER WORLDS
from May 1950
BURCH, WALTER
Man Who Was, The. .s . . . .
. . . . Amz May 27 188
BURG, FRITZ
Silicon Empire, The. .s . . . .
. . . . Amz Aug 33 456
BURGEL, BRUNO H.
Cosmic Cloud, The. .n. .*(tr fr the*
German by Konrad Schmidt &
Fletcher Pratt) . . . . . WQ Fal 31 6
BURKE, LYLE
Blueprint for Destruction. .s . . . .
. . . . FA Apr 50 138
BURKE, THOMAS
Hollow Man, The. .s . . . . AFR #4 36
BURKHOLDER, A. L.
Dimensional Fate. .s . . . .
. . . . WS Aug 34 262
Mad World, The. .s . . . .
. . . . .WS Jan 36 800
BURKS, ARTHUR J. *See also pseuds*
ESTIL CRITCHIE (0), BURKE
MacARTHUR (0)
Biog sketch, photo. . . TW Jun 39 88
Challenge of Atlantis, The. . . . . .
. .s . . . . TW Oct 38 50
Changeling, The. .nt . . . .
. . . . UK Apr 39 73
Citadel of Science. .s . . . .
. . . . TW Jan 41 14
Dictator of the Atoms. .nt . . . . . .
. . . . TW Oct 36 92
Discarded Veil, The. .s . . . .
. . . . TW Feb 39 88
Dominion. .nt . . . . . SF Jul 43 10
Done in Oil. .nt . . . . ASF Jun 39 79
Earth, the Marauder. .n 3 pt . . . .
. . . . .ASF Jul 30 18
Exodus. .nt . . . . MSS Nov 38 8

Far Detour, The. .n . . . .
. . . . SFQ Win 42 4
Fatal Quadrant, The. .nt . . . .
. . . . ASF Feb 38 36
First Shall Be Last, The. .s . . . . .
. . . . .ASF Jan 39 141
Follow the Bouncing Ball . . . . . .
. .s . . . . . . ASF Mar 39 45
Golden Horseshoe, The. .nt . . . . .
. . . . ASF Nov 37 12
Great Mirror, The. .n . . . .
. . . . .SFQ Sum 42 4
Hell Ship. .nt . . . . . . ASF Aug 38 6
Jason Sows Again. .n 2 pt . . . . . .
. . . . ASF Mar 38 64
"JOSH McNAB" series includes:
HELL SHIP
THE FIRST SHALL BE LAST
FOLLOW THE BOUNCING BALL
DONE IN OIL
Lords of the Stratosphere. .nt . . .
. . . . ASF Mar 33 22
Mad Marionettes. .s . . . .
. . . . Mir Apr 31 116
Man Who Fought Destiny,
The. .s . . . . CF Win 42 98
Manape the Mighty. .nt . . . .
. . . . .ASF Jun 31 308
Mind Master, The. .n 2 pt . . . . . .
. . . . .ASF Jan 32 28
Monsters of Moyen. .nt . . . .
. . . . ASF Apr 30 18
My Bride Belongs To the
Ages. .s . . . . MSS Dec 39 80
My Lady of the Tunnel. .s . . . . . .
. . . . ASF Nov 33 101
Pioneer, The. .s . . . . . Sti Jun 41 6
Snare for Tomorrow, A. .s . . . . . .
. . . . .TW Nov 40 110
Survival. .n . . . . MSS Aug 38 4
Thieves of Time. .s . . . .
. . . . .TW Apr 48 60
Trapper, The. .nt . . .ASF Sep 38 118
Trin. .nt. . . . . MSS Nov 50 6
Vanishers, The. .nt . . . .
. . . . .SSS May 50 104
West Point of Tomorrow. .nt . . . .
. . . . TW Sep 40 87
White Catastrophe. .s . . . .
. . . . TW Jun 49 100
Yesterday's Doors. .nt . . . .
. . . . TW Oct 48 65
BURROUGHS, EDGAR RICE *See*
also pseud NORMAN BEAN (0)
Biog sketch . . . . .FA Jul 39 89

AUTHOR
Title. .Length . . . . Magazine, Date, Page

Biog sketch, photo. . . . .
. . . . Amz May 41 138
MASTERS OF FANTASY biog . .
. . . . FFM Oct 48 117
A Tribute to Edgar Rice Burroughs
by Darrell C. Richardson. .a. . . . .
. . . . OW Jul 50 2
Black Pirates of Barsoom. .n . . . .
. . . . Amz Jun 41 8
"CARSON OF VENUS" series
includes:
SLAVES OF THE FISH MEN
GODDESS OF FIRE
THE LIVING DEAD
WAR ON VENUS
"JOHN CARTER OF MARS" series
includes:
THE MASTER MIND OF MARS
JOHN CARTER AND THE GIANT
OF MARS
THE CITY OF MUMMIES
BLACK PIRATES OF BARSOOM
YELLOW MEN OF MARS
INVISIBLE MEN OF MARS
SKELETON MEN OF JUPITER
City of Mummies, The. .nt . . . . .
. . . . Amz Mar 41 8
Goddess of Fire. .nt . . . .
. . . . .FA Jul 41 8
Invisible Men of Mars. .nt . . . . . .
. . . . Amz Oct 41 8
John Carter and the Giant of
Mars. .nt . . . . Amz Jan 41 8
Land That Time Forgot, The. . . . .
. .n 3 pt . . . . . . Amz Feb 27 982
Living Dead, The. .nt . . . .
. . . . FA Nov 41 8
Master Mind of Mars, The. .n . . . .
. . . . .AA 27 6
Men of the Bronze Age. .nt . . . . .
. . . . Amz Mar 42 74
"PELLUCIDAR" series includes:
THE RETURN TO PELLUCIDAR
MEN OF THE BRONZE AGE
TIGER GIRL
Return to Pellucidar, The. .nt . . .
. . . . Amz Feb 42 26
Scientists Revolt, The. .nt . . . . . .
. . . . .FA Jul 39 6
Skeleton Men of Jupiter. .nt . . . .
. . . . Amz Feb 43 8
Slaves of the Fish Men. .nt . . . . .
. . . . FA Mar 41 8
Tiger Girl. .nt . . . . . Amz Apr 42 48
War on Venus. .nt . . . . FA Mar 42 8
Yellow Men of Mars. .nt . . . .
. . . . Amz Aug 41 6
BURROUGHS, HULBERT
Biog sketch, photo. . . . .
. . . . TW Jun 39 41

AUTHOR
Title. .Length . . . . Magazine, Date, Page

with JOHN COLEMAN BURROUGHS
Bottom of the World, The. .n. . . .
. . . . .SS Sep 41 14
Lightning Men, The. .nt . . . .
. . . . TW Feb 40 12
Man Without a World, The. .s. . . .
. . . . TW Jun 39 38
BURROUGHS, JOHN COLEMAN
Biog sketch, photo. . . . .
. . . . TW Jun 39 41
with HULBERT BURROUGHS
Bottom of the World, The. .n. . . .
. . . . .SS Sep 41 14
Lightning Men, The. .nt . . . .
. . . . TW Feb 40 12
Man Without a World, The . . . . .
. .s . . . . TW Jun 39 38
BURTON A. E.
Discovery of Nil. .s . . . .
. . . . .Fant #2 39 93
BURTON, WALTER E.
Test of Airplane Lightning Hazards,
A. .a . . . . AW Mar 30 818
BURTT, J. LEWIS
Daughter of Luna. .s . . . .
. . . . Amz Aug 37 65
Daughter of Luna. .s . . . .
. . . . Amz Apr 38 91
(These two are not the same story, but
two stories in the same series)
LEMURIAN DOCUMENTS, THE
1. Pygmalion. .s . . . .
. . . . .Amz Jan 32 920
2. The Gorgons. .s . . . .
. . . . Amz Mar 32 1128
3. Daedalus and Icarus. .s . . . . .
. . . . Amz May 32 144
4. Phaeton. .s . . . .
. . . . Amz Jun 32 222
5. The Sacred Cloak of
Feathers. .s. . . . Amz Jul 32 338
6. Prometheus. .s . . . .
. . . . Amz Sep 32 524
Martian Mail, The. .s . . . .
. . . . Amz Apr 35 85
Never-Dying Light, The. .s. . . . . .
. . . . Amz Aug 35 96
When the Meteor Struck. .s . . . . .
. . . . Amz Jun 36 75
When the Universe Shrank. . . . . .
. .n 2 pt . . . . . . Amz Oct 33 519
White Dwarf, The. .s . . . .
. . . . .Amz May 34 91
BUSWELL, LOUIS
Clouds of Death. .s . . . .
. . . . Amz Jun 29 272

AUTHOR
Title. .Length . . . . Magazine, Date, Page

BUTLER, ELLIS PARKER
Experiment in Gyro-Hats,
An. .s . . . . Amz Jun 26 267
Solander's Radio Tomb. .s. . . . . .
. . . . Amz Jun 27 268
BUTLER, WALTER C. *pseud of*
FREDERICK FAUST
BYRNE, LEON
Monsters of the Mountain. .s . . . .
. . . . MSS Aug 38 90
BYRNE, S.(TUART) J.(AMES) *See*
Also pseuds JOHN BLOOD-
STONE (0), MARX KAYE (h) (1)
Colossus. .n . . . . . . .OW May 50 80
Colossus II. .nt . . . . . OW Jul 50 22
Colossus III .n. . . . . . OW Sep 50 96
Music of the Spheres, The. .ss . . .
. . . . Amz Aug 35 45
Prometheus II. .n. . . . Amz Feb 48 8
BYRON, THOMAS P.
Place of Monsters, A. .s. . . . .
. . . . FFM Mar 40 113

C

CABOT, JOHN YORK *pseud of*
DAVID WRIGHT O'BRIEN
Bill of Rights, 5,000 A.D. . . .ss. .
. . . . FA Jun 41 130
Blitzkrieg in the Past. .nt . . . . . .
. . . . .Amz Jul 42 8
Case of Jonathan Lane, The. . . . .
. .s . . . . Amz Aug 42 44
Daughter of Genghis Khan . . . . .
. .nt . . . . FA Jan 42 8
Fantastic Twins, The. .s . . . .
. . . . FA Mar 42 72
Great Train Robbery, The. . . . . .
. .s . . . . FA Feb 43 160
Hammer of the Gods. .s . . . .
. . . . .Amz Jan 41 118
Last Analysis, The. .s . . . .
. . . . Amz Feb 41 56
Last Case of Jules de Granjerque,
The. .s. . . . . FA Apr 43 128
Legend of Mark Shane, The. . . . .
. .s . . . . FA Apr 42 224
Man the World Forgot, The. . . . .
. .s . . . . FA Apr 40 18
Man Who Changed History,
The. .nt . . . . Amz Feb 42 64
Man Who Forgot, The. .s. . . . . . .
. . . . .Amz May 41 94

AUTHOR
Title..Length .... Magazine, Date, Page

Man Who Got Everything,
The. .s . . . . Amz Aug 41 100
Marlow's Malicious Mirror. .s . . . .
. . . . FA Dec 42 188
Matches and Kings. .s . . . .
. . . . Amz Sep 44 186
Miracle at Dunkirk. .s . . . .
. . . . FA Sep 41 88
Mr. Hibbard's Magic Hat . . . .
. .s . . . . FA Jun 42 74
Murder in the Past. .s . . . .
. . . . Amz Mar 41 68
Nicolbee's Nightmare. .s . . . .
. . . . Amz Nov 41 62
Odds On Sergeant Shane, The . . .
. .s . . . . Amz Dec 41 98
Rats in the Belfry. .s . . . .
. . . . Amz Jan 43 84
Sergeant Shane Goes to War . . . .
. .s . . . . Amz Jun 42 152
Sergeant Shane of the Space
Marines. .s . . . . . Amz Oct 41 94
Talu's Fan. .nt . . . . FA Nov 42 122
Tenant on the 13th Floor,
The. .s . . . . FA Feb 42 124
That Dreadful Night. .s . . . .
. . . . FA Sep 42 162
Thought Robot, The. .s . . . .
. . . . FA Mar 41 78
3 Terrible People. .nt . . . .
. . . . .FA Jul 41 90
Time on Your Hands. .nt . . . . . .
. . . . FA Apr 44 84
Trail of the Magic Slippers. . . . . .
. .nt . . . . FA Mar 43 176
Truthful Liar, The. .s . . . .
. . . . FA Oct 41 128
24 Terrible Hours. .s . . . .
. . . . Amz May 42 250
with WILLIAM P. McGIVERN
Daughter of the Snake God . . . . .
. .nt . . . . .FA May 42 8
CAESARI artist
Cover for NEW WORLDS . . . . . .
. . . .#2 1946
CAHILL, JOED
Pleasure Age, The. .s . . . .
. . . . TW Feb 47 58
CALHOUN, DOROTHY DONNELL
Afraid of His Shadow. .ss . . . . . .
. . . . FFM Aug 41 118
CALLAHAN, WILLIAM pseud of
RAYMOND Z. GALLUN
Machine That Thought, The . . . .
. .s . . . . SF Mar 39 63

AUTHOR
Title..Length .... Magazine, Date, Page

CALLE, PAUL artist
Cover for GALAXY SCIENCE
FICTION NOVELS . . . #2 (1950)
Cover for WORLDS BEYOND . . .
. . . . Dec 1950
CAMERON, LEIGH pseud of
SEWELL PEASLEE WRIGHT
CAMPBELL, CLYDE CRANE pseud of
HORACE L. GOLD
Age. .nt . . . . ASF Apr 35 119
Avatar, The. .nt . . . .
. . . . ASF Jul 35 128
Fog. .s . . . . .ASF Jun 35 135
Gold. .s . . . . .ASF Jan 35 51
Inflexure. .nt . . . .
. . . . ASF Oct 34 8
CAMPBELL, J.(OHN) S.(COTT)
Beyond Pluto. .n . . . .
. . . . .WQ Sum 32 438
Film of Death. .s . . . .
. . . . ASF Mar 48 141
Infinite Brain, The. .s . . . .
. . . . SW May 30 1076
Invulnerable Scourge, The. .s . . . .
. . . . WS Nov 30 524
Seeing Ear, The. .s . . . .
. . . . TW Feb 37 82
CAMPBELL, JOHN W., Jr. See also
pseuds ARTHUR McCANN (13),
DON A. STUART (16), KARL
VAN CAMPEN (1)
Editor ASTOUNDING SCIENCE
FICTION from October 1937
issue
Editor all issues of UNKNOWN and
UNKNOWN WORLDS, March
1939–Oct 1943
Editor FROM UNKNOWN
WORLDS, 1948
Atomic Power Plant. .a . . . .
. . . . ASF Feb 47 100
Battery of Hate, The. .s . . . .
. . . . Amz Nov 33 52
Beachhead for Science. .a . . . . . .
. . . . ASF May 44 103
Beyond the End of Space . . . . .
. .n 2 pt . . . . . Amz Mar 33 1096
Bikini A and B. .a . . . .
. . . . ASF Dec 46 99
Black Star Passes, The. .n . . . . .
. . . . .AQ Fal 30 492
Brain Pirates, The. .s . . . .
. . . . TW Oct 38 74
Brain Stealers of Mars, The . . . . .
. .nt . . . . TW Dec 36 14

AUTHOR
Title..Length .... Magazine, Date, Page

Brookhaven Sketches. .a . . . .
. . . . .ASF Jul 49 4
Contest of the Planets, The
Conquest of the Planets, The Mother
World. .n 3 pt . . . . Amz Jan 35 11
(Title is given as "Contest, etc." on
the first installment; as "Conquest,
etc." on the second and third
installments.)
Derelicts of Ganymede, The . . . .
. .s . . . . .WS Jan 32 938
Double Minds, The. .nt . . . .
. . . . .TW Aug 37 54
Electronic Siege, The. .s . . . .
. . . . WS Apr 32 1246
Immortality Seekers, The. .nt . . .
. . . . TW Oct 37 40
Invaders from the Infinite. .n . . . .
. . . . AQ Spr-Sum 32 146
Inverted Alchemy. .a . . . .
. . . . ASF Jun 48 66
Islands of Space. .n . . . .
. . . . AQ Spr 31 146
Last Evolution, The. .s . . . .
. . . . Amz Aug 32 414
Metal Horde, The. .s . . . .
. . . . Amz Apr 30 6
Mightiest Machine, The. . . . .
. .n 5 pt . . . . . . ASF Dec 34 10
"PENTON AND BLAKE" series
includes:
THE BRAIN STEALERS OF MARS
THE DOUBLE MINDS
THE IMMORTALITY SEEKERS
THE TENTH WORLD
THE BRAIN PIRATES
Piracy Preferred. .nt . . . .
. . . . Amz Jun 30 228
Planet of Eternal Night. .nt . . . . .
. . . . TW Oct 39 95
Solarite. .nt . . . .
. . . . Amz Nov 30 706
Space Rays. .s . . . . . WS Dec 32 584
STUDY OF THE SOLAR SYSTEM, A
1. Accuracy. .a . . . ASF Jun 36 96
2. Two Scales. .a . . .ASF Jul 36 39
3. Mercury. .a . . . . ASF Aug 36 91
4. Veiled Planet, The (Venus) . .
. .a . . . . . . ASF Sep 36 99
5. Double World, The (Earth and
Moon). .a . . . .ASF Oct 36 125
6. Red Death (Mars .).a . . . . . .
. . . . ASF Nov 36 43
7. Single Clue, The. .a . . . .
. . . . ASF Dec 36 89
8. Cosmic Gossip. .a . . . .
. . . . .ASF Jan 37 122

AUTHOR
Title. .Length . . . . Magazine, Date, Page

9. Other Eyes Watching
    (Jupiter). .a . . . .
    . . . . ASF Feb 37 34
10. Cosmic Cactus *(Jupiter's Satel-
    lites)*. .a . . . . ASF Mar 37 88
11. Beyond the Life Line. .a . . .
    . . . . ASF Apr 37 81
12. Weather Report *(Uranus)* . .
    . .a . . . . . . ASF May 37 57
13. Cosmic Discovery. .a . . . . .
    . . . . .ASF Jun 37 106
14. Interplanetary Dividends. . .
    . .a . . . . . . .ASF Jul 37 44
15. Smallpox of Space. .a . . . . .
    . . . . ASF Aug 37 62
16. Bluff. .a . . . . . ASF Sep 37 90
17. Sleet Storm. .a . . . .
    . . . . .ASF Oct 37 151
18. Atomic Generator. .a . . . . .
    . . . . ASF Nov 37 69
Tenth World, The. .s . . . .
. . . . TW Dec 37 36
Uncertainty. .n 2 pt . . . .
. . . . Amz Oct 36 14
Voice in the Void, The. .s . . . . . .
. . . . .AQ Sum 30 390
"WADE ARCOTT & MOREY"
  series includes:
  PIRACY PREFERRED
  SOLARITE
  THE BLACK STAR PASSES
  ISLANDS OF SPACE
  INVADERS FROM THE INFINITE
We're Not All Human. .a . . . . . .
. . . . .ASF Sep 41 121
When the Atoms Failed. .s . . . . .
. . . . .Amz Jan 30 910
CAMPBELL, W. J.
Man on the Bench, The. .s . . . . . .
. . . . .Amz Jan 28 941
CANEDO *artist*
*Cover for ASTOUNDING SCIENCE
  FICTION*
Aug 1948
CANEY *artist*
Cover for TALES OF WONDER
Win 1939
CARGHILL, RALPH *pseud of
  ARTHUR JEAN COX*
CARLETON, H. B. *house pseud*
Biog sketch . . . . . . FA Mar 43 217
by HOWARD BROWNE
They Gave Him a Rope. .nt . . . . .
. . . . FA Mar 43 74
Real author unknown
Hard Guy. .ss . . . . Amz Nov 42 225

CARLIN, RUPPERT
I Murdered You. .ss . . . .
. . . . Amz Jun 49 48
Why the Sky is Blue. .ss . . . .
. . . . .Amz Jul 49 74
CARLISLE, EDWARD
Annus Mirabilus. .nt . . . .
. . . . Amz Apr 38 98
CARLISLE, JAMES HENRY, III
Biog sketch . . . . . . TW Fal 43 43
Bubble People, The. .s . . . .
. . . . TW Fal 43 41
CARLISLE, LOGAN
Airwayman, The. .s . . . .
. . . . Amz Apr 36 127
CARLSON *artist*
*Cover for ASTOUNDING SCIENCE
  FICTION*
May 1939
CARNELL, JOHN (EDWARD) *See
  pseud TED CARNELL*
*Editor of all issues of NEW
  WORLDS,*
1946 –
CARNELL, TED *pseud of JOHN
  EDWARD CARNELL*
PROBABILITY ZERO
  Time Marches On. .ss . . . .
  . . . . ASF Aug 42 99
CARPENTER, S. C.
Super Velocitor, The. .s . . . .
. . . . SW Dec 29 624
                      SS Mar 43 108
CARR, DR. ARCH
Cardiaca Vera. .s . . . .
. . . . ASF Mar 35 132
Wanderer of the Void. .s . . . .
. . . . TW Apr 37 64
with CARL BUCHANAN
Discus Men of Ekta. .nt . . . .
. . . . ASF Feb 35 10
Warriors of Eternity. .nt . . . .
. . . . ASF Aug 34 74
CARROLL, DUANE N.
Into the Mesozoic. .s . . . .
. . . . AQ Fal–Win 32 426
When Reptiles Ruled. .ss . . . . . .
. . . . .WS Jan 34 618
CARROLL, JOHN S. *pseud*
Hsilgne Esrever *(on story)*
Reverse English *(in ToC)*. .s . . . . .
. . . . TW Oct 48 125
CARSON, SAM
Space Blackout. .s . . . .
. . . . Com May 41 105

Sphere of the Never-Dead. .s . . . .
. . . . PS Sum 40 28
CARTER, FRANK
Undertones of Death. .s . . . .
. . . . AD Sep 30 822
CARTER, MANFRED A.
Colony of the Unfit. .nt . . . .
. . . . .PS Win 44 84
CARTER, PAUL
Last Objective, The. .nt . . . .
. . . . ASF Aug 46 46
CARTER, PHILIP
Ounce of Prevention. .s . . . .
. . . . .F&SF Sum 50 59
CARTIER, ED(D.) *artist*
*Cover for ASTOUNDING SCIENCE
  FICTION*
Oct 1950
Covers for UNKNOWN
Dec 1939
Feb, Mar, Apr, Jun 1940
*Cover for FROM UNKNOWN
  WORLDS*
1948
CARTMILL, CLEVE *See also pseud
  MICHAEL CORBIN (1)*
Bargain, The. .s . . . . UK Aug 42 107
Bells On His Toes. .s . . . .
. . . . .F&SF Fal 49 6
Bit of Tapestry. .n . . . . UK Dec 41 9
Cabal. .s . . . . SSS Jan 49 110
Captain Famine. .s . . . .
. . . . TW Dec 50 80
Clean-Up. .s . . . . . . UK Oct 43 145
Darker Light, The. .s . . . .
. . . . SSS May 43 74
Dead Run. .s . . . . . . TW Feb 50 51
Deadline. .nt . . . . ASF Mar 44 154
Forever Tomorrow. .s . . . .
. . . . .Ash Apr 43 74
Hell Hath Fury. .n . . . .
. . . . .UK Aug 43 9
High Jack and Dame. .s . . . .
. . . . TW Oct 49 90
Huge Beast. .s . . . .F&SF Sum 50 18
Let's Disappear. .s . . . .
. . . . ASF May 43 124
Link, The. .s . . . . . ASF Aug 42 84
Little Joe. .s . . . .
. . . . TW Apr 50 105
Murderer's Apprentice. .s . . . . . .
. . . . SF Apr 43 35
No Graven Image. .nt . . . .
. . . . UK Feb 43 79
No Hiding Place. .nt . . . .
. . . . TW Jun 50 52

AUTHOR
   Title. .Length . . . . Magazine, Date, Page

No News Today. .s. . . . .
. . . . UK Oct 41 59
Number Nine. .s . . . ASF Feb 50 98
Oscar. .ss . . . . UK Feb 41 135
Overthrow. .nt . . . . . ASF Nov 42 9
Persecutors, The. .nt . . . .
. . . . .SSS Feb 43 28
Prelude to Armageddon. .n . . . . .
. . . . .UK Apr 42 8
Punching Pillows. .s . . . .
. . . . ASF Jun 50 33
Salvage. .s . . . . TW Aug 49 111
Shape of Desire, The. .s . . . . . .
. . . . UK Jun 41 101
Some Day We'll Find You. . . . . .
. .nt . . . . ASF Dec 42 38
Thicker Than Water. .s . . . .
. . . . TW Dec 49 123
Visiting Yokel. .s. . . TW Aug 43 107
Wheesht!. .nt . . . . . . UK Jun 43 9
With Flaming Swords. .nt . . . . . .
. . . . .ASF Sep 42 109
CARTUR, PETER
   Nor Moon by Night. .ss. . . . . . .
. . . . FFM Oct 50 116
Target. .s . . . . ASF Oct 47 60
CARVER, WILM
   Biog sketch . . . . . . TW Oct 42 73
Jones' Physique. .s. . . . .
. . . . TW Spr 46 77
Time to Regret. .s . . . .
. . . . TW Oct 42 71
World of Living Dead. .s . . . . . .
. . . . TW Jun 43 108
You'll See a Pink House . . . .
. .s . . . . TW Win 45 85
CASEY, KENT pseud
   Ceres Affair, The. .s . . . .
. . . . .ASF Oct 38 136
Flareback. .s. . . . . ASF Mar 38 132
Good Old Brig. .s. . . . .
. . . . .ASF Jul 38 52
Melody and Moons. .s. . . . .
. . . . ASF May 39 93
Star Crash. .s . . . . . ASF Mar 39 95
Static. .s . . . . ASF May 38 95
They Had Rhythm. .s. . . . .
. . . . ASF Dec 38 141
Thundering Peace. .s . . . .
. . . . ASF Dec 39 35
CASEY, RICHARD house pseud
   Carrion Crypt. .s . . . . FA Jul 47 166
Don't Look Behind You. .s . . . . .
. . . . Amz Sep 45 158
Dragons Behind Us. .s. . . . .
. . . . FA Apr 45 106

AUTHOR
   Title. .Length . . . . Magazine, Date, Page

Fingerprints of Fear. .s . . . .
. . . . FA Oct 45 82
Horn O'Plenty. .s. . . . .
. . . . FA Jun 44 184
Lark on the Ark. .s . . . .
. . . . FA Feb 46 72
Miracle of Herbert Plunk,
   The. .s . . . . FA Nov 47 148
My World Died Tonight. .s . . . . .
. . . . FA May 48 160
Pearl-Handled Poison. .s . . . . . .
. . . . FA Dec 43 68
Tomorrow I Die. .s . . . .
. . . . FA Aug 48 154
Valley of Delirium. .nt . . . .
. . . . Amz Mar 45 150
CASTLE, ROBERT pseud of
   EDMOND HAMILTON
Conqueror's Voice, The. .s . . . . .
. . . . SF Mar 39 34
Short-Wave Madness. .s . . . .
. . . . .SF Jun 39 57
CAVE, ARTHUR
   Weather Master, The. .s. . . . . . .
. . . . Amz Jul 35 124
CAVE, HUGH B. See also pseuds
   ALLEN BECK (0), GEOFFREY
   VACE (0)
Corpse on the Grating. .s . . . . . .
. . . . ASF Feb 30 187
Murder Machine, The. .s . . . .
. . . . .ASF Sep 30 377
CECIL, HENRY pseud of DAVID H.
   KELLER
CHADWICK, PAUL
   Crusaders of Space. .s. . . . .
. . . . AQ Sep 32 384
Day They Landed, The. .s . . . . . .
. . . . MSS Nov 50 101
Satanic Cysts, The. .s . . . .
. . . . TW Aug 38 35
Thing That Killed, The. .s . . . . . .
. . . . .TW May 40 72
CHALLIS, GEORGE pseud of
   FREDERICK FAUST
Smoking Land, The. .n . . . .
. . . . .AMF Feb 50 8
CHAMBERLAIN, J. LESLIE
   Sword of Akalah, The. .s. . . . . . .
. . . . Amz Jun 36 123
CHAMBERLIN, PHILIP DENNIS
   Tale of the Atom, The. .s . . . . . .
. . . . .Amz Jan 35 132
CHAMBERS, ROBERT W.(ILLIAM)
   MASTERS OF FANTASY
   biog . . . . FFM Dec 47 103

AUTHOR
   Title. .Length . . . . Magazine, Date, Page

Demoiselle d'Ys, The. .s . . . .
. . . . FFM Nov 42 133
In the Court of the Dragon . . . . .
. .s . . . . AFR #5 92
Mask, The. .s . . . . FFM Dec 43 109
Messenger, The. .s . . . .
. . . . FFM Apr 48 102
Passeur. .s . . . . . . FFM Apr 47 110
Yellow Sign, The. .s. . . . .
. . . . FFM Sep 43 130
. . . . AFR #2 81
CHAMPION, MARK
   Unforseen, The. .s . . . .
. . . . ASF Nov 46 38
CHAN, RAYMOND
   Incomplete Angler, The. .s . . . . .
. . . . FA Apr 45 62
CHANDLER, A. BERTRAM See also
   pseud GEORGE WHITLEY (7)
Alter Ego. .s . . . . ASF Mar 45 118
Bad Patch. .s. . . . . .ASF Jan 47 155
Coefficient X. .s . . . . NW Spr 50 80
Dawn of Nothing. .s . . . .
. . . . ASF Aug 48 46
False Dawn. .nt . . . .ASF Oct 46 126
Fire Brand!. .s. . . . MSS Nov 50 109
Giant Killer. .s . . . . . ASF Oct 45 7
Golden Journey, The. .nt . . . . . .
. . . . .ASF Jun 45 138
Haunt. .s . . . . . . F&SF Sum 50 123
Lady Dog. .s. . . . . ASF Mar 46 119
Mutiny on Venus. .nt . . . .
. . . . .PS Win 48 38
New Wings. .s . . . . . ASF Apr 48 71
Perfect Machine, The. .a . . . .
. . . . .ASF Jan 45 107
Position Line. .s . . . . .NW #4 49 73
Preview of Peril. .s. . . . PS Fal 48 67
Raiders of the Solar Frontier. . . .
. .nt . . . . .OTWA Dec 50 4
Special Knowledge. .n . . . .
. . . . ASF Feb 46 7
Stability. .s . . . . . . ASF Jul 46 130
Terror of the Mist Maidens. .s . . . .
. . . . OTWA Jul 50 88
"This Means War!". .s. . . . .
. . . . ASF May 44 29
Tides of Time, The. .s . . . .
. . . . FA Jun 48 150
Tower of Darkness. .s . . . .
. . . . ASF Nov 46 78
CHANDLER, LAWRENCE house
   pseud
   by HOWARD BROWNE
Forgotten Worlds. .n . . . .
. . . . .FA May 48 8

AUTHOR
  Title. .Length . . . . Magazine, Date, Page

CHANDLER, RAYMOND
  Bronze Door, The. .s . . . .
  . . . . UK Nov 39 90
CHAPMAN, JOHN L.
  Another's Eyes. .ss. . . . .
  . . . . SSS Jan 41 104
  Crystal World. .s . . . . Cos Mar 41 47
  Cycle. .s. . . . . . . MSS Nov 40 106
  In the Earth's Shadow. .s . . . . . .
  . . . . Com Dec 40 117
  Into the Sun. .ss . . . .
  . . . . Com May 41 116
  Lunar Gun. .ss . . . . . Sti Feb 41 25
  Stroke. .ss . . . . . . SFQ Sum 42 142
  Time, Inc. . .s. . . . . .Cos May 41 69
  Upon the Dark Moon. .ss . . . . . .
  . . . . SF Dec 39 76
CHAPPELOW, EDWARD E.
  Air Trap, The. .s . . . .
  . . . . .AW May 30 966
  In Two Worlds. .s . . . .
  . . . . SW Oct 29 448
  Planet's Air Master, The. .s . . . . .
  . . . . .AW Aug 29 160
  Return of the Air Master,
  The. .s. . . . . AW Mar 30 774
CHAPPLE, PAUL K.
  Growth Promotor, The. .ss . . . . .
  . . . . WS Nov 34 702
CHARLES, DAVID
  PROBABILITY ZERO
  Finance. .ss . . . . .ASF Sep 43 101
CHARTERIS, LESLIE pseud of
    LESLIE C. B. LIN
  Darker Drink, The. .s . . . .
  . . . . TW Oct 47 66
CHESNUTT, CLARA E.
  Escape from Ceres. .s . . . .
  . . . . Amz Oct 35 114
CHESTERTON, G.(ILBERT) K.
  Angry Street—A Bad Dream,
  The. .ss . . . . . . FFM Feb 47 108
  Man Who Was Thursday, The. . . .
  . .n . . . . .FFM Mar 44 8
CHIBBETT, H. S. W.
  Turnabout. .s . . . . FB #3 39
CHRISTOPHER, JOHN pseud of
    C. S. YOUD
CHUTE, VERNE
  Mad Domneys, The. .s . . . .
  . . . . SS Fal 44 82
CLAIRE, MOLLIE
  Peril in Dragonia. .nt . . . .
  . . . . FA Apr 49 114

AUTHOR
  Title. .Length . . . . Magazine, Date, Page

CLARK, EDDIN
  Double! Double! . .nt. . . . .
  . . . . ASF Sep 38 88
CLARK, GEORGE E.
  Test-Tube Monster, The. .s . . . . .
  . . . . .MSS May 40 55
CLARK, JOHN D., Ph.D.
  Minus Planet. .nt. . . ASF Apr 37 86
  Space Blister. .s. . . ASF Aug 37 107
CLARK, ROSCOE, F.R.C.S.
  Experiment. .s . . . . . TW Apr 39 29
CLARKE, ARTHUR C. See also
    pseuds E. G. O'BRIEN (1),
    CHARLES WILLIS (2)
  Against the Fall of Night. .n . . . .
  . . . . SS Nov 48 11
  Exile of the Eons. .s. . . . .
  . . . . .SSS Mar 50 86
  Fires Within, The. .s. . . . .
  . . . . SS Sep 49 121
  Forgotten Enemy, The. .s . . . . . .
  . . . . .NW #5 49 48
  Guardian Angel. .s . . . .
  . . . . FFM Apr 50 98
                        NW Win 50 2
  Hide and Seek. .s. . . ASF Sep 49 68
  History Lesson. .s . . . .
  . . . . SS May 49 137
  Inheritance. .s. . . . .ASF Sep 48 145
  Lion of Comarre. .nt . . . .
  . . . . .TW Aug 49 44
  Loophole. .s. . . . . . ASF Apr 46 57
  Man's Empire of Tomorrow. . . . .
  . .a . . . . ToW Win 38 74
  Rescue Party. .nt . . . .
  . . . . ASF May 46 36
  Reversed Man, The. .s. . . . .
  . . . . TW Jun 50 43
  Shape of Ships to Come, The. . . .
  . .a . . . . .NW #4 49 40
  Technical Error. .s . . . .
  . . . . Fant Dec 46 58
  Thirty Seconds—Thirty
  Days. .s . . . . TW Dec 49 106
  Transience. .ss. . . . . SS Jul 49 125
  Walk in the Dark, A. .s . . . . . .
  . . . . TW Aug 50 134
  Wall of Darkness, The. .s. . . . . .
  . . . . SSS Jul 49 66
  We Can Rocket to the Moon—
  Now!. .a . . . . . . .ToW Sum 39 84
CLAUSEN, CARL
  Grim Inheritance, The. .s . . . . . .
  . . . . Amz Aug 29 456

AUTHOR
  Title. .Length . . . . Magazine, Date, Page

CLEATOR, P. E.
  Biog sketch . . . . . .Fant #1 38 128
  Barrier, The. .s . . . .
  . . . . Fant Apr 47 59
  By Rocket Ship to the
  Planets. .a . . . . . . .Fant #1 38 53
  Martian Madness. .s . . . .
  . . . . WS Mar 34 840
  Spaceward. .a . . . . . .TW Aug 37 90
  Supernova. .s . . . . . Fant Dec 46 40
CLEGGETT, G. L.
  Mystery of the Cat's Back,
  The. .s. . . . . .Amz Jul 49 88
CLEMENT, HAL pseud of HARRY
    CLEMENT STUBBS
  Answer. .s . . . . ASF Apr 47 93
  Assumption Unjustified. .nt. . . . .
  . . . . ASF Oct 46 58
  Attitude. .nt. . . . . . ASF Sep 43 9
  Cold Front. .nt . . . . .ASF Jul 46 7
  Fireproof. .s . . . . . ASF Mar 49 67
  Impediment. .nt . . . .
  . . . . ASF Aug 42 106
  Needle. .n 2 pt . . . . .ASF May 49 7
  PROBABILITY ZERO
  Avenue of Escape. .ss . . . .
  . . . . ASF Nov 42 126
  Proof. .s. . . . . .ASF Jun 42 101
  Technical Error. .nt . . . .
  . . . . ASF Jan 44 7
  Trojan Fall. .s . . . . . ASF Jun 44 57
  Uncommon Sense. .s . . . .
  . . . . ASF Sep 45 47
CLICK, J. HAROLD
  Dimension Segregator, The . . . . .
  . .s . . . . Amz Aug 29 422
CLIVE, DENNIS pseud All or most
    of the following stories are by
    JOHN RUSSELL FEARN, tho this
    by-line may also have been used as
    a house name.
  Flat Folk of Vulcan, The. .s. . . . .
  . . . . .Fut Nov 40 52
  Frigid Moon. .s . . . . .Fut Nov 39 78
  Laughter Out of Space. .nt . . . . .
  . . . . Fut Jul 40 24
  Valley of Pretenders. .s. . . . .
  . . . . SF Mar 39 46
  Voice Commands, The. .s . . . . . .
  . . . . SF Jun 40 8
CLOTHIER artist
  Covers for NEW WORLDS
  #5 1949
  Spr, Sum, Win 1950

AUTHOR
  Title. .Length . . . . Magazine, Date, Page

CLOUKEY, CHARLES *pseud of*
  CHARLES CLOUTIER
Anachronism. .s . . . .
  . . . . Amz Dec 30 840
In the Spacesphere. .s. . . . .
  . . . . WS Jun 31 10
Paradox. .s. . . . . . .AQ Sum 29 386
Paradox +. .s. . . . . Amz Jul 30 312
Rhythm. .s. . . . . . . Amz Apr 30 55
Sub-Satellite. .s . . . .
  . . . . Amz Mar 28 1194
Super-Radio. .s . . . .
  . . . . .Amz Jul 28 294
Swordsman of Sarvon, The . . . . .
  . .n 3 pt . . . . . Amz Aug 32 392
Synthetic. .s . . . . Amz May 30 130
CLOUTIER, CHARLES *See pseud*
  CHARLES CLOUKEY
COATES, ROBERT M.
Return of the Gods, The. .s . . . . .
  . . . . .F&SF Win-Spr 50 17
COBB, IRVIN S.
Blood Brother of the Swamp Cats
  (orig title: FISHHEAD). .s . . . .
  . . . . FS Nov 50 39
Fishhead. .s . . . . . FFM Jun 42 123
COBLENTZ, STANTON A.
Biog sketch . . . . .Amz Jan 39 131
Biog sketch . . . . .ToW Spr 39 125
Biog sketch, photo. . . . .
  . . . . TW Jun 39 86
Biog sketch, photo. . . . .
  . . . . Amz Sep 41 123
After the Atom. .p. . . . .
  . . . . FFM Apr 50 115
After 12,000 Years. .n . . . .
  . . . . AQ Spr 29 148
Ard of the Sun People. .s . . . . . .
  . . . . Amz Feb 43 144
Beyond the Universe. .s . . . .
  . . . . Amz Dec 34 70
Blue Barbarians, The. .n . . . . . .
  . . . . .AQ Sum 31 290
Circe of Science, A. .s. . . . .
  . . . . Amz May 30 170
Confession of Dr. DeKalb,
  The. .s. . . . . .ASF Jan 34 31
Cosmic Deflector, The. .s . . . . . .
  . . . . .Amz Jan 43 170
Crystal Planetoids, The. .n. . . . . .
  . . . . .Amz May 42 78
Death in the Tubeway. .s . . . . . .
  Amz Jan 39 116
Denitro. .s . . . . . . Amz Feb 37 107
Enchantress of Lemuria . . . .
  . .n . . . . Amz Sep 41 8

AUTHOR
  Title. .Length . . . . Magazine, Date, Page

Episode in Space, An. .s . . . .
  . . . . ASF May 35 43
Exiles from the Universe. .s . . . . .
  . . . . Amz Feb 38 125
Fire Gas. .s. . . . .
  . . . . FFM Apr 40 113
Flight Through Tomorrow . . . . .
  . .s . . . . FB #1 29
Gas-Weed, The. .s . . . .
  . . . . Amz May 29 138
  . . . . ToW Spr 39 90
Glowworm Flower, The. .s . . . . .
  . . . . ASF Jun 36 22
Gravity, Unaffected. .s . . . .
  . . . . ASF Sep 37 50
Green Plague, The. .s . . . .
  . . . . ASF Apr 34 30
Golden Planetoid, The. .s . . . . . .
  . . . . Amz Aug 35 48
Headhunters of Nuamerica. .s . . .
  . . . . Com Mar 41 57
In Caverns Below. .n 3 pt . . . . .
  . . . . WS Mar 35 1160
  . . . . FSQ Fal 50 11
In the Footsteps of the Wasp . . . .
  . .s . . . . Amz Aug 34 90
Into Plutonian Depths. .n . . . . . .
  . . . . WQ Spr 31 294
Lord of Tranerica. .n . . . .
  . . . . DS Feb 39 12
Making of Misty Isle, The . . . . . .
  . .s . . . . SW Jun 29 75
  . . . . SS May 42 112
Man from Tomorrow, The. .n . . .
  . . . . .AQ Spr–Sum 33 434
Man from Xenern, The. .s . . . . . .
  . . . . .TW Aug 39 13
Manna from Mars. .s. . . . .
  . . . . ASF Mar 34 46
Men Without Shadows, The . . . . .
  . .s . . . . Amz Oct 33 491
  . . . . ToW Win 39 71
Missionaries of Mars. .s . . . .
  . . . . ToW Spr 40 60
Missionaries from the Sky . . . . .
  . .s . . . . Amz Nov 30 744
Nemesis of the Astropede,
  The. .s. . . . . TW Fal 45 53
Odyssey of Battling Bert,
  The. .s. . . . . . Amz Dec 44 124
Older Than Methuselah. .s . . . . .
  . . . . Amz May 35 67
Over the Space-Waves. .ss . . . . . .
  . . . . .SS Mar 41 111
Phantom Armada, The . . . .
  . .s . . . . FA May 42 192

AUTHOR
  Title. .Length . . . . Magazine, Date, Page

Planet of the Knob Heads . . . . . .
  . .s . . . . SF Dec 39 10
Planet of Youth, The. .s . . . .
  . . . . WS Oct 32 390
  . . . . ToW Win 38 4
Purple Conspiracy, The. . . . .
  . .s . . . . . . FA Nov 39 26
Radio Mind-Ray, The. . . . .
  . . . . .ASF Jul 34 90
Radio Telescope, The. .s . . . .
  . . . . Amz Jun 29 198
  . . . . ToW Aut 40 44
Reclaimers of the Ice. .n. . . . . . .
  . . . . AQ Spr 30 148
Reign of the Long Tusks,
  The. .s. . . . . ASF Feb 37 29
Riches for Pluto. .s . . . .
  . . . . ASF Dec 34 98
Rout of the Fire Imps. .s. . . . . . .
  . . . . MSS Nov 38 63
Scarlet Rollers, The. .s . . . .
  . . . . FA Sep 42 48
Sidereal Time-Bomb, The . . . . . .
  . .s . . . . .SS Win 44 100
Stygian Terror, The. .s . . . .
  . . . . FA Nov 42 158
Sun Doom, The. .s. . . . .
  . . . . FA Jun 43 64
Sunken World, The. .n . . . .
  . . . . .AQ Sum 28 292
  . . . . AQ Fal 34 28
Sunward. .s . . . . . .TW Apr 40 32
Through the Time Radio. .s. . . . .
  . . . . MSS Aug 38 83
Time Trap. .nt . . . .
  . . . . .Fant Aug 47 5
Titan of the Jungle. .nt . . . .
  . . . . .TW Sum 46 13
Triple-Geared. .s . . . .
  . . . . ASF Apr 35 41
Truth About the Psycho-Tector,
  The. .s. . . . . ASF Oct 34 86
Universe Ranger, The. .s . . . .
  . . . . FB #6 21
Wand of Creation, The. .s . . . . . .
  . . . . Amz Aug 29 435
Weather Adjudicator, The. .s . . . .
  . . . . MSS Feb 39 90
COCKCROFT, W. P. *see also W. P.*
  COCKROFT
Green Spheres. .s . . . . .NW #2 46 56
COCKROFT, W. P. *see also W. P.*
  COCKCROFT
Biog sketch . . . . . .ToW Spr 39 126
Alien Room, The. .s . . . .
  . . . . WS Dec 34 776

AUTHOR
  Title. .Length . . . . Magazine, Date, Page

Revolt on Venus. .s . . . .
. . . . ToW #1 37 40
Riddle of Tanye, The. .s . . . .
. . . . .Cos May 41 48
Thing in the Ice, The. .s . . . .
. . . . ToW Spr 39 37
CODER, S. MAXWELL
Ether Ship of Oltor, The. .s . . . . .
. . . . .Amz Jul 27 318
COHEN, CHESTER   See pseud
CHESTER B. CONANT (2)
COLBY, LINCOLN S.
Radio Detective, The. .s . . . .
. . . . Amz May 31 125
COLEY, ROBERT
Don't Go Haunting. .s . . . .
. . . . UK Jun 39 73
COLERIDGE, JOHN pseud of EARL
ANDREW BINDER and OTTO
OSCAR BINDER in collaboration.
Artificial Universe. .s . . . .
. . . . SFQ Win 41 138
Black Comet, The. .s . . . .
. . . . .SF Jun 39 105
Doom from the Void. .s . . . .
. . . . .SF Jun 40 75
Life Beyond, The. .nt . . . .
. . . . SF Mar 41 10
Martian Martyrs. .s . . . .
. . . . SF Mar 39 18
Mogu of Mars, The. .nt . . . .
. . . . SF Aug 39 37
Mystery from The Stars . . . .
. .s . . . . .Fut Nov 39 58
New Life, The. .s . . . .
. . . . SF Mar 40 25
Poison Realm, The. .s . . . .
. . . . Fut Jul 40 83
Polar Doom. .s . . . .
. . . . SFQ Sum 40 121
World of Illusion. .s . . . .
. . . . .Fut Nov 40 40
COLLADAY, MORRISON
Blattids, The. .s . . . .
. . . . Amz Dec 31 844
Burning Swamp, The. .s . . . .
. . . . Amz Aug 31 446
Cosmic Gun, The. .s . . . .
. . . . WS May 31 1410
Earthspot. .s . . . . WS May 34 1120
Giant in the Earth. .s . . . .
. . . . WS Apr 33 850
Planetoid of Doom, The. .s . . . . .
. . . . WS Dec 32 574
Return of the Cosmic Gun,
The. .s . . . . WS Oct 31 582

SCIENTIFIC MYSTERIES
How Long Has the Earth To
Live?. .a . . . . . . Amz Jan 41 54
Silent Scourge, The. .s . . . .
. . . . WS Dec 30 680
COLLAS, PHIL
Inner Domain, The. .nt . . . .
. . . . Amz Oct 35 85
COLLIER, HARRY pseud of
HARRY WALTON
Suitor by Proxy, A. .s . . . .
. . . . WS Apr 35 1308
COLLIER, JOHN
Evening Primrose. .s . . . .
. . . . AFR #3 107
COLLINS, CLARK
He Took It With Him. .s . . . .
. . . . FA Apr 50 104
COLLINS, DEAN
Stallion's Trappings. .ss . . . .
. . . . Amz Mar 33 1135
COLLINS, GILBERT
Starkenden Quest, The. .n . . . . . .
. . . . FFM Oct 49 10
COLLINS, W. F.
Twenty Years from Today. .ss . . .
. . . . Amz Feb 31 1024
COLTER, HAROLD MOORHOUSE
Absolute Zero. .s . . . .
. . . . .Amz Jan 29 937
CONANT, CHESTER B. pseud of
CHESTER COHEN
Forbidden Flight. .ss . . . .
. . . . Fut Oct 41 104
Galactic Gear. .s . . . . Fut Apr 42 77
CONANT, ROBERT WILLIAM
Nature's "Fluorescent" Lights . . .
. .a . . . . FA May 42 222
CONKLIN, GROFF See also pseud
W. B. DE GRAEFF (1)
GALAXY'S FIVE STAR SHELF
Book review dept of GALAXY
SCIENCE FICTION from Oct
1950 (first issue)
CONN, ALAN pseud of ALAN
CONNELL
Fate. .ss . . . . WS Mar 36 952
CONNELL, A(LAN) See also pseud
ALAN CONN
Dream's End. .s . . . . WS Nov 35 646
Duplicate, The. .s . . . .
. . . . WS Mar 36 936
Espionage in Space. .s . . . .
. . . . .PS Win 41 76
Reign of the Reptiles, The. . . . .
. .s . . . . WS Aug 35 262

CONNINGTON, J. J.
Nordenholt's Million. .n . . . .
. . . . FFM Dec 48 14
CONOVER, WILLIAM
Biog sketch . . . .
. . . . .PS Fal 43 72
Soul Eaters, The. .nt . . . .
. . . . .PS Fal 44 2
CONRAD, GREGG
Mental Assassins, The. .nt . . . . . .
. . . . .FA May 50 8
CONSTANTINESCU, CLINTON
War of the Universe, The. .nt . . . .
. . . . .AQ Fal 31 534
CONWAY, BOWEN pseud of JOHN
MICHEL
Boomerang. .ss . . . .
. . . . SFQ Sum 42 138
File 384. .s . . . .
. . . . .Fut Apr 42 39
CONWAY, W. KERMIT, III
Biog sketch . . . . PS Sum 45 42
COOKE, ARTHUR pseud for an
extremely complex collaboration
by E. BALTER, CYRIL KORN-
BLUTH, ROBERT W. LOWNDES,
JOHN MICHEL and DONALD A.
WOLLHEIM.
Psychological Regulator, The. . . .
. .nt . . . . Com Mar 41 40
COOKE, DAVID C.
Package of Power. .s . . . .
. . . . SFQ Sum 40 111
Women's World. .s . . . .
. . . . SF Dec 39 78
COOKE, MILLEN See also pseud
ALEXANDER BLADE (h) (1)
Affair of Mathew Eldon, The. . . .
. .s . . . . Amz May 46 104
Champion for Tibet, A. .a . . . . . .
. . . . Amz May 46 148
Descent from Mera. .n . . . .
. . . . OW Jan 50 106
Edmund Latimer's Milking
Machine. .s . . . . .OW May 50 148
Egg of Time. .s . . . .
. . . . Amz Mar 48 124
I, John Cotter. .s . . . .
. . . . Amz Apr 47 74
M—m—m—m—m—m! .s . . . .
. . . . Amz Oct 46 68
Truth About Tibet, The. .a . . . . .
. . . . Amz Nov 46 159
COOLE, WALTER ANTON, M.D.
Surgical Error, A. .s . . . .
. . . . ASF Nov 37 106

AUTHOR
   Title. .Length . . . . Magazine, Date, Page

COPPEL, ALFRED (JR.)
Age of Unreason. .s . . . .
. . . . ASF Dec 47 32
Captain Midas. .s . . . .
. . . . PS Fal 49 61
Earthbound. .s . . . . . FA Dec 50 96
First Man on the Moon, The . . . .
. .s . . . . PS Spr 50 36
Flight from Time. .s . . . .
. . . . .PS Win 49 36
Goldfish Bowl. .s . . . . FB #6 74
Half-Life. .s . . . . SSS Sep 50 30
Jinx Ship to the Rescue. .s . . . .
. . . . .PS Win 48 27
Last Two Alive, The. .nt . . . . . .
. . . . PS Nov 50 76
Metal Smile, The. .s . . . .
. . . . SSS Jul 50 78
My Brother's Keeper. .s . . . .
. . . . Amz Jun 50 36
Rebel of the Valkyr, The . . . . . .
. .nt . . . . PS Fal 50 4
Runaway. .s . . . . PS Spr 49 31
Secret Weapon. .s . . . .
. . . . .ASF Jul 49 93
Star Tamer. .s . . . . .SSS Nov 50 48
Starbusters, The. .s . . . .
. . . . PS Sum 49 60
Terror, The. .s. . . . .
. . . . .Fut Nov 50 62
Warrior Maid of Mars. .nt . . . . . .
. . . . PS Sum 50 4
CORBETT, CHAN pseud of NATHAN
   SCHACHNER
Beyond Infinity. .nt . . . .
. . . . ASF Jan 37 8
Ecce Homo. .s. . . . . ASF Jun 36 56
Intra-Planetary. .s . . . .
. . . . ASF Oct 35 95
Nova in Messier 33. .nt . . . .
. . . . ASF May 37 138
Thought Web of Minipar,
   The. .s . . . . . . ASF Nov 36 112
When the Sun Dies. .s . . . .
. . . . ASF Mar 35 50
When Time Stood Still. .s . . . . . .
. . . . .ASF Jun 37 112
CORBETT, JOHN M.
Black River, The. .s . . . .
. . . . WS Dec 34 784
Caves of Pele, The. .s . . . .
. . . . Amz May 32 152
CORBIN, MICHAEL pseud of
   CLEVE CARTMILL
Guardian. .s . . . .
. . . . UK Feb 43 102

AUTHOR
   Title. .Length . . . . Magazine, Date, Page

CORD, BARRY pseud of PETER B.
   GERMANO
Lost Planet, The. .nt . . . .
. . . . TW Mar 41 16
Martian Heritage. .s . . . .
. . . . TW Dec 42 66
CORD, HARRY
with OTIS ADELBERT KLINE
Meteor-Men of Mars. .s . . . .
. . . . .PS Win 42 98
CORSON, WILLIAM
Klystron Fort. .s . . . .
. . . . ASF Aug 41 48
CORWIN, CECIL pseud of CYRIL
   KORNBLUTH
City in the Sofa, The. .s . . . .
. . . . Cos Jul 41 54
Crisis! . .s . . . . . . .SFQ Spr 42 130
Golden Road, The. .s . . . .
. . . . Sti Mar 42 34
Mr. Packer Goes to Hell. .s . . . . .
. . . . .Sti Jun 41 66
Reversible Revolutions, The . . . .
. .s . . . . Cos Mar 41 107
Rocket of 1955, The. .s . . . .
. . . . Sti Apr 41 53
Thirteen O'Clock. .s . . . .
. . . . Sti Feb 41 70
What Sorghum Says. .s . . . .
. . . . .Cos May 41 101
COSTELLO, P. F. house pseud used
   by CHESTER S. GEIER and others
Cosmic Punch of Lefty O'Rourke,
   The. .s . . . . Amz Feb 42 162
Curse of El Dorado, The. .s . . . . .
. . . . FA Apr 44 176
Death Makes a Mistake. .s . . . . . .
. . . . Amz Jan 43 70
Dictagraphs of Death. .s . . . .
. . . . Amz May 41 136
Duncan's Dreadful Doll. .s . . . . . .
. . . . .FA Jul 42 170
Flame for the Future. .s . . . .
. . . . Amz Oct 41 108
Flight of the Sirius. .s . . . .
. . . . Amz Jun 43 40
Gloves of Gino, The. .s . . . .
. . . . Amz Jun 50 41
Illusion Seekers. .nt . . . .
. . . . Amz Aug 50 8
Kiss and Kill. .s . . . . Amz Dec 50 44
Lady and the Vampire, The. . . . .
. .s . . . . FA Feb 42 40
Man Who Cried "Werewolf" . . . .
. .s . . . . FA Mar 43 60

AUTHOR
   Title. .Length . . . . Magazine, Date, Page

People of the Pyramids. .s . . . . . .
. . . . FA Dec 41 116
Perfect Hideout, The. .s . . . .
. . . . FA Oct 41 104
Phantom City of Luna. .nt . . . . .
. . . . .Amz Jan 44 102
Planet of Lost Men. .s . . . .
. . . . Amz Dec 41 110
Professor Thorndyke's
   Mistake. .s . . . . . . Amz Sep 44 82
Rehearsal for Danger. .s . . . .
. . . . .Amz Jan 42 190
Reluctant Genii, The. .s . . . .
. . . . FA Jul 50 130
Silver Raiders of Sirius. .nt . . . . .
. . . . Amz Jul 43 164
Spawn of Hell. .s . . . .
. . . . FA Feb 43 148
Squares from Space. .s . . . .
. . . . Amz Sep 50 78
They Forgot to Remember Pearl
   Harbor. .s . . . . . . Amz Jun 42 54
Tireless Leg, The. .s . . . .
. . . . FA Nov 42 176
Vengeance on Venus. .s . . . .
. . . . Amz Sep 42 116
Visitor to Earth. .s . . . .
. . . . Amz Feb 43 48
When Destiny Dealt. .s . . . .
. . . . FA Sep 42 214
Yellow Mud for Cowards. .s. . . . .
. . . . Amz Sep 41 110
COTTON, JOHN pseud of JOHN
   RUSSELL FEARN
After Doomsday. .nt . . . .
. . . . .Fut Mar 40 66
Onslaught from Below, The. . . . .
. .s . . . . .Fut Nov 40 96
Outlaw of Saturn. .s . . . .
. . . . SF Mar 39 94
COUNSELMAN, MARY ELIZABETH
Cat-Woman, The. .s . . . . AFR #8 40
House of Shadows, The. .s . . . . . .
. . . . .AFR #13 98
COUPLING, J. J. pseud of JOHN R.
   PIERCE
Activity. .a . . . . . . ASF Nov 46 100
Broad Band. .a . . . ASF Aug 47 116
Chance Remarks. .a . . . .
. . . . .ASF Oct 49 104
Ergodic Prediction. .a . . . .
. . . . ASF Feb 50 128
How To Build a Thinking
   Machine. .a . . . . . ASF Aug 50 117
It Isn't So Easy. .a . . . .
. . . . ASF May 45 124

AUTHOR
Title. .Length . . . . Magazine, Date, Page

Less Light, Please. .a . . . .
. . . . ASF Mar 47 90
Little Enough. .a . . . .
. . . . ASF Apr 45 100
Little Blue Cells, The. .a . . . .
. . . . ASF Feb 49 85
Maggie. .a. . . . . . . ASF Feb 48 77
News from Our Sun. .a . . . .
. . . . ASF Jun 47 76
Period Piece. .s . . . . ASF Nov 48 71
Phoney Atoms. .a . . . .
. . . . ASF May 46 105
Portrait of a Voice. .a . . . .
. . . . ASF Jul 46 101
Science for Art's Sake. .a . . . . . .
. . . . ASF Nov 50 83
Stuck in the Mud. .a. . . . .
. . . . ASF Nov 47 97
Universes to Order. .a . . . .
. . . . ASF Feb 44 102
COURTNEY, BOB
Aid to the Enemy. .a . . . .
. . . . Amz Jun 43 56
COX, ARTHUR JEAN See also
pseuds RALPH CARGHILL (0),
JEAN COX (0)
Linguistics and Time. .a . . . .
. . . . ASF Aug 50 128
Varieties of Culture. .a . . . .
. . . . ASF Dec 50 87
COX, CHARLES ROY
with HARL VINCENT (H. V.
Schoepflin)
Sky Cops. .s . . . . . Amz Dec 31 813
COX, JEAN pseud of ARTHUR
JEAN COX
CRAIG, A. A. pseud of POUL
ANDERSON
CRAIG, JOHN C.
Age of the Cephalods. .s . . . .
. . . . .Ash Dec 40 82
CRAIG, WEBSTER pseud of ERIC
FRANK RUSSELL
Homo Saps. .s . . . . ASF Dec 41 102
CRAMER, STERLING S.
Death from Within. .s . . . .
. . . . WS Jun 35 48
CRAVEY, JERRY E.
Stamp of Doom, The. .s . . . .
. . . . AD Aug 30 694
CRIMP, H. M.
Call to Migrate, The. .s . . . .
. . . . Amz Dec 32 833
Mosquito Army, The. .s . . . .
. . . . Amz Apr 35 12

AUTHOR
Title. .Length . . . . Magazine, Date, Page

CRITCHIE, ESTIL pseud of ARTHUR
J. BURKS
CRONIN, BERNARD See pseud ERIC
NORTH (2)
CROSS, POLTON pseud of JOHN
RUSSELL FEARN
Biog sketch . . . . . . Amz Jun 38 6
Chameleon Planet. .nt .Ash Feb 40 6
Chaos. .s . . . . SS Nov 47 77
Degenerates, The. .nt . . . .
. . . . ASF Feb 38 6
Destroyer from the Past. .s . . . . .
. . . . Amz May 42 230
Devouring Tide, The. .s. . . . . . .
. . . . .TW Sum 44 82
Last Secret Weapon, The. . . . . . .
. .nt . . . . MSS Apr 41 8
Man from Hell, The. .nt . . . .
. . . . .FA Nov 39 6
Man Who Bought Mars, The. . . . .
. .nt . . . . FA Jun 41 76
Mark Grayson Unlimited. .s . . . .
. . . . TW Spr 45 78
Martian Avenger. .s . . . .
. . . . Amz Apr 39 76
Master of the Golden City,
The. .nt . . . . Amz Jun 38 44
Mental Ultimate, The. .s . . . .
. . . . .ASF Jan 38 142
Other Eyes Watching. .n . . . .
. . . . SS Spr 46 13
Outcasts of Eternity. .nt . . . .
. . . . FA Sep 42 188
Prisoner of Time. .nt . . . .
. . . . SSS May 42 10
Science from Syracuse. .s . . . . . .
. . . . SF Mar 41 61
Space Trap. .s . . . . . TW Fal 45 40
Twilight Planet. .s . . . .
. . . . .TW Sum 46 63
Ultra Evolution. .s . . . .
. . . . SS Jan 48 84
Vicious Circle, The. .s . . . .
. . . . SS Sum 46 79
NW #2 46 26
Wanderer of Time. .s . . . .
. . . . SS Sum 44 69
Wedding of the Forces. .s . . . . . .
. . . . .Fut Nov 40 86
Wings Across the Cosmos . . . . . .
. .s . . . . TW Jun 38 73
World Beneath Ice. .nt . . . .
. . . . Amz Aug 39 28
World That Dissolved, The . . . . .
. .s . . . . Amz Feb 39 104

AUTHOR
Title. .Length . . . . Magazine, Date, Page

World Without Chance. .s . . . . . .
. . . . .TW Feb 39 98
World Without Death. .nt . . . . . .
. . . . Amz Jun 39 6
CROUCH, CHARLES ALBAN
Lost Key, The. .s . . . .
. . . . Fant Aug 47 42
CROUTCH, LESLIE A.
Day the Bomb Fell, The. .s . . . . .
. . . . Amz Nov 50 100
Eemanu Grows Up. .s . . . .
. . . . FFM Jun 48 112
Salvage Job. .s . . . . . Fut Dec 41 95
CROZETTI, LOYD artist
Covers for FANTASY BOOK
#3 (1948)
CUMMINGS, RAY(mond K.) See
also pseud GABRIEL WILSON
(1)
Biog sketch . . . . . FM Sep 40 132
Biog sketch, photo. . . . .
. . . . FA Jun 41 135
Biog sketch, photo. . . . .
. . . . .SS Jun 43 125
Aerita of the Light Country. . . . .
. .nt . . . . .SSS Aug 41 10
Ahead of His Time. .s . . . .
. . . . TW Jun 48 92
Almost Human. .s . . . .
. . . . .SSS Mar 41 98
Around the Universe. .nt. . . . . . .
. . . . Amz Oct 27 626
Fut Dec 41 10
Arton's Metal. .s . . . SSS May 40 73
Atom Prince, The. .nt. . . . .
. . . . SF Dec 39 52
Bandits of Time. .nt . . . .
. . . . Amz Dec 41 62
Battle of the Solar System. .s . . . .
. . . . TW Spr 44 94
Beyond the End of Time. .s . . . . .
. . . . .SSS Nov 42 124
Beyond the Stars. .n . . . .
. . . . .Fut Feb 42 10
Beyond the Vanishing Point . . . .
. .nt . . . . ASF Mar 31 314
Blood of the Moon. .nt. . . . .
. . . . .TW Aug 36 12
Brand New World, A. .n . . . .
. . . . FFM Sep 42 6
Brigands of the Moon. .n 4 pt . . .
. . . . ASF Mar 30 306
SFQ Fal 42 4
Coming of the Giant Germs. . . . .
. .nt . . . . Uc Apr 41 8

AUTHOR
Title. .Length . . . . Magazine, Date, Page

Crimes of the Year 2000. .s . . . . .
. . . . FFM Dec 41 109
No. 2: The Television Alibi . . . .
. .s . . . . FFM Jun 42 129
Curious Case of Norton Hoorne,
The. .s . . . . AFR #13 14
Decadence. .s . . . . . TW Dec 41 70
Door at the Opera, The. .s . . . . .
. . . . Ash Dec 40 77
Elixir of Doom. .nt . . . . . .
. . . . TW Apr 37 98
End of His Service, The. .s . . . . .
. . . . CF Win 42 87
Exile of Time, The. .n 4 pt . . . . .
. . . . ASF Apr 31 26
Flame Breathers, The. .nt . . . . . .
. . . . .PS Mar 43 71
Fragment of Diamond Quartz,
A. .s . . . . SSS Jan 50 60
Fugitive. .s . . . . TW Feb 42 34
Gadget Girl, The. .s . . . .
. . . . TW Fal 44 80
Girl from Infinite Smallness,
The. .s . . . . PS Spr 40 30
Girl in the Golden Atom,
The. .nt . . . . FFM Sep–Oct 39 75
Gods of Space. .s . . . . . PS Spr 42 42
Golden Temple, The. .s . . . .
. . . . TW Jun 43 102
Great Adventure, The. .s . . . . . .
. . . . TW Dec 38 51
Great Transformation, The . . . .
. .s . . . . WS Feb 31 936
Ice Over America. .s . . . .
. . . . TW Aug 40 62
Imp of the Theremin. .s . . . . . .
. . . . Ash Apr 41 64
Into the Fourth Dimension . . . . .
. .n . . . . SFQ Win 41–42 4
Jetta of the Lowlands. . . . .
. .n 3 pt . . . . ASF Sep 30 310
Juggernaut of Space. .nt . . . . . .
. . . . PS Fal 45 2
Little Monsters Come, The . . . . .
. .nt . . . . .PS Win 48 84
Machine That Had No Flaws,
The. .s . . . . SS Sep 40 106
Machines of Destiny. .s . . . .
. . . . .Ash Nov 41 96
Magnus' Disintegrator. .s . . . . . .
. . . . .Ash Feb 41 73
Man from 2890, The. .s . . . . . .
. . . . .Ash Apr 43 58
Man on the Meteor, The . . . . . .
. .n . . . . Fut Oct 41 10

Man Who Mastered Time,
The. .n . . . . FN Mar 50 10
Man Who Saved New York,
The. .s . . . . SF Jul 43 69
Man Who Saw Too Much,
The. .s . . . . TW Oct 38 100
Mark of the Meteor, The . . . . . .
. .s . . . . WQ Win 31 220
Miracle. .s . . . . . Ash Oct 42 93
Monster of the Asteroid . . . . . .
. .s . . . . .PS Win 41 102
Monster of the Moon. .s . . . . . .
. . . . .SSS Nov 41 127
Onslaught of the Druid Girls . . . .
. .nt . . . . FA Jun 41 6
Other Man's Blood, The. .nt . . . .
. . . . FFM Dec 40 56
Out of Smallness. .s . . . .
. . . . TW Jun 41 53
Patriotism Plus. .s . . . .
. . . . Fut Feb 43 91
People of the Golden Atom,
The. .n . . . . FN Sep 10 6
Personality Plus. .s . . . .
. . . . Ash Oct 40 66
Phantom of the Seven Stars. . . . .
. .nt . . . . .PS Win 40 74
Phantoms of Reality. .nt . . . . . .
. . . . .ASF Jan 30 46
Planet Smashers, The. .nt . . . . . .
. . . . OTWA Jul 50 6
Portrait. .s . . . . . . UK Sep 39 121
Priestess of the Moon. .nt . . . . . .
. . . . Amz Dec 40 42
Rain of Fire. .s . . . .Fut Aug 42 52
Regeneration. .s . . . . TW Apr 42 90
Revolt in the Ice Empire (on story)
Revolt in the Ice Kingdom (in
ToC). .s . . . . PS Fal 40 101
Science of Time Travel, The . . . .
. .a . . . . ASF Feb 50 114
Secret of the Sun. .s . . . .
. . . . TW Aug 39 90
Shadow Girl, The. .n . . . .
. . . . SFQ Spr 42 4
Shadow Gold. .nt . . . .
. . . . TW Oct 36 14
Shadow People, The. .s . . . .
. . . . .Ash Mar 42 86
Shadow World. .s . . . .
. . . . TW Dec 39 80
Simple Life, The. .s . . . .
. . . . SS May 48 61
Space Flight of Terror. .nt . . . . . .
. . . . .SF Jan 41 10

Space-Liner X87. .nt . . . .
. . . . .PS Sum 40 2
Space–Time–Size Machine,
The. .s . . . . TW Oct 37 30
Space-Wolf. .s . . . . . PS Sum 41 95
Star Arrow. .s . . . . . TW Feb 43 58
Star-Master, The. .s . . . .
. . . . .PS Sum 42 42
Story of the Cover, The. .a . . . . .
. . . . TW Jun 39 37
Tarrano the Conqueror. .n . . . . . .
. . . . .SFQ Sum 41 4
Thing from Mars, The. .s . . . . . .
. . . . .TW Aug 38 78
This Atom, Earth . . . .
. .guest ed . . . . SS May 39 13
Thought Machine, The. .s . . . . . .
. . . . MSS Apr 41 48
Thought-Woman, The. .s . . . . . .
. . . . SSS Jul 40 85
Three Eyed Man, The. .s . . . . . .
. . . . AFR #14 30
Trapped in Eternity. .s . . . .
. . . . TW Dec 36 29
"TUBBY" series includes:
AROUND THE UNIVERSE
THE SPACE-TIME-SIZE MACHINE
WORLD UPSIDE DOWN
TUBBY–TIME TRAVELER
TUBBY–ATOM SMASHER
BATTLE OF THE SOLAR SYSTEM
THE GADGET GIRL
TUBBY–MASTER OF THE ATOM
THE THREE EYED MAN
Tubby–Atom Smasher. .s . . . . . .
. . . . .TW Aug 43 86
Tubby–Master of the Atom . . . .
. .s . . . . TW Fal 46 92
Tubby–Time Traveler. .s . . . . . .
. . . . .TW Dec 42 47
Ultimatum from Mars, An. . . . . .
. .s . . . . ASF Aug 39 131
Up and Atom. .s . . . . .SS Sep 47 87
Vanishing Men, The. .s . . . .
. . . . TW Sep 40 56
Voyage 13. .s . . . . . .ASF Jul 38 6
Wandl, The Invader. .n 4 pt . . . . .
. . . . ASF Feb 32 168
SFQ Spr 43 4
War-Nymphs of Venus, The . . . .
. .nt . . . . .PS Spr 41 2
White Invaders, The. .nt . . . . . .
. . . . ASF Dec 31 310
Wings of Icarus. .n . . . .
. . . . .SS Jun 43 13
World Beyond, The. .nt . . . .
. . . . .Amz Jul 42 90

AUTHOR
 Title. .Length . . . . Magazine, Date, Page

World Upside Down. .s . . . .
 . . . . TW Dec 40 83
X1-2-200. .s . . . .
 . . . . ASF Sep 38 59
Zeoh-X. .s . . . . TW Apr 39 106
with WILLIAM THURMOND
Derelict of Space, The. .s . . . . . .
 . . . . WQ Fal 31 98
 WSA 50 140
CUMMINGS, MRS. RAY See pseud
 GABRIEL WILSON (1)
CUMMINS, DAVE
Brain Control. .s . . . .
 . . . . ASF May 37 132
CURRIER, FRANCIS M.
translations from the German of:
Airports for World Traffic *by H.
 Dominik*. .a . . . . . AW Jan 30 610
Berlin to New York in One Hour *by
 Max Valier*. .a . . . . AW Feb 30 744
Between Earth and Moon *by Otfrid
 Von Hanstein*. .n . . . . WQ Fal 30 6
Can Man Free Himself from Gravity
 by Dr. Th. Wolff. .a . . . .
 . . . . SW Feb 30 788
Daring Trip to Mars, A *by Max
 Valier*. .s . . . . WS Jul 31 254
Electopolis *by Otfrid Von
 Hanstein*. .n . . . . WQ Sum 30 482
Garfield's Invention *by Leo am
 Bruhl*. .s . . . . WS Jan 34 642
Problems of Space Flying, The *by
 Capt. Hermann Noordung, A.D.,
 M.E.* . .a 2 pt . . . . . SW Jul 29 170
Secret of the Microcosm, The *by F.
 Golub*. .ss. . . . . . . WS Jan 34 622
Shot Into Infinity, The *by Otto W.
 Gail*. .n . . . . WQ Fal 29 6
Stone from the Moon, The *by Otto
 Willi Gail*. .n . . . . . WQ Spr 30 294
Utopia Island *by Otfrid von
 Hanstein*. .n . . . . WS May 31 1352
CURRY, G. S.
What's Wrong in the Patent
 System? . .a . . . . . ASF Oct 47 87
CURRY, TOM
From an Amber Block. .s . . . . . .
 . . . . .ASF Jul 30 50
Giants of the Ray. .s . . . .
 . . . . .ASF Jun 30 368
Hell's Dimension. .s . . . .
 . . . . ASF Apr 31 51
Rays of Death. .n 2 pt . . . .
 . . . . .SD Spr 30 340
Soul-Snatcher, The. .s . . . .
 . . . . ASF Apr 30 101

AUTHOR
 Title. .Length . . . . Magazine, Date, Page

CURTIS, BETSY
Divine Right. .s . . . .
 . . . . .F&SF Sum 50 96
Old Ones, The. .nt . . . .
 . . . . Im Dec 50 98
CUTHBERT, CHESTER D.
Last Shrine, The. .s . . . .
 . . . . .WS Jul 34 194
Sublime Vigil, The. .s . . . .
 . . . . WS Feb 34 698

D

DALE, GEORGE E. *pseud of ISAAC
 ASIMOV*
PROBABILITY ZERO
Time Pussy. .ss . . . .
 . . . . ASF Apr 42 113
DALY, HAMLIN *pseud of E.
 HOFFMAN PRICE*
DANE, CLEMENCE
Third person Singular. .nt . . . . . .
 . . . . FFM Oct 46 64
DANIELS, DAVID R.
Branches of Time, The. .s . . . . . .
 . . . . WS Aug 35 294
Death Cloud. .nt . . . ASF Feb 36 46
Far Way, The. .s . . . ASF Jul 35 119
Into the Depths. .s . . . .
 . . . . .ASF Jun 35 146
Stars. .s . . . . ASF May 35 37
Way of the Earth, The. .nt . . . . . .
 . . . . .ASF Oct 35 136
DANIELS, J. STALLWORTH
Horrible Transformation, The . . .
 . .s . . . . SW May 30 1130
DANIELS, NORMAN A.
Biog sketch, photo. . . . .
 . . . . .SS Mar 43 128
Great Ego, The. .n . . . .SS Spr 44 11
Lady is a Witch, The. .n . . . .
 . . . . .SS Mar 50 11
Road Beyond, The. .s . . . .
 . . . . .UK Aug 41 81
Speak of the Devil. .n . . . .
 . . . . .SS Mar 43 15
DANNER, WILLIAM M.
PROBABILITY ZERO
True Fidelity. .ss . . . .
 . . . . ASF Dec 42 104
DANZELL, GEORGE *pseud of
 NELSON S. BOND*
Castaway, The. .s . . . .
 . . . . .PS Win 40 36

AUTHOR
 Title. .Length . . . . Magazine, Date, Page

DARE, JOHN C.
Cosmic Power. .s . . . Amz Apr 31 28
DAVIDSON, GENE A. *pseud of
 DAVID LESPERANCE*
DAVIDSON, HUGH *pseud of
 EDMOND HAMILTON*
DAVIES, HOWELL See pseud
 ANDREW MARVELL (1)
DAVIES, LINTON
War-Lords of the Moon. .s . . . . . .
 . . . . .PS Win 39 81
DAVIES, WALTER C. *pseud of
 CYRIL KORNBLUTH*
Forgotten Tongue. .s . . . .
 . . . . .Sti Jun 41 23
Interference. .s . . . . . Cos Jul 41 35
New Directions. .a . . . .
 . . . . .Cos Mar 41 122
DAVIS, BOB
WEIRD TRAVEL TALES
 1. A Chat with the Skipper
 Concerning Clairvoyance. . . .
 . .ss. . . . . FFM Jan 40 78
 2. Tragic Fate of Those Who
 Sought the Lost Lemon
 Mine. .ss . . . . . FFM Apr 40 64
DAVIS, CHAN
Aristocrat, The. .nt . . . .
 . . . . ASF Oct 49 6
Journey and the Goal, The .s . . . .
 . . . . ASF May 47 99
Letter to Ellen. .s . . . .
 . . . . ASF Jun 47 42
Nightmare, The. .s . . . .
 . . . . .ASF May 46 7
To Still the Drums. .s . . . .
 . . . . .ASF Oct 46 159
DAVIS, CHARLES BEN
PROBABILITY ZERO
You Said It. .ss . . . .
 . . . . .ASF Sep 43 100
DAVIS, CHARLES H.
Who Goes There? . .s . . . .
 . . . . .PS Spr 50 53
DAWSON, PETER *pseud of
 FREDERICK FAUST*
DE CAMP L.(YON) SPRAGUE *See
 also pseuds LYMAN R. LYON (1),
 J. WELLINGTON WELLS (0)*
Ananias. .s . . . . . .DS Apr–May 39 68
Animal-Cracker Plot, The. .s . . . .
 . . . . .ASF Jul 49 67
Asokore Power. .s . . . .
 . . . . .SSS Nov 40 26
Best-Laid Scheme, The. .s . . . . . .
 . . . . ASF Feb 41 107

AUTHOR
  Title. .Length .s . . . Magazine, Date, Page

BLACK, JOHNNY series includes:
  THE COMMAND
  THE INCORRIGIBLE
  THE EMANCIPATED
  THE EXHALTED
Blue Giraffe, The. .s . . . .
  . . . . ASF Aug 39 113
Colorful Character, The. .s . . . . .
  . . . . TW Dec 49 133
Command, The. .s . . . .
  . . . . ASF Oct 38 70
Contraband Cow, The. .s. . . . . . .
  . . . . .ASF Jul 42 38
Design for Life. .a 2 pt . . . .
  . . . . ASF May 39 103
Divide and Rule. .n 2 pt . . . .
  . . . . UK Apr 39 125
Emancipated, The. .s . . . .
  . . . . ASF Mar 40 50
Exhalted, The. .s . . . ASF Nov 40 64
Finished. .s. . . . . ASF Nov 49 146
Get Out and Get Under . . . .
  . .a 2 pt . . . . ASF Dec 42 76
Ghosts of Melvin Pye, The. . . . .
  .s . . . . TW Dec 46 66
Git Along! . .s. . . . . ASF Aug 50 61
Gnarly Man, The. .s . . . .
  . . . . UK Jun 39 97
Great Floods, The. .a . . . .
  . . . . .ASF Oct 49 112
Hand of Zei, The. .n 4 pt . . . . . .
  . . . . ASF Oct 50 6
Hardwood Pile, The. .nt . . . .
  . . . . UK Sep 40 100
Hibited Man, The. .s. . . . .
  . . . . TW Oct 49 42
Hyperpilosity. .s . . . ASF Apr 38 39
Incorrigible, The. .s . . . .
  . . . . .ASF Jan 39 82
Inspector's Teeth, The. .s . . . . . .
  . . . . ASF Apr 50 104
Invaders from Nowhere. .nt. . . . .
  . . . . .SSS Aug 41 71
Isolinguals, The. .s . . . .
  . . . . .ASF Sep 37 108
Juice. .s . . . . SSS May 40 62
Justinian Jugg's Patent. .a . . . . . .
  . . . . ASF Dec 40 68
Lands of Yesterday. .a . . . .
  . . . . GSF Nov 50 48
Language for Time
  Travelers. .a . . . . . ASF Jul 38 63
Lest Darkness Fall. .n . . . .
  . . . . .UK Dec 39 9
Living Fossil. .s . . . . ASF Feb 39 33
Long Tailed Huns, The . . . .
  . .a 2 pt . . . . .ASF Jan 42 86

AUTHOR
  Title. .Length . . . . Magazine, Date, Page

Mayan Elephants, The. .a . . . . . .
  . . . . ASF Jun 50 85
Merman, The. .s . . . .
  . . . . ASF Dec 38 80
Mr. Arson. .s. . . . .
  . . . . UK Dec 41 116
Nothing in the Rules. .nt. . . . . . .
  . . . . .UK Jul 39 89
               UK 48 36
PROBABILITY ZERO
  Some Curious Effects of Time
  Travel. .ss. . . . . ASF Apr 42 111
  The Anecdote of the Negative
  Wugug. .ss . . . . ASF Aug 42 101
  The Anecdote of the Movable
  Ears. .ss. . . . . . ASF Feb 43 91
  Queen of Zamba, The. . . . . . .
  . . n 2 pt . . . . . . ASF Aug 49 6
  Reluctant Shaman, The. .s. . . . .
  . . . . TW Apr 47 90
  Sea King's Armored Division,
  The. .a 2 pt . . . . ASF Sep 41 46
  Science of Whithering, The . . . .
  . .a 2 pt . . . . . . ASF Jul 40 108
  Solomon's Stone. .n. . . . .
  . . . . UK Jun 42 8
  Space Suit, The. .a . . . .
  . . . . ASF Mar 48 108
  Stolen Dormouse, The . . . .
  . .n 2 pt . . . . ASF Apr 41 9
  Summer Wear. .s . . . .
  . . . . SS May 50 127
  There Ain't No Such! . . . .
  . .a 2 pt . . . . . . ASF Nov 39 92
  Throwback. .s. . . . .
  . . . . ASF Mar 49 48
  Undesired Princess. .n. . . . . . .
  . . . . .UK Feb 42 7
  Warrior Race, The . . . .
  . .s . . . . .ASF Oct 40 136
  Wheels of If, The. .n. . . . .
  . . . . UK Oct 40 9
  Why Do They Do It? . . . .
  . .a . . . . .ASF Sep 50 121
  Wide-Open Planet. .nt. . . . . . .
  . . . . .Fut Sep–Oct 50 8
  Wisdom of the East . . . .
  . .s . . . . UK Aug 42 90
with H. L. GOLD
None But Lucifer. .n . . . .
  . . . . UK Sep 39 9
with L. RON HUBBARD
Last Drop, The. .s . . . .
  . . . . .Ash Nov 41 87
with P. SCHUYLER MILLER
Genus Homo. .n . . . . .SSS Mar 41 8

AUTHOR
  Title. .Length . . . . Magazine, Date, Page

with FLETCHER PRATT
Castle of Iron, The. .n . . . .
  . . . . .UK Apr 41 9
GAVAGAN'S BAR
  1. Elephas Frumenti. .s . . . . . .
  2. The Gift of God. .s . . . . . .
  . . . . F&SF Win–Spr 50 95
  The Better Mousetrap. .s. . . . . .
  . . . . F&SF Dec 50 27
Land of Unreason, The. .n. . . . . .
  . . . . UK Oct 41 8
"MATHEMATICS OF MAGIC"
  series includes:
  THE ROARING TRUMPET
  THE MATHEMATICS OF MAGIC
  THE CASTLE OF IRON
Mathematics of Magic, The . . . . .
  . .n . . . . .UK Aug 40 9
Roaring Trumpet, The. .n . . . . . .
  . . . . .UK May 40 9
DE COURCY, JOHN and DOROTHY
  (Mr. & Mrs. John de Courcy)
Alchemy. .s . . . . .OTWA Dec 50 83
Captain Ham. .s. . . . . OW Oct 50 36
Chess and Double Chess. .s . . . . .
  . . . . Amz Mar 47 40
Come Into My Garden. .s . . . . . .
  . . . . FA Nov 47 84
Devil to Pay, The. .s. . . . .
  . . . . FA Dec 47 72
Don't Mention It. .s . . . .
  . . . . Amz May 46 134
Evensong. .s . . . . . . .FA Jan 48 112
Golden Mask of Agharti, The. . . .
  . .nt . . . . FA Jan 50 86
Goma's Follicles. .s . . . .
  . . . . PS Sum 48 86
Man from Agharti, The. .n. . . . . .
  . . . . .Amz Jul 48 8
Man Who Went Nowhere,
  The. .s. . . . . Amz Nov 46 102
Miracle Man. .nt . . . Amz Apr 47 46
Morton's Fork. .nt. . . . .
  . . . . Amz Sep 46 116
Night Has a Thousand Eyes,
  The. .s. . . . . .PS Win 49 42
Once To Die. .s . . . . FA Sep 47 126
Rat Race. .s . . . . .SS Sep 48 72
Some Are Not Men. .nt. . . . .
  . . . . Amz Aug 46 102
Traitor to War. .s. . . . .
  . . . . Amz Aug 49 76
DEE, ROGER *pseud of ROGER D.*
  AYCOCK
Last Return. .s . . . . . SSS Jul 50 62
Slave of Eternity. .s . . . .
  . . . . SSS May 50 84

AUTHOR
Title. .Length . . . . Magazine, Date, Page

Ultimatum. .s . . . . . . .PS Spr 50 98
Unwelcome Tenant. .ss . . . .
. . . . .PS Sum 50 96
Wheel Is Death, The. .ss . . . .
. . . . .PS Fal 49 75
DEEGAN, FRANCES M.
Cat-Snake, The. .s . . . FA Apr 48 66
Gallery of Glacial Doom. .s . . . . .
. . . . Amz Dec 45 146
Keep It Simple. .s . . . .
. . . . Amz May 50 104
Little Drops of Water. .s . . . .
. . . . Amz Feb 46 132
Martian and the Milkmaid. .s . . . .
. . . . FA Oct 44 136
Moon Pirates, The. .s . . . .
. . . . Amz Jun 50 106
Radiant Rock, The. .s. . . . .
. . . . Amz Jun 45 100
Shouldn't Happen to a Dog . . . .
. .s . . . . FA Aug 50 126
Something for Herbert. .s . . . . . .
. . . . Amz Sep 45 96
Third Bolt, The. .s . . . .
. . . . Amz Oct 47 24
Wizard of Blue Gap, The. . . . . .
. .s . . . . FA Dec 50 104
DEEPING, WARWICK
Man Who Went Back, The . . . . .
. .n . . . . .FFM Dec 47 6
deFORD, MIRIAM ALLEN
Last Generation, The. .s . . . .
. . . . F&SF Win–Spr 50 50
deGRAEFF, W. B. pseud of GROFF
CONKLIN
Congress Is Too Busy (for the
Atom). .a . . . . . .ASF Sep 46 100
de KOVEN, WILLIAM
Bighead. .nt . . . . . . NW Win 50 52
DeKY, THORNTON
Ultimate Experiment, The. . . . . .
. .ss. . . . . .Com Jul 41 120
DE LISLE, WILLIAM
Degenerate Mr. Smith, The . . . . .
. .s . . . . Amz Aug 43 138
When the Darkness Came . . . . . .
. .nt . . . . Amz Sep 43 8
DEL REY, LESTER (R. ALVAREZ
del Rey) See pseud PHILIP
ST. JOHN (B) ERIC VAN
LHYN (0)
Coopersmith, The. .s . . . .
. . . . UK Sep 39 110
Dark Mission. .s. . . . ASF Jul 40 117
Day Is Done, The. .s . . . .
. . . . ASF May 39 39

Doubled in Brass. .s . . . .
. . . . UK Jan 40 107
Faithful, The. .s . . . ASF Apr 38 78
Forsaking All Others. .s . . . .
. . . . .UK Aug 39 89
Habit. .s. . . . . . . ASF Nov 39 119
Helen O'Loy. .s . . . .
. . . . ASF Dec 38 118
Hereafter, Inc. . .s . . . .
. . . . UK Dec 41 106
Imitation of Death. .s . . . .
. . . . Fut May–Jun 50 76
Into Thy Hands. .nt. . . . .
. . . . ASF Aug 45 47
Kindness. .s . . . . . ASF Oct 44 80
Luck of Ignatz, The. .nt . . . . . .
. . . . .ASF Aug 39 9
Lunar Landing. .nt. . . . .
. . . . ASF Oct 42 9
My Name Is Legion. .s . . . .
. . . . ASF Jun 42 69
Nerves. .n. . . . . . . ASF Sep 42 54
No Head for My Bier. .s . . . .
. . . . FA Sep 50 94
Omega and the Wolf Girl. . . . . . .
. .s . . . . OTWA Jul 50 30
Over the Top. .s . . . .
. . . . ASF Nov 49 41
Pipes of Pan, The. .s. . . . .
. . . . .UK May 40 110
Reincarnate. .nt . . . .
. . . . ASF Apr 40 100
Shadows of Empire. .s . . . .
. . . . F&SF Jul–Aug 50 57
Smallest God, The. .nt . . . .
. . . . .ASF Jan 40 43
Stars Look Down, The. .nt . . . . .
. . . . .ASF Aug 40 9
Though Dreamers Die. .s . . . .
. . . . ASF Feb 44 34
Though Poppies Grow. .nt. . . . . .
. . . . UK Aug 42 115
When the World Tottered. .n . . . .
. . . . FA Dec 50 6
Whom the Gods Love. .s . . . .
. . . . ASF Jun 43 60
Wings of Night, The. .s . . . .
. . . . ASF Mar 42 46
DE MAUPASSANT, GUY
Horla, The. .s . . . . FFM Sep 42 129
DE MEXICO, N. R.
Devil's Fiddle, The. .s . . . .
. . . . TW Jun 43 58
DENHOLM, MARK
Solar Assignment. .s . . . .
. . . . .NW #1 46 23

AUTHOR
Title. .Length . . . . Magazine, Date, Page

DENNIS artist
Cover for NEW WORLDS
#4 1949
DENNIS, BRUCE pseud of DAVID
WRIGHT O'BRIEN
Incredible Antique, The. .nt . . . .
. . . . FA Dec 42 126
Where in the Warehouse. .s . . . . .
. . . . FA Apr 43 50
with GERALD VANCE pseud
Giant from Jupiter, The. .nt . . . .
. . . . FA Jun 42 8
DENNIS, WALTER See also pseud
DENNIS McDERMOTT
with ERNEST TUCKER
Gladiators, The. .s . . . .
. . . . SS Jan 43 106
DE PINA, ALBERT
Keeper of the Deathless
Sleep. .nt . . . . .PS Win 44 36
Minions of the Crystal
Sphere. .nt . . . . PS Sum 44 2
Moon of Danger. .nt. . . . .
. . . . PS Sum 47 46
Priestess of Pakmari. .s . . . .
. . . . .TW Sum 44 64
Silver Plague, The. .nt. . . . .
. . . . .PS Spr 45 48
Star Guardsman, The. .nt . . . . . .
. . . . .PS Win 43 86
with HENRY HASSE
Alcatraz of the Starways. .nt . . . .
. . . . PS May 43 2
Star of Panadur. .s . . . .
. . . . .PS Mar 43 65
DE RESZKE, EUGENE
Clasp of Doom, The. .s . . . .
. . . . AD Oct 30 870
Painted Murder, The. .s. . . . .
. . . . AD Aug 30 678
DE RICHTER, CHARLES
Fall of the Eiffel Tower, The (tr fr
French by Fletcher Pratt) . . . . .
. .n 3 pt . . . . WS Sep 34 390
DERLETH, AUGUST (W.) See Also
pseud TALLY MASON (0)
Carousel. .s. . . . .
. . . . FA Apr 45 54
Fifth Child, The. .s . . . .
. . . . FA Sep 50 126
Headlines for Tod Shane. .s . . . . .
. . . . .FA Jul 42 222
Island Out of Space, The. .s. . . . .
. . . . Amz Jun 50 166
Lonesome Place, The. .s . . . .
. . . . FFM Feb 48 114

AUTHOR
  Title..Length . . . . Magazine, Date, Page

Mr. Ames' Devil. .s. . . . .
. . . . FA Aug 42 80
Mrs. Corter Makes Up Her
  Mind. .s. . . . . . . .FA May 42 216
Room in a House, A. .s. . . . . . .
. . . . .F&SF Fal 50 44
Shuttered House, The. .s. . . . . . .
. . . . .AFR #1 45
Thing That Walked on the Wind,
  The. .s. . . . . AFR #13 74
DERREAUX, GASTON
  Flame Queen, The. .n. . . . .
. . . . .Amz May 49 8
  Sun King, The. .s. . . Amz Apr 49 52
DE SOTO *artist*
  Cover for FAMOUS FANTASTIC
      MYSTERIES
    Oct 1950
  Cover for FANTASTIC NOVELS
    Nov 1950
DEUTSCH, A. J.
  Subway Named Mobius, A . . . . .
. .s . . . . ASF Dec 50 72
DE VET, CHARLES V.
  I Take This Earthman. .s. . . . . . .
. . . . FA Nov 50 84
  Unexpected Weapon, The . . . . . .
. .s . . . . Amz Sep 50 50
DEXTER, MARTIN *pseud of*
      FREDERICK FAUST
DEXTER, PETER *pseud of*
      RICHARD S. SHAVER
  Gamin, The. .nt. . . . .OW Mar 50 68
  Palace of Darkness. .nt . . . .
. . . . OW Sep 50 54
DICKINSON, H. O.
  Giant Bacillus, The. .nt. . . . . . .
. . . . .ToW Sum 38 74
  Sex Serum, The. .s. . . . .
. . . . WS Oct 35 588
DICKSON, GORDON
  with POUL ANDERSON
  Trespass! . .s. . . . . .FSQ Spr 50 131
DIFFIN, CHARLES WILLARD *See*
    pseud C. D. WILLARD
  Blue Magic. .n 4 pt. . . . .
. . . . ASF Nov 35 76
  Brood of the Dark Moon. . . . . . .
. .n 4 pt. . . . . . . ASF Aug 31 168
  Dark Moon. .nt . . . .
. . . . ASF May 31 148
  Finding of Haldgren, The . . . . . .
. .nt . . . . ASF Apr 32 20
  Hammer of Thor, The. .s. . . . . . .
. . . . ASF Mar 32 358

AUTHOR
  Title..Length . . . . Magazine, Date, Page

Holocaust. .s. . . . . .ASF Jun 31 356
Land of the Lost. .n 2 pt. . . . . . .
. . . . ASF Dec 33 2
Long Night, The. .nt . . . .
. . . . ASF May 34 129
Moon Master, The. .nt . . . .
. . . . .ASF Jun 30 384
Pirate Planet, The. .n 4 pt . . . . . .
. . . . ASF Nov 30 168
Power and the Glory, The . . . . .
. .s . . . . ASF Jul 30 104
                        AFR #13 57
Spawn of the Stars. .s. . . . .
. . . . ASF Feb 30 166
Two Thousand Miles Below. . . . .
. . .n 4 pt. . . . . . .ASF Jun 32 311
When the Mountain Came to
  Miramar. .s. . . . . ASF Mar 31 297
DIRK, R. K.
  Happy to Die. .s . . . .
. . . . FA Feb 49 104
  On the Back of a Beetle. .nt. . . . .
. . . . .FA May 49 82
DOANE, WARREN F.
  Alchemy of Ian Bjornsen,
    The. .s. . . . . . . .Amz Jan 34 115
DOCKWEILER, JOSEPH HAROLD
  "HARRY" *See DIRK WYLIE &*
    PAUL DENNIS LAVOND (4)
DOLD, DOUGLAS M.
  Valley of Sin. .n . . . .
. . . . Mir Apr–May 31 10
DOLD, (WILLIAM) ELLIOTT (JR.)
  artist and author
  Cover for COSMIC STORIES
    Jul 1941
  Covers for MIRACLE SCIENCE
    AND FANTASY STORIES
    Apr–May, Jun–Jul 1931
  Bowl of Death, The. .n . . . .
. . . . .Mir Jun–Jul 31 154
DOMINIK, H.
  Airports for World Traffic *(tr fr*
    the German by Francis W.
    Currier). .a. . . . . . AW Jan 30 610
DOMITZ, HAROLD
  Visitor from the Twentieth Century,
    A. .s . . . . Amz May 28 170
DORNISCH, ALCUIN
  Solarius. .ss . . . . . Amz Dec 32 802
DOUGHTY, DON J.
  Adoption. .s . . . . . . NW Spr 50 38
DOUGLAS, NORMAN
  Unnatural Feud, An. .s . . . .
. . . . FFM Apr 42 110

AUTHOR
  Title..Length . . . . Magazine, Date, Page

DOUGLAS, WILLIAM WITHERS
  Ice Man, The. .s. . . . .
. . . . Amz Feb 30 1020
DOW, PACKARD
  Winged Menace, The. .s. . . . . . .
. . . . WQ Spr 31 416
DOWD, CONSTANCE R.
  First Hundred Years You Get
    Nowhere, The. .a. . . . .
. . . . Amz Mar 184
DOWNIE, J. VALE
  Tombi Sink. .s . . . . . UK Aug 40 84
DOYLE, (Sir) A.(rthur) CONAN
  Horror of the Heights, The. .s . . .
. . . . FFM Dec 47 108
DRAGONETTE, REE (Rita
    Drayanette)
  Eye to the Future. .s . . . .
. . . . ASF Feb 47 51
DRAKE, A. *artist*
  Covers for PLANET STORIES
    Win 1939
    Sum 1940
DRENNAN, PAUL
  Head Hunters Fooled and
    Foiled. .s . . . . . Amz Aug 33 410
DRESSLER, DR. DANIEL
  Brain Accelerator, The. .s . . . . . .
. . . . Amz Nov 29 696
  White Army, The. .s. . . . .
. . . . Amz Sep 29 528
DREW, DOUGLAS
  Carbon Eater, The. .nt . . . .
. . . . ASF Jun 40 51
  Nightmare Island. .nt . . . .
. . . . ASF Oct 36 98
DREXEL, JAY B. *pseud of JEROME*
    BIXBY
  Cargo to Callisto. .s . . . .
. . . . PS Nov 50 37
  Crowded Colony, The. .s. . . . . . .
. . . . PS Fal 50 36
DRIGIN, S. R. *artist*
  Covers for FANTASY
    #1 1938
    #2, #3 1939
DRYFOOS, DAVE
  "Lest Ye Be Judged. . ." . .s . . . .
. . . . FA Oct 50 98
DU BOIS, THEODORA
  Devil's Spoon, The. .n . . . .
. . . . .FFM Jun 48 8

AUTHOR
  Title. .Length . . . . Magazine, Date, Page

DUCLOS, MAURICE
  Biog sketch . . . . . . .FA May 39 86
  Into Another Dimension. .s. . . . .
    . . . . FA Nov 39 42
  Sabotage on Mars. .nt. . . . .
    . . . . FA Jun 40 70
  Sleeping Goddess, The. .s . . . . . .
    . . . . .FA May 39 44
  Spawn of the Ray. .s . . . .
    . . . . Amz Feb 38 55
DUFFIN, HOWARD M. *artist*
  Atomic Power Plant. . . . .
    . .bacover. . . . . Amz Oct 39
  Evolution Gone Mad . . . .
    . .bacover. . . . .s. . . . Amz Feb 40
DUGAN, ARTHUR
  Bacterial Time Bomb. .a . . . .
    . . . . ASF Dec 49 93
  Case of the Missing Octane,
    The. .a. . . . . . . ASF Mar 49 102
DUNKELBERGER, WALT
  Biog sketch . . . . . . .PS Spr 46 47
DUNN, H. H.
  Test Tube Bloodhounds. .s . . . . .
    . . . . SD Mar 30 232
  Traced by a Scratch. .s . . . .
    . . . . .AD Jul 30 599
DUNN, J. ALLAN
  On the Knees of the Gods . . . . . .
    . .n 3 pt . . . . UK Jan 40 132
  Right Ear of Malchus, The. . . . . .
    . .s . . . . UK Jun 39 67
DUNSANY, LORD (Edward John
    Morton Drax Plunkett, Baron
    Dunsany)
  MASTERS OF FANTASY
  biog . . . . FFM Jun 49 113
  Hashish Man, The. .s . . . .
    . . . . FFM Dec 45 108
  Highwayman, The. .s . . . .
    . . . . FFM Dec 44 116
  Hoard of the Gibbelins, The . . .
    . .ss. . . . . .AFR #4 62
  Madness of Andelsprutz,
    The. .ss . . . . AFR #9 118
  Postman of Otford, The. .ss . . .
    . . . . FFM Sep 44 108
  Slugly Beast, The. .s. . . . .
    . . . . .AFR #7 54
  Three Infernal Jokes, The . . . .
    . .s . . . . AFR #1 125
  Wonderful Window, The. .ss . . .
    . . . . .AFR #12 80
DUTHIE, JOHN
  Electrolytic Onslaught. .s . . . . . .
    . . . . ASF Jun 35 98

DUTTON, PATRICK
  Beautiful Bacillus, The. .s . . . . . .
    . . . . Amz Jun 31 262
DWYER, JAMES FRANCIS
  Cave of the Invisible, The. .s . . . .
    . . . . .AFR #14 40
DYE, CHARLES
  Last Orbit, The. .s . . . .
    . . . . Amz Feb 50 68
DYE, GEORGE A.
  Mystery of Planet Deep, The . . . .
    . .s . . . . WS Aug 33 102

E

EADIE, MARION F.
  Beast of the Crater. .s. . . . .
    . . . . ToW Spr 42 41
EASTON, NORMA LAZELL
  Avenger, The. .nt. . . . .
    . . . . Amz Nov 49 116
EATON, BURNHAM
  Three, The. .p. . . . FFM Aug 49 116
EBEL, FRED
  Man No One Could Lift, The. . . .
    . .s . . . . AD Oct 30 916
EBERLE, MERAB
  Mordant, The. .s . . . .
    . . . . Amz Mar 30 1181
ECHOLS, ALLAN K.
  Island of Doctor X, The. .nt . . . .
    . . . . TW Dec 36 90
  Love's Lethal Ingredient. .s . . . . .
    . . . . MSS Dec 39 59
EDDINGTON, SIR ARTHUR S.
  Eclipses of the Sun. .a . . . .
    . . . . TW Apr 38 32
EDHOLM, CHARLTON L.
  Ping-Ting. .s . . . . .ASF Oct 33 122
EDMONDS, PAUL *pseud of HENRY
    KUTTNER*
  Improbability. .s . . . . Ash Jun 40 74
  Lifestone, The. .s. . . ASF Feb 40 70
  Mad Virus, The. .s . . . SF Jul 40 29
  Night of Gods. .nt . . .Ash Dec 42 11
  Telepathy Is News. .s . . . .
    . . . . .SF Jun 39 89
  Tree of Life, The. .s . . . .
    . . . . .Ash Sep 41 44
EDWARDS, DOLTON
  Meihem In Ce Clasrum. .a . . . . . .
    . . . . ASF Sep 46 94
EDWARDS, D. M.
  Spheres. .nt . . . . . ASF Dec 40 44

EDWARDS, GAWAIN *pseud of G.
    EDWARDS PENDRAY*
  Mutiny in Space, The. .nt . . . . . .
    . . . . WS Sep 31 500
  . .nt 2 pt . . . . CF Win 41 101
  Rescue from Jupiter, A. . . . .
    . .n 2 pt. . . . . . . SW Feb 30 774
  Return from Jupiter, The . . . . . .
    . .n 2 pt . . . . . . WS Mar 31 1062
EDWARDS, GEORGE
  Biog sketch, photo. . . . .
    . . . . .TW Aug 43 78
  Amnesiac, The. .s . . . .
    . . . . .TW Aug 43 78
EDWARDS, JOHN
  Masters of the Earth. .nt . . . .
    . . . . Amz Jun 32 200
  Menace from Space, The. .nt . . . .
    . . . . WS Apr 34 980
                        ToW Aut 38 4
  Planet of Perpetual Night,
    The. .nt . . . . Amz Feb 37 15
  Universe of Babel. .s . . . .
    . . . . ToW Win 38 33
ELDON, CLEO *pseud of DON
    WILCOX*
  Sapphire Enchantress. .nt . . . . . .
    . . . . FA Dec 45 84
ELLERMAN, GENE *pseud of BASIL
    WELLS*
  Crusader. .s . . . . FB #5 67
  Prison Rats. .ss . . . . . . FB #4 39
  Raiders of the Second Moon . . . .
    . .s . . . . PS Sum 45 43
  World of Misers. .s . . . . FB #6 103
ELLIOTT, FRANCIS
  Biog sketch . . . . . . PS Sum 44 57
ELLIS, CRAIG *house pseud*
  by LEE ROGOW
  Dr. Varsag's Experiments. .s . . . .
    . . . . .Amz Jan 40 112
  by DAVID VERN
  Dr. Varsag's Second Experiment . .
    . .n . . . . Amz Aug 43 76
ELLIS, SOPHIE WENZEL
  Creatures of the Light. .s . . . . . .
    .ASF Feb 30 196
  Shadow World, The. .s . . . .
    . . . . Amz Dec 32 824
  Slaves of the Dust. .s . . . .
    . . . . ASF Dec 30 295
ELSTAR, DOW *pseud of RAYMOND
    Z. GALLUN*
  Avalanche. .s . . . . ASF Dec 35 109
  Second Cataclysm, The. .s . . . . . .
    . . . . ASF Mar 37 94

AUTHOR
  Title. .Length . . . . Magazine, Date, Page

  Something from Jupiter. .nt . . . .
  . . . . ASF Mar 38 6
  Thunder Voice. .s . . . .
  . . . . ASF Feb 38 142
with ROBERT S. McREADY
  Stardust Gods. .nt . . . .
  . . . . .ASF Oct 37 122
EMANUEL, VICTOR ROUSSEAU
  See pseuds VICTOR ROUSSEA
  (11), CLIVE TRENT (0)
EMERSON, HARVEY
  Biog sketch . . . . Amz Oct 38 142
  Artificial Hell. .s . . . .
  . . . . Amz Oct 38 96
ENDERSBY, VICTOR A.
  After 5000 Years. .s. . . . .
  . . . . .WS Jul 30 136
  Day of Judgement, The. .ss . . . .
  . . . . SW Apr 30 1015
  Disowned. .s. . . . . ASF Sep 32 20
  Gimlet, The. .s . . . .
  . . . . Amz May 30 140
  Job of Blending, A. .ss . . . .
  . . . . Amz Mar 34 124
  When the Top Wobbled. .nt. . . . .
  . . . . Amz Feb 36 78
ENDORE, GUY
  Day of the Dragon, The. .nt . . . .
  . . . . .AFR #2 50
  Men of Iron. .s . . . .F&SF Fal 49 80
ENFERD, KNUT
  Day of the Druid. .s . . . .
  . . . . Amz Nov 48 126
ENGELHARDT, FREDERICK
  General Swamp, C. L. C. . . . . . .
  . .n 2 pt . . . . ASF Aug 39 41
  History Class, 2133 A. D. . . . . .
  . .s . . . . TW Jan 41 111
  Kraken, The. .s . . . . . UK Jun 40 82
  This Ship Kills. .s. . . . .
  . . . . ASF Nov 39 107
  Vanderdecken. .s. . . . UK Dec 39 96
ENGLAND, GEORGE ALLAN
  Biog sketch . . . . . .FFM Aug 40 79
  Afterglow. .n . . . . . .FFM Dec 41 6
  Beyond the Great Oblivion . . . . .
  . .n . . . . .FFM Jun 41 6
"DARKNESS AND DAWN" trilogy
  includes:
  DARKNESS AND DAWN
  BEYOND THE GREAT OBLIVION
  AFTERGLOW
  Darkness and Dawn. .n. . . . .
  . . . . .FFM Aug 40 6
  Elixier of Hate, The. .n. . . . .
  . . . . FFM Oct 42 6
  AMF Oct 50 10

AUTHOR
  Title. .Length . . . . Magazine, Date, Page

  Flying Legion, The. .n 4 pt . . . . .
  . . . . AW Jan 30 582
  FN Jan 50 8
  Golden Blight, The. .n . . . .
  . . . . FN Mar 49 10
  Man With the Glass Heart,
  The. .s. . . . . . .FFM Nov 39 75
  Thing from Outside, The. .s. . . .
  . . . . Amz Apr 26 67
ENGLAND, GORDON PHILIP
  They Buried Her Body. .s . . . . . .
  . . . . FA Feb 48 152
EPPERLY, R. E. *artist*
  Cover for FANTASTIC
  ADVENTURES
  Apr 1945
ERMAN, JACQUES DeFOREST
  pseud of FORREST J.
  ACKERMAN
with WILFRED OWEN MORLEY
  pseud (R. W. Lowndes)
  Dhactwhu!—Remember? .s . . . .
  . . . . .SSS Apr 49 84
ERNST, PAUL
  Death Dives Deep. .nt. . . . .
  . . . . TW Aug 36 94
  From the Wells of the Brain. . . .
  . .s . . . . ASF Oct 33 48
  Hidden In Glass. .s. . . . .
  . . . . Amz Apr 31 58
  Incredible Formula, The. .s . . . .
  . . . . Amz Jun 31 218
  Invincible Midge, The. .s . . . . . .
  . . . . TW Apr 37 32
  FSQ Fal 50 87
  Marooned Under the Sea. .nt . . . .
  . . . . .ASF Sep 30 346
  Microscopic Giants, The. .s . . . . .
  . . . . TW Oct 36 78
  SS May 48 108
  Mind Magnet, The. .s . . . .
  . . . . TW Dec 37 74
  Nothing Happens on the
  Moon. .s . . . . . . ASF Feb 39 97
  Planetoid of Peril, The. .s . . . . . .
  . . . . ASF Nov 31 151
  Protoplasmic Station. .nt . . . . . .
  . . . . TW Feb 37 14
  Radiant Shell, The. .s . . . .
  . . . . .ASF Jan 31 120
  Raid on the Termites, The. . . . . .
  . .nt . . . . .ASF Jun 32 354
  Red Hell of Jupiter, The. .nt . . . .
  . . . . ASF Oct 31 70
  Rift in Infinity. .s . . . .
  . . . . TW Aug 37 96

AUTHOR
  Title. .Length . . . . Magazine, Date, Page

  Stolen Element, The. .s. . . . . . .
  . . . . .ASF Sep 34 107
  Terror in Utopia. .s . . . .
  . . . . TW Jun 38 106
  Thing in the Pond, The. .s . . . . . .
  . . . . ASF Jun 34 48
  32nd of May, The. .s . . . .
  . . . . ASF Apr 35 110
  World Behind the Moon, The. . . .
  . .s . . . . ASF Apr 31 64
ESCHBACH, LLOYD ARTHUR
  (alternate spelling; see L. A.
  ESHBACH)
ESHBACH (ESCHBACH), L.(LOYD
  A.(RTHUR)
  Brain of Ali Kahn, The. .s . . . . . .
  . . . . WS Oct 34 556
  Dust. .s . . . . MSS Aug 39 91
  God of Light. .s. . . . .
  . . . . .TW Sum 44 93
  God That Science Made, The . . . .
  . .s . . . . SF Aug 39 86
  Gray Plague, The. .s. . . . .
  . . . . ASF Nov 30 210
  Hyper Sense, The. .s. . . . .
  . . . . SS Jan 41 85
  Invisible Destroyer, The. .s . . . . .
  . . . . .AW May 30 1004
  Kingdom of Thought, The. . . . . .
  . .nt . . . . Amz Aug 35 10
  Light from Infinity, The. .s . . . . .
  . . . . Amz Mar 32 1094
  Man With the Silver Disc,
  The. .s. . . . . . . SD Feb 30 128
  Meteor Miners, The. .s . . . .
  . . . . Amz Dec 35 15
  Mutineers of Space. .s. . . . .
  . . . . DS Feb 39 69
  Out of the Past. .s . . . .
  . . . . ToW Aut 38 31
  Out of the Sun. .s . . . . . . FB #4 52
  Outpost on Ceres, The. .s . . . . . .
  . . . . Amz Oct 36 121
  Overlord of Earth. .s . . . .
  . . . . MSS Nov 50 48
  Shadows from Hesplon, The . . . .
  . .nt . . . . SF Oct 40 8
  Three Wise Men. .s. . . SS Nov 39 92
  Time Conqueror, the. .s . . . .
  . . . . WS Jul 32 126
  Valley of Titans, The. .nt . . . . . .
  . . . . Amz Mar 31 1062
  Voice from the Ether, A. . . . . . .
  . .s . . . . Amz May 31 174
ESTES, O. G., JR.
  Little Johnny. .ss. . . . . . . FB #2 11

AUTHOR
Title. .Length . . . . Magazine, Date, Page

ETTINGER, R. C. W.
Penultimate Trump, The. .s . . . . .
. . . . .SS Mar 48 104
Skeptic, The. .s . . . . . TW Feb 50 85
EUSTACE, C. J.
Ten Days to Live. .s . . . .
. . . . .AQ Sum 28 418
EVAN, EVIN *pseud of*
FREDERICK FAUST
EVANS, DON
Last Hope, The. .nt . . . .
. . . . ASF Sep 39 45
Summons, The. .s . . . .
. . . . UK Jun 39 39
UK 48 123
EVANS, E. EVERETT
Blurb. .s. . . . . FB #3 27
Guaranteed. .ss . . . . .SS Jan 48 93
Little Miss Ignorance. .s . . . . .
. . . . OW Sep 50 40
EVANS, EVAN *pseud of*
FREDERICK FAUST
EVANS, GERALD
Pebbles of Dread. .s . . . .
. . . . TW Aug 40 51
Upward Bound. .s . . . TW Oct 40 82
EVANS, I. O.
Can We Conquer Space? . .a . . . . .
. . . . .ToW Sum 38 68
Can We Conquer Time? . .a . . . . .
. . . . .ToW Sum 40 56
EVANS, JOHN *pseud of HOWARD*
BROWNE

F

FABERS, DAN
Red Ray, The. .s . . . .
. . . . AQ Apr 30 278
FAIRMAN, PAUL W.
Broken Doll, The. .s. . . . .
. . . . .FA Jul 50 84
No Teeth for the Tiger. .s . . . . . .
. . . . Amz Feb 50 82
FALCONER, KENNETH *pseud of*
CYRIL KORNBLUTH
Masquerade. .s . . . . . Sti Mar 42 49
Words of Guru, The. .s . . . .
. . . . .Sti Jun 41 88
FARLEY, RALPH MILNE *pseud*
of ROGER SHERMAN HOAR
*B*iog sketch . . . . . Amz Aug 38 145
Biog sketch, photo. . . . .
. . . . TW Jun 39 88

Biog sketch, photo. . . . .
. . . . Amz Nov 39 134
Black Light. .s . . . . . ASF Aug 36 87
Conquest of the Impossible . . . . .
. .guest ed. . . . . . . SS Nov 39 89
Danger from the Deep, The . . . . .
. .s . . . . ASF Aug 31 149
Degravitator, The. .s . . . .
. . . . Amz Mar 32 1136
Flashlight Brigade, The. .s . . . . . .
. . . . AD Jun 30 504
Golden City, The. .n . . . .
. . . . .FFM Dec 42 6
Hidden Universe, The. . . . .
. .n 2 pt . . . . Amz Nov 39 24
Holy City of Mars. .nt . . . .
. . . . .FA May 42 78
Immortality of Alan
Whidden. .s . . . . Amz Feb 42 146
Liquid Life. .nt . . . . . TW Oct 36 60
Living Mist, The. .nt . . . .
. . . . Amz Aug 40 46
Month a Minute, A. .s. . . . .
. . . . TW Dec 37 14
Pe–Ra, Daughter of the Sun. . . . .
. .nt . . . . .Amz Jul 39 44
Radio Beasts, The. .n . . . .
. . . . FN Jan 41 6
"RADIO MAN" series includes:
THE RADIO MAN
THE RADIO BEASTS
THE RADIO PLANET
THE RADIO MAN RETURNS
Radio Man, The. .n 3 pt . . . .
. . . . FFM Dec 39 6
Radio Man Returns, The. . . . . . .
. .s . . . . Amz Jun 39 96
Radio Planet, The. .n . . . .
. . . . .FFM Apr 42 6
Rescue Into the Past. .s. . . . .
. . . . Amz Oct 40 34
Time Capsule, The. .s . . . .
. . . . .Ash Apr 41 26
Time for Sale. .s . . . .
. . . . Amz Aug 38 32
Time-Wise Guy, The. .s. . . . .
. . . . .Amz May 40 6
Vanishing Man, The. .s . . . .
. . . . AD Aug 30 706
with AL. P. NELSON
City of Lost Souls. .nt . . . .
. . . . .FA Jul 41 66
with STANLEY G. WEINBAUM
Revolution of 1950. .nt 2 pt . . . .
. . . . .n . . Amz Oct 38 106
Smothered Seas. .nt . . . .
. . . . ASF Jan 36 8

AUTHOR
Title. .Length . . . . Magazine, Date, Page

FARNSWORTH, DUNCAN *pseud of*
DAVID WRIGHT O'BRIEN
Afraid to Live. .s . . . . FA Mar 42 84
Cupid Takes a Holiday. .nt . . . . .
. . . . FA Jun 42 28
Flight from Farisha. .nt . . . .
. . . . Amz Nov 42 168
Genius of Mr. Pry, The. .s . . . . . .
. . . . FA Nov 41 112
Goddess of Love, The. .s . . . .
. . . . FA Oct 41 118
I'll See You Again. .s . . . .
. . . . Amz Sep 44 194
Lord of the Crystal Bow. .n . . . . .
. . . . .Amz May 42 8
Man Who Murdered Himself,
The. .s . . . . FA May 41 110
Mystery of the Mummy. .s . . . . .
. . . . Amz Sep 41 124
Outsiders, The. .nt. . . . .
. . . . FA Feb 42 88
Pepper Pot Planet. .s . . . .
. . . . Amz Jun 41 120
Problem on Mars. .s . . . .
. . . . FA Aug 41 64
Q Ship of Space. .s. . . . .
. . . . .Amz Jan 42 206
Rayhouse in Space. .s. . . . .
. . . . Amz Dec 41 82
Return of the Spacehawk. .s . . . .
. . . . Amz May 41 192
Suicide Ship to Earth. .s . . . .
. . . . Amz Feb 42 176
Twenty-Fifth Century
Sherlock. .s . . . . FA Mar 41 128
V is for Vengeance. .s . . . .
. . . . .FA Jan 42 102
FARNSWORTH, MONA
All Roads. .s . . . . . . UK Aug 40 118
Are You There? . .s . . . .
. . . . UK Nov 40 120
Joker, The. .s . . . . .UK Jul 39 115
Whatever. .s . . . . .UK May 39 97
Who Wants Power? . .s . . . .
. . . . UK Mar 39 95
FARNSWORTH, R. L.
First Target in Space. .a . . . .
. . . . .SS Sep 48 98
Rocket Target No. 2. .a . . . .
. . . . SS May 49 93
FARRELL, JOHN WADE *pseud of*
JOHN D. MacDONALD
All Our Yesterdays. .s . . . .
. . . . .SSS Apr 49 42
Sleepers, The. .s . . . .
. . . . .SSS Nov 49 96

AUTHOR
    Title. .Length . . . . Magazine, Date, Page

    Spin, Devil! ..s . . . .
    . . . . SSS Jan 50 81
FARRELL, JOSEPH
    Bard of Ceres, The. .s . . . .
    . . . . SS Spr 44 111
    Black-Out. .s . . . . . . .PS Win 43 57
    Hero, The. .s . . . . . ASF Oct 48 52
    Juke Box Asteroid. .s . . . .
    . . . . TW Spr 44 66
    Men Without a World. .s . . . .
    . . . . PS Fal 44 23
    Mind Stealers of Pluto. .s . . . . . .
    . . . . PS Win 44 2
    Secret Weapon. .s . . . SS Fal 44 114
FARRERE, CLAUDE
    House of the Secret, The (La Maison
    des Hommes Vivants). .n . . . . . .
    . . . . FFM Feb 46 66
FAST, HOWARD MELVIN
    Wrath of the Purple. .s . . . .
    . . . . Amz Oct 32 602
FAUST, FREDERICK See pseuds
    FRANK AUSTIN (0), GEORGE
    OWEN BAXTER (0), LEE BOLT
    (0), MAX BRAND (5), WALTER
    C. BUTLER (0), GEORGE
    CHALLIS (1), PETER DAWSON
    (0), MARTIN DEXTER (0),
    EVIN EVAN (0), EVAN EVANS
    (0), JOHN FREDERICK (0),
    FREDERICK FROST (0), DENNIS
    LAWTON (0), DAVID MANNING
    (0), PETER HENRY MORLAND
    (0), HUGH OWEN (0), NICHOLAS
    SILVER (0), HENRY URIEL (0).
    For complete listing of his works
    see MAX BRAND, THE MAN AND
    HIS WORK by Darrell C. Richard-
    son, Fantasy Pub. Co., Inc., Los
    Angeles.
FAWCETT, COL. P. H.
    Callahuaya's Curse. .s . . . .
    . . . . .ASF Oct 33 140
FEARN, JOHN RUSSELL See also
    pseuds GEOFFREY ARMSTRONG
    (1), THORNTON AYRE (33),
    DENNIS CLIVE (h?) (5), JOHN
    COTTON (h?) (3), POLTON
    CROSS (28), VARGO STATTEN
    (0), EPHRIAN WINIKI (h?) (4)
    Biog sketch . . . . . . Amz Jun 38 7
    Biog sketch . . . . . Fant #1 38 128
    Biog sketch . . . . . . Fant #2 39 92
    Biog sketch . . . . ToW Aut 39 127
    Biog sketch, photo. . . . .
    . . . . SS Fal 45 95

AUTHOR
    Title. .Length . . . . Magazine, Date, Page

    After the Atom. .s . . . .
    . . . . SS May 48 117
    Aftermath. .n . . . . . . SS Fal 45 11
    Arbiter, The. .s . . . . SS May 47 90
    Before Earth Came. .nt . . . .
    . . . . .ASF Jul 34 8
    Black Empress, The. .nt . . . .
    . . . . Amz Jan 39 86
    Blue Infinity, The. .nt . . . .
    . . . . ASF Sep 35 70
    Brain of Light, The. .nt. . . . . . .
    . . . . ASF May 34 45
    Brain of Venus. .nt . . . .
    . . . . TW Feb 37 42
    Climatica. .nt . . . . . Fant #2 39 100
    Cosmic Derelict, The. .s . . . . . .
    . . . . .PS Spr 41 57
    Cosmic Juggernaut, The . . . .
    . .s . . . . PS Sum 40 82
    Dark Eternity. .nt . . . .
    . . . . ASF Dec 37 14
    Death at the Observatory . . . . . .
    . .s . . . . CF Sum 40 106
    . . . . FSQ Spr 50 99
    Deserted Universe. .nt . . . .
    . . . . .ASF Sep 36 137
    Dynasty of the Small. .nt . . . . . .
    . . . . ASF Nov 36 59
    Earth's Mausoleum. .nt. . . . . . .
    . . . . ASF May 35 52
    He Conquered Venus. .s . . . .
    . . . . .Ash Jun 40 6
    He Never Slept. .s . . . .
    . . . . ASF Jun 34 56
    Intelligence Gigantic, The . . . . . .
    . .n 2 pt . . . . Amz Jun 33 235
    Interlink. .s . . . . . . TW Fal 45 72
    Last Conflict. .nt. . . . .
    . . . . Fant Dec 46 4
    Last Hours, The. .nt . . . .
    . . . . Amz Aug 42 90
    Liners of Time. .n 4 pt . . . .
    . . . . .Amz May 35 28
    Lords of 9016. .s. . . . .
    . . . . TW Apr 36 80
    Dust, The. .nt . . . .
    . . . . ASF Mar 34 55
    . . . . ToW Aut 39 102
    Martian Miniature. .s . . . .
    . . . . .Amz May 42 66
    Mathematica. .nt . . . .
    . . . . ASF Feb 36 64
    Mathematica Plus. .nt . . . .
    . . . . ASF May 36 90
    Menace from the Microcosm . . . .
    . .nt . . . . TW Jun 37 14

AUTHOR
    Title. .Length . . . . Magazine, Date, Page

    Metamorphosis. .nt . . . .
    . . . . .ASF Jan 37 90
    Misty Wilderness, The. .s . . . . . .
    . . . . SS Sep 39 102
    Multillionth Chance, The . . . . . .
    . .nt . . . . TW Fal 46 9
    Phantom from Space. .s . . . .
    . . . . .SSS Mar 40 57
    Queen of Venus. .n . . . .
    . . . . MSS Nov 40 8
    Red Heritage. .nt. . . . .
    . . . . .ASF Jan 38 76
    Red Magician, The. .nt . . . .
    . . . . .Fant #1 38 58
    Secret of the Buried City . . . . . .
    . .nt . . . . .Amz May 39 6
    Seed from Space. .nt . . . .
    . . . . .ToW #1 37 17
    She Walked Alone. .s . . . .
    . . . . .FA Jul 39 66
    Subconscious. .nt . . . .
    . . . . Amz Aug 36 57
    Summons from Mars, A. .s . . . . .
    . . . . Amz Jun 38 82
    Superhuman. .s . . . . SS May 41 84
    Sweet Mystery of Life. .s . . . . . .
    . . . . .NW #1 46 36
    . . . . TW Feb 47 74
    Thoughts That Kill. .s . . . .
    . . . . .SF Oct 39 105
    Through Earth's Core. .s . . . . . .
    . . . . .ToW #2 38 86
    Ultimate Analysis, The. .s . . . . .
    . . . . TW Fal 44 89
    Unbroken Chain, The. .s . . . . . .
    . . . . .SS Spr 46 90
    War of the Scientists. .nt. . . . . . .
    . . . . Amz Apr 40 50
    Worlds Within. .nt . . . .
    . . . . ASF Mar 37 12
    Zagribud. .n 3 pt . . . Amz Dec 37 58
FEDOR, A.
    with HENRY HASSE
    End of Tyme, The. .s . . . .
    . . . . WS Nov 33 337
    Man Who, The. .s. . . MSS Nov 40 78
    Return of Tyme, The. .s . . . .
    . . . . WS Aug 34 294
FENNEL, ERIK
    Biog sketch . . . . . . .PF Fal 47 88
    Atavism. .s. . . . . . . .PS Spr 47 95
    Beneath the Red World's
    Crust. .nt . . . . PS Fal 47 90
    Black Priestess of Varda. .nt . . . .
    . . . . PS Win 47 4
    Madmen of Mars. .s . . .PS Spr 50 40

AUTHOR
Title. .Length . . . . Magazine, Date, Page

Synthetic Hero. .s . . . . PS Fal 48 96
War of Intangibles. .nt . . . .
. . . . .ASF Jun 48 118
FERRY, FRANK
Biog sketch, photo. . . . .
. . . . .TW Sum 44 47
Horatius at the Bridge. .s . . . .
. . . . .TW Sum 44 45
FEZANDIE, CLEMENT
DR. HACKENSAW'S SECRETS
The Secret of the Invisible
Girl. .s . . . . Amz Jul 26 376
Some Minor Inventions. .s . . . . .
. . . . Amz Jun 26 280
FIELDS, RALPH B.
Inside Mount Lassen. .a . . . .
. . . . Amz Dec 46 155
FIERST, A. L.
Man of Bronze, The. .s . . . .
. . . . WQ Win 31 206
FINLAY, VIRGIL *artist*
Biog sketch, portrait . . . .
. . . . TW Jun 39 90
Cover for ASTONISHING STORIES
June 1942
Cover for ASTOUNDING SCIENCE
FICTION
Aug 1939 (?)
Covers for FAMOUS FANTASTIC
MYSTERIES
Mar, Aug, Oct 1940
Feb, Apr, Jun, Aug, Oct,
Dec 1941
Feb, Apr, Jun, Jul, Aug, Sep,
Oct, Nov, Dec 1942
Mar, Sep 1943
Dec 1946
Feb, June, Aug, Dec 1947
Feb, Jun 1948
Covers for FANTASTIC NOVELS
Jul, Nov 1940
Jan, Apr 1941
Nov 1948
Mar, Nov 1949
Cover for PLANET STORIES
Sum 1941
Covers for SUPER SCIENCE
STORIES
May 1942
Feb, May 1943
FISCHER, FRED W.
with JOSEPH GILBERT
Escape. .nt . . . . . . ASF Apr 43 43
FISHER, PHILIP (M.), (JR.)
Beyond the Pole. .nt . . . .
. . . . FFM Jun 42 96

Devil of the Western Sea, The . . .
. .nt . . . . .FFM Apr 40 6
Fungus Isle. .nt . . . .
. . . . FFM Oct 40 67
Lady of the Moon, The. .s . . . . .
. . . . .ASF Sep 35 105
Lights. .s . . . . FFM Dec 39 78
Ship of Silent Men, The. .nt . . . .
. . . . FFM Feb 41 87
Strange Case of Lemuel Jenkins,
The. .nt . . . . AFR #2 27
FISHER, STEVE
Returned from Hell. .n . . . .
. . . . .UK May 39 9
FISK, CLINTON EARLE
Moon Doom, The, Part 4. .n . . . .
. . . . WS Jun 33 82
FISKE, TARLETON *pseud of*
ROBERT BLOCH
Biog sketch, gag photo . . . .
. . . . FA Aug 43 203
Almost Human. .s . . . .
. . . . FA Jun 43 184
Black Brain, The. .s . . . .
. . . . FA Mar 43 218
Fairy Tale. .s . . . .
. . . . FA Aug 43 184
Mystery of the Creeping Underwear,
The. .s . . . . FA Oct 43 132
Phantom from the Film. .s . . . . .
. . . . Amz Feb 43 208
Skeleton in the Closet, The . . . . .
. .s . . . . FA May 43 116
FITZGERALD, WILLIAM *pseud of*
WILL F. JENKINS
Assignment on Pasik. .s . . . .
. . . . TW Feb 49 122
Cure for a Ylith. .s . . . .
. . . . .SS Nov 49 113
Deadly Dust, The. .nt . . . .
. . . . TW Aug 47 11
Devil of East Lupton, Vermont,
The. .s . . . . TW Aug 48 96
Gregory Circle, The. .s . . . .
. . . . TW Apr 47 50
Nameless Something, The . . . . . .
. .s . . . . TW Jun 47 66
Seven Temporary Moons, The . . .
. .s . . . . TW Feb 48 56
FITZPATRICK, ROBERT FLEMING
"I Paint from Death". .nt . . . . . .
. . . . Amz Aug 49 24
FLAGG, FRANCIS *pseud of*
GEORGE HENRY WEISS
Adventure in Time, An. .s . . . . . .
. . . . SW Apr 30 1018

After Armageddon. .s . . . .
. . . . WS Sep 32 340
SS Fal 46 72
Blue Dimension, The. .s . . . .
. . . . Amz Jun 28 224
Chemical Brain, The. .s . . . .
. . . . ToW Win 38 53
Cities of Ardathia, The. .nt . . . . .
. . . . Amz Mar 32 1064
Dancer in the Crystal, The. .s . . . .
. . . . AFR #11 111
Heads of Apex, The. .s . . . .
. . . . ASF Oct 31 24
Land of the Bipos, The. .s . . . . . .
. . . . SW Feb 30 806
Lizard Men of Bu-Lo, The. .s . . . .
. . . . WS Oct 30 402
Machine Man of Ardathia,
The. .s . . . . Amz Nov 27 798
ToW Aut 40 35
AFR #8 27
Master Ants, The. .s . . . .
. . . . Amz May 28 158
Mentanicals, The. .s . . . .
. . . . Amz Apr 34 60
AFR #10 59
Resistant Ray, The. .s . . . .
. . . . .Amz Jul 32 346
Seed of the Toc-Toc Birds,
The. .s . . . . .ASF Jan 31 81
Superman of Dr. Jukes, The . . . .
. .s . . . . WS Nov 31 744
SS Fal 45 66
Synthetic Monster, The. .s . . . . . .
. . . . WS Mar 31 1152
with FORREST J. ACKERMAN
Earth's Lucky Day. .s . . . .
. . . . WS Mar 35 926
with WEAVER WRIGHT (Forrest
J. Ackerman)
Time Twister, The. .s . . . .
. . . . TW Oct 47 61
FLEMING, ROSCOE B.
Menace of the Little, The . . . . . .
. .nt . . . . .AQ Sum 31 378
FLEMING-ROBERTS, G. T.
Golden Barrier, The. .s . . . .
. . . . TW Dec 40 54
FLEMING, STUART *pseud of*
DAMON KNIGHT
Avenger, The. .s . . . .
. . . . .PS Spr 44 31
Doorway to Kal-Jmar. .s . . . .
. . . . .PS Win 44 19
New Day on Aurrora. .s . . . .
. . . . SSS May 43 98

AUTHOR
    Title. .Length . . . . Magazine, Date, Page

FLEMING, WARD
  Mystery on Pluto. .s . . . .
  . . . . FA Feb 50 126
FLINT, HOMER EON
  Lord of Death, The. .nt . . . .
  . . . . FFM Dec 39 42
  Nth Man, The. .nt . . . .
  . . . . AQ Spr 28 196
  with AUSTIN HALL
  Biog sketch: HALL AND FLINT by
    Phil Richards . . . . FFM Feb 41 84
  Blind Spot, The. .n. .*(The first 27*
  of 48 chapters were printed in
  3 instalments, then dropped when
  published complete in FANTASTIC
  NOVELS) . . . . . . FFM Mar 40 6
  Blind Spot, The. .n . . . .FN Jul 40 2
FOHN, L. JOE
  Watch That Window. .s . . . .
  . . . . UK Sep 40 122
FORD, EDSEL
  Timeless. .ss . . . . FB #5 19
FORD, GARRET
  Editor FANTASY BOOK from #1 –
FORESTER, C. S.
  Peacemaker, The. .n. . . . .
  . . . . .FFM Feb 48 6
FORMAN, JAN
  Mr. Ellerbee Transplanted. .s . . . .
  . . . . ASF Oct 37 39
FORT, CHARLES
  Lo! . .non-fic book 8 pt . . . .
  . . . . ASF Apr 34 146
FORTE, (JOHN R., JR.) *artist*
  Covers for FUTURE FICTION
    Aug 1941
  Covers for FUTURE COMBINED
    WITH SCIENCE FICTION
    Apr, Jun, Aug 1942
FOSTER, D. J.
  Alien Error, The. .s . . . .
  . . . . ToW Spr 39 76
  Island in the Air, The. .s . . . .
  . . . . ToW Aut 39 50
  Ship of Cold Death. .s . . . .
  . . . . .Fut Nov 40 24
FOX, CARDNER F.
  Biog sketch . . . . . PS Sum 47 117
  Engines of the Gods. .nt . . . .
  . . . . .PS Spr 46 2
  Heart of Light. .s . . . .
  . . . . .Amz Jul 46 94
  Last Monster, The. .s . . . .
  . . . . .PS Fal 45 38
  Man Nth. .s . . . . .PS Win 45 98

AUTHOR
    Title. .Length . . . . Magazine, Date, Page

  Man the Sun Gods Made, The . . .
  . .nt . . . . PS Win 46 4
  Sword of the Seven Suns. .nt . . . .
  . . . . .PS Spr 47 58
  Temptress of the Time Flow . . . .
  . .nt . . . . MSS Nov 50 72
  Vassals of the Lode-Star . . . .
  . .nt . . . . PS Sum 47 2
  Werewile of the Crystal
    Crypt. .s . . . . . . PS Sum 48 106
  When Kohonnes Screamed. .s. . . .
  . . . . PS Fal 48 43
  with JOHN GUINTA artist
  Crom the Barbarian . . . .
  . .comic. . . . . . OTWA Jul 50 72
  Spider God of Akka, The . . . . . .
  . .comic. . . . . . .OTWA Dec 50 72
FOX, GEORGE R.
  Electronic Wall, The. . . . .
  . .s . . . . Amz Jun 27 234
FRANCIS, LEE *house pseud*
by HOWARD BROWNE
  Man from Yesterday, The . . . . . .
  . .n . . . . FA Aug 48 8
Authors' real names unknown
  Biog sketch, photo. . . . .
  . . . . Amz Aug 43 203
  Appointment With the Past . . . . .
  . .nt . . . . FA Feb 44 142
  Backward Passage. .s . . . .
  . . . . FA Sep 49 68
  Change for the Bitter. .s . . . .
  . . . . FA Apr 45 100
  Chemical Vampire, The. .s. . . . . .
  . . . . Amz Mar 49 8
  Citadel of Hate. .nt . . . .
  . . . . FA Jun 43 154
  Coffin of Hope. .nt . . . .
  . . . . .Amz Jul 49 28
  Comet from Yesterday . . . .
  . .nt . . . . Amz Mar 45 106
  Cursed Caverns of Ra. .nt . . . . . .
  . . . . Amz Sep 45 64
  Daughter of Destiny. .nt . . . .
  . . . . Amz Apr 43 190
  Flight Into Fog. .nt . . . .
  . . . . FA Apr 48 116
  Forgotten Hades. .nt . . . .
  . . . . Amz May 48 140
  Hell is a Circle. .s. . . . .
  . . . . FA Nov 47 160
  Hitler's Right Eye. .s . . . .
  . . . . FA Jun 44 120
  Man from Yesterday, The . . . . . .
  . .n . . . . .FA Aug 48 8

AUTHOR
    Title. .Length . . . . . Magazine, Date, Page

  Man Who Could Not Die,
    The. .s . . . . FA Jan 50 34
  Midgets and Mighty Men. .nt . . . .
  . . . . FA May 49 44
  Murder Solves a Problem. .s. . . . .
  . . . . Amz Nov 47 88
  Outlaws of Corpus. .nt . . . .
  . . . . FA Dec 48 8
  Phantom of the Forest. .s . . . . . .
  . . . . Amz Nov 48 50
  Sentimental Monster. .s . . . .
  . . . . Amz Dec 46 136
  Shadow of the Spider. .s. . . . . . .
  . . . . Amz Mar 43 202
  Stone Goddess of Yunan. . . . . . .
  . .nt . . . . Amz Aug 43 154
  Tears for the Crocodile. .s . . . . . .
  . . . . FA Dec 45 166
  Terror on the Telephone. .s . . . . .
  . . . . Amz Sep 47 58
  When the Spirit Moves me . . . . . .
  . .s . . . . .FA May 47 90
  Witch of Blackfen Moore. .nt . . . .
  . . . . FA Dec 43 10
  Zero A.D. . .n . . . .
  . . . . FA Mar 48 90
FRANKLIN, PAUL *pseud of BRYCE*
  WALTON
FREDERICK, J. GEORGE
  Einstein Express, The. .n 2 pt . . .
  . . . . ASF Apr 35 10
  Planet Juggler, The. .nt. . . . .
  . . . . .FFM Mar 40 42
FREDERICK, JOHN *pseud of*
  FREDERICK FAUST
FREEMAN, DR. R. AUSTIN
  Blue Spangle, The. .s . . . .
  . . . . AD Jun 30 536
FRESKA, FRIEDRICH
  Druso *(Tr fr German by Fletcher*
  Pratt). .n 3 pt . . . WS May 34 1066
FRENTZ, ROY B.
  Repair Job. .s . . . . . Amz Oct 50 46
FREW, JOHN *artist*
  Cover for ASTOUNDING SCIENCE
    FICTION
    Jan 1939
FRIEDENSON, CAPT. MEYER
  Biog sketch, photo. . . . .
  . . . . Amz Mar 44 13
  Superman, The. .ss . . . .
  . . . . Amz Mar 44 14
FRIEND, OSCAR J. *See also pseuds*
  OWEN FOX JEROME (3), FORD
  SMITH (7)

AUTHOR
Title. .Length . . . . Magazine, Date, Page

*Editor THRILLING WONDER
    STORIES*
  Aug 41 thru Fal 44 issues
Editor STARTLING STORIES
  Jul 41 issue to mid 1944
Editor CAPTAIN FUTURE
  from 1940 to 1944
Biog sketch, photo. . . . .
  . . . . TW Apr 40 95
Ali Baba, Junior. .s . . . .
  . . . . CF Win 43 103
Blind Victory. .s . . . TW Feb 41 104
Coup d'Etat. .s . . . . . TW Dec 39 68
Experiment With Destiny . . . . . .
  . .s . . . . TW Oct 39 64
Glamour Girl—2040. .ss . . . .
  . . . . SS May 40 108
Impossible Highway, The. .s . . . .
  . . . . TW Aug 40 80
Kid from Mars, The. .n . . . .
  . . . . .SS Sep 40 12
Mind Over Matter. .s . . . .
  . . . . SS Jan 40 112
Molecule Monsters, The . . . .
  . . . . TW Oct 42 77
Of Jovian Build. .s . . . .
  .TW Oct 38 63
Roar of the Rocket. .nt . . . .
  . . . . TW Apr 40 91
Robot A-1. .s . . . . SS Jul 39 37
Station Death. .s . . . .SS Mar 40 106
Stolen Spectrum, The. . . . .
  . . . . TW Sep 40 108
This Is Hell. .s . . . . . TW Feb 42 108
*THRILLS IN SCIENCE dept in
    STARTLING STORIES.* Most
  issues Jan 42 to Sum 45
Venusian Quartz. .s . . . .
  . . . . .CF Sum 43 112
Water World, The. .n . . . .
  . . . . SS May 41 14
Worm Turns, The. .s. . . . .
  . . . . SS Jul 40 109
FRITCHEY, ALFRED
Before the Ice Age. .s . . . .
  . . . . Amz Dec 28 826
FROST, FREDERICK *pseud of
    FREDERICK FAUST*
FUQUA, ROBERT *artist*
Covers for AMAZING STORIES
  Oct, Nov, Dec 1938
  Jan, Feb, Mar, Apr, May, Jul,
    Aug, Sep, Oct 1939
  Jan, Jul, Sep, Nov, Dec 1940
  Sep, Nov 1941
  Mar, Apr, 1942

AUTHOR
Title. .Length . . . . Magazine, Date, Page

  Mar, Apr, Aug 1943
  Jan 1944
*Covers for FANTASTIC
    ADVENTURES*
  May, Nov 1939
  Feb, Mar 1940
  May, Sep 1941
  Feb 1942 *(with H. W.
    MacCAULEY)*
STORIES OF THE STARS
  Death of the Moon . . . .
    . . . . .bacover . . . . .Amz Jan 44
FURTH, CARLTON *pseud of
    JOE GIBSON*
FYFE, H.(ORACE) B. *See also pseud
    ANDREW MacDUFF (0)*
Bureau of Slick Tricks. .nt . . . . .
  . . . . ASF Dec 48 70
Compromise. .s . . . .
  . . . . ASF Dec 50 51
Conformity Expected. .s . . . . . .
  . . . . ASF Mar 50 140
In Value Deceived. .s . . . .
  . . . . ASF Nov 50 38
Locked Out. .s . . . . ASF Feb 40 42
Sinecure 6. .s . . . . . .ASF Jan 47 55
Special Jobbery. .nt . . . .
  . . . . ASF Sep 49 41
Spy Scare. .s . . . . .ASF Sep 50 142
Well-Oiled Machine, The. .s . . . .
  . . . . F&SF Dec 50 105
with F. H. HAUSER
  Hold That Comet. .s . . . .
    . . . . .Ash Dec 40 64

G

GADDIS, VINCENT
Energy from Beyond. .a . . . .
  . . . . Amz May 46 156
Giants on the Earth. .a . . . .
  . . . . Amz Dec 45 162
Medicine Man Magic. .a. . . . . . .
  . . . . FA Feb 46 170
Mystery of Magic Drugs, The . . . .
  . .a . . . . Amz Sep 49 147
New Evidence for Atlantis. .a. . . .
  . . . . Amz Aug 46 151
Puzzles from Earth's Past. .a . . . .
  . . . . Amz Aug 46 156
Shaverian Sidelights. .a . . . .
  . . . . .Amz Jan 49 130
Tales from Tibet. .a . . . .
  . . . . Amz Feb 46 170

AUTHOR
Title. .Length . . . . Magazine, Date, Page

Truth About Tibet, The . . . .
  . .a . . . . Amz Jul 46 168
Weird Wonders of the War. . . . . .
  . .a . . . . .Amz Jan 49 137
When Flesh Defies Fire. .a . . . . .
  . . . . Amz May 46 160
World's Most Famous Illusion,
    The. .a . . . . FA Jun 48 158
plus numerous shorter "fillers"
GADE, HENRY *house pseud
by RAYMOND A. PALMER*
Invincible Crime Buster, The . . . .
  . .nt . . . . .Amz Jul 41 102
Liners of Space. .s . . . .
  . . . . Amz Dec 39 108
Pioneer—1957. .s . . . . FA Nov 39 68
*Authors' real names unknown
Biog sketch, photo.* . . . .
  . . . . FA Nov 39 86
Heroes Die Hard. .s . . . .
  . . . . FA Dec 43 128
My Name Is Madness. .nt . . . . . .
  . . . . FA Nov 49 78
plus numerous "fillers"
GAIL, O.(TTO) W.(ILLI)
Shot into Infinity, The *(tr fr German
    by Francis Currier).* .n . . . .
  . . . . WQ Fal 29 6
    SFQ Win 41 1
Stone from the Moon, The *(tr fr
    German by Francis Currier)* . . . .
  . .n . . . . WQ Mar 30 294
GALE, FLOYD
Treachery on Planetoid 41. .s . . . .
  . . . . Amz Jun 40 100
GALLUN, RAYMOND Z. *See also
    pseuds ARTHUR ALLPORT (1),
    WILLIAM CALLAHAN (1), DOW
    ELSTAR (5), E. V. RAYMOND (1)
Biog sketch, photo.* . . . .
  . . . . TW Mar 40 33
Biog sketch, photo. . . . .
  . . . . Amz Mar 42 229
Biog sketch, photo. . . . .
  . . . . Amz Jun 42 261
Achilles Heel, The. .s . . . .
  . . . . Amz Nov 40 124
Atomic Fire. .s . . . . Amz Apr 31 64
Beast of the Void, A. .s . . . .
  . . . . ASF Sep 36 48
Blue Haze on Pluto. .s . . . .
  . . . . ASF Jun 35 90
Bluff Play. .s. . . . . . TW Dec 50 113
Buried Moon. .s. . . . ASF Feb 36 37
Child of the Stars. .nt . . . .
  . . . . ASF Apr 36 10

AUTHOR
Title. .Length . . . . Magazine, Date, Page

Coffins to Mars. .nt . . . .
. . . . TW Jun 50 88
Comet's Captive. .s . . . .
. . . . ASF Jun 37 35
Crystal Ray, The. .s . . . .
. . . . .AW Nov 29 452
Dark Sun. .s . . . . TW Jun 37 56
Davey Jones' Ambassador . . . . . .
. .nt . . . . ASF Dec 35 10
Dawn-World Echoes. .nt . . . .
. . . . .ASF Jul 37 96
Death and the Dictator. .s . . . . . .
. . . . .SF Oct 40 42
Derelict. .s . . . . ASF Oct 35 23
Dictator for All Time, A . . . .
. .s . . . . MSS Nov 40 56
Eternal Wall, The. .s . . . .
. . . . Amz Nov 42 144
Eyes That Watch. .s . . . .
. . . . Com Dec 40 107
Fires of Genesis. .nt . . . .
. . . . ASF Mar 37 124
Flight of the RX–1, The . . . . . .
. .s . . . . Amz Jul 33 371
Gears for Nemesis. .s . . . .
. . . . SS Jan 42 106
Godson of Almarlu. .nt . . . .
. . . . ASF Oct 36 8
Guardian Angel. .s . . . .
. . . . SSS May 40 24
Hell-Stuff for Planet X . . . .
. .s . . . . .SS Jun 43 89
Hotel Cosmos. .s . . . ASF Jul 38 141
Invaders of the Forbidden
  Moon. .nt . . . . PS Sum 41 2
Iszt—Earthman. .nt . . . .
. . . . ASF Apr 38 86
Long Winter, The. .s . . . .
. . . . ASF May 40 112
Lotus Engine, The. .s . . . .
. . . . .SSS Mar 40 26
Luminous Mine, The. .s . . . .
. . . . .ASF Jan 37 80
Lunar Chrysalis, The. .s . . . .
. . . . Amz Sep 31 528
Lunar Parasites. .s . . . .
. . . . .CF Sum 40 100
Machine from Ganymede,
  The. .s . . . . . . ASF Nov 34 112
Mad Robot. .s . . . . . ASF Mar 36 66
Magician of Dream Valley. .s . . . .
. . . . ASF Oct 38 12
Masson's Secret. .s . . . .
. . . . .ASF Sep 39 101
Menace in Miniature, A. .s . . . . . .
. . . . ASF Oct 37 88

AUTHOR
Title. .Length . . . . Magazine, Date, Page

Mercutian Adventure. .s . . . .
. . . . ASF Feb 38 98
Meteor Legacy. .s . . . .
. . . . ASF Aug 41 37
Mind Over Matter. .s . . . .
. . . . .ASF Jan 35 116
Moon Mistress. .s. . . . .
. . . . WS May 32 1330
Moon Plague. .nt . . . .WS Jan 34 626
Nemesis from Lilliput. . . . .
. .ss. . . . . SS May 40 113
N'goc. .s . . . . . . ASF Mar 35 145
"OLD FAITHFUL" series includes:
  OLD FAITHFUL
  THE SON OF OLD FAITHFUL
  CHILD OF THE STARS
Old Faithful. .nt . . . .
. . . . ASF Dec 34 106
Operation Pumice. .s . . . .
. . . . TW Apr 49 37
Path, The. .s . . . .
. . . . ASF Nov 36 38
Raiders of Saturn's Rings,
  The. .s . . . . PS Fal 41 70
Red Shards on Ceres. .s. . . . .
. . . . TW Dec 37 27
                        FSQ Spr 50 69
Renegade from Saturn. .s . . . . . .
. . . . TW Mar 40 32
Revolt of the Star Men, The . . . .
. .nt . . . . WQ Win 32 222
Sarker's Joke Box. .s . . . .
. . . . Amz Mar 42 110
Saturn's Ringmaster. .s . . . .
. . . . TW Dec 36 80
Scarab, The. .s . . . . ASF Aug 36 80
Scientist Disowned. .s. . . . .
. . . . Amz Jun 42 102
Secret of the Comet. .s . . . .
. . . . TW Jan 41 50
Seeds of the Dusk. .nt . . . .
. . . . ASF Jun 38 76
Shadow of the Veil. .s . . . .
. . . . ASF Feb 39 109
Son of Old Faithful, The. .nt . . . .
. . . . .ASF Jul 35 8
Space Dwellers, The. .s . . . .
. . . . SW Nov 29 522
                        SS Fal 43 106
Space Flotsam. .s. . . ASF Feb 34 59
Space Oasis. .s. . . . . PS Aug 42 30
Step Further Out, A. .nt . . . .
. . . . .SSS Mar 50 48
Stepson of Space. .s . . . .
. . . . .Ash Oct 40 36
Strange Creature. .s . . . .
. . . . SF Aug 39 59

AUTHOR
Title. .Length . . . . Magazine, Date, Page

Tangled Paths. .s . . . . .TW Jul 40 84
Telepathic Piracy. .s . . . .
. . . . ASF Mar 35 142
Terror Out of the Past. .nt . . . . .
. . . . Amz Mar 40 100
Wall of water, The. .s . . . .
. . . . SFQ Win 41 129
Wand of Creation, The. .s . . . . . .
. . . . ASF Sep 34 98
Waves of Compulsion. .s . . . .
. . . . WS Mar 32 1138
Weapon, The. .s. . . . .
. . . . ASF May 36 79
World Wrecker, The. .s . . . .
. . . . .ASF Jun 34 104
with JOHN MICHEL
Menace from Mercury, The . . . . .
. .s . . . . .WQ Sum 32 544
GALT, JOSEPH R.
Half-Way Street. .s . . . .
. . . . Amz Feb 49 134
GARBY, LEE HAWKINS
with EDWARD ELMER SMITH, Ph.D.
Skylark of Space, The. .n 3 pt . . .
. . . . Amz Aug 28 390
GARDNER, NOEL pseud of HENRY
    KUTTNER
Shining Man, The. .nt . . . .
. . . . .FA May 40 40
Uncanny Power of Edwin Cobalt,
  The. .ss . . . . FA Oct 40 98
GARDNER, THOMAS S.(amuel)
Cosmic Tragedy. .ss . . . .
. . . . Com Mar 41 116
Insect World, The. .s . . . .
. . . . WS Apr 35 1315
                        ToW Aut 41 53
Last Woman, The. .s. . . . .
. . . . WS Apr 32 1238
                        SS Win 44 72
Traitor, The. .ss. . . . .
. . . . .SF Jun 39 103
World of Singing Crystals,
  The. .s . . . . . . WS Mar 36 902
GARFIELD, FRANCES (Mrs. Manly
    Wade Wellman)
Biog sketch . . . . . Amz Dec 39 132
Gulpers Versus Earthmen. .s . . . .
. . . . Amz Dec 39 68
GARFINKEL, SAMUEL
Act of Retipu, The. .s . . . .
. . . . .Amz Jan 31 946
GARRETT, GORDON
PROBABILITY ZERO
The Absence of Heat. .ss . . . . . .
. . . . .ASF Jun 44 131

AUTHOR
Title. .Length . . . . Magazine, Date, Page

GARSON, CLEE *pseud of DAVID
WRIGHT O'BRIEN–possibly
others*
Club of the Damned. .s . . . .
. . . . FA Feb 43 202
Direct Wire. .s. . . . .
. . . . Amz Jan 43 58
Madagascar Ghost. .s . . . .
. . . . FA Dec 42 174
Merchant of Venus, The. .nt . . . .
. . . . FA Apr 43 100
Money Machine, The. .nt . . . . . .
. . . . Amz Mar 43 134
Other Abner Small, The. .s . . . . .
. . . . FA Mar 43 96
Saunders' Strange Second
Sight. .s . . . . .FA Jan 43 182
Sharbeau's Startling Statue . . . . .
. .s . . . . FA Nov 42 166
GARSON, VASELEOS
Little Pets of Arkkhan, The. . . . .
. .s . . . . PS Sum 47 75
One Against the Stars. .s. . . . . . .
. . . . PS Sum 44 104
Prodigal Weapon. .s . . . .
. . . . PS Sum 45 30
Running of the Zar, The. .s . . . . .
. . . . .PS Win 47 67
Shadow-Gods, The. .s. . . . .
. . . . PS Sum 46 101
Test for the Pearl. .s. . . . .
. . . . PS Fal 47 76
GARTH, WILL *house pseud*
by OTTO BINDER
Rays of Blindness. .s . . . .
. . . . TW Apr 38 106
by EDMOND HAMILTON
Great Illusion, The. .s. . . . .
. . . . TW Jun 38 97
by HENRY KUTTNER
Hands Across the Void. .s . . . . . .
. . . . TW Dec 38 15
by MORT WEISINGER
Incident on Titan. .s. . . . .
. . . . TW Jun 41 93
Turnabout. .s . . . . . .SS Mar 39 117
Authors' real names unknown
Bloodless Peril, The. .s . . . .
. . . . TW Dec 37 100
Memory Blocks. .ss . . . .
. . . . .CF Spr 41 109
Men of Honor. .s. . . . .
. . . . .CF Spr 40 115
GATES, FRANK
Man Who Died by Proxy,
The. .s. . . . . . Amz May 27 145

GATTER, GEORGE F.
Emotion Gas, The. .s . . . .
. . . . WS Mar 36 966
GAUGHAN, JACK *artist*
*Cover for FANTASY BOOK
#6 (1950)*
GEE, JACKSON
Extra Man, An. .s . . . .
. . . . .ASF Oct 30 118
GEER, OMAR
Twirl My Turbine, Man Alive. . . .
. .s . . . . Amz Mar 45 180
GEIER, CHESTER S. *See also pseuds
GUY ARCHETTE (19), WARREN
KASTEL (8). Also has stories
under house names; ALEXANDER
BLADE, P. F. COSTELLO, S. M.
TENNESHAW, GERALD VANCE
and PETER WORTH.*
Biog sketch, photo. . . . .
. . . . Amz Apr 43 231
Biog sketch, photo. . . . .
. . . . .FA Dec 45 2
Cold Ghost. .s. . . . . Amz Nov 48 26
Crystal and a Spell, A. . . . .
. .s . . . . FA May 46 108
Death Sentence. .s. . . . .
. . . . Amz Dec 46 26
Death's Head. .s . . . . FA Nov 48 60
Disappearance. .s. . . . .
. . . . .ASF Jul 45 115
Enigma of the City. .nt. . . . .
. . . . Amz Apr 43 136
Environment. .s. . . ASF May 44 161
Fido. .s . . . . UK Oct 43 125
Fire Globe, The. .nt. .*(by-lined
GEIER in ToC; GUY ARCHETTE
on story)* . . . . . Amz Oct 49 90
Flight of the Starling. .nt . . . . . .
. . . . Amz Jan 48 8
Forever is Too Long. .n . . . .
. . . . FA Mar 47 8
Four Who Returned. .nt . . . .
. . . . Amz Feb 46 138
Getaway. .s . . . . . Amz Oct 46 56
Happiness Is Nowhere. .s. . . . . . .
. . . . FA Nov 46 112
Haunted Metropolis. .nt . . . .
. . . . Amz Nov 46 64
Hidden City. .n. . . . .
. . . . .Amz Jul 47 8
If You Believe. .s. . . . .
. . . . .FA Jul 43 94
Jewel of Death. .s . . . FA Dec 45 36
Length of Rope, A. .s. . . . .
. . . . UK Apr 41 120

Light of Life. .s . . . .
. . . . Amz Dec 47 46
Minions of the Tiger. .n . . . .
. . . . FA Sep 46 8
Mirage World. .s . . . .
. . . . Amz Dec 45 74
Planet of Creation. .s . . . .
. . . . .PS Spr 47 52
Return of Sinbad, The. .n . . . . . .
. . . . FA Jan 49 8
Secret of the Robot. .s. .*(by-lined
GEIER in ToC; GUY ARCHETTE
on story)* . . . . . . Amz Apr 48 76
Shadow for Sale. .s . . . .
. . . . FA Jun 48 112
Sky Imp. .s. . . . . . FA Jun 43 10
Soul Stealers, The. .nt . . . .
. . . . Im Oct 50 6
Sphere of Sleep, The. .s . . . .
. . . . Amz Dec 42 178
Spirit of the Keys. .s . . . .
. . . . FA Mar 48 56
Time Out of Mind. .s . . . .
. . . . .FA Nov 47 98
Venus Evil, The. .s. . . . .
. . . . .PS Sum 47 68
Weep No More, My Robot. . . . . .
. .s . . . . Amz Jun 45 54
Window to the Past. .s . . . .
. . . . FA Aug 50 70
with RICHARD S. SHAVER
Battle in Eternity. .nt. . . . .
. . . . Amz Nov 49 58
Fountain of Change. .nt . . . .
. . . . FA Dec 48 38
Ice City of the Gorgon. .n . . . . . .
. . . . Amz Jun 48 8
with TAYLOR VICTOR SHAVER
Strange Disappearance of Guy
Sylvester, The. .s . . . .
. . . . Amz Mar 49 24
GELULA, ABNER J.
Biog sketch . . . . Amz Jun 39 132
Automaton. .nt. . . Amz Nov 31 680
Hibernation. .s . . . . Amz Jul 33 302
Peace Weapons. .s . . . .
. . . . Amz Jun 34 35
Valley of the Blind. .s. . . . .
. . . . .AQ Spr–Sum 33 559
Vengeance of a Scientist, The . . .
. .s . . . . WS Feb 34 708
Whistling Death, The. .nt . . . . . .
. . . . Amz Jun 39 36
GERGEN, JOHN
with POUL ANDERSON
Entity. .s . . . . ASF Jun 49 58

AUTHOR
Title. .Length . . . . Magazine, Date, Page

GERIS, TOM ERWIN *pseud of MORT WEISINGER*
Lever of Destruction. .s . . . .
. . . . SF Dec 39 87
GERMANO, PETER B. *See pseud BARRY CORD (2)*
GERNSBACK, HUGO
Editor AMAZING STORIES
Apr 26 *thru* Apr 29 *issues*
Editor AMAZING STORIES ANNUAL
(only issue)
Editor AMAZING STORIES QUARTERLY
Fal 28 *thru* Win 29 *issues*
Editor AIR WONDER STORIES
(all issues)
Editor SCIENCE WONDER STORIES
(all issues)
Editor SCIENCE WONDER QUARTERLY
(all issues)
Editor WONDER STORIES
(all issues)
Editor WONDER STORIES QUARTERLY
(all issues)
Airplane of the Future, The. . . . .
. .a . . . . AW Sep 29 196
Baron Munchausen's Scientific
Adventures. .n 6 pt . . . .
. . . . Amz Feb 28 1060
Electric Duel, The. .ss. . . . .
. . . . Amz Sep 27 543
Killing Flash, The. .ss . . . .
. . . . SW Nov 29 496
Infinite Brain, The. .ss . . . .
. . . . Fut Jun 42 40
Magnetic Storm, The. .s . . . .
. . . . Amz Jul 26 350
Ralph 124C 41+. .n . . . .
. . . . AQ Win 29 4
GERSON, IRVING
In All Probability. .ss . . . .
. . . . Amz Jul 48 106
GIBSON, B. B.
Why Are You What You
Are? . .a . . . . . . Amz Sep 42 225
GIBSON, HOBART M.
WHAT MAN CAN IMAGINE
Immortality Needs Your
Help. .a . . . . . Amz Feb 46 166
GIBSON, JOE *See also pseuds JOHN BRIDGER (1), CARLTON FURTH (0)*

"I Like You, Too—". .s . . . .
. . . . TW Oct 48 52
GIESY, J. U.
Blind Man's Buff. .s . . . .
. . . . FFM Sep–Oct 39 118
Gravity Experiment, The . . . . . .
. .s . . . . FFM Dec 39 118
Jason, Son of Jason. .n . . . .
. . . . FN May 48 36
Mouthpiece of Zitu, The. .n. . . . .
. . . . FFM Nov 42 6
Palos of the Dog Star Pack . . . . .
. .n . . . . FFM Oct 41 6
GIFFIN, LEWIS A.
(Untitled story). .ss . . . .
. . . . SS Mar 40 104
GIFFORD, GUY *cartoonist*
THE RINGER FAMILY. .series of
of cartoons in PS irregularly from
Sum 42 *to* Spr 46
GILBERT, JOHN DEWITT
Ship That Died, The. .s . . . .
. . . . FN Jan 41 118
GILBERT, JOSEPH
Conquest. .ss . . . . . . TW Oct 42 87
Eternal Quest, The. .s . . . .
. . . . Ash Oct 42 60
Man Who Knew Roger Stanley,
The. .s. . . . . Ash Mar 42 43
PROBABILITY ZERO
Destiny and Uncle Louie. . . . . .
. .ss. . . . . ASF Aug 42 100
Twilight of Tomorrow. .s . . . . . .
. . . . .Fut Aug 42 47
with FRED W. FISCHER
Escape. .nt . . . . . . ASF Apr 43 43
GILBERT, KENNETH
Winged Doom, The. .s . . . .
. . . . Amz Oct 27 668
GILES, GEOFFREY *pseud of WALTER GILLINGS*
Lost Planet. .a . . . .
. . . . Fant Dec 46 56
GILES, GORDON A. *pseud of OTTO BINDER*
Biog sketch . . . . . Amz Oct 38 140
Atom Smasher, The. .s . . . .
. . . . Amz Oct 38 30
Diamond Planetoid. .s . . . .
. . . . ASF May 37 99
Flight of the Starshell. .s . . . . . .
. . . . TW Feb 39 50
"VIA—" series includes the following
"Via—" stories plus "Via Jupiter"
under the EANDO BINDER
by-line.

Via Asteroid. .s . . . . . TW Feb 38 29
Via Catacombs. .s . . . TW Nov 40 66
Via Death. .s. . . . . . .TW Aug 38 95
Via Etherline. .s . . . . TW Oct 37 79
Via Intelligence. .s . . . .
. . . . .TW Dec 40 42
Via Mercury. .s . . . . . TW Oct 40 67
Via Pyramid. .s . . . . . TW Jan 40 29
Via Sun. .s . . . . . . .TW Mar 40 45
Via Venus. .s . . . . . . TW Oct 39 33
Vision of the Hydra. .s . . . .
. . . . .TW Aug 37 82
Wayward World. .s . . . .
. . . . ASF Feb 38 106
Winking Lights of Mars, The . . .
. .s . . . . Amz Feb 41 120
GILFORD, BERNARD C.
Liquid Man, The. .n . . . .
. . . . FA Sep 41 8
GILLINGS, WALTER *See also pseuds GEOFFREY GILES (1), THOMAS SHERIDAN (3)*
Editor TALES OF WONDER
(all issues)
Editor FANTASY (post-war)
from Dec 46 thru Aug 47 issues
Are You There, Mars? . .a . . . . . .
. . . . Fant Aug 47 48
Moon Men, The . .a . . . .
. . . . Fant Dec 46 34
Space-ship Ahoy. .a . . . .
. . . . Fant Apr 47 38
GILMORE, ANTHONY *pseud of HARRY BATES & DESMOND WINTER HALL*
"HAWK CARSE" series includes:
HAWK CARSE
THE AFFAIR OF THE BRAINS
THE BLUFF OF THE HAWK
THE PASSING OF KU SUI
THE RETURN OF HAWK CARSE
by HARRY BATES
Return of Hawk Carse, The . . . . .
. .n . . . . .Amz Jul 42 158
by HARRY BATES and DESMOND W. HALL
Affair of the Brins, The. .nt . . . . .
. . . . ASF Mar 32 314
Bluff of the Hawk, The. .nt . . . . .
. . . . ASF May 32 256
Coffin Ship, The. .nt . . . .
. . . . ASF Oct 33 66
Four Miles Within. .nt . . . .
.ASF Apr 31 76
Hawk Carse. .nt. . . . .
. . . . ASF Nov 31 166
Passing of Ku Sui, The. .s . . . . . .
. . . . ASF Nov 32 320

AUTHOR
  Title. .Length . . . . Magazine, Date, Page

Tentacles from Below, The . . . . .
  . .nt . . . . ASF Feb 31 172
GILMORE, INEZ HAYNES
  Angel Island. .n. . . . FFM Feb 49 10
GILMOUR, A.(LBERT) A. (O.)
  Against Tetrach. .s. . . . .
    . . . . PS Fal 47 54
  Two-Way Time. .s . . . Fut Apr 43 46
GIPSON, LEONARD
  Sports of the Future. .a . . . .
    . . . . Amz Sep 40 128
GLADNEY, GRAVES *artist*
  Covers for ASTOUNDING SCIENCE
    FICTION
    Mar, Jun, Jul 1939
  Covers for UNKNOWN
    Apr, Aug, Nov 1939
GLAMIS, WALTER *pseud of*
  NATHAN SCHACHNER
  Orange God, The. .s . . . .
    . . . . ASF Oct 33 2
GLASSER, ALLEN
  Across the Ages. .s . . . .
    . . . . Amz Aug 33 466
with A. ROWLEY HILLIARD
  Martian, The. .s . . . .
    . . . . WQ Win 32 270
GLEASON, C. STERLING
  Radiation of the Chinese Vegetable,
    The. .s . . . . SW Dec 29 618
                          SS Win 45 80
GLUECKSTEIN, ROBERT W.
  cartoonist
  Biog sketch, photo. . . . .
    . . . . Amz Nov 41 140
                          FA Dec 41 140
                          Amz Apr 42 265
GOBLE, H. C.
  Remember Cassandra. .a . . . .
    . . . . Amz Jun 48 164
GOLD, H.(orace) L.(eonard) *See also*
  pseuds CLYDE CRANE CAMP-
  BELL (5), LEIGH KEITH (1)
  Editor GALAXY SCIENCE
    FICTION
    Oct 50—*(all issues)*
  Editor GALAXY SCIENCE
    FICTION NOVELS from #1 —
  Black Absolute. .ss. . . CF Fal 40 109
  Day Off. .s . . . . UK Nov 39 79
  Grifter's Asteroid. .s. . . . .
    . . . . PS May 43 87
  Hero. .s . . . . TW Oct 39 85
  Jewel of Mars. .ss. . . . .
    . . . . .CF Spr 40 100

AUTHOR
  Title. .Length . . . . Magazine, Date, Page

Matter of Form, A. .nt . . . .
  . . . . ASF Dec 38 9
Out of the Depths. .s . . . .
  . . . . .TW Jul 40 44
Perfect Murder. .ss. . . . .
  . . . . TW Mar 40 74
Problem in Murder. .nt . . . .
  . . . . ASF Mar 39 119
Trouble With Water. .s . . . .
  . . . . UK Mar 39 117
                          UK 48 62
Warm, Dark Places. .s . . . .
  . . . . UK Oct 40 114
Without Rocket from Earth. . . . .
  . .s . . . . TW Dec 41 110
with L. SPRAGUE de CAMP
  None But Lucifer. .n . . . .
    . . . . .UK Sep 39 9
GOLDSMITH, NORMAN R.
  Starting Point. .a . . . .
    . . . . .ASF Jan 41 90
GOLLOMB, JOSEPH
  True Adventures of a Super-
    Scientific Detective. .s . . . .
    . . . . SD Feb 30 138
GOLUB, F.
  Secret of the Microcosm, The . . .
    . .s. .*(tr fr German by Francis W.*
    Currier) . . . . .WS Jan 34 622
GORDON, DAVID
  By the Rules. .nt . . . .
    . . . . .OW Oct 50 6
GORDON, HARRY
  Gateway to Destruction. .s . . . . .
    . . . . FA Sep 49 112
GORDON, MILLARD VERNE *pseud*
  of DONALD A. WOLLHEIM
  Blind Flight. .s . . . . . Sti Mar 42 21
  Bomb. .ss. . . . . . . SFQ Win 42 81
  Cosmophobia. .ss. . . . Sti Apr 41 60
  Oomph Beasts, The. .s . . . .
    . . . . Fut Dec 42 99
  Planet of Illusion, The. .ss . . . . .
    . . . . Cos Mar 41 119
  Purple Dandelions, The. .ss . . . .
    . . . . Cos Mar 41 105
  Revolving World. .ss. . . . .
    . . . . .SF Sep 41 47
  Saknarth. .ss. . . . . .SFQ Spr 42 118
  Space Lens, The. .s . . . .
    . . . . WS Sep 35 452
                          FSQ Fal 50 134
  Storm Warning. .s . . . Fut Oct 42 43
  World in Balance, The . . . .
    . .s . . . . Fut Jun 42 76

AUTHOR
  Title. .Length . . . . Magazine, Date, Page

GORDON, PETER
  Anything Can Happen. .s . . . . . .
    . . . . ASF Oct 33 40
GOTTESMAN, S. D. *pseud of CYRIL*
  KORNBLUTH, alone and in
  collaboration with others.
by CYRIL KORNBLUTH
  Core, The. .nt . . . . . .Fut Apr 42 10
  Dead Center. .nt . . . . . Sti Feb 41 6
  Dimension of Darkness. .s . . . . . .
    . . . . .Cos May 41 27
  Fire Power. .s . . . . Cos Jul 41 6
  Kazam Collects. .s . . .Sti Jun 41 102
  King Cole of Pluto. .s . . . .
    . . . . SSS May 40 90
  Perfect Invasion, The. .s . . . .
    . . . . Sti Mar 42 4
  Return from M–15. .nt . . . .
    . . . . .Cos Mar 41 58
  Sir Mallory's Magnitude. .s . . . . .
    . . . . .SFQ Win 41–42 88
by CYRIL KORNBLUTH and
  FREDERIK POHL
  Before the Universe. .nt . . . .
    . . . . SSS Jul 40 96
  Best Friend. .s . . . . SSS May 41 85
  Mars-Tube. .s . . . . . .Ash Sep 41 10
  Nova Midplane. .s . . . .
    . . . . .SSS Nov 40 102
  Trouble in Time. .s . . . .
    . . . . .Ash Dec 40 34
by CYRIL KORNBLUTH, ROBERT
  W. LOWNDES and FREDERIK
  POHL
  Castle on Outerplanet, The . . . . .
    . .s . . . . Sti Apr 41 28
  Extrapolated Dimwit, The. . . . . .
    . .nt . . . . Fut Oct 42 10
GRABER, EDWIN L.
  Flame-Jewel of the Ancients . . . .
    . .nt . . . . .PS Spr 50 60
GRAHAM, FELIX *pseud of*
  FREDRIC BROWN
  Hat Trick, The. .s . . . .
    . . . . UK Feb 43 110
GRAHAM, HOWARD W., Ph.D. *pseud*
  of HOWARD WANDREI
  Guns of Eternal Day. .s. . . . .
    . . . . ASF Jul 34 123
  Other, The. .s . . . . ASF Dec 34 31
  Time Haven. .s . . . . ASF Sep 34 42
  Wall, The. .s . . . . . . ASF May 34 22
GRAHAM, REX
  Customs Declaration. .nt . . . . . .
    . . . . ASF Mar 49 82

AUTHOR
  Title. .Length . . . . Magazine, Date, Page

GRAHAM, ROGER P. *See Also*
  pseuds CRAIG BROWNING (19),
  ROG PHILLIPS (44), A. R.
  STEBER (h)
  Frame Concept of Numbers, Time
    and Space, The. .a . . . .
    . . . . Amz Sep 46 158
  Unforseen. .s . . . . . .FA Jan 49 136
GRANOSKI, CLARENCE
  Ephony's Spectacles. .s. . . . .
    . . . . .SFQ Win 41–42 79
  Femintown, Mars. .s. . . . .
    . . . . .SFQ Spr 41 141
GRANT, GILBERT
  Make Mine a Mermaid. .s. . . . . . .
    . . . . .Amz Jul 50 136
  Mechanical Genius, The. .s . . . . .
    . . . . FA Jun 50 140
  Mr. Destiny Follows Through . . .
    . .nt . . . . FA Mar 50 58
  One Way. .s . . . . . . FA Nov 50 108
  This Table Reserved. .s. . . . .
    . . . . Amz Sep 50 146
GRANT, HAL
  Ancient Horror, The. .s. . . . .
    . . . . Amz Apr 38 56
GRAUMAN, GEORGE
  Supermen Incorporated. .n . . . . .
    . . . . Amz Jun 49 94
GRAY, KENNETH
  Smaller Than You Think. . . . . . .
    . .s . . . . ASF Aug 48 32
GRAY, RUSSELL
  Fresh Fiancés for the Devil's
    Daughter. .nt . . . . MSS May 40 87
GRAY, WILL H.
  Bees from Borneo, The. .s . . . . . .
    . . . . Amz Feb 31 988
  Star of Dead Love, The. .s. . . . . .
    . . . . Amz May 27 200
  Tide Projectile Transportation
    Co., The. .s . . . . . Amz Sep 27 54
GREENE, GRAHAM
  End of the Party, The. .s. . . . . . .
    . . . . WB Dec 50 32
GREENE, L. PATRICK
  Out of the Desert. .s. . . . .
    . . . . FFM Oct 41 116
GREENFIELD, TAYLOR H.
  Sword and the Atopen, The. . . . .
    . .s . . . . .Amz Jan 30 904
GREGOR, LEE *pseud of MILTON*
  A. ROTHMAN
  Asteroid. .s. . . . . . .Ash Feb 40 62
  Flight to Galileo. .s . . . .
    . . . . Ash Oct 40 88

Heavy Planet. .s. . . . ASF Aug 39 33
Power Plant. .s . . . .
    . . . . .SFQ Win 41–42 71
Shawn's Sword. .s . . . .
    . . . . .ASF Oct 39 110
GREGORY, FRANKLIN
  Screaming Shapes, The. .nt . . . . .
    . . . . Amz Aug 50 58
GREGORY, JACKSON, JR.
  Secret of the Cyclotron . . . .
    . .s . . . . TW Feb 40 32
GREGORY, JOHN MILLER
  Fish-Men of Arctica. .nt . . . .
    . . . . .Mir Jun–Jul 31 238
GRENDON, EDWARD
  Figure, The. .s. . . . . ASF Jul 47 46
  Trip One. .s . . . . . . ASF Jul 49 85
GRENDON, STEPHEN
  Bishop's Gambit. .s . . . .
    . . . . AFR #3 95
GREY, CAROL *pseud of ROBERT*
  W. LOWNDES
  Leapers, The. .s . . . . . Fut Dec 42 40
  Passage to Sharanee. .s . . . .
    . . . . Fut Apr 42 88
GREY, HECTOR GAVIN
  Arrested by Radio. .a . . . .
    . . . . .AD Jul 30 591
  Telegraphic Finger Print, The. . . .
    . .a . . . . AD Jun 30 549
  Tracked by Ultra-Violet. .a . . . . .
    . . . . AD Aug 30 692
GRIMSHAW, BEATRICE
  Cave, The. .s. . . . . . . AFR #13 13
GRINNELL, DAVID
  Top Secret. .ss . . . .F&SF Fal 50 31
GRONER, AUGUSTA
  City of the Dead. .n . . . .
    . . . . .FFM Apr 48 8
GROSS *artist*
  Covers for PLANET STORIES
  Win 1943
  Sum 1944
GROSS, JEROME
with RICHARD PENNY
  Emperors of Space. .s. . . . .
    . . . . WS Nov 31 762
GROSSER, E. A.
  Blue Boy. .s . . . . SSS Jan 41 94
  Brain of Many Bodies, The . . . . .
    . .s . . . . .SF Oct 40 54
  Children of Zeus. .s . . . .
    . . . . Ash Jun 40 64
  Finity. .s . . . . ASF Nov 41 70
  Habits Via Radio. .s . . . .
    . . . . .SF Jan 41 60

Living Ghost, The. .s . . . .
    . . . . UK Mar 40 93
Mister Island. .s. . . . .
    . . . . Ash Oct 40 23
Opportunists, The. .s . . . .
    . . . . .ASF Jan 41 116
Out of Nowhere. .s . . . .
    . . . . Fut Oct 41 84
Psychomorph, The. .s. . . . .
    . . . . UK Feb 40 89
                              UK 48 112
Radiant Avenger, The. .s. . . . . . .
    . . . . .Fut Apr 41 38
Time Exposure. .s . . .Fut Aug 42 76
Willie Wins a War. .s . . . .
    .SSS Aug 41 61
GROVER, LEONARD
  Plunge of the Knupfen, The. . . . .
    . .s . . . . FFM Feb 40 116
GROVES, J. W.
  Regrowth. .s. . . . . . SS Jan 50 133
  Robots Don't Bleed. .s . . . .
    . . . . NW Win 50 42
  Sphere of Death, The. .s . . . .
    . . . . Amz Oct 31 656
GRUBER, FRANK
  Gun, The. .s . . . . AFR #7 111
GUERNSEY, H. W. *pseud of*
  HOWARD WANDREI
  African Trick, The. .s . . . .
    . . . . UK Apr 40 81
  Black Farm, The. .s . . . .
    . . . . UK Mar 40 75
  Danger: Quicksand. .s. . . . .
    . . . . UK Sep 39 79
  Hexer, The. .s . . . . . UK Jun 39 121
                              UK 48 118
  Macklin's Little Friend. .s . . . . . .
    . . . . ASF Nov 36 83
  Missing Ocean, The. .s . . . .
    . . . . .UK May 39 47
  Monocle, The. .nt . . . .
    . . . . UK Nov 39 107
GUINTA, JOHN *artist*
with GARDNER FOX (text)
  Crom the Barbarian. .comic. . . . . .
    . . . . OTWA Jul 50 72
  Spider God of Akka, The. .comic
    . . . . .OTWA Dec 50 72
GUNN, JAMES E. *See pseud*
  EDWIN JAMES (4)
GUNN, LYLE D.
  If the Earth's Magnetic Field
    Failed. .a . . . . FA Nov 39 82
  Time Twin, The. .s. . . . .
    . . . . .TW Aug 39 26

AUTHOR
Title. .Length . . . . Magazine, Date, Page

GURDON, J. E.
Biog sketch . . . . . Fant #1 38 128
Leashed Lightning. .s . . . .
. . . . Fant #1 38 37
Man Outside, The. .s . . . .
. . . . Fant #3 39 50
GURWIT, S. GORDON
World Flight. .s . . . . .ASF Jan 34 73
GUTH, HENRY
Doom Ship. .s . . . . . .SSS Nov 40 86
Earthbound. .s . . . . . .PS Win 47 84
Planet in Reverse. .s . . . .
. . . . PS Spr 48 59
Signal Red. .s . . . . PS Fal 49 69
GUTHRIE, Lt. COMDR. WARREN,
USNR
Operation Asdevlant. .a . . . .
. . . . SS Jul 47 71

H

HADDEN *artist*
Cover for AMAZING STORIES
Jun 43
HAGGARD, H. RIDER
Allan and the Ice Gods. .n . . . . .
. . . . FFM Apr 47 6
Ancient Allan, The. .n . . . .
. . . . FFM Dec 45 10
Morning Star. .n . . . . FFM Feb 50 8
HAGGARD, J. HARVEY
Biog sketch, photo. . . . .
. . . . Amz Feb 39 132
Adventure on Eros, An. .s . . . . . .
. . . . WS Sep 31 546
Castaways on Deimos. .s . . . .
. . . . WS Aug 33 128
Children of the Ray. .s . . . .
. . . . WS Mar 34 826
. . . . FSQ Spr 50 142
Denizons of Zeron. .s . . . .
. . . . .ASF Jan 37 115
Derelicts of Uranus. .s . . . .
. . . . .Com May 41 54
Episode on Io, An. .s . . . .
. . . . WS Feb 34 736
Evolution Satellite. .nt 2 pt . . . . .
. . . . WS Dec 33 422
Faster Than Light. .s . . . .
. . . . WS Oct 30 432
From the Vacuum of Space. . . . .
. .s . . . . ASF Dec 37 136
Fruit of the Moon-Weed. .s . . . . .
. . . . ASF Nov 35 44

Girl of the Silver Sphere. .s . . . . .
. . . . PS Fal 47 115
He Who Masters Time. .s . . . . . .
. . . . TW Feb 37 58
Healing Rays in Space. .s . . . . . .
. . . . Com Mar 41 72
Human Ants. .s . . . WS May 35 1440
Human Machines. .s . . . .
. . . . ASF Dec 35 70
Jupiter Napoleon. .ss . . . .
. . . . .OTWA Dec 50 39
Light That Kills, The. .s . . . .
. . . . Amz Feb 39 74
Little Green Stone, A. .s . . . .
. . . . ASF Mar 36 30
Lost in Space. .s . . . .
. . . . ASF Aug 35 53
Messenger to Infinity. .s . . . .
. . . . SFQ Win 42 144
Moon Crystals. .s . . . .ASF Jan 36 30
Phantom Star. .s . . .ASF Oct 35 132
Professor Splits, The. .s . . . .
. . . . .Ash Feb 41 6
Relativity to the Rescue. .nt . . . .
. . . . Amz Apr 35 100
Renegade. .ss . . . . . . TW Jun 37 88
Round About Rigel. .s . . . .
. . . . TW Aug 37 74
Task of Tau. .s . . . . PS Sum 48 103
Through the Einstein Line. . . . . .
. .s . . . . WS Nov 33 394
Universe in Darkness. .s . . . .
. . . . .Fut Nov 40 8
World Reborn. .n . . . .
. . . . .Fut Nov 39 10
Year of Unreason, The. .s . . . . . .
. . . . TW Jun 38 84
HAHN, GEORGE R.
Gangway for Homer. .s . . . .
. . . . .SFQ Spr 42 122
HALE, EDWARD EVERETT
Good Natured Pendulum,
The. .s . . . . Amz May 33 177
HALE, STEPHEN G.
Laughing Death, The. .s . . . .
. . . . Amz Apr 31 42
Worlds Adrift. .nt . . . .
. . . . Amz May 32 158
HALE, RANDALL
PROBABILITY ZERO
De Gustibus. .ss. . . . .
. . . . ASF Jul 42 110
HALL, AUSTIN
Biog Sketch . . . . FFM Apr 40 112
Almost Immortal. .nt . . . .
. . . . .FFM Nov 39 82

Into the Infinite. .n 4 pt . . . .
. . . . .FFM Oct 42 83
Man Who Saved theEarth,
The. .nt . . . . Amz Apr 26 75
                        AA 27 82
                        FFM Feb 40 6
Rebel Soul, The. .nt . . . .
. . . . .FFM Aug 40 80
Spot of Life, The. .n . . . .
. . . . .FFM Feb 41 6
with HOMER EON FLINT
Biog sketch: HALL AND FLINT by
Phil Richards . . . . FFM Feb 41 84
Blind Spot, The. .n. .*(The first 27*
of 48 chapters were printed in 3
instalments, then dropped when
published complete in FANTASTIC
NOVELS) . . . . . . .FFM Mar 40 6
Blind Spot, The. .n . . . .FN Jul 40 2
HALL, CHARLES F.
Man Who Lived Backwards, The. .
. .s . . . . .ToW Sum 38 21
Time Drug, The. .s . . . .
. . . . ToW Win 38 62
HALL, D.(esmond) W.(inter) *See*
also pseuds ANTHONY GILMORE
(7), H. G. WINTER (4)
Raiders Invisible. .s . . . .
. . . . ASF Nov 31 200
Scientist Rises, A. .s . . . .
. . . . ASF Nov 32 165
Werewolves of War. .s . . . .
. . . . ASF Feb 31 153
HALL, GEORGE W.
PROBABILITY ZERO
Applesauce. .ss . . . .
. . . . ASF Dec 44 131
HALL, JAMES *pseud of HENRY*
KUTTNER
Dictator of the Americas. .s . . . . .
. . . . MSS Aug 38 65
HALL, T. PROCTOR
Doctor O'Glee's Experiments. . . .
. .nt . . . . .AQ Sum 29 398
HAMILTON, EDMOND *See also*
pseuds ROBERT CASTLE (2),
HUGH DAVIDSON (0), WILL
GARTH (h) (1), BRETT
STERLING (h) (4), ROBERT
WENTWORTH (1)
Biog sketch . . . .
. . . . Amz Nov 38 143
Biog sketch, photo. . . . .
. . . . TW Jun 39 88
Biog sketch, photo. . . . .
. . . . .SS Win 46 95

AUTHOR
Title. .Length . . . . Magazine, Date, Page

Accursed Galaxy, The. .s . . . . . .
. . . . .ASF Jul 35 64
Alien Earth. .s . . . . . TW Apr 49 54
CAPTAIN FUTURE
Captain Future and the Space
Emperor. .n . . . . . CF Win 40 12
Calling Captain Future . . . . . .
. .n . . . . .CF Spr 40 12
Captain Future's Challenge . . . .
. .n . . . . .CF Sum 40 14
The Triumph of Captain
Future. .n . . . . . .CF Fal 40 14
Captain Future and the Seven
Space Stones. .n . . . .
. . . . CF Win 41 14
Star Trail to Glory. .n. . . . . . .
. . . . .CF Spr 41 14
The Magician of Mars. .n . . . . . .
. . . . .CF Sum 41 14
The Lost World of Time. .n . . . .
. . . . .CF Fal 41 14
The Quest Beyond the Stars . . .
. .n . . . . CF Win 42 15
Outlaws of the Moon. .n . . . . . .
. . . . .CF Spr 42 14
The Comet Kings. .n . . . .
. . . . .CF Sum 42 11
Planets of Peril. .n . . . .
. . . . .CF Fal 42 13
The Face of the Deep. . . . . . .
. .n . . . . CF Win 43 15
*(See title index for additional
CAPTAIN FUTURE stories at this
point in the series and under
other by-lines)*
Outlaw World. .n . . . .
. . . . .SS Win 46 11
The Return of Captain
Future. .nt . . . . . . SS Jan 50 94
Children of the Sun. .s . . . .
. . . . SS May 50 98
The Harpers of Titan. .s . . . . . .
. . . . .SS Sep 50 96
Pardon My Iron Nerves. . . . . . .
. .s . . . . SS Nov 50 78
Cities in the Air. .n 2 pt . . . .
. . . . .AW Nov 29 390
City at World's End, The. . . . . .
. .n . . . . SS Jul 50 11
Come Home from Earth . . . . . .
. .s . . . . TW Feb 47 91
Comet Doom, The. .nt . . . .
. . . . .Amz Jan 28 926
ToW Aut 39 4
Conquest of Two Worlds, A. . . . .
. .s . . . . WS Feb 32 1046
SS Jan 48 70

AUTHOR
Title. .Length . . . . Magazine, Date, Page

Cosmic Hiss, The. .s . . . .
. . . . TW Dec 38 90
Cosmic Pantograph, The. .s . . . . .
. . . . WS Oct 35 554
Cosmic Quest. .s . . . .
. . . . TW Oct 36 33
Daughter of Thor, The. .nt . . . . .
. . . . .FA Aug 42 10
Day of the Micro-Men. .s . . . . . .
. . . . .SF Sep 41 50
Dead Planet, The. .s . . . .
. . . . .SS Spr 46 84
Deconventionalizers, The . . . . . .
. .s . . . . .TW Sum 45 59
Devolution. .s . . . . Amz Dec 36 90
Dictators of Creation. .nt . . . . . .
. . . . TW May 40 50
Doom Over Venus. .nt . . . .
. . . . TW Feb 40 85
Dweller in the Darkness. .s . . . . .
. . . . .SF Oct 39 56
Easy Money. .s . . . .
. . . . TW Apr 38 55
Ephemerae, The. .s . . . .
. . . . ASF Dec 38 50
Eternal Cycle, The. .s . . . .
. . . . WS Mar 35 1184
Evans of the Earth Guard . . . . . .
. .s . . . . AW Apr 30 902
Exile. .ss . . . . SSS May 43 88
Fear Neutralizer, The. .s . . . . . .
. . . . .SS Mar 39 108
Forgotten World. .nt . . . .
. . . . TW Win 46 13
Free-Lance of Space, The . . . . . .
. .s . . . . Amz May 44 122
Gift from the Stars. .nt . . . .
. . . . TW Dec 40 91
Hidden World. .n . . . . WQ Fal 29 84
FSQ Spr 50 11
Holmes' Folly. .s . . . . TW Oct 37 59
Horror in the Telescope. .s . . . . .
. . . . .ToW Sum 38 33
Horror Out of Carthage . . . .
. .nt . . . . FA Sep 39 6
Horse That Talked, The . . . .
. .nt . . . . .FA Jan 41 108
Indestructible Man, The. .s . . . . .
. . . . TW Spr 46 32
Intelligence Undying. .s . . . .
. . . . Amz Apr 36 13
Interplanetary Graveyard. .s . . . .
. . . . .Fut Mar 40 56
Invaders from the Monster
World. .nt . . . .
. . . . Amz Jun 45 68

AUTHOR
Title. .Length . . . . Magazine, Date, Page

Invisible Master, The. .nt . . . . . .
. . . . SD Apr 30 300
Island of Unreason, The. .s . . . . .
. . . . WS May 33 970
SS Spr 45 90
Isle of Changing Life, The . . . . .
. .s . . . . TW Jun 40 33
Knowledge Machine, The. .s . . . .
. . . . TW Jun 48 109
Lilene, the Moon Girl. .nt . . . . . .
. . . . Amz May 40 66
Locked Worlds. .s . . . .
. . . . AQ Spr 29 222
Lost City of Burma. .n . . . .
. . . . FA Dec 42 38
Lost Treasure of Mars. .s . . . .
. . . . Amz Aug 40 68
Man Who Evolved, The. .s . . . . . .
. . . . WS Apr 31 1266
SS Nov 40 110
Man Who Lived Twice, The . . . . .
. .s . . . . Amz Nov 38 76
Man Who Saw the Future,
The. .s . . . . Amz Oct 30 600
ToW Sum 40 24
Man Who Solved Death, The . . . .
. .s . . . . SF Aug 39 92
Man With X-Ray Eyes, The . . . . .
. .s . . . . WS Nov 33 386
SS Sum 46 62
Master of the Genes. .s . . . .
. . . . .WS Jan 35 958
Million Years Ahead, A. . . . .
. .s . . . . TW Apr 37 92
Monsters of Mars. .nt . . . .
. . . . ASF Apr 31 4
Murder Asteroid. .ss. . . . .
. . . . TW Oct 40 80
Murder in the Clinic, The. .nt. . . .
. . . . SD May 30 390
Murder in the Void. .s . . . .
. . . . TW Jun 38 14
Mutiny on Europa. .nt . . . .
. . . . TW Dec 36 94
Mystery Moon. .nt. . . . .
. . . . Amz Jan 41 72
Night the World Ended, The . . . .
. .s . . . . TW Sep 40 82
No-Man's-Land of Time. .s . . . . .
. . . . SF Apr 43 45
Other Side of the Moon, The . . . .
. .nt . . . . .AQ Fal 29 516
Prisoner of Mars, The. .n . . . . . .
. . . . SS May 39 14
Proxy Planeteers. .s . . . .
. . . . SS Jul 47 88

AUTHOR
    Title. .Length . . . . Magazine, Date, Page

Quest in Time, The. .nt. . . . . . .
. . . . FA Jun 42 150
Reign of the Robots, The. .s . . . .
. . . . WS Dec 31 848
Revolt on the Tenth World . . . . .
. .s . . . . Amz Nov 40 60
Sargasso of Space, The. .s . . . . . .
. . . . .ASF Sep 31 390
Sea Terror, The. .nt . . . .
. . . . ToW Aut 38 72
Second Satellite, The. .s . . . .
. . . . ASF Aug 30 175
Son of Two Worlds. .n . . . .
. . . . .TW Aug 41 14
Space Beings, The. .s . . . .
. . . . ToW Win 38 39
Space Mirror. .s. . . . .TW Aug 37 43
Space Rocket Murders. .nt . . . . .
. . . . Amz Oct 32 582
Space Visitors, The. .s . . . .
. . . . .AW May 30 804
                     SS Sep 39 110
Star Kings, The. .n. . . . .
. . . . Amz Sep 47 8
Star of Life, The. .n . . . .
. . . . SS Jan 47 13
Star-Stealers, The. .nt. . . . .
. . . . AFR #6 65
Three Planeteers, The. .n. . . . . . .
. . . . SS Jan 40 12
Through Invisible Barriers. . . . . .
. .nt . . . . TW Oct 42 15
Transuranic. .s . . . . TW Feb 48 72
Treasure on Thunder Moon. . . . .
. .n . . . . Amz Apr 42 198
Trouble on Triton. .s . . . .
. . . . SS Fal 45 75
Truth Gas, The. .s . . . .
. . . . WS Feb 35 1060
Under the White Star. .s . . . .
. . . . SF Mar 39 6
Universe Wreckers, The. . . . .
. .n 3 pt . . . . . . Amz May 30 102
Valley of Creation, The . . . .
. .n . . . . SS Jul 48 9
Valley of Invisible Men. .nt . . . . .
. . . . Amz Mar 39 22
Wacky World. .s . . . .
. . . . Amz Mar 42 198
When Space Burst. .s . . . .
. . . . .TW Dec 37 90
World Atavism. .s . . . .
. . . . Amz Aug 30 428
World With a Thousand Moons,
    The. .nt . . . . Amz Dec 42 64

AUTHOR
    Title. .Length . . . . Magazine, Date, Page

Yank at Valhalla, A. .n . . . .
. . . . .SS Jan 41 14
HAMILTON, PETER
Meteor Makers, The. .s . . . .
. . . . PS May 43 78
HAMLING, WILLIAM LAWRENCE
Associate Editor AMAZING
    STORIES
    Aug 46 *thru* Dec 47 *issues*
Managing Editor AMAZING
    STORIES
    Jan 48 *thru* Jan 51 *issues*
Associate Editor FANTASTIC
    ADVENTURES
    Sep 46 *thru* Oct 47 *issues*
Managing Editor FANTASTIC
    ADVENTURES
    Nov 47 *thru* Feb 51 *issues*
Biog sketch . . . . Amz May 39 128
Biog sketch, photo. . . . .
. . . . Amz Sep 44 185
Biog sketch, photo. . . . .
. . . . FA Sep 46 2
Animated Tenpin, The. .s . . . . . .
. . . . Amz Sep 45 30
Bag and Baggage. .s . . . .
. . . . FA Oct 45 76
Jimmy Takes a Trip. .s . . . .
. . . . FA Jul 46 116
Man Who Spoke Too Late,
    The. .s . . . . FA Oct 44 194
Mirror, The. .s. . . . . FA Sep 46 80
Orphan of Atlans .n . . . .
. . . . Amz Feb 47 8
Overlord of Venus. .s . . . .
. . . . Amz Sep 44 174
Peril from the Outlands . . . .
. .s . . . . Amz Jun 45 154
Planet of the Duplicates. .s . . . . .
. . . . Amz Dec 45 62
Problem in Lumbering, A . . . . . .
. .s . . . . FA Dec 45 140
Prop, The. .s. . . . . Amz Aug 47 44
Rejuvenation Asteroid. .s . . . . . .
. . . . Amz Jan 47 28
Shadow of the Sphinx. .n . . . . . .
. . . . .FA Nov 46 8
with MARK REINSBERG
War With Jupiter. .s . . . .
. . . . .Amz May 39 74
HAMMOND, H. R. *artist*
Cover for AMAZING STORIES
    Apr 1940
12,000 Years Ago . . . .
. .bacover pic . . . . . Amz May 40

AUTHOR
    Title. .Length . . . . Magazine, Date, Page

Earth's Core, The. .bacover . . . . .
. . . . Amz Mar 40
HAMMOND, KEITH *pseud of*
    HENRY KUTTNER and C. L.
    MOORE
Biog sketch . . . . . . .SS Mar 46 111
Call Him Demon. .s . . . .
. . . . TW Fal 46 46
Dark Dawn. .s. . . . .
. . . . .TW Aug 47 89
Lord of the Storm. .n. . . . .
. . . . .SS Sep 47 11
Valley of the Flame. .n. . . . .
. . . . .SS Mar 46 13
HAMMOND, W. F.
Grey Shadow, The. .s . . . .
. . . . .AD Jul 30 586
Lakh-Dal, Destroyer of Souls. . . .
. .s . . . . Amz Mar 28 1184
HANSEN, L.(ouise) TAYLOR
City on the Cloud, The. .s . . . . . .
. . . . WS Oct 30 426
Enigma of the Oceans, The
    .a . . . . Amz Dec 47 168
Ghost Ship of Aztlan, The. .s . . . .
. . . . SS Jul 42 110
Lords of the Underworld. .nt. . . .
. . . . Amz Apr 41 8
Man from Space, The. .s . . . .
. . . . Amz Feb 30 1034
MYSTERIES OF GEOLOGY
    The Enigma of the Pacific. . . . .
    . .a . . . . Amz May 48 168
Prince of Liars, The. .s . . . .
. . . . Amz Oct 30 582
PROBLEMS OF SCIENCE dept
    The Enigma of Rifting. .a . . . . .
    . . . . Amz Mar 48 154
    The Enigma of Compression . . .
    . .a . . . . Amz Apr 48 161
SCIENTIFIC MYSTERIES dept
    Gondwanaland. .a . . . .
    . . . . Amz Sep 41 130
    Votan, The Clever Builder. . . . .
    . .a . . . . Amz Dec 41 126
    The Spider Totem. .a . . . .
    . . . . .Amz Jan 42 230
    Mystery of Man's Migration. . . .
    . .a . . . . Amz Jun 42 258
    The White Race—Does It
    Exist? . .a . . . . . Amz Jul 42 210
    The Mystery of Man's Color . . .
    . .a . . . . Amz Aug 42 150
    The Mystery of the Neanderthal
    Man. .a . . . . Amz Sep 42 42

AUTHOR
Title. .Length . . . . Magazine, Date, Page

How Old Is Mankind? . .a . . . . .
. . . . Amz Oct 42 224
Did the American Indian Once
Invade Europe? . .a . . . .
. . . . Amz Nov 42 228
Riddle of the African Bushman .
. .a . . . . Amz Dec 42 224
Mystery of the Earth's Rift
Valleys. .a . . . . .Amz Jan 43 222
Mystery of the Earth's Long-
Headed Races. .a . . . .
. . . . Amz Feb 43 230
Totem of the Eagle. .a . . . .
. . . . Amz Mar 43 224
Who Were the People of the
Dragon? . .a . . . Amz Apr 43 226
What Do We Celebrate at
Christmas? . .a . . . .
. . . . Amz May 43 138
The Mystery Behind the Atlantic
"Twins". .a . . . Amz Jun 43 194
Mystery of Pan, Saturn and
Ammon-Ra. .a . . . .
. . . . .Amz Jul 43 196
Does the Atlantic Hide a Sunken
Land? . .a . . . . Amz Aug 43 198
Mystery of the Megaliths. .a . . . .
. . . . Amz Sep 43 196
The Mysterious Tuaraks . . . . . .
. . . . Amz Nov 43 186
The American Dragon. .a . . . . .
. . . . .Amz Jan 44 186
Tracking Down the Dragon . . . .
. .a . . . . Amz Mar 44 186
Footprints of the Dragon . . . . .
. .a . . . . Amz May 44 194
Ancient American Nations . . . .
. .a . . . . Amz Sep 44 198
Ancient Americans—The Aztecs
and Toltecs. .a . . . .
. . . . Amz Dec 44 192
A Scientific Jig-Saw Puzzle . . . .
. .a . . . . Amz Mar 45 196
The Mystery of the Natchez . . .
. .a . . . . Amz Jun 45 184
The Turtle Totem. .a . . . .
. . . . Amz Sep 45 106
The Black Tortoise. .a . . . .
. . . . Amz Dec 45 158
The Bearded White Prophet. . . .
. .a . . . . Amz Feb 46 162
Where Was the War of the Wind
God? . .a . . . . . Amz May 46 152
The Ghost of the Venus
Calendar. .a . . . Amz Jun 46 170

The Ghost of Pan. .a . . . .
. . . . Amz Aug 46 144
Shadow of Ancient India . . . . .
. . . . Amz Sep 46 154
More Shadows of Ancient
India. .a . . . . . Amz Oct 46 158
Totem of the Fish. .a . . . .
. . . . Amz Nov 46 162
Tribal Memories of the
Navaho. .a . . . . Amz Dec 46 148
The Totem of the Wolf. .a . . . .
. . . . .Amz Jan 47 154
The Mystery of the Apache
Tradition. .a . . . Amz Feb 47 166
The Totem of the Snake . . . . . .
. . . . Amz Mar 47 152
The Sun-Moon War. .a . . . .
. . . . Amz Apr 47 152
The Empire of the Moon. . . . . .
. . . . Amz May 47 154
The Empire of the Sun. .a . . . . .
. . . . Amz Jun 47 130
Untangling the Origin of the
Nahuas. .a . . . . Amz Aug 47 156
The Atlantic Empire of the
Quinames. .a . . . Amz Sep 47 166
The Land of Maize. .a . . . .
. . . . Amz Oct 47 154
Fascinating Matto Grosso . . . . .
. . . . .Amz Jan 48 142
Wherein the Stage Is Set for a
Titanic Drama. .a . . . .
. . . . Amz Feb 48 136
Was There a Great Flood? . . . .
. . . . Amz Mar 48 148
The Degenerating Karibs. . . . . .
. . . . Amz Apr 48 156
Totem of the Tiger. .a . . . .
. . . . Amz Jun 48 150
The Mysterious Easterners. .a . . .
. . . . .Amz Jul 48 148
The City of the Seven Caves . . .
. .a . . . . Amz Aug 48 150
The Search for the City of Seven
Caves. .a . . . . . Amz Nov 48 142
The Puzzling American
Pageant. .a . . . . Amz Dec 48 94
Undersea Tube, The. .s . . . .
. . . . Amz Nov 29 720
What the Sodium Lines
Revealed. .s . . . . . AQ Win 29 120
HAPPEL, R. V.
Triple Ray, The. .s . . . .
. . . . .AQ Fal 30 529

AUTHOR
Title. .Length . . . . Magazine, Date, Page

HARBAUGH, CHARLES W.
Star of Treasure. .nt. . . . .
. . . . TW Spr 44 13
HARBERS, HENRY
Lost Martian, The. .s . . . .
. . . . SW Dec 29 636
HARDART, F. E.
Beast of Space, The. .s . . . .
. . . . .Com Jul 41 82
Devil's Pocket, The. .s . . . .
. . . . .Ash Jun 40 35
HARDING, ALLISON V.
Guard in the Dark. .s . . . .
. . . . .AFR #14 51
HARMON, H. H. *pseud of ROBERT
MOORE WILLIAMS*
Secret of the Lightning. .s . . . . . .
. . . . FA Sep 49 100
Swamp Girl of Venus. .s . . . .
. . . . Amz Sep 49 44
HARNESS, CHARLES (L.)
Even Steven. . . . .s . . . .
. . . . .OW Nov 50 138
Flight Into Yesterday. .n. . . . . . .
. . . . SS May 49 9
Fruits of the Agathon. .s . . . . . .
. . . . TW Dec 48 64
Heritage. .nt . . . . . .F&SF Fal 50 93
New Reality, The. .nt . . . .
. . . . TW Dec 50 56
Stalemate in Space. .s . . . .
. . . . PS Sum 49 84
Time Trap. .nt . . . . . ASF Aug 48 7
HARRIS, ARTHUR T. *house pseud*
Biog sketch, gag photo . . . .
. . . . .FA Jul 42 230
Abner Schlap's Strange
Insight. .s . . . . .FA Jul 41 56
Armageddon of Johann Schmidt,
The. .s . . . . .Amz Jan 41 108
Caution: Dead Man at Work . . . .
. .s . . . . Amz Feb 47 150
Ernest's Evil Entity. .s . . . .
. . . . FA Oct 48 108
Mr. Duffy's Other Life. .s . . . . . .
. . . . FA May 41 124
Plastic Genie, The. .s . . . .
. . . . TW Apr 42 101
Throne of Valhalla, The . . . .
. .s . . . . Amz Sep 41 92
Traitor, The. .s . . . . . .FA Jul 42 98
HARRIS, CLARE WINGER
Ape Cycle, The. .s . . . .
. . . . WQ Spr 30 388

AUTHOR
Title. .Length . . . . Magazine, Date, Page

Artificial Man, The. .s. . . . .
. . . . WQ Fal 29 78
Diabolical Drug, The. .s . . . .
. . . . Amz May 29 156
Evolutionary Monstrosity, The. . .
. .s . . . . AQ Win 29 70
Fate of the Poseidonia, The. . . . .
. .s . . . . Amz Jun 27 245
Fifth Dimension, The. .s . . . .
. . . . Amz Dec 28 823
Menace of Mars, The. .s . . . .
. . . . Amz Oct 28 582
Miracle of the Lily, The . . . .
. .s . . . . Amz Apr 28 48
                          AFR #75
with MILES J. BREUER, M.D.
Baby on Neptune, A. .s. . . . .
. . . . Amz Dec 29 790
Child of Neptune. .s. . . . .
. . . . ToW Spr 41 54
HARRIS, HUGH KING
Dimension Twister, The. .s . . . . .
. . . . WS Apr 33 886
HARRIS, JOHN B.(EYNON) *See also*
pseuds JOHN BEYNON (18),
WYNDHAM PARKES (1), JOHN
WYNDHAM (1)
Exiles on Asperus. .nt. . . . .
. . . . WQ Win 33 166
Invisible Monsters. .s . . . .
. . . . WS Dec 33 448
Last Lunarians, The. .s . . . .
. . . . .ToW Sum 38 95
Lost Machine, The. .s. . . . .
. . . . Amz Apr 32 40
Man from Beyond, The. .s. . . . . .
. . . . WS Sep 34 420
                          FSQ Sum 50 130
Man from Earth, The. .s . . . .
. . . . ToW Spr 40 42
Moon Devils, The. .s. . . . .
. . . . WS Apr 34 968
                          WSA 50 149
Spheres of Hell. .s . . . .
. . . . WS Oct 33 230
Third Vibrator, The. .s . . . .
. . . . .WS May 33 938
                          ToW Aut 38 94
Venus Adventure, The. .s . . . . . .
. . . . WS May 32 1352
Wanderers of Time. .s. . . . .
. . . . WS Mar 33 776
Worlds to Barter. .s . . . .
. . . . WS May 31 1422

AUTHOR
Title. .Length . . . . Magazine, Date, Page

HARRISON, EDWARD LEE
Air Spy, The. .s. . . . .
. . . . AW Oct 29 322
HARRISON, J. S.
Atala Rim. .s . . . . Amz Nov 46 128
HARRISION, KENNETH L.
Biog sketch . . . . . . TW Dec 40 74
Blonde, the Time Machine and
   Johnny Bell, The. .s. . . . .
. . . . TW Dec 40 74
HARRY, JOHN E.
Hunted Ones, The. .nt . . . .
. . . . SSS Feb 42 109
Our Director. .s. . . . .Ash Apr 41 47
Our Director Meets Trouble. . . . .
. .s . . . . .Ash Dec 42 63
Outlaws on Venus. .s . . . .
. . . . SSS Jul 40 43
HART, DALE
Tongue of the Dragon. .s. . . . . . .
. . . . AFR #5 77
HART, JAMES S.
Traitor, The. .s . . . .F&SF Fal 50 17
HARTMAN, C. L. *artist*
Covers for AMAZING STORIES
Feb, May 1940
HARVEY, WILLIAM FRYER
Sambo. .s. . . . . .AFR #5 30
HASSAN, SILAKI ALI *pseud of*
U. G. MIHALAKIS
Caliph of Yafri. .nt . . . .
. . . . UK Sep 39 91
Dolphin's Doubloons, The. . . . . .
. .s . . . . UK Oct 41 122
Wisdom of an Ass, The. .nt . . . . .
. . . . UK Feb 40 67
HASSE, HENRY
Biog Sketch . . . . . . PS Spr 47 101
Angular Stone, The. .nt . . . .
. . . . SSS May 43 8
City of the Living Flame. .nt . . . .
. . . . PS Aug 42 92
Bread-Flame of M'Tonak. .nt. . . .
. . . . .PS Fal 46 2
Eternal Zemmd Must Die. .nt. . . .
. . . . .PS Spr 49 2
Farewell to Fuzzies. .s . . . .
. . . . .Ash Sep 41 29
Final Glory. .ss . . . . . .PS Spr 47 91
He Who Shrank. .nt . . . .
. . . . Amz Aug 36 13
Mars Warning. .s . . . .SSS Aug 42 34
Miracle in Time, A. . . . .
. . . . .Ash Jun 40 83

AUTHOR
Title. .Length . . . . Magazine, Date, Page

Missing Day, The. .s . . . .
. . . . SSS May 42 30
Mission Unknown. .n . . . .
. . . . SSS May 41 8
Out of This World. .s . . . .
. . . . PS Sum 42 58
Passage to Planet X. .s . . . .
. . . . .PS Win 45 70
Proktols of Neptune. .nt . . . .
. . . . PS Sum 41 104
Revenge of the Vera. .s. . . . .
. . . . .PS Fal 43 81
Star of Satan, The. .s . . . .
. . . . .PS Fal 41 50
Survival. .s . . . .
. . . . .OW Mar 50 24
Thief of Mars. .s . . . .
. . . . .PS Win 41 57
Tomb of the Seven Taajos. .nt . . .
. . . . Amz Feb 50 106
Trail of the Astrogar. .nt. . . . . . .
. . . . Amz Oct 47 42
Walls of Acid. .s . . . . . . FB #1 32
with RAY BRADBURY
Final Victim. .s. . . Amz Feb 46 114
Gabriel's Horn. .s. . . . .
. . . . .CF Spr 43 105
Pendulum. .s. . . . .SSS Nov 41 102
with ALBERT de PINA
Alcatraz of the Starways. .nt . . . .
. . . . PS May 43 2
Star of Panadur. .s. . . . .
. . . . .PS Mar 43 65
with A. FEDOR
End of Tyme, The. .s . . . .
. . . . WS Nov 33 336
Man Who, The. .s. . . . .
. . . . MSS Nov 40 78
Return of Tyme, The. .s . . . .
. . . . WS Aug 34 294
with EMIL PETJA (published under
the Hasse by-line—Petja not
credited)
Don't Come to Mars! . .s. . . . . . .
. . . . FA Apr 50 86
HASTA, M. H.
Talking Brain, The. .s . . . .
. . . . Amz Aug 26 440
HASTINGS, HUDSON *pseud of*
HENRY KUTTNER and C. L.
MOORE
Big Night, The. .s. . . . .
. . . . TW Jun 47 38
Noon. .s. . . . . .TW Aug 47 31

AUTHOR
Title. .Length . . . . Magazine, Date, Page

HATCHER, JACK
Fuel for the Future. .a . . . .
. . . . ASF Mar 40 68
Transmutation, 1939. .a . . . .
. . . . .ASF Jan 40 69
HATFIELD, HAROLD S.
Doorway to Destruction. .ss . . . .
. . . . .PS Win 42 55
HAUCKE, FRED artist
Cover for ASTOUNDING SCIENCE
FICTION
Aug 1944
HAUSER, F. H.
with H. B. FYFE
Hold That Comet. .s . . . .
. . . . .Ash Dec 40 64
HAUSER, HEINRICH See also pseud
ALEXANDER BLADE (h) (1)
Agharti. .n . . . .
. . . . Amz Jun 46 6
Titan's Battle. .n . . . .
. . . . Amz Mar 47 50
HAWKINS, JOHN
Ark of Fire. .n . . . .
. . . . FFM Mar 43 12
Direct Action. .s . . . ASF Nov 41 81
Everything's Jake. .s. . . . .
. . . . UK Aug 42 54
HAWKINS, WARD
Biog sketch, photo. . . . .
. . . . TW Jun 39 87
Conquest by Fire. .nt . . . .
. . . . TW Apr 40 48
Men Must Die. .s . . . . TW Apr 39 48
SS Mar 50 88
HAWKINS, WILLARD
Chalice of Circe, The. .nt . . . . . .
. . . . FA Apr 50 64
Dwindling Sphere, The. .s . . . . .
. . . . ASF Mar 40 99
Look to the Stars. .n . . . .
. . . . .Im Oct 50 82
Man Who Was Millions, The. . . . .
. .nt . . . . .SF Jun 41 10
Master of Emotions. .s . . . .
. . . . .SF Sep 41 64
Power for Zenovia. .nt . . . .
. . . . TW Jun 41 14
Rannie, The. .nt . . . .
. . . . .SSS May 41 106
Romance Across the Ages. .s . . . .
. . . . .TW Jul 40 54
HAWKINS, WINTHROP W.
Regenerative Wonder, The. .s . . . .
. . . . Amz Feb 34 58

AUTHOR
Title. .Length . . . . Magazine, Date, Page

HAYS, RUSSELL
Beetle Experiment, The. .s . . . . .
. . . . Amz Jun 29 207
Purple Plague, The. .nt . . . .
. . . . Amz Feb 31 994
HEALD, HAZEL
Man of Stone, The. .s . . . .
. . . . WS Oct 32 440
HEALD, L. V.
Pain Machine, The. .s . . . .
. . . . Fant Dec 46 70
HECKMAN, ROYAL W.
Asteroid Pirates. .s . . . .
. . . . ASF Aug 38 112
Silver Sphere, The. .s . . . .
. . . . ASF Nov 38 128
HEFFRLIN, H. C.
Static Was Licked Twenty Years
Ago. .a . . . . Amz Oct 46 166
HEINER, FRANK G.
Secret of Lord Fennel, The . . . . .
. .s . . . . Amz Nov 46 84
HEINLEIN, ROBERT (A.) See also
pseuds ANSON MacDONALD (7),
LYLE MONROE (5), JOHN
RIVERSIDE (1), CALEB
SAUNDERS (1)
"—And He Built a Crooked
House" . . .s . . . . . ASF Feb 41 68
Blowups Happen. .nt . . . .
. . . . ASF Sep 40 51
Columbus Was a Dope. .ss . . . . . .
. . . . SS May 47 67
Common Sense. .n. . . . .
. . . . .ASF Oct 41 102
Coventry. .nt . . . . . ASF Jul 40 56
Devil Makes the Law, The. .n. . . .
. . . . UK Sep 40 9
Gulf. .n 2 pt . . . . . . ASF Nov 49 53
If This Goes ON—. .n 2 pt . . . . .
. . . . ASF Feb 40 9
Jerry Is a Man. .s . . . .
. . . . TW Oct 47 46
Life-Line. .s . . . . . . ASF Aug 39 83
Logic of Empire. .nt. . . . .
. . . . ASF Mar 41 9
Methuselah's Children . . . .
. .n 3 pt . . . . .ASF Jul 41 9
Misfit. .s . . . . ASF Nov 39 53
Requiem. .s . . . . . . .ASF Jan 40 80
Roads Must Roll, The. .nt . . . . . .
. . . . ASF Jun 40 9
Shooting "Destination Moon" . . .
. .a . . . . .ASF Jul 50 6
They. .s . . . . UK Apr 41 84
Universe. .nt. . . . . . ASF May 41 9

AUTHOR
Title. .Length . . . . Magazine, Date, Page

HELD, S. S.
Death of Iron, The. .n 3 pt. .(tr fr
the French by Fletcher Pratt). . .
. . . . WS Sep 32 294
HELLER, CLARENCE EDWARD
Flamingo. .s . . . . . Amz Jul 30 324
HENDRED, PAUL
People of the Deep. .s. . . . .
. . . . Fant #2 39 43
HENRY, MARION
Renegade, The. .s . . . ASF Jul 43 87
HENRY, SPEYTON
Strange Mental Phenomena . . . . .
. .a . . . . SF Mar 40 39
HENTON, WILLIAM HASKELL artist
Cover for FANTASTIC
ADVENTURES
Aug 1948
HERBERT, BENSON
Biog sketch . . . . . Amz Dec 38 144
Biog sketch, photo. . . ToW Spr 42 3
Control Drug, The. .s . . . .
. . . . WS Nov 34 668
Earth Shall Die, The. .nt . . . . . .
. . . . ToW Spr 42 6
Invaders from Venus. .s . . . .
. . . . .ToW #2 (38) 56
Patrolman E–6 Gets His Man . . . .
. .s . . . . Amz Dec 38 90
Perfect World, The. .n 3 pt . . . . .
. . . . WS Oct 35 518
Shot from the Sky, The. .ss . . . . .
. . . . WS Feb 34 753
World Within, The. .s . . . .
. . . . WS Aug 31 312
World Without, The. .s . . . .
. . . . WS Feb 31 996
SS Sep 40 90
HERMANSON, ULF
House in the Clouds, The. .s . . . .
. . . . WS Nov 30 514
HERRICK, THORNECLIFF house
pseud used in PLANET COMICS by
JEROME BIXBY and others.
HESS, JACK
Project. .s . . . . . . Amz Oct 49 116
HESTER, R. FREDERICK
Gypsies of Thos, The. .s . . . .
. . . . Amz May 35 115
HEWELCKE, GEOFFREY
Ten Million Miles Sunward . . . . .
. .nt . . . . Amz Mar 28 1126
HICKEY, H. B. pseud of HERB
LIVINGSTON
Beyond the Thunder. .s . . . .
. . . . Amz Dec 38 74

AUTHOR
  Title. .Length . . . . Magazine, Date, Page

  Checkmate to Demos. .s . . . .
  . . . . FA Mar 49 118
  Cosmic Cleanup. .s. . . . .
  . . . . .Amz Jul 50 124
  Curse of Ra, The. .nt . . . .
  . . . . FA Apr 48 80
  Daughters of Doom. .s . . . .
  . . . . Amz Apr 49 60
  Drums of Murd, The. .nt . . . . . .
  . . . . .FA Jan 48 132
  Eye of Wilbur Mook, The. .s . . . .
  . . . . Amz Nov 48 8
  Finished by Hand. .s . . . .
  . . . . FA May 46 166
  Hildy Finds His Wings. .s. . . . . . .
  . . . . FA Sep 48 90
  Ice Cream Tree, The. .s. . . . .
  . . . . .FA Jul 50 92
  Little Knowledge, A. .s. . . . .
  . . . . FA Jan 47 64
  Man from Arbutus, The. .s . . . . .
  . . . . Amz Mar 50 58
  Mr. Wilson's Watch. .s. . . . .
  . . . . .Amz Jan 47 144
  Perfect Imitation, The. .s . . . . . .
  . . . . Amz May 46 142
  Photo Finish. .s. . . . FA Oct 47 118
  Place Like Eden, A. .s. . . . .
  . . . . FA Dec 48 116
  Shades of Henry Morgan. . . . . . .
  . .nt . . . . FA May 47 146
  Smiling Wife, The. .s . . . .
  . . . . FA Nov 46 128
  To Dust Returneth. .nt. . . . .
  . . . . FA Feb 48 70
  To the Victors. .s. . . . FA Dec 50 70
  Valiant is the Word. .s . . . .
  . . . . FA Oct 50 104
  You Only Live Twice. .s . . . .
  . . . . Amz Mar 50 112
HIGHSTONE, H. A.
  Frankenstein—Unlimited. .s. . . . .
  . . . . ASF Dec 36 38
  Millions In It. .s. . . . .
  . . . . .OW Nov 50 76
HILBRETH, BOB artist
  Cover for AMAZING STORIES
  Dec 1946
HILL, ALMA
  Norte Americanos, You Are
  Doomed! . .s. . . . . .OW Mar 50 14
HILL, H. HAVERSTOCK
  Terror Out of Space. .n 4 pt . . . .
  . . . . Amz Feb 34 12

AUTHOR
  Title. .Length . . . . Magazine, Date, Page

HILLIARD, A. ROWLEY
  Avenging Ray, The. .nt. . . . .
  . . . . WQ Spr 31 374
  Breath of the Comet. .s. . . . . . .
  . . . . .ASF Jan 34 102
  Death from the Stars. .s . . . . . .
  . . . . WS Oct 31 612
  . . . . SS Sep 41 98
  Green Torture, The. .s . . . .
  . . . . WS Mar 31 1162
  . . . . SS Jan 43 88
  Island of the Giants, The. . . . . .
  . .s . . . . WS Aug 31 362
  Reign of the Star-Death. .s . . . . .
  . . . . WS Apr 32 1220
  Space Coffin, The. .s . . . .
  . . . . WS Aug 32 230
  with ALLEN GLASSER
  Martian, The. .s. . . . .
  . . . . .WQ Win 32 270
HINTON, EDWARD H.
  Monsters of Callisto. .s . . . .
  . . . . WS Oct 33 198
HIRSCH, ALCAN, Ph.D.
  Within Sight of Hell. .s . . . .
  . . . . Amz Dec 33 67
HOADLEY, H. O.(RLO) See also
  pseud GENE MITCHELL (1)
  PROBABILITY ZERO
  Picture from Tokyo. .ss . . . . . .
  . . . . .ASF Jan 44 165
HOAG, R. B., M.D.
  New Theory of Geology,
  A. .a . . . . Amz Feb 48 140
HOAR, ROGER SHERMAN See
  pseuds RALPH MILNE FARLEY
  (25), BENNINGTON ORTH (0),
  LT. JOHN PEASE (2), GENERAL
  "X" (0)
HODGE, FREDERICK ARTHUR
  Modern Atlantis, A. .n . . . .
  . . . . AQ Spr 28 148
HODGES, A. L.
  Astounding Announcement,
  An. .ss. . . . . Amz Jun 35 96
  Mystery of Professor Brown,
  The. .ss . . . . . . Amz Aug 30 415
  Pea Vine Mystery, The. .ss. . . . .
  . . . . Amz May 30 182
  Dead Sailor, The. .ss. . . . .
  . . . . Amz May 30 182
HODGKINS, RUSSELL J.
  Continental Engineers. .a . . . . . .
  . . . . .SF Jun 40 26

AUTHOR
  Title. .Length . . . . Magazine, Date, Page

HODGSON, WILLIAM HOPE
  Boats of the Glen Carrig, The. . . .
  . .n . . . . FFM Jun 45 10
  Derelict, The. .s . . . FFM Dec 43 94
  . . . . AFR #4 66
  Ghost Pirates, The. .n . . . .
  . . . . FFM Mar 44 88
  Stone Ship, The. .nt. . . . .
  . . . . .AFR #9 87
  Voice in the Night, The. .s. . . . .
  . . . . .AFR #1 57
HOFFMAN, SAMUEL
  Biog sketch . . . . TW Jun 42 51
  Last Disappearance. .s . . . .
  . . . . TW Jun 42 48
HOLBROOK, JOHN pseud of JACK
  VANCE
  Ultimate Quest. .s . . . .
  . . . . .SSS Sep 50 40
HOLBY, FRANK
  PROBABILITY ZERO
  The Strange Case of the Missing
  Hero. .ss . . . . . ASF Jul 42 109
  The Thirty First of June. .ss . . .
  . . . . ASF Sep 44 91
HOLDEN, FOX B.
  Biog Sketch, photo . . . .
  . . . . TW Win 45 65
  PROBABILITY ZERO
  Noise is Beautiful. .ss . . . .
  . . . . ASF Feb 43 90
  Sidewinders from Sirius. .s . . . . .
  . . . . PS Nov 50 28
  Stop Thief! . .ss. . . . . TW Win 45 63
HOLDING, ELISABETH SANXAY
  Friday, The Nineteenth. .s. . . . . .
  . . . . .F&SF Sum 50 3
HOLLEY, TIMOTHY V.
  Sailplanes of the Future. .a . . . . .
  . . . . Amz Aug 41 128
HOLLOWAY, WILLIAM
  Environment. .s. . . . FN Nov 48 112
  Wrath of Amen-Ra, The. .s . . . . .
  . . . . .FN Jan 49 102
HOLMAN, GEORGE
  PROBABILITY ZERO
  Sourdough. .ss . . . .
  . . . . .ASF Jan 44 163
  Contagion. .ss . . . .ASF Jun 44 130
  Agricultural Geology. .ss. . . . . .
  . . . . ASF Dec 44 128
HOLMBERG MILLICENT
  To Whom It May Concern. .s. . . .
  . . . . Amz Jun 46 118

AUTHOR
Title. .Length . . . . Magazine, Date, Page

HOLMES, A. R. *pseud of HARRY BATES*
Slave Ship from Space, The. . . . .
. .s . . . . ASF Jul 31 68
HOLMES, H. H. *pseud of WILLIAM ANTHONY PARKER WHITE*
Q. U. R. . .s . . . . . ASF Mar 43 79
Review Copy. .s . . . .
. . . . .F&SF Fal 49 70
Robinc. .s . . . . ASF Sep 43 76
Sanctuary. .s. . . . . ASF Jun 43 86
HOPE, ANTHONY
My Astral Body. .s . . . .
. . . . F&SF Win–Spr 50 89
HOPKINSON, O. W., JR.
Conquest. .s . . . . . . ASF Sep 47 26
Psych's War. .nt. . . ASF Apr 47 63
HORN, HOLLOWAY
Man from Cincinnati, The. . . . . .
. .s . . . . ASF Nov 33 70
HORN, PETER *house pseud used by DAVID VERN and HENRY KUTTNER and possibly one other.*
Biog sketch . . . . Amz Mar 40 129
by HENRY KUTTNER
50 Miles Down. .s . . . .
. . . . .FA May 40 74
by DAVID VERN (slight possibility that one of the following is by another)
Giants Out of the Sun. .nt. . . . . .
. . . . Amz May 40 14
Vagabonds of the Void. .nt . . . . .
. . . . Amz Mar 40 66
HORNIG, CHARLES D. *See Also pseud DERWIN LESSER (4)*
Editor FUTURE FICTION
Nov 39 *thru* Nov 40 *issues*
Editor SCIENCE FICTION
Mar 39 *thru* Sep 41 *issues*
Editor SCIENCE FICTION QUARTERLY
#1 *and* #2
Managing Editor WONDER STORIES
Nov 33 *thru* Apr 36 *issues*
Esperanto, Tongue of
Tomorrow. .a . . . . .SF Jun 39 62
Psychology of Anger, The. . . . .
. .a . . . . SF Aug 39 57
Strange Visitors. .a. . . .SF Oct 39 60
HOUGHTON, JOSEPH F.
Andromeda Menace, The . . . . .
. .s . . . . WS Dec 31 860
HOWARD, G. N.
Depth. .s . . . . . . ASF Mar 46 156

AUTHOR
Title. .Length . . . . Magazine, Date, Page

HOWARD, ROBER E.(rvin)
Blonde Goddess of Bal-Sagoth,
The. .nt . . . . AFR #12 3
Cairn on the Headland, The. . . . .
. .s . . . . AFR #6 3
Mirror of Tuzun Thune, The . . . .
. .s . . . . .AFR #2 73
Queen of the Black Coast. .nt . . .
. . . . .AFR #8 3
Temptress of the Tower of
Torture and Sin. .s . . . .
. . . . AFR #14 3
Witch Shall Be Born, A. .nt . . . . .
. . . . AFR #10 3
HOWARD, WARREN F. *pseud of FREDERIK POHL*
Voyage in Time, A. .ss . . . .
. . . . SSS Mar 41 110
HOWARD–BURLEIGH, F. S.
Don Mackinder's Model. .s . . . . .
. . . . ASF Oct 33 55
HUBBARD, L. RON *See also pseuds RENE LAFAYETTE (17), KURT VON RACHEN (5)*
Analytical Mind, The. .a . . . .
. . . . .ASF Oct 50 139
Automagic Horse, The. .nt . . . . .
. . . . ASF Oct 49 75
Battle of Wizards. .s . . . . . FB #5 4
Battling Bolto. .s . . . .TW Aug 50 84
Beast, The. .s . . . . .ASF Oct 42 100
Beyond All Weapons. .s . . . .
. . . . SSS Jan 50 70
Borrowed Glory. .s . . . . ;
. . . . UK Oct 41 85
Can of Vacuum, A. .s . . . .
. . . . ASF Dec 49 81
Case of the Friendly Corpse,
The. .n . . . . .UK Aug 41 9
Crossroads, The. .s . . . .
. . . . UK Feb 41 71
Danger in the Dark. .s . . . .
. . . . .UK May 39 59
Dangerous Dimension, The . . . .
. .s . . . . ASF Jul 38 100
Death's Deputy. .n. . . . .
. . . . .UK Feb 40 9
Devil's Rescue, The. .s . . . .
. . . . UK Oct 40 99
Dianetics, the Evolution of a
Science. .a . . . . . . ASF May 50 43
End Is Not Yet, The. . . . .
. .n 3 pt. . . . . ASF Aug 47 6
Fear. .n . . . . UK Jul 40 9
Final Blackout. .n 3 pt . . . .
. . . . ASF Apr 40 9

AUTHOR
Title. .Length . . . . Magazine, Date, Page

Final Enemy. .s . . . . SSS Sep 50 119
Ghoul, The. .n . . . . . .UK Aug 39 9
Great Secret, The. .s . . . .
. . . . SF Apr 43 81
Greed. .s . . . . . ASF Apr 50 53
He Didn't *Like* Cats. .s . . . . .
. . . . UK Feb 42 83
Invaders, The. .nt . . . .
. . . . .ASF Jan 42 62
Kingslayer, The. .nt . . . .
. . . . .2CSAB Win 50 102
Masters of Sleep, The. .n. . . . . . .
. . . . FA Oct 50 6
Matter of Matter, A. .s . . . .
. . . . ASF Aug 49 59
Obsolete Weapon, The. .s . . . . . .
. . . . ASF May 48 48
Planet Makers, The. .s . . . .
. . . . TW Oct 49 123
Professor Was a Thief, The . . . . .
. .nt . . . . ASF Feb 40 130
Room, The. .s . . . . . UK Apr 42 93
Slaver, The. .s . . . . ASF Jun 42 31
Slaves of Sleep. .n . . . .
. . . . UK Jul 39 9
Space Can. .s . . . . . .ASF Jul 42 71
Strain. .s . . . . ASF Apr 42 72
To the Stars. .n 2 pt . . . .
. . . . ASF Feb 50 5
Tough Old Man. .s . . . .
. . . . .SS Nov 50 116
Tramp, The. .n 3 pt . . . .
. . . . ASF Sep 38 71
240,000 Miles Straight Up. .s. . . .
. . . . TW Dec 48 42
Typewriter in the Sky . . . .
. n 2 pt . . . . .UK Nov 40 9
Ultimate Adventure, The. .n . . . .
. . . . .UK Apr 39 9
When Shadows Fall. .s . . . .
. . . . SS Jul 48 83
with L. SPRAGUE de CAMP
Last Drop, The. .s . . . .
. . . . .Ash Nov 41 87
HUECKELS, JACK G.
Advanced Chemistry. .s . . . .
. . . . Amz Mar 27 1127
HUFF, MELBOURNE
Robot Terror, The. .s . . . .
.SD Mar 30 216
HUGI, MAURICE G. *A real person, under whose name ERIC FRANK RUSSELL sold one story. All others were by Hugi.*
Creature of Eternity. .s . . . .
. . . . .ToW Sum 39 89

AUTHOR
Title. .Length . . . . Magazine, Date, Page

Fantasia Dementia. .s . . . .NW #3 42
Invaders from the Atom. .nt . . . .
. . . . .ToW #1 37 92
Lure of Science Fiction, The . . . .
. .a . . . . ToW Sum 39 125
Mill of the Gods, The. .nt . . . . .
. . . . NW #1 46 2
Super-Senses. .s. . . . .
. . . . .ToW #2 (38) 74
by ERIC FRANK RUSSELL
Mechanical Mice, The. .nt . . . . . .
. . . . .ASF Jan 41 54
HULL, E.(dna) M.(AYNE) *(Mrs. A. E.*
van Vogt)
Abdication. .s . . . . . ASF Apr 43 72
"ARTHUR BLORD" series includes:
    ABDICATION
    COMPETITION
    THE DEBT
    THE CONTRACT
    ENTER THE PROFESSOR
    BANKRUPTCY PROCEEDINGS
Bankruptcy Proceedings. .nt . . . .
. . . . ASF Aug 46 120
Competition. .s . . . . ASF Jun 43 44
Contract, The. .nt . . . .
. . . . ASF Mar 44 7
Debt, The. .nt . . . . . ASF Dec 43 7
Enter the Professor. .nt. . . . . . .
. . . . .ASF Jan 45 45
Flight That Failed, The. .s . . . . .
. . . . ASF Dec 42 29
Patient, The. .s . . . . UK Oct 43 121
Ultimate Wish, The. .s . . . .
. . . . UK Feb 43 71
Winged Man, The. .n 2 pt . . . . . .
. . . . ASF May 44 37
Wishes We Make, The. .s . . . .
. . . . UK Jun 43 35
HUNTER, DON *artist*
Cover for GALAXY SCIENCE
    FICTION
HUME, CYRIL
Atlantis Exile. .s . . . .
. . . . FFM Dec 47 104
HUNT, ROY
Cover for FANTASY BOOK
    #2 (1947)
HUNTER, E. WALDO *pseud of*
THEODORE STURGEON
Nightmare Island. .nt . . . .
. . . . UK Jun 41 132
Purple Light, The. .ss . . . .
. . . . .ASF Jun 41 117
HUNTER, GENE
Bargain With Beelzebub. .ss . . . . .
. . . . FB #2 12

HUXLEY, JULIAN
Tissue Culture King, The. .s . . . .
. . . . Amz Aug 27 451
HYERS, H. H.
Tides and Gravity, The. .a . . . . . .
. . . . Amz Sep 49 142
HYNE, CUTCLIFFE
Lost Continent, The. .n . . . .
. . . . FFM Dec 44 10

I

IAMS, JACK
Hat in the Hall, The. .s . . . .
. . . . F&SF Sum 50 25
INGELS *artist*
Cover for PLANET STORIES
    Spr 1944
IRVINE, CLYDE
Devil's Bodyguard, The. .s . . . . . .
. . . . FFM Dec 40 99
IRVING, MINNA
Moon Woman, The. .s . . . .
. . . . Amz Nov 29 746
IRWIN, G. H. *house pseud used by*
RAYMOND A. PALMER,
RICHARD S. SHAVER and
possibly others.
by RAYMOND A. PALMER
Justice of Martin Brand, The . . . .
. .n . . . . OW Jul 50 60
Vengeance of Martin Brand,
The. .n 2 pt . . . . . Amz Aug 42 10
by RICHARD S. SHAVER
Lair of the Grimalkin. .n . . . . . .
. . . . FA Apr 48 8
Where No Foot Walks. .nt . . . . . .
. . . . .OW Nov 49 42
Author's real name unknown
You Can Say That Again. .s . . . . .
. . . . FA Dec 43 112
ISIP, M. *artist*
Cover for UNKNOWN
    May 1940

J

JACKSON, CLIVE (G. B.)
Still Small Voice, The. .ss . . . . . .
. . . . AFR #14 63
Swordsmen of Varnis, The . . . . .
. .ss . . . . OW Sep 50 38

JACKSON, J. AUSTIN
Haunted House. .s . . . .
. . . . Fant Apr 47 30
JACKSON, JAY *artist*
Biog sketch, photo. . . . .
. . . . FA Oct 41 139
JACKSON STUART
Lovely Ghost, The. .s . . . .
. . . . ASF Nov 33 21
JACKSON, WOOD
Bat-Men of Mars, The. . . . .
. .n 3 pt . . . . . . AW May 30 1026
JACOBI, CARL
Biog sketch, photo. . . . .
. . . . TW Jun 39 87
Assignment on Venus. .s . . . . . .
. . . . PS Fal 43 73
Canal. .s . . . . .SS Spr 44 78
Cosmic Castaway. .nt . . . .
. . . . PS Mar 43 2
Cosmic Doodler, The. .s . . . . . .
. . . . SS Fal 44 65
Cosmic Teletype. .s . . . .
. . . . TW Oct 38 35
Doctor Universe. .s . . . .
. . . . PS Fal 44 35
Double Trouble. .s . . . .
. . . . PS Spr 44–45 69
Enter the Nebula. .s . . . .
. . . . PS Fal 46 34
Gentlemen, the Scavengers! . . . .
. .s . . . . TW Apr 48 80
Historian, The. .ss . . . .
. . . . SS May 50 137
Lodana. .s . . . . .SS Sep 47 80
Moss Island. .s. . . . . AQ Win 32 136
Random Quantity, The. .s . . . . . .
. . . . .AFR #5 54
Sky Trap. .s . . . . SF Mar 40 96
Tepondicon. .s . . . . . .PS Win 46 40
Tomb from Beyond, The. .s. . . . .
. . . . WS Nov 33 354
War of the Weeds, The. .s . . . . . .
. . . . TW Feb 39 41
World in a Box, The. .s . . . .
. . . . TW Feb 37 103
with CLIFFORD D. SIMAK
Street That Wasn't There,
The. .s . . . . .Com Jul 41 18
                        AFR #13 116
JAKES, JOHN W.
Dreaming Trees, The. .s . . . .
. . . . FA Nov 50 98
Your Number Is Up! . .s . . . .
. . . . Amz Dec 50 64

AUTHOR
Title. .Length . . . . Magazine, Date, Page

JAMES, D. L.
Alchemy of Outer Space. .s . . . . .
. . . . TW Feb 38 90
Beyond the Sun. .s. . . . .
. . . . ASF Mar 39 141
Cosmo-Trap, The. .s. . . . .
. . . . ASF Apr 36 98
Crystals of Madness. .s . . . .
. . . . TW Oct 36 107
Exit from Asteroid 60. .s . . . . . .
. . . . .PS Win 40 65
Moon of Delirium. .s . . . .
. . . . .ASF Jan 40 30
Philosophers of Stone. . . . .
. .s . . . . ASF Jun 38 62
Tickets to Paradise. .s. . . . .
. . . . Com Dec 40 53
JAMES, E. R.
Prefabrication. .s. . . . .
. . . . Fant Apr 47 46
Rebels, The. .s . . . . .NW #4 49 59
JAMES, EDWIN *pseud of JAMES E.*
GUNN
Communications. .nt . . . .
. . . . SS Sep 49 100
Man With Common Sense,
The. .s. . . . . . . .Amz Jul 50 112
Paradox. .s. . . . . . TW Oct 49 135
Private Enterprise. .s . . . .
. . . . .ASF Jul 50 63
JAMES, FRANCIS
Priest of Quiche, A. .s. . . . .
. . . . .FN May 50 88
JAMES, HENRY *pseud of L. C.*
KELLENBERGER
Mernos. .s . . . . . . Amz Feb 29 100
JAMES, KENNETH
Burroughs Passes. .s . . . .
. . . . ASF Oct 33 35
JAMES, M. F.
Destruction of Amul, The. . . . . .
. .s . . . . .ASF Jan 37 35
Expedition from Kytlm, The. . . .
. .s . . . . ASF Dec 36 111
JAMES, MAURICE
with T. HOWARD JAMES
Mystery Metal, The. .s . . . .
. . . . SW Mar 30 898
JAMES, M.(ontague) R.(hodes)
MASTERS OF FANTASY
biog . . . . FFM Apr 50 113
Episode of Cathedral History,
An. .s . . . . AFR #12 102
Warning to the Curious, A. . . . .
. .s . . . . AFR #4 112

AUTHOR
Title. .Length . . . . Magazine, Date, Page

JAMES, PHILIP
Carillion of Skulls. .s . . . .
. . . . UK Feb 41 122
JAMES, T. HOWARD
with MAURICE JAMES
Mystery Metal, The. .s . . . .
. . . . SW Mar 30 898
JAMESON, MALCOLM *See also*
pseuds COLIN KEITH (5), MARY
MacGREGOR (1)
Biog sketch, photo. . . . .
. . . . Amz Aug 40 133
Biog sketch, photo. . . . .
. . . . .SS Win 44 128
Obituary . . . . .ASF Jul 45 43
Admiral's Inspection. .nt. . . . . .
. . . . ASF Apr 40 123
Alien Envoy. .nt . . . .
. . . . ASF Nov 44 116
Anachron, Inc. . .nt. . . . .
. . . . ASF Oct 42 56
Anarch, The. .nt . . . .
. . . . ASF Feb 44 123
Barrius, Imp. . .s. . . . .
. . . . .ASF Jan 43 69
Blind Alley. .nt. . . . UK Jun 43 48
Blind Man's Buff. .nt . . . .
. . . . ASF Oct 44 7
Blockade Runner. .s. . . . .
. . . . ASF Mar 41 44
Brains for Bricks. .s . . . .
. . . . ASF Apr 45 124
Brimstone Bill. .s. . . . ASF Jul 42 27
Bullard Reflects. .s. . . . .
. . . . ASF Dec 41 66
Bureaucrat, The. .nt. . . . .
. . . . ASF Apr 44 117
Catalyst Poison. .s . . . .
. . . . ASF Apr 39 31
Children of the "Betsy B." . . . . .
. .s . . . . ASF Mar 39 109
Dead End. .s. . . . . . TW Mar 41 91
Death by Proxy. .s. . . . .
. . . . .SS Spr 45 79
Devil's Powder. .s . . . .
. . . . ASF Jun 41 69
Dispersion. .a . . . . ASF Mar 42 104
Doubled and Redoubled. .s . . . . .
. . . . UK Feb 41 87
Even the Angels. .s. . . . .
. . . . UK Aug 41 151
Eviction by Isotherm. .s . . . . . .
. . . . ASF Aug 38 134
Fighters Never Quit. .s . . . .
. . . . UK Aug 42 84

AUTHOR
Title. .Length . . . . Magazine, Date, Page

4½B, Eros. .s . . . . . . .PS Spr 41 69
Giant Atom, The. .n. . . . .
. . . . .SS Win 44 15
Giftie Gien, The. .s . . . .
. . . . UK Apr 43 94
Goddess' Legacy, The. .s. . . . . .
. . . . UK Oct 42 100
God's Footstool. .a . . . .
. . . . ASF Feb 43 76
Heaven Is What You Make It . . . .
. .nt . . . . . . .UK Aug 43 85
Hobo God. .s . . . . . ASF Sep 44 72
In His Own Image. .s . . . .
. . . . UK Feb 42 106
Joshua's Battering Ram . . . .
. .s . . . . .Ash Jun 40 22
Keep 'Em Under. .a . . . .
. . . . ASF Nov 43 108
Land of the Burning Sea. . . . . . .
. .nt . . . . .TW Aug 42 13
Leech, The. .nt . . . .ASF Jan 44 46
Lilies of Life. .s . . . .
. . . . ASF Feb 45 29
Lotus Juice. .s. . . . . TW Apr 43 75
Military Explosives. .a . . . .
. . . . .ASF Jan 42 57
Mill of the Gods. .s . . . .
. . . . .ASF Jan 39 130
Monster Out of Space, The . . . . .
. .nt . . . . .Amz Jul 40 74
Murder in the Time World. . . . . .
. .s . . . . Amz Aug 40 82
Not According to Dante. .s . . . . .
. . . . UK Jun 41 59
Old Ones Hear, The. .s . . . .
. . . . UK Jun 42 101
Orders. .s . . . . ASF Dec 45 47
Philtered Power. .s. . . . .
. . . . UK Mar 40 63
Pride. .s . . . . ASF Sep 42 92
PROBABILITY ZERO
Pig Trap. .ss . . . . ASF Apr 42 112
Eureka! . .ss . . . . ASF Nov 42 126
Downfall. .ss. . . . . ASF Apr 43 87
The Vacumulator. .ss . . . .
. . . . .ASF Jan 44 166
Prospectors of Space. .s . . . .
. . . . TW Sep 40 43
Question of Salvage, A . . . .
. .nt . . . . ASF Oct 39 69
Quicksands of Youthwardness . . .
. .n 3 pt . . . . Ash Oct 40 6
Seaward. .s. . . . . . ASF Nov 38 82
Slacker's Paradise. .s. . . . .
. . . . ASF Apr 41 82

AUTHOR
   Title. .Length . . . . Magazine, Date, Page

Space-War Strategy. .a . . . .
. . . . .SSS Mar 41 94
Space-War Tactics. .a . . . .
. . . . ASF Nov 39 68
Stellar Showboat. .s . . . .
. . . . PS Fal 42 78
Taa the Terrible. .s. . . . .
. . . . .Ash Dec 42 32
Tarnished Utopia. .n . . . .
. . . . .SS Mar 42 14
Tidal Waves. .a . . . . ASF Oct 43 30
Time Column. .n . . . . TW Dec 41 15
Tricky Tonnage. .s. . . . .
. . . . ASF Feb 44 56
Vengeance in Her Bones. .s . . . . .
. . . . AFR #10 81
Vulcan: Ice King. .a . . . .
. . . . ASF Nov 42 88
What Do You Mean by
   Up? . .a . . . . .Ash Apr 41 44
When Is When? . .s. . . . .
. . . . ASF Aug 43 143
White Mutiny. .s . . . ASF Oct 40 43
Wreckers of the Star Patrol . . . . .
   . .nt . . . . .SSS Aug 42 48
You Can't Win. .s . . . .
. . . . ASF Nov 41 59
JANUS, WARWICK
Paladins of the Sky. .s . . . .
. . . . .AQ Fal 31 571
JARVIS, E. K. house pseud used by
   ROBERT MOORE WILLIAMS and
   possibly others
Curse of Many Hands, The. .nt . . .
. . . . FA Apr 43 30
All Else Is Dust. .nt . . . .
. . . . Amz Mar 50 72
Dolls of Death. .nt. . . . .
. . . . Amz Sep 44 96
Fugitive, The. .s . . . .
. . . . FA Feb 43 216
Giants Beyond Pluto. .s . . . .
. . . . Amz Sep 42 76
Hickson's Strange Adventure. . . .
   . .s . . . . FA Mar 47 120
Infinite Invasion, The. .nt . . . . .
. . . . FA Sep 42 108
Let's Do It My Way. .s . . . .
. . . . Amz May 50 128
Man Who Was Two Men, The. . . .
   . .s . . . . Amz Jun 42 180
Men Scared of Nothing. .s . . . . . .
. . . . .FA Jul 42 210
Metal Monster, The. .nt . . . .
. . . . Amz Mar 43 8

AUTHOR
   Title. .Length . . . . Magazine, Date, Page

Murder Ray, The. .nt . . . .
. . . . FA Apr 49 38
Mystery of the Lost Race. .nt . . .
. . . . FA Oct 42 8
Mystery of the Midgets. .s . . . . .
. . . . .Amz Jul 48 60
Vengeance of the Golden
   God. .nt. . . . . Amz Dec 50 6
Wheel from Space, The. .s . . . . .
. . . . FA Aug 49 118
"You Can't Escape from
   Mars!". .nt . . . . . . Amz Sep 50 6
JEANS, SIR JAMES
Giant and Dwarf Stars. .a . . . . . .
. . . . TW Feb 38 64
JENKINS, AINSLEE
In the Shadow of the Tii. .s . . . . .
. . . . ASF Nov 33 43
JENKINS, HARRY, JR.
Biog sketch, photo. . . . .
. . . . Amz Feb 43 221
Pawn for a King, A. .s . . . .
. . . . Amz Feb 43 222
JENKINS, WILL(iam) F.(itzgerald)
   See also pseuds WILLIAM
   FITZGERALD (7), MURRAY
   LEINSTER (75)
From Beyond the Stars. .s. . . . . .
. . . . TW Jun 47 82
Logic Named Joe, A. .s . . . .
. . . . ASF Mar 46 139
JENSEN, L. M.
   PROBABILITY ZERO
Take-Off. .ss. . . . ASF Dec 42 107
JERGOVIC, MAX
   with MANLY WADE WELLMAN
Rebels of the Moon. .s . . . .
. . . . WQ Spr 32 354
JEROME, OWEN FOX pseud of
   OSCAR J. FRIEND
British Thermal Units. .s. . . . . . .
. . . . TW Jun 42 83
Meteorite Enigma. .s . . . .
. . . . .SS Sep 42 93
Sun Engine. .s. . . . . . TW Aug 43 98
JESSEL, JOHN pseud of STANLEY
   G. WEINBAUM
Adaptive Ultimate, The. .nt . . . .
. . . . ASF Nov 35 108
JOHNSON, A. H.
Amir's Magic, The. .s . . . .
. . . . Amz Mar 32 1086
Phagocytes. .s . . . Amz Feb 29 1018
Raid of the Mercury, The. .s . . . .
. . . . .Amz Jul 31 364

AUTHOR
   Title. .Length . . . . Magazine, Date, Page

Superman, The. .nt . . . .
. . . . Amz Aug 31 454
Thunderer, The. .s . . . .
. . . . AW Jan 30 634
JOHNSON, E. D.
Hole That Grew, The. .s . . . . . .
. . . . .AQ Spr–Sum 32 280
JOHNSON, E. H.
Golden Vapor, The. .s . . . .
. . . . AQ Win 28 127
JOHNSON, FRANK
Colossus from Space. .s . . . .
. . . . TW Oct 40 44
Kids Don't Know Everything. . . .
   . .s . . . . SS Sep 42 106
Private Brown's Blitzkrieg. .s . . . .
. . . . .TW Aug 42 99
JOHNSON, L. J.
Satellites of Death. .s . . . .
. . . . .ToW Sum 38 43
JOHNSON, LESLIE T.
   with ERIC FRANK RUSSELL
Seeker of Tomorrow. .nt. . . . . .
. . . . ASF Jul 37 124
JOHNSTON, A. H. cartoonist
   with E. J. BELLIN pseud (story)
Dead Man's Tale. .comic . . . . . .
. . . . .OTWA Dec 50 59
JOHNSTON, E. M.
   with CLARK ASHTON SMITH
Planet Entity, The. .s . . . .
. . . . WQ Fal 31 110
JONES, ARTHUR FREDERICK
Inquisition of 6061, The. .s . . . . .
. . . . WS Dec 33 441
JONES, FRANK
Arctic God. .s . . . .
. . . . Amz May 42 192
JONES, L. RAYMOND artist
   Cover for AMAZING STORIES
   Feb 1942
JONES, NEIL R.
Biog sketch . . . . . Amz Dec 38 143
Biog sketch, photo. . . . .
. . . . Amz Apr 41 131
Asteroid of Death, The. .s . . . . . .
. . . . WQ Fal 31 76
Astounding Exodus, The. .nt . . . .
. . . . TW Apr 37 76
Captives of the Durna Rangue . . .
   . .nt . . . . SSS Mar 41 114
Cat-Men of Aemt, The. .nt . . . . .
. . . . .Ash Aug 40 42
Cosmic Derelict. .nt . . . .
. . . . .Ash Feb 41 82

AUTHOR
Title. .Length . . . . Magazine, Date, Page

Dark Swordsman of Saturn,
The. .s . . . . PS Sum 40 106
Death's Head Meteor, The. .s . . . .
. . . . AW Jan 30 628
Doomsday on Ajiat. .s . . . .
. . . . Ash Oct 42 74
"DURNA RANGUE" series includes:
  LITTLE HERCULES
  DURNA RANGUE NEOPHYTE
  KISS OF DEATH
  INVISIBLE ONE
  CAPTIVES OF THE DURNA
    RANGUE
  PRIESTESS OF THE SLEEPING
    DEATH
  VAMPIRE OF THE VOID
Durna Rangue Neophyte. .nt . . . .
. . . . .ASF Jun 37 134
Electrical Man, The. .nt . . . . . .
. . . . SD May 30 400
Escape from Phobos. .s . . . .
. . . . WS Feb 33 690
Hermit of Saturn's Ring. .s . . . . .
. . . . PS Fal 40 80
Into the Hydrosphere. .s . . . .
. . . . Amz Oct 33 554
Jameson Satellite, The. .s . . . . . .
. . . . Amz Jul 31 334
Invisible One. .nt . . . .SSS Sep 40 6
Kiss of Death. .s . . . .
. . . . Amz Dec 38 108
Labyrinth. .nt . . . . . Amz Apr 36 84
Liquid Hell. .s . . . . . . Fut Jul 40 8
Little Hercules. .nt . . . .
. . . . ASF Sep 36 62
Martian and Troglodite. .s . . . . . .
. . . . Amz May 33 124
Metal Moon, The. .nt . . . .
. . . . SSS Sep 49 102
Mind Masters, The. .nt . . . .
. . . . SSS Sep 50 70
Moon Pirates, The. .nt 2 pt . . . . .
. . . . Amz Sep 34 11
Music Monsters, The. .nt . . . . . .
. . . . Amz Apr 38 15
On the Planet Fragment. .nt . . . .
. . . . Amz Oct 37 97
Parasite Planet. .nt . . . .
. . . . .SSS Nov 40 104
Planet of the Double Sun,
The. .s . . . . . . Amz Feb 32 1020
Priestess of the Sleeping Death. . .
. .s . . . . Amz Apr 41 88
"PROFESSOR JAMESON" series
  includes:
  THE JAMESON SATELLITE
  THE PLANET OF THE DOUBLE SUN
  THE RETURN OF THE TRIPEDS
  INTO THE HYDROSPHERE

AUTHOR
Title. .Length . . . . Magazine, Date, Page

  TIME'S MAUSOLEUM
  THE SUNLESS WORLD
  ZORA OF THE ZOROMES
  SPACE WAR
  LABYRINTH
  TWIN WORLDS
  ON THE PLANET FRAGMENT
  THE MUSIC MONSTERS
  THE CAT-MEN OF AEMT
  COSMIC DERELICT
  SLAVES OF THE UNKNOWN
  DOOMSDAY ON AJIAT
  THE METAL MOON
  PARASITE PLANET
  WORLD WITHOUT DARKNESS
  THE MIND MASTERS
Ransom for Toldeo, The. .nt . . . .
. . . . .Com May 41 80
Return of the Tripeds, The . . . . .
. .s . . . . Amz May 32 120
Shadows of the Night. .s . . . .
. . . . AD Oct 30 882
Slaves of the Unknown. .s . . . . .
. . . . .Ash Mar 42 10
Space War. .nt . . . . . .Amz Jul 35 9
Spacewrecked on Venus. .s . . . . .
. . . . WQ Win 32 260
Spoilers of the Spaceways. .s . . . .
. . . . .PS Win 42 40
Suicide Durkee's Last Ride . . . . .
. .s . . . . Amz Sep 32 534
Sunless World, The. .nt . . . .
. . . . Amz Dec 34 26
Swordsmen of Saturn. .n . . . .
. . . . SF Oct 39 8
Time's Mausoleum. .s . . . .
. . . . Amz Dec 33 10
Twin Worlds. .nt . . . Amz Apr 37 17
Vampire of the Void. .s . . . . .
. . . . .PS Spr 41 38
World Without Darkness. .s . . . . .
. . . . SSS Mar 50 100
Zora of the Zoromes. .nt . . . . . .
. . . . Amz Mar 35 88
JONES, RALPH T.
Man Beast of Toree, The. .s . . . . .
. . . . WQ Fal 31 84
                        SS Jul 41 102
JONES, RAYMOND F.
Biog sketch . . . . . PS Sum 47 117
Alien Machine, The. .s . . . .
. . . . TW Jun 49 74
Black Market. .nt . . . .
. . . . ASF Apr 46 133
Cat and the King, The. .nt . . . . . .
. . . . ASF Aug 46 73
Children's Room, The. .nt . . . . . .
. . . . FA Sep 47 136
Correspondence Course. .s . . . . .
. . . . ASF Apr 45 61

AUTHOR
Title. .Length . . . . Magazine, Date, Page

Cybernetic Brains, The. .n . . . . .
. . . . .SS Sep 50 11
Deadly Host. .s . . . .ASF Sep 45 115
Discontinuity. .nt . . . .
. . . . ASF Oct 50 76
. . .Divided We Fall. .n . . . .
. . . . Amz Dec 50 96
Encroachment. .s . . . .SS Mar 50 112
Fifty Million Monkeys. .nt . . . . .
. . . . ASF Oct 43 39
Forecast. .nt . . . . . . ASF Jun 46 6
Greater Conflict, The. .nt . . . . . .
. . . . TW Feb 50 92
Martian Circe, The. .nt . . . .
. . . . PS Sum 47 94
Model Shop, The. .nt . . . .
. . . . ASF Jun 47 54
Outpost Infinity. .nt . . . .
. . . . .SSS Jan 50 8
Pacer. .s . . . . ASF May 43 71
Person from Porlock, The . . . . . .
. .nt . . . . ASF Aug 47 96
Pete Can Fix It. .nt . . . .
. . . . ASF Feb 47 64
Pigeon Sense. .a . . . .
. . . . ASF Mar 45 100
Portrait of Narcissus. .s . . . .
. . . . .OW May 50 56
Production Test. .s . . . .
. . . . ASF Oct 49 39
Regulations Provide. .s . . . .
. . . . ASF Mar 50 39
Renaissance. .n 4 pt . . . .
. . . . .ASF Jul 44 6
Seven Jewels of Chamar, The. . . .
. .nt . . . . .PS Win 46 90
Shroud of Secrecy, The. .s . . . . . .
. . . . TW Dec 49 64
Starting Point. .s . . . .
. . . . ASF Feb 42 68
Stone and a Spear, A . . . .
. .nt . . . . GSF Dec 50 66
Sunday Is Three Thousand Years
Away. .nt . . . . TW Jun 50 11
Swimming Lesson. .nt . . . .
. . . . ASF Apr 43 9
Test of the Gods. .s . . . .
. . . . ASF Sep 41 85
Tools of the Trade. .nt . . . .
. . . . ASF Nov 50 48
Toymaker, The. .nt . . . .
. . . . ASF Sep 46 6
JONES, ROBERT GIBSON *artist*
Covers for AMAZING STORIES
Nov 1942
Sep, Nov 1943

AUTHOR
  Title. .Length . . . . Magazine, Date, Page

  Mar, Jun, Sep, Dec 1945
  Sep, Oct 1946
  Feb, Mar, Jun, Oct, Nov, Dec 1947
  Mar, Apr, May, Jun, Aug, Sep,
    Nov 1948
  Feb, Jul, Dec 1949
  Feb, Mar, Apr, Jun, Jul, Aug, Sep,
    Oct, Nov 1950
  *Covers for FANTASTIC
    ADVENTURES*
  Aug 1942
  Jan, Feb, Mar, Jul, Aug, Oct,
    Dec 1943
  Jun 1944
  Jan 1945
  Jan, Mar, May, Sep, Oct, Nov,
    Dec 1947
  Jan, Feb, Mar, Apr, May, Jun, Sep,
    Oct 1948
  Jan, May, Sep, Nov 1949
  Feb, Mar, Apr, Jun, Jul, Sep, Oct,
    Nov, Dec 1950
JONES, THOMAS RICHARD
  Reprisal. .s . . . . . . Amz Oct 28 637
JUDD, CYRIL *pseud of CYRIL
    KORNBLUTH and JUDITH
    MERRIL in Collaboration*
JUHRE, WILLIAM *artist*
  Cover for AMAZING STORIES
  Jun 1939
  End of the World, The . . . .
    . .bacover pic . . . . . Amz May 39
JUVE, HENDRIK DAHL
  In Martian Depths. .s . . . .
    . . . . WS Sep 32 320
  Martian Revenge, The. .s . . . . . .
    . . . . WS Aug 30 196
  Monsters of Neptune, The. . . . . .
    . .s . . . . .WQ Sum 30 536
  Silent Destroyer, The. .s . . . .
    . . . . AW Aug 29 102
  Sky Maniac, The. .s . . . .
    . . . . AW Oct 29 294
  Streamers of Death. .s . . . .
    . . . . SW Feb 30 790
  Struggle for Neptune, The. . . . . .
    . .s . . . . WQ Fal 30 94
  Vanishing Fleet, The. .s . . . .
    . . . . AW Feb 30 678

AUTHOR
  Title. .Length . . . . Magazine, Date, Page

K

KAEMPFFERT, WALDEMAR
  Diminishing Draft, The. .s . . . . . .
    . . . . FFM Dec 39 28
KAFKA, FRANZ
  Hunter Gracchus, The. .s . . . . . .
    . . . . WB Dec 50 49
KAHN, BERNARD I.
  Command. .nt. . . . .
    . . . . .ASF Jan 47 121
  For the Public. .nt . . . .
    . . . . ASF Dec 46 73
  Pinch of Culture, A. .nt . . . .
    . . . . ASF Aug 50 78
KALETSKY, MILTON
  Biog sketch . . . . . Amz Apr 40 135
  Biog sketch, photo. . . . .
    . . . . FA May 40 86
  Beam, The. .ss. . . . .
    . . . . Amz Sep 34 116
  Election Campaign on Saturn. . . .
    . .s . . . . .Amz Jul 42 48
  End of the Universe, The. .ss . . . .
    . . . . WS Apr 34 1008
  Have We a Sixth Sense? . .a . . . . .
    . . . . FA Aug 40 134
  Heavy Cargo. .ss . . . . .SF Sep 41 82
  Homer Higginbotham, Rain
    Maker. .s . . . . . . Amz Jun 41 114
  Planet of Errors, The. .ss . . . . . .
    . . . . Amz Dec 40 70
  Ray of Hypnosis, The. .ss . . . . . .
    . . . . .Amz Jul 40 94
  Revolt of the Ants. .s . . . .
    . . . . Amz Apr 40 76
  Space-Ship Derby. .s . . . .
    . . . . SFQ Sum 40 101
  Star of Blue. .s . . . . . SF Mar 41 54
  Water, Water Everywhere. .a . . . .
    . . . . .Ash Apr 40 105
  Wizard of Baseball, The. .s . . . . .
    . . . . .FA May 40 68
  X-Ray Murder. .ss . . . .
    . . . . Amz Sep 40 64
KALLAND, JOHN FRANCIS
  Restitution. .s . . . . Amz Dec 35 118
  Sages of Eros, The. .s . . . .
    . . . . Amz Feb 32 992
KAMINS, BERNIE
  Astral Rhythm. .s . . . .
    . . . . FA Mar 48 66
  Well-Wisher, The. .s . . . .
    . . . . FA Oct 48 120

AUTHOR
  Title. .Length . . . . Magazine, Date, Page

KARDEN, RAY
  PROBABILITY ZERO
  Cash on the Dimension. .ss . . . .
    . . . . .ASF Jan 44 167
KASTEL, WARREN *pseud used
    primarily by CHESTER S. GEIER
    and possibly others*
  Air race. .s . . . . .FA Jul 48 136
  Beacons Must Burn, The. .s . . . . .
    . . . . FA Oct 49 136
  Demonstration Flight. .s . . . .
    . . . . FA Aug 49 130
  Illusion on Callisto. .s . . . .
    . . . . Amz May 48 110
  Jirandel. .s . . . . FA Jan 50 50
  Lightning Loot. .s . . . .
    . . . . FA Sep 49 50
  Lunar Monkey Business. .s . . . . .
    . . . . Amz Jun 48 76
  Ominous Bequest, The. .s . . . . . .
    . . . . FA Jun 48 140
KATELEY, WALTER
  Arctic Rescue, The. .s . . . .
    . . . . .AW May 30 974
  Beings of the Boundless Blue . . . .
    . .s . . . . Amz May 31 130
  Children of the Great Magma. . . .
    . .nt . . . . Amz Aug 33 412
  Denizen of the Underworld,
    A. .s . . . . SD Apr 30 323
  Eye of the Vulture, The. .s . . . . .
    . . . . Amz Nov 28 738
  Fourteenth Earth, The. .s . . . . . .
    . . . . Amz Feb 28 1092
  From Eros to Earth. .s . . . .
    . . . . SW Oct 29 436
  Godl Triumvirate, The. .s . . . . . .
    . . . . SW Nov 29 514
  Hollister Experiment, The. . . . . .
    . .s . . . . AQ Win 29 112
  Incredible Monstrosity, The. . . . .
    . .s . . . . WS Jun 30 24
  Insects Extraordinary. .s . . . .
    . . . . .AQ Win 32 84
  Remote Control. .s . . . .
    . . . . Amz Apr 30 22
  Room for the Super Race . . . . . .
    . .nt . . . . Amz Aug 32 430
  Steam God, The. .s . . . .
    . . . . Amz Oct 29 640
  Subjugating the Earth. .nt . . . . . .
    . . . . Amz Jun 34 64
  Under Arctic Ice. .s . . . .
    . . . . WS Jun 32 46
  World of a Hundred Men,
    The. .s . . . . SW Feb 30 818

AUTHOR
   Title. .Length . . . . Magazine, Date, Page

KAW
   Time Eliminator, The. .s . . . . . .
   . . . . Amz Dec 26 802
KAYE, MARX *house pseud*
by S. J. BYRNE
   Mystery of the Peruvian
   Giants. .a . . . . . Amz Jun 47 162
Author's real name unknown
   Forten Aspects of the Flying
   Discs. .a . . . . . . Amz Jun 48 154
KEELER, HARRY STEPHEN
   John Jones' Dollar. .s . . . .
   . . . . Amz Apr 27 25
KEENE, DAY
   "What So Proudly We Hail. . ." . .
   . .s . . . . Im Dec 50 44
KIERSTEAD, B. S.
   Island of Science. .s . . . .
   . . . . Amz Dec 33 102
KEITH, COLIN *pseud of MALCOLM
   JAMESON*
   "If You're Smart–". .s . . . .
   . . . . ASF Apr 42 51
   PROBABILITY ZERO
   Efficiency. .ss . . . . . ASF Feb 43 89
   Sand. .s . . . . ASF Nov 42 80
   Sorcerer's Apprentice, The. .s . . .
   . . . . ASF Dec 41 56
   Soup King. .s . . . . . ASF Jan 42 27
KEITH, J. E.
   Between Dimensions. .s . . . .
   . . . . WS Oct 31 624
   21931. .s . . . . . . Amz Feb 36 119
KEITH, LEIGH *pseud H. L. Gold*
   No Medals. .s . . . . . ASF Mar 35 45
KELLEAM, JOSEPH E.
   Eagles Gather, The. .s . . . .
   . . . . ASF Apr 42 93
   From the Dark Waters. .s . . . . . .
   . . . . AFR #6 59
   Last of the Asterites, The . . . . . .
   . .s . . . . ASF May 40 52
   Rust. .s . . . . .ASF Oct 39 133
KELLENBERGER, L. C. *See pseud
   HENRY JAMES (1)*
KELLER, DAVID H., (M.D.) *See also
   pseuds HENRY CECIL (0), AMY
   WORTH (0)*
   Biog sketch, photo . . . .
   . . . . TW Jun 39 95
   Biog sketch . . . . .ToW Sum 39 125
   Air Lines. .s . . . . . .Amz Jan 30 963
   Ambidexter, The. .s . . . .
   . . . . Amz Apr 31 36
   Biological Experiment, A. .s . . . .
   . . . . Amz Jun 28 232

Bloodless War, The. .s . . . .
   . . . . AW Jul 29 52
Boneless Horror, The. .s . . . .
   . . . . SW Jul 29 133
                         SS Nov 41 98
Boomeranging 'Round the Moon'.
   . .s . . . . .AQ Fal 30 524
Burning Water. .s . . . AD Jun 30 518
Calypso's Island. .s . . . .
   . . . . Sti Apr 41 84
Cerebral Library, The . . . .
   . .s . . . . Amz May 31 116
Conquerors, The. .n 2 pt . . . .
   . . . . SW Dec 29 582
Doorbell, The. .s . . . .
   . . . . WS Jun 34 52
Eternal Professors, The. .s . . . . . .
   . . . . Amz Aug 29 414
                         ToW Aut 38 61
Euthanasia Limited. .s . . . .
   . . . . .AQ Fal 29 506
Evening Star, The. .n 2 pt . . . . . .
   . . . . SW Apr 30 966
Feminine Metamorphosis,
   The. .s . . . . SW Aug 29 246
Fireless Age, The. .n 2 pt . . . . . .
   . . . . Amz Aug 37 33
Flying Fool, The. .s . . . .
   . . . . Amz Jul 29 310
Flying Threat, The. .nt . . . .
   . . . . AQ Spr 30 242
Free As the Air. .s . . . .
   . . . . Amz Jun 31 228
Growing Wall, The. .nt . . . .
   . . . . SFQ Win 42 54
Half-Mile Hill. .s . . . .
   . . . . .AQ Sum 31 371
Human Termites, The. . . . .
   . .n 3 pt . . . . SW Sep 29 294
   4 pt . . . . CF Win 40 99
Island of White Mice. .nt . . . .
   . . . . Amz Feb 35 82
Ivy War, The. .s . . . .
   . . . . Amz May 30 160
Key to Cornwall, The. .s . . . .
   . .s . . . . Sti Feb 41 93
Life Detour, The. .s . . . .
   . . . . WS Feb 35 1072
                         SS Jul 47 64
Life Everlasting. .n 2 pt . . . .
   . . . . .Amz Jul 34 9
Literary Corkscrew, The. .s . . . . .
   . . . . WS Mar 34 866
                         SS May 41 112
Living Machine, The. .s . . . .
   . . . . WS May 35 1464

Lost Language, The. .s . . . .
   . . . . Amz Jan 34 87
Menace, The. .nt . . . . .*(This is
   actually 4 short stories: THE
   MENACE, THE GOLD SHIP,
   THE TAINTED FLOOD and
   THE INSANE AVALANCHE
   published together)* . . . .
   . . . . .AQ Sum 28 382
                         AQ Win 33 91
Menacing Claws. .s . . . .
   . . . . AD Sep 30 798
Metal Doom, The. .n 3 pt . . . . . .
   . . . . Amz May 32 104
Moon Artist, The. .s . . . .
   . . . . .Sti Jun 41 113
Moon Rays, The. .s . . . .
   . . . . WQ Jun 30 558
No More Friction. .s. . . . .
   . . . . TW Jun 39 93
No More Tomorrows. .s . . . .
   . . . . Amz Dec 32 804
One-Way Tunnel. .s . . . .
   . . . . .WS Jan 35 934
Pent House, The. .s . . . .
   . . . . Amz Feb 32 989
Pit of Doom, The. .s. . . . .
   . . . . .Fut Feb 42 88
Psychophonic Nurse, The . . . . . .
   . .Amz Nov 28 710
Rat Racket, The. .s . . . .
   . . . . Amz Nov 31 698
Red Death, The. .nt . . . .
   . . . . Cos Jul 41 76
Revolt of the Pedestrians,
   The. .s . . . . . . Amz Feb 28 1048
Scientific Widowhood, A. .s . . . .
   . . . . SD Feb 30 114
Service First. .s . . . . AQ Win 30 136
Sleeping War, The. .s . . . .
   . . . . WS Feb 31 980
Speed Will Be My Bride. .s . . . . .
   . . . . Uc Apr 41 94
Steam Shovel, The. .s . . . .
   . . . . Amz Sep 31 510
Stenographer's Hands. .s . . . .
   . . . . .AQ Fal 28 522
                         ToW #2 (38) 40
                         AFR #2 7
"TAINE OF SAN FRANCISCO"
   series include:
   THE MENACE
   THE FEMININE METAMORPHOSIS
   EUTHANASIA LIMITED
   A SCIENTIFIC WIDOWHOOD
   BURNING WATER
   MENACING CLAWS
   THE CEREBRAL LIBRARY

AUTHOR
Title. .Length . . . . Magazine, Date, Page

THE TREE OF EVIL
ISLAND OF WHITE MICE
Thing in the Cellar, The. .a . . . . .
. . . . AFR #6 42
Thirty and One, The. .s . . . .
. . . . MSS Nov 38 53
Threat of the Robot, The. .s . . . .
. . . . SW Jun 29 63
Tree of Evil, The. .s . . . .
. . . . WS Sep 34 446
Tree Terror, The. .s . . . .
. . . . Amz Oct 33 545
Twentieth Century Homunculus,
A. .s . . . . Amz Feb 30 1012
Unlocking the Past. .s . . . .
. . . . Amz Sep 28 513
Unto Us a Child is Born. .s . . . . .
. . . . Amz Jul 33 297
White City, The. .s . . . .
. . . . Amz May 35 11
White Collars. .s . . . .AQ Jul 29 380
Worm, The. .s . . . Amz Mar 29 1066
Yeast Men, The. .s . . . .
. . . . Amz Apr 28 26
                        ToW Sum 39 70
                        AFR #14 79
with DAVID LASSER
Time Projector, The. .n 2 pt . . . .
. . . . WS Jul 31 152
KELLEY, HUBERT
with FRED T. BARTON
Raiders of the Air. .ss . . . .
. . . . .FFM May–Jun 40 75
KELLEY, THOMAS P.
He Who Saw Tomorrow. .nt . . . .
. . . . .FA Jul 46 92
KELLY, FRANK K.
Crater 17, Near Tycho. .nt . . . . .
. . . . ASF Jun 34 68
Crisis With Mars, The. .s . . . .
. . . . WQ Fal 32 60
Exiles of Mars. .s . . . .
. . . . WQ Jun 32 484
                        WSA 50 184
Famine on Mars. .nt . . . .
. . . . ASF Sep 34 72
Into the Meteorite Orbit . . . .
. .s . . . . Amz Dec 33 76
Light Bender, The. .s . . . .
. . . . WS Jun 31 34
                        FSQ Sum 50 99
Moon Tragedy, The. .s . . . .
. . . . WS Oct 33 240
Radio World, The. .s . . . .
. . . . WS Feb 32 1058

AUTHOR
Title. .Length . . . . Magazine, Date, Page

Red April, 1965. .s . . . .
. . . . WS Mar 32 1154
Star Ship Invincible. .nt . . . .
. . . . .ASF Jan 35 10
KENDIG, JULIAN, JR.
Eternal Mask, The. .nt . . . .
. . . . Amz Feb 33 1017
Fourth Dimensional Space
Penetrator . . . . . .Amz Jan 30 958
KENEALY, NICHOLAS E.
Biog sketch, photo. . . TW Jan 40 79
Conquistadores from Beyond. . . .
. .s . . . . TW Jan 40 78
KENNEDY, FRED
Trial by Television. .s . . . .
. . . . Amz Dec 31 828
KENNEDY, JOE
Biog sketch . . . . PS Spr 45 68
KENNELLY, JOSEPH
Death from the Seas. .s . . . .
. . . . .WS Jan 31 810
KENNY, YALE
Cassius Siddle's Great Illusion . . .
. .s . . . . FA Jun 42 204
KENT, GROVER
Death's Double. .s . . . .
. . . . Amz Jun 49 82
KENT, KELVIN *pseud used by
ARTHUR K. BARNES and
HENRY KUTTNER individually
and in collaboration on the PETE
MANX stories.*
by ARTHUR K. BARNES
De Wolfe of Wall Street . . . .
. .s . . . . TW Feb 43 49
Greeks Had a War for It, The . . . .
. .s . . . . TW Jan 41 36
Grief of Bagdad. .s . . . .
. . . . TW Jun 43 76
Knight Must Fall. .s . . . .
. . . . TW Jun 40 84
*(Kuttner did some minor rewrite on
the early portion of this.)*
by HENRY KUTTNER
Comedy of Eras, The. .s . . . .
. . . . TW Sep 40 32
Dames Is Poison. .s . . . .
. . . . TW Jun 42 92
Hercules Muscles In. .s . . . .
. . . . TW Feb 41 90
Man About Time. .s . . . .
. . . . TW Oct 40 54
Swing Your Lady. .s. . . . .
. . . . TW Win 44 85
World's Pharaoh. .s . . . .
. . . . TW Dec 39 57

AUTHOR
Title. .Length . . . . Magazine, Date, Page

*by ARTHUR K. BARNES and
HENRY KUTTNER*
Roman Holiday. .s . . . .
. . . . TW Aug 39 76
                        SS Jan 50 80
Science Is Golden. .s . . . .
. . . . TW Apr 40 80
KENT, MALLORY *pseud of ROBERT
W. LOWNDES*
Collector, The. .ss . . . Fut Oct 42 97
Peacemakers, The. .ss . . . .
. . . . .Fut Aug 42 98
Quarry. .ss . . . . . . .Fut Dec 41 91
KENYON, ROBERT O. *pseud of
HENRY KUTTNER*
Dark Heritage, The. .s . . . .
. . . . MSS Aug 38 73
KERMAC, ANTON
President's Daughter, The . . . . . .
. .ss . . . . FanF May 50 67
KERRUISH, JESSIE DOUGLAS
Undying Monster, The. .n . . . . . .
. . . . FFM Jun 46 12
KEY, GEORGE EUGENE
Mind Machine, The. .s . . . .
. . . . .AD Jul 30 616
Red Ace, The. .s . . . .
. . . . AW Feb 30 692
Temple of Dust, The. .s . . . .
. . . . AD Sep 30 774
KIDWELL, ROBERT PAUL
Shaverian Hypothesis, The . . . . .
. .a . . . . .Amz Jan 48 150
KIEMLE, H. W. *artist*
Biog sketch . . . . . . .PS Win 45 115
KING, C. DALY *See also pseud
JEREMIAH PHELAN (0)*
Dianetics: a book review. . . . . . .
. . . . F&SF Dec 50 99
KING, D. C.
PROBABILITY ZERO
A Snitch in Time. .ss . . . .
. . . . ASF Apr 43 89
KING, RAY
Lust Rides the Roller Coaster . . .
. .s . . . . MSS Dec 39 70
Man Who Killed the World,
The. .ss . . . . .PS Spr 40 94
KINGSLEY, ROY, Ph.D.
Forty Billion Winks. .a . . . .
. . . . .TW Apr 43 89
KIRBY, JASON
Floating Island of Madness,
The. .s . . . . .ASF Jan 33 326
KIRCHHOFF, BJARNE
Day of Wrath. .s . . . . PS Sum 48 69

AUTHOR
Title. .Length . . . . Magazine, Date, Page

KIRKHAM, HENRY F.
End of Time, The. .s . . . .
. . . . WS Dec 30 658
Lords of the Deep. .s . . . .
. . . . WS Nov 30 544
Time Oscillator, The. .s. . . . . . .
. . . . SW Dec 29 602
KLASS, MORTON
Invitation from the Stars. .s . . . . .
. . . . Fut Sep–Oct 50 51
KLASS, PHILIP See pseud WILLIAM
TENN (11)
KLEIER, JOE
Head, The. .s . . . . Amz Aug 28 418
KLIMARIS, J. S. pseud of WALTER
KUBILIUS
Case of the Baby Dinosaur,
The. .s. . . . . Fut Oct 42 70
Case of the Vanishing Cellars,
The. .s. . . . . .Fut Aug 42 84
KLINE, ALLEN S.
with OTIS ADELBERT KLINE
Secret Kingdom, The. .n 3 pt. . . .
. . . . Amz Oct 29 616
KLINE, OTIS ADELBERT
Biog sketch, photo. . . . .
. . . . TW Jun 39 35
Biog sketch, photo. . . . .
. . . . TW Aug 39 101
Iron World, The. .s. . . . .
. . . . .TW Aug 37 12
Malignant Entity, The. .s. . . . . .
. . . . Amz Jun 26 272
                     AQ Fal 34 120
Man from the Moon, The . . . . . .
. .s . . . . Amz Oct 30 646
                     AFR #9 54
Man in Room 18, The. .s. . . . . . .
. . . . AD Oct 30 912
Metal Monster, The. .nt . . . .
. . . . .Amz Jul 31 344
Meteor-Men of Mars. .s . . . .
. . . . .PS Win 42 98
Prophets of Science. .guest
editorial. . . . . SS Jan 39 15
Race Around the Moon. .nt. . . . .
. . . . TW Aug 39 95
Radio Ghost, The. .s . . . .
. . . . Amz Sep 27 531
Revenge of the Robot. .s. . . . . . .
. . . . TW Aug 36 38
Robot Beasts, The. .s . . . .
. . . . TW Jan 41 68
Stolen Centuries. .s . . . .
. . . . TW Jun 39 30

Stranger from Smallness. .nt . . . .
. . . . .SSS Aug 41 114
Thing That Walked in the Rain,
The. . . . . Amz Mar 31 1124
Treasure Accursed. .s . . . .
. . . . .FanF May 50 121
Vision of Venus, A. .s. . . . .
. . . . Amz Dec 33 97
with ALLEN S. KLINE
Secret Kingdom, The. .n 3 pt. . . .
. . . . Amz Oct 29 616
KNIGHT, DAMON See also pseuds
STUART FLEMING (3), DONALD
LAVERTY (1)
Editor WORLDS BEYOND
Dec 50 thru Feb 51 issues (all
issues)
Biog sketch . . . . . . PS Sum 48 37
Blackout. .ss. . . . . . SF Jul 43 55
Devil's Pawn. .ss . . . . Fut Oct 42 84
Gravity Trap. .s. . . SSS Jul 49 112
Not With a Bang. .s . . . .
. . . . . . F&SF Win–Spr 50 123
Resilience. .ss . . . . . Sti Feb 41 35
Star Beast, The. .s . . . .PS Spr 49 59
Third Little Green Man, The . . . .
. .s . . . . PS Sum 48 27
To Serve Man. .s . . . GSF Nov 50 91
with JAMES BLISH
Secret People, The. .s . . . .
. . . . .Fut Nov 50 46
Tiger Ride. .s . . . . .ASF Oct 48 142
Weakness of Rvog, The. .s . . . . . .
. . . . TW Feb 49 76
KNIGHT, NORMAN L.
Bombardment in Reverse . . . . . .
. .s . . . . ASF Feb 40 124
Crisis in Utopia. .n 2 pt. . . . .
. . . . .ASF Jul 40 9
Frontier of the Unknown . . . . . .
. .n 2 pt. . . . . .ASF Jul 37 8
Fugitive from Vangard. .s . . . . . .
. . . . .ASF Jan 42 76
Isle of the Golden Swarm. .s . . . .
. . . . ASF Jun 38 97
Kilgallen's Lunar Legacy. . . . . . .
. .s . . . . ASF Aug 42 92
Once in a Blue Moon. .nt . . . . . .
. . . . .Fut Aug 42 10
Saurian Valedictory. .s . . . .
. . . . .ASF Jan 39 33
Short-Circuited Probability . . . . .
. .s . . . . ASF Sep 41 61
Testament of Akubii, The. .s . . . .
. . . . ASF Jun 40 90

KNIGHT, QUEEN'S pseud
Is This a Four-Dimensional
Universe? . .a . . . Amz Feb 48 152
KNIGHT, RAYMOND
Just Around the Corner . . . .
. .1 act play . . . . . Amz Jul 28 358
KNIGHT, THOMAS H.
Great Green Things. .s . . . .
. . . . WS Apr 31 1288
Man Who Was Dead, The. .s. . . . .
. . . . ASF Apr 30 9
Revenge of the Chosen, The . . . .
. .s . . . . WQ Fal 30 128
KOBER, KEN
Sudden Death from Sound . . . . .
. .a . . . . .FA May 42 51
KOBER, WILLIAM
Man Who Lived Twice, The. . . . .
. .s . . . . Amz Nov 32 708
KOHN, ARNOLD artist
Covers for AMAZING STORIES
May, Jun, Nov 1946
Aug 1947
Jul 1948
Apr, Jun, Aug, Nov 1949
Jan, May 1950
Covers for FANTASTIC
ADVENTURES
Jul 1945
Jul, Sep 1946
Nov 1948
Feb, Mar, Aug 1949
with MALCOLM SMITH
Cover for OTHER WORLDS
Oct 1950
KORNBLUTH, C.(YRIL) M. See also
pseuds ARTHUR COOKE (1),
CECIL CORWIN (8), WALTER C.
DAVIES (3), KENNETH FAL-
CONER (2), S. D. GOTTESMAN
(16), CYRIL JUDD (0), PAUL
DENNIS LAVOND (4), SCOTT
MARINER (1), IVAR TOWERS
(1). See also DIRK WYLIE (1
collab)
Iteration. .ss . . . . .Fut Sep–Oct 50 60
Little Black Bag, The. .nt . . . . . .
. . . . .ASF Jul 50 132
Mindworm, The. .s. . . WB Dec 50 54
Only Thing We Learn, The. .s. . . .
. . . . SS Jul 49 129
Silly Season, The. .s . . . .
. . . . .F&SF Fal 50 3
Words of Guru, The. .s . . . .
. . . . .AFR #5 119

AUTHOR
Title. .Length . . . . Magazine, Date, Page

KOSTKOS, HENRY J.
Black Death. .s . . . . ASF Mar 34 76
Death in the Stratosphere. .s . . . .
. . . . Amz Aug 37 11
Earth Rehabilitators Consolidated.
. . n 3 pt . . . . Amz Mar 35 13
Emperor's Heart, The. .s . . . . . .
. . . . ASF Jun 34 93
Man Who Stopped the Earth,
The. .ss . . . . . . Amz Mar 34 120
Men Created for Death. .s . . . . . .
. . . . Amz Dec 34 76
Meteor-Men of Plaa, The. .nt . . . .
. . . . Amz Aug 33 392
North God's Temple. .s. . . . . . .
. . . . Amz Aug 34 99
Price of Escape, The. .s. . . . . . .
. . . . .SF Jun 40 88
Six Who Were Masked. .s. . . . . .
. . . . Amz Oct 36 70
Sleep Scourge, The. .s. . . . .
. . . . WS Dec 34 838
We of the Sun. .s. . . Amz Feb 36 68
KRAUS, JOSEPH H.
Phantom Monsters. .ss . . . .
. . . . WS Apr 35 1305
KREPPS, ROBERT W. *See also*
pseud GEOFF ST. REYNARD
(12)
Nickle Saved. . .", "A. .s . . . . . .
. . . . FA Mar 49 100
KRIMMEL, HERMAN E.
FANTASTIC HUMANS
Wolf Children. .a . . . FA Apr 40 60
Idiots Savants. .a . . . FA Jun 40 51
KRULFELD, MYER
Higgledy's Pig. .s . . . .SSS Aug 41 92
Invasion's End. .s. . . . TW Feb 39 64
Lunar Pit, The. .s. . . . TW Jun 40 44
Mission. .s . . . . . . ASF Sep 41 74
Mudman. .s . . . . . ASF Jun 42 92
Thing from Antares, The. .s. . . . .
. . . . TW Feb 40 61
KRUPA, JULIAN *artist*
Covers for AMAZING STORIES
Jun 1940
Sep 1944
Apr, Jul 1947
Biog sketch, photo. . . . .
. . . . Amz Dec 38 142
Biog sketch, photo. . . . .
. . . . FA Oct 40 135
Arctic Radio Farm. . . . .
. .bacover pic . . . . . Amz Sep 39
Cities of Tomorrow . . . .
. .bacover. . . . . Amz Aug 39

AUTHOR
Title. .Length . . . . Magazine, Date, Page

Colonizing the Ocean Bottom . . .
. .bacover pic . . . . . . Amz Apr 40
Future Ocean Liner . . . .
. .bacover. . . . . Amz Feb 39
Space Devastator. .bacover . . . .
. . . . .Amz Jul 39
Spaceship of 2038. .bacover . . . .
. . . . Amz Dec 38
Stratosphere Airliner of 1988 . . .
. .bacover pic . . . . . Amz Nov 38
When Meteorites Crash. . . . . . .
. .bacover. . . . . Amz Jun 40
KRUSE, CLIFTON B.
Code of the Spaceways. .s . . . . . .
. . . . ASF Jul 36 106
Death Protozoan, The. .s . . . . . .
. . . . Amz Feb 34 99
Dr. Lu-Mie. .s . . . .
. . . . .ASF Jul 34 42
Don Kelz of the L.S.P. . .s . . . .
. . . . ASF Feb 36 88
Door, The. .s . . . .
. . . . .SFQ Spr 43 108
Drums, The. .s . . . .
. . . . ASF Mar 36 115
Flight of the Typhoon. .s . . . . . .
. . . . .ASF Oct 36 140
Fractional Ego. .s . . . .
. . . . ASF Feb 37 106
Heat Destroyers, The. .s . . . . . .
. . . . WS Dec 33 466
Incredible Visitor, The . . . .
. .s . . . . ASF May 38 32
Menace from Saturn. .s. . . . . . .
. . . . ASF Jul 35 76
Osa the Killer. .s . . . .
. . . . .ASF Jan 35 91
Planet Leave. .s . . . . . Cos Mar 41 77
Princess of Pallis, A. .s . . . .
. . . . ASF Oct 35 95
Secret of the Canali, The. .s. . . . .
. . . . .ASF Jul 38 20
Stranger from Fomalhaut. .s . . . .
. . . . .ASF Jan 36 106
Voice Out of Space, The. .s . . . . .
. . . . .ASF Jan 38 34
W62 to Mercury. .s . . . .
. . . . ASF Sep 35 30
W–62's Last Flight, The. .s . . . . .
. . . . ASF May 36 115
KSANDRA, CHARLES F.
Biog sketch, photo. . . . .
. . . . TW Oct 39 77
Forever is Today. .s . . . .
. . . . .TW Sum 46 92
Hades. .s . . . . TW Oct 39 76

AUTHOR
Title. .Length . . . . Magazine, Date, Page

KUBERT, J. *cartoonist*
with EDWARD BELLIN pseud (story)
Man-Eating Lizards, The . . . .
. .comic . . . . . . OTWA Jul 50 61
with JOHN MICHEL (story)
Corsairs of the Coalsack, The. . . .
. .comic . . . . . .OTWA Dec 50 51
Lunar Station. .comic. . . . .
. . . . OTWA Jul 50 51
KUBILIUS, WALTER *See also*
pseud J. S. KLIMARIS (2)
Atrakin and the Man. .s . . . .
. . . . .SSS Feb 42 76
Caridi Shall Not Die. .s. . . . .
. . . . .SFQ Win 41–42 115
Fut Nov 50 80
Come to Mars. .s . . . .Ash Feb 43 78
Day has Come, The. .s . . . .
. . . . Sti Mar 42 26
AFR #12 116
Galactic Ghost. .s . . . .PS Win 42 91
Handful of Stars, A. .s . . . .
. . . . SSS Jan 49 76
Journey's End. .s. . . . .
. . . . .SSS May 43 118
Parrots of Venus. .s . . . .
. . . . .SSS Nov 42 69
Planet Alone. .s. . . . . Fut Feb 43 49
Remember Me, Kama! . .ss . . . . .
. . . . .Ash Oct 42 31
Trail's End. .s . . . . . .Sti Jun 41 57
Unusual Case, The. .ss . . . .
. . . . Cos Jul 41 74
Voice in the Void. .s . . . .
. . . . .Ash Mar 42 77
When the Earth Shook. .s . . . . . .
. . . . Fut Oct 42 103
KUEHN, ALFRED G.
Biog sketch, photo. . . TW Fal 44 51
Bloated Brain. .s . . . . TW Fal 44 49
KUMMER, FREDERIC ARNOLD,
JR. *See also pseuds JOHN*
ARNOLD (0), MARTIN VAETH
(1)
Biog sketch . . . . . Amz Oct 38 141
Biog sketch, photo. . . . .
. . . . Amz Mar 39 124
Biog sketch . . . . . . .FA May 39 85
Biog sketch, photo. . . . .
. . . . TW Jun 39 88
Biog sketch, photo. . . . .
. . . . FA Mar 40 92
Adventure in Lemuria. .s. . . . . . .
.FA May 39 60
Blitzkrieg–1950. .s . . . .
. . . . Amz Sep 40 84

AUTHOR
Title. .Length . . . . Magazine, Date, Page

Dark Invasion. .n. . . . MSS Aug 39 6
Day of the Comet. .nt . . . .
. . . . SSS Jul 40 6
Day of the Titans. .s. . . . .
. . . . Fut Dec 41 74
Deadly Slime, The. .s . . . .
. . . . Amz Jun 39 62
Delvers in Destiny. .s . . . .
. . . . TW Spr 45 67
Earth Stealers, The. .s. . . . .
. . . . Uc Apr 41 40
Exterminators, The. .s . . . .
. . . . TW Aug 38 48
Flying Dutchman of Space, The. .
. .s . . . . Amz Oct 38 84
Foreign Legion of Mars, The . . . .
. .s . . . . Amz May 39 98
Forgiveness of Tenchu Taen,
The. .s . . . . . ASF Nov 38 119
Hell Ship of Space. .s . . . .
. . . . Amz Nov 40 108
Ice Plague, The. .s . . . .
. . . . Amz Oct 39 72
Insect Invasion, The. .s . . . .
. . . . FA Sep 39 80
Intrigue in Lemuria. .s . . . .
. . . . .FA Jul 39 56
Invisible Invasion. .s. . . . .
. . . . Amz Apr 39 40
Isles of the Blest. .n . . . .
. . . . .Fut Mar 40 8
Legion of the Dead. .s . . . .
. . . . Amz Nov 39 100
Lorelei of Space. .nt. . . . .
. . . . ASF Feb 39 117
Pied Piper of Mars. .s . . . .
. . . . .PS Spr 42 80
Pirates of Eros. .s. . . . .
. . . . Amz Nov 38 90
Princess of Power. .s. . . . .
. . . . MSS May 40 72
Revolt Against Life. .s . . . .
. . . . TW Jan 40 12
Salvage of Space. .s . . . .
. . . . .Ash Apr 40 55
Sargasso of the Stars. .s. . . . . . .
. . . . PS Sum 41 46
Satellite of Fear. .s. . . . .
. . . . .PS Spr 41 96
Signboard of Space. .s . . . .
. . . . TW Dec 39 12
. . . . SS May 50 80
Slaves of Rhythm. .s . . . .
. . . . Amz Jan 40 98
Spaceship from Korl. .s. . . . . . .
. . . . .SSS Feb 42 58

Spring Machine, The. .s . . . .
. . . . .SSS Feb 42 68
Star Pirate. .s . . . . . . PS Sum 40 69
Stranger from the Stars. .s . . . . .
. . . . TW Mar 41 66
Stronger, The. .s . . . .
. . . . .DS Apr–May 39 94
Telepathic Tomb, The. .s . . . . . .
. . . . TW Feb 39 72
Time Merchant, The. .s. . . . .
. . . . FA Jan 40 48
Treasure on Asteroid X, The . . . .
. .s . . . . Amz Jan 39 60
Tyrant of Mars, The. .s . . . .
.TW Sep 40 12
Vengeance from the Void. .s . . . .
. . . . Amz Mar 39 86
Volcano Slaves of Mu. .s . . . .
. . . . FA Mar 40 54
Wedding of the Moons. .s . . . . . .
. . . . .Ash Aug 40 73
White Land of Venus. .s . . . .
. . . . .Ash Feb 40 26
Worlds Within Worlds. .nt . . . . . .
. . . . TW Mar 40 85
with DIRK WYLIE (& Frederik Pohl)
When Time Went Mad. .nt . . . . . .
. . . . TW Feb 50 11

KUTTNER, HENRY *See also pseuds*
EDWARD J. BELLIN (h) (1),
PAUL EDMONDS (6), NOEL
GARDNER (2), WILL GARTH (h)
(1), JAMES HALL (1), KEITH
HAMMOND (4), HUDSON
HASTINGS (2), PETER HORN
(h) (1), KELVIN KENT (8),
ROBERT O. KENYON (1), C. H.
LIDDELL (2), SCOTT MORGAN
(1), K. H. MAEPEN (0),
LAWRENCE O'DONNELL (2),
LEWIS PADGETT (32),
WOODROW WILSON SMITH (1),
CHARLES STODDARD (h) (0)
Virtually everything written since
their marriage in June, 1940 has
been to some extent a collaboration
with Kuttner's wife, C. L. MOORE.
Biog Sketch, photo . . . .
. . . . TW Jun 39 87
Biog sketch, photo. . . . .
. . . . TW Oct 39 23
Biog sketch . . . . . . SS Sum 46 112
Absalom. .s . . . . SS Fal 46 90
All Is Illusion. .s . . . . UK Apr 40 95
As You Were. .nt. . . . . .TW Aug 50 9
Atomic! . .s . . . . TW Aug 47 48

Avengers of Space. .nt . . . .
. . . . MSS Aug 38 98
Baby Face. .s . . . . . . TW Spr 45 88
Beauty and the Beast. .s . . . .
. . . . TW Apr 40 67
Before I Wake. . . . .s. . . . .
. . . . FFM Mar 45 106
Better Than One. .s . . .CF Spr 43 92
Beyond Annihilation. .s . . . .
. . . . TW Apr 39 37
Black Sun Rises, The. .nt . . . . . .
. . . . .SSS Jan 49 8
Cold War. .s . . . . TW Oct 49 102
Compliments of the Author. . . . .
. .nt . . . . UK Oct 42 111
Crypt-City of the Deathless
One. .nt. . . . . PS Win 43 3
Crystal Circe, The. .s . . . .
. . . . Ash Jun 42 66
Dark Angel, The. .s . . .SS Mar 46 89
Dark World, The. .n . . . SS Sum 46 9
Design for Dreaming. .nt. . . . . . .
. . . . UK Feb 42 113
Devil We Know, The. .s. . . . .
. . . . .UK Aug 41 90
. . . . UK 48 102
Disinherited, The. .s . . . .
. . . . ASF Aug 38 146
Dr. Cyclops. .s . . . . . TW Jun 40 14
Don't Look Now. .s. . . . .
. . . . .SS Mar 48 13
Doom World. .s . . . . TW Aug 38 12
Dream's End. .s . . . . . SS Jul 47 80
Elixir of Invisibility, The. . . . . . .
. .s . . . . FA Oct 40 114
Exit the Professor. .s . . . .
. . . . TW Oct 47 83
Eyes of Thar, The. .s . . . .
. . . . PS Fal 44 45
False Dawn. .s. . . . TW Jun 42 107
Ghost. .s . . . . ASF May 43 60
God Named Kroo, A. .nt . . . .
. . . . TW Win 44 13
Gnome There Was, A. .s . . . .
. . . . UK Oct 41 108
Happy Ending. .s . . . .TW Aug 48 46
"HOLLYWOOD ON THE MOON"
series includes:
HOLLYWOOD ON THE MOON
DOOM WORLD
THE STAR PARADE
THE ENERGY EATERS*
SUIDIDE SQUAD
THE SEVEN SLEEPERS*
PERCY THE PIRATE
*With ARTHUR K. BARNES, combined
with the "Gerry Carlisle" series.

AUTHOR
Title. .Length . . . . Magazine, Date, Page

Hollywood on the Moon. .nt . . . .
. . . . TW Apr 38 12
                              SS Jul 49 108
I Am Eden. .nt . . . . . TW Dec 46 11
Infinite Moment, The. .nt . . . . . .
. . . . TW Apr 42 17
Land of Time to Come, The . . . .
. .n . . . . TW Apr 41 14
Lands of the Earthquake. . . . . . .
. .n . . . . SS May 47 11
Later Than You Think. .s . . . . . .
. . . . FA Mar 42 60
LittleThings, The. .s . . . .
. . . . TW Fal 46 85
Mask of Circe, The. .n . . . .
. . . . SS May 48 11
Million Years to Conquer, A . . . .
. .n . . . . SS Nov 40 16
Misguided Halo, The. .s . . . . . .
. . . . UK Aug 39 125
Music Hath Charms. .s . . . .
. . . . .SS Win 44 89
No Greater Love. .nt . . . .
. . . . UK Apr 43 105
No Man's World. .s . . . .
. . . . TW Aug 40 42
Nothing But Gingerbread
Left. .s . . . . .ASF Jan 43 60
Pegasus. .s . . . .FFM May–Jun 40 78
Percy the Pirate. .s . . . .
. . . . .TW Sum 45 79
Pile of Trouble. .s . . . .
. . . . TW Apr 48 51
Portal in the Picture, The . . . . . .
. .n . . . . .SS Sep 49 9
Power and the Glory, The . . . . . .
. .nt . . . . TW Dec 47 13
PROBABILITY ZERO
Blue Ice. .ss . . . . . ASF Feb 43 88
Corpus Delicti. .ss . . . .
. . . . ASF Apr 43 85
Problem in Ethics. .s . . . .
. . . . SF Jul 43 58
Reader, I Hate You! . .s . . . . . .
. . . . SSS May 43 48
Red Gem of Mercury. .s . . . .
. . . . .SSS Nov 41 109
Remember Tomorrow. .nt . . . . . .
. . . . TW Jan 41 87
Reverse Atom. .s . . . .TW Nov 40 40
Secret of the Earth Star . . . .
. .nt . . . . Amz Aug 42 110
See You Later. .s . . . TW Jun 49 116
Silent Eden. .s . . . . . .SS Mar 42 88
Soldiers of Space. .s . . . .
. . . . .Ash Feb 43 87

AUTHOR
Title. .Length . . . . Magazine, Date, Page

Star Parade, The. .nt . . . .
. . . . TW Dec 38 26
Suicide Squad. .s . . . . TW Dec 39 42
Sword of Tomorrow. .nt . . . . . .
. . . . TW Fal 45 11
Threshold. .s . . . . . . UK Dec 40 92
Thunder in the Void. .nt . . . . . .
. . . . .Ash Oct 42 10
Time Axis, The. .n . . . .
. . . . SS Jan 49 13
Time Trap, The. .n . . . .
. . . . MSS Nov 38 72
To Dust Returneth. .s . . . .
. . . . CF Win 44 93
Too Many Cooks. .s . . . .
. . . . TW Dec 42 80
Trouble on Titan. .s . . . .
. . . . TW Feb 47 36
Tube to Nowhere. .s . . . .
. . . . TW Jun 41 63
Voice of the Lobster, The . . . . . .
. .nt . . . . TW Feb 50 114
Volluswen. .s . . . . . . SF Apr 43 86
War-Gods of the Void. .nt . . . . . .
. . . . .PS Fal 42 2
Way of the Gods. .nt . . . .
. . . . TW Apr 47 11
We Guard the Black Planet . . . . .
. .nt . . . . .SSS Nov 42 10
Wet Magic. .nt . . . . . .UK Feb 43 9
What Hath Me? . .nt . . . .
. . . . PS Spr 46 50
When New York Vanished. . . . . .
. .n . . . . .SS Mar 40 14
When the Earth Lived. .s . . . . . .
. . . . TW Oct 37 90
                              SS Jul 48 92
World Without Air. .s . . . .
. . . . FA Aug 40 108
with ARTHUR K. BARNES
Energy Eaters, The. .s. . . . .
. . . . TW Oct 39 16
                              SS Sep 50 124
Seven Sleepers, The. .nt . . . .
. . . . .TW May 40 93
with C. L. MOORE
Earth's Last Citadel. .n . . . .
. . . . .FN Jul 50 12
KYLE, DAVID A.
Golden Nemesis. .s . . . .
. . . . Sti Feb 41 28

AUTHOR
Title. .Length . . . . Magazine, Date, Page

L

LACHER, R.
with NATHAN SCHACHNER
Memory of the Atoms, The . . . . .
. .s . . . . .WS Jan 33 614
LAFAYETTE, RENE
LaFAYETTE, RENE pseud of L. RON
HUBBARD
Beyond the Black Nebula. .s . . . .
. . . . SS Sep 49 126
"CONQUEST OF SPACE" series
includes:
FORBIDDEN VOYAGE
THE MAGNIFICENT FAILURE
THE INCREDIBLE DESTINATION
THE UNWILLING HERO
BEYOND THE BLACK NEBULA
THE EMPEROR OF THE UNIVERSE
THE LAST ADMIRAL
Conroy Diary, The. .s . . . .
. . . . ASF May 49 134
Emperor of the Universe, The . . .
. .s . . . . .SS Nov 49 132
Expensive Slaves, The. .s . . . . . .
. . . . ASF Nov 47 63
Forbidden Voyage. .s . . . .
. . . . SS Jan 49 142
Great Air Monopoly, The. .nt . . .
. . . . ASF Sep 48 71
Her Majesty's Aberration. .s . . . .
. . . . ASF Mar 48 126
Incredible Destination, The . . . . .
. .s . . . . SS May 49 96
Indigestible Triton, The. .n . . . . .
. . . . UK Apr 40 9
Last Admiral, The. .s . . . .
. . . . SS Jan 50 112
1 Magnificent Failure, The. .s. . . .
. . . . SS Mar 49 104
"OLD DOC METHUSELAH" series
includes:
OLD DOC METHUSELAH
THE EXPENSIVE SLAVES
HER MAJESTY'S ABERRATION
THE GREAT AIR MONOPOLY
PLAGUE
A SOUND INVESTMENT
OLE MOTHER METHUSELAH
Old Doc Methuselah. .nt . . . .
. . . . ASF Oct 47 6
Ole Mother Methuselah. .nt . . . . .
. . . . .ASF Jan 50 80
One Was Stubborn. .s . . . .
. . . . ASF Nov 40 82
Plague. .nt . . . . ASF Apr 49 6
Sound Investment, A. .nt . . . . . .
. . . . ASF Jun 49 36

AUTHOR
  Title. .Length . . . . Magazine, Date, Page

  Unwilling Hero, The. .s . . . .
  . . . . SS Jul 49 98
LAKE, BABETTE ROSMOND
  Are You Run-Down, Tired— . . . .
  . .s . . . . UK Oct 42 82
LAMBERT, ARTHUR *pseud of*
  ARTHUR LAMBERT WIDNER
  Perfect Incinerator, The . . . .
  . .ss . . . . SFQ Win 42 139
LANDON, PERCEVAL
  Thurnley Abbey. .s . . . .
  . . . . .F&SF Fal 49 18
LANE, SPENCER *house pseud*
  Angel in the Dust Bowl. .s . . . . .
  . . . . ASF Dec 37 95
  Niedbalski's Mutant. .s . . . .
  . . . . ASF May 38 129
  Origin of Thought. .s . . . .
  . . . . .ASF Jun 36 100
LANG, ALLEN K.
  Machine Of Klamugra. .s . . . .
  . . . . PS Nov 50 46
LASH, KERRY
  Vendetta on Venus. .s . . . .
  . . . . .SSS Aug 41 52
LASSER DAVID
  Managing Editor AMAZING
    DETECTIVE TALES
  Aug 30 *thru* Oct 30 *issues*
  Managing Editor AIR WONDER
    STORIES
  (all issues)
  Managing Editor SCIENCE
    WONDER STORIES
  (all issues)
  Managing Editor WONDER
    STORIES
  Jun 30 *thru* Oct 33 *issues*
  Managing Editor WONDER
    STORIES QUARTERLY
  (all issues)
  with DAVID H. KELLER, M. D.
  Time Projector, The. .n 2 pt . . . .
  . . . . .WS Jul 31 152
LATHAM, PHILIP *pseud of ROBERT*
  S. RICHARDSON
  Aphrodite Project, The. .s . . . . . .
  . . . . ASF Jun 49 73
  Blindness, The. .nt . . . .
  . . . . .ASF Jul 46 84
  N Day. .s . . . . .ASF Jan 46 46
  Xi Effect, The. .s . . . . ASF Jan 50 6
LAURENCE, LEE
  History in Reverse . . . .
  . .radio script . . . . Amz Oct 39 8

AUTHOR
  Title. .Length . . . . Magazine, Date, Page

LAVERTY, DONALD *pseud of*
  JAMES BLISH and DAMON
  KNIGHT
  No Winter, No Summer. .s . . . . .
  . . . . TW Oct 48 140
LAVOND, PAUL DENNIS *house*
  pseud
  by CYRIL KORNBLUTH, ROBERT
  W. LOWNDES, FREDERIK
  POHL & DIRK WYLIE
  Einstein's Planetoid. .s . . . .
  . . . . .SFQ Spr 42 100
  Exiles of New Planet. .s . . . .
  . . . . .Ash Apr 41 74
  by CYRIL KORNBLUTH &
  FREDERIK POHL
  Callistan Tomb. .s . . . .
  . . . . .SFQ Spr 41 108
  Prince of Pluto, A. .s . . . .
  . . . . .Fut Apr 41 85
  by ROBERT W. LOWNDES
  Doll Master, The. .ss . . . .
  . . . . .Sti Apr 41 115
  by ROBERT W. LOWNDES,
  FREDERIK POHL & DIRK
  WYLIE
  Something from Beyond. .ss . . . .
  . . . . Fut Dec 41 100
  by FREDERIK POHL & DIRK
  WYLIE
  Star of the Undead. .s . . . .
  . . . . FB #2 14
  (ROBERT W. LOWNDES also had a
  hand in this but most of his work was
  eliminated in Wylie's final re-write).
LAWLOR, HAROLD
  Biog sketch, photo. . . . .
  . . . . FA Apr 42 233
  Daughters of Darkness. .s . . . . . .
  . . . . FA Apr 43 86
  Dinky Winky Woo. .s . . . .
  . . . . FA Aug 43 168
  Eternal Princess, The. .s . . . .
  . . . . FA Apr 42 108
  Irresistible Perfume, The . . . .
  . .s . . . . FA May 43 102
  Manchu Coffin, The. .s . . . .
  . . . . FA Dec 42 204
LAWRENCE, RAYMOND EMERY
  Posterity Fund, The. .s . . . .
  . . . . Amz May 29 162
LAWRENCE, (STEPHEN) *pseud of*
  L.(awrence) STERNE STEVENS
  artist
  Cover for ASTONISHING STORIES
  Dec 1942

AUTHOR
  Title. .Length . . . . Magazine, Date, Page

  Covers for FAMOUS FANTASTIC
    MYSTERIES
  Dec 1943
  Mar, Jun, Sep, Dec 1944
  Mar, Jun, Sep, Dec 1945
  Feb, Apr, Jun, Aug, Oct 1946
  Apr, Oct 1947
  Apr, Aug, Oct, Dec 1948
  Feb, Apr, Jun, Aug, Oct, Dec 1949
  Feb, Apr 1959
  Covers for FANTASTIC NOVELS
  Mar, May, Jul, Sep 1948
  Jan, May, Jul, Sep 1949
  Jan, Jul 1950
  Covers for SUPER SCIENCE
    STORIES
  Nov 1942
  Jan, Apr, Jul, Sep 1949
  Jan, May, Jul 1950
LAWTON, DENNIS *pseud of*
  FREDERICK FAUST
LAZENBY, NORMAN
  Cireesians, The. .s . . . .NW #4 49 27
  Matter of Size, A. .s . . . .
  . . . . Fant Dec 46 79
  Survival. .s . . . . . . Fant Apr 47 77
LEA, MACK CHAPMAN
  Gorgons, The. .s . . . .
  . . . . .ASF Sep 48 119
LEATH, ROBERT NEAL
  Karpen the Jew. .s . . . .
  . . . . FFM Sep–Oct 39 63
LEE, MATT *pseud of SAM*
  MERWIN, JR.
  Appointment in New Utrecht . . .
  . .s . . . . .SS Mar 50 129
  Exit Line. .s . . . . . . .SS Sep 50 119
  Problem in Astrogation, A. .s . . . .
  . . . . TW Apr 48 99
LEE, THORNE
  Ghost Planet. .s . . . . .SS Jun 43 104
  Man Who Lost His Shadow,
  The. .nt . . . . FA Jun 44 84
LEFTWICH, EDMUND H.
  Bell-Tone, The. .ss . . . .
  . . . . .Com Jul 41 117
LEHMAN, PAUL *artist*
  Cover for FANTASTIC
    ADVENTURES
  Dec 1945
LEIBER, FRITZ, (JR.)
  Black Eye, The. .s . . . .
  . . . . SS May 50 117
  Bleak Shore, The. .s . . . .
  . . . . UK Nov 40 111

AUTHOR
Title. .Length . . . . Magazine, Date, Page

Business of Killing. .s . . . .
. . . . ASF Sep 44 59
Coming Attraction. .s . . . .
. . . . GSF Nov 50 75
Conjure Wife. .n . . . . . UK Apr 43 9
Destiny Times Three. .n 2 pt . . . .
. . . . ASF Mar 45 6
Dreams of Albert Moreland,
The. .s . . . . AFR #7 40
Enchanted Forest, The. .s . . . . . .
. . . . .ASF Oct 50 110
Gather, Darkness! . .n 3 pt . . . . .
. . . . .ASF May 43 9
Hill and the Hole, The . . . .
. . . . UK Aug 42 78
Howling and the Hole, The . . . . .
. .s . . . . UK Jun 41 90
Later Than You Think. .s . . . . . .
. . . . .GSF Oct 50 108
Let Freedom Ring. .n . . . .
. . . . Amz Apr 50 90
Lion and the Lamb, The . . . .
. .nt . . . . ASF Sep 50 6
Man Who Never Grew Young,
The. .s . . . . AFR #9 48
Martians, Keep Out!. .s . . . .
. . . . Fut Jul-Aug 50 45
Mutant's Brother, The. .s . . . . . .
. . . . ASF Aug 43 53
Sanity. .s . . . . . . ASF Apr 44 160
Ship Sails at Midnight, The . . . . .
. .s . . . . FA Sep 50 54
Smoke Ghost. .s . . . UK Oct 41 100
Sunken Land, The. .s . . . .
. . . . UK Feb 42 97
Taboo. .s . . . . ASF Feb 44 85
They Never Come Back. .nt . . . . .
. . . . .Fut Aug 41 10
Thieves' House. .nt . . . .
. . . . UK Feb 43 34
Thought. .s . . . . . . .ASF Jul 44 84
Two Sought Adventure. .nt . . . . .
. . . . UK Aug 39 99
Wanted—An Enemy. .s . . . .
. . . . ASF Feb 45 49
You're All Alone. .n . . . .
. . . . .FA Jul 50 8
LEINSTER, MURRAY *pseud of*
F. JENKINS
Biog sketch . . . . . . ToW Win 39 92
Adapter. .s . . . . . . .ASF Mar 46 49
Beyond the Sphinxes' Cave . . . . .
. .nt . . . . ASF Nov 33 2
Be Young Again! . .s . . . .
. . . . Fut Jul–Aug 50 28

AUTHOR
Title. .Length . . . . Magazine, Date, Page

Black Galaxy, The. .n . . . .
. . . . .SS Mar 49 13
Boomerang Circuit, The . . . .
. .nt . . . . TW Jun 47 11
Borneo Devils. .s . . . .
. . . . Amz Feb 33 989
Day of the Deepies, The. .s . . . . .
. . . . FFM Oct 47 98
Dead City. .nt . . . . .TW Sum 46 42
De Profundis. .s . . . .
. . . . TW Win 45 92
Disciplinary Circuit, The . . . . . .
. .nt . . . . TW Win 46 44
End, The. .nt . . . . . . TW Dec 46 36
Eternal Now, The. .s . . . .
. . . . TW Fal 44 11
Ethical Equations, The. .s . . . . . .
. . . . .ASF Jun 45 117
Fear Planet, The. .s . . . .
. . . . SSS Jan 50 48
Fifth-Dimension Catapult,
The. .nt . . . . .ASF Jan 31 72
Fifth-Dimension Tube, The . . . . .
. .nt . . . . .ASF Jan 33 366
First Contact. .nt . . . .
. . . . .ASF Jan 33 366
First Contact. .nt . . . .
. . . . .ASF May 45 7
Four Little Ships. .s . . . .
. . . . ASF Nov 42 36
Fourth-Dimensional Demonstrator,
The. .s . . . . ASF Dec 35 100
Friends. .s . . . . .SS Jan 47 86
Fury from Lilliput. .nt . . . .
. . . . .TW Aug 49 9
Ghost Planet, The. .nt . . . .
. . . . TW Dec 48 13
"—If You Can Get It.". .s . . . . . .
. . . . ASF Nov 43 155
Incident on Calypso. .s . . . .
. . . . SS Fal 45 57
Incredible Invasion, The . . . .
. .n 5 pt . . . . ASF Aug 36 6
Interference. .s . . . .
. . . . ASF Oct 45 49
Invasion. .s . . . . . ASF Mar 33 118
Laws of Chance, The. .n . . . .
. . . . .SS Mar 47 13
Life-Work of Professor Muntz,
The. .s . . . . TW Jun 49 128
Like Dups. .s . . . . . TW Spr 46 93
Lonely Planet, The. .s . . . .
. . . . TW Dec 49 80
Lost Race, The. .s . . . .
. . . . TW Apr 49 112

AUTHOR
Title. .Length . . . . Magazine, Date, Page

Mad Planet, The. .nt . . . .
. . . . Amz Nov 26 736
. . . . ToW Spr 39 4
. . . . FN Nov 48 82
Man in the Iron Cap, The. .n . . . .
. . . . SS Nov 47 11
Manless Worlds, The. .nt . . . .
. . . . .TW Feb 47 11
Mole Pirate, The. .nt . . . .
. . . . ASF Nov 34 10
Morale. .s . . . . . . ASF Dec 31 402
Murder Madness. .n 4 pt . . . .
. . . . ASF May 30 166
Night Before the End of the World,
The. .s . . . . FFM Aug 48 114
Nobody Saw the Ship. .s . . . .
. . . . Fut May–Jun 50 40
Other World, The. .n . . . .
. . . . SS Nov 49 11
Pipeline to Pluto. .s . . . .
. . . . ASF Aug 45 68
Plague. .nt . . . . ASF Feb 5
Plague. .nt . . . . . ASF Feb 44 52
Planet of Sand. .nt . . . .
. . . . FFM Feb 48 90
Planet of the Small Men. .nt . . . .
. . . . TW Apr 50 11
Plants, The. .s . . . . .ASF Jan 46 138
Pocket Universes. .s . . . .
. . . . TW Fal 46 70
Politics. .s . . . . . . Amz Jun 32 268
Power, The. .s . . . . . ASF Sep 45 83
Power Planet, The. .nt . . . .
. . . . Amz Jun 31 198
. . . . AFR #1 7
Propagandist. .s . . . .
. . . . ASF Aug 47 139
Proxima Centauri. .nt . . . .
. . . . ASF Mar 35 10
Queen's Astrologer, The. .s . . . . .
. . . . TW Oct 49 83
Racketeer Ray, The. .s . . . .
. . . . Amz Feb 32 1004
Red Dust, The. .nt . . . .
. . . . .Amz Jan 27 878
. . . . ToW Win 39 6
. . . . FN May 49 58
Regulations. .s . . . . .TW Aug 48 39
Runaway Skyscraper, The. .s . . . .
. . . . Amz Jun 26 250
Sidewise in Time. .nt . . . .
. . . . ASF Jun 34 10
Skit-Tree Planet. .s . . . .
. . . . TW Apr 47 41
Space-Can. .s . . . . . TW Jun 47 117

AUTHOR
Title. .Length . . . . Magazine, Date, Page

Story of Rod Cantrell, The . . . . .
. .s . . . . SS Jan 49 88
Strange Case of John Kingman,
The. .s. . . . . ASF May 48 34
Tanks. .s . . . . .ASF Jan 30 100
Things Pass By. .nt. . . . .
. . . . .TW Sum 45 11
This Star Shall Be Free. .s . . . . . .
. . . . .SSS Nov 49 48
Tight Place. .s . . . . . ASF Jul 45 131
Time to Die. .s . . . .
. . . . .ASF Jan 47 141
Trog. .n . . . . ASF Jun 44 7
Wabbler, The. .s . . . .
. . . . ASF Oct 42 85
West Wind. .nt . . . .
. . . . ASF Mar 48 77
LEIPIAR, LOUISE See pseud L.
MAJOR REYNOLDS (1)
LEITERIED, ROBERT H.
Prisms of Space. .s . . . .
. . . . ASF Nov 33 27
Prisoners on the Electron. .s . . . . .
. . . . ASF Oct 30 75
Where Gravity Ends. .s . . . .
. . . . AW Sep 29 214
LEMKE, HENRY E.
Last of the Swarm, The. .s . . . . .
. . . . WS Oct 33 256
LEMKIN, WILLIAM, (Ph.D.)
Atomic Adventure, An. .nt . . . . .
. . . . WQ Sep 30 60
Beyond the Stratosphere. . . . . . .
. .n 2 pt . . . . Amz Jun 36 13
Blue Water. .s . . . . . AQ Win 32 96
Cold Light. .s . . . . Amz Nov 29 706
Cupid of the Laboratory. .nt . . . .
. . . . Amz Aug 37 79
Doom of Lun-Dhag, The. .nt . . . .
. . . . Amz Nov 32 678
Eclipse Special, The. .nt . . . .
. . . . Amz Dec 30 774
Isle of the Gargoyles. .nt. . . . . . .
. . . . .WS Jan 36 820
Matter of Nerves, A. .nt . . . .
. . . . Amz Jun 32 232
Vitamin Z. .s . . . Amz Feb 30 1056
LEMON, DON M.
Scarlet Planet, The. .n . . . .
. . . . WQ Win 31 150
LENAHAN, JOHN P.
Voice from Beyond, A. .s . . . . . .
. . . . FA Sep 46 88
LES TINA, DOROTHY
When You Think That. . .Smile!. .
. .s . . . . .Fut Feb 43 55

AUTHOR
Title. .Length . . . . Magazine, Date, Page

LESPERANCE, DAVID See pseud
GENE A. DAVIDSON (0)
LESSER, DERWIN pseud of
CHARLES D. HORNIG
Fatal Glance, The. .ss . . . .
. . . . WS Feb 35 1058
Hazards of Space Flight. .a . . . . .
. . . . SF Mar 39 80
Science of Dreams. .a . . . .
. . . . .SF Oct 39 80
Science and Truth. .a . . . .
. . . . SF Aug 39 30
LESSER, MILTON See also pseuds
STEPHEN MARLOW (0), S. M.
TENNESHAW (h) (1)
Biog sketch . . . . . . .PS Mar 43 64
All Heroes Are Hated. .nt . . . . . .
. . . . Amz Nov 50 8
It's Raining Frogs. .nt. . . . .
. . . . Im Dec 50 74
LESTER, IRVIN
with FLETCHER PRATT
Danger. .s . . . . Amz Jul 29 364
Great Steel Panic, The . . . .
. .s . . . . Amz Sep 28 522
Octopus Cycle, The. .s . . . .
. . . . .Amz May 28 110
Reign of the Ray. .n 2 pt . . . . . .
. . . . SW Jun 29 7
Roger Bacon Formula, The . . . . .
. .s . . . . .Amz Jan 29 940
LEVERAGE, HENRY
Black Cabinet, The. .s . . . .
. . . . AD Sep 30 780
Black Light. .s . . . .
. . . . SD Apr 30 330
Sealed Room, The. .s . . . .
. . . . AD Jun 30 541
LEWIS, D. B. pseud of JEROME
BIXBY
LEWIS, GEORGE D.
Von Hulckman's Pets. .s . . . .
. . . . Amz Sep 49 120
LEWIS, HELMAR
Biog sketch, photo. . . . .
. . . . Amz Jul 43 200
Aura of Death, The. .s . . . .
. . . . Amz Nov 43 156
Curse of the Phantom Legion. . . .
. .s . . . . FA Jun 44 190
Headless Horror, The. .nt . . . . . .
. . . . Amz May 44 134
Journey in Time to Cleopatra . . .
. .nt . . . . Amz Mar 44 124
Man Who Lost His Face, The . . . .
. .s . . . . .Amz Jul 43 88

AUTHOR
Title. .Length . . . . Magazine, Date, Page

Whips of Doom, The. .s . . . .
. . . . Amz Dec 44 132
LEWIS, HENRY S.
Death Ray. .s . . . . . .SS Nov 42 114
Secret Weapon. .ss . . . CF Fal 42 103
LEWIS, RICHARD O.
Biog sketch, photo. . . . .
. . . . Amz Feb 40 134
Adam's Eve. .s . . . . Amz May 43 62
Alla-Beg's Genii. .s . . . .
. . . . SS May 42 89
Dr. Kelton—Body Snatcher . . . . .
. .s . . . . FA Jan 41 98
Fate Changer, The. .s . . . .
. . . . Amz Sep 39 125
Hell in Eden. .s . . . .
. . . . FA Jan 40 64
Incredible Theory of Dr. Penwing,
The. .s. . . . . Amz Aug 40 28
Man Who Came Back, The. .s. . . .
. . . . FA Jun 40 104
Moon Madness. .s . . . .
. . . . Amz Aug 42 198
Nazi Diamond. .s. . . . .
. . . . Amz Nov 42 204
Strange Voyage of Dr. Penwing,
The. .s. . . . . Amz Mar 40 40
Thirteenth Mr. Tumps, The . . . . .
. .s . . . . Amz Feb 40 76
Thought-World Monsters,
The. .s. . . . . MSS Nov 40 67
Vitality for Murder. .s . . . .
. . . . .FA Jul 42 110
Zurk. .s . . . . .PS Win 41 92
LEY, WILLY See also pseud
ROBERT WILLEY (4)
Biog sketch . . . . . . .Fant #2 39 92
Photo . . . . .TW Nov 40 34
Atlantropa; The Improved
Continent. .a . . . . MSS Feb 39 99
Birth of a Superstition, The. . . . .
. .a . . . . ASF May 42 98
Bombing Is a Fine Art. .a . . . . . .
. . . . ASF Aug 42 75
Botanical Invasion. .a . . . .
. . . . ASF Feb 40 91
"Brickwall" in the Sky, The . . . .
. .a . . . . ASF Nov 48 78
Calling All Martians. .a . . . .
. . . . .TW Nov 40 34
Channel Tunnel, The. .a . . . .
. . . . .SS Nov 50 135
Conquest of the Deep, The . . . . .
. .a . . . . TW Jun 38 36
Dawn of the Conquest of Space,
The. .a. . . . . . . ASF Mar 37 104

AUTHOR
    Title. .Length . . . . Magazine, Date, Page

Death Under the Sea. .a . . . .
 . . . . ASF Sep 42 44
Earth's Second Moon. .a . . . .
 . . . . .ASF Oct 39 141
Eight Days in the Story of
 Rocketry. .a . . . . . TW Dec 37 56
Eighty Percent. .a . . . .
 . . . . .UK May 40 122
Electric Battery 2000 Years Ago,
 An. .a . . . . ASF Mar 39 43
End of the Rocket Society,
 The. .a 2 pt . . . . . ASF Aug 43 64
Ersatz World, The. .a . . . .
 . . . . .SSS May 40 118
Extraterrestrial Bacteria. .a . . . . .
 . . . . ASF Dec 43 110
FANTASTIC HOAXES
 The Fischer Hoax. .a . . . .
 . . . . FA Jan 40 28
 Dr. Koch's Sea Serpent. .a. . . . .
 . . . . FA Feb 40 26
 The Baloon Hoax. .a . . . .
 . . . . FA Mar 40 28
 George Psalmanazar. .a . . . .
 . . . . FA Apr 40 40
 Atlantis Hoax of Dr.
  Schliemann. .a . . . FA Aug 40 46
 John Jacob Scheuchzer. . . . . . .
 . .a . . . . FA Oct 40 74
Fatal Coloration, The. .a. . . . . . .
 . . . . ASF Apr 42 98
Few Notes on the Reliability of
 Newspaper Clippings Without
 Additional Remarks About Charles
 Fort and Others. .a . . . .
 . . . . UK Mar 40 156
Flying Saucers; Friend, Foe or
 Fantasy. .a . . . . . . GSF Oct 50 67
Fusible Alloys. .a. . . . ASF Jul 37 71
Galileo's Revolution. .a. . . . .
 . . . . .SSS Aug 41 100
Geography for Time Travelers . . .
 . .a . . . . ASF Jul 39 122
". . .Giants in Those Days. . ." . . .
 . .a . . . . ASF Nov 45 111
Homemade Gun of Jamrud,
 The. .a. . . . . . . ASF Apr 41 126
Ice Age Ahead? . .a . . . .
 . . . . ASF Feb 39 86
Impossibilities. .a. . . . Fant #3 39 45
Improving Upon V–2. .a . . . .
 . . . . .ASF Jan 47 100
It Happens Twice At Least . . . . .
 . .a . . . . UK Jan 40 119
Kitchen of the Future, The . . . . .
 . . .a . . . . TW Oct 41 96

LANDSCAPES OF OTHER
  WORLDS
 Mars–Planet of War. .a . . . .
 . . . . Amz Apr 42 256
 Luna–Goddess of Love. .a . . . .
 . . . . Amz May 42 256
 Venus–World of Mystery . . . . .
 . .a . . . . Amz Jun 42 176
 Saturn–World of Rings. . . . . . .
 . . . . .Amz Jul 42 154
 Mercury–The Fire World . . . . .
 . . . . Amz Aug 42 86
 Jupiter–The Giant World . . . . .
 . .a.Amz Sep 42 220
 Neptune–World of Ice. .a . . . . .
 . . . . Amz Oct 42 202
Magic Bullet, The. .a . . . .
 . . . . ASF Apr 40 85
Matter of Taste, A. .a . . . .
 . . . . .ASF Jan 44 86
Moon Mysteries. .a. . . . .
 . . . . ASF Dec 44 104
Old Ones, The. .a. . . . .
 . . . . ASF May 43 88
Orbits, Take-Offs and
 Landings. .a . . . . ASF Aug 38 125
Other End of the Trajectory,
 The. .a. . . . . ASF Jul 48 63
Our Turbulent Atmosphere . . . . .
 . .a 2 pt . . . . ASF Mar 50 124
Paris Gun, The. .a . . ASF Oct 42 50
Plurality of Worlds, The. .a . . . . .
 . . . . ASF Feb 44 112
POWER PLANTS OF
  TOMORROW
 Harnessing the Sun's Rays. . . . .
 . .a . . . . .ASF Jan 38 63
 Harnessing the Earth's Heat. . . .
 . .a . . . . ASF Feb 38 123
 Putting the Moon on the
  Job. .a. . . . . . ASF Mar 38 108
 Prelude to Engineering. .a . . . . . .
 . . . . ASF Aug 41 110
 Pseudoscience in Naziland. . . . . .
 . .a . . . . ASF May 47 90
 Push for Pushbutton Warfare . . . .
 . .a . . . . ASF Sep 47 87
ROAD TO SPACE TRAVEL, THE
 The Last Twelve Years. .a . . . . .
 . . . . .SS Mar 49 68
 The Next Twelve Years. .a. . . . .
 . . . . SS May 49 116
 Station in Space. .a . . . .
 . . . . SS Jul 49 73
 Medicine and Space Travel . . . .
 . .a . . . . .SS Sep 49 137

Rocket Artillery. .a . . . .
 . . . . ASF Apr 44 104
Round-the-World Bomber,
 The. .a. . . . . . . .TW Aug 50 99
Science and "Truth" (Pravda) . . .
 . .a . . . . ASF Dec 49 96
Sea of Mystery. .a . . . .
 . . . . ASF Jun 43 97
Search for Zero, The. .a 2 pt . . . .
 . . . . .ASF Oct 40 122
Secret Giant, The. .a . . . .
 . . . . ASF Jul 45 101
See Earth First. .guest ed . . . . . .
 . . . . SS Jul 39 13
Sergeant Terry Bull's Terrible
 Weapons. .a . . . . ASF Dec 41 76
Seven Follies of Science, The. . . .
 . .a . . . . .Amz Jan 43 228
Space War. .a . . . . . ASF Aug 39 72
Stations in Space. .a. . . . .
 . . . . Amz Feb 40 122
Stepping-Stone to the Stars . . . . .
 . .a . . . . SSS May 43 92
Terminal in Space. .a . . . .
 . . . . Fant #2 39 53
"They Were Dead–". .a . . . .
 . . . . .ASF Jun 44 103
"They Were Dead–" (Addenda to
 previous article). .a . . . .
 . . . . .ASF Jan 45 146
"Torpedo!". .a . . . .
 . . . . ASF Jul 44 113
Twenty-Foot Miss. .a . . . .
 . . . . GSF Dec 50 86
Tyranosaurus Was No Killer. . . . .
 . .a . . . . ASF Apr 43 81
V–2–Rocket Cargo Ship. .a . . . . .
 . . . . ASF May 45 100
Vanishing Meteorites, The. .a . . . .
 . .a . . . . .SSS Nov 42 119
Visitors from the Void . . . .
 . .a . . . . ASF May 37 91
War Rockets. .a. . . . .
 . . . . Amz May 40 126
What's Wrong With Rockets? . . . .
 . .a . . . . Amz Mar 40 39
Witnesses of the Past. .a . . . .
 . . . . .ASF Jun 38 136
Wooden Ships of the Air. .a . . . . .
 . . . . .ASF Oct 44 104
LEYDENFROST artist
Covers for PLANET STORIES
 Spr, Fal 1942
LICHTENSTEIN, WILLIAM
Moon Doom, The (Part 2). .n. . . .
 . . . . WS Apr 33 880

AUTHOR
Title. .Length . . . . Magazine, Date, Page

LIDDELL, C. H. *pseud of HENRY
   KUTTNER & C. L. MOORE*
Biog sketch . . . . . . .PS Nov 50 106
Carry Me Home. .nt . . . .
. . . . PS Nov 50 4
Sky Is Falling, The. .s . . . .
. . . . .PS Fal 50 42
LIN, LESLIE C. B. *See pseud
   LESLIE CHARTERIS (1)*
LINN, RALPH
Element 87. .s. . . . Amz Jun 30 222
LISTON, B. E.
Grave for Gullible, A. .s . . . .
. . . . .FA Jul 45 56
LISTON, E. J.
Castle of Terror. .s . . . .
. . . . Amz Nov 48 36
LIVINGSTON, BERKELEY *See also
   pseuds ALEXANDER BLADE (h)
   (?), MORRIS J. STEELE (h) (1?)*
Biog sketch . . . . . . FA Jun 43 196
Biog sketch, photo. . . . .
. . . . Amz Mar 44 184
Bat Out of Hell. .s . . . .
. . . . FA Oct 44 102
City of Sand. .n . . . . FA Mar 49 52
Cokie Goes Treasure Hunting. . . .
. .s . . . . Amz Mar 44 172
Command Performance. .s. . . . . .
. . . . Amz Nov 46 142
Constant Drip, The. .s . . . .
. . . . Amz May 44 174
Crumbling World, The. .s . . . . . .
. . . . .FA Jan 50 138
Cult of the Eagle. .nt . . . .
. . . . .FA Jul 46 146
Death of a B.E.M. .s . . . .
. . . . Amz Oct 48 18
Dimensions Unlimited. .n . . . . . .
. . . . .FA Nov 48 8
Drink Like a Fish. .s . . . .
. . . . Amz Apr 48 62
Everything But the Sink . . . .
. .s . . . . Amz Mar 48 132
Gehenna, Incorporated. .s . . . . . .
. . . . .Amz Jan 50 130
Gift, The. .nt . . . . Amz Aug 46 82
Gift, The. .s . .*(Not the same story
   as the other of the same
   title)* . . . . FA Dec 47 106
Gimme Finds the Gimmick . . . . .
. .s . . . . FA Dec 48 132
Homer and the Herring. .s . . . . .
. . . . FA Apr 44 66
I'll Be Fleeced. .s . . . .
. . . . Amz Jun 45 164

AUTHOR
Title. .Length . . . . Magazine, Date, Page

I'll Be There With Music. .s . . . . .
. . . . FA Jun 43 38
I'll Take the Subway. .nt . . . . . .
. . . . FA Sep 46 98
Invasion of the Plant Men . . . . . .
. .nt . . . . FA Sep 49 8
Island of Eternal Storm. .nt . . . .
. . . . .Amz Jan 44 150
It's Raining Dimes. .s . . . .
. . . . FA Jul 45 124
Key, The. .s . . . . . FA Sep 48 102
Knotted String, A. .nt . . . .
. . . . FA Oct 47 50
Lamp of Vengeance, The. .n . . . .
. . . . .FA Nov 47 8
Land of the Damned. .n . . . .
. . . . Amz Feb 47 86
Life Symbol, The. .nt . . . .
. . . . FA Feb 46 48
Lotus Temple, The. .s . . . .
. . . . .FA Jul 45 178
Me and My Shadow. .s . . . .
. . . . Amz Dec 45 106
Mr. Jones' Eternal Camera. . . . . .
. .s . . . . Amz Nov 49 100
Moving Finger, The. .s . . . .
. . . . FA Nov 46 92
Oogie Finds Love. .s . . . .
. . . . Amz Nov 48 114
Phantom Hands, The. .s . . . .
. . . . Amz Feb 48 98
Queen of the Panther World . . . .
. .n . . . . .FA Jul 48 8
Shackled Statue, The. .s . . . .
. . . . FA Jan 45 52
Shroud-Sewers, The. .s . . . .
. . . . FA Sep 47 160
Sword and the Pool, The. . . . . . .
. .n . . . . FA May 46 120
Tiger Woman of Shadow
   Valley. .s . . . . Amz Oct 49 8
Triumph of the Pig, The. .s . . . . .
. . . . Amz Jul 48 112
Truk Island. .n . . . .
. . . . Amz Dec 44 144
Truthful Pencil, The. .s . . . .
. . . . FA Jun 44 106
What's In a Name. .s . . . .
. . . . FA Feb 44 36
LIVINGSTON, HERB *See pseud
   H. B. HICKEY (22)*
LOCARD, EDMOND
Hunting Vipers. .s . . . .
. . . . SD May 30 440
Most Dangerous Forgeries,
   The. .s . . . . AD Oct 30 898

AUTHOR
Title. .Length . . . . Magazine, Date, Page

LOCKE, A. T.
Machine That Knew Too Much,
   The. .s . . . . ASF Dec 33 29
Vandals of the Stars. .s . . . .
. . . . ASF Mar 30 390
LOCKE, E. L.
Cybernetics. .a . . . .
. . . . ASF Sep 49 78
Electrical Robot Brain, The . . . . .
. .a 2 pt . . . . ASF May 48 79
Electronics—New Style. .a . . . . .
. . . . ASF Dec 48 91
Finan-Seer, The. .s . . . .
. . . . .ASF Oct 49 132
Modern Calculators. .a . . . .
. . . . .ASF Jan 49 87
New Dielectrics. .a . . . .
. . . . ASF Aug 48 72
New Natural Law, A. .a . . . . . .
. . . . ASF Nov 48 100
Piezoelectricity. .a . . . .
. . . . ASF Apr 50 146
LOCKE, RICHARD ADAMS
Moon Hoax, The. .a . . . .
. . . . Amz Sep 26 556
LOCKE, WILLIAM P.
Moon Beasts, The. .s . . . .
. . . . SW Aug 29 198
LOEHE, RICHARD *artist*
Cover for AMAZING STORIES
Sep 1949
LOHRMAN, PAUL *house pseud
by RICHARD S. SHAVER*
World of the Lost, The. .n . . . . . .
. . . . FA Mar 50 78
Authors' real names unknown
Let the Gods Decide. .s . . . .
. . . . Amz Apr 50 46
Man Who Would Not Burn,
   The. .s . . . . FA Jun 50 134
They're Alive On Mars. .s . . . . .
. . . . .Amz Jul 50 56
Unremembered, The. .s . . . . . .
. . . . Amz May 50 170
LONDON, JACK
Scarlet Plague, The. .nt . . . .
. . . . FFM Feb 49 92
Shadow and the Flash, The . . . . .
. .s . . . . FFM Jun 48 102
Star Rover, The. .n . . . .
. . . . .FFM Feb 47 8
LONG, A.(MELIA) R.(EYNOLDS)
Castaways in Space. .s . . . .
. . . . .SF Jun 40 57
Cosmic Fever. .s . . . .
. . . . ASF Feb 37 138

AUTHOR
Title. .Length . . . . Magazine, Date, Page

Death by Fire. .s . . . . SF Mar 39 106
Leak in the Fountain of Youth,
A. .s . . . . ASF Aug 36 48
Mind Master, The. .s . . . .
. . . . ASF Dec 37 41
Mystery of the Phantom Shot,
The. .s . . . . .AD Jul 30 600
Omega. .s . . . . Amz Jul 32 370
                        AFR #10 116
Reverse Philogeny. .s . . . .
. . . . ASF Jun 37 72
Scandal in the Fourth
Dimension. .s . . . . ASF Feb 34 94
When the Half Gods Go. .s . . . .
. . . . ASF Jul 39 111
LONG, FRANK BELKNAP, (JR.)
See also pseud LESLIE
NORTHERN (h) (2)
Biog sketch, photo. . . . .
. . . . TW Jun 39 86
Biog sketch, photo. . . . .
. . . . SS Sum 45 95
Alias the Living. .s . . . .
. . . . .ASF Jan 44 115
And We Sailed the Mighty Dark . .
. .s . . . . .SS Mar 48 76
Atomic Station. .s . . . .
. . . . TW Win 46 83
Beyond the Vortex. .s . . . .
.TW Fal 44 55
Black Vortex, The. .nt . . . .
. . . . TW Jun 37 104
Blue Earthman, The. .s . . . .
. . . . ASF Apr 35 32
Bridgehead. .nt . . . .
. . . . ASF Aug 44 120
Brown. .s . . . . ASF Jul 41 144
Castaways in Two
Dimensions. .s . . . . TW Win 45 37
Census Taker. .s . . . UK Apr 42 100
Circle of Youth. .s . . . .
. . . . .SSS Feb 43 72
Collector's Item. .s . . . .
. . . . ASF Oct 47 68
Cones. .nt . . . . . . ASF Feb 36 122
Critters, The. .s . . . ASF Nov 45 127
Dark Command. .s . . . .
. . . . .SS Win 45 66
Dark Vision. .s . . . . UK Mar 39 107
Destination Unknown. .s. . . . . . .
. . . . .Ash Dec 42 48
Dweller in Outer Darkness, The . .
. .s . . . . TW Aug 39 60
Elemental, The. .s . . . .UK Jul 39 79
Ether Robots, The. .nt . . . .
. . . . TW Dec 42 15

Exiles of the Stratosphere. .s . . . .
. . . . .ASF Jul 35 35
Filch. .s . . . . ASF Mar 45 56
Fisherman's Luck. .s . . . .
. . . . .UK Jul 40 102
Flame Midget, The. .s . . . .
. . . . ASF Dec 36 28
Flame of Life. .s . . . .
. . . . .SF Oct 39 92
Fuzzy Head. .s . . . . TW Dec 48 144
Galactic Heritage. .s . . . .
. . . . TW Oct 48 43
Glory Flight, The. .s . . . .
. . . . .SS Mar 43 82
Grab Bags Are Dangerous . . . . .
. .s . . . . UK Jun 42 66
Great Cold, The. .s. . . . .
. . . . ASF Feb 35 39
Green Glory. .s . . . .ASF Jan 35 43
Guest in the House. .s. . . . .
. . . . ASF Mar 46 67
Heavy Man, The. .s . . . .
. . . . TW Apr 43 94
Hollow World, The. .n . . . .
. . . . SS Sum 45 11
Horizontals, The. .s . . . .
. . . . .SSS Nov 40 48
House of Rising Winds, The. . . . .
. .s . . . . SS May 48 70
Humpty Dumpty Had a Great
Fall. .s . . . . SS Nov 48 74
If You Don't Watch Out—. .s . . . .
. . . . TW Dec 50 107
Invaders from the Outer Suns . . .
. .nt . . . . TW Feb 37 66
Invasion. .s . . . . SS Jul 50 133
It Will Come to You. .s. . . . . . .
. . . . UK Dec 42 106
It's a Tough Life. .a . . . .
. . . . ASF Nov 42 101
"JOHN CARSTAIRS, botanical
DETECTIVE" series includes:
PLANTS MUST GROW
SNAP DRAGON
PLANTS MUST SLAY
SATELLITE OF PERIL
THE ETHER ROBOTS
THE HEAVY MAN
WOBBLIES IN THE MOON
THE HOLLOW WORLD
Johnny on the Spot. .ss . . . .
. . . . UK Dec 39 123
Last Men, The. .s . . . ASF Aug 34 55
Lichen from Eros, The. .s . . . . . .
. . . . ASF Nov 35 97
Long, Long Ago. .s . . . .
. . . . .CF Fal 41 97

Lost Planet. .s . . . . . ASF Nov 34 65
Love Slave and the Scientists,
The. .s. . . . . .AFR #13 3
Man from Nowhere, The. .s . . . .
. . . . UK Jun 40 112
Man With a Thousand Legs,
The. .nt . . . . .AFR #8 45
Mercurian, The. .s . . . PS Win 41 69
Mind Out of Time. .s . . . .
. . . . TW Oct 38 89
Miniature Menace, The. .s . . . . . .
. . . . Fut May–Jun 50 50
Plague from Tomorrow, The . . . .
. .s . . . . .Ash Sep 41 75
Plants Must Grow. .s . . . .
. . . . TW Oct 41 64
Plants Must Slay. .s . . . .
. . . . TW Apr 42 55
Prison Bright, Prison Deep. . . . . .
. .s . . . . ASF Aug 50 108
Prisoners in Flatland. .s. . . . .
. . . . .SS Sep 41 89
Red Moon. .s . . . . . . TW Jun 40 56
Red Storm on Jupiter. .s. . . . . . .
. . . . ASF May 36 32
Refugees, The. .s . . . . UK Feb 42 92
Roaring Blot, The. .nt . . . .
. . . . ASF Mar 36 12
Satellite of Peril. .s . . . .
. . . . .TW Aug 42 88
Shadow Dwellers, The . . . .
. .s . . . . .TW Sum 45 52
Shadow Over Venus. .s . . . .
. . . . .SS Mar 46 73
Sky Rock. .s . . . . . ASF Sep 35 59
Sky Trap, The. .s. . . . .
. . . . .Com Jul 41 46
Snapdragon. .s . . . . . TW Dec 41 93
Son of His Father. .s . . . .
. . . . .SS Jun 43 76
Spawn of the Further Dark . . . . .
. .s . . . . SS Spr 44 100
Spawn of the Red Giants. .nt. . . .
. . . . ASF May 37 110
Star Comrades. .s . . . .
. . . . SF Apr 43 95
Stellar Vampires. .s . . . .
. . . . SF Jul 45 79
Step Into My Garden. .s . . . .
. . . . UK Aug 42 98
Stitch in Time, A. .s . . . .
. . . . .SSS Mar 40 108
Temporary Warp. .s . . . .
. . . . ASF Aug 37 37
Thought Materializer, The. . . . . .
. .s . . . . WQ Spr 30 414

AUTHOR
Title. .Length . . . . Magazine, Date, Page

Time Trap. .s . . . . . .PS Win 48 109
Timeless Man, The. .s . . . .
. . . . .SSS Nov 49 40
To Follow Knowledge. .s . . . . .
. . . . ASF Dec 42 86
Trap, The. .s . . . . . ASF May 45 36
Two Against Neptune. .s. . . . . .
. . . . TW Jun 41 74
Vapor Death, The. .s . . . .
. . . . ASF Oct 34 39
Vibration Wasps, The. .s . . . .
. . . . Com Jan 41 82
We, the Invisible. .s . . . .
. . . . .TW Feb 38 98
Were-Snake, The. .s . . . .
. . . . .AFR #7 99
White Barrier. .nt. . . . .
. . . . TW Apr 39 88
Willie. .s. . . . . . . .ASF Oct 43 118
Wobblies in the Moon. .s. . . . . .
. . . . TW Jun 43 44
Woman Out of Time. .s. . . . . . .
. . . . .Ash Aug 40 62
World of Wulkins, The. .s . . . . . .
. . . . TW Apr 48 102
LONG, JULIUS
He Walked by Day. .s. . . . .
. . . . AFR #13 63
LONG, WESLEY pseud of GEORGE
O. SMITH
Circle of Confusion. .nt . . . .
. . . . ASF Mar 44 45
Climate—Incorporated. .s . . . . . .
. . . . .TW Aug 48 78
Fixer, The. .nt . . . . ASF May 45 68
Latent Image. .nt. . . . .
. . . . .ASF May 44 7
Nomad. .n 3 pt . . . . . ASF Dec 44 7
One of Three. .n . . . . .SS Mar 48 13
Redevelopment. .nt . . . .
. . . . ASF Nov 44 136
LOOMIS, BATTEL
Talking Hill, A. .a . . . .
. . . . ASF Apr 37 108
Invasion Squad. .s . . . .
. . . . WB Dec 50 100
LOOMIS, NOEL (Miller) See also
pseud BENJ. MILLER (4)
Biog sketch, photo. . . . .
. . . . SS Jul 42 8
Biog sketch, photo. . . . .
. . . . .SS Win 45 112
City of Glass. .n . . . .
. . . . SS Jul 42 12
Electron Eat Electron. .s. . . . . . .
. . . . .PS Spr 46 70

Iron Men. .n . . . . . . .SS Win 45 11
Long Dawn, The. .s . . . .
. . . . .SSS Jan 50 98
Mr. Zytztz Goes to Mars. .nt . . . .
. . . . .TW Aug 48 9
Parking Unlimited. .s . . . .
. . . . Fut May–Jun 50 70
Rocket Pants. .s . . . TW Spr 46 64
Schizophrenic. .s . . . . TW Dec 48 58
Softie. .s . . . . TW Oct 48 133
Turnover Time. .s . . . .
. . . . .SS Mar 49 129
Ultimate Planet, The. .nt. . . . . .
. . . . TW Apr 49 13
Zero. .s . . . . .TW Sum 46 84
LORRAINE, ALDEN pseud of
FORREST J. ACKERMAN
Micro Man, The. .ss . . . .
. . . . .NW #2 46 52
LORRAINE, LILITH
Conductor of SONGS OF THE
SPACEWAYS, poetry dept of
FANTASY BOOK from #3
Celestial Visitor, The. .s . . . .
. . . . WS Mar 35 1190
Into the 28th Century. .s . . . . . .
. . . . WQ Win 30 250
Isle of Madness, The. .s. . . . .
. . . . WS Nov 35 652
Jovian Jest, The. .s. . . . .
. . . . ASF May 30 228
Titan's Goblet. .p . . . .
. . . . .SSS Sep 50 39
LOUIS, RICHARD
Lie, The. .ss . . . . . . UK Oct 42 97
LOVECRAFT, H.(oward)
P.(hillips)
MASTERS OF FANTASY
biog . . . . FFM Aug 47 113
At the Mountains of Madness. . . .
. .n 3 pt . . . . ASF Feb 36 8
Beyond the Wall of Sleep . . . . . .
. .s . . . . .AFR #6 21
Colour Out of Space, The . . . . . .
. .s . . . . Amz Sep 27 556
FFM Oct 41 98
Outsider, The. .s . . . .
. . . . FFM Jun 50 114
Shadow Out of Time, The. . . . . .
. .n . . . . .ASF Jun 36 110
Silver Key, The. .s . . . .
. . . . AFR #3 44
Statement of Randolph Carter,
The. .s. . . . . AFR #10 53
Temple, The. .s . . . .
. . . . .AFR #8 89

LOVERING, PAUL H.
Inevitable Conflict, The . . . .
. .n 2 pt . . . . . . Amz Dec 31 776
When the Earth Grew Cold . . . . .
. .nt . . . . .AQ Fal 29 556
LOW, PROFESSOR A. M.
Life on Mars. .a. . . . .
. . . . ToW Aut 39 67
LOWER, H.(AROLD) A.
Hunting Big Game. .a . . . .
. . . . .ASF Oct 39 123
Raiders from Space. .ss . . . .
. . . . SW Mar 30 896
Telescopes vs. Cameras. .a . . . . . .
. . . . .ASF Jan 39 96
LOWNDES, ROBERT W. See also
pseuds ARTHUR COOKE (1),
S. D. GOTTESMAN (2), CAROL
GREY (1), MALLORY KENT (3),
PAUL DENNIS LAVOND (4),
JOHN MacDOUGAL (1),
WILFRED OWEN MORLEY (10),
RICHARD MORRISON (1),
LAWRENCE WOODS (2)
Editor of FUTURE FICTION
Apr 41 thru Feb 43 issues
Editor of SCIENCE FICTION
Apr 43 and Jul 43 issues
Editor of FUTURE COMBINED
WITH SCIENCE FICTION
May–Jun 50 –––
Editor of SCIENCE FICTION
QUARTERLY
Spr 41 –––
Abyss, The. .s . . . . .Sti Feb 41 118
Green Cloud Came, A. .ss . . . . . .
. . . . Com Jan 41 97
Grey One, The. .s . . . .Sti Jun 41 83
Martians Are Coming, The. . . . . .
. .s . . . . Cos Mar 41 36
Other, The. .ss . . . . . Sti Apr 41 92
Outpost at Altark, The . . . .
. .ss . . . . .SSS Nov 40 112
with JOHN B. MICHEL
Inheritors, The. .s . . . .
. . . . Fut Oct 42 54
AFR #11 90
LUDWIG, EDWARD W.
Inheritance. .s . . . . .Im Oct 50 150
LUDWIG, KATHLEEN
Dr. Immortelle. .s . . . .
. . . . .AQ Fal 30 560
LULL, ROBERT WILBUR
with LILLIAN M. AINSWORTH
Astral Gentleman, An. .s . . . .
. .FFM Jan 40 80

AUTHOR
   Title. .Length . . . . Magazine, Date, Page

LUROS, (MILTON) *artist*
   Covers for ASTONISHING STORIES
      Feb, Apr 1943
   Covers for FUTURE (SCIENCE)
      FICTION
      Feb 1943
      Nov 1950
   Covers for SCIENCE FICTION
      Apr, Jul 1943
   Covers for SCIENCE FICTION
      QUARTERLY
      Win 1942
      Spr 1943
LYNCH, ARTHUR H.
   Editor AMAZING STORIES
      May 29 *thru* Oct 29 *issues*
   Editor AMAZING STORIES
      QUARTERLY
      Sum 29 *issue only*
LYNCH, BOHUN
   Menace from the Moon. .s. . . . . .
      . . . . Fant Aug 47 66
LYON, LYMAN R. *pseud of L.*
   SPRAGUE DE CAMP
   Employment. .s. . . . ASF May 39 79
LYONS, MARCUS *pseud of JAMES*
   BLISH

M

MacARTHUR, BURKE *pseud of*
   ARTHUR J. BURKS
MacBETH, CLAYTON JAMES
   PROBABILITY ZERO
   Universal Solvent. .ss . . . .
      . . . . .ASF Sep 43 104
McCANN, ARTHUR *pseud of JOHN*
   W. CAMPBELL, JR.
   Atomic Ringmaster. .a . . . .
      . . . . ASF Mar 40 112
   Cosmic Ray Shields. .a . . . .
      . . . . ASF Nov 37 113
   Dead—and Embalmed. .a. . . . . . .
      . . . . .ASF Jan 41 160
   Giant Stars. .a. . . . ASF Jul 38 113
   Gypped! . .a. . . . . ASF Feb 41 116
   Hot Filament. .a . . . .
      . . . . ASF May 50 156
   Ignition Point. .a. . . . .
      . . . . ASF Apr 38 149
   Isotope 235. .a . . . . ASF Aug 39 70
   Master Chemist. .a. . . . .
      . . . . ASF Dec 43 101

AUTHOR
   Title. .Length . . . . Magazine, Date, Page

   Shhhhh———Don't Mention It! . .
      . .a . . . . ASF Aug 40 104
   Stored Power. .a . . . .
      . . . . ASF Dec 38 151
   Stress Fluid. .a . . . . ASF Jun 37 45
   Tough Guy. .a. . . . ASF Feb 40 101
McCARTHY, DAVID
   Undesirable Alien. .s . . . .
      . . . . .ASF Jan 50 24
McCAULEY, H.(AROLD) W. *artist*
   Biog sketch, photo. . . . .
      . . . . FA Oct 42 225
   Covers for AMAZING STORIES
      Nov 1939
      Mar 1940
      May, Aug 1942
      May, Jul 1943
      Aug 1946
      Jan 1947
      Dec 1948
      May, Oct 1949
   Covers for FANTASTIC
      ADVENTURES
      Sep 1939
      Jan, Aug 1940
      Jan, Jun, Oct 1941
      Jan, Sep, Nov, Dec 1942
      May, Jun 1943
      May 1946
      Jul 1947
      Aug 1950
   Cover for IMAGINATION
      Dec 1950
   Future Rocket Train . . . .
      . .bacover. . . . . .Amz Jan 39
   Future Sky Fighter . . . .
      . .bacover. . . . . Amz Apr 39
   This Amazing Universe . . . .
      . .bacover. . . . . Amz Jun 38
   Undersea Salvager . . . .
      . .bacover. . . . . Amz Mar 39
   with ROBERT FUQUA
   Cover for FANTASTIC
      ADVENTURES
      Feb 1942
   with J. ALLEN ST. JOHN
   Cover for FANTASTIC
      ADVENTURES
      Jul 1941
McCLARY, THOMAS CALVERT
   See also pseud CALVIN PEREGOY
   Case of Jack Freysling, The. . . . .
      . .s . . . . .ASF Oct 44 121
   Food for the First Planet. .a . . . .
      . . . . ASF Aug 38 40

AUTHOR
   Title. .Length . . . . Magazine, Date, Page

   New Frontiers. .a. . . . .
      . . . . ASF Feb 37 89
   Parole. .s . . . . UK Jun 39 115
   Rebirth. .n 2 pt. . . . .
      . . . . ASF Feb 34 10
   Super Fast Eyes. .a . . . .
      . . . . .ASF Sep 37 122
   Three Thousand Years . . . .
      . .n 3 pt. . . . . ASF Apr 38 6
   Tommyknocker, The. .n 2 pt. . . . .
      . . . . UK Oct 40 129
McCLINTIC, WINONA
   In the Days of Our Fathers . . . . .
      . .s . . . . .F&SF Fal 49 123
MACCLURE, VICTOR
   Ark of the Covenant. .n 4 pt . . . .
      . . . . AW Jul 29 6
McCLUSKY, THORP
   Biog sketch . . . . . Amz Aug 38 145
   Biog sketch . . . . . Amz Nov 38 142
   Crawling Terror, The. .s . . . .
      . . . . .AFR #6 3
   Kidnappers of Space. .s. . . . . . .
      . . . . Amz Aug 38 110
   Little Planet. .s . . . . . .SF Oct 39 83
   Monstrosity of Evolution . . . . . .
      . .nt . . . . Amz Nov 38 38
McCOMAS, J. FRANCIS *See also*
   pseud WEBB MARLOWE (2)
   Co-Editor of MAGAZINE OF
      FANTASY (AND SCIENCE
      FICTION)
   From Fal 49 *issue (all issues)*
McCORMACK, FORD
   Skin Deep. .s . . . . . .ASF Jul 50 78
McCORMAC, JOHN
   Enchanted Week End, The . . . . .
      . .nt . . . . UK Oct 39 115
                              UK 48 6
McCOWN, WILLIAM
   Death in Time. .s . . . .
      . . . . Amz May 43 212
MacCREIGH, JAMES *pseud of*
   FREDERIK POHL
   Conspiracy on Callisto. .s . . . . .
      . . . . .PS Win 43 38
   Darkside Destiny. .s. . . . .
      . . . . .SSS Apr 49 75
   Daughters of Eternity. .s. . . . . .
      . . . . .Ash Mar 42 66
   Donovan Had a Dream. .nt . . . . .
      . . . . TW Oct 47 11
   Doublecross. .s . . . . .PS Win 44 112
   Dweller in the Ice, The. . . . .
      . .s . . . . .SSS Jan 41 63

AUTHOR
Title. .Length . . . . Magazine, Date, Page

Earth, Farewell! . .s . . . .
. . . . .Ash Feb 43 30
Hitch in Time, A. .s . . . .
. . . . TW Jun 47 61
It's a Young World. .nt . . . .
. . . . .Ash Apr 41 84
King's Eye, The. .s . . . .
. . . . .Ash Feb 41 63
Let the Ants Try. .s . . . .
. . . . .PS Win 49 63
Wings of the Lightning Land . . . .
. .nt . . . . .Ash Nov 41 11
with ISAAC ASIMOV
Little Man on the Subway,
The. .s . . . . FB #6 4
McCUNE, CARLOS
Biog sketch, photo. . . . .
. . . . FA Jul 43 200
Caverns of Time. .n . . . .
. . . . FA Jul 43 108
McDERMOTT, DENNIS *pseud used*
by WALTER L. DENNIS, PAUL
McDERMOTT & P. SCHUYLER
MILLER
by WALTER L. DENNIS & PAUL
McDERMOTT
with P. SCHUYLER MILLER
Duel on the Asteroid, The. . . . . .
. .s . . . . .WS Jan 32 950
by P. SCHUYLER MILLER
Red Spot of Jupiter, The. .s. . . . .
. . . . .WS Jul 31 214
McDERMOTT, PAUL *See pseud*
DENNIS McDERMOTT (1)
MacDONALD, ANSON *pseud of*
ROBERT A. HEINLEIN
Beyond This Horizon—. . . . .
. .n 2 pt . . . . ASF Apr 42 9
By His Bootstraps. .nt . . . .
. . . . ASF Oct 41 9
Goldfish Bowl. .nt . . . .
. . . . ASF Mar 42 77
Sixth Column. .n 3 pt . . . .
. . . . ASF Jan 41 9
Solution Unsatisfactory. .nt . . . . .
. . . . ASF May 41 56
Waldo. .n . . . . ASF Aug 42 9
"—We Also Walk Dogs". .s . . . . . .
. . . . ASF Jul 41 126
MacDONALD, JOHN D. *See also*
pseuds JOHN WADE FARRELL
(3), PETER REED (4)
Amphiskios. .s . . . .
. . . . .TW Aug 49 70
Appointment for Tomorrow . . . .
. .s . . . . .SSS Nov 49 82

AUTHOR
Title. .Length . . . . Magazine, Date, Page

Big Contest, The. .s . . . .
. . . . WB Dec 50 41
By the Stars Forgot. .s . . . .
. . . . SSS May 50 36
Child Is Crying, A. .s . . . .
. . . . TW Dec 48 131
Condition of Beauty, A. .s. . . . .
. . . . .SS Sep 49 79
Cosmetics. .s. . . . . ASF Feb 48 68
Dance of a New World. .s . . . . . .
. . . . .ASF Sep 48 133
Death Quotient. .nt . . . .
. . . . .SSS Apr 49 8
Final Mission. .s . . . . PS Nov 50 57
First One, The. .ss . . . .
. . . . SS Jan 50 139
Flaw. .s . . . . .SS Jan 49 83
Half-Past Eternity. .nt . . . .
. . . . SSS Jul 50 12
Hunted, The. .s . . . . SSS Jul 49 52
Immortality. .ss. . . . SS May 49 113
Journey for Seven. .nt . . . .
. . . . TW Apr 50 48
Like a Keepsake. .s . . . .
. . . . TW Jun 49 95
Mechanical Answer, The . . . .
. .s . . . . ASF May 48 64
Minion of Chaos. .nt . . . .
. . . . .SSS Sep 49 8
Ring Around the Redhead. . . . . .
. .s . . . . SS Nov 48 98
School for the Stars. .s . . . .
. . . . .ASF Oct 48 100
Shadow on the Sand. .n . . . .
. TW Oct 50 11
Shenadun. .s. . . . . . .SS Sep 48 102
Spectator Sport. .ss . . . .
. . . . TW Feb 50 81
That Mess Last Year. .s. . . . .
. . . . TW Oct 48 38
Trojan Horse Laugh. .nt . . . .
. . . . ASF Aug 49 73
Ultimate One, The. .ss . . . .
. . . . .SSS Mar 50 72
Vanguard of the Lost. .s . . . .
. . . . FA May 50 60
Wine of the Dreamers. .n. . . . . . .
. . . . SS May 50 11
MacDONALD, PHILIP
Private———Keep Out! . .s . . . . . .
. . . . .F&SF Fal 49 32
MacDOUGAL, JOHN *pseud of JAMES*
BLISH & ROBERT W. LOWNDES
in collaboration
Chaos, Co-ordinated. .nt . . . . . .
. . . . ASF Oct 46 36

AUTHOR
Title. .Length . . . . Magazine, Date, Page

McDOWD, KENNIE
Marble Virgin, The. .s . . . .
. . . . SW Jun 29 53
. . . . SS Jul 42 86
McDOWELL, EMMETT
Biog sketch . . . . . . .PS Spr 48 126
Beyond the Yellow Fog. .nt. . . . .
.PS Jan 47 2
Black Silence. .nt. . . . .
. . . . .PS Spr 46 88
Blue Venus, The. .nt . . . .
.PS Spr 46 88
Citadel of the Green Death . . . . .
. .nt . . . . .PS Fal 48 4
Great Green Blight, The. .nt . . . .
. . . . PS Win 45 2
Hereafter. .nt . . . . . Amz Apr 50 62
Love Among the Robots. .s . . . . .
. . . . .PS Win 46 29
Moon of Treason. .s . . . .
. . . . PS Sum 50 72
Outcasts of Solar III. .nt . . . .
. . . . .PS Spr 48 6
Realities Unlimited. .s . . . .
. . . . SS Jul 48 70
Red Witch of Mercury. .nt. . . . . .
. . . . .PS Sum 45 2
Sword of Fire. .nt . . . .
. . . . .PS Win 49 70
Veiled Island. .nt. . . .ASF Jan 46 63
Wandering Egos, The. .n . . . .
. . . . Amz Apr 48 104
McDOWELL, ROBERT E.
Happy Castaway, The. .s. . . . . . .
. . . . .PS Spr 45 41
MacDUFF, ANDREW *pseud of*
HORACE B. FYFE
MACFADYEN, A. (B. L.), JR.
Closed Doors. .s . . . UK Mar 39 137
Endless Chain, The. .nt . . . .
. . . . ASF Apr 37 56
Jason Comes Home. .s . . . .
. . . . ASF Aug 38 28
Last Selenite, The. .s . . . .
. . . . ASF Nov 36 48
Space Signals. .s . . . ASF Dec 37 82
Time Decelerator, The. .s . . . . . .
. . . . .ASF Jul 36 28
MACFADYEN, BURT
Helping Hand, The. .s . . . .
. . . . .ASF Jan 48 62
MACFARLANE, W.
How Can You Lose? . .s . . . .
. . . . .ASF Jan 49 51
To Watch the Watchers. .s . . . . .
. . . . ASF Jun 49 28

AUTHOR
Title. .Length . . . . Magazine, Date, Page

McGIVERN, WILLIAM P. *See also*
pseuds ALEXANDER BLADE
(h) (?)
Biog sketch, photo. . . . .
. . . . FA Mar 41 136
Adopted Son of the Stars. .s . . . .
. . . . FA Mar 41 98
Al Addin and the Infra-Red
Lamp. .nt. . . . . . . FA Nov 41 74
Avengers, The. .n. . . . Amz Jun 42 8
Battle of Manetong, The. .s . . . . .
. . . . FA Jun 42 86
Bertie and the Black Arts. .s . . . .
. . . . FA Apr 42 206
Chameleon Man, The. .s . . . .
. . . . .Amz Jan 43 210
Contract of Carson Carruthers,
The. . . . . FA Jan 42 90
Convoy in Space. .nt . . . .
. . . . Amz Sep 42 96
Convoy to Atlantis. .n . . . .
. . . . .Amz Nov 41 8
Dark Wish. .s . . . . . FA Sep 48 78
Death of Asteroid 13, The. . . . . .
. .s . . . . .Amz Jul 48 78
Doorway of Vanishing Men . . . . .
. .s . . . . .FA Jul 41 126
Double Cross in Double Time . . .
. .s . . . . FA Feb 48 120
Dynamouse, The. .s . . . .
. . . . FA Jan 41 46
Enchanted Bookshelf. .nt . . . . . .
. . . . FA Mar 43 112
Fate of the Asteroid, The . . . . . .
. .s . . . . Amz May 41 120
Galaxy Raiders, The. .nt . . . .
. . . . Amz Feb 50 8
Genie of Bagdad. .nt . . . .
. . . . FA Jun 43 108
Ghost That Haunted Hitler,
The. .nt . . . . .FA Dec 42 8
Goddess of the Fifth Plane . . . . .
. .nt . . . . FA Sep 42 8
Goddess of the Golden
Flame. .nt . . . . .FA Jul 47 8
Horse on Thorndyke, A. .nt. . . . .
. . . . FA Apr 44 126
Howie Lemp Meets an
Enchantress. .s . . . . FA Feb 42 52
Kidnapped Into the Future . . . . .
. .s . . . . Amz Feb 42 8
Killer's Turnabout. .ss . . . .
. . . . Amz Apr 41 120
Mad Robot, The. .nt . . . .
. . . . Amz Jan 44 10

Masterful Mind of Mortimer Meek,
The. .nt . . . . .FA May 41 60
Musketeers in Paris, The. .nt . . . .
. . . . FA Feb 44 92
Mystery on Base Ten. .s . . . .
. . . . .Amz Jan 42 218
Orders for Willy Weston. .s . . . . .
. . . . .FA Jan 48 120
Peter Fereny's Death Cell . . . . .
. .s . . . . FA Aug 41 124
Picture of Death, The. .s . . . .
FA Nov 42 146
Quandary of Quintus Quaggle,
The. .s . . . . Amz Jun 41 88
Rewbarb's Remarkable Radio . . .
. .s . . . . FA Dec 41 102
Ring of Faith, The. .s . . . .
. . . . FA Nov 48 122
Russian Ziegfeld. .a . . . .
. . . . Amz Aug 41 108
Safari to the Lost Ages. .nt . . . . .
. . . . FA Jul 42 118
Sidetrack in Time. .s . . . .
. . . . .Amz Jul 41 90
Sidney, the Screwloose
Robot. .s . . . . . . FA Jun 41 116
Survival. .s . . . . . . .FA Jul 50 102
Thinking Cap, The. .nt . . . .
. . . . Amz Sep 44 38
Thunder Over Washington. .s . . . .
. . . . FA Oct 41 48
Tink Fights the Gremlins . . . . . .
. .nt . . . . FA Oct 43 102
Tink Takes a Fling. .s . . . .
. . . . FA Jun 42 136
Tink Takes a Hand. .s . . . .
. . . . FA Oct 41 94
Tink Takes Command. .s. . . . . . .
. . . . FA Aug 42 48
Visible Invisible Man, The . . . . . .
. .nt . . . . . . Amz Dec 40 74
Voice, The. .s . . . .
. . . . Amz Oct 42 206
Voice from a Star. .s . . . .
. . . . Amz Oct 47 138
Wandering Swordsmen, The. . . . .
. .s . . . . FA Apr 48 148
Willful Puppets, The. .nt . . . .
. . . . FA Feb 43 170
World Beyond Belief. .nt. . . . . . .
. . . . FA Aug 43 40
with JOHN YORK CABOT pseud
(DAVID WRIGHT O'BRIEN)
Daughter of the Snake God . . . . .
. .nt . . . . .FA May 42 8

with DAVID WRIGHT O'BRIEN
John Brown's Body. .s . . . .
. . . . Amz May 40 112
Mr. Muddle Does as He Pleases. . .
. .nt . . . . Amz Aug 41 64
Victory from the Void. .nt . . . . .
. . . . Amz Mar 43 158
McGOWAN, DAVID C.
Decoy in Space. .s . . . .
. . . . .Amz Jul 49 48
McGREEVEY, JOHN
Brave Walk Alone, The. .s . . . . . .
. . . . .Im Dec 50 142
MacGREGOR, MARY *pseud of*
MALCOLM JAMESON
Transients Only. .s . . . .
. . . . UK Dec 42 71
MacHARG, WILLIAM B.
with EDWIN BALMER
Duel in the Dark, The. .s . . . .
. . . . AD Sep 30 790
Eleventh Hour, The. .s . . . .
. . . . Amz Feb 27 1042
SD May 30 428
Fast Watch, The. .s . . . .
. . . . .SD Jan 30 21
Hammering Man, The. .s . . . .
. . . . Amz Mar 27 1118
SD Apr 30 314
Man Higher Up, The. .s . . . .
. . . . Amz Dec 26 792
SD Feb 30 122
Man in the Room, The. .s . . . . . .
. . . . Amz Apr 27 43
SD Mar 30 224
Matter of Mind Reading, A . . . . .
. .s . . . . AD Jun 30 496
Private Bank Puzzle, The. .s . . . . .
. . . . .AD Jul 30 608
Vapors of Death. .s . . . .
. . . . AD Aug 30 712
MACHEN, ARTHUR
MASTERS OF FANTASY
biog . . . . .FFM Dec 48 12
Novel of the Black Seal, The . . . .
. .s . . . . FFM Jun 46 109
Novel of the White Powder,
The. .s . . . . FFM Sep 44 111
Strange Occurence in
Clerkenwell. .s . . . .
. . . . FFM Feb 50 108
M'INTOSH, J. T. *pseud of JAMES*
MacGREGOR
Curfew Tolls, The. .s . . . .
. . . . ASF Dec 50 42

AUTHOR
Title..Length . . . . Magazine, Date, Page

AUTHOR
Title..Length . . . . Magazine, Date, Page

AUTHOR
Title..Length . . . . Magazine, Date, Page

MacISAAC, FRED
Hothouse World, The. .n . . . . . .
. . . . FN Nov 50 12
McKAY, H.(ARNOLD B.)
Flannelcake's Invention. .s . . . . .
. . . . AW Dec 29 530
Flying Buzz-Saw, The. .s . . . . . .
. . . . AW Apr 30 898
McKAY, HERBERT C.
Radiation in Uniform. .a . . . . . .
. . . . ASF Apr 38 116
Rainbow Bridge, The. .a . . . . . .
. . . . ASF Feb 38 65
Spectral Adventures. .a . . . .
. . . . ASF Dec 37 46
McKENNA, BOB
with RICHARD S. SHAVER
Cult of the Witch Queen. .n . . . . .
. . . . .Amz Jul 46 8
Return of Sathanas, The. .n . . . . .
. . . . Amz Nov 46 8
McKENZIE, A. R.
Biog sketch, photo. . . . .
. . . . Amz May 42 267
Juggernaut Jones, Commando . . .
. .s . . . . .Amz Jul 43 112
Juggernaut Jones, Draftee. .s . . . .
. . . . Amz May 43 142
Juggernaut Jones, Expressman . . .
. .s . . . . Amz Nov 42 132
Juggernaut Jones, Pirate. .s . . . . .
. . . . Amz Nov 43 168
Juggernaut Jones, Salesman. . . . .
. .s . . . . Amz May 42 166
Juggernaut Jones, Trucker. . . . . .
. .s . . . . Amz Jun 42 128
Juggernaut Jones, Warrior. . . . . .
. .s . . . . Amz Apr 43 110
Luvium. .s . . . . . Amz Nov 31 706
Luvium, The Invincible City . . . .
. .nt . . . . Amz Sep 43 30
Luvium Under the Sand. .nt . . . .
. . . . Amz Jun 36 88
MACKINTOSH, CHARLES HENRY
Men on the Morning Star. .s . . . . .
. . . . SSS Sep 40 57
MacLAUGHLAN, LORNE
Electrical Mathematicians. .a . . . .
. . . . ASF May 49 93
Noise from Outside. .a . . . .
. . . . ASF Apr 47 44
Servomechanisms. .a . . . .
. . . . .ASF Jan 48 89
McLAUGHLIN, VERNARD
Hands, The. .s . . . . . Fut Feb 43 43
Silence, The. .s . . . . . .Sti Jun 41 94

MacLEAN, GORDON Listed as
author or co-author (with ROD
RUTH) or parts of the ROMANCE
OF THE ELEMENTS series, which
see.
MacLEAN, KATHERINE
And Be Merry. .s . . ASF Feb 50 107
Contagion. .nt . . . .GSF Oct 50 114
Defense Mechanism. .s . . . .
. . . . .ASF Oct 49 155
Incommunicado. .nt . . . .
. . . . ASF Jun 50 6
McLOCIARD, GEORGE
Monorail. .s . . . . . Amz Dec 28 832
Smoke Rings. .ss . . . .
. . . . Amz Feb 28 1103
Television Hill. .n 2 pt . . . .
. . . . Amz Feb 31 966
Terror of the Streets, The. .s . . . .
. . . . Amz Apr 29 18
McMORROW, WILL
Biog sketch . . . . FFM Dec 40 104
Sun Makers, The. .n . . . .
. . . . .FFM Dec 40 6
Venus or Earth? . .nt . . . .
. . . . FFM Apr 41 72
World of Indexed Numbers,
A. .nt . . . . .FFM May–Jun 40 87
MacNAMARA, PAUL
Last Man in New York, The. . . . .
. .s . . . . TW Fal 44 32
McNEIL, A. M.
Noise Killer, The. .s . . . .
. . . . Amz May 30 151
MACOM, ARTHUR
Andryne. .s . . . . . . SSS May 42 82
McRAE, D. B.
Gravitomobile, The. .s . . . .
. . . . .Amz Jul 27 347
McREADY, ROBERT S.
with DOW ELSTAR pseud (Raymond
Z. Gallun)
Stardust Gods. .nt . . . .
. . . . .ASF Oct 37 122
MADDOCKS, G. L.
Macrocosmic. .s . . . .
. . . . SS May 42 103
MAEPENN, K. H. pseud of HENRY
KUTTNER
MAGARIAN, ALBERT &
FLORENCE artists
Biog sketch, photos . . . .
. . . . .FA Jan 42 139
MAGUIRE, JOHN G.
Story of the Cover, The. .ss . . . . .
. . . . TW Dec 39 90

MAHAFFEY, BEATRICE
Managing Editor OTHER WORLDS
from Mar 50 issue
Managing Editor IMAGINATION
Oct 50 and Dec 50 issues
MALLOCH, G.(eorge) R.(eston)
Biog sketch . . . . . . .Fant #2 39 92
Winged Terror. .nt . . . .
. . . . .Fant #2 39 2
MANCHESTER, BRUCE
We, the Other People. .s . . . .
. . . . MSS Apr 41 96
MANLEY, EDGAR A.
with WALTER THODE
Time Annihilator. .s . . . .
. . . . WS Nov 30 488
MANN, JACK pseud of E. CHARLES
VIVIAN
Ninth Life, The. .n . . . .
. . . . .AMF Apr 50 10
MANNING, DAVID pseud of
FREDERICK FAUST
MANNING, LAURENCE
Call of the Mech-Men, The. .s . . . .
. . . . WS Nov 33 366
Caverns of Horror. .s . . . .
. . . . WS Mar 34 850
Living Galaxy, The. .s . . . .
. . . . WS Sep 34 436
Man Who Woke, The. .s . . . .
. . . . WS Mar 33 756
2. Master of the Brain. .s . . . .
. . . . WS Apr 33 838
3. The City of Sleep. .s . . . . . .
. . . . WS May 33 926
4. The Individualists. .s . . . . . .
. . . . WS Jun 33 58
5. The Elixir. .s . . . .
. . . . WS Aug 33 150
Man Who Awoke, The . . . .
. .n 3 pt . . . . CF Sum 41 111
Moth Message, The. .s . . . .
. . . . WS Dec 34 808
Prophetic Voice, The. .s . . . .
. . . . WS Apr 35 1330
Seeds from Space. .s . . . .
. . . . WS Jun 35 8
"STRANGER CLUB" series includes:
THE CALL OF THE MECH-MEN
CAVERNS OF HORROR
VOICE OF ATLANTIS
THE MOTH MESSAGE
SEEDS FROM SPACE
Voice of Atlantis. .s . . . .
. . . . .WS Jul 34 156
Voyage of the Asteroid, The . . . .
. .nt . . . . .WQ Sum 32 508

AUTHOR
    Title. .Length . . . . Magazine, Date, Page

    World of the Mist. .n 2 pt . . . . .
    . . . . WS Sep 35 390
    Wreck of the Asteroid, The . . . . .
    . .n 3 pt . . . . WS Dec 32 551
with FLETCHER PRATT
    City of the Living Dead, The . . . .
    . .nt . . . . SW May 30 1110
                              SS Jul 40 94
                              AFR #2 108
    Expedition to Pluto. .nt . . . .
    . . . . .PS Win 39 52
MANTELL, E.
    Men from Gayln, The. .s . . . .
    . . . . WS Aug 34 310
MARCELLINUS, AMMIANUS
    Thought Machine, The. .s . . . . . .
    . . . . Amz Feb 27 1052
MARCHIONI, MARK *artist*
    Biog sketch, photo. . . . .
    . . . . TW Jun 39 90
MARINER, SCOTT *pseud of CYRIL
    KORNBLUTH & FREDERIK
    POHL in collaboration*
    Old Neptunian Custom, An . . . . .
    . .s . . . . .SSS Aug 42 74
MARIUS
    Sixth Glacier, The. .n 2 pt . . . . . .
    . . . . .Amz Jan 29 900
    Vandals from the Moon. .s . . . . .
    . . . . .Amz Jul 28 302
MARKS, CHARLES I.
    Conqueror, The. .s . . . .
    . . . . FA Apr 45 184
MARKS, WINSTON K.
    Mad Hatter. .s . . . . .UK May 40 78
    Maniac Perverse. .s . . . .
    . . . . ASF Oct 41 80
MARLOWE, STEPHEN *pseud of
    MILTON LESSER*
MARLOWE, WEBB *pseud of J.
    FRANCIS McCOMAS*
    Contract for a Body. .nt . . . . . .
    . . . . .FA Jul 48 108
    Flight Into Darkness. .s . . . .
    . . . . ASF Feb 43 40
MARSHALL, EDISON (TELSA)
    Dian of the Lost Land. .n . . . . . .
    . . . . .FFM Apr 49 8
    Ogden's Strange Story. .n . . . . . .
    . . . . FFM Dec 49 10
    Who Is Charles Avison? . .s . . . . .
    . . . . FFM Dec 39 110
MARSHALL, J.(AMES) P.
    Warriors of Space. .s . . . .
    . . . . SW Jun 29 39

AUTHOR
    Title. .Length . . . . Magazine, Date, Page

    World in the Balance, The. .s . . . .
    . . . . .FFM Nov 39 32
MARTIN, AL H.
    Jovian Horde, The. .nt . . . .
    . . . . .WQ Sum 32 554
MARTIN, G. M.
    City of the Dead. .nt . . . .
    . . . . Amz Jan 50 38
MARTIN, HARRY
    Rice's Ray. .s . . . . .Amz Jan 28 958
MARTIN, STUART
    Sleep of Ages, The. .s . . . .
    . . . . FFM Dec 40 88
MARTIN, WALTER LIVINGSTON
    Horror House. .s . . . .AD Jul 30 594
    Zina the Killer. .ss . . . .
    . . . . WQ Fal 31 108
MARVELL, ANDREW *pseud of
    HOWELL DAVIES*
    Minimum Man. .n . . . .
    . . . . .FFM Aug 47 6
MASON, C. P. *See also pseud
    EPAMINONDAS T. SNOOKS (3)*
    Hypercosmos. .a . . . . TW Dec 38 46
    Rambling Through the Solar
    System. .s . . . . . . TW Oct 38 44
    Time-Table for Earth. .a . . . .
    . . . . TW Aug 41 102
MASON, ELMER BROWN
    Albino Otter, The. .s . . . .
    . . . . .FN Jul 49 108
    Black Butterflies. .nt . . . .
    . . . . .FFM Apr 49 88
    Lost—One Mylodon. .s . . . .
    . . . . .FN Jul 50 108
    White Gorilla, The. .s . . . .
    . . . . FN Nov 49 114
MASON, F. V. W.
    Phalanxes of Atlans. .n 2 pt . . . . .
    . . . . ASF Feb 31 228
MASON, JOHN HOLLIS
    Mission. .ss . . . . . .SFQ Spr 42 141
    Sacrifice. .ss.Fut Feb 42 97
MASON, TALLY *pseud of AUGUST
    DERLETH*
MATHESON, DONALD *(in Table of
    Contents)*
MATHESON, FLORENCE *(on Story)*
    Molecule Trapper, The. .ss . . . . . .
    . . . . Amz Sep 34 133
MATHESON, RICHARD
    Born of Man and Woman. .s . . . .
    . . . . F&SF Sum 50 108
    Third from the Sun. .s . . . .
    . . . . GSF Oct 50 61

AUTHOR
    Title. .Length . . . . Magazine, Date, Page

    Waker Dreams, The. .s . . . .
    . . . . GSF Dec 50 93
MATHISON, VOLNEY G.
    Mongolians' Ray, The. .s . . . . . .
    . . . . Amz Jun 29 258
MATTHEWS, W.(ILLIAM) J.
    Biog sketch . . . . . . .PS Spr 48 126
    Derelict, The. .s . . . . . PS Fal 46 49
    Space-Trap at Banya Tor. .s . . . . .
    . . . . .PS Spr 48 68
    Death from Orion, The. .s . . . . . .
    . . . . .PS Win 48 66
MAUGHAN, RALPH
    Choice, The. .ss . . . Amz Jun 34 101
MAUROIS, ANDRE
    War Against the Moon, The . . . . .
    . .s . . . . .F&SF Sum 50 29
    Weigher of Souls, The. .nt . . . . . .
    . . . . FFM Oct 50 86
MAVITY, HUBERT *pseud of
    NELSON S. BOND*
    Message from the Void, The . . . .
    . .s . . . . DS Feb 39 85
MAXON, P. B.
    Waltz of Death, The. .n 3 pt . . . .
    . . . . WS May 35 1416
MAXWELL, ALFRED E.
    Biog sketch . . . . . . .PS Mar 43 64
    Alpha Say, Beta Do. .s . . . .
    . . . . PS Sum 50 63
MAXWELL, JOSLYN
    Outpost on the Moon, The . . . . .
    . .n 3 pt . . . . WS Dec 30 630
MAXWELL, PAUL *artist*
    Suspended Animation . . . .
    . .bacover. . . . . .Amz Jan 40
MAYOPGA, GABRIEL *artist*
    *Covers for ASTONISHING
    STORIES*
    Jun, Aug(?), Oct 1940
    *Cover for SUPER SCIENCE
    STORIES*
    May 1940
    *Cover for THRILLING WONDER
    STORIES*
    Jan 1941
MEAD, GILBERT
    Maybe It's True. .a . . . .
    . . . . .Amz Nov 49 35
    Music of Doom, The. .s . . . .
    . . . . Amz Oct 49 124
    Time Is a Coffin. .s . . . .
    . . . . Amz Sep 50 134
    White God of Chicken Itza,
    The. .nt . . . . FA Nov 49 118

AUTHOR
Title. .Length . . . . Magazine, Date, Page

AUTHOR
Title. .Length . . . . Magazine, Date, Page

AUTHOR
Title. .Length . . . . Magazine, Date, Page

MEADOWCROFT, KIRK
Invisible Bubble, The. .s . . . .
. . . . Amz Sep 28 508
MEEK, (CAPT.) S.(terner St.) P.(aul)
*See also pseud STERNER ST.
PAUL (1)*
Attack from Space, The. .s . . . . .
. . . . .ASF Sep 30 390
Awlo of Ulm. .nt. . . . .
. . . . Amz Sep 31 486
B. C. 30,000. .s . . . . ASF Apr 32 5
Beyond the Heaviside Layer . . . .
. .s . . . . .ASF Jul 30 5
Black Lamp, The. .s . . . .
. . . . ASF Feb 31 212
Cave of Horror, The. .s . . . .
. . . . .ASF Jan 30 32
Cold Light. .s . . . .
. . . . ASF May 30 295
"DR. BIRD & OPERATIVE
CARNES" series includes:
THE PERFECT COUNTERFEIT
THE CAVE OF HORROR
THE THIEF OF TIME
COLD LIGHT
THE RAY OF MADNESS
THE GLAND MURDERS
STOLEN BRAINS
THE SEA TERROR
THE BLACK LAMP
THE EARTH'S CANCER
WHEN CAVERNS YAWNED
THE PORT OF MISSING PLANES
THE SOLAR MAGNET
POISONED AIR
THE GREAT DROUTH
VANISHED GOLD
Drums of Tapajos. .n 3 pt . . . . . .
. . . . Amz Nov 30 678
Earth's Cancer, The. .s . . . .
. . . . Amz Mar 31 116
Futility. .s . . . . . . .Amz Jul 29 316
Giant son the Earth. .n 2 pt. . . . .
. . . . ASF Dec 31 366
Gland Murders, The. .s . . . .
. .. . AD Jun 30 508
Great Drought, The. .s . . . .
. . . . ASF May 32 218
Last War, The. .nt . . . .
. . . . Amz Aug 30 438
Mentality Machine, The . . . .
. . . . ToW Spr 39 44
Murgatroyd Experiment, The. . . .
. .s . . . . .AQ Win 29 78
Osmotic Theorem, The. . . . .
. .s . . . . .WQ Win 30 234
Perfect Counterfeit, The. .s . . . . .
. . . . .SD Jan 30 28
Poisoned Air. .s . . . .
. . . . ASF Mar 32 295

Port of Missing Planes, The . . . . .
. .s . . . . ASF Aug 31 255
Radio Robbery, The. .s . . . .
. . . . Amz Feb 30 1046
AQ Fal 34 110
Ray of Madness, The. .s . . . . .
. . . . ASF Apr 30 112
Red Peril, The. .s . . . .
. . . . Amz Sep 29 486
Sea Terror, The. .s . . . .
. . . . ASF Dec 30 336
Solar Magnet, The. .s . . . .
.ASF Oct 31 113
Stolen Brains. .s . . . . ASF Oct 30 7
Submicroscopic. .s. . . . .
. . . . Amz Aug 31 390
Synthetic Entity, The. .s . . . . . .
. . . . .WS Jan 33 638
ToW Sum 40 72
Thief of Time, The. .s . . . .
.ASF Feb 30 259
Tragedy of Spider Island,
The. .s . . . . WS Sep 30 324
Trapped in the Depths. .s . . . . . .
. . . . WS Jun 30 38
Troyana. .n 3 pt . . . .
. . . . Amz Feb 32 968
Vanishing Gold. .s . . . .
. . . . WS May 32 1320
When Caverns Yawned. .s . . . . . .
. . . . ASF May 31 198
MEISSNER, AUGUST
Flea Circus, The. .s . . . .
. . . . .Amz Jan 49 118
MELHORN, R. I.
Infra-Calorescence. .s . . . .
. . . . Amz Oct 32 622
MENASCO, NORMAN
Trigger Tide. .s . . . . ASF Oct 50 63
MEREDITH, D. W.
Next Friday Morning. .s . . . .
. . . . ASF Feb 49 135
MERIWETHER, LEE
Roman Resurrection, A. .s . . . . .
. . . . .FFM Aug 42 115
MERLYN, ARTHUR *pseud of*
JAMES BLISH
Sunken Universe. .s . . . .
. . . . SSS May 42 49
SSS Nov 50 98
MERRIL, JUDITH *See also pseud*
CYRIL JUDD (0)
Barrier of Dread. .s . . . .
. . . . Fut Jul–Aug 50 72
Death Is the Penalty. .s. . . . . . .
. . . . .ASF Jan 49 56

That Only a Mother. .s . . . .
.ASF Jun 48 88
MERRITT, A.(braham)
Biog sketch . . .FFM May–Jun 40 44
Obituary . . . . .FFM Mar 44 86
MASTERS OF FANTASY
biog . . . . FFM Oct 47 97
Biog sketch, portrait . . . .
. . . . .AMF Oct 50 91
Burn, Witch, Burn. .n . . . .
. . . . .FFM Jun 42 6
Conquest of the Moon Pool,
The. .n 6 pt . . . . .FFM Nov 39 6
(complete). . . FFN Sep 48 6
(combined with THE MOON POOL
under that title). .n 3 pt . . . . . .
. . . . Amz May 28 110
Creep, Shadow! .n . . . .
. . . . .FFM Aug 42 6
AMF Dec 49 10
Drone Man, The. .s . .TW Aug 36 29
Drone, The *(The Drone Man)*. . . .
. .s . . . . .AFR #6 49
Dwellers in the Mirage, The . . . .
. .n . . . . FN Apr 41 6
FN Sep 49 8
Face in the Abyss, The. .n . . . . . .
. . . . AA 27 54
FFM Oct 40 6
AMF Jul 50 12
Metal monster, The. .n . . . .
. . . . .FFM Aug 41 6
Moon Pool, The *(incorporating the*
novelet THE MOON POOL and the
novel THE CONQUEST OF THE
MOON POOL into one) . . . . . .
. .n 3 pt . . . . . . Amz May 27 110
Moon Pool, The. .nt . . . .
. . . . .FFM Sep–Oct 39 2
FN May 48 8
People of the Pit, The. .s . . . .
. . . . Amz Mar 27 1130
AA 27 89
FN Jan 41 106
Rhythm of the Spheres. .s. . . . . .
. . . . TW Oct 36 52
AFR #3 7
Seven Footprints to Satan. . . . . .
. .n . . . . FN Jan 49 8
Ship of Ishtar, The. .n . . . .
. . . . .FN Mar 48 8
Snake Mother, The. .n . . . .
. . . . .FN Nov 40 6
Three Lines of Old French. .s. . . .
. . . . .FFM May–Jun 40 31
AMF Feb 50 102

AUTHOR
Title. .Length . . . . Magazine, Date, Page

Through the Dragon Glass. .s . . . .
. . . . FN Sep 40 118
When Old Gods Wake. .s . . . .
. . . .'. . . . . .AFR #7 94
Woman of the Wood, The . . . . . .
. .s . . . . AFR #1 68
MERWIN, SAM, JR. *See also pseuds*
MATT LEE (3), CARTER
SPRAGUE (6)
Biog sketch, Photo. . . . .
. . . . TW Oct 39 49
Editor FANTASTIC STORY
QUARTERLY
Spr 51 *(first issue) to mid-1951*
Editor STARTLING STORIES
1944 *thru* Sep 51 *issue*
Editor THRILLING WONDER
STORIES
Win 45 *thru* Oct 51 *issues*
Editor WONDER STORY ANNUAL
1950
Admiral's Walk, The. .s . . . .
. . . . TW Dec 47 61
Carriers, The. .s . . . . TW Feb 49 90
"Dreaming" Down Axis
Planes. .s . . . . . . .TW Sum 44 42
Exiled from Earth. .s . . . .
.TW Dec 40 31
Forgotten Envoy. .s . . . .
. . . . SS May 49 122
Jimson Island Giant, The. .s . . . .
. . . . .SS Win 46 77
Judas Ram. .s . . . . . GSF Dec 50 32
No Greater Worlds. .ss . . . .
. . . . TW Spr 45 85
Scourge Below, The. .s . . . .
. . . . TW Oct 39 46
Sky-Going Aircraft Carrier,
The. .a . . . . TW Aug 43 103
Tenth Degree, The. .s . . . .
.TW Oct 50 104
MEYERINCK, GUSTAVUS
Fatal Word, The. .s . . . .
. . . . OW Jan 50 78
MICHALSKE, E. M.
Greatest Painter in the World,
The. .s . . . . FA Feb 49 120
MICHEL, JOHN (B.) *See also pseuds*
BOWEN CONWAY (1), ARTHUR
COOKE (1), HUGH RAYMOND
(17), LAWRENCE WOODS (1)
Goblins Will Get You, The. .s . . . .
. . . . AFR #8 100
with RAYMOND Z. GALLUN
Menace from Mercury, The . . . . .
. .s . . . . .WQ Sum 32 544

AUTHOR
Title. .Length . . . . Magazine, Date, Page

with J. KUBERT cartoonist
Corsairs from the Coalsack,
The. .comic . . . .OTWA Dec 50 51
Lunar Station. .comic. . . . .
. . . . OTWA Jul 50 51
with ROBERT W. LOWNDES
Inheritors, The. .s . . . .
. . . . Fut Oct 42 54
                              AFR #11 90
MIHAILAKIS, ULYSSES GEORGE
See pseud SILAKI ALI HASSAN
Machine of Destiny, The. .s . . . . .
. . . . .WQ Sum 31 514
MILES, PAUL
Bill Caldron Goes to the
Future. .s . . . . . Amz Mar 43 196
MILLARD, JOSEPH J.
Biog sketch, photo. . . . .
. . . . Amz Oct 41 139
Conquest of Venus, The . . . .
.TW Apr 43 56
Crash on Viar. .s . . . TW Feb 41 113
Crystal Invaders, The. .s . . . .
. . . . TW Jan 41 78
Earth Saver, The. .s . . . .
. . . . SS Nov 42 90
Earthquake Girl, The. .nt . . . . . .
. . . . FA Oct 41 8
Gods Hate Kansas, The. .n. . . . . .
. . . . SS Nov 41 16
Mister John Doe, Earthman. . . . .
. .s . . . . .SS Mar 42 108
Paganini—Man or Devil? . .a . . . .
. . . . FA Oct 40 130
SCIENTIFIC MYSTERIES
The Fate of the Mammoth . . . .
. .a . . . . Amz Oct 40 68
The Mystery of the Moon . . . . .
. .a . . . . Amz Nov 40 58
Bomb Sight of the Gods . . . . . .
. .a . . . . Amz Dec 40 98
The Great Pyramid of
Gizeh. .a . . . . . Amz Feb 41 70
Earth's Amazing
Atmosphere. .a . . . .
. . . . Amz Apr 41 124
Plants That Think. .a . . . .
. . . . Amz May 41 132
Lightning. .a . . . .
. . . . Amz Jun 41 132
Size. .a . . . . Amz Jul 41 132
Are There Strange Life Forms
on Earth Unknown? . .a . . . . .
. . . . Amz Aug 41 124
Mystery of Life. .a . . . .
. . . . Amz Oct 41 134

AUTHOR
Title. .Length . . . . Magazine, Date, Page

Matto Grosso. .a . . . .
. . . . Amz Nov 41 112
Vanished Civilizations . . . .
. . . . Amz Feb 42 228
The Sea Serpent. .a . . . .
. . . . Amz Mar 42 226
Thunder to Venus. .nt . . . .
. . . . TW Jun 42 11
with A. R. STEBER pseud
(Raymond A. Palmer)
Lone Wolf of Space. .nt . . . .
. . . . .Amz May 41 50
MILLER *artist*
Covers for ASTOUNDING SCIENCE
FICTION
Jun, Aug, Sep 1950
MILLER, BENJ. *pseud of NOEL*
LOOMIS
Date Line. .s . . . . . TW Oct 48 117
Horse on Me, A. .s . . . .
. . . . TW Dec 48 89
Monsters from the West. .s . . . . .
. . . . TW Feb 49 98
On the House. .s . . . . TW Apr 49 82
MILLER, P. SCHUYLER *See also*
pseud DENNIS McDERMOTT (1)
Arrhenius Horror, The. .nt . . . . .
. . . . Amz Sep 31 514
                              AFR #4 7
As Never Was. .s . . . .ASF Jan 44 31
Atom Smasher, The. .s . . . .
. . . . .Amz Jan 34 127
Bird Walk. .s . . . . ASF Apr 41 112
Cave, The. .s . . . . . .ASF Jan 43 83
Chrysalis, The. .s . . . .
. . . . ASF Apr 36 44
Cleon of Yzdral. .s . . . .
. . . . .Amz Jul 31 320
Coils of Time. .nt . . . .
. . . . .ASF May 39 9
Counterfeiting a Golden Age . . . .
. .guest editorial . . . SS May 41 83
Cuckoo. .nt . . . . . . ASF May 44 77
Dust of Destruction. .s . . . .
. . . . WS Feb 31 918
Facts of Life, The. .s . . . .
. . . . .Com May 41 25
Flayed Wolf, The. .s . . . .
. . . . .UK Jul 40 112
Forgotten Man of Space, The. . . .
. .s . . . . WS Apr 33 872
                              SS Win 46 66
Fricassee in Four Dimensions. . . .
. .s . . . . ASF Dec 43 55
Frog, The. .s . . . . . . UK Oct 42 59
Gleeps. .s . . . . .ASF Jul 43 99

AUTHOR
Title. .Length . . . . Magazine, Date, Page

Hounds of Kalimar, The . . . . . .
. . . . UK Jun 43 138
In the Good Old Summertime . . .
. .s . . . . ASF Mar 40 36
Jeremiah Jones, Alchemist . . . . .
. .s . . . . Amz May 33 142
Living Isotopes. .s . . . .
. . . . SSS May 40 80
Man from Mars, The. .s . . . .
. . . . .WQ Sum 31 524
                    SS Mar 39 96
Old Man Mulligan. .nt. . . . .
. . . . ASF Dec 40 9
Over the River. .s. . . . .
. . . . UK Apr 41 96
People of the Arrow, The. .s . . . .
. . . . .Amz Jul 35 63
Pleasure Trove. .nt. . . . .
. . . . ASF Aug 39 139
Pool of Life, The. .nt . . . .
. . . . Amz Oct 34 12
PROBABILITY ZERO
 A Matter of Eclipses. .ss . . . . . .
. . . . ASF Nov 42 129
Red Flame of Venus. .s. . . . . . .
. . . . WS Sep 32 346
Red Plague, The. .s . . . .
. . . . .WS Jul 30 171
Sands of Time. .nt . . . .
. . . . ASF Apr 37 116
Smugglers of the Moon. .s . . . . . .
. . . . SSS May 41 72
Tetrahedra of Space. .s . . . .
. . . . WS Nov 31 728
                    SS Sep 48 82
Thing on Outer Shoal, The . . . . .
. .s . . . . ASF Sep 47 62
Through the Vibrations. .nt. . . . .
. . . . Amz May 31 102
                    AFR #9 18
Trouble on Tantalus. .nt. . . . . . .
. . . . ASF Feb 41 48
Ultimate Image, The. .s. . . . . . .
. . . . Com Dec 40 23
with L. SPRAGUE de CAMP
Genus Homo. .n . . . . .SSS Mar 41 8
*with DENNIS McDERMOTT pseud
(Walter L. Dennis & Paul
McDermott)*
Duel on the Asteroid, The. .s. . . .
. . . . .WS Jan 32 950
MILLER, R. DeWITT
Beyond Hell. .nt . . . .
. . . . Uc Apr 41 58
Great Eye, The. .a . . . .
. . . . ASF Jun 38 54

Hour of Judgement. .nt . . . . . .
. . . . MSS Aug 39 70
Master Shall Not Die, The . . . .
. .s . . . . ASF Mar 38 38
Ra, the Inscrutable. .a . . . .
. . . . .ASF Oct 37 101
Shapes, The. .s . . . . ASF Feb 36 60
Virus, The. .s . . . . . .ASF Jul 36 65
Within the Pyramid. .s . . . .
. . . . ASF Mar 37 41
MILLS, CHARLIE
Roadside Strategy. .ss. . . . .
. . . . Amz Jul 34 130
MILLS, HERBERT
What Price Clues? . .a . . . .
. . . . AD Sep 30 812
MILO *artist*
*Cover for FANTASY BOOK
#1 (1947)*
MILOCHE, FRANK
Empire of Glass, The. .s . . . .
. . . . WQ Spr 31 366
MILTON, DANE
Hormone, The. .s. . . . .
. . . . ASF Nov 34 59
MINES, SAMUEL
Donkeys to Baldpate. .s . . . .
. . . . .TW Aug 47 84
Find the Sculptor. .s . . . .
. . . . TW Apr 46 58
Matter of Size, A. .s . . . .
. . . . TW Feb 47 53
They Wouldn't Dare. .s . . . .
. . . . TW Dec 47 43
MITCHELL, CURTIS
*Editor FANTASY (FICTION)
(STORIES)*
May 50 *and* Nov 50 *issues (all)*
MITCHELL, GENE *pseud of H.
ORLO HOADLEY*
Refraction and Lenses. .a . . . . . .
. . . . ASF Aug 44 105
MITCHELL, J. LESLIE
Three Go Back. .n . . . .
. . . . .FFM Dec 43 8
MOFFATT, LEN J.
Alpha Centauri Curtain Call. . . . .
. .s . . . . .OTWA Dec 50 100
MONROE, LYLE *pseud of ROBERT
A. HEINLEIN*
Let There be Light. .s. . . . .
. . . . SSS May 40 34
Lost Legion. .n . . . .SSS Nov 41 10
"My Object All Sublime". .s . . . .
. . . . .Fut Feb 42 82
Pied Piper. .s. . . . . .Ash Mar 42 54

with ELMA WENTZ
Beyond Doubt. .s . . .Ash Apr 41 35
MONTAGUE, JAMES
Forbidden Light. .nt . . . .
. . . . ASF Dec 35 116
MOORE, C.(atherine) L. (Mrs. Henry
Kuttner) *See also pseuds KEITH
HAMMOND (4), HUDSON
HASTINGS (2), C. H. LIDDELL
(2), LAWRENCE O'DONNELL
(8), LEWIS PADGETT (32). She
has also collaborated on virtually
all stories under HENRY
KUTTNER'S by-line and
pseudonyms ever since their
marriage in June, 1940.*
Black Thirst. .nt . . . . .AFR #3 56
Bright Illusion, The. .nt . . . .
. . . . .ASF Oct 34 120
Daemon. .s . . . . . . FFM Oct 46 98
Doorway Into Time. .s . . . .
. . . . FFM Sep 43 116
Fruit of Knowledge. .nt . . . .
. . . . UK Oct 40 73
Greater Glories. .nt . . . .
. . . . .ASF Sep 35 111
Greater Than Gods. .nt. . . . . . .
.ASF Jul 39 136
Judgement Night. .n 2 pt . . . . . .
. . . . ASF Aug 43 9
No Woman Born. .nt . . . .
. . . . ASF Dec 44 134
Scarlet Dream. .nt . . . . .AFR #5 7
Shambleau. .nt . . . . . . .AFR #7 3
There Shall Be Darkness. .nt . . . .
. . . . ASF Feb 42 9
Tryst in Time. .nt . . . .
. . . . ASF Dec 36 10
with HENRY KUTTNER
Earth's Last Citadel. .n . . . .
. . . . .FN Jul 50 12
MOORE, DONALD BAKER
Foundling. .s . . . . . ASF Dec 50 66
MOORE, HAL
Albino Canary, The. .s . . . FB #5 14
MOORE, ROBERT *pseud of
ROBERT MOORE WILLIAMS*
Zero as a Limit. .s . . . ASF Jul 37 34
MOORE, W.
Pool of Infinity. .s . . . .NW #4 49 93
MOORE, WARD
Sword of Peace. .nt . . . .
. . . . Amz Mar 50 124
MOORE, WILLIAM RUSSELL
Warriors of Zantos. .ss . . . .
. . . . Amz Jun 33 233

AUTHOR
Title. .Length . . . . Magazine, Date, Page

MORAN, NEIL
Tooth, The. .s . . . . . ASF Apr 34 87
MORAVSKY, MARIA
Calling of the Harp. .s . . . .
. . . . SS Jul 41 84
MOREY, LEO artist
Biog sketch, photo. . . . .
. . . . TW Jun 39 89
Covers for AMAZING STORIES
Jul, Aug, Oct, Nov, Dec 1929
Jan, Feb, Mar, Apr, May, Jun, Jul,
Aug, Sep, Oct, Nov, Dec 1930
Jan, Feb, Mar, Apr, May, Jun, Jul,
Aug, Sep, Oct, Nov, Dec 1931
Jan, Feb, Mar, Apr, May, Jun, Jul,
Aug, Sep, Oct, Nov, Dec 1932
Aug–Sep, Oct, Nov, Dec 1933
Jan, Feb, Mar, Apr, May, Jun, Jul,
Aug, Sep, Oct, Nov, Dec 1934
Jan, Feb, Mar, Apr, May, Jun, Jul,
Aug, Oct, Dec 1935
Feb, Apr, Jun, Aug, Oct, Dec 1936
Feb, Apr, Jun, Aug, Oct, Dec 1937
Feb, Apr 1938
Aug (w/ Julian S. Krupa), Oct 1940
Feb 1941
Covers for AMAZING STORIES
    QUARTERLY
Sum, Fal, Win 1930
Spr, Sum, Fal 1931
Win, Spr–Sum, Fal–Win 1932
Spr–Sum, Win 1933
Fal 1934
Covers for ASTONISHING STORIES
Feb 1941
Oct 1942
Covers for COMET
Dec 1940
Mar, Jul 1941
Cover for COSMIC STORIES
Mar 1941
Cover for FANTASTIC
    ADVENTURES
Jul 1939
Cover for FUTURE c/w SCIENCE
    FICTION
Sep–Oct 1950
Cover for STIRRING SCIENCE
    STORIES
Feb 1941
Cover for SUPER SCIENCE
    STORIES
Nov 1940
MORGAN, BASSETT
Bimini. .s . . . . AFR #10 36
Tiger Dust. .s . . . . AFR #12 84

MORGAN, JAQUE
SCIENTIFIC ADVENTURES OF
    MR. FOSDICK, THE
Mr. Fosdick Invents the Seidlitz-
mobile. .s . . . . . Amz Jun 26 233
The Feline Light and Power Co. Is
Organized. .s . . . . Amz Jul 26 319
                        AA 27 117
The International Electro-Galvanic
Undertaking Corporation . . . .
. .s . . . . Amz Aug 26 417
MORGAN, SCOTT pseud of HENRY
    KUTTNER
Trophy. .s . . . . TW Win 44 62
MORLAND, PETER HENRY pseud
    of FREDERICK FAUST
MORLEY, WILFRED OWEN pseud
    of ROBERT W. LOWNDES
Does Not Imply. .s . . . .
. . . . Fut Feb 43 76
Highway. .s . . . . . . SFQ Fal 42 139
Lemmings, The. .s . . . .
. . . . .SSS May 42 102
Long Wall, The. .s . . . Sti Mar 42 55
Matter of Philosophy, A . . . . . .
. .ss . . . . .SF Sep 41 85
Message for Jean, A. .s . . . .
. . . . Fut Jun 42 94
My Lady of the Emerald . . . . . .
. .s . . . . .Ash Nov 41 60
No Star Shall Fall. .ss . . . .
. . . . .Fut Dec 41 60
Slim People, The. .ss . . . .
. . . . .Fut Aug 42 91
with JACQUES DeFOREST ERMAN
    pseud (Forrest J. Ackerman)
Dhactwhu!–Remember? . .s . . . .
. . . . .SSS Apr 49 84
MORRIS, A.
Cancer—The Fantastic. .a . . . . . .
. . . . FA Aug 42 227
Devil of Doom, The. .nt . . . .
. . . . FA Jan 49 64
Human Body a Mighty Fortress,
The. .a . . . . Amz Jun 43 187
MORRIS, EARLE H.
Starvation in Space. .s . . . .
. . . . AQ Win 32 122
MORRIS, EDWARD
with JOHN BERTIN
Rebellion on Venus. .s . . . .
. . . . .WQ Sum 32 494
MORRISON, RICHARD pseud of
    ROBERT W. LOWNDES
Deliverers, The. .ss . . . .
. . . . SFQ Win 42 142

MORRISON, ROBERT
Dead on Arrival. .s . . . .
. . . . Amz Aug 48 138
MORRISON, WILLIAM pseud of
    JOSEPH SAMACHSON
Biog sketch, photo. . . . .
. . . . SS Sep 42 127
Ancient, The. .s . . . . FSQ Fal 50 139
Bad Medicine. .s . . . . TW Feb 41 81
Barbarians, The. .s . . . .
. . . . .Fut Aug 41 85
Christmas on Mars. .s . . . .
. . . . TW Dec 41 83
Companions of Sirius, The. .s . . . .
. . . . CF Win 44 106
Crossroads of the Universe. .s . . . .
. . . . SS Jul 41 95
Disappointment. .s . . . .
. . . . SS Jul 50 138
Forgotten Past. .s . . . . SS Jan 43 82
Free Land. .s . . . . . . TW Aug 49 89
Garments of Doom. .ss . . . .
. . . . .SSS Feb 43 63
Get Your Extra Here! . .s . . . . . .
. . . . SS Sum 44 60
Great Invasion, The. .s . . . .
. . . . .SS Mar 43 98
Hop O' My Thumb. .s . . . .
. . . . SSS May 50 94
Invincible Wrestler, The. .s . . . .
. . . . TW Apr 43 108
Light in Darkness. .s . . . .
. . . . .TW Fal 43 103
Lion-Hearted, The. .s . . . .
. . . . .CF Sum 42 80
Man in the Moon, The. .s . . . . . .
. . . . SS Jul 42 96
Masters of Chance. .s . . . .
. . . . .TW Aug 41 76
Monkey and the Typewriter,
The. .s . . . . SS Fal 43 97
Plastic Pigskin Daze. .s . . . .
. . . . TW Mar 41 83
Back, The. .s . . . . . . ASF Sep 50 46
Skin Dupe. .s . . . . . . TW Dec 49 98
Stars Over Santa Claus. .s . . . . . .
. . . . .SS Jan 50 71
Strangest Bedfellows, The. .s . . . .
. . . . TW Jun 50 125
Treasure, The. .s . . . CF Win 43 108
Two Worlds To Save. .n . . . .
. . . . .SS Sep 42 13
Undersea Snatch. .s . . . .
. . . . .CF Fal 41 107
Wheezers, The. .s . . . .
. . . . .CF Sum 43 91

AUTHOR
Title. .Length . . . . Magazine, Date, Page

AUTHOR
Title. .Length . . . . Magazine, Date, Page

AUTHOR
Title. .Length . . . . Magazine, Date, Page

MORROW, LOWELL HOWARD
Air Terror, The. .s . . . .
. . . . AW Sep 29 266
Blue Demon, The. .s . . . .
. . . . AW Dec 29 486
Islands in the Air. .s . . . .
. . . . AW Jul 29 32
Omega, The Man. .s . . . .
. . . . .Amz Jan 33 929
Rescue in Space, A. .s. . . . . . .
. . . . WS Sep 30 346
Through the Meteors. .s . . . .
. . . . AW Apr 30 870

MORSE, PHILIP M.
Pandora's Icebox. .a . . . .
. . . . .ASF Jun 39 120

MOSKOWITZ, SAM
Biog sketch . . . . .PS Win 41 91
FANTASY BOOK REVIEWS dept in
FANTASTIC NOVELS; irregularly
from Jan 49
Man of the Stars. .s . . . .
. . . . .PS Win 41 30
Way Mack, The. .nt . . . .
. . . . Com Jan 41 60
World of Mockery. .s . . . .
. . . . PS Sum 41 74

MULFORD, STOCKTON *artist*
Cover for AMAZING STORIES
Jul 1941
Covers for FANTASTIC
ADVENTURES
May, Jun 1940

MULLEN, STANLEY
Lady Into Hell-Cat. .s. . . . .
. . . . PS Spr 49 66
Living Vortex, The. .nt . . . .
. . . . FA Apr 50 42
Mirror Maze. .s . . . .
. . . . FFM Jun 49 114
Moonworm's Dance. .s . . . .
. . . . SSS Jan 40 34
S.O.S. Aphrodite!. .s . . . .
. . . . PS Sum 49 45
Spaceman, Beware!. .s . . . .
. . . . SSS Jul 49 85
Star-Brother. .s . . . .
. . . . SSS Sep 49 88
Suicide Command. .s . . . .
. . . . PS Sum 50 86

MUND, EDWARD S.
Brain Leeches. .s . . . ASF Jul 35 109

MUNN, H. WARNER
Dreams May Come. .s . . . .
. . . . UK Oct 39 67

MUNRO, DUNCAN H. *pseud of*
ERIC FRANK RUSSELL
Muten. .s . . . . . . .ASF Oct 48 126
U-Turn. .s . . . . . . ASF Apr 50 133

MURRAY, RICHARD RUSH
Radicalite. .s. . . . . .Amz Jan 33 948
Stellarite. .s . . . . Amz Mar 33 1122

MUSA
Stellarite. .s . . . . Amz Mar 33 1122

MUSSACHIA, JOHN B. *artist*
Cover for SCIENCE FICTION
QUARTERLY
Sum 1942

MYERS, CHARLES F.
Biog sketch, photo. . . . .
. . . . FA Feb 49 2
I'll Dream of You. .s . . . .
. . . . FA Jan 47 19
Shades of Toffee, The. .n . . . . . .
. . . . FA Jun 50 8
Spirit of Toffee, The. .nt . . . .
. . . . FA Nov 48 72
Toffee Haunts a Ghost. .nt . . . . .
. . . . FA Nov 47 108
Toffee Takes a Trip. .nt . . . .
. . . . .FA Jul 47 50
Toffee Turns the Trick. .nt . . . . . .
. . . . FA Feb 49 46
You Can't Scare Me! . .nt. . . . . .
. . . . FA Mar 47 80

MYERS, RAY AVERY
Into the Subconscious. .s . . . . . .
. . . . SW Oct 29 426

N

NATHANSON, I.(SAAC) (R.)
Antarctic Transformation,
The. .nt . . . . . . Amz Nov 31 720
Conquest of the Earth, The . . . . .
. .s . . . . Amz Apr 30 42
Falling Planetoid, The. .s . . . . . .
. . . . SW Apr 30 986
Gold. .s . . . . Amz Jan 34 95
Last Neanderthal Man, The . . . . .
. .s . . . . Amz Feb 37 116
Modern Comedy of Science,
A. .s . . . . Amz Apr 36 27
Moon People of Jupiter. .nt . . . . .
. . . . AQ Spr 31 230
Passing Star, The. .s . . . .
. . . . Amz Sep 30 506
Pithecanthropus Island . . . .
. .s . . . . WQ Win 31 228

Shot Into Space. .s . . . .
. . . . Amz Aug 34 111
World Aflame, The. .nt . . . .
. . . . Amz Jan 35 44

NAYLOR, RAMON *artist*
Cover for AMAZING STORIES
Jan 1948
Covers for FANTASTIC
ADVENTURES
Jul 1948
Jan 1950

NEAL, HARRY *pseud of JEROME*
BIXBY

NEARING, H., JR.
Poetry Machine, The. .s . . . .
. . . . .F&SF Fal 50 53

NELSON, AL P.
with RALPH MILNE FARLEY
pseud (Roger Sherman Hoar)
City of Lost Souls. .nt . . . .
. . . . .FA Jul 41 66

NELSON, BEN
Ponape—The Real "Moon
Pool". .a . . . . . . .FN Jan 49 116

NEVILLE, KRIS *See also*
HENDERSON STARKE (1)
Cold War. .s . . . .
. . . . .ASF Oct 49 121
Every Work Into Judgement . . . .
. .s . . . . F&SF Win–Spr 50 29
First, The. .s . . . . . . .SSS Sep 50 53
Forbidden Fruit. .s . . . .
. . . . OTWA Jul 50 111
Hand from the Stars, The. .s . . . .
. . . . SSS Jul 49 116
If This Be Utopia. .s. . . . .
. . . . Amz May 50 60
One Leg is Enough. .s. . . . .
. . . . Amz Jul 50 166
Satellite Secret. .s . . . .
. . . . Amz Apr 50 166
Take Two Quiggies. .nt. . . . .
. . . . F&SF Dec 50 3
Wind in Her Hair. .s . . . .
. . . . .Im Oct 50 40

NEVIN, JAMES B.
Whereabouts of Mr. Moses Bailey,
The. .s . . . . FFM Jun 41 117

NEVINS, W. VARICK, III
Cosmic Calamity. .ss . . . .
. . . . WS Jun 34 61
Emotion Meter, The. .ss . . . .
. . . . .WS Jan 35 954
Mystery of the −/−, The. . . . . . .
. .s . . . . WS Jun 35 40

AUTHOR
  Title. .Length . . . . Magazine, Date, Page

Sense Twister, The. .s. . . . .
. . . . WS Aug 34 350
NEWMAN, R. *cartoonist*
Biog sketch, caricature . . . .
. . . . Amz Aug 41 132
NEWTON, DOUGLAS
Sunken Cities. .nt . . . .
. . . . FFM May–Jun 40 6
NEWTON, (E.) EDSEL
Flaming Cloud, The. .s . . . .
. . . . .WS Jan 31 802
Freedom of the Skies. .s . . . .
. . . . AW Dec 29 518
Hour the Conqueror Came,
The. .s. . . . . WQ Win 31 252
House of Monstrosities. .s . . . . . .
. . . . WS Dec 34 802
Sargasso Monster, The. .s . . . . . .
. . . . WS Apr 31 1252
Space Hermit, The. .s . . . .
. . . . Amz Jul 29 326
Torpedo Terror, The. .s . . . .
. . . . WS Sep 30 356
NICHOLS, H. L.
Yesterday's Revenge. .s. . . . .
. . . . .Com Jan 41 114
"NICK" *artist*
Covers for TALES OF WONDER
Win, Spr, Aut 1941
Spr 1942
NIHLEAN, RUSSELL E.
Tanya's Night to Howl. .s . . . . . .
. . . . FA Aug 48 148
NITKIN, NATHANIEL
Fruits of Prejudice, The . . . .
. .s . . . . .CF Fal 42 92
Man Who Was King, The. .s . . . . .
. . . . SS Jan 43 94
Return of the Ice Age, The . . . . .
. .s . . . . .CF Spr 44 95
NOORDUNG, CAPT. HERMANN,
A.D., M.E.
Problems of Space Flying,
The. .a. . . *(tr fr German by Francis
M. Currier)* . . . . . . .SW Jul 29 170
NORMAN, JAMES
Biog sketch, photo. . . . .
. . . . Amz Mar 41 133
Blue Tropics, The. .s . . . .
. . . . FA Apr 40 6
Death Walks in Washington . . . . .
. .nt . . . . FA Mar 41 50
Double Trouble for Oscar . . . . . .
. .nt . . . . FA Oct 42 124
Lost Colony in the Superstitions,
The. .s. . . . . Amz Mar 41 114

AUTHOR
  Title. .Length . . . . Magazine, Date, Page

Lost Treasure of Angkor. .nt . . . .
. . . . Amz Jun 41 44
Machine from the Past, The. . . . .
. .s . . . . FA May 41 116
Mystery on Planetoid Ten . . . . . .
. .nt . . . . .Amz Jul 41 46
Oscar and the Talking
Totems. .nt . . . . . FA Apr 42 130
"OSCAR, DETECTIVE OF MARS"
series includes:
OSCAR, DETECTIVE OF MARS
DEATH WALKS IN WASHINGTON
OSCAR SAVES THE UNION
OSCAR AND THE TALKING TOTEMS
DOUBLE TROULBE FOR OSCAR
Oscar, Detective of Mars. .s . . . . .
. . . . FA Oct 40 58
Oscar Saves the Union. .nt . . . . .
. . . . FA Sep 41 52
Planet for Your Thoughts, A . . . .
. .s . . . . .PS Win 41 44
Sutton's Strange Voyage. .s . . . . .
. . . . Amz May 42 142
NORSE, LLOYD
Biog sketch, photo. . . . .
. . . . TW Dec 42 59
Scientific Spooks. .s . . . .
. . . . TW Dec 42 56
NORTH, ANDREW *pseud of
ANDRÉ NORTON*
Gifts of Asti, The. .s . . . . . FB #3 8
People of the Crater, The. .nt . . . .
. . . . FB #1 4
NORTH, BRENT
Girls for Satan's Utopia. .s . . . . . .
. . . . MSS Dec 39 105
NORTH, ERIC *pseud of BERNARD
CRONIN*
Green Flame, The. .n . . . .
. . . . AMF Jul 50 64
Three Against the Stars. .n . . . . .
. . . . .FN May 50 14
NORTHERN, LESLIE *house pseud
used by FRANK BELKNAP
LONG and others (?)*
by FRANK BELKNAP LONG
Purple Dusk, The. .s . . . .
. . . . .TW Sum 45 68
They Sculp. .s . . . . . TW Win 45 76
Authors' real names unknown
Fatal Thoughts. .s . . . SS Sum 45 74
Skyrover. .s . . . . .SS Win 45 87
NORTON, ANDRÉ *See pseud
ANDREW NORTH*
NORTON, HENRY (A.)
Man in the Moon, The. .s . . . . . .
. . . . ASF Feb 43 70

AUTHOR
  Title. .Length . . . . Magazine, Date, Page

Prison in Space. .s . . . .
. . . . Amz Aug 43 58
Sammy Calls a Noobus. .s . . . . . .
. . . . .FA Jan 43 220
NOWLAN, PHIL(IP FRANCIS) *See
also pseud FRANK PHILLIPS (1)*
Biog sketch, photo. . . . .
. . . . FA Feb 40 86
Obituary, photo . . . FA Jun 40 134
Airlords of Han, The. .nt . . . . . .
. . . . Amz Mar 29 1106
Armageddon–2419 A.D. . . . . . .
. .nt . . . . Amz Aug 28 422
"BUCK ROGERS" series includes:
ARMAGEDDON–2419 A.D.
THE AIRLORDS OF HAN
Prince of Mars Returns, The . . . .
. .n 2 pt . . . . FA Feb 40 28
Space Guards. .nt . . . .
. . . . .ASF May 40 9
Time Jumpers, The. .s . . . .
. . . . Amz Feb 34 108

O

OBERFIELD, WILLIAM
Enormous Word, The. .s . . . . . .
. . . . PS Sum 50 43
Escape from Pluto. .s . . . .
. . . . PS Fal 47 84
O'BRIEN, DAVID WRIGHT *See also
pseuds ALEXANDER BLADE (h)
(?), JOHN YORK CABOT (34),
BRUCE DENNIS (2), DUNCAN
FARNSWORTH (18), CLEE
GARSON (8), RICHARD
VARDON (1)*
Biog sketch . . . . . Amz Apr 40 135
Biog sketch, Photo. . . . .
. . . . Amz Nov 40 138
Beauty and the Beasties, The . . . .
. .s . . . . FA Dec 41 86
Beyond the Time Door. .s . . . . . .
. . . . FA Mar 41 90
Bring Back My Body. .s . . . .
. . . . Amz Mar 43 116
Christopher Crissom's Cravat . . . .
. .nt . . . . .FA May 46 70
Creegar Dares to Die. .n . . . . . .
. . . . FA Aug 42 88
Curious Coat, The. .s . . . .
. . . . FA May 43 130
Devil's Planet, The. .n. . . . .
. . . . Amz Sep 43 108

AUTHOR
  Title. .Length . . . . Magazine, Date, Page

Ferdinand Finknodle's Perfect
  Day. .s. . . . . Amz Sep 41 74
Fish Men of Venus. .nt . . . .
  . . . . Amz Apr 40 30
Floating Robot, The. .nt. . . . . . .
  . . . . FA Jan 41 10
Furlough from Eternity. .n . . . . .
  . . . . FA Apr 43 144
Hokum Hotel. .nt . . . FA Jul 42 184
Incredible Mr. Kismet, The . . . . .
  . .s . . . . FA Jun 42 94
Living Manikins, The. .nt . . . . . .
  . . . . FA Feb 42 66
Man Who Lived Next Week,
  The. .nt . . . . Amz Mar 41 46
Mister Anonymous. .nt. . . . . . .
  . . . . FA Dec 45 108
Mister Trouble. .s . . .FA Jan 43 106
Painting of the Prophet. .s. . . . .
  . . . . .FA May 47 74
Pegasus Plays Priorities. .nt . . . .
  . . . . FA Dec 42 102
Periscope Prey. .s. . . . .
  . . . . Amz Apr 43 216
Place Is Familiar, The. .nt . . . . . .
  . . . . FA Feb 44 50
Private Prune Speaking. .nt . . . . .
  . . . . Amz Sep 44 62
Resurrection from Hell. .s . . . . .
  . . . . FA Sep 42 172
Return of Joan of Arc. .s . . . . . .
  . . . . FA May 42 224
Room With a View. .nt. . . . . . .
  . . . . Amz May 46 112
Secret of the Lost Planet. .nt . . . .
  . . . . Amz May 41 152
Skidmore's Strange Experiment . .
  . .s . . . . .Amz Jan 41 124
Softly Silken Wallet, The. .s. . . . .
  . . . . FA Jul 46 128
Spook for Yourself. .s . . . .
  . . . . FA Jan 42 70
Squadron of the Damned. .nt. . . .
  . . . . .Amz Jul 42 114
Stenton's Shadow. .s . . . .
  . . . . FA Jun 43 56
Strange Voyage of Hector Squinch,
  The. .nt . . . . FA Aug 40 58
Suicide Squadrons of Space. .nt . .
  . . . . Amz Aug 40 6
10 Seconds from Nowhere. .s. . . .
  . . . . .Amz Jul 41 96
Trapped on Titan. .s. . . . .
  . . . . Amz Jun 40 68
Treasure Trove in Time. .s . . . . .
  . . . . Amz Nov 40 44

Truth Is a Plague. .s . . . .
  . . . . Amz Feb 40 58
Yesterday's Clock. .nt . . . .
  . . . . FA Feb 43 106
with WILLIAM P. McGIVERN
John Brown's Body. .s . . . .
  . . . . Amz May 40 112
Mr. Muddle Does As He
  Pleases. .nt . . . . . Amz Aug 41 64
Victory in the Void. .nt . . . .
  . . . . Amz Mar 43 158
O'BRIEN, DEAN D. pseud of EARL
  BINDER and OTTO BINDER in
  collaboration
Guyon 45X. .s . . . . .SSS Mar 40 40
O'BRIEN, E. G. pseud of ARTHUR
  C. CLARKE
Fires Within, The. .s. . . . .
  . . . . Fant Aug 47 72
O'BRIEN, FITZ-JAMES
Diamond Lens, The. .s . . . .
  . . . . Amz Dec 26 834
                       Amz Oct 33 600
Lost Room, The. .s . . . .
  . . . . S&SF Fal 49 47
What Was It?. .s. . . . .
  . . . . FFM Dec 49 106
Wondersmith, The. .nt . . . .
  . . . . F&SF Dec 50 52
O'DONNELL, JOHN SHAMUS
Naval Control. .s . . . .
  . . . . AQ Win 32 141
O'DONNELL, LAWRENCE pseud
  of C. L. MOORE and occasionally
  HENRY KUTTNER
by HENRY KUTTNER
This is the House. .s . . . .
  . . . . ASF Feb 46 80
by HENRY KUTTNER and C. L.
  MOORE
Fury. .n 3 pt . . . . . .ASF May 47 6
by C. L. MOORE
Children's Hour, The. .nt . . . . . .
  . . . . ASF Mar 44 86
Clash by Night. .n . . . .
  . . . . ASF Mar 43 9
Code, The. .nt. . . . .
  . . . . .ASF Jul 45 7
Heir Apparent. .nt . . . .
  . . . . .ASF Jul 50 19
Paradise Street. .nt. . . . .
  . . . . ASF Sep 50 63
Promised Land. .nt . . . .
  . . . . ASF Feb 50 137
Vintage Season. .s . . . .
  . . . . ASF Sep 46 54

OFFENBECKER, LARRY
Mutiny. .s . . . . .PS Fal 45 29
OGDEN, H. B.
Weapon, The. .s. . . .SSS May 42 115
OGE-MAKE
Fire Trail, The. .s. . .Amz Jan 48 128
                       FA Jan 48 66
O'HARA, KENNETH pseud of
  BRYCE WALTON
O'HEARN, MARIAN
Soldiers of the Black Goat. .n . . .
  . . . . UK Jan 40 9
Spark of Allah, The. .nt 3 pt . . . .
  . . . . .UK Jul 40 129
OHMERT J. G.
Celestial Pioneers. .nt . . . .
  . . . . .AQ Spr–Sum 33 538
OLES, FLOYD
Hoffman's Widow. .s . . . .
  . . . . Amz Feb 36 112
OLIVER, CHAD
Biog sketch . . . . . . PS Spr 44 113
Land of Lost Content, The . . . . .
  . .s . . . . .SSS Nov 50 74
OLIVER, OWEN
Platinum. .s . . . . . . FN Sep 49 114
OLSEN, ALFRED JOHN, JR. See
  pseud BOB OLSEN (27)
OLSEN, BOB pseud of ALFRED
  JOHN OLSEN, JR.
Ant With the Human Soul, The . .
  . .nt . . . . . . .AQ Spr–Sum 32 230
Captain Brink of the Space
  Marines. .s . . . . . Amz Nov 32 722
Cosmic Trash. .ss. . . . .
  . . . . SW Apr 30 1014
Crime Crusher, The. .nt . . . .
  . . . . Amz Jun 33 255
Educated Pill, The. .s . . . .
  . . . . .Amz Jul 28 365
Flight in 1999. .s . . . .
  . . . . AW Sep 29 256
Four Dimensional Auto-Parker,
  The. .s. . . . . . . .Amz Jul 34 113
Four Dimensional Escape,
  The. .s. . . . . . . Amz Dec 33 44
Four Dimensional Robberies . . . .
  . .s . . . . Amz May 28 102
Four-Dimensional Roller-Press,
  The. .s. . . . . . . Amz Jun 27 302
Four Dimensional Surgery. .s. . . .
  . . . . Amz Feb 28 1078
Four Dimensional Transit . . . . . .
  . .nt . . . . .AQ Fal 28 530
Isle of Juvenescence, The. .nt. . . .
  . . . . Amz Jun 36 42

AUTHOR
   Title. .Length . . . . Magazine, Date, Page

Man Who Annexed the Moon,
   The. .nt . . . . . Amz Feb 31 1026
Master of Mystery, The. .nt . . . . .
   . . . . Amz Oct 31 626
Noekken of Norway. .s . . . .
   . . . . Amz Nov 34 61
Out Robot Maid. .ss . . . .
   . . . . Fut Nov 40 72
Peril Among the Drivers. .nt . . . .
   . . . . Amz Mar 34 36
Phantom Teleview, The. .s. . . . . .
   . . . . SW Nov 29 486
                        SS Mar 40 92
Pool of Death, The. .nt . . . .
   . . . . .Amz Jan 33 890
Purple Monsters, The. .s . . . .
   . . . . Amz Aug 32 458
Rhythm Rides the Rocket. .s . . . .
   . . . . .SF Oct 40 28
Scourge of a Single Cell, The . . . .
   . .s . . . . SF Mar 40 56
Seven Sunstrokes. .nt . . . .
   . . . . Amz Apr 32 16
Six-Legged Gangsters. .s . . . .
   . . . . Amz Jun 35 98
Space Marines and the Slavers,
   The. .nt . . . . . . Amz Dec 36 61
Superperfect Bride, The. .s . . . . .
   . . . . .Amz Jul 29 300
OLSEN, JAMES P.
   Cavern World, The. .s . . . .
      . . . . .ASF Jun 30 340
ONIONS, OLIVER
   Rooum. .s . . . .
      . . . . .S&SF Fal 49 95
ORBAN artist
   Covers for ASTOUNDING SCIENCE
      FICTION
   Dec 1948
   May, Sep 1949
ORLOVSKY, V.
   Revolt of the Atoms, The . . . . . .
      . .s . . . . Amz Apr 29 6
ORNDORFF, FRANK
   Terrors of the Upper Air,
      The. .s . . . . AQ Win 28 138
ORTH, BENNINGTON pseud of
   ROGER SHERMAN HOAR
OSBORNE, CHESTER G.
   Tone Machine, The. .s . . . .
      . . . . WS May 34 1134
OSBORNE, RICHARDSON (in ToC)
OSBORNE, ROBERTSON (on Story)
   Action on Azura. .nt . . . .
      . . . . PS Fal 49 78

AUTHOR
   Title. .Length . . . . Magazine, Date, Page

OTT, ANTHONY B.
   Biological Barrier, The. .s . . . . . .
      . . . . FA Nov 49 64
   Revolt in Pacifico. .s . . . .
      . . . . .FA Jan 50 120
OVERHOLSER, WAYNE D.
   Meet My Brother—Mr.
      Ghost! ..s . . . . . . Uc Apr 41 101
OVERTON, MAX pseud of DON
   WILCOX
   Deadly Yappers, The. .s . . . .
      .FA Sep 42 92
   Robotcycle for Two. .s . . . .
      . . . . Amz Sep 42 130
OWEN, FRANK
   Golden Hour of Kwoh Fan,
      The. .s . . . . AFR #11 22
   Silent Trees, The. .s . . . .
      . . . . .AFR #3 19
   Study in Amber, A. .s . . . .
      . . . . .AFR #5 100
OWEN, HUGH pseud of FREDERICK
   FAUST
OWEN, LESLIE
   Tomorrow's Mail. .s . . . .
      . . . . FA Mar 43 204
OWENS, LEE
   FABLES FROM THE FUTURE dept
      of fillers. .once only . . . .
         . . . . FA Mar 50 156
   FACTS OF THE FUTURE dept of
      fillers. .once only . . . .
         . . . . FA Feb 50 156
   FANTASTIC FACTS dept of
      fillers. .irregularly from . . . .
         . . . . FA Mar 48 170

P

PACE, TOM
   Death Star. .s . . . . . . .PS Spr 45 77
   Example. .ss . . . . . . .PS Win 46 73
PADGETT, LEWIS pseud of HENRY
   KUTTNER & C. L. MOORE
   "BALDY" series includes:
   THE PIPER'S SON
   THREE BLIND MICE
   THE LION AND THE UNICORN
   BEGGARS IN VELVET
   Beggars in Velvet. .nt . . . .
      . . . . ASF Dec 45 7
   Camouflage. .nt. . . .ASF Sep 45 135
   Cure, The. .s . . . . . ASF May 46 25
   Deadlock. .s . . . . . . ASF Aug 42 54

AUTHOR
   Title. .Length . . . . Magazine, Date, Page

   Endowment Policy. .s. . . . .
      . . . . ASF Aug 43 118
   Ex Machina. .nt. . . . ASF Apr 48 7
   Fairy Chessmen, The . . . .
      . .n 2 pt . . . . ASF Jan 46 7
   "GALLOWAY GALLEGHER"
      series includes:
      TIME LOCKER
      THE WORLD IS MINE
      THE PROUD ROBOT
      GALLEGHER PLUS
      EX MACHINA
   Gallegher Plus. .nt . . . .
      . . . . ASF Nov 43 120
   Iron Standard, The. .nt . . . .
      . . . . ASF Dec 43 74
   Jesting Pilot. .s . . . .
      . . . . ASF May 47 79
   Line to Tomorrow. .s . . . .
      . . . . ASF Nov 45 54
   Lion and the Unicorn, The . . . . .
      . .nt . . . . ASF Jul 45 144
   Margin for Error. .nt . . . .
      . . . . ASF Nov 47 129
   Mimsy Were the Borogoves . . . . .
      . .nt . . . . ASF Feb 43 52
   Open Secret. .s . . . . ASF Apr 43 33
   Piggy Bank. .nt . . . .
      . . . . ASF Dec 42 114
   Piper's Son, The. .nt . . . .
      . . . . .ASF Feb 45 6
   Prisoner in the Skull, The . . . . . .
      . .nt . . . . ASF Feb 49 100
   Private Eye. .nt . . . .
      . . . . ASF Jan 49 7
   Project. .s . . . . ASF Apr 47 74
   Proud Robot, The. .nt . . . .
      . . . . ASF Oct 43 95
   Rain Check. .s . . . . . ASF Jul 46 47
   Shock. .s . . . . ASF Mar 43 40
   Three Blind Mice. .nt . . . .
      . . . . ASF Jun 45 68
   Time Enough. .s . . . .
      . . . . ASF Dec 46 124
   Time Locker. .s . . . ASF JAn 43 100
   Tomorrow and Tomorrow. . . . . .
      . .n 2 pt . . . . ASF Jan 47 6
   Twonky, The. .s . . . ASF Sep 42 34
   We Kill People. .s . . . .
      . . . . ASF Mar 46 82
   What You Need. .s . . . .
      . . . . .ASF Oct 45 133
   When the Bough Breaks. .nt . . . . .
      . . . . ASF Nov 44 75
   World Is Mine, The. .nt . . . .
      . . . . ASF Jun 43 9

AUTHOR
Title. .Length . . . . Magazine, Date, Page

PAETZKE, ROY
Earth's Maginot Line. .ss. . . . . . .
. .Com May 41 119
PAGE, NORVELL W.
But Without Horns. .n . . . .
. . . . UK Jun 40 9
Flame Winds. .n . . . . UK Jun 39 9
Sons of the Bear-God. .n. . . . . . .
. . . . .UK Nov 39 9
PALLANT, NORMAN C.
Three Suns, The. .s . . . .
. . . . Fant Aug 47 56
PALMER, RAYMOND A. *See also
pseuds HENRY GADE (h) (3),
G. H. IRWIN (h) (2), FRANK
PATTON (h) (6), WALLACE
QUITMAN (1), ALFRED R.
STEBER (h) (6), MORRIS J.
STEELE (h) (3), RAE WINTERS
(0)*
Editor of AMAZING STORIES
Jun 38 *thru* Dec 49 *issues*
*Editor of FANTASTIC
ADVENTURES*
May 39 *(first) thru* Dec 49 *issues*
*Editor OTHER WORLDS
(anonymously in the first issue;
credited from the second issue)*
Nov 49—
Editor IMAGINATION
Oct 50 *and* Dec 50
Catalyst Planet. .s . . .TW Aug 38 65
Matter Is Conserved. .s . . . .
. . . . ASF Apr 38 27
Symphony of Death, The. .s . . . . .
. . . . Amz Dec 35 92
Three from the Test Tube. .s . . . .
. . . . WS Nov 36 674
Time Ray of Jandra, The. .s. . . . .
. . . . WS Jun 30 46
Time Tragedy, The. .s. . . . .
. . . . WS Dec 34 822
PALMER, STUART
Bride for the Devil, A. .s . . . .
. . . . .F&SF Fal 49 87
PARKE, WALTER *artist*
Cover for AMAZING STORIES
Jul 1946
*Cover for FANTASTIC
ADVENTURES*
Feb 1946
**PARKER, HARRY D., A.S.M.E.,
S.O.A.E.**
4th-Dimensional Possibilities . . . .
. .a . . . . ASF Dec 36 115

Gravitational Deflector, The . . . .
. .s . . . . WQ Fal 29 130
PARKER, HUGH FRAZIER
Sword of Johnny Damokles,
The. .s. . . . . .PS Mar 43 24
PARKES, WYNDHAM *pseud of
JOHN B. HARRIS*
Child of Power. .s . . . .
. . . . Fant #3 39 89
PARKHURST *artist*
Covers for PLANET STORIES
Fal, Win 1944
Spr, Sum, Fal, Win 1945
Spr, 1946
PARKINSON, R. D.
Rays from the Asteroid, The . . . .
. .WS Nov 35 695
PARLETT, ARTHUR C. (JR.)
Maxwell's Demon and Monsieur
Ranque. .a . . . . . .ASF Jan 50 105
9F[19]. .a . . . . ASF Apr 49 146
This Is Hot! . .a . . . . ASF Jul 50 94
PARNELL, FRANCIS *pseud of
FESTUS PRAGNELL*
Monsters of the Moon. .s. . . . . .
. . . . .ToW #1 37 66
PASSANTE, DOM
Across the Ages. .s. . . . .
. . . . Fut Oct 41 87
Men Without a World. .s . . . . . .
. . . . SF Mar 40 8
Moon Heaven. .nt . . . .SF Jun 39 64
PATTEE *artist*
*Cover for ASTOUNDING SCIENCE
FICTION*
Nov 1950
PATTON, FRANK *house pseud used
mostly by RAYMOND A.
PALMER*
by RAYMOND A. PALMER
Doorway to Hell. .n 2 pt. . . . . . .
. . . . .FA Feb 42 8
Jewels of the Toad. .s. . . . .
. . . . .FA Oct 43 8
Mahaffey's Mystery. .s . . . .
. . . . OW Mar 50 122
Patriot Never Dies, A. .nt . . . . . .
. . . . Amz Aug 43 12
Test Tube Girl, The. .nt . . . .
. . . . Amz Jan 42 8
War Worker 17. .s . . . .
. . . . Amz Sep 43 72
by RICHARD S. SHAVER
When the Moon Bounced. .nt. . . .
. . . . .Amz May 49 58

Authors' real names unknown
Biog sketch, photo. . . . .
. . . . Amz Sep 43 87
Biog sketch, photo. . . . .
. . . . FA Oct 43 199
Astral Assassin. .s . . . .
. . . . .Amz Jul 43 192
Cloak of Satan. .s . . . .
. . . . FA Dec 43 136
PATZER, SYDNEY
Great Invasion, The. .s . . . .
. . . . .WQ Sum 31 552
Lunar Consul, The. .n 2 pt . . . . .
. . . . WS Nov 33 294
PAUL, FRANK R. *artist*
Biog sketch, photo. . . . .
. . . . .WS Jan 33 668
Biog sketch, photo. . . . .
. . . . TW Jun 39 87
*Covers for AIR WONDER
STORIES*
Jul, Aug, Sep, Oct, Nov, Dec
1929
Jan, Feb, Mar, Apr, May 1930
Covers for AMAZING STORIES
Apr, May, Jun, Jul, Aug, Sep, Oct,
Nov, Dec 1926
Jan, Feb, Mar, Apr, May, Jun, Jul,
Aug, Sep, Oct, Nov, Dec 1927
Jan, Feb, Mar, Apr, May, Jun, Jul,
Aug, Sep, Oct, Nov, Dec 1928
Jan, Feb, Mar, Apr, May, Jun 1929
*Cover for AMAZING STORIES
ANNUAL*
1927
*Covers for AMAZING STORIES
QUARTERLY*
Win, Spr, Sum, Fal 1928
Win, Spr, Sum 1929
Covers for COMET
Jan, May 1941
*Cover for DYNAMIC SCIENCE
STORIES*
Feb 1939
*Covers for FAMOUS FANTASTIC
MYSTERIES*
Apr, May–Jun, Dec 1940
*Cover for FANTASTIC
ADVENTURES*
Apr 1940
Cover for FANTASTIC NOVELS
Sep 1940
Covers for FUTURE FICTION
Nov 1940
Apr 1941

AUTHOR
Title. .Length . . . . Magazine, Date, Page

*Cover for MARVEL SCIENCE
    STORIES*
Nov 1938
Cover for PLANET STORIES
Fal 1940
Covers for SCIENCE FICTION
Mar, Jun, Aug, Oct, Dec 1939
Mar, Jun, Oct 1940
Jan, Mar, Jun, Sep 1941
*Covers for SCIENCE FICTION
    QUARTERLY*
Win, Spr, Sum 1941
*Covers for SCIENCE WONDER
    STORIES*
Jun, Jul, Aug, Sep, Oct, Nov, Dec
    1929
Jan, Feb, Mar, Apr, May 1930
*Cover for SCIENTIFIC DETECTIVE
    MONTHLY*
Apr 1930
Covers for WONDER STORIES
Jul, Aug, Sep, Oct, Nov, Dec 1930
Jan, Feb, Mar, Apr, May, Jun, Jul,
    Aug, Sep, Oct, Nov, Dec 1931
Jan, Feb, Mar, Apr, May, Jun, Jul,
    Aug, Sep, Oct, Dec 1932
Jan, Feb, Mar, Apr, May, Jun, Aug,
    Oct, Nov, Dec 1933
Jan, Feb, Mar, Apr, May, Jun, Jul,
    Aug, Sep, Oct, Nov, Dec 1934
Jan, Feb, Mar, Apr, May, Jun, Jul,
    Aug, Sep, Oct, Nov–Dec 1935
Jan–Feb, Mar–Apr 1936
*Covers for SCIENCE WONDER
    QUARTERLY*
Fal 1929
Win, Spr 1930
*Covers for WONDER STORIES
    QUARTERLY*
Sum, Fal 1930
Win, Spr, Sum, Fal 1931
Win, Spr, Sum, Fal 1932
Win 1933
As Mars Sees Us. .bacover pic. . . .
. . . . .Amz Jul 40
As Mars Sees Us. .Bacover pic . . .
. . . . Amz Mar 42
"CITY" series includes:
A City on Mars. .bacover. . . . . .
. . . . Amz Dec 40
A City on Venus. .bacover. . . . .
. . . . .Amz Jan 41
A City on Jupiter. .bacover . . . .
. . . . Amz Feb 41
A City on Neptune. .bacover . . .
. . . . Amz Mar 41

A City on Uranus. .bacover . . . .
. . . . Amz Apr 41
A City on Pluto. .bacover . . . . .
. . . . Amz Jun 41
A City on Io. .bacover pic . . . . .
. . . . .Amz Jul 41
A City on Saturn. .bacover . . . .
. . . . Amz Aug 41
A City on Mercury. .bacover . . .
. . . . Amz Sep 41
A City on the Moon. . . . .
. .bacover. . . . . . . Amz Oct 41
A City on Titan. .bacover . . . . .
. . . . Amz Nov 41
A City on Callisto. .bacover. . . .
. . . . Amz Dec 41
A City on Europa. .bacover . . . .
. . . . .Amz Jan 42
A City on Ganymede . . . .
. .bacover. . . . . . . Amz Feb 42
Future City on Earth . . . .
. .bacover. . . . . . . Amz Apr 42
Future Space Suit . . . .
. .bacover. . . . . . . Amz Jun 39
"LIFE ON. . ." series includes:
Life on Mercury . . . .
. .bacover pic . . . . . FA Sep 39
Life on Saturn . . . .
. .bacover pic . . . . . FA Nov 39
Life on Jupiter . . . .
. .bacover pic . . . . . .FA Jan 40
Life on Pluto. .bacover pic . . . .
. . . . FA Feb 40
Life on Neptune . . . .
. .bacover pic . . . . . FA Mar 40
Life on Uranus . . . .
. .bacover pic . . . . . FA Apr 40
Life on Io. .bacover pic. . . . . . .
. . . . FA May 40
Life on Callisto . . . .
. .bacover. . . . . . . Amz Aug 40
Life on Europa . . . .
. . . bacover pic . . . Amz Sep 40
Life on Ganymede. . . . .
. .bacover. . . . . . . Amz Oct 40
Life on Titan . . . .
. .bacover pic . . . . Amz Nov 40
Man from Mars, The. . . . .
. .bacover. . . . . FA May 39
Man from Venus, The. . . . .
. .bacover. . . . . .FA Jul 39
"MYTHOLOGY" series includes:
Zeus–The Thunder God . . . . . .
. . . . .FA Jul 42
Vulcan–God of Heavy Industry .
. .bacover pic . . . . . FA Aug 42

Atlas–The God of Strength. . . .
. . . . FA Sep 42
Perseus–Slayer of the
    Medusa. .bacover pic . . . . . .
. . . . FA Oct 42
Prometheus. .bacover pic . . . . .
. . . . FA Nov 42
Apollo–God of Hygiene . . . . . .
. . . . FA Dec 42
Mercury, God of the Winged
    Sandals. .bacover pic . . . . . .
. . . . .FA Jan 43
Icarus and Daedalus, First
    Aviators. .bacover pic. . . . . .
. . . . FA Feb 43
Phaeton, Son of Apollo . . . . . .
. .bacover. . . . . FA Mar 43
Hercules–The God of
    Strength. .bacover pic. . . . . .
. . . . FA Apr 43
The Sphinx of Thebes . . . .
. .bacover pic . . . . . FA Oct 43
Jason–The Superman. . . . .
. .bacover pic . . . . . FA Apr 44
Bellerphon and the Chimera . . .
. . . . FA Jun 44
New York Invaded. . . . .
. .bacover pic . . . . . Amz May 41
"STORIES OF THE STARS"
Canis Major, The Great Dog. . . .
. . . . Amz Feb 43
Vega, In Lyra, The Harp . . . . . .
. .bacover pic . . . . . Amz Apr 43
Procyon, In Canis Minor . . . . . .
. .bacover pic . . . . . Amz May 43
The Great Nebula in Orion . . . .
. . . . Amz Jun 43
Rigel. .bacover pic . . . .
. . . . Amz Aug 43
Betelgeuse, In Orion. . . . .
. .bacover pic . . . . . Amz Sep 44
Spica. .bacover pic. . . Amz Mar 45
Gemini. .bacover pic . . .FA Jul 45
Great Nebula in
    Andromeda . . . . FA Oct 45
Aldebaran. .bacover pic . . . . . .
. . . . FA Dec 45
Alphecca. .bacover pic . . . .
. . . . FA Feb 46
Mizar in Ursa Major . . . .
. .bacover pic . . . . . .FA May 46
Antares in Scorpius . . . .
. .bacover. . . . . .FA Jul 46
Altair (Constellation of
    Aquila). .bacover pic . . . . . .
. . . . Amz Aug 46

AUTHOR
Title. .Length . . . . Magazine, Date, Page

PAUL, HERB
Angel with Purple Hair,
The. .s . . . . F&SF Dec 50 85
PAYNE, PAUL L.
Editor PLANET STORIES
Fal 46 *thru* Spr 50 *issues*
PEACOCK, W.(ILBUR) S.(COTT)
Biog sketch . . . . . . PS Aug 42 51
Editor of PLANET STORIES
Fal 42 *thru* Fal 45 *issues*
Chimera World. .s . . . .PS Win 44 62
Destination–Death. .s . . . .
. . . . .PS Win 43 51
Life Cycle. .ss . . . . . .SF Oct 40 72
Planet of No-Return. .s . . . .
. . . . .PS Win 42 28
Prey of the Space Falcon . . . . . .
. .nt . . . . PS Fal 43 2
Spider Men of Gharr. .nt . . . . . .
. . . . PS Sum 45 54
Thing of Venus, The. .s . . . .
. . . . PS Spr 42 66
Too Perfect. .s . . . . . Fut Feb 43 60
Uranian Justice. .ss . . . .
. . . . .CF Fal 40 104
Victory of Klon, The. .s . . . .
. . . . PS Fal 41 46
PEARCE, GEORGE P.
Girl and the Glacier, The. .s . . . . .
. . . . Amz May 33 170
PEARSON, MARTIN *pseud of*
DONALD A. WOLLHEIM
"*AJAX CLAKINS*" *series includes:*
POGO PLANET
DESTINY WORLD
NYE DAY
AJAX OF AJAX
Ajax of Ajax. .s . . . . .Fut Aug 42 40
Cosmos Eye. .s . . . .SFQ Spr 41 101
Destiny World. .s . . . .
. . . . Fut Dec 41 70
Embassy, The. .s . . . ASF Mar 42 72
Hidden Conflict, The. .s . . . .
. . . . SFQ Fal 42 115
Key to the Dark Planet, The . . . .
. .s . . . . Fut Dec 42 10
Millionth Year, The. .s . . . .
. . . . SF Apr 43 55
Mimic. .s . . . . .Ash Dec 42 58
Mye Day. .s . . . . . . Fut Apr 42 30
Nothing. .ss . . . . . . Ash Oct 42 56
Planet Called Aquella, The . . . . .
. .ss . . . . .SSS Nov 42 115
Planet Passage. .ss . . . .
. . . . Fut Oct 42 39
Pogo Planet. .s . . . . . Fut Oct 41 82

AUTHOR
Title. .Length . . . . Magazine, Date, Page

Second Satellite, The. .s . . . .
. . . . .Fut Feb 43 10
So You Want To Be a
Space-Flier? . .a . . .Cos May 41 116
Unfinished City, The. .ss . . . .
. . . . Sti Mar 42 60
Up There. .ss . . . . .SFQ Sum 42 85
World on the Edge of the Universe,
The. .s . . . . SFQ Sum 41 133
PEASE, LT. JOHN *pseud of ROGER*
SHERMAN HOAR
Biog sketch . . . . Amz Jun 38 7
Horror's Head. .s . . . Amz Oct 38 42
Invisible Bomber, The. .s . . . . . .
. . . . Amz Jun 38 130
PEASE, M. C.
Convergence to Death. .s . . . . .
. . . . .ASF Jul 49 60
Devious Weapon. .s . . . .
. . . . ASF Apr 49 34
Reversion. .s . . . . . .ASF Jan 50 45
PECHTEL, CURTIS
Miracle of Dr. Beaujean . . . .
. .s . . . . .FA Jan 45 176
PELCHER, ANTHONY
Invisible Death. .s . . . .
. . . . .ASF Jan 30 118
Mad Music. .s . . . . ASF Feb 30 248
Soulless Entity. .s . . . .
. . . . .WS Jan 31 844
Vampires of Venus. .s . . . .
. . . . ASF Apr 30 47
PELKIE, J. W.
Biog sketch, photo. . . . .
. . . . FA Oct 45 2
In the Sphere of Time. .nt . . . . . .
. . . . PS Sum 48 76
King of the Dinosaurs. .n . . . .
. . . . FA Oct 45 6
Toka and the Man Bats. .n . . . . . .
. . . . FA Feb 46 108
Toka Fights the Big Cats. .n . . . . .
. . . . FA Dec 47 8
PELLETIER, E. E.
What's New? . .s . . . .FA Jul 45 110
"Wa–al, Bust Mah Britches!" . . . .
. .s . . . . Amz Apr 48 30
PENDRAY, G. EDWARDS *See pseud*
GAWAIN EDWARDS
PENNY, RICHARD
with JEROME GROSS
Emperors of Space. .s . . . .
. . . . WS Nov 31 762
PERDUE, ELMER
Swing Low. .ss . . . .
. . . . .Sti Apr 41 119

AUTHOR
Title. .Length . . . . Magazine, Date, Page

PEREGOY, CALVIN *pseud of*
THOMAS CALVERT McCLARY
Dr. Conklin–Pacifist. .s . . . .
. . . . ASF Aug 34 34
Short–Wave Castle. .s . . . .
. . . . ASF Feb 34 47
Shortwave Experiment. .s . . . . . .
. . . . ASF Feb 35 83
Terrible Sense, The. .s . . . .
. . . . ASF Aug 38 99
PERIL, MILTON R.
Dynasty of the Blue-Black Rays,
The. . . . . Amz Oct 30 634
Lost City, The. .n 3 pt . . . .
. . . . .Amz May 34 10
Radium Doom, The. .nt . . . .
. . . . Amz Dec 37 90
PERRI, LESLIE *pseud of DORIS*
WILSON
Space Episode. .ss . . . .
. . . . Fut Dec 41 106
PERRY, JAMES D.
Death Between the Planets. .s . . .
. . . . WS Nov 33 342
Waters Under the Earth, The . . . .
. .s . . . . .SSS Feb 42 82
PETERS, WOODS
Great Catastrophe of 2947,
The. .s . . . . Amz May 31 166
When Inca-Land Revolted. .s . . . .
. . . . Amz Aug 30 458
PETERSON, JOHN VICTOR *See also*
pseud VICTOR VALDING (1)
Lie on the Beam. .s . . . .
. . . . Com Mar 41 105
Lightning's Course, The. .s . . . . .
. . . . Com Jan 41 4
Martyrs Don't Mind Dying . . . . .
. .s . . . . ASF Mar 38 97
Ra for the Rajah. .s . . . .
. . . . ASF May 38 108
Reinmuth Rider, The. .s . . . .
. . . . TW Jun 39 31
PETERSON, PHYLLIS LEE
Pamela Pays the Piper. .s . . . . . .
. . . . .F&SF Fal 50 60
PETAJA, EMIL (Theodore) *See also*
pseud THEODORE PINE (0)
Biog sketch, photo. . . . .
. . . . Amz Jun 43 198
Ancestral Thread, The. .s . . . . . .
. . . . Amz May 47 20
Dinosaur Goes Hollywood. .s . . . .
. . . . Amz Nov 42 122
Man Who Hated War, The. .s . . . .
. . . . Amz Dec 44 24

AUTHOR
Title. .Length . . . . Magazine, Date, Page

Me the People. .s . . . .
. . . . Amz Jun 43 116
Midas Morgan's Golden Touch . . .
. .s . . . . Amz May 44 162
Time Will Tell. .s . . . .
. . . . Amz Jun 42 94
PETTICOLAS, ARTHUR
Dinosaur Destroyer. .n . . . .
. . . . Amz Jan 49 8
PHELAN, JEREMIAH *pseud of*
C. DALY KING
PHILLIPS A.(LEXANDER) (M.)
Beast of the Island. .nt . . . .
. . . . Amz Sep 39 8
Chapter from the Beginning, A. . .
. .s . . . . ASF Mar 40 84
Death of the Moon, The. .s . . . . .
. . . . Amz Feb 29 1024
Enemy of Knowledge, An. .n. . . .
. . . . ASF Apr 47 114
Extra Bricklayer, The. .s. . . . . . .
. . . . UK Sep 40 85
Martian Gesture. .nt. . . . .
. . . . WS Oct 35 560
SS Jan 49 112
Mislaid Charm, The. .n . . . .
. . . . .UK Feb 41 9
Revolt. .nt . . . .
. . . . ASF Apr 39 89
Space Flame, The. .s . . . .
. . . . .PS Spr 40 84
Time-Travel Happens. .a . . . .
. . . . UK Dec 39 112
PHILLIPS, FRANK *pseud of PHIL*
NOWLAN
Onslaught from Venus, The. . . . .
. .nt . . . . SW Sep 29 326
PHILLIPS, PETER *Ziff-Davis may*
have used this as a house name. At
press time, no information was
available on the author of the
stories appearing elsewhere.
Dreams Are Sacred. .nt . . . .
. . . . ASF Sep 48 51
Manna. .nt . . . . . . ASF Feb 49 62
P–Plus. .nt . . . .
. . . . ASF Aug 49 112
Plagiarist. .s . . . . . NW Sum 50 54
Unknown Quantity. .s . . . .
. . . . .NW #5 49 54
"Well I'll Be Hexed". .nt. . . . . . .
. . . . FA Aug 50 90
PHILLIPS, ROG *pseud of ROGER P.*
GRAHAM
Biog sketch, photo. . . . .
. . . . .Amz May 46 2

CLUB HOUSE, THE dept of fanzine
reviews and fan news, irregular
from . . . . Amz Mar 48 160
And Eve Was. .nt. . . . .
. . . . Amz Nov 47 60
Atom War. .s . . . . Amz May 46 74
Awakening, The. .s . . . .
. . . . Amz Aug 49 6
Battle of the Gods. .nt . . . .
. . . . Amz Sep 46 78
Beyond the Matrix of Time . . . . .
. .nt . . . . Amz Nov 49 38
Can Opener, The. .s . . . .
. . . . FA Jan 49 86
Cube Root of Conquest, The . . . .
. .s . . . . Amz Oct 48 6
Despoilers, The. .nt . . . .
. . . . Amz Oct 47 78
Detour from Tomorrow . . . .
. .s . . . . FA Mar 50 34
Dual Personality. .nt . . . .
. . . . FA Sep 46 150
Fatal Technicality, The. .s. . . . . .
. . . . .OW Mar 50 56
Hate. .nt . . . . Amz Jan 48 50
High Ears. .nt . . . . FA Oct 47 142
Holes In My Head. .s . . . .
. . . . OW Oct 50 54
House, The. .s. . . . Amz Feb 47 140
"If You Were Me. . .". .s . . . . . .
. . . . Amz Jun 50 86
Incompatible. .s . . . . FA Sep 49 84
Involuntary Immortals, The. . . . .
. .n . . . . FA Dec 49 8
Let Freedom Ring. .nt . . . .
. . . . Amz Dec 45 124
Lost Bomb, The. .nt. . . . .
. . . . .Amz May 50 70
Love My Robot. .s . . . SS Nov 50 97
Matrix. .n. . . . . . . Amz Oct 49 22
M'Bong–Ah. .n . . . . Amz Feb 49 8
Miracle of Elmer Wilde, The . . . .
. .nt . . . . .OW Nov 49 84
Mutants, The. .nt. . . . .
. . . . .Amz Jul 46 40
One for the Robot—Two for the
Same. .nt . . . . . . .Im Oct 50 58
Planet of the Dead. .nt . . . .
. . . . FA Oct 49 36
Pranksters, The. .s . . . .
. . . . Amz Feb 50 134
Quite Logical. .s . . . . TW Apr 49 68
Rescue Beacon. .(by-lined ROG
PHILLIPS in ToC; CRAIG
BROWNING on story). .s . . . . .
. . . . .OW Nov 50 86

Robot Men of Bubble City,
The. .n . . . . .FA Jul 49 6
She. .nt . . . . FA Apr 49 88
Shortcut, the. .s . . . .
. . . . .Amz Jul 49 62
So Shall Ye Reap! . .n . . . .
. . . . .Amz Aug 47 8
Starship from Sirius. .n. . . . .
. . . . Amz Aug 48 66
Supernal Note, The. .s . . . .
. . . . Amz Jul 48 124
Tangential Semanticist, The. . . . .
. .s . . . . FA Aug 49 38
This Time . . . . OW Jan 50 60
Twice to Die. .nt . . . .
. . . . FA Feb 48 92
Uninvited Jest, The. .s . . . .
. . . . Amz Sep 47 44
Unthinkable. .s . . . .
. . . . Amz Apr 49 34
Unthinking Destroyer, The . . . . .
. .s . . . . Amz Dec 48 66
Vacation in Shasta. .nt . . . .
. . . . FA Feb 46 26
Weapon from the Stars. .nt . . . . .
. . . . Amz Oct 50 6
PHILLIPS, VIC
Czech Interlude. .ss . . . .
. . . . UK Dec 41 124
Defense Line. .nt. . . . .
. . . . ASF Dec 41 115
Emergency. .s . . . . .ASF Sep 40 143
Maiden Voyage. .nt . . . .
. . . . .ASF Jan 39 51
Once Around the Moon. .s . . . . .
. . . . ASF Jun 37 90
Rocket's Swan Song. .s. . . . .
. . . . .SFQ Spr 41 124
Salvage. .nt. . . . . . . ASF Nov 40 9
with SCOTT ROBERTS
Fish Story. .s . . . . ASF May 41 101
Monopoly. .s . . . . ASF Apr 42 116
Putsch. .s . . . . ASF Mar 41 86
PIERCE, JOHN (Robinson) *See also*
pseud J. J. COUPLING (17)
Adrift in the Void. .s . . . .
. . . . WS Jun 34 64
Invariant. .s . . . . . ASF Apr 44 94
Pre-vision. .s . . . . . ASF Mar 36 105
PROBABILITY ZERO
About Quarrels, About the
Past. .ss . . . . . . ASF Jul 42 112
Relics from the Earth, The . . . . .
. .ss . . . . SW Mar 30 894
Unthinking Cap. .s . . . .
. . . . .ASF Jul 43 39

AUTHOR
    Title. .Length . . . . Magazine, Date, Page

PILLSWORTH, EDWARD S.
  Spawn of Infinitude. .s . . . .
    . . . . FN Sep 40 133
PINE, THEODORE *pseud of EMIL
  PETAJA alone except for one
  story in collaboration with HENRY
  HASSE*
PIPER, H. BEAM
  Flight from Tomorrow. .s . . . . . .
    . . . . Fut Sep–Oct 50 36
  He Walked Around the Horses . . .
    . .s . . . . ASF Apr 48 53
  Last Enemy. .n . . . .
    . . . . ASF Aug 50 5
  Mercenaries, The. .nt . . . .
    . . . . ASF Mar 50 78
  Police Operation. .nt . . . .
    . . . . .ASF Jul 48 8
  Time and Time Again. .s . . . .
    . . . . ASF Apr 47 27
PIPER, MAJOR VERNON
  Secrets of the Flying Saucers Told at
  Last. .nt. . . . . . . .FanS Nov 50 4
PLAISTED, MAX
  ZARNAK (comic)
    1. The Plunder Plague . . . .
      . . . . TW Aug 36 65
    2. The Metal World . . . .
      . . . . TW Oct 36 89
    3. Madness on Mercury . . . . . .
      . . . . TW Dec 36 87
    4. The Human Guinea Pig. . . . .
      . . . . TW Feb 37 63
    5. Etarre . . . . TW Apr 37 73
    6. The Supreme One, Master of
      Mercury. . . . . TW Jun 37 101
    7. The Strange Deluge . . . .
      . . . . TW Aug 37 79
    8. Harnessed Elements. . . . . . .
      . . . . TW Oct 37 87
PLANET PRINCE, THE *pseud of
  J. HARVEY HAGGARD (for 1
  poem in AMAZING)*
PLIMMER, DENIS
  Man from the Wrong Time-Track,
  The. .s . . . . Uc Apr 41 85
PLUNKETT, CYRIL
  X-Gas, The. .s . . . . . AW Mar 30 812
PODOLSKY, EDWARD
  Death by Radio. .s . . . .
    . . . . Amz Dec 32 809
  Life on Other Planets? . .a . . . . .
    . . . . PS Sum 40 105
POE, EDGAR ALLAN
  MASTERS OF FANTASY
  biog . . . . FFM Dec 49 113

Balloon Hoax, The. .s . . . .
    . . . . Amz Apr 27 58
Descent into the Maelstrom,
  A. .s . . . . Amz Feb 34 123
Facts in the Case of M. Valdemar,
  The. .s . . . . Amz Apr 26 92
Gold-Bug, The. .s . . . .
    . . . . Amz Apr 34 109
Ms. Found in a Bottle. .s . . . . . .
    . . . . Amz Mar 34 127
Mellonta Tauta. .s . . . .
    . . . . Amz Nov 33 124
Mesmeric Revelation. .s . . . .
    . . . . Amz May 26 124
Sphinx, The. .s . . . . Amz Jul 26 357
Thousand and Second Tale of
  Scheherazade, The. .s . . . .
    . . . . Amz May 28 126
Von Kempelen and His
  Discovery. .s . . . . Amz Jul 27 363
POHL, FREDERIK *See pseuds
  ELTON V. ANDREWS (0), S. D.
  GOTTESMAN (7), PAUL DENNIS
  LAVOND (h) (6), JAMES
  MacCREIGH (12), SCOTT
  MARINER (1), WARREN F.
  HOWARD (1). See also DIRK
  WYLIE (6)*
  Editor of ASTONISHING STORIES
  Feb 40 *thru* Sep 41 *issues*
  *Assistant Editor ASTONISHING
  STORIES*
  Nov 41 *thru* Apr 43
  *Editor SUPER SCIENCE (STORIES)
  (NOVELS)*
  Mar 40 *thru* Aug 41
  *Assistant Editor SUPER SCIENCE
  STORIES*
  Nov 41 *thru* May 43
  *SCIENCE FICTIONEER, THE book
  review dept* . . . .
    . . . . *regularly from* SSS Jan 49 91
POLK, EDGAR
  Pink Humans Aren't Real! . . . . .
    . .s . . . . FA Feb 49 84
POLLARD, JOHN X. *house pseud
by HOWARD BROWNE*
  Strange Mission of Arthur Pendran,
  The. .n . . . . FA Jun 44 10
POLLOCK, FRANK LILLIE
  Finis. .s . . . . .FFM May–Jun 40 116
                FN Jul 48 118
POMEROY, JOHN H.
  PROBABILITY ZERO
  Icicle Built for Groo. .ss . . . . . .
    . . . . ASF Sep 44 87

Progress Report. .a . . . .
    . . . . ASF Sep 49 31
POOL, CHARLES B.
  Justice of the Atoms. .s . . . .
    . . . . .WS Jul 35 170
POWELL, FRANCIS WILSON
  Pop Gun. .s . . . . . . Amz Aug 43 40
  PROBABILITY ZERO
  That's a Lot of Hot Air. . . . . . .
    . .ss . . . . ASF Dec 44 128
POWELL, JEP
  *Biog sketch, pen & ink
  portrait* . . . . FA Aug 41 132
                Amz Sep 40 132
  Amazons of a Weird Creation. . . .
    . .nt . . . . FA Jun 41 96
  Chilly, But Cheering. .a . . . .
    . . . . FA Feb 42 38
  Is the Death Ray Here? . .a . . . . .
    . . . . TW Dec 42 76
  Man, An Unnecessary Evil. .a . . . .
    . . . . FA Aug 41 129
  Murdered—Yet Alive. .s . . . .
    . . . . .FA Jul 41 44
  Mutiny in Space. .s . . . .
    . . . . Amz Sep 41 62
  Planet of Love, The. .s . . . .
    . . . . Amz Mar 42 212
  Rain, Raids and Rays. .s . . . .
    . . . . .CF Sum 43 102
  Synthetic Woman, The. .nt . . . . .
    . . . . Amz Sep 40 100
  Venusian Slave Smugglers . . . . . .
    . .nt . . . . Amz Aug 42 176
  Water, Water Everywhere. .a . . . .
    . . . . FA Dec 41 136
POWELL, TED
  Sign and the Message, The. . . . . .
    . .s . . . . .SS Mar 50 105
POWERS, PAUL S.
  Terror in the Dust. .s . . . .
    . . . . .TW Sum 44 55
POWERS, WILLIAM T.
  Meteor. .s . . . . .ASF Sep 50 107
PRAGNELL, FESTUS *See pseud
  FRANCIS PARNELL (1)*
  Biog Sketch . . . . . Amz Dec 38 143
  Biog sketch . . . . . Amz Jun 40 131
  Biog sketch, photo. . . . .
    . . . . FA Aug 40 135
  Collision in Space. .nt. . . . .
    . . . . .Amz Jul 43 126
  Conspirators on Phobos. .s . . . . .
    . . . . Amz Jun 43 22
  Devil Birds of Deimos. .nt . . . . . .
    . . . . Amz Apr 42 168

AUTHOR
 Title. .Length . . . . Magazine, Date, Page

Essense of Life, The. .s . . . .
 . . . . Amz Aug 33 436
 ToW Aut 38 105
Ghost of Mars. .nt . . . Amz Dec 38 8
Green Man of Graypec, The. . . . .
 . .n 3 pt . . . . WS Jul 35 136
"HARGREAVES, DON" series
 includes:
 GHOST OF MARS
 WARLORDS OF MARS
 KIDNAPPED IN MARS
 OUTLAW OF MARS
 DEVIL BIRDS OF DEIMOS
 INTO THE CAVES OF MARS
 TWISTED GIANT OF MARS
 CONSPIRATORS OF PHOBOS
 MADCAP OF MARS
Into the Caves of Mars. .nt . . . . .
 . . . . Amz Aug 42 154
Isotope Men, The. .s . . . .
 . . . . WS Aug 33 136
 SS Nov 48 110
Kidnapped in Mars. .nt . . . .
 . . . . Amz Oct 41 60
Machine God Laughs, The. . . . . .
 . .nt 3 pt . . . . FB #2 32
Madcap of Mars. .nt . . . .
 . . . . Amz Sep 43 172
Man of the Future. .s . . . .
 . . . . ToW #1 37 57
Men of the Dark Comet. .s . . . . .
 . . . . WS Jun 33 40
Outlaw of Mars. .nt . . . .
 . . . . Amz Jan 42 142
Twisted Giant of Mars. .nt. . . . .
 . . . . Amz May 43 32
Visit to Venus, A. .s . . . .
 . . . . WS Aug 34 270
 FSQ Spr 50 106
War of the Human Cats. .s . . . . . .
 . . . . FA Aug 40 90
Warlords of Mars. .s . . . .
 . . . . Amz Jun 40 48
with R. F. STARZL
Venus Germ, The. .s . . . .
 . . . . WS Nov 32 486

PRATT, FLETCHER
Dr. Grimshaw's Sanatarium . . . . .
 . .s . . . . Amz May 34 79
Mad Destroyer, The. .s . . . .
 . . . . WQ Spr 30 406
Onslaught from Rigel, The . . . . .
 . .n . . . . WQ Win 32 150
 WSA 50 5
Pardon My Mistake. .ss . . . .
 . . . . TW Dec 46 92

AUTHOR
 Title. .Length . . . . Magazine, Date, Page

War of the Giants, The . . . .
 . .s . . . . WS May 31 1440
translations from the French of:
Death of Iron, The by S. S.
 Held. .n 3 pt . . . . . WS Sep 32 294
Fall of the Eiffel Tower, The by
 Charles De Richter. .n 3 pt . . . .
 . . . . WS Sep 34 390
Radio Terror, The by Eugene
 Thebault. .n 3 pt . . . . WS Jun 33 6
translations from the German of:
Druso by Freidrich Freksa. . . . . .
 . .n 3 pt . . . . WS May 34 1066
Hidden Colony, The by Otfrid von
 Hanstein. .n 3 pt . . . .
 . . . . .WS Jan 35 904
with L. SPRAGUE de CAMP
Better Mousetrap, The. .s . . . . . .
 . . . . F&SF Dec 50 27
Castle of Iron, The. .n . . . .
 . . . . UK Apr 41 9
GAVAGAN'S BAR
 1. Elephas Frumenti . . . .
 2. The Gift of God. .s . . . .
 . . . . . . F&SF Win–Spr 50 95
"INCOMPLETE ENCHANTER"
 series includes:
 THE ROARING TRUMPET
 THE MATHEMATICS OF MAGIC
 THE CASTLE OF IRON
Land of Unreason, The. .n. . . . . .
 . . . . UK Oct 41 9
Mathematics of Magic, The . . . . .
 . .n . . . . .UK Aug 40 9
Roaring Trumpet, The. .n . . . . . .
 . . . . .UK May 40 9
with IRVIN LESTER
Danger. .s . . . . Amz Jul 29 364
Great Steel Panic, The. .s . . . . . .
 . . . . Amz Sep 28 522
Octopus Cycle, The. .s . . . .
 . . . . Amz May 28 110
Reign of the Ray, The . . . .
 . .n 2 pt . . . . SW Jun 29 7
Roger Bacon Formula, The . . . . .
 . .s . . . . .Amz Jan 29 940
with LAURENCE MANNING
City of the Living Dead, The . . . .
 . .s . . . . SW May 30 1100
 SS Jul 40 94
 AFR #2 108
Expedition to Pluto. .nt . . . .
 . . . . .PS Win 39 52
with B. F. RUBY
Thing in the Woods, The. . . . . . .
 . .s . . . . Amz Feb 35 112

AUTHOR
 Title. .Length . . . . Magazine, Date, Page

with KONRAD SCHMIDT
translation from the German of:
Cosmic Cloud, The by Bruno H.
 Burgel. .n . . . . .WQ Sep 31 6
with I. M. STEPHENS
Pineal Stimulator, The. .s . . . . . .
 . . . . Amz Nov 30 738
Voice Across the Years, A. . . . . .
 . .n . . . . AQ Win 32 2

PRECIADO, A. A.
Rubber Future is a Snap, The . . .
 . .a . . . . TW Feb 43 100

PRESCOTT, LEE
Golden Pennies, The. .nt . . . .
 . . . . Amz Aug 49 52
Sleepwalker of Sandwich . . . . . .
 . .s . . . . FA Nov 49 104

PRESTAGIACOMO, A
Biog sketch . . . . . . Fant #1 38 128
Menace of the Metal-Men. .nt. . . .
 . . . . .Fant #1 38 2

PRESTON, ROBERT PAGE
Land of Twilight. .n 3 pt. . . . . . .
 . . . . Amz Nov 34 73

PRESTON, WALTER R.
Lunar Sanctuary. .s . . . .
 . . . . SFQ Win 42 114

PRICE, E. HOFFMAN See also
 pseud HAMLIN DALY (0)
Strange Gateway. .s . . . .
 . . . . UK Apr 39 113
Well of the Angels. .s . . . .
 . . . . .UK May 40 91

PRINGLE, ALFRED
Into the Valley of Death. .s . . . . .
 . . . . Amz Feb 30 1080

PROUT, BEN
Singing Weapon, The. .s . . . .
 . . . . Amz May 27 180

PURCELL, ARTHUR
Positive Inertia. .s . . . .
 . . . . ASF Oct 36 43

PURCELL, BRYCE
Cut Out This Aztec Heart (The
 Aztec Heart). .s . . . .
 . . . . .FanS Nov 50 111

PUTNAM, EDMUND W.
Translation of John Forsythe,
 The. .s . . . . Amz Sep 30 518

PUTNAM, KENNETH
Confusion Cargo. .s . . .PS Spr 48 84
Dud. .s . . . . TW Apr 48 88
Me, Myself and I. .s . . . .
 . . . . .PS Win 47 48

AUTHOR
    Title. .Length . . . . Magazine, Date, Page

Q

QUICK, DOROTHY
  Blue and Silver Brocade. .s . . . . .
  . . . . UK Oct 39 103
  "PATCHWORK QUILT" series
      includes:
      BLUE AND SILVER BROCADE
      TRANSPARENT STUFF
      TWO FOR A BARGAIN
  Transparent Stuff. .s . . . .
  . . . . UK Jun 40 97
  Two for a Bargain. .nt . . . .
  . . . . UK Dec 40 104
  Year from Tonight, A. .s . . . . . .
  . . . . FA Jan 45 92
QUINN, SEABURY
  Glamour. .s . . . . AFR #11 3
QUITMAN, WALLACE *pseud of*
  RAYMOND A. PALMER
  Outlaw of Space. .ss . . . .
  . . . . Amz Aug 38 128

R

RAFFERTY, DR. AMADEUS
  Man's Journey to the Stars . . . . .
  . .a . . . . TW Apr 48 77
RALEIGH, WALTER
  with LT. APOLLO SOUCEK
  How High Can Man Fly? . .a . . . .
  . . . . AW Apr 30 940
RANDOM, ELMER
  Golden Age. .s . . . . . UK Dec 42 82
RAPHAEL, LEONARD
  Man Who Saw Through Time,
  The. .s . . . . FA Sep 41 134
RAY, RICE
  Today's Yesterday. .s . . . .
  . . . . .WS Jan 34 608
RAY, ROBERT
  If Tomorrow Be Lost. .ss . . . . . .
  . . . . FA Jun 50 130
RAYCRAFT, STAN *pseud of*
  RICHARD S. SHAVER
  Pillars of Delight. .nt . . . .
  . . . . Amz Dec 49 8
RAYER, F. G.
  Adaptability. .s . . . . . NW Spr 50 62
  Basic Fundamental. .s . . . .
  . . . . Fant Aug 47 78
  Deus Ex Machina. .s . . . .
  . . . . .NW Win 50 30

From Beyond the Dawn. .s . . . . .
  . . . . .NW #3 96
Necessity. .s . . . . .NW #5 49 74
Quest. .s . . . . NW Sum 50 80
RAYMOND, E. V. *pseud of*
  RAYMOND Z. GALLUN
  Nova Solis. .s . . . . . ASF Dec 35 34
RAYMOND, HUGH *pseud of JOHN*
  MICHEL
  Claggett's Folly. .s . . . .
  . . . . Fut Dec 42 53
  Eight Ball. .s . . . . . UK Jun 43 120
  Full Circle. .s . . . . . Fut Feb 43 84
  Glory Road. .s . . . .SFQ Fal 42 129
  Goblins Will Get You, The. .s . . . .
  . . . . Sti Mar 42 45
  He Wasn't There! . .s . . . .
  . . . . .Ash Feb 41 22
  Hell in the Village. .s . . . .
  . . . . SFQ Win 42 129
  Last Viking, The. .s . . . .
  . . . . .Cos Mar 41 96
  Path of Empire. .s . . . .
  . . . . SFQ Sum 41 138
  Power. .s . . . . .Cos May 41 37
  Powerful Ones, The. .s . . . .
  . . . . Fut Oct 42 31
  Real McCoy, The. .s . . . .
  . . . . Fut Jun 42 84
  Rebirth of Tomorrow. .s . . . . . .
  . . . . Sti Apr 41 6
  Spokesman for Terra. .ss . . . . . .
  . . . . .Sti Jun 41 29
  Washington Slept Here. .s . . . . . .
  . . . . .Fut Aug 42 68
  When Half-Worlds Meet. .s . . . . .
  . . . . Cos Jul 41 21
  Year of Uniting, The. .s . . . .
  . . . . .SFQ Win 41–42 124
RAYMOND, K.(AYE)
  Air Space. .s . . . . . . ASF Sep 37 97
  Comet, The. .s . . . . ASF Feb 37 98
  Great Thought, The. .s . . . .
  . . . . ASF Mar 37 80
  Into the Infinitesimal. .nt . . . . . .
  . . . . WS Jun 34 6
REA, MARGARETTA W.
  Delilah. .s . . . . . . .Amz Jan 33 942
READ, RANSOM F.
  Movies Via Radio. .a . . . .
  . . . . SF Dec 39 95
RECOUR, CHARLES
  Amoeba 'Roid. .s . . . .
  . . . . Amz Jul 48 134
  And the Rockets Came. .s . . . . .
  . . . . .Amz Jul 49 78

Cybernetic Brain, The. .s . . . . . .
  . . . . FA Dec 49 138
Hammer on the Moon, The . . . . .
  . .s . . . . FA Jan 49 98
Lunar Legacy, The. .s . . . .
  . . . . Amz Feb 49 124
"Out of this Dust . . ." . .s . . . . .
  . . . . FA Feb 49 36
Sanctuary. .s . . . . . . FA Jan 50 58
Signal Point in Space. .s . . . .
  . . . . FA Jun 49 102
Survivors in Space. .s . . . .
  . . . . .FA May 49 130
Swordsman of Pira. .n . . . .
  . . . . Amz Mar 49 82
That We May Rise Again. .s . . . . .
  . . . . .Amz Jul 48 94
RECTOR, CHARLES H.
  Crystals of Growth. .s . . . .
  . . . . Amz Dec 27 874
REDMAN, AMABEL
  Out of the Dark. .s . . . .
  . . . . FFM Oct 40 100
REED, ANTON
  Next Time I'll Get You. .s . . . . . .
  . . . . Amz Oct 42 94
REED, BALIR
  Dimension: Praecox. .s . . . .
  . . . . SS May 49 107
REED, DAVID B. *pseud of DAVID*
  VERN
  Biog sketch . . . .
  . . . . FA May 41 131
  Biog sketch, photo. . . . .
  . . . . FA Feb 43 227
  Brothers Shenanigan, The . . . . . .
  . .nt . . . . Amz Jun 46 64
  Court of Kublai Khan, The . . . . .
  . .nt . . . . FA Mar 48 8
  Death Plays a Game. .nt . . . .
  . . . . FA Dec 41 10
  Empire of Jegga. .n . . . .
  . . . . Amz Nov 43 10
  Girl from Venus, The. .s . . . .
  . . . . Amz Jun 41 72
  Kid Poison. .nt . . . . Amz Aug 41 42
  Machine Brain, The. .s . . . .
  . . . . .TW Jul 40 31
  Magic Flute, The. .s . . . .
  . . . . .FA May 42 178
  Moons of Death. .s . . . .
  . . . . .FA May 41 94
  Murder in Space. .n . . . .
  . . . . .Amz May 44 8
  Penace Cruise. .nt . . . .
  . . . . .ASF Jul 42 46

AUTHOR
Title. .Length . . . . Magazine, Date, Page

Planet of Ghosts. .n . . . .
. . . . Amz Mar 42 124
Return of the Whispering
Gorilla. .n . . . . FA Feb 43 8
Where Is Roger Davis. .nt . . . . . .
. . . . .Amz May 39 34
World of Miracles The . . . .
. . . . Amz Oct 41 44
REED, PETER *pseud of JOHN D.*
MacDONALD
Delusion Drive. .s . . . .
. . . . .SSS Apr 49 100
Escape to Fear. .s . . . .
. . . . SSS Jul 50 72
Gift of Darkness. .s . . . .
. . . . SSS May 50 76
Miniature, The. .s . . . .
. . . . .SSS Sep 49 46
REED, WARREN A.
Little Yowlie. .ss . . . .
. . . . .FA Jul 43 90
REEDS, F. ANTON
Forever Is Not So Long . . . .
. .s . . . . ASF May 42 34
Pin the Medals on Poe. .s . . . . . .
. . . . .Ash Sep 41 61
Wee Bonnie Poupon, The . . . . . .
. .s . . . . OW Mar 50 140
REESE, GEORGE
That Guy, Satan, Sends Me! . . . .
. .s . . . . .FA Jan 49 118
REEVE, ARTHUR B.
Editorial Commissioner of
SCIENTIFIC DETECTIVE
MONTHLY
Jan 30 *thru* May 30 *issues (all)*
Editorial Commissioner of AMAZ-
ING DETECTIVE TALES
Jun 30 *thru* Oct 30 *issues (all)*
Azure Ring, The. .s . . . .
. . . . SD May 30 418
Bacteriological Detective,
The. .s. . . . . SD Feb 30 104
Body That Wouldn't Burn,
The. .s. . . . . AD Sep 30 804
"CRAIG KENNEDY" series includes:
THE MYSTERY OF THE BULAWAYO
DIAMOND
THE BACTERIOLOGICAL
DETECTIVE
THE SEISMOGRAPH ADVENTURE
THE TERROR IN THE AIR
THE AZURE RING
THE DIAMOND MAKER
THE WHITE SLAVE
THE SCIENTIFIC CRACKSMAN
THE BODY THAT WOULDN'T BURN
THE MAN WHO WAS DEAD

Diamond Maker, The. .s . . . .
. . . . AD Jun 30 488
Man Who Was Dead, The. .s. . . . .
. . . . AD Oct 30 890
Mystery of the Bulawayo Diamond,
The. .s. . . . . SD Jan 30 8
Scientific Cracksman, The. . . . . .
. .s . . . . AD Aug 30 688
Seismograph Adventure, The . . . .
. .s . . . . SD Mar 30 200
Terror in the Air, The. .s . . . .
. . . . SD Apr 30 294
What Are the Great Detective
Stories and Why? . .a . . . .
. . . . SD Jan 30 6
White Slave, The. .s . . . .
. . . . .AD Jul 30 626
REEVES, JUDSON W. *See pseud*
ALADRA SEPTAMA
REGIS, JUL
Paradise of the Ice Wilderness,
The. .s. . . . . . . Amz Oct 27 701
REID, J. DAVID
Great Invasion of 1955, The . . . .
. .s . . . . Amz Oct 32 662
REID, VINCENT
Future's Fair, The. .s . . . .
. . . . Ash Oct 40 48
REINSBERG, MARK
Biog sketch . . . . . Amz May 39 127
with W. LAWRENCE HAMLING
War With Jupiter. .s . . . .
. . . . .Amz May 39 74
REISS, MALCOLM
Editor of PLANET STORIES
Win 39 *thru* Sum 42 *issues*
REMENTER, EDWARD L.
Space Bender, The. .s . . . .
. . . . Amz Dec 28 838
Time Deflector, The. .nt . . . .
. . . . Amz Dec 29 806
REMSON, HAL
Vast Beyond the Concept . . . . . .
. .s . . . . MSS Feb 39 120
RENARD, MAURICE
Five After Five. .s . . . .
. . . . TW Apr 41 65
RENSHAW, F. STANLEY
Ancients of Easter Island . . . . . .
. .s . . . . Amz Apr 33 46
REPP, ED EARL
Biog sketch, photo. . . . .
. . . . Amz Oct 38 140
Annihilator Comes, The. .s . . . . .
. . . . WS Aug 30 212

AUTHOR
Title. .Length . . . . Magazine, Date, Page

Armageddon, 1948. .nt . . . .
. . . . Amz Nov 41 116
Beast of Ban-du-lu, The. .s . . . . .
. . . . .WS May 31 1448
Beyond Gravity. .s . . . .
. . . . .AW Aug 29 114
Beyond the Aurora. .s . . . .
. . . . .AW Nov 29 430
Black Pool, The. .s . . . .
. . . . Amz Nov 43 190
Body Pirate, The. .s . . . .
. . . . Amz Mar 35 121
Brigade of the Damned. .s . . . . . .
. . . . Amz Jun 39 110
Buccaneer of the Star Seas . . . . .
. .s . . . . PS Fal 40 41
Carewe Murder Mystery, The. . . .
. .n 2 pt . . . . AD Sep 30 814
City That Walked, The. .s . . . . . .
. . . . Amz Mar 39 112
Curse of Montezuma, The . . . . . .
. .s . . . . .Amz May 39 86
Deadly Paint of Harley Gale,
The. .nt . . . . Amz Apr 39 54
Deep Sea Justice. .s . . . .
. . . . .AQ Sum 31 414
Destiny Made to Order. .s . . . . . .
. . . . .SF Jan 41 32
Dwellers of the Darkness. .s . . . . .
. . . . Amz Oct 42 106
Flight of the Eastern Star. .s . . . .
. . . . AW Dec 29 498
From Out of the Earth. .s . . . . . .
. . . . WS Mar 31 1168
Gland Superman, The. .nt . . . . . .
. . . . Amz Oct 38 8
Gulf Stream Gold. .s . . . .
. . . . SW May 30 1062
Invaders from Sirius. .s . . . .
. . . . .FA Jul 39 74
Invisible Raiders, The. .s . . . .
. . . . AW Oct 29 352
Invisible World, The. .nt . . . .
. . . . Amz Oct 40 48
"JOHN HALE" series includes:
THE SCIENTIFIC GHOST
THE CURSE OF MONTEZUMA
BRIGADE OF THE DAMNED
JOHN HALE CONVICTS A KILLER
JOHN HALE'S HOLLYWOOD
MYSTERY
John Hale Convicts a Killer . . . . .
. .s . . . . .Amz Jul 39 94
John Hale's Hollywood
Mystery. .s . . . . Amz Aug 39 106
Light That Killed, The. .s . . . . . .
. . . . Amz Mar 43 98

90 REPP—RICHARDSON   INDEX TO THE SCIENCE FICTION MAGAZINES

AUTHOR
Title. .Length . . . . Magazine, Date, Page

Lost on the Sea Bottom. .s . . . . .
. . . . Amz Feb 39 114
Martian Terror. .s . . . .
. . . . .PS Spr 40 46
Master of the Living Dead . . . . .
. .nt . . . . .Amz Jan 44 130
Metal World, The. .s . . . .
. . . . SW Oct 29 390
Norris Tapley's Sixth Sense . . . . .
. .s . . . . FA Apr 40 78
Phantom of Terror, The. .s . . . . .
. . . . Amz Apr 33 60
Planet of Black Terror. .nt . . . . .
. . . . Amz Jun 40 110
Radium Pool, The. .n 2 pt . . . . .
. . . . SW Aug 29 218
Red Dimension, The. .s . . . .
. . . . .SW Jan 30 696
                           SS Sum 45 66
Rescue from Venus. .n . . . .
. . . . SFQ Spr 41 4
Scientific Ghost, The. .s . . . . . .
. . . . Amz Jan 39 72
Second Missile, The . . . .
. .s . . . . Amz Dec 30 800
Secret of Planetoid 88, The . . . . .
. .n . . . . Amz Dec 41 10
Sky Ruler, The. .s . . . .
. . . . AW May 30 1014
Sky Terror, The. .s. . . . .
. . . . .SF Sep 41 31
Song of Death. .s. . . . .
. . . . Amz Nov 38 26
Spawn of Jupiter. .nt . . . .
. . . . Amz Mar 44 150
Sphinx of the Spaceways . . . . . .
. .nt . . . . SF Aug 39 10
Stellar Missile, The. . . . .
. .s . . . . SW Nov 29 498
Storm Buster, The. .s . . . .
. . . . AW Jan 30 614
Synthetic Man, The. .s . . . .
. . . . WS Dec 30 698
Under the North Pole. .s . . . . . .
. .nt . . . . .DS Apr–May 39 80
When Time Rolled Back. .s . . . . .
. . . . Com May 41 69
Wisdom of the Dead. .s. . . . . . .
. . . . SF Mar 41 75
World in the Atom, The . . . .
. .s . . . . FA Jun 40 52
World of the Living Dead . . . . . .
. .n 3 pt . . . . . . Amz Nov 32 734
Worlds at War. .s . . . .
. . . . .FA May 40 56

AUTHOR
Title. .Length . . . . Magazine, Date, Page

REYNOLDS, JOHN MURRAY
Goddess of the Moon. .nt . . . . . .
. . . . .PS Spr 40 2
Golden Amazons of Venus,
The. .n . . . . PS Win 39 3
REYNOLDS, L. MAJOR *pseud of*
LOUISE LEIPIAR
Chrysalis. .s . . . . . . FA Dec 50 80
REYNOLDS, MACK *See also*
pseud DALLAS ROSS (2)
Devil Finds Work, The. .s . . . . . .
. . . . FA Dec 50 90
Discord Makers, The. .s. . . . . . .
. . . . OTWA Jul 50 102
Down the River. .s . . . .
. . . . SS Sep 50 113
Fido. .s . . . . FA May 50 78
Isolationist. .s . . . . FA Apr 50 96
Long Beer—Short Horn. .s. . . . . .
. . . . FA Nov 50 76
Luvver. .s. . . . . . FA Jun 50 118
Man in the Moon, The. .s . . . . . .
. . . . .Amz Jul 50 40
One of Our Planets is Missing. . . .
. .s . . . . Amz Nov 50 108
Precognition. .s . . . . TW Jun 50 120
Spark, The. .ss . . . . . TW Dec 50 94
Tall Tale. .s . . . . . . .SS Nov 50 130
Tourists to Terra. .s . . . .
. . . . Im Dec 50 36
United We Stand. .s . . . .
. . . . Amz May 50 164
Word from the Void, The . . . . . .
. .ss. . . . . .SSS Sep 50 99
with FREDRIC BROWN
Six-Legged Svengali. .s . . . .
. . . . .WB Dec 50 2
RHODES, DOUGLAS NELSON
FANTASTIC HOAXES
The Hail-Storm Gun. .a. . . . . . .
. . . . FA Mar 41 76
RHODES, W. H.
Case of Summerfield, The . . . . . .
. .nt . . . . F&SF Sum 50 70
RICE, JANE
Crest of the Wave, The . . . .
. .s . . . . UK Jun 41 71
Dream, The. .s . . . . .UK Jul 40 84
Elixir, The. .nt . . . . UK Dec 42 114
Forbidden Trail, The. .nt . . . . . .
. . . . UK Apr 41 130
Golden Bridle, The. .nt. . . . .
. . . . UK Apr 43 79
House, The. .s . . . .
. . . . .UK Dec 41 85

AUTHOR
Title. .Length . . . . Magazine, Date, Page

Idol of the Flies, The. .s . . . .
. . . . UK Jun 42 90
Magician's Dinner. .nt. . . . .
. . . . UK Oct 42 65
Pobby. .nt . . . . . . UK Apr 42 110
Refugee, The. .nt. . . . .
. . . . UK Oct 43 111
                           UK 48 30
RICE, LOUISE
with TONJOROFF–ROBERTS
Astounding Enemy, The. .nt . . . .
. . . . AQ Win 30 78
RICH, H. THOMPSON
Beast Plants, The. .s . . . .
. . . . .FFM Apr 40 66
Diamond Thunderbolt, The. . . . .
. .s . . . . .ASF Jul 31 46
Flying City, The. .s . . . .
. . . . ASF Aug 30 260
Spawn of the Comet. .s . . . .
. . . . ASF Nov 31 236
Sunken Empire, The. .s. . . . . . .
. . . . .ASF Jan 31 24
RICHARDS, HAROLD F., Ph.D.
Vibrator of Death, The. .s . . . . .
. . . . AQ Spr 28 259
RICHARDS, PHIL
Hall and Flint. .biog. . . . .
. . . . FFM Feb 41 84
RICHARDSON, DARRELL C.
Tribute to Edgar Rice Burroughs,
A. .a . . . . OW Jul 50 2
RICHARDSON, R.(OBERT) S. *See*
also pseud PHILIP LATHAM (3)
Advance in the Red. .a . . . .
. . . . ASF Aug 45 100
Calendar for Mars. .a . . . .
. . . . ASF Aug 47 133
Engineering in Extremes. .a . . . .
. . . . .ASF Jun 45 136
Extra-Solar Planets. .a . . . .
. . . . .ASF Sep 44 106
Headstones for Astronomers . . . .
. .a . . . . ASF Jul 44 104
Helpful Pleiades, The. .a . . . .
. . . . ASF Feb 45 104
Inside Out Matter. .a . . . .
. . . . ASF Dec 41 112
Late-Model Stars. .a . . . .
. . . . ASF Oct 42 90
Lots of Gold—But Get It! .a. . . .
. . . . ASF Aug 45 154
Luna Observatory No. 1. .a . . . . .
. . . . ASF Feb 40 113
Man on Mira. .a . . . . ASF Apr 48 88

AUTHOR
Title. .Length . . . . Magazine, Date, Page

No Handicap Allowed. .a . . . . . .
. . . . ASF Jun 42 63
Other Side of Astronomy,
The. .a. . . . . ASF Sep 39 85
Paper Planets. .a . . . .
. . . . .ASF Sep 48 100
Postwar Plan for Mars. .a. . . . . .
. . . . .ASF Jan 44 101
Prediction—Past Tense. .a . . . . . .
. . . . .ASF Jun 45 100
Prominences. .a. . . . ASF Oct 45 99
Second Approximation. .a. . . . . .
. . . . .ASF Sep 46 109
Space Fix. .a 2 pt . . . .
. . . . ASF Mar 43 68
Space Has a Spectrum. .a . . . . . .
. . . . ASF Mar 41 104
Stars Also Have Rings. .a. . . . . .
. . . . ASF Jul 42 78
Time for a Universe. .a . . . .
. . . . ASF Nov 44 99
Time of Your Life, The. .a . . . . .
. . . . ASF Nov 49 110
Trepidation. .a . . . ASF Apr 41 106
Turn on the Moon—Make It
Hotter. .a. . . . . . ASF Nov 43 101
Universes for Lenses. .a. . . . . . .
. . . . ASF Sep 40 41
Vermin of the Sky. .a. . . . .
. . . . ASF Jul 41 105
Wanted: Suggestions. .a . . . .
. . . . ASF Dec 40 103
World of 61 Cygni C, The . . . . . .
. .a . . . . ASF Jul 43 67
RIMEL, DUANE W.
City Under the Sea, The . . . .
. .s . . . . Fut Jul 40 55
RISK, PETER
Warrior's Age. .s . . . ASF Oct 42 32
RITTER, SIMPSON
SCIENCE FICTION QUIZ
dept . . . . SSS Jan 49 51
RIVERSIDE, JOHN *pseud of*
ROBERT A. HEINLEIN
Unpleasant Profession of Jonathan
Hoag, The. .n . . . . . UK Oct 42 9
ROAMAN, J.
Undersea Express, The. .s . . . . . .
. . . . Amz Dec 27 870
ROBBINS, R. J.
with WILL SMITH
Soul Master, The. .s . . . .
. . . . ASF Mar 30 350
ROBBINS, TOD
Living Portrait, The. .nt . . . .
. . . . FN Nov 49 76

AUTHOR
Title. .Length . . . . Magazine, Date, Page

Terrible Three, The. .n . . . .
. . . . .FN Nov 48 8
Toys of Fate, The. .s . . . .
. . . . FN Mar 49 102
Whimpus, The. .nt . . . .
. . . . FFM Sep–Oct 39 37
Who Wants a Green Bottle? . . . .
. .s . . . . FN Nov 40 113
Wild Wullie, The Master. .s . . . . .
. . . . FFM Sep 42 114
ROBERTS, SCOT
with Vic PHILLIPS
Fish Story. .s . . . . ASF May 41 101
Monopoly. .s . . . . ASF Apr 42 116
Putsch. .s . . . . ASF Mar 41 86
ROBERTS, W. J. *artist*
Covers for TALES OF WONDER
Sum, Aut, Win 1938
Spr 1939
Spr, Aut 1940
ROBIN, RALPH
Pygmies of Phobos, The . . . .
. .s . . . . Amz Apr 36 116
ROBINSON, FRANK M.
Maze, The. .s . . . . . ASF Jun 50 69
ROCCA, SAMUEL F.
New Face—Same Heel. .nt . . . . . .
. . . . Amz Sep 48 40
ROCKLYNNE, ROSS
Biog sketch . . . . . . Amz Jun 38 6
Biog sketch . . . . . . FA May 39 85
Biog sketch . . . . Amz Jun 40 131
Biog sketch, pen & ink
portrait . . . . SS Nov 42 128
Biog sketch . . . . . PS May 43 106
Biog sketch, photo. . . . .
. . . . SS Fal 43 125
Abyss of Darkness. .s . . . .
. . . . .Ash Dec 42 86
And Then There Was One . . . . . .
. .s . . . . ASF Feb 40 53
Anton Moves the Earth. .nt . . . . .
. . . . ASF Nov 36 124
At the Center of Gravity. .s . . . . .
. . . . ASF Jun 36 67
Atom of Death. .s . . . .PS Win 40 46
Backfire. .s. . . . . . .ASF Jan 43 34
Beyond the Boiling Zone . . . . . .
. .s . . . . .SS Win 44 79
Big Man. .s . . . . . . Amz Apr 41 70
Bottled Men, The. .nt . . . .
. . . . ASF Jun 46 66
Bubble Dwellers, The. .nt . . . . . .
. . . . PS Fal 45 78
Captives of the Weir-Wind . . . . .
. .nt . . . . PS Sum 46 54

AUTHOR
Title. .Length . . . . Magazine, Date, Page

Collision Course. .s . . . .
. . . . .SSS Jan 41 8
Cosmic Yo-Yo. .s. . . . .
. . . . PS Sum 45 97
Creator, The. .s . . . . .Fut Dec 42 62
Daughter of Darkness. . . . .
. .s . . . . .Ash Nov 41 68
Day of the Cloud, The. .n . . . . . .
. . . . SS Nov 42 15
Distress Signal. .s. . . . .PS Spr 47 35
Diversifal, The. .s. . . . .PS Win 45 54
Electrical Butterflies, The . . . . . .
. .s . . . . FA Mar 42 46
Empress of Mars, The. .nt . . . . . .
. . . . .FA May 39 26
                    FA Oct 42 184
Escape Through Space . . . .
. .s . . . . Amz Jun 38 30
Exile to Centauri. .nt . . . .
. . . . TW Aug 43 13
Exiles of the Desert Star. . . . .
. .s . . . . .PS Spr 41 80
Extra Earth. .s . . . . SS Sum 46 88
For Sale—One World. .s . . . .
. . . . .SSS Feb 43 11
Forbidden Dream, The. .s . . . . . .
. . . . PS Sum 40 41
Giant of Ganymede, The. . . . . . .
. .s . . . . Amz Dec 46 36
Giant Runt, The. .nt . . . .
. . . . .TW Sum 44 11
Gift Horse. .nt . . . ASF Aug 45 116
Gods Gil Made, The . . . .
. .s . . . . .UK Nov 40 68
Good Egg, The. .s . . . TW Fal 46 37
Ice World, The. .s . . .TW Sum 46 72
Immortal, The. .s. . . . Com Mar 41 4
Infidels, The. .s . . . . ASF Sep 45 63
Interlude. .s . . . . . . ASF Dec 42 67
Into the Darkness. .nt. . . . .
. . . . .Ash Jun 40 44
Intruders from the Stars. .n . . . . .
. . . . Amz Jan 44 44
Invisible Army, The. .s . . . .
. . . . TW Win 44 50
Jackdaw. .nt. . . . . . ASF Aug 42 61
Jaywalker. .s. . . . . . GSF Dec 50 51
Jupiter Trap. .s . . . . ASF Aug 37 46
Last Outpost, The. .nt . . . .
. . . . .ASF Jul 45 67
Man of Iron. .s . . . .
. . . . ASF Aug 35 94
Man Who Never Lived, The . . . . .
. .s . . . . Amz Sep 40 70
Mathematical Kid, The. . . . .
. .s . . . . Amz Jun 40 96

AUTHOR
Title..Length .... Magazine, Date, Page

Matter of Length, A. .s . . . .
. . . . .ASF Jan 46 118
Men and the Mirror, The. . . . . . .
. .nt . . . . .ASF Jul 38 74
Moth, The. .s . . . . . ASF Jul 39 91
Mutiny Aboard the "Terra". . . . .
. .s . . . . PS Sum 41 80
Pirates of the Time Trail. .n . . . .
. . . . SS Fal 43 15
Powerful Pipsqueak, The. .s . . . . .
. . . . Amz Sep 43 158
Pressure. .s . . . . ASF Jun 39 65
Prophecy of Doom. .s . . . .
. . . . Fut Jul 40 43
Quietus. .s . . . . ASF Sep 40 86
Reflection That Lived, The . . . . .
. .s . . . . FA Jun 40 42
Return from Zero. .s . . . .
. . . . .SSS Aug 42 130
Sandhound, The. .s . . . .
. . . . PS May 43 38
Sandhound Strikes, The . . . .
. .nt . . . . .PS Spr 45 2
Six Tuesdays. .s . . . . . PS Fal 46 85
Slaves of the Ninth Moon. .s . . . .
. . . . .PS Mar 43 100
Storm in Space. .s . . . .
. . . . TW Dec 42 90
Tantallus Death, The. .s . . . .
. . . . .PS Spr 40 61
Task to Lalri. .s . . . . . PS Sum 42 2
Time Wants a Skeleton. .nt . . . . .
. . . . ASF Jun 41 9
Trans-Plutonian Trap. .nt . . . . . .
. . . . .SSS Mar 40 80
Unguh Made a Fire. .s . . . .
. . . . ASF Apr 40 38
Vanishing Witness, The. .s . . . . . .
. . . . FA Jan 41 62
Venus Sky-Trap. .s . . . .
. . . . TW Spr 45 48
Victory Drums. .s . . . .CF Spr 44 79
Voice, The. .s . . . . . TW Oct 41 86
Warrior Queen of Lolarth . . . . . .
. .n . . . . .Amz May 43 88
Water for Mars. .nt . . . .
. . . . ASF Apr 37 10
Who Was Dilmo Deni? . .s . . . . . .
. . . . ASF Nov 38 108
Wicked People, The. .s . . . .
. . . . .SSS Feb 42 96
ROGERS, HUBERT artist
Covers for ASTOUNDING SCIENCE
FICTION
Feb, Sep, Oct, Nov 1939
Feb, Apr, May, Jun, Jul, Aug, Sep,

AUTHOR
Title..Length .... Magazine, Date, Page

Oct, Nov, Dec 1904
Jan, Feb, Mar, Apr, May, Jun, Jul,
Aug, Sep, Oct, Nov, Dec 1941
Jan, Feb, Mar, Apr, May, Jun, Jul,
Aug 1942
Mar, May, Aug, Nov 1947
Jan, Mar, Oct, Nov 1948
Jan, Feb, Jul, Aug, Nov 1949
Feb, Mar, Apr 1950
Cover for SUPER SCIENCE
STORIES
Aug 1942
ROGERS, JOEL TOWNSLEY
Beyond Space and Time. .s . . . . .
. . . . SSS Sep 50 102
Through the Blackboard. .nt . . . .
. . . . TWO Jun 43 13
ROGERS, MARGARET
I Have Been in the Caves. .nt . . . .
. . . . Amz Jan 47 8
ROGERS, MELVA
To Give Them Welcome. .nt . . . .
. . . . OW Jan 50 84
ROHMER, SAX *pseud ARTHUR S.*
WARD
Curse of a Thousand Kisses,
The. .s . . . . .AFR #7 29
In the Valley of the Sorceress . . .
. .s . . . . AFR #12 48
ROMANS, R. H.
Around the World in 24
Hours. .s . . . . . . AW Oct 29 306
Moon Conquerors, The. .n . . . . .
. . . . WQ Win 30 150
SFQ Sum 40 4
War of the Planets, The. .n . . . . .
. . . . .WQ Sum 30 438
RONAN, MARGARET
Finger! Finger! . .s . . . .
. . . . UK Oct 41 81
ROONEY, RAY
Eye of Madness, The. .s . . . .
. . . . ASF Apr 37 73
ROSBOROUGH, L. B.
Hastings—1066. .s . . . .
. . . . Amz Jun 34 53
ROSCOE, THEODORE
He Love Was Jungle Gold *(Leopard*
Teeth). .nt . . . . . .FanS Nov 50 49
Little Doll Died, The. .nt . . . . . .
. . . . .AMF Apr 50 94
She Said, "Take Me If You Dare"
(On Account of a Woman) . . . .
. .nt . . . . FanF May 50 3

AUTHOR
Title..Length .... Magazine, Date, Page

ROSE, (DR.) WALTER, (L.D.S.,
R.C.S.)
By Jove!. .n 3 pt . . . Amz Feb 37 75
Lurking Death, The. .s . . . .
. . . . Amz Feb 36 11
ROSMOND, BABETTE
One Man's Harp. .s . . . .
. . . . UK Aug 43 120
UK 48 98
ROSS, DALLAS *pseud of MACK*
REYNOLDS
Give the Devil His Due. .s . . . . . .
. . . . FA Oct 50 84
You Might Say Virginia
Dared. .s . . . . . Amz Sep 50 70
ROSS, E. L.
Faceted Eyes. .s . . .ASF Oct 35 127
ROSS, JOHN C.
Squirrel People, The. .nt . . . .
. . . . Amz Sep 48 8
ROSSI, WILLIAM A.
Mutiny in Hell. .s . . . .
. . . . .SSS Nov 40 92
ROTHMAN, MILTON A. *See Also*
pseud LEE GREGOR
ROUSE, WILLIAM MERRIAM
Destroyer, The. .s . . . .
. . . . ASF Nov 30 198
ROUSSEAU, VICTOR *pseud of*
V. R. EMANUEL
Atom Smasher, The. .nt . . . .
. . . . ASF May 30 234
Beetle Horde, The. .nt 2 pt . . . . .
. . . . ASF Jan 30 8
Eye of Balamok, The. .n . . . .
. . . . .FN May 49 8
Invisible Death, The. .nt . . . .
. . . . ASF Oct 30 24
Lord of Space, The. .s . . . .
. . . . ASF Aug 30 158
Moon Patrol. .s . . . . . TW Oct 41 75
Outlaws of the Sun. .nt. . . . .
. . . . Mir Apr–May 31 78
Revolt on Inferno. .nt . . . .
. . . . .Mir Jun–Jul 31 195
Seal Maiden, The. .s . . . .
. . . . AMF Feb 50 116
Stone Men of Ignota, The . . . . . .
. .s . . . . .Fut Aug 41 68
Wall of Death, The. .s . . . .
. . . . ASF Nov 30 151
ROZEN *artist*
Cover for CAPTAIN FUTURE
Win 1940
Covers for PLANET STORIES
Mar, May, Fal 1943

AUTHOR
 Title. .Length . . . . Magazine, Date, Page

RUBY, B. F.
 Pellucid Horror, The. .s. . . . . . .
 . . . . Amz Aug 33 450
with FLETCHER PRATT
 Thing in the Woods, The. .s. . . . .
 . . . . Amz Feb 35 112
RUCH, MONROE K.
 Moon Destroyers, The. .s . . . . . .
 . . . . WQ Win 32 212
RUD, ANTHONY
 Molten Bullet, The. .s. . . . .
 .TW Jun 37 31
            FSQ Spr 50 61
RUDMORE, C.
 Coded Speech. .a. . ASF Aug 49 134
 Story of Modulation, The . . . . . .
 . .a . . . . ASF Jul 47 86
 Talking on Pulses. .a. . . . .
 . . . . ASF Jul 49 105
RUFF, J. W.
 Phantom of Galon, The. .s. . . . . .
 . . . . AW Dec 29 508
RUGER, JNO. artist
 Covers for AMAZING DETECTIVE
   TALES
 Jun, Jul, Sep 1930
 Covers for SCIENTIFIC
   DETECTIVE MONTHLY
 Jan, Mar, May 1930
RUPERT, M. F.
 Via the Hewitt Ray. .s . . . .
 . . . . WQ Spr 30 370
RUPPERT, CHESTER
 Last Stronghold, The. .nt . . . . . .
 . . . . Amz May 49 96
RUSSELL, ERIC FRANK See also
   MAURICE G. HUGI (1) and pseuds
   WEBSTER CRAIG (1), DUNCAN
   H. MUNRO (2)
 Biog sketch . . . . . . Fant #1 38 128
 Biog sketch . . . . . . .Fant #2 39 92
 Biog sketch, photo. . . . .
 . . . . ToW Aut 40 79
 Controller. .nt. . . . . ASF Mar 44 66
 Dear Devil. .nt . . . . . OW May 50 6
 Describe a Circle. .nt . . . .
 . . . . ASF Mar 42 116
 Dreadful Sanctuary. .n 3 pt . . . . .
 . . . . ASF Jun 48 8
 Exposure. .s . . . . . ASF Jul 50 107
 First Person Singular. .nt. . . . . .
 . . . . TW Oct 50 78
 Follower. .s . . . . . . ASF Nov 50 68
 Glass Eye, The . . . . ASF Mar 49 40
 Great Radio Peril, The. .s . . . . . .
 . . . . ASF Apr 37 47

AUTHOR
 Title. .Length . . . . Magazine, Date, Page

 "Hobbyist". .nt. . . . .
 . . . . ASF Sep 47 33
 I, Spy! . .s . . . . ToW Aut 40 54
 Impulse. .s . . . . . . .ASF Sep 38 110
 Invisible. .s. . . . . CF Win 40 92
 Jay Score. .s . . . . . ASF May 41 88
 Kid from Kalamazoo, The . . . . . .
 . .nt . . . . FA Aug 42 202
 Late Night Final. .nt . . . .
 . . . . ASF Dec 48 39
 Machinery. .s . . . . . . TW Dec 50 43
 Mana. .s. . . . . ASF Dec 37 37
 Mechanistria. .nt . . . .ASF Jan 42 35
 Metamorphosite. .n . . . .
 . . . . ASF Dec 46 6
 Mightier Yet. .s . . . . .Fant # 39 76
 Mr. Wisel's Secret. .ss . . . .
 . . . . Amz Feb 42 212
 Over the Border. .a . . . .
 . . . . UK Sep 39 129
 Present from Joe, A. .s . . . .
 . . . . ASF Feb 49 50
 Prr–r–eet, The. .s . . . . ToW #1 37 76
 Relic. .nt . . . . Fant Apr 47 5
 Resonance. .nt . . . . . ASF Jul 45 44
 Saga of Pelican West, The. .nt . . .
 . . . . ASF Feb 37 12
 Seat of Oblivion. .s . . . .
 . . . . ASF Nov 41 110
 Sinister Barrier. .n . . . .
 . . . . .UK Mar 39 9
         GSFN #1 7
 Shadow Man. .ss . . . .Fant #1 38 49
 Spontaneous Frognation. .a. . . . .
 . . . . .UK Jul 40 83
 Symbiotica. .nt . . . .ASF Oct 43 128
 Timid Tiger, The. .s . . . .
 . . . . ASF Feb 47 121
 Undecided, The. .nt . . . .
 . . . . ASF Apr 49 44
 Vampire from the Void. .s. . . . . .
 . . . . .Fant #2 39 79
 With a Blunt Instrument. .s . . . . .
 . . . . UK Dec 41 97
 World's Eighth Wonder, The . . . .
 . .s . . . . .ToW Sum 38 4
with LESLIE T. JOHNSON
 Seeker of Tomorrow. .nt. . . . . . .
 . . . . ASF Jul 37 124
RUTH, ROD artist
 Cover for AMAZING STORIES
 Dec 1941
 Covers for FANTASTIC
   ADVENTURES
 Aug, Dec 1941
 Feb 1943

AUTHOR
 Title. .Length . . . . Magazine, Date, Page

ROMANCE OF THE ELEMENTS
pictorial feature in FANTASTIC
ADVENTURES quite regular from
1939 to 1947. Credited irregularly
to ROD RUTH alone and occa-
sionally in collaboration with
GORDON MacLEAN. See Title
Index for complete listing.
RYAN, FRANKLIN W.
 Last Earl, The. .s . . .Amz Jan 33 917
RYAN, J B.
 Mosaic, The. .s . . . . .ASF Jul 40 39
RYTER, STANLEY
 Future War Tank. . . . .
 . .bacover pic . . . . . . Amz Dec 39

S

SAARI, OLIVER (E.)
 Around Infinity. .s. . . . .
 . . . . CF Win 40 118
 Cannibals, The. .s . . . Fut Dec 42 76
 Door, The. .ss . . . . . ASF Nov 41 93
 Life Jewel, The. .s . . . .
 . . . . .SFQ Spr 41 115
 Secret of the Crypt. .s . . . .
 . . . . .SSS Nov 40 82
 Shadowless World, The. .s . . . . . .
 . . . . .Fut Aug 41 96
 Sigma Lyra Passes. .s . . . .
 . . . . SSS Jul 40 71
 Stellar Exodus, The. .s . . . .
 . . . . ASF Feb 37 144
 Time Bender, The. .s . . . .
 . . . . ASF Aug 37 69
 Two Sane Men. .s . . . .
 . . . . ASF Jun 37 80
 Under the Sand Seas. .s. . . . .
 . . . . SSS Jan 41 107
SABE, QUIEN
 City of Eric, The. .s . . . .
 . . . . AQ Spr 29 270
SACHS, BERNARD
 Memory Machine, The . . . .
 . .s . . . . .WS Jul 35 180
ST. CLAIR, MARGARET See also
   pseud IDRIS SEABRIGHT (1)
 Biog sketch, photo. . . . .
 . . . . .FA Nov 46 2
 Biog sketch . . . . . . .SS Mar 47 111
 Aleph Sub One. .s . . . .
 . . . . SS Jan 48 62
 Bride of Eternity. .s . . . .
 . . . . .SSS Sep 49 36

AUTHOR
Title. .Length . . . . Magazine, Date, Page

Child of Void. .s . . . .SSS Nov 49 62
Counter Charm, The. .s. . . . . . .
. . . . FFM Aug 49 110
Dobridust, The. .s . . . TW Feb 48 41
Dreadful Dreamer. .s . . . .
. . . . SSS Jul 49 80
Everlasting Food, The. .nt. . . . . .
. . . . TW Dec 50 120
Flowering Evil. .s. . . . PS Sum 50 30
Garden of Evil. .s. . . . PS Sum 49 77
Gardener, The. .s. . . . TW Oct 49 56
Hathor's Pets. .s . . . . SS Jan 50 126
Hierophants, The. .s. . . . .
. . . . .TW Apr 49 77
Himalaychalet, The. .s . . . .
. . . . TW Feb 49 110
Jamieson. .s . . . . FFM Dec 49 114
Meem. .s . . . . PS Fal 50 58
Metal Lark, The. .s. . . . .
. . . . TW Jun 48 71
Neo-Geoduck, The. .s. . . . .
.TW Aug 49 129
"OONA & JIK" series includes:
    THE SOMA RACKS
    SUPER WHOST
    ALEPH SUB ONE
    THE DOBRIDUST
    THE METAL LARK
    THE HIMALAYCHALET
    THE NEO-GEODUCK
Piety. .s . . . . TW Dec 47 85
Pillows, The. .s . . . . TW Jun 50 133
Probate. .ss. . . . . . . TW Oct 47 80
Quis Custodiet. . .? . .s. . . . . . .
. . . . SS Jul 48 109
Rocket to Limbo. .s. . . . .
. . . . FA Nov 46 70
Rotohouse, The. .s. . . . .
. . . . TW Aug 48 119
Sacred Martian Pig, The . . . .
. .nt . . . . SS Jul 49 78
Soma Racks, The. .s. . . . .
. . . . .SS Mar 47 65
Stroller, The. .s. . . . . TW Aug 47 79
Super Whost. .s. . . . . . SS Jul 47 97
When the Sun Shines. .s . . . . . .
. . . . FA Oct 47 134
World of Arlesia. .s . . . .
. . . . F&SF Win–Spr 50 108
ST. JOHN, J. ALLEN artist
Covers for AMAZING STORIES
    Jan, Mar, Apr, May, Jun, Aug,
        Oct 1941
    Jul, Dec 1942
    Mar 1944
    Jan 1949

AUTHOR
Title. .Length . . . . Magazine, Date, Page

Covers for FANTASTIC
    ADVENTURES
    Oct 1940
    Mar, Jul (w/H. W. McCauley,)
        Nov 1941
    Mar, Jul, Oct 1942
    Apr, Oct, 1944
    Oct 1945
    Nov 1946
Centaur—Steed of the Gods,
    The. .bacover pic. . . . . FA May 43
ST. JOHN, PHILIP pseud LESTER
Del Rey
Anything. .s . . . . . . UK Oct 39 80
                        UK 48 71
Done Without Eagles. .s . . . . . .
. . . . ASF Aug 40 70
One-Eyed Man, The. .s . . . .
. . . . ASF May 45 48
ST. JOHN-LOE, G.
Where Four Roads Met. .s . . . . .
. . . . .ASF Oct 33 132
ST. PAUL, STERNER pseud of
CAPT. S. P. MEEK
Into Space. .s . . . . ASF Feb 30 221
ST. REYNARD, GEOFF(REY)
    pseud of ROBERT W. KREPPS
Androcles and the Buccaneer. . . .
. .s . . . . FA Jan 47 68
Blue Bottle Fly. .s . . . .
. . . . FA Apr 49 78
By Yon Bonnie Banks. .nt . . . . .
. . . . ASF Nov 45 65
Elements of Jedar. .s . . . .
. . . . .FA May 50 44
Five Years in the Marmalade . . . .
. .s . . . . .FA Jul 49 58
Make Yourself a Wish. .s. . . . . .
. . . . FA Mar 48 48
Mr. Beller and the Winged
    Horse. .nt. . . . . . . FA Oct 47 70
Mistress of the Djinn. .n . . . . . .
. . . . .FA Nov 50 8
Plaid Pterodactyl, The . . . .
. .s . . . . FA Mar 49 106
Through a Dean Man's Eyes. . . . .
. .s . . . . FA Oct 45 68
Usurpers, The. .nt . . . . FA Jan 50 8
Warder and the Wampum,
    The. .s. . . . . FA Dec 47 164
Wink Van Ripple. .s . . . .
. . . . FA Dec 45 128
SALE, RICHARD
Benevolent Ghost and Captain
    Lowrie, The (Till Doomsday). . .
. .s . . . . FanF May 50 71

AUTHOR
Title. .Length . . . . Magazine, Date, Page

Perseus Had a Helmet. .s . . . . . .
. . . . .F&SF Fal 49 108
SALISBURY, NATHANIEL
Moon Doom, The, Part 1 . . . . . .
. .n 4 pt . . . . WS Feb 33 708
SALTER, GEORGE artist
Covers for MAGAZINES OF
    FANTASY AND SCIENCE
    FICTION
    Win–Spr, Sum, Fal 1950
SAMACHSON, JOSEPH See pseuds
    WILLIAM MORRISON (28),
    BRETT STERLING (h) (12)
SAMALMAN, ALEXANDER
Changer of History, The. .s . . . . .
. . . . TW Feb 38 58
Life on the Moon. .ss . . . .
.TW Dec 46 95
Lost Hour, The. .ss . . . .
. . . . SS May 39 116
Medical Note. .s . . . .
. . . . TW Feb 42 103
SAMPLINER, LOUIS H. See pseud
    ALEXANDER BLADE (h) (1)
SANDERS, WARREN E.
Memory Stream, The. .s . . . .
. . . . Amz Apr 33 54
Sheridan Becomes Ambassador . .
. .s . . . . .Amz Jul 32 356
Sterile World, The. .s . . . .
. . . . WQ Spr 32 408
SANDROF, IVAN
Out of the Years. .s . . . .
. . . . TW Mar 41 102
Scientific Miler of Bowler U.,
    The. . . . . FA Oct 40 104
SANDS, DAVE house pseud used
    elsewhere by BRYCE WALTON
    and others
SANTRY artist
Cover for ASTOUNDING SCIENCE
    FICTION
    Apr 1949
SARGENT, SAMUEL M., JR.
Dr. Brittlestone's Method. .s . . . .
. . . . .Amz May 28 120
Telepathic Pick Up, The. .s . . . . .
. . . . Amz Dec 26 828
SATURN, SERGEANT editorial
    pseud given as conductor of
    editorial depts from beginning of
    1941 to Spring 1947 issues of
    THRILLING WONDER,
    STARTLING STORIES and
    CAPTAIN FUTURE

AUTHOR
Title..Length . . . . Magazine, Date, Page

EB *pseud of*
ROBERT A. HEINLEIN
Elsewhere. .nt. . . . . ASF Sep 41 96
SAUNDERS, NORMAN *artist*
Cover for DYNAMIC SCIENCE
STORIES
Apr–May 1939
Covers for FAMOUS FANTASTIC
MYSTERIES
Jun, Aug 1950
Covers for FANTASTIC NOVELS
Mar, May, Sep 1950
Covers for MARVEL SCIENCE
STORIES
Aug 1938
Apr–May 1939
Nov 1950
Covers for A. MERRITT'S
FANTASY MAGAZINE
Feb (?), Apr, Jul, Oct 1950
Covers for PLANET STORIES
Sum 1942
Cover for SUPER SCIENCE
STORIES
Mar 1950
SAWTELLE, WILLIAM CARTER
house pseud
Slaves of the Crystal Brain. .n . . .
. . . . .Amz May 50 8
SCHACHNER, NAT(HAN) *See also*
pseuds CHAN CORBETT (7),
WALTER GLAMIS (1)
Biog sketch . . . . FA Sep 39 91
FA Aug 41 133
Ancestral Voices. .s . . . .
. . . . ASF Dec 33 70
Beyond All Weapons. .nt. . . . . . .
. . . . ASF Nov 41 130
Beyond Which Limits. .s . . . .
. . . . ASF Feb 37 77
City of the Corporate Mind . . . . .
. .nt . . . . ASF Dec 39 45
City of the Cosmic Rays. .nt . . . .
. . . . .ASF Jul 39 47
City of the Rocket Horde . . . . . .
. .nt . . . . ASF Dec 37 112
City Under the Sea: .nt. . . . .
. . . . FA Sep 39 58
Cold. .nt . . . . ASF Mar 40 9
Crystalized Thought. .nt. . . . . . .
.ASF Aug 37 73
Earthspin. .nt . . . . . ASF Jun 37 8
Eight Who Came Back. .nt. . . . .
. . . . .FA Nov 41 44
Emissaries of Space. .n . . . .
. . . . WQ Fal 32 6

Entropy. .nt . . . . . . ASF Mar 36 76
Eternal Dictator, The. .s . . . .
. . . . WS Feb 33 678
Eternal Wanderer, The. .nt . . . . .
. . . . ASF Nov 36 14
Fire Imps of Vesuvius. .s . . . .
. . . . .ASF Oct 33 102
Great Thirst, The. .nt . . . .
. . . . ASF Nov 34 74
He from Procyon. .n . . . .
. . . . ASF Apr 34 92
100th Generation, The. .s . . . . . .
. . . . ASF May 34 85
I Am Not God. .n 2 pt . . . .
. . . . ASF Oct 35 64
Infra-Universe. .n 2 pt . . . .
. . . . ASF Dec 36 118
Island of the Individualists . . . . .
. .nt . . . . ASF May 38 42
Isotope Men, The. .nt. . . . .
. . . . .ASF Jan 36 40
Jurisdiction. .nt. . . . . ASF Aug 41 9
Living Equation, The. .s . . . .
. . . . ASF Sep 34 6
Lost in the Dimensions. .s . . . . . .
. . . . ASF Nov 37 54
Master Gerald of Cambray. . . . . .
. .nt . . . . UK Jun 40 125
Mind of the World. .nt . . . .
. . . . ASF Mar 35 64
Negative Space. .nt . . . .
. . . . ASF Apr 38 48
Old Fireball. .nt . . . ASF Jun 41 79
Orb of Probability, The. .nt. . . . .
. . . . .ASF Jun 35 110
Pacifica. .nt . . . . . . .ASF Jul 36 74
Palooka from Jupiter. .s . . . .
. . . . ASF Feb 39 73
"PAST, PRESENT & FUTURE"
series includes:
PAST, PRESENT AND FUTURE
CITY OF THE ROCKET HORDE
ISLAND OF INDIVIDUALISTS
CITY OF THE COSMIC RAYS
CITY OF THE CORPORATE MIND
Past, Present and Future. .nt . . . .
. . . . ASF Sep 37 60
Pirates of the Gorm. .s . . . .
. . . . ASF May 32 149
Redmask of the Outlands. .nt . . .
. . . . ASF Jan 34 2
Return of Circe, The. .n . . . .
. . . . .FA Aug 41 8
Return of the Murians, The . . . . .
. .nt . . . . ASF Aug 36 60
Reverse Universe. .nt . . . .
. . . . ASF Jun 36 8

Revolt of the Scientists. . . . .
. .s . . . . WS Apr 33 806
2. The Great Oil War. .s . . . .
. . . . WS May 33 946
3. The Final Triumph. .s. . . . .
. . . . WS Jun 33 26
Robot Technocrat, The. .s . . . . .
. . . . WS Mar 33 742
Runaway Cargo. .s . . . .
. . . . ASF Oct 40 88
Saphrophyte Men of Venus,
The. .s . . . . ASF Oct 36 84
Simultaneous Worlds. .n 2 pt . . . .
. . . . ASF Nov 38 9
Slaves of Mercury. .nt. . . . .
. . . . ASF Sep 32 78
Shining One, The. .s . . . .
. . . . .ASF May 37 78
Son of Redmask, The. .nt . . . . . .
. . . . ASF Aug 35 100
Space Double. .s . . . ASF May 40 83
Sterile Planet. .nt. . . . ASF Jul 37 52
Stratosphere Towers. .nt. . . . . . .
. . . . ASF Aug 34 94
Sun-World of Soldus, The . . . . . .
. .nt . . . . .ASF Oct 38 106
Time Express, The. .s . . . .
. . . . WS Dec 32 562
Time Impostor, The. .s . . . .
.ASF Mar 34 128
Ultimate Metal, The. .s . . . .
. . . . ASF Feb 35 90
When the Future Dies. .s . . . . . .
. . . . ASF Feb Jun 39 29
World Gone Mad. .s . . . .
. . . . Amz Oct 35 122
Worlds Don't Care. .nt . . . .
. . . . ASF Apr 39 9
with R. LACHER
Memory of the Atoms, The . . . . .
. .s . . . . .WS Jan 33 614
with ARTHUR LEO ZAGAT
Back to 20,000 A.D. . .s . . . . . .
. . . . WS Mar 31 1120
Death-Cloud, The. .s . . . .
. . . . ASF May 31 256
Emperor of the Stars, The. . . . . .
. .s . . . . WS Apr 31 1210
Exiles of the Moon. .n 3 pt . . . . .
. . . . WS Sep 31 440
In 20,000 A.D. . .s . . . .
. . . . WS Sep 30 310
Menace from Andromeda,
The. .s . . . . Amz Apr 31 78
Revolt of the Machines, The . . . .
. .s . . . . .ASF Jul 31 88

AUTHOR
  Title. .Length . . . . Magazine, Date, Page

Tower of Evil, The. .s . . . .
. . . . .WQ Sum 30 468
Venus Mines, Incorporated. .s . . .
. . . . WS Aug 31 294
                        SS Jan 47 72
SCHEER, GEORGE H., JR.
  Another Dimension. .nt . . . . .
. . . . Amz Oct 35 36
  Beam Transmission. .nt. . . . . .
. . . . .Amz Jul 34 78
  Crystaline Salvation, The. .nt. . . .
. . . . Amz Jun 37 92
  Last Ice, The. .nt . . . .
. . . . Amz Oct 37 71
SCHEER, JAMES F.
  Do Cave Men Still Live?. .a . . . . .
. . . . Amz Feb 40 125
SCHEFTLEMAN, EUGENE H.
  Waterspout, The. .s . . . .
. . . . WS Dec 34 828
SCHERE, M(OSES)
  Anachronistic Optics. .s . . . .
. . . . ASF Feb 38 26
  Bargain in Bodies, A. .s . . . .
. . . . UK Jun 43 71
  Brain-Storm Vibration, The. . . . .
. .s . . . . ASF May 38 138
  Let Cymbals Ring! . .s . . . .
. . . . ASF Dec 38 126
  Meteoric Magnet, The. .s . . . .
. . . . AW Apr 30 908
  Mind Worms. .s . . . .
. . . . PS Spr 48 43
SCHEULER, EDMUND
  Crawling Terrors. .s . . . .
. . . . Amz Jun 37 120
SCHIRRING, ALICE–MARY
  Child's Play. .s . . . .
. . . . .AFR #9 110
SCHLOSSEL, J.
  Extra-Galactic Invaders. .nt . . . . .
. . . . AQ Spr 31 260
  Second Swarm, The. .nt . . . .
. . . . AQ Spr 28 266
  To the Moon by Proxy. .s . . . . . .
. . . . Amz Oct 28 598
SCHMIDT, KONRAD
  Translation from the German of:
  Interplanetary Bridges *by Ludwig
    Anton*. .n . . . . . .WQ Win 33 102
  with LAURENCE MANNING
  Translation from the German of:
  In the Year 8000 *by Otfrid Von
    Hanstein*. .n 3 pt . . . .
. . . . .WS Jul 32 102

with FLETCHER PRATT
Translation from the German of:
  Cosmic Cloud, The *by Bruno H.
    Burgel*. .nt . . . . WQ Fal 31 6
SCHMIDT, L.(EO) A.
  Biog sketch . . . . . Amz Dec 38 144
  Dr. MacDonough's Encephalo-
    semanticommunicator. .s . . . . .
. . . . Amz Mar 45 188
  Return of Man, The. .s . . . .
. . . . Amz Feb 42 134
with A. R. TOFTE
  Purge of the Deaf. .s . . . .
. . . . Amz Dec 38 56
SCHMITZ, JAMES H.
  Agent of Vega. .n . . .ASF Jul 49 10
  Greenface. .s . . . . . UK Aug 43 140
  Second Night of Summer. .nt. . . .
. . . . GSF Dec 50 4
  Truth About Cushgar, The . . . . .
  . .nt . . . . ASF Nov 50 6
  Witches of Karres, The. .nt . . . . .
. . . . ASF Dec 49 7
SCHNEEMAN, CHARLES *artist*
  *Covers for ASTOUNDING SCIENCE
    FICTION*
  May, Dec 1938
  Apr 1939
  Jan 1940
SCHOENFELD, HOWARD
  Built Up Logically. .s . . . .
. . . . .F&SF Fal 50 33
SCHOEPFLIN, HARL VINCENT *See
  pseud HARL VINCENT (74)*
SCHOMBERG, ALEX *artist*
  Biog sketch, photo. . . . .
. . . . TW Jun 39 89
SCHOOLCRAFT, J. L.
  Death's Secret. .nt . . . .FN Jul 50 68
SCHWARTZ, JULIUS
  Can We Fortell the Future? . . . . .
  . .a . . . . FA Jul 42 116
  FANTASTIC HOAXES
  The Cardiff Giant. .a . . . .
. . . . .FA Jul 39 54
  John Worrel Keely's Atomic
    Power Plant. .a . . . FA Sep 39 56
  The Calaveras Skull Hoax . . . . .
. . . . FA Nov 39 54
  The Comet Seeker Hoax. .a . . . .
. . . . FA May 40 38
  Cagliostro. .a . . . .
. . . . FA Jun 40 90
  Barnum. .a . . . . . . FA Jan 41 76
                        Amz May 41 48

SCHWARTZMAN, LAURENCE
with JACK WILLIAMSON
  Red Slag of Mars. .s . . . .
. . . . WQ Spr 32 394
SCOTT, E. M.
  Voyage to Kemptonia, The . . . . .
  . .s . . . . Amz Oct 28 642
  What Happened to Professor
    Stockley? . .s . . . Amz Dec 31 836
SCOTT, H. W. *artist*
  Covers for UNKNOWN
  Mar, May, Jun, Jul, Sep 1939
  Jan 1940
SCOTT, (J. W.) *artist*
  Covers for FUTURE FICTION
  Nov 1939
  Mar, Jul 1940
  *Covers for MARVEL (SCIENCE)
    STORIES*
  Aug 1939
  Nov 1940
  Apr 1941
SEABRIGHT, IDRIS *pseud of
  MARGARET ST. CLAIR*
  Listening Child, The. .s . . . .
. . . . F&SF Dec 50 37
SEABROOK, WILLIAM
  Wow. .s . . . . WB Dec 50 108
SEARIGHT, RICHARD F.
  Cosmic Horror, The. .s . . . .
. . . . WS Aug 33 120
SEARS, EDWARD S.
  Atomic Riddle, The. .s . . . .
. . . . AQ Win 28 44
  Shadow on the Spark, The . . . . .
  . .s . . . . Amz Aug 27 498
  Singing Moonbeams, The . . . . . .
  . .s . . . . .AQ Sum 29 418
SELBY, PATRICK S.
  Space Ship 13. .s . . . . .NW #2 46 20
SELL, WILLIAM
  Other Tracks. .s . . . . ASF Oct 38 56
SELWYN, CARL
  Biog sketch . . . . . . .PS Win 47 118
  Citadel of Death, The. .nt . . . . . .
. . . . PS Fal 44 72
  Earth Is Missing. .nt . . . .
. . . . .PS Win 47 90
  Exiles of the Three Red
    Moons. .s . . . . PS Sum 40 54
  Hunter of the King Planet,
    The. .s.TW Aug 42 105
  Ice Planet. .nt . . . . . .Com May 41 4
  Man Who Could Stand Up,
    The. .SF Apr 43 68

AUTHOR
    Title. .Length . . . . Magazine, Date, Page

Revolt on the Earth-Star. .s . . . . .
. . . . .PS Spr 40 71
Space Bat. .s . . . . . . .PS Win 46 48
Strange Death of Richard Sefton,
    The. .s . . . . Amz Jan 40 62
Venus Has Green Eyes. .s . . . . . .
. . . . PS Fal 40 92
SEPTAMA, ALADRA *pseud of*
    JUDSON W. REEVES
Beast Men of Ceres, The. .nt . . . .
. . . . AQ Win 29 90
Cry from the Ether, The. .nt . . . .
. . . . AQ Spr 29 246
Dragons of Space. .nt . . . .
. . . . AQ Spr 30 218
Princess of Arelli, The. .nt . . . . .
. . . . .AQ Sum 30 402
Tani of Ekkis. .nt . . . .
. . . . AQ Win 30 104
Terrors of Arelli. .nt. . . . .
. . . . .AQ Fal 30 530
SEQUOYAH, REV. CHIEF
America's Mysterious Race of
    Indian Giants. .a . . . .
. . . . Amz Dec 46 157
Spirit of the Serpent God. .a . . . .
. . . . Amz Jun 48 158
SERVISS, GARRETT P.(UTAM)
Columbus of Space, A . . . .
. .n 3 pt . . . . . . Amz Aug 26 388
Moon Metal, The. .s . . . .
. . . . .Amz Jul 26 322
                            FFM Nov 39 40
Second Deluge, The . . . .
. .n 3 pt . . . . . . Amz Nov 26 676
                            AQ Win 33 2
                            FN Jul 48 6
SETTLES, JAMES B. *artist*
Covers for AMAZING STORIES
    Sep 1942
    Dec 1944
    Oct 1948
    Dec 1950
*Covers for FANTASTIC
    ADVENTURES*
    Jun, Jul 1949
Aircraft of Uranus . . . .
. .bacover . . . . Amz Aug 42
Airship of Io. .bacover pic . . . . .
. . . . Amz Nov 42
Airship of Venus . . . .
. .bacover pic . . . . . Amz May 42
Appointment With the Past . . . . .
. .(story illustration) . . . .
. .bacover pic . . . . . . FA Feb 44

AUTHOR
    Title. .Length . . . . Magazine, Date, Page

Archers of Mons, The . . . .
. .bacover . . . . FA Dec 47
Atomic Airship of Mars . . . .
. .bacover . . . . Amz Jun 42
Cable Train of Tomorrow . . . . .
. .bacover . . . . Amz Sep 45
Ether Powered Ship of
    Europa . . . . Amz Nov 43
Flying Wing of Pluto . . . .
. .bacover . . . . Amz Oct 42
Glider of Ganymede . . . .
. .bacover . . . . Amz Dec 42
IMPOSSIBLE BUT TRUE
    (Alaskan Mirage). .bacover . . . .
. . . . FA Feb 48
    The Bomb Out of Space . . . . .
. .bacover . . . . FA Apr 48
    The Incredible Wheels . . . . . .
. .bacover . . . . FA May 48
    The Mystery of the Ball of
    Fire. .bacover pic . . . Amz Nov 47
Jet-Boat of Tomorrow . . . .
. .bacover . . . . FA Apr 45
Jet-Propelled Mono Train . . . . .
. .bacover . . . . Amz Dec 45
Kite Ship of the Moon . . . .
. .bacover . . . . .FA Jan 45
Mica Sailboat of Mercury . . . . .
. bacover . . . . Amz Jun 45
Plastic Airship of Europa . . . . .
. .bacover . . . . Amz Sep 42
Radium Airship of Saturn . . . . . .
. .bacover . . . . .Amz Jul 42
Rocket Warship. .bacover pic . . . .
. . . . Amz May 44
Sailing Ship of Venus . . . .
. .bacover . . . . .Amz Jan 43
Satellite Space Ship Station . . . . .
. . . . Amz May 46
Ship of Callisto. .bacover pic . . . .
. . . . Amz Mar 44
Ship of Jupiter. .bacover pic . . . .
. . . . Amz Sep 43
Son of the Sun. .bacover pic . . . .
. . . . FA Nov 47
Spaceship Seen Over Idaho . . . . .
. .bacover . . . . .Amz Jan 48
Space Ships in Antarctica . . . . .
. .bacover . . . . Amz Feb 48
Space Ships at Angkor Wat? . . . .
. . . . Amz Apr 48
Spaceships in Ancient Egypt . . . .
. . . . Amz May 48
Space Ship in the Jungle . . . . . .
. .bacover . . . . Amz Jul 48

AUTHOR
    Title. .Length . . . . Magazine, Date, Page

Submarine of Neptune . . . .
. .bacover . . . . Amz Mar 43
Super Train of Tomorrow . . . . .
. .bacover . . . . Amz Dec 44
Trade Your Trouble for a
    Bubble. .bacover pic . . . .
. . . . Amz Feb 46
Warship of Mars. .bacover pic . . .
. . . . .Amz Jul 43
*WONDERS OF THE ANCIENT
    WORLD*
    Building the Great Pyramid . . . .
. . . . Amz Jun 46
    The Colossus of Rhodes . . . . . .
. .bacover . . . . .Amz Jul 46
SHANKS, EDWARD
People of the Ruins. .n . . . .
. . . . FFM Jun 47 6
SHARP, D. D.
At Bay in the Void. .s . . . .
. . . . WS Feb 33 698
Captive of the Crater. .s . . . .
. . . . WS Jun 33 20
Children of the Gods. .s . . . .
. . . . TW Jun 43 35
Day of the Beast, The. .s . . . . . .
. . . . SW May 30 1094
                            SS Fal 44 74
Death on the Siderite. .s . . . .
. . . . TW Feb 42 93
Doomed by the Planetoid . . . . . .
. .nt . . . . ASF May 36 58
Eternal Man, The. .s . . . .
. . . . SW Aug 29 230
                            SS Jan 39 100
                            WSA 50 116
Eternal Man Revives, The . . . . . .
. .s . . . . .WQ Sum 30 584
Faster Than Light. .s . . . .
. . . . MSS Feb 39 73
Girl from Venus, The. .s . . . .
. . . . MSS Apr 41 53
Higher Jurisdiction. .ss . . . .
. . . . WS Dec 34 782
Indesinent Stykal, The . . . .
. .s . . . . .ASF Jun 37 126
Lodestone, The. .s . . .Ash Aug 40 82
Messenger from Space,
    The. .s . . . . .WS Jan 33 628
Pillage of the Space-Marine . . . . .
. .s . . . . .CF Spr 43 78
Satellite of Doom, The . . . .
. .s . . . . .WS Jan 31 774
Substitute for War. .s . . . .
. . . . MSS Nov 40 90

AUTHOR
Title..Length . . . . Magazine, Date, Page

Three Worlds to Conquer . . . . . .
. .s . . . . WQ Win 31 262
SHARP, ENOCH
Unfinished Business. .s . . . .
. . . . FA Aug 48 138
SHARPE, D. RICHARD pseud of
RICHARD S. SHAVER
First Rocket. .s . . . . Amz Aug 47 72
SHAVER, RICHARD S.(harpe)
See also EDWIN BENSON (1) and
pseuds WES AMHERST (1),
ALEXANDER BLADE (h) (1),
PETER DEXTER (2), G. H.
IRWIN (h) (2), PAUL LOHRMAN
(h) (1), FRANK PATTON (h) (1),
STAN RAYCRAFT (1), D.
RICHARD SHARPE (1)
Adam from the Sixth, An. .s . . . .
. . . . FA May 46 96
Cave City of Hell. .nt . . . .
. . . . Amz Sep 45 6
Crystalline Sarcophagus, The . . . .
. .s . . . . .Amz May 47 10
Cyclopeans, The. .nt . . . .
. . . . FA Jun 49 112
Cyclops, The. .a . . . .
. . . . Amz Jan 48 72
Daughter of the Night. .nt. . . . . .
. . . . Amz Dec 48 8
Earth Slaves to Space. .n . . . . . .
. . . . Amz Sep 46 8
Erdis Cliff. .n . . . .
. . . . Amz Sep 49 62
Exiles of the Elfmounds . . . .
. .nt . . . . .Amz Jul 49 8
Fall of Lemuria, The. .nt. . . . . . .
. . . . .OW Nov 49 4
Formula from the
Underworld. .s . . . Amz Jun 47 10
Gods of Venus. .n . . . .
. . . . Amz Mar 48 8
"I Remember Lemuria". .n . . . . .
. . . . Amz Mar 45 12
If We Get a Chance. .a . . . .
. . . . .Amz Jul 48 156
Invasion of the Micro-Men. . . . . .
. .nt . . . . Amz Feb 46 6
Joe Dannon, Pioneer. .nt. . . . . . .
. . . . Amz Mar 47 10
Lady. .s . . . . .OW Mar 50 40
Land of Kui, The. .s . . . .
. . . . Amz Dec 46 8
Luder Valley. .nt. . . Amz Jun 46 98
Masked World, The. .n . . . .
. . . . .Amz May 46 6

AUTHOR
Title. .Length . . . . Magazine, Date, Page

Medieval Illicit. .a . . . .
. . . . .Amz Jan 48 157
Mer-Witch of Ether "18" . . . . . .
. .s . . . . Amz Aug 47 82
Mind Rovers, The. .nt. . . . .
. . . . Amz Jan 47 96
Mirrors of the Queen. .s . . . .
. . . . .FA Jul 48 90
Of Gods and Goats. .nt. . . . . . .
. . . . Amz Dec 47 58
Princess and Her Pig, The . . . . . .
. .s . . . . FA Mar 47 158
Proof. .a . . . .
. . . . Amz Jun 47 136
Quest of Brail. .n. . . . .
. . . . Amz Dec 45 8
Red Legion, The. .nt . . . .
. . . . Amz Jun 47 90
Sea People, The. .nt . . . .
. . . . .Amz Aug 46 8
SHAVER MYSTERY, THE (All-
Shaver issue recapitulating and
bringing up to date the Shaver
Mystery) . . . . Amz Jun 47
Slaves of the Worm. .n . . . .
. . . . FA Feb 48 8
Tale of the Last Man, The. .ss . . .
. . . . .FA Jul 46 142
Tale of the Red Dwarf, The. . . . .
. .nt . . . . .FA May 47 8
Thin Woman, The. .s . . . .
. . . . FA Mar 48 78
Titan's Daughter. .n. . . . .
. . . . Amz Sep 48 64
Thought Records of Lemuria. .nt .
. . . . Amz Jun 45 16
We Dance for the Dom. .nt . . . . .
. . . . Amz Jan 50 8
Witch of the Andes. .nt. . . . . . .
. . . . FA Oct 47 8
Witch's Daughter. .nt . . . .
. . . . Amz Jun 47 62
Zigor Mephisto's Collection of
Mentalia. .nt. . . . Amz Jun 47 30
with CHESTER S. GEIER
Battle in Eternity. .nt. . . . .
. . . . Amz Nov 49 58
Fountain of Change. .nt . . . .
. . . . FA Dec 48 38
Ice City of the Gorgon. .n . . . . . .
. . . . Amz Jun 48 8
with BOB McKENNA
Cult of the Witch Queen. .n. . . . .
. . . . .Amz Jul 46 8
Return of Sathanas, The . . . .
. .n . . . . .Amz Nov 46 8

AUTHOR
Title. .Length . . . . Magazine, Date, Page

SHAVER, TAYLOR VICTOR
with CHESTER S. GEIER
Strange Disappearance of Guy
Sylvester, The. .s . . . .
. . . . Amz Mar 49 24
SHAW, DICK cartoonist
Biog sketch, self-portrait. . . . . . .
. . . . Amz May 41 225
SHAW, LARRY B. See pseud TERRY
THOR (2)
Biog sketch . . . . PS Fal 45 64
Simworthy's Circus. .s . . . .
. . . . .WB Dec 50 18
SHEA, MICHAEL D.
Brothers, The. .ss. . .SSS May 41 102
SHEDENHELM, WILLIAM
Patch. .s. . . . . PS Fal 50 93
SHEEHAN, PERLEY POORE
Belated Tears of Louis Marcel,
The. . . . . FFM Mar 40 108
Monsieur De Guise. .ss . . . .
. . . . .FN Jul 40 142
SHELDON, WALT See pseud
SELDON WALTERS (1)
Bit of Forever, A. .s . . . .
. . . . SSS Jul 50 64
Celestial Landfall. .s . . . .
. . . . .OTWA Dec 50 90
Chore for a Spaceman. .s. . . . . . .
. . . . TW Dev 50 97
Country Beyond the Curve,
The. .nt. . . . . . . Amz Oct 50 68
Detonator. .s . . . . . . FA Sep 50 44
Eyes Are Watching, The. .nt . . . .
. . . . .Amz Jul 50 90
Music of the Spheres. .s . . . .
. . . . SS Jul 50 113
Operation Decoy. .s. . . . .
. . . . FA Jun 50 110
Perfect Servant. .s . . . .
. . . . SS Jul 48 115
Rope for Lucifer, A. .s . . . .
. . . . F&SF Win–Spr 50 37
Salad Citizens, The. .s. . . . .
. . . . TW Oct 50 133
Spacemate. .s . . . .
. . . . .TW Aug 50 93
Time Cave. .s . . . .
. . . . TW Apr 50 131
SHELTON, JERRY
Battle of the Brains. .s . . . .
. . . . TW Spr 46 13
Culture. .s . . . . ASF Sep 44 42
Devils from Darkonia. .nt . . . . . .
. . . . TW Spr 45 11

AUTHOR
Title. .Length . . . . Magazine, Date, Page

PROBABILITY ZERO
   Light Trap. .s . . . .ASF Jan 44 164
   Swamper. .nt . . . . . ASF Apr 46 62
   You Are Forbidden! . .s . . . . . .
      . . . . TW Jun 47 89
SHELTON, MILES *pseud of DON*
   WILCOX
   Ebbtide Jones' Atom
      Constrictor. .nt . . . FA Aug 41 100
   Ebbtide Jones on the
      Warpath. .s . . . . . FA Jun 42 218
   Fair Exchange. .s . . . FA Oct 44 148
   Gift of Magic, The. .s . . . .
   Girl in the Whirlpool, The. .s . . . .
      . . . . FA Aug 40 120
   Ocean Den of Mercury, The. . . . .
      . .n . . . . Amz Jun 48 100
   Perfect Trap, The. .s . . . .
      . . . . Amz Apr 42 84
   Woman's Island. .nt . . . .
      . . . . FA Dec 45 46
   Whirlpool in Space, The . . . .
      . .s . . . . Amz Nov 39 59
SHEPPARD, W. L., JR.
   Hair-Raising Tale, A. .ss . . . . . .
      . . . . .WS Jul 34 191
SHERIDAN, MAX C.
   Biog sketch, photo. . . . .
      . . . . TW Jun 39 86
   Formula for Life. .s . . . .
      . . . . TW Sep 40 66
   Human Equation, The. .s . . . . . .
      . . . . .TW Feb 39 15
   Interference. .s . . . . Amz Mar 35 44
   Venusian Tragedy. .s . . . .
      . . . . .SSS Sep 40 78
   Zones of Space. .s . . . .
      . . . . TW Feb 38 38
SHERIDAN, THOMAS *pseud of*
   WALTER L. GILLINGS
   Going Down! . .a . . . .
      . . . . Fant Dec 46 68
   Midget from Mars, The. .s . . . . . .
      . . . . .ToW Sum 38 108
   Skylight. .a. . . . . . Fant Apr 47 70
SHERIN, RONALD M.
   Lost Comet, The. .s . . . .
      . . . . Amz Jun 27 260
   When the World Went Mad . . . . .
      . .s . . . . .AQ Fal 28 554
SHERMAN, HAROLD M.
   All Aboard for the Moon . . . . . .
      . .n . . . . Amz Apr 47 10
   Green Man, The. .n . . . .
      . . . . Amz Oct 46 8

Green Man Returns, The. . . . . . .
   . .n . . . . Amz Dec 47 8
This Way to Heaven. .n. . . . .
   . . . . FA Oct 48 8
SHERMAN, L. R.
   Throw-Back, The. .s . . . .
      . . . . .FN Jul 49 98
SHERRED, T. L.
   E for Effort. .nt . . . .
      . . . . ASF May 47 119
SHERRY, (BOB) (ROBERT C.)
   artist
   Covers for ASTONISHING STORIES
   Dec 1940
   Apr(?), Sep(?) 1941
   *Covers for FUTURE FANTASY
      AND SCIENCE FICTION*
   Dec 1942
SHIEL, M. P.
   MASTERS OF FANTASY
   biog . . . . FFM Feb 49 91
   Purple Cloud, The. .n . . . .
      . . . . FFM Jun 49 10
SHIRAS, WILMAR H.
   In Hiding. .nt . . . .
      . . . . ASF Nov 48 40
   New Foundations. .nt. . . . .
      . . . . ASF Mar 50 5
   Opening Doors. .nt . . . .
      . . . . ASF Mar 49 9
SHIRLEY, VIVIAN
   Out of Tomorrow. .s . . . .
      . . . . OW Nov 50 132
SHOOK, C.
   Band Played On, The. .s . . . . . .
      . . . . .Ash Jun 42 90
SHORT, STANLEY R.
   Coronaviser, The. .a . . . .
      . . . . .ASF Sep 40 132
   Klystron, The. .a . . . .
      . . . . ASF Feb 41 98
SHULMAN, EDWARD
   PROBABILITY ZERO
   The Case of the Invincible
      Pirate. .ss . . . . . ASF Sep 44 92
SHURTLEFF, BERNARD L.
   Biog sketch . . . .
      . . . . FA Feb 40 86
   New York Fights the
      Termanites. .nt . . . . . FA Feb 40 8
   North of Matto Grosso. .nt . . . . .
      . . . . .Amz Jul 32 310
   Silence Is–Deadly. .nt . . . .
      . . . . ASF Apr 42 58
   Underground City, The. .nt . . . . .
      . . . . Amz Sep 39 38

SIBLEY, DON *artist*
   *Cover for GALAXY SCIENCE
      FICTION*
   Nov 1950
SIBSON, FRANCIS (H.)
   Son of Space. .s . . . . Fant #1 38 86
   Unthinkable. .n . . . . FFM Dec 46 10
SIEGEL, LARRY
   Another Chance for Casey. .s . . . .
      . . . . F&SF Dec 50 120
SILBERBERG, MRS. WILLIAM
   See pseud LESLIE F. STONE (17)
SILVER, NICHOLAS *pseud of*
   FREDERICK FAUST
SIMAK, CLIFFORD D.
   Biog sketch, photo. . . . .
      . . . . TW Jun 39 85
   Aesop. .nt . . . . ASF Dec 47 7
   Asteroid of Gold, The. .s . . . . . .
      . . . . WS Nov 32 514
   Bathe Your Bearings in
      Blood. .s . . . . Amz Dec 50 80
   Call from Beyond, The. .nt . . . . .
      . . . . SSS May 50 56
   Census. .nt . . . . ASF Sep 44 6
   City. .nt . . . . ASF May 44 136
   Clerical Error. .s . . . .
      . . . . ASF Aug 40 94
   Cosmic Engineers. .n 3 pt . . . . . .
      . . . . ASF Feb 39 45
   Desertion. .s . . . . . ASF Nov 44 64
   Earth for Inspiration. .s . . . .
      . . . . TW Apr 41 99
   Eternity Lost. .nt . . . .
      . . . . ASF Jul 49 117
   Hellhounds of the Cosmos. . . . . .
      . .s . . . . .ASF Jun 32 336
   Hermit of Mars. .nt . . . .
      . . . . ASF Jun 39 9
   Hobbies. .nt . . . . . . ASF Nov 46 49
   Huddling Place. .s . . . .
      . . . . ASF Jul 44 133
   Hunch. .nt . . . . .ASF Jul 43 9
   Hunger Death. .nt . . . .
      . . . . ASF Oct 38 23
   Infiltration. .s . . . . . . SF Jul 43 43
   Limiting Factor. .s . . . .
      . . . . .SS Nov 49 123
   Lobby. .s . . . . ASF Apr 44 144
   Loot of Time, The. .nt . . . .
      . . . . TW Dec 38 58
      . . . . SS Mar 49 88
   Madness from Mars. .s . . . .
      . . . . TW Apr 39 76
   Masquerade. .s . . . .
      . . . . ASF Mar 41 57

AUTHOR
Title. .Length . . . . Magazine, Date, Page

Message from Mars. .s . . . .
. . . . PS Fal 43 30
Mr. Meek—Musketeer. .s . . . .
. . . . PS Sum 44 58
Mr. Meek Plays Polo. .s . . . .
. . . . PS Fal 44 56
Mutiny on Mercury. .s . . . .
. . . . WS Mar 32 1166
Ogre. .nt . . . .
. . . . .ASF Jan 44 123
Paradise. .nt . . . .
. . . . ASF Jun 46 46
Reunion on Ganymede. .s . . . . . .
. . . . ASF Nov 38 66
Rim of the Deep. .nt . . . .
. . . . ASF May 40 63
Rule 18. .nt . . . .
. . . . .ASF Jul 38 32
Seven Came Back. .s . . . .
. . . . Amz Oct 50 102
Shadow of Life. .nt . . . .
. . . . ASF Mar 43 50
Space-Beasts, The. .s . . . .
. . . . .Ash Apr 40 6
Spaceship in a Flask. .s . . . .
. . . . .ASF Jul 41 45
Sunspot Purge. .s . . . .
. . . . ASF Nov 40 49
Time Quarry. .n 3 pt . . . .
. . . . GSF Oct 50 4
Tools. .s . . . ASF Jul 42 118
Voice in the Void, The. .s . . . . . .
. . . . WQ Spr 32 382
"WEBSTER FAMILY" series includes:
  CITY
  HUDDLING PLACE
  CENSUS
  DESERTION
  PARADISE
  HOBBIES
  AESOP
World of the Red Sun, The . . . . .
. .s . . . . WS Dec 31 878
with CARL JACOBI
Street That Wasn't There,
  The. .s . . . . .Com Jul 41 18
                          AFR #13 116
SIMMONS, HENRY HUGH
HICKS' INVENTIONS WITH
  A KICK
Automatic Self Serving Dining
  Table. .s . . . . . . Amz Apr 27 52
The Automatic Apartment . . . .
  . .s . . . . Amz Aug 27 493
The Electro-Hydraulic Bank
  Protector. .s . . . Amz Dec 27 860
The Perambulating Home. .s . . .
  . . . . Amz Aug 28 450

AUTHOR
Title. .Length . . . . Magazine, Date, Page

SIMMONS, HENRY T.
Z-Day on Centauri. .nt . . . .
. . . . PS Sum 48 4
SIMMONS, JOE
Living Test Tube, The. .s . . . . . .
. . . . Amz Nov 28 744
SIODMAK, CURT
Donovan's Brain. .n . . . .
. . . . .FFM Aug 50 54
Eggs from Lake Tanganyika,
  The. .s . . . . . Amz Jul 26 346
SKEEN, WARD
170 Miles a Minute. .s . . . .
. . . . Amz Jun 35 114
SKIDMORE, JO(E)(SEPH)
  W.(ILLIAM)
Adventures of Posi and Nega . . . .
  . .s . . . . Amz Jan 34 67
Beetle in the Amber, The . . . . . .
  . .s . . . . Amz Nov 33 80
Dramatis Personnae. .s . . . .
  . . . . .AQ Fal 31 522
Epos of Posi and Nega, An . . . . .
  . .s . . . . .Amz Jan 35 112
First Flight, The. .s . . . .
  . . . . Amz Nov 34 92
Legend of Posi and Nega, A . . . . .
  . .s . . . . Amz Oct 35 13
Maelstrom of Atlantis, The . . . . .
  . .n 2 pt . . . . Amz Feb 36 25
Murder by Atom. .nt . . . .
  . . . . Amz Jun 37 13
Romance of Posi and Nega,
  The. .s . . . . Amz Sep 32 512
Saga of Posi and Nega, A . . . . . .
  . .s . . . . Amz May 35 93
Seven Perils to Quinches. .s . . . . .
  . . . . Amz Feb 35 62
Souls Aspace. .ss . . . .
  . . . . Amz Feb 33 1005
Velocity of Escape, The . . . .
  . .nt . . . . . . .Amz Aug 34 55
World Unseen, A. .n 2 pt. . . . .
  . . . . .WS Jan 36 774
SKINNER, E. D.
Corpse That Lived, The. .s . . . . . .
  . . . . .Amz Jan 30 950
Electro-Episoded in A.D. 2025. . .
  . .s . . . . Amz Aug 27 469
Suitcase Airplanes. .s . . . .
  . . . . .AW Nov 29 424
SLACHTA, PAUL
Twenty-First Century Limited,
  The. .s . . . . Amz Dec 29 828

AUTHOR
Title. .Length . . . . Magazine, Date, Page

SLACK *artist*
Cover for NEW WORLDS
  #3 (1947)
SLEDGE, BROOX
Biog sketch, photo. . . . .
  . . . . .TW Feb 42 87
Rendezvous in the Void. .s . . . . .
  . . . . .TW Feb 42 84
SLOAN, RALPH
Ordeal in Space. .s . . . .
  . . . . PS Fal 49 53
SLOAN, T. O'CONNER
Managing Editor of AMAZING
  STORIES
Apr 26 *thru* Oct 29 issues
Editor of AMAZING STORIES
Nov 29 *thru* Apr 38 issues
Editor of AMAZING STORIES
  QUARTERLY
Fal 29 *thru* Fal 34 issues
SLOAT, EDWIN K.
Biog sketch . . . . . .Amz Jul 39 132
Beyond the Planetoids. .s . . . . . .
  . . . . Amz Aug 32 422
Deadly Swarm, The. .s . . . .
  . . . . Ash Aug 40 6
Flight to Venus. .s . . . .
  . . . . Amz Dec 28 780
Loot of the Void. .s . . . .
  . . . . ASF Sep 32 4
Master of Storms, The. .s . . . . . .
  . . . . .WS Jul 32 148
Nova, The. .s . . . .
  . . . . ASF Dec 39 86
Space Rover, The. .s . . . .
  . . . . ASF Feb 32 222
Three Suns of Eve, The. . . . .
  . .s . . . . Amz May 33 152
Vibration, The. .s . . . .
  . . . . Amz Dec 32 845
When Time Stood Still. .s . . . . . .
  . . . . .Amz Jul 39 76
World Without Name, The. . . . . .
  . .s . . . . WS Mar 31 1092
                          SS Jul 39 96
SMALE, FRED C.
"V" Force, The. .s . . . .
  . . . . FFM Jan 40 120
SMITH, CARLTON
As It Was. .s . . . . PS Sum 42 82
Pumpkin Eater. .s . . . PS Sum 46 36
SMITH, CHESTER
Pattern for Destiny. .s . . . .
  . . . . .Amz Jan 49 104

AUTHOR
Title. .Length . . . . Magazine, Date, Page

SMITH, CLARK ASHTON
MASTERS OF FANTASY
biog . . . . FFM Aug 49 109
Biog sketch . . . . . .ToW Sum 40 95
Adventure in Futurity, An . . . . .
. .s . . . . WS Apr 31 1230
Amazing Planet, The. .nt. . . . . .
. . . . .WQ Sum 31 534
Beyond the Singing Flame. . . . . .
. .s . . . . WS Nov 31 752
. . . . SS Sum 44 90
Chain of Aforgomon, The . . . . . .
. .s . . . . AFR #12 34
City of the Singing Flame,
The. .s. . . . . WS Jul 31 202
City of Singing Flame. . . . .
. . . . ToW Spr 40 6
. . . . SS Jan 41 98
Coming of the White Worm,
The. .s. . . . . . . .Sti Apr 41 105
Dark Age, The. .s. . . . .
. . . . TW Apr 38 95
Demon of the Flower, The. .s . . .
. . . . ASF Dec 33 131
Devotee of Evil, The. .s. . . . . . .
. . . . .Sti Feb 41 109
Dimension of Chance, The . . . . .
. .s . . . . WS Nov 32 520
. . . . ToW Win 41 61
. . . . SS Spr 46 72
Dweller in Martian Depths. . . . .
. .s . . . . WS Mar 33 768
Empire of the Necromancers,
The. .s. . . . . .AFR #7 85
Escape to Mlok. .s . . . .
. . . . ToW Aut 41 57
Eternal World, The. .s. . . . . . .
. . . . WS Mar 32 1130
Flight into Super-Time. . . . . . .
. .s . . . . WS Aug 32 218
Flight Through Time. .s . . . . . .
. . . . ToW Spr 42 54
Flower-Women, The. .s. . . . . . .
. . . . .AFR #9 3
Great God Awto, The. .s. . . . . .
. . . . TW Feb 40 111
Invisible City, The. .s . . . .
. . . . WS Jun 32 6
. . . . ToW Win 39 50
Light from Beyond, The. . . . . . .
. .s . . . . WS Apr 33 822
Marooned in Andromeda . . . . . .
. .s . . . . WS Oct 30 390
Master of the Asteroid . . . .
. .s . . . . WS Oct 32 435
. . . . ToW Sum 40 46

AUTHOR
Title. .Length . . . . Magazine, Date, Page

Murder in the Fourth
Dimension. .s . . . . AD Oct 30 908
. . . . ToW Spr 40 40
Planet of the Dead, The. .s . . . .
. . . . AFR #4 101
Plutonian Drug, The. .s. . . . . . .
. . . . Amz Sep 34 41
Primal City, The. .s . . . .
. . . . Com Dec 40 102
Vaults of Yoh-Vombis, The. . . . .
. .s . . . . AFR #1 101
Visitors from Mlok, The . . . . . .
. .s . . . . WS May 33 962
World of Horror. .s . . . .
. . . . ToW Aut 39 92
with E. M. JOHNSTON
Planet Entity, The. .s . . . .
. . . . WQ Fal 31 110
SMITH, CORDWAINER
Scanners Live in Vain. .n. . . . . .
. . . . FB #6 32
SMITH, E.(DWARD) E.(LMER),
(Ph.D.)
Biog sketch, photo. . . . .
. . . . TW Jun 39 76
Catastrophe. .a . . . .
. . . . ASF May 38 118
Children of the Lens. .n 4 pt . . . .
. . . . ASF Nov 47 7
Galactic Patrol. .n 6 pt . . . .
. . . . ASF Sep 37 8
Grey Lensman. .n 4 pt . . . .
. . . . ASF Oct 39 9
"LENSMEN" series includes:
TRIPLANETARY
GALACTIC PATROL
GREY LENSMAN
SECOND STAGE LENSMEN
CHILDREN OF THE LENS
Robot Nemesis. .s . . . TW Jun 39 72
. . . . SS Jul 50 120
Second Stage Lensmen. . . . . . .
. .n 4 pt . . . . ASF Nov 41 9
SKYLARK series includes:
THE SKYLARK OF SPACE
SKYLARK THREE
THE SKYLARK OF VALERON
Skylark of Space, The . . . .
. .n 3 pt . . . . . . Amz Aug 28 390
Skylark of Valeron, The . . . . . .
. .n 7 pt . . . . ASF Aug 34 8
Skylark Three. .n 3 pt . . . .
. . . . Amz Aug 30 388
Spacehounds of IPC. . . . .
. .n 3 pt . . . . . . .Amz Jul 31 294
*"STORM CLOUD, VORTEX
BLASTER" series:*
THE VORTEX BLASTER
STORM CLOUD ON DEKA
THE VORTEX BLASTER MAKES WAR

AUTHOR
Title. .Length . . . . Magazine, Date, Page

Storm Cloud on Deka. .nt . . . . . .
. . . . .Ash Jun 42 40
Triplanetary. .n 4 pt . . . .
. . . . Amz Jan 34 10
Vortex Blaster, The. .s . . . .
. . . . .Com Jul 41 2
Vortex Blaster Makes War,
The. .s. . . . . . . .Ash Oct 42 38
SMITH, EVERETT C.
with R. F. STARZL
Metal Moon, The. .s . . . .
. . . . WQ Win 32 246
SMITH, FORD *pseud of OSCAR
J. FRIEND*
Are You There, Charlie? . .ss. . . .
. . . . .SS Spr 45 72
Cosmic Chain, The. .ss . . . .
. . . . .SS Win 45 96
Gas Attack. .ss . . . . TW Spr 44 47
Helicopter Invasion. .ss. . . . . . .
. . . . .TW Sum 44 70
I Get Off Here. .s. . . . .
. . . . TW Win 45 68
Serum Rubber Man, The. .s . . . .
. . . . SS Sum 44 83
Venusian Nightmare. .s. . . . . . .
. . . . TW Win 44 44
SMITH, GARRET
Between Worlds. .n . . . .FN Jul 49 8
On the Brink of 2000. .nt . . . . . .
. . . . FFM Jan 40 6
Treasures of Tantalus. .n 2 pt. . . .
. . . . Amz Oct 27 676
SMITH, GEORGE O. *See also pseud
WESLEY LONG (7)*
Alien. .s. . . . . . . .ASF Oct 46 115
Answer, The. .s . . . . ASF Feb 47 84
Beam Pirate. .nt . . . ASF Oct 44 32
Blind Time. .s . . . . . ASF Sep 46 40
Calling the Empress. .s . . . .
. . . . ASF Jun 43 68
Catspaw, The. .nt . . . ASF Sep 48 7
Cosmic Jackpot, The. .s . . . . . .
. . . . TW Oct 48 109
Death Crystal, The. .nt . . . .
. . . . SSS May 50 14
Dog's Life, A. .s . . . .
. . . . TW Apr 48 118
Dynasty of the Lost. .nt . . . .
. . . . Fut Apr–May 50 8
Elusive Microvolt, The. .a . . . . . .
. . . . .ASF Sep 45 101
Fine Feathers. .nt . . . .
. . . . .ASF Jan 46 152
Fire in the Heavens. .n . . . .
. . . . SS Jul 49 9

AUTHOR
Title. .Length . . . . Magazine, Date, Page

Firing Line. .nt . . . . ASF Dec 44 69
Identity. .nt . . . . . ASF Nov 45 145
Impossible Pirate, The. .s . . . . . .
. . . . ASF Dec 46 59
In the Cards. .s . . . . . TW Aug 47 64
Incredible Invasion, The. .s . . . . .
. . . . ASF Mar 48 62
Journey. .s . . . . SS May 48 101
Kingdom of the Blind, The . . .
. .n . . . . SS Jul 47 11
Long Way, The. .nt . . . .
. . . . ASF Apr 44 67
Lost Art. .nt . . . . . ASF Dec 43 33
Meddler's Moon. .nt . . . .
. . . . ASF Sep 47 6
Minus Danger! . .nt . . . .
. . . . SSS Sep 49 66
Mobius Trail, The. .nt . . . .
. . . . TW Dec 48 105
Obey That Impulse. .a . . . .
. . . . ASF Jul 47 84
Off the Beam. .nt . . . .
. . . . ASF Feb 44 6
Pandora's Millions. .nt . . . .
. . . . ASF Jun 45 7
Pattern for Conquest . . . .
. .n 3 pt . . . . ASF Mar 46 6
PROBABILITY ZERO
Der Fuehrer's Base. .ss . . . .
. . . . ASF Sep 43 99
Problem in Solid. .nt . . . .
. . . . ASF Oct 47 39
QRM—Interplanetary. .nt . . . . . .
. . . . .ASF Oct 42 109
Quarantine. .s . . . .
. . . . TW Dec 47 48
Quest to Centaurus. .s . . . .
. . . . TW Apr 47 74
Rat Race. .s . . . .
. . . . ASF Aug 47 55
Recoil. .nt . . . . ASF Nov 43 5
Special Delivery. .nt . . . .
. . . . ASF Mar 45 72
Trans-Galactic Twins, The. . . . . .
. .nt . . . . TW Jun 48 9
Trouble. .nt . . . . . . ASF Jul 46 60
Trouble Times Two. .s . . . .
. . . . ASF Dec 45 125
Two Worlds for One. .s . . . .
. . . . Fut Jul–Aug 50 66
Unapproachable. .a . . . .
. . . . ASF Apr 46 112
Undamned, The. .nt . . . .
. . . . .ASF Jan 47 72
Vanishing Yankee, The. .a . . . . . .
. . . . ASF Mar 44 103

AUTHOR
Title. .Length . . . . Magazine, Date, Page

"VENUS EQUILATERAL" series
includes:
QRM—INTERPLANETARY
CALLING THE EMPRESS
RECOIL
LOST ART
OFF THE BEAM
THE LONG WAY
BEAM PIRATE
FIRING LINE
SPECIAL DELIVERY
PANDORA'S MILLIONS
IDENTITY
Vocation. .s . . . . . . ASF Apr 45 80
World-Mover, The. .nt . . . .
. . . . .Fut Nov 50 8
SMITH, LANGDON
Evolution. .poem. . . . .
. . . . FFM Apr 41 101
SMITH, LAWRENCE
Buried in Space. .s . . . .
. . . . Amz Oct 34 130
SMITH, MALCOLM artist
Covers for AMAZING STORIES
Jan, Oct 1942
May 1944
Feb 1946
Sep 1947
Feb 1948
Covers for FANTASTIC
ADVENTURES
Apr, May, Jun 1942
Apr 1943
Dec 1948
Covers for OTHER WORLDS
Nov 1949
Jan, Mar, May, Jul, Sep, Oct
(w/Arnold Kohn) 1950
IMPOSSIBLE BUT TRUE
The Thing on the Moon . . . . . .
. .bacover pic . . . . . . .FA Jan 48
WARRIORS OF OTHER WORLDS
Uranus. .bacover pic. . . FA Jun 43
Venus. .bacover pic . . . . FA Jul 43
Callisto. .bacover pic . . . .
. . . . FA Aug 43
Mercury. .bacover pic. . . . . . .
. . . . FA Dec 43
Saturn. .bacover pic . . . FA Oct 44
SMITH, MILTON K.
Mystery of Element 117, The . . .
. .nt . . . . Amz Dec 49 102
SMITH, WAYLAND
Machine Stops, The. .n . . . .
. . . . .FFM Mar 45 8
SMITH, WILL
with R. J. ROBBINS
Soul Master, The. .s . . . .
. . . . ASF Mar 30 350

AUTHOR
Title. .Length . . . . Magazine, Date, Page

SMITH, WOODROW WILSON pseud
of HENRY KUTTNER
Juke-Box. .s . . . . TW Feb 47 83
SMYTHE, FRANK J.
PROBABILITY ZERO
My Word. .ss. . . . ASF Dec 42 107
SNEDDON, ROBERT W.
Both Feet in Eternity (Half Past
Twelve in Eternity). .s . . . .
. . . . .FanS Nov 50 105
Half-Past Twelve in Eternity . . . .
. .s . . . . .FFM Aug 40 118
SNIFFEN artist
Cover for ASTOUNDING SCIENCE
FICTION
Feb 1947
SNOOKS, EPAMINONDAS T. pseud
of C. P. MASON
Brahma-Kalpa or The Expanding
Universe. .ss . . . . . WS May 33 945
Traders in Treasures. .s . . . . . .
. . . . WS May 34 1114
Why the Heavens Fell. .s . . . .
. . . . WS May 32 1374
SNYDER, ALEXANDER
Blasphemer's Plateau. .s . . . .
. . . . Amz Oct 26 656
Coral Experiment, The. .s . . . . . .
. . . . Amz Sep 29 522
SOMMERS, ASHUR VAN A.
Science, the Police and the
Criminal. .a . . . . . SD Apr 30 336
SONBERGH, GILBERT RAE
Laboratory of the Mighty
Mites. .s . . . . Amz Jun 43 8
SONDEREGGER, LEO
Biog sketch, photo. . . . .
. . . . TW Mar 40 79
Thought Materializer, The. .s . . . .
. . . . TW Mar 40 78
SONDERLUND, NILS O.
Angel from Hell, The. .n . . . . . .
. . . . MSS Dec 39 10
Mistress of Machine-Age
Madness. .nt . . . . . MSS May 40 8
SONNEMAN, W.(ILLIAM) K.
Council of Drones, The. .nt . . . . .
. . . . Amz Oct 36 41
Greta, Queen of Queens. .nt . . . .
. . . . Amz Feb 38 14
Master Minds of Venus, The . . . .
. .nt . . . .
SOUTH, CLARK pseud of DWIGHT
V. SWAIN
Devil's Lady, The. .s . . . .
. . . . FA Oct 42 164

AUTHOR
   Title. .Length . . . . Magazine, Date, Page

Outlaw Echo, The. .s . . . .
. . . . FA Dec 42 162
Time Mirror, The. .nt . . . .
. . . . Amz Dec 42 116
SOUCEK, LT. APOLLO
with WALTER RALEIGH
How High Can Man Fly? . .a . . . .
. . . . AW Apr 30 940
SPARKS, DAVID R.
Ape Men of Xlotli, The. .nt . . . . .
.ASF Dec 30 370
Winged Men of Orcon, The . . . . .
. .nt . . . . .ASF Jan 31 54
SPEAKER, DAVID M.
Disintegrating Ray, The . . . .
. .s . . . . Amz Feb 28 1088
Message from Space, The . . . . . .
. .s . . . . .Amz Jul 30 330
Supermen, The. .s . . . .
. . . . Amz Oct 33 592
SPEER, JACK
PROBABILITY ZERO
The Image of Annihilation . . . .
. .ss. . . . . ASF Aug 42 100
SPENCER, PARKE pseud of
SEWELL PEASLEE WRIGHT
SPENCER, PAUL
You Must Feel Again. .s . . . .
. . . . .FanS Nov 50 81
SPOHR, CARL W.
Final War, The. .n 2 pt . . . .
. . . . WS Mar 32 1110
SPRAGUE, CARTER pseud of SAM
MERWIN, JR.
Borghese Transparency, The . . . .
. .s . . . . TW Apr 50 134
Climate–Disordered. .ss . . . . . .
. . . . .SS Mar 48 101
Journey for One. .s . . . .
. . . . SS Nov 49 76
Long Flight, The. .s . . . .
. . . . .FSQ Fal 50 147
Rocket's Red Glare, The. .a . . . . .
. . . . SS Jun 43 100
Star Slavers, The. .s . . . .
. . . . .FSQ Spr 50 76
SPRIGG, T. STANHOPE
Editor of Pre-War FANTASY
No. 1 38 thru No. 3 39 issues
STACPOOLE, H. deVERE
Middle Bedroom, The. .s . . . . . .
. . . . FN Sep 40 128
FN Mar 48 124
STALEY, M. L.
Stolen Mind, The. .s . . . .
. . . . .ASF Jan 30 75

AUTHOR
   Title. .Length . . . . Magazine, Date, Page

STANDISH, LYNN
SCIENTIFIC ODDITIES dept . . .
irregularly from Mar 48 to Apr 49
VIGNETTES OF FAMOUS
SCIENTISTS
Benjamin Silliman. .biog . . . . .
. . . . Amz Sep 44 37
STANGLAND, ARTHUR G.
Ancient Brain, The. .s . . . .
. . . . SW Oct 29 400
SS Nov 42 100
Bon Voyage! . .s . . . .Ash Aug 40 24
Buckethead. .s . . . SSS Jan 41 24
Castaways of Space. .s . . . .
. . . . .WS Jul 32 118
Crossroads of Space. .s . . . .
. . . . WS Sep 32 310
Eye of Two Worlds, The. .s . . . . .
. . . . WS Jun 31 44
Fatal Equation, The. .s . . . .
. . . . WS Apr 33 830
50th Century Revolt. .s . . . .
. . . . WS Apr 32 1206
Jake and the Fifth Columnist. . . .
. .s . . . . .SFQ Spr 43 118
Lake of Life, The. .s. . . . .
. . . . WS Nov 32 504
Last of the Lemurians, The . . . . .
. .s . . . . .WS Jan 33 648
Menace from the Skies, The. . . . .
. .ss. . . . . SW Apr 30 1016
Outcast in Space. .s . . . .
. . . . .WQ Sum 31 560
Outcasts from Mars. .s . . . .
. . . . WS Oct 32 406
Plant Men, The. .s . . . TW Apr 45 41
Space Satan. .s . . . . . .SF Jan 41 83
Spaceman's Savvy. .s . . . .
. . . . TW Apr 42 109
35th Millennium, The. .s. . . . . . .
. . . . WS Aug 31 330
STANTON, L. JEROME
Measuring Rod. .a . . . .
. . . . .ASF Jun 46 100
Radar: The Waves That
"Feel". .a . . . . . . ASF Aug 46 100
STAPLEDON, OLAF
MASTERS OF FANTASY
biog . . . . FFM Feb 50 121
STAPLETON, DOUGLAS
How Much to Thursday? . . . . . .
. .s . . . . TW Dec 42 105
STARKE, KENDERSON pseud of
KRIS NEVILLE
Dumb Supper. .s . . . .
. . . . F&SF Sum 50 47

AUTHOR
   Title. .Length . . . . Magazine, Date, Page

STARR, JOHN pseud of ROGER
D. AYCOCK
STARR, PAUL
Invading Blood Stream, The . . . .
. .s . . . . ASF Dec 33 40
STARZL, R. F.
Dimension of the Conquered . . . .
. .s . . . . . . .ASF Oct 34 138
Earthman's Burden, The . . . .
. .s . . . . . . .ASF Jun 31 375
Eye of Prometheus, The. .s . . . . .
. . . . .SD Jan 30 38
Globoid Terror, The. .s . . . .
. . . . Amz Nov 30 700
Hornets of Space. .s . . . .
. . . . WS Nov 30 564
SS Mar 42 100
If the Sun Died. .s . . . .
. . . . ASF Aug 31 198
In the Orbit of Saturn. .s. . . . . . .
. . . . ASF Oct 31 7
King of the Black Bowl, The . . . .
. .s . . . . WS Sep 30 334
Last Planet, The. .s . . . .
. . . . WS Apr 34 1010
FSQ Sum 50 108
Madness of the Dust. .s. . . . .
. . . . Amz May 30 154
Man Who Changed the Future,
The. .s . . . . WS Jun 31 54
Martian Cabal, The. .nt . . . .
. . . . ASF May 32 168
Out of the Sub-Universe. .s . . . . .
. . . . .AQ Sum 28 378
Planet of Despair, The. .s . . . . . .
. . . . .WS Jul 31 190
Planet of Dread, The. .s . . . .
. . . . ASF Aug 30 147
Power Satellite, The. .s . . . .
. . . . WS Jun 32 60
Radiant Enemies, The. .s. . . . . . .
. . . . .FFM Nov 39 118
Red Germ of Courage, The . . . . .
. .s . . . . FFM Jan 40 65
Terrors of Aryl, The. .s . . . .
. . . . WS Mar 31 1102
20th Century Medusa, A . . . .
. .s . . . . WS Sep 31 476
with F. PRAGNELL
Venus Germ, The. .s . . . .
. . . . WS Nov 32 486
with EVERETT C. SMITH
Metal Moon, The. .s . . . .
. . . . WQ Win 32 246
STATTEN, VARGO pseud of JOHN
RUSSELL FEARN

AUTHOR
Title. .Length . . . . Magazine, Date, Page

STEBER, A.(LFRED) R. *pseud*
originally of RAYMOND A.
PALMER, later used also by
ROGER P. GRAHAM
by ROGER P. GRAHAM
Man Named Mars, A. .n . . . .
. . . . OW Oct 50 106
by RAYMOND A. PALMER
Biog sketch . . . . . Amz Aug 38 145
Biog sketch . . . . . Amz Mar 40 129
Biog sketch . . . . . Amz Jul 40 131
Biog sketch, photo (gag) . . . . . .
. . . . Amz Mar 45 199
Black World. .n 2 pt. . . . .
. . . . Amz Mar 40 8
Blinding Ray, The. .s . . . .
. . . . Amz Aug 38 46
Moon of Double Trouble . . . . . .
. .nt . . . . Amz Mar 45 82
When the Gods Make War . . . . .
. .nt . . . . .Amz Jul 40 6
with THORNTON AYRE pseud
(John Russell Fearn)
Mystery of the Martian
Pendulum. .s. . . . Amz Oct 41 116
with JOSEPH J. MILLARD
Lone Wolf of Space. .nt . . . .
. . . . .Amz May 41 50
STEELE, MORRIS J. *house pseud*
used by RAYMOND A. PALMER
and others
by BERKELEY LIVINGSTON
Wooden Ham, The. .s . . . .
. . . . FA Dec 43 62
by RAYMOND A. PALMER
Biog sketch . . . . . Amz Dec 38 144
Polar Prison. .s . . . .
. . . . Amz Dec 38 126
Phantom Enemy, The. .s. . . . . . .
. . . . Amz Feb 39 86
Weapon for a Wac. .s . . . .
. . . . Amz Sep 44 128
Author's real name unknown
Martian Masterpiece, The . . . . . .
. .s . . . . Amz Mar 45 72
STEIN, MODEST *artist*
Cover for ASTOUNDING SCIENCE
FICTION
Nov 1942
Cover for UNKNOWN
Oct 1939
STEPHENS, I. M.
with FLETCHER PRATT
Pineal Stimulator, The. .s . . . . . .
. . . . Amz Nov 30 738

Voice Across the Years, A. . . . . .
. .n . . . . .AQ Win 32 2
STERLING, BRETT *house pseud*
originated to cover varied author-
ship of CAPTAIN FUTURE stories;
later used on others.
by RAY BRADBURY
Referent. .s . . . . . . TW Oct 48 148
by EDMOND HAMILTON
CAPTAIN FUTURE
The Star of Dread. .n . . . .
.CF Sum 43 13
Magic Moon. .n . . . . CF Win 44 15
Red Sun of Danger. .n . . . .
. . . . SS Spr 45 11
Never the Twain Shall Meet . . . . .
. .s . . . . TW Fal 46 60
by JOSEPH SAMACHSON
CAPTAIN FUTURE
Days of Creation. .n . . . .
. . . . .CF Spr 44 11
Worlds to Come. .n . . . .
. . . . .CF Spr 43 15
STERLING, KENNETH
Bipeds of Bjhulhu, The. .ss . . . . .
. . . . .WS Jan 36 817
Brain Eaters of Pluto, The. . . . . . .
. .s . . . . WS Mar 34 822
Red Moon. .s . . . .
. . . . WS Nov 35 668
STERNIG, LARRY
Breath of Beelzebub. .s. . . . .
. . . . .PS Win 46 83
Clutch of Morpheus. .s . . . .
. . . . TW Win 46 92
Hesitant Angel, The. .s . . . .
. . . . FA Oct 47 108
Total Recall. .s . . . .
. . . . PS Fal 46 65
Venusian Invader. .s . . . .
. . . . .PS Win 45 90
STEVENS, FRANCIS
Behind the Curtain. .s. . . . .
. . . . FFM Jan 40 37
Citadel of Fear, The. .n . . . .
. . . . .FFM Feb 42 6
Claimed. .n . . . . . . .FFM Apr 41 6
Elf-Trap, The. .s . . . .
. . . . FN Nov 49 100
Friend Island. .s . . . .
. . . . FN Sep 50 110
Serapion. .n . . . . . . .FFM Jul 42 78
STEVENS, L.(awrence) STERN
artist See pseud (STEPHEN)
LAWRENCE

STEWART, WILL *pseud of JACK*
WILLIAMSON
Collision Orbit. .nt. . . . .
. . . . .ASF Jul 42 80
Minus Sign. .n . . . . . ASF Nov 42 43
Opposites—React! . .n 2 pt. . . . .
. . . . ASF Jan 43 9
Seetee Shock. .n 3 pt . . . .
. . . . ASF Feb 49 8
STILSON, CHARLES B.
Minos of Sardanes. .n . . . .
. . . . FN Nov 49 10
Polaris and the Goddess
Glorian. .n . . . . . . FN Sep 50 10
Polaris—Of the Snows. .n . . . . . .
. . . . FFM Jul 42 6
Sky Woman, The. .s . . . .
. . . . FFM Feb 40 33
Soul Trap, The *(Liberty or*
Death). .s . . . . .FN Jul 50 96
STIMSON, A. C.
Land of Mighty Insects, The . . . .
. .nt . . . . WS Apr 34 934
STOCKHEKER, R. W.
Fission Man, The. .s . . . .
. . . . SS Jan 49 135
Jet Jockeys, The. .s . . . .
. . . . .TW Aug 47 39
STOCKTON, FRANK R.
Philosophy of Relative Existences",
"The. .s . . . . .AFR #6 96
STODDARD, CHARLES *house pseud*
Atlantis Here We Come. .a . . . . . .
. . . . TW Apr 43 104
Atom Smashers, The. .a . . . .
. . . . TW Jun 41 90
Invisible Vandals, The. .s. . . . . . .
. . . . SS Fal 44 97
Martian Menu. .s . . . CF Sum 41 106
Rule of Math. .a . . . .TW Aug 42 82
Rule of Thumb. .a . . . .
. . . . TW Dec 41 104
STOKER, BRAM
Burial of the Rats, The. .s . . . . . .
. . . . FFM Oct 46 112
Secret of the Growing Gold,
The. .s . . . . FFM Aug 46 116
STOKES, SIMPSON
Down on the Farm. .s . . . .
. . . . TW Apr 37 60
STONE, BILL *photographer*
Cover for FANTASY FICTION
May 1950
Cover for FANTASY STORIES
Nov 1950

AUTHOR
Title. .Length . . . . Magazine, Date, Page

Cover for MAGAZINE OR
  FANTASY
Fall 1949
STONE, BURT B.
Keepers of the Flame, The . . . . .
  . .nt . . . . .FA May 49 8
STONE, (DAVE) (DAVID) *artist*
Cover for GALAXY SCIENCE
  FICTION
Oct 1950
Cover for GALAXY SCIENCE
  FICTION NOVELS
#1 (1950)
STONE, ELINORE COWAN
Devil Fish, The. .s . . . .
  . . . . AMF Oct 50 92
STONE, LESLIE F. *pseud of MRS.*
  WILLIAM SILBERBERG
Across the Void. .n 3 pt . . . .
  . . . . Amz Apr 31 6
Conquest of Gola, The . . . .
  . .s . . . . WS Apr 31 1278
Cosmic Joke. .s . . . . .WS Jan 35 970
Fall of Mercury, The. .nt. . . . . . .
  . . . . Amz Dec 35 27
Gravity Off. .s . . . . .Fut Jul 40 100
Great Ones, The. .s . . . .
  . . . . .ASF Jul 37 75
Gulliver, 3000 A.D. . .s . . . .
  . . . . WS May 33 902
Hell Planet, The. .s. . . . .
  . . . . WS Jun 32 14
Human Pets of Mars, The . . . . . .
  . .nt . . . . Amz Oct 36 83
Letter of the Twenty-Fourth
  Century. .ss . . . . Amz Dec 29 860
Man Who Fought a Fly, The . . . .
  . .s . . . . Amz Oct 32 610
Man With the Four Dimensional
  Eyes, The. .s. . . . . WS Aug 35 286
Men With Wings. .s. . . . .
  . . . . AW Jul 29 58
Out of the Void. .n 2 pt . . . .
  . . . . Amz Aug 29 440
Rape of the Solar System,
  The. .s. . . . . Amz Dec 34 12
Through the Veil. .s. . . . .
  . . . . Amz May 30 174
Women With Wings. .s . . . .
  . . . . .AW May 30 984
STONE, ROCKY
Ancient Geometrical Monument,
  The. .a 8 pt. .*(monthly* July
  thru Dec 49 *then skip to* May
  & Jul 50 issues on the final
  installments). . . . . .Amz Jul 49 132

STONEHAM, C. T.
Lion's Way, The. .n . . . .
  . . . . FFM Oct 48 10
STOREY, RICHARD
Menace of the Mists. .s . . . .
  . . . . PS May 43 107
STORM, RUSSELL *pseud of*
  ROBERT MOORE WILLIAMS
And No Tomorrow. .ss . . . .
  . . . . Amz Feb 50 146
Caveman Meets Blonde. .s . . . . . .
  . . . . Amz May 42 152
Gold Rush on Callisto. .s. . . . . . .
  . . . . Amz Apr 43 176
Mr. Throop's Incredible
  Hand. .s. . . . . . . FA Oct 42 208
Thunor Flees the Devils. .s . . . . .
  . . . . FA Feb 40 48
Trouble in Avalon. .s . . . .
  . . . . FA Jun 40 30
Warburton's Invention. .nt . . . . .
  . . . . Amz Sep 44 154
STOWELL, EUGENE
Giant Puffball, The. .ss . . . .
  . . . . .AQ Sum 31 429
STRANGER, RALPH
Biog sketch . . . . . . .Fant #3 39 74
Cold Comet, The. .s. . . . .
  . . . . .Fant #3 39 69
Message from Mars, The . . . .
  . .s . . . . WS Jun 32 28
STRATHGLASS, ALLAN
Doctor's Experiment, The. . . . . . .
  . .s . . . . Amz Mar 31 1140
STRATTON, GEORGE FREDERICK
Sam Graves' Gravity Nullifier. . . .
  . .s . . . . Amz Aug 29 465
STRIBLING, T. S.
Green Splotches, The. .nt . . . . . .
  . . . . Amz Mar 27 1086
Mogglesby. .nt . . . . . .AFR #11 41
STRINGER, ARTHUR
Woman Who Couldn't Die,
  The. .n . . . . FFM Oct 50 12
STUART, ALBERT B., M.D.
High Tension. .s . . . .
  . . . . Amz Aug 26 446
STUART, A. R.
Beer-Trust Busters. .s . . . .
  . . . . PS Fal 45 53
STUART, DON A. *pseud of JOHN*
  W. CAMPBELL, JR.
Atomic Power. .s . . . ASF Dec 34 88
Blindness. .s . . . . . . ASF Mar 35 99
Cloak of Aesir. .nt . . . .
  . . . . ASF Mar 39 9

Dead Knowledge. .nt . . . .
  . . . . .ASF Jan 38 44
Elder Gods, The. .n . . . .
  . . . . UK Oct 39 9
Elimination. .s . . . . ASF May 36 45
Escape, The. .nt . . . .
  . . . . ASF May 35 118
Forgetfulness. .nt . . . .
  .ASF Jun 37 52
Frictional Losses. .nt . . . .
  . . . . .ASF Jul 36 44
Invaders, The. .nt . . ASF Jun 35 54
"MACHINE" series includes:
  THE MACHINE
  THE INVADERS
  REBELLION
Machine, The. .s . . . ASF Feb 35 70
Night. .nt. . . . . ASF Oct 35 8
Out of Night. .nt. . . ASF Oct 37 10
Rebellion. .nt . . . . . .ASF Jul 35 64
Twilight. .s . . . . . . ASF Nov 34 44
Who Goes There? . .nt . . . .
  . . . . ASF Aug 38 60
STUBBS, HARRY CLEMENT *See*
  pseud HAL CLEMENT (12)
STURGEON, THEODORE *See also*
  pseuds E. WALDO HUNTER (2),
  E. HUNTER WALDO (1)
Artnan Process. .nt . . . .
  . . . . ASF Jun 41 50
Biddiver. .s . . . . . ASF Aug 41 120
Blabbermouth. .s. . . Amz Feb 47 66
Brat. .s . . . . UK Dec 41 69
Butyl and the Breather. .s . . . . . .
  . . . . .ASF Oct 40 105
Cargo. .nt. . . . . UK Nov 40 82
Chromium Helmet, The. .nt. . . . .
  . . . . .ASF Jun 46 132
Completely Automatic. .s . . . . . .
  . . . . ASF Feb 41 84
Derm Fool. .s . . . . UK Mar 40 114
Dreaming Jewels, The. .n . . . . . .
  . . . . .FA Feb 50 8
Ether Breather. .s . . . .
  . . . . .ASF Sep 39 119
God in a Garden, A . . . .
  . . . . UK Oct 39 75
Golden Egg, The. .s . . . .
  .UK Aug 41 132
Green-Eyed Monster, The . . . . . .
  . .s . . . . UK Jun 43 126
Haunt, The. .s . . . . UK Apr 41 106
He Shuttles. .s . . . . UK Apr 40 113
Hurkle Is a Happy Beast, The. . . .
  . .s . . . . .F&SF Fal 49 62
It. .nt . . . . UK Aug 40 97
Jumper, The. .s . . . . UK Aug 42 46

AUTHOR
Title. .Length . . . . Magazine, Date, Page

Killdozer! . .n . . . . . ASF Nov 44 7
Largo. .s . . . . FA Jul 47 122
Love of Heaven, The. .s . . . .
. . . . ASF Nov 48 28
Maturity. .nt. . . . . . ASF Feb 47 7
Medusa. .s . . . . . . ASF Feb 42 80
Memorial. .s . . . . . ASF Apr 46 158
Memory. .s. . . . . . . TW Aug 48 56
Messenger. .s. . . . . TW Feb 49 115
Mewhu's Jet. .nt . . . . ASF Nov 46 7
Microcosmic God. .nt. . . . .
. . . . ASF Apr 41 46
Minority Report. .s . . . .
. . . . .ASF Jun 49 130
Poker Face. .s . . . . . ASF Mar 41 75
Prodigy. .s . . . . . . ASF Apr 49 71
Shottle Bop. .nt . . . UK Feb 41 100
Sky Was Full of Ships, The . . . . .
. .s . . . . TW Jun 47 55
Stars Are the Styx, The . . . .
. .nt . . . . GSF Oct 50 72
That Low. .ss . . . . FFM Oct 48 118
There Is No Defense. .nt. . . . . . .
. . . . ASF Feb 48 7
Thunder and Roses. .nt. . . . . . .
. . . . ASF Nov 47 76
Tiny and the Monster. .nt . . . . . .
. . . . ASF May 47 50
Two Percent Inspiration. .s . . . . .
. . . . ASF Oct 41 86
Unite and Conquer. .nt. . . . . . .
. . . . ASF Oct 48 63
What Dead Men Tell. .nt . . . . . .
. . . . ASF Nov 49 122
Yesterday Was Monday. . . . . . .
. .s . . . . UK Jun 41 112
                        UK 48 54
with JAMES H. BEARD
Bones, The. .s . . . . . UK Aug 43 107
Hag Seleen, The. .s. . . . .
. . . . .UK Dec 42 96
SULLIVAN, EDWARD S.
Let Clarence Do It. .ss . . . .
. . . . FFM Dec 48 112
SULLIVAN, H. L. G.
Moon Waits, The. .nt . . . .
. . . . Amz Nov 34 14
SUMNER, C. R.
Flower of Evil, The. .nt . . . .
. . . . AD Oct 30 900
SURDEZ, GEORGES
Translation from the French of:
Five After Five by Maurice
Renard. .s . . . . . . TW Apr 41 65
SUTHERLAND, HALLIDAY
Biog sketch . . . . . .Fant #2 39 92

Valley of Doom. .s. . . . .
. . . . .Fant #2 39 31
SUTTON, RANSOME
Island of Terror, The. .s . . . . . .
. . . . WQ Fal 30 80
SWAIN, DWIGHT V. See Also
pseud CLARK SOUTH (3)
Bottle Imp, The. .nt . .. .
. . . . FA Sep 42 140
Crusade Across the Void. .n. . . . .
. . . . Amz Oct 42 8
Drummers of Daugavo. .n . . . . . .
. . . . FA Mar 43 8
Hands of Ali Jinnah, The . . . . . .
. .nt . . . . FA Dec 47 82
Henry Horn's Blitz Bomb . . . . . .
. .s . . . . Amz Jun 42 112
Henry Horn's Racing Ray . . . . .
. .s.FA Feb 42 112
Henry Horn's Super-Solvent . . . .
. .s . . . . FA Nov 41 128
Henry Horn's X-Ray Eye
Glasses. .s. . . . . Amz Dec 42 194
Long Remember. .s . . . .
. . . . FA Dec 42 86
Peace Mission to Planetoid X . . . .
. .nt . . . . Amz Sep 42 150
Perfect Husband, The. .s . . . . . .
. . . . FA Jan 43 92
Persian Carpet, The. .n . . . .
. . . . Amz Feb 43 156
Powers of Darkness, The. . . . . . .
. .s . . . . .Amz Jul 42 58
Shayla's Garden. .nt. . . . .
. . . . FA Nov 42 194
Skin-Deep Beauty, The. .s . . . . .
. . . . FA Jun 42 122
SWIATEK, EDMOND artist
Cover for AMAZING STORIES
Mar 1949
Covers for FANTASTIC
ADVENTURES
Apr, Oct, Dec 1949
SWISHER, R. D., (Ph.D.)
Plan for a Universe. .a . . . .
. . . . ASF Apr 46 120
What Are Positrons? . .a . . . . . .
. . . . ASF Aug 37 117
SYKES, HAROLD S.
Ancient Ones, The. .s . . . .
. . . . SSS Jul 50 92
Beacon of Airport Seven,
The. .s. . . . . AW Jul 29 42
Insatiable Entity, The. . . . .
. .s . . . . SW Mar 30 902
Myriad, The. .s . . . . Amz Oct 37 16

T

TAINE, JOHN pseud of ERIC
TEMPLE BELL
MASTERS OF FANTASY
biog . . . . FFM Apr 49 87
Biog sketch, photo. . . . .
. . . . TW Jun 39 17
Before the Dawn. .n. . . . .
. . . . .FFM Feb 46 10
Black Goldfish. .nt 2 pt . . . .
. . . . .FB #4 4
Greatest Adventure, The. . . . . . .
. .n . . . . .FFM Jun 44 8
Iron Star, The. .n. . . . .
. . . . .FFM Sep 43 8
Purple Sapphire, The. .n . . . .
. . . . .FFM Aug 48 8
Seeds of Life. .n . . . .
. . . . .AQ Fal 31 434
Time Stream, The. .n 3 pt . . . . . .
. . . . WS Dec 31 824
Tomorrow. .n . . . .
. . . . .MSS Apr–May 39 12
Twelve Eighty-Seven . . . .
. .n 5 pt . . . . .ASF May 35 8
Ultimate Catalyst, The. .s . . . . . .
. . . . TW Jun 39 13
                        SS Nov 49 84
White Lily. .n . . . . . . AQ Win 30 4
Why Science Fiction?. . . . .
. .guest editorial . . . .SS Mar 39 15
TANNER, CHARLES R.
Biog sketch . . . . Amz Jun 38 6
Biog sketch, photo. . . . .
. . . . Amz Feb 41 129
Cham of the Hills. .nt. . . . .
. . . . .SSS Aug 42 106
Color of Space, The. .ss . . . .
. . . . SW Mar 30 892
Flight of the Mercury, The . . . . .
. .s . . . . .WS Jul 30 116
Improbable, The. .s . . . .
. . . . .Cos May 41 80
Johnny Goodturn. .s . . . .
. . . . .OW Nov 50 144
Luck of Enoch Higgins, The . . . .
. .s . . . . FA Aug 42 176
Mr. Garfinkel and the
Lepra-Cohen. .s. . . OW Sep 50 142
Mutiny in the Void. .s . . . .
. . . . PS Fal 43 45
Out of the Jar. .s . . . .
. . . . .Sti Feb 41 101

AUTHOR
Title. .Length . . . . Magazine, Date, Page

Revolt of the Machine Men,
The. .s . . . . . . .SSS Nov 42 32
Stillwell Degravitator, The. .s. . . .
. . . . Amz Feb 41 108
Tumithak in Shawm. .nt . . . .
.Amz Jun 33 201
Tumithak of the Corridors . . . . .
. .nt . . . . .Amz Jan 32 898
Tumithak of the Towers of
Fire. .nt. . . . . . .SSS Nov 41 78
Vanishing Diamonds, The. .s . . . .
. . . . Amz Jun 38 72

TANNER, ROBERT L.
Immortality No Longer a
Myth? . .a . . . . . Amz Nov 46 155

TARBELL, LEE
Valley of the Croen. .n . . . .
. . . . Amz Apr 49 74

TASHMAN, GEORGE
Caduceus of Hermes, The. .s . . . .
. . . . Amz Oct 46 48
Most Ingenious Paradox, A . . . . .
. .s . . . . Amz Dec 44 78

TAURASI, JAMES V.
FANDOM'S CORNER dept of
fanews and fanzine
reviews. .starting . . . . SSS Jan 49 6

TAYLOR, J. GIBSON
Last Sacrifice. .s . . . ASF Dec 33 84

TAYLOR, JOHN M.
Beings of the Ooze. .s . . . .
. . . . SF Mar 41 39
Old Martian Proverb, An. . . . . . .
. .s . . . . .SF Jun 41 49

TAYLOR, MERLIN MOORE
White Gold Pirate, The . . . .
. .s . . . . Amz Apr 27 30

TEASON, JAMES artist
Cover for AMAZING STORIES
May 1947

TEMPLE, WILLIAM F.
Biog sketch . . . . Amz Feb 39 134
Bone of Contention, The . . . . . .
. .s . . . . TW Oct 50 122
Brain Beast, The. .nt . . . .
. . . . SSS Jul 49 8
Date to Remember, A. .s. . . . . .
. . . . TW Aug 49 121
Experiment in Genius. . . . .
. .s . . . . .ToW Sum 40 33
For Each Man Kills. .s . . . .
. . . . Amz Mar 50 92
Forget-Me-Not. .nt. . . . .
. . . . OW Sep 50 18
4 Sided Triangle, The. .s . . . . . .
. . . . Amz Nov 39 6

Lunar Lilliput. .nt . . . .
. . . . ToW #2 38 100
Martian's Fancy. .s. . . . .
. . . . NW Sum 50 38
Miracle Town. .s . . . . TW Oct 48 86
Mr. Craddock's Amazing
Experience. .s. . . . Amz Feb 39 42
Monster on the Border, The. . . . .
. .s . . . . .SSS Nov 40 60
Smile of the Sphinx, The . . . . . .
. .s . . . . ToW Aut 38 42
WB Dec 50 68
Three Pylons, The. .s . . . .
. . . . .NW #1 46 43
Way of Escape. .s. . . . TW Jun 48 46
Wisher Take All. .ss . . . .
. . . . OW Jul 50 20

TEMPLETON, WILLIAM F.
Mr. Primrose Goes to the
Devil. .s . . . . FN May 50 118

TENCH, C. V.
Compensation. .s. . . .ASF Jan 30 92

TENN, WILLIAM pseud of PHILIP
KLASS
Alexander the Bait. .s . . . .
. . . . ASF May 46 79
Brooklyn Project. .s. . . . .
. . . . PS Fal 48 90
Child's Play. .nt. . . . .
. . . . ASF Mar 47 139
Consulate. .s. . . . . . TW Jun 48 56
Errand Boy. .s. . . . ASF Jun 47 89
House Dutiful, The. .s . . . .
.ASF Apr 48 36
Human Angle, The. .ss . . . .
. . . . FFM Oct 48 112
Ionian Cycle, The. .s . . . .
. . . . TW Aug 48 104
Last Bounce, The. .nt. . . . .
. . . . FA Sep 50 70
Puzzle of Priipiirii, The. .s . . . . .
. . . . OTWA Jul 50 42
Remarkable Flirgleflip, The. . . . .
. .s . . . . .FA May 50 88

TENNESHAW, S. M. house pseud
used by CHESTER S. GEIER,
MILTON LESSER and others.
by MILTON LESSER
Who's That Knocking at my
Door? . .s . . . . . . Amz Nov 50 44
Authors' real names unknown:
Come Along With Me. .nt . . . . . .
. . . . FA Sep 47 78
Diana and the Golden Ring . . . . .
. .s . . . . FA Mar 50 8
Doom Globe. .s. . . Amz May 48 100

Holey Land. .s . . . .
. . . . Amz Aug 48 8
Lunar Point of View, The. .s . . . .
. . . . FA Apr 50 112
Magician of Misty Cave, The . . . .
. .nt . . . . FA Feb 49 8
Monster, The. .nt. . . . .
. . . . Amz Apr 49 8
Outcast, The. .s. . . . .
. . . . Amz Jun 49 36
Pied Piper of Space, The. .s . . . . .
. . . . Amz Jun 48 66
Queen of the Ice Men. .nt . . . . . .
. . . . .FA Nov 49 8
Tavern Knight, The. .s . . : . . . . .
. . . . FA Jun 48 102
Who Sups With the Devil. . . . . . .
. .s . . . . FA Apr 48 54

THADEUS, VICTOR
Chemical Magnet, The. .s . . . . . .
. . . . Amz Aug 27 486

THEBAULT, EUGENE
Radio Terror, The (trans fr French
by Fletcher Pratt). .n 3 pt . . . . .
. . . . WS Jun 33 6

THIESSEN, V. E.
Asteroid Justice. .s. . . . .
. . . . PS Fal 47 46
Prisoner in Time. .s . . . .
. . . . FFM Apr 47 114
Reach for the Stars. .s . . . .
. . . . .FanS Nov 50 71
Spiders of Saturn. .s. . . . .
. . . . Amz Feb 50 94

THIESSON, W. E.
Afraid. .s . . . . SS Fal 46 81

THODE, WALTER
with EDGAR A. MANLEY
Time Annihilator, The. .s . . . . . .
. . . . WS Nov 30 488

THOMAS, DORIS pseud of DORIS
VANCEL
Biog sketch, photo. . . . .
. . . . FA Apr 43 230
Bracelet, The. .nt. . . . .
. . . . FA Apr 43 206

THOMAS, K.
Knowledge Without Learning. . . .
. .s . . . . .NW #1 46 30

THOMAS, SELDEN G.
PROBABILITY ZERO
The Floater. .ss . . . .
. . . . ASF Jul 42 114

THOMPSON, D. B.
Eccentric Orbit. .s . . . .
. . . . ASF Mar 41 113

AUTHOR
Title. .Length . . . . Magazine, Date, Page

THOMPSON, ROBERT G.
Brontosaurus, The. .ss . . . .
. . . . Sti Apr 41 55
THOMSON artist
Cover for ASTOUNDING SCIENCE
FICTION
Sep 38
THOR, TERRY pseud of LARRY B.
SHAW
Secret Weapon. .s . . . . . . FB #3 20
THURMOND, WILLIAM
with RAY CUMMINGS
Derelict of Space, The. .s . . . . . .
. . . . WQ Fal 31 98
WSA 50 140
TIMMINS, WILLIAM artist
Covers for ASTOUNDING SCIENCE
FICTION
Sep, Dec 1942
Jan, Feb, Mar, Apr, May, Jun, Jul,
Aug, Sep, Oct, Nov, Dec 1943
Jan, Feb, Mar, Apr, May, Jun, Aug,
Sep, Oct, Nov, Dec 1944
Jan, Feb, Mar, Apr, May, Jun,
(Jul)*, Aug, Sep, Oct, Nov,
Dec 1945
Jan, Feb, Mar, Apr, May, Jun, Jul,
Aug, Sep, Oct, Nov 1946
Jan, Apr, Jul 1947
Jun 1948
Dec 1950
*Credited to TIMMINS but actually is a
photo montage.
TINDE, ERIC
Boomerang. .s . . . . ASF Nov 47 112
TODD, STEWART (by-line listed in
ToC; STEWART TOLAND on
story)
Question Is Answered, The . . . . .
. .s . . . . UK Nov 39 133
TOFTE, ARTHUR R.
Biog sketch . . . . . Amz Aug 38 145
Biog sketch . . . . . Amz Dec 38 144
Biog sketch, photo. . . . .
. . . . .FA May 39 84
Meteor Monsters, The. .s . . . . . .
. . . . Amz Aug 38 74
Power and the People, The. .s . . .
. . . . .Fut Nov 40 61
Revolt of the Robots. .s . . . .
. . . . .FA May 39 6
Warriors of Mars. .nt . . . .
. . . . Amz Aug 39 6
with L. A. SCHMIDT
Purge of the Deaf. .s . . . .
. . . . Amz Dec 38 56

AUTHOR
Title. .Length . . . . Magazine, Date, Page

TOLAND, STEWART (by-line listed
on story; STEWART TODD in
ToC)
Question Is Answered, The . . . . .
. .s . . . . UK Nov 39 133
TONJOROFF-ROBERTS
with LOUISE RICE
Astounding Enemy, The. .nt . . . .
. . . . AQ Win 30 78
TOOKE, ALFRED I.
Reaping the Whirlwind. .s . . . . . .
. . . . Amz Dec 30 850
TOOKER, RICHARD
Biog sketch . . . . . Amz Nov 38 142
Antares Tryst. .s . . . .
. . . . Amz Aug 37 113
Darcondra. .s . . . .
. . . . TW Jun 37 63
Day of the Brown Horde,
The. .n . . . . FFM Sep 44 8
Green Doom, The. .s . . . .
. . . . ASF Dec 35 44
Lilliput in Equusia. .a . . . .
. . . . TW Oct 42 98
Man of Tomorrow, The. .a . . . . .
. . . . TW Jun 43 97
Mongrovian Caravan. .s . . . .
. . . . TW Fal 44 70
Moon of Arcturus. .nt . . . .
. . . . Amz Jun 35 41
Ray of Eternity. .s. . . . .
. . . . Amz Nov 38 8
Song from the Dark Star,
The. .s . . . . .ASF Sep 36 125
Tomb of Time, The. .nt . . . .
. . . . Amz Mar 33 1062
Toward the Superman. .a . . . . . .
. . . . ASF Mar 39 88
Tyrant of the Red World. . . . . . .
. .s . . . . WS Aug 32 198
ToW Aut 40 6
TORLEY, LUKE pseud of JAMES
BLISH
TOWERS, IVAR house pseud
by CYRIL KORNBLUTH and
RICHARD WILSON
Stepsons of Mars. .nt . . . .
. . . . .Ash Apr 40 78
by RICHARD WILSON
Man Without a Planet, The . . . . .
. .ss . . . . .SSS Nov 42 86
TRACY, DON
Day to Come, The. .nt . . . .
. . . . .TW Nov 40 89
Gift of Urs, The. .s. . . . .
. . . . TW Apr 40 39

AUTHOR
Title. .Length . . . . Magazine, Date, Page

Pettigrew Lives Again. .s . . . .
. . . . TW Aug 41 110
Super-Athlete. .s . . . . TW Apr 42 66
Tomorrow's Hero. .s . . . .
. . . . .TW May 40 39
TREMAINE, F. ORLIN See also
pseuds ANNE BEALE (0),
ARTHUR LANE (0), GUTHRIE
PAINE (0), WARREN B. SAND
(0), ALFRED SANTOS (0),
WARNER VAN LORNE (1 story
only)
Editor of ASTOUNDING STORIES
Oct 33 thru May 38 issues
Editorial Director ASTOUNDING
STORIES
Oct 37 thru May 38 issues
Editor of COMET
Dec 40 thru Jul 41 issues (all
issues)
Biog sketch . . . . FA Sep 39 91
From Peas to Horses to Men . . . .
. .a . . . . TW Feb 49 61
Golden Girl of Kalendar. .nt . . . .
. . . . FA Sep 39 24
Jalu of Radiant Valley. .nt . . . . .
. . . . FA Mar 40 30
Leader for Korcin, A. .s . . . .
. . . . .Fut Dec 42 22
Man of the Future, The. .a . . . . .
. . . . TW Apr 49 105
Son of the Stars. .s. . . . .
. . . . .SSS Apr 49 110
True Confession. .s . . . .
. . . . TW Feb 40 74
World on a Pogo Stick. .a . . . . . .
. . . . TW Dec 48 82
TRENT, CLIVE pseudo of VICTOR
ROUSSEAU EMANUEL
TUCKER, ARTHUR WILSON
See also pseuds BOB TUCKER (6),
WILSON TUCKER (1)
TUCKER, BOB pseud of ARTHUR
WILSON TUCKER
Exit. .s . . . . .Ash Apr 43 90
Gentlemen—The Queen. .s. . . . . .
. . . . .SFQ Fal 42 107
Interstellar Way-Station. .s . . . . .
. . . . SSS May 41 94
Princess of Detroit, The. .s . . . . .
. . . . Fut Jun 42 42
Prison Planet. .s. . . . .
. . . . PS Fal 42 69
PROBABILITY ZERO
That Myserious Bomb Raid . . . .
. .ss. . . . . ASF Jul 42 111

AUTHOR
Title. .Length . . . . Magazine, Date, Page

Miraculous Fluid. .ss . . . .
. . . . ASF Apr 43 86
TUCKER, DENNIS
PROBABILITY ZERO
The Green Sphere. .ss. . . . . . .
. . . . ASF Nov 42 128
TUCKER, ERNEST
with WALT DENNIS
Gladiators, The. .s . . . SS Jan 43 106
TUCKER, REV. LOUIS, D.D.
Cubic City, The. .s. . . . .
. . . . SW Sep 29 316
SS Sep 42 84
TUCKER, WILSON *pseud of*
ARTHUR WILSON TUCKER
Job Is Ended, The. .s . . . .
. . . . .OW Nov 50 56
TURNER *artist*
Cover for TALES OF WONDER
Sum 1940

U

ULLRICH, J. ROGERS
Inverted World, The. .s. . . . . . .
. . . . WQ Spr 31 392
Moon Strollers, The. .s . . . .
. . . . Amz May 29 146
Stolen Chrysalis, The. .s . . . . . .
. . . . Amz Jul 31 372
URIEL, HENRY *pseud of*
FREDERICK FAUST

V

VACE, GEOFFREY *pseud of HUGH*
B. CAVE
VAETH, MARTIN *pseud of*
FREDERIC ARNOLD
KUMMER, JR.
After the Plague. .s . . . .
. . . . .Ash Feb 40 88
VAID, SANFORD
Other, The. .s . . . . . SSS Jan 49 52
VALDING, VICTOR *pseud of JOHN*
VICTOR PETERSON & ALLAN
INGVALD BENSON
Atmospherics. .s . . . ASF Sep 39 33
VALIER, MAX
Berlin to New York in One Hour
(tr fr German by Francis M.
Currier). .a . . . . . AW Feb 30 744

Daring Trip to Mars, A *(tr fr German*
by Francis Currier) .s. . . . . . .
. . . . .WS Jul 31 254
VAN CAMPEN, KARL *pseud of*
JOHN W. CAMPBELL
Irrelevant, The. .s . . . .
. . . . ASF Dec 34 41
VANCE, A.(RLYN) H.
Biog sketch . . . . . Amz Aug 38 146
Germs of Death. .s. . . . .
. . . . Amz Aug 38 98
When the Earth Stood Still . . . . .
. .s . . . . Amz Dec 36 118
VANCE, GERALD *house pseud used*
by CHESTER S. GEIER and others
Brothers Under the Skin. .nt . . . .
. . . . Amz Nov 50 72
Captain Stinky. .s . . . .
. . . . Amz Jun 42 168
Captain Stinky's Luck. .s . . . . . .
. . . . Amz Sep 42 64
Devil in a Box, The. .nt. . . . . . .
. . . . Amz Nov 50 118
Double-Cross on Mars. .s. . . . . .
. . . . Amz Sep 44 134
Double in Death. .s . . . .
. . . . FA Apr 42 120
Happy Death of Algernon
Applenod, The. .s . . . .
. . . . FA Nov 42 220
Larson's Luck. .s. . . . .
. . . . Amz Jan 43 98
Monsoons of Death. .s . . . .
. . . . Amz Dec 42 208
Needle Points to Death, The . . . .
. .s . . . . .Amz Jan 44 176
Plot of Gold. .s . . . . FA Nov 42 220
Psyche Steps Out, The. .nt . . . . .
. . . . Amz May 50 138
Reggie and the Vampire. .s . . . . .
. . . . FA Sep 48 118
Science of Suckers, The. .a . . . . .
. . . . Amz Nov 41 55
Time of My Life. .s . . . .
. . . . Amz Jun 50 148
with BRUCE DENNIS pseud (David
Wright O'Brien)
Giant from Jupiter, The. .nt . . . .
. . . . FA Jun 42 8
VANCE, JACK *See also pseud*
JOHN HOLBROOK (1)
Biog sketch . . . . . .TW Sum 45 97
Cosmic Hotfoot. .s. . . . .
. . . . .SS Sep 50 82
Five Gold Bands, The. .n. . . . . . .
. . . . SS Nov 50 11

Hard Luck Diggings. .s . . . .
. . . . SS Jul 48 102
Howling Bounders, The. .s. . . . .
. . . . .SS Mar 49 115
I'll Build Your Dream Castle . . . .
. .s . . . . ASF Sep 47 72
King of Thieves, The. .s . . . .
. . . . SS Nov 49 98
Loom of Darkness, The. .s. . . . . .
. . . . .WB Dec 50 117
"MAGNUS RIDOLPH" series
includes:
HARD LUCK DIGGINGS
SANATORIS SHORT-OUT
THE UNSPEAKABLE McINCH
THE SUB-STANDARD SARDINES
THE HOWLING BOUNDERS
THE KING OF THIEVES
THE SPA OF THE STARS
COSMIC HOTFOOT
New Bodies for Old. .nt . . . .
. . . . .TW Aug 50 46
Phalid's Fate. .s . . . . TW Dec 46 74
Planet of the Black Dust. .s . . . . .
. . . . SS Sum 46 70
Potters of Firsk, The. .s . . . .
. . . . ASF May 50 88
Sanatoris Short-Cut. .s . . . .
. . . . .SS Sep 48 113
Spa of the Stars, The. .s . . . .
. . . . SS Jul 50 78
Sub-Standard Sardines, The. . . . .
. .s . . . . .SS Jan 49 98
Unspeakable McInch, The . . . . . .
. .s . . . . .SS Nov 48 139
World-Thinker, The. .s . . . .
. . . . .TW Sum 45 36
VAN DINE, S. S.
Bishop Murder Case, The . . . . . .
. .n 3 pt . . . . .SD Jan 30 52
VAN DONGEN *artist*
Cover for SUPER SCIENCE
STORIES
Sep, Nov 1950
VAN HOUTEN, RAYMOND
Last Martian, The. .s . . . .
. . . . .PS Spr 42 92
VAN DRESSER, PETER
Introduction to a Nameless
Science. .a . . . . .ASF Jun 40 100
South Polar Beryllium,
Limited. .s . . . . . Amz Aug 30 416
Why Rockets Don't Fly. .a . . . . .
. . . . ASF Oct 38 81
VAN DUSEN, ASHUR
Police Checkmate New Move of
Scientific Criminals. .a . . . .
. . . . .AD Jul 30 625

AUTHOR
  Title. .Length . . . Magazine, Date, Page

VAN LHYN, ERIC, *pseud of*
  ~~VAN LORNE, WARNER~~ *pseud used
  by F. ORLIN TREMAINE for one
  story, after which it was used as a
  personal pseudonym by one other
  writer, real name unknown.*
by *F. ORLIN TREMAINE*
Upper Level Road, The. .s . . . . .
  . . . . ASF Aug 35 41
Author's real name unknown
Australano. .nt . . . . . ASF Jul 36 6
Blue-Men of Yrano, The. .nt . . . .
  . . . . ASF Jan 39 9
Desert City. .s . . . . ASF Mar 37 48
Follow the Rocket Trail . . . . . .
  . .s . . . . ASF Sep 36 89
Glagula. .nt . . . . . ASF Jun 36 78
Liquid Power. .nt . . . ASF Jul 35 46
Marinorro. .s . . . . . ASF Nov 37 42
Ormoly of Roonerion. .nt . . . . . .
  . . . . ASF Jan 38 6
Other Space. .nt . . . . ASF May 37 8
Resilient Planet. .s . . . .
  . . . . ASF Aug 38 48
Strange City. .nt . . . ASF Jan 36 116
Vibratory. .s . . . . . ASF Mar 38 119
Wanted: 7 Fearless Engineers. . . .
  . .nt . . . . Amz Feb 39 8
White Adventure. .s . . . .
  . . . . ASF Apr 36 55
Winter on the Planet. .s . . . .
  . . . . ASF Apr 37 139
World of Purple Light. .nt . . . . . .
  . . . . ASF Dec 36 48
VAN NAME, E.(dgar) J. *See pseud*
  JIM VANNY
Sunlight Master, The. .s . . . .
  . . . . Amz Apr 35 31
VANNE, EMMA
Moaning Lily, The. .s . . . .
  . . . . WS May 35 1458
VANNY, JIM *pseud of EDGAR J.
  VAN NAME*
Exiles of Venus, The. .s . . . .
  . . . . WS Jun 31 64
Liners of Space. .s . . . .
  . . . . AW Feb 30 704
Radium Master, The. .s . . . .
  . . . . WS Aug 30 240
War of the Great Ants, The . . . . .
  . .s . . . . WS Jul 30 140
van VOGT, A.(lfred) E.
Asylum. .nt . . . . . . ASF May 42 8
Automaton. .s . . . . . . OW Sep 50 6
Barbarian, The. .nt . . . .
  . . . . ASF Dec 47 44

Beast, The. .n . . . . . ASF Nov 43 48
Black Destroyer. .nt . . . .
  . . . . ASF Jul 39 9
Book of Ptath, The. .n . . . .
  . . . . UK Oct 43 9
Can of Paint, A. .s . . . .
  . . . . ASF Sep 44 29
Cataaaa, The. .s . . . . MSS Nov 50 38
Cataaaaa, The. .s . . . . . . FB #1 37
Centaurus II. .nt . . . . ASF Jun 47 6
Changeling, The. .n . . . .
  . . . . ASF Apr 44 7
Child of the Gods. .nt . . . .
  . . . . ASF Aug 46 145
"CLANE" series includes:
  A SON IS BORN
  CHILD OF THE GODS
  HAND OF THE GODS
  HOME OF THE GODS
  THE BARBARIAN
  THE WIZARD OF LINN
Concealment. .s . . . . ASF Sep 43 88
Co-operate—Or Else! . .nt . . . . . .
  . . . . ASF Apr 42 78
Defense. .ss . . . . AFR #4 128
"DELLIAN ROBOT" series includes:
  CONCEALMENT
  THE STORM
  THE MIXED MEN
Discord in Scarlet. .nt . . . .
  . . . . ASF Dec 39 9
Dormant. .s . . . . . . SS Nov 48 88
Earth Killers, The. .nt . . . .
  . . . . SSS Apr 49 50
Enchanted Village. .s . . . .
  . . . . OW Jul 50 6
Far Centaurus. .s . . . .
  . . . . ASF Jan 44 68
Film Library. .s . . . .
  . . . . ASF Jul 46 148
Final Command. .s . . . .
  . . . . ASF Nov 49 91
Ghost, The. .nt . . . . UK Aug 42 61
Great Engine, The. .nt . . . .
  . . . . ASF Jul 43 44
Great Judge, The. .ss . . . .
  . . . . FB #3 4
Green Forest, The. .nt . . . .
  . . . . ASF Jun 49 6
Hand of the Gods. .nt . . . .
  . . . . ASF Dec 46 142
Harmonizer, The. .s . . . .
  . . . . ASF Nov 44 169
Heir Apparent. .nt . . . .
  . . . . ASF Jun 45 32
Home of the Gods. .nt . . . .
  . . . . ASF Apr 47 6
Juggernaut. .s . . . . . ASF Aug 44 55

Letter from the Stars . . . .
  . .s . . . . OTWA Jul 50 25
M 33 in Andromeda. .s . . . .
  . . . . ASF Aug 43 129
Mixed Men, The. .nt . . . .
  . . . . ASF Jan 45 7
Monster, The. .s . . . ASF Aug 48 56
Not Only Dead Men. .s . . . .
  . . . . ASF Nov 42 114
Not the First. .s . . . .
  . . . . ASF Apr 41 94
Players of $\overline{A}$, The . . . .
  . .n 4 pt . . . . ASF Oct 48 7
Process. .s . . . . . . F&SF Dec 50 46
Project Spaceship. .s . . . .
  . . . . TW Aug 49 96
Purpose, The. .nt . . . .
  . . . . ASF May 45 139
Recruiting Station. .n . . . .
  . . . . ASF Mar 42 8
Repetition. .nt . . . . ASF Apr 40 51
Rogue Ship. .nt . . . . SSS Mar 50 10
Rulers, The. .s . . . . . ASF Jar 44 27
Rull, The . . . . ASF May 48 7
Sea Thing, The. .s . . . .
  . . . . UK Jan 40 81
Search, The. .nt . . . .
  . . . . ASF Jan 43 44
Second Solution, The. .s . . . .
  . . . . ASF Oct 42 41
Secret Unattainable. .nt . . . .
  . . . . ASF Jul 42 9
Seesaw, The. .s . . . . ASF Jul 41 60
Shadow Men, The. .n . . . .
  . . . . SS Jan 50 11
Ship of Darkness, The. .s . . . . . .
  . . . . FB #2 4
Slan. .n 4 pt . . . . . . ASF Sep 40 9
Son Is Born, A. .s . . . .
  . . . . ASF May 46 61
Sound, The. .nt . . . . ASF Feb 50 56
Storm, The. .nt . . . . . ASF Oct 43 9
Vault of the Beast. .nt . . . .
  . . . . ASF Aug 40 50
War of Nerves. .s . . . .
  . . . . OW May 50 36
Weapon Makers, The. .n 3 pt . . . .
  . . . . ASF Feb 43 9
"WEAPON SHOP" series includes:
  THE SEESAW
  THE WEAPON SHOP
  THE WEAPON MAKERS
  THE WEAPON SHOPS OF ISHER
Weapon Shop, The. .nt . . . .
  . . . . ASF Dec 42 9
Weapon Shops of Isher, The . . . .
  . .n . . . . TW Feb 49 11

AUTHOR
Title. .Length . . . . Magazine, Date, Page

Witch, The. .s . . . . . UK Feb 43 118
Wizard of Linn, The. .n 3 pt . . . .
. . . . ASF Apr 50 6
World of A. .n 3 pt . . . .
. . . . ASF Aug 45 7
VARDON, RICHARD *pseud of*
DAVID WRIGHT O'BRIEN
Have You Seen Me? . .s . . . .
. . . . FA Jun 43 142
VAUGHAN, RICHARD
Exile of the Skies, The . . . .
. .n 3 pt . . . . .WS Jan 34 550
. .n *(complete)* . . . . FSQ Sum 50 11
Woman from Space, The. .s . . . . .
. . . . WQ Spr 32 364
VERN, DAVID *See also pseuds*
ALEXANDER BLADE (h) (?),
CRAIG ELLIS (h) (1), PETER
HORN (h) (2), DAVID V. REED
(15), CLYDE WOORUFF (1)
VERNE, JULES
Desert of Ice, The. .n 2 pt . . . . .
. . . . Amz Jun 29 241
Dr. Ox's Experiment. .s . . . .
. . . . Amz Aug 26 420
Drama in the Air, A. .s . . . .
. . . . Amz Nov 26 758
English at the North Pole,
The. .n 2 pt . . . . Amz May 29 104
Master of the World, The . . . . . .
. .n 2 pt . . . . . Amz Feb 28 1026
Measuring a Meridian. .n 4 pt . . . .
. . . . Amz May 34 107
Off on a Comet *or* Hector
Servadac. .n 2 pt . . . .
. . . . Amz Apr 26 4
Purchase of the North Pole,
The. .n 2 pt . . . . Amz Sep 26 510
Robur the Conqueror *or* The Clipper
of the Clouds. .n 2 pt . . . .
. . . . Amz Dec 27 826
Trip to the Center of the Earth,
A. .n 3 pt . . . . . Amz May 26 100
Watch's Soul, The. .s . . . .
. . . . Amz Dec 33 111
Winter Amid the Ice, A *or* The
Cruise of the Jeune-Hardie . . . .
. .nt . . . . AQ Jan 34 74
VERNON, LEO
Rocket Flight. .a . . . .
. . . . .ASF Jan 38 106
Tools for Brains. .a . . . .
. . . . .ASF Jul 39 80
Unseen Tools. .a . . . ASF Jun 40 79
VERRILL, A.(lpheus) HYATT
Biog sketch . . . . . . .FA May 39 85

AUTHOR
Title. .Length . . . . Magazine, Date, Page

Astounding Discoveries of Doctor
Mentiroso, The. .s . . . .
. . . . Amz Nov 27 746
Beyond the Green Prism . . . . . .
. .n 2 pt . . . . . . .Amz Jan 30 886
Beyond the Pole. .n 2 pt . . . . . .
. . . . Amz Oct 26 580
Bridge of Light, The. .n . . . .
. . . . .AQ Fal 29 436
Death Drum, The. .nt . . . .
. . . . Amz May 33 104
Death from the Skies . . . .
. .nt . . . . Amz Oct 29 583
                    ToW Spr 41 4
Dirigibles of Death, The. .nt . . . .
. . . . AQ Win 30 124
Exterminator, The. .ss . . . .
. . . . Amz Feb 31 1020
Feathered Detective, The . . . . . .
. .s . . . . Amz Apr 30 31
Inner World, The. .n 3 pt . . . . . .
. . . . Amz Jun 35 69
Inner World, The *(The Voice from
the Inner World).* .s . . . .
. . . . .ToW Spr 39 101
Into the Green Prism. .n 2 pt . . . .
. . . . Amz Mar 29 1064
King of the Monkey Men,
The. .nt . . . . AQ Spr 28 230
Man Who Could Vanish, The . . . .
. .s . . . . .Amz Jan 27 900
                    AA 27 104
Monsters of the Ray. .nt . . . . . .
. . . . .AQ Sum 30 364
Mummy of Ret-Seh, The. .s . . . . .
. . . . .FA May 39 70
Non-Gravitational Vortex,
The. .nt . . . . . . Amz Jun 30 198
Plague of the Living Dead,
The. .s . . . . .Amz Apr 27 6
Psychological Solution, The. . . . .
. .s . . . . .Amz Jan 28 946
Through the Andes. .n 3 pt . . . . .
. .n . . . . Amz Sep 34 49
Through the Crater's Rim . . . . . .
. .s . . . . Amz Dec 26 806
Treasure of the Golden God,
The. .n 2 pt . . . . .Amz Jan 33 870
Ultra-Elixir of Youth, The. . . . . .
. .s . . . . Amz Aug 27 476
Vampires of the Desert . . . .
. .s . . . . Amz Dec 29 774
Visit to Suari, A. .s . . . .
. . . . .Amz Jul 30 292
Voice from the Inner World,
The. .s . . . . .Amz Jul 27 328

AUTHOR
Title. .Length . . . . Magazine, Date, Page

When the Moon Ran Wild. .n . . . .
. . . . AQ Win 31 90
World of the Giant Ants, The. . . .
. .n . . . . .AQ Fal 28 436
VINCENT, HARL *pseud of H. V.*
SCHOEPFLIN
Biog sketch . . . . . Amz Dec 38 144
Ambassador from Mars, The . . . .
. .s . . . . Amz Sep 28 486
Barrier, The. .s . . . Amz Sep 34 119
Barton's Island. .s . . . .
. . . . Amz Aug 29 390
                    AQ Fal 34 6
Before the Asteroids. .s. . . . .
. . . . SW Mar 30 870
Callisto at War. .s. . . . .
. . . . Amz Mar 30 1150
Cat's Eye. .s . . . . . Amz Apr 34 10
Cavern of Thunders. .nt . . . .
. . . . Amz Jul 33 345
Colloidal Nemesis, The. .s . . . . . .
. . . . Amz Dec 29 800
Copper-Clad World, The. .nt . . . .
. . . . .ASF Sep 31 296
Cosmic Rhythm. .nt. . . . .
. . . . ASF Oct 34 94
Creatures of Vibration. .s . . . . . .
. . . . .ASF Jan 32 11
Deputy Correspondent. .s . . . . . .
. . . . ASF Jun 40 38
Devil Flower, The. .s . . . .
. . . . .FA May 39 80
Energy. .s. . . . . . . .ASF Jan 35 79
Explorers of Callisto, The . . . . . .
. .s . . . . Amz Feb 30 998
Faster Than Light. .n . . . .
. . . . AQ Fal–Win 32 290
Free Energy. .s . . . Amz Sep 30 529
Golden Girl of Munan, The . . . . .
. .s . . . . Amz Jun 28 252
Grave of the Achilles. .s . . . .
. . . . CF Win 41 109
Gravity Island. .s . . . .SSS Mar 40 68
Gray Denim. .s . . . ASF Dec 30 354
High Frequency War. .s. . . . .
. . . . ASF Feb 40 102
Invisible Ships. .s . . . .
. . . . AQ Apr 31 250
Life Inside a Wall. .s . . . .
. . . . .SFQ Sum 40 142
Lightning Strikes Once. .s . . . . . .
. . . . MSS Aug 39 100
Lost City of Mars. .nt . . . .
. . . . ASF Feb 34 67
Lunar Station. .s . . . .
. . . . Com Jan 41 34

AUTHOR
Title. .Length . . . . Magazine, Date, Page

Master Control. .nt . . . .
. . . . .Ash Apr 40 34
Master of Dreams. .nt. . . . .
. . . . Amz Jan 34 37
Matter of Ethics, A. .s . . . .
. . . . Amz Oct 31 650
Menace from Below, The. .s. . . . .
. . . . .SW Jul 29 143
Microcosmic Buccaneers. . . . . . .
. .nt . . . . Amz Nov 29 678
Moon Weed, The. .s . . . .
. . . . ASF Aug 31 236
Morons, The. .nt . . . .
. . . . ASF Jun 39 45
Mystery of the Collapsing
Skyscrapers, The. .nt . . . .
. . . . Amz Aug 39 74
Neutral Vessel. .nt. . . . .
. . . . ASF Jan 40 9
Newscast. .s . . . .
. . . . MSS Apr–May 39 119
Old Crompton's Secret. .s . . . . .
. . . . ASF Feb 30 153
Once in a Blue Moon. .s . . . . . .
. . . . AQ Win 32 74
Other World. .s . . . . Ash Oct 40 78
Parasite. .nt . . . . . .Amz Jul 35 71
Plane Compass, The. .s . . . .
. . . . ASF Jun 35 42
Power. .nt . . . . . . .Amz Jan 32 872
Power Plant. .nt . . . .
. . . . ASF Nov 39 129
Prince Deru Returns. .nt. . . . . . .
. . . . Amz Dec 38 70
Prowler of the Wastelands . . . . . .
. .s . . . . ASF Apr 35 72
Return of the Prowler. .s. . . . . . .
. . . . ASF Nov 38 36
Return to Subterrania, The . . . . .
. .s . . . . SW Apr 30 992
Rex. .s. . . . . .ASF Jun 34 143
Roadways of Mars. .s . . . .
. . . . Amz Dec 32 812
Seventh Generation, The. . . . . . .
. .s . . . . AQ Win 29 54
Silver Dome. .s . . . ASF Aug 30 192
Tanks Under the Sea. .s . . . .
. . . . .Amz Jan 31 896
Telegraph Plateau. .nt. . . . .
. . . . ASF Nov 33 115
Terror of Air-Level Six, The . . . .
. .nt . . . . .ASF Jul 30 62
Terrors Unseen. .s . . . .
. . . . ASF Mar 31 360
Thia of the Drylands. .s . . . .
. . . . Amz Jul 32 296

AUTHOR
Title. .Length . . . . Magazine, Date, Page

Through the Air Tunnel . . . . . .
. .s . . . . AW Oct 29 314
Too Many Boards. .s . . . .
. . . . Amz Apr 31 70
Trouble Shooter. .s . . . .
. . . . SSS Jul 40 54
Undersea Prisoner. .s . . . .
. . . . Amz Feb 40 40
Vagabonds of Space. .nt . . . . . .
. . . . ASF Nov 30 244
Valley of the Rukh. .s . . . .
. . . . Amz Feb 35 38
Venus Liberated. .n . . . .
. . . . .AQ Sum 29 292
Voice from the Void. .s . . . .
. . . . Amz Jun 42 244
Vulcan's Workshop. .s . . . .
. . . . .ASF Jun 32 293
Wanderer of Infinity . . . .
. .s . . . . ASF Mar 33 100
War of the Planets, The. . . . . . .
. .s . . . . .Amz Jan 29 872
Water-Bound World. .s . . . . . .
. . . . AQ Spr–Sum 32 264
When the Comet Returned . . . . .
. .nt . . . . Amz Apr 33 8
Whisper of Death. .s. . . . .
. . . . Amz Nov 33 11
Yellow Air Peril, The. .s . . . .
. . . . AW Sep 29 198
with CHAS. ROY COX
Sky Cops. .s . . . .
. . . . Amz Dec 31 818
VIVIAN, E. CHARLES *See also*
pseud JACK MANN (1)
City of Wonder, The. .n . . . .
. . . . FFM Oct 47 6
Valley of Silent Men, The . . . . . .
. .n . . . . .FFM Aug 49 8
VON COSEL, KARL TANZLER
Secret of Elena's Tomb, The . . . .
. .n . . . . FA Sep 47 8
VON DREY, HOWARD *pseud of*
HOWARD WANDREI
God Box, The. .s . . . .
. . . . ASF Apr 34 75
VON HANSTEIN, OTFRID
Between Earth and Moon *(tr fr*
German by Francis Currier). . . .
. .n . . . . WQ Fal 30 6
Electropolis *(tr fr German by*
Francis Currier). . . . .
. .n . . . . .WQ Sum 30 482
Hidden Colony, The *(tr fr German*
by Fletcher Pratt). .n 3 pt . . . . .
. . . . .WS Jan 35 904

AUTHOR
Title. .Length . . . . Magazine, Date, Page

In the Year 8000 *(tr fr German*
by Konrad Schmidt & Laurence
Manning). .n 2 pt. . . . .
. . . . .WS Jul 32 102
Utopia Island *(tr fr German by*
Francis Currier). .n 2 pt . . . . . .
. . . . .WS May 31 1352
VON MUNCHAUSEN, A. *artist*
Cover for ASTOUNDING SCIENCE
FICTION
Oct 1942
VON RACHEN, KURT *pseud of*
L. RON HUBBARD
Idealist, The. .s . . . .
. . . . .ASF Jul 40 94
Kilkenny Cats, The. .s . . . .
. . . . ASF Sep 40 98
Mutineers, The. .nt . . . .
. . . . ASF Apr 41 127
Rebels, The. .nt. . . . .
. . . . ASF Feb 42 49
Traitor, The. .s . . . . .ASF Jan 41 74

W

WADE, ROBERT
Coffin of Life and Death. .s . . . . .
. . . . FA Apr 48 100
WAGENER, SIEGFRIED
Cosmic Cocktail, The. .s . . . .
. . . . WS Mar 36 908
WAINRIGHT, CARTER T.
Her Majesty, The Queen. .a . . . . .
. . . . FA Oct 43 194
WAIT, ROBERT A.
Clavilux. .s . . . . . . Amz Jun 29 214
Cosmic Steeple-Chase. .nt . . . . . .
. . . . Amz Apr 32 48
Invisible Finite, The. .s . . . .
. . . . Amz May 29 172
Lanterns of God. .s . . . .
. . . . Amz Mar 30 1168
WAKEFIELD, H. RUSSELL
Central Figure, The. .s . . . .
. . . . AFR #1 116
Professor Pownall's Oversight. . . .
. .s . . . . F&SF Sum 50 111
WALDEYER, GRAPH
Biog sketch, photo. . . . .
. . . . .TW Aug 39 51
Answer Out of Space, The. . . . . .
. .s . . . . SF Jul 43 97
Beings Like These. .s . . . .
. . . . SSS Jan 41 76

AUTHOR
    Title. .Length . . . . Magazine, Date, Page

    Cosmic Cube. .s. . . . . TW Aug 39 50
    Dummy That Saved Earth,
      The. .s. . . . . .CF Spr 42 108
    4-D Doodler, The. .s . . . .
      . . . . .Com Jul 41 90
WALDO, E. HUNTER *pseud of*
    THEODORE STURGEON
    Ultimate Egoist, The. .s . . . .
      . . . . UK Feb 41 57
WALDROF, F. N.
with POUL ANDERSON
    Tomorrow's Children. .nt . . . . . .
      . . . . ASF Mar 47 56
WALKER, CEDRIC
    Guinea-Pig, The. .s. . . . .
      . . . . MSS Nov 50 62
WALKER, DERALD S.
    Phytic Empire, The. .s . . . .
      . . . . Amz Jun 35 122
WALLACE, JOHN
    Perfectionist Perdition. .s . . . . . .
      . . . . MSS Dec 39 96
WALLIS, B.(RUCE)
    From Time's Dawn. .s . . . .
      . . . . .FN May 50 96
with G.(EO) C. WALLIS
    Mother World, The. .nt. . . . . . .
      . . . . .AQ Spr–Sum 33 497
    World at Bay, The. .n 2 pt. . . . . .
      . . . . Amz Nov 28 678
WALLIS, G.(EORGE) C.
    Biog sketch . . . . . ToW Win 38 126
    Biog sketch . . . . . . .Fant #3 39 74
    Across the Abyss. .s. . . . .
      . . . . ToW Sum 39 100
    Cosmic Cloud, The. .s. . . . .
      . . . . ToW Aut 41 37
    Crystal Menace, The. .s. . . . .
      . . . . ToW Aut 39 73
    Invaders from the Void. .s. . . . . .
      . . . . Fant #3 39 106
    Orbit Jumper, The. .s. . . . .
      . . . . ToW Win 38 100
    Power Supreme, The. .s . . . .
      . . . . ToW Win 41 42
    Red Spheres, The. .s. . . . .
      . . . . ToW Spr 41 46
    Under the Dying Sun. .s . . . .
      . . . . .ToW Sum 40 62
    Voyage of Sacrifice. .s . . . .
      . . . . ToW Spr 39 51
with (BRUCE) WALLIS
    Mother World, The. .nt. . . . . . .
      . . . . .AQ Spr–Sum 33 497
    World at Bay, The. .n 2 pt. . . . . .
      . . . . Amz Nov 28 678

AUTHOR
    Title. .Length . . . . Magazine, Date, Page

WALLRICH, WILLIAM
    Scissors, The. .s. . . . .OW May 50 156
WALSBY, CHARNOCK
    Biog sketch . . . . . .ToW Spr 39 126
    Last Man, The. .ss . . . .
      . . . . Com Jan 41 94
    Warning from Luna. .s . . . .
      . . . . ToW Spr 39 64
WALSH, J. M.
    Biog sketch . . . . . ToW Win 38 125
    Biog sketch . . . . . . .Fant #3 39 74
    After 1,000,000 Years. .s . . . . . .
      . . . . WS Oct 31 658
    After a Million Years. .s . . . .
      . . . . ToW Aut 39 30
    Stick Men, The. .s . . . Fant #3 39 21
    Struggle for Pallas, The. .s. . . . . .
      . . . . WQ Fal 31 126
    Vandals of the Void. .n. . . . .
      . . . . .WQ Sum 31 438
    Vanguard to Neptune, The . . . . . .
      . .n . . . . WQ Spr 32 294
    When the Earth Tilted. .s . . . . . .
      . . . . WS May 32 1342
      . . . . .ToW Win 38 80
WALTERS, SELDON *pseud of WALT*
    SHELDON
    "All You Do Is Tranz the
      Framis!". .s . . . . . .Amz Jul 50 78
WALTON, BRYCE *See also pseuds*
    PAUL FRANKLIN (0), KENNETH
    O'HARA (0), DAVE SANDS
    (h) (0)
    Biog sketch . . . . . . PS Sum 46 118
    Assignment in the Dawn. . . . . . .
      . .s . . . . PS Fal 47 67
    City of the Singing Cubes,
      The. .s. . . . . . .OTWA Dec 50 42
    Design for Doomsday. .nt . . . . . .
      . . . . PS Spr 48 94
    Earth Needs a Killer. .nt . . . .
      . . . . Fut Jul–Aug 50 8
    Green Dream, The. .s . . . .
      . . . . .PS Win 49 55
    In His Image. .ss . . . .
      . . . . .PS Win 48 34
    Mo-Sanshon!. .s. . . . .
      . . . . .PS Apr 47 32
    Moon of Memory. .s. . . . .
      . . . . .Fut Nov 50 68
    Princess of Chaos. .s. . . . .
      . . . . PS Spr 47 102
    Prisoner of the Brain- Mistress . . .
      . .s . . . . PS Sum 46 82
    Savage Galahad. .s . . . .
      . . . . .PS Win 46 77

AUTHOR
    Title. .Length . . . . Magazine, Date, Page

    Sleeper Is a Rebel, The. . . . .
      . .nt . . . . .TW Feb 48 13
    Strange Alliance. .s . . . . . FB #1 22
    Survivors, The. .s. . . . .
      . . . . SSS Jul 49 104
    Ulimate World, The. .s . . . .
      . . . . .PS Win 45 63
    Victorious Failure. .s . . . .
      . . . . .TW Apr 47 66
    World of No Return. .s. . . . .
      . . . . .SSS Sep 49 56
WALTON, HARRY *See also pseud*
    HARRY COLLIER (1)
    Asteroid H277-Plus. .s . . . .
      . . . . PS Sum 40 98
    Below–Absolute. .s . . . .
      . . . . ASF Jun 38 22
    Bomb from Beranga. .s. . . . .
      . . . . FFM Mar 40 69
    Boomerang. .s. . . . .ASF Jun 44 119
    Cache, The. .s . . . . ASF Apr 39 110
    Cross of Mercrux. .nt . . . .
      . . . . .SSS Feb 42 11
      . . . . FN Nov 50 94
    Doom Ship. .nt. . . . .
      . . . . .ASF Jan 41 128
    Episode on Dhee Minor . . . .
      . .s . . . . ASF Oct 39 96
    Fatal Asteroid. .s. . . . .
      . . . . TW Jun 41 106
    Housing Shortage. .s. . . . .
      . . . . .ASF Jan 47 37
    In the Ancient Way. .s . . . .
      . . . . .TW Aug 41 91
    Insomnia, Inc. . .nt . . . .
      . . . . ASF Aug 47 68
    Man Who Didn't Breathe,
      The. .s. . . . . . . .Ash Nov 41 49
    Moon of Exile. .s. . . . .
      . . . . ASF Aug 40 115
    Quicksilver, Unlimited . . . .
      . .s . . . . .ASF Jul 37 116
    Radiation Trap. .s . . . .
      . . . . .Ash Sep 41 90
    Schedule. .s . . . . . . ASF Jun 45 54
    Scrambler, The. .s . . . .
      . . . . ASF Apr 41 70
    Spawn of the Venus Sea . . . .
      . .s . . . . .PS Fal 41 96
    Subcruiser. .s . . . . ASF May 41 109
    Swamp Train. .s . . . .
      . . . . UK Jan 40 71
    Timeless Ones, The. .s . . . .
      . . . . .SSS Jul 40 30
    War God's Gamble. .s. . . . .
      . . . . .SSS Feb 43 128

AUTHOR
Title. .Length . . . . Magazine, Date, Page

WALWORTH, JOHN STUART
Invasion of the Bone Men . . . . . .
. .s . . . . Amz Jan 49 78
WANDREI, DONALD
Atom Smasher, The. .ss . . . .
. . . . ASF Apr 34 85
Black Fog. .s. . . . . . TW Feb 37 33
Blinding Shadows. .s . . . .
. . . . ASF May 34 11
Colossus. .nt. . . . . . .ASF Jan 34 41
Colossus Eternal. .nt . . . .
. . . . ASF Dec 34 50
Don't Dream. .s. . . . .
. . . . UK Aug 39 75
Earth Minus. .nt . . . .
. . . . ASF Sep 35 40
Farewell to Earth. .nt . . . .
. . . . ASF Dec 33 98
Finality Unlimited. .nt . . . .
. . . . ASF Sep 36 8
Infinity Zero. .s. . . .ASF Oct 36 130
Life Current. .s . . . ASF Apr 35 102
Man Who Never Lived, The . . . . .
. .s . . . . ASF Mar 34 39
Murray's Light. .s . . ASF Jun 35 33
Nerveless Man, The. .s . . . .
. . . . ASF Jul 34 54
Painted Mirror, The. .s . . . .
. . . . AFR #9 121
Race Through Time, A. . . . .
. .s . . . . ASF Oct 33 18
Raiders of the Universes . . . . . .
. .s . . . . ASF Sep 32 63
                                    AFR #13 83
Scientist Divides, A. .s . . . .
. . . . ASF Sep 34 53
Whisperers, The. .s. . . . .
. . . . ASF May 35 133
Witch-Makers, The. .s . . . .
. . . . FFM Sep–Oct 39 100
WANDREI, HOWARD ELMER
See pseuds HOWARD GRAHAM
(4), H. W. GUERNSEY (7),
HOWARD VON DREY (1)
WARD, ARTHUR S. See pseud
SAX ROHMER (2)
WARD, PETER pseud of
FREDERICK FAUST
WARLAND, ALLEN pseud of
DONALD A. WOLLHEIM
Baby Dreams. .s . . . .
. . . . .SFQ Win 41–42 107
WARNER, HARRY, JR.
PROBABILITY ZERO
Sleep That Slaughtered, The . . .
. .ss. . . . . ASF Nov 42 127

AUTHOR
Title. .Length . . . . Magazine, Date, Page

WASHBURN, RUTH
Biog sketch, photo. . . . .
. . . . TW Spr 44 75
Unsung Hero. .s. . . . .
. . . . TW Spr 44 73
WATES, CYRIL G.
Face of Isis, The. .s . . . .
. . . . Amz Mar 29 1084
Gold Dust and Star Dust. . . . . . .
. .s . . . . Amz Sep 29 510
Modern Prometheus, A. .n. . . . . .
. . . . .AQ Fal 30 436
Visitation, The. .s . . . .
. . . . Amz Jun 27 241
WATSON, GEORGE COOKMAN
Cauphul, The City Under the
Sea. .s . . . . .Amz Jan 29 918
WATSON, WEBSTER
When the Moon Moons. .ss . . . . .
. . . . Amz Nov 33 114
WEBB, A. C., M.D.
Double Lightning, The. .s . . . . . .
. . . . AD Jun 30 530
Underground Waters. .s. . . . . . .
. . . . WQ Win 30 268
WEBSTER, ROBERT N. pseud listed
as
Editor of OTHER WORLDS
Nov 49 (first) thru Jan 50 issues
WEDE
Death Creeps the Moon. .s . . . . .
. . . . Amz Dec 36 102
WEDLAKE, C. J.
Peril Orbit. .s . . . . . PS Sum 49 72
WEINBAUM, HELEN
Bargain With Colossus. .s. . . . . .
. . . . SF Mar 41 91
Devil Dogs of Space. .nt . . . . . .
. . . . .SF Sep 41 87
Double Destiny. .nt . . . .
. . . . SFQ Win 41 109
Genius Bureau, The. .s . . . .
. . . . .Fut Apr 41 28
Honeycombed Satellite. .s. . . . . .
. . . . .TW Jul 40 70
Radium Rugs, The. .s . . . .
. . . . SSS Sep 40 102
with (brother) STANLEY G.
WEINBAUM
Tidal Moon. .s. . . . . TW Dec 38 78
WEINBAUM, STANLEY G.(rauman)
See also pseud JOHN JESSEL
(1)
Biog sketch . . . . . Amz Oct 38 141
Biog sketch . . . . . Amz Nov 48 144
Obituary, photo . . . TW Jun 39 103

AUTHOR
Title. .Length . . . . Magazine, Date, Page

Black Flame, The. .n . . SS Jan 39 16
Brink of Infinity, The. .s . . . . . .
. . . . TW Dec 36 56
                                    SS Mar 48 116
Circle of Zero, The. .s . . . .
. . . . .TW Aug 36 48
                                    SS Sep 47 70
Dawn of Flame. .nt . . . .
. . . . TW Jun 39 99
Flight on Titan. .s . . . .
. . . . .ASF Jan 35 100
Ideal, The. .s. . . . . WS Sep 35 416
                                    SS Jun 43 66
                                    FSQ Spr 50 86
Lotus Eaters, The. .nt. . . . .
. . . . ASF Apr 35 52
Mad Moon, The. .nt . . . .
. . . . ASF Dec 35 52
Martian Odyssey, A . . . .
. . . . .WS Jul 34 174
                                    SS Nov 39 106
New Adam, The. .n 2 pt . . . .
. . . . Amz Feb 43 62
Parasite Planet, The. .nt . . . . . .
. . . . ASF Feb 35 50
Planet of Doubt, The . . . .
. .nt . . . . .ASF Oct 35 106
Point of View, The. .s . . . .
. . . . .WS Jan 35 806
                                    SS Spr 44 88
Proteus Island. .nt . . . .
. . . . ASF Aug 36 96
Pygmalion's Spectacles. .s . . . . .
. . . . WS Jun 35 28
                                    SS May 39 100
Red Peri, The. .nt . . . .
. . . . ASF Nov 35 10
Redemption Cairn. .nt . . . .
. . . . ASF Mar 36 42
Shifting Seas. .s . . . .
. . . . Amz Apr 37 115
Valley of Dreams. .s. . . . .
. . . . WS Nov 34 676
                                    SS May 40 94
"VAN MANDERPOOTZ" series
includes:
THE WORLDS OF IF
THE IDEAL
THE POINT OF VIEW
Worlds of If, The. .s . . . .
. . . . WS Aug 35 276
                                    SS Mar 41 90
                                    Fant Dec 46 46
with RALPH MILNE FARLEY
pseud (Roger Sherman Hoar)
Revolution of 1950. .nt 2 pt . . . .
. . . . Amz Oct 38 106

AUTHOR
  Title. .Length . . . . Magazine, Date, Page

  Smothered Seas. .nt . . . .
  . . . . ASF Jan 36 8
with (sister) HELEN WEINBAUM
  Tidal Moon. .s . . . . . TW Dec 38 78
WEINER, SAM
  Astounding Clue, The. .s . . . . . .
  . . . . AD Aug 30 684
WEISINGER, MORT *See also pseuds*
  WILL GARTH (h) (2), TOM
  ERWIN GERIS (1)
  Editor THRILLING WONDER
    STORIES
  Aug 36 *thru* Jun 41 *issues*
  Editor STARTLING STORIES
  Jan 39 *(first) thru* May 41 *issues*
  Editor CAPTAIN FUTURE
  Win 40 *(first) thru* mid-1941
  Nth Degree, The. .s . . . .
  . . . . TW Aug 36 61
  Pigments Is Pigments. .s . . . .
  . . . . WS Mar 35 1208
  Prenatal Plagiarism, The. .ss . . . . .
  . . . . .WS Jan 35 932
  Price of Peace, The. .s . . . .
  . . . . Amz Nov 33 115
  Thompson's Time Traveling
    Theory. .s . . . . . Amz Mar 44 118
  THRILLS IN SCIENCE dept in
    STARTLING STORIES Jan 39
    thru Nov 41 issues
  Time on My Hands. .ss . . . .
  . . . . TW Jun 38 104
WEISS, HERB
  Way Station. .s . . . . .UK Jul 39 109
WEISS, GEORGE HENRY *See*
  pseud FRANCIS FLAGG (18)
WELCH, EARL
  Electrical Yardsticks. .a . . . .
  . . . . .ASF Jan 46 101
WELLMAN, MANLY WADE *See*
  also pseud GABRIEL BARCLAY
  (h) (1)
  Biog Sketch . . . . . .Amz Jan 39 130
  Biog sketch, photo. . . . .
  . . . . TW Jun 39 85
  Biog sketch, photo. . . . .
  . . . . Amz May 40 131
  Biog sketch, photo. . . . .
  . . . . SS Sum 44 109
  Asteroid Castaways. .s . . . .
  . . . . TW Jun 42 54
  . . .Backward, O Time! . .s . . . . .
  . . . . TW Oct 49 117
  Battle in the Dawn. .nt . . . .
  . . . . Amz Jan 39 30

AUTHOR
  Title. .Length . . . . Magazine, Date, Page

  Bratton's Idea. .s . . . .
  . . . . Com Dec 40 85
  Brothers of Fate. .ss . . . .
  . . . . .SF Jun 39 87
  Day of the Conquerors, The . . . .
  . .nt . . . . TW Jan 40 89
  Devil Is Not Mocked, The . . . . .
  . .s . . . . UK Jun 43 115
  Devil's Asteroid. .s . . . .
  . . . . .Com Jul 41 28
  Devil's Planet. .n . . . . . SS Jan 42 15
  Disc-Men of Jupiter, The. . . . . . .
  . .s . . . . WS Sep 31 522
  . . . . SS May 47 70
  Dream-Dust from Mars. .s . . . . . .
  . . . . TW Feb 38 14
  Einstein Slugger, The. .s . . . .
  . . . . TW Dec 39 30
  Forces Must Balance. .nt . . . .
  . . . . ASF Sep 39 9
  Frontier Planet. .nt . . . .
  . . . . TW Feb 43 15
  Gambler's Asteroid. .s . . . .
  . . . . TW Spr 44 87
  Giants from Eternity. .n . . . .
  . . . . SS Jul 39 14
  Glimpse. .s . . . . TW Apr 38 74
  "HOK" series includes:
    BATTLE IN THE DAWN
    HOK GOES TO ATLANTIS
    HOK DRAWS THE BOW
    HOK AND THE GIFT OF HEAVEN
    HOK VISITS THE LAND OF
      LEGENDS
  Hok and the Gift of Heaven. . . . .
  . .s . . . . Amz Mar 41 76
  Hok Draws the Bow. .nt . . . .
  . . . . .Amz May 40 88
  Hok Goes to Atlantis. .nt . . . . . .
  . . . . Amz Dec 39 42
  Hok Visits the Land of
    Legends. .nt . . . . . FA Apr 42 154
  Hole in the Sky, The. .s . . . .
  . . . . .CF Sum 42 95
  Insight. .s . . . . . .DS Apr–May 39 59
  Island in the Sky. .n . . . .
  . . . . TW Oct 41 14
  It Happened in Space. .s . . . .
  . . . . Amz Jun 42 140
  Kelpie, The. .s . . . . . AFR #12 61
  Legion of the Dark. .s . . . .
  . . . . SSS May 43 56
  Life Machines, The. .s . . . .
  . . . . TW Dec 40 16
  Lost Rocket. .s . . . .
  . . . . .ASF Jan 41 103
  Men Against the Stars. .s . . . .
  . . . . ASF Jun 38 6

AUTHOR
  Title. .Length . . . . Magazine, Date, Page

  Nuisance Value. .n 2 pt. . . . .
  . . . . ASF Dec 38 61
  Outlaws on Callisto. .nt . . . .
  . . . . ASF Apr 36 108
  Pithecanthropus Rejectus . . . . . .
  . .s . . . . .ASF Jan 38 68
  Planet of Change, The. .s . . . . . .
  . . . . TW Mar 40 56
  Robot and the Lady, The. .ss . . . .
  . . . . TW Oct 38 110
  Rocket of Metal Men. .s . . . .
  . . . . .Ash Dec 40 26
  Rule of the Bee. .s . . . .
  . . . . ASF Oct 37 51
  Sky Will Be Ours, The. .s . . . . . .
  . . . . SS Jan 49 94
  Sojarr of Titan. .n . . . .
  . . . . .SS Mar 41 16
  Solar Invasion, The *(CAPTAIN*
    FUTURE). .n . . . . . SS Fal 46 13
  Space Shore. .s . . . . .TW Aug 41 65
  Space Station No. 1. .s . . . .
  . . . . FFM Sep Oct 39 27
  Strangers on the Heights. .n . . . . .
  . . . . SS Sum 44 11
  Suicide Rocket. .s . . . .
  . . . . Amz Mar 42 62
  That's Just Like a Martian. .s . . . .
  . . . . TW Fal 43 94
  There Was No Paradise. .s . . . . . .
  . . . . .TW Aug 40 14
  Thirtieth Century Duel. .s . . . . . .
  . . . . .Fut Apr 41 10
  Timeless Tomorrow, The . . . .
  . .s . . . . .TW Dec 47 68
  Tongue Cannot Tell, The . . . . . .
  . .s . . . . TW Oct 47 90
  Treasure Asteroid. .s . . . .
  . . . . ASF Sep 38 6
  Twice in Time. .n . . . .
  . . . . SS May 40 14
  Undermost. .s . . . . . . TW Spr 46 46
  Venus Enslaved. .nt . . . .
  . . . . PS Sum 42 90
  Warrior of Two Worlds. .nt . . . . .
  . . . . PS Sum 44 74
  West Point, 3000 A.D. . . . .
  . .n 2 pt. . . . . . . Amz Nov 40 12
  When It Was Moonlight. .s . . . . . .
  . . . . UK Feb 40 124
  When Planets Clashed. .s . . . .
  . . . . WQ Spr 31 400
  . . . . SS Mar 47 70
  Where Angels Fear. . . . .s . . . . .
  . . . . UK Mar 39 131

AUTHOR
    Title. .Length . . . . Magazine, Date, Page

Wings of the Storm. .s . . . .
. . . . ASF Mar 38 88
Worlds of the Tomorrow,
    The. .nt . . . . TW Oct 40 93
with MAX JERGOVIC
Rebels of the Moon. .s . . . .
. . . . WQ Spr 32 354
WELLS, BASIL See also pseud
    GENE ELLERMAN (4)
Among the Scented Ones. .s . . . .
. . . . .PS Win 47 75
Animat. .s . . . . .PS Spr 49 77
Biped. .ss . . . . Cos Mar 41 117
Caverns of Ith. .s . . . . . . FB #2 22
Empire of Dust. .s . . . . . . FB #5 23
Factory in the Sky. .s . . . .
. . . . Ash Sep 41 68
Fog of the Forgotten. .s . . . .
. . . . .PS Win 46 63
Giant, The. .s . . . . . Sti Mar 42 15
Hairy One, The. .s . . . .
. . . . .PS Win 44 76
Half-Man, The. .s . . . .
. . . . SFQ Fal 42 119
Human Mice of Kordar. .s . . . . . .
. . . . .Sti Jun 41 32
New Moon. .s . . . . . .Cos May 41 90
Power for Darm. .s . . . .
. . . . FB #6 89
Queen of the Blue World. .s . . . .
. . . . .PS Win 41 22
Quest of Thig. .s . . . . PS Fal 42 23
Quest's End. .s . . . . . PS Spr 44 65
Rebel Slug, The. .s . . . .
. . . . Fut Apr 42 35
Rebirth of Man. .s . . . .
. . . . SSS Sep 40 94
Scrambled Worlds. .s . . . .
. . . . .PS Spr 47 83
Survival. .s . . . . .PS Spr 46 30
Swift People, The. .s . . . .
. . . . Fut Feb 43 100
Under Martian Sands. .s . . . .
. . . . .OTWA Dec 50 24
Valkyrie from the Void . . . .
. .s . . . . PS Fal 48 102
Wall of Darkness. .s . . . . FB #4 26
WELLS, HAL K.
Biog sketch, photo. . . . .
. . . . SS Jul 42 10
Blood on the Sun. .n . . . .
. . . . SS May 42 14
Cavern of the Shining Ones,
    The. .s . . . . . . ASF Nov 32 149
Devil Crystals of Arret. .s . . . . . .
. . . . .ASF Sep 31 344

AUTHOR
    Title. .Length . . . . Magazine, Date, Page

Dimension-Hazard. .s . . . .
. . . . .SSS Nov 40 40
Flame Worms of Yokku. .s . . . . .
. . . . Amz Mar 33 1137
Gate to Xoran, The. .s . . . .
. . . . .ASF Jan 31 46
Man-Jewels for Xothar. .nt . . . . .
. . . . TW Oct 36 38
Moon of Mad Atavism. .s . . . . . .
. . . . .TW Feb 39 32
Purple Brain, The. .s . . . .
. . . . ASF Dec 33 57
When the Moon Turned
    Green. .s . . . . . ASF May 31 241
White Brood, The. .s . . . .
. . . . TW Nov 40 52
Zehru of Xollar. .s . . . .
. . . . ASF Feb 32 264
WELLS, H.(erbert) G.(eorge)
MASTERS OF FANTASY
    biog . . . . FFM Jun 48 101
MEMORIAL TO H. G. WELLS . .
    . .pict feat . . . . . . PS Spr 47 119
Aepyonis Island. .s . . . .
. . . . Amz Oct 27 662
Country of the Blind, The. .s . . . .
. . . . Amz Dec 27 850
Crystal Egg, The. .s . . . .
. . . . Amz May 26 128
Diamond Maker, The. .s . . . .
. . . . SW Jun 29 35
Empire of the Ants, The. .s . . . . .
. . . . Amz Aug 26 410
First Men in the Moon, The. . . . .
    . .n 3 pt . . . . . . Amz Dec 26 774
Flowering of the Strange Orchid,
    The. .s . . . . . . Amz Mar 28 1161
In the Abyss. .s . . . Amz Sep 26 484
Invisible Man, The. .n 2 pt. . . . . .
. . . . Amz Jun 28 198
Island of Dr. Moreau, The . . . . .
    . .n 2 pt . . . . . . Amz Oct 26 636
        (Complete). . . FFM Oct 46 8
Lord of the Dynamos, The . . . . .
    . .s . . . . Amz Feb 29 975
Man Who Could Work Miracles,
    The. .s . . . . . .Amz Jul 26 312
Moth, The. .s . . . . Amz Aug 28 461
New Accelerator, the. .s . . . .
. . . . Amz Apr 26 57
Plattner Story, The. .s . . . .
. . . . .Amz Jul 27 355
Pollock and the Porroh Man . . . .
    . .s . . . . Amz Feb 28 1072
Queer Story of Brownlow's
    Newspaper, The. .s. . . . AFR #3 27

AUTHOR
    Title. .Length . . . . Magazine, Date, Page

Remarkable Case of Davidson's
    Eyes, The. .s . . . . Amz Apr 27 21
Star, The. .s . . . . Amz Jun 26 242
Stolen Body, The. .s . . . .
. . . . .Amz Jan 28 998
Story of the Days to Come, A . . .
    . .n 2 pt . . . . Amz Apr 28 6
Story of the Late Mr. Elvesham,
    The. .s . . . . Amz Jun 27 253
Story of the Stone Age, A . . . . . .
    . .nt . . . . Amz Nov 27 726
Time Machine, The. .nt . . . .
. . . . Amz May 27 148
            FFM Aug 50 10
Truth About Pyecraft, The . . . . .
    . .s . . . . AFR #1 92
Under the Knife. .s . . . .
. . . . Amz Mar 27 1112
            AA 27 120
War of the Worlds, The. . . . .
    . .n 2 pt . . . . . . Amz Aug 27 422
When the Sleeper Wakes. .n . . . . .
. . . . .AQ Win 28 55
WELLS, HUBERT GEORGE pseud
    of FORREST J. ACKERMAN
Earth Can Be Fair. .ss . . . .
. . . . OW Oct 50 26
WELLS, J. WELLINGTON pseud of
    L. SPRAGUE de CAMP (for
    book reviews in UK)
WENTWORTH, ROBERT pseud of
    EDMOND HAMILTON
World Without Sex. .s . . . .
. . . . MSS May 40 41
WENTZ, ELMA
with LYLE MONROE pseud (Robert
    A. Heinlein)
Beyond Doubt. .s . . .Ash Apr 41 35
WENTZ, ROBY
Change. .s . . . . UK Oct 43 135
Day After Tomorrow. .nt . . . . . .
. . . . ASF Mar 42 55
House of Tomorrow. .s . . . .
. . . . ASF May 44 118
Nose for News, A. .s. . . . .
. . . . ASF Jun 42 56
WERNHAM, GUY
Outcasts. .s . . . . . . ASF Nov 34 98
WERTENBAKER, G. PEYTON
Chamber of Life, The. .s . . . .
. . . . Amz Oct 29 628
Coming of the Ice, The . . . .
    . .s . . . . Amz Jun 26 232
Elaine's Tomb. .s . . . AQ Win 30 74
Man from the Atom, The . . . . . .
    . .n 2 pt . . . . Amz Apr 26 62

AUTHOR
  Title. .Length . . . . Magazine, Date, Page

Ship That Turned Aside, The. . . . .
  . .s . . . . Amz Mar 30 1130
WESSO(LOWSK), H.(ans)
  W.(aldemar) *artist*
  Biog sketch, photo. . . . .
  . . . . TW Jun 39 89
  Cover for AMAZING STORIES
    QUARTERLY
    Fal 1929
  Cover for ASTONISHING STORIES
    Mar 1942
  Covers for ASTOUNDING
    (STORIES) (SCIENCE FICTION)
    Jan, Feb, Mar, Apr, May, Jun, Jul,
      Aug, Sep, Oct, Nov, Dec 1930
    Jan, Feb, Mar, Apr, May, Jun, Jul,
      Aug, Sep, Oct, Nov, Dec 1931
    Jan, Feb, Mar, Apr, May, Jun, Sep,
      Nov 1932
    Jan, Mar 1933
    Jan, Sep, Nov 1937
    Jan, Mar, Jun, Aug 1938
  Cover for MARVEL SCIENCE
    STORIES
    Feb 1939
  Covers for THRILLING WONDER
    STORIES
    Aug 1937
    Jun 1941
WEST, JACK
  Biog sketch, photo. . . . .
  . . . . Amz Oct 40 131
  Jules Verne Fantasy, A. .a . . . . .
  . . . . FA Aug 42 222
  Nature's Bullets. .a. . . . .
  . . . . Amz Jun 42 126
  Land-Going Fish. .a . . . .
  . . . . .FA Jul 42 106
  Revolt on Io. .nt . . . .
  . . . . Amz Oct 40 106
  SCIENTIFIC MYSTERIES
  Life from Electricity. .a . . . . . .
  . . . . Amz Mar 41 44
  When the Ice Terror Came. . . . .
  . .s . . . . Amz Apr 40 118
WEST, JOHN FOSTER
  Biog sketch, photo. . . . .
  . . . . TW Win 44 127
  Moon Trap. .s . . . . . TW Win 44 73
  Duel in Black. .s . . . .
  . . . . .PS Win 47 113
WEST, WALLACE
  Cannonball Road, The. .s . . . . . .
  . . . . .FA Jan 45 108
  Dragon's Teeth. .s . . . .
  . . . . ASF Sep 34 63

En Route to Pluto. .s . . . .
  . . . . ASF Aug 36 39
End of Time, The. .s . . . .
  . . . . ASF Mar 33 64
Last Man, The. .s. . . . .
  . . . . Amz Feb 29 1030
Lure of Polaris, The. .nt . . . . . .
  . . . . .TW Oct 49 9
Nocturne. .s . . . . . TW Apr 50 116
Outlaw Queen of Venus . . . .
  . .nt . . . . FA Feb 44 8
Phantom Dictator, The. . . . .
  . .s . . . . ASF Aug 35 123
Plane People. .nt . . . ASF Nov 33 74
Retreat from Utopia, The . . . . . .
  . .s . . . . ASF Mar 34 143
Sculptors of Life. .s . . . .
  . . . . ASF Dec 39 71
Tanner of Kiev, The. .s . . . .
  . . . . FA Oct 44 82
Weariest River, The. .nt . . . . . .
  . . . . .TW Aug 50 104
WESTON, ED
  Cosmic Caravan. .s. . . . .
  . . . . TW Fal 45 60
WESTON, SAM
  In the Day of the Cold . . . .
  . .s . . . . .ASF Jan 40 92
WESTWOOD, N. J.
  Aimless Asteroid. .s . . . .
  . . . . TW Feb 43 75
  Glory of the U.S.L., The. . . . . . .
  . .s . . . . TW Jun 42 72
  Minnie of Mars. .s . . . .
  . . . . TW Aug 42 70
WETJEN, ALBERT RICHARD
  Ship of Silence, The. .s . . . .
  . . . . .AFR # 13 104
WHITE, CECIL B.
  Lost Continent, The. .s . . . .
  . . . . Amz Jul 27 339
  Retreat to Mars, The . . . .
  . .s . . . . Amz Aug 27 460
  Return of the Martians, The . . . .
  . .s . . . . Amz Apr 28 70
WHITE, PARKER *pseud of*
  WILLIAM ANTHONY PARKER
  WHITE
WHITE, NORMAN
  Story of Roger Bacon, The . . . . .
  . .a . . . . Amz Mar 43 220
WHITE, W. MALCOLM
  Pallas Rebellion. .ss . . . .
  . . . . OTWA Jul 50 70
  War of the Marsh-Men. .ss . . . . . .
  . . . . .OTWA Dec 50 70

WHITE, WILLIAM ANTHONY
  PARKER *See pseuds ANTHONY*
  BOUCHER (14), H. H. HOLMES
  (4), PARKER WHITE (0)
WHITEHEAD, HENRY S.
  Bothon. .nt . . . . . Amz Aug 46 122
  Scar Tissue. .s . . . . Amz Jul 46 146
  Shadows, The. .s . . . . AFR #14 110
  Trap, The. .nt . . . . . . AFR #6 102
WHITEHORN, CHESTER
  Editor of PLANET STORIES
  Win 45 *thru* Sum 46 *issues*
  Coming of the Gods. .s . . . .
  . . . . PS Sum 45 107
WHITENACK, D., JR.
  PROBABILITY ZERO
  O'Ryan, The Invincible. . . . . . .
  . .ss . . . . ASF Dec 42 106
WHITESIDE, STANLEY
  Information Please. .ss . . . .
  . . . . TW Win 46 79
WHITLEY, GEORGE *pseud of A.*
  BERTRAM CHANDLER
  And Not in Peace. .s. . . . .
  . . . . FFM Dec 46 112
  Boomerang. .s. . . . FFM Aug 47 114
  Castaway. .s . . . . . . NW Spr 50 52
  Moon of Madness. .s. . . . .
  . . . . .PS Spr 49 40
  One Came Back. .s. . . . .
  . . . . TW Fal 45 79
  Second Meeting. .s. . . . .
  . . . . .F&SF Fal 50 84
  Traveler's Tale. .s. . . . .
  . . . . .SS Jan 47 93
WHITTINGTON, GEORGE (A.)
  Battlefield in Black. .s . . . .
  . . . . PS Fal 45 65
  Invaders from Infinity. .s . . . . .
  . . . . .PS Win 44 29
  Mists of Mars. .s . . . .
  . . . . PS Sum 45 78
  Space-Lane of No-Return . . . . . .
  . .s . . . . PS Sum 46 47
WIDNER, ARTHUR LAMBERT
  See pseud ARTHUR
  LAMBERT (1)
WIGGIN, John
  Cave Dwellers of Saturn. .nt . . . .
  . . . . .PS Win 39 96
WILCOX, DON *See also pseuds*
  BUZZ-BOLT ATOMCRACKER (1)
  (1), CLEO ELDON (0), MAX
  OVERTON (2), MILES
  SHELTON (8)
  Biog sketch . . . . . . Amz Jul 39 133

AUTHOR
Title. .Length . . . . Magazine, Date, Page

Biog sketch, photo. . . . .
. . . . .Amz Jan 41 120
Angel With Four Faces, An . . . . .
. .nt . . . . FA Sep 42 58
Battering Rams of Space. .n. . . . .
. . . . Amz Feb 41 8
"BEN GLEED" series includes:
 BEN GLEED, KING OF SPEED
 THE IRON MEN OF SUPER CITY
 THE FIEND OF NEW LONDON
Ben Gleed, King of Speed. .s . . . .
. . . . Amz Dec 39 24
Bull Moose of Babylon. .nt . . . .
. . . . FA Apr 42 70
Cats of Kadenza. .n . . . .
. . . . FA Oct 44 10
Champlin Fights the Purple
 God. .nt. . . . . . . Amz Sep 40 28
Chariot of Death. .n. . . . .
. . . . FA Aug 43 66
Craig's Book. .n. . . . .FA Jul 43 10
Desert of the Damned. .n . . . . . .
. . . . Amz May 47 62
Devil's Pigs, The. .s . . . .
. . . . FA Jan 45 12
Dictator of Peace. .nt . . . .
. . . . Amz Nov 39 70
Disciples of Destiny. .n 2 pt. . . . .
. . . . Amz Mar 42 8
Dwellers of the Deep. .n . . . .
. . . . FA Apr 42 8
Eagle Man, The. .n. . . . .
. . . . .FA Jul 42 8
Earth Stealers. .n. . . Amz Jun 43 60
Fiend of New London, The. . . . .
. .s . . . . Amz Feb 42 194
Giants of Mogo, The. .n . . . .
. . . . Amz Nov 47 8
Great Brain Panic, The. .n. . . . . .
. . . . .Amz Jul 43 32
Great Gods and Little
 Termites. .s . . . . Amz Dec 46 52
Hollow Planet, The. .n . . . .
. . . . Amz Oct 42 144
Ice Queen, The. .n . . . FA Jan 43 8
Invasion Dust. .s . . . .
. . . . Amz Dec 44 108
Invisible Raiders of Venus. . . . . .
. .s . . . . Amz Apr 41 106
Invisible Wheel of Death, The . . .
. .nt . . . . Amz Jan 41 44
Iron Men of Super City, The . . . .
. .nt . . . . Amz May 41 104
Kettle in the Pit, The. .s . . . .
. . . . Amz Oct 47 8
Land of the Big Blue Apples,
 The. .n . . . . .FA May 46 6

Lavender Vine of Death, The. . . .
. .n . . . . FA Sep 48 8
Leopard Girl, The. .n . . . .
. . . . FA Oct 42 50
Let War Gods Clash. .s . . . .
. . . . FA Feb 40 70
Lost Race Comes Back, The . . . .
. .n . . . . .Amz May 41 8
Madamoiselle Butterfly. .nt . . . .
. . . . FA May 42 146
Magnetic Miss Meteor. .nt . . . . . .
. . . . Amz Mar 44 50
Man from the Future, The. . . . .
. .s . . . . FA Nov 41 100
Man from the Magic River. . . . .
. .nt . . . . FA Jun 44 126
Man Who Turned to Smoke,
 The. .s . . . . FA Jun 42 192
March of the Mercury Men . . . .
. .nt . . . . Amz Aug 46 46
Mirrors of Madness. .nt . . . .
. . . . .Amz Jul 40 48
Mr. Eee Conducts a Tour . . . . . .
. .s . . . . FA Dec 41 52
Mystery of the Mind Machine . . .
. .n . . . . Amz Aug 40 100
Pit of Death, The. .s . . . .
. . . . .Amz Jul 39 108
Princess of the Sea. .n. . . . .
. . . . FA Jan 47 8
Queen of the Living Puppets . . . .
. .nt . . . . FA Oct 41 64
Rainbow of Death. .nt . . . .
. . . . .FA Jan 42 110
Red Door, The. .nt . . . .
. . . . FA Nov 46 140
Rikits of Mars, The. .n . . . .
. . . . Amz Jan 48 80
Robot Peril, The. .nt . . . .
. . . . FA Jan 40 6
Scarlet Swordsman, The . . . . . .
. .nt . . . . Amz Jun 45 120
Secret of Sutter's Lake, The . . . .
. .n . . . . Amz Jan 47 38
Secret of the Serpent. .n . . . . . .
. . . . FA Jan 48 8
Secret of the Stone Doll . . . . . .
. .nt . . . . FA Mar 41 106
Secret League of Six. .s. . . . . . .
. . . . FA Aug 41 86
Serpent Has Five Fangs, The . . . .
. .nt . . . . FA Dec 45 6
Singing Skulls, The. .nt . . . .
. . . . FA Apr 45 66
Slave Raiders from Mercury. . . . .
. .nt . . . . Amz Jun 40 6

Stevedore of Jupiter, The . . . . . .
. .s . . . . Amz Nov 41 70
Taggart's Terrible Turban . . . . . .
. .n . . . . .FA Jan 45 122
Taxi to Jupiter. .s . . . .
. . . . Amz Aug 41 110
Three Eyes in the Dark. . . . .
. .s . . . . .FA May 41 44
Voice from Venus, The. . . . .
. .nt . . . . Amz Sep 45 40
Voyage That Lasted 600 Years,
 The. .nt. . . . . . . Amz Oct 40 82
When the Moon Died. .nt . . . . . .
. . . . Amz Sep 39 64
Whispering Gorilla, The. .nt . . . .
. . . . .FA May 40 6
Wives in Duplicate. .s . . . .
. . . . Amz Aug 39 62
World of the Paper Dolls. . . . . . .
. .n . . . . FA Oct 43 22
WILEY, JOHN
Venus Trouble. .nt. . . . .
. . . . OW Oct 50 78
Venus Trouble Shooter. .nt . . . . .
. . . . .OW Nov 49 120
WILKIN, R. A. *artist*
Cover for NEW WORLDS
#1 1946
WILKINS, RALPH (W.)
Campus Murder Mystery, The . . .
. .s . . . . .SD Jan 30 14
Death in a Drop. .s . . . .
. . . . AD Oct 30 876
Empire in the Sky, The. . . . .
. .s . . . . WS Oct 30 418
Impossible Crime, The. .s . . . . . .
. . . . .AD Jul 30 632
When Space Ripped Open . . . . . .
. .s . . . . AW Nov 29 412
WILKINSON, NEAL B.
Decision Illogical. .s . . . .
. . . . .ASF Jul 48 36
WILLARD, C. D. *pseud of CHARLES WILLARD DIFFIN*
Eye of Allah, The. .s . . . .
. . . . .ASF Jan 31 58
Out of the Dreadful Depths. . . . .
. .s . . . . .ASF Jun 30 293
WILLEY, ROBERT *pseud of WILLY LEY*
At the Perihelion. .nt . . . .
. . . . ASF Feb 37 41
Fog. .nt . . . . ASF Dec 40 80
Invasion, The. .s . . . .SSS Sep 40 25
Orbit XXIII-H. .nt . . . .
. . . . ASF Sep 38 17

AUTHOR
Title. .Length . . . . Magazine, Date, Page

WILLIAMS, LLOYD
Shipwrecked Bogey Man, The . . .
. .s . . . . OTWA Jul 50 83
WILLIAMS, NICK BODDIE
Terrible Morning, The. .s. . . . . . .
. . . . NW #3 29
WILLIAMS, RALPH
Emergency Landing. .ss . . . .
. . . . ASF Jul 40 52
WILLIAMS, ROBERT MOORE *See
also pseuds JOHN S. BROWN-
ING (1), H. H. HARMON (2),
E. K. JARVIS (h) (17?), ROBERT
MOORE (1), RUSSELL STORM
(7)*
Biog sketch . . . . Amz Jun 38 6
Biog sketch, photo. . . . .
. . . . TW Jun 39 86
Biog sketch, photo. . . . .
. . . . Amz Jun 39 132
Biog sketch . . . . . Amz Jul 39 132
Biog sketch, photo. . . . .
. . . . SS Jan 43 129
Accidental Murders, The. . . . . . .
. .s . . . . Amz Feb 41 98
Battle Before Dawn. .s . . . .
. . . . Amz Mar 44 104
Bees of Death, The. .n . . . .
. . . . FA Oct 49 86
Beyond That Curtain. .s . . . .
. . . . TW Dec 37 65
Blitz Against Japan. .nt. . . . .
. . . . Amz Sep 42 10
Bridge of Life. .s . . . .
. . . . Amz May 46 92
Bridge to Earth, The . . . .
. .n . . . . SS Sep 39 16
Castaway. .s . . . . . . ASF Feb 41 37
Challenge, The. .s . . . .
. . . . TW Oct 50 69
Counterfeiter, The. .s . . . .
. . . . FA Nov 46 78
Crime Clean-Up in Center
City. .s . . . . FA Apr 42 54
Danger Is My Destiny. .nt . . . . . .
. . . . Amz Apr 50 136
Dark Reality. .s. . . . Com Mar 41 88
Death Desert. .s. . . . .
. . . . Amz Nov 41 84
Death Over Chicago. .nt . . . .
. . . . FA Jan 40 30
Death Sentence. .s. . . . .
. . . . UK Mar 39 151
Dr. Destiny, Master of the
Dead. .nt . . . . FA Jun 40 6
Doom Ship. .nt . . . . . FA Feb 50 94

AUTHOR
Title. .Length . . . . Magazine, Date, Page

Elixir of Peace, The. .s . . . .
. . . . Amz Dec 49 124
Eternal Light, The. .s . . . .
. . . . TW Jan 40 66
Fate and the Fly. .s . . . .
. . . . FA Feb 42 132
Fifth Column of Mars. .nt . . . . . .
. . . . Amz Sep 40 6
Final Frontier, The. .s . . . .
. . . . SS Jan 50 88
Fisherman, The. .s . . . .
. . . . FA Feb 43 98
Flight of the Dawn Star . . . .
. .s . . . . ASF Mar 38 26
Girl Who Read Minds, The . . . . .
. .s . . . . Amz Sep 49 8
Golden Princess, The. .nt . . . . . .
. . . . FA Aug 40 6
Homeward Bound. .s . . . .
. . . . SS Nov 49 109
House of Fire, The. .nt. . . . .
. . . . FA Jan 42 40
Huntress of Akkan, The. .n . . . . .
. . . . Amz Feb 46 54
Incredible Slingshot Bombs,
The. .s. . . . . . . Amz May 42 130
Impossible Invention, The. .s . . . .
. . . . Ash Jun 42 30
Isle of Doom, The. .nt . . . .
. . . . FA Jan 48 80
Jimmy Dolan's Radio Ray. .s. . . .
. . . . Amz Jul 43 96
Johnny Had a Gun. .s. . . . .
. . . . ASF Dec 42 98
Jongor of Lost Land. .n . . . .
. . . . FA Oct 40 10
Land of Golden Men. .s . . . .
. . . . Amz Jun 49 70
Like Alarm Bells Ringing . . . . . .
. .s . . . . Amz Jan 47 84
Lord of the Silent Death. . . . . . .
. .s . . . . Com Dec 40 7
Lost Warship, The. .n . . . .
. . . . Amz Jan 43 8
Lundstret's Invention. .s . . . .
. . . . Amz Jun 39 76
Machine, The. .nt . . . .
. . . . Amz May 43 8
Magic of Joe Wilks, The . . . .
. .nt . . . . FA Sep 49 128
Man from the Stars, The. . . . . . .
. .s . . . . TW Fal 43 50
Man Next Door, The . . . .
. .s . . . . Amz Jul 46 156
Man of Two Worlds. .nt . . . .
. . . . FA Mar 47 134

AUTHOR
Title. .Length . . . . Magazine, Date, Page

Man Who Looked Like Steinmetz,
The. .s. . . . . TW Jun 38 44
Man Who Ruled the World,
The. .s. . . . . Amz Jun 38 10
Martian Adventure. .nt. . . . .
. . . . FA Oct 44 162
Metal Martyr, The. .s . . . .
. . . . Amz Jul 50 66
Miracle Man. .s . . . . FA Feb 48 134
Miracle of Bulldozer Mikke,
The. .s. . . . . Amz Dec 45 92
Miracle of Kicker McGuire,
The. .s. . . . . FA May 43 208
Missing: Millions in Radium. . . . .
. .s . . . . Amz Nov 39 116
Mr. Murchison's Ghost. .s . . . . . .
. . . . FA Aug 41 74
Mystery of Shaft 13, The . . . .
. .s . . . . FA Jul 42 158
No Heroes Wanted. .s. . . . .
. . . . SS Sep 41 107
Observer, The. .s . . . . FA Jan 45 80
On Pain of Death. .nt . . . .
. . . . ASF Jun 42 40
One Way Star Ride. .s. . . . .
. . . . TW Oct 40 33
Pacifist of Hell's Island. .nt . . . . .
. . . . Amz Jun 43 130
Piping Death, The. .s . . . .
. . . . UK May 39 87
Planet of Doomed Men. . . . .
. .nt . . . . Amz Jan 42 100
Planet of the Gods. .nt . . . .
. . . . Amz Dec 42 150
Pruning Man, The. .s . . . .
. . . . FA Oct 48 136
Quest of Zipantoric. .s . . . .
. . . . DS Feb 39 88
Quest on Io. .s . . . . . PS Fal 40 33
Raiders out of Space . . . .
. .nt . . . . Amz Oct 40 10
Red Earth of Mars, The . . . .
. .nt . . . . ASF Jul 40 130
Reformation of Joseph Reed,
The. .s. . . . . FA Dec 41 68
Return of Jongor, The. .n . . . . . .
. . . . FA Apr 44 12
Return of Satan. .nt. . . . .
. . . . Amz Oct 39 28
Road Block. .s . . . . . SS Nov 50 106
Robots Return. .s . . . .
. . . . ASF Sep 38 140
Rocket Race to Luna. .s . . . .
. . . . Amz Sep 39 112
Rockets over Europe . . . .
. .s . . . . Amz Feb 40 28

AUTHOR
   Title. .Length . . . . Magazine, Date, Page

Rockey Gordon's Billion Dollar
   Trap. .s . . . . . . Amz May 41 180
SCIENTIFIC MYSTERIES
The Lost Race of Illinois. . . . . . .
   . .a . . . . Amz Apr 42 262
Lost Races of America . . . .
   . .a . . . . Amz May 42 264
Secret of the Golden Jaguar. . . . .
   . .nt . . . . FA May 42 54
Secret of the Pyramid. .nt . . . . . .
   . . . . .Amz Jul 39 8
Seekers, The. .s . . . . . SS May 48 92
Son of Death, The. .nt . . . .
   . . . . FA Aug 42 134
Song of the Shadow Death . . . . .
   . .s . . . . TW Aug 38 106
Sons of the Prophet. .nt . . . .
   .FA Aug 49 54
Soul Makers, The. .s . . . .
   . . . . .SSS Nov 50 58
Sound of Bugles, The. .s . . . .
   . . . . .SS Mar 49 74
Star Base X. .nt . . . . Amz Sep 44 8
Stubborn Men, The. .ss . . . .
   . . . . SS Nov 48 71
Survivors from 9000 B.C. . . . . .
   . .n . . . . .Amz Jul 41 8
This Way Out. .nt . . . .
   . . . . Amz Sep 50 94
Tides of Time, The. .s . . . .
   . . . . TW Apr 40 12
Time Tolls for Toro. .nt . . . .
   . . . . Amz Aug 50 124
To Fight Another Day. .s . . . . . .
   . . . . .ASF Jun 41 106
To the End of Time. .s . . . .
   . . . . SSS Jul 50 108
To Watch by Night. .n . . . .
   . . . . .FA Jul 46 8
Voyage into the Lightning. . . . .
   . .nt . . . . Amz Feb 42 98
Warning from the Past, The . . . . .
   . .s . . . . TW Aug 39 34
Watching Eyes, The. .s . . . .
   .FA May 48 142
Weapon, The. .s. . . . .Amz Jul 47 76
When Two Worlds Meet . . . .
   . .nt . . . . Amz Apr 50 8
Where Tall Towers Gleam . . . . . .
   . .s . . . . FA Aug 50 116
Who Was Thomas Morrow? . . . .
   . .s . . . . TW Apr 41 109
World Beyond the Sky . . . .
   . .n . . . . SS Jan 43 15
World of Reluctant Virgins,
   The. .s. . . . . . . Amz Nov 50 60

AUTHOR
   Title. .Length . . . . Magazine, Date, Page

World Without Men . . . .
   . .nt . . . . Amz Jun 50 60
You Ought to Be Dead . . . .
   . .s . . . . Amz Aug 41 86
WILLIAMSON, IAN
   Chemical Plant. .s . . . .
   . . . . NW Win 50 82
WILLIAMSON, JACK See also
   pseud WILL STEWART (4)
   Biog sketch, photo. . . . .
   . . . . TW Jun 39 63
   Biog sketch . . . . ToW Aut 39 128
   Biog sketch, photo. . . . .
   . . . . TW Jun 40 101
After World's End. .n . . . .
   . . . . MSS Feb 39 8
Alien Intelligence, The . . . .
   . .n 2 pt . . . . SW Jul 29 102
   (in 3 pt) . . . .CF Spr 42 96
. . .and Searching Mind . . . .
   . .n 3 pt . . . . . ASF Mar 48 7
As In the Beginning. .ss. . . . . . .
   . . . . .Fut Mar 40 85
Backlash. .s . . . .
   . . . . ASF Aug 41 148
Blue Spot, The. .n 2 pt . . . .
   . . . . .ASF Jan 37 48
Born of the Sun. .nt . . . .
   . . . . ASF Mar 34 11
Breakdown. .nt . . . . . ASF Jan 42 9
Cometeers, The. .n 4 pt . . . .
   . . . . .ASF May 36 6
Conscience, Ltd. . .s . . . .
   . . . . UK Aug 43 70
Cosmic Express, The. .s . . . .
   . . . . Amz Nov 30 752
Crucible of Power, The. . . . .
   . .nt . . . . ASF Feb 39 9
Darker Than You Think . . . .
   . .n . . . . UK Dec 40 9
Dead Spot, The. .s . . . .
   . . . . MSS Nov 38 41
Dead Star Station. .s . . . .
   . . . . ASF Nov 33 54
Doom from Planet 4, The . . . . . .
   . .s . . . . .ASF Jul 31 5
Electron Flame, The. .s. . . . . . .
   . . . . WQ Fal 32 84
Equalizer, The. .n . . . .
   . . . . ASF Mar 47 6
Flame from Mars, The. .s . . . . . .
   . . . . .ASF Jan 34 88
Fortress of Utopia, The . . . .
   . .n . . . . SS Nov 39 14
Galactic Circle, The. .nt . . . .
   . . . . ASF Aug 35 6

AUTHOR
   Title. .Length . . . . Magazine, Date, Page

Gateway to Paradise. .n . . . .
   . . . . SS Jul 41 14
Girl in the Bottle, The . . . .
   . .nt . . . . .SSS Sep 40 36
Green Girl, The. .n 2 pt . . . .
   . . . . Amz Mar 30 1110
Hindsight. .s . . . .
   . . . . ASF May 40 98
Ice Entity, The. .nt . . . .
   . . . . .TW Feb 37 86
In the Scarlet Star. .s . . . .
   . . . . Amz Mar 33 113
Infinite Enemy, The. .s. . . . .
   . . . . TW Apr 38 38
Iron God, The. .nt . . . .
   . . . . MSS Apr 41 70
Islands of the Sun. .n 2 pt . . . . . .
   . . . . ASF Sep 35 6
Lady of Light, The. .nt . . . .
   . . . . Amz Sep 32 486
Lake of Light, The. .s . . . .
   . . . . ASF Apr 31 100
"LEGION OF SPACE" series
   includes:
   THE LEGION OF SPACE
   THE COMETEERS
   ONE AGAINST THE LEGION
Legion of Space, The. .n 6 pt. . . .
   . . . . ASF Apr 34 10
   (Complete). . . . GSFN #2
Legion of Time. .n 3 pt. . . . . . .
   . . . . ASF May 38 4
Metal Man, The. .s . . . .
   . . . . Amz Dec 28 792
   AFR #6 31
   ToW Aut 39 42
Meteor Girl, The. .s . . . .
   . . . . ASF Mar 31 404
Moon and Mr. Wick, The. . . . . . .
   . .s . . . . FSQ Sum 50 149
Moon Era, The. .s . . . .
   . . . . WS Feb 32 1016
   ToW Aut 41 7
One Against the Legion . . . .
   . .n 3 pt . . . . ASF Apr 39 43
Passage to Saturn. .s . . . .
   . . . . TW Jun 39 61
Prince of Space, The. .nt . . . .
   . . . . .Amz Jan 31 870
Pygmy Planet. .s . . . .
   . . . . ASF Feb 32 151
Racketeers in the Sky. .nt . . . . . .
   . . . . AMF Oct 50 100
Reign of Wizardry, The. . . . .
   . .n 3 pt . . . . .UK Mar 40 9
Released Entropy. .n 2 pt . . . . . .
   . . . . .ASF Aug 37 8

AUTHOR
Title. .Length . . . . Magazine, Date, Page

Salvage in Space. .s . . . .
. . . . ASF Mar 33 6
Second Shell, The. .s . . . .
. . . . AW Nov 29 442
Star of Dreams, The. .nt . . . .
. . . . Com Mar 41 18
Stone from the Green Star,
The. .n 2 pt . . . . Amz Oct 31 584
Sun Maker, The. .nt . . . .
. . . . TW Jun 40 95
Terror Out of Time. .s . . . .
. . . . ASF Dec 33 116
Through the Purple Cloud. . . . . .
. .s . . . . WS May 31 1398
                              SS Nov 47 68
Twelve Hours to Live. .s . . . .
. . . . WS Aug 31 354
                              SS Mar 46 84
Unpredictable. .a 2 pt. . . . .
. . . . ASF Feb 46 100
Vanguard of Science . . . .
. .guest editorial . . . . SS Sep 39 15
With Folded Hands. .nt. . . . . . .
. . . . .ASF Jul 47 6
Xandulu. .n 3 pt . . . .
. . . . WS Mar 34 806
with MILES J. BREUER, M.D.
Birth of a New Republic, The . . .
. .n . . . . AQ Win 30 4
with LAURENCE SCHWARTZMAN
Red Slag of Mars. .s . . . .
. . . . WQ Spr 32 394
WILLIS, CHARLES *pseud of*
ARTHUR C. CLARKE
Castaway. .s . . . . . . Fant Apr 47 72
Inheritance. .ss . . . . .NW #3 54
WILSON, CLYDE
Roamer of the Stars. .s . . . .
.TW Apr 38 66
WILSON, DORIS (Mrs. Richard W.)
See LESLIE PERRI
WILSON, GABRIEL *pseud of RAY*
CUMMINGS & MRS. RAY
CUMMINGS in collaboration
Earrh—Venus 12. .s . . . .
. . . . TW Dec 36 103
WILSON, RICHARD *See pseud IVAR*
TOWERS (h) (2)
Four Star Planet. .s . . . .
. . . . .Fut Apr 42 66
Man from Siykul, The. .s. . . . . .
. . . . .PS Win 42 77
Message, The. .s. . . . .
. . . . .Ash Mar 42 82
Murder from Mars. .s . . . .
. . . . .Ash Apr 40 24

Purple Bat, The. .s . . . .
. . . . TW Oct 41 108
Transitory Island. .s . . . .
. . . . .Cos May 41 107
Wide-Open Ship. .s. . . . .
. . . . Fut Oct 42 88
WILSON, ROBERT
Vandals of the Void. .nt . . . . . .
. . . . .PS Spr 45 84
WILSON, ROBERT H.
Flight into Time, A . . . .
. .s . . . . WS Feb 31 944
Out Around Rigel. .s . . . .
. . . . ASF Dec 31 295
WILSTACH, JOHN
Biog sketch, pic. . . . . FA Apr 45 193
Escape from Doom. .n . . . .
. . . . FA Apr 45 10
WINIKI, EPHRAIM *pseud of JOHN*
RUSSELL FEARN (and possibly
others)
Earth Asunder. .s. . . . .
. . . . .SF Oct 39 62
Eclipse Bears Witness. .s . . . .
. . . . SF Mar 40 42
Jewels from the Moon, The . . . .
. .s . . . . SF Aug 39 69
Leeches from Space. .s . . . .
. . . . .SF Mar 39 114
WINKS, JACK
Adrift on a Meteor. .s . . . .
. . . . Amz Aug 33 430
First Ornithopter, The . . . .
. .s . . . . .Amz Jan 30 943
WINN, CHARLES C.
Infinite Vision, The. .s . . . .
. . . . .Amz May 26 136
WINSELL, HODGE
Starting Over, The. .s . . . .
. . . . OW Oct 50 70
WINSOR, G. McLEOD
Station X. .n 3 pt . .Amz Jul 25 292
WINSTEAD, D. E., M. D.
Ultra Gamma Wave, The . . . .
. .s . . . . .Amz May 34 43
WINTER, H. G. *pseud of HARRY*
BATES and DESMOND WINTER
HALL in collaboration
Hands of Aten, The. .nt . . . .
. . . . .ASF Jul 31 20
Midget from the Island. .nt . . . . .
. . . . ASF Aug 31 214
Seed of the Arctic Ice. . . . .
. .s . . . . ASF Feb 32 202
Under Arctic Ice. .nt . . . .
. . . . .ASF Jan 33 298

AUTHOR
Title. .Length . . . . Magazine, Date, Page

WINTER(S), J.(OSEPH) A., M.D.
Endocrinology Is Tough . . . .
. .a . . . . .ASF Oct 48 114
Expedition Mercy. .nt . . . .
. . . . ASF Nov 48 7
Expedition Polychrome. .s . . . . .
. . . . .ASF Jan 49 33
General Adaptation Syndrome,
The. .a. . . . . ASF Nov 50 76
WINTERBOTHAM, R.(USSELL) R.
Biog sketch . . . . . .Amz Jan 39 130
Biog sketch, photo. . . . .
. . . . Amz Apr 39 122
Biog sketch . . . . FA Jan 40 84
Captives of the Void. .s. . . . . . .
. . . . FA Jan 40 58
Cepheid Planet. .s . . . .
. . . . SSS Nov 40 8
Clouds over Uranus. .s . . . .
. . . . ASF Mar 37 111
Dead Man's Planet. .s . . . .
. . . . PS Fal 41 62
Disappearing Sam. .s . . . .
. . . . MSS Aug 39 62
Einleill. .s. . . . . . . .ASF Jul 37 90
Element of Logic, The. .s . . . . . .
. . . . .Ash Aug 40 34
Equation for Time. .s . . . .
.Com Dec 40 65
Fourth Dynasty, The. .s . . . .
. . . . ASF Dec 36 82
Genesis! . .s . . . . PS Sum 41 63
Interplanetary Graveyard . . . . . .
. .s . . . . Amz Jan 39 22
Invent or Die. .s . . . .
. . . . .Ash Sep 41 55
Jitterbug. .s . . . . .Sti Jun 41 48
Linked Worlds. .s. . . . .
. . . . .ASF Jan 37 40
Madness on Luna. .s. . . . .
. . . . Amz Apr 39 32
Message from Venus. .s . . . .
. . . . Com Jan 41 21
Monster That Threatened the
Universe, The. .s . . . .PS Spr 41 30
Old Man Mars. .s . . . .Fut Apr 42 59
Oridin's Formula. .s . . . .
. . . . .PS Mar 43 39
Procession of Suns. .s . . . .
. . . . ASF May 38 63
Psycho Power Quest, The . . . . . .
. .s . . . . ASF Feb 36 140
Second Moon, The. .s . . . .
. . . . MSS Feb 39 105
Secret of the Rocks, The. .s . . . .
. . . . ASF Dec 37 104

AUTHOR
Title. .Length . . . . Magazine, Date, Page

Specialization. .s . . . ASF Aug 37 31
Spore Trappers. .nt . . . .
. . . . ASF May 37 62
Star That would Not Behave,
The. .s . . . . ASF Aug 35 86
Status Quo. .s . . . . . Fut Apr 41 97
Thought-Feeders, The. .s . . . . . .
. . . . Fut Oct 41 72
Thought-Men of Mercury,
The. .s . . . . PS Fal 42 44
Time Maker, The. .s . . . .
. . . . .Fut Aug 41 43
Train That Vanished, The . . . . . .
. .s . . . . ASF Jul 36 118
Whispering Spheres, The . . . .
. .s . . . . .Com Jul 41 100
WINTERS, RAE *pseud of*
RAYMOND A. PALMER
WINTLE, W. JAMES
Spectre Spiders, The . . . .
. .s . . . . FFM Feb 47 114
WIRE, DON
Oil. .s . . . . ASF Feb 39 137
WITHROW, LAURA
Kiss of Death, The. .s . . . .
. . . . FFM Feb 40 111
WITWER, BENJAMIN
Radio Mates. .s . . . . Amz Jul 27 368
WOLFE, CHARLES S.
Educated Harpoon, The. .s . . . . .
. . . . Amz Dec 26 831
Master Key, The. .s . . . .
. . . . Amz Apr 28 67
Whispering Ether. .s . . . .
. . . . Amz Jun 26 247
WOLFF, DR. TH.
Can Man Free Himself from Gravity?
(tr fr German by Francis W.
Currier). .a . . . . . . SW Feb 30 788
WOLLHEIM, DONALD A. *See pseuds*
ARTHUR COOKE (1), MILLARD
VERNE GORDON (11), MARTIN
PEARSON (18), ALLEN
WARLAND (1), LAWRENCE
WOODS (5), "X" (1)
Editor AVON FANTASY READER
#1———(all issues)
Editor COSMIC STORIES
Mar 41 *thru* Jul 41 *issues (all)*
Editor OUT OF THIS WORLD
ADVENTURES
Jul 50 *thru* Dec 50 *issues (all)*
Editor STIRRING SCIENCE
STORIES
Feb 41 *thru* Mar 41 *issues (all)*
Aquella. .s . . . . AFR #7 80

AUTHOR
Title. .Length . . . . Magazine, Date, Page

Blueprint. .ss . . . . . . Sti Apr 41 23
Bones. .s . . . . Sti Feb 41 88
Castaway. .ss . . . . .SSS May 40 112
Haters, The. .ss . . . . . UK Oct 40 70
Man from Ariel, The. .ss . . . . . .
. . . . .WS Jan 34 604
Man from the Future, The. .ss . . .
. . . . Cos Mar 41 55
Mimic. .s . . . . FN Sep 50 118
AFR #3 89
Planet That Time Forgot,
The. .s . . . . .PS Fal 40 70
Storm Warning. .s . . . AFR #10 107
WOOD, JAMIESON
Black Arrow, The. .n . . . .
. . . . FA Jun 48 8
WOODBURY, DAVID O.
Aground in Space. .s . . . .
. . . . ASF Aug 34 45
Electric Snare, The. .s. . . . .
. . . . .ASF Jul 34 98
WOODRUFF, CLYDE *pseud of*
DAVID VERN
Man With Five Lives, The . . . . . .
. .n . . . . .FA Jan 43 102
WOODS, LAWRENCE *pseud of*
DONALD A. WOLLHEIM alone
and with revisions by ROBERT W.
LOWNDES and JOHN MICHEL
by DONALD A. WOLLHEIM &
ROBERT W. LOWNDES
Black Flames. .s . . . . Sti Apr 41 68
Colossus of Maia, The. .s. . . . . . .
. . . . Cos Jul 41 45
by DONALD A. WOLLHEIM &
JOHN B. MICHEL
Earth Does Not Reply. .s . . . . . .
. . . . SFQ Sum 41 123
by DONALD A. WOLLHEIM
Million Years and a Day, A . . . . .
. .ss . . . . .Fut Aug 41 80
Strange Return. .s . . . .
. . . . Sti Feb 41 51
WOOLRICH, CORNELL
Speak to Me of Death. .nt . . . . . .
. . . . FanF May 50 91
WOOLSTON, STANLEY
PROBABILITY ZERO
The Human Bomb. .ss . . . .
. . . . ASF Dec 42 104
WOOSTER, HAROLD
PROBABILITY ZERO
Y = Sin X
WORRELL, EVERIL
Canal, The. .s . . . . . . AFR #8 107

AUTHOR
Title. .Length . . . . Magazine, Date, Page

WORTH, AMY *pseud of DAVID*
H. KELLER, M.D.
WORTH, PETER *house pseud used*
by CHESTER S. GEIER and others
I Died Tomorrow. .nt. . . . .
. . . . FA May 49 104
Lunar Holiday. .s . . . .
. . . . FA Nov 49 52
Null F. .s . . . . FA Feb 50 116
Read It and Weep. .s . . . .
. . . . Amz Jun 50 124
Robot and the Pearly Gates,
The. .s . . . . Amz Jan 49 90
Typewriter from the Future . . . .
. .nt . . . . Amz Feb 50 44
Window to the Future. .s . . . . . .
. . . . Amz May 49 118
WRIGHT, ROSCOE E.
PROBABILITY ZERO
Ultimate Opposition. .ss . . . . . .
. . . . ASF Apr 43 89
WRIGHT, SEWELL PEASLEE *See*
also pseuds THOMAS ANDREWS
(0), LEIGH CAMERON (0),
PARKE SPENCER (0)
"COMMANDER JOHN HANSON"
series includes:
THE FORGOTTEN PLANET
THE TERRIBLE TENTACLES OF
L–472
THE DARK SIDE OF ANTRI
THE GHOST WORLD
THE MAN FROM 2071
THE GOD IN THE BOX
THE TERROR FROM THE DEPTHS
VAMPIRES OF SPACE
PRIESTESS OF THE FLAME
THE DEATH-TRAPS OF FX–31
Dark Side of Antri, The. .s . . . . .
. . . . ASF Jan 31 9
Death-Traps of FX–31, The. . . . .
. .s . . . . ASF Mar 33 82
Forgotten Planet, The. .s . . . . . .
. . . . .ASF Jul 30 88
AFR #13 25
From the Ocean's Depths. .s . . . .
. . . . ASF Mar 30 376
Ghost World, The. .s . . . .
. . . . ASF Apr 31 118
God in the Box, The. .s. . . . .
. . . . .ASF Sep 31 407
Infra-Medians, The. .s . . . .
. . . . ASF Dec 31 389
Into the Ocean's Depths. .s . . . . .
. . . . ASF May 30 151
Man from 2071, The. .s . . . .
. . . . .ASF Jun 31 295
Priestess of the Flame. .s. . . . . . .
. . . . .ASF Jun 32 401

AUTHOR
   Title. .Length . . . . Magazine, Date, Page

   Terrible Tentacles of L-472,
      The. .s . . . . .ASF Sep 30 332
   Terror from the Depths, The . . . .
      . .s . . . . ASF Nov 31 222
   Vampires of Space. .s . . . .
      . . . . ASF Mar 32 402
WRIGHT, S.(ydney) FOWLER
   MASTERS OF FANTASY
   biog . . . . FFM Feb 48 113
   Biog sketch . . . . Fant #3 39 74
   Adventure of Wyndham Smith,
      The. .n . . . . FFM Jun 50 12
   Automata. .s. . . . . .AFR #2 97
   Island of Captain Sparrow,
      The. .n . . . . FFM Apr 46 10
   Original Sin. .s . . . .
      . . . . AFR #13 68
   Whom the Rat Bites. .s . . . .
      . . . . Fant #3 39 33
WRIGHT, WEAVER pseud of
   FORREST J. ACKERMAN
   Micro-Man. .s . . . . FB #1 26
with FRANCIS FLAGG pseud
   (George Henry Weiss)
   Time Twister, The. .s . . . .
      . . . . TW Oct 47 61
WULFRES, ROGER
   Air Plant Men, The. .s . . . .
      . . . . WS Dec 30 738
WYCOFF, J. EARLE
   Seeing Blindness, The. .s . . . .
      . . . . ASF Feb 36 33
WYLIE, DIRK Born JOSEPH
   HAROLD DOCKWEILER, he
   took the name DIRK WYLIE
   for all purposes. Many stories
   appearing under his name were
   collaborations as below.
by CYRIL KORNBLUTH,
   FREDERIK POHL and DIRK
   WYLIE
   Vacant World. .s . . . . SSS Jan 41 46
by FREDERIK POHL and DIRK
   WYLIE
   Asteroid of the Damned. .s . . . . .
      . . . . PS Sum 42 31
   Highwayman of the Void. .nt. . . .
      . . . . PS Fal 44 94
   Outpost of the Eons. .nt . . . . . .
      . . . . .Ash Apr 43 32
   Sky Test. .s . . . . . . .SSS Nov 42 50
with FREDERIC ARNOLD
   KUMMER, JR.
   When Time Went Mad. .nt. . . . . .
      . . . . TW Feb 50 11

AUTHOR
   Title. .Length . . . . Magazine, Date, Page

WYLIE, PHILIP
   Epistle to the Thessalonians,
      An. .s . . . . WB Dec 50 11
WYNDHAM, JOHN pseud of JOHN
   BEYNON HARRIS
   Eternal Eve, The. .nt . . . .
      . . . . Amz Sep 50 114

X

X pseud of DONALD A. WOLLHEIM
   (for this one story only)
   !!! . .ss. . . . . Sti Apr 41 39
X, GENERAL pseud of ROGER
   SHERMAN HOAR

Y

YAMIN, MICHAEL
   Dreamers, The. .s . . . .
      . . . . ASF Dec 47 67
YERXA, FRANCES
   Freddie Funk's Flippant Fairies . .
      . .s . . . . FA Sep 48 130
   I Wake Up Dreaming. .s . . . . . .
      . . . . FA Jun 48 126
   Negative Problem. .s . . . .
      . . . . Amz Aug 47 58
   One More Spring. .s . . . .
      . . . . Amz Sep 47 74
YERXA, LEROY See also pseuds
   ALEXANDER BLADE (h) (1+),
   RICHARD CASEY (h) (?) also
   numerous stories under other hse
   pseuds.
   Biog sketch, photo. . . . .
      . . . . Amz Aug 42 232
   All Kinds of People. .s . . . .
      . . . . FA Apr 45 96
   "Anything You Say, Dear" . . . . .
      . .s . . . . Amz Feb 46 44
   Bridge of Banishment. .nt . . . . . .
      . . . . Amz May 43 154
   Bury Me Deep. .nt . . . .
      . . . . FA Jun 44 160
   Corporal Webber's Last
      Stand. .s . . . . FA Oct 42 118
   Cosmic Sisters, The. .nt . . . .
      . . . . Amz Sep 46 54
   Crossed Wires. .nt . . . .
      . . . . Amz Mar 44 80

AUTHOR
   Title. .Length . . . . Magazine, Date, Page

   Death Rides at Night. .nt . . . . . .
      . . . . Amz Aug 42 66
   Double for Destiny. .n . . . .
      . . . . Amz Dec 46 64
   Dummy of Death. .s . . . .
      . . . . FA Oct 45 90
   Emperor's Eye, The. .nt . . . .
      . . . . FA May 47 116
   Freddie Funk's Forest Forge . . . .
      . .s . . . . FA Jan 45 66
   Freddie Funk's Forgetful
      Elephant. .s . . . . . FA Apr 44 112
   Freddie Funk's Madcap Mermaid . .
      . .s . . . . FA Jan 43 82
   Freddie Funk's Seven League
      Boots. .s . . . . FA Dec 43 46
   Garden of Hel, The. .s . . . .
      . . . . FA May 43 164
   Johnny Rain-Maker. .s . . . .
      . . . . Amz Nov 43 180
   Lost Legions of Carthage. .nt. . . .
      . . . . FA Jun 43 72
   Louie's Cat Eye. .s . . . .
      . . . . FA Dec 42 218
   Lying Lie-Detector, The . . . . . .
      . .s . . . . Amz Mar 45 132
   Man With Two Minds, The . . . . .
      . .s . . . . .Amz Jul 46 86
   Moon Slave. .s . . . .
      . . . . FA Feb 46 6
   Mysterious Crater. .s . . . .
      . . . . Amz Sep 45 110
   "Nazi, Are You Resting
      Well?". .s . . . . FA Jul 43 176
   Oliver Performs a Miracle . . . . . .
      . .s . . . . Amz Oct 42 216
   One-Way Ticket to Nowhere . . . .
      . .s . . . . Amz Dec 42 96
   Phantom Commando. .s . . . .
      . . . . FA Aug 43 142
   Phantom Transport. .nt . . . .
      . . . . Amz Feb 43 112
   Queen of the Flaming
      Diamond. .nt . . . .Amz Jan 43 184
   Side Street. .s . . . . Amz Nov 46 114
   Spawn of the Glacier. .nt . . . . . .
      . . . . FA Dec 43 152
   Spirit of Egypt, The. .s . . . .
      . . . . Amz Aug 43 194
   Story Escapes Me, The. .s . . . . . .
      . . . . FA Dec 45 148
   Strange Tea of Ting Sun Fu,
      The. .nt. . . . . . . Amz Mar 49 48
   Taming of the Tyrant. .nt . . . . . .
      . . . . FA Sep 46 128

AUTHOR
Title. .Length . . . . Magazine, Date, Page

Thought in Time, A. .s . . . .
. . . . FA Feb 44 128
Through the Asteroids—To
Hell! . .s . . . . PS Fal 46 71
Valley of the Black Sun. .s . . . . .
. . . . Amz Apr 43 124
Warlord of Peace. .s . . . .
. . . . Amz Mar 47 32
Warrior Maids of Libya. .nt . . . . .
. . . . FA Oct 43 148
YOUD, CHRISTOPHER (S.) *See also*
pseud JOHN CHRISTOPHER
Christmas Tree. .s . . . .
. . . . ASF Feb 49 155
Colonial. .nt . . . .
. . . . ASF Apr 49 81
YOUNG, ARNOLD
Just Plain Wizardry. .ss . . . .
. . . . Amz Dec 44 122
YOUNG, RAYMOND A.
Thief in Time, A. .ss . . . .
. . . . WS Jul 35 202
                              FSQ Sum 50 146
YOUNG, ROGER FLINT
Forbidden Fruit. .s . . . .
. . . . Amz Aug 50 116
Inoculation. .s . . . .
. . . . FA Mar 50 46
Not to be Opened—. .nt . . . .
. . . . .ASF Jan 50 33
Suburban Frontiers. .nt . . . .
. . . . ASF Feb 50 77

AUTHOR
Title. .Length . . . . Magazine, Date, Page

Z

ZAGAT, ARTHUR L.(EO)
Beyond the Spectrum. .s . . . . . .
. . . . ASF Aug 34 61
Cavern of the Shining Pool,
The. .s . . . . TW Oct 37 66
Faceless Men, The. .nt . . . .
. . . . TW Apr 48 13
Flight of the Silver Eagle. . . . . . .
. .nt . . . . TW Apr 37 44
Great Dome on Mercury, The . . .
. .s . . . . ASF Apr 32 120
Green Bay, The. .s . . . .
. . . . TW Aug 38 82
Grim Rendezvous. .s . . . .
. . . . TW Dec 46 56
Land Where Time Stood Still,
The. .nt . . . . TW Aug 36 78
Lanson Screen, The. .nt . . . .
. . . . TW Dec 36 42
Living Flame, The. .nt . . . .
. . . . ASF Feb 34 102
Lost in Time. .nt . . . .
. . . . TW Jun 37 40
No Escape from Destiny. .s . . . . .
. . . . SS May 48 80
Slaves of the Lamp. .n 2 pt . . . . .
. . . . ASF Aug 46 7
Spoor of the Bat. .nt . . . .
. . . . .ASF Jul 34 62
Sunward Flight. .nt . . . .
. . . . .SSS Feb 43 82
Venus Station. .nt . . . .
. . . . SF Apr 43 12

AUTHOR
Title. .Length . . . . Magazine, Date, Page

When the Sleepers Woke . . . .
. .s . . . . ASF Nov 32 171
with NAT(HAN) SCHACHNER
Back to 20,000 A.D. . .s . . . . . .
. . . . WS Mar 31 1120
Death-Cloud, The. .s . . . .
. . . . ASF May 31 256
Emperor of the Stars, The . . . . . .
. .s . . . . WS Apr 31 1210
Exiles of the Moon. .n 3 pt . . . . .
. . . . WS Sep 31 440
In 20,000 A.D. . .s . . . .
. . . . WS Sep 30 310
Menace from Andromeda, The . . .
. .s . . . . Amz Apr 31 78
Revolt of the Machines, The . . . .
. .s . . . . .ASF Jul 31 88
Tower of Evil, The. .s . . . .
. . . . .WQ Sum 30 468
Venus Mines Incorporated. .s . . . .
. . . . WS Aug 31 294
                              SS Jan 47 72
ZAKHARTCHENCKO, VASSILIJ
with VICTOR BOLKHOVEITINOV
World of Nightmare Fantasies,
The. .a . . . . .ASF Jun 49 158
ZBOYAN *artist*
Cover for ASTOUNDING SCIENCE
FICTION
Dec 1949
ZISKA, K. F.
Man of Ages. .s . . . . ASF Oct 34 48
Succubus. .s . . . . . . ASF May 34 33
ZORBAS, ERNEST
Tower Mystery, The. .s . . . .
. . . . .AD Jul 30 582

Alphabetical Index by Titles

A

Title. .Author. .Length . . . . Magazine. .Date. .Page No.

ABDICATION by E. M. Hull. .s . . . . ASF Apr 43 56
ABNER SCHLAP'S STRANGE INSIGHT by Arthur
T. Harris *h pseud*. . .s . . . . .FA Jul 41 56
ABSALOM by Henry Kuttner. .s . . . . SS Fal 46 90
ABSOLUTE ZERO by Harold Moohouse Colter. .s . . . .
. . . . .Amz Jan 29 937
ABYSS, THE by Robert W. Lowndes. .s . . .Sti Feb 41 118
ABYSS OF DARKNESS by Ross Rocklynn. .nt . . . . . .
. . . . .Ash Dec 42 86
ACCIDENTAL MURDERS, THE by Robert Moore
Williams. .s . . . . Amz Feb 41 98
ACCURSED GALAXY, THE by Edmond Hamilton. . . .
. .s . . . . .ASF Jul 35 64
ACHILLES HEEL, THE by Raymond Z. Gallun. .s . . . .
. . . . Amz Nov 40 124
ACROSS THE ABYSS by Geo. C. Wallis. .s . . . .
. . . . .ToW Sum 39 100
ACROSS THE AGES by Allen Glasser. .s . . . .
. . . . Amz Aug 33 466
ACROSS THE AGES by Dom Passante. .s . . . .
. . . . Fut Oct 41 87
ACROSS THE VOID by Leslie F. Stone *ps (Mrs.
Wm. Silberberg)*. .n 3 pt . . . . Amz Apr 31 6
ACT OF RETIPUJ, THE by Samuel Garfinkel. .s. . . . .
. . . . .Amz Jan 31 946
ACTION ON AZURA by Robertson Osburn *(ToC gives . .
author as Richardson Osborne)*. .nt . . . . . PS Fal 49 78
ACTIVITY by J. J. Coupling *ps (John R. Pierce)*. .a . . . .
. . . . ASF Nov 46 100
ADAM AND NO EVE by Alfred Bester. .s . . . .
. . . . ASF Sep 41 34
ADAM FROM THE SIXTH, AN by Richard S.
Shaver. .s. .FA May 46 96
ADAM LINK, CHAMPION ATHLETE by Eando Binder
ps (Otto Binder). .nt . . . . .Amz Jul 40 28
ADAM LINK FACES A REVOLT by Eando Binder *ps
(Otto Binder)*. .nt . . . . .Amz May 41 70
ADAM LINK FIGHTS A WAR by Eando Binder *ps
(Otto Binder)*. .nt . . . . Amz Dec 40 10
ADAM LINK IN BUSINESS by Eando Binder *ps
(Otto Binder)*. .s . . . . Amz Jan 40 44
ADAM LINK IN THE PAST by Eando Binder *ps
(Otto Binder)*. .nt . . . . Amz Feb 41 62
ADAM LINK, ROBOT DETECTIVE by Eando Binder
ps (Otto Binder). .nt . . . . .Amz May 40 42
ADAM LINK SAVES THE WORLD by Eando Binder
ps (Otto Binder). .nt . . . . Amz Apr 42 10

ADAM LINK'S VENGEANCE by Eando Binder *ps
(Otto Binder)*. .nt . . . . Amz Feb 40 8
ADAM'S EVE by Richard O. Lewis. .s . . . .
. . . . .Amz May 43 62
ADAPTABILITY by F. G. Rayer. .s . . . .
. . . . NW Spr 50 62
ADAPTATION by John Beynon *(Harris)*. .s . . . .
. . . . ASF Jul 49 144
ADAPTER by Murray Leinster *ps (Will F. Jenkins)*. .s . .
. . . . ASF Mar 46 49
ADAPTIVE ULTIMATE, THE by John Jessel *ps
(Stanley G. Weinbaum)*. .nt . . . . ASF Nov 35 108
ADMIRAL'S INSPECTION by Malcolm Jameson. .nt. . .
. . . . ASF Apr 40 123
ADMIRAL'S WALK, THE by Sam Merwin, Jr. . .s . . . . .
. . . . .TW Dec 47 61
ADOPTED SON OF THE STARS by William P.
McGivern. .s . . . . FA Mar 41 98
ADOPTION by Don J. Doughty. .s . . . . NW Spr 50 38
ADRIFT IN THE VOID by John Pierce, B. S. . .s . . . . .
. . . . WS Jun 34 64
ADRIFT ON A METEOR by Jack Winks. .s . . . .
. . . . Amz Aug 33 430
ADVANCE IN THE RED by R. S. Richardson. .a . . . . .
. . . . ASF Aug 45 100
ADVANCED CHEMISTRY by Jack G. Hueckels. .s . . . .
. . . . Amz Mar 27 1127
ADVENT by William Bade. .s . . . . .ASF Jan 48 76
ADVENTURE IN FUTURITY, AN by Clark Ashton
Smith. .s . . . . WS Apr 31 1230
ADVENTURE IN LEMURIA by Frederic Arnold
Kummer, Jr. . .s . . . . .FA May 39 60
ADVENTURE IN TIME, AN by Francis Flagg *ps
(George Henry Weiss)*. .s . . . . SW Apr 30 1018
ADVENTURE OF WYNDHAM SMITH, THE by S. Fowler
Wright. .n. FFM Jun 50 12
ADVENTURE ON EROS, AN by J. Harvey
Haggard. .s . . . . WS Sep 31 547
ADVENTURES OF POSI AND NEGA by Joe W.
Skidmore. .s . . . . Amz Jan 34 67
AEPYORNIS ISLAND by H. G. Wells. .s . . . .
. . . . Amz Oct 27 662
AERITA OF THE LIGHT COUNTRY by Ray
Cummings. .nt . . . . .SSS Aug 41 10
AESOP by Clifford D. Simak. .nt . . . . ASF Dec 47 7
AFFAIR OF MATTHEW ELDON, THE by Millen
Cooke. .s . . . . Amz May 46 104

125

Title. .Author. .Length . . . . Magazine. .Date. .Page No.

AFFAIR OF THE BRAINS, THE by Anthony Gilmore
  ps (Harry Bates & D. W. Hall). .nt . . . .
  . . . . ASF Mar 32 314
AFRAID by W. E. Thiessen. .s . . . . SS Fal 46 81
AFRAID OF HIS SHADOW by Dorothy Donnell
  Calhoun. .ss . . . . FFM Aug 41 118
AFRAID TO LIVE by Duncan Farnsworth ps (David
  Wright O'Brien). .s . . . . FA Mar 42 84
AFRICAN TRICK, THE by H. W. Guernsey ps (Howard
  Wandrei). .s . . . . UK Apr 40 81
AFTER 1,000,000 YEARS by J. M. Walsh. .s . . . .
  . . . . WS Oct 31 658
AFTER A MILLION YEARS by J. M. Walsh. .s . . . . .
  . . . . ToW Aut 39 30
AFTER AN AGE by Eando Binder pse (Otto Binder). . .
  . .s . . . . Amz Nov 42 8
AFTER ARMAGEDDON by Francis Flagg ps (George
  Henry Weiss). .s . . . . WS Sep 32 340
                                                  SS Fal 46 73
AFTER DOOMSDAY by John Cotton ps (John Russell
  Fearn). .nt . . . . Fut Mar 40 66
AFTER 5000 YEARS by Victor A. Endersby. .s . . . . . .
  . . . . WS Jul 30 136
AFTER THE ATOM by John Russell Fearn. .s . . . .
  . . . . SS May 48 117
AFTER THE ATOM by Stanton A. Coblentz. .p . . . . . .
  . . . . FFM Apr 50 115
AFTER THE PLAGUE by Martin Vaeth ps (Frederic
  Arnold Kummer, Jr.). .s . . . . Ash Feb 40 88
AFTER 12,000 YEARS by Stanton A. Coblentz. .n. . . .
  . . . . AQ Spr 29 148
AFTER WORLD'S END by Jack Williamson. .n . . . . . .
  . . . . MSS Feb 39 8
AFTERGLOW, THE by George Allan England. .n . . . . .
  . . . . FFM Dec 41 6
AFTERMATH by John Russell Fearn. .n . . . .
  . . . . SS Fal 45 11
AGAINST TETRARCH by A. A. O. Gilmour. .s . . . . . .
  . . . . PS Fal 47 54
AGAINST THE FALL OF NIGHT by Arthur C. . . . . . .
  Clarke. .n . . . . SS Nov 48 11
AGAINST THE STONE BEASTS by James Blish. .s. . . .
  . . . . PS Fal 48 74
AGE by Clyde Crane Campbell ps (H. L. Gold). .nt . . . .
  . . . . ASF Apr 35 119
AGE OF THE CEPHALODS by John C. Craig. .s . . . . . .
  . . . . Ash Dec 40 82
AGE OF UNREASON by Alfred Coppel, Jr. . .s . . . . . .
  . . . . ASF Dec 47 32
AGENT OF VEGA by James H. Schmitz. .n . . . .
  . . . . ASF Jul 49 10
AGHARTI by Heinrich Hauser. .n . . . . . . Amz Jun 46 6
AGROUND IN SPACE by David O. Woodbury. .s . . . .
  . . . . ASF Aug 34 45
AHEAD OF HIS TIME by Ray Cummings. .s . . . .
  . . . . TW Jun 48 92

Title. .Author. .Length . . . . Magazine. .Date. .Page No.

AID TO THE ENEMY by Bob Courtney. .s . . . .
  . . . . Amz Jun 43 56
AIMLESS ASTEROID by M. J. Westwood. .s . . . .
  . . . . TW Feb 43 75
AIR LINES by David H. Keller, M.D. . .s . . . .
  . . . . .Amz Jan 30 936
AIR-PLANT MEN, THE by Roger Wulfres. .s . . . .
  . . . . WS Dec 30 738
AIR RACE by Warren Kastel ps (Chester S. Geier). .s. . .
  . . . . .FA Jul 48 136
AIR SPACE by K. Raymond. .s . . . . ASF Sep 37 97
AIR SPY, THE by Edward Lee Harrison. .s . . . .
  . . . . AW Oct 29 322
AIR TERROR, THE by Lowell Howard Morrow. .s. . . .
  . . . . AW Sep 29 266
AIR TRAP, THE by Edward E. Chappelow. .s . . . . . .
  . . . . .AW May 30 966
AIRCRAFT OF URANUS by James B. Settles . . . .
  . .bacover pic . . . . Amz Aug 42
AIRLORDS OF HAN, THE by Philip Francis
  Nowlan. .nt . . . . Amz Mar 29 1106
AIRPLANE OF THE FUTURE, THE by Hugo
  Gernsback. .a . . . . AW Sep 29 196
AIRPORTS FOR WORLD TRAFFIC by H. Domink
  (tr fr German by Francis M. Currier). .a . . . .
  . . . . AW Jan 30 610
AIRSHIP OF VENUS by James B. Settles . . . .
  . .bacover pic . . . . Amz May 42
AIRSHIP OF IO by James B. Settles . . . .
  . .bacover pic . . . . Amz Nov 42
AIRWAYMAN, THE by Logan Carlisle. .s . . . .
  . . . . Amz Apr 36 127
AIRWHALE, THE by James Blish. .s . . . .
  . . . . .Fut Aug 42 93
AJAX OF AJAX by Martin Pearson. .s . . . .
  . . . . .Fut Aug 42 40
AL ADDIN AND THE INFRA-RED LAMP by . . . .
  William P. McGivern. .nt . . . . FA Nov 41 74
AL HADDON'S LAMP by Nelson S. Bond. .nt . . . .
  . . . . UK Jun 42 110
ALAS, ALL THINKING by Harry Bates. .nt . . . .
  . . . . ASF Jun 35 6
ALBINO CANARY, THE by Hal Moore. .s . . . .
  . . . . .FB # 5 14
ALBINO OTTER, THE by Elmer Brown Mason. .s . . . .
  . . . . .FN Jul 49 108
ALACATRAZ OF THE STARWAYS by Albert de Pina &
  Henry Hasse. .nt . . . . PS May 43 2
ALCHEMY by John & Dorothy de Courcy. .s . . . .
  . . . . .OTWA Dec 50 83
ALCHEMY OF IAN BJORNSEN, THE by Warren F.
  Doane. .s . . . . .Amz Jan 34 115
ALCHEMY OF OUTER SPACE by D. L. James. .s . . . .
  . . . . TW Feb 38 90
ALEPH SUB ONE by Margaret St. Clair. .s . . . .
  . . . . .SS Jan 48 62

Title. .Author. .Length . . . . Magazine. .Date. .Page No.

ALEXANDER THE BAIT by William Tenn *ps (Philip Klass)*. .s . . . . ASF May 46 79
ALI BABA, JUNIOR by Oscar J. Friend. .ss . . . . CF Win 43 103
ALIAS THE LIVING by Frank B. Long. .s . . . . .ASF Jan 44 115
ALIEN by George O. Smith. .s . . . . .ASF Oct 46 115
ALIEN EARTH by Edmond Hamilton. .s . . . . TW Apr 49 54
ALIEN ENVOY by Malcolm Jameson. .nt . . . . ASF Nov 44 116
ALIEN ERROR, THE by D. J. Foster. .s . . . . ToW Spr 39 76
ALIEN INTELLIGENCE, THE by Jack Williamson . . . .
. .n 2 pt . . . . SW Jul 29 102
. .n 3 pt . . . . .CF Spr 42 98
ALIEN MACHINE, THE by Raymond F. Jones. .s. . . . . TW Jun 49 74
ALIEN ROOM, THE by W. P. Cockroft. .s . . . . WS Dec 34 776
ALIEN VIBRATION, THE by Hannes Bok. .s . . . . Fut Feb 42 74
ALL ABOARD FOR THE MOON by Harold M. Sherman. .n . . . . Amz Apr 47 10
ALL ELSE IS DUST by E. K. Jarvis *h ps*. .nt . . . . Amz Mar 50 72
ALL GOOD BEMS by Frederic Brown. .s . . . . TW Apr 49 124
ALL HEROES ARE HATED! by Milton Lesser. .nt . . . . .Amz Nov 50 8
ALL IS ILLUSION by Henry Kuttner. .s . . . . UK Apr 40 95
ALL KINDS OF PEOPLE by Leroy Yerxa. .s . . . . FA Apr 45 96
ALL OUR YESTERDAYS by John Wade Farrell *ps (John D. McDonald)*. .s . . . . .SSS Apr 49 42
ALL ROADS by Mona Farnsworth. .s . . . . UK Aug 40 118
"ALL YOU DO IS TRANZ THE FRAMMIS!" . . . . by Seldon Walters *ps (Walt Sheldon)*. .s . . . . .Amz Jul 50 78
ALLA-BEG'S GENII by Richard O. Lewis. .s . . . . SS May 42 89
ALLAN AND THE ICE-GODS by H. Rider Haggard . . . .
. .n . . . . .FFM Apr 47 6
ALMOST HUMAN by Ray Cummings. .s . . . . .SSS Mar 41 98
ALMOST HUMAN by Tarleton Fiske *ps (Robert Bloch)*. .s . . . . FA Jun 43 184
ALMOST IMMORTAL by Austin Hall. .nt . . . . .FFM Nov 39 82
ALPHA CENTAURI CURTAIN CALL by Len J. Moffatt. .s . . . . .OTWA Dec 50 100
ALPHA SAY, BETA DO by Alfred E. Maxwell. .s . . . . PS Sum 50 63

Title. .Author. .Length . . . . Magazine. .Date. .Page No.

ALTER EGO by A. Bertram Chandler. .s . . . . ASF Mar 45 118
AMAZING FACTS dept of fillers. Occasional in Amz
AMAZING INVENTION OF WILBERFORCE WEEMS, THE by Nelson S. Bond. .s . . . . FA Sep 39 48
AMAZING PLANET, THE by Clark Ashton Smith. .nt . . . . .WQ Sum 31 534
AMAZING PROPHECIES
  THE MYSTERIOUS PREDICTIONS OF MICHEL NOSTRADAMUS by Joseph J. Millard. .a . . . . Amz May 41 190
AMAZING SCIENCE ADVENTURES dept of fillers by P. E. Jones & Forrest J. Ackerman . . . . MSS Nov 50 69
AMAZON FIGHTS AGAIN, THE by Thornton Ayre *ps (John Russell Fearn)*. .nt . . . . FA Jun 40 112
AMAZONS OF A WEIRD CREATION by Jep Powell. .nt . . . . FA Jun 41 96
AMBASSADOR FROM MARS, THE by Harl Vincent *(Schoepflin)*. .s . . . . Amz Sep 28 486
AMBIDEXTER, THE by David H. Keller, M.D. . .s . . . . Amz Apr 31 36
AMERICAN JULES VERNE, AN. .a . . . . Amz Jun 28 270
AMERICA'S MYSTERIOUS RACE OF INDIAN GIANTS by Rev. Chief Sequoyah. .a . . . . Amz Dec 46 157
AMIR'S MAGIC, THE by A. H. Johnson. .s . . . . Amz Mar 32 1086
AMNESIAC, THE by George Edwards. .s . . . . .TW Aug 43 78
AMOEBA 'ROID by Charles Recour. .s . . . . .Amz Jul 48 134
AMONG THE SCENTED ONES by Basil Wells. .s . . . . .PS Win 47 75
AMPHISKIOS by John D. MacDonald. .s . . . . .TW Aug 49 70
ANACHRON, INC. by Malcolm Jameson. .nt . . . . ASF Oct 42 56
ANACHRONISM by Charles Cloukey. .s . . . . Amz Dec 30 840
ANACHRONISTIC OPTICS by M. Schere. .s . . . . ASF Feb 38 26
ANALYTICAL MIND, THE by L. Ron Hubbard. .a . . . . .ASF Oct 50 139
ANANIAS by L. Sprague de Camp. .s . . . . DS Apr-May 39 68
ANANIAS GLAND, THE by W. Alexander. .s . . . . Amz Nov 28 707
ANARCH, THE by Malcolm Jameson. .nt . . . . ASF Feb 44 123
ANASTOMOSIS by Clyde Beck. .s . . . . SS Nov 47 86
ANCESTRAL THREAD, THE by Emil Petaja. .s . . . . Amz May 47 20

Title. .Author. .Length . . . . Magazine. .Date. .Page No.

Title. .Author. .Length . . . . Magazine. .Date. .Page No.

ANCESTRAL VOICES by Nat Schachner. .s . . . .
. . . . ASF Dec 33 70
ANCIENT, THE by William Morrison ps (Joseph
Samachson). .s . . . . FSQ Fal 50 139
ANCIENT ALLAN, THE by H. Rider Haggard. .n . . . . .
. . . . FFM Dec 45 10
ANCIENT BRAIN, THE by A. G. Stangland. .s. . . . . . .
. . . . SW Oct 29 400
SS Nov 42 100
ANCIENT GEOMETRICAL MONUMENT by Rocky
Stone. .a 8 pt (Jul thru Dec 49, May & July 50) . . . .
. . . . Amz Jul 49 132
ANCIENT HORROR, THE by Hal Grant. .s. . . . .
. . . . Amz Apr 28 56
ANCIENT ONES, THE by Harold S. Sykes. .s. . . . . . .
. . . . SSS Jul 50 92
ANCIENTS OF EASTER ISLAND by F. Stanley
Renshaw. .s . . . . Amz Apr 33 46
—AND ALL FOR ONE" by Jerome Bixby. .s . . . .
. . . . .OW May 50 68
AND BE MERRY. . . by Katherine MacLean. .s. . . . . .
. . . . ASF Feb 50 107
AND EVE WAS by Rog Phillips ps (Roger P.
Graham). .nt. . . . . Amz Nov 47 60
"—AND HE BUILT A CROOKED HOUSE—" by
Robert A. Heinlein. .s. . . . . ASF Feb 41 68
AND NO TOMORROW by Russell Storm ps (Robert
Moore Williams). .ss . . . . Amz Feb 50 146
AND NOT IN PEACE by George Whitley ps (A.
Bertram Chandler). .s . . . . FFM Dec 46 112
. . .AND NOW YOU DON'T by Isaac Asimov . . . .
. .n 3 pt . . . . ASF Nov 49 5
AND RETURN by Eando Binder ps (Otto Binder). . . . .
. .s .Com Jan 41 100
. . .AND SEARCHING MIND by Jack Williamson . . . . .
. .n 3 pt . . . . ASF Mar 48 7
AND THE GODS LAUGHED by Fredric Brown . . . . . .
. .s . . . . PS Spr 44 105
. . .AND THE MOON BE STILL AS BRIGHT by Ray
Bradbury. .s . . . . TW Jun 48 78
AND THE ROCKETS CAME by Charles Recour. .s . . . .
. . . . .Amz Jul 49 78
AND THEN THERE WAS ONE by Ross Rocklynne . . .
. .s . . . . ASF Feb 40 53
AND WE SAILED THE MIGHTY DARK by Frank
Belknap Long. .s . . . . .SS Mar 48 76
ANDROCLES AND THE BUCCANEER by
Geoffrey St. Reynard ps (Robert W. Krepps). .s . . . .
. . . . FA Jan 47 68
ANDROMEDA MENACE, THE by Joseph F.
Houghton. .s. . . . . WS Dec 31 860
ANDRYNE by Arthur Macom. .s . . . . . . SSS May 42 82
ANGEL FROM HELL, THE by Nils O.
Sonderlund. .n . . . . MSS Dec 39 10
ANGEL IN THE DUST BOWL by Spencer Lane
h ps. .s. . . . . ASF Dec 37 95

ANGEL ISLAND by Inez Haynes Gillmore. .n . . . . . .
. . . . FFM Feb 49 10
ANGEL WITH FOUR FACES, AN by Don
Wilcox. .nt . . . . FA Sep 42 58
ANGEL WITH PURPLE HAIR, THE by Herb
Paul. .s . . . . F&SF Dec 50 85
ANGELIC ANGLEWORM, THE by Frederic
Brown. .nt . . . . UK Feb 43 49
ANGRY STREET—A BAD DREAM by G. K.
Chesterton. .s . . . . FFM Feb 47 108
ANGULAR STONE, THE by Henry Hasse. .nt . . . .
. . . . SSS May 43 8
ANIMAL-CRACKER PLOT, THE by L. Sprague . .
de Camp. .s . . . . .ASF Jul 49 67
ANIMAT by Basil Wells. .s . . . . PS Spr 49 77
ANIMATED TENPIN, THE by William Lawrence
Hamling. .s. . . . . Amz Sep 45 30
ANNIHILATOR COMES, THE by Ed Earl Repp. .s . . . .
. . . . WS Aug 30 212
ANNUS MIRABILIS by Edward Carlisle. .nt . . . .
. . . . Amz Apr 38 98
ANOTHER CHANCE FOR CASEY by Larry
Siegel. .s . . . . F&SF Dec 50 120
ANOTHER DIMENSION by George H. Scheer, Jr. . . . .
. .nt . . . . Amz Oct 35 36
ANOTHER'S EYES by John L. Chapman. .ss . . . .
. . . . SSS Jan 41 104
ANSWER by Hal Clement ps (Harry Clement
Stubbs). .s . . . . ASF Apr 47 93
ANSWER, THE by George O. Smith. .s . . . .
. . . . ASF Feb 47 84
ANSWER OUT OF SPACE, THE by Graph
Waldeyer. .s . . . . SF Jul 43 97
ANT WITH THE HUMAN SOUL, THE
by Bob Olsen ps (Alfred John Olsen). .nt . . . .
. . . . AQ Spr-Sum 32 230
ANTARCTIC TRANSFORMATION, THE by I. R.
Nathanson. .nt . . . . Amz Nov 31 720
ANTARES TRYST by Richard Tooker. .s . . . .
. . . . Amz Aug 37 113
ANTI-WEAPON, THE by Eando Binder ps (Otto
Binder). .s . . . . ASF Feb 38 127
ANTON MOVES THE EARTH by Ross Rocklynne. . . .
. .nt . . . . ASF Nov 36 124
ANYTHING by Philip St. John. .s . . . . . . UK Oct 39 89
UK 48 71
ANTHING CAN HAPPEN by Peter Gordon. .s . . . . . .
. . . . ASF Oct 33 40
"ANYTHING YOU SAY, DEAR" by Leroy Yerxa . . . .
. .s . . . . Amz Feb 46 44
APE CYCLE, THE by Clare Winger Harris. .s . . . .
. . . . WQ Spr 30 288
APE MEN OF XLOTLI, THE by David R.
Sparks. .nt . . . . ASF Dec 30 370
APHRODITE PROJECT, THE by Philip Latham
ps (Robert S. Richardson). .s . . . . . . ASF Jun 49 73

Title. .Author. .Length. . . . . Magazine. .Date. .Page No.

APOLLO by Frank R. Paul. .bacover pic . . . . . FA Dec 42
APPENDIX AND THE SPECTACLES, THE by Miles
J. Breuer, M.D. . .s. . . . . Amz Dec 28 774
APPOINTMENT FOR TOMORROW by John D.
MacDonald. .s. . . . . .SSS Nov 49 82
APPOINTMENT IN NEW UTRECT by Matt Lee. . . . .
ps (Sam Merwin, Jr.). .s . . . . .SS Mar 50 129
APPOINTMENT IN SPACE by John Broome. .s . . . . . .
. . . . TW Aug 41 85
APPOINTMENT WITH THE PAST by Lee Francis
h ps. .nt. FA Feb 44 142
APPRENTICE, THE by Miles M. Acheson. .s . . . .
. . . . ASF May 50 30
AQUELLA by Donald A. Wollheim. .s. . . . . .AFR #7 80
ARBITER, THE by John Russell Fearn. .s . . . .
. . . . SS May 47 90
ARCHERS OF MONS, THE by James B. Settles . . . . . .
. .bacover. . . . . FA Dec 47
ARCTIC GOD by Frank Jones. .s . . . . . Amz May 42 192
ARCTIC RADIO FARMS by Julian S. Krupa . . . .
. .bacover pic . . . . Amz Sep 39
ARCTIC RESCUE, THE by Walter Kately. .s . . . .
. . . . .AW May 30 974
ARD OF THE SUNSET PEOPLE by Stanton A.
Coblentz. .s . . . . Amz Feb 43 144
ARE YOU RUN-DOWN, TIRED— by Babette
Rosmond Lake. .s . . . . UK Oct 42 82
ARE YOU THERE? by Mona Farnsworth. .s . . . .
. . . . UK Nov 40 120
ARE YOU THERE, CHARLIE? by Ford Smith ps
(Oscar J. Friend). .ss . . . . .SS Spr 45 72
ARE YOU THERE, MARS? by Walter Gillings. .a . . . . .
. . . . Fant Aug 47 48
ARENA by Fredric Brown. .nt. . . . . ASF Jun 44 70
ARIEL'S SONG ill by Virgil Finlay. . . . . FFM Sep 42 113
ARISTOCRAT, THE by Chan Davis. .nt . . . .
. . . . ASF Oct 49 6
ARK OF FIRE by John Hawkins. .n . . . . . FFM Mar 43 12
ARK OF THE COVENANT, THE by Victor
MacClure. .n 4 pt. . . . . AW Jul 29 6
ARMAGEDDON by Fredric Brown. .s. . . . UK Aug 41 119
ARMAGEDDON by Craig Browning ps (Roger P.
Graham). .n . . . . .Amz May 48 8
ARMAGEDDON, 1948 by Ed Earl Repp. .nt . . . .
. . . . Amz Nov 41 116
ARMAGEDDON OF JOHANN SCHMIDT by
Arthur T. Harris h ps. .s . . . . .Amz Jan 41 108
ARMAGEDDON—2419 by Philip Francis Nowlan. .nt . .
. . . . Amz Aug 28 422
AROUND INFINITY by Oliver E. Saari. .s. . . . .
. . . . CF Win 40 118
AROUND THE UNIVERSE by Ray Cummings. .n . . . .
. . . . Amz Oct 27 626
Fut Dec 41 10
AROUND THE WORLD IN 24 HOURS by R. H.
Romans. .s . . . . AW Oct 29 306

Title. .Author. .Length . . . . Magazine. .Date. .Page No.

ARRESTED BY RADIO by Hector Gavin Grey. .s. . . . .
. . . . .AD Jul 30 591
ARRHENIUS HORROR, THE by P. Schuyler Miller . . .
. .s . . . . Amz Sep 31 514
AFR #4 7
ARTIFICIAL HELL by Harvey Emerson. .s . . . .
. . . . Amz Oct 38 96
ARTIFICIAL MAN, THE by Clare Winger
Harris. .s . . . . WQ Fal 29 78
ARTIFICIAL UNIVERSE by John Coleridge ps
(Earl Binder & Otto Binder). .s. . . . . . SFQ Win 41 138
ARTNAN PROCESS by Theodore Sturgeon. .nt . . . . . .
. . . . ASF Jun 41 50
ARTON'S METAL by Ray Cummings. .s . . . .
. . . . SSS May 40 73
AS IN THE BEGINNING by Jack Williamson. .ss . . . . .
. . . . Fut Mar 40 85
AS IT WAS by Carlton Smith. .s. . . . . . . PS Sum 42 82
AS MARS SEES US by Frank R. Paul. . . . .
. .bacover pic . . . . .Amz Jul 40
AS MARS SEES US by Frank R. Paul. . . . .
. .bacover pic . . . . Amz Mar 42
(These are two different pics with the same
title)
AS NEVER WAS by P. Schuyler Miller. .s . . . .
. . . . .ASF Jan 44 31
AS YOU WERE by Henry Kuttner. .nt . . . . .TW Aug 50 9
ASLEEP IN ARMAGEDDON by Ray Bradbury. .s . . . .
. . . . .PS Win 48 58
AFR #11 79
ASOKORE POWER by L. Sprague de Camp. .s . . . . . .
. . . . .SSS Nov 40 26
ASSIGNMENT IN THE DAWN by Bryce Walton. .s. . . .
. . . . PS Fal 47 67
ASSIGNMENT ON PASIK by William Fitzgerald
ps (Will F. Jenkins). .s . . . . .TW Feb 49 122
ASSIGNMENT ON VENUS by Carl Jacobi. .s. . . . . . .
. . . . PS Fal 43 73
ASSUMPTION UNJUSTIFIED by Hal Clement
ps (Harry Clement Stubbs). .nt. . . . . . . ASF Oct 46 58
ASTEROID by Lee Gregor ps (Milton A.
Rothman). .s . . . . .Ash Feb 40 62
ASTEROID CASTAWAYS by Manley Wade
Wellman. .s. . . . . TW Jun 42 54
ASTEROID H277-PLUS by Harry Walton. .s . . . .
. . . . PS Sum 40 98
ASTEROID JUSTICE by V. E. Thiessen. .s . . . .
. . . . PS Fal 47 46
ASTEROID OF DEATH, THE by Neil R. Jones . . . . . .
. .s . . . . WQ Fal 31 76
ASTEROID OF GOLD, THE by Clifford D.
Simak. .s . . . . WS Nov 32 514
ASTEROID OF THE DAMNED by Dirk Wylie
(w/Frederik Pohl). .s . . . . PS Sum 42 31
ASTEROID PIRATES by Royal W. Heckman. .s . . . . . .
. . . . ASF Aug 38 112

Title. .Author. .Length . . . . Magazine. .Date. .Page No.

ASTOUNDING ANNOUNCEMENT, AN by A. L.
Hodges. .ss . . . . Amz Jun 35 96
ASTOUNDING CLUE, THE by Sam Weiner. .s . . . . . .
. . . . AD Aug 30 684
ASTOUNDING DISCOVERIES OF DOCTOR
MENTIROSO, THE by A. Hyatt Verrill. .s . . . .
. . . . Amz Nov 27 746
ASTOUNDING ENEMY, THE by Louise Rice &
Tonjoroff-Roberts. .nt . . . . AQ Win 30 78
ASTOUNDING EXODUS, THE by Neil R. Jones . . . . .
. .nt . . . . TW Apr 37 76
ASTRAL ASSASSIN by Frank Patton h ps. .s . . . .
. . . . Amz Jul 43 192
ASTRAL GENTLEMAN, AN by Robert Wilbur
Lull & Lillian M. Ainsworth. .s . . . . . . FFM Jan 40 80
ASTRAL RHYTHM by Bernie Kamins. .s . . . .
. . . . FA Mar 48 66
ASYLUM by A. E. van Vogt. .nt . . . . ASF May 42 8
AT BAY IN THE VOID by D. D. Sharp. .s . . . .
. . . . WS Feb 33 698
AT THE CENTER OF GRAVITY by Ross
Rocklynne. .s . . . . ASF Jun 36 67
AT THE FARMHOUSE by E. F. Benson. .s . . . .
. . . . FFM Dec 46 102
AT THE MOUNTAINS OF MADNESS by H. P.
Lovecraft. .n 3 pt . . . . ASF Feb 36 8
AT THE PERIHELION by Robert Willey ps (Willy
Ley). .nt . . . . ASF Feb 37 41
ATALA RIM by J. S. Harrison. .s . . . . . . Amz Nov 46 128
ATAVISM by Erik Fennel. .s . . . . PS Spr 47 95
ATLANTIS EXILE by Cyril Hume. .s . . . .
. . . . FFM Dec 47 104
ATLANTIS HERE WE COME! by Charles Stoddard . . .
h ps. .a . . . . TW Apr 43 104
ATLANTIS HOAX OF DR. SCHLIEMANN
(FANTASTIC HOAXES) by Willy Ley. .a . . . .
. . . . FA Aug 40 46
ATLANTROPA; THE IMPROVED CONTINENT
by Willy Ley. .a. . . . . MSS Feb 39 99
ATLAS by Frank R. Paul. .bacover pic . . . . . FA Sep 42
ATMOSPHERICS by Victor Valding ps (Allen
Ingvald Benson & John Victor Peterson). .s . . . .
. . . . ASF Sep 39 33
ATOM OF DEATH by Ross Rocklynne. .s . . .PS Win 40 46
ATOM PRINCE, THE by Ray Cummings. .nt . . . .
. . . . SF Dec 39 52
ATOM SMASHER, THE by Gordon A. Giles ps
(Otto Binder). .s . . . . Amz Oct 38 30
ATOM SMASHER, THE by P. Schuyler Miller. .s . . . . .
. . . . .Amz Jan 34 127
ATOM SMASHER, THE by Victor Rousseau
(Emanuel). .nt . . . . ASF May 30 234
ATOM-SMASHER, THE by Donald Wandrei. .ss . . . . .
. . . . ASF Apr 34 85
ATOM SMASHERS, THE by Charles Stoddard
h ps. .a . . . . TW Jun 41 90

ATOM WAR by Rog Phillips ps (Roger P. Graham) . . . .
. .s . . . . Amz May 46 74
ATOMIC! by Henry Kuttner. .s . . . . .TW Aug 47 48
ATOMIC ADVENTURE, AN by William
Lemkin, Ph.D. . .nt . . . . WQ Fal 30 60
ATOMIC AIRSHIP OF MARS by James B. Settles. . . . .
. .bacover. . . . . Amz Jun 42
ATOMIC ERROR by Forrest J. Ackerman. .ss . . . .
. . . . OW Jul 50 18
ATOMIC FIRE by Raymond Gallun. .s . . . .
. . . . Amz Apr 31 64
ATOMIC PILE, THE (in ToC) "FROM ATOMIC
BOMBS—TO ATOMIC INDUSTRIES!" (on text) . . .
. .a . . . . ASF Oct 46 99
ATOMIC POWER by Don A. Stuart ps (John W.
Campbell, Jr.). .s . . . . ASF Dec 34 88
ATOMIC POWER PLANT by Howard M. Duffin. . . . . .
. .bacover pic . . . . Amz Oct 39
ATOMIC POWER PLANT by John W. Campbell, Jr. . . .
. .a . . . . ASF Feb 47 100
ATOMIC RIDDLE, THE by Edward S. Sears. .s . . . . . .
. . . . AQ Win 28 44
ATOMIC RINGMASTER by Arthur McCann ps
(John W. Campbell, Jr.). .a . . . . ASF Mar 40 112
ATOMIC STATION by Frank Belknap Long. .s . . . . . .
. . . . TW Win 46 83
ATRAKIN AND THE MAN by Walter Kubilius. .s . . . . .
. . . . .SSS Feb 42 76
ATTACK FROM SPACE, THE by Captain S. P.
Meek. .s . . . . .ASF Sep 30 390
ATTITUDE by Hal Clement ps (Harry Clement
Stubbs). .nt . . . . ASF Sep 43 9
AURA OF DEATH, THE by Helmar Lewis. .s. . . . . . .
. . . . Amz Nov 43 156
AUSTRALANO by Warner Van Lorne ps. .nt . . . .
. . . . .ASF Jul 36 6
AUTHOR UNKNOWN by Albert Bernson. .s . . . .
. . . . FA Jul 50 126
AUTHOR'S ADVENTURE by Arthur L. Bain. .ss . . . . .
. . . . Amz Apr 33 75
AUTHOR'S CORNER biog & guest ed dept in ToW
Win 38 thru Aut 40
AUTOMAGIC HORSE, THE by L. Ron Hubbard . . . . .
. .nt . . . . ASF Oct 49 75
AUTOMATA by S. Fowler Wright. .s . . . . . . .AFR #2 97
AUTOMATIC APARTMENT, THE (HICKS'
INVENTIONS WITH A KICK) by Henry Hugh
Simmons. .s . . . . Amz Aug 27 493
AUTOMATIC SELF SERVING DINING TABLE,
THE (HICKS' INVENTIONS WITH A KICK) . . . . . .
by Henry Hugh Simmons. .s . . . . . . Amz Apr 27 52
AUTOMATON by Abner J. Gelula. .nt . . . .
. . . . Amz Nov 31 680
AUTOMATON by A. E. van Vogt. .s . . . . . .OW Sep 50 6
AVALANCH by Dow Elstar ps (Raymond Z.
Gallun). .s . . . . ASF Dec 35 109

Title. .Author. .Length . . . . Magazine. .Date. .Page No.

AVATAR, THE by Clyde Crane Campbell *ps (H. L. Gold)*. .nt . . . . ASF Jul 35 128
AVENGER, THE by Norma Lazell Easton. .nt . . . . . .
. . . . Amz Nov 49 116
AVENGER, THE by Stuart Fleming *ps (Damon Knight)*. .s . . . . PS Spr 44 31
AVENGERS, THE by William P. McGivern. .n . . . .
. . . . Amz Jun 42 8
AVENGERS OF SPACE by Henry Kuttner. .nt . . . . . .
. . . . MSS Aug 38 98
AVENGING RAY, THE by A. Rowley Hilliard. .nt . . . .
. . . . WQ Spr 31 374
AWAKENING, THE by Rog Phillips *ps (Roger P. Graham)*. .s . . . . Amz Aug 49 6
AWLO OF ULM by Capt. S. P. Meek. .nt . . . .
. . . . Amz Sep 31 486
AZURE RING, THE by Arthur B. Reeve. .s . . . .
. . . . SD May 30 418

B

B. C. 30,000 by Capt. S. P. Meek. .s . . . . . ASF Apr 32 5
BABY DREAMS by Allen Warland *ps (Donald A. Wollheim)*. .s . . . . SFQ Win 41–42 107
BABY FACE by Henry Kuttner. .s . . . . TW Spr 45 88
BABY ON NEPTUNE, A by Clare Winger Harris & Miles J. Breuer, M.D. . .s . . . . Amz Dec 29 790
BACK TO 20,000 A. D. by Nat Schachner & Arthur L. Zagat. .s . . . . WS Mar 31 1120
BACKFIRE by Ross Rocklynne. .s . . . . . . .ASF Jan 43 34
BACKLASH by Jack Williamson. .s . . . . . ASF Aug 41 148
. . .BACKWARD, O TIME! by Manly Wade Wellman . . .
. .s . . . . TW Oct 49 117
BACKWARD PASSAGE by Lee Francis *h ps*. .s . . . . . .
. . . . FA Sep 49 68
BACTERIAL TIME BOMB by Arthur Dugan. .a . . . . . .
. . . . ASF Dec 49 93
BACTERIOLOGICAL DETECTIVE, THE by Arthur B. Reeve. .s . . . . SD Feb 30 104
BAD MEDICINE by William Morrison *ps (Joseph Samachson)*. .s . . . . TW Feb 41 81
BAD PATCH by A. Bertram Chandler. .s . . . .
. . . . .ASF Jan 47 155
BAG AND BAGGAGE by William Lawrence Hamling. .s. . . . . FA Oct 45 76
BALDY series LEWIS PADGETT auth
BALLAD OF BLASTER BILL, THE by Nelson S. Bond. .p . . . . .PS Sum 1 27
BALLAD OF VENUS NELL, THE by Nelson S. Bond. .p . . . . PS Spr 42 56
BALLOON HOAX, THE *(FANTASTIC HOAXES)* by Willy Ley. .a . . . . FA Mar 40 28
BALLOON HOAX, THE by Edgar Allen Poe. .s . . . . . .
. . . . Amz Apr 27 58

Title. .Author. .Length . . . . Magazine. .Date. .Page No.

BAND PLAYED ON, THE by C. Shook. .s . . . .
. . . . .Ash Jun 42 90
BANDITS OF TIME by Ray Cummings. .nt . . . .
. . . . Amz Dec 41 62
BANKRUPTCY PROCEEDINGS by E. Mayne Hull . . . .
. .nt . . . . ASF Aug 46 120
BARBARIAN, THE by A. E. van Vogt. .nt . . . .
. . . . ASF Dec 47 44
BARBARIANS, THE by William Morrison *ps (Joseph Samachson)*. .s . . . . .Fut Aug 41 85
BARD OF CERES, THE by Joseph Farrell. .s . . . .
. . . . SS Spr 44 111
BARGAIN, THE by Cleve Cartmill. .s . . . . UK Aug 42 107
BARGAIN IN BODIES, A by Moses Schere. .s . . . . . .
. . . . UK Jun 43 71
BARGAIN WITH BEELZEBUB by Gene Hunter. .ss . . .
. . . . FB #2 12
BARGAIN WITH COLOSSUS by Helen Weinbaum .
. .s . . . . SF Mar 41 91
BARNUM, PHINEAS TAYLOR *(FANTASTIC HOAXES)* by Julius Schwartz. .a . . . . . . FA Jan 41 76
                                          Amz May 41 48
BARON MUNCHAUSEN'S SCIENTIFIC ADVENTURES by Hugo Gernsback. .n 6 pt. . . . . . .
. . . . Amz Feb 28 1060
BARRIER, THE by Anthony Boucher *ps (William Anthony Parker White)*. .nt . . . . ASF Sep 42 9
BARRIER, THE by P. E. Cleator. .s . . . .
. . . . Fant Apr 47 59
BARRIER, THE by Harl Vincent *(Schoepflin)* . . . .
. .s . . . . Amz Sep 34 119
BARRIER OF DREAD by Judith Merril. .s . . . .
. . . . Fut Jul-Aug 50 72
BARRIUS, IMP. by Malcolm Jameson. .s . . . .
. . . . .ASF Jan 43 69
BARSOOM series See EDGAR RICE BURROUGHS auth
BARTON'S ISLAND by Harl Vincent *(Schoepflin)* . . . .
. .s . . . . Amz Aug 29 390
                                            AQ Fal 34 6
BASIC FUNDAMENTAL by F. G. Rayer. .s . . . .
. . . . .Fant Aug 47 78
BAT-MEN OF MARS, THE by Wood Jackson. . . . .
. .n 3 pt . . . . .AW May 30 1026
BAT OUT OF HELL by Berkeley Livingston. .s . . . . . .
. . . . FA Oct 44 102
BATHE YOUR BEARINGS IN BLOOD by Clifford Simak. .s . . . . Amz Dec 50 80
BATTERING RAMS OF SPACE by Don Wilcox. .n. . . .
. . . . Amz Feb 41 8
BATTERY OF HATE by John W. Campbell, Jr. . .s . . . .
. . . . Amz Nov 33 52
BATTLE BEFORE DAWN by Robert Moore Williams. .s . . . . Amz Mar 44 104
BATTLE IN ETERNITY by Richard S. Shaver & Chester S. Geier. .nt . . . . Amz Nov 49 58

Title. .Author. .Length . . . . Magazine. .Date. .Page No.

BATTLE IN THE DAWN by Manly Wade Wellman. .nt. .
. . . . Amz Jan 39 30
BATTLE OF MANETONG, THE by William P.
McGivern. .s. . . . . FA Jun 42 86
BATTLE OF THE BRAINS by Jerry Shelton. .s . . . . .
. . . . TW Spr 46 13
BATTLE OF THE GODS by Rog Phillips ps (Roger P.
Graham). .nt. . . . . Amz Sep 46 78
BATTLE OF THE SOLAR SYSTEM by Ray Cummings
. .s . . . . TW Spr 44 94
BATTLE OF THE UNBORN by James Blish. .s. . . . . .
. . . . .Fut May-Jun 50 65
BATTLE OF WIZARDS by L. Ron Hubbard. .s . . . . . .
. . . . FB #5 4
BATTLEFIELD IN BLACK by George A. Whittington. .
. .s . . . . PS Fal 45 65
BATTLING BOLTO by L. Ron Hubbard. .s . . . .
. . . . TW Aug 50 84
BE YOUNG AGAIN! by Murray Leinster ps (Will F.
Jenkins). .s. . . . . Fut Jul-Aug 50 28
BEACHHEAD FOR SCIENCE by John W.
Campbell, Jr. . .a . . . . ASF May 44 103
BEACON OF AIRPORT SEVEN, THE by Harold S.
Sykes. .s . . . . AW Jul 29 42
BEACONS MUST BURN, THE by Warren Kastel ps. . . .
. .s . . . . FA Oct 49 136
BEAM, THE by Milton Kaletsky. .s. . . . . Amz Sep 34 116
BEAM PIRATE by George O. Smith. .nt . . ASF Oct 44 32
BEAM TRANSMISSION by George H. Scheer, Jr. . . . .
. .nt . . . . .Amz Jul 34 78
BEAST, THE by L. Ron Hubbard. .s . . . .ASF Oct 42 100
BEAST, THE by A. E. van Vogt. .nt . . . . . ASF Nov 43 48
BEAST-JEWEL OF MARS, THE by Leigh Brackett . . . .
. .nt . . . . PS Win 48 4
BEAST-MEN OF CERES, THE by Aladra Septama . . . .
. .nt . . . . AQ Win 29 90
BEAST OF BAN-DU-LU, THE by Ed Earl Repp. .s . . . .
. . . . WS May 31 1448
BEAST OF SPACE, THE by F. E. Hardart. .s . . . .
. . . . .Com Jul 41 82
BEAST OF THE CRATER by Mario F. Eadie. .s . . . . .
. . . . ToW Spr 42 41
BEAST OF THE ISLAND by Alexnader M. Philips . . . .
. .nt . . . . Amz Spe 39 8
BEAST OF THE VOID, A by Ramond Z. Gallun. .s. . . .
. . . . ASF Sep 36 48
BEAST PLANTS, THE by H. Thompson Rich. .s. . . . .
. . . . FFM Apr 40 66
BEAUTIFUL BACILLUS, THE by Patric Dutton. .s . . .
. . . . Amz Jun 31 262
BEAUTY by Hannes Bok. .s . . . . Fut Oct 42 49
BEAUTY AND THE BEAST by Henry Kuttner. .s. . . . .
. . . . TW Apr 40 67
BEAUTY AND THE BEASTIES by David Wright
O'Brien. .s . . . . FA Dec 41 86

Title. .Author. .Length . . . . Magazine. .Date. .Page No.

BEER-TRUST BUSTERS by A. R. Stuart. .s . . . .
. . . . PS Fal 45 53
BEES FROM BORNEO, THE by Will H. Gray. .s. . . . .
. . . . Amz Feb 31 988
BEES OF DEATH, THE by Robert Moore Williams . . . .
. .n . . . . FA Oct 49 86
BEETLE EXPERIMENT, THE by Russell Hays. .s. . . . .
. . . . Amz Jun 29 207
BEETLE HORDE, THE by Victor Rousseau
(Emanuel). .n 2 pt. . . . . ASF Jan 30 8
BEETLE IN THE AMBER, THE by Joe W. Skimore . . .
. .s . . . . Amz Nov 33 80
BEFORE EARTH CAME by John Russell Fearn . . . . . .
. .nt . . . . .ASF Jul 34 8
BEFORE I WAKE. . . by Henry Kuttner. .s . . . .
. . . . FFM Mar 45 106
BEFORE THE ASTEROIDS by Harl Vincent
(Schoepflin). .s . . . . SW Mar 30 870
BEFORE THE DAWN by John Taine ps (Eric
Temple Bell). .n . . . . FFM Feb 46 10
BEFORE THE ICE AGE by Alfred Fritchey. .s . . . . . .
. . . . Amz Dec 28 826
BEFORE THE UNIVERSE by S. D. Gottesman ps
(Cyril Kornbluth & Frederik Pohl). .nt . . . .
. . . . SSS Jul 40 96
BEGGARS IN VELVET by Lewis Padgett ps
(Henry Kuttner & C. L. Moore). .nt . . . .
. . . . ASF Dec 45 7
BEHIND THE ATE BALL (A MARTIAN
ODDITY) (by Forrest J. Ackerman). .ss. . . . .
. . . . MSS Nov 40 128
BEHIND THE CURTAIN by Francis Stevens. .s . . . . . .
. . . . FFM Jan 40 37
BEINGS LIKE THESE by Graph Waldeyer. .s. . . . . . .
. . . . .SSS Jan 41 76
BEINGS OF THE BOUNDLESS BLUE by Walter
Kately. .s. . . . . Amz May 31 130
BEINGS OF THE OOZE by John M. Taylor. .s . . . . . .
. . . . SF Mar 41 39
BELATED TEARS OF LOUIS MARCEL, THE
by Perley Poore Sheehan. .s. . . . . . . FFM Mar 40 108
BELL-TONE, THE by Edmund H. Leftwich. .ss
. . . . Com Jul 41 117
BELLEROPHON AND THE CHIMERA by Frank
R. Paul. .bacover. . . . . FA Jun 44
BELLS ON HIS TOES by Cleve Cartmill. .s . . . .
. . . . .F&SF Fal 49 6
BELOW—ABSOLUTE by Harry Walton. .s. . . . .
. . . . ASF Jun 38 22
BELOW THE INFRA RED by George Paul Bauer . . . . .
. .nt . . . . Amz Dec 27 882
BEN GLEED, KING OF SPEED by Don Wilcox . . . . . .
. .s . . . . Amz Dec 39 24
BENEAH THE RED WORLD'S CRUST by Eric
Fennel. .nt. . . . . .PS Fal 47 90

Title. .Author. .Length . . . . Magazine. .Date. .Page No.

BENEVOLENT GHOST AND CAPTAIN LOWRIE,
THE *(Till Doomsday)* by Richard Sale. .s . . . .
. . . . FanF May 50 71
BEQUEST OF THE ANGEL by James Blish. .s . . . .
. . . . SSS May 40 46
BERLIN TO NEW YORK IN ONE HOUR by Max
Valier *(tr fr German by Francis M. Currier)*. .a . . . . .
. . . . AW Feb 30 744
BERTIE AND THE BLACK ARTS by William P.
McGivern. .s . . . . FA Apr 42 206
BEST FRIEND by S. D. Gottesman *ps (Cyril Kornbluth.
& Frederik Pohl)*. .s . . . . SSS May 41 85
BEST-LAID SCHEME, THE by L. Sprague de
Camp. .s . . . . ASF Feb 41 107
BETATRON, THE. .a. . . . . ASF Apr 46 108
BETTER MOUSETRAP, THE by L. Sprague de Camp
& Fletcher Pratt. .s . . . . F&SF Dec 50 27
BETTER THAN ONE by Henry Kuttner. .s . . . .
. . . . .CF Spr 43 92
BETWEEN DIMENSIONS by J. E. Keith. .s . . . .
. . . . WS Oct 31 624
BETWEEN EARTH AND MOON by Otfrid von Hanstein
(tr fr German by Francis Currier). .n . . . .
. . . . WQ Fal 30 6
BETWEEN WORLDS by Garrett Smith. .n . . . .
. . . . .FN Jul 49 8
BEYOND ALL WEAPONS by L. Ron Hubbard. .s . . . .
. . . . SSS Jan 50 70
BEYOND ALL WEAPONS by Nat Schachner. .nt . . . . .
. . . . ASF Nov 41 130
BEYOND ANNIHILATION by Henry Kuttner. .s . . . . .
. . . . TW Apr 39 37
BEYOND DOUBT by Lyle Monroe *ps (Robert A.
Heinlein)* & Elma Wentz. .s . . . . .Ash Apr 41 35
BEYOND GRAVITY by Ed Earl Repp. .s . . . .
. . . . AW Aug 29 114
BEYOND HELL by R. DeWitt Miller. .nt . . . .
. . . . Uc Apr 41 58
BEYOND INFINITY by Chan Corbett *ps (Nathan
Schachner)*. .nt . . . . ASF Jan 37 8
BEYOND LIGHT by Nelson S. Bond. .s. . . . .
. . . . .PS Win 40 53
BEYOND PLUTO by John Scott Campbell. .n . . . .
. . . . .WQ Sum 32 438
BEYOND SPACE AND TIME by Joel Townsley
Rogers. .s. . . . . SSS Sep 50 102
BEYOND THAT CURTAIN by Robert Moore
Williams. .s. . . . . TW Dec 37 65
BEYOND THE AURA by Ed Earl Repp. .s . . . .
. . . . .AW Nov 29 430
BEYOND THE BLACK NEBULA by Rene
LaFayette *ps (L. Ron Hubbard)*. .s . . . . .SS Sep 49 126
BEYOND THE BOILING ZONE by Ross
Rocklynne. .s . . . . .SS Win 44 79
BEYOND THE END OF SPACE by John W.
Campbell, Jr. . .n 2 pt . . . . Amz Mar 33 1096

BEYOND THE END OF TIME by Ray Cummings. . . . .
. .s .SSS Nov 42 124
BEYOND THE GREAT OBLIVION by George
Allan England. .n. . . . . FFM Jun 41 6
BEYOND THE GREEN PRISM by A. Hyatt
Verrill. .n 2 pt. . . . . .Amz Jan 30 886
BEYOND THE HEAVISIDE LAYER by Captain
S. P. Meek. .s . . . . .ASF Jul 30 5
BEYOND THE MATRIX OF TIME by Rog Phillips
ps (Roger P. Graham). .nt . . . . Amz Nov 49 38
BEYOND THE PLANETOIDS by Edwin K. Sloat . . . . .
. .s . . . . Amz Aug 32 422
BEYOND THE POLE by Philip M. Fisher. .nt. . . . . . .
. . . . FFM Jun 42 96
BEYOND THE POLE by A. Hyatt Verrill. .n 2 pt . . . . .
. . . . Amz Oct 26 580
BEYOND THE SCREEN by John Beynon
(Harris). .nt . . . . .Fant #1 38 92
BEYOND THE SINGING FLAME by Clark Ashton
Smith. .s . . . . WS Nov 31 752
SS Sum 44 90
BEYOND THE SPECTRUM by Arthur Leo Zagat . . . . .
. .s . . . . ASF Aug 34 61
BEYOND THE SPHINXES' CAVE by Murray
Leinster *ps (Will F. Jenkins)*. .nt. . . . . . .ASF Nov 33 2
BEYOND THE STAR CURTAIN by Garth Bentley. . . .
. .s . . . . WS Oct 31 640
FSQ Fal 50 116
BEYOND THE STARS by Ray Cummings. .n . . . .
. . . . .Fut Feb 42 10
BEYOND THE STRATOSPHERE by William
Lemkin, Ph.D. . .n 2 pt . . . . Amz Jun 36 13
BEYOND THE SUN by D. L. James. .s . . . .
. . . . ASF Mar 39 141
BEYOND THE THUNDER by H. B. Hickey *ps
(Herb Livingston)*. .s . . . . Amz Dec 48 74
BEYOND THE TIME DOOR by David Wright
O'Brien. .s . . . . FA Mar 41 90
BEYOND THE UNIVERSE by Stanton A.
Coblentz. .s . . . . Amz Dec 34 70
BEYOND THE VANISHING POINT by Ray
Cummings. .nt . . . . ASF Mar 31 314
BEYOND THE VEIL OF SCIENCE by Alexander
Blade *h ps*. .a . . . . .Amz Jan 49 134
BEYOND THE VEIL OF TIME by B. H. Barney. . . . . .
. .nt . . . . .AQ Fal-Win 32 394
BEYOND THE VORTEX by Frank Belknap Long. . . . .
. .s . . . . TW Fal 44 55
BEYOND THE WALL OF SLEEP by H. P.
Lovecraft. .s . . . . .AFR #6 21
BEYOND THE YELLOW FOG by Emmett
McDowell. .nt. . . . . .PS Spr 47 2
BEYOND THIS HORIZON—by Anson MacDonald . . . .
. .n 2 pt . . . . ASF Apr 42 9
BEYOND WHICH LIMITS by Nat Schachner. .s . . . . . .
. . . . ASF Feb 37 77

Title. .Author. .Length . . . . Magazine. .Date. .Page No.

BIDDIVER by Theodore Sturgeon. .s . . . ASF Aug 41 120
BIG AND THE LITTLE, THE by Isaac Asimov. .nt . . . .
. . . . ASF Aug 44 7
BIG CLOUD, THE by Coutts Brisbane. .s . . . . .
. . . . .ToW Sum 39 42
BIG CONTEST, THE by John D. MacDonald. .s . . . . . .
. . . . WB Dec 50 41
BIG MAN by Ross Rocklynn. .s . . . . Amz Apr 41 70
BIG NIGHT, THE by Hudson Hastings ps (Henry
Kuttner & C. L. Moore). .s . . . . TW Jun 47 38
BIGHEAD by William de Koven. .nt . . . . . NW Win 50 52
BIGGS, LAUNCELOT series See NELSON S. BOND
BIKINI A AND B by John W. Campbell, Jr. . .a . . . . . .
. . . . ASF Dec 46 99
BILL CALDRON GOES TO THE FUTURE by Paul
Miles. .s . . . . Amz Mar 43 196
BILL OF RIGHTS, 5000 A. D. by John York
Cabot ps (David Wright O'Brien). .ss . . . .
. . . . FA Jun 41 130
BIMINI by Bassett Morgan. .s . . . . AFR #10 36
BINDLESTIFF by James Blish. .nt . . . . . . ASF Dec 50 6
BIOLOGICAL BARRIER, THE by Anthony B. Ott. . . .
. .s . . . . FA Nov 49 64
BIOLOGICAL EXPERIMENT, A by David H.
Keller, M.D. . .s . . . . Amz Jun 28 232
BIPED by Basil Wells. .ss. . . . . Cos Mar 41 117
BIPED, REEGAN, THE by Alfred Bester. .s . . . .
. . . . .SSS Nov 41 66
BIPEDS OF BJHULHU by Kenneth Sterling. .ss . . . . . .
. . . . .WS Jan 36 817
BIRD, DR. & OPERATIVE CARNES series See
CAPT. S. P. MEEK auth
BIRD WALK by P. Schuyler Miller. .s . . . ASF Apr 41 112
BIRDS OF A FEATHER by Lester Barclay. .s . . . .
. . . . FA May 50 134
BIRTH OF A NEW REPUBLIC, THE by Miles J.
Breuer & Jack Williamson. .n . . . . AQ Win 30 4
BIRTH OF A SUPERSTITION, THE by Willy Ley. .a . .
. . . . ASF May 42 98
BISHOP MURDER CASE, THE by S. S. Van Dyne . . . .
. .n 3 pt . . . . .SD Jan 30 52
BISHOP'S GAMBIT by Stephen Grendon. .s . . . .
. . . . AFR #3 95
BIT OF FOREVER, A by Walt Sheldon. .s . . . .
. . . . SSS Jul 50 84
BIT OF TAPESTRY by Cleve Cartmill. .n . . . UK Dec 41 9
BLABBERMOUTH by Theodore Sturgeon. .s . . . .
. . . . Amz Feb 47 66
BLACK ABSOLUTE by H. L. Gold. .ss . . . . CF Fal 40 109
BLACK ARROW by Jamieson Wood. .n . . . . FA Jun 48 8
BLACK BRAIN, THE by Tarleton Fiske ps (Robert
Bloch). .s . . . . FA Mar 43 218
BLACK BUTTERFLIES by Elmer Brown Mason. . . . .
. .nt . . . . FFM Apr 49 88
BLACK CABINET, THE by Henry Leverage. .s . . . . . .
. . . . AD Sep 30 780

BLACK COMET, THE by John Coleridge ps (Earl
Binder & Otto Binder). .s . . . . .SF Jun 39 105
BLACK DEATH by Henry J. Kostkos. .s . . . .
. . . . ASF Mar 34 76
BLACK DESTROYER by A. E. van Vogt. .nt . . . .
. . . . .ASF Jul 39 9
BLACK EMPRESS, THE by John Russell Fearn . . . . . .
. .nt . . . . Amz Jan 39 86
BLACK EWE, THE by Fritz Leiber, Jr. . .s . . . .
. . . . SS May 50 117
BLACK FARM, THE by H. W. Guernsey ps
(Howard Wandrei). .s . . . . UK Mar 40 75
BLACK FLAME, THE by Stanley G. Weinbaum. .n . . . .
. . . . SS Jan 39 16
BLACK FLAMES by Lawrence Woods ps (Robert
W. Lowndes & Donald A. Wollheim). .s . . . .
. . . . Sti Apr 41 68
BLACK FOG by Donald Wandrei. .s . . . . . TW Feb 37 33
BLACK FRIAR OF THE FLAME by Isaac Asimov . . . .
. .nt . . . . .PS Spr 42 2
BLACK GALAXY, THE by Murray Leinster ps (Will
F. Jenkins). .n . . . . .SS Mar 49 13
BLACK GOLDFISH by John Taine ps (Eric Temple
Bell). .nt 2 pt . . . . FB #4 4
BLACK HAND, THE by Charles Gardner Bowers. .s . . .
. . . . .Amz Jan 31 909
BLACK, JOHNNY series See L. SPRAGUE DE CAMP
auth
BLACK LAMP, THE by Captain S. P. Meek. .s . . . . . .
. . . . ASF Feb 31 212
BLACK LIGHT by Ralph Milne Farley ps (Roger
Sherman Hoar). .s . . . . ASF Aug 36 87
BLACK LIGHT by Henry Leverage. .s . . . . SD Apr 30 330
BLACK LOTUS by Robert Bloch. .s . . . . FB #1 19
BLACK MARKET by Raymond F. Jones. .nt . . . .
. . . . ASF Apr 46 133
BLACK-OUT by Joseph Farrell. .s . . . . . . .PS Win 43 57
BLACK POOL, THE by Ed Earl Repp. .s . . . .
. . . . Amz Nov 43 190
BLACK PIRATES OF BARSOOM by Edgar Rice
Burroughs. .nt . . . . Amz Jun 41 8
BLACK PRIESTESS OF VARDA by Erik Fennel . . . . .
. .nt . . . . PS Win 47 4
BLACK RIVER, THE by John M. Corbett. .s . . . .
. . . . WS Dec 34 784
BLACK SILENCE by Emmett McDowell. .nt . . . .
. . . . PS Fal 47 4
BLACK STAR PASSES, THE by John W.
Campbell, Jr. . .n . . . . .AQ Fal 30 492
BLACK SUN RISES, THE by Henry Kuttner. .nt . . . . .
. . . . SSS Jan 49 8
BLACK THIRST by C. L. Moore. .nt . . . . . . AFR #3 56
BLACK VORTEX, THE by Frank Belknap Long, Jr.
. .nt . . . . TW Jun 37 104
BLACK WORLD by A. R. Steber h ps (Raymond A.
Palmer). .n . . . . Amz Mar 40 8

Title. .Author. .Length . . . . Magazine. .Date. .Page No.

BLACKOUT by Damon Knight. .ss . . . . SF Jul 43 55
BLADE OF GRASS, A by Ray Bradbury. .s . . . .
. . . . TW Dec 49 59
BLASPHEMER'S PLATEAU by Alexander Snyder. .s . .
. . . . Amz Oct 26 656
BLATTIDS, THE by Morrison Colladay. .s . . . .
. . . . Amz Dec 31 844
BLEAK SHORE, THE by Fritz Leiber, Jr. . .s . . . .
. . . . UK Nov 40 111
BLIND ALLEY by Isaac Asimov. .s . . . . ASF Mar 45 139
BLIND ALLEY by Malcolm Jameson. .nt . . . .
. . . . UK Jun 43 48
BLIND FLIGHT by Millard Verne Gordon ps
(Donald A. Wollheim). .s . . . . Sti Mar 42 21
BLIND MAN'S BUFF by J. U. Giesy. .s . . . .
. . . . FFM Sep-Oct 39 118
BLIND MAN'S BUFF by Malcolm Jameson. .nt . . . . .
. . . . ASF Oct 44 7
BLIND REASONING by Roi Auckland. .s . . . .
. . . . ASF Feb 34 127
BLIND SPOT, THE by Austin Hall & Homer Eon Flint .
. .n . . .(The first 27 out of 48 chapters were published
in Three installments starting in . . . . . . FFM Mar 40 6
then dropped when it was published complete
in . . . . .FN Jul 40 2
BLIND TIME by George O. Smith. .s . . . . ASF Sep 46 40
BLIND VICTORY by Oscar J. Friend. .s . . TW Feb 41 104
BLINDING RAY, THE by Alfred R. Steber ps
(Raymond A. Palmer). .nt . . . . Amz Aug 38 46
BLINDING SHADOWS by Donald Wandrei. .s . . . .
. . . . ASF May 34 11
BLINDNESS by Don A. Stuart ps (John W.
Campbell, Jr.). .s . . . . ASF Mar 35 99
BLINDNESS, THE by Phillip Latham ps (Robert S.
Richardson). .nt . . . . .ASF Jul 46 84
BLITZ AGAINST JAPAN by Robert Moore
Williams. .nt . . . . Amz Sep 42 10
BLITZKRIEG IN THE PAST by John York Cabot
ps (David Wright O'Brien). .nt . . . . .Amz Jul 42 8
BLITZKRIEG—1950 by Frederic Arnold
Kummer, Jr. . .s . . . . Amz Sep 40 84
BLOATED BRAIN by Alfred G. Kuehn. .s . . . .
. . . . TW Fal 44 49
BLOCKADE RUNNER by Malcolm Jameson. .s . . . . . .
. . . . ASF Mar 41 44
BLONDE GODDESS OF BAL-SAGOTH, THE
by Robert E. Howard. .nt . . . . .AFR #12 3
BLONDE, THE TIME MACHINE AND JOHNNY
BELL, THE by Kenneth L. Harrison. .s . . . .
. . . . TW Dec 40 74
BLOOD OF THE MOON by Ray Cummings. .nt . . . . . .
. . . . TW Aug 36 12
BLOOD ON THE SUN by Hal K. Wells. .n . . . .
. . . . SS May 42 14
BLOOD-BROTHER OF THE SWAMP CATS
(Fishhead) by Irvin S. Cobb. .s . . . . . .FanS Nov 50 39

Title. .Author. .Length . . . . Magazine. .Date. .Page No.

BLOODLESS PERIL, THE by Will Garth h ps. .s . . . . .
. . . . TW Dec 37 100
BLOODLESS WAR, THE by David H. Keller, M.D. . . .
. .s . . . . AW Jul 29 52
BLORD, ARTUR series See E. MAYNE HULL auth
BLOWUPS HAPPEN by Robert Heinlein. .nt . . . .
. . . . ASF Sep 40 51
BLUE AND SILVER BROCADE by Dorothy Quick . . .
. .s . . . . UK Oct 39 103
BLUE BARBARIANS, THE by Stanton A. Coblentz . . .
. .n . . . . .AQ Sum 31 290
BLUE BEAM OF PESTILENCE, THE by Eando
Binder ps (Earl Binder and Otto Binder). .s . . . .
. . . . Amz Dec 37 114
BLUE BEHEMOTH, THE by Leigh Brackett. .s . . . . . .
. . . . PS May 43 54
BLUE BOTTLE FLY by Geoff St. Reynard ps
(Robert W. Krepps). .s . . . . FA Apr 49 78
BLUE BOY by E. A. Grosser. .s . . . . SSS Jan 41 94
BLUE DEMON, THE by Lowell Howard Morrow. .s . . .
. . . . AW Dec 29 486
BLUE DIMENSION, THE by Francis Flagg ps
(George Henry Weiss). .s . . . . Amz Jun 28 224
BLUE EARTHMAN, THE by Frank Belknap
Long, Jr. . .s . . . . ASF Apr 35 32
BLUE FLAMINGO, THE by Hannes Bok. .n . . . .
. . . . .SS Jan 48 13
BLUE GIRAFFE, THE by L. Sprague de Camp. .s . . . . .
. . . . ASF Aug 39 113
BLUE HAZE ON PLUTO by Raymond Z. Gallun. .s . . .
. . . . ASF Jun 35 90
BLUE INFINITY, THE by John Russell Fearn. .nt . . . . .
. . . . ASF Sep 35 70
BLUE MAGIC by Charles Willard Diffin. .n 4 pt . . . . .
. . . . ASF Nov 35 76
BLUE-MEN OF YRANO, THE by Warner Van
Lorne ps. .nt . . . . ASF Jan 39 9
BLUE SPANGLE, THE by Dr. R. Austin Freeman. . . . .
. .s . . . . AD Jun 30 536
BLUE SPOT, THE by Jack Williamson. .n 2 pt . . . .
. . . . .ASF Jan 37 48
BLUE TROPICS, THE by James Norman. .s . . . .
. . . . FA Apr 40 6
BLUE VENUS, THE by Emmett McDowell. .nt . . . . . .
. . . . .PS Spr 46 88
BLUE WATER by William Lemkin, Ph.D. . .s. . . . . . .
. . . . AQ Win 32 96
BLUEPRINT by Donald A. Wollheim. .ss . . . .
. . . . Sti Apr 41 23
BLUEPRINT FOR DESTRUCTION by Lyle Burke. .s . .
. . . . FA Apr 50 138
BLUFF OF THE HAWK, THE by Anthony Gilmore
ps (Harry Bates & D. W. Hall). .s . . . .
. . . . ASF May 32 256
BLUFF PLAY by Raymond Z. Gallun. .s . . . .
. . . . TW Dec 50 113

Title. .Author. .Length . . . . .Magazine. .Date. .Page No.

BLURB by E. Everett Evans. .s . . . . FB #3 27
BOATS OF THE GLEN CARRIG, THE by William
    Hope Hodgson. .n . . . . FFM Jun 45 10
BODY PIRATE, THE by Ed Earl Repp. .s . . . .
    . . . . Amz Mar 35 121
BODY THAT WOULDN'T BURN, THE by Arthur
    B. Reeve. .s . . . . AD Sep 30 804
BOMB by Millard Verne Gordon ps (Donald A.
    Wollheim). .ss . . . . SFQ Win 42 81
BOMB FROM BERANGA by Harry Walton. .s . . . .
    . . . . FFM Mar 40 69
BOMBARDMENT IN REVERSE by Norman L.
    Knight. .s . . . . ASF Feb 40 124
BOMBING IS A FINE ART by Willy Ley. .a . . . .
    . . . . ASF Aug 42 75
BON VOYAGE! by Arthur G. Stangland. .s . . . .
    . . . . .Ash Aug 40 25
BONE OF CONTENTION, THE by William F.
    Temple. .s . . . . TW Oct 50 122
BONELESS HORROR, THE by David H. Keller,
    M.D. . .s . . . . SW Jul 29 133
                                                  SS Nov 41 98
BONES by Donald A. Wollheim. .s . . . . . . Sti Feb 41 88
BONES, THE by Theodore Sturgeon & James H.
    Beard. .s . . . . UK Aug 43 107
BOOK MARK, THE Letter dept in FANTASY
    BOOK from #2
BOOK OF PTATH, THE by A. E. van Vogt. .n . . . .
    . . . . UK Oct 43 9
BOOK OF WORLDS, THE by Dr. Miles J.
    Breuer. .s . . . . Amz Jul 29 294
                                                  ToW Win 41 36
BOOK SHELF, THE Book review dept in
    FANTASY BOOK from #2
BOOMERANG by Bowen Conway ps (John Michel) . . .
    . .ss . . . . SFQ Sum 42 138
BOOMERANG by Eric Tinde. .s . . . . . . ASF Nov 47 112
BOOMERANG by Harry Walton. .s . . . .
    . . . . .ASF Jun 44 119
BOOMERANG by George Whitley ps (A. Bertram
    Chandler). .s . . . . FFM Aug 47 114
BOOMERANG CIRCUIT, THE by Murray Leinster
    ps (Will F. Jenkins). .nt . . . . TW Jun 47 11
BOOMERANGING 'ROUND THE MOON by David
    H. Keller, M.D. . .s . . . . .AQ Fal 30 524
BORE, THE by James Blish. .s . . . . FSQ Sum 50 124
BORGHESE TRANSPARENCY, THE by Carter
    Sprague ps (Sam Merwin, Jr.). .s . . . . . . TW Apr 50 134
BORN OF MAN AND WOMAN by Richard
    Matheson. .ss . . . . F&SF Sum 50 108
BORN OF THE SUN by Jack Williamson. .nt . . . .
    . . . . ASF Mar 34 11
BORNEO DEVILS by Murray Leinster ps (Will F.
    Jenkins). .s . . . . Amz Feb 33 989
BORROWED GLORY by L. Ron Hubbard. .s . . . .
    . . . . UK Oct 41 85

Title. .Author. .Length . . . . .Magazine. .Date. .Page No.

BOTANICAL INVASION by Willy Ley. .a . . . .
    . . . . ASF Feb 40 91
BOTTLE, THE by Guy Archette ps (Chester S.
    Geier). .s . . . . FA Dec 49 98
BOTH FEET IN ETERNITY (Half Past Twelve in
    Eternity) by Robert w. Sneddon. .s . . . .
    . . . . .FanS Nov 50 105
BOTHON by Henry S. Whitehead. .nt . . . .
    . . . . Amz Aug 46 122
BOTTLE IMP, THE by Dwight V. Swain. .nt . . . .
    . . . . FA Sep 42 140
BOTTLED MEN, THE by Ross Rocklynn. .nt. . . . .
    . . . . ASF Jun 46 66
BOTTOM OF THE WORLD, THE by John
    Coleman Burroughs & Hulbert Burroughs. .n . . . . . .
    . . . . .SS Sep 41 14
BOUNDING CROWN, THE by James Blish. .s . . . .
    . . . . SSS Jan 49 60
BOWL OF DEATH, THE by Elliot Dold. .n . . . .
    . . . . .Mir Jun-Jul 31 154
BOX, THE by James Blish. .s . . . . TW Apr 49 130
BRACELET, THE by Doris Thomas ps (Doris
    Vancel). .nt . . . . FA Apr 43 206
BRAHMA-KALPA—OR THE EXPANDING
    UNIVERSE by Epaminondas T. Snooks ps
    (C. P. Mason). .ss . . . . .WS May 33 945
BRAIN, THE by Alexander Blade h ps (Heinrich
    Hauser). .n . . . . Amz Oct 48 64
BRAIN ACCELERATOR, THE by Dr. Daniel
    Dressler. .s . . . . Amz Nov 29 696
BRAIN BEAST, THE by William F. Temple. .nt . . . . . .
    . . . . SSS Jul 49 8
BRAIN CONTROL by Dave Cummins. .s . . . .
    . . . . ASF May 37 132
BRAIN EATERS OF PLUTO, THE by Kenneth
    Sterling. .s . . . . WS Mar 34 822
BRAIN LEECHES by Edward S. Mund. .s . . . .
    . . . . ASF Jul 35 109
BRAIN OF ALI KAHN, THE by L. A. Eshbach . . . . . .
    . .s . . . . WS Oct 34 556
BRAIN OF LIGHT, THE by John Russell Fearn . . . . . .
    . .nt . . . . ASF May 34 45
BRAIN OF MANY BODIES, THE by E. A. Grosser. . . .
    . .s . . . . .SF Oct 40 54
BRAIN OF VENUS by John Russell Fearn. .nt . . . .
    . . . . TW Feb 37 42
BRAIN PIRATES, THE by John W. Campbell, Jr. . . . .
    . .s . . . . TW Oct 38 74
BRAIN STEALERS OF MARS, THE by John W.
    Campbell, Jr. . .nt . . . . .TW Dec 36 14
BRAIN-STORM VIBRATION, THE by M. Schere. . . . .
    . .s . . . . ASF May 38 138
BRAINS FOR BRICKS by Malcolm Jameson. .s . . . . . .
    . . . . ASF Apr 45 124
BRAINSTORM by Alexander Blade h ps. .nt . . . .
    . . . . FA Dec 48 74

Title. .Author. .Length . . . . Magazine. .Date. .Page No.

BRANCHES OF TIME, THE by David R. Daniels. .s . . .
. . . . WS Aug 35 294
BRAND NEW WORLD, A by Ray Cummings. .n . . . . . .
. . . . FFM Sep 42 6
BRAT by Theodore Sturgeon. .s. . . . . UK Dec 41 69
BRATTON'S IDEA by Manly Wade Wellman. .s . . . . .
. . . . Com Dec 40 85
BRAVE WALK ALONE, THE by John McGreevey. .s . .
. . . . .Im Dec 50 142
BREAKDOWN by Jack Williamson. .nt . . . . ASF Jan 42 9
BREATH OF BEELZEBUB by Larry Sternig. .s . . . . .
. . . . .PS Win 46 83
BREATH OF THE COMET by A. Rowley Hilliard. . . . .
. .s . . . . .ASF Jan 34 102
BREATH OF UTOPIA by Miles J. Breuer. .s. . . . .
. . . . ToW Spr 42 31
"BRICKWALL" IN THE SKY, THE by Willy Ley . . . .
. .a . . . . ASF Nov 48 78
BRIDE FOR THE DEVIL, A by Stuart Palmer. .s . . . . .
. . . . .F&SF Fal 49 87
BRIDE OF ETERNITY by Margaret St. Clair. .s . . . . . .
. . . . SSS Sep 49 36
BRIDGE OF BANISHMENT by Leroy Yerxa. .nt . . . . .
. . . . Amz May 43 154
BRIDGE OF LIFE by Robert Moore Williams. .s. . . . . .
. . . . Amz May 46 92
BRIDGE OF LIGHT THE by A. Hyatt Verrill. .n . . . . .
. . . . .AQ Fal 29 436
BRIDGE TO EARTH, THE by Robert Moore
Williams. .n . . . . .SS Sep 39 16
BRIDGEHEAD by Frank Belknap Long. .nt. . . . .
. . . . ASF Aug 44 120
BRIDLE AND SADDLE by Isaac Asimov. .nt. . . . . . .
. . . . ASF Jun 42 9
BRIGADE OF THE DAMNED by Ed Earl Repp. .s . . . .
. . . . Amz Jun 39 110
BRIGANDS OF THE MOON by Ray Cummings . . . . . .
. .n 4 pt. . . . . ASF Mar 30 306
                    (Complete) . . . . . .SFQ Fal 42 4
BRIGHT ILLUSION, THE by C. L. Moore. .nt . . . . . .
. . . . .ASF Oct 34 120
BRIMSTONE BILL by Malcolm Jameson. .s. . . . .
. . . . ASF Jul 42 27
BRING BACK MY BODY by David Wright
O'Brien. .s . . . . Amz Mar 43 116
BRINK OF INFINITY, THE by Stanley G.
Weinbaum. .s . . . . TW Dec 36 56
                                        SS Mar 48 116
BRITISH THERMAL UNITS by Owen Fox Jerome
ps (Oscar J. Friend). .s . . . . TW Jun 42 83
BROAD BAND by J. J. Coupling ps (John R. Pierce) . . .
. .a . . . . ASF Aug 47 116
BROKEN AXIOM, THE by Alfred Bester. .s. . . . . . .
. . . . TW Apr 39 64
BROKEN DOLL, THE by Paul W. Fairman. .s . . . . . .
. . . . .FA Jul 50 84

Title. .Author. .Length . . . . Magazine. .Date. .Page No.

BRONTOSAURUS, THE by Robert G. Thompson . . . .
. .ss. . . . . Sti Apr 41 55
BRONZE DOOR, THE by Raymond Chandler. .s . . . . .
. . . . .UK Nov 39 90
BRONZE DOOR, THE by Jerry Benedict. .s. . . . .
. . . . Amz May 33 164
BROOD OF HELIOS by John Bertin. .n 3 pt . . . .
. . . . WS May 32 1302
BROOD OF THE DARK MOON by Charles
Willard Diffin. .n 4 pt. . . . . ASF Aug 31 168
BROOKHAVEN SKETCHES by John W.
Campbell, Jr. . .a . . . . .ASF Jul 49 4
BROOKLYN PROJECT by William Tenn ps
(Phillip Klass). .s . . . . PS Fal 48 90
BROTHER MICHEL by Nelson S. Bond. .s . . . .
. . . . FA May 42 202
BROTHERS, THE by Michael D. Shea. .ss . . . .
. . . . .SSS May 41 102
BROTHERS OF FATE by Manly Wade Wellman. . . . . .
. .ss. . . . . .SF Jun 39 87
BROTHERS SHENANIGAN, THE by David V.
Reed ps (David Vern). .nt . . . . Amz Jun 46 64
BROTHERS UNDER THE SKIN by Gerald
Vance h ps. .nt . . . . Amz Nov 50 72
BROWN by Frank Belknap Long. .s . . . . . ASF Jul 41 144
BUBASTIS OF EGUPT by Craig Browning ps (Roger
P. Graham). .nt . . . . .OW Nov 50 6
BUBBLE DWELLERS, THE by Ross Rocklynne. . . . . .
. .nt . . . . PS Fal 45 78
BUBBLE PEOPLE, THE by James Henry
Carlisle III. .s . . . . TW Fal 43 41
BUCCANEER OF THE STAR SEAS by Ed Earl
Repp. .s . . . . PS Fal 40 41
BUCKETHEAD by Arthur G. Stangland. .s . . . .
. . . . .SSS Jan 41 24
BUILT UP LOGICALLY by Howard Schoenfeld. .s . . . .
. . . . .F&SF Fal 50 33
BULL MOOSE OF BABYLON by Don Wilcox. .nt . . . .
. . . . FA Apr 42 70
BULLARD REFLECTS by Malcolm Jameson. .s . . . . . .
. . . . ASF Dec 41 66
BUREAU OF SLICK TRICKS by H. B. Fyfe. .nt . . . . .
. . . . ASF Dec 48 70
BUREAUCRAT, THE by Malcolm Jameson. .nt . . . . . .
. . . . ASF Apr 44 117
BURIAL OF THE RATS, THE by Bram Stoker. .s. . . . .
. . . . FFM Oct 46 112
BURIED IN SPACE by Lawrence Smith. .s . . . .
. . . . Amz Oct 34 130
BURIED MOON by Raymond Z. Gallun. .s . . . .
. . . . ASF Feb 36 37
BURIED TREASURE by Miles J. Breuer, M.D.
. .s . . . . Amz Apr 29 38
BURN, WITCH, BURN By A. Merritt. .n . . . FFM Jun 42 6
BURNING BRIGHT by John S. Browning ps
(Robert Moore Williams). .s. . . . . .ASF Jul 48 45

Title. .Author. .Length . . . . Magazine. .Date. .Page No.

BURNING SWAMP, THE by Morrison Colladay. .s . . . .
. . . . Amz Aug 31 446
BURNING WATER by David H. Keller, M.D. . .s . . . .
. . . . AD Jun 30 518
BURNT PLANET, THE by William Brittain. .ss. . . . . .
. . . . .PS Win 48 80
BURROUGHS PASSES by Kenneth James. .s. . . . . . .
. . . . ASF Oct 33 35
BURY ME DEEP by Leroy Yerxa. .nt . . . .
. . . . FA Jun 44 160
BUSINESS OF KILLING by Fritz Leiber, Jr. . .s . . . . .
. . . . ASF Sep 44 59
BUT WITHOUT HORNS by Norvell W. Page. .n . . . . . .
. . . . UK Jun 40 9
BUTYL AND THE BREATHER by Theodore
Sturgeon. .s . . . . .ASF Oct 40 105
BY HIS BOOTSTRAPS by Anson McDonald ps
(Robert A. Heinlein). .nt . . . . ASF Oct 41 9
BY JOVE! by Walter Rose, L.D.S., R.C.S. . .n 3 pt . . . .
. . . . Amz Feb 37 75
BY ROCKET-SHIP TO THE PLANETS by P. E.
Cleator, F.R.S.A., A.M.R.I.E. . .a . . . . . Fant #1 38 53
BY THE RULES by David Gordon. .nt . . . . .OW Oct 50 6
BY THE STARS FORGOT by John D. MacDonald . . . .
. .s . . . . SSS May 50 36
BY YON BONNIE BANKS by Geoff St. Reynard
ps (Robert W. Krepps). .nt . . . . ASF Nov 45 65

C

CABAL by Cleve Cartmill. .s . . . . SSS Jan 49 110
CABLE TRAIN OF TOMORROW by James B.
Settles. .bacover . . . . Amz Sep 45
CACHE, THE by Harry Walton. .s . . . . . ASF Apr 39 110
CADUCEUS OF HERMES, THE by George
Tashman. .s . . . . Amz Oct 46 48
CAGLIOSTRO (FANTASTIC HOAXES) by Julius
Schwartz. .a . . . . FA Jun 40 90
CAIRN ON THE HEADLAND, THE by Robert E.
Howard. .s . . . . .AFR #7 63
CALAVERAS SKULL HOAX, THE (FANTASTIC
HOAXES) by Julius Schwartz. .a . . . . . . FA Nov 39 54
CALENDAR FOR MARS by R. S. Richardson. .a . . . . .
. . . . ASF Aug 47 133
CALIF OF YAFRI by Silaki Ali Hassan. .nt . . . .
. . . . UK Sep 39 91
CALKINS, AJAX series See MARTIN PEARSON author
CALL FROM BEYOND, THE by Clifford D. Simak. . . .
. .nt . . . . SSS May 50 56
CALL HIM DEMON by Keith Hammond ps (Henry
Kuttner & C. L. Moore). .s . . . . TW Fal 46 46
CALL OF DUTY by J. J. allerton. .s . . . . FA Apr 50 122
CALL OF DUTY by Laurence Bour, Jr. . .s . . . .
. . . . UK Feb 40 56

CALL OF THE MECH-MEN, THE by Laurence
Manning. .s. . . . . WS Nov 33 366
CALL TO MIGRATE, THE by H. M. Crimp. .s . . . . . .
. . . . Amz Dec 32 833
CALLAHUAYA'S CURSE by Col. H. P.
Fawcett. .s . . . . .ASF Oct 33 140
CALLING ALL FANTASY FANS editorial page
of AMF from . . . . Dec 49
CALLING ALL MARTIANS by Willy Ley. .a . . . .
. . . . TW Nov 40 34
CALLING CAPTAIN FUTURE by Edmond
Hamilton. .n . . . . .CF Spr 40 12
CALLING OF THE HARP by Maria Moravsky. .s . . . . .
. . . . SS Jul 41 84
CALLING THE EMPRESS by George O. Smith. .s. . . . .
. . . . ASF Jun 43 68
CALLISTAN CABAL by James Blish. .s . . . .
. . . . Sti Apr 41 42
CALLISTAN MENACE, THE by Isaac Asimov . . . .
. .s . . . . .Ash Apr 40 66
CALLISTAN TOMB by Paul Dennis Lavond
h ps (Cyril Kornbluth & Frederik Pohl). .s . . . .
. . . . .SFQ Spr 41 108
CALLISTRO AT WAR by Harl Vincent
(Schoepflin). .s . . . . Amz Mar 30 1150
CALYPSO'S ISLAND by David H. Keller. .s. . . . .
. . . . Sti Apr 41 84
CAMOUFLAGE by Lewis Padgett ps (Henry
Kuttner & C. L. Moore). .nt . . . . .ASF Sep 45 135
CAMPUS MURDER MYSTERY, THE by Ralph
W. Wilkins. .s . . . . .SD Jan 30 14
CAN MAN FREE HIMSELF FROM GRAVITY?
by Dr. Th. Wolff (tr fr German by Francis M.
Currier). .a . . . . SW Feb 30 788
CAN OF PAINT, A by A. E. van Vogt. .s . . . .
. . . . ASF Sep 44 29
CAN OF VACUUM, A by L. Ron Hubbard. .s . . . .
. . . . ASF Dec 49 81
CAN OPENER, THE by Rog Phillips ps (Roger P.
Graham). .s . . . . FA Jan 49 86
CAN V-2 BE IMPROVED? by David A.
Anderton. .a . . . . .ASF Sep 47 106
CAN WE CONQUER SPACE? by I. O. Evans. .a . . . . . .
. . . . .ToW Sum 38 68
CAN WE CONQUER TIME? by I. O. Evans. .a . . . . . .
. . . . .ToW Sum 40 56
CAN WE FORTELL THE FUTURE? by Julius
Schwartz. .a . . . . .FA Jul 42 116
CANAL by Carl Jacobi. .s . . . . SS Spr 44 78
CANAL, THE by Everil Worrell. .s . . . . . . AFR #8 107
CANAL BUILDERS, THE by Robert Abernathy. . . . . .
. .s . . . . .ASF Jan 45 33
CANCER THE FANTASTIC by A. Morris. .a . . . .
. . . . FA Aug 42 227
CANNIBALS, THE by Oliver E. Saari. .s . . . .
. . . . .Fut Dec 42 76

Title. .Author. .Length . . . . Magazine. .Date. .Page No.

CANNONBALL ROAD, THE by Wallace West. .s . . . . .
. . . . .FA Jan 45 108
CAPTAIN BRINK OF THE SPACE MARINES by Bob
Olsen ps (Alfred John Olsen, Jr.). .s . . Amz Nov 32 722
CAPTAIN CHAOS by Nelson S. Bond. .s . . . PS Sum 42 70
CAPTAIN FAMINE by Cleve Cartmill. .s . . . TW Dec 50 80
CAPTAIN FUTURE series (in the order of their
publication)
CAPTAIN FUTURE AND THE SPACE EMPEROR
by Edmond Hamilton. .n. . . . . CF Win 40 12
CALLING CAPTAIN FUTURE by Edmond
Hamilton. .n. . . . . .CF Spr 40 12
CAPTAIN FUTURE'S CHALLENGE by Edmond
Hamilton. .n. . . . . .CF Sum 40 14
THE TRIUMPH OF CAPTAIN FUTURE by
Edmond Hamilton. .n. . . . . .CF Fal 40 14
CAPTAIN FUTURE AND THE SEVEN SPACE
STONES by Edmond Hamilton. .n . . . . CF Win 41 14
STAR TRAIL TO GLORY by Edmond Hamilton . . .
. .n . . . . .CF Spr 41 14
THE MAGICIAN OF MARS by Edmond
Hamilton. .n. . . . . .CF Sum 41 14
THE LOST WORLD OF TIME by Edmond
Hamilton. .n. . . . . .CF Fal 41 14
THE QUEST BEYOND THE STARS by
Edmond Hamilton. .n. . . . . CF Win 42 15
OUTLAWS OF THE MOON by Edmond
Hamilton. .n. . . . . .CF Spr 42 14
THE COMET KINGS by Edmond Hamilton. . . . . .
. .n .CF Sum 42 11
PLANETS IN PERIL by Edmond Hamilton . . . . . .
. .n . . . . .CF Fal 42 13
THE FACE OF THE DEEP by Edmond
Hamilton. .n. . . . . CF Win 43 15
WORLDS TO COME by Brett Sterling h ps
(Joseph Samachson). .n. . . . . .CF Spr 43 15
THE STAR OF DREAD by Brett Sterling
h ps (Edmond Hamilton). .n . . . . .CF Sum 43 13
MAGIC MOON by Brett Sterling ps (Edmond
Hamilton). .n . . . . CF Win 44 15
DAYS OF CREATION by Brett Sterling h ps
(Joseph Samachson). .n. . . . . .CF Spr 44 11
RED SUN OF DANGER by Brett Sterling h ps
(Edmond Hamilton). .n. . . . . SS Spr 45 11
OUTLAW WORLD by Edmond Hamilton. .n . . . . . .
. . . . .SS Win 46 11
THE SOLAR INVASION by Manly Wade
Wellman. .n . . . . SS Fal 46 13
THE RETURN OF CAPTAIN FUTURE by
Edmond Hamilton. .s . . . . SS Jan 50 94
CHILDREN OF THE SUN by Edmond
Hamilton. .s . . . . SS May 50 98
THE HARPERS OF TITAN by Edmond
Hamilton. .s . . . . .SS Sep 50 96
PARDON MY IRON NERVES by Edmond
Hamilton. .s . . . . SS Nov 50 78

Title. .Author. .Length . . . . Magazine. .Date. .Page No.

CAPTAIN FUTURE AND THE SEVEN SPACE
STONES by Edmond Hamilton. .n . . . . . CF Win 41 14
CAPTAIN FUTURE AND THE SPACE EMPEROR
by Edmond Hamilton. .n . . . . CF Win 40 12
CAPTAIN FUTURE'S CHALLENGE by Edmond
Hamilton. .n. . . . . .CF Sum 40 14
CAPTAIN HAM by John & Dorothy de Courcy. .s . . . .
. . . . OW Oct 50 36
CAPTAIN MIDAS by Alfred Coppel, Jr. . .s. . . . . .
. . . . .PS Fal 49 61
CAPTAIN STINKY by Gerald Vance h ps. .s . . . .
. . . . Amz Jun 42 168
CAPTAIN STINKY'S LUCK by Gerald Vance
h ps. .s. . . . . Amz Sep 42 64
CAPTIVE OF THE CRATER by D. D. Sharp. .s . . . . . .
. . . . WS Jun 33 20
CAPTIVES OF THE DURNA RANGUE by Neil
R. Jones. .nt. . . . . .SSS Mar 41 114
CAPTIVES OF THE VOID by R. R. Winterbotham. . . .
. .s . . . . FA Jan 40 58
CAPTIVES OF THE WEIR-WIND by Ross
Rocklynn. .nt. . . . . PS Sum 46 54
CAPTURED CROSS-SECTION, THE by Miles J.
Breuer, M.D. . .s. . . . . Amz Feb 29 968
AFR #12 67
CARBON-COPY KILLER by Alexander Blade
h ps (Howard Browne). .nt . . . . .Amz Jul 43 12
CARBON EATER, THE by Douglas Drew. .nt . . . .
. . . . ASF Jun 40 51
CARDIACA VERA by Dr. Arch Carr. .s . . . .
. . . . ASF Mar 35 132
CARDIFF GIANT, THE (FANTASTIC HOAXES)
by Julius Schwartz. .a. . . . . .FA Jul 39 54
CAREWE MURDER MYSTERY, THE by Ed Earl
Repp. .n . . . . AD Sep 30 814
CARGO by Theodore Sturgeon. .nt . . . . . .UK Nov 40 82
CARGO TO CALLISTO by Jay B. Drexel ps
(Jerome Bixby). .s. . . . . PS Nov 50 37
CARIDI SHALL NOT DIE by Walter Kubilius. .s . . . . .
. . . . SFQ Win 41–42 115
Fut Nov 50 80
CARILLION OF SKULLS by Philip James. .s. . . . . . .
. . . . UK Feb 41 122
CARLISLE, GERRY series See ARTHUR K. BARNES
author
CARNES, OPERATIVE & DR. BIRD series See
CAPT. S. P. MEEK auth
CARNIVAL OF MADNESS by Ray Bradbury. .s. . . . . .
. . . . TW Apr 50 95
CAROUSEL by August Derleth. .s . . . . . . FA Apr 45 54
CARRIERS, THE by Sam Merwin, Jr. . .s . . . .
. . . . TW Feb 49 90
CARRION CRYPT by Richard Casey h ps. .s . . . .
. . . . FA Jul 47 166
CARRY ME HOME by C. H. Liddell ps (Henry
Kuttner & C. L. Moore). .nt. . . . . PS Nov 50 4

Title. .Author. .Length . . . . Magazine. .Date. .Page No.

CARSON OF VENUS series See EDGAR RICE
   BURROUGHS author
CARSTAIRS, JOHN, BOTANICAL DETECTIVE series
   See FRANK BELKNAP LONG author
CARTER, JOHN, OF MARS series See EDGAR RICE
   BURROUGHS author
CARTWRIGHT'S CAMERA by Nelson S. Bond. .s . . . .
. . . . UK Nov 40 104
CASE OF JACK FREYSLING, THE by Thomas
   Calvert McClary. .s. . . . . .ASF Oct 44 121
CASE OF JONATHAN LANE, THE by John York
   Cabot ps (David Wright O'Brien). .s. . . . Amz Aug 42 34
CASE OF SUMMERFIELD, THE by W. H. Rhodes . . . .
. .nt . . . . F&SF Sum 50 70
CASE OF THE BABY DINOSAUR, THE by J. S.
   Klimaris ps (Walter Kubilius). .s . . . . . . Fut Oct 42 70
CASE OF THE FRIENDLY CORPSE, THE by L. Ron
   Hubbard. .n . . . . .UK Aug 41 9
CASE OF THE MESOZOIC MONSTERS, THE by
   Thornton Ayre ps (John Russell Fearn). .nt . . . .
. . . . Amz May 42 210
CASE OF THE MISSING OCTANE, THE by
   Arthur Dugan. .a . . . . ASF Mar 49 102
CASE OF THE MURDERED SAVANTS, THE by
   Thornton Ayre ps (John Russell Fearn). .nt . . . .
. . . . Amz Apr 40 6
CASE OF THE VANISHING CELLARS, THE by
   J. S. Klimaris ps (Walter Kubilius). .s. . . . .
. . . . .Fut Aug 42 84
CASSANDRA by John K. Aiken. .n . . . . NW #5 49 2
CASSIUS SIDDLE'S GREAT ILLUSION by Yale
   Kenny. .s. . . . . FA Jun 42 204
CASTAWAY, THE by George Danzell ps (Nelson S.
   Bond). .s . . . . .PS Win 40 36
CASTAWAY by George Whitley ps (A. Bertram
   Chandler). .s. . . . . NW Spr 50 52
CASTAWAY by Robert Moore Williams. .s . . . .
. . . . ASF Feb 41 37
CASTAWAY by Charles Willis ps (Arthur C. Clarke) . . .
. .s . . . . Fant Apr 47 72
CASTAWAY by Donald A. Wollheim. .ss . . . .
. . . . .SSS May 40 112
CASTAWAYS IN SPACE by Amelia Reynolds
   Long. .s. . . . . .SF Jun 40 57
CASTAWAYS IN TWO DIMENSIONS by Frank
   Belknap Long. .s . . . . TW Win 45 37
CASTAWAYS OF EROS by Nelson S. Bond. .nt . . . . . .
. . . . .PS Win 43 62
CASTAWAYS OF SPACE by Arthur G. Stangland. . . . .
. .s . . . . WS Jul 32 118
CASTAWAYS ON DEIMOS by J. Harvey Haggard. . . . .
. .s . . . . WS Aug 33 128
CASTLE OF IRON, THE by L. Sprague de Camp &
   Fletcher Pratt. .n. . . . . .UK Apr 41 9
CASTLE OF TERROR by E. J. Liston. .s . . . .
. . . . Amz Nov 48 36

CASTLE ON OUTERPLANET, THE by S. D.
   Gottesman ps (Cyril Kornbluth, Robert W.
   Lowndes & Frederik Pohl). .s . . . . Sti Apr 41 28
CAT AND THE KING, THE by Raymond F. Jones . . . .
. .nt . . . . ASF Aug 46 73
CAT-MEN OF AEMT, THE by Neil R. Jones. .nt . . . . .
. . . . ASH Aug 40 42
CAT-SNAKE, THE by Frances M. Deegan. .s . . . .
. . . . FA Apr 48 66
CAT-WOMAN, THE by Mary Elizabeth
   Counselman. .s . . . . .AFR #8 40
CATAAAAA, THE by A. E. van Vogt. .s . . . . . FB #1 37
CATAAAA, THE by A. E. van Vogt. .s . . . MSS Nov 50 38
CATALYST PLANET by Raymond A. Palmer. .s . . . . . .
. . . . .TW Aug 38 65
CATALYST POISON by Malcolm Jameson. .s . . . .
. . . . ASF Apr 39 31
CATASTROPHE! by Edward E. Smith, Ph.D. . .a . . . .
. . . . ASF May 38 118
CATCH THAT RABBIT by Isaac Asimov. .s . . . .
. . . . ASF Feb 44 159
CATERPILLARS by E. F. Benson. .s . . . FFM Jun 47 116
CAT'S EYE by Harl Vincent (Schoepflin). .s . . . .
. . . . Amz Apr 34 10
CATS OF KADENZA by Don Wilcox. .n . . . FA Oct 44 10
CATSPAW, THE by George O. Smith. .nt . . . .
. . . . ASF Sep 48 7
CAUPHUL, THE CITY UNDER THE SEA by George
   Cookman Watson. .s. . . . . .Amz Jan 29 918
CAUTION: DEAD MAN AT WORK by Arthur T.
   Harris h ps. .s . . . . Amz Feb 47 150
CAVE, THE by Beatrice Grimshaw. .s . . . . . AFR #13 13
CAVE, THE by P. Schuyler Miller. .s . . . . .ASF Jan 43 83
CAVE CITY OF HEL by Richard S. Shaver. .nt . . . . . .
. . . . Amz Sep 45 6
CAVE DWELLERS OF SATURN by John Wiggin . . . . .
. .nt . . . . .PS Win 39 96
CAVE OF HORROR, THE by Captain S. P. Meek . . . . .
. .s .ASF Jan 30 32
CAVE OF THE INVISIBLE, THE by James Francis
   Dwyer. .s . . . . AFR #14 40
CAVEMAN MEETS BLONDE by Russell Storm ps
   (Robert Moore Williams). .s . . . . Amz May 42 152
CAVERN OF THE SHINING ONES, THE by Hal
   K. Wells. .s . . . . ASF Nov 32 149
CAVERN OF THE SHINING POOL, THE by
   Arthur Leo Zagat. .s. . . . . TW Oct 37 66
CAVERN OF THUNDERS by Harl Vincent
   (Schoepflin). .nt . . . . .Amz Jul 33 345
CAVERN WORLD, THE by James P. Olsen. .s . . . .
. . . . .ASF Jun 30 310
CAVERNS OF HORROR by Laurence Manning. .s . . . .
. . . . WS Mar 34 850
CAVERNS OF ITH by Basil Wells. .s. . . . . FB #2 22
CAVERNS OF TIME by Carlos McCune. .n . . . .
. . . . .FA Jul 43 108

Title. .Author. .Length . . . . Magazine. .Date. .Page No.

CAVES OF PELE, THE by John M. Corbett. .s . . . . . .
. . . . Amz May 32 152
CELESTIAL LANDFALL by Walt Sheldon. .s . . . .
. . . . .OTWA Dec 50 90
CELESTIAL PIONEERS by J. G. Ohmert. .nt . . . .
. . . . AQ Spr-Sum 33 538
CELESTIAL VISITOR, THE by Lilith Lorraine. .s . . . .
. . . . WS Mar 35 1190
CENSUS by Clifford D. Simak. .nt . . . . . . ASF Sep 44 6
CENSUS TAKER by Frank Belknap Long. .s . . . .
. . . . UK Apr 42 100
CENTAUR, THE by J. Allen St. John. .bacover pic . . . .
. . . . FA May 43
CENTAURUS II by A. E. van Vogt. .nt . . . . ASF Jun 47 6
CENTRAL FIGURE, THE by H. Russell Wakefield . . . .
. .s . . . . AFR #1 116
CEPHEID PLANET by R. R. Winterbotham. .s . . . . . .
. . . . SSS Nov 40 8
CEREBRAL LIBRARY, THE by David H.
Keller, M.D. . .s . . . . Amz May 31 116
CERES AFFAIR, THE by Kent Casey. .s . . . .
. . . . .ASF Oct 38 137
CHAIN OF AFORGOMON, THE by Clark Ashton
Smith. .s . . . . AFR #12 34
CHALICE OF CIRCE, THE by Willard Hawkins. .nt . . .
. . . . FA Apr 50 64
CHALLENGE, THE by Robert Moore Williams. .s . . . . .
. . . . TW Oct 50 69
CHALLENGE OF ATLANTIS, THE by Arthur J.
Burks. .s . . . . TW Oct 38 50
CHALLENGE OF THE COMET, THE by Arthur K.
Barnes. .s . . . . WS Feb 32 1036
CHAM OF THE HILLS by Charles R. Tanner. .nt . . . . .
. . . . .SSS Aug 42 106
CHAMBER OF LIFE, THE by G. Peyton
Wertenbaker. .s . . . . Amz Oct 29 628
CHAMELEON MAN, THE by William P. McGivern . . . .
. .s . . . . .Amz Jan 43 210
CHAMELEON PLANET by Polton Cross ps (John
Russell Fearn). .nt . . . . .Ash Feb 40 6
CHAMPION FOR TIBET, A by Millen Cooke. .a . . . . . .
. . . . Amz May 46 148
CHAMPLIN FIGHTS THE PURPLE GOD by Don
Wilcox. .nt . . . . Amz Sep 40 28
CHANCE OF A GHOST, THE by Robert Bloch. .s . . . .
. . . . FA Mar 43 142
CHANCE REMARKS by J. J. Coupling ps (John R.
Pierce). .a . . . . .ASF Oct 49 104
CHANGE by Roby Wentz. .s . . . . UK Oct 43 135
CHANGE FOR THE BITTER by Lee Francis
h ps. .s . . . . FA Apr 45 100
CHANGELING by Ray Bradbury. .s . . . . . SSS Jul 49 98
CHANGELING, THE by Arthur J. Burks. .nt . . . .
. . . . UK Apr 39 73
CHANGELING, THE by A. E. van Vogt. .n . . . .
. . . . ASF Apr 44 7

Title. .Author. .Length . . . . Magazine. .Date. .Page No.

CHANGER OF HISTORY, THE by Alexander
Samalman. .s . . . . .TW Feb 38 58
CHANNEL TUNNEL, THE by Willy Ley. .a . . . .
. . . . .SS Nov 50 135
CHAOS by Polton Cross ps (John Russell
Fearn). .s . . . . SS Nov 47 77
CHAOS, CO-ORDINATED by John MacDougal
ps (James Blish & Robert W. Lowndes). .nt . . . .
. . . . ASF Oct 46 36
CHAPTER FROM THE BEGINNING, A by
A. M. Phillips. .s . . . . ASF Mar 40 84
CHARIOT OF DEATH by Don Wilcox. .n . . . .
. . . . FA Aug 43 66
CHARMING MR. GRANT, THE by Lester
Barclay. .s . . . . FA Nov 48 134
CHAT WITH THE SKIPPER CONCERNING
CLAIRVOYANCE, A (WEIRD TRAVEL
TALES) by Bob Davis. .ss . . . . FFM Jan 40 78
CHECKMATE TO DEMOS by H. B. Hickey ps
(Herb Livingston). .s . . . . FA Mar 49 118
CHEMICAL BRAIN, THE by Francis Flagg ps
(George Henry Weiss). .s . . . . ToW Win 38 53
CHEMICAL MAGNET, THE by Victor Thaddeus . . . . .
. .s . . . . Amz Aug 27 486
CHEMICAL MURDER, THE by Eando Binder
ps (Earl Binder & Otto Binder). .s . . . . . Amz Apr 37 91
CHEMICAL PLANT by Ian Williamson. .s . . . .
. . . . .NW Win 50 82
CHEMICAL VAMPIRE, THE by Lee Francis
h ps. .s. . . . . Amz Mar 49 8
CHEMISTRY MURDER CASE, THE by Miles J.
Breuer, M.D. . .s . . . . Amz Oct 35 73
CHESS AND DOUBLE CHESS by John &
Dorothy de Courcy. .s . . . . Amz Mar 47 40
CHESSBOARD OF MARS by Eando Binder ps
(Otto Binder). .nt . . . . TW Jun 37 72
CHICAGO INVADED—BY THE MEN FROM
MARS. .a . . . . Amz Mar 41 130
CHICAGO 2042 A. D. by Paul Bolton. .s . . . .
. . . . WS Oct 32 416
CHILD IS CRYING, A by John D. MacDonald . . . .
. .s . . . . TW Dec 48 131
CHILD OF NEPTUNE (A Baby On Neptune) by Miles
J. Breuer & Clare Winger Harris. .s . . . . ToW Spr 41 54
CHILD OF POWER by Wyndham Parkes ps (John
Beynon Harris). .s . . . . .Fant #3 39 89
CHILD OF THE GODS by A. E. van Vogt. .nt . . . .
. . . . ASF Aug 46 145
CHILD OF THE GREEN LIGHT by Leigh
Brackett. .s. . . . . .SSS Feb 42 44
CHILD OF THE STARS by Raymond Z. Gallun . . . . . .
. .nt . . . . ASF Apr 36 10
CHILD OF THE SUN by Leigh Brackett. .s . . . .
. . . . PS Spr 42 102
CHILD OF VOID by Margaret St. Clair. .s . . . .
. . . . .SSS Nov 49 62

Title. .Author. .Length . . . . Magazine. .Date. .Page No.

CHILDREN OF THE "BETSY B." by Malcolm
    Jameson. .s. . . . . ASF Mar 39 109
CHILDREN OF THE GODS by D. D. Sharp. .s . . . .
    . . . . TW Jun 43 35
CHILDREN OF THE GOLDEN AMAZON by Thornton.
    Ayre ps (John Russell Fearn). .nt . . . . . . FA Apr 43 8
CHILDREN OF THE GREAT MAGMA by Walter
    Kateley. .nt . . . . Amz Aug 33 412
CHILDREN OF THE LENS by E. E. Smith. .n 4 pt . . . .
    . . . . ASF Nov 47 7
CHILDREN OF THE RAY by J. Harvey Haggard. .s . . .
    . . . . WS Mar 34 826
                                              FSQ Spr 50 142
CHILDREN OF THE SUN by Edmond Hamilton . . . . .
    . .s . . . . SS May 50 98
CHILDREN OF ZEUS by E. A. Grosser. .s . . . .
    . . . . Ash Jun 40 64
CHILDREN'S HOUR, THE by Lawrence O'Donnell
    ps (C. L. Moore). .nt . . . . ASF Mar 44 86
CHILDREN'S ROOM, THE by Raymond F. Jones . . . .
    . .nt . . . . FA Sep 47 136
CHILD'S PLAY by Alice-Mary Schnirring. .s . . . . . .
    . . . . AFR #9 110
CHILD'S PLAY by William Tenn ps (Philip Klass) . . . .
    . .nt . . . . ASF Mar 47 139
CHILLY, BUT CHEERING by Jep Powell. .a . . . .
    . . . . FA Feb 42 38
CHIMERA WORLD by Wilbur S. Peacock. .s . . . .
    . . . . .PS Win 44 62
CHOICE, THE by Ralph Maughan. .ss . . . Amz Jun 34 101
CHORE FOR A SPACEMAN by Walt Sheldon. .s . . . . .
    . . . . TW Dec 50 97
CHRISTMAS ON GANYMEDE by Isaac Asimov. .s . . . .
    . . . . SS Jan 42 83
CHRISTMAS ON MARS by William Morrison
    ps (Joseph Samachson). .s . . . . TW Dec 41 83
CHRISTMAS TREE by Christopher Youd. .s . . . .
    . . . . ASF Feb 49 155
CHRISTOPHER CRISSOM'S CRAVAT by David
    Wright O'Brien. .nt . . . . FA May 46 70
CHROMIUM HELMET, THE by Theodore
    Sturgeon. .nt . . . . .ASF Jun 46 132
CHRONICLER, THE by A. E. van Vogt. .n 2 pt . . . . . .
    . . . . ASF Oct 46 7
"CHRONOKINESIS OF JONATHAN HULL," THE
    by Anthony Boucher ps (William Anthony
    Parker White). .s .s . . . . .ASF Jun 46 118
CHRYSALIS by Ray Bradbury. .s . . . . . . .Amz Jul 46 70
CHRYSALIS, THE by P. Schuyler Miller. .s . . . .
    . . . . ASF Apr 36 44
CHRYSALIS by L. Major Reynolds ps (Louise
    Leipiar). .s . . . . FA Dec 50 80
CINEROBOT, INC. by Robert Arthur. .s . . . .
    . . . . TW Feb 43 105
CIRCE OF SCIENCE, A by Stanton A. Coblentz. .s . . . .
    . . . . Amz May 30 170

Title. .Author. .Length . . . . Magazine. .Date. .Page No.

CIRCLE OF CONFUSION by Wesley Long ps
    (George O. Smith). .nt . . . . ASF Mar 44 45
CIRCLE OF YOUTH by Frank Belknap Long. .s . . . . .
    . . . . .SSS Feb 43 72
CIRCLE OF ZERO, THE by Stanley G. Weinbaum . . . .
    . .s . . . . .TW Aug 36 48
                                              SS Sep 47 70
CIREESIANS, THE by Norman Lazenby. .s . . . .
    . . . . .NW #4 49 27
CITADEL OF DEATH, THE by Carl Selwyn. .nt . . . . .
    . . . . PS Fal 44 72
CITADEL OF FEAR, THE by Francis Stevens. .n . . . . .
    . . . . .FFM Feb 42 6
CITADEL OF HATE by Lee Francis h ps. .nt . . . .
    . . . . FA Jun 43 154
CITADEL OF LOST AGES, THE by Leigh
    Brackett. .nt . . . . .TW Dec 50 9
CITADEL OF LOST SHIPS by Leigh Brackett. .nt . . . .
    . . . . .PS Mar 43 44
CITADEL OF SCIENCE by Arthur J. Burks. .s . . . . . .
    . . . . TW Jan 41 14
CITADEL OF THE GREEN DEATH by Emmett
    McDowell . .nt . . . . PS Fal 48 4
CITADEL OF THOUGHT by James Blish. .s . . . .
    . . . . Sti Feb 41 38
CITIES IN THE AIR by Edmond Hamilton. .n 2 pt . . . .
    . . . . .AW Nov 29 390
CITIES OF ARDATHIA, THE by Francis Flagg ps
    (George Henry Weiss). .nt . . . . Amz Mar 32 1064
CITIES OF TOMORROW by Julian S. Krupa . . . .
    . .bacover pic . . . . Amz Aug 39
CITY by Clifford D. Simak. .nt . . . . ASF May 44 136
CITY AT WORLD'S END by Edmond Hamilton. .n. . . .
    . . . . SS Jul 50 11
CITY IN THE SOFA, THE by Cecil Corwin ps
    (Cyril Kornbluth). .s . . . . Cos Jul 41 54
CITY INSIDE THE MOON by Frank R. Paul
    . .bacover pic . . . . Amz Oct 41
CITY OF ERIC by Quien Sabe. .s . . . . AQ Spr 29 270
CITY OF GLASS by Noel Loomis. .n . . . . . . SS Jul 42 12
CITY OF LOST SOULS by Ralph Milne Farley ps
    (Roger Sherman Hoar) & Al. P. Nelson. .nt. . . . . . .
    . . . . .FA Jul 41 66
CITY OF MACHINES by Frank Edward Arnold . . . . . .
    . .nt . . . . .ToW Sum 39 54
CITY OF MUMMIES, THE by Edgar Rice
    Burroughs. .nt. . . . . Amz Mar 41 8
CITY OF OBLIVION, THE by Bradner Buckner. .s . . . .
    . . . . .Amz May 39 56
CITY OF SAND by Berkeley Livingston. .n . . . .
    . . . . FA Mar 49 52
CITY OF SINGING CUBES, THE by Bryce Walton . . . .
    . .s . . . . .OTWA Dec 50 42
CITY OF SINGING FLAME (The City of the
    Singing Flame) by Clark Ashton Smith. .nt. . . . . . .
    . . . . ToW Spr 40 6

Title. .Author. .Length . . . . Magazine. .Date. .Page No.

CITY OF SLEEP, THE by Laurence Manning. .s . . . . . .
. . . . WS May 33 926
CITY OF THE CORPORATE MIND by Nat
Schachner. .nt. . . . . ASF Dec 39 45
CITY OF THE COSMIC RAYS by Nat Schachner . . . . .
. .nt . . . . ASF Jul 39 47
CITY OF THE DEAD by Augusta Groner. .n . . . .
. . . . FFM Apr 48 8
CITY OF THE DEAD by G. M. Martin. .nt. . . . .
. . . . Amz Jan 50 38
CITY OF THE FUTURE by Frank R. Paul. . . . .
. .bacover pic . . . . Amz Apr 42
CITY OF THE LIVING DEAD, THE by Laurence
Manning & Fletcher Pratt. .s . . . . SW May 30 1100
SS Jul 40 94
AFR #2 108
CITY OF THE LIVING FLAME by Henry Hasse. . . . . .
. .nt . . . . PS Aug 42 92
CITY OF THE ROCKET HORDE by Nat
Schachner. .nt. . . . . ASF Dec 37 112
CITY OF THE SINGING FLAME by Clark Ashton
Smith. .nt . . . . WS Jul 31 202
(as CITY OF SINGING FLAME) . . . . . . ToW Spr 40 6
SS Jan 41 98
CITY OF WONDER, THE by E. Charles Vivian. .n . . . .
. . . . FFM Oct 47 6
CITY ON JUPITER, A by Frank R. Paul . . . .
. .bacover pic . . . . Amz Feb 41
CITY ON MARS, A by Frank R. Paul. .bacover pic . . . .
. . . . Amz Dec 40
CITY OF NEPTUNE, A by Frank R. Paul . . . .
. .bacover pic . . . . Amz Mar 41
CITY ON PLUTO, A by Frank R. Paul. .bacover pic . . .
. . . . Amz Jun 41
CITY ON THE CLOUD, THE by L. Taylor Hansen . . . .
. .s . . . . WS Oct 30 426
CITY ON URANUS, A by Frank R. Paul. . . . .
. .bacover pic . . . . Amz Apr 41
CITY ON VENUS, A by Frank R. Paul . . . .
. .bacover pic . . . . Amz Jan 41
CITY THAT WALKED, THE by Ed Earl Repp. .s . . . . .
. . . . Amz Mar 39 112
CITY UNDER THE SEA, THE by Duane W. Rimel . . . .
. .s . . . . Fut Jul 40 55
CITY UNDER THE SEA by Nat Schachner. .s . . . .
. . . . FA Sep 39 58
CLAGGETT'S FOLLY by Hugh Raymond ps (John
Michel). .s . . . . Fut Dec 42 53
CLAIMED by Francis Stevens. .n . . . . FFM Apr 41 6
CLANE series See A. E. VAN VOGT author
CLASH BY NIGHT by Lawrence O'Donnell ps
(C. L. Moore). .nt . . . . ASF Mar 43 9
CLASP OF DOOM, THE by Eugene De Reszke. .s . . . . .
. . . . AD Oct 30 870
CLAVILUX by Robert A. Wait. .s . . . . . Amz Jun 29 214
CLEAN-UP by Cleve Cartmill. .s . . . . UK Oct 43 145

CLEON OF YZDRAL by P. Schuyler Miller. .s . . . .
. . . . Amz Jul 31 320
CLERICAL ERROR by Clifford D. Simak. .s . . . .
. . . . ASF Aug 40 95
CLIMATE DISORDERED by Carter Sprague ps
(Sam Merwin, Jr.). .ss. . . . . .SS Mar 48 101
CLIMATE—INCORPORATED by Wesley Long ps
(George O. Smith). .s . . . . .TW Aug 48 78
CLIMATICA by John Russell Fearn. .nt . . Fant #2 39 100
CLIPPER OF THE CLOUDS, THE or ROBUR THE
CONQUEROR by Jules Verne. .n 2 pt. . . . .
. . . . Amz Dec 27 826
CLOAK, THE by Robert Bloch. .s . . . . . . .UK May 39 75
UK 48 48
CLOAK OF AESIR by Don A. Stuart ps (John W.
Cambell, Jr.). . .nt. . . . . ASF Mar 39 9
CLOAK OF SATAN by Frank Patton h ps. .s . . . .
. . . . FA Dec 43 136
CLOSED DOORS by A. B. L. Macfadyen, Jr. . .s . . . . .
. . . . UK Mar 39 137
CLOUDS OF DEATH by Louis Buswell. .s . . . .
. . . . Amz Jun 29 272
CLOUDS OVER URANUS by R. R. Winterbotham . . . .
. .s . . . . ASF Mar 37 111
CLUB HOUSE, THE dept of fanzine reviews and
fanews conducted by Rog Phillips. Quite regular
from . . . . Amz Mar 48
CLUB OF THE DAMNED by Clee Garson ps (David . . .
Wright O'Brien). .s . . . . FA Feb 43 202
CLUTCH OF MORPHEUS by Larry Sternig. .s . . . . . .
. . . . TW Win 46 92
CODE, THE by Lawrence O'Donnell ps (C. L.
Moore). .nt. . . . . .ASF Jul 45 7
CODE OF THE SPACEWAYS by Clifton B. Kruse. . . . .
. .s . . . . ASF Jul 36 106
CODED SPEECH by C. Rudmore. .a. . . . ASF Aug 49 134
COEFFICIENT X by A. Bertram Chandler. .s . . . .
. . . . NW Spr 50 80
COFFIN OF HOPE by Lee Francis h ps. .nt . . . .
. . . . .Amz Jul 49 28
COFFIN OF LIFE AND DEATH by Robert Wade. . . . .
. .s . . . . FA Apr 48 100
COFFIN SHIP, THE by Anthony Gilmore ps (Harry
Bates & D. W. Hall). .nt . . . . ASF Oct 33 66
COFFINS TO MARS by Raymond Z. Gallun. .nt . . . . .
. . . . TW Jun 50 88
COILS OF TIME by P. Schuyler Miller. .nt . . . .
. . . . .ASF May 39 9
COKIE GOES TREASURE HUNTING by Berkeley
Livingston. .s . . . . Amz Mar 44 172
COLD by Nat Schachner. .nt . . . . ASF Mar 40 9
COLD COMET, THE by Ralph Stranger. .s . . . .
. . . . .Fant #3 39 69
COLD FRONT by Hal Clement ps (Harry Clement
Stubbs). .nt . . . . .ASF Jul 46 7
COLD GHOST by Chester S. Geier. .s . . . . Amz Nov 48 26

Title. .Author. .Length . . . . Magazine. .Date. .Page No.

COLD LIGHT by William Lemkin, Ph.D. . .s . . . .
. . . . Amz Nov 29 706
COLD LIGHT by Captain S. P. Meek. .s . . . .
. . . . ASF Mar 30 297
COLD WAR by Henry Kuttner. .s . . . . . . TW Oct 49 102
COLD WAR by Kris Neville. .s . . . . .ASF Oct 49 121
COLLECTOR, THE by Mallory Kent ps (Robert W.
Lowndes). .ss . . . . Fut Oct 42 97
COLLECTOR'S ITEM by Frank B. Long. .s . . . .
. . . . ASF Oct 47 68
COLLEGE OF SCIENTIFICTIONAL KNOWLEDGE by.
Forrest J. Ackerman quiz dept. . . . . . .FanS Nov 50 80
COLLISION COURSE by Ross Rocklynne. .s . . . . .
. . . . SSS Jan 41 8
COLLISION IN SPACE by Festus Pragnell. .nt . . . . .
. . . . .Amz Jul 43 126
COLLISION ORBIT by Clyde Beck. .s . . . . PS Sum 50 48
COLLISION ORBIT by Will Stewart ps (Jack
Williamson). .nt. . . . . ASF Jul 42 80
COLLOIDAL NEMESIS, THE by Harl Vincent
(Schoepflin). .s . . . . Amz Dec 29 800
COLONIAL by Christopher Youd. .nt. . . . ASF Apr 49 81
COLONIZING THE OCEAN BOTTOM by Julian S.
Krupa. .bacover. . . . . Amz Apr 40
COLONY OF THE UNFIT by Manfred A. Carter . . . . .
. .nt .PS Win 44 84
COLOR OF SPACE, THE by Charles R. Tanner. .ss . . . .
. . . . SW Mar 30 892
COLORFUL CHARACTER, THE by L. Sprague de
Camp. .s . . . . TW Dec 49 133
COLOSSUS by S. J. Byrne. .n . . . . .OW May 50 80
COLOSSUS II by S. J. Byrne. .nt . . . . OW Jul 50 22
COLOSSUS III by S. J. Byrne. .n . . . . OW Sep 50 96
COLOSSUS by Donald Wandrei. .nt . . . . . .ASF Jan 34 41
COLOSSUS ETERNAL by Donald Wandrei. .nt . . . . . .
. . . . ASF Dec 34 50
COLOSSUS FROM SPACE by Frank Johnson. .s . . . . .
. . . . TW Oct 40 44
COLOSSUS OF CHAOS by Nelson S. Bond. .nt . . . . . .
. . . . PS Nov 42 2
COLOSSUS OF MAIA, THE by Lawrence Woods
ps (Robert W. Lowndes & Donald A. Wollheim) . . . .
. .s . . . . Cos Jul 41 45
COLOUR OUT OF SPACE, THE by H. P.
Lovecraft. .s . . . . Amz Sep 27 556
FFM Oct 41 98
COLUMBUS OF SPACE, A by Garrett P. Serviss. . . . .
. .n 3 pt. . . . . Amz Aug 26 388
COLUMBUS WAS A DOPE by Robert A. Heinlein . . . .
. .ss . . . . SS May 47 67
COLUMN OF LIFE, THE by Lester Barclay. .s . . . . . .
. . . . FA Dec 49 120
COME ALONG WITH ME by S. M. Tenneshaw. . . . . .
h ps. .nt. . . . . FA Sep 47 78
COME HOME FROM EARTH by Edmond
Hamilton. .s . . . . .TW Feb 47 91

COME INTO MY GARDEN by John & Dorothy
de Courcy. .s . . . . FA Nov 47 84
COME TO MARS by Walter Kubilius. .s . . . .Ash Feb 43 78
COMEDY OF ERAS, THE by Kelvin Kent ps (Henry
Kuttner). .s . . . . TW Sep 40 32
COMET, THE by K. Raymond. .s . . . . . . ASF Feb 37 98
COMET DOOM, THE by Edmond Hamilton. .s . . . . . .
. . . . .Amz Jan 28 926
ToW Aut 39 4
COMET FROM YESTERDAY by Lee Francis h ps . . . .
. .nt . . . . Amz Mar 45 106
COMET KINGS, THE by Edmond Hamilton. .n . . . . . .
. . . . .CF Sum 42 11
COMET PASSES, A by Eando Binder ps (Otto
Binder). .s . . . . TW Oct 37 102
COMET-SEEKER HOAX, THE (FANTASTIC
HOAXES) by Julius Schwartz. .a . . . . . .FA May 40 38
COMETEERS, THE by Jack Williamson. .n 4 pt . . . . . .
. . . . ASF May 36 6
COMET'S CAPTIVE by Raymond Z. Gallun. .s . . . . . .
. . . . ASF Jun 37 35
COMING ATTRACTION by Fritz Leiber. .s . . . .
. . . . GSF Nov 50 75
COMING OF THE GODS by Chester Whitehorn. .s . . . .
. . . . PS Sum 45 107
COMING OF THE GIANT GERMS by Ray
Cummings. .nt . . . . Uc Apr 41 8
COMING OF THE ICE, THE by G. Peyton
Wertenbaker. .s . . . . Amz Jun 26 232
COMING OF THE WHITE WORM, THE by Clark
Ashton Smith. .s . . . . .Sti Apr 41 105
COMMAND, THE by L. Sprague de Camp. .s . . . .
. . . . ASF Oct 38 70
COMMAND by Bernard I. Kahn. .nt . . . . .ASF Jan 47 121
COMMAND PERFORMANCE by Berkeley
Livingston. .s . . . . Amz Nov 46 142
COMMON SENSE by Robert Heinlein. .n . . . .
. . . . .ASF Oct 41 102
COMMUNICATIONS by Edwin James ps (James E.
Gunn). .nt .SS Sep 49 100
COMPANIONS OF SIRIUS by William Morrison
ps (Joseph Samachson). .s . . . . CF Win 43 106
COMPANY OR THE WEATHER, THE by Miles J.
Breuer, M.D. . .ss . . . . Amz Jun 37 51
COMPENSATION by C. V. Tench. .s . . . .
. . . . .ASF Jan 30 92
COMPETITION by E. M. Hull. .s . . . . ASF Jun 43 44
COMPLEAT WEREWOLF, THE by Anthony
Boucher ps (William Anthony Parker White). .nt . . . .
. . . . UK Apr 42 68
UK 48 77
COMPLETELY AUTOMATIC by Theodore
Sturgeon. .s . . . . ASF Feb 41 84
COMPLIMENTS OF THE AUTHOR by Henry
Kuttner. .nt . . . . UK Oct 42 111
COMPROMISE by H. B. Fyfe. .s . . . . ASF Dec 50 51

Title. .Author. .Length . . . . Magazine. .Date. .Page No.

CONCEALMENT by A. E. van Vogt. .s . . . ASF Sep 43 88
CONCRETE MIXER, THE by Ray Bradbury. .s . . . . . .
. . . . TW Apr 49 94
CONDITION OF BEAUTY, A by John D.
MacDonald. .s . . . . .SS Sep 49 79
CONES by Frank Belknap Long. .nt . . . . ASF Feb 36 122
CONFESSION OF DR. DeKALB by Stanton A.
Coblentz. .s . . . . .ASF Jan 34 31
CONFESSIONS OF A MECHANICAL MAN by
Buzz-Bolt Atomcracker ps (Don Wilcox). .nt . . . . . .
. . . . Amz May 47 36
CONFORMITY EXPECTED by H. B. Fyfe. .s. . . . . . .
. . . . ASF Mar 50 140
CONFUSION CARGO by Kenneth Putnam. .s . . . .
. . . . .PS Spr 48 84
CONGRESS IS TOO BUSY (FOR THE ATOM) by
W. B. deGraeff ps (Groff Conklin). .a . .ASF Sep 46 100
CONJURE WIFE by Fritz Leiber, Jr. . .n . . . UK Apr 43 9
CONQUEROR, THE by Charles I. Marks. .s . . . .
. . . . FA Apr 45 184
CONQUERORS, THE by David H. Keller, M.D. . . . . .
. .n 2 pt . . . . SW Dec 29 582
CONQUERORS' ISLE by Nelson Bond. .s . . . . AFR #4 48
CONQUEROR'S VOICE, THE by Robert Castle ps
(Edmond Hamilton). .s. . . . . SF Mar 39 35
CONQUEST by Joseph Gilbert. .ss . . . . . . TW Oct 42 87
CONQUEST by O. W. Hopkinson, Jr. . .s . . . .
. . . . ASF Sep 47 26
CONQUEST BY FIRE by Ward Hawkins. .nt . . . .
. . . . TW Apr 40 48
CONQUEST OF GOLA, THE by Leslie F. Stone ps
(Mrs. William Silberberg). .s. . . . . . . WS Apr 31 1278
CONQUEST OF LIFE, THE by Eando Binder ps
(Otto Binder). .s . . . . .TW Aug 37 28
                                        SS May 49 80
CONQUEST OF SPACE series See RENE LaFAYETTE
auth
CONQUEST OF THE DEEP, THE by Willy Ley. .a . . . .
. . . . TW Jun 38 96
CONQUEST OF THE EARTH, THE by Isaac R.
Nathanson. .s . . . . Amz Apr 30 42
CONQUEST OF THE IMPOSSIBLE, THE by Ralph
Milne Farley ps (Roger Sherman Hoar). .Guest ed . . .
. . . . SS Nov 39 89
CONQUEST OF THE MOON POOL, THE by
A. Merritt. .n 6 pt . . . . .FFM Nov 39 6
                       (complete). . . . . FN Sep 48 6
(combined with THE MOON POOL). .n 3 pt . . . . . .
. . . . Amz May 27 110
CONQUEST OF THE PLANETS—MOTHER WORLD
by John W. Campbell, Jr. . .n 3 pt. .(first installment
gives title as "CONTEST OF THE PLANETS"). . . . .
. . . . Amz Jan 35 11
CONQUEST OF TWO WORLDS, A by Edmond
Hamilton. .s . . . . WS Feb 32 1046
                                        SS Jan 48 70

Title. .Author. .Length . . . . Magazine. .Date. .Page No.

CONQUEST OF VENUS, the by Joseph J. Millard. . . . .
. .nt . . . . .TW Apr 43 56
CONQUISTADORES FROM BEYOND by Nicholas
E. Kenealy. .s . . . . TW Jan 40 78
CONROY DIARY, THE by Rene Lafayette ps (L. Ron
Hubbard). .s . . . . ASF May 49 134
CONSCIENCE, LTD. by Jack Williamson. .s . . . .
. . . . UK Aug 43 70
CONSPIRACY ON CALLISTO by James MacCreigh
ps (Frederik Pohl). .s . . . . .PS Win 43 38
CONSPIRATORS OF PHOBOS by Festus Pragnell . . . .
. .s . . . . Amz Jun 43 22
CONSTANT DRIP, THE by Berkeley Livingston. .s . . . .
. . . . Amz May 44 174
CONSULATE by William Tenn ps (Philip Klass). .s . . . .
. . . . TW Jun 48 56
CONTAGION by Katherine MacLean. .nt . . . .
. . . . .GSF Oct 50 114
CONTEST OF THE PLANETS, THE—MOTHER
WORLD by John W. Campbell, Jr. (title given
as "CONQUEST OF THE PLANETS" on 2nd &
3rd installments). .n 3 pt. . . . . Amz Jan 35 11
CONTINENTAL ENGINEERS by Russell J.
Hodgkins. .a . . . . .SF Jun 40 26
CONTRABAND COW, THE by L. Sprague de
Camp. .s . . . . ASF Jul 42 38
CONTRACT, THE by E. Mayne Hull. .nt . . . .
. . . . ASF Mar 44 7
CONTRACT FOR A BODY by Webb Marlowe ps
(J. Francis McComas). .nt . . . . .FA Jul 48 108
CONTRACT OF CARSON CARRUTHERS, THE by
William P. McGivern. .s. . . . . FA Jan 42 90
CONTRIBUTORS TO "FANTASY" dept of biog
sketches in pre-war Fantasy #1 38 thru #3 39
CONTROL DRUG, THE by Benson Herbert. .s. . . . . . .
. . . . WS Nov 34 668
CONTROLLER by Eric Frank Russell. .nt . . . .
. . . . ASF Mar 44 66
CONVERGENCE TO DEATH by M. C. Pease. .s . . . . . .
. . . . .ASF Jul 49 60
CONVOY IN SPACE by William P. McGivern. .nt . . . .
. . . . Amz Sep 42 96
CONVOY TO ATLANTIS by William P. McGivern. .n . .
. . . . Amz Nov 41 8
CO-OPERATE—OR ELSE by A. E. van Vogt. .nt . . . . .
. . . . ASF Apr 42 78
COPPER—CLAD WORLD, THE by Harl Vincent. .nt . . .
. . . . .ASF Sep 31 296
COPPERSMITH, THE by Lester del Rey. .s . . . .
. . . . UK Sep 39 110
CORAL EXPERIMENT, THE by Alexander Snyder. . . .
. .s . . . . Amz Sep 29 522
CORE, THE by S. D. Gottesman ps (Cyril
Kornbluth). .nt . . . . .Fut Apr 42 10
CORONAVISER, THE by Stanley R. Short. .a . . . .
. . . . .ASF Sep 40 132

Title. .Author. .Length . . . . Magazine. .Date. .Page No.

CORPORAL WEBBER'S LAST STAND by Leroy
Yerxa. .s . . . . FA Oct 42 118
CORPSE ON THE GRATING, THE by Hugh B. Cave. .s.
. . . . ASF Feb 30 187
CORPSE THAT LIVED, THE by E. D. Skinner. .s. . . .
. . . . .Amz Jan 30 950
CORRESPONDENCE COURSE by Raymond F.
Jones. .s. . . . . ASF Apr 45 61
CORSAIRS FROM THE COALSACK, THE by John
Michel (text) & J. Kubert (pics). .comic. . . . .
. . . . .OTWA Dec 50 51
COSMETICS by John D. MacDonald. .s. . . ASF Feb 48 68
COSMIC CALAMITY by W. Varick Nevins III. .ss . . . .
. . . . WS Jun 34 61
COSMIC CARAVAN by Ed Weston. .s . . . . TW Fal 45 60
COSMIC CASTAWAY by Carl Jacobi. .nt . . . PS Mar 43 2
COSMIC CHAIN, THE by Ford Smith ps (Oscar J.
Friend). .ss. . . . . .SS Win 45 96
COSMIC CLEANUP by H. B. Hickey ps (Herb
Livingston). .s. . . . . .Amz Jul 50 124
COSMIC CLOUD, THE by Bruno H. Burgel (tr fr
German by Konrad Schmidt & Fletcher Pratt). .n . . .
. . . . WQ Fal 31 6
COSMIC CLOUD, THE by Geo. C. Wallis. .s. . . . . . .
. . . . ToW Aut 41 37
COSMIC COCKTAIL by Siegfried Wagener. .s. . . . . .
. . . . WS Mar 36 908
COSMIC CUBE by Graph Waldeyer. .s. . . . .TW Aug 39 50
COSMIC DEFLECTOR, THE by Stanton A.
Coblentz. .s . . . . .Amz Jan 43 170
COSMIC DERELICT, THE by John Broome. .s. . . . . .
. . . . PS Sum 42 20
COSMIC DERELICT, THE by John Russell Fearn. . . . .
. .s .PS Spr 41 57
COSMIC DERELICT by Neil R. Jones. .nt . . . .
. . . . .Ash Feb 41 82
COSMIC DOODLER, THE by Carl Jacobi. .s . . . .
. . . . SS Fal 44 65
COSMIC ENCORES editorial & letter dept of
FSQ from . . . . .Spr 50 6
COSMIC ENGINEERS by Clifford D. Simak . . . .
. .n 3 pt. . . . . ASF Feb 39 45
COSMIC EXPRESS, THE by Jack Williamson. .s . . . . .
. . . . Amz Nov 30 752
COSMIC FEVER by A. R. Long. .s . . . . ASF Feb 37 138
COSMIC GUN, THE by Morrison F. Colladay. .s . . . . .
. . . . WS May 31 1410
COSMIC HISS, THE by Edmond Hamilton. .s. . . . . . .
. . . . TW Dec 38 90
COSMIC HORROR, THE by Richard F. Searight. .s. . . .
. . . . WS Aug 33 120
COSMIC HOTFOOT by Jack Vance. .s . . . . .SS Sep 50 82
COSMIC JACKPOT, THE by George O. Smith. .s . . . . .
. . . . TW Oct 48 109
COSMIC JOKE by Leslie F. Stone ps (Mrs.
William Silberberg). .s. . . . . .WS Jan 35 970

COSMIC JUGGERNAUT, THE by John Russell
Fearn. .s . . . . PS Sum 40 82
COSMIC MENACE by A. W. Bernal. .s . . .AQ Sum 31 408
COSMIC PANTOGRAPH, THE by Edmond
Hamilton. .s . . . . WS Oct 35 554
COSMIC POWER by John C. Dare. .s . . . . Amz Apr 31 28
COSMIC PUNCH OF LEFTY O'ROURKE, THE
by P. F. Costello h ps. .s . . . . Amz Feb 42 162
COSMIC QUEST by Edmond Hamilton. .s. . . . .
. . . . TW Oct 36 33
COSMIC RAY SHIELDS by Arthur McCann ps
(John W. Campbell, Jr.). .a . . . . ASF Nov 37 113
COSMIC RHYTHM by Harl Vincent. .nt . . . .
. . . . ASF Oct 34 94
COSMIC SISTERS, THE by Leroy Yerxa. .nt . . . .
. . . . Amz Sep 46 54
COSMIC STAGE by Robert Arthur. .s . . . . .SS Sep 39 90
                                        FSQ Spr 50 125
COSMIC STEEPLECHASE by Robert A. Wait. .nt . . . . .
. . . . Amz Apr 32 48
COSMIC TELETYPE by Carl Jacobi. .s . . . . TW Oct 38 35
COSMIC TRAGEDY by Thomas S. Gardiner. .ss . . . . .
. . . . Com Mar 41 116
COSMIC TRASH by Bob Olsen ps (Alfred John
Olsen, Jr.). .ss . . . . SW Apr 30 1014
COSMIC YO-YO by Ross Rocklynne. .s. . . . .
. . . . PS Sum 45 97
COSMO-TRAP, THE by D. L. James. .s . . . ASF Apr 36 98
COSMOPHOBIA by Millard Verne Gordon ps
(Donald A. Wollheim). .ss . . . . Sti Apr 41 60
COSMOS EYE by Martin Pearson ps (Donald A.
Wollheim). .ss. . . . . .SFQ Spr 41 101
COUNCIL OF DRONES, THE by W. K.
Sonnemann. .nt . . . . Amz Oct 36 41
COUNTER CHARM, THE by Margaret St. Clair. .s . . . .
. . . . .FFM Aug 49 110
COUNTERFEITER, THE by Robert Moore
Williams. .s. . . . . FA Nov 46 78
COUNTERFEITING THE GOLDEN AGE by
P. Schuyler Miller. .guest editorial. . . . . SS May 41 83
COUNTRY BEYOND THE CURVE, THE by . . . .
Walt Sheldon. .nt. . . . . Amz Oct 50 68
COUNTRY OF THE BLIND, THE by H. G. Wells . . . .
. .s . . . . Amz Dec 27 850
COUP D'ETAT by Oscar J. Friend. .s . . . . . TW Dec 39 68
COURT OF KUBLAI KHAN, THE by David V.
Reed ps (David Vern). .nt . . . . FA Mar 48 8
COVENTRY by Robert Heinlein. .nt . . . . .ASF Jul 40 56
CRAIG'S BOOK by Don Wilcox. .n . . . . . .FA Jul 43 10
CRASH BEAM by John Barret. .ss . . . . . . .PS Fal 47 37
CRASH ON VIAR by Joseph J. Millard. .s . . . .
. . . . TW Feb 41 113
CRATER CITY ON SATURN by Frank R. Paul . . . . . .
. .bacover pic . . . . Amz Aug 41
CRATER 17, NEAR TYCHO by Frank K. Kelly . . . . .
. .nt . . . . ASF Jun 34 68

Title. .Author. .Length . . . . Magazine. .Date. .Page No.

CRAWLING HORROR, THE by Thorp McClusky. .s . . .
. . . . .AFR #6 3
CRAWLING TERRORS by Edmund Schueler. .s . . . . .
. . . . Amz Jun 37 120
CREATURE OF ETERNITY by Maurice G. Hugi. .s . . .
. . . . .ToW Sum 39 89
CREATURES OF THE LIGHT by Sophie Wenzel
Ellis. .s . . . . ASF Feb 30 196
CREATURES OF VIBRATION by Harl Vincent
(Schoepflin). .s . . . . .ASF Jan 32 11
CREATURES THAT TIME FORGOT, THE by Ray
Bradbury. .nt . . . . PS Fal 46 94
CREEGAR DARES TO DIE by David Wright
O'Brien. .n . . . . FA Aug 42 88
CREEP, SHADOW! by A. Merritt. .n . . . . .FFM Aug 42 6
AMF Dec 49 10
CREST OF THE WAVE, THE by Jane Rice. .s . . . .
. . . . UK Jun 41 71
CRIME CLEAN-UP IN CENTER CITY by Robert
Moore Williams. .s . . . . FA Apr 42 54
CRIME CRUSHER, THE by Bob Olsen ps (Alfred
John Olsen, Jr.). .nt . . . . Amz Jun 33 255
CRIMES OF THE YEAR 2000 by Ray Cummings. . . . .
. .s . . . . FFM Dec 41 109
No. 2: The Television Alibi. .s . . . . . . FFM Jun 42 129
CRISIS! by Cecil Corwin ps (Cyril Kornbluth). .s . . . . .
. . . . SFQ Spr 42 130
CRISIS IN UTOPIA by Norman L. Knight. .n 2 pt. . . . .
. . . . .ASF Jul 40 9
CRISIS ON TITAN by James R. Adams. .s . . . .
. . . . .PS Spr 46 79
CRISIS WITH MARS, THE by Frank K. Kelly. .s . . . . .
. . . . WQ Fal 32 60
CRITICAL COMMENTARY letter dept of Fantasy . . . .
. . . .#2 39 & #3 39
CRITTERS, THE by Frank Belknap Long. .s . . . .
. . . . ASF Nov 45 127
CROM THE BARBARIAN by Gardner Fox (story) &
John Guinta (pictures). .comic. . . . . . OTW Jul 50 72
CROSS OF MERCRUX by Harry Walton. .nt . . . .
. . . . .SSS Feb 42 11
FN Nov 50 94
CROSSED WIRES by Leroy Yerxa. .nt . . . Amz Mar 44 80
CROSSROADS, THE by L. Ron Hubbard. .s . . . .
. . . . UK Feb 41 71
CROSSROADS OF SPACE by Arthur G. Stangland. . . .
. .s . . . . WS Sep 32 310
CROSSROADS OF THE UNIVERSE by William
Morrison ps (Joseph Samachson). .s . . . . . SS Jul 41 95
CROWDED COLONY, THE by Jay B. Drexel ps
(Jerome Bixby). .s . . . . .PS Fal 50 36
CRUCIBLE OF POWER, THE by Jack Williamson. . . . .
. .nt . . . . .ASF Feb 39 9
CRUISE OF THE JEUNE-HARDIE, THE or A
WINTER AMONG THE ICE by Jules Verne. .s . . . . .
. . . . AQ Win 33 74

Title. .Author. .Length . . . . Magazine. .Date. .Page No.

CRUMBLING WORLD, THE by Berkeley
Livingston. .s . . . . .FA Jan 50 138
CRUSADE ACROSS THE VOID by Dwight V.
Swain. .n . . . . Amz Oct 42 8
CRUSADER by Gene Ellerman ps (Basil Wells). .s . . . . .
. . . . FB #5 67
CRUSADERS OF SPACE by Paul Chadwick. .s . . . . . .
. . . . .AQ Fal-Win 32 384
CRY FROM THE ETHER, THE by Aladra
Septama. .nt . . . . AQ Spr 29 246
CRYPT-CITY OF THE DEATHLESS ONE by
Henry Kuttner. .nt . . . . PS Win 43 3
CRYSTAL AND A SPELL, A by Chester S.
Geier. .s . . . . FA May 46 108
CRYSTAL CIRCE, THE by Henry Kuttner. .s . . . .
. . . . Ash Jun 42 66
CRYSTAL EGG, THE by H. G. Wells. .s . . . .
. . . . Amz May 26 128
CRYSTAL EMPIRE, THE by Sidney D.
Berlow. .s . . . . .WS Jan 32 962
CRYSTAL INVADERS, THE by Joseph J.
Millard. .s . . . . TW Jan 41 78
CRYSTAL MENACE, THE by Geo. C. Wallis. .s . . . . . .
. . . . ToW Aut 39 73
CRYSTAL PLANETOIDS, THE by Stanton A.
Coblentz. .n . . . . .Amz May 42 78
CRYSTAL RAY, THE by Raymond Z. Gallun. .s . . . . .
. . . . .AW Nov 29 452
CRYSTAL WORLD by John L. Chapman. .s . . . .
. . . . .Cos Mar 41 47
CRYSTALIZED THOUGHT by Nat Schachner. .nt . . . .
. . . . ASF Aug 37 73
CRYSTALLINE SALVATION, THE by George H.
Scheer, B.Sc., E. E. . .nt . . . . Amz Jun 37 92
CRYSTALLINE SARCOPHAGUS by Richard S.
Shaver. .s . . . . .Amz May 47 10
CRYSTALLIS, GLASS CITY OF IO by Frank R.
Paul. .bacover . . . . .Amz Jul 41
CRYSTALS OF GROWTH by Charles H. Rector. .s . . . .
. . . . Amz Dec 27 874
CRYSTALS OF MADNESS by D. L. James. .s . . . .
. . . . TW Oct 36 107
CUBE FROM SPACE by Leigh Brackett. .nt . . . .
. . . . .SSS Aug 42 11
CUBE ROOT OF CONQUEST, THE by Rog Phillips
ps (Roger P. Graham). .s . . . . Amz Oct 48 6
CUBIC CITY, THE by Louis Tucker. .s . . . SW Sep 29 316
SS Sep 42 84
CUCKOO by P. Schuyler Miller. .nt . . . . . ASF May 44 77
CULT OF THE EAGLE by Berkeley Livingston. .nt. . . .
. . . . .FA Jul 46 146
CULT OF THE WITCH QUEEN, THE by Richard
S. Shaver & Bob McKenna. .n . . . . .Amz Jul 46 8
CULTURE by Jerry Shelton. .s . . . . ASF Sep 44 42
CUPID OF THE LABORATORY by William
Lemkin. .nt . . . . .Amz Aug 37 79

Title. .Author. .Length . . . . Magazine. .Date. .Page No.

CUPID TAKES A HOLIDAY by Duncan Farnsworth
ps (David Wright O'Brien). .nt . . . . FA Jun 42 28
CURE, THE by Lewis Padgett ps (Henry Kuttner &
C. L. Moore). .s . . . . ASF May 46 25
CURE FOR A YLITH by William Fitzgerald ps (Will
F. Jenkins). .s . . . . .SS Nov 49 113
CURFEW TOLLS, THE by J. T. M'Intosh ps (James
MacGregor). .s . . . . ASF Dec 50 42
CURIOUS CASE OF NORTON HOORNE, THE by
Ray Cummings. .s . . . . AFR #13 43
CURIOUS COAT, THE by David Wright O'Brien. .s. . . .
. . . . FA May 43 130
CURSE OF A THOUSAND KISSES, THE by Sax
Rohmer. .s . . . . .AFR #7 29
CURSE OF EL DORADO, THE by P. F. Costello
h ps. .s. . . . . FA Apr 44 176
CURSE OF MANY HANDS, THE by E. K. Jarvis
h ps. .nt. . . . . FA Apr 43 30
CURSE OF MONTEZUMA, THE by Ed Earl
Repp. .s. . . . . .Amz May 39 86
CURSE OF RA, THE by H. B. Hickey ps (Herb
Livingston). .nt. . . . . FA Apr 48 80
CURSE OF THE PHANTOM LEGION by
Helmar Lewis. .s . . . . FA Jun 44 190
CURSE OF YIG, THE by Zealia Brown Bishop. .s. . . . .
. . . . AFR #14 66
CURSED CAVERNS OF RA by Lee Francis h ps . . . . .
. .nt . . . . Amz Sep 45 64
CUSTOMS DECLARATION by Rex Graham. .nt . . . . .
. . . . ASF Mar 49 82
CUT OUT THIS AZTEC HEART (The Aztec
Heart) by Brice Purcell. .s . . . . .FanS Nov 50 111
CYBERNETIC BRAIN, THE by Charles Recour . . . . . .
. .s . . . . FA Dec 49 138
CYBERNETIC BRAINS, THE by Raymond F.
Jones. .n . . . . .SS Sep 50 11
CYBERNETICS by E. L. Locke. .a . . . . . ASF Sep 49 78
CYCLE by John L. Chapman. .s . . . . . . MSS Nov 40 106
CYCLOPEANS, THE by Richard S. Shaver. .nt . . . . . .
. . . . FA Jun 49 112
CYCLOPS, THE by Richard S. Shaver. .a. . . . .
. . . . Amz Jan 49 72
CZECH INTERLUDE by Vic Phillips. .s . . UK Dec 41 114

D

DAEDALUS AND ICARUS (THE LEMURIAN
DOCUMENTS No. 3) by J. Lewis Burtt. .s. . . . . . .
. . . . Amz May 32 144
DAEMON by C. L. Moore. .s . . . . FFM Oct 46 98
DAMES IS POISON by Kelvin Kent ps (Henry
Kuttner). .s . . . . TW Jun 42 92
DANCE OF A NEW WORLD by John D.
MacDonald. .s. . . . . .ASF Sep 48 133

DANCER IN THE CRYSTAL, THE by Francis
Flagg ps (George Henry Weiss). .s . . . . . AFR #11 111
DANCING GIRL OF GANYMEDE, THE by Leigh
Brackett. .s . . . . .TW Feb 50 62
DANGER by Irvin Lester & Fletcher Pratt. .s . . . .
. . . . .Amz Jul 29 364
DANGER FROM THE DEEP, THE by Ralph Milne
Farley ps (Roger Sherman Hoar). .s. . . ASF Aug 31 149
DANGER IN THE DARK by L. Ron Hubbard. .s . . . . .
. . . . .UK May 39 59
DANGER IS MY DESTINY by Robert Moore
Williams. .nt . . . . Amz Apr 50 136
DANGER: QUICKSAND by H. W. Guernsey ps (Howard
Wandrei).ss . . . . UK Sep 39 79
DANGEROUS DIMENSION, THE by L. Ron
Hubbard. .s . . . . ASF Jul 38 100
DARCONDRA by Richard Tooker. .s . . . . . TW Jun 37 63
DARING TRIP TO MARS, A by Max Valier. .s . . . . . .
. . . . .WS Jul 31 254
DARK AGE, THE by Clark Ashton Smith. .s . . . .
. . . . TW Apr 38 95
DARK ANGEL, THE by Henry Kuttner. .s . . . .
. . . . .SS Mar 46 89
DARK COMMAND by Frank Belknap Long. .s . . . . . .
. . . . .SS Win 45 66
DARK DAWN by Keith Hammond ps (Henry Kuttner
& C. L. Moore). .s . . . . .TW Aug 47 89
DARK ETERNITY by John Russell Fearn. .nt . . . .
. . . . ASF Dec 37 14
DARK HERITAGE, THE by Robert O. Kenyon
ps [Henry Kuttner). .s . . . . MSS Aug 38 73
DARK INVASION by Frederic Arnold
Kummer, Jr. . .n . . . . .MSS Aug 39 6
DARK MISSION by Lester del Rey. .s . . . . ASF Jul 40 117
DARK MOON by Charles W. Diffin. .nt. . . . .
. . . . ASF May 31 148
DARK REALITY by Robert Moore Williams. .s . . . . . .
. . . . Com Mar 41 88
DARK SIDE OF ANTRI, THE by Sewell Peaslee
Wright. .s. . . . . ASF Jan 31 9
DARK SUN by Raymond Z. Gallun. .s . . . .
. . . . TW Jun 37 56
DARK SWORDSMEN OF SATURN, THE by Neil
R. Jones. .s. . . . . PS Sum 40 106
DARK VISION by Frank Belknap Long. .s . . . .
. . . . UK Mar 39 107
DARK WATERS by M. Ludington Cain. .p . . . .
. . . . FFM Oct 47 111
DARK WISH by William P. McGivern. .s . . . .
. . . . FA Sep 48 78
DARK WORLD, THE by Henry Kuttner. .n . . . .
. . . . SS Sum 46 9
DARKER DRINK, THE by Leslie Charteris ps
(Leslie C. B. Lin). .s . . . . .TW Oct 47 66
DARKER LIGHT, THE by Cleve Cartmill. .s . . . .
. . . . SSS May 43 74

Title. .Author. .Length . . . . Magazine. .Date. .Page No.

DARKER THAN YOU THINK by Jack Williamson . . . .
. .n . . . . UK Dec 40 9
DARKNESS AND DAWN by George Allan England. . . .
. .n .FFM Aug 40 6
DARKSIDE DESTINY by James MacCreigh ps
(Frederik Pohl). .s . . . . .SSS Apr 49 75
DARWINIAN POOL ROOM by Isaac Asimov. .s . . . . .
. . . . .GSF Oct 50 152
DATE LINE by Benj. Miller ps (Noel Loomis). .s. . . . .
. . . . TW Oct 48 117
DATE TO REMEMBER, A by William F. Temple . . . .
. .s . . . . TW Aug 49 121
DAUGHTER OF DARKNESS by Ross Rocklynne . . . .
. .s . . . . .Ash Nov 41 68
DAUGHTER OF DESTINY by Lee Francis h ps . . . . .
. .nt . . . . Amz Apr 43 190
DAUGHTER OF GENGHIS KHAN by John York
Cabot ps (David Wright O'Brien). .nt. . . . . FA Jan 42 8
DAUGHTER OF LUNA by J. Lewis Burtt. .s . . . .
. . . . Amz Aug 37 65
DAUGHTER OF LUNA by J. Lewis Burtt (a different
story, a sequel to the above). .s . . . . . Amz Apr 38 91
DAUGHTER OF THE NIGHT by Richard S.
Shaver. .nt . . . . Amz Dec 48 8
DAUGHTER OF THE SNAKE GOD by John York
Cabot ps (David Wright O'Brien) & William P.
McGivern. .nt . . . . .FA May 42 8
DAUGHTER OF THOR, THE by Edmond
Hamilton. .nt . . . . FA Aug 42 10
DAUGTHERS OF DARKNESS by Harold Lawlor. . . . .
. .s . . . . FA Apr 43 86
DAUGHTERS OF DOOM by H. B. Hickey ps (Herb
Livingston). .s. . . . . Amz Apr 49 60
DAUGHTERS OF ETERNITY by James McCreigh
ps (Frederik Pohl). .s . . . . .Ash Mar 42 66
DAVY JONES' AMBASSADOR by Raymond Z.
Gallun. .nt . . . . ASF Dec 35 10
DAWN BREAKS RED, THE by John Brody. .nt . . . . .
. . . . NW Sum 50 4
DAWN OF FLAME by Stanley G. Weinbaum. .nt . . . . .
. . . . TW Jun 39 99
DAWN OF NOTHING by A. Bertram Chandler. .s . . . .
. . . . ASF Aug 48 46
DAWN OF THE CONQUEST OF SPACE, THE by
Willy Ley. .a. . . . . ASF Mar 37 104
DAWN TO DUSK by Eando Binder ps (Earl Binder
& Otto Binder). .n 3 pt . . . . WS Nov 34 646
DAWN WORLD ECHOES by Raymond Z. Gallun . . . . .
. .nt .ASF Jul 37 96
DAY AFTER TOMORROW by Roby Wentz. .nt . . . . .
. . . . ASF Mar 42 55
DAY HAS COME, THE by Walter Kubilius. .s . . . .
. . . . Sti Mar 42 26
                                              AFR #12 116
DAY IS DONE, THE by Lester del Rey. .s . . . .
. . . . ASF May 39 39

Title. .Author. .Length . . . . Magazine. .Date. .Page No.

DAY OF JUDGEMENT, THE by Victor A.
Endersby. .ss . . . . SW Apr 30 1015
DAY OF THE BEAST, THE by D. D. Sharp. .s . . . .
. . . . SW May 30 1094
                                              SS Fal 44 74
DAY OF THE BROWN HORDE, THE by Richard
Tooker. .n . . . . FFM Sep 44 8
DAY OF THE CLOUD, THE by Ross Rocklynne. .n . . .
. . . . SS Nov 42 15
DAY OF THE COMET by Frederic Arnold
Kummer, Jr. . .nt . . . . SSS Jul 40 6
DAY OF THE CONQUERORS, THE by Manly
Wade Wellman. .nt . . . . TW Jan 40 89
DAY OF THE DEEPIES, THE by Murray Leinster
ps (Will F. Jenkins). .s . . . . FFM Oct 47 98
DAY OF THE DRAGON, THE by Guy Endore. .nt . . . .
. . . . .AFR #2 50
DAY OF THE DRUID by Knut Enferd. .s . . . .
. . . . Amz Nov 48 126
DAY OF THE HUNTERS by Isaac Asimov. .s . . . .
. . . . .Fut Nov 50 74
DAY OF THE MICRO-MEN by Edmond Hamilton . . . .
. .s .SF Sep 41 50
DAY OF THE TITANS by Arthur K. Barnes. .s . . . . . .
. . . . TW Feb 40 46
DAY OF THE TITANS by Frederic A. Kummer, Jr. . . .
. .s .Fut Dec 41 74
DAY OF WRATH by Bjarne Kirchhoff. .s . . . .
. . . . PS Sum 48 69
DAY OFF by H. L. Gold. .s . . . . .UK Nov 39 79
DAY THE BOMB FELL, THE by Leslie A. Croutch. . . .
. .s . . . . Amz Nov 50 100
DAY THEY LANDED, THE by Paul Chadwick. .s . . . . .
. . . . MSS Nov 50 101
DAY TIME STOPPED MOVING, THE by Bradner
Buckner. .s . . . . Amz Oct 40 70
DAY TO COME, THE by Don Tracy. .nt . . .TW Nov 40 89
DAY WE CELEBRATE, THE by Nelson S. Bond. .s . . . .
. . . . .ASF Jan 41 42
DAYMARE by Frederic Brown. .nt . . . . . . TW Fal 43 15
DAYS OF CREATION by Brett Sterling h ps
(Joseph Samachson). .n . . . . .CF Spr 44 11
DE PROFUNDIS by Murray Leinster ps (Will F.
Jenkins). .s. . . . . TW Win 45 92
DE WOLFE OF WALL STREET by Kelvin Kent ps
(Arthur K. Barnes). .s. . . . . TW Feb 43 49
DEAD—AND EMBALMED! by Arthur McCann. .a . . . .
. . . . .ASF Jan 41 160
DEAD CENTER by S. D. Gottesman ps (Cyril
Kornbluth). .nt . . . . Sti Feb 41 6
DEAD CITY by Murray Leinster ps (Will F.
Jenkins). .nt . . . . .TW Sum 46 42
DEAD END by Malcolm Jameson. .s . . . . . TW Mar 41 91
DEAD HAND by Isaac Asimov. .n . . . . ASF Apr 45 6
DEAD KNOWLEDGE by Don A. Stuart ps (John
W. Campbell, Jr.). .nt . . . . .ASF Jan 38 44

Title. .Author. .Length. . . . . Magazine. .Date. .Page No.

DEAD MAN'S PLANET by R. R. Winterbotham. .s. . . .
. . . . PS Fal 41 62
DEAD MAN'S TALE by E. J. Bellin *h ps (text)* &
A. H. Johnson *(pics)*. .comic . . . . . . .OTWA Dec 50 59
DEAD ON ARRIVAL by Robert Morrison. .s. . . . . . .
. . . . Amz Aug 48 138
DEAD PLANET, THE by Edmond Hamilton. .s . . . . . .
. . . . .SS Spr 46 84
DEAD RUN by Cleve Cartmill. .s . . . . TW Feb 50 51
DEAD SAILOR, THE by A. L. Hodges. .ss. . . . . . .
. . . . Amz May 30 182
DEAD SPOT, THE by Jack Williamson. .s . . . .
. . . . MSS Nov 38 41
DEAD-STAR ROVER, THE by Robert Abernathy . . . .
.nt . . . . PS Win 49 2
DEAD STAR STATION by Jack Williamson. .s. . . . . .
. . . . ASF Nov 33 55
DEADLINE by Cleve Cartmill. .nt . . . . . ASF Mar 44 154
DEADLOCK by Lewis Padgett *ps (Henry Kuttner*
& C. L. Moore). .s . . . . ASF Aug 42 54
DEADLY DUST, THE by William Fitzgerald *ps (Will*
F. Jenkins). .nt . . . . .TW Aug 47 11
DEADLY HOST by Raymond F. Jones. .s . . . .
. . . . .ASF Sep 45 115
DEADLY PAINT OF HARLEY GALE, THE by Ed
Earl Repp. .nt . . . . Amz Apr 39 54
DEADLY SLIME, THE by Frederic Arnold
Kummer, Jr. . .s . . . . Amz Jun 39 62
DEADLY SWARM, THE by Edwin K. Sloat. .s . . . .
. . . . Ash Aug 40 6
DEADLY YAPPERS, THE by Max Overton. .s . . . .
. . . . FA Sep 42 92
DEAR DEVIL by Eric Frank Russell. .nt . . . .
. . . . OW May 50 6
DEATH AND THE DICTATOR by Raymond Z.
Gallun. .s. . . . . .SF Oct 40 42
DEATH AT THE OBSERVATORY by John Russell
Fearn. .s . . . . CF Sum 40 106
. . . . FSQ Spr 50 99
DEATH BETWEEN THE PLANETS by James D.
Perry. .s. . . . . WS Nov 33 342
DEATH BY FIRE by Amelia Reynolds Long. .s . . . . . .
. . . . .SF Mar 39 106
DEATH BY PROXY by Malcolm Jameson. .s . . . .
. . . . .SS Spr 45 79
DEATH BY RADIO by Edward Podolsky. .s . . . .
. . . . Amz Dec 32 809
DEATH-BY-RAIN by Ray Bradbury. .s. . . . PS Sum 50 35
DEATH CLOUD by David R. Daniels. .nt . . . .
. . . . ASF Feb 36 46
DEATH CLOUD, THE by Nat Schachner & Arthur
Zagat. .s. . . . . ASF May 31 256
DEATH CREEPS THE MOON by Wede. .s. . . . .
. . . . Amz Dec 36 102
DEATH CRYSTAL, THE by George O. Smith. .nt. . . . .
. . . . SSS May 50 14

DEATH DESERT by Robert Moore Williams. .s . . . . . .
. . . . Amz Nov 41 84
DEATH DIVES DEEP by Paul Ernst. .nt . . . .
. . . . .TW Aug 36 94
DEATH DRUM, THE by A. Hyatt Verrill. .nt. . . . . . .
. . . . Amz May 33 104
DEATH FROM ORION, THE by W. J.
Matthews. .s. . . . . .PS Win 48 66
DEATH FROM THE SEAS by Joseph Kennelly . . . . . .
. .s .WS Jan 31 810
DEATH FROM THE SKIES by A. Hyatt
Verrill. .nt . . . . Amz Oct 29 583
ToW Spr 41 4
DEATH FROM THE STARS by A. Rowley
Hilliard. .s . . . . WS Oct 31 612
SS Sep 41 98
DEATH FROM WITHIN by Sterling S.
Cramer. .s . . . . WS Jun 35 48
DEATH IN A DROP by Ralph W. Wilkins. .s . . . .
. . . . AD Oct 30 876
DEATH IN THE STRATOSPHERE by Henry J.
Kostkos. .s. . . . . Amz Aug 37 11
DEATH IN THE TUBEWAY by Stanton A.
Coblentz. .s . . . . .Amz Jan 39 116
DEATH IN TIME by William McCown. .s. . . . .
. . . . Amz May 43 212
DEATH IS THE PENALTY by Judith Merril . . . .
. .s .ASF Jan 49 56
DEATH MAKES A MISTAKE by P. F. Costello . . . . . .
. .s . . . . Amz Jan 43 70
DEATH OF A B.E.M. by Berkeley Livingston. .s. . . . . .
. . . . Amz Oct 48 18
DEATH OF ASTEROID 13, THE by William P.
McGivern. .s. . . . . .Amz Jul 48 78
DEATH OF IRON, THE by S. S. Held *(tr fr French*
by Fletcher Pratt). .n 3 pt . . . . WS Sep 32 294
DEATH OF THE MOON, THE by Alexander
Phillips. .s . . . . Amz Feb 29 1024
DEATH ON THE SIDERITE by D. D. Sharp. .s . . . . . .
. . . . .TW Feb 42 93
DEATH OVER CHICAGO by Robert Moore
Williams. .nt . . . . FA Jan 40 30
DEATH PLAYS A GAME by David V. Reed
ps (David Vern). .nt . . . . FA Dec 41 10
DEATH PROTOZOAN, THE by Clifton B.
Kruse. .s . . . . Amz Feb 34 99
DEATH QUOTIENT by John D. MacDonald . . . .
. .nt .SSS Apr 49 8
DEATH RAY by Henry S. Lewis. .ss. . . . .
. . . . .SS Nov 42 114
DEATH RIDES AT NIGHT by Leroy Yerxa. .nt . . . . . .
. . . . Amz Aug 42 66
DEATH SEEMS SO FINAL by Alexander Blade
h ps. .s. . . . . .Amz Jan 47 136
DEATH SENTENCE by Isaac Asimov. .s . . . .
. . . . ASF Nov 43 32

Title. .Author. .Length . . . . Magazine. .Date. .Page No.

DEATH SENTENCE by Chester S. Geier. .s . . . .
. . . . Amz Dec 46 26
DEATH SENTENCE by Robert Moore Williams. .s . . . .
. . . . UK Mar 39 151
DEATH STAR by Tom Pace. .s . . . . PS Spr 45 77
DEATH TIME by D. M. Bricker. .s . . . . . UK Apr 39 101
DEATH TRAPS OF FX–31, THE by Sewell Peaslee
Wright. .s . . . . ASF Mar 33 82
DEATH UNDER THE SEA by Willy Ley. .a . . . .
. . . . ASF Sep 42 44
DEATH WALKS IN WASHINGTON by James
Norman. .nt . . . . FA Mar 41 50
DEATH WEARS A ROSE by Alexander Blade h ps . . . .
. .s . . . . FA Jan 47 78
DEATH-WISH by Ray Bradbury. .s. . . . . . . PS Fal 50 29
DEATH'S DEPUTY by L. Ron Hubbard. .n . . . .
. . . . UK Feb 40 9
DEATH'S DOUBLE by Grover Kent. .s . . . Amz Jun 49 82
DEATH'S HEAD by Chester S. Geier. .s . . . FA Nov 48 60
DEATH'S HEAD METEOR, THE by Neil R. Jones . . . .
. .s . . . . AW Jan 30 628
DEATH'S SECRET by J. L. Schoolcraft. .nt . . . .
. . . . FN Jul 50 68
DEBT, THE by E. Mayne Hull. .nt . . . . ASF Dec 43 7
DECADENCE by Ray Cummings. .s . . . . . . TW Dec 41 70
DECISION ILLOGICAL by Neal B. Wilkinson. .s . . . . .
. . . . ASF Jul 48 36
DECONVENTIONALIZERS, THE by Edmond
Hamilton. .s . . . . .TW Sum 45 59
DECOY IN SPACE by David C. McGowan. .s . . . .
. . . . Amz Jul 49 48
DEEP SEA JUSTICE by Ed Earl Repp. .s. . . . .
. . . . AQ Sum 31 414
DEFENSE by A. E. van Vogt. .ss . . . . AFR #4 128
DEFENSE LINE by Vic Phillips. .nt . . . . ASF Dec 41 115
DEFENSE MECH by Ray Bradbury. .s . . . . .PS Spr 46 42
DEFENSE MECHANISM by Katherine MacLean. .s. . . .
. . . . .ASF Oct 49 155
DEGENERATE MR. SMITH, THE by William
De Lisle. .s . . . . Amz Aug 43 138
DEGENERATES, THE by Polton Cross ps (John
Russell Fearn). .nt . . . . ASF Feb 38 6
DEGRAVITOR, THE by Ralph Milne Farley ps
(Roger Sherman Hoar). .s . . . . Amz Mar 32 1136
DELILAH by Margaretta W. Rea. .s . . . .Amz Jan 33 942
DELIVERERS, THE by Richard Morrison ps
(Robert W. Lowndes). .ss . . . . SFQ Win 42 142
DELLIAN ROBOT series See A. E. VAN VOGT author
DELUSION DRIVE by Peter Reed ps (John D.
MacDonald). .s . . . . .SSS Apr 49 100
DELVERS IN DESTINY by Frederic Arnold
Kummer, Jr. . .s . . . . TW Spr 45 67
DEMOISELLE D'YS, THE by Robert W.
Chambers. .s . . . . .FFM Nov 42 133
DEMON OF THE FLOWER, THE by Clark
Ashton Smith. .s . . . . ASF Dec 33 131

Title. .Author. .Length . . . . Magazine. .Date. .Page No.

DEMONS OF DARKSIDE, THE by Leigh
Brackett. .s . . . . .SS Jan 41 107
DEMONS OF RHADI-MU, THE by Miles
J. Breuer, M.D. . .s . . . . .AQ Fal 31 506
DEMONSTRATION FLIGHT by Warren
Kastel ps. .s . . . . FA Aug 49 130
DENITRO by Stanton A. Coblentz. .s . . . .
. . . . Amz Feb 37 107
DENIZEN OF THE UNDERWORLD, A by Walter
Kateley. .s . . . . SD Apr 30 323
DENIZONS OF ZERON by J. Harvey Haggard . . . .
. .s .ASF Jan 37 115
DEPTH by G. N. Howard. .s . . . . ASF Mar 46 156
DEPUTY CORRESPONDENT by Harl Vincent
(Schoepflin). .s . . . . ASF Jun 40 38
DERELICT by Raymond Z. Gallun. .s. . . . ASF Oct 35 23
DERELICT, THE by William Hope Hodgson. .s. . . . . .
. . . . FFM Dec 43 94
AFR #4 66
DERELICT, THE by William J. Matthews. .s . . . .
. . . . PS Fal 46 49
DERELICT OF SPACE by John Beynon
(Harris). .s . . . . .Fant #3 39 2
DERELICT OF SPACE, THE by William
Thurmond & Ray Cummings. .s . . . . WQ Fal 31 98
WSA 50 140
DERELICTS OF GANYMEDE, THE by John W.
Campbell, Jr. . .s. . . . . .WS Jan 32 939
DERELICTS OF URANUS by J. Harvey Haggard . . . . .
. .s .Com May 41 54
DERM FOOL by Theodore Sturgeon. .s . . . .
. . . . UK Mar 40 114
DESCENT FROM MERA by Millen Cooke. .n . . . .
. . . . OW Jan 50 106
DESCENT INTO THE MAELSTROM, A by Edgar
Allen Poe. .s. . . . . Amz Feb 34 123
DESCRIBE A CIRCLE by Eric Frank Russell. .nt . . . . .
. . . . ASF Mar 42 116
DESERT CITY by Warner Van Lorne ps. .s . . . .
. . . . ASF Mar 37 48
DESERT OF ICE, THE by Jules Verne. .n 2 pt . . . .
. . . . Amz Jun 29 241
DESERT OF THE DAMNED by Don Wilcox. .n . . . . . .
. . . . Amz May 47 62
DESERTED UNIVERSE by John Russell Fearn . . . . . .
. .nt .ASF Sep 36 137
DESERTION by Clifford D. Simak. .s . . . .
. . . . ASF Nov 44 164
DESIGN FOR DOOMSDAY by Bryce Walton. .nt . . . . .
. . . . .PS Spr 48 94
DESIGN FOR DREAMING by Henry Kuttner. .nt . . . .
. . . . UK Feb 42 113
DESIGN FOR LIFE by L. Sprague de Camp. .a 2 pt . . .
. . . . ASF May 39 103
DESPOILERS, THE by Rog Phillips ps (Roger
P. Graham). .nt . . . . Amz Oct 47 78

Title. .Author. .Length . . . . Magazine. .Date. .Page No.

DESTINATION—DEATH by Wilbur S. Peacock. .s . . . .
. . . . .PS Win 43 51
DESTINATION MOON by Forrest J. Ackerman. .a . . . .
. . . . .OW May 50 147
DESTINATION UNKNOWN by Frank Belknap
Long. .s .Ash Dec 42 48
DESTINY MADE TO ORDER by Ed Earl Repp. .s . . . .
. . . . .SF Jan 41 32
DESTINY TIMES THREE by Fritz Leiber, Jr. . . . . . .
. .n 2 pt . . . .s . . . . ASF Mar 45 6
DESTINY WORLD by Martin Pearson ps (Donald
A. Wollheim). .ss . . . . Fut Dec 41 70
DESTROYER, THE by William Merriam Rouse. .s . . . .
. . . . ASF Nov 30 198
DESTROYER FROM THE PAST by Polton Cross
ps (John Russell Fearn). .s . . . . Amz May 42 230
DESTRUCTION OF AMUL, THE by M. F. James . . . . .
. .s . . . . .ASF Jan 37 35
DETONATOR by Walt Sheldon. .s . . . . . . FA Sep 50 44
DETOUR FROM TOMORROW by Rog Phillips ps
(Roger P. Graham). .s . . . . FA Mar 50 34
DEUS EX MACHINA by F. G. Rayer. .s . . . NW Win 50 30
DEVIL BIRDS OF DEIMOS by Festus Pragnell. .nt . . . .
. . . . Amz Apr 42 168
DEVIL CRYSTALS OF ARRET by Hal K. Wells. . . . . .
. .s . . . . .ASF Sep 31 344
DEVIL DOGS OF SPACE by Helen Weinbaum. .nt . . . .
. . . . .SF Sep 41 87
DEVIL FINDS WORK, THE by Mack Reynolds. .s . . . .
. . . . FA Dec 50 90
DEVIL FISH, THE by Elinore Cowan Stone. .s . . . . . .
. . . . AMF Oct 50 92
DEVIL FLOWER, THE by Harl Vincent
(Schoepflin). .s . . . . FA May 39 80
DEVIL IN A BOX, THE by Gerald Vance
h ps. .nt . . . . Amz Nov 50 118
DEVIL IS NOT MOCKED, THE by Manly
Wade Wellman. .s . . . . UK Jun 43 115
DEVIL MAKES THE LAW, THE by Robert A.
Heinlein. .n . . . . UK Sep 40 9
DEVIL OF DOOM, THE by A. Morris. .nt . . . .
. . . . FA Jan 49 64
DEVIL OF EAST LUPTON, VERMONT, THE by
William Fitzgerald ps (Will F. Jenkins). .s . . . .
. . . . .TW Aug 48 96
DEVIL OF THE WESTERN SEA, THE by Philip
M. Fisher. .nt . . . . .FFM Apr 40 6
DEVIL RITTER by Max Brand ps (Frederick
Faust). .nt . . . . .FN May 49 90
DEVIL TO PAY, THE by John & Dorothy de
Courcy. .s . . . . FA Dec 47 72
DEVIL WE KNOW, THE by Henry Kuttner. .s . . . . . .
. . . . .UK Aug 41 90
                                              UK 48 102
DEVIL WITH YOU!", "THE by Robert Bloch . . . .
. .n . . . . .FA Aug 50 8

DEVIL'S ASTEROID by Manly Wade Wellman. .s . . . . .
. . . . .Com Jul 41 28
DEVIL'S BODYGUARD, THE by Clyde Irvine . . . . . .
. .s . . . . FFM Dec 40 99
DEVIL'S FIDDLE, THE by N. R. de Mexico. .s . . . . . .
. . . . TW Jun 43 58
DEVILS FROM DARKONIA by Jerry Shelton . . . .
. .nt . . . . TW Spr 45 11
DEVIL'S INVENTION, THE by Alfred Bester. .s . . . . .
. . . . ASF Aug 50 133
DEVIL'S LADY, THE by Clark South ps (Dwight
V. Swain). .s . . . . FA Oct 42 164
DEVIL'S PAWN by Damon Knight. .ss . . . . Fut Oct 42 84
DEVIL'S PIGS, THE by Don Wilcox. .s . . . . FA Jan 45 12
DEVIL'S PLANET, THE by David Wright O'Brien. . . . .
. .n . . . . Amz Sep 43 108
DEVIL'S PLANET by Manly Wade Wellman. .n . . . . .
. . . . .SS Jan 42 15
DEVIL'S POCKET, THE by F. E. Hardart. .s . . . .
. . . . .Ash Jun 40 35
DEVIL'S POWDER by Malcolm Jameson. .s . . . .
. . . . ASF Jun 41 69
DEVIL'S RESCUE, THE by L. Ron Hubbard. .s . . . . . .
. . . . UK Oct 40 99
DEVIL'S SPOON, THE by Theodora Du Bois. .n . . . . .
. . . . .FFM Jun 48 8
DEVIOUS WEAPON by M. C. Pease. .s . . . ASF Apr 49 34
DEVOLUTION by Edmond Hamilton. .s . . . .
. . . . Amz Dec 36 90
DEVOTEE OF EVIL, THE by Clark Ashton
Smith. .s . . . . .Sti Feb 41 109
DEVOURING TIDE, THE by Polton Cross ps (John
Russell Fearn). .s . . . . .TW Sum 44 82
DIABOLICAL DRUG, THE by Clare Winger Harris . . . .
. .s . . . . Amz May 29 156
DIAMOND LENS, THE by Fitz-James O'Brien. .s . . . .
. . . . Amz Dec 26 834
                                         Amz Oct 33 600
DIAMOND MAKER, THE by Arthur B. Reeve. .s . . . . .
. . . . AD Jun 30 488
DIAMOND MAKER, THE by H. G. Wells. .s . . . .
. . . . SW Jun 29 35
DIAMOND OF DOOM by Alexander Blade h ps. .n . . . .
. . . . .FA Jul 45 10
DIAMOND PLANETOID, THE by Gordon A. Giles
ps (Otto Binder). .s . . . . ASF May 37 99
DIAMOND THUNDERBOLT, THE by H.
Thompson Rich. .s . . . . .ASF Jul 31 46
DIAN OF THE LOST LAND by Edison Marshall. . . . . .
. .n .FFM Apr 49 8
DIANA AND THE GOLDEN RING by S. M.
Tenneshaw h ps. .s . . . . FA Mar 50 8
DIANETICS: A BOOK REVIEW by C. Daly
King, Ph.D. . . . . F&SF Dec 50 99
DIANETICS—THE EVOLUTION OF A SCIENCE by
L. Ron Hubbard. .long article . . . . . . ASF May 50 43

Title. .Author. .Length . . . . Magazine. .Date. .Page No.

DICTAGRAPHS OF DEATH by P. F. Costello. .s . . . . .
. . . . Amz May 41 136
DICTATOR FOR ALL TIME, A by Raymond Z.
Gallun. .s . . . . MSS Nov 40 56
DICTATOR OF PEACE by Don Wilcox. .nt . . . .
. . . . Amz Nov 39 70
DICTATOR OF TIME by Nelson S. Bond. .nt . . . . . .
. . . . PS Spr 40 98
DICTATOR OF THE AMERICAS by James Hall ps
(Henry Kuttner). .s . . . . MSS Aug 38 65
DICTATOR OF THE ATOMS by Arthur J. Burks. .nt . .
. . . . TW Oct 36 92
DICTATORS OF CREATION by Edmond Hamilton . . .
. .nt . . . . .TW May 40 50
DIMENSION—HAZARD by Hal K. Wells. .s . . . .
. . . . .SSS Nov 40 40
DIMENSION OF CHANCE, THE by Clark Ashton
Smith. .s . . . . WS Nov 32 520
ToW Win 41 61
SS Spr 46 72
DIMENSION OF DARKNESS by S. D. Gottesman
ps (Cyril Kornbluth). .s . . . . .Cos May 41 27
DIMENSION OF THE CONQUERED by R. F.
Starzl. .s . . . . .ASF Oct 34 138
DIMENSION: PRAECOX by Blair Reed. .s . . . .
. . . . SS May 49 107
DIMENSION SEGREGATOR, THE by J. Harold
Click. .s . . . . Amz Aug 29 422
DIMENSION TWISTER, THE by Hugh King
Harris. .s . . . . WS Apr 33 886
DIMENSIONAL FATE by A. L. Burkholder. .s . . . . . .
. . . . WS Aug 34 262
DIMENSIONS UNLIMITED by Berkeley
Livingston. .n . . . . .FA Nov 48 8
DIMINISHING DRAFT, THE by Waldemar
Kaempffert. .s . . . . FFM Dec 39 28
DINKY WINKY WOO by Harold Lawlor. .s . . . .
. . . . FA Aug 43 168
DINOSAUR DESTROYER by Arthur Petticolas. .n . . . .
. . . . Amz Jan 49 8
DINOSAUR GOES HOLLYWOOD by Emil Petaja. . . .
. .s . . . . Amz Nov 42 122
DIRECT ACTION by John Hawkins. .s . . . .
. . . . ASF Nov 41 81
DIRECT WIRE by Clee Garson ps (David Wright
O'Brien). .s . . . . Amz Jan 43 58
DIRIGIBLES OF DEATH, THE by A. Hyatt Verrill. . . .
. .nt . . . . AQ Win 30 124
DISAPPEARANCE by Chester S. Geier. .s . . . .
. . . . .ASF Jul 45 115
DISAPPEARING PAPERS, THE by Miles J.
Breuer. .ss .Fut Nov 39 74
DISAPPEARING SAM by R. R. Winterbotham. . . . . . .
. .s . . . . MSS Aug 39 62
DISAPPOINTMENT by William Morrison. .s . . . .
. . . . SS Jul 50 138

Title. .Author. .Length . . . . Magazine. .Date. .Page No.

DISC-MEN OF JUPITER, THE by Manly Wade
Wellman. .nt . . . . WS Sep 31 522
SS May 47 70
DISCARDED VEIL, THE by Arthur J. Burks. .s . . . . . .
. . . . .TW Feb 39 88
DISCIPLES OF DESTINY by Don Wilcox. .n 2 pt. . . . .
. . . . Amz Mar 42 8
DISCIPLINARY CIRCUIT, THE by Murray
Leinster ps (Will F. Jenkins). .nt . . . . . . .TW Win 46 44
DISCONTINUITY by Raymond F. Jones. .nt . . . .
. . . . ASF Oct 50 76
DISCORD IN SCARLET by A. E. van Vogt. .nt . . . . . .
. . . . ASF Dec 39 9
DISCORD MAKERS, THE by Mack Reynolds. .s . . . . .
. . . . OTWA Jul 50 102
DISCOVERY OF NIL by A. E. Burton. .s . . . .
. . . . .Fant #2 39 93
DISCUS MEN OF EKTA by Carl Buchanan &
Dr. Arch Carr. .nt . . . . ASF Feb 35 10
DISCUSSIONS Letter dept in Amz & one issue
of AQ
DISINHERITED, THE by Henry Kuttner. .s . . . .
. . . . ASF Aug 38 146
DISINTEGRATING RAY, THE by David M.
Speaker. .s . . . . Amz Feb 28 1088
DISOWNED by Victor Endersby. .s . . . . . ASF Sep 32 20
DISPERSION by Malcolm Jameson. .a . . . .
. . . . ASF Mar 42 104
DISSECTING TABLE, THE book review dept of
Worlds Beyond fr #1
DISTRESS SIGNAL by Ross Rocklynne. .s . . . .
. . . . .PS Spr 47 35
DIVERSIFAL, THE by Ross Rocklynne. .s . . . .
. . . . .PS Win 45 54
DIVIDE AND RULE by L. Sprague de Camp . . . .
. .n 2 pt . . . . UK Apr 39 125
. . .DIVIDED WE FALL by Raymond F. Jones . . . . . .
. .n . . . . Amz Dec 50 96
DIVINE RIGHT by Betsy Curtis. .s . . . . . F&SF Sum 50 96
DHACTWHU!—REMEMBER? by Wilfred Owen Morley
ps (Robert W. Lowndes) & Jacques DeForest Erman
ps (Forrest J. Ackerman). .s . . . .
. . . . .SSS Apr 49 84
DO CAVE MEN STILL LIVE? by James F.
Scheer. .a . . . . Amz Feb 40 125
DOBRIDUST, THE by Margaret St. Clair. .s . . . .
. . . . .TW Feb 48 41
DR. BRITTLESTONE'S METHOD by Samuel M. . . . .
Sargent, Jr. . .s . . . . Amz May 28 120
DR. CONKLIN—PACIFIST by Calvin Peregoy
ps (Thomas Calvert McClary). .s . . . . . . ASF Aug 34 34
DR. CYCLOPS by Henry Kuttner. .s . . . . . TW Jun 40 14
DR. DESTINY, MASTER OF THE DEAD by
Robert Moore Williams. .nt . . . . FA Jun 40 6
DR. GRIMSHAW'S SANATORIUM by Fletcher
Pratt. .s . . . . Amz May 34 79

Title. .Author. .Length . . . . Magazine. .Date. .Page No.

DR. HACKENSAW'S SECRETS by Clement Fezandie
   The Secret of the Invisible Girl. .s . . . . . Amz Jul 26 376
   Some Minor Inventions. .s . . . . Amz Jun 26 280
DR. IMMORTELLE by Kathleen Ludwick *(on story.*
   ToC gives author as KATHLEEN LUCKWICK). .s . . .
   . . . . .AQ Fal 30 560
DR. KELTON—BODY SNATCHER by Richard O.
   Lewis. .s . . . . FA Jan 41 98
DR. KOCH'S SEA SERPENT *(FANTASTIC*
   HOAXES) by Willy Ley. .a . . . . . . FA Feb 40 26
DR. LOUDON'S ARMAGEDDON by Alexander
   Blade *h ps (Louis H. Sampliner).* .s . . . Amz Sep 41 134
DR. LU-MIE by Clifton B. Kruse. .s . . . . . . ASF Jul 34 42
DR. MacDONOUGH'S ENCEPHALOSEMANTI-
   COMMUNICATOR by Leo A. Schmidt. .s . . . .
   . . . . Amz Mar 45 188
DOCTOR O'GLEE'S EXPERIMENT by T. Proctor
   Hall. .nt . . . . .AQ Sum 29 398
DR. OX'S EXPERIMENT by Jules Verne. .s . . . .
   . . . . Amz Aug 26 420
DOCTOR UNIVERSE by Carl Jacobi. .s . . . . PS Fal 44 35
DR. VARSAG'S EXPERIMENT by Craig Ellis
   h ps (Lee Rogow). .s . . . . .Amz Jan 40 112
DR. VARSAG'S SECOND EXPERIMENT by Craig
   Ellis *h ps (David Vern).* .n . . . . Amz Aug 43 76
DR. ZANGER'S CATS by J. J. Allerton. .nt . . . .
   . . . . .FA Jul 45 86
DOCTOR'S EXPERIMENT, THE by Allan
   Strathglass. .s . . . . Amz Mar 31 1140
DOES NOT IMPLY by Wilfred Owen Morley *ps*
   (Robert W. Lowndes). .s . . . . Fut Feb 43 76
DOG'S LIFE, A by George O. Smith. .s . . . TW Apr 48 118
DOG'S SIXTH SENSE, THE by W. Alexander. .s . . . . .
   . . . . Amz Sep 29 540
DOLL MASTER, THE by Paul Dennis Lavond *h ps*
   (Robert W. Lowndes). .ss . . . . .Sti Apr 41 115
DOLLS OF DEATH by Pvt. E. K. Jarvis *h ps* . . . .
   .nt . . . . Amz Sep 44 96
DOLPHIN'S DUBLOONS, THE by Silaki Ali
   Hassan. .s . . . . UK Oct 41 122
DOMAIN OF ZERO by Thornton Ayre *ps (John*
   Russell Fearn). .s . . . . PS Fal 40 57
DOMINION by Arthur J. Burks. .nt . . . . . . SF Jul 43 10
DON KELZ OF THE I.S.P. by Clifton B. Kruse. .s . . . .
   . . . . ASF Feb 36 88
DON MACKINDER'S MODEL by F. S.
   Howard-Burleigh. .s . . . . ASF Oct 33 55
DONE IN OIL by Arthur J. Burks. .nt . . . . ASF Jun 39 79
DONE WITHOUT EAGLES by Philip St. John. .s . . . . .
   . . . . ASF Aug 40 70
DONKEYS TO BALDPATE by Samuel Mines. .s . . . . . .
   . . . . TW Aug 47 84
DONOVAN HAD A DREAM by James MacCreigh.
   ps (Frederik Pohl). .nt . . . . TW Oct 47 11
DONOVAN'S BRAIN by Curt Siodmak. .n . . . .
   . . . . .FFM Aug 50 54

Title. .Author. .Length . . . . Magazine. .Date. .Page No.

DON'T COME TO MARS! by Henry Hasse. .s . . . .
   . . . . FA Apr 50 86
DON'T DREAM by Donald Wandrei. .s . . . .
   . . . . UK Aug 39 75
DON'T GO HAUNTING by Robert Coley. .s . . . .
   . . . . UK Jun 39 73
DON'T LOOK BEHIND YOU by Richard Casey
   h ps. .s . . . . Amz Sep 45 158
DON'T LOOK NOW by Henry Kuttner. .s . . . .
   . . . . .SS Mar 48 69
DON'T MENTION IT by John & Dorothy
   de Courcy. .s . . . . Amz May 46 134
DOODAD by Ray Bradbury. .s . . . . ASF Sep 43 49
DOOM FROM PLANET 4, THE by Jack
   Williamson. .s . . . . .ASF Jul 31 5
DOOM FROM THE VOID by John Coleridge *ps*
   (Earl Binder & Otto Binder). .s . . . . .SF Jun 40 75
DOOM GLOBE by S. M. Tenneshaw *h ps.* .s . . . .
   . . . . Amz May 48 100
DOOM OF LUN-DHAG by William Lemkin, Ph.D. . . . .
   . .nt . . . . Amz Nov 32 678
DOOM OVER VENUS by Edmond Hamilton. .nt . . . . .
   . . . . TW Feb 40 85
DOOM SHIP by Henry Guth. .s . . . . .SSS Nov 50 86
DOOM SHIP by Harry Walton. .nt . . . . . .ASF Jan 41 128
DOOM SHIP by Robert Moore Williams. .nt . . . .
   . . . . FA Feb 50 94
DOOM WORLD by Henry Kuttner. .s . . . . .TW Aug 38 12
DOOMED BY THE PLANETOID by D. D. Sharp
   . .nt . . . . ASF May 36 58
DOOMSDAY ON AJIAT by Neil R. Jones. .s . . . .
   . . . . .Ash Oct 42 74
DOOR, THE by Clifton B. Kruse. .s . . . . .SFQ Spr 43 108
DOOR, THE by Oliver Saari. .s . . . . ASF Nov 41 93
DOOR AT THE OPERA, THE by Ray Cummings . . . . .
   . .s . . . . .Ash Dec 40 77
DOORBELL, THE by David H. Keller, M.D. . .s . . . . . .
   . . . . WS Jun 34 52
DOORWAY INTO TIME by C. L. Moore. .s . . . .
   . . . . FFM Sep 43 116
DOORWAY OF VANISHING MEN by William P.
   McGivern. .s . . . . .FA Jul 41 128
DOORWAY TO DESTRUCTION by Garold S.
   Hatfield. .ss . . . . .PS Win 42 55
DOORWAY TO HELL by Frank Patton *h ps*
   (Raymond A. Palmer). .n 2 pt . . . . FA Feb 42 8
DOORWAY TO KAL-JMAR by Stuart Fleming *ps*
   (Damon Knight). .s . . . . .PS Win 44 19
DORMANT by A. E. van Vogt. .s . . . . SS Nov 48 88
DOSAGE by Bill Brudy. .s . . . . .TW May 40 84
DOUBLE CROSS IN DOUBLE TIME by William
   P. McGivern. .s . . . . FA Feb 48 120
DOUBLE-CROSS ON MARS by Sgt. Gerald Vance
   h ps. .s . . . . Amz Sep 44 134
DOUBLE! DOUBLE! by Eddin Clark. .nt . . . .
   . . . . ASF Sep 38 88

Title. .Author. .Length . . . . Magazine. .Date. .Page No.

DOUBLE DESTINY by Helen Weinbaum. .nt . . . .
. . . . SFQ Win 41 109
DOUBLE-DYED VILLAINS, THE by Poul
Anderson. .nt . . . . ASF Sep 49 6
DOUBLE FOR DESTINY by Leroy Yerxa. .n. . . . . . .
. . . . Amz Dec 46 64
DOUBLE IN DEATH by Gerald Vance h ps. .s . . . . . .
. . . . FA Apr 42 120
DOUBLE LIGHTNING, THE by A. C. Webb, M. D. . . .
. .s . . . . AD Jun 30 530
DOUBLE MINDS, THE by John W. Campbell, Jr. . . . .
. .nt . . . . .TW Aug 37 54
DOUBLE OR NOTHING by Eando Binder ps (Otto
Binder). .s . . . . TW Oct 42 104
DOUBLE TROUBLE by Carl Jacobi. .s . . . . .PS Spr 45 67
DOUBLE TROUBLE FOR OSCAR by James Norman . .
. .nt . . . . FA Oct 42 124
DOUBLE-CROSS by James MacCreigh ps (Frederik
Pohl). .s. . . . . .PS Win 44 112
DOUBLED AND REDOUBLED by Malcolm Jameson . .
. .s . . . . UK Feb 41 87
DOUBLED IN BRASS by Lester del Rey. .s . . . .
. . . . UK Jan 40 107
DOUBT, THE by Ben Aronin. .s . . . . . . Amz May 32 180
DOWN ON THE FARM by Simpson Stokes. .s . . . .
. . . . TW Apr 37 60
DOWN THE DIMENSIONS by Nelson S. Bond. .s . . . . .
. . . . ASF Apr 37 102
DOWN THE RIVER by Mack Reynolds. .s. . SS Sep 50 113
DOWN TO EARTH Letter dept of Future. . . . .
. . . . from May-Jun 50
DRAGON-QUEEN OF JUPITER, THE by Leigh
Brackett. .s. . . . . PS Sum 41 35
DRAGONS BEHIND US by Richard Casey h ps. .s . . . .
. . . . FA Apr 45 106
DRAGONS OF SPACE by Aladra Septama. .nt . . . . . .
. . . . AQ Spr 30 218
DRAGON'S TEETH by John K. Aiken. .nt . . . .NW #3 2
DRAGON'S TEETH by Wallace West. .s . . ASF Sep 34 63
DRAMA IN THE AIR, A by Jules Verne. .s . . . .
. . . . Amz Nov 26 758
DRAMATIS PERSONAE by Joe W. Skidmore. .s . . . . .
. . . . .AQ Fal 31 522
DRAUGHT OF IMMORTALITY by A. W. Bernal. .s . . .
. . . . Amz Dec 35 74
DREAD-FLAME OF M'TONAK by Henry Hasse. . . . . .
. .nt . . . . .PS Fal 46 2
DREADFUL DREAMER by Margaret St. Clair. .s . . . . .
. . . . SSS Jul 49 80
DREADFUL SANCTUARY by Eric Frank Russell . . . .
. .n 3 pt . . . . ASF Jun 48 8
DREADNOUGHTS OF DOOM by Henry Andrew
Ackerman. .s . . . . .SSS May 42 124
DREAM, THE by Jane Rice. .s . . . . .UK Jul 40 84
DREAM DUST FROM MARS by Manly Wade
Wellman. .s. . . . . TW Feb 38 14

DREAMERS, THE by Michael Yamin. .s . . . .
. . . . ASF Dec 47 67
"DREAMING" DOWN AXIS PLANES by Sam
Merwin, Jr. . .a. . . . . .TW Sum 44 42
DREAMING JEWELS, THE by Theodore Sturgeon . . . .
. .n . . . . FA Feb 50 8
DREAMING TREES, THE by John W. Jakes. .s . . . . .
. . . . .FA Nov 50 98
DREAMS ARE SACRED by Peter Phillips. .nt . . . . . .
. . . . ASF Sep 48 51
DREAM'S END by A. Connell. .s . . . . WS Nov 35 646
DREAM'S END by Henry Kuttner. .s . . . . . . SS Jul 47 80
DREAMS MAY COME by H. Warner Munn. .s . . . .
. . . . UK Oct 39 67
DREAMS OF ALBERT MORELAND, THE by
Fritz Leiber, Jr. . .s. . . . . .AFR #7 40
DRINK LIKE A FISH by Berkeley Livingston. .s. . . . .
. . . . Amz Apr 48 62
DRIVING POWER, THE by Miles J. Breuer, M.D. . . . .
. .s . . . . .Amz Jul 30 306
DRONE, THE (THE DRONE MAN) by A. Merritt. . . . .
. .s . . . . .AFR #6 49
DRONE MAN, THE by A. Merritt. .s . . . . .TW Aug 36 29
DRUMMERS OF DAUGAVO by Dwight V. Swain . . . .
. .n . . . . FA Mar 43 8
DRUMS, THE by Clifton B. Kruse. .s . . . .
. . . . ASF Mar 36 115
DRUMS OF MURD, THE by H. B. Hickey ps (Herb
Livingston). .nt . . . . .FA Jan 48 132
DRUMS OF TAPAJOS, THE by Capt. S. P. Meek
. .n 3 pt . . . . Amz Nov 30 678
DRUSO by Friedrich Freska (tr fr German by . ,
Fletcher Pratt). .n 3 pt . . . . WS May 34 1066
DUAL PERSONALITY by Rog Phillips ps (Roger P. . .
Graham). .nt . . . . FA Sep 46 150
DUAL WORLD, THE by Arthur K. Barnes. .nt . . . . . .
. . . . TW Jun 38 54
DUD by Kenneth Putnam. .s . . . . TW Apr 48 88
DUAL IN BLACK by John Foster West. .s . . . .
. . . . .PS Win 47 113
DUAL IN THE DARK by Edwin Balmer & William
B. MacHarg. .s. . . . . AD Sep 30 790
DUAL IN THE SPACE LANES by William C.
Beckett. .s . . . . ASF Mar 38 56
DUEL ON THE ASTEROID, THE by P. Schuyler
Miller & Dennis McDermott ps (Walter L. Dennis. . . .
& Paul McDermott). .s . . . . .WS Jan 32 950
DUMB SUPPER by Henderson Starke ps (Kris
Neville). .s . . . . F&SF Sum 50 47
DUMMY OF DEATH by Leroy Yerxa. .s . . . FA Oct 45 90
DUMMY THAT SAVED THE EARTH, THE by
Graph Waldeyer. .s. . . . . .CF Spr 42 108
DUNCAN'S DREADFUL DOLL by P. F. Costello
h ps. .s . . . . FA Jul 42 170
DUPLICATE, THE by A. Connell. .s . . . . . WS Mar 36 936
DURNA RANGUE series See NEIL R. JONES auth

Title. .Author. .Length . . . . Magazine. .Date. .Page No.

DURNA RANGUE NEOPHYTE by Neil R. Jones . . . . .
. .nt .ASF Jun 37 134
DUSK ON THE MOON by Hannes Bok. .nt . . . .
. . . . Fut Feb 43 20
DUST by Lloyd Arthur Eshbach. .s . . . . . MSS Aug 39 91
DUST OF DESTRUCTION by P. Schuyler Miller . . . . .
. .s . . . . WS Feb 31 918
DWELLER IN OUTER DARKNESS, THE by Frank
Belknap Long, Jr. . .s . . . . TW Aug 39 60
DWELLER IN MARTIAN DEPTHS by Clark Ashton
Smith. .s . . . . WS Mar 33 768
DWELLER IN THE DARKNESS by Edmond
Hamilton. .s . . . . .SF Oct 39 56
DWELLER IN THE ICE, THE by James MacCreigh . . . .
ps (Frederik Pohl). .s . . . . SSS Jan 41 63
DWELLERS IN SILENCE by Ray Bradbury. .s . . . . . .
. . . . .PS Spr 49 51
DWELLERS IN THE DUST by Forrest J.
Ackerman. .s . . . . FB #4 31
DWELLERS IN THE MIRAGE, THE by A. Merritt . . . .
. .n . . . . FN Apr 41 6
                                        FN Sep 49 8
DWELLERS OF THE DARKNESS by Ed Earl
Repp. .s . . . . Amz Oct 42 106
DWELLERS OF THE DEEP by Don Wilcox. .n . . . . . .
. . . . FA Apr 42 8
DWINDLING SPHERE, THE by Willard E.
Hawkins. .s . . . . ASF Mar 40 99
DYNAMITE PLANET by Guy Archette ps (Chester
S. Geier). .nt . . . . Amz Oct 49 68
DYNAMOUSE, THE by William P. McGivern. .s . . . . . .
. . . . FA Jan 41 46
DYNASTY OF THE BLUE-BLACK RAYS by Milton
R. Peril. .s . . . . Amz Oct 30 634
DYNASTY OF THE DEVIL by Alexander Blade. . . . . .
. .nt . . . . Amz Jun 49 6
DYNASTY OF THE LOST by George O. Smith. .nt. . . .
. . . . .Fut May-Jun 50 8
DYNASTY OF THE SMALL by John Russell Fearn . . .
. .nt . . . . ASF Nov 36 59

E

E FOR EFFORT by T. L. Sherred. .nt. . . ASF May 47 119
EAGLE MAN, THE by Don Wilcox. .n . . . . .FA Jul 42 8
EAGLES GATHER, THE by Joseph E. Kelleam. .s . . . .
. . . . ASF Apr 42 93
EARTH ASUNDER by Ephriam Winiki. .s . . . .
. . . . .SF Oct 39 62
EARTH CAN BE FAIR by Hubert George Wells ps
(Forrest J. Ackerman). .s . . . . OW Oct 50 26
EARTH DOES NOT REPLY by Lawrence Woods ps
(John B. Michel & Donald A. Wollheim). .s . . . .
. . . . SFQ Sum 41 123

Title. .Author. .Length . . . . Magazine. .Date. .Page No.

EARTH, FAREWELL! by James MacCreigh ps
(Frederik Pohl). .s . . . . .Ash Feb 43 30
EARTH FOR INSPIRATION by Clifford D. Simak . . . .
. .s . . . . TW Apr 41 99
EARTH IS MISSING by Carl Selwyn. .nt. . . .PS Win 47 90
EARTH KILLERS, THE by A. E. van Vogt. .nt . . . . . .
. . . . .SSS Apr 49 50
EARTH MEN, THE by Ray Bradbury. .s . . .TW Aug 48 69
EARTH MINUS by Donald Wandrei. .nt . . . .
. . . . ASF Sep 35 40
EARTH NEEDS A KILLER by Bryce Walton. .nt . . . . .
. . . . Fut Jul-Aug 50 8
EARTH REHABILITATORS, CONSOLIDATED by
Henry J. Kostkos. .n 2 pt . . . . Amz Mar 35 13
EARTH-SAVER, THE by Joseph J. Millard. .s . . . . . .
. . . . SS Nov 42 90
EARTH SHALL NOT DIE!, THE by Benson
Herbert. .nt . . . . ToW Spr 42 6
EARTH SLAVES TO SPACE by Richard S.
Shaver. .n. . . . . Amz Sep 46 8
EARTH STEALERS, THE by Frederic Arnold
Kummer, Jr. . .s . . . . Uc Apr 41 40
EARTH STEALERS by Don Wilcox. .n . . . Amz Jun 43 60
EARTH, THE MARAUDER by Arthur J. Burks . . . . . .
. .n 3 pt . . . . .ASF Jul 30 18
EARTH-VENUS 12 by Gabriel Wilson ps (Mr. &
Mrs. Ray Cummings). .s . . . . TW Dec 36 103
EARTHBOUND. . . by Alfred Coppel . .s . . . FA Dec 50 96
EARTHBOUND by Henry Guth. .s . . . . . . .PS Win 47 84
EARTHMAN'S BURDEN by R. F. Starzl. .s . . . .
. . . . .ASF Jun 31 375
EARTHQUAKE GIRL, THE by Joseph J. Millard . . . . .
. .nt . . . . FA Oct 41 8
EARTH'S CANCER, THE by Capt. S. P. Meek,
U.S.A. . .s . . . . Amz Mar 31 1116
EARTH'S CORE, THE by H. R. Hammond . . . .
. .bacover pic . . . . Amz Mar 40
EARTH'S LAST CITADEL by C. L. Moore &
Henry Kuttner. .n . . . . .FN Jul 50 12
EARTH'S LUCKY DAY by Francis Flagg ps
(George Henry Weiss) & Forrest J. Ackerman . . . . . .
. .s . . . . WS Mar 36 927
EARTH'S MAGINOT LINE by Roy Paetzke. .ss . . . . . .
. . . . Com May 41 119
EARTH'S MAUSOLEUM by John Russell Fearn. . . . . .
. .nt . . . . ASF May 35 52
EARTH'S SECOND MOON by Willy Ley. .a . . . .
. . . . .ASF Oct 39 141
EARTHSPIN by Nat Schachner. .nt . . . . . ASF Jun 37 8
EARTHSPOT by Morrison Colladay. .s . . . .
. . . . WS May 34 1120
EASY MONEY by Edmond Hamilton. .s . . . TW Apr 38 55
EBBTIDE JONES' ATOM CONSTRICTOR by
Miles Shelton ps (Don Wilcox). .nt . . . . FA Aug 41 100
EBBTIDE JONES ON THE WARPATH by Miles
Shelton ps (Don Wilcox). .s . . . . FA Jun 42 218

Title. .Author. .Length . . . . Magazine. .Date. .Page No.

ECCE HOMO by Chan Corbett *ps (Nathan Schachner)*. .
. .s . . . . ASF Jun 36 56
ECCENTRIC ORBIT by D. B. Thompson. .s . . . .
. . . . ASF Mar 41 113
ECLIPSE BEARS WITNESS by Ephriam Winiki *ps*
(John Russell Fearn). .s . . . . SF Mar 40 42
ECLIPSE SPECIAL, THE by William Lemkin, Ph.D.   . .
. .nt . . . . Amz Dec 30 774
ECLIPSES OF THE SUN by Sir Arthur S. Eddington. . .
. .a . . . . TW Apr 39 32
EDGE OF NIGHT by John K. Aiken. .s . . . . .NW #4 49 43
EDITOR'S NOTEBOOK, THE Editorial dept of
FANTASTIC ADVENTURES
EDITOR'S NOTEBOOK, THE Editorial dept of
FANTASY BOOK
EDMUND LATIMER'S MILKING MACHINE by
Millen Cooke. .s . . . . .OW May 50 148
EDUCATED HARPOON, THE by Charles S. Wolfe . . . .
. .s . . . . Amz Dec 26 831
EDUCATED PILL, THE by Bob Olsen *ps (Alfred*
John Olsen, Jr.). .s . . . . Amz Jul 28 365
EEMANU GROWS UP by Leslie A. Croutch. .s . . . . . .
. . . . FFM Jun 48 112
EGGS FROM LAKE TANGANYIKA, THE by
Curt Siodmak. .s . . . . .Amz Jul 26 346
EGG OF TIME, THE by Millen Cooke. .s. Amz Mar 48 124
EGO OF THE ANT, THE by Alfred Gordon Bennett . . .
. .ss . . . . ToW Win 38 96
EIGHT BALL by Hugh Raymond *ps (John Michel)* . . . .
. .s . . . . UK Jun 43 120
EIGHT DAYS IN THE STORY OF ROCKETRY by
Willy Ley. .a . . . . TW Dec 37 56
EIGHT WHO CAME BACK by Nat Schachner. .nt . . . . .
. . . . FA Nov 41 44
EIGHTY-FIVE AND EIGHTY-SEVEN by Eando Binder
ps (Earl Binder & Otto Binder). .s . . . . . Amz Oct 34 84
EIGHTY PERCENT by Willy Ley. .a . . . . UK May 40 122
EINLEILL by R. R. Winterbotham. .s . . . . ASF Jul 37 90
EINSTEIN EXPRESS, THE by J. George Frederick . . . .
. .n 2 pt . . . . ASF Apr 35 10
EINSTEIN INSHOOT, THE by Nelson S. Bond. .s . . . . .
. . . . ASF Nov 38 103
EINSTEIN SEE-SAW, THE by Miles J. Breuer. .s . . . . .
. . . . ASF Apr 32 74
EINSTEIN SLUGGER, THE by Manly Wade Wellman . .
. .s . . . . TW Dec 39 30
EINSTEIN'S PLANETOID by Paul Dennis Lavond
h ps (Cyril Kornbluth, Robert W. Lowndes &
Frederik Pohl). .s . . . . .SFQ Spr 42 100
ELAINE'S TOMB by G. Peyton Wertenbaker. .s . . . . . .
. . . . AQ Win 31 74
ELDER GODS, THE by Don A. Stuart *ps (John W.*
Campbell, Jr.). .n . . . . UK Oct 39 9
ELECTION CAMPAIGN ON SATURN by Milton
Kaletsky. .s . . . . .Amz Jul 42 48

Title. .Author. .Length . . . . Magazine. .Date. .Page No.

ELECTRIC BATTERY 2000 YEARS AGO, AN
by Willy Ley. .a . . . . ASF Mar 39 43
ELECTRIC DUEL, THE by Hugo Gernsback. .ss . . . . .
. . . . Amz Sep 27 543
ELECTRIC SNARE, THE by David O. Woodbury. .s . . .
. . . . .ASF Jul 34 98
ELECTRICAL BUTTERFLIES, THE by Ross
Rocklynne. .s . . . . FA Mar 42 46
ELECTRICAL MAN, THE by Neil R. Jones. .nt . . . . . .
. . . . SD May 30 400
ELECTRICAL MATHEMATICIANS by Lorne
Maclaughlin. .a . . . . ASF May 49 93
ELECTRICAL ROBOT BRAIN, THE by E. L.
Locke. .a 2 pt . . . . ASF May 48 79
ELECTRICAL YARDSTICKS by Earl Welch. .a . . . . . .
. . . . .ASF Jan 46 101
ELECTRO-EPISODE IN A.D. 2025 by E. D.
Skinner. .s . . . . Amz Aug 27 469
ELECTRO HYDRAULIC BANK PROTECTOR, THE
(HICK'S INVENTIONS WITH A KICK) by
Henry Hugh Simmons. .s . . . . Amz Dec 27 860
ELECTROLYTIC ONSLAUGHT by John Duthie. .s . . .
. . . . ASF Jun 35 98
ELECTRON EAT ELECTRON by Noel Loomis. .s . . . .
. . . . .PS Spr 46 70
ELECTRON FLAME, THE by Jack Williamson. .s . . . . .
. . . . WQ Fal 32 84
ELECTRONIC SIEGE, THE by John W. Campbell, Jr.   .
. .s . . . . WS Apr 32 1246
ELECTRONIC WALL, THE by George R. Fox. .s . . . . .
. . . . Amz Jun 27 234
ELECTRONICS—NEW STYLE by E. M. Locke. .a . . . .
. . . . ASF Dec 48 91
ELECTROPOLIS by Otfrid von Hanstein *(tr fr German*
by Francis Currier). .n . . . . .WQ Sum 30 482
ELEMENT 87 by Ralph Linn. .s . . . . . . Amz Jun 30 222
ELEMENT OF LOGIC, THE by R. R. Winterbotham. . .
. .s .Ash Aug 40 34
ELEMENTAL, THE by Frank Belknap Long, Jr. . .s . . .
. . . . .UK Jul 39 79
ELEMENTALS OF JEDAR by Geoff St. Reynard *ps*
(Robert W. Krepps). .s . . . . .FA May 50 44
ELEPHANT EARTH by Gabriel Barclay *h ps (Manly . . .*
Wade Wellman). .s . . . . .Ash Feb 40 54
ELEPHAS FRUMENTI by L. Sprague de Camp &
Fletcher Pratt. .s . . . . .F&SF Win-Spr 50 95
ELEVENTH HOUR, THE by Edwin Balmer & Wm. B.   .
MacHarg. .s . . . . Amz Feb 27 1042
                                          SD May 30 428
ELF-TRAP, THE by Francis Stevens. .s . . . FN Nov 49 100
ELIMINATION by Don A. Stuart *ps (John W.*
Campbell, Jr.). .s . . . . ASF May 36 45
ELIXIR, THE *(Pt. 5 THE MAN WHO AWOKE)* by
Laurence Manning. .s . . . . WS Aug 33 150
ELIXIR, THE by Jane Rice. .nt . . . . UK Dec 42 114

Title. .Author. .Length . . . . Magazine. .Date. .Page No.

ELIXIR OF DOOM by Ray Cummings. .nt . . . .
. . . . TW Apr 37 98
ELIXIR OF HATE, THE by George Allan England. .n . .
. . . . FFM Oct 42 6
                                        AMF Oct 50 10
ELIXIR OF INVISIBILITY, THE by Henry Kuttner . . .
. .s . . . . FA Oct 40 114
ELIXIR OF PEACE, THE by Robert Moore Williams. . .
. .s . . . . Amz Dec 49 124
ELIXIR OF PROGRESS, THE by Philip J. Bartel. .s . . .
. . . . WS Apr 35 1286
ELSEWHEN by Anthony Boucher ps (William
Anthony Parker White). .nt . . . . .ASF Jan 43 112
ELSEWHERE by Caleb Saunders. .nt . . . . ASF Sep 41 96
ELUSIVE MICROVOLT, THE by George O. Smith . . . .
. .a . . . . .ASF Sep 45 101
EMANCIPATED, THE by L. Sprague de Camp. .s . . . . . .
. . . . ASF Mar 40 50
EMBASSY, THE by Martin Pearson ps (Donald A.
Wollheim). .s . . . . ASF Mar 42 72
EMERGENCY by Vic Phillips. .s . . . . . . .ASF Sep 40 143
EMERGENCY LANDING by Ralph Williams. .ss . . . . .
. . . . ASF Jul 40 52
EMERGENCY REFUELING by James Blish. .ss . . . . . .
. . . . SSS Mar 40 101
EMISSARIES OF SPACE by Nathan Schachner. .n . . . .
. . . . WQ Fal 32 6
EMOTION GAS, THE by George F. Gatter. .s. . . . . . .
. . . . WS Mar 36 966
EMOTION METER, THE by W. Varick Nevins III . . . . .
. .ss . . . . .WS Jan 35 954
EMOTION SOLUTION by Arthur K. Barnes. .s . . . . . .
. . . . WS Mar 36 954
EMPEROR OF THE STARS, THE by Nat Schachner
& Arthur L. Zagat. .s . . . . WS Apr 31 1210
EMPEROR OF THE UNIVERSE by Rene LaFayette. . .
ps (L. Ron Hubbard). .s . . . . .SS Nov 49 132
EMPEROR'S EYE, THE by Leroy Yerxa. .nt . . . .
. . . . FA May 47 116
EMPEROR'S HEART, THE by Henry J. Kostkos. .s . . .
. . . . ASF Jun 34 93
EMPERORS OF SPACE by Jerome Gross &
Richard Penny. .s . . . . WS Nov 31 762
EMPIRE IN THE SKY, THE by Ralph W. Wilkins. .s . . .
. . . . WS Oct 30 418
EMPIRE OF DUST by Basil Wells. .s . . . . FB #5 23
EMPIRE OF GLASS, THE by Frank Miloche. .s . . . . . .
. . . . WQ Spr 31 366
EMPIRE OF JEGGA by David V. Reed ps (David
Vern). .n . . . . Amz Nov 43 10
EMPIRE OF THE ANTS, THE by H. G. Wells. .s . . . . . .
. . . . Amz Aug 26 410
EMPIRE OF THE NECROMANCERS, THE by
Clark Ashton Smith. .s . . . . .AFR #7 85
EMPLOYMENT by Lyman R. Lyon ps (L. Sprague
de Camp). .s . . . . ASF May 39 79

EMPRESS OF MARS, THE by Ross Rocklynne. .nt . . . .
. . . . FA May 39 26
                                        FA Oct 42 184
EN ROUTE TO PLUTO by Wallace West. .s . . . .
. . . . ASF Aug 36 39
ENCHANTED BOOKSHELF by William P.
McGivern. .nt . . . . FA Mar 43 112
ENCHANTED FOREST, THE by Fritz Leiber. .s . . . . .
. . . . .ASF Oct 50 110
ENCHANTED VILLAGE by A. E. van Vogt. .s . . . .
. . . . OW Jul 50 6
ENCHANTED WEEK END, THE by John
MacCormac. .nt . . . . UK Oct 39 115
                                        UK 48 6
ENCHANTRESS OF LEMURIA by Stanton A.
Coblentz. .n . . . . Amz Sep 41 8
ENCHANTRESS OF VENUS by Leigh Brackett. .nt . . .
. . . . PS Fal 49 4
ENCROACHMENT by Raymond F. Jones. .s . . . .
. . . . .SS Mar 50 112
END, THE by Murray Leinster ps (Will F. Jenkins) . . . .
. .nt . . . . TW Dec 46 36
END IS NOT YET, THE by L. Ron Hubbard. .n 3 pt . . .
. . . . ASF Aug 47 6
END OF HIS SERVICE, THE by Ray Cummings. .s. . . .
. . . . CF Win 42 87
END OF THE PARTY, THE by Graham Greene. .s . . . .
. . . . WB Dec 50 32
END OF THE ROCKET SOCIETY, THE by Willy Ley. .
. .a 2 pt . . . . ASF Aug 43 64
END OF THE UNIVERSE, THE by Milton Kaletsky . . .
. .s . . . . WS Apr 34 1008
END OF THE WORLD, THE IT CAN HAPPEN
TOMMORROW! by William Juhre. .bacover pic . . . .
. . . . Amz May 39
END OF TIME, THE by Henry F. Kirkham. .s . . . .
. . . . WS Dec 30 658
END OF TIME, THE by Wallace West. .s . . . .
. . . . ASF Mar 33 64
END OF TYME, THE by A. Fedor & Henry Hasse. . . . .
. .s . . . . WS Nov 33 336
END OF YOUR ROPE by Robert Bloch. .s . . . .
. . . . .FA Jul 50 110
ENDLESS CHAIN, THE by A. Macfadyen, Jr. . .nt . . . .
. . . . ASF Apr 37 56
ENDOCHRONIC PROPERTIES OF RESUBLIMATED .
THEOTIMOLINE, THE by Isaac Asimov. .a . . . .
. . . . ASF Mar 48 120
ENDOCRINOLOGY IS TOUGH by Joseph A.
Winter(s), M.D. . .a . . . . .ASF Oct 48 114
ENDOWMENT POLICY by Lewis Padgett ps (Henry
Kuttner & C. L. Moore). .s . . . . ASF Aug 43 118
ENEMY OF KNOWLEDGE, AN by A. M. Phillips . . . . .
. .n . . . . ASF Apr 47 114
ENERGY by Harl Vincent. .s . . . .
. . . . .ASF Jan 35 79

Title. .Author. .Length . . . . Magazine. .Date. .Page No.

ENERGY EATERS, THE by Arthur K. Barnes &
  Henry Kuttner. .s . . . . TW Oct 39 16
  SS Sep 50 124
ENERGY FROM BEYOND by Vincent H. Gaddis. .a . . .
  . . . . Amz May 46 156
ENGINEERING IN EXTREMES by R. S. Richardson . .
  . .a .ASF Jun 45 136
ENGINES OF THE GODS by Gardner F. Fox. .nt . . . . .
  . . . . .PS Spr 46 2
ENGLISH AT THE NORTH POLE, THE by Jules
  Verne. .n 2 pt . . . . Amz May 29 104
ENIGMA OF THE CITY by Chester S. Geier. .nt . . . . .
  . . . . Amz Apr 43 136
ENIGMA OF THE OCEANS, THE by L. Taylor
  Hansen. .a . . . . Amz Dec 47 168
ENORMOUS WORD, THE by William Oberfield. .s . . . .
  . . . . PS Sum 50 43
ENSLAVED BRAINS by Eando Binder ps (Earl
  Binder & Otto Binder). .n 3 pt . . . . . . .WS Jul 34 134
ENTER THE NEBULA by Carl Jacobi. .s. . . . .
  . . . . PS Fal 46 24
ENTER THE PROFESSOR by E. Mayne Hull. .nt . . . .
  . . . . .ASF Jan 45 45
ENTROPY by Nat Schachner. .nt . . . . . . ASF Mar 36 76
ENTITY by Poul Anderson & John Gergen. .s. . . . . .
  . . . . ASF Jun 49 58
ENVIRONMENT by Chester S. Geier. .s . . . .
  . . . . ASF May 44 161
ENVIRONMENT by William Holloway. .s . . . .
  . . . . FN Nov 48 112
EPHEMERAE, THE by Edmond Hamilton. .s. . . . . . .
  . . . . ASF Dec 38 50
EPHONY'S SPECTACLES by Clarence
  Granowski. .s . . . . .SFQ Win 41–42 79
EPISODE OF CATHEDRAL HISTORY, AN by
  M. R. James. .s . . . . AFR #12 102
EPISODE IN SPACE, AN by Stanton A.
  Coblentz. .s . . . . .ASF May 35 43
EPISODE ON DHEE MINOR by Harry Walton. .s . . . . .
  . . . . ASF Oct 39 96
EPISODE ON IO, AN by J. Harvey Haggard. .s . . . . . .
  . . . . WS Feb 34 736
EPISTLE TO THE THESSALONIANS, AN by Philip
  Wylie. .s. . . . . .WB Dec 50 11
EPOS OF POSI AND NEGA, AN by Joe W.
  Skidmore. .s. . . . . .Amz Jan 35 112
EQUALIZER, THE by Jack Williamson. .n. . . . .
  . . . . ASF Mar 47 6
EQUATION FOR TIME by R. R. Winterbotham. .s . . . .
  . . . . Com Dec 40 65
ERDIS CLIFF by Richard S. Shaver. .n . . . .
  . . . . Amz Sep 49 62
ERGODIC PREDICTION by J. J. Coupling. .a . . . .
  . . . . ASF Feb 50 128
ERNEST'S EVIL ENTITY by Arthur T. Harris
  h ps. .s. . . . . FA Oct 48 108

Title. .Author. .Length . . . . Magazine. .Date. .Page No.

EROS TO EARTH by Walter Kately. .s . . . .
  . . . . SW Oct 29 436
ERRAND BOY by William Tenn ps (Philip Klass) . . . . .
  . .s . . . . ASF Jun 47 89
ERSATZ WORLD, THE by Willy Ley. .a . . . .
  . . . . .SSS May 40 118
ESCAPE by Joseph Gilbert and Fred W. Fisher. .nt . . . .
  . . . . ASF Apr 43 43
ESCAPE, THE by Don A. Stuart ps (John W.
  Campbell, Jr.). .nt . . . . ASF May 35 118
ESCAPE FROM CERES by Clara E. Chesnutt. .s. . . . . .
  . . . . Amz Oct 35 114
ESCAPE FROM DOOM by John Wilstach. .n . . . .
  . . . . FA Apr 45 10
ESCAPE FROM PHOBOS by Neil R. Jones. .s . . . .
  . . . . WS Feb 33 690
ESCAPE FROM PLUTO by William Oberfield. .s. . . . . .
  . . . . .PS Fal 47 84
ESCAPE THROUGH SPACE by Ross Rocklynne. .s . . .
  . . . . Amz Jun 38 30
ESCAPE TO FEAR by Peter Reed. .s . . . . . SSS Jul 50 72
ESCAPE TO MLOK by Clark Ashton Smith. .s . . . .
  . . . . ToW Aut 41 57
ESPERANTO—TONGUE OF TOMORROW by Charles .
  D. Hornig. .s. . . . . .SF Jun 39 62
ESPIONAGE IN SPACE by Alan Connell. .s. . . . .
  . . . . .PS Win 41 76
ESSENCE OF LIFE, THE by F. Pragnell. .s . . . .
  . . . . Amz Aug 33 436
  ToW Aut 38 105
ETAOIN SHRDLU by Fredric Brown. .s . . . UK Feb 42 67
ETERNAL CYCLE, THE by Edmond Hamilton. .s . . . .
  . . . . WS Mar 35 1184
ETERNAL DICTATOR, THE by Nathan Schachner . . .
  . .s . . . . WS Feb 33 678
ETERNAL EVE, THE by John Wyndham ps (John
  Beynon Harris). .nt . . . . Amz Sep 50 114
ETERNAL LIGHT, THE by Robert Moore Williams . . .
  . .s . . . . TW Jan 40 66
ETERNAL MAN, THE, by D. D. Sharp. .s . . . .
  . . . . SW Aug 29 230
  SS Jan 39 100
  WSA 50 116
ETERNAL MAN REVIVES, THE by D. D. Sharp . . . . .
  . .s . . . . .WQ Sum 30 548
ETERNAL MASK, THE by Julian Kendig, Jr. . .nt . . . .
  . . . . Amz Feb 33 1017
ETERNAL MOMENT, THE by Robert Arthur. .s . . . . .
  . . . . .SS Mar 41 103
ETERNAL NOW, THE by Murray Leinster ps (Will
  F. Jenkins). .s. . . . . TW Fal 44 11
ETERNAL PRIESTESS, THE by Harold Lawlor. .s . . . .
  . . . . FA Apr 42 108
ETERNAL PROFESSORS, THE by David H.
  Keller, M.D. . .s . . . . Amz Aug 29 414
  ToW Aut 38 61

Title. .Author. .Length . . . . Magazine. .Date. .Page No.

ETERNAL QUEST, THE by Joseph Gilbert. .s . . . .
. . . . Ash Oct 42 61
ETERNAL WALL, THE by Raymond Z. Gallun. .s . . . .
. . . . Amz Nov 42 144
ETERNAL WANDERER, THE by Nat Schachner. .nt . .
. . . . ASF Nov 36 14
ETERNAL WORLD, THE by Clark Ashton Smith. . . . .
. .s . . . . WS Mar 32 1130
ETERNAL ZEMMD MUST DIE by Henry Hasse . . . . . .
. .nt . . . . .PS Spr 49 2
ETERNITY LOST by Clifford D. Simak. .nt. . . . .
. . . . ASF Jul 49 117
ETHER BREATHER by Theodore Sturgeon. .s. . . . . . .
. . . . .ASF Sep 39 119
ETHER-POWER SHIP OF EUROPA by James B.
Settles. .bacover . . . . Amz Nov 43
ETHER ROBOTS, THE by Frank Belknap Long. . . . . .
. .nt . . . . TW Dec 42 15
ETHER SHIP OF OLTOR, THE by S. Maxwell
Coder. .s . . . . Amz Jul 27 318
ETHER VIBRATES, THE Letter dept of
STARTLING STORIES
ETHICAL EQUATIONS, THE by Murray Leinster
ps (Will F. Jenkins). .s . . . . .ASF Jun 45 117
EUROPA ENCHANTMENT by Henry Andrew
Ackermann. .ss . . . . SSS Jul 40 112
EUTHANASIA LIMITED by David H. Keller, M.D. . . .
. .s . . . . .AQ Fal 29 506
EVANS OF THE EARTH GUARD by Edmond
Hamilton. .s . . . . AW Apr 30 902
EVEN A WORM by J. S. Bradford. .nt . . . .
. . . . FFM Jun 45 78
EVEN STEVEN. . . by Charles Harness. .s . . . .
. . . . .OW Nov 50 138
EVEN THE ANGELS by Malcolm Jameson. .s . . . .
. . . . UK Aug 41 151
EVENING PRIMROSE by John Collier. .s . . . .
. . . . AFR #3 107
EVENING STAR, THE by David H. Keller, M.D. . . . . .
. .n 2 pt . . . . SW Apr 30 966
EVENSONG by John & Dorothy de Courcy. .s . . . .
. . . . .FA Jan 48 112
EVERLASTING FOOD, THE by Margaret
St. Clair. .nt . . . . TW Dec 50 120
EVERY WORK INTO JUDGEMENT by Kris
Neville. .s . . . . .F&SF Win-Spr 50 29
EVERYTHING BUT THE SINK by Berkeley
Livingston. .s . . . . Amz Mar 48 132
EVERYTHING'S JAKE by John Hawkins. .s . . . .
. . . . UK Aug 42 54
EVICTION BY ISOTHERM by Malcolm Jameson . . . . .
. .s . . . . ASF Aug 38 134
EVIDENCE by Isaac Asimov. .nt . . . . . . .ASF Sep 46 121
EVITABLE CONFLICT, THE by Isaac Asimov. . . . . . .
. .nt . . . . ASF Jun 50 48

EVOLUTION by Langdon Smith. .p . . . . FFM Apr 41 101
EVOLUTION GONE MAD by Howard M. Duffin . . . . .
. .bacover pic . . . . Amz Feb 40
EVOLUTION SATELLITE by J. Harvey Haggard . . . . .
. .nt 2 pt . . . . WS Dec 33 422
EVOLUTIONARY MONSTROSITY, THE by Clare
Winger Harris. .s . . . . AQ Win 29 70
EVOLUTION'S END by Robert Arthur. .s . . . .
. . . . TW Apr 41 75
EX MACHINA by Lewis Padgett *ps (Henry Kuttner
& C. L. Moore).* .nt . . . . ASF Apr 48 7
EXAMPLE by Tom Pace. .ss . . . . .PS Win 46 73
EXHALTED, THE by L. Sprague de Camp. .s . . . .
. . . . ASF Nov 40 64
EXILE by Edmond Hamilton. .ss . . . . SSS May 43 88
EXILE OF THE EONS by Arthur C. Clarke. .s . . . .
. . . . .SSS Mar 50 86
EXILE OF THE SKIES, THE by Richard Vaughan . . . .
. .n 3 pt . . . . .WS Jan 34 550
                                      FSQ Sum 50 11
EXILE OF TIME, THE by Ray Cummings. .n 4 pt . . . . .
. . . . ASF Apr 31 26
EXILE TO CENTAURI by Ross Rocklynne. .nt . . . . . .
. . . . .TW Aug 43 13
EXILED FROM EARTH by Sam Merwin, Jr. . .s . . . . .
. . . . TW Dec 40 31
EXILES, THE by Ray Bradbury. .s . . . .
. . . . .F&SF Win-Spr 50 74
EXILES FROM THE UNIVERSE by Stanton A.
Coblentz. .s . . . . Amz Feb 38 125
EXILES OF MARS by Frank K. Kelly. .s . . . .
. . . . .WQ Sum 32 484
                                      WSA 50 184
EXILES OF NEW PLANET by Paul Dennis Lavond
*h ps (Cyril Kornbluth, Robert W. Lowndes &
Frederik Pohl).* .s . . . . .Ash Apr 41 74
EXILES OF THE DESERT STAR by Ross Rocklynne . .
. .s . . . . .PS Spr 41 80
EXILES OF THE ELFMOUNDS by Richard S. Shaver . .
. .nt . . . . .Amz Jul 49 8
EXILES OF THE MOON by Nat Schachner & Arthur
L. Zagat. .n 3 pt . . . . WS Sep 31 440
EXILES OF THE STRATOSPHERE by Frank Belknap
Long, Jr. . .s . . . . .ASF Jul 35 35
EXILES OF THE THREE RED MOONS by Carl Selwyn
. .s . . . . PS Sum 40 54
EXILES OF VENUS by Jim Vanny. .s . . . . . WS Jun 31 64
EXILES ON ASPERUS by John Beynon Harris. .nt . . . .
. . . . WQ Win 33 166
EXIT by Bob Tucker *ps (Arthur Wilson Tucker).* .s . . . .
. . . . .Ash Apr 43 90
EXIT FROM ASTEROID 60 by D. L. James. .s . . . .
. . . . .PS Win 40 65
EXIT LINE by Matt Lee *ps (Sam Merwin, Jr.).* .s . . . .
. . . . .SS Sep 50 119

Title. .Author. .Length . . . . Magazine. .Date. .Page No.

EXIT THE PROFESSOR by Henry Kuttner. .s . . . .
. . . . TW Oct 47 83
EXODUS by Arthur J. Burks. .nt . . . . MSS Nov 38 8
EXPEDITION by Anthony Boucher ps (William Anthony
  Parker White). .s . . . . TW Aug 43 49
EXPEDITION FROM KYTLM, THE by M. F. James . . .
  . .s . . . . ASF Dec 36 111
EXPEDITION MERCY by J. A. Winter, M.D. . .nt . . . .
. . . . ASF Nov 48 7
EXPEDITION POLYCHROME by J. A. Winter, M. D.
  . .s .ASF Jan 49 33
EXPEDITION TO PLUTO by Fletcher Pratt & Laurence
  Manning. .nt. . . . . .PS Win 39 52
EXPENSIVE SLAVES, THE by Rene Lafayette. .s . . . .
. . . . ASF Nov 47 63
EXPERIMENT by Roscoe Clark, F.R.C.S. . .s . . . . .
. . . . TW Apr 39 29
EXPERIMENT IN GENIUS by William F. Temple. .s . . .
. . . . .ToW Sum 40 33
EXPERIMENT IN GYRO HATS, AN by Ellis Parker
  Butler. .s . . . . Amz Jun 26 266
EXPERIMENT OF DR. SARCONI, THE by Harry Bates
  . .nt . . . . .TW Jul 40 93
EXPERIMENT WITH DESTINY by Oscar J. Friend. .s. .
. . . . TW Oct 39 64
EXPLORERS OF CALLISTO, THE by Harl Vincent . . .
  (Schoepflin). .s . . . . Amz Feb 30 998
EXPOSURE by Eric Frank Russell. .s . . . .
. . . . ASF Jul 50 107
EXTERMINATOR, THE by A. Hyatt Verrill. .ss . . . . .
. . . . Amz Feb 31 1020
EXTERMINATORS, THE by Frederic Arnold
  Kummer, Jr. . .s . . . . .TW Aug 38 48
EXTEROCEPTOR DECEPTOR, THE by Craig Browning.
  ps (Roger P. Graham). .s . . . . FA Jan 50 74
EXTRA BRICKLAYER, THE by A. M. Phillips. .s. . . .
. . . . UK Sep 40 85
EXTRA EARTH by Ross Rocklynne. .s. . . . SS Sum 46 88
EXTRA-GALACTIC INVADERS by J. Schlossel. . . . .
  . .nt . . . . AQ Spr 31 260
EXTRA MAN, AN by Jackson Gee. .s . . . .ASF Oct 30 118
EXTRA-SOLAR PLANETS by R. S. Richardson. .a . . . .
. . . . .ASF Sep 44 106
EXTRAPOLATED DIMWIT, THE by S. D. Gottesman
  ps (Cyril Kornbluth, Robert W. Lowndes & Frederick
  Pohl). .nt. . . . . Fut Oct 42 10
EXTRATERRESTRIAL BACTERIA by Willy Ley. .a . .
. . . . ASF Dec 43 110
EYE OF ALLAH, THE by C. D. Willard. .s . . . .
. . . . .ASF Jan 31 58
EYE OF BALAMOK, THE by Victor Rousseau
  (Emanuel). .n . . . . .FN May 49 8
EYE OF MADNESS, THE by Ray Rooney. .s. . . . . . .
. . . . ASF Apr 37 73
EYE OF PROMETHEUS, THE by R. F. Starzl. .s . . . . .
. . . . .SD Jan 30 38

Title. .Author. .Length . . . . Magazine. .Date. .Page No.

EYE OF THE PAST by Eando Binder ps (Otto Binder) .
  . .s . . . . ASF Mar 38 142
EYE OF THE VULTURE, THE by Walter Kateley. .s. . .
. . . . Amz Nov 28 738
EYE OF THE WORLD, THE by Alexander Blade
  h ps (Don Wilcox). .n 2 pt. . . . . FA Jun 49 8
EYE OF TWO WORLDS, THE by Arthur G. Stangland
  . .s . . . . WS Jun 31 44
EYE OF WILBUR MOOK, THE by H. B. Hickey ps
  (Herb Livingston). .s . . . . .Amz Nov 48 8
EYE TO THE FUTURE by Ree Dragonette. .s . . . . . .
. . . . ASF Feb 47 51
EYES ARE WATCHING, THE by Walt Sheldon. .nt . . .
. . . . .Amz Jul 50 90
EYES OF THAR, THE by Henry Kuttner. .s . . . .
. . . . PS Fal 44 45
EYES THAT WATCH by Raymond Z. Gallun. .s . . . . .
. . . . Com Dec 40 107

F

F.O.B. VENUS by Nelson S. Bond. .s . . . . . FA Nov 39 34
FABLES FROM THE FUTURE by Lee Owens. . . . . . .
  . .dept. . . . . .from FA Mar 50
FACE BEYOND THE VEIL, THE by Franklin Bahl. . . .
  . .nt . . . . FA Apr 50 8
FACE IN THE ABYSS, THE by A. Merritt. .n . . . .
. . . . AA 27 54
                                      FFM Oct 40 6
                                      AMF Jul 50 12
FACE IN THE SKY by Thornton Ayre ps (John Russell
  Fearn). .nt . . . . Amz Sep 39 90
FACE OF ISIS, THE by Cyril G. Wates. .s . . . .
. . . . Amz Mar 29 1084
FACE OF THE DEEP, THE by Edmond Hamilton . . . .
  . .n . . . . CF Win 43 15
FACELESS MEN, THE by Arthur Leo Zagat. .nt . . . . .
. . . . .TW Apr 48 13
FACES THRU THE AGES. .bacover pic . . . . Amz Oct 38
FACETED EYES by E. L. Ross. .s . . . . . .ASF Oct 35 127
FACTORY IN THE SKY by Basil E. Wells. .s . . . .
. . . . .Ash Sep 41 68
FACTS IN THE CASE OF M. VALDEMAR, THE by
  Edgar Allen Poe. .s . . . . Amz Apr 26 92
FACTS OF LIFE, THE by P. Schuyler Miller. .s . . . . . .
. . . . .Com May 41 25
FACTS OF THE FUTURE by Lee Owens. .dept . . . . . .
. . . . FA Feb 50 156
FAILURE ON TITAN by Robert Abernathy. .s . . . . . .
. . . . .PS Win 47 56
FAIR EXCHANGE by Miles Shelton ps (Don Wilcox) . .
  . .s . . . . FA Oct 44 148
FAIRY CHESSMEN, THE by Lewis Padgett ps (Henry
  Kuttner & C. L. Moore). .n 2 pt . . . . ASF Jan 46 7

Title. .Author. .Length . . . . Magazine. .Date. .Page No.

FAIRY TALE by Tarleton Fiske *ps (Robert Bloch)*. . . .
. .s . . . . FA Aug 43 184
FAITHFUL, THE by Lester del Rey. .s . . . .
. . . . ASF Apr 38 78
FALL OF LEMURIA, THE by Richard S. Shaver . . . . .
. .nt . . . . .OW Nov 49 4
FALL OF MERCURY, THE by Leslie F. Stone *ps (Mrs. .*
William Silberberg). .nt . . . . Amz Dec 35 27
FALL OF THE EIFFEL TOWER, THE by Charles
de Richter *(tr fr French by Fletcher Pratt)*. .n 3 pt. . .
. . . . WS Sep 34 390
FALLING PLANETOID, THE by I. R. Nathanson. . . . .
. .s . . . . SW Apr 30 986
FALSE DAWN by A. Bertram Chandler. .nt . . . .
. . . . .ASF Oct 46 126
FALSE DAWN by Henry Kuttner. .s . . . . . TW Jun 42 107
FAMILY TREE OF THE ANIMAL KINGDOM, THE
by T. Rorr. .a . . . . FA May 43 226
FAMINE ON MARS by Frank K. Kelly. .nt . . . .
. . . . ASF Sep 34 72
FANATICS OF MERCURY by Henry Andrew
Ackermann. .s. . . . . Fut Dec 42 86
FANDOM'S CORNER by James V. Taurasi. *.dept of*
fanews & fanzine reviews . . . .*from* SSS Jan 49 6
FANE OF THE BLACK PHARAOH by Robert
Bloch. .s . . . . AFR #5 37
FANTASIA DEMENTIA by Maurice G. Hugi. .s . . . . . .
. . . . .NW #3 42
FANTASTIC FACTS by Lee Owens. *.dept*. . . . .
. .*irregularly in* FA . . . . *between* Mar 48 & Jan 50
FANTASTIC HOAXES
THE MOON HOAX OF RICHARD ADAMS LOCKE
. .a . . . . FA May 39 58
THE CARDIFF GIANT by Julius Schwartz. .a . . . . .
. . . . .FA Jul 39 54
JOHN WORRELL KEELY'S ATOMIC VIBRATION
POWER by Julius Schwartz. .a . . . . . . FA Sep 39 56
THE CALAVERAS SKULL HOAX by Julius
Schwartz. .a . . . . FA Nov 39 54
THE FISCHER HOAX by Willy Ley. .a . . . .
. . . . FA Jan 40 28
DR. KOCH'S SEA SERPENT by Willy Ley. .a . . . . . .
. . . . FA Feb 40 26
THE BALOON HOAX by Willy Ley. .a . . . .
. . . . FA Mar 40 28
GEORGE PSALMANAZAR by Willy Ley. .a . . . . . .
. . . . FA Apr 40 40
COMET-SEEKER HOAX by Julius Schwartz. .a . . . .
. . . . FA May 40 38
CAGLIOSTRO by Julius Schwartz. .a . . . .
. . . . FA Jun 40 90
ATLANTIS HOAX OF DR. SCHLIEMANN by
Willy Ley. .a . . . . FA Aug 40 46
JOHN JACOB SCHEUCHZER by Willy Ley. .a . . . .
. . . . FA Oct 40 74

Title. .Author. .Length . . . . Magazine. .Date. .Page No.

BARNUM, (PHINEAS TAYLOR) by Julius
Schwartz. .a . . . . FA Jan 41 76
Amz May 41 48
HAIL-STORM GUN by Douglas Nelson Rhodes
. .a . . . . FA Mar 41 76
FANTASTIC INVENTIONS
PERPETUAL MOTION MACHINES. .a . . . .
. . . . .FA May 39 25
FANTASTIC HUMANS
WOLF CHILDREN by Herman E. Krimmel. .a . . . . .
. . . . FA Apr 40 60
IDIOTS SAVANTS by Herman E. Krimmel. .a . . . . .
. . . . FA Jun 40 51
FANTASTIC TWINS, THE by John York Cabot *ps*
(David Wright O'Brien). .s . . . . FA Mar 42 72
FANTASY BOOK REVIEWS by Sam Moskowitz . . . . .
review dept in FA . . . . *irregularly from* Jan 49
FANTASY CIRCLE by Forrest J. Ackerman & Barbara
Bovard. *.dept* . . . . .Ash Feb 43 85
FAR CENTAURUS by A. E. van Vogt. .s . . . .
. . . . .ASF Jan 44 68
FAR DETOUR, THE by Capt. Arthur J. Burks, U.S.M.C.
. .n . . . . SFQ Win 42 4
FAR WAY, THE by David R. Daniels. .s . . . .
. . . . ASF Jul 35 119
FAREWELL TO EARTH by Donald Wandrei. .nt . . . . .
. . . . ASF Dec 33 98
FAREWELL TO FUZZIES by Henry Hasse. .s . . . .
. . . . .Ash Sep 41 29
FAREWELL TO THE MASTER by Harry Bates. .nt . . .
. . . . ASF Oct 40 58
FAST WATCH, THE by Edwin Balmer & W. B.
MacHarg. .s . . . . .SD Jan 30 21
FASTER THAN LIGHT by J. Harvey Haggard. .s . . . . .
. . . . WS Oct 30 432
FASTER THAN LIGHT by D. D. Sharp. .s . . . .
. . . . MSS Feb 39 73
FASTER THAN LIGHT by Harl Vincent *(Schoepflin)* . .
. .n . . . . .AQ Fal-Win 32 290
FATAL ASTEROID by Harry Walton. .s . . . .
. . . . TW Jun 41 106
FATAL COLORATION, THE by Willy Ley. .a . . . .
. . . . ASF Apr 42 98
FATAL EQUATION, THE by Arthur G. Stangland. .s . .
. . . . WS Apr 33 830
FATAL GLANCE, THE by Derwin Lesser *ps (Charles D.*
Hornig). .ss . . . . WS Feb 35 1058
FATAL QUADRANT, THE by Arthur J. Burks. .nt . . . .
. . . . ASF Feb 38 36
FATAL TECHNICALITY, THE by Rog Phillips *ps*
(Roger P. Graham). .s . . . . .OW Mar 50 56
FATAL THOUGHTS by Leslie Northern *h ps*. .s . . . . .
. . . . SS Sum 45 74
FATAL WORD, THE by Gustavus Meyrinck. .s . . . . . .
. . . . OW Jan 50 78

Title. .Author. .Length. . . . . Magazine. .Date. .Page No.

FATE by Alan Conn *ps (Alan Connell)*. .ss. . . . .
. . . . WS Mar 36 952
FATE AND THE FLY by Robert Moore Williams. .s . . .
. . . . FA Feb 42 132
FATE CHANGER, THE by Richard O. Lewis. .s . . . . .
. . . . Amz Sep 39 125
FATE OF THE ASTEROID, THE by William P.
McGivern. .s . . . . Amz May 41 120
FATE OF THE POSEIDONIA, THE by Clare Winger
Harris. .s . . . . Amz Jun 27 245
FEAR by L. Ron Hubbard. .n . . . . UK Jul 40 9
FEAR NEUTRALIZER, THE by Edmond Hamilton . . .
. .s . . . . SS Mar 39 108
FEAR PLANET, THE by Murray Leinster *ps (Will F.
Jenkins)*. .s. . . . . SSS Jan 50 48
FEAR PLANET, THE by Robert Bloch. .s . . . .
. . . . SSS Feb 43 116
FEATHERED DETECTIVE, THE by A. Hyatt
Verrill. .s . . . . Amz Apr 30 31
FEEP, LEFTY series See ROBERT BLOCH author
FELINE LIGHT AND POWER COMPANY IS
ORGANIZED, THE *(THE SCIENTIFIC ADVENTURES
OF MR. FOSDICK)* by Jaque Morgan. .s . . . .
. . . . Amz Jul 26 319
. . . . AA 27 117
FEMININE METAMORPHOSIS, THE by David H.
Keller, M.D. . .s . . . . SW Aug 29 246
FEMINTOWN, MARS by Clarence Granowski. .s. . . . .
. . . . .SFQ Spr 41 141
FERDINAND FINKNODLE'S PERFECT DAY by David
Wright O'Brien. .s . . . . Amz Sep 41 74
FERTILITY OF DALRYMPLE TODD, THE by Nelson
S. Bond. .s . . . . FA Aug 40 48
FEW NOTES ON THE RELIABILITY OF NEWSPAPER
CLIPPINGS WITHOUT ADDITIONAL REMARKS
ABOUT CHARLES FORT AND OTHERS by Willy
Ley. .a. . . . . UK Mar 40 156
FIDO by Chester S. Geier. .s . . . . UK Oct 43 125
FIDO by Mack Reynolds. .s. . . . . .FA May 50 78
FIEND OF NEW LONDON, THE by Don Wilcox. .s . . .
. . . . Amz Feb 42 194
FIFTH CHILD, THE by August Derleth. .s. . . . .
. . . . FA Sep 50 126
FIFTH COLUMN OF MARS by Robert Moore
Williams. .nt . . . . Amz Sep 40 6
FIFTH DIMENSION, THE by Clare Winger Harris. . . . .
. .s . . . . Amz Dec 28 823
FIFTH DIMENSION CATAPULT, THE by Murray
Leinster *ps (Will F. Jenkins)*. .nt. . . . . .ASF Jan 31 72
FIFTH DIMENSION TUBE, THE by Murray Leinster
ps (Will F. Jenkins). .nt. . . . . .ASF Jan 33 366
FIFTH FREEDOM by John Alvarez. .s . . . .
. . . . ASF May 43 109
50th CENTURY REVOLT by Arthur G. Stangland. .s . .
. . . . WS Apr 32 1206

Title. .Author. .Length. . . . . Magazine. .Date. .Page No.

50 MILES DOWN by Peter Horn *h ps (Henry Kuttner)*. .
. .s . . . . .FA May 40 74
FIFTY MILLION MONKEYS by Raymond F. Jones . . .
. .nt . . . . ASF Oct 43 39
FIGHTERS NEVER QUIT by Malcolm Jameson. . . . .
. .s . . . . .UK Aug 42 84
FIGHTING HEART, THE by W. Alexander. .s . . . . . .
. . . . Amz Feb 28 1099
FIGURE, THE by Edward Grendon. .s . . . .
. . . . .ASF Jul 47 46
FILCH by Frank Belknap Long. .s . . . . . ASF Mar 45 56
FILE 384 by Bowen Conway *ps (John Michel)* . . . .
. .s . . . . .Fut Apr 42 39
FILM LIBRARY by A. E. van Vogt. .s . . . .
. . . . ASF Jul 46 148
FILM OF DEATH by J. Scott Campbell. .s. . . . .
. . . . ASF Mar 48 141
FINAL BLACKOUT by L. Ron Hubbard. .n 3 pt . . . . .
. . . . ASF Apr 40 9
FINAL COMMAND by A. E. van Vogt. .s . . . .
. . . . ASF Nov 49 91
FINAL ENEMY by L. Ron Hubbard. .s. . . . .
. . . . SSS Sep 50 119
FINAL FRONTIER, THE by Robert Moore
Williams. .s. . . . . SSS Jan 50 88
FINAL GLORY by Henry Hasse. .ss . . . . . .PS Spr 47 91
FINAL MISSION by John D. MacDonald. .ss . . . .
. . . . PS Nov 50 57
FINAL STRUGGLE, THE by Francesco Bivona. .s . . . .
. . . . WS Oct 34 550
FINAL TRIUMPH, THE *(Part 3 of THE REVOLT OF
THE SCIENTISTS)* by Nat Schachner. .s . . . .
. . . . WS Jun 33 26
FINAL VICTIM by Henry Hasse & Ray Bradbury. .s . . .
. . . . Amz Feb 46 114
FINAL WAR, THE by Carl W. Spohr. .n 2 pt . . . .
. . . . WS Mar 32 1110
FINALITY UNLIMITED by Donald Wandrei. .nt . . . . .
. . . . ASF Sep 36 8
FINAN-SEER, THE by E. L. Locke. .s . . . .
. . . . .ASF Oct 49 132
FIND THE SCULPTOR by Samuel Mines. .s. . . . .
. . . . TW Spr 46 58
FINDING OF HALDGREN, THE by Charles
Willard Diffin. .nt . . . . ASF Apr 32 20
FINE FEATHERS by George O. Smith. .nt . . . .
. . . . .ASF Jan 46 152
FINGER! FINGER! by Margaret Ronan. .s . . . .
. . . . UK Oct 41 81
FINGER OF THE PAST, THE by Miles J.
Breuer, M.D. . .s . . . . Amz Nov 32 703
FINGERPRINTS OF FEAR by Richard Casey *h ps* . . . .
. .s . . . . FA Oct 45 82
FINGERS OF THE MIST by Peter Brough. .s . . . .
. . . . Amz Jun 29 264

Title. .Author. .Length . . . . Magazine. .Date. .Page No.

FINIS by Frank Lillie Pollock. .s . . . FFM May-Jun 40 116
FN Jul 48 118
FINISHED by L. Sprague de Camp. .s . . . ASF Nov 49 146
FINISHED BY HAND by H. B. Hickey ps (Herb
Livingston). .s. . . . . FA May 46 166
FINITY by E. A. Grosser. .s . . . . ASF Nov 41 70
FIRE BRAND! by A. Bertram Chandler. .s. . . . .
. . . . MSS Nov 50 109
FIRE GAS by Stanton A. Coblentz. .s. . . . .
. . . . FFM Apr 40 113
FIRE GLOBE, THE by Guy Archette (on Story) (ps of
CHESTER S. GEIER, to whom it is credited in
ToC). .nt . . . . Amz Oct 49 90
FIRE IMPS OF VESUVIUS by Nat Schachner. .s . . . . .
. . . . .ASF Oct 33 102
FIRE IN THE HEAVENS by George O. Smith. .n . . . . .
. . . . SS Jul 49 9
FIRE-POWER by S. D. Gottesman ps (Cyril
Kornbluth). .s. . . . . Cos Jul 41 6
FIRE TRAIL, THE by Oge-Make. .s . . . . .Amz Jan 48 128
FA Jan 48 66
FIRELESS AGE, THE by David H. Keller, M. D. . . . . .
. .n 2 pt. . . . . Amz Aug 37 33
FIREPROOF by Hal Clement ps (Harry Clement
Stubbs). .s . . . . ASF Mar 49 67
FIRES OF GENESIS by Raymond Z. Gallun. .nt . . . . .
. . . . ASF Mar 37 124
FIRES WITHIN, THE by E. G. O'Brien ps (Arthur C.
Clarke). .s . . . . Fant Aug 47 72
by Arthur C. Clarke . . . . . SS Sep 49 121
FIRING LINE by George O. Smith. .nt . . . ASF Dec 44 69
FIRST, THE by Kris Neville. .s . . . . SSS Sep 50 53
FIRST CONTACT by Murray Leinster ps (Will F. Jenkins)
. .nt . . . . ASF May 45 7
FIRST FLIGHT, THE by Joe W. Skidmore. .s. . . . . . .
. . . . Amz Nov 34 92
FIRST HUNDRED YEARS YOU GET NOWHERE, THE
by Constance R. Dowd. .a. . . . . Amz Mar 45 184
FIRST MAN ON THE MOON, THE by Alfred Coppel . .
. .ss. . . . . PS Spr 50 36
FIRST MARTIAN, THE by Eando Binder ps (Earl Binder
& Otto Binder). .s . . . . Amz Oct 32 651
FIRST MEN IN THE MOON, THE by H. G. Wells. . . .
. .n 3 pt. . . . . Amz Dec 26 774
FIRST ONE, THE by John D. MacDonald. .ss. . . . . . .
. . . . SS Jan 50 139
FIRST ORNITHOPTER, THE by Jack Winks. .s . . . . . .
. . . . .Amz Jan 30 943
FIRST PERSON SINGULAR by Eric Frank Russell. . . .
. .nt . . . . TW Oct 50 78
FIRST ROCKET by D. Richard Sharpe ps (Richard S.
Shaver). .s . . . . .Amz Aug 47 72
FIRST SHALL BE LAST, THE by Arthur J. Burks . . . .
. .s .ASF Jan 39 141
FIRST TARGET IN SPACE by R. L. Farnsworth . . . . .
. .a .SS Sep 48 98

FISCHER HOAX, THE (FANTASTIC HOAXES) by
Willy Ley. .a. . . . . FA Jan 40 28
FISH-MEN OF ARCTICA by John Miller Gregory. . . . .
. .nt . . . . Mir Jun-Jul 31 238
FISH MEN OF VENUS by David Wright O'Brien. .nt . . .
. . . . Amz Apr 40 30
FISH STORY by Vic Phillips & Scott Roberts. .s . . . . .
. . . . ASF May 41 101
FISHERMAN, THE by Robert Moore Williams. .s . . . . .
. . . . FA Feb 43 98
FISHERMAN'S LUCK by Frank Belknap Long. .s. . . . .
. . . . .UK Jul 40 102
FISHHEAD by Irvin S. Cobb. .s . . . . . . FFM Jun 42 123
(repr as Blood Brother of the Swamp Cats). . . . . . .
. . . . .FanS Nov 50 39
FISSION MAN, THE by R. W. Stockheker. .s . . . .
. . . . SS Jan 49 135
FITZGERALD CONTRACTION, THE by Miles J.
Breuer, M.D. . .s . . . . .SW Jan 30 678
SS Jan 42 94
FIVE AFTER FIVE by Maurice Renard (tr fr French
by Georges Surdez). .s . . . . TW Apr 41 65
FIVE FATHOMS OF PEARLS by James H. Beard. . . . .
. .s . . . . UK Dec 39 88
FIVE GOLD BANDS, THE by Jack Vance. .n. . . . . . .
. . . . SS Nov 50 11
FIVE STEPS TO TOMORROW by Eando Binder ps
(Otto Binder). .n . . . . SS Jul 40 12
FIVE YEARS IN THE MARMALADE by Geoff St.
Reynard ps (Robert W. Krepps). .s . . . . . .FA Jul 49 58
FIXER, THE by Wesley Long ps (George O. Smith). . . .
. .nt . . . . ASF May 45 68
FLAME BREATHERS, THE by Ray Cummings. .nt . . .
. . . . .PS Mar 43 71
FLAME FOR THE FUTURE by P. F. Costello h ps . . . .
. .s . . . . Amz Oct 41 108
FLAME FROM MARS, THE by Jack Williamson. .s. . . .
. . . . .ASF Jan 34 88
FLAME FROM NOWHERE, THE by Eando Binder ps
(Otto Binder). .s . . . . Amz Apr 39 88
FLAME-JEWEL OF THE ANCIENTS by Edwin L.
Graber. .nt. . . . . .PS Spr 50 60
FLAME MIDGET, THE by Frank Belknap Long, Jr. . .
. .s . . . . ASF Dec 36 28
FLAME OF LIFE by Frank Belknap Long, Jr. . .s. . . . .
. . . . .SF Oct 39 92
FLAME QUEEN, THE by Gaston Derreaux. .n . . . . . .
. . . . .Amz May 49 8
FLAME WINDS by Norvell W. Page. .n . . . .
. . . . UK Jun 39 9
FLAME-WORMS OF YOKKU by Hal K. Wells. .s . . . . .
. . . . Amz Mar 33 1137
FLAMING CLOUD, THE by Edsel Newton. .s . . . .
. . . . .WS Jan 31 802
FLAMINGO by Charles Edward Heller. .s . . . .
. . . . .Amz Jul 30 324

Title. .Author. .Length . . . . Magazine. .Date. .Page No.

FLANNELCAKE'S INVENTION by H. McKay. .s . . . . .
. . . . AW Dec 29 530
FLAREBACK by Kent Casey. .s . . . . . . ASF Mar 38 132
FLASHLIGHT BRIGADE, THE by Ralph Milne Farley
ps (Roger Sherman Hoar). .s . . . . AD Jun 30 504
FLAT FOLK OF VULCAN, THE by Dennis Clive *ps*
(John Russell Fearn). .s . . . . .Fut Nov 40 52
FLAW by John D. MacDonald. .s . . . . SS Jan 49 83
FLAYED WOLF, THE by P. Schuyler Miller. .s . . . . . .
. . . . .UK Jul 40 112
FLEA CIRCUS, THE by August Meissner. .s . . . .
. . . . .Amz Jan 49 118
FLESH AGAINST SPIRIT by Alexander Blade *h ps*
(Richard S. Shaver). .s . . . . Amz Mar 48 140
FLIGHT FROM FARISHA by Duncan Farnsworth
ps (David Wright O'Brien). .nt . . . . . Amz Nov 42 168
FLIGHT FROM TIME by Alfred Coppel. .s . . . .
. . . . .PS Win 49 36
FLIGHT FROM TOMORROW by H. Beam Piper . . . . .
. .s . . . . Fut Sep-Oct 50 36
FLIGHT IN 1999 by Bob Olsen *ps (Alfred John*
Olsen, Jr.). .s . . . . AW Sep 29 256
FLIGHT INTO DARKNESS by Webb Marlowe
ps (J. Francis McComas). .s . . . . Amz Feb 43 40
FLIGHT INTO FOG by Lee Francis *h ps*. .nt . . . .
. . . . FA Apr 48 116
FLIGHT INTO SUPER-TIME by Clark Ashton
Smith. .s . . . . WS Aug 32 218
FLIGHT INTO TIME, A by Robert H. Wilson. .s . . . . .
. . . . .WS Feb 31 944
FLIGHT INTO YESTERDAY by Charles L.
Harness. .n . . . . SS May 49 9
FLIGHT OF THE DAWN STAR by Robert Moore
Williams. .s . . . . ASF Mar 38 26
FLIGHT OF THE EASTERN STAR by Ed Earl
Repp. .s . . . . AW Dec 29 498
FLIGHT OF THE MERCURY, THE by Charles R.
Tanner. .s . . . . .WS Jul 30 116
FLIGHT OF THE RX-1, THE by Raymond Z.
Gallun. .s . . . . .Amz Jul 33 371
FLIGHT OF THE SILVER EAGLE by Arthur Leo
Zagat. .s . . . . TW Apr 37 44
FLIGHT OF THE SIRIUS by P. F. Costello *h ps*. .s . . . .
. . . . Amz Jun 43 40
FLIGHT OF THE STARLING by Chester S. Geier . . . .
. .nt . . . . Amz Jan 48 8
FLIGHT OF THE STARSHELL by Gordon A. Giles
ps (Otto Binder). .s . . . . .TW Feb 39 50
FLIGHT OF THE TYPHOON by Clifton B. Kruse. .s . . .
. . . . .ASF Oct 36 140
FLIGHT ON TITAN by Stanley G. Weinbaum. .s . . . . .
. . . . .ASF Jan 35 100
FLIGHT THAT FAILED, THE by E. M. Hull. .s . . . . . .
. . . . ASF Dec 42 29
FLIGHT THROUGH TIME by Clark Ashton Smith. .s . .
. . . . ToW Spr 42 54

Title. .Author. .Length . . . . Magazine. .Date. .Page No.

FLIGHT THROUGH TOMORROW by Stanton A.
Coblentz. .s . . . . FB #1 29
FLIGHT TO FOREVER by Poul Anderson. .nt . . . . . .
. . . . .SSS Nov 50 12
FLIGHT TO GALILEO by Lee Gregor *ps (Milton A.*
Rothman). .s . . . . .Ash Oct 40 88
FLIGHT TO VENUS by Edwin K. Sloat. .s . . . .
. . . . Amz Dec 28 780
FLOATING ISLAND OF MADNESS, THE by
Jason Kirby. .s . . . . .ASF Jan 33 326
FLOATING ROBOT, THE by David Wright
O'Brien. .nt . . . . FA Jan 41 10
FLOWER OF EVIL, THE by C. R. Sumner. .nt . . . . . .
. . . . AD Oct 30 900
FLOWER-WOMEN, THE by Clark Ashton Smith. .s . . .
. . . . .AFR #9 3
FLOWERING EVIL by Margaret St. Clair. .s . . . .
. . . . PS Sum 50 30
FLOWERING OF THE STRANGE ORCHID, THE by
H. G. Wells. .s . . . . Amz Mar 28 1161
FLYING BUZZ-SAW, THE by Harold B. McKay. .s . . . .
. . . . AW Apr 30 898
FLYING CITY, THE by H. Thompson Rich. .s . . . . . .
. . . . ASF Aug 30 260
FLYING DUTCHMAN OF SPACE, THE by Frederic
Arnold Kummer, Jr. . .s . . . . Amz Oct 38 84
FLYING EYE, THE by Robert Arthur. .s . . . .
. . . . FanF May 50 51
FLYING FOOL, THE by David H. Keller, M. D. . .s . . .
. . . . .Amz Jul 29 310
FLYING LEGION, THE by George Allen England. . . . .
. .n 4 pt . . . . AW Jan 30 582
                    (complete). . . . . . . FN Jan 50 8
FLYING SAUCERS: FRIEND, FOE OR FANTASY?
by Willy Ley. .a . . . . GSF Oct 50 67
FLYING THREAT, THE by David H. Keller, M. D. . . .
. .nt . . . . AQ Spr 30 242
FLYING WING OF PLUTO by James B. Settles . . . . . .
. .bacover. . . . . Amz Oct 42
FOG by C. C. Campbell *ps (Horace L. Gold)*. .s . . . .
. . . . .ASF Jun 35 135
FOG by Robert Willey *ps (Willy Ley)*. .nt . . . .
. . . . ASF Dec 40 80
FOG OF THE FORGOTTEN by Basil Wells. .s . . . . . .
. . . . .PS Win 46 63
FOG OVER VENUS by Arthur K. Barnes. .nt . . . .
. . . . TW Win 45 11
FOLLOW THE BOUNCING BALL by Arthur J.
Burks. .s . . . . ASF Mar 39 45
FOLLOW THE ROCKET TRAIL by Warner Van
Lorne. .s . . . . ASF Sep 36 89
FOLLOWER by Eric Frank Russell. .s . . . . ASF Nov 50 68
FOOD FOR THE FIRST PLANET by Thomas Calvert
McClary. .a . . . . ASF Aug 38 40
FOOTSTEPS INVISIBLE by Robert Arthur. .s . . . .
. . . . .AMF Dec 49 118

Title. .Author. .Length. . . . . Magazine. .Date. .Page No.   Title. .Author. .Length. . . . . Magazine. .Date. .Page No.

FOR EACH MAN KILLS by William F. Temple. .s . . . .
. . . . Amz Mar 50 92
FOR SALE–ONE WORLD by Ross Rocklynne. .s. . . .
. . . . .SSS Feb 43 11
FOR THE PUBLIC by Bernard I. Kahn. .nt . . . . .
. . . . ASF Dec 46 73
FORBIDDEN DREAM, THE by Ross Rocklynne. .s . . .
. . . . PS Sum 40 41
FORBIDDEN FLIGHT by Chester B. Conant ps (Chester
Cohen). .ss . . . . Fut Oct 41 104
FORBIDDEN FRUIT by Kris Neville. .s . . . .
. . . . OTWA Jul 50 111
FORBIDDEN FRUIT by Roger Flint Young. .s. . . . . .
. . . . Amz Aug 50 116
FORBIDDEN LIGHT by James Montague. .nt . . . . . .
. . . . ASF Dec 35 116
FORBIDDEN TRAIL, THE by Jane Rice. .nt . . . . . .
. . . . UK Apr 41 130
FORBIDDEN VOYAGE by Rene LaFayette ps (L. Ron
Hubbard). .s. . . . . SS Jan 49 142
FORCES MUST BALANCE by Manly Wade Wellman. . .
.nt . . . . ASF Sep 39 9
FORECAST by Raymond F. Jones. .nt . . . . ASF Jun 46 6
FOREIGN BODY by John Brody. .ss . . . . .NW #2 46 48
FOREIGN LEGION OF MARS, THE by Frederic Arnold
Kummer, Jr. . .s . . . . Amz May 39 98
FOREVER AND THE EARTH by Ray Bradbury. .s . . . .
. . . . .PS Spr 50 26
FOREVER IS NOT SO LONG by F. Anton Reeds. .s. . .
. . . . ASF May 42 34
FOREVER IS TODAY by Charles F. Ksanda. .s . . . . . .
. . . . .TW Sum 46 92
FOREVER IS TOO LONG by Chester S. Geier. .n. . . . .
. . . . FA Mar 47 8
FOREVER TOMORROW by Cleve Cartmill. .s . . . . . .
. . . . .Ash Apr 43 74
FORGET-ME-NOT by William F. Temple. .nt . . . .
. . . . OW Sep 50 18
FORGETFULNESS by Don A. Stuart ps (John W.
Campbell, Jr.). .nt . . . . ASF Jun 37 52
FORGIVENESS OF TENCHU TAEN, THE by Frederic
Arnold Kummer, Jr. . .s. . . . . ASF Nov 38 119
FORGOTTEN ENEMY, THE by Arthur C. Clarke. .s. . .
. . . . .NW #5 49 48
FORGOTTEN ENVOY by Sam Merwin, Jr. . .s . . . . .
. . . . SS May 49 122
FORGOTTEN FUTURE by Arthur K. Barnes. .s . . . .
. . . . .SF Jan 41 47
FORGOTTEN HADES by Lee Francis h ps. .nt . . . . .
. . . . Amz May 48 140
FORGOTTEN MAN OF SPACE, THE by P. Schuyler
Miller. .s . . . . WS Apr 33 872
SS Win 46 66
FORGOTTEN PAST by William Morrison ps (Joseph
Samachson). .s . . . . SS Jan 43 82

FORGOTTEN PLANET, THE by Sewell Peaslee
Wright. .s . . . . .ASF Jul 30 88
AFR #13 25
FORGOTTEN TONGUE by Walter C. Davies ps (Cyril
Kornbluth). .s . . . . .Sti Jun 41 23
FORGOTTEN WORLD, THE by E. Bauer. .s . . . .
. . . . Amz Aug 31 436
FORGOTTEN WORLD by Edmond Hamilton. .nt. . . .
. . . . TW Win 46 13
FORGOTTEN WORLDS by Lawrence Chandler h ps
(Howard Browne). .n . . . . .FA May 48 8
FORM OF HUNGER, THE by Craig Browning ps (Roger
P. Graham). .s. . . . . FA Oct 49 70
FORMULA FOR CONQUEST by James R. Adams. .s . .
. . . . PS Fal 45 110
FORMULA FOR LIFE by Max C. Sheridan. .s . . . . . .
. . . . TW Sep 40 66
FORMULA FROM THE UNDERWORLD by Richard S.
Shaver. .s . . . . Amz Jun 47 10
FORSAKING ALL OTHERS by Lester del Rey. .s . . . .
. . . . UK Aug 39 89
FORTEAN ASPECTS OF THE FLYING DISCS by Marx
Kaye h ps. .a . . . . Amz Jun 48 154
FORTRESS OF UTOPIA, THE by Jack Williamson . . . .
. .n . . . . SS Nov 39 14
FORTY BILLION WINKS by Roy Kingsley, Ph.D.   . . .
. .a . . . . TW Apr 43 89
FOSDICK, THE SCIENTIFIC ADVENTURES OF MR.
See JACQUE MORGAN author
FOUNDATION series See ISAAC ASIMOV author
FOUNDATION by Isaac Asimov. .nt . . . . . ASF May 42 38
FOUNDLING by Donald Baker Moore. .s . . . .
. . . . ASF Dec 50 66
FOUNTAIN, THE by Nelson S. Bond. .n . . . . UK Jun 41 9
FOUNTAIN OF CHANGE by Chester S. Geier & Richard
S. Shaver. .nt . . . . FA Dec 48 38
4½B, EROS by Malcolm Jameson. .s . . . . . . .PS Spr 41 69
4-D DOODLER, THE by Graph Waldeyer. .s . . . .
. . . . .Com Jul 41 90
FOUR DIMENSIONAL AUTO-PARKER, THE by Bob
Olsen ps (Alfred John Olsen, Jr.). .s . . .Amz Jul 34 113
FOUR DIMENSIONAL ESCAPE, THE by Bob Olsen
ps (Alfred John Olsen, Jr.). .s. . . . . . . Amz Dec 33 44
FOUR DIMENSIONAL ROBBERIES by Bob Olsen ps
(Alfred John Olsen, Jr.). .s . . . . Amz May 28 102
FOUR-DIMENSIONAL ROLLER-PRESS, THE by Bob
Olsen ps (Alfred John Olsen, Jr.). .s . . Amz Jun 27 302
FOUR DIMENSIONAL SURGERY by Bob Olsen ps
(Alfred John Olsen, Jr.). .s . . . . Amz Feb 28 1078
FOUR DIMENSIONAL TRANSIT by Bob Olsen ps (Alfred
John Olsen, Jr.). .nt . . . . .AQ Fal 28 530
FOUR LITTLE SHIPS by Murray Leinster ps (Will F.
Jenkins). .s . . . . ASF Nov 42 36
FOUR MILES WITHIN by Anthony Gilmore ps (Harry
Bates & Desmond W. Hall). .nt . . . . . . ASF Apr 31 76

Title. .Author. .Length . . . . Magazine. .Date. .Page No.

4-SIDED TRIANGLE, THE by William F. Temple. .s . . .
. . . . Amz Nov 39 6
FOUR STAR PLANET by Richard Wilson. .s . . . .
. . . . Fut Apr 42 66
FOUR WHO RETURNED by Chester S. Geier. .nt. . . .
. . . . Amz Feb 46 138
FOURTEENTH EARTH, THE by Walter Kateley. .s . . .
. . . . Amz Feb 28 1092
FOURTH-DIMENSIONAL DEMONSTRATOR, THE by
Murray Leinster ps (Will F. Jenkins). .s . . . .
. . . . ASF Dec 35 100
FOURTH-DIMENSIONAL POSSIBILITIES by Harry D.
Parker, A.S.M.E., S.O.A.E. . .a . . . . . ASF Dec 36 115
FOURTH-DIMENSIONAL SPACE PENETRATOR by
Julian Kendig, Jr. . .s . . . . .Amz Jan 30 958
FOURTH DYNASTY, THE by R. R. Winterbotham . . .
. .s . . . . ASF Dec 36 82
FRACTIONAL EGO by Clifton B. Kruse. .s . . . .
. . . . ASF Feb 37 106
FRAGILE! GLASS! . .a . . . .
. . . . ASF Feb 45 99
FRAGMENT OF DIAMOND QUARTZ, A by Ray
Cummings. .s . . . . SSS Jan 50 60
FRAME CONCEPT OF NUMBERS, TIME AND SPACE,
THE by Roger P. Graham. .a . . . .
. . . . Amz Sep 46 158
FRANKINSTEIN-UNLIMITED by H. A. Highstone. . . .
. .s . .s. . . . . ASF Dec 36 38
FREDDIE FUNK'S FLIPPANT FAIRIES by Frances
Yerxa. .s . . . . FA Sep 48 130
FREDDIE FUNK'S FOREST FORGE by Leroy
Yerxa. .s . . . . FA Jan 45 66
FREDDIE FUNK'S FORGETFUL ELEPHANT by Leroy
Yerxa. .s . . . . FA Apr 4 12
FREDDIE FUNK'S MADCAP MERMAID by Leroy
Yerxa. .s . . . . FA Jan 43 82
FREDDIE FUNK'S SEVEN LEAGUE BOOTS by Leroy
Yerxa. .s . . . . FA Dec 43 46
FREE AS THE AIR by David H. Keller, M.D. . .s . . . . .
. . . . Amz Jun 31 228
FREE ENERGY by Harl Vincent (Schoepflin). .s . . . . .
. . . . Amz Sep 30 529
FREE-LANCE OF SPACE, THE by Edmond Hamilton .
. .s . . . . Amz May 44 122
FREE LAND by William Morrison ps (Joseph
Samachson). .s . . . . .TW Aug 49 89
FREEDOM OF THE SKIES by Edsel Newton. .s . . . . .
. . . . AW Dec 29 518
FRESH FIANCES FOR THE DEVIL'S DAUGHTER by
Russell Gray. .nt . . . . MSS May 40 87
FRICASSEE IN FOUR DIMENSIONS by P. Schuyler
Miller. .s . . . . ASF Dec 43 55
FRICTIONAL LOSSES by Don A. Stuart ps (John W.
Campbell, Jr.). .nt . . . . .ASF Jul 36 44
FRIDAY, THE NINETEENTH by Elisabeth Sanxay
Holding. .s . . . . .F&SF Sum 50 3

Title. .Author. .Length . . . . Magazine. .Date. .Page No.

FRIEND ISLAND by Francis Stevens. .s . . . .
. . . . FN Sep 50 110
FRIENDLY WOLF, THE by Craig Browning ps (Roger
P. Graham). .s. . . . . FA Feb 50 138
FRIENDS by Murray Leinster ps (Will F. Jenkins). .s . . .
. . . . SS Jan 47 86
FRIGHTENED PLANET, THE by Sidney Austen. .s . . .
. . . . Amz Oct 48 28
FRIGID MOON by Dennis Clive ps (J. R. Fearn). .s . . . .
. . . . .Fut Nov 39 77
FROG, THE by P. Schuyler Miller. .s . . . . . UK Oct 42 59
FROM AN AMBER BLOCK by Tom Curry. .s . . . .
. . . . .ASF Jul 30 50
FROM BEYOND THE DAWN by F. G. Rayer. .s. . . . .
. . . . .NW #3 36
FROM BEYOND THE STARS by Will F. Jenkins. .s . . .
. . . . TW Jun 47 82
FROM EROS TO EARTH by Walter Kateley. .s . . . . . .
. . . . SW Oct 29 436
FROM OUT OF THE EARTH by Ed Earl Repp. .s . . . .
. . . . WS Mar 31 1168
FROM THE OCEAN'S DEPTHS by Sewell Peaslee
Wright. .s. . . . . ASF Mar 30 376
FROM PEAS TO HORSES TO MEN by F. Orlin
Tremaine. .a . . . . .TW Feb 49 61
FROM THE BOOKSHELF Book review dept of Fut
from Jul-Aug 50
FROM THE DARK WATERS by Joseph E. Kelleam . . .
. .s . . . . .AFR #6 59
FROM THE VACUUM OF SPACE by J. Harvey
Haggard. .s . . . . ASF Dec 37 136
FROM THE WELLS OF THE BRAIN by Paul Ernst. .s. .
. . . . ASF Oct 33 48
FROM THESE ASHES by Fredric Brown. .s . . . .
. . . . Amz Aug 50 46
FROM TIME'S DAWN by B. Wallis. .s . . . . .FN May 50 96
FRONTIER OF THE UNKNOWN by Norman L.
Knight. .n 2 pt . . . . .ASF Jul 37 8
FRONTIER PLANET by Manly Wade Wellman. .nt . . . .
. . . . .TW Feb 43 15
FROWNZLY FLORGELS, THE by Fredric Brown . . . .
. .s . . . . OW Oct 50 30
FRUIT OF KNOWLEDGE, THE by C. L. Moore. . . . . .
. .nt . . . . UK Oct 40 73
FRUIT OF THE FORBIDDEN TREE by Leslie Burton
Blades. .s . . . . FFM Nov 39 109
FRUIT OF THE MOON-WEED by J. Harvey Haggard . .
. .s . . . . ASF Nov 35 44
FRUITS OF PREJUDICE, THE by Nathaniel
Nitkin. .s . . . . .CF Fal 42 92
FRUITS OF THE AGATHON by Charles L. Harness . . .
. .s . . . . TW Dec 48 64
FRYING PAN, THE Fanzine review dept of TW
from Oct 48
FUEL FOR THE FUTURE by Jack Hatcher. .a . . . . . .
. . . . ASF Mar 40 68

Title. .Author. .Length . . . . Magazine. .Date. .Page No.

FUGITIVE by Ray Cummings. .s . . . . TW Feb 42 34
FUGITIVE, THE by E. K. Jarvis *h ps*. .s . . . .
. . . . FA Feb 43 216
FUGITIVES FROM EARTH by Nelson S. Bond. .s . . . .
. . . . Amz Dec 39 8
FUGITIVE FROM VANGARD by Norman L. Knight . .
. .s . . . . .ASF Jan 42 76
FULL CIRCLE by Hugh Raymond *ps (John Michel)* . . .
. .s . . . . Fut Feb 43 84
FUNGUS ISLE by Philip M. Fisher. .nt . . . FFM Oct 40 67
FURLOUGH FROM ETERNITY by David Wright
O'Brien. .n . . . . FA Apr 43 144
FURY by Lawrence O'Donnell *ps (Henry Kuttner &
C. L. Moore)*. .n 3 pt . . . . ASF May 47 6
FURY FROM LILLIPUT by Murray Leinster *ps (Will F.
Jenkins)*. .nt . . . . .TW Aug 49 9
FUSIBLE ALLOYS by Willy Ley. .a . . . . . ASF Jul 37 71
FUTILITY by Gerald H. Adams. .ss . . . . WS Mar 36 964
FUTILITY by Captain S. P. Meek, USA. .s . . . .
. . . . Amz Jul 29 316
FUTURE OCEAN LINER by Julian S. Krupa. . . . . . .
. .bacover pic . . . . Amz Feb 39
FUTURE ROCKET TRAIN by H. W. MacCauley . . . .
. .bacover pic . . . . .Amz Jan 39
FUTURE SKY FIGHTER by H. W. McCauley . . . .
. .bacover pic . . . . Amz Apr 39
FUTURE SPACE SUIT by Frank R. Paul. . . . .
. .bacover pic . . . . Amz Jun 39
FUTURE WAR TANK by Stanley Ryter . . . .
. .bacover pic . . . . Amz Dec 39
FUTURE'S FAIR, THE by Vincent Reid. .s . . . .
. . . . Ash Oct 40 48
FUZZY HEAD by Frank Belknap Long. .s . . . .
. . . . TW Dec 48 144

G

GABRIEL'S HORN by Ray Bradbury & Henry Hasse. . .
. .s . . . . .CF Spr 43 105
GADGET GIRL, THE by Ray Cummings. .s . . . .
. . . . TW Fal 44 80
GALACTIC CIRCLE, THE by Jack Williamson. .nt . . . .
. . . . ASF Aug 35 6
GALACTIC GEAR by Chester B. Conant *ps (Chester
Cohen)*. .s . . . . .Fut Apr 42 77
GALACTIC GHOST by Walter Kubilius. .s . . . .
. . . . .PS Win 42 91
GALACTIC HERITAGE by Frank Belknap Long. .s . . .
. . . . TW Oct 48 43
GALACTIC PATROL by E. E. Smith, Ph.D. . . . .
. .n 4 pt . . . . ASF Sep 37 8
GALAXIES OF STARS. .a . . . . ASF Sep 44 99
GALAXY RAIDERS, THE by William P. McGivern . . . .
. .nt . . . . Amz Feb 50 8

GALAXY'S FIVE STAR SHELF by Groff Conklin
Book review dept of GSF *from* Oct 50 *(first issue)*
GALILEO'S REVOLUTION by Willy Ley. .a . . . .
. . . . .SSS Aug 41 100
*GALLEGHER, GALLOWAY series See LEWIS PADGETT
ps author*
GALLEGHER PLUS by Lewis Padgett *ps (Henry
Kuttner & C. L. Moore)*. .nt . . . . ASF Nov 43 120
GALLERY OF GLACIAL DOOM by Frances M.
Deegan. .s . . . . Amz Dec 45 146
GAMBLER'S ASTEROID by Manly Wade Wellman . . . .
. .s . . . . TW Spr 44 87
GAMIN, THE by Peter Dexter *ps (Richard S. Shaver)*. . .
. .nt . . . . .OW Mar 50 68
GANGWAY FOR HOMER by George R. Hahn. .s . . . . .
. . . . .SFQ Spr 42 122
GARDEN OF EVIL by Margaret St. Clair. .s . . . .
. . . . PS Sum 49 77
GARDEN OF HELL, THE by Leroy Yerxa. .s . . . .
. . . . FA May 43 164
GARDENER, THE by Margaret St. Clair. .s . . . .
. . . . TW Oct 49 56
GARFIELD'S INVENTION by Leo Am Bruhl. .s . . . . .
. . . . .WS Jan 34 642
GARMENTS OF DOOM by William Morrison *ps
(Joseph Samachson)*. .ss . . . . .SSS Feb 43 63
GAS ATTACK by Ford Smith *ps (Oscar J. Friend)* . . . .
. .ss . . . . TW Spr 44 47
GAS-WEED, THE by Stanton A. Coblentz. .s . . . .
. . . . Amz May 29 138
ToW Spr 39 90
GATE TO XORAN, THE by Hal K. Wells. .s . . . .
. . . . .ASF Jan 31 46
GATEWAY by Robert Arthur. .s . . . .
. . . . UK Mar 40 104
GATEWAY TO DARKNESS by Fredric Brown. .nt . . . .
. . . . .SSS Nov 49 10
GATEWAY TO DESTRUCTION by Harry Gordon . . . .
. .s . . . . FA Sep 49 112
GATEWAY TO GLORY by Fredric Brown. .nt . . . . . .
. . . . Amz Oct 50 120
GATEWAY TO PARADISE by Jack Williamson . . . . . .
. .n . . . . SS Jul 41 14
GATHER, DARKNESS! by Fritz Leiber, Jr. . . . .
. .n 3 pt . . . . .ASF May 43 9
GATHER 'ROUND THE FLOWING BOWLER by
Robert Bloch. .s . . . . FA May 42 130
GAVAGAN'S BAR
  1. ELEPHAS FRUMENTI by L. Sprague de Camp &
  Fletcher Pratt
  2. THE GIFT OF GOD by L. Sprague de Camp &
  Fletcher Pratt. .short stories. . . .F&SF Win-Spr 50 95
GEARS FOR NEMESIS by Raymond Z. Gallun. .s . . . .
. . . . SS Jan 42 106
GEHENNA, INCORPORATED by Berkeley Livingston .
. .s . . . . .Amz Jan 50 130

Title. .Author. .Length . . . . Magazine. .Date. .Page No.

GEMS OF LIFE by Eando Binder *ps (Otto Binder)* . . . .
. .s . . . . TW May 40 30
GENERAL ADAPTATION SYNDROME, THE by Joseph
A. Winter, M.D. . .a . . . . ASF Nov 50 76
GENERAL SWAMP, C. I. C. by Frederick Engelhardt . .
. .n 2 pt . . . . ASF Aug 39 41
GENESIS by R. R. Winterbotham. .s . . . . . PS Sum 41 63
GENIE OF BAGDAD by William P. McGivern. .nt . . . . .
. . . . FA Jun 43 108
GENIE WITH THE LIGHT BROWN HAIR by Robert
Bloch. .s . . . . FA May 43 148
GENIUS by Poul Anderson. .nt . . . . ASF Dec 48 6
GENIUS BUREAU, THE by Helen Weinbaum. .s . . . . .
. . . . .Fut Apr 41 28
GENIUS OF LANCELOT BIGGS, THE by Nelson S.
Bond. .s . . . . FA Jun 40 92
GENIUS OF MR. PRY, THE by Duncan Farnsworth
ps (David Wright O'Brien). .s . . . . FA Nov 41 112
GENTLE BRAIN, THE by Arthur Allport *ps (Raymond Z.
Gallun)*. .s . . . . SFQ Sum 40 130
GENTLE PIRATES, THE by John Berryman. .s . . . . . .
. . . . ASF Nov 42 93
GENTLEMEN—THE QUEEN by Bob Tucker *ps (Arthur
Wilson Tucker)*. .s . . . . SFQ Fal 42 107
GENTLEMEN, THE SCAVENGERS! by Carl Jacobi . . .
. .s . . . . TW Apr 48 80
GENUS HOMO by L. Sprague de Camp & P. Schuyler
Miller. .n . . . . .SSS Mar 41 8
GEOGRAPHY FOR TIME TRAVELERS by Willy Ley .
. .a . . . . ASF Jul 39 122
GEOMETRICS OF JOHNNY DAY, THE by Nelson S.
Bond. .s . . . . ASF Jul 41 114
GERMS OF DEATH by A. H. Vance. .s . . . .
. . . . Amz Aug 38 98
GET OUT AND GET UNDER by L. Sprague de
Camp. .a . . . . ASF Dec 42 76
GET YOUR EXTRA HERE! by William Morrison *ps
(Joseph Samachson)*. .s . . . . SS Sum 44 60
GETAWAY by Chester S. Geier. .s . . . . . Amz Oct 46 56
GHOST by Henry Kuttner. .s . . . . ASF May 43 60
GHOST, THE by A. E. van Vogt. .nt . . . . .UK Aug 42 61
GHOST OF MARS by Festus Pragnell. .nt . . . .
. . . . Amz Dec 38 8
GHOST OF ME, THE by Anthony Boucher *ps
(William Anthony Parker White)*. .s . . . . UK Jun 42 82
GHOST PIRATES, THE by William Hope Hodgson . . . .
. .n . . . . FFM Mar 44 88
GHOST PLANET by Thorne Lee. .s . . . . . .SS Jun 43 104
GHOST PLANET, THE by Murray Leinster *ps (Will F.
Jenkins)*. .nt . . . . TW Dec 48 13
GHOST SHIP OF AZTLAN, THE by L. Taylor Hansen .
. .s . . . . SS Jul 42 110
GHOST THAT HAUNTED HITLER, THE by William P.
McGivern. .nt . . . . .FA Dec 42 8
GHOST WORLD, THE by Sewell Peaslee Wright. .s . . . .
. . . . ASF Apr 31 118

Title. .Author. .Length . . . . Magazine. .Date. .Page No.

GHOSTS OF MELVIN PYE, THE by L. Sprague de
Camp. .s . . . . TW Dec 46 66
GHOUL, THE by L. Ron Hubbard. .n . . . . . .UK Aug 39 9
GIANT, THE by Basil Wells. .s . . . . Sti Mar 42 15
GIANT AND DWARF STARS by Sir James Jeans. .a . . .
. . . . TW Feb 38 64
GIANT ATOM, THE by Malcolm Jameson. .n . . . .
. . . . .SS Win 44 15
GIANT BACILLUS, THE by H. O. Dickinson. .nt . . . . .
. . . . .ToW Sum 38 74
GIANT FROM JUPITER, THE by Gerald Vance *h ps* &
Bruce Dennis *ps (David Wright O'Brien)*. .nt . . . . . .
. . . . FA Jun 42 8
GIANT IN THE EARTH by Morrison Colladay. .s . . . . .
. . . . WS Apr 33 850
GIANT KILLER y A. Bertram Chandler. .nt . . . .
. . . . ASF Oct 45 7
GIANT OF GANYMEDE by Ross Rocklynne. .s . . . . . .
. . . . Amz Dec 46 36
GIANT PUFFBALL, THE by Eugene Stowell. .ss . . . . .
. . . . .AQ Sum 31 429
GIANT RUNT, THE by Ross Rocklynne. .nt . . . .
. . . . .TW Sum 44 11
GIANT STARS by Arthur McCann *ps (John W.
Campbell, Jr.)*. .a . . . . ASF Jul 39 113
GIANTS BEYOND PLUTO by E. K. Jarvis *h ps*. .s . . . . .
. . . . Amz Sep 42 76
GIANTS FROM ETERNITY by Manly Wade Wellman . .
. .n . . . . SS Jul 39 14
". .GIANTS IN THOSE DAYS. ." by Willy Ley. .a . . . . .
. . . . ASF Nov 45 111
GIANTS OF MOGO, THE by Don Wilcox. .n . . . .
. . . . .Amz Nov 47 8
GIANTS OF THE RAY by Tom Curry. .s . . . .
. . . . .ASF Jun 30 368
GIANTS ON THE EARTH by Captain S. P. Meek . . . . .
. .n 2 pt . . . . ASF Dec 31 366
GIANTS ON THE EARTH by Vincent H. Gaddis . . . . .
. .a . . . . Amz Dec 45 162
GIANTS OUT OF THE SUN by Peter Horn *h ps (David
Vern)*. .nt . . . . .Amz May 40 14
GIANTS RETURN, THE by Robert Abernathy. .s . . . . .
. . . . PS Fal 49 43
GIFT, THE by Berkeley Livingston. .nt . . . .
. . . . Amz Aug 46 82
GIFT, THE by Berkeley Livingston. .s. *(This is a different
story from the one above with the same title)* . . . . .
. . . . FA Dec 47 106
GIFT FROM THE STARS by Edmond Hamilton. .nt. . .
. . . . TW Dec 40 91
GIFT HORSE by Ross Rocklynne. .nt . . . .
. . . . ASF Aug 45 116
GIFT OF DARKNESS by Peter Reed *ps (John D.
MacDonald)*. .s . . . . SSS May 50 76
GIFT OF GOD, THE *(GAVAGAN'S BAR)* by L. Sprague
de Camp & Fletcher Pratt. .s . . . .F&SF Win-Spr 50 100

Title. .Author. .Length . . . . Magazine. .Date. .Page No.

GIFT OF MAGIC, THE by Miles Shelton *ps (Don Wilcox)* . .s . . . . FA Jan 40 76
GIFTIE GIEN, THE by Malcolm Jameson. .s . . . . UK Apr 43 94
GIFTS OF ASTI, THE by Andrew North. .s . . . . FB #3 8
GIFTS OF URS, THE by Don Tracy. .s . . . . TW Apr 40 39
GIMLET, THE by Victor Endersby. .s . . . Amz May 30 140
GIMME FINDS THE GIMMICK by Berkeley Livingston. .s . . . . FA Dec 48 132
GIPSIES OF THOS, THE by Frederick Hester. .s. . . . . Amz May 35 115
GIRL AND THE GLACIER, THE by George P. Pearce. . . .s . . . . Amz May 33 170
GIRL FROM INFINITE SMALLNESS, THE by Ray Cummings. .s . . . . PS Spr 40 30
GIRL FROM MARS by Robert Bloch. .s . . . FA Mar 50 28
GIRL FROM VENUS, THE by David V. Reed *ps (David Vern)*. .s . . . . Amz Jun 41 72
GIRL FROM VENUS, THE by D. D. Sharp. .s . . . . MSS Apr 41 53
GIRL IN THE BOTTLE, THE by Jack Williamson. .nt . . . . SSS Sep 40 36
GIRL IN THE GOLDEN ATOM, THE by Ray Cummings. . .nt . . . . FFM Sep-Oct 39 75
GIRL IN THE WHIRLPOOL, THE by Miles Shelton *ps (Don Wilcox)*. .s . . . . FA Aug 40 120
GIRL OF THE SILVER SPHERE by J. Harvey Haggard. . .s . . . . PS Fal 47 115
GIRL WHO READ MINDS, THE by Robert Moore Williams. .nt . . . . Amz Sep 49 8
GIRLS FOR SATAN'S UTOPIA by Brent North. .s . . . . MSS Dec 39 105
GIT ALONG! by L. Sprague de Camp. .s . . . . ASF Aug 50 61
GIVE THE DEVIL HIS DUE by Dallas Ross *ps (Mack Reynolds)*. .s . . . . FA Oct 50 84
GLADIATORS, the by Walt Dennis & Ernest Tucker. . . . .s . . . . SS Jan 43 106
GLAGULA by Warner Van Lorne *ps*. .nt . . ASF Jun 36 78
GLAMOUR by Seabury Quinn. .s . . . . AFR #11 3
GLAMOUR GIRL—2040 by Oscar J. Friend. .ss . . . . SS May 40 108
GLAND MEN OF THE ISLAND, THE by Malcolm R. Afford. .s . . . . .WS Jan 31 828
GLAND MURDERS, THE by Captain S. P. Meek. .s . . . . AD Jun 30 508
GLAND SUPERMAN, THE by Ed Earl Repp. .nt . . . . Amz Oct 38 8
GLASS CITY OF EUROPA by Frank R. Paul. . . . . . .bacover pic . . . . .Amz Jan 42
GLASS EYE, THE by Eric Frank Russell. .s . . . . ASF Mar 49 40
GLEED, BEN series See DON WILCOX author
GLEEPS by P. Schuyler Miller. .s . . . . . . ASF Jul 43 99
GLIDER OF GANYMEDE by James B. Settles. . . . . . . .bacover. . . . . Amz Dec 42

Title. .Author. .Length . . . . Magazine. .Date. .Page No.

GLIMPSE by Manly Wade Wellman. .s. . . . . TW Apr 38 74
GLOBOID TERROR, THE by R. F. Starzl. .s . . . . Amz Nov 30 700
GLORY FLIGHT, THE by Frank Belknap Long . . . . .s . . . . .SS Mar 43 82
GLORY OF THE U. S. L., THE by N. J. Westwood. . . . . . .s . . . . TW Jun 42 72
GLORY ROAD by Hugh Raymond *ps (John Michel)* . .s . . . . .SFQ Fal 42 129
GLOVES OF GINO, THE by P. F. Costello *h ps* . . . . .s . . . . Amz Jun 50 44
GLOWWORM FLOWER, THE by Stanton A. Coblentz . . .s . . . . ASF Jun 36 22
GNARLY MAN, THE by L. Sprague de Camp. .s . . . . UK Jun 39 97
GNOME THERE WAS, A Henry Kuttner. .s . . . . UK Oct 41 108
GNURRS COME FROM THE VOODVORK OUT, THE by R. Bretnor. .s . . . . F&SF Win-Spr 50 3
GOBLINS WILL GET YOU, THE by Hugh Raymond *ps (John Michel)*. .s . . . . Sti Mar 42 45
by John Michel. . . . . . AFR #8 100
GOD BOX, THE by Howard Von Drey *ps (Howard Wandrei)*. .s . . . . ASF Apr 34 75
GOD IN A GARDEN, A by Theodore Sturgeon. .s. UK Oct 39 75
GOD IN THE BOX, THE by Sewell Peaslee Wright . . . . . .s . . . . .ASF Sep 31 407
GOD NAMED KROO, A by Henry Kuttner. .nt . . . . TW Win 44 13
GOD OF LIGHT by Lloyd Arthur Eshbach. .s . . . . .TW Sum 44 93
GOD THAT SCIENCE MADE, THE by Lloyd Arthur Eshbach. .s. . . . . SF Aug 39 86
GODDESS' LEGACY, THE by Malcolm Jameson. .s . . . . UK Oct 42 100
GODDESS OF FIRE by Edgar Rice Burroughs. .nt .FA Jul 41 8
GODDESS OF LOVE, THE by Duncan Farnsworth *ps (David Wright O'Brien)*. .s . . . . FA Oct 41 118
GODDESS OF THE FIFTH PLANE by William P. McGivern. .nt . . . . FA Sep 42 8
GODDESS OF THE GOLDEN FLAME by William P. McGivern. .nt . . . . .FA Jul 47 8
GODDESS OF THE MOON by John Murray Reynolds. . . .nt . . . . .PS Spr 40 2
GODDESS OF THE VOLCANO by Craig Browning *ps (Roger P. Graham)*. .nt . . . . Amz Jun 50 8
GOD'S FOOTSTOOL BY Malcolm Jameson. .a . . . . ASF Feb 43 76
GODS GIL MADE, THE by Ross Rocklynne. .s . . . . UK Nov 40 68
GODS HATE KANSAS, THE by Joseph J. Millard. . . . . . .n . . . . SS Nov 41 16
GODS OF SPACE by Ray Cummings. .s . . . .PS Spr 42 42

Title. .Author. .Length . . . . Magazine. .Date. .Page No.

GODS OF THE JUNGLE by Nelson S. Bond. .n 2 pt . . .
. . . . Amz Jun 42 194
GODS OF VENUS by Richard S. Shaver. .n . . . .
. . . . Amz Mar 48 8
GODSON OF ALMARLU by Raymond Z. Gallun . . . . .
. .nt . . . . ASF Oct 36 8
GOING DOWN! by Thomas Sheridan ps (Walter L.
Gillings). .a . . . . Fant Dec 46 68
GOLD by Clyde Crane Campbell ps (H. L. Gold). .s . . . .
. . . . .ASF Jan 35 51
GOLD by Isaac Nathanson. .s . . . . Amz Jan 34 95
GOLD-BUG, THE by Edgar Allan Poe. .s . . . .
. . . . Amz Apr 34 109
GOLD DRESS, THE by Stephen Vincent Benet . . . . . .
. .s . . . . .AFR #5 62
GOLD DUST AND STAR DUST by Cyril G. Wates . . . .
. .s . . . . Amz Sep 29 510
GOLD RUSH ON CALLISTO by Russell Storm ps (Robert
Moore Williams). .s . . . . Amz Apr 43 176
GOLD SHIP, THE by David H. Keller. .s . . . .
. . . . .AQ Jul 28 391
GOLD TRIUMVIRATE, THE by Walter Kateley. .s . . . .
. . . . SW Nov 29 514
GOLDEN AGE, THE by Elmer Ransom. .s . . . .
. . . . UK Dec 42 82
GOLDEN AMAZON, THE by Thornton Ayre ps (John
Russell Fearn). .s . . . . .FA Jul 39 32
GOLDEN AMAZON RETURNS, THE by Thornton Ayre
ps (John Russell Fearn). .nt . . . . FA Jan 41 78
GOLDEN AMAZONS OF VENUS, THE by John Murray
Reynolds. .n. . . . . PS Win 39 3
GOLDEN BARRIER, THE by G. T. Fleming-Roberts . .
. .s . . . . TW Dec 40 54
GOLDEN BLIGHT, THE by George Allan England . . . .
. .n . . . . FN Mar 49 10
GOLDEN BRIDLE, THE by Jane Rice. .nt . . . .
. . . . UK Apr 43 79
GOLDEN CITY, THE by Ralph Milne Farley ps (Roger
Sherman Hoar). .n . . . . FFM Dec 42 6
GOLDEN CITY ON TITAN by Frank R. Paul. . . . . . .
. .bacover pic . . . . Amz Nov 41
GOLDEN EGG, THE by Theodore Sturgeon. .s . . . . . .
. . . . UK Aug 41 132
GOLDEN GIRL OF KALENDAR by F. Orlin Tremaine .
. .nt . . . . FA Sep 39 24
GOLDEN GIRL OF MUNAN, THE by Harl Vincent
(Schoepflin). .s . . . . Amz Jun 28 252
GOLDEN HORSESHOE, THE by Arthur J. Burks. .nt . .
. . . . ASF Nov 37 12
GOLDEN HOUR OF KWOH FAN, THE by Frank Owen
. .s . . . . AFR #11 22
GOLDEN JOURNEY, THE by (A.) Bertram Chandler . .
. .nt . . . . .ASF Jun 45 138
GOLDEN MASK OF AGHARTI, THE by John & Dorothy
de Courcy. .nt. . . . . FA Jan 50 86
GOLDEN NEMESIS by David A. Kyle. .s . . . Sti Feb 41 28

Title. .Author. .Length . . . . Magazine. .Date. .Page No.

GOLDEN OPPORTUNITY OF LEFTY FEEP, THE by
Robert Bloch. .s . . . . FA Nov 42 106
GOLDEN PENNIES, THE by Lee Prescott. .nt . . . . . .
. . . . Amz Aug 49 52
GOLDEN PLANETOID, THE by Stanton A. Coblentz. .
. .s . . . . Amz Aug 35 48
GOLDEN PRINCESS, THE by Robert Moore Williams
. .nt . . . . FA Aug 40 6
GOLDEN ROAD, THE by Cecil Corwin ps (Cyril
Kornbluth). .s. . . . . Sti Mar 42 34
GOLDEN TEMPLE, THE by Ray Cummings. .s . . . . . .
. . . . TW Jun 43 102
GOLDEN VAPOR, THE by E. H. Johnson. .s . . . .
. . . . AQ Win 28 127
GOLDFISH BOWL by Alfred J. Coppel, Jr. . .s . . . . . .
. . . . FB #6 74
GOLDFISH BOWL by Anson MacDonald ps (Robert A.
Heinlein). .nt . . . . ASF Mar 42 77
GOMA'S FOLLICLES by John & Dorothy de Courcy . .
. .s . . . . PS Sum 48 96
GOOD EGG, THE by Ross Rocklynne. .s. . . TW Fal 46 37
GOOD KNIGHT'S WORK, A by Robert Bloch. .s . . . . .
. . . . UK Oct 41 66
GOOD NATURED PENDULUM, THE by Edward
Everett Hale. .s . . . . Amz May 33 177
GOOD OLD BRIG by Kent Casey. .s . . . . . ASF Jul 38 52
GOON FROM RANGOON, THE by Robert Bloch. .s . . .
. . . . .FA Jul 43 160
GORGONS, THE (No. 2 of THE LEMURIAN DOCU-
MENTS) by J. Lewis Burtt. .s . . . . . Amz Mar 32 1128
GORGONS, THE by Mack Chapman Lea. .s . . . .
. . . . .ASF Sep 48 119
GOSTAK AND THE DOSHES, THE by Miles J.
Breuer, M.D. . .s . . . . Amz Mar 30 1142
AFR #10 92
GRAB BAGS ARE DANGEROUS by Frank Belknap
Long. .s . . . . UK Jun 42 66
GRAVE FOR GULLIBLE, A by B. E. Liston. .s . . . . . .
. . . . .FA Jul 45 56
GRAVE OF THE ACHILLES by Harl Vincent
(Schoepflin). .s . . . . CF Win 41 109
GRAVITATIONAL DEFLECTOR, THE by Harry D.
Parker. .s . . . . WQ Fal 29 130
GRAVITOMOBILE, THE by D. B. McRae. .s . . . .
. . . . .Amz Jul 27 347
GRAVITY EXPERIMENT, THE by J. U. Giesy. .s . . . .
. .nt . . . . FFM Dec 39 118
GRAVITY ISLAND by Harl Vincent (Schoepflin). . . . .
. .s . . . . .SSS Mar 40 68
GRAVITY KING, THE by Clelland J. Ball. .s . . . .
. . . . .AQ Fal 28 564
GRAVITY OFF by Leslie F. Stone ps (Mrs. William
Silberberg). .s . . . . .Fut Jul 40 100
GRAVITY TRAP by Damon Knight. .s . . . SSS Jul 49 112
GRAVITY, UNAFFECTED by Stanton A. Coblentz . . .
. .s . . . . ASF Sep 37 50

Title. .Author. .Length . . . . Magazine. .Date. .Page No.

GRAY DENIM by Harl Vincent (Schoepflin). .s . . . . . .
. . . . ASF Dec 30 354
GRAY PLAGUE, THE by L. A. Eshbach. .s . . . . .
. . . . ASF Nov 30 210
GREAT ADVENTURE, THE by Ray Cummings. . . . . .
. .s . . . . TW Dec 38 51
GREAT AIR MONOPOLY, THE by Rene Lafayette
ps (L. Ron Hubbard). .nt . . . . ASF Sep 48 71
GREAT BRAIN PANIC, THE by Don Wilcox. .n. . . . . .
. . . . .Amz Jul 43 32
GREAT CATASTROPHE OF 2947, THE by Woods
Peters. .s . . . . Amz May 31 166
GREAT COLD, THE by Frank Belknap Long. .s . . . . . .
. . . . ASF Feb 35 39
GREAT DOME ON MERCURY, THE by Arthur L. Zagat.
. .s . . . . ASF Apr 32 120
GREAT DROUGHT, THE by Capt. S. P. Meek. .s . . . . .
. . . . ASF May 32 218
GREAT EGO, THE by Norman A. Daniels. .n. . . . . . .
. . . . SS Spr 44 11
GREAT ENGINE, THE by A. E. van Vogt. .nt . . . .
. . . . .ASF Jul 43 44
GREAT EYE, THE by R. DeWitt Miller. .a. . . . .
. . . . ASF Jun 38 54
GREAT FLOODS, THE by L. Sprague de Camp. .a . . . .
. . . . .ASF Oct 49 112
GREAT GOD AWTO, THE by Clark Ashton Smith . . . .
. .s . . . . TW Feb 40 111
GREAT GODS AND LITTLE TERMITES by Don
Wilcox. .s. . . . . Amz Dec 46 52
GREAT GREEN BLIGHT, THE by Emmett McDowell .
. .nt . . . . PS Win 45 2
GREAT GREEN THINGS by Thomas H. Knight. .s . . . .
. . . . WS Apr 31 1288
GREAT ILLUSION, THE by Will Garth h ps (Edmond
Hamilton). .s . . . . TW Jun 38 97
GREAT INVASION, THE by Sidney Patzer. .s . . . . . .
. . . . .WQ Sum 31 552
GREAT INVASION, THE by William Morrison ps (Joseph
Samachson). .s . . . . .SS Mar 43 98
GREAT INVASION OF 1955, THE by J. David Reid. . .
. .s . . . . Amz Oct 32 662
GREAT JUDGE, THE by A. E. van Vogt. .ss . . . . FB #3 4
GREAT MIRROR, the by Arthur J. Burks. .n. . . . . . .
. . . . .SFQ Sum 42 4
GREAT OIL WAR, THE (Part 2 of THE REVOLT OF THE
SCIENTISTS) by Nat Schachner. .s. . . . WS May 33 946
GREAT ONES, THE by Leslie F. Stone ps (Mrs. Wm.
Silberberg). .s. . . . . .ASF Jul 37 75
GREAT RADIO PERIL, THE by Eric Frank Russell . . .
. .s . . . . ASF Apr 37 47
GREAT SECRET, THE by L. Ron Hubbard. .s. . . . . . .
. . . . SF Apr 43 81
GREAT STEEL PANIC, THE by Irvin Lester & Fletcher
Pratt. .s. . . . . Amz Sep 28 522

Title. .Author. .Length . . . . Magazine. .Date. .Page No.

GREAT THIRST, THE by Nat Schachner. .nt. . . . . . .
. . . . ASF Nov 34 74
GREAT THOUGHT, THE by K. Raymond. .s. . . . . . .
. . . . ASF Mar 37 80
GREAT TRAIN ROBBERY, THE by John York Cabot
ps (David Wright O'Brien). .s . . . . FA Feb 43 160
GREAT TRANSFORMATION, THE by Ray Cummings.
. .s . . . . WS Feb 31 936
GREATER CONFLICT, THE by Raymond F. Jones . . .
. .nt . . . . TW Feb 50 92
GREATER GLORIES by C. L. Moore. .nt . . . .
. . . . .ASF Sep 35 111
GREATER THAN GODS by C. L. Moore. .nt. . . . . . .
. . . . ASF Jul 39 136
GREATEST ADVENTURE, THE by John Taine ps (Eric
Temple Bell). .n . . . . FFM Jun 44 8
GREATEST PAINTER IN THE WORLD, THE by E. M.
Michalske. .s. . . . . FA Feb 49 120
GREED by L. Ron Hubbard. .s . . . .
. . . . ASF Apr 50 53
GREEKS HAD A WAR FOR IT, THE by Kelvin Kent
ps (Arthur K. Barnes). .s . . . . TW Jan 41 36
GREEN CLOUD CAME, A by Robert W. Lowndes. .ss. .
. . . . Com Jan 41 97
GREEN CLOUD OF SPACE, THE by Eando Binder
ps (Earl Binder & Otto Binder). .s. . . . WS May 34 1140
GREEN DOOM, THE by Richard Tooker. .s. . . . .
. . . . ASF Dec 35 44
GREEN DREAM, THE by Bryce Walton. .s . . . .
. . . . .PS Win 49 55
GREEN-EYED MONSTER, THE by Theodore
Sturgeon. .s . . . . UK Jun 43 126
GREEN FLAME, THE by Eric North ps (Bernard
Cronin). .n . . . . AMF Jul 50 64
GREEN FOREST, THE by A. E. van Vogt. .nt . . . .
. . . . ASF Jun 49 6
GREEN GIRL, THE by Jack Williamson. .n 2 pt . . . . . .
. . . . Amz Mar 30 1110
GREEN GLORY by Frank Belknap Long, Jr. . .s . . . . .
. . . . .ASF Jan 35 43
GREEN HELL by Arthur K. Barnes. .s . . . . TW Jun 37 91
GREEN INTELLIGENCE, THE by Harley S. Aldinger. .
. .s . . . . SW Nov 29 550
GREEN MAN, THE by Harold M. Sherman. .n . . . . . .
. . . . Amz Oct 46 8
GREEN MAN RETURNS, THE by Harold M. Sherman .
. .n . . . . Amz Dec 47 8
GREEN MAN OF GRAYPEC, THE by Festus Pragnell. .
. .n 3 pt. . . . . WS Jul 35 136
GREEN PLAGUE, THE by Stanton A. Coblentz. .s. . . .
. . . . ASF Apr 34 30
GREEN RAY, THE by Arthur Leo Zagat. .s. . . . .
. . . . .TW Aug 38 82
GREEN SPHERES by W. P. Cockroft. .s . . . .
. . . . .NW #2 46 56

Title. .Author. .Length . . . . Magazine. .Date. .Page No.

GREEN SPLOTCHES, THE by T. S. Stribling. .nt . . . . .
. . . . Amz Mar 27 1086
GREEN TORTURE, THE by A. Rowley Hilliard. .s . . . .
. . . . WS Mar 31 1162
                                        SS Jan 43 88
GREENFACE by James H. Schmitz. .s . . . .
. . . . UK Aug 43 140
GREGORY CIRCLE, THE by William Fitzgerald ps (Will
F. Jenkins). .s . . . . TW Apr 47 50
GRETA, QUEEN OF QUEENS by W. K. Sonnemann. . .
. .nt . . . . Amz Feb 38 14
GREY LENSMAN by E. E. Smith, Ph.D. . .n 4 pt . . . .
. . . . ASF Oct 39 9
GREY ONE, THE by Robert W. Lowndes. .s . . . .
. . . . .Sti Jun 41 83
GREY SHADOW, THE by W. F. Hammond. .s . . . .
. . . . AD Jul 30 586
GRIEF OF BAGDAD by Kelvin Kent ps (Arthur K.
Barnes). .s . . . . TW Jun 43 76
GRIFTERS' ASTEROID by H. L. Gold. .s . . . .
. . . . PS May 43 97
GRIM INHERITANCE, THE by Carl Clausen. .s . . . . .
. . . . Amz Aug 29 456
GRIM RENDEZVOUS by Arthur Leo Zagat. .s . . . . . .
. . . . TW Dec 46 56
GROWING WALL, THE by David H. Keller. .nt . . . . . .
. . . . SFQ Win 42 54
GROWTH PROMOTOR, THE by Paul K. Chapple . . . . .
. .ss . . . . WS Nov 34 702
GUARANTEED by E. Everett Evans. .ss . . . . SS Jan 48 93
GUARD IN THE DARK by Allison V. Harding. .s . . . .
. . . . AFR #14 51
GUARDIAN by Michael Corbin ps (Cleve Cartmill) . . . .
. .s . . . . UK Feb 43 102
GUARDIAN ANGEL by Raymond Z. Gallun. .s . . . . . .
. . . . SSS May 40 24
GUARDIANS OF THE VOID by Arthur K. Barnes . . . .
. .s . . . . WQ Fal 32 72
GUEST IN THE HOUSE by Frank Belknap Long . . . . .
. .s . . . . ASF Mar 46 67
GUINEA PIG by Arthur K. Barnes. .s . . . . . .CF Spr 42 87
GUINEA-PIG, THE by Cedric Walker. .s . . MSS Nov 50 62
GUINEA PIG, PH. D. by Alfred Bester. .s . . . .
. . . . .SS Mar 40 116
GULF by Robert A. Heinlein. .n 2 pt . . . . ASF Nov 49 53
GULF STREAM GOLD by Ed Earl Repp. .s . . . .
. . . . SW May 30 1062
GULLIVER, 3000 A.D. by Leslie F. Stone ps (Mrs.
William Silberberg). .s . . . . .WS May 33 902
GULPERS VERSUS EARTHMEN by Frances Garfield. .
. .s . . . . Amz Dec 39 68
GUN, THE by Frank Gruber. .s . . . . AFR #7 111
GUNS OF ETERNAL DAY by Howard W. Graham, Ph.D.
ps (Howard Wandrei). .s . . . . ASF Jul 34 123
GUYON 45X by Dean D. O'Brien ps (Earl Binder & Otto
Binder). .s . . . . .SSS Mar 40 40

Title. .Author. .Length . . . . Magazine. .Date. .Page No.

GYPPED! by Arthur McCann ps (John W. Campbell, Jr.)
. .a . . . . ASF Feb 41 116
GYPSY by Poul Anderson. .s . . . . .ASF Jan 50 66

H

HABIT by Lester del Rey. .s . . . . ASF Nov 39 119
HABITS VIA RADIO by E. A. Grosser. .s . . .SF Jan 41 60
HADES by Charles F. Ksanda. .s . . . . TW Oct 39 76
HAG SELEEN, THE by Theodore Sturgeon & James H.
Beard. .s . . . . UK Dec 42 96
HAIL-STORM GUN, THE (FANTASTIC HOAXES)
by Douglas Nelson Rhodes. .a . . . . FA Mar 41 76
HAIR RAISING TALE, A by W. L. Sheppard, Jr. . . . .
. .ss . . . . .WS Jul 34 191
HAIRY ONES, THE by Basil Wells. .s . . . . .PS Win 44 76
HALE, JOHN series See ED EARL REPP author
HALF-BREED by Isaac Asimov. .s . . . . . . .Ash Feb 40 38
HALF-BREEDS ON VENUS by Isaac Asimov. .s . . . . .
. . . . .Ash Dec 40 6
HALF-LIFE by Alfred Coppel. .s . . . . .SSS Sep 50 30
HALF-MAN, THE by Basil Wells. .s . . . .
. . . . SFQ Fal 42 119
HALF-MILE HILL by David H. Keller. .s . . . .
. . . . .AQ Jul 31 371
HALF-PAST ETERNITY by John D. MacDonald. .nt . . .
. . . . SSS Jul 50 12
HALF-PAST TWELVE IN ETERNITY by Robert W.
Sneddon. .ss . . . . FFM Aug 40 118
(under title BOTH FEET IN ETERNITY) . . . .
. . . . .FanS Nov 50 105
HALF-WAY STREET by Joseph R. Galt. .s . . . .
. . . . Amz Feb 49 134
HALFLING, THE by Leigh Brackett. .s . . . .
. . . . .Ash Feb 43 11
HALL & FLINT by Phil Richards. .biog. . . . .
. . . . FFM Feb 41 84
HAMMER OF THE GODS by John York Cabot ps (David
Wright O'Brien). .s . . . . .Amz Jan 41 118
HAMMER OF THOR, THE by Charles Willard
Diffin. .s . . . . ASF Mar 32 358
HAMMER ON THE MOON, THE by Charles Recour. .s .
. . . . FA Jan 49 98
HAMMERING MAN, THE by Edwin Balmer & Wm. B.
MacHarg. .s . . . . Amz Mar 27 1118
                                        SD Apr 30 314
HAND FROM THE STARS, THE by Kris Neville. .s . . .
. . . . SSS Jul 49 116
HAND OF THE GODS by A. E. van Vogt. .nt . . . .
. . . . ASF Dec 46 142
HAND OF ZEI, THE by L. Sprague de Camp . . . .
. .n 4 pt . . . . ASF Oct 50 6
HANDFUL OF STARS, A by Walter Kubilius. .s . . . . .
. . . . SSS Jan 49 76

Title. .Author. .Length . . . . Magazine. .Date. .Page No.

HANDS, THE by Venard McLaughlin. .s . . . Fut Feb 43 43
HANDS ACROSS THE VOID by Will Garth *h ps (Henry Kuttner).* .s . . . . TW Dec 38 15
HANDS OF ALI JINNAH, THE by Dwight V. Swain . . .
. .nt . . . . FA Dec 47 82
HANDS OF ATEN, THE by H. G. Winter *ps (Harry Bates & D. W. Hall).* .nt . . . . ASF Jul 31 20
HANDYMAN, THE by Lester Barclay. .s . . . FA Oct 50 90
HANSON, COMMANDER JOHN series See SEWELL PEASLEE WRIGHT auth
HAPPINESS IS NOWHERE by Chester S. Geier. .s . . . .
. . . . FA Nov 46 112
HAPPY CASTAWAY, THE by Robert E. McDowell. . . .
. .s . . . . PS Spr 45 41
HAPPY DEATH OF ALGERNON APPLENOD, THE by Gerald Vance *h ps.* .s . . . . FA Nov 48 112
HAPPY ENDING by Henry Kuttner. .s . . . . TW Aug 48 46
HAPPY TO DIE by R. K. Dirk. .s . . . . . . FA Feb 49 104
HARD LUCK DIGGINGS by Jack Vance. .s . . . .
. . . . SS Jul 48 102
HARD GUY by H. B. Carleton *h ps.* .ss . . . .
. . . . Amz Nov 42 225
HARDWOOD PILE, THE by L. Sprague de Camp . . . .
. .nt . . . . UK Sep 40 100
HARGREAVES, DON series See FESTUS PRAGNELL author
HARMONIZER, THE by A. E. van Vogt. .s . . . . . .
. . . . ASF Nov 44 169
HARNESSING EARTH'S HEAT *(POWER PLANTS OF TOMORROW No. 2)* by Willy Ley. .a . . . .
. . . . ASF Feb 38 123
HARNESSING THE SUN'S RAYS *(POWER PLANTS OF TOMORROW No. 1)* by Willy Ley. .a . . . .
. . . . .ASF Jan 38 63
HARPERS OF TITAN, THE by Edmond Hamilton . . . .
. .s . . . . .SS Sep 50 96
HASHISH MAN, THE by Lord Dunsany. .ss . . . .
. . . . FFM Dec 45 108
HASTINGS—1066 by L. B. Rosborough. .s . . . .
. . . . Amz Jun 34 53
HAT IN THE HALL, THE by Jack Iams. .ss . . . .
. . . . F&SF Sum 50 25
HAT TRICK, THE by Felix Graham *ps (Fredric Brown).* .s . . . . UK Feb 43 110
HATE by Rog Phillips *ps (Roger P. Graham).* .nt . . . . . .
. . . . Amz Jan 48 50
HATERS, THE by Donald A. Wollheim. .ss . . . .
. . . . UK Oct 40 70
HATHOR'S PETS by Margaret St. Clair. .s . . . .
. . . . SS Jan 50 126
HAUNT by A. Bertram Chandler. .s . . . .
. . . . F&SF Sum 50 123
HAUNT, THE by Theodore Sturgeon. .s . . . .
. . . . UK Apr 41 106
HAUNTED HOUSE by Guy Archette *ps (Chester S. Geier).* .s . . . . FA Jun 49 90

HAUNTED HOUSE by J. Austin Jackson. .s . . . .
. . . . Fant Apr 47 30
HAUNTED METROPOLIS by Chester S. Geier. .nt . . . .
. . . . Amz Nov 46 64
HAVE YOU SEEN ME? by Richard Vardon *ps (David Wright O'Brien).* .s . . . . FA Jun 43 142
HAVE WE A SIXTH SENSE? by Milton Kaletsky. .a . . .
. . . . FA Aug 40 134
HAWK CARSE by Anthony Gilmore *ps (Harry Bates & Desmond W. Hall).* .nt . . . . ASF Nov 31 166
HAZARDS OF SPACE FLIGHT by Derwin Lesser *ps (Charles D. Hornig).* .a . . . . SF Mar 39 80
HAZING, THE by Isaac Asimov. .s . . . . . . TW Oct 42 89
HE CONQUERED VENUS by John Russell Fearn. . . . .
. .s . . . . .Ash Jun 40 6
HE DIDN'T *LIKE* CATS by L. Ron Hubbard. .s . . . . . .
. . . . UK Feb 42 83
HE FROM PROCYON by Nat Schachner. .n . . . .
. . . . ASF Apr 34 92
HE NEVER SLEPT by John Russell Fearn. .s . . . .
. . . . ASF Jun 34 56
HE SHUTTLES by Theodore Sturgeon. .s . . . .
. . . . UK Apr 40 113
HE TOOK IT WITH HIM by Clark Collins. .s . . . .
. . . . FA Apr 50 104
HE WALKED AROUND THE HORSES by H. Beam Piper. .s . . . . ASF Apr 48 53
HE WALKED BY DAY by Julius Long. .s . . . AFR #13 63
HE WASN'T THERE! by Hugh Raymond *ps (John Michel).* .s .Ash Feb 41 22
HE WHO MASTERS TIME by J. Harvey Haggard. .s . . .
. . . . TW Feb 37 58
HE WHO SAW TOMORROW by Thomas P. Kelley . .nt . . . . .FA Jul 46 92
HE WHO SHRANK by Henry Hasse. .nt . . . .
. . . . Amz Aug 36 13
HEAD, THE by Joe Kleier. .s . . . . Amz Aug 28 418
HEAD HUNTERS FOOLED AND FOILED by Paul Drennan. .ss . . . . Amz Aug 33 410
HEADACHES FOR RADARS. .a . . . . ASF Apr 46 99
HEADHUNTERS OF NUAMERICA by Stanton A. Coblentz. .s . . . . Com Mar 41 57
HEADLESS HORROR, THE by Helmar Lewis. .nt . . . .
. . . . Amz May 44 134
HEADLESS MILLER OF KOBOLD'S KEEP, THE by Irvin Ashkenazy. .s . . . . AFR #14 95
HEADLINES FOR TOD SHANE by August W. Derleth. .s . . . . FA Jul 42 222
HEADS OF APEX, THE by Francis Flagg *ps (George Henry Weiss).* .s. . . . . ASF Oct 31 24
HEADSTONES FOR STRONOMERS by R. S. Richardson. .a. . . . . ASF Jul 44 104
HEALING RAYS IN SPACE by J. Harvey Haggard . . . .
. .s . . . . Com Mar 41 72
HEART OF LIGHT by Gardner F. Fox. .s . . . .
. . . . .Amz Jul 46 94

Title. .Author. .Length . . . . Magazine. .Date. .Page No.

HEAT DESTROYERS, THE by Clifton Bryan Kruse . . .
. .s . . . . WS Dec 33 466
HEAT RAY, THE by O. L. Beckwith. .s . . . .
. . . . AW Apr 30 890
HEAVEN IS WHAT YOU MAKE IT by Malcolm
Jameson. .nt. . . . . UK Aug 43 85
HEAVEN ONLY KNOWS by Joe Archibald. .s . . . . . .
. . . . FFM Sep 45 112
HEAVY CARGO by Milton Kaletsky. .ss . . . .SF Sep 41 82
HEAVY MAN, THE by Frank Belknap Long. .s . . . . . .
. . . . TW Apr 43 94
HEAVY PLANET by Lee Gregor ps (Milton A.
Rothman). .s . . . . ASF Aug 39 33
HECTOR SERVADAC or OFF ON A COMET by Jules
Verne. .n 2 pt . . . . Amz Apr 26 4
HEIR APPARENT by Lawrence O'Donnell ps (C. L.
Moore). .nt. . . . . ASF Jul 50 19
HEIR APPARENT by A. E. van Vogt. .nt . . . .
. . . . ASF Jun 45 32
HELEN O'LOY by Lester del Rey. .s . . . ASF Dec 38 118
HELICOPTER INVASION by Ford Smith ps (Oscar J.
Friend). .ss. . . . . .TW Sum 44 70
HELL HATH FURY by Cleve Cartmill. .n . . . .
. . . . .UK Aug 43 9
HELL IN EDEN by Richard O. Lewis. .s . . . FA Jan 40 64
HELL IN THE VILLAGE by Hugh Raymond ps (John
Michel). .s . . . . SFQ Win 42 129
HELL IS A CIRCLE by Lee Francis h ps. .s . . . .
. . . . FA Nov 47 160
HELL IS FOREVER by Alfred Bester. .n. . . . .
. . . . .UK Aug 42 8
HELL PLANET, THE by Leslie F. Stone ps (Mrs. Wm.
Silberberg). .s . . . . WS Jun 32 14
HELL SHIP by Arthur J. Burks. .nt . . . . . . ASF Aug 38 6
HELL SHIP OF SPACE by Frederic Arnold
Kummer, Jr. . .s . . . . Amz Nov 40 108
HELL-STUFF FOR PLANET X by Raymond Z. Gallun .
. .s . . . . .SS Jun 43 89
HELLHOUNDS OF THE COSMOS by Clifford D.
Simak. .s . . . . .ASF Jun 32 336
HELL'S DIMENSION by Tom Curry. .s. . . . .
. . . . ASF Apr 31 51
HELPFUL PLEIADES, THE by R. S. Richardson . . . . .
. .a . . . . ASF Feb 45 104
HELPING HAND, THE by Poul Anderson. .nt . . . . . .
. . . . .ASF May 50 6
HELPING HAND, THE by Burt Macfadyen. .s . . . . . .
. . . . .ASF Jan 48 62
HENRY HORN'S BLITZ BOMB by Dwight V. Swain. . .
. .s . . . . Amz Jun 42 112
HENRY HORN'S RACING RAY by Dwight V.
Swain. .s . . . . FA Feb 42 112
HENRY HORN'S SUPER-SOLVENT by Dwight V.
Swain. .s . . . . FA Nov 41 128
HENRY HORN'S X-RAY EYE GLASSES by Dwight
V. Swain. .s . . . . Amz Dec 42 194

Title. .Author. .Length . . . . Magazine. .Date. .Page No.

HER LOVE WAS JUNGLE GOLD (LEOPARD TEETH)
by Theodore Roscoe. .nt . . . . .FanS Nov 50 49
HER MAJESTY, THE QUEEN by Carter T. Wainwright .
. .a . . . . FA Oct 43 194
HER MAJESTY'S ABERRATION by Rene Lafayette . .
. .s . . . . ASF Mar 48 126
HERCULES, THE GOD OF STRENGTH by Frank R.
Paul. .bac. . . . . FA Apr 43
HERCULES MUSCLES IN by Kelvin Kent ps (Henry
Kuttner). .s . . . . .TW Feb 41 90
HEREAFTER by Emmett McDowell. .nt. . . . .
. . . . Amz Apr 50 62
HEREAFTER, INC. by Lester del Rey. .s . . . .
. . . . UK Dec 41 106
HEREDITY by Isaac Asimov. .s . . . . .Ash Apr 41 8
HERITAGE by Robert Abernathy. .nt . . .ASF Jun 42 114
HERITAGE by Charles L. Harness. .nt . . . .
. . . . .F&SF Fal 50 93
HERITAGE OF THE EARTH, THE by Harley S.
Aldinger. .s. . . . . Amz Feb 32 1036
HERMIT OF MARS by Clifford D. Simak. .nt . . . . . .
. . . . ASF Jun 39 9
HERMIT OF SATURN'S RINGS by Neil R. Jones. .s. . .
. . . . .PS Fal 40 80
HERO, THE by Joseph Farrell. .s . . . . . . ASF Oct 48 52
HERO by H. L. Gold. .s . . . . .TW Oct 39 85
HEROES DIE HARD by Henry Gade h ps. .s . . . .
. . . . FA Dec 43 128
HESITANT ANGEL, THE by Larry Sternig. .s . . . . . .
. . . . FA Oct 47 108
HEXER, THE by H. W. Guernsey ps (Howard Wandrei) .
. .s . . . . UK Jun 39 121
                                          UK 48 118
HIBERNATION by Abner J. Gelula. .s . . .Amz Jul 33 302
HIBITED MAN, THE by L. Sprague de Camp. .s . . . . . .
. . . . TW Oct 49 42
HICKS' INVENTIONS WITH A KICK by Henry Hugh
Simmons
    THE AUTOMATIC SELF SERVING DINING TABLE
    . .s . . . . Amz Apr 27 52
    THE AUTOMATIC APARTMENT. .s . . . .
    . . . . Amz Aug 27 493
    THE ELECTRO HYDRAULIC BANK PROTECTOR.
    . .s . . . . Amz Dec 27 860
    THE PERAMBULATING HOME. .s . . . .
    . . . . Amz Aug 28 450
HICKSON'S STRANGE ADVENTURE by E. K. Jarvis
h ps. .s. . . . . FA Mar 47 120
HIDDEN CITY by Chester S. Geier. .n . . . . .Amz Jul 47 8
HIDDEN COLONY, THE by Otfrid von Hanstein (tr fr
German by Fletcher Pratt). .n 3 pt . . . . .WS Jan 35 904
HIDDEN CONFLICT, THE by Martin Pearson ps (Donald
A. Wollheim). .ss . . . . .SFQ Fal 42 115
HIDDEN IN GLASS by Paul Ernst. .s . . . . Amz Apr 31 58
HIDDEN UNIVERSE, THE by Ralph Milne Farley ps
(Roger Sherman Hoar). .n 2 pt . . . . . . Amz Nov 39 24

Title. .Author. .Length . . . . Magazine. .Date. .Page No.

HIDDEN WORLD, THE by Edmond Hamilton. .n. . . .
. . . . WQ Fal 29 84
                                          FSQ Spr 50 11
HIDE AND SEEK by Arthur C. Clarke. .s . . . .
. . . . ASF Sep 49 68
HIEROPHANTS, THE by Margaret St. Clair. .s . . . . . .
. . . . TW Apr 49 77
HIGGLEDY'S PIG by Meyer Krulfeld. .s . . . .
. . . . .SSS Aug 41 92
HIGH EARS by Rog Phillips. .nt . . . . . . FA Oct 47 142
HIGH FREQUENCY WAR by Harl Vincent. .s . . . . . .
. . . . ASF Feb 40 102
HIGH JACK AND DAME by Cleve Cartmill. .s . . . . . .
. . . . TW Oct 49 90
HIGH TENSION by Albert B. Stuart, M.D. . .s . . . . . .
. . . . Amz Aug 26 446
HIGH VACUA by Henry Bott. .a . . ASF Nov 41 97
HIGHWAYMAN OF THE VOID by Dirk Wylie. .nt . . . .
. . . . PS Fal 44 94
HIGHER JURISDICTION by D. D. Sharp. .ss . . . .
. . . . WS Dec 34 782
HIGHWAY by Wilfred Owen Morley ps (Robert W.
Lowndes). .s . . . . SFQ Fal 42 139
HIGHWAYMAN, THE by Lord Dunsany. .s . . . .
. . . . FFM Dec 44 116
HILDY FINDS HIS WINGS by H. B. Hickey. .s . . . . .
. . . . FA Sep 48 90
HILL AND THE HOLE, THE by Fritz Leiber, Jr. . . . .
. .s . . . . .UK Aug 42 78
HIMALAYCHALET, THE by Margaret St. Clair. .s . . . .
. . . . TW Feb 49 110
HINDSIGHT by Jack Williamson. .s . . . . . ASF May 40 98
HIS AUNT THIAMIN by Alan Barrister. .s . . . .
. . . . .SSS Nov 42 94
HISTORIAN, THE by Carl Jacobi. .ss . . . .
. . . . SS May 50 137
HISTORY by Isaac Asimov. .s . . . . .SSS Mar 41 86
HISTORY CLASS, 2133 A.D. by Frederick
Engelhardt. .s . . . . TW Jan 41 111
HISTORY IN REVERSE by Lee Laurence. . . . .
. .radio script . . . . Amz Oct 39 8
HISTORY LESSON by Arthur C. Clarke. .s . . . .
. . . . SS May 49 137
HITCH IN TIME, A by James MacCreigh ps (Frederik
Pohl). .s . . . . TW Jun 47 61
HITLER'S RIGHT EYE by Lee Francis h ps. .s . . . . . .
. . . . FA Jun 44 120
HO-MING GLAND, THE by Malcolm Afford. .s . . . . . .
. . . . Amz Feb 33 1006
HOARD OF THE GIBBELINS, THE by Lord Dunsany .
. .s . . . . AFR #4 62
HOBBIES by Clifford D. Simak. .nt . . . . . ASF Nov 46 49
"HOBBYIST" by Eric Frank Russell. .nt . . ASF Sep 47 33
HOBO GOD by Malcolm Jameson. .s. . . . . ASF Sep 44 72
HOFFMAN'S WIDOW by Floyd Oles. .s . . . .
. . . . Amz Feb 36 112

Title. .Author. .Length . . . . Magazine. .Date. .Page No.

HOK AND THE GIFT OF HEAVEN by Manly Wade
Wellman. .s. . . . . Amz Mar 41 76
HOK DRAWS THE BOW by Manly Wade Wellman . . . .
. .nt . . . . Amz May 40 88
HOK GOES TO ATLANTIS by Manly Wade Wellman . .
. .nt . . . . Amz Dec 39 42
HOK VISITS THE LAND OF LEGENDS by Manly Wade
Wellman. .nt. . . . . FA Apr 42 154
HOKUM HOTEL by David Wright O'Brien. .nt . . . . . .
. . . . .FA Jul 42 184
HOLD THAT COMET by F. H. Hauser & H. B. Fyfe . . .
. .s . . . . .Ash Dec 40 64
HOLE IN THE SKY, THE by Manly Wade Wellman. .s. .
. . . . .CF Sum 42 95
HOLE THAT GREW, THE by E. D. Johnson. .s . . . . . .
. . . . AQ Spr-Sum 32 280
HOLES IN MY HEAD by Rog Phillips. .s. . . OW Oct 50 54
HOLEY LAND by S. M. Tenneshaw h ps. .s . . . .
. . . . Amz Aug 48 8
HOLLISTER EXPERIMENT, THE by Walter Kateley . .
. .s . . . . AQ Win 29 112
HOLLOW MAN, THE by Thomas Burke. .s . . .AFR #4 36
HOLLOW OF THE MOON by Gabriel Barclay h ps. .s . .
. . . . SSS May 40 6
HOLLOW PLANET, THE by Don Wilcox. .n . . . .
. . . . Amz Oct 42 144
HOLLOW WORLD, THE by Frank Belknap Long. .n . . .
. . . . SS Sum 45 11
HOLLYWOOD ON THE MOON by Forrest J.
Ackerman. .a . . . . Amz Jun 50 186
HOLLYWOOD ON THE MOON series See HENRY
KUTTNER author
HOLLYWOOD ON THE MOON by Henry Kuttner . . . .
. .nt . . . . TW Apr 38 12
                                        SS Jul 49 108
HOLMES' FOLLY by Edmond Hamilton. .s . . . .
. . . . TW Oct 37 59
HOLOCAUST by Charles Willard Diffin. .s . . . .
. . . . .ASF Jun 31 356
HOLY CITY OF MARS by Ralph Milne Farley ps (Roger
Sherman Hoar). .nt . . . . .FA May 42 78
HOME OF THE GODS by A. E. van Vogt. .nt . . . .
. . . . ASF Apr 47 6
HOMECOMING by Ray Bradbury. .s . . . . . . AFR #3 117
HOMEMADE GUN OF JAMRUD, THE by Willy Ley. . .
. .a . . . . ASF Apr 41 126
HOMER AND THE HERRING by Berkeley Livingston .
. .s . . . . FA Apr 44 66
HOMER HIGGINBOTTOM, RAINMAKER by Milton
Kaletsky. .s . . . . Amz Jun 41 114
HOMESTEADER, THE by James Blish. .s . TW Jun 49 135
HOMEWARD BOUND by Robert Moore Williams. .ss . .
. . . . .SS Nov 49 109
HOMO SAPS by Webster Craig ps (Eric Frank Russell) . .
. .s . . . . ASF Dec 41 102
HOMO SOL by Isaac Asimov. .s . . . . .ASF Sep 40 117

Title. .Author. .Length . . . . Magazine. .Date. .Page No.

HONEYCOMBED SATELLITE by Helen Weinbaum . . .
. .s . . . . .TW Jul 40 70
HONEYMOON IN HELL by Fredric Brown. .nt . . . . . .
. . . . GSF Nov 50 4
HOP O' MY THUMB by William Morrison ps (Joseph
Samachson). .s . . . . SSS May 50 94
HORATIUS AT THE BRIDGE by Frank Ferry. .s . . . . .
. . . . .TW Sum 44 45
HORIZONTALS, THE by Frank Belknap Long. .s . . . . .
. . . . .SSS Nov 40 48
HORLA, THE by Guy de Maupassant. .s . . . .
. . . . FFM Sep 42 129
HORMONE, THE by Dane Milton. .s . . . . ASF Nov 34 59
HORMONE MENACE, THE by Eando Binder ps (Otto
Binder). .nt . . . . TW Aug 36 34
HORN O' PLENTY by Richard Casey h ps. .s . . . .
. . . . FA Jun 44 184
HORNETS OF SPACE by R. F. Starzl. .s . . . .
. . . . WS Nov 30 564
                                        SS Mar 42 100
HORRIBLE TRANSFORMATION, THE by J. Stallworth
Daniels. .s . . . . SW May 30 1130
HORROR HOUSE by Walter Livingston Martin. .s. . . . .
. . . . .AD Jul 30 594
HORROR IN THE TELESCOPE, THE by Edmond
Hamilton. .s . . . . .ToW Sum 38 33
HORROR OF THE HEIGHTS, THE by A. Conan Doyle.
. .s . . . . FFM Dec 47 108
HORROR OUT OF CARTHAGE by Edmond Hamilton .
. .nt . . . . FA Sep 39 6
HORROR'S HEAD by Lieut. John Pease ps (Roger
Sherman Hoar). .s . . . . Amz Oct 38 42
HORSE ON LEFTY FEEP, A by Robert Bloch. .s . . . . .
. . . . FA Oct 43 86
HORSE ON ME, A by Benj. Miller ps (Noel Loomis) . . .
. .s . . . . TW Dec 48 89
HORSE ON THORNDYKE, A by William P. McGivern. .
. .nt . . . . FA Apr 44 126
HORSE THAT TALKED, THE by Edmond Hamilton . .
. .nt .FA Jan 41 108
HORSESENSE HANK series See NELSON S. BOND
author
HORSESENSE HANK DOES HIS BIT by Nelson S.
Bond. .s . . . . Amz May 42 178
HORSESENSE HANK IN THE PARALLEL WORLDS by
Nelson S. Bond. .nt . . . . Amz Aug 42 212
HOSTAGE OF TOMORROW by Robert Abernathy. . . .
. .nt . . . . .PS Spr 49 86
HOT CARGO by Bill Brudy. .s . . . . TW Oct 41 99
HOT FILAMENT by Arthur McCann ps (John W.
Campbell, Jr.). .a . . . . ASF May 40 156
HOTEL COSMOS by Raymond Z. Gallun. .s . . . .
. . . . ASF Jul 38 140
HOTHOUSE PLANET, THE by Arthur K. Barnes . . . . .
. .s . . . . TW Oct 37 12
                                        SS Sep 49 84

Title. .Author. .Length . . . . Magazine. .Date. .Page No.

HOTHOUSE WORLD, THE by Fred MacIsaac. .n . . . . .
. . . . FN Nov 50 12
HOUNDS OF KALIMAR, THE by P. Schuyler Miller. . .
. .s . . . . UK Jun 43 138
HOUR OF JUDGEMENT by R. DeWitt Miller. .nt . . . . .
. . . . MSS Aug 39 70
HOUR THE CONQUEROR CAME, THE by Edsel
Newton. .s . . . . .WQ Win 31 252
HOUSE, THE by Rog Phillips ps (Roger P. Graham) . . .
. .s . . . . Amz Feb 47 140
HOUSE, THE by Jane Rice. .s . . . . UK Dec 41 85
HOUSE DUTIFUL, THE by William Tenn ps (Philip
Klass). .s . . . . ASF Apr 48 36
HOUSE IN THE CLOUDS, THE by Ulf Hermanson. . . .
. .s . . . . WS Nov 30 514
HOUSE OF FIRE, THE by Robert Moore Williams . . . .
. .nt . . . . FA Jan 42 40
HOUSE OF MONSTROSITIES by Edsel Newton. .s. . . .
. . . . WS Dec 34 802
HOUSE OF RISING WINDS, THE by Frank Belknap
Long. .s . . . . SS May 48 70
HOUSE OF SHADOWS, THE by Mary Elizabeth
Counselman. .s . . . . .AFR #13 98
HOUSE OF SHADOWS, THE (La Maison des Hommes
Vivants)by Claude Farrere (tr fr French). .n . . . . . .
. . . . FFM Feb 46 66
HOUSE OF TOMORROW by Roby Wentz. .s . . . .
. . . . ASF May 44 118
HOUSE THAT WALKED, THE by Dave Barnes ps (Arthur
K. Barnes). .s . . . . ASF Sep 36 37
HOUSING SHORTAGE by Harry Walton. .s. . . . .
. . . . .ASF Jan 47 37
HOW CAN YOU LOSE? by W. Macfarlane. .s . . . .
. . . . .ASF Jan 49 51
HOW HIGH CAN MAN FLY? by Lt. Apollo Soucek
& Walter Raleigh. .a . . . . AW Apr 30 940
HOW MUCH TO THURSDAY? by Douglas
Stapleton. .s . . . . TW Dec 42 105
HOW TO BUILD A THINKING MACHINE by J. J.
Coupling ps (John R. Pierce). .a . . . . . ASF Aug 50 117
HOWIE LEMP MEETS AN ENCHANTRESS by William
P. McGivern. .s . . . . FA Feb 42 52
HOWLING BOUNDERS, THE by Jack Vance. .s . . . . . .
. . . . .SS Mar 49 115
HOWLING TOWER, THE by Fritz Leiber, Jr. . .s . . . . .
. . . . UK Jun 41 90
HSILGNE ESREVER (on story) by John S. Carroll
(ToC gives title as REVERSE ENGLISH). .s . . . .
. . . . TW Oct 48 125
HUDDLING PLACE by Clifford D. Simak. .s . . . .
. . . . .ASF Jul 44 133
HUGE BEAST by Cleve Cartmill. .s . . . . F&SF Sum 50 18
HUMAN ANGLE, THE by William Tenn ps (Philip Klass).
. .s . . . . FFM Oct 48 112
HUMAN ANTS by J. Harvey Haggard. .s . . . .
. . . . WS May 35 1440
HUMAN BODY A MIGHTY FORTRESS, THE by A.
Morris. .a . . . . Amz Jun 43 187

Title. .Author. .Length . . . . Magazine. .Date. .Page No.

HUMAN EQUATION, THE by Max C. Sheridan. .s . . . .
. . . . TW Feb 39 15
HUMAN MACHINES by J. Harvey Haggard. .s . . . .
. . . . ASF Dec 35 70
HUMAN MICE OF KORDAR by Basil Wells. .s . . . . . .
. . . . .Sti Jun 41 32
HUMAN PETS OF MARS, THE by Leslie F. Stone ps
(Mrs. William Silberberg). .nt . . . . Amz Oct 36 83
HUMAN TERMITES, THE by David H. Keller, M.D. . .
. .n 3 pt . . . . SW Sep 29 294
. .n 4 pt . . . . CF Win 40 99
HUMPTY DUMPTY HAD A GREAT FALL by Frank
Belknap Long. .s . . . . SS Nov 48 74
HUNCH by Clifford D. Simak. .nt . . . . . . .ASF Jul 43 9
HUNGER DEATH by Clifford D. Simak. .nt . . . . . .
. . . . ASF Oct 38 23
HUNGRY GUINEA-PIG, THE by Miles J. Breuer, M.D.
. .s .Amz Jan 30 926
HUNTED, THE by John D. MacDonald. .s . . SSS Jul 49 52
HUNTED ONES, THE by John E. Harry. .nt . . . .
. . . . .SSS Feb 42 109
HUNTER GRACCHUS, THE by Franz Kafka. .s . . . . . .
. . . . WB Dec 50 49
HUNTER OF THE KING PLANET, THE by Carl
Selwyn. .s . . . . TW Aug 42 105
HUNTING BIG GAME by Harold A. Lower. .a . . . .
. . . . .ASF Oct 39 123
HUNTING VIPERS (SCIENTIFIC ACTUALITIES) by
Edmond Locard. .a . . . . SD May 30 440
HUNTRESS OF AKKAN, THE by Robert Moore
Williams. .n . . . . Amz Feb 46 54
HURKLE IS A HAPPY BEAST, THE by Theodore
Sturgeon. .s . . . . .F&SF Fal 49 62
HYPER-SENSE, THE by Lloyd Arthur Eshbach. .s . . . .
. . . . SS Jan 41 85
HYPERCOSMOS by C. P. Mason. .a . . . . . TW Dec 38 46
HYPERPILOSITY by L. Sprague de Camp. .s . . . .
. . . . ASF Apr 38 39

I

I AM EDEN by Henry Kuttner. .nt . . . . . . TW Dec 46 11
I AM NOT GOD by Nat Schachner. .n 2 pt . . . .
. . . . ASF Oct 35 64
I DIED TOMORROW by Peter Worth. .nt . . . .
. . . . FA May 49 104
I GET OFF HERE by Ford Smith ps (Oscar J. Friend) . .
. .s . . . . TW Win 45 68
I HAVE BEEN IN THE CAVES by Margaret Rogers. .nt.
. . . . Amz Jan 47 8
I, JOHN COTTER by Millen Cooke. .s . . . .
. . . . Amz Apr 47 74
"I LIKE YOU, TOO—" by Joe Gibson. .s . . . .
. . . . TW Oct 48 52

I, MARS by Ray Bradbury. .s . . . . .SSS Apr 49 35
I MURDERED YOU by Ruppert Carlin. .ss . . . .
. . . . Amz Jun 49 48
"I PAINT FROM DEATH" by Robert Fleming
Fitzpatrick. .nt . . . . Amz Aug 49 24
"I REMEMBER LEMURIA!" by Richard S. Shaver . . . .
. .n . . . . Amz Mar 45 12
I, ROBOT by Eando Binder ps (Otto Binder). .s . . . . . .
. . . . Amz Jan 39 8
I, ROCKET by Ray Bradbury. .s . . . Amz May 44 108
I, SPY! by Eric Frank Russell. .s . . . . ToW Aug 40 54
I TAKE THIS EARTHMAN by Charles V. De Vet . . . . .
. .s . . . . FA Nov 50 84
I WAKE UP DREAMING by Frances Yerxa. .s . . . . . .
. . . . FA Jun 48 126
ICARUS AND DAEDALUS, FIRST AVIATORS by
Frank R. Paul. .bacover pic . . . . FA Feb 43
ICE AGE AHEAD? by Willy Ley. .a . . . . . ASF Feb 39 86
ICE CITY OF THE GORGON by Richard S. Shaver &
Chester S. Geier. .n . . . . Amz Jun 48 8
ICE CREAM TREE, THE by H. B. Hickey ps (Herb
Livingston). .s . . . . .FA Jul 50 92
ICE ENTITY, THE by Jack Williamson. .nt . . . .
. . . . TW Feb 37 86
ICE, F.O.B., MARS by Eando Binder ps (Otto
Binder). .s . . . . .CF Spr 41 100
ICE MAN, THE by William Withers Douglas. .s . . . . . .
. . . . Amz Feb 30 1020
ICE OVER AMERICA by Ray Cummings. .s . . . .
. . . . .TW Aug 40 62
ICE PLAGUE, THE by Frederic Arnold Kummer, Jr. . .
. .s . . . . Amz Oct 39 72
ICE PLANET by Carl Selwyn. .nt. . . . . . .Com May 41 4
ICE QUEEN, THE by Don Wilcox. .n . . . . . . FA Jan 43 8
ICE WORLD, THE by Ross Rocklynne. .s . . . .
. . . . .TW Sum 46 72
IDEAL, THE by Stanley G. Weinbaum. .s . . . .
. . . . WS Sep 35 416
SS Jun 43 66
FSQ Spr 50 86
IDEALIST, THE by Kurt von Rachen ps (L. Ron
Hubbard). .s . . . . .ASF Jul 40 94
IDENTITY by George O. Smith. .nt . . . . ASF Nov 45 145
IDOL OF THE FLIES, THE by Jane Rice. .s . . . .
. . . . UK Jun 42 90
IF by Jack Binder. .pictorial feature
IF ANOTHER ICE AGE GRIPS THE EARTH . . . . .
. . . . TW Jun 37 87
IF ATOMIC POWER COULD BE HARNESSED . . . .
. . . . TW Aug 37 73
IF THE EARTH STOPPED TURNING . . . .
. . . . TW Oct 37 101
IF A SECOND DELUGE FLOODED THE EARTH . .
. . . . TW Dec 37 89
IF EVOLUTION SPEEDED UP . . . .
. . . . TW Feb 38 89

Title. .Author. .Length . . . . Magazine. .Date. .Page No.

IF THE OCEANS DRIED . . . . TW Apr 38 104
IF SCIENCE CONQUERS GRAVITY . . . TW Jun 38 82
IF MAN MASTERED TELEPATHY. . . . TW Aug 38 76
IF SCIENCE REACHED THE EARTH'S CORE . . . .
. . . . TW Oct 38 98
IF YOU WERE STRANDED IN TIME . . . .
. . . . TW Dec 38 76
IF THERE WERE NO FRICTION . . . . . TW Feb 39 86
IF THE SUN WENT OUT . . . . TW Apr 39 74
IF THE MOON FELL . . . . TW Jun 39 118
IF INSECTS RULED HUMANITY . . . . . TW Aug 39 74
IF AN ADVANCING SUN MENACED EARTH . . . .
. . . . TW Oct 39 62
IF A DARK NEBULA ENVELOPED EARTH . . . . .
. . . . TW Dec 39 66
IF SCIENCE CONQUERED DEATH . . . TW Jan 40 64
IF THE STARS VANISHED . . . . TW Feb 40 72
IF WARS WERE FOUGHT WITH ADVANCED
SCIENCE. . . . . TW Mar 40 72
IF EARTH'S AXIS SHIFTED . . . . TW Apr 40 78
IF INTELLIGENT ROBOTS ARE ACHIEVED. . . . .
. . . . TW May 40 48
IF SCIENCE SOLVED THE SECRETS OF GLAND
CONTROL. . . . . TW Jun 40 70
IF UTOPIA WERE ACHIEVED . . . . . . .TW Jul 40 68
IF ANOTHER RACE LIVES AT THE EARTH'S
CORE . . . . TW Aug 40 60
IF PLANT-LIFE REVOLTED . . . . TW Sep 40 80
IF THE EARTH'S MAGNETIC FIELD FAILED by
Lyle D. Gunn. .a . . . . FA Nov 39 82
IF THE SUN DIED by R. F. Starzl. .s . . . ASF Aug 31 198
IF THIS BE UTOPIA by Kris Neville. .s . . . . . .
. . . . Amz May 50 60
IF THIS GOES ON— by Robert Heinlein. .n 2 pt. . . . . .
. . . . ASF Feb 40 9
IF TOMORROW BE LOST by Robert Ray. .s . . . .
. . . . FA Jun 50 130
IF WE GET A CHANCE by Richard S. Shaver. .a . . . . .
. . . . Amz Jul 48 156
IF YOU BELIEVE by Chester S. Geier. .s . . . .
. . . . .FA Jul 43 94
"—IF YOU CAN GET IT." by Murray Leinster ps (Will
F. Jenkins). .s . . . . ASF Nov 43 155
IF YOU DON'T WATCH OUT— by Frank Belknap
Long. .s . . . . TW Dec 50 107
"IF YOU WERE ME. . ." by Rog Phillips ps (Roger P.
Graham). .s . . . . Amz Jun 50 86
"IF YOU'RE SMART—" by Colin Keith ps (Malcolm
Jameson). .s . . . . ASF Apr 42 51
IGNITION POINT by Arthur McCann ps (John W.
Campbell, Jr.). .s . . . . ASF Apr 38 149
I'LL BE FLEECED by Berkeley Livingston. .s . . . .
. . . . Amz Jun 45 164
I'LL BE SEEING YOU by Lester Barclay. .s . . . .
. . . . FA Oct 44 118

Title. .Author. .Length . . . . Magazine. .Date. .Page No.

I'LL BE THERE WITH MUSIC by Berkeley
Livingston. .s . . . . FA Jun 43 38
I'LL BUILD YOUR DREAM CASTLE by Jack Vance . .
. .s . . . . ASF Sep 47 72
I'LL DREAM OF YOU by Charles F. Myers. .s . . . .
. . . . FA Jan 47 46
I'LL SEE YOU AGAIN by Cpl. Duncan Farnsworth
ps (David Wright O'Brien). .ss . . . . . . Amz Sep 44 194
I'LL TAKE THE SUBWAY by Berkeley Livingston . . . .
. .nt . . . . FA Sep 46 98
ILLUSION OF CALLISTO by Warren Kastel ps. .s . . . .
. . . . Amz May 48 110
ILLUSION SEEKERS, THE by P. F. Costello h ps. . . . .
. .nt . . . . .Amz Aug 50 8
I'M A STRANGER HERE MYSELF by John Bridger
ps (Joe Gibson). .nt . . . . Amz Aug 50 148
IMAGINARY, THE by Isaac Asimov. .s . . . .SSS Nov 42 74
IMITATION OF DEATH by Lester del Rey. .s . . . .
. . . . .Fut May-Jun 50 76
IMMORTAL, THE by Ross Rocklynne. .s . . . .
. . . . Com Mar 41 4
IMMORTAL MENACE, THE by Craig Browning ps
(Roger P. Graham). .s . . . . Amz Feb 49 112
IMMORTALITY by John D. MacDonald. .ss . . . .
. . . . SS May 49 113
IMMORTALITY NEEDS YOUR HELP (WHAT MAN
CAN IMAGINE) by Hobart M. Gibson. .a . . . .
. . . . Amz Feb 46 166
IMMORTALITY NO LONGER A MYTH? by Robert L.
Tanner. .a . . . . Amz Nov 46 155
IMMORTALITY OF ALAN WHIDDEN, THE by Ralph
Milne Farley ps (Roger Sherman Hoar). .s . . . .
. . . . Amz Feb 42 146
IMMORTALITY SEEKERS, THE by John W.
Campbell, Jr. . .nt . . . . TW Oct 37 40
IMP OF THE THEREMIN by Ray Cummings. .s . . . . . .
. . . . .Ash Apr 41 64
IMPEDIMENT by Hal Clement ps (Harry Clement
Stubbs). .nt . . . . ASF Aug 42 106
IMPERFECT GUESS, THE by Philip Barshofsky ps. . . .
. .s . . . . WS Mar 36 942
IMPOSSIBILITIES by Willy Ley. .a . . . . . .Fant #3 39 45
IMPOSSIBLE by Ray Bradbury. .s . . . . . . .SSS Nov 49 72
IMPOSSIBLE BUT TRUE
THE MYSTERY OF THE BALL OF FIRE by James
B. Settles. .bacover pic . . . . Amz Nov 47
THE RAIN OF FISH. .bacover pic . . . . . . Amz Dec 47
THE THING ON THE MOON by Malcolm Smith . . .
. .bacover . . . . .FA Jan 48
(Alaskan Mirage) by James B. Settles. .bacover pic. . .
. . . . FA Feb 48
THE BOMB OUT OF SPACE by James B. Settles . . .
. .bacover . . . . FA Apr 48
THE INCREDIBLE WHEELS by James B. Settles . . .
. .bacover . . . . .FA May 48

Title. .Author. .Length . . . . Magazine. .Date. .Page No.

IMPOSSIBLE CRIME, THE by Ralph W. Wilkins. .s . . . .
. . . . AD Jul 30 632
IMPOSSIBLE HIGHWAY, THE by Oscar J. Friend. .s . .
. . . . TW Aug 40 80
IMPOSSIBLE INVENTION, THE by Robert Moore
Williams. .s . . . . Ash Jun 42 30
IMPOSSIBLE PIRATE, THE by George O. Smith. .s . . .
. . . . ASF Dec 46 59
IMPOSSIBLE WORLD, THE by Eando Binder ps (Otto
Binder). .n . . . . SS Mar 39 16
IMPROBABILITY by Paul Edmonds h ps (Henry
Kuttner). .s . . . . Ash Jun 40 44
IMPROBABLE, THE by Charles R. Tanner. .s. . . . . . .
. . . . .Cos May 41 80
IMPROVING UPON V–2 by Willy Ley. .a . . . .
. . . . ASF Jan 47 100
IMPULSE by Eric Frank Russell. .s . . . . .ASF Sep 38 110
IN ALL PROBABILITY by Irving Gerson. .ss . . . .
. . . . Amz Jul 48 106
IN CAVERNS BELOW by Stanton A. Coblentz . . . . . .
. .n 3 pt . . . . WS Mar 35 1160
                    (Complete) . . . . . . .FSQ Fal 50 11
IN HIDING by Wilmar H. Shiras. .nt . . . . . ASF Nov 48 40
IN HIS IMAGE by Bryce Walton. .ss . . . . . .PS Win 48 34
IN HIS OWN IMAGE by Malcolm Jameson. .s. . . . . .
. . . . UK Feb 42 106
IN MARTIAN DEPTHS by Hendrik Dahl Juve. .s . . . . .
. . . . WS Sep 32 320
IN THE ABYSS by H. G. Wells. .s . . . . . Amz Sep 26 484
IN THE ANCIENT WAY by Harry Walton. .s . . . .
. . . . .TW Aug 41 91
IN THE CARDS by George O. Smith. .s. . . . TW Aug 47 64
IN THE COURT OF THE DRAGON by Robert W.
Chambers. .s. . . . . .AFR #5 92
IN THE DAY OF THE COLD by Sam Weston. .s. . . . . .
. . . . .ASF Jan 40 92
IN THE DAYS OF OUR FATHERS by Winona
McClintic. .s. . . . . F&SF Fal 49 123
IN THE EARTH'S SHADOW by John L. Chapman. .s . .
. . . . Com Dec 40 117
IN THE FOOTSTEPS OF THE WASP by Stanton A.
Coblentz. .s . . . . Amz Aug 34 90
IN THE GOOD OLD SUMMERTIME by P. Schuyler
Miller. .s . . . . ASF Mar 40 36
IN THE ORBIT OF SATURN by R. F. Starzl. .s . . . . . .
. . . . .ASF Oct 31 7
IN THE SCARLET STAR by Jack Williamson. .s. . . . .
. . . . Amz Mar 33 1113
IN THE SHADOW OF THE TII by Ainslee Jenkins . . . .
. .s . . . . ASF Nov 33 42
IN THE SPACESPHERE by Charles Cloukey. .s . . . . . .
. . . . WS Jun 31 10
IN THE SPHERE OF TIME by J. W. Pelkie. .nt. . . . . .
. . . . .PS Sum 48 76
IN THE VALLEY OF THE SORCERESS by Sax
Rohmer ps. .s . . . . AFR #12 48

Title. .Author. .Length . . . . Magazine. .Date. .Page No.

IN THE YEAR 8000 by Otfrid Von Hanstein (tr fr
German by Konrad Schmidt & Laurence Manning) . .
. .n 2 pt . . . . .WS Jul 32 102
IN 20,000 A.D. by Nat Schachner & Arthur L.
Zagat. .s . . . . WS Sep 30 310
IN TWO WORLDS by Edward E. Chappelow. .s . . . . .
. . . . SW Oct 29 448
IN VALUE DECEIVED by H. B. Fyfe. .s . . . .
. . . . ASF Nov 50 38
INCIDENT ON CALYPSO by Murray Leinster ps (Will
F. Jenkins). .s . . . . SS Fal 45 57
INCIDENT ON TITAN by Will Garth h ps (Mort
Weisinger). .s . . . . TW Jun 41 93
INCOMMUNICADO by Katherine MacLean. .nt . . . . . .
. . . . ASF Jun 50 6
INCOMPATIBLE by Rog Phillips ps (Roger P.
Graham). .s . . . . FA Sep 49 84
INCOMPLETE ANGLER, THE by Raymond Chan . . . .
. .ss . . . . FA Apr 45 62
INCORRIGIBLE, THE by L. Sprague de Camp. .s . . . . .
. . . . .ASF Jan 39 82
INCREDIBLE ANTIQUE, THE by Bruce Dennis. .nt . . .
. . . . FA Dec 42 126
INCREDIBLE DESTINATION, THE by Rene
Lafayette. .s . . . . SS May 49 96
INCREDIBLE FORMULA, THE by Paul Ernst. .s . . . . .
. . . . Amz Jun 31 218
INCREDIBLE INVASION, THE by Murray Leinster
ps (Will F. Jenkins). .n 5 pt . . . . ASF Aug 36 6
INCREDIBLE INVASION, THE by George O. Smith. . . .
. .s . . . . ASF Mar 48 62
INCREDIBLE MR. KISMET, THE by David Wright
O'Brien. .s . . . . FA Jun 42 94
INCREDIBLE MONSTROSITY, THE by Walter
Kateley. .s . . . . WS Jun 30 24
INCREDIBLE SLINGSHOT BOMBS, THE by Robert
Moore Williams. .s . . . . Amz May 42 130
INCREDIBLE THEORY OF DR. PENWING, THE by
Richard O. Lewis. .s . . . . Amz Aug 40 28
INCREDIBLE VISITOR, THE by Clifton B. Kruse . . . .
. .s . . . . ASF May 38 32
INDESINENT STYKAL, THE by D. D. Sharp. .s. . . . . .
. . . . .ASF Jun 37 126
INDESTRUCTIBLE, THE by Robert Arthur. .s . . . . . .
. . . . TW Mar 41 48
INDESTRUCTIBLE MAN, THE by Edmond Hamilton. .
. .s . . . . TW Spr 46 32
INDIGESTIBLE TRITON, THE by Rene Lafayette ps
(L. Ron Hubbard). .n . . . . .UK Apr 40 9
INDIVIDUALISTS, THE (THE MAN WHO AWOKE
Part 4) by Laurence Manning. .s . . . .
. . . . WS Jun 33 58
INDULGENCE OF NEGU MAH, THE by Robert
Arthur. .s. . . . . .Com Jul 41 75
INEVITABLE CONFLICT, THE by Paul H. Lovering. . .
. .n 2 pt . . . . Amz Dec 31 776

Title. .Author. .Length . . . . Magazine. .Date. .Page No.

INEXORABLE LAWS, THE by John Brody. .s . . . . . .
. . . . .NW #3 58
INFERIORITY COMPLEX, THE by Miles J.
Breuer, M.D. . .s . . . . Amz Sep 30 535
INFIDELS, THE by Ross Rocklynne. .s. . . ASF Sep 45 63
INFILTRATION by Clifford D. Simak. .s . . . SF Jul 43 43
INFINITE BRAIN, THE by John C. Campbell ps (John
Scott Campbell). .s . . . . SW May 30 1076
INFINITE BRAIN, THE by Hugo Gernsback. .ss . . . . . .
. . . . Fut Jun 42 40
INFINITE ENEMY, THE by Jack Williamson. .s . . . . . .
. . . . TW Apr 38 38
INFINITE EYE, THE by Philip Jacques Bartel ps. .s . . .
. . . . .Fut Nov 39 94
INFINITE INVASION, THE by E. K. Jarvis h ps . . . . . .
. .nt . . . . FA Sep 42 108
INFINITE MOMENT, THE by Henry Kuttner. .nt . . . .
. . . . TW Apr 42 17
INFINITE VISION, THE by Charles C. Winn. .s . . . . . .
. . . . Amz May 26 136
INFINITY ZERO by Donald Wandrei. .s . . . .
. . . . .ASF Oct 36 130
INFLEXURE by Clyde Crane Campbell ps (H. L. Gold)
. .nt . . . . ASF Oct 34 8
INFORMATION PLEASE by Stanley Whiteside. .ss. . . .
. . . . TW Win 46 79
INFRA-CALORESCENCE by R. I. Melhorn. .s . . . .
. . . . Amz Oct 32 622
INFRA-MEDIANS, THE by Sewell Peaslee Wright. .s . . .
. . . . ASF Dec 31 389
INFRA-UNIVERSE by Nat Schachner. .n 2 pt . . . . . .
. . . . ASF Dec 36 118
INHABITANT OF CARCOSA, AN by Ambrose
Bierce. .ss. . . . . .AFR #8 123
INHERITANCE by Charles Willis ps (Arthur C. Clarke) .
. .s . . . . .NW #3 54
by Arthur C. Clarke. .s . . . .ASF Sep 48 145
INHERITANCE by Edward W. Ludwig. .s . . . .
. . . . .Im Oct 50 150
INHERITORS, THE by John B. Michel & Robert W.
Lowndes. .s . . . . Fut Oct 42 54
AFR #11 90
INNER DOMAIN, THE by Phil Collas. .nt . . . .
. . . . Amz Oct 35 85
INNER WORLD, THE by A. Hyatt Verrill. .n 3 pt. . . . .
. . . . Amz Jun 35 69
INNER WORLD, THE (The Voice from the Inner World)
by A. Hyatt Verrill. .s. . . . . .ToW Spr 39 101
INOCULATION by Roger Flint Young. .s . . . .
. . . . FA Mar 50 46
INQUISITION OF 6061, THE by Arthur Fredrick
Jones. .s. . . . . WS Dec 33 440
INSANE AVALANCHE, THE (THE MENACE Part 4)
by David H. Keller, M.D. . .s . . . . . . .AQ Sum 28 407
INSANE PLANET, THE by Alexander Blade h ps. .nt . .
. . . . Amz Feb 49 86

Title. .Author. .Length . . . . Magazine. .Date. .Page No.

INSANE ROBOT, THE by Craig Browning ps (Roger P.
Graham). .s . . . . FA Nov 49 34
INSATIABLE ENTITY, THE by Harold S. Sykes. .s . . .
. . . . SW Mar 30 902
INSECT INVASION, THE by Frederic Arnold
Kummer, Jr. . .s. . . . . FA Sep 39 80
INSECT THREAT, THE by Alfred Gordon Bennett,
F.R.S.A. . .a . . . . ToW Win 39 64
INSECT WORLD, THE by Thomas S. Gardner. .s . . . . .
. . . . WS Apr 35 1316
ToW Aug 41 53
INSECTS EXTRAORDINARY by Walter Kateley. .s . . .
. . . . AQ Win 32 84
INSIDE MOUNT LASSEN by Ralph B. Fields. .a . . . . .
. . . . Amz Dec 46 155
INSIDE OUT MATTER by R. S. Richardson. .a . . . . . .
. . . . ASF Dec 41 112
INSIGHT by Manly Wade Wellman. .s . . . .
. . . . DS Apr-May 39 59
INSOMNIA, INC. by Harry Walton. .nt . . . ASF Aug 47 68
INSPECTOR'S TEETH, THE by L. Sprague de Camp. . .
. .s . . . . ASF Apr 50 104
INTELLIGENCE GIGANTIC, THE by John Russell
Fearn. .n 2 pt . . . . Amz Jun 33 235
INTELLIGENCE UNDYING by Edmond Hamilton. . . .
. .s . . . . Amz Apr 36 13
INTERFERENCE by Walter C. Davies ps (Cyril
Kornbluth). .s. . . . . Cos Jul 41 35
INTERFERENCE by Murray Leinster ps (Will F.
Jenkins). .s. . . . . .ASF Oct 45 49
INTERFERENCE by Max C. Sheridan. .s . . . .
. . . . Amz Mar 35 44
INTERLINK by John Russell Fearn. .s . . . . TW Fal 45 72
INTERLUDE by Ross Rocklynne. .s . . . . . ASF Dec 42 67
INTERNATIONAL ELECTRO-GALVANIC UNDER-
TAKING CORPORATION, THE (THE SCIENTIFIC
ADVENTURES OF MR. FOSDICK) by Jacque
Morgan. .s . . . . Amz Aug 26 417
INTERPLANETARY BRIDGES by Ludwig Anton (tr fr
German by Konrad Schmidt). .n. . . . . .WQ Win 33 102
INTERPLANETARY COMMUNICATION by Howard M.
Duffin. .bacover pic. . . . . Amz Nov 39
INTERPLANETARY GRAVEYARD by Edmond
Hamilton. .s . . . . .Fut Mar 40 56
INTERPLANETARY GRAVEYARD by R. R.
Winterbotham. .s. . . . . Amz Jan 39 22
INTERPLANETARY REPORTER by Leigh Brackett . .
. .s . . . . SS May 41 100
INTERSTELLAR WAY STATION by Bob Tucker ps
(Arthur Wilson Tucker). .s. . . . . SSS May 41 94
INTO ANOTHER DIMENSION by Maurice Duclos . . . .
. .s . . . . FA Nov 39 42
INTO PLUTONIAN DEPTHS by Stanton A. Coblentz . .
. .n . . . . WQ Spr 31 294
INTO SPACE by Sterner St. Paul ps (Capt. Sterner St.
Paul Meek). .s. . . . . ASF Feb 30 221

Title. .Author. .Length . . . . Magazine. .Date. .Page No.

INTO THE CAVES OF MARS by Festus Pragnell. .nt . .
. . . . Amz Aug 42 154
INTO THE DARKNESS by Ross Rocklynne. .nt . . . . . .
. . . . Ash Jun 40 44
INTO THE DEPTHS by David R. Daniels. .s . . . .
. . . . .ASF Jun 35 146
INTO THE FOURTH DIMENSION by Ray Cummings. .
. .n . . . . .SFQ Win 41–42 4
INTO THE GREEN PRISM by A. Hyatt Verrill. . . . . . .
. .n 2 pt . . . . Amz Mar 29 1046
INTO THE HYDROSPHERE by Neil R. Jones. .s . . . . .
. . . . Amz Oct 33 554
INTO THE INFINITE by Austin Hall. .n 4 pt . . . .
. . . . FFM Oct 42 83
INTO THE INFINITESIMAL by Kaye Raymond . . . . .
. .nt . . . . WS Jun 34 6
INTO THE MESOZOIC by Duane N. Carroll. .s . . . . . .
. . . . .AQ Fal-Win 32 426
INTO THE METEORITE ORBIT by Frank K. Kelly . . .
. .s . . . . Amz Dec 33 76
INTO THE OCEAN'S DEPTHS by Sewell Peaslee
Wright. .s . . . . ASF May 30 151
INTO THE SUBCONSCIOUS by Ray Avery Myers . . . .
. .s . . . . SW Oct 29 426
INTO THE SUN by John L. Chapman. .ss . . . .
. . . . Com May 41 116
INTO THE 28th CENTURY by Lillith Lorraine . . . . . .
. .s . . . . WQ Win 30 250
INTO THE VALLEY OF DEATH by Alfred Pringle. . . .
. .s . . . . Amz Feb 30 1080
INTO THY HANDS by Lester del Rey. .nt . . . .
. . . . ASF Aug 45 47
INTRA-PLANETARY by Chan Corbett ps (Nathan
Schachner). .s . . . . ASF Oct 35 51
INTRIGUE IN LEMURIA by Frederic Arnold
Kummer, Jr. . .s . . . . .FA Jul 39 56
INTRODUCTION TO A NAMELESS SCIENCE by
Peter van Dresser. .a . . . . .ASF Jun 40 100
INTRUDERS FROM THE STARS by Ross
Rocklynne. .n . . . . Amz Jan 44 44
INVADER FROM INFINITY by George Whittington. . .
. .s .PS Win 44 29
INVADERS, THE by L. Ron Hubbard. .nt . . . .
. . . . .ASF Jan 42 62
INVADERS, THE by Don A. Stuart ps (John W.
Campbell, Jr.). .nt . . . . ASF Jun 35 54
INVADERS FROM NOWHERE by L. Sprague de
Camp. .nt . . . . .SSS Aug 41 71
INVADERS FROM SIRIUS by Ed Earl Repp. .s . . . . .
. . . . .FA Jul 39 74
INVADERS FROM THE ATOM by Maurice G.
Hugi. .nt . . . . .ToW #1 37 92
INVADERS FROM THE INFINITE by John W.
Campbell, Jr. . .n . . . . AQ Spr-Sum 32 146
INVADERS FROM THE MONSTER WORLD by
Edmond Hamilton. .nt . . . . Amz Jun 45 68

Title. .Author. .Length . . . . Magazine. .Date. .Page No.

INVADERS FROM THE OUTER SUNS by Frank Belknap
Long, Jr. . .nt . . . . TW Feb 37 66
INVADERS FROM THE VOID by Russell Branch. . . . .
. .nt . . . . Amz Aug 50 80
INVADERS FROM THE VOID by Geo. C. Wallis . . . .
. .s . . . . Fant #3 39 106
INVADERS FROM VENUS by Benson Herbert, M.Sc. . .
. .s .ToW #2 38 56
INVADERS OF THE FORBIDDEN MOON by Raymond
Z. Gallun. .nt . . . . PS Sum 41 2
INVADING BLOOD STREAM, THE by Paul Starr . . . .
. .s . . . . ASF Dec 33 40
INVARIANT by John Pierce. .s . . . . ASF Apr 44 94
INVASION by Murray Leinster ps (Will F. Jenkins) . . . .
. .s . . . . ASF Mar 33 118
INVASION by Frank Belknap Long. .s . . . . SS Jul 50 133
INVASION by Robert Willey ps (Willy Ley). .s . . . . . .
. . . . .SSS Sep 40 25
INVASION DUST by Don Wilcox. .s . . . .
. . . . Amz Dec 44 108
INVASION OF THE BONE MEN by John Stuart
Walworth. .s . . . . Amz Jan 49 78
INVASION OF THE MICRO-MEN by Richard S.
Shaver. .nt . . . . Amz Feb 46 6
INVASION OF THE PLANT MEN by Berkeley
Livingston. .nt . . . . FA Sep 49 8
INVASION OF THE RAINDROPS by Edwin Benson. . .
. .nt . . . . FA Jan 45 26
INVASION SQUAD by Battell Loomis. .s . . . .
. . . . WB Dec 50 100
INVASION'S END by Myer Krulfeld. .s . . . .
. . . . .TW Feb 39 64
INVENT OR DIE by R. R. Winterbotham. .s . . . .
. . . . .Ash Sep 41 55
INVERTED ALCHEMY. .a . . . . ASF Jun 48 96
INVERTED WORLD, THE by J. Rogers Ullrich . . . . . .
. .s . . . . WQ Spr 31 392
INVINCIBLE CRIME BUSTER, THE by Henry Gade
h ps (Raymond A. Palmer). .nt . . . . . . Amz Jul 41 102
INVINCIBLE MIDGE, THE by Paul Ernst. .s . . . .
. . . . TW Apr 37 32
FSQ Fal 50 87
INVINCIBLE WRESTLER, THE by William Morrison
ps (Joseph Samachson). .s . . . . TW Apr 43 108
INVISIBLE by Eric Frank Russell. .s . . . . . CF Win 40 92
INVISIBLE ARMY, THE by Ross Rocklynne. .s . . . . . .
. . . . TW Win 44 50
INVISIBLE BOMBER, THE by Lieut. John Pease ps
(Roger Sherman Hoar). .s . . . . Amz Jun 38 130
INVISIBLE BUBBLE, THE by Kirk Meadowcroft. .s . . .
. . . . Amz Sep 28 508
INVISIBLE CITY, THE by Clark Ashton Smith. .s . . . .
. . . . WS Jun 32 6
ToW Win 39 50
INVISIBLE CONTINENT by Russell Blaiklock. .nt . . . .
. . . . Fut Jun 42 10

Title. .Author. .Length . . . . Magazine. .Date. .Page No.   Title. .Author. .Length . . . . Magazine. .Date. .Page No.

INVISIBLE DEATH by Anthony Pelcher. .s . . . .
. . . . .ASF Jan 30 118
INVISIBLE DEATH, THE by Victor Rousseau
(Emanuel). .nt . . . . ASF Oct 30 24
INVISIBLE DESTROYER, THE by L. A. Eschbach. . . . .
. .s . . . . AW May 30 1004
INVISIBLE FINITE, THE by Robert A. Wait. .s . . . . .
. . . . Amz May 29 172
INVISIBLE INVASION by Frederic Arnold
Kummer, Jr. ..s . . . . Amz Apr 39 40
INVISIBLE MAN, THE by H. G. Wells. .n 2 pt . . . .
. . . . Amz Jun 28 198
INVISIBLE MASTER, THE by Edmond Hamilton . . . .
. .nt . . . . SD Apr 30 300
INVISIBLE MEN OF MARS by Edgar Rice Burroughs. .
. .nt . . . . Amz Oct 41 8
INVISIBLE MONSTERS by John Beynon Harris. .s . . . .
. . . . WS Dec 33 448
INVISIBLE MONSTER by John Beynon (Harris). .s . . . .
. . . . .ToW Sum 40 6
INVISIBLE ONE by Neil R. Jones. .nt . . . . .SSS Sep 40 6
INVISIBLE RAIDERS, THE by Ed Earl Repp. .s . . . . .
. . . . AW Oct 29 352
INVISIBLE RAIDERS OF VENUS by Don Wilcox . . . .
. .s . . . . Amz Apr 41 106
INVISIBLE ROBINHOOD, THE by Eando Binder
ps (Otto Binder). .s . . . . FA May 39 16
INVISIBLE SHIPS by Harl Vincent (Schoepflin). .s . . . .
. . . . AQ Spr 31 250
INVISIBLE VANDALS, THE by Charles Stoddard
h ps. .s . . . . SS Fal 44 97
INVISIBLE WHEEL OF DEATH, THE by Don Wilcox. .
. .nt . . . . Amz Jan 41 44
INVISIBLE WORLD, THE by Ed Earl Repp. .nt . . . . . .
. . . . Amz Oct 40 48
INVITATION FROM THE STARS by Morton Klass . . .
. .s . . . . Fut Sep-Oct 50 51
INVOLUNTARY IMMORTALS, THE by Rog Phillips . .
. .n . . . . FA Dec 49 8
INVULNERABLE SCOURGE, THE by John S.
Campbell. .s . . . . WS Nov 30 524
IONIAN CYCLE, THE by William Tenn ps (Philip
Klass). .s . . . . TW Aug 49 104
IRON GOD, THE by Jack Williamson. .nt . . . .
. . . . MSS Apr 41 70
IRON MEN by Noel Loomis. .n . . . . .SS Win 45 11
IRON MEN OF SUPER CITY, THE by Don Wilcox. . . .
. .nt . . . . Amz May 41 104
IRON STANDARD, THE by Lewis Padgett ps (Henry
Kuttner & C. L. Moore). .nt . . . . ASF Dec 45 74
IRON STAR, THE by John Taine ps (Eric Temple
Bell). .n . . . . FFM Sep 43 8
IRON WORLD, THE by Otis Adelbert Kline. .s . . . . . .
. . . . .TW Aug 37 12
IRRELEVANT, THE by Karl van Campen ps (John W.
Campbell, Jr.). .s . . . . ASF Dec 34 41

IRRESISTIBLE PERFUME, THE by Harold Lawlor . . .
. .s . . . . FA May 43 102
IRRITATED PEOPLE, THE by Ray Bradbury. .s . . . . .
. . . . TW Dec 47 90
IS THE DEATH RAY HERE? by Jep Powell. .a . . . . . .
. . . . TW Dec 42 76
IS THIS A FOUR-DIMENSIONAL UNIVERSE? (on
article)
IS THIS A FOUR DIMENSIONAL WORLD? (in ToC)
by Queen's Knight. .a . . . . Amz Feb 48 152
IS THIS THE NIGHT? by Alexander Blade h ps (Leroy
Yerxa). .ss . . . . Amz Mar 45 102
ISLAND IN THE AIR by D. J. Foster. .s . . . .
. . . . ToW Aut 39 50
ISLAND IN THE MARSH by Thornton Ayre ps (John
Russell Fearn). .s . . . . SS Nov 40 96
ISLAND IN THE SKY by Manly Wade Wellman. .n . . . .
. . . . TW Oct 41 14
ISLAND OF CAPTAIN SPARROW, THE by S. Fowler
Wright. .n . . . . FFM Apr 46 10
ISLAND OF DR. MOREAU, THE by H. G. Wells . . . . .
. .n 2 pt . . . . Amz Oct 26 636
(complete) . . . . . . .FFM Oct 46 8
ISLAND OF DOCTOR X, THE by Allan K. Echols . . . .
. .nt . . . . .TW Dec 36 90
ISLAND OF ETERNAL STORM by Berkeley
Livingston. .nt . . . . .Amz Jan 44 150
ISLAND OF SCIENCE by B. S. Kierstead. .s . . . .
. . . . Amz Dec 33 102
ISLAND OF TERROR, THE by Ransome Sutton . . . . .
. .s . . . . WQ Fal 30 80
ISLAND OF THE GIANTS, THE by A. Rowley
Hilliard. .s . . . . WS Aug 31 362
ISLAND OF THE INDIVIDUALISTS by Nat
Schachner. .nt . . . . ASF May 38 42
ISLAND OF UNREASON, THE by Edmond Hamilton. .
. .s . . . . WS May 33 970
SS Spr 45 90
ISLAND OF WHITE MICE by David H. Keller, M.D. . .
. .nt . . . . Amz Feb 35 82
ISLAND OUT OF SPACE, THE by August Derleth . . . .
. .s . . . . Amz Jun 50 166
ISLANDS IN THE AIR by Lowell Howard Morrow . . . .
. .s . . . . AW Jul 29 32
ISLANDS OF SPACE by John W. Campbell, Jr. . . . . .
. .n . . . . AQ Spr 31 146
ISLANDS OF THE SUN by Jack Williamson. .n 2 pt . . .
. . . . ASF Sep 35 6
ISLE OF CHANGING LIFE, THE by Edmond
Hamilton. .s . . . . TW Jun 40 33
ISLE OF DOOM, THE by Robert Moore Williams . . . . .
. .nt . . . . FA Jan 48 80
ISLE OF JUVENESCENCE, THE by Bob Olsen ps
(Alfred John Olsen, Jr.). .nt . . . . Amz Jun 36 42
ISLE OF MADNESS, THE by Lillith Lorraine. .s . . . . .
. . . . WS Nov 35 652

Title. .Author. .Length . . . . Magazine. .Date. .Page No.

ISLE OF THE GARGOYLES by William Lemkin,
    Ph.D. . .nt . . . . .WS Jan 36 820
ISLE OF THE GOLDEN SWARM by Norman L.
    Knight. .s . . . . ASF Jun 38 97
ISLES OF THE BLEST by Frederic Arnold Kummer,
    Jr. . .n . . . . .Fut Mar 40 8
ISOLATIONIST by Mack Reynolds. .s . . . . FA Apr 50 96
ISOLINGUALS, THE by L. Sprague de Camp. .s . . . . .
    .ASF Sep 37 108
ISOTOPE MEN, THE by Festus Pragnell. .s . . . .
    . . . . WS Aug 33 136
                                            SS Nov 48 110
ISOTOPE MEN, THE by Nat Schachner. .nt . . . .
    . . . . .ASF Jan 36 40
ISOTOPE 235 by Arthur McCann ps (John W.
    Campbell, Jr.). .a . . . . ASF Aug 39 70
ISZT—EARTHMAN by Raymond Z. Gallun. .nt . . . . .
    . . . . ASF Apr 38 86
IT by Theodore Sturgeon. .nt . . . . .UK Aug 40 97
IT HAPPENED IN SPACE by Manly Wade Wellman. . . .
    . .s . . . . Amz Jun 42 140
IT HAPPENED TOMORROW by Robert Bloch. .nt . . . .
    .Ash Feb 43 46
IT HAPPENS TWICE AT LEAST by Willy Ley. .a . . . .
    . . . . UK Jan 40 119
IT ISN'T SO EASY by J. J. Coupling ps (John R.
    Pierce). .a . . . . ASF May 45 124
IT WILL COME TO YOU by Frank Belknap Long. . . . .
    . .s . . . . UK Dec 42 106
ITERATION by C. M. Kornbluth. .s . . . .
    . . . . Fut Sep-Oct 50 60
IT'S A TOUGH LIFE by Frank Belknap Long. .a . . . . .
    . . . . ASF Nov 42 101
IT'S A SMALL WORLD by Robert Bloch. .nt . . . .
    . . . . Amz Mar 44 16
IT'S A YOUNG WORLD by James MacCreigh ps
    (Frederik Pohl). .nt . . . . .Ash Apr 41 84
IT'S RAINING DIMES by Berkeley Livingston. .s . . . . .
    .FA Jul 45 124
IT'S RAINING FROGS by Milton Lesser. .nt . . . .
    . . . . Im Dec 50 74
IVY WAR, THE by David H. Keller, M.D. . .s. . . . . . .
    . . . . Amz May 30 160

J

JACKDAW by Ross Rocklynne. .nt . . . . . ASF Aug 42 61
JAKE AND THE FIFTH COLUMNIST by Arthur G.
    Stangland. .s . . . . .SFQ Spr 43 118
JALU OF RADIANT VALLEY by F. Orlin Tremaine . .
    . .nt . . . . FA Mar 40 30
JAMESON, PROFESSOR series See NEIL R. JONES
    author

Title. .Author. .Length . . . . Magazine. .Date. .Page No.

JAMESON SATELLITE, THE by Neil R. Jones. .s . . . . .
    . . . . .Amz Jul 31 334
JAMIESON by Margaret St. Clair. .ss. . . . FFM Dec 49 114
JASON by Frank R. Paul. .bacover pic . . . . . . FA Apr 44
JASON COMES HOME by A. B. L. Macfadyen, Jr.   . . .
    . .s . . . . ASF Aug 38 28
JASON, SON OF JASON by J. U. Giesy. .n . . . .
    . . . . .FN May 48 36
JASON SOWS AGAIN by Arthur J. Burks. .n 2 pt . . . .
    . . . . ASF Mar 38 64
JAY SCORE by Eric Frank Russell. .s . . . . ASF May 41 88
JAYWALKER by Ross Rocklynne. .s . . . . GSF Dec 50 51
JENNY—THE FLYING FORD by Elroy Arno. .s . . . . .
    . . . . Amz Nov 43 162
JEREMIAH JONES, ALCHEMIST by P. Schuyler
    Miller. .s . . . . .Amz May 33 142
JERK, THE GIANT KILLER by Robert Bloch. .s . . . . .
    . . . . FA Oct 42 148
JERRY IS A MAN by Robert A. Heinlein. .s . . . .
    . . . . TW Oct 47 46
JESSIFER RIDES AGAIN by Nelson S. Bond. .s . . . . .
    . . . . TW Oct 42 56
JESTING PILOT by Lewis Padgett ps (Henry Kuttner
    & C. L. Moore). .s . . . . .ASF May 47 79
JESUS SHOES by Allan R. Bosworth. .s . . . UK Apr 42 65
                                            UK 48 128
JET-BOAT OF TOMORROW by James B. Settles . . . . .
    . .bacover . . . . FA Apr 45
JET JOCKEYS, THE by R. W. Stockheker. .s . . . .
    .TW Aug 47 39
JET LANDING by Francis Ashton. .ss. . . . NW Spr 50 77
JET PROPELLED MONO TRAIN by James B.
    Settles. .bac . . . . Amz Dec 45
JETTA OF THE LOWLANDS by Ray Cummings . . . . .
    . .n 3 pt . . . . .ASF Sep 30 310
JEWEL OF BAS by Leigh Brackett. .nt . . . . .PS Spr 44 3
JEWEL OF DEATH by Chester S. Geier. .s . . . .
    . . . . FA Dec 45 36
JEWEL OF MARS by H. L. Gold. .s . . . . . .CF Spr 40 100
JEWELS FROM THE MOON, THE by Ephriam Winiki
    ps (John Russell Fearn). .s. . . . . . . SF Aug 39 69
JEWELS OF THE TOAD by Frank Patton h ps (Raymond
    A. Palmer). .s . . . . FA Oct 43 8
JIMMY DOLAN'S RADIO RAY by Robert Moore
    Williams. .s . . . . .Amz Jul 43 96
JIMMY TAKES A TRIP by William Lawrence Hamling. .
    . .s . . . . .FA Jul 46 116
JIMSON ISLAND GIANT, THE by Sam Merwin, Jr.   . .
    . .ss . . . . .SS Win 46 77
JINX, THE by Alexander Blade h ps. .ss . . . .
    . . . . .Amz May 49 54
JINX SHIP TO THE RESCUE by Alfred Coppel, Jr. . . .
    . .s .PS Win 48 27
JIRANDEL by Warren Kastel ps. .s . . . . . . FA Jan 50 50
JITTERBUG by R. R. Winterbotham. .s . . . .Sti Jun 41 48

Title. .Author. .Length . . . . Magazine. .Date. .Page No.

JOB IS ENDED, THE by Wilson Tucker ps (Arthur Wilson
   Tucker). .s . . . . .OW Nov 50 56
JOB OF BLENDING, A by Victor Endersby. .ss . . . . . .
   . . . . Amz Mar 34 124
JOE CARSON'S WEAPON by James R. Adams. .s. . . .
   . . . . PS Spr 45 108
JOE DANNON, PIONEER by Richard S. Shaver. .nt . . .
   . . . . Amz Mar 47 10
JOHN BROWN'S BODY by David Wright O'Brien &
   William P. McGivern. .s. . . . . Amz May 40 112
JOHN CARTER AND THE GIANT OF MARS by Edgar
   Rice Burroughs. .nt . . . . Amz Jan 41 8
JOHN HALE CONVICTS A KILLER by Ed Earl Repp. .
   . .s . . . . .Amz Jul 39 94
JOHN HALE'S HOLLYWOOD MYSTERY by Ed Earl
   Repp. .s. . . . . Amz Aug 39 106
JOHN JONES'S DOLLAR by Harry Stephen Keeler . . .
   . .s . . . . Amz Apr 27 25
JOHN OVINGTON RETURNS by Max Brand ps
   (Frederick Faust). .s. . . . . FFM Jun 41 106
   (titled THE STRANGE LOVES OF BEATRICE
   JERVAN) . . . . FanF May 50 36
JOHNNY GOODTURN by Charles R.Tanner. .s . . . . . .
   . . . . .OW Nov 50 144
JOHNNY HAD A GUN by Robert Moore Williams. .s. . .
   . . . . ASF Dec 42 98
JOHNNY ON THE SPOT by Frank Belknap Long, Jr. .
   . .ss. . . . . UK Dec 39 123
JOHNNY RAIN-MAKER by Leroy Yerxa. .s . . . .
   . . . . Amz Nov 43 180
JOKE FOR HARRY, A by Richard Ashby. .ss . . . . . .
   . . . . Amz Sep 49 116
JOKER, THE by Mona Farnsworth. .s. . . . .UK Jul 39 115
JONAH OF THE JOVE-RUN by Ray Bradbury. .s. . . .
   . . . . .PS Spr 48 50
JONES BUYS WAR BLONDES by Elroy Arno. .s . . . . .
   . . . . FA Dec 43 98
JONES GETS THE WILLIES by Elroy Arno. .s. . . . . .
   . . . . FA Mar 43 160
JONES' PHYSIQUE by Wilm Carver. .s. . . . TW Spr 46 77
JONGOR OF LOST LAND by Robert Moore
   Williams. .n . . . . FA Oct 40 10
JOSHUA by R. Creighton Buck. .ss. . . . . UK Jun 41 126
JOSHUA'S BATTERING RAM by Malcolm
   Jameson. .s. . . . . .Ash Jun 40 22
JOURNEY by George O. Smith. .s . . . . . . SS May 48 101
JOURNEY AND THE GOAL, THE by Chan Davis . . . .
   . .s . . . . ASF May 47 99
JOURNEY FOR ONE by Carter Sprague ps (Sam
   Merwin, Jr.). .s . . . . SS Nov 49 76
JOURNEY FOR SEVEN by John D. MacDonald. . . . . .
   . .nt . . . . TW Apr 50 48
JOURNEY IN TIME TO CLEOPATRA by Helmar
   Lewis. .nt . . . . Amz Mar 44 124
JOURNEY'S END by Walter Kubilius. .s . . . .
   . . . . .SSS May 43 118

Title. .Author. .Length . . . . Magazine. .Date. .Page No.

JOVIAN HORDE, THE by Al H. Martin. .nt. . . . .
   . . . . .WQ Sum 32 554
JOVIAN JEST, THE by Lillith Lorraine. .s. . . . .
   . . . . ASF May 30 228
JUDAS RAM by Sam Merwin, Jr. . .s . . . .
   . . . . GSF Dec 50 32
JUDGEMENT NIGHT by C. L. Moore. .n 2 pt . . . .
   . . . . ASF Aug 43 9
JUDGEMENT SUN, THE by Eando Binder ps (Otto
   Binder). .nt . . . . TW Apr 37 14
JUDGING OF THE PRIESTESS, THE by Nelson S.
   Bond. .nt. . . . . FA Apr 40 42
JUDSON'S ANNIHILATOR by John Beynon (Harris) . .
   . . . . Amz Oct 39 104
JUGGERNAUT by A. E. van Vogt. .s . . . . ASF Aug 44 55
JUGGERNAUT JONES, COMMANDO by A. R.
   McKenzie. .s . . . . .Amz Jul 43 112
JUGGERNAUT JONES, DRAFTEE by A. R.
   McKenzie. .s . . . . Amz May 43 142
JUGGERNAUT JONES, EXPRESSMAN by A. R.
   McKenzie. .s . . . . Amz Nov 42 132
JUGGERNAUT JONES, PIRATE by A. R. McKenzie . .
   . .s . . . . Amz Nov 43 168
JUGGERNAUT JONES, SALESMAN by A. R.
   McKenzie. .s . . . . .Amz May 42 166
JUGGERNAUT JONES, TRUCKER by A. R.
   McKenzie. .s . . . . Amz Jun 42 128
JUGGERNAUT JONES, WARRIER by A. R.
   McKenzie. .s . . . . Amz Apr 43 110
JUGGERNAUT OF SPACE by Ray Cummings. .nt . . . .
   . . . . .PS Fal 45 2
JUICE by L. Sprague de Camp. .s . . . . SSS May 40 62
JUKE-BOX by Woodrow Wilson Smith ps (Henry
   Kuttner). .s . . . . .TW Feb 47 83
JUKE BOX ASTEROID by Joseph Farrell. .s . . . .
   . . . . TW Spr 44 66
JULES VERNE EXPRESS, THE by Eando Binder ps
   (Otto Binder). .s . . . . .TW Apr 39 13
JULES VERNE FANTASY, A by Jack West. .a. . . . . .
   . . . . FA Aug 42 222
JUMPER, THE by Theodore Sturgeon. .s. . .UK Aug 42 46
JUPITER NAPOLEON by J. Harvey Haggard. .ss. . . . . .
   . . . . .OTWA Dec 50 39
JUPITER–THE GIANT WORLD (LANDSCAPES OF
   OTHER WORLDS) by Willy Ley. .a . . . .
   . . . . Amz Sep 42 220
JUPITER TRAP by Ross Rocklynne. .s. . . ASF Aug 37 46
JURISDICTION by Nat Schachner. .nt . . . . ASF Aug 41 9
JUST A MATTER OF TIME by Roger Angell. .s . . . . . .
   . . . . .F&SF Fal 50 73
JUST AROUND THE CORNER by Raymond Knight . .
   . .play . . . . .Amz Jul 28 358
JUST PLAIN WIZARDRY by Arnold Young. .s . . . . . .
   . . . . Amz Dec 44 122
JUSTICE OF MARTIN BRAND, THE by G. H. Irwin
   h ps (Raymond A. Palmer). .n . . . . OW Jul 50 60

Title. .Author. .Length . . . . Magazine. .Date. .Page No.

JUSTICE OF THE ATOMS by Charles B. Pool. .s . . . . .
. . . . WS Jul 35 170
JUSTICE SATELLITE by Guy Archette ps (Chester S.
Geier). .nt . . . . Amz May 48 120
JUSTINIAN JUGG'S PATENT by L. Sprague de Camp .
. .a . . . . ASF Dec 40 68

K

KALEIDOSCOPE by Ray Bradbury. .s . . . TW Oct 49 129
KARPEN THE JEW by Robert Neal Leath. .s . . . .
. . . . FFM Sep-Oct 39 63
KAZAM COLLECTS by S. D. Gottesman ps (Cyril
Kornbluth). .s . . . . .Sti Jun 41 102
KEEP 'EM UNDER by Malcolm Jameson. .a . . . .
. . . . ASF Nov 43 108
KEEP IT SIMPLE by Frances M. Deegan. .s . . . .
. . . . Amz May 50 104
KEEPER OF THE DEATHLESS SLEEP by Albert de
Pina. .nt .PS Win 44 36
KEEPER OF THE FLAME, THE by Burt B. Stone . . . .
. .nt . . . . .FA May 49 8
KELPIE, THE by Manly Wade Wellman. .s . . . .
. . . . AFR #12 61
KENNEDY, CRAIG series See ARTHUR B. REEVE
author
KETTLE IN THE PIT, THE by Don Wilcox. .s . . . .
. . . . Amz Oct 47 8
KEY, THE by Berkeley Livingston. .s . . . . FA Sep 48 102
KEY TO CORNWALL, THE by David H. Keller. .s . . . .
. . . . Sti Feb 41 93
KEY TO THE DARK PLANET, THE by Martin
Pearson ps (Donald A. Wollheim). .s . . . . Fut Dec 42 10
KID FROM KALAMAZOO, THE by Eric Frank
Russell. .nt . . . . FA Aug 42 202
KID FROM MARS, THE by Oscar J. Friend. .n . . . . . .
. . . . .SS Sep 40 12
KID POISON by David V. Reed ps (David Vern) . . . . . .
. .nt . . . . Amz Aug 41 42
KIDNAPPED IN MARS by Festus Pragnell. .nt . . . .
. . . . Amz Oct 41 60
KIDNAPPED INTO THE FUTURE by William P.
McGivern. .s . . . . Amz Feb 42 8
KIDNAPPERS OF SPACE by Thorp McClusky. .s . . . . .
. . . . Amz Aug 38 110
KIDS DON'T KNOW EVERYTHING by Frank
Johnson. .s . . . . .SS Sep 42 106
KILGALLEN'S LUNAR LEGACY by Norman L.
Knight. .s . . . . ASF Aug 42 92
KILKENNY CATS, THE by Kurt von Rachen ps
(L. Ron Hubbard). .s . . . . ASF Sep 40 98
KILLDOZER! by Theodore Sturgeon. .n . . . .
. . . . ASF Nov 44 7

Title. .Author. .Length . . . . Magazine. .Date. .Page No.

KILLER'S TURNABOUT by William P. McGivern. . . . .
. .ss. . . . . Amz Apr 41 120
KILLING FLASH, THE by Hugo Gernsback. .ss . . . . . .
. . . . SW Nov 29 496
KINDNESS by Lester del Rey. .s . . . . ASF Oct 44 80
KING AND THE PAWN, THE by Seven Anderton. . . . .
. .nt .AQ Fal-Win 32 354
KING ARTHUR'S KNIGHT IN A YANKEE COURT
by A. W. Bernal. .nt . . . . Amz Apr 41 48
KING COLE OF PLUTO by S. D. Gottesman ps (Cyril
Kornbluth). .nt . . . . SSS May 40 90
KING OF THE BLACK BOWL, THE by R. F. Starzl . . .
. .s . . . . WS Sep 30 334
KING OF THE DINOSAURS by J. W. Pelkie. .n . . . . . .
. . . . FA Oct 45 6
KING OF THE GRAY SPACES by Ray Bradbury . . . . .
. .s . . . . FFM Dec 43 120
KING OF THE MONKEY MEN, THE by A. Hyatt
Verrill. .nt . . . . AQ Spr 28 230
KING OF THE STARS by William L. Bade. .s . . . .
. . . . SSS Jul 50 48
KING OF THIEVES, THE by Jack Vance. .s . . . .
. . . . SS Nov 49 98
KINGDOM OF THE ANTS by Gerald Bowman. .s . . . .
. . . . SS Sep 40 113
KINGDOM OF THE BLIND, THE by George O.
Smith. .n . . . . SS Jul 47 11
KINGDOM OF THOUGHT, THE by L. A. Eshbach. . . .
. .nt . . . . Amz Aug 35 10
KING'S EYE, THE by James MacCreigh ps (Frederik
Pohl). .s. . . . . .Ash Feb 41 63
KINGSLAYER, THE by L. Ron Hubbard. .nt . . . .
. . . . .2CSAB Win 50 102
KINNISON, KIMBALL (LENSMAN series) See. E. E.
SMITH author
KISS AND KILL by P. F. Costello h ps. .s . . . .
. . . . Amz Dec 50 44
KISS OF DEATH by Neil R. Jones. .s . . . Amz Dec 38 108
KISS OF DEATH, THE by Laura Withrow. .s . . . .
. . . . FFM Feb 40 111
KITCHEN OF THE FUTURE, THE by Willy Ley . . . . .
. .a . . . . TW Oct 41 96
KITE SHIP OF THE MOON by James B. Settles . . . . . .
. .bacover. .FA Jan 45
KLYSTRON, THE by Stanley R. Short. .a . . . .
. . . . ASF Feb 41 98
KLYSTRON FORT by William Corson. .s . . . .
. . . . ASF Aug 41 48
KNIGHT MUST FALL by Kelvin Kent ps (Arthur K.
Barnes). .s . . . . TW Jun 40 84
KNOCK by Fredric Brown. .s . . . . TW Dec 48 138
KNOTTED STRING, . .A by Berkeley Livingston . . . . .
. .nt . . . . FA Oct 47 50
KNOWLEDGE MACHINE, THE by Edmond
Hamilton. .s . . . . TW Jun 48 109

Title. .Author. .Length . . . . Magazine. .Date. .Page No.

KNOWLEDGE WITHOUT LEARNING by K. Thomas. .
. .s . . . . .NW #1 46 30
KRAKEN, THE by Frederick Engelhardt. .s . . . . . .
. . . . UK Jun 40 82

L

LABORATORY CO-OPERATOR—3 by B. L. Bowman .
. .s . . . . .ASF Jan 36 76
LABORATORY OF THE MIGHTY MITES by Gilbert
Rae Sonbergh. .s . . . . Amz Jun 43 8
LABYRINTH by Neil R. Jones. .nt . . . . . Amz Apr 36 84
LADY by Richard S. Shaver. .s . . . . .OW Mar 50 40
LADY AND THE VAMPIRE, THE by P. F. Costello . . .
. .s . . . . FA Feb 42 40
LADY DOG by A. Bertram Chandler. .s . . . .
. . .s. . . .s. . . . . .s. . . . . ASF Mar 46 119
LADY INTO HELL-CAT by Stanley Mullen. .s . . . .
. . . . .PS Spr 49 66
LADY IS A WITCH, THE by Norman A. Daniels. . . . .
. .n . . . . .SS Mar 50 11
LADY OF LIGHT, THE by Jack Williamson. .nt . . . . .
. . . . Amz Sep 32 486
LADY OF THE ATOMS by Miles J. Breuer. .s . . . . . .
. . . . ToW Aut 41 47
LADY OF THE MOON, THE by Philip M. Fisher . . . . .
. .s .ASF Sep 35 105
LAIR OF THE GRIMALKIN by G. H. Irwin h ps
(Richard S. Shaver). .n . . . . FA Apr 48 8
LAKE OF LIFE, THE by Arthur G. Stangland. .s . . . .
. . . . WS Nov 32 504
LAKE OF LIGHT, THE by Jack Williamson. .s . . . . . .
. . . . ASF Apr 31 100
LAKE OF THE GONE FOREVER, THE by Leigh
Brackett. .nt . . . . TW Oct 49 63
LAKH-DAHL, DESTROYER OF SOULS by W. F.
Hammond. .s . . . . Amz Mar 28 1193
LAMP OF NO LIGHT by Alexander Blade h ps. . . . . . .
. .s . . . . .FA May 49 70
LAMP OF VENGEANCE, THE by Berkeley
Livingston. .n . . . . FA Nov 47 8
LANCELOT BIGGS COOKS A PIRATE by Nelson S.
Bond. .s . . . . FA Feb 40 40
LANCELOT BIGGS, MASTER NAVIGATOR by
Nelson S. Bond. .s . . . . FA May 40 30
LAND-GOING FISH by Jack West. .a . . . . . FA Jul 42 106
LAND OF BIG BLUE APPLES, THE by Don
Wilcox. .n . . . . .FA May 46 6
LAND OF KUI, THE by Richard S. Shaver. .s . . . .
. . . . Amz Dec 46 8
LAND OF LOST CONTENT, THE by Chad Oliver . . . .
. .s . . . . .SSS Nov 50 74
LAND OF MIGHTY INSECTS, THE by A. C.
Stimson. .nt . . . . WS Apr 34 934

Title. .Author. .Length . . . . Magazine. .Date. .Page No.

LAND OF NO RETURN by Nelson S. Bond. .nt . . . . . .
. . . . .Ash Apr 43 10
LAND OF THE BIPOS, THE by Francis Flagg ps
(George Henry Weiss). .s . . . . SW Feb 30 806
LAND OF THE BURNING SEA by Malcolm
Jameson. .nt . . . . .TW Aug 42 13
LAND OF THE DAMNED by Berkeley Livingston . . . .
. .n . . . . Amz Feb 47 86
LAND OF THE GOLDEN MEN by Robert Moore
Williams. .s . . . . Amz Jun 49 70
LAND OF THE LOST by Charles Willard Diffin . . . . . .
. .n 2 pt . . . . ASF Dec 33 2
LAND OF THE SHADOW DRAGONS by Eando Binder
ps (Otto Binder). .nt . . . . .FA May 41 8
LAND OF TIME TO COME, THE by Henry
Kuttner. .n . . . . TW Apr 41 14
LAND OF TWILIGHT by Robert Page Preston . . . .
. .n 3 pt . . . . Amz Nov 34 73
LAND OF UNREASON, THE by L. Sprague de Camp
& Fletcher Pratt. .n . . . . UK Oct 41 8
LAND OF WOODEN MEN by John Broome. .nt . . . . . .
. . . . FA Apr 40 24
LAND THAT TIME FORGOT, THE by Edgar Rice
Burroughs. .n 3 pt . . . . Amz Feb 27 982
LAND WHERE TIME STOOD STILL, THE by Arthur
Leo Zagat. .nt . . . . .TW Aug 36 78
LANDS OF THE EARTHQUAKE by Henry Kuttner . . .
. .n . . . . SS May 47 11
LANDS OF YESTERDAY by L. Sprague de Camp . . . .
. .a . . . . GSF Nov 50 48
LANGUAGE FOR TIME TRAVELERS by L. Sprague
de Camp. .a . . . . .ASF Jul 38 63
LANSON SCREEN, THE by Arthur Leo Zagat. .nt . . . .
. . . . TW Dec 36 42
LANTERNS OF GOD by Robert A. Wait. .s . . . .
. . . . Amz Mar 30 1168
LANDSCAPES OF OTHER WORLDS by Willy Ley
MARS—PLANET OF WAR. .a . . . . . . Amz Apr 42 256
LUNA—GODDESS OF LOVE. .a . . . . Amz May 42 256
VENUS—WORLD OF MYSTERY. .a . . . .
. . . . Amz Jun 42 176
SATURN—WORLD OF RINGS. .a . . . . Amz Jul 42 154
MERCURY—THE FIRE WORLD. .a . . . .
. . . . Amz Aug 42 86
JUPITER—THE GIANT WORLD. .a . . . .
. . . . Amz Sep 42 220
NEPTUNE—WORLD OF ICE. .a . . . . Amz Oct 42 202
LARGO by Theodore Sturgeon. .s . . . . . . .FA Jul 47 122
LARK ON THE ARK by Richard Casey h ps. .s . . . . . .
. . . . FA Feb 46 72
LARSON'S LUCK by Gerald Vance h ps. .s . . . .
. . . . Amz Jan 43 98
LAST ADMIRAL, THE by Rene LaFayette ps (L. Ron
Hubbard). .s . . . . .SS Jan 50 112
LAST ANALYSIS, THE by John York Cabot ps (David
Wright O'Brien). .s . . . . Amz Feb 41 56

Title. .Author. .Length . . . . Magazine. .Date. .Page No.

Title. .Author. .Length . . . . Magazine. .Date. .Page No.

LAST BOUNCE, THE by William Tenn *ps (Philip Klass)*. .nt . . . . FA Sep 50 70

LAST CASE OF JULES DE GRANJERQUE, THE by John York Cabot *ps (David Wright O'Brien)*. .s . . . . FA Apr 43 128

LAST CONFLICT by John Russell Fearn. .nt . . . . Fant Dec 46 4

LAST DISAPPEARANCE by Samuel Hoffman. .s . . . . TW Jun 42 48

LAST DROP, THE by L. Sprague de Camp & L. Ron Hubbard. .s . . . . .Ash Nov 41 87

LAST EARL, THE by Franklin W. Ryan. .s . . . . .Amz Jan 33 817

LAST ENEMY by H. Beam Piper. .n . . . . . ASF Aug 50 5

LAST EVOLUTION, THE by John W. Campbell, Jr. . . . .s . . . . Amz Aug 32 414

LAST GENERATION?, THE by Miriam Allen deFord. .s . . . . .F&SF Win-Spr 50 50

LAST HOPE, THE by Don Evans. .nt . . . . ASF Sep 39 45

LAST HOURS, THE by John Russell Fearn. .nt . . . . Amz Aug 42 90

LAST ICE, THE by George H. Scheer, B.Sc., E. E. . . . . .nt . . . . Amz Oct 37 71

LAST LAUGH by Robert Bloch. .s . . . . . . SS Nov 41 91

LAST LUNARIANS, THE by John B. Harris . . . . .s . . . . .ToW Sum 38 95

LAST MAN, THE by Charnock Walsby. .ss . . . . Com Jan 41 94

LAST MAN, THE by Wallace G. West. .s . . . . Amz Feb 29 1030

LAST MAN IN NEW YORK, THE by Paul MacNamara. .s . . . . TW Fal 44 32

LAST MARTIAN, THE by Fredric Brown. .s . . . . .GSF Oct 50 145

LAST MARTIAN, THE by Raymond Van Houten. . . . . . .s . . . . PS Spr 42 92

LAST MEN, THE by Frank Belknap Long, Jr. . . . . .s . . . . ASF Aug 34 55

LAST MONSTER, THE by Gardner F. Fox. .s . . . . PS Fal 45 38

LAST NEANDERTHAL MAN, THE by Isaac R. Nathanson. .s . . . . Amz Feb 37 116

LAST OBJECTIVE, THE by Paul Carter. .nt . . . . ASF Aug 46 46

LAST OF THE ASTERITES, THE by Joseph E. Kelleam. .s. . . . . .ASF May 40 52

LAST OF THE LEMURIANS, THE by Arthur G. Stangland. .s. . . . . .WS Jan 33 648

LAST OF THE SWARM, THE by Henry E. Lemke . . . . . . .s . . . . WS Oct 33 256

LAST ORBIT, THE by Charles Dye. .s . . . Amz Feb 50 68

LAST OUTPOST, THE by Ross Rocklynne. .nt . . . . .ASF Jul 45 67

LAST PLANET, THE by R. F. Starzl. .s . . . . WS Apr 34 1010
                                                    FSQ Sum 50 108

LAST RETURN by Roger Dee *ps (Roger D. Aycock)*. . . . . .s . . . . SSS Jul 50 62

LAST SACRIFICE by J. Gibson Taylor. .s . . . . ASF Dec 33 84

LAST SECRET WEAPON, THE by Polton Cross *ps (John Russell Fearn)*. .nt . . . . MSS Apr 41 8

LAST SELENITE, THE by A. Macfadyen, Jr. . .s . . . . ASF Nov 36 48

LAST SHRINE, THE by Chester D. Cuthbert. .s . . . . .WS Jul 34 194

LAST STRONGHOLD, THE by Chester Ruppert . . . . . .nt . . . . .Amz May 49 96

LAST TWO ALIVE, THE by Alfred Coppel. .nt . . . . PS Nov 50 76

LAST VIKING, THE by Hugh Raymond *ps (John Michel)*. .s . . . . .Cos Mar 41 96

LAST WAR, THE by Capt. S. P. Meek. .nt . . . . Amz Aug 30 438

LAST WOMAN, THE by Thomas D. Gardner. .s . . . . WS Apr 32 1238
                  by Thomas S. Gardner. .s . . . . .SS Win 44 72

LATE MODEL STARS by R. S. Richardson. .a . . . . ASF Oct 42 90

LATE NIGHT FINAL by Eric Frank Russell. .nt . . . . ASF Dec 48 39

LATENT IMAGE by Wesley Long. .nt . . . . ASF May 44 7

LATER THAN YOU THINK by Henry Kuttner. .s . . . . FA Mar 42 60

LATER THAN YOU THINK by Fritz Leiber. .s . . . . .GSF Oct 50 108

LAUGHING DEATH, THE by Alexander Blade *h ps* . . . . . .s . . . . .Amz Jul 50 152

LAUGHING DEATH, THE by Stephen G. Hale. .s . . . . Amz Apr 31 42

LAUGHTER OUT OF SPACE by Dennis Clive *ps (John Russell Fearn)*. .nt . . . . Fut Jul 40 24

LAVENDER VINE OF DEATH, THE by Don Wilcox . . . . .n . . . . FA Sep 48 8

LAW OF THE UNIVERSE, THE by Coutts Brisbane . . . . . .s . . . . ToW Win 41 54

LAWS OF CHANCE, THE by Murray Leinster *ps (Will F. Jenkins)*. .n . . . . .SS Mar 47 13

LAZARUS COME FORTH by Ray Bradbury. .s . . . . .PS Win 44 105

LEADER FOR KORCIN, A by F. Orlin Tremaine. .s . . . . .Fut Dec 42 22

LEAK IN THE FOUNTAIN OF YOUTH, A by A. R. Long. .s . . . . ASF Aug 36 48

LEAPERS, THE by Carol Grey *ps (Robert W. Lowndes)*. .s . . . . .Fut Dec 42 40

LEASHED LIGHTNING by J. E. Gurdon. .s . . . . .Fant #1 38 37

LEECH, THE by Malcolm Jameson. .nt . . . . .ASF Jan 44 46

LEECHES FROM SPACE by Ephriam Winiki *ps (John Russell Fearn)*. .s . . . . .SF Mar 39 114

Title. .Author. .Length . . . . Magazine. .Date. .Page No.

LEFTY FEEP AND THE RACING ROBOT by Robert
Bloch. .s . . . . FA Apr 43 70
LEFTY FEEP AND THE SLEEPY-TIME GAL by Robert
Bloch. .s . . . . FA Dec 42 146
LEFTY FEEP CATCHES HELL by Robert Bloch. .s . . .
. . . . .FA Jan 43 192
LEFTY FEEP DOES TIME by Robert Bloch. .nt. . . . . .
. . . . FA Apr 44 156
LEFTY FEEP GETS HENPECKED by Robert Bloch. . .
. .s . . . . FA Apr 45 116
LEFTY FEEP'S ARABIAN NIGHTMARE by Robert
Bloch. .s . . . . FA Feb 44 178
LEGACY by Nelson S. Bond. .s . . . . ASF Dec 40 33
LEGEND OF MARK SHANE, THE by John York Cabot
ps (David Wright O'Brien). .s . . . . FA Apr 42 224
LEGEND OF POSI AND NEGA, A by Joseph Wm.
Skidmore. .s . . . . Amz Oct 35 13
LEGION OF SPACE, THE by Jack Williamson . . . . . .
. .n 6 pt. . . . . ASF Apr 34 10
(complete) . . . . GSFN #2
LEGION OF THE DARK by Manly Wade Wellman. .s . .
. . . . SSS May 43 56
LEGION OF THE DEAD by Frederic Arnold Kummer,
Jr. . .s. . . . . Amz Nov 39 100
LEGION OF TIME by Jack Williamson. .n 3 pt. . . . . .
. . . . ASF May 38 4
LEMMINGS, THE by Wilfred Owen Morley ps (Robert
W. Lowndes). .s. . . . . .SSS May 42 102
LEMURIAN DOCUMENTS, THE by J. Lewis Burtt, B. Sc.
No. 1 PYGMALION. .s . . . . .Amz Jan 32 920
No. 2 THE GORGONS. .s . . . . Amz Mar 32 1128
No. 3 DAEDALUS AND ICARUS. .s . . . .
. . . . Amz May 32 144
No. 4 PHAETON. .s . . . . Amz Jun 32 222
No. 5 THE SACRED CLOAK OF FEATHERS. . . . .
. .s . . . . .Amz Jul 32 338
No. 6 PROMETHEUS. .s . . . . Amz Sep 32 524
LENGTH OF ROPE, A by Chester S. Geier. .s . . . . . .
. . . . UK Apr 41 120
LENSMAN series See E. E. SMITH author
LEOPARD GIRL, THE by Don Wilcox. .n . . . .
. . . . FA Oct 42 50
LESS LIGHT, PLEASE by J. J. Coupling ps (John R.
Pierce). .a. . . . . ASF Mar 47 90
LEST DARKNESS FALL by L. Sprague de Camp. .n. . .
. . . . .UK Dec 39 9
"LEST YE BE JUDGED. . ." by Dave Dryfoos. .s . . . . .
. . . . FA Oct 50 98
LET CLARENCE DO IT by Edward S. Sullivan . . . . . .
. .ss . . . . FFM Dec 48 112
LET CYMBALS RING! by M. Schere. .s . . . .
. . . . ASF Dec 38 126
LET FREEDOM RING by Fritz Leiber, Jr. . .n . . . . . .
. . . . Amz Apr 50 90
LET FREEDOM RING by Rog Phillips ps (Roger P.
Graham). .nt. . . . . Amz Dec 45 124

Title. .Author. .Length . . . . Magazine. .Date. .Page No.

LET THE ANTS TRY by James MacCreigh ps (Frederik
Pohl). .s. . . . . .PS Win 49 63
LET THE FINDER BEWARE! by James Blish. .n . . . . .
. . . . TW Dec 49 11
LET THE GODS DECIDE by Paul Lohrman h ps . . . . .
. .s . . . . Amz Apr 50 46
LET THERE BE LIGHT by Lyle Monroe ps (Robert A.
Heinlein). .s . . . . SSS May 40 34
LET WAR GODS CLASH by Don Wilcox. .s. . . . .
. . . . FA Feb 40 70
LET'S DISAPPEAR by Cleve Cartmill. .nt . . . .
. . . . ASF May 43 124
LET'S DO IT MY WAY by E. K. Jarvis h ps. .s . . . . . .
. . . . Amz May 50 128
LETTER FROM THE STARS by A. E. van Vogt. .s. . . .
. . . . OTWA Jul 50 25
LETTER OF THE TWENTY-FOURTH CENTURY by
Leslie F. Stone ps (Mrs. Wm. Silberberg). .ss . . . .
. . . . Amz Dec 29 860
LETTER PAGE dept of Imagination from Oct 50
LETTER TO A PHOENIX by Fredric Brown. .s . . . . . .
. . . . ASF Aug 49 146
LETTER TO AN INVISIBLE WOMAN by Hannes
Bok. .ss . . . . UK Oct 42 79
LETTER TO ELLEN by Chan Davis. .s . . . ASF Jun 47 42
LETTER TO THE EDITOR (anon). .s . . . . FA Feb 44 120
LETTERS dept in OTHER WORLDS from *Nov 49
(first issue*)
LETTERS FROM THE READERS dept in Imagination
from Dec 50
LEVER OF DESTRUCTION by Tom Erwin Geris ps
(Mort Weisinger). .s . . . . SF Dec 39 87
LIAR! by Isaac Asimov. .s . . . . ASF May 41 43
LICHEN FROM EROS, THE by Frank Belknap Long,
Jr. . .s. . . . . ASF Nov 35 97
LIE, THE by Richard Louis. .ss . . . . UK Oct 42 97
LIE ON THE BEAM by John Victor Peterson. .s . . . . .
. . . . Com Mar 41 105
LIFE BATTERY, THE by Eando Binder ps (Otto
Binder). .s . . . . SS Jul 39 113
LIFE BEYOND, THE by John Coleridge ps (Earl
Binder & Otto Binder). .nt . . . . SF Mar 41 10
LIFE CURRENT by Donald Wandrei. .s . . . .
. . . . ASF Apr 35 102
LIFE CYCLE by Wilbur S. Peacock. .ss . . . .
. . . . .SF Oct 40 72
LIFE DETOUR, THE by David H. Keller, M.D. . .s . . . .
. . . . WS Feb 35 1072
SS Jul 47 64
LIFE DISINHERITED by Eando Binder ps (Otto
Binder). .nt . . . . ASF Mar 37 58
LIFE ETERNAL by Eando Binder ps (Otto Binder). . . .
. .s . . . . TW Feb 38 70
LIFE EVERLASTING by David H. Keller, M.D. . . . . . .
. .n 2 pt. . . . . .Amz Jul 34 9
LIFE FOR SALE by Alfred Bester. .nt . . .Amz Jan 42 166
. . . . .Amz Jan 42 166

Title. .Author. .Length . . . . Magazine. .Date. .Page No.

LIFE INSIDE A WALL by Harl Vincent (Schoepflin). . .
. .s . . . . SFQ Sum 40 142
LIFE JEWEL, THE by Oliver Saari. .s . . . .SFQ Spr 41 115
LIFE LINE, THE. .bacover pic. . . . . Amz Aug 38
LIFE MACHINE, THE by Lester Barclay. .nt . . . .
. . . . Amz Dec 44 84
LIFE-LINE by Robert Heinlein. .s . . . . . ASF Aug 39 83
LIFE MACHINE, THE by Manly Wade Wellman. .s . . . .
. . . . TW Dec 40 16
LIFE ON CALLISTO by Frank R. Paul. .bacover pic . . .
. . . . Amz Aug 40
LIFE ON EUROPA by Frank R. Paul. .bacover pic . . . .
. . . . Amz Sep 40
LIFE ON GANYMEDE by Frank R. Paul. .bacover pic. .
. . . . Amz Oct 40
LIFE ON IO by Frank R. Paul. .bacover pic . . . .
. . . . FA May 40
LIFE ON JUPITER by Frank R. Paul. .bacover pic . . . .
. . . . .FA Jan 40
LIFE ON MARS by Professor A. M. Low. .a . . . .
. . . . ToW Aut 39 67
LIFE ON MERCURY by Frank R. Paul. .bacover pic . . .
. . . . FA Sep 39
LIFE ON NEPTUNE by Frank R. Paul. .bacover pic . . .
. . . . FA Mar 40
LIFE ON OTHER PLANETS? by Edward Podolsky. . . .
. .a . . . . PS Sum 40 105
LIFE ON PLUTO by Frank R. Paul. .bacover pic. . . . .
. . . . FA Feb 40
LIFE ON SATURN by Frank R. Paul. .bacover pic . . . .
. . . . FA Nov 39
LIFE ON THE MOON by Alexander Samalman. .ss . . . .
. . . . TW Dec 46 95
LIFE ON TITAN by Frank R. Paul. .bacover pic . . . . .
. . . . Amz Nov 40
LIFE ON URANUS by Frank R. Paul. .bacover pic . . . .
. . . . FA Apr 40
LIFE SYMBOL, THE by Berkeley Livingston. .nt . . . . .
. . . . FA Feb 46 48
LIFESTONE, THE by Paul Edmonds ps (Henry
Kuttner). .s . . . . .Ash Feb 40 70
LIFE-WORK OF PROFESSOR MUNTZ, THE by Murray
Leinster ps (Will F. Jenkins). .s. . . . . . TW Jun 49 128
LIGHT BENDER, THE by Frank K. Kelly. .s . . . .
. . . . WS Jun 31 34
                                        FSQ Sum 50 99
LIGHT FROM BEYOND, THE by Clark Ashton
Smith. .s . . . . WS Apr 33 822
LIGHT FROM INFINITY, THE by L. A. Eshbach. .s . . .
. . . . Amz Mar 32 1094
LIGHT IN DARKNESS by William Morrison ps (Joseph
Samachson). .s . . . . .TW Fal 43 103
LIGHT OF LIFE by Chester S. Geier. .s. . . Amz Dec 47 46
LIGHT THAT KILLED, THE by Ed Earl Repp. .s . . . . .
. . . . Amz Mar 43 98

LIGHT THAT KILLS, THE by J. Harvey Haggard. .s . . .
. . . . Amz Feb 39 74
LIGHTNING LOOT by Warren Kastel ps. .s . . . .
. . . . FA Sep 49 50
LIGHTNING MEN, THE by John Coleman Burroughs
& Hulbert Burroughs. .nt . . . . .TW Feb 40 12
LIGHTNING STRIKES ONCE by Harl Vincent
(Schoepflin). .s . . . . MSS Aug 39 100
LIGHTNING'S COURSE, THE by John Victor
Peterson. .s. . . . . Com Jan 41 4
LIGHTS by Phillip Fisher. .s . . . . FFM Dec 39 78
LIGHTSHIP, HO! by Nelson S. Bond. .s . . . .
. . . . .ASF Jul 39 67
LIKE A KEEPSAKE by John D. MacDonald. .s. . . . . .
. . . . TW Jun 49 95
LIKE ALARM BELLS RINGING by Robert Moore
Williams. .s . . . . Amz Jan 47 84
LIKE DUPS by Murray Leinster ps (Will F. Jenkins) . . .
. .s . . . . TW Spr 46 93
LILENE, THE MOON GIRL by Edmond Hamilton . . . .
. .nt . . . . .Amz May 40 66
LILLIES OF LIFE by Malcolm Jameson. .s . . . .
. . . . ASF Feb 45 29
LILLIPUT IN EQUUSIA by Richard Tooker. .a . . . . . .
. . . . TW Oct 42 98
LIMITING FACTOR by Clifford D. Simak. .s . . . .
. . . . .SS Nov 49 123
LINE TO TOMORROW by Lewis Padgett ps (Henry
Kuttner & C. L. Moore). .s . . . . ASF Nov 45 54
LINERS OF SPACE by Henry Gade h ps (Raymond A.
Palmer). .s . . . . Amz Dec 39 108
LINERS OF SPACE by Jim Vanny. .s . . . .
. . . . AW Feb 30 704
LINERS OF TIME by John Russell Fearn. .n 4 pt . . . .
. . . . .Amz May 35 28
LINGUISTICS AND TIME by Arthur J. Cox. .a . . . . .
. . . . ASF Aug 50 128
LINK, THE by Cleve Cartmill. .s . . . . . . ASF Aug 42 84
LINK, ADAM series See EANDO BINDER ps (Otto
Binder) author
LINK TO THE PAST, A by Charles G. Blandford. .a . . .
. . . . Amz Sep 27 598
LINKED WORLDS by R. R. Winterbotham. .s . . . .
. . . . .ASF Jan 37 40
LION AND THE LAMB, THE by Fritz Leiber. .nt . . . .
. . . . ASF Sep 50 6
LION AND THE UNICORN, THE by Lewis Padgett ps
Henry Kuttner & C. L. Moore). .nt . . . . ASF Jul 45 144
LION-HEARTED, THE by William Morrison ps (Joseph
Samachson). .s . . . . .CF Sum 42 80
LION OF COMARRE by Arthur C. Clarke. .nt . . . . . .
. . . . .TW Aug 49 44
LION'S WAY, THE by C. T. Stoneham. .n . . . .
. . . . FFM Oct 48 10
LIQUID HELL by Neil R. Jones. .s . . . . Fut Jul 40 8

Title. .Author. .Length . . . . Magazine. .Date. .Page No.

LIQUID LIFE by Ralph Milne Farley ps (Roger Sherman
    Hoar). .nt. TW Oct 36 60
LIQUID MAN, THE by Bernard C. Gifford. .n . . . .
    . . . . FA Sep 41 8
LIQUID POWER by Warner van Lorne ps. .nt. . . . .
    . . . . ASF Jul 35 46
LISTENING CHILD, THE by Idris Seabright ps (Margaret
    St. Clair). .s . . . . F&SF Dec 50 37
LITERARY CORKSCREW, THE by David H. Keller,
    M.D. . .s . . . . WS Mar 34 866
                                          SS May 41 112
LITTLE BLACK BAG, THE by C. M. Kornbluth. .nt . . .
    . . . . ASF Jul 50 132
LITTLE BLUE CELLS, THE by J. J. Coupling. .a . . . . .
    . . . . ASF Feb 49 85
LITTLE DOLL DIED, THE by Theodore Roscoe . . . . .
    . .nt . . . . AMF Apr 50 94
LITTLE DROPS OF WATER by Francis M. Deegan. . . .
    . .s . . . . Amz Feb 46 132
LITTLE ENOUGH by J. J. Coupling ps (John R.
    Pierce). .a. . . . . ASF Apr 45 100
LITTLE GREEN STONE, A by J. Harvey Haggard . . . .
    . .s . . . . ASF Mar 36 30
LITTLE HERCULES by Neil R. Jones. .nt . . . .
    . . . . ASF Sep 36 62
LITTLE JOE by Cleve Cartmill. .s . . . . . . TW Apr 50 105
LITTLE JOHNNY by O. G. Estes, Jr. . .ss . . . .
    . . . . FB #2 11
LITTLE KNOWLEDGE, A by H. B. Hickey ps (Herb
    Livingston). .s. . . . . FA Jan 47 64
LITTLE LOST ROBOT by Isaac Asimov. .nt . . . .
    . . . . ASF Mar 47 111
LITTLE MAN ON THE SUBWAY, THE by Isaac Asimov
    & James MacCreigh ps (Frederik Pohl). .s. . . . . FB #6 4
LITTLE MAN WHO WASN'T ALL THERE, THE by
    Robert Bloch. .s . . . . FA Aug 42 188
LITTLE MAN WHO WASN'T THERE, THE by Arthur
    K. Barnes. .s. . . . . TW Mar 41 59
LITTLE MISS IGNORANCE by E. Everett Evans. .s . . .
    . . . . OW Sep 50 40
LITTLE MONSTERS COME, THE by Ray Cummings . .
    . .nt . . . . .PS Win 48 84
LITTLE PEOPLE, THE by Eando Binder ps (Otto
    Binder). .nt . . . . FA Mar 40 8
LITTLE PETS OF ARKKHAN, THE by Vaseleos
    Garson. .s. . . . . PS Sum 47 75
LITTLE PLANET by Thorp McCluskey. .s . . . .
    . . . . .SF Oct 39 83
LITTLE THINGS, THE by Henry Kuttner. .s . . . .
    . . . . TW Fal 46 85
LITTLE YOWLIE by Warren A. Reed. .ss . . . .
    . . . . .FA Jul 43 90
LIVE IN AN ORBIT AND LIKE IT! (on cover)
LIVE IN AN ORBIT AND LOVE IT! (on story & ToC) by
    Craig Browning ps (Roger P. Graham). .s . . . .
    . . . . OW Mar 50 108

Title. .Author. .Length . . . . Magazine. .Date. .Page No.

LIVING DEAD, THE by Edgar Rice Burroughs. .nt . . . .
    . . . . .FA Nov 41 8
LIVING EQUATION, THE by Nat Schachner. .s. . . . . .
    . . . . ASF Sep 34 6
LIVING FLAME, THE by Arthur Leo Zagat. .nt . . . . .
    . . . . ASF Feb 34 102
LIVING FOSSIL by L. Sprague de Camp. .s . . . .
    . . . . ASF Feb 39 33
LIVING GALAXY, THE by Laurence Manning. .s. . . . .
    . . . . WS Sep 34 436
LIVING GHOST, THE by E. A. Grosser. .s. . . . .
    . . . . UK Mar 40 93
LIVING ISOTOPES by P. Schuyler Miller. .s . . . .
    . . . . SSS May 40 80
LIVING LIES, THE by John Beynon (Harris). .nt . . . . .
    . . . . NW #2 46 2
                                          OW Nov 59 96
LIVING MACHINE, THE by David H. Keller, M.D. . . .
    . .s . . . . WS May 35 1464
LIVING MANIKINS, THE by David Wright O'Brien . . .
    . .nt . . . . FA Feb 42 66
LIVING MIST, THE by Ralph Milne Farley ps (Roger
    Sherman Hoar). .nt . . . . Amz Aug 40 46
LIVING PORTRAIT, THE by Tod Robbins. .nt . . . . . .
    . . . . FN Nov 49 76
LIVING TEST TUBE, THE by Joe Simmons. .s . . . . . .
    . . . . Amz Nov 28 744
LIVING VORTEX, THE by Stanley Mullen. .nt . . . . . .
    . . . . FA Apr 50 42
LIZARD MEN OF BUH-LO, THE by Francis Flagg ps
    (George Henry Weiss). .s . . . . WS Oct 30 402
LO! by Charles Fort. .a 8 pt . . . . ASF Apr 34 146
LOBBY by Clifford D. Simak. .s. . . . .
    . . . . ASF Apr 44 144
LOCKED CITY by Thornton Ayre. .nt . . . .
    . . . . Amz Oct 38 58
LOCKED OUT by H. B. Fyfe. .s. . . . . . . ASF Feb 40 42
LOCKED WORLDS by Edmond Hamilton. .s. . . . .
    . . . . AQ Spr 29 222
LODANA by Carl Jacobi. .s. . . . . .SS Sep 47 80
LODESTONE, THE by D. D. Sharp. .s . . . .
    .Ash Aug 40 82
LOGIC by Poul Anderson. .nt . . . . .ASF Jul 47 51
LOGIC NAMED JOE, A by Will F. Jenkins. .s. . . . . . .
    . . . . ASF Mar 46 139
LOGIC OF EMPIRE by Robert Heinlein. .nt . . . .
    . . . . ASF Mar 41 9
LONE WOLF OF SPACE by Joseph J. Millard & A. R.
    Steber h ps (Raymond A. Palmer). .nt . . . .
    .Amz May 41 50
LONELY ONES, THE by Ray Bradbury. .s . . . .
    . . . . SS Jul 49 135
LONELY PLANET, THE by Murray Leinster ps (Will F.
    Jenkins). .s. . . . . TW Dec 49 80
LONESOME PLACE, THE by August Derleth. .s. . . . .
    . . . . FFM Feb 48 114

Title. .Author. .Length . . . . Magazine. .Date. .Page No.

LONG BEER—SHORT HORN by Mack Reynolds . . . . .
. .s . . . . FA Nov 50 76
LONG DAWN, THE by Noel Loomis. .s. . . . SSS Jan 50 98
LONG FLIGHT, THE by Carter Sprague *ps (Sam
Merwin, Jr.)* .s . . . . FSQ Fal 50 147
LONG, LONG AGO by Frank Belknap Long. .s . . . . .
. . . . .CF Fal 41 97
LONG NIGHT, THE by Charles Willard Diffin . . . .
. .nt . . . . ASF May 34 129
LONG REMEMBER by Dwight V. Swain. .s . . . .
. . . . FA Dec 42 86
LONG RETURN, THE by Poul Anderson. .nt. . . . . . .
. . . . Fut Sep-Oct 50 64
LONG-TAILED HUNS, THE by L. Sprague de Camp. . .
. .a 2 pt . . . . .ASF Jan 42 86
LONG WALL, THE by Wilfred Owen Morley *ps
(Robert W. Lowndes)*. .s . . . . Sti Mar 42 55
LONG WAY, THE by Francis L. Ashton. .s . . . . . .
. . . . SSS May 50 42
LONG WAY, THE by George O. Smith. .nt . . . . . .
. . . . ASF Apr 44 67
LONG WAY BACK, THE by John Barrett. .s . . . . .
. . . . TW Feb 48 84
LONG WINTER, THE by Raymond Z. Gallun . . . .
. .s . . . . ASF May 40 112
LOOK TO THE STARS by Willard Hawkins. .n. . . . . .
. . . . .Im Oct 50 82
LOOM OF DARKNESS, THE by Jack Vance . . . .
. .s . . . . WB Dec 50 117
LOOPHOLE by Arthur C. Clarke. .s . . . . ASF Apr 46 57
LOOT OF THE VOID by Edwin K. Sloat. .s . . . .
. . . . ASF Sep 32 4
LOOT OF TIME, THE by Clifford D. Simak. . . . . . .
. .nt . . . . TW Dec 38 58
SS Mar 49 88
LORD OF DEATH, THE by Homer Eon Flint. .nt. . . . .
. . . . FFM Dec 39 42
LORD OF SPACE, THE by Victor Rousseau
(Emanuel). .s . . . . ASF Aug 30 158
LORD OF THE CRYSTAL BOW by Duncan
Farnsworth *ps (David Wright O'Brien)*. .n. . . . . . .
. . . . .Amz May 42 8
LORD OF THE DYNAMOS, THE by H. G. Wells . . . .
. .s . . . . Amz Feb 29 975
LORD OF THE EARTHQUAKE by Leigh Brackett . . . .
. .nt . . . . .SF Jun 41 60
LORD OF THE LIGHTNING by Arthur K. Barnes . . . .
. .s . . . . WS Dec 31 868
LORD OF THE SILENT DEATH by Robert
Moore Williams. .s . . . . Com Dec 40 7
LORD OF THE STORM by Keith Hammond *ps
(Henry Kuttner & C. L. Moore)*. .n . . . .
. . . . .SS Sep 47 11
LORD OF THE WINDS, THE by Augusto
Bissiri. .s . . . . Amz Dec 26 820

Title. .Author. .Length . . . . Magazine. .Date. .Page No.

LORD OF TRANERICA, THE by Stanton A.
Coblentz. .n . . . . DS Feb 39 12
LORDS OF 9016 by John Russell Fearn. .s . . . .
. . . . TW Apr 38 80
LORDS OF THE DEEP by Henry F. Kirkham . . . .
. .s . . . . WS Nov 30 544
LORDS OF THE STRATOSPHERE by Arthur J.
Burks. .nt. . . . . ASF Mar 33 22
LORDS OF THE UNDERWORLD by L. Taylor
Hansen. .nt . . . . Amz Apr 41 8
LORELEI DEATH, THE by Nelson S. Bond. .nt . . . . .
. . . . PS Win 41 2
LORELEI OF SPACE by Frederic Arnold Kummer,
Jr. . .nt . . . . ASF Feb 39 117
LORELEI OF THE RED MIST by Leigh Brackett &
Ray Bradbury. .nt . . . . PS Sum 46 2
LORELEI STREET by Craig Browning *ps (Roger P.
Graham)*. .s . . . . FA Sep 50 112
LOST ART by George O. Smith. .nt . . . .
. . . . ASF Dec 43 33
LOST BOMB, THE by Rog Phillips *ps (Roger P.
Graham)*. .nt. . . . . .Amz May 50 70
LOST CITY, THE by Milton R. Peril. .n 3 pt . . . .
. . . . .Amz May 34 10
LOST CITY OF BURMA by Edmond Hamilton . . . . . .
. .n . . . . FA Dec 42 38
LOST CITY OF MARS by Harl Vincent (Schoepflin). . .
. .nt . . . . ASF Feb 34 67
LOST COLONY IN THE SUPERSTITIONS by James
Norman. .s . . . . Amz Mar 41 114
LOST COMET, THE by Ronald M. Sherin. .s . . . .
. . . . Amz Jun 27 260
LOST CONTINENT, THE by Cecil B. White. .s . . . . .
. . . . .Amz Jul 27 339
LOST CONTINENT, THE by Cutcliffe Hyne. .n . . . . .
. . . . FFM Dec 44 10
LOST GARDEN, THE by Max Brand *ps (Frederick
Faust)*. .s . . . . FFM Dec 41 96
LOST HOUR, THE by Alexander Samalman. .ss . . . . .
. . . . SS May 39 116
LOST IN SPACE by J. Harvey Haggard. .s . . . .
. . . . ASF Aug 35 53
LOST IN THE DIMENSIONS by Nat Schachner. .s . . . .
. . . . ASF Nov 37 54
LOST IN TIME by Arthur Leo Zagat. .nt. . . TW Jun 37 40
LOST KEY, THE by Charles Alban Crouch. .s . . . .
. . . . Fant Aug 47 42
LOST LANGUAGE, THE by David H. Keller, M.D. . . .
. .s . . . . Amz Jan 34 87
LOST LEGION by Lyle Monroe *ps (Robert A.
Heinlein)*. .n . . . . .SSS Nov 41 10
LOST LEGIONS OF CARTHAGE by Leroy Yerxa . . . .
. .nt . . . . FA Jun 43 72
LOST MACHINE, THE by John B. Harris. .s . . . .
. . . . Amz Apr 32 40

Title. .Author. .Length . . . . Magazine. .Date. .Page No.

LOST MARTIAN, THE by Henry Harber. .s . . . .
. . . . SW Dec 29 636
LOST ON THE SEA BOTTOM by Ed Earl Repp. .s . . . .
. . . . Amz Feb 39 114
LOST—ONE MYLODON by Elmer Brown Mason . . . . .
. .s . . . . FN Jul 50 108
LOST PLANET, THE by Barry Cord ps (Peter B.
Germano). .nt . . . . TW Mar 41 16
LOST PLANET by Geoffrey Giles ps (Walter Gillings) . .
. .a . . . . Fant Dec 46 56
LOST PLANET by Frank Belknap Long, Jr. . .s . . . . . .
. . . . ASF Nov 34 65
LOST POWER, THE by Guy Archette ps (Chester S.
Geier). .s . . . . Amz Mar 49 42
LOST RACE, THE by Murray Leinster ps (Will F.
Jenkins). .s . . . . TW Apr 49 112
LOST RACE COMES BACK, THE by Don Wilcox. . . . .
. .n . . . . Amz May 41 8
LOST ROCKET by Manly Wade Wellman. .s . . . .
. . . . ASF Jan 41 103
LOST ROOM, THE by Fitz-James O'Brien. .s . . . .
. . . . F&SF Fal 49 47
LOST TREASURE OF ANGKOR by James Norman . . .
. .nt . . . . Amz Jun 41 44
LOST TREASURE OF MARS by Edmond Hamilton . . .
. .s . . . . Amz Aug 40 68
LOST ULYSSES by William L. Bade. .nt . . . .
. . . . ASF May 49 109
LOST WARSHIP, THE by Robert Moore Williams. . . . .
. .nt . . . . Amz Jan 43 8
LOST WORLD OF TIME, THE by Edmond Hamilton . .
. .n . . . . CF Fal 42 14
LOTOS EATERS, THE by Bolling Branham. .s . . . .
. . . . TW Aug 43 58
LOTS OF GOLD—BUT GET IT by R. S. Richardson . . .
. .a . . . . ASF Aug 45 154
LOTUS EATERS, THE by Stanley G. Weinbaum . . . . .
. .nt . . . . ASF Apr 35 52
LOTUS-ENGINE, THE by Raymond Z. Gallun. .s . . . . .
. . . . SSS Mar 40 26
LOTUS JUICE by Malcolm Jameson. .s . . . . TW Apr 43 75
LOTUS TEMPLE, THE by Berkeley Livingston. .s . . . .
. . . . FA Jul 45 178
LOUIE'S CAT EYE by Leroy Yerxa. .s . . . FA Dec 42 218
LOVE AMONG THE ROBOTS by Emmett
McDowell. .s . . . . PS Win 46 29
LOVE MY ROBOT by Rog Phillips ps (Roger P.
Graham). .s . . . . SS Nov 50 97
LOVE OF HEAVEN, THE by Theodore Sturgeon. .s . . .
. . . . ASF Nov 48 28
LOVE SLAVE AND THE SCIENTISTS, THE by
Frank Belknap Long, Jr. . .s . . . . AFR #13 3
LOVE SONG OF LANCELOT BIGGS, THE by Nelson
S. Bond. .s . . . . Amz Sep 42 46
LOVELY GHOST, THE by Stuart Jackson. .s . . . .
. . . . ASF Nov 33 21

LOVE'S LETHAL INGREDIENT by Allan K. Echols. . .
. .s . . . . MSS Dec 39 59
LUCK OF ENOCH HIGGINS, THE by Charles R.
Tanner. .s . . . . FA Aug 42 176
LUCK OF IGNATZ, THE by Lester del Rey. .nt . . . . . .
. . . . ASF Aug 39 9
LUDER VALLEY by Richard S. Shaver. .nt . . . .
. . . . Amz Jun 46 98
LUMINOUS MINE by Raymond Z. Gallun. .s . . . .
. . . . ASF Jan 37 80
LUNA OBSERVATORY No. 1 by R. S. Richardson . . .
. .a . . . . ASF Feb 40 113
LUNA CHRYSALIS, THE by Raymond Z. Gallun. . . . .
. .s . . . . Amz Sep 31 528
LUNAR CONCESSION by Thornton Ayre ps (John
Russell Fearn). .nt . . . . SF Sep 41 10
NW #2 46 34
LUNAR CONSUL, THE by Sidney Patzer. .n 2 pt . . . . .
. . . . WS Nov 33 294
LUNAR GUN by John L. Chapman. .ss . . . . Sti Feb 41 25
LUNAR HOLIDAY by Peter Worth h ps. .s . . . .
. . . . FA Nov 49 52
LUNAR INTRIGUE by Thornton Ayre ps (John Russell
Fearn). .s . . . . FA Nov 39 56
LUNAR LANDING by Lester del Rey. .nt . . . .
. . . . ASF Oct 42 9
LUNAR LEGACY by Charles Recour. .s . . . .
. . . . Amz Feb 49 124
LUNAR LILLIPUT by William F. Temple. .nt . . . .
. . . . ToW #2 38 100
LUNAR LOOT by Edwin Benson. .s . . . . . FA Mar 40 64
LUNAR MISSILE, THE by Coutts Brisbane. .s . . . .
. . . . ToW Spr 40 32
LUNAR MONKEY BUSINESS by Warren Kastel ps. .s . .
. . . . Amz Jun 48 76
LUNAR PARASITES by Raymond Z. Gallun. .s . . . . . .
. . . . CF Sum 40 100
LUNAR PIT, THE by Myer Krulfeld. .s . . . . TW Jun 40 44
LUNAR POINT OF VIEW, THE by S. M. Tenneshaw
h ps. .s . . . . FA Apr 50 112
LUNAR SANCTUARY by Walter R. Preston. .s . . . . . .
. . . . SFQ Win 42 114
LUNAR STATION by John Michel (story) & J. Kubert
(pics). .comic . . . . OTWA Jul 50 51
LUNAR STATION by Harl Vincent (Schoepflin). .s . . . .
. . . . Com Jan 41 34
LUNAR VENGEANCE by Thornton Ayre ps (John
Russell Fearn). .nt . . . . Amz Sep 43 88
LUNDSTRET'S INVENTION by Robert Moore
Williams. .s . . . . Amz Jun 39 76
LURE OF POLARIS, THE by Wallace West. .nt . . . . . .
. . . . TW Oct 49 9
LURKING DEATH, THE by Dr. Walter Rose. .s . . . . . .
. . . . Amz Feb 36 11
LUST RIDES THE ROLLER COASTER by Ray King . .
. .s . . . . MSS Dec 39 70

Title. .Author. .Length . . . . Magazine. .Date. .Page No.

LUVIUM by A. R. McKenzie. .s . . . . Amz Nov 31 706
LUVIUM, THE INVINCIBLE CITY by A. R. . . . . . .
   McKenzie. .nt . . . . Amz Sep 43 30
LUVIUM UNDER THE SAND by A. R. McKenzie . . .
   .nt . . . . Amz Jun 36 88
LUVVER by Mack Reynolds. .s . . . . FA Jun 50 118
LUXURY LINER by Nelson S. Bond. .nt . . . .
   . . . . TW Feb 42 15
LYING LIE-DETECTOR, THE by Leroy Yerxa. .s . . . .
   . . . . Amz Mar 45 132

M

M 33 IN ANDROMEDA by A. E. van Vogt. .s . . . .
   . . . . ASF Aug 43 129
MACHINE, THE by Don A. Stuart ps (John W.
   Campbell, Jr.). .s . . . . ASF Feb 35 70
MACHINE, THE by Robert Moore Williams. .nt . . . . . .
   . . . . .Amz May 43 8
MACHINE BRAIN, THE by David V. Reed ps (David
   Vern). .s . . . . .TW Jul 40 31
MACHINE FROM GANYMEDE, THE by Raymond Z.
   Gallun. .s . . . . ASF Nov 34 112
MACHINE FROM THE PAST, THE by James Norman. .
   . .s . . . . FA May 41 116
MACHINE-GOD LAUGHS, THE by Festus Pragnell. . . .
   . .nt 3 pt . . . . FB #2 32
MACHINE MAN OF ARDATHIA, THE by Francis Flagg
   (George Henry Weiss). .s . . . . Amz Nov 27 798
                                              ToW Aut 40 35
                                              AFR #8 27
MACHINE OF DESTINY, THE by Ulysses George
   Mihalakis. .s . . . . .WQ Sum 31 514
MACHINE OF KLAMUGRA by Allen K. Lang. .s . . . . .
   . . . . PS Nov 50 46
MACHINE STOPS, THE by Wayland Smith. .n . . . . . .
   . . . . .FFM Mar 45 8
MACHINE THAT CHANGED HISTORY, THE by
   Robert Bloch. .s . . . . SF Jul 43 88
MACHINE THAT HAD NO FLAWS, THE by Ray
   Cummings. .s . . . . .SS Sep 40 106
MACHINE THAT KNEW TOO MUCH, THE by A. T.
   Locke. .s . . . . ASF Dec 33 28
MACHINE THAT THOUGHT, THE by William
   Callahan ps (Raymond Z. Gallun). .s . . . . SF Mar 39 63
MacHINERY by Eric Frank Russell. .s . . . .
   . . . . TW Dec 50 43
MACHINES OF DESTINY by Ray Cummings. .s . . . . . .
   . . . . .Ash Nov 41 96
MACKLIN'S LITTLE FRIEND by H. W. Guernsey
   ps (Howard Wandrei). .s . . . . ASF Nov 36 83
McNAB, JOSH series See ARTHUR J. BURKS author
MACROCOSMIC by G. L. Maddocks. .s . . . .
   . . . . SS May 42 103

Title. .Author. .Length . . . . Magazine. .Date. .Page No.

MAD DESTROYER, THE by Fletcher Pratt. .s . . . . . .
   . . . . WQ Spr 30 406
MAD DOMNEYS, THE by Verne Chute. .s . . . .
   . . . . SS Fal 44 82
MAD HATTER by Winston K. Marks. .s . . .UK May 40 78
MAD MARIONETTES by Arthur J. Burks. .s . . . .
   . . . . Mir Apr 31 116
MAD MOLECULE, THE by Alfred Bester. .s . . . .
   . . . . TW Jan 41 29
MAD MOON, THE by Stanley G. Weinbaum. .nt . . . . . .
   . . . . ASF Dec 35 52
MAD MUSIC by Anthony Pelcher. .s . . . ASF Feb 30 248
MAD PLANET, THE by Murray Leinster ps (Will F.
   Jenkins). .s . . . . Amz Nov 26 736
                                              ToW Spr 39 4
                                              FN Nov 48 82
MAD ROBOT by Raymond Z. Gallun. .s . . . .
   . . . . ASF Mar 36 66
MAD ROBOT, THE by William P. McGivern. .nt . . . . . .
   . . . . Amz Jan 44 10
MAD SCIENTIST, THE by Robert Bloch. .s . . . .
   . . . . FA Sep 47 108
MAD VIRUS, THE by Paul Edmonds ps (Henry
   Kuttner). .s . . . . .SF Jun 40 29
MAD WORLD, THE by A. L. Burkholder. .s . . . .
   . . . . .WS Jan 36 800
MADAGASCAR GHOST by Clee Garson. .s . . . .
   . . . . FA Dec 42 174
MADAMOISELLE BUTTERFLY by Don Wilcox . . . . .
   . .nt . . . . FA May 42 146
MADCAP METALLOIDS, THE by W. V. Athanas . . . . .
   . .s . . . . PS Sum 49 37
MADCAP OF MARS by Festus Pragnell. .nt . . . .
   . . . . Amz Sep 43 172
MADMEN OF MARS by Eric Fennel. .s . . . .
   . . . . PS Spr 50 40
MADNESS FROM MARS by Clifford D. Simak. .s . . . . .
   . . . . TW Apr 39 76
MADNESS OF ANDELSPRUTZ, THE by Lord
   Dunsany. .ss . . . . .AFR #9 118
MADNESS OF LANCELOT BIGGS, THE by Nelson S.
   Bond. .s . . . . FA Apr 40 70
MADNESS OF THE DUST by R. F. Starzl. .s . . . .
   . . . . Amz May 30 154
MADNESS ON LUNA by R. R. Winterbotham. .s . . . . .
   . . . . Amz Apr 39 32
MAELSTROM OF ATLANTIS, THE by Joseph Wm.
   Skidmore. .n 2 pt . . . . Amz Feb 36 25
MAGGIE by J. J. Coupling ps (John R. Pierce). .a . . . . .
   . . . . ASF Feb 48 77
MAGIC BULLET, THE by Willy Ley. .a . . ASF Apr 40 85
MAGIC CITY by Nelson S. Bond. .nt . . . . . ASF Feb 41 9
MAGIC FLUTE, THE by David V. Reed ps (David
   Vern). .s . . . . FA May 42 178
MAGIC MOON by Brett Sterling h ps (Edmond
   Hamilton). .n . . . . CF Win 44 15

Title. .Author. .Length . . . . Magazine. .Date. .Page No.

MAGIC OF JOE WILKS, THE by Robert Moore
Williams. .nt . . . . FA Sep 49 128
MAGICIAN OF DREAM VALLEY by Raymond Z.
Gallun. .s . . . . ASF Oct 38 12
MAGICIAN OF MARS, THE by Edmond Hamilton. . . .
. .n . . . . .CF Sum 41 14
MAGICIAN OF MISTY CAVE, THE by S. M.
Tenneshaw h ps. .nt . . . . .FA Feb 49 8
MAGICIAN'S DINNER by Jane Rice. .nt . . . .
. . . . UK Oct 42 65
MAGNETIC CITY ON GANYMEDE by Frank R. Paul. .
. .bacover . . . . Amz Feb 42
MAGNETIC MISS METEOR by Don Wilcox. .nt . . . . . .
. . . . Amz Mar 44 50
MAGNETIC STORM, THE by Hugo Gernsback. .s . . . .
. . . . Amz Jul 26 350
MAGNIFICENT FAILURE, THE by Rene Lafayette
ps (L. Ron Hubbard). .s . . . . .SS Mar 49 104
MAGNIFICENT POSSESSION, THE by Isaac
Asimov. .s . . . . Fut Jul 40 71
MAGNUS' DISINTEGRATOR by Ray Cummings. .s . . .
. . . . .Ash Feb 41 73
MAHAFFEY'S MYSTERY by Frank Patton h ps
(Raymond A. Palmer). .s . . . . OW Mar 50 122
MAIDEN VOYAGE by Vic Phillips. .nt . . . .
. . . . .ASF Jan 39 51
MAIL FROM PLANET TERRA   letter dept of OTWA
MAISON DES HOMMES VIVANTS, LA by Claude
Farrere (orig title of THE HOUSE OF THE
SECRET). .n . . . . FFM Feb 46 66
MAKE MINE A MERMAID by Gilbert Grant. .s . . . . . .
. . . . .Amz Jul 50 136
MAKE YOURSELF A WISH by Geoff St. Reynard
ps (Robert W. Krepps). .s . . . . .FA Mar 48 48
MAKING OF MISTY ISLE, THE by Stanton A.
Coblentz. .s . . . . SW Jun 29 75
SS May 42 112
MAKING OF THE BOMB, THE (Excerpt from THE
SMYTH REPORT). .a . . . . ASF Dec 45 100
MALIGNANT ENTITY, THE by Otis Adelbert Kline. . .
. .s . . . . Amz Jun 26 272
AQ Fal 34 120
MALIGNANT FLOWER, THE by Anthos. .s . . . .
. . . . Amz Sep 27 526
MAN, THE by Ray Bradbury. .s . . . . TW Feb 49 69
MAN ABOUT TIME by Kelvin Kent ps (Henry
Kuttner). .s . . . . TW Oct 40 54
MAN, AN UNNECESSARY EVIL by Jep Powell. . . . .
. .a . . . . FA Aug 41 129
MAN-BEAST OF TOREE, THE by Ralph T. Jones . . . .
. .s . . . . WQ Fal 31 84
SS Jul 41 102
MAN-EATING LIZARDS, THE by Edward Bellin h ps
(story) & J. Kubert (pictures). .comic . . . .
. . . . OTWA Jul 50 61

MAN FROM AGHARTI, THE by John & Dorothy
de Courcy. .n . . . . .Amz Jul 48 8
MAN FROM ARBUTUS, THE by H. B. Hickey ps (Herb
Livingston). .s . . . . Amz Mar 50 58
MAN FROM ARIEL, THE by Donald A. Wollheim . . . .
. .ss . . . . .WS Jan 34 604
MAN FROM BEYOND, THE by John Beynon Harris. . .
. .s . . . . WS Sep 34 420
FSQ Sum 50 130
MAN FROM CINCINNATI, THE by Holloway Horn . . .
. .s . . . . ASF Nov 33 70
MAN FROM EARTH, THE by John B. Harris. .s . . . . .
. . . . ToW Spr 40 42
MAN FROM HELL, THE by Polton Cross ps (John
Russell Fearn). .nt . . . . .FA Nov 39 6
MAN FROM MARS, THE by P. Schuyler Miller. .s . . . .
. . . . .WQ Sum 31 524
SS Mar 39 96
MAN FROM MARS, THE by Frank R. Paul . . . .
. .bacover pic . . . . FA May 39
MAN FROM NOWHERE, THE by Frank Belknap
Long, Jr. . .s . . . . UK Jun 40 112
MAN Nth by Gardner F. Fox. .s . . . .
. . . . .PS Win 45 98
MAN FROM SPACE, THE by L. Taylor Hansen. .s . . . .
. . . . Amz Feb 30 1034
MAN FROM SIYKUL, THE by Richard Wilson. .s . . . .
. . . . PS Win 42-3 77
MAN FROM THE ATOM, THE by G. Peyton
Wertenbaker. .nt 2 pt . . . . Amz Apr 26 62
MAN FROM THE FUTURE, THE by Don Wilcox. . . . .
. .s . . . . FA Nov 41 100
MAN FROM THE FUTURE, THE by Donald A.
Wollheim. .ss . . . . .Cos Mar 41 55
MAN FROM THE MAGIC RIVER by Don Wilcox. . . . .
. .nt . . . . FA Jun 44 126
MAN FROM THE MOON, THE by Otis Adelbert
Kline. .s . . . . Amz Oct 30 646
AFR #9 54
MAN FROM THE STARS, THE by Robert Moore
Williams. .s . . . . TW Fal 43 50
MAN FROM THE WRONG TIME TRACK by Dennis
Plimmer. .s . . . . Uc Apr 41 85
MAN FROM TOMORROW, THE by Stanton A.
Coblentz. .n . . . . AQ Spr-Sum 33 434
MAN FROM 2090, THE by Ray Cummings. .s . . . .
. . . . .Ash Apr 43 58
MAN FROM 2071, THE by Sewell Peaslee Wright . . . . .
. .s .ASF Jun 31 295
MAN FROM VENUS, THE by Frank R. Paul . . . .
. .bacover pic . . . . FA Jul 39
MAN FROM XENERN, THE by Stanton A.
Coblentz. .s . . . . .TW Aug 39 13
MAN FROM YESTERDAY, THE by Lee Francis h ps
(Howard Browne). .n . . . . .FA Aug 48 8

Title. .Author. .Length . . . . Magazine. .Date. .Page No.

MAN HIGHER UP, THE by Edwin Balmer & William B.
MacHarg. .s . . . . Amz Dec 26 792
SD Feb 30 122
MAN IN ROOM 18, THE by Otis Adelbert Kline. .s. . . .
. . . . AD Oct 30 912
MAN IN THE IRON CAP, THE by Murray Leinster *ps*
(Will F. Jenkins). .n . . . . SS Nov 47 11
MAN IN THE MOON, THE by Lester Barclay. .s. . . . . .
. . . . Amz Apr 48 90
MAN IN THE MOON, THE by William Morrison *ps*
(Joseph Samachson). .s. . . . . SS Jul 42 96
MAN IN THE MOON, THE by Henry Norton. .s. . . . . .
. . . . ASF Feb 43 70
MAN IN THE MOON, THE by Mack Reynolds. .s . . . . .
. . . . .Amz Jul 50 40
MAN IN THE ROOM, THE by Edwin Balmer & Wm. B.
MacHarg. .s . . . . Amz Apr 27 43
SD Mar 30 224
MAN-JEWELS FOR XOTHAR by Hal K. Wells. .nt . . . .
. . . . TW Oct 36 38
MAN NAMED MARS, A by A. R. Steber *h ps (Roger P.
Graham)*. .n . . . . OW Oct 50 106
MAN NEXT DOOR, THE by Robert Moore Williams. . .
. .s . . . . .Amz Jul 46 156
MAN NO ONE COULD LIFT, THE by Fred Ebel . . . . .
. .s . . . . AD Oct 30 916
MAN OF AGES by K. F. Ziska. .s. . . . . . ASF Oct 34 48
MAN OF BRONZE, THE by A. L. Fierst. .s . . . .
. . . . WQ Win 31 206
MAN OF IRON by Ross Rocklynne. .s . . . ASF Aug 35 94
MAN OF STONE, THE by Hazel Heald. .s . . . .
. . . . WS Oct 32 440
MAN OF THE FUTURE by Festus Pragnell. .s . . . . . .
. . . . .ToW #1 37 57
MAN OF THE FUTURE, THE by F. Orlin
Tremaine. .a . . . . TW Apr 49 105
MAN OF THE STARS by Sam Moskowitz. .s . . . .
. . . . .PS Win 41 30
MAN OF TOMORROW, THE by Richard Tooker. .a . . .
. . . . TW Jun 43 97
MAN OF TWO WORLDS by Robert Moore Williams . . .
. .nt . . . . FA Mar 47 134
MAN ON MIRA by R. S. Richardson. .a . . . .
. . . . ASF Apr 48 88
MAN ON THE BENCH, THE by W. J. Campbell . . . . .
. .s .Amz Jan 28 941
MAN ON THE METEOR, THE by Ray Cummings. . . . .
. .n . . . . Fut Oct 41 10
MAN OUTSIDE, THE by J. E. Gurdon. .s . . . .
. . . . Fant #3 39 50
MAN THE SUN GODS MADE, THE by Gardner F.
Fox. .nt. . . . . PS Win 46 4
MAN THE WORLD FORGOT, THE by John York Cabot
ps (David Wright O'Brien). .s . . . . FA Apr 40 18
MAN UPSTAIRS, THE by Ray Bradbury. .s. . . . .
. . . . .AFR #4 90

Title. .Author. .Length . . . . Magazine. .Date. .Page No.

MAN WITH A THOUSAND LEGS, THE by Frank
Belknap Long, Jr. . .nt . . . . .AFR #8 45
MAN WHO, THE by A. Fedor & Henry Hasse. .s . . . . . .
. . . . MSS Nov 40 78
MAN WHO ANNEXED THE MOON, THE by Bob Olsen
ps (Alfred John Olsen, Jr.). .nt . . . . Amz Feb 31 1026
MAN WHO AWOKE, THE by Laurence Manning. .s . . . .
. . . . WS Mar 33 756
II—MASTER OF THE BRAIN. .s . . . . . WS Apr 33 838
III—THE CITY OF SLEEP. .s . . . . WS May 33 926
IV—THE INDIVIDUALISTS. .s . . . . WS Jun 33 58
V—THE ELIXIR. .s . . . . WS Aug 33 150
(The above stories combined as a: n 3 pt . . . .
. . . . CF Sum 41 111
MAN WHO BOUGHT MARS, THE by Polton Cross *ps*
(John Russell Fearn). .nt . . . . FA Jun 41 76
MAN WHO CAME BACK, THE by Richard O. Lewis . . .
. .s . . . . FA Jun 40 104
MAN WHO CHANGED HISTORY, THE by John York
Cabot *ps (David Wright O'Brien)*. .nt . . . Amz Feb 42 64
MAN WHO CHANGED THE FUTURE, THE by R. F.
Starzl. .s . . . . WS Jun 31 54
MAN WHO COULD NOT DIE, THE by Lee Francis
h ps. .s. . . . . FA Jan 50 34
MAN WHO COULD STAND UP, THE by Carl Selwyn . .
. .s . . . . SF Apr 43 68
MAN WHO COULD VANISH, THE by A. Hyatt
Verrill. .s . . . . .Amz Jan 27 900
AA 27 104
MAN WHO COULD WORK MIRACLES, THE by H. G.
Wells. .s . . . . .Amz Jul 26 312
MAN WHO CRIED "WEREWOLF", THE by P. F.
Costello *h ps*. .s. . . . . FA Mar 43 60
MAN WHO DIDN'T BREATHE, THE by Harry Walton .
. .s .Ash Nov 41 49
MAN WHO DIED BY PROXY, THE by Frank Gates . . .
. .s . . . . Amz May 27 145
MAN WHO EVOLVED, THE by Edmond Hamilton. . . .
. .s . . . . WS Apr 31 1266
SS Nov 40 110
MAN WHO FORGOT, THE by John York Cabot *ps (David
Wright O'Brien)*. .s . . . . .Amz May 41 94
MAN WHO FOUGHT A FLY, THE by Leslie F. Stone
ps (Mrs. Wm. Silberberg). .s . . . . Amz Oct 32 610
MAN WHO FOUGHT DESTINY, THE by Arthur J.
Burks. .s . . . . CF Win 42 98
MAN WHO GOT EVERYTHING, THE by John York
Cabot *ps (David Wright O'Brien)*. .s. . . Amz Aug 41 100
MAN WHO HATED WAR, THE by Emil Petaja. .s . . . . .
. . . . Amz Dec 44 24
MAN WHO KILLED THE WORLD, THE by Ray King. .
. .ss. .PS Spr 40 94
MAN WHO KNEW ALL THE ANSWERS, THE by Donald
Bern. .ss. . . . . Amz Aug 40 124
MAN WHO KNEW ROGER STANLEY, THE by Joseph
Gilbert. .s . . . . .Ash Mar 42 43

Title. .Author. .Length . . . . Magazine. .Date. .Page No.

MAN WHO LAUGHED AT TIME, THE by Alexander
Blade *h ps*. .nt. . . . . FA Aug 49 6
MAN WHO LAUGHS, THE by Norman J. Bonney. .s. . .
. . . . WS Oct 30 438
MAN WHO LIVED BACKWARDS, THE by Charles F.
Hall. .s. . . . . .ToW Sum 38 21
MAN WHO LIVED NEXT WEEK, THE by David Wright
O'Brien. .nt . . . . Amz Mar 41 46
MAN WHO LIVED TWICE, THE by Edmond Hamilton .
. .s . . . . Amz Nov 38 76
MAN WHO LIVED TWICE, THE by William Kober. . . .
. .s . . . . Amz Nov 32 708
MAN WHO LOOKED LIKE STEINMETZ, THE by
Robert Moore Williams. .s . . . . TW Jun 38 44
MAN WHO LOST HIS FACE, THE by Helmar Lewis . . .
. .s . . . . .Amz Jul 43 88
MAN WHO LOST HIS SHADOW, THE by Thorne
Lee. .nt . . . . FA Jun 44 84
MAN WHO MASTERED TIME, THE by Ray
Cummings. .n . . . . FN Mar 50 10
MAN WHO MURDERED HIMSELF, THE by Duncan
Farnsworth *ps (David Wright O'Brien)*. .s . . . . . .
. . . . FA May 41 110
MAN WHO NEVER GREW YOUNG, THE by Fritz
Leiber, Jr. . .s. . . . . .AFR #9 48
MAN WHO NEVER LIVED, THE by Ross Rocklynne . .
. .s . . . . Amz Sep 40 70
MAN WHO NEVER LIVED, THE by Donald Wandrei . .
. .s . . . . ASF Mar 34 39
MAN WHO RULED THE WORLD, THE by Robert
Moore Williams. .s . . . . Amz Jun 38 10
MAN WHO SAVED NEW YORK, THE by Ray
Cummings. .s . . . . SF Jul 43 69
MAN WHO SAVED THE EARTH, THE by Austin
Hall. .nt. Amz Apr 26 75
                                                AA 27 82
                                                FFM Feb 40 6
MAN WHO SAW THE FUTURE, THE by Edmond
Hamilton. .s . . . . Amz Oct 30 600
                                                ToW Sum 40 24
MAN WHO SAW THROUGH TIME, THE by Leonard
Raphael. .s. . . . . FA Sep 41 134
MAN WHO SAW TOO LATE, THE by Eando Binder
ps (Otto Binder). .s . . . . FA Sep 39 70
MAN WHO SAW TOO MUCH, THE by Ray
Cummings. .s . . . . TW Oct 38 100
MAN WHO SAW TWO WORLDS, THE by Thornton
Ayre *ps (John Russell Fearn)*. .nt . . . . . Amz Jan 40 76
MAN WHO SHRANK, THE by George B. Beattie . . . . .
. .s . . . . WS Apr 32 1257
MAN WHO SOLD THE EARTH, THE by Thornton
Ayre *ps (John Russell Fearn)*. .s . . . . . . .SF Oct 40 84
MAN WHO SOLVED DEATH, THE by Edmond
Hamilton. .s . . . . SF Aug 39 32
MAN WHO SPOKE TOO LATE, THE by William
Lawrence Hamling. .s . . . . FA Oct 44 194

MAN WHO STOPPED THE DUST, THE by John
Russell Fearn. .nt . . . . ASF Mar 34 55
                                                ToW Aut 39 102
MAN WHO STOPPED THE EARTH, THE by Henry J.
Kostkos. .ss . . . . Amz Mar 34 120
MAN WHO TURNED TO SMOKE, THE by Don
Wilcox. .s. . . . . FA Jun 42 192
MAN WHO WALKED THROUGH MIRRORS, THE by
Robert Bloch. .s . . . . .Amz Aug 39 52
MAN WHO WAS, THE by Walter Burch. .s . . . .
. . . . Amz May 27 188
MAN WHO WAS DEAD, THE by Thomas H. Knight . . .
. .s . . . . ASF Apr 30 9
MAN WHO WAS DEAD, THE by Arthur B. Reeve. . . . .
. .s . . . . AD Oct 30 890
MAN WHO WAS KING, THE by Nathaniel Nitkin. . . . .
. .s . . . . .SS Jan 43 94
MAN WHO WAS MILLIONS, THE by Willard E.
Hawkins. .nt . . . . .SF Jun 41 10
MAN WHO WAS THURSDAY, THE by G. K.
Chesterton. .n . . . . .FFM Mar 44 8
MAN WHO WAS TWO MEN, THE by E. K. Jarvis
h ps. .s. . . . . Amz Jun 42 180
MAN WHO WASN'T HIMSELF, THE by Alexander Blade
h ps. .s. . . . . Amz Dec 41 130
MAN WHO WEIGHED MINUS 12, THE by Nelson S.
Bond. .s. FA Mar 40 48
MAN WHO WENT BACK, THE by Warwick Deeping . . .
. .n . . . . .FFM Dec 47 6
MAN WHO WENT NOWHERE, THE by John &
Dorothy de Courcy. .s . . . . Amz Nov 46 102
MAN WHO WOULD NOT BURN, THE by Paul Lohrman
h ps. .s. . . . . FA Jun 50 134
MAN WITH COMMON SENSE, THE by Edwin James
ps (James E. Gunn). .s . . . . .Amz Jul 50 112
MAN WITH FIVE LIVES, THE by Clyde Woodruff *ps
(David Vern)*. .n . . . . .FA Jan 43 102
MAN WITH THE FOUR DIMENSIONAL EYES, THE
by Leslie F. Stone *ps (Mrs. Wm. Silberberg)*. .s . . . . .
. . . . WS Aug 35 286
MAN WITH THE GLASS HEART, THE by George Allan
England. .s . . . . .FFM Nov 39 75
MAN WITH THE SILVER DISC, THE by L. A.
Eshbach. .s . . . . SD Feb 30 128
MAN WITH THE STRANGE HEAD, THE by Dr. Miles J.
Breuer. .s . . . . .Amz Jan 27 940
MAN WITH TWO MINDS, THE by Leroy Yerxa. .s . . . .
. . . . .Amz Jul 46 86
MAN WITH X-RAY EYES, THE by Edmond Hamilton .
. .s . . . . WS Nov 33 386
                                                SS Sum 46 62
MAN WITHOUT A PLANET, THE by Ivar Towers *h ps* .
. .s . . . . .SSS Nov 42 86
MAN WITHOUT A WORLD, THE by John Coleman
Burroughs & Hulbert Burroughs. .s . . . .
. . . . TW Jun 39 38

Title. .Author. .Length . . . . Magazine. .Date. .Page No.

MANA by Eric Frank Russell. .s . . . . ASF Dec 37 37
MANAPE THE MIGHTY by Arthur J. Burks. .nt . . . . .
. . . . .ASF Jun 31 308
MANCHU COFFIN, THE by Harold Lawlor. .s . . . . . .
. . . . FA Dec 42 204
MANIC PERVERSE by Winston K. Marks. .s . . . .
. . . . ASF Oct 41 80
MANLESS WORLDS, THE by Murray Leinster ps (Will
F. Jenkins). .nt . . . . TW Feb 47 11
MANNA by Peter Phillips. .nt . . . . ASF Feb 49 62
MANNA FROM MARS by Stanton A. Coblentz. .s . . . .
. . . . ASF Mar 34 46
MAN'S EMPIRE OF TOMORROW by Arthur C. Clarke
. .a . . . . ToW Win 38 74
MAN'S JOURNEY TO THE STARS by Dr. Amadeus
Rafferty. .a . . . . TW Apr 48 77
MANTONG, THE LANGUAGE OF LEMURIA. .a . . . .
. . . . Amz Mar 45 71
MS. FOUND IN A BOTTLE by Edgar Allan Poe. .s . . . .
. . . . Amz Mar 34 127
MANUSCRIPT FOUND IN THE DESERT, THE by
Frank J. Brueckel, Jr. . .ss . . . . SW Mar 30 895
MANX, PETE series See KELVIN KENT pseud author
MAP OF FATE, THE by Cpl. Donald Bern. .s . . . . .
. . . . Amz Dec 44 72
MARAI'S WIFE by Edwin Benson ps (Richard S.
Shaver). .s . . . . OW Mar 50 152
MARBLE VIRGIN, THE by Kennie McDowd. .s . . . . . .
. . . . SW Jun 29 53
SS Jul 42 86
MARCH OF THE MERCURY MEN by Don Wilcox. . . .
. .nt . . . . Amz Aug 46 46
MARGIN FOR ERROR by Lewis Padgett ps (Henry
Kuttner & C. L. Moore). .nt . . . . ASF Nov 47 129
MARINORRO by Warner Van Lorne ps. .s . . . .
. . . . ASF Nov 37 42
MARIONETTES, INC. by Ray Bradbury. .ss . . . .
. . . . .SS Mar 49 125
MARK GRAYSON UNLIMITED by Polton Cross ps
(John Russell Fearn). .s . . . . TW Spr 45 78
MARK OF THE METEOR, THE by Ray Cummings. . . .
. .s . . . . WQ Win 31 220
MARLOW'S MALICIOUS MIRROR by John York Cabot
ps (David Wright O'Brien). .s . . . . FA Dec 42 188
MAROONED IN ANDROMEDA by Clark Ashton Smith
. .s . . . . WS Oct 30 390
MAROONED OFF VESTA by Isaac Asimov. .s . . . . . .
. . . . Amz Mar 39 66
MAROONED UNDER THE SEA by Paul Ernst. .nt . . . .
. . . . .ASF Sep 30 346
MARS IS HEAVEN! by Ray Bradbury. .s . . . .
. . . . PS Fal 48 56
MARS IS—HELL! by Forrest J. Ackerman. .a . . . .
. . . . PS Nov 50 3
MARS—PLANET OF WAR (LANDSCAPES OF OTHER
WORLDS) by Willy Ley. .a . . . . Amz Apr 42 256

Title. .Author. .Length . . . . Magazine. .Date. .Page No.

MARS–TUBE by S. D. Gottesman ps (Cyril Kornbluth
& Frederik Pohl). .s . . . . .Ash Sep 41 10
MARS WARNING by Henry Hasse. .s . . . . .SSS Aug 42 34
MARTIAN, THE by Allen Glasser & A. Rowley
Hilliard. .s . . . . WQ Win 32 270
MARTIAN ADVENTURE by Pvt. Robert Moore
Williams. .nt . . . . FA Oct 44 162
MARTIAN AND THE MILKMAID, THE by Frances M.
Deegan. .s . . . . FA Oct 44 136
MARTIAN AND TROGLODYTE by Neil R. Jones . . . .
. .s . . . . Amz May 33 124
MARTIAN AVENGER by Polton Cross ps (John Russell
Fearn). .s . . . . Amz Apr 39 76
MARTIAN CABAL, THE by R. F. Starzl. .nt . . . .
. . . . ASF May 32 168
MARTIAN CIRCE, THE by Raymond F. Jones. .nt . . . .
. . . . PS Sum 47 94
MARTIAN FANTASY by Henry Andrew Ackermann . .
. .s . . . . .Sti Jun 41 16
MARTIAN GESTURE by Alexander M. Phillips. .nt . . .
. . . . WS Oct 35 560
SS Jan 49 112
MARTIAN GUNS by Stanley D. Bell. .s. . . .WS Jan 32 920
Fut Apr 41 50
MARTIAN HERITAGE by Barry Cord ps (Peter B.
Germano). .s. . . . . TW Dec 42 66
MARTIAN MADNESS by P. E. Cleator. .s . . . .
. . . . WS Mar 34 840
MARTIAN MAIL, THE by J. Lewis Burtt, B.Sc. . . . . .
. .s . . . . Amz Apr 35 85
MARTIAN MARTYRS by John Coleridge ps (Earl
Binder & Otto Binder). .s . . . . SF Mar 39 18
MARTIAN MENU by Charles Stoddard h ps. .s . . . . . .
. . . . CF Sum 41 106
MARTIAN MINIATURE by John Russell Fearn. .s . . . .
. . . . Amz May 42 66
MARTIAN NEMESIS, THE by George B. Beattie. .s . . .
. . . . WQ Win 31 238
MARTIAN ODYSSEY by Stanley G. Weinbaum. .s . . . .
. . . . .WS Jul 34 174
SS Nov 39 106
MARTIAN QUEST by Leigh Brackett. .s . . . .
. . . . ASF Feb 40 78
MARTIAN REVENGE, THE by Hendrik Dahl Juve. . . .
. .s . . . . WS Aug 30 198
MARTIAN SPACESHIPS INVADE NEW YORK by Frank
R. Paul. .bacover pic . . . . Amz May 41
MARTIAN TERROR by Ed Earl Repp. .s . . .PS Spr 40 46
MARTIANS ARE COMING, THE by Robert W.
Lowndes. .s . . . . .Cos Mar 41 36
MARTIAN'S FANCY by William F. Temple. .s . . . . . .
. . . . NW Sum 50 38
MARTIANS, KEEP OUT! by Fritz Leiber, Jr. . . . .
. .s . . . . Fut Jul-Aug 50 45
MARTIAN'S MASTERPIECE, THE by Sgt. Morris J.
Steele h ps. .s . . . . Amz Mar 45 72

Title. .Author. .Length . . . . Magazine. .Date. .Page No.

MARTYRS DON'T MIND DYING by John Victor
Peterson. .s . . . . ASF Mar 38 97
MASK, THE by Robert W. Chambers. .s . . . .
. . . . FFM Dec 43 109
MASK OF CIRCE, THE by Henry Kuttner. .n . . . .
. . . . SS May 48 11
MASKED WORLD, THE by Richard S. Shaver. .n . . . .
. . . . .Amz May 46 6
MASQUERADE by Kenneth Falconer ps (Cyril
Kornbluth). .s . . . . Sti Mar 42 49
MASQUERADE by Clifford D. Simak. .s . . . .
. . . . ASF Mar 41 57
MASSON'S SECRET by Raymond Z. Gallun. .s . . . . . .
. . . . .ASF Sep 39 101
MASTER ANTS, THE by Francis Flagg ps (George
Henry Weiss). .s . . . . Amz May 28 158
MASTER CHEMIST by Arthur McCann ps (John W.
Campbell, Jr.). .a . . . . ASF Dec 43 101
MASTER CONTROL by Harl Vincent (Schoepflin). . . .
. .nt .Ash Apr 40 34
MASTER, GERALD OF CHAMBRAY by Nat
Schachner. .nt . . . . UK Jun 40 125
MASTER KEY, THE by Charles S. Wolfe. .s . . . .
. . . . Amz Apr 28 67
MASTER MIND OF MARS, THE by Edgar Rice
Burroughs. .n . . . . .AA 27 6
MASTER MINDS OF VENUS, THE by William K.
Sonnemann. .nt . . . . Amz Sep 34 71
MASTER OF DREAMS by Harl Vincent
(Schoepflin). .nt . . . . Amz Jan 34 37
MASTER OF EMOTION by Willard E. Hawkins. .s . . . .
. . . . .SF Sep 41 64
MASTER OF MYSTERY, THE by Bob Olsen ps (Alfred
John Olsen, Jr.). .nt . . . . Amz Oct 31 626
MASTER OF STORMS, THE by Edwin K. Sloat . . . . . .
. .s .WS Jul 32 148
MASTER OF TELEPATHY by Eando Binder ps (Otto
Binder). .s . . . . Amz Dec 38 38
MASTER OF THE ASTEROID by Clark Ashton
Smith. .s . . . . WS Oct 32 434
ToW Sum 40 46
MASTER OF THE BRAIN (THE MAN WHO AWOKE
Pt. 2) by Laurence Manning. .s . . . . . . WS Apr 33 838
MASTER OF THE GENES by Edmond Hamilton . . . . .
. .s . . . . .WS Jan 35 958
MASTER OF THE GOLDEN CITY, THE by Polton Cross
ps (John Russell Fearn). .nt . . . . Amz Jun 38 44
MASTER OF THE LIVING DEAD by Ed Earl Repp . . .
. .nt .Amz Jan 44 130
MASTER OF THE WORLD, THE by Jules Verne . . . . .
. .n 2 pt . . . . Amz Feb 28 1026
MASTER SHALL NOT DIE, THE by R. DeWitt
Miller. .s . . . . ASF Mar 38 38
MASTERFUL MIND OF MORTIMER MEEK, THE by
William P. McGivern. .nt . . . . .FA May 41 60

Title. .Author. .Length . . . . Magazine. .Date. .Page No.

MASTERS OF CHANCE by William Morrison ps (Joseph
Samachson). .s . . . . .TW Aug 41 76
MASTERS OF FANTASY by Neil Austin (with text by
Forrest J. Ackerman). .pictorial feature (biographical)
HOWARD PHILLIPS LOVECRAFT . . . .
. . . . .FFM Aug 47 113
A. MERRITT . . . . FFM Oct 47 97
ROBERT WILLIAM CHAMBERS . . . FFM Dec 47 103
SYDNEY FOWLER WRIGHT . . . . . FFM Feb 48 113
ALGERNON BLACKWOOD . . . . FFM Apr 48 121
HERBERT GEORGE WELLS . . . . . . FFM Jun 48 101
STEPHEN VINCENT BENET (w/William Rose
Benet) . . . . FFM Aug 48 113
EDGAR RICE BURROUGHS . . . . . . FFM Oct 48 117
ARTHUR MACHEN . . . . FFM Dec 48 12
M. P. SHIEL . . . . FFM Feb 49 91
JOHN TAINE . . . . FFM Apr 49 87
DUNSANY . . . . FFM Jun 48 113
CLARK ASHTON SMITH. . . . . FFM Aug 49 109
RAY BRADBURY . . . . FFM Oct 49 119
EDGAR ALLAN POE . . . . FFM Dec 49 113
OLAF STAPLEDON . . . . FFM Feb 50 121
M. R. JAMES . . . . FFM Apr 50 113
MASTERS OF MADNESS by Brad Buckner. . . . .
. .s .SF Jan 41 92
MASTERS OF SLEEP, THE by L. Ron Hubbard. .n . . .
. . . . FA Oct 50 6
MASTERS OF THE EARTH by John Edwards. .nt . . . .
. . . . Amz Jun 32 200
MATCHES AND KINGS by John York Cabot ps (David
Wright). .s . . . . Amz Sep 44 186
MATHEMATICA by John Russell Fearn. .nt . . . .
. . . . ASF Feb 36 64
MATHEMATICA PLUS by John Russell Fearn. .nt . . . .
. . . . ASF May 36 90
MATHEMATICAL KID, THE by Ross Rocklynne. . . . .
. .s . . . . Amz Jun 40 86
MATHEMATICS OF MAGIC, THE by L. Sprague de
Camp & Fletcher Pratt. .n . . . . .UK Aug 40 9
MATRIX by Rog Phillips ps (Roger P. Graham) . . . . . .
. .n . . . . Amz Oct 49 22
MATTER IS CONSERVED by Raymond A. Palmer. . . .
. .s . . . . ASF Apr 38 27
MATTER OF ETHICS, A by Harl Vincent
(Schoepflin). .s . . . . Amz Oct 31 650
MATTER OF FORM, A by Horace L. Gold. .nt . . . . . .
. . . . ASF Dec 38 9
MATTER OF LENGTH, A by Ross Rocklynne. .s . . . . .
. . . . .ASF Jan 46 118
MATTER OF MATTER, A by L. Ron Hubbard. .s . . . .
. . . . ASF Aug 49 59
MATTER OF MIND READING, A by Edwin Balmer &
William B. MacHarg. .s . . . . AD Jun 30 496
MATTER OF NERVES, A by William Lemkin,
Ph. D. . .nt . . . . Amz Jun 32 232

Title. .Author. .Length . . . . Magazine. .Date. .Page No.

MATTER OF PHILOSOPHY, A by Wilfred Owen Morley
 ps (Robert W. Lowndes). .ss . . . . .SF Sep 41 85
MATTER OF SIZE, A by Harry Bates. .nt . . . .
 . . . . ASF Apr 34 38
MATTER OF SIZE, A by Norman Lazenby. .s . . . .
 . . . . Fant Dec 46 79
MATTER OF SIZE, A by Samuel Mines. .s . . . .
 . . . . TW Feb 47 53
MATTER OF SPEED, A by Harry Bates. .nt . . . .
 . . . . .ASF Jun 41 128
MATTER OF TASTE, A by Willy Ley. .a . . . .
 . . . . .ASF Jan 44 86
MATTERS OF FACT ed dept of post-war Fantasy
 (all issues)
MATURITY by Theodore Sturgeon. .nt. . . . ASF Feb 47 7
MAXWELL'S DEMON AND MONSIEUR RANQUE by
 Arthur C. Parlett. .a . . . . .ASF Jan 50 105
MAYAN ELEPHANTS, THE by L. Sprague de Camp. . .
 . .a . . . . ASF Jun 50 85
MAYBE IT'S TRUE by Gilbert Grant. .a . . . .
 . . . . Amz Nov 49 35
MAZE, THE by Frank M. Robinson. .s . . . .
 . . . . ASF Jun 50 69
M'BONG–AH by Rog Phillips ps (Roger P.
 Graham). .n . . . . Amz Feb 49 8
ME AND MY SHADOW by Berkeley Livingston . . . . . .
 . .s . . . . Amz Dec 45 106
ME, MYSELF AND I by Kenneth Putnam. .s . . . .
 . . . . .PS Win 47 48
ME THE PEOPLE by Emil Petaja. .s . . . . Amz Jun 43 116
MEASURING A MERIDIAN by Jules Verne . . . .
 . .n 4 pt . . . . Amz May 34 107
MEASURING ROD by L. Jerome Stanton. .a . . . .
 . . . . .ASF Jun 46 100
MECANICA by Frank Edward Arnold. .nt . . . .
 . . . . .Cos Mar 41 6
MECHANICAL ANSWER by John D. MacDonald . . . . .
 . .s . . . . ASF May 48 64
MECHANICAL BLOOD HOUND, THE by Frank
 Bridge ps (Francis J. Brueckel). .s . . . . WQ Spr 30 384
MECHANICAL GENIUS, THE by Gilbert Grant . . . . .
 . .s . . . . FA Jun 50 140
MECHANICAL HEART, THE by H. I. Barrett. .s . . . . .
 . . . . .AQ Fal 31 564
MECHANICAL MICE, THE by Maurice G. Hugi
 ps (Eric Frank Russell). .nt . . . . .ASF Jan 41 54
MECHANISTRIA by Eric Frank Russell. .nt . . . .
 . . . . .ASF Jan 42 35
MECHANOCRACY by Miles J. Breuer, M.D. . . . . . .
 . .s . . . . Amz Apr 32 6
MEDDLER'S MOON by George O. Smith. .nt . . . .
 . . . . ASF Sep 47 6
MEDICAL NOTE by Alexander Samalman. .s . . . .
 . . . . TW Feb 42 103
MEDICINE MAN MAGIC by Vincent H. Gaddis . . . . .
 . .a . . . . FA Feb 46 170

Title. .Author. .Length . . . . Magazine. .Date. .Page No.

MEDIEVAL ILLICIT by Richard S. Shaver. .a . . . .
 . . . . .Amz Jan 48 157
MEDUSA by Theodore Sturgeon. .s . . . . . ASF Feb 42 80
MEEM by Margaret St. Clair. .s . . . . .PS Fal 50 58
MEET ME IN TOMORROW by Guy Archette ps
 (Chester S. Geier). .s . . . . Im Dec 50 6
MEET MY BROTHER–MR. GHOST! by Wayne D.
 Overholser. .s . . . . .Uc Apr 41 101
MEET MY MUMMY by Elroy Arno. .nt. . . .FA May 47 46
MEET THE AUTHOR biog dept in STARTLING
 STORIES occasional
MEET THE AUTHORS biog dept in Amz & FA
 irregular
MEG, THE PRIESTESS series See NELSON S. BOND
 author
MEIHEM IN CE KLASRUM by Dolton Edwards. .a . . . .
 . . . . ASF Sep 46 94
MELLONTA TAUTA by Edgar Allan Poe. .s . . . .
 . . . . Amz Nov 33 124
MELODY AND MOONS by Kent Casey. .s. . . . .
 . . . . ASF May 39 92
MEMORIAL by Theodore Sturgeon. .s . . . .
 . . . . ASF Apr 46 158
MEMORY by Theodore Sturgeon. .s . . . . . .TW Aug 48 56
MEMORY BLOCKS by Will Garth h ps. .ss. . . . .
 . . . . .CF Spr 41 109
MEMORY MACHINE, THE by Bernard Sachs. .s . . . . .
 . . . . .WS Jul 35 180
MEMORY OF THE ATOMS, THE by Nathan
 Schachner & R. Lacher. .s . . . . .WS Jan 33 614
MEMORY STREAM, THE by Warren E. Sanders. .s . . . .
 . . . . Amz Apr 33 54
MEMOS ON MERCURY by Eando Binder ps (Otto
 Binder). .s . . . . .CF Sum 41 94
MEN AGAINST THE STARS by Manly Wade Wellman .
 . .s . . . . ASF Jun 38 6
MEN AND THE MIRROR, THE by Ross Rocklynne . . .
 . .nt .ASF Jul 38 74
MEN CREATED FOR DEATH by Henry J. Kostkos . . .
 . .s . . . . Amz Dec 34 76
MEN FROM GAYLN, THE by E. Mantell. .s . . . .
 . . . . WS Aug 34 310
MEN MUST DIE by Ward Hawkins. .s . . . . . TW Apr 39 48
                                                 SS Mar 50 88
MEN OF HONOR by Will Garth h ps. .s. . . .CF Spr 40 115
MEN OF IRON by Guy Endore. .s . . . . . .F&SF Fal 49 80
MEN OF THE BRONZE AGE by Edgar Rice
 Burroughs. .nt. . . . . Amz Mar 42 74
MEN OF THE DARK COMET by Festus Pragnell . . . . .
 . .s . . . . WS Jun 33 40
MEN OF THE MORNING STAR by Charles Henry
 Mackintosh. .s. . . . . .SSS Sep 40 57
MEN SCARED OF NOTHING by E. K. Jarvis h ps . . . .
 . .s . . . . FA Jul 42 210
MEN WITH WINGS by Leslie F. Stone ps (Mrs. Wm.
 Silberberg). .s . . . . AW Jul 29 58

Title. .Author. .Length . . . . Magazine. .Date. .Page No.

MEN WITHOUT A WORLD by Joseph Farrell . . . .
. .s . . . . PS Fal 44 23
MEN WITHOUT A WORLD by Dom Passante . . . . . .
. .s . . . . SF Mar 40 8
MEN WITHOUT SHADOWS, THE by Stanton A.
Coblentz. .s . . . . Amz Oct 33 491
ToW Win 39 71
MEN WITHOUT SLEEP by Edwin Bruell. .s . . . . '
. . . . WS May 33 982
MENACE, THE by David H. Keller, M.D. *(Four
connected short stories published together: THE
MENACE, THE GOLD SHIP, THE TAINTED
FLOOD, THE INSANE AVALANCHE).* .nt . . . .
. . . . AQ Sum 28 392
AQ Win 33 91
MENACE FROM ANDROMEDA, THE by Nat
Schachner & Arthur L. Zagat. .s . . . . . Amz Apr 31 78
MENACE FROM BELOW, THE by Harl Vincent
(Schoepflin). .s . . . . SW Jul 29 143
MENACE FROM MERCURY, THE by John Michel &
Raymond Gallun. .s . . . . .WQ Sum 32 544
MENACE FROM SATURN by Clifton B. Kruse. .s . . . .
. . . . ASF Jul 35 76
MENACE FROM SPACE, THE by John Edwards . . . . .
. .nt . . . . WS Apr 34 980
ToW Aut 38 4
MENACE FROM THE MICROCOSM by John Russell
Fearn. .nt. . . . . TW Jun 37 14
MENACE FROM THE MOON by Bohun Lynch . . . . . .
. .s . . . . Fant Aug 47 66
MENACE FROM THE SKIES, THE by Arthur G.
Stangland. .s. . . . . SW Apr 30 1016
MENACE IN MINIATURE, A by Raymond Z. Gallun . .
. .s . . . . ASF Oct 37 88
MENACE OF MARS, THE by Clare Winger Harris. . . . .
. .s . . . . Amz Oct 28 582
MENACE OF THE LITTLE, THE by Roscoe B.
Fleming. .nt . . . . .AQ Sum 31 378
MENACE OF THE METAL-MEN by A. Prestigiacomo. .
. .nt .Fant #1 38 2
MENACE OF THE MISTS by Richard Storey. .s . . . . . .
. . . . PS May 43 107
MENACING CLAWS by David H. Keller, M.D. . . . . . .
. .s . . . . AD Sep 30 798
MENTAL ASSASSINS, THE by Gregg Conrad. .nt . . . .
. . . . .FA May 50 8
MENTAL GANGSTER, THE by Thornton Ayre *ps
(John Russell Fearn).* .s . . . . FA Aug 42 64
MENTAL ULTIMATE, THE by Polton Cross *ps (John
Russell Fearn).* .s. . . . . .ASF Jan 38 142
MENTALITY MACHINE, THE by S. P. Meek. .s. . . . . .
. . . . ToW Spr 39 44
MENTANICALS, THE by Francis Flagg *ps (George
Henry Weiss).* .s. . . . . Amz Apr 34 60
AFR #10 59

MER-WITCH OF ETHER "18" by Richard S. Shaver. . .
. .s . . . . .Amz Aug 47 82
MERCENARIES, THE by H. Beam Piper. .nt . . . .
. . . . ASF Mar 50 57
MERCHANT OF VENUS, THE by Richard Ashby . . . .
. .nt . . . . .OW Nov 50 36
MERCHANT OF VENUS, THE by Clee Garson *ps
(David Wright O'Brien).* .nt . . . . FA Apr 43 100
MERCURIAN, THE by Frank Belknap Long. .s . . . . . .
. . . . .PS Win 41 69
MERCURIAN MENACE, THE by Nelson S. Bond. . . . .
. .s . . . . DS Feb 39 59
MERCURY, GOD OF THE WINGED SANDALS by
Frank R. Paul. .bacover pic . . . . .FA Jan 43
MERCUTIAN ADVENTURE by Raymond Z. Gallun. . .
. .s . . . . ASF Feb 38 98
MERMAID OF MARACOT DEEP, THE by Alexander
Blade *h ps.* .nt. . . . . FA Mar 49 8
MERMAN, THE by L. Sprague de Camp. .s . . . .
. . . . ASF Dec 38 80
MERNOS by Henry James *ps (L. C. Kellenberger)* . . . . .
. .s . . . . Amz Feb 29 1000
MESMERIC REVELATION by Edgar Allan Poe. .s . . . .
. . . . Amz May 26 124
MESSAGE, THE by Richard Wilson. .ss. . . . .
. . . . .Ash Mar 42 82
MESSAGE FOR JEAN, A by Wilfred Owen Morley *ps
(Robert W. Lowndes).* .s . . . . Fut Jun 42 94
MESSAGE FROM MARS, THE by Ralph Stranger . . . .
. .s . . . . WS Jun 32 28
MESSAGE FROM MARS by Clifford D. Simak. .s . . . . .
. . . . PS Fal 43 30
MESSAGE FROM SPACE, THE by David M. Speaker . .
. .s . . . . .Amz Jul 30 330
MESSAGE FROM THE ULTRA-VIOLET, A by H.
Ashton-Wolfe. .s . . . . .SD Jan 30 46
MESSAGE FROM THE VOID, THE by Hubert Mavity
ps (Nelson S. Bond). .s . . . . DS Feb 39 85
MESSAGE FROM VENUS by R. R Winterbotham . . . .
. .s . . . . Com Jan 41 21
MESSAGE TO THE FUTURE. .a . . . . Amz Jan 39 19
MESSENGER, THE by Robert W. Chambers. .s . . . . . .
. . . . FFM Apr 48 102
MESSENGER by Theodore Sturgeon. .s . . . .
. . . . TW Feb 49 115
MESSENGER FROM SPACE, THE by D. D. Sharp . . . .
. .s .WS Jan 33 628
MESSENGER TO INFINITY by J. Harvey Haggard . . . .
. .s . . . . SFQ Win 42 144
METAL DOOM, THE by David H. Keller, M.D. . . . . . .
. .n 3 pt . . . . Amz May 32 104
METAL HORDE, THE by John W. Campbell, Jr. . . . . .
. .s . . . . Amz Apr 30 6
METAL LARK, THE by Margaret St. Clair. .s . . . .
. . . . TW Jun 48 71

Title. .Author. .Length . . . . .Magazine. .Date. .Page No.

METAL MAN, THE by Jack Williamson. .s. . . . .
. . . . Amz Dec 28 792
                                                ToW Aug 39 42
                                                AFR #6 31
METAL MARTYR, THE by Robert Moore Williams . . .
. .s . . . . .Amz Jul 50 66
METAL MONSTER, THE by Otis Adelbert Kline . . . .
. .nt . . . . Amz Jul 31 344
METAL MONSTER, THE by A. Merritt. .n . . . .
. . . . .FFM Aug 41 6
METAL MOON, THE by Neil R. Jones. .nt . . . .
. . . . SSS Sep 49 102
METAL MOON, THE Everett C. Smith & R. F.
Starzl. .s . . . . WQ Win 32 246
METAL SMILE, THE by Alfred Coppel. .s. . . . .
. . . . SSS Jul 50 78
METAL WORLD, THE by Ed Earl Repp. .s . . . .
. . . . SW Oct 29 390
METAMORPHOSIS by John Russell Fearn. .nt. . . . . .
. . . . .ASF Jan 37 90
METAMORPHOSITE by Eric Frank Russell. .n. . . . . .
. . . . ASF Dec 46 6
METEOR by William T. Powers. .s . . . .
. . . . .ASF Sep 50 107
METEOR GIRL, THE by Jack Williamson. .s . . . .
. . . . ASF Mar 31 404
METEOR LEGACY by Raymond Z. Gallun. .s . . . . . .
. . . . ASF Aug 41 37
METEOR MAKERS, THE by Peter Hamilton. .s . . . . .
. . . . PS May 43 78
METEOR-MEN OF MARS by Harry Cord & Otis
Adelbert Kline. .s . . . . .PS Win 42 98
METEOR-MEN OF PLAA, THE by Henry Kostkos . . . .
. .nt . . . . Amz Aug 33 392
METEOR MINERS, THE by L. A. Eshbach. .s . . . .
. . . . Amz Dec 35 15
METEOR MONSTERS, THE by Arthur R. Tofte . . . . .
. .s . . . . Amz Aug 38 74
METEORIC MAGNET, THE by Moses Schere . . . . . .
. .s . . . . AW Apr 30 908
METEORIC MR. MYRTLE by Robert Arthur. .s. . . . . .
. . . . .TW Aug 42 56
METEORITE ENIGMA by Owen Fox Jerome ps
(Oscar J. Friend). .s . . . . .SS Sep 42 93
METHUSELAH, OLD DOC series see RENE
LAFAYETTE ps author
METHUSELAH'S CHILDREN by Robert Heinlein . . . .
. .n 3 pt . . . . .ASF Jul 41 9
MEWHU'S JET by Theodore Sturgeon. .nt. . . . .
. . . . ASF Nov 46 7
MICA SAILBOAT OF MERCURY by James B.
Settles. .bacover . . . . Amz Jun 45
MICRO MAN, THE by Alden Lorraine ps (Forrest J.
Ackerman). .ss . . . . .NW #2 46 52
by Weaver Wright ps (Forrest J. Ackerman) . . . FB #1 26

Title. .Author. .Length . . . . .Magazine. .Date. .Page No.

MICROBES FROM SPACE by Thornton Ayre ps (John
Russell Fearn). .s . . . . Amz Jun 39 86
MICROCOSMIC BUCCANEERS by Harl Vincent
(Schoepflin). .nt . . . . Amz Nov 29 678
MICROCOSMIC GOD by Theodore Sturgeon. .nt . . . . .
. . . . ASF Apr 41 46
MICROSCOPIC GIANTS, THE by Paul Ernst. .s . . . . . .
. . . . TW Oct 36 78
                                                SS May 48 108
MIDAS MORGAN'S GOLDEN TOUCH by Emil
Petaja. .s . . . . Amz May 44 162
MIDDLE BEDROOM, THE by H. deVere Stacpoole . . .
. .ss . . . . FN Sep 40 128
                                                FN Mar 48 124
MIDGET FROM MARS, THE by Thomas Sheridan
ps (Walter L. Gillings). .s . . . . .ToW Sum 38 108
MIDGET FROM THE ISLAND, THE by H. G. Winter
ps (Harry Bates & Desmond Winter Hall). .nt . . . . . .
. . . . ASF Aug 31 214
MIDGETS AND MIGHTY MEN by Lee Francis h ps . . .
. .nt .FA May 49 44
MIGHTIER YET by Eric Frank Russell. .s . . . .
. . . . Fant #3 39 76
MIGHTIEST MACHINE, THE by John W. Campbell,
Jr. . .n 5 pt . . . . ASF Dec 34 10
MILITARY EXPLOSIVES by Malcolm Jameson. .a . . . .
. . . . .ASF Jan 42 57
MILL OF THE GODS, THE by Maurice G. Hugi . . . . .
. .nt . . . . NW #1 46 2
MILL OF THE GODS by Malcolm Jameson. .s . . . .
. . . . .ASF Jan 39 131
MILLION DOLLAR GLAND, THE by W. Alexander . . .
. .s . . . . Amz Dec 34 129
MILLION YEAR PICNIC, THE by Ray Bradbury . . . . .
. .s . . . . PS Sum 46 95
MILLION YEARS AHEAD, A by Edmond Hamilton. . .
. .s . . . . TW Apr 37 92
MILLION YEARS AND A DAY, A by Lawrence
Woods ps (Donald A. Wollheim). .ss . . . .Fut Aug 41 80
MILLION YEARS TO CONQUER, A by Henry
Kuttner. .n . . . . SS Nov 40 16
MILLIONS FOR DEFENSE by Miles J. Breuer,
M.D. . .s . . . . Amz Mar 35 77
MILLIONS IN IT by H. A. Highstone. .s . . .OW Nov 50 76
MILLIONTH YEAR, THE by Martin Pearson ps
(Donald A. Wollheim). .s . . . . SF Apr 43 55
MIMIC by Martin Pearson ps (Donald A. Wollheim) . . . .
. .s . . . . .Ash Dec 42 58
by Donald A. Wollheim. .s . . . . .AFR #3 89
by Donald A. Wollheim. .s . . . . FN Sep 50 118
MIMSY WERE THE BOROGOVES by Lewis Padgett ps
(Henry Kuttner & C. L. Moore). .nt . . . ASF Feb 43 52
MIND MACHINE, THE by George Eugene Key. . . . . .
. .s . . . . .AD Jul 30 616
MIND MAGNET, THE by Paul Ernst. .s. . . . TW Dec 37 74

Title. .Author. .Length . . . . Magazine. .Date. .Page No.

MIND MASTER, THE by Arthur J. Burks. .n 2 pt . . . . .
. . . . .ASF Jan 32 28
MIND MASTER, THE by Amelia Reynolds Long . . . . .
. .s . . . . ASF Dec 37 41
MIND MASTERS, THE by Neil R. Jones. .nt . . . .
. . . . SSS Sep 50 70
MIND OF THE WORLD by Nat Schachner. .nt . . . . . .
. . . . ASF Mar 35 64
MIND OUT OF TIME by Frank Belknap Long. .s . . . . .
. . . . TW Oct 38 89
MIND OVER MATTER by Oscar J. Friend. .s. . . . . .
. . . . SS Jan 40 112
MIND OVER MATTER by Raymond Z. Gallun . . . . . .
. .s . . . . .ASF Jan 35 116
MIND ROVERS, THE by Richard S. Shaver. .nt . . . . . .
AMZ Jan 47 96
MIND STEALERS OF PLUTO by Joseph Farrell . . . . .
. .s . . . . PS Win 44 2
MIND WORMS by Moses Schere. .s. . . . . . .PS Spr 48 43
MINDWORM, THE by C. M. Kornbluth. .s. . . . .
. . . . WB Dec 50 54
MINER CRISIS ON IO by Guy Archette ps
(Chester S. Geier). .s . . . . Amz Oct 47 122
MINIATURE, THE by Peter Reed ps (John D.
MacDonald). .s . . . . SSS Sep 49 46
MINIATURE MENACE, THE by Frank Belknap
Long. .s . . . . .Fut May-Jun 50 50
MINIMUM MAN or TIME TO BE GONE by Andrew
Marvell ps (Howell Davies). .n . . . . . . .FFM Aug 47 6
MINIONS OF CHAOS by John D. MacDonald. .nt . . . .
. . . . .SSS Sep 49 8
MINIONS OF THE CRYSTAL SPHERE by Albert
de Pina. .nt . . . . PS Sum 44 2
MINIONS OF THE TIGER by Chester S. Geier. .n . . . .
. . . . FA Sep 46 8
MINNIE OF MARS by N. J. Westwood. .s . . . .
. . . . .TW Aug 42 70
MINORITY REPORT by Theodore Sturgeon. .s . . . . . .
. . . . .ASF Jun 49 130
MINOS OF SARDANES by Charles B. Stilson. .n . . . . .
. . . . FN Nov 49 10
MINUS DANGER! by George O. Smith. .nt . . . .
. . . . SSS Sep 49 66
MINUS PLANET by John D. Clark, Ph.D. . .nt . . . . . .
. . . . ASF Apr 37 86
MINUS SIGN by Will Stewart ps (Jack Williamson) . . . .
. .n . . . . ASF Nov 42 43
MIRACLE by Ray Cummings. .s . . . . Ash Oct 42 93
MIRACLE AT DUNKIRK by John York Cabot ps
(David Wright O'Brien). .s . . . . FA Sep 41 88
MIRACLE IN TIME by Henry Hasse. .s . . . .
. . . . Ash Jun 40 83
MIRACLE MAN by John & Dorothy de Courcy . . . . . .
. .nt . . . . Amz Apr 47 46
MIRACLE MAN by Robert Moore Williams. .s . . . .
. . . . FA Feb 48 134

MIRACLE OF BULLDOZER MIKE, THE by Robert
Moore Williams. .s . . . . Amz Dec 45 92
MIRACLE OF DR. BEAUJEAN, THE by Curtis
Pechtel. .s . . . . .FA Jan 45 176
MIRACLE OF ELMER WILDE by Rog Phillips ps (Roger
P. Graham). .nt . . . . .OW Nov 49 84
MIRACLE OF HERBERT PLUNK, THE by Richard
Casey h ps. .s . . . . FA Nov 47 148
MIRACLE OF KICKER McGUIRE by Robert Moore
Williams. .s . . . . FA May 43 208
MIRACLE OF THE LILY, THE by Clare Winger
Harris. .s . . . . Amz Apr 28 48
AFR #5 75
MIRACLE TOWN by William F. Temple. .s . . . .
. . . . TW Oct 48 86
MIRAGE WORLD by Chester S. Geier. .s. . . . .
. . . . Amz Dec 45 74
MIRROR, THE by William Lawrence Hamling. .s . . . . .
. . . . FA Sep 46 80
MIRROR MAZE by Stanley Mullen. .s . . . .
. . . . FFM Jun 49 114
MIRRORS OF MADNESS by Don Wilcox. .nt . . . .
. . . . .Amz Jul 40 48
MIRRORS OF THE QUEEN by Richard S. Shaver . . . .
. .s . . . . .FA Jul 48 90
MIRRORS OF TUZUN THUNE, THE by Robert E.
Howard. .s . . . . .AFR #2 73
MISBEGOTTEN MISSIONARY by Isaac Asimov. .s. . . .
. . . . GSF Nov 50 34
MISFIT by Robert Heinlein. .s . . . . ASF Nov 39 53
MISGUIDED HALO by Henry Kuttner. .s . . . .
. . . . UK Aug 39 125
MISLAID CHARM, THE by A. M. Phillips. .n . . . .
. . . . .UK Feb 41 9
MISSING DAY, THE by Henry Hasse. .s . . . .
. . . . SSS May 42 30
MISSING HOURS, THE by Morton Brotman. .s . . . . . .
. . . . WS Apr 35 1320
MISSING: MILLIONS IN RADIUM by Robert Moore
Williams. .s . . . . Amz Nov 39 116
MISSING OCEAN, THE by H. W. Guernsey ps
(Howard Wandrei). .s . . . . .UK May 39 47
MISSING YEAR, THE by Eando Binder ps (Otto
Binder). .s . . . . Amz Oct 39 54
MISSION by M. Krulfeld. .s . . . . ASF Sep 41 74
MISSION by John Hollis Mason. .ss . . . . .SFQ Spr 42 141
MISSION FROM ARCTURUS by Robert Abernathy. . .
. .s . . . . .SFQ Spr 43 130
MISSION UNKNOWN by Henry Hasse. .n . . . .
. . . . SSS May 41 8
MISSIONARIES FROM THE SKY by Stanton A.
Coblentz. .s . . . . Amz Nov 30 744
MISSIONARIES OF MARS by Stanton A.
Coblentz. .s . . . . ToW Spr 40 60
MISSIVES AND MISSILES letter dept of Super
Science Stories

Title. .Author. .Length . . . . Magazine. .Date. .Page No.

MISTAKE INSIDE by James Blish. .s . . . . .SS Mar 48 90
MR. AMES' DEVIL by August Derleth. .s . . . .
. . . . FA Aug 42 80
MISTER ANONYMOUS by David Wright O'Brien . . . . .
. .nt . . . . FA Dec 45 108
MR. ARSON by L. Sprague de Camp. .s . . . .
. . . . UK Dec 41 116
MR. BELLER AND THE WINGER HORSE by Geoff
St. Reynard ps (Robert W. Krepps). .nt . . . .
. . . . FA Oct 47 70
MR. BIGGS GOES TO TOWN by Nelson S. Bond . . . . .
. .s . . . . Amz Oct 42 126
MR. BOWEN'S WIFE REDUCES by Miles J. Breuer,
M.D. . .s . . . . Amz Feb 38 118
MR. CRADDOCK'S AMAZING EXPERIENCE by William
F. Temple. .s . . . . Amz Feb 39 42
MR. DESTINY FOLLOWS THROUGH by Gilbert
Grant. .nt . . . . FA Mar 50 58
MR. DIMMITT SEEKS REDRESS by Miles J. Breuer,
M.D. . .s . . . . Amz Aug 36 91
MR. DUFFY'S OTHER LIFE by Arthur T. Harris
h ps. .s. . . . . FA May 41 124
MR. EEE CONDUCTS A TOUR by Don Wilcox. .s . . . .
. . . . FA Dec 41 52
MR. ELLERBEE TRANSPLANTED by Jan Forman . . .
. .s . . . . ASF Oct 37 39
MR. FOSDICK INVENTS THE SEIDLITZMOBILE (THE
SCIENTIFIC ADVENTURES OF MR. FOSDICK) by
Jacque Morgan. .s . . . . Amz Jun 26 238
MR. GARFINKEL AND THE LEPRA-COHEN by
Charles R. Tanner. .s . . . . OW Sep 50 142
MR. HIBBARD'S MAGIC HAT by John York Cabot ps
(David Wright O'Brien). .s . . . . FA Jun 42 74
MISTER ISLAND by E. A. Grosser. .s . . . . . Ash Oct 40 23
MR. JINX by Robert Arthur. .s . . . . UK Aug 41 107
MISTER JOHN DOE, EARTHMAN by Joseph J.
Millard. .s. . . . . .SS Mar 42 108
MR. JONES' ETERNAL CAMERA by Berkeley
Livingston. .s . . . . Amz Nov 49 100
MR. LAHR SAYS HIS PRAYERS by Alexander
Blade h ps. .s . . . . Amz Oct 50 56
MR. MEEK—MUSKETEER by Clifford D. Simak . . . . .
. .s . . . . PS Sum 44 58
MR. MEEK PLAYS POLO by Clifford D. Simak . . . . . .
. .s . . . . PS Fal 44 56
MR. MUDDLE DOES AS HE PLEASES by William P.
McGivern & David Wright O'Brien. .nt . . . .
. . . . Amz Aug 41 64
MR. MURCHISON'S GHOST by Robert Moore
Williams. .s . . . . FA Aug 41 74
MR. PACKER GOES TO HELL by Cecil Corwin
ps (Cyril Kornbluth). .s . . . . .Sti Jun 41 66
MR. PRIMROSE GOES TO THE DEVIL by William F.
Templeton. .s . . . . FN May 50 118
MR. PYM MAKES A DEAL by John Broome. .s . . . . . .
. . . . FA May 42 116

Title. .Author. .Length . . . . Magazine. .Date. .Page No.

MR. THROOP'S INCREDIBLE HAND by Russell
Storm ps (Robert Moore Williams). .s . . . .
. . . . FA Oct 42 208
MISTER TROUBLE by David Wright O'Brien. .s . . . . .
. . . . .FA Jan 43 206
MR. WILSON'S MATCH by H. B. Hickey ps (Herb
Livingston). .s . . . . .Amz Jan 47 144
MR. WISEL'S SECRET by Eric Frank Russell. . . . . . .
. .ss . . . . Amz Feb 42 212
MR. ZYTZTZ GOES TO MARS by Noel Loomis. . . . .
. .nt . . . . .TW Aug 48 9
MRS. AMWORTH by E. F. Benson. .s . . . .
. . . . FFM Jun 50 106
MRS. CORTER MAKES UP HER MIND by August W.
Derleth. .s . . . . FA May 42 216
MISTRESS OF MACHINE-AGE MADNESS by Nils O.
Sonderlund. .nt . . . . MSS May 40 8
MISTRESS OF THE DARK by Elroy Arno. .nt . . . . . .
. . . . FA May 43 184
MISTRESS OF THE DJINN by Geoff St. Reynard ps
(Robert W. Krepps). .n . . . . .FA Nov 50 8
MISTS OF MARS by George A. Whittington. .s . . . . . .
. . . . PS Sum 45 78
MISTY WILDERNESS, THE by John Russell Fearn. . . .
. .s . . . . .SS Sep 39 102
MITKEY RIDES AGAIN by Fredric Brown. .s . . . .
. . . . PS Nov 50 61
MIXED MEN, THE by A. E. van Vogt. .nt . . . .
. . . . ASF Jan 45 7
M—M—M—M—M—M! by Millen Cooke. .s . . . .
. . . . Amz Oct 46 68
MO—SANSHON! by Bryce Walton. .s . . . .
. . . . PS Sum 47 32
MOANING LILY, THE by Emma Vanne. .s . . . .
. . . . WS May 35 1458
MOBIUS TRAIL, THE by George O. Smith. .nt . . . . . .
. . . . TW Dec 48 105
MODEL SHOP, THE by Raymond F. Jones. .nt . . . . . .
. . . . ASF Jun 47 54
MODERN ATLANTIS, A by Frederick Arthur
Hodge. .n . . . . AQ Spr 28 148
MODERN CALCULATORS by E. L. Locke. .a . . . .
. . . . .ASF Jan 49 87
MODERN COMEDY OF SCIENCE, A by Isaac R.
Nathanson. .s . . . . Amz Apr 36 27
MODERN PROMETHEUS, A by Cyril G. Wates. .n . . . .
. . . . .AQ Fal 30 436
MOGGLESBY by T. S. Stribling. .nt . . . . . . AFR #11 41
MOGU OF MARS, THE by John Coleridge ps (Earl
Binder & Otto Binder). .nt . . . . SF Aug 39 37
MOLE-MEN OF MERCURY, THE by Arthur K.
Barnes. .s . . . . WS Dec 33 476
MOLE PIRATE, THE by Murray Leinster ps (Will F.
Jenkins). .nt . . . . ASF Nov 34 10
MOLECULE MONSTERS, THE by Oscar J. Friend . . . .
. .s . . . . TW Oct 42 77

Title. .Author. .Length . . . . .Magazine. .Date. .Page No.

MOLECULE TRAPPER, THE by Florence Matheson *(on story)* Donald Matheson *(in ToC)*. .ss . . . .
. . . . Amz Sep 34 133
MOLTEN BULLET, THE by Anthony Rud. .s . . . .
. . . . TW Jun 37 31
                                                FSQ Spr 50 61
MOMUS' MOON by Eando Binder *ps (Otto Binder)*. . . .
. .s . . . . Com Dec 40 75
MONEY MACHINE, THE by Clee Garson *ps (David Wright O'Brien)*. .nt. . . . . Amz Mar 43 134
MONGOLIAN'S RAY, THE by Volney G. Mathison . . .
. .s . . . . Amz Jun 29 258
MONGROVIAN CARAVAN by Richard Tooker. .s . . . .
. . . . TW Fal 44 70
MONKEY AND THE TYPEWRITER, THE by William Morrison *ps (Joseph Samachson)*. .s . . . . . SS Fal 43 97
MONOCLE, THE by H. W. Guernsey *ps (Howard Wandrei)*. .nt . . . . UK Nov 39 107
MONOPOLY by Vic Phillips & Scott Roberts. .s . . . . . .
. . . . ASF Apr 42 116
MONORAIL by George McLociard. .s . . . .
. . . . Amz Dec 28 832
MONSIEUR DE GUISE by Perley Poore Sheehan . . . .
. .ss . . . . FN Jul 40 142
MONSTER, THE by S. M. Tenneshaw *h ps*. .nt . . . . . .
. . . . Amz Apr 49 8
MONSTER, THE by A. E. van Vogt. .s . . . ASF Aug 48 56
MONSTER FROM MARS, THE by Alexander Blade *h ps*. .nt. . . . . Amz Apr 48 8
MONSTER FROM NOWHERE, THE by Nelson S. Bond. .s. .FA Jul 39 46
MONSTER MAKER, THE by Ray Bradbury. .s. . . . . . .
. . . . .PS Spr 44 39
MONSTER OF THE ASTEROID by Ray Cummings . . .
. .s .PS Win 41 102
MONSTER OF THE MOON by Ray Cummings. .s. . . . .
. . . . .SSS Nov 41 127
MONSTER ON THE BORDER, THE by William F. Temple. .s .SSS Nov 40 60
MONSTER OUT OF SPACE, THE by Malcolm Jameson. .nt. . . . . .Amz Jul 40 74
MONSTER THAT THREATENED THE UNIVERSE, THE by R. R. Winterbotham. .s . . . . . . .PS Spr 41 30
MONSTERS FROM THE WEST by Benj. Miller *ps (Noel Loomis)*. .s. . . . . TW Feb 49 98
MONSTERS OF CALLISTO by Edward H. Hinton . . . .
. .s . . . . WS Oct 33 198
MONSTERS OF MARS by Edmond Hamilton. .nt. . . . .
. . . . ASF Apr 31 4
MONSTERS OF MOYEN by Arthur J. Burks. .nt . . . . .
. . . . ASF Apr 30 18
MONSTERS OF NEPTUNE, THE by Hendrik Dahl Juve. .s . . . . .WQ Sum 30 536
MONSTERS OF THE MOON by Francis Parnell . . . . .
. .s . . . . .ToW #1 37 66

MONSTERS OF THE MOUNTAIN by Leon Byrne . . . .
. .s . . . . MSS Aug 38 90
MONSTERS OF THE RAY by A. Hyatt Verrill. .nt . . . .
. . . . .AQ Sum 30 364
MONSTROSITY OF EVOLUTION by Thorp McClusky. .nt. . . . . Amz Nov 38 38
MONTH A MINUTE, A by Ralph Milne Farley *ps (Roger Sherman Hoar)*. .s . . . . TW Dec 37 14
MOON AND MR. WICK, THE by Jack Williamson. . . . .
. .s . . . . FSQ Sum 50 149
MOON ARTIST, THE by David H. Keller. .s. . . . .
. . . . .Sti Jun 41 113
MOON BEASTS, THE by William P. Locke. .s . . . .
. . . . SW Aug 29 198
MOON CONQUERORS, THE by R. H. Romans . . . . . .
. .n . . . . WQ Win 30 150
                                                SFQ Sum 40 4
MOON CRYSTALS by J. Harvey Haggard. .s . . . .
. . . . .ASF Jan 36 30
MOON DESTROYERS, THE by Monroe K. Ruch. . . . . .
. .s . . . . WQ Win 32 212
MOON DEVILS, THE by John Beynon Harris. .s . . . . .
. . . . WS Apr 34 968
                                                WSA 50 149
MOON DOOM, THE *(Novel in 4 pt, each by a different author)*
Part 1 by Nathaniel Salisbury. . . . . . . WS Feb 33 708
Part 2 by William Lichenstein . . . . . . WS Apr 33 880
Part 3 by Wesley P. Baird . . . . .WS May 33 978
Part 4 by Clinton Earle Fisk . . . . WS Jun 33 82
MOON ERA, THE by Jack Williamson. .s. . . . .
. . . . WS Feb 32 1016
                                                ToW Aut 41 7
MOON HEAVEN by Dom Passante. .nt. . . . .
. . . . .SF Jun 39 64
MOON HOAX, THE by Richard Adams Locke. .a . . . . .
. . . . Amz Sep 26 556
MOON HOAX OF RICHARD ADAMS LOCKE, THE *(FANTASTIC HOAXES)*. .a . . . . .FA May 39 58
MOON MADNESS by Richard O. Lewis. .s. . . . .
. . . . Amz Aug 42 198
MOON MASTER, THE by Charles W. Diffin. .s. . . . . . .
. . . . .ASF Jun 30 384
MOON MEN, THE by Frank J. Brueckel, Jr. . .s . . . . . .
. . . . Amz Nov 28 718
MOON MEN, THE by Walter Gillings. .a . . . .
. . . . Fant Dec 46 34
MOON METAL, THE by Garrett P. Serviss. .s. . . . .
. . . . .Amz Jul 26 322
                                                FFM Nov 39 40
MOON MINES, THE by Eando Binder *ps (Earl Binder & Otto Binder)*. .s . . . . WS Apr 33 858
MOON MISTRESS, THE by Raymond Z. Gallun. .s . . . .
. . . . WS May 32 1330
MOON MYSTERIES by Willy Ley. .a . . . ASF Dec 44 104

Title. .Author. .Length . . . . Magazine. .Date. .Page No.

MOON OF ARCTURUS by Richard Tooker. .nt . . . . . .
. . . . Amz Jun 35 41
MOON OF BATTLE by J. J. Allerton. .n . . . .
. . . . Amz Dec 49 40
MOON OF DANGER by Albert de Pina. .nt . . . .
. . . . PS Sum 47 46
MOON OF DELIRIUM by D. L. James. .s . . . .
. . . . .ASF Jan 40 30
MOON OF DOOM, THE by Earl L. Bell. .n . . . .
. . . . .AQ Win 28 4
MOON OF DOUBLE TROUBLE by A. R. Steber h ps
(Raymond A. Palmer). .nt . . . . Amz Mar 45 82
MOON OF EXILE by Harry Walton. .s . . . .
. . . . ASF Aug 40 115
MOON OF INTOXICATION by Eando Binder ps
(Otto Binder). .s . . . . TW Jun 39 53
MOON OF MAD ATAVISM by Hal K. Wells. .s . . . . . .
. . . . TW Feb 39 32
MOON OF MADNESS by George Whitley ps (A.
Bertram Chandler). .s . . . . .PS Spr 49 40
MOON OF MEMORY by Bryce Walton. .s . . . .
. . . . .Fut Nov 50 68
MOON OF TREASON by Emmett McDowell. .s . . . . . .
. . . . PS Sum 50 72
MOON PATROL by Victor Rousseau (Emanuel). .s . . . .
. . . . TW Oct 41 75
MOON PEOPLE OF JUPITER by Isaac R.
Nathanson. .nt . . . . AQ Spr 31 230
MOON PIRATES, THE by Francis M. Deegan. .s . . . . .
. . . . Amz Jun 50 106
MOON PIRATES, THE by Neil R. Jones. .n 2 pt . . . . .
. . . . Amz Sep 34 11
MOON PLAGUE, THE by Raymond Z. Gallun. .nt . . . .
. . . . .WS Jan 34 626
MOON POOL, THE (combining the nt "THE MOON
POOL" and the n "THE CONQUEST OF THE MOON
POOL") by A. Merritt. .n 3 pt . . . . . . Amz May 27 110
MOON POOL, THE by A. Merritt. .nt . . . .
. . . . FFM Sep-Oct 39 2
FN May 48 8
MOON RAYS, THE by David H. Keller, M.D. . .s . . . . .
. . . . .WQ Sum 30 558
MOON SLAVE by Leroy Yerxa. .s . . . . FA Feb 6 6
MOON STROLLERS, THE by J. Rogers Ullrich. .s . . . .
. . . . Amz May 29 146
MOON THAT VANISHED, THE by Leigh Brackett. . . .
. .nt . . . . TW Oct 48 13
MOON TRAGEDY, THE by Frank K. Kelly. .s . . . . . .
. . . . WS Oct 33 240
MOON TRAP by John Foster West. .s . . . . . TW Win 44 73
MOON WAITS, THE by H. L. G. Sullivan. .nt . . . .
. . . . Amz Nov 34 14
MOON WEED, THE by Harl Vincent (Schoepflin). . . . .
. .s . . . . ASF Aug 31 236
MOON WOMAN, THE by Minna Irving. .s . . . .
. . . . .s. . . . . Amz Nov 29 746

MOONS OF DEATH by David V. Reed ps (David
Vern). .s . . . . .FA May 41 94
MOONWORM'S DANCE by Stanley Mullen. .s . . . .
. . . . SSS Jan 49 34
MORALE by Murray Leinster ps (Will F. Jenkins) . . . . .
. .s . . . . ASF Dec 31 402
MORDANT, THE by Merab Eberle. .s . . . .
. . . . Amz Mar 30 1181
MORGUE SHIP by Ray Bradbury. .s . . . . . PS Sum 44 51
MORNING STAR by H. Rider Haggard. .n . . . .
. . . . .FFM Feb 50 8
MORONS, THE by Harl Vincent (Schoepflin). .nt . . . . .
. . . . ASF Jun 39 45
MORTON'S FORK by Dorothy & John de Courcy . . . .
. .nt . . . . Amz Sep 46 116
MOSAIC, THE by J. B. Ryan. .s . . . . .ASF Jul 40 39
MOSQUITO ARMY, THE by H. M. Crimp. .s . . . .
. . . . Amz Apr 35 12
MOSS ISLAND by Carl Jacobi. .s . . . . . . AQ Win 32 136
MOST DANGEROUS OF FORGERIES, THE (SCIENTIFIC
ACTUALITIES) by Edmond Locard. .s . . . .
. . . . AD Oct 30 898
MOST INGENIOUS PARADOX, A by George
Tashman. .s . . . . .Amz Dec 44 78
MOTH, THE by Ross Rocklynne. .s . . . . . ASF Jul 39 91
MOTH, THE by H. G. Wells. .s . . . . Amz Aug 28 461
MOTH MESSAGE by Laurence Manning. .s . . . .
. . . . WS Dec 34 808
MOTHER EARTH by Isaac Asimov. .nt . . . .
. . . . .ASF May 49 59
MOTHER WORLD (THE CONTEST OF THE PLANETS)
by John W. Campbell, Jr. . .n 3 pt . . . . Amz Jan 35 11
MOTHER WORLD, THE by Bruce & G. C. Wallis . . . . .
. .nt . . . . AQ Spr-Sum 33 497
MOUSE by Fredric Brown. .s . . . . TW Jun 49 89
MOUTHPIECE OF ZITU, THE by J. U. Giesy. .n . . . . .
. . . . .FFM Nov 42 6
MOVIES VIA RADIO by Ransom F. Read. .a . . . .
. . . . SF Dec 39 95
MOVING FINGER, THE by Berkeley Livingston. .s . . . .
. . . . FA Nov 46 92
MUDMAN by M. Krulfeld. .s . . . . ASF Jun 42 92
MULE, THE by Isaac Asimov. .n 2 pt . . . .
. . . . .ASF Nov 45 7
MULTILLIONTH CHANCE, THE by John Russell
Fearn. .nt . . . . TW Fal 46 9
MUMMY OF RET-SEH, THE by A. Hyatt Verrill. .s . . .
. . . . .FA May 39 70
MURDER ASTEROID by Edmond Hamilton. .ss . . . . .
. . . . TW Oct 40 80
MURDER BY ATOM by Joseph Wm. Skidmore. .nt. . . .
. . . . Amz Jun 37 13
MURDER FROM MARS by Richard Wilson. .s . . . . . .
. . . . .Ash Apr 40 24
MURDER FROM THE MOON by Robert Bloch. .s . . . .
. . . . Amz Nov 42 154

Title. .Author. .Length . . . . Magazine. .Date. .Page No.

MURDER IN SPACE by David V. Reed ps (David
Vern). .n .s. . . . . .Amz May 44 8
MURDER IN THE CLINIC, THE by Edmond
Hamilton. .nt . . . . SD May 30 390
MURDER IN THE FOURTH DIMENSION by Clark
Ashton Smith. .s . . . . AD Oct 30 908
                                            ToW Spr 41 40
MURDER IN THE PAST by John York Cabot ps (David
Wright O'Brien). .s. . . . . Amz Mar 41 68
MURDER IN THE TIME WORLD by Malcolm
Jameson. .s. . . . . Amz Aug 40 82
MURDER IN THE VOID by Edmond Hamilton. .s . . . .
. . . . TW Jun 38 14
MURDER MACHINE, THE by Hugh B. Cave. .s . . . . . .
. . . . .ASF Sep 30 377
MURDER MADNESS by Murray Leinster ps (Will F.
Jenkins). .n 4 pt . . . . ASF May 30 166
MURDER ON THE ASTEROID by Eando Binder ps
(Earl Binder & Otto Binder). .s. . . . . . . WS Jun 33 70
MURDER RAY, THE by E. K. Jarvis h ps. .nt . . . .
. . . . FA Apr 49 38
MURDER SOLVES A PROBLEM by Lee Francis h ps . .
. .s . . . . Amz Nov 47 88
MURDERED—YET ALIVE by Jep Powell. .s . . . .
. . . . .FA Jul 41 44
MURDERER'S APPRENTICE by Cleve Cartmill. .s. . . .
. . . . SF Apr 43 34
MURDERER'S BASE by William Brittain. .s . . . .
. . . . PS Sum 48 60
MURDERS ON THE MOON SHIP, THE by G. B.
Beattie. .s. . . . . WS Feb 31 958
MURGATROYD EXPERIMENT, THE by Capt. S. P.
Meek, U.S.A. . .s. . . . . AQ Win 29 78
MURRAY'S LIGHT by Donald Wandrei. .s . . . .
. . . . ASF Jun 35 33
MUSIC HATH CHARMS by Henry Kuttner. .s . . . .
. . . . .SS Win 44 89
MUSIC MONSTERS, THE by Neil R. Jones. .nt . . . . . .
. . . . Amz Apr 38 15
MUSIC OF DOOM, THE by Gilbert Mead. .s . . . .
. . . . Amz Oct 49 124
MUSIC OF THE SPHERES, THE by Stuart James
Byrne. .ss. . . . . Amz Aug 35 45
MUSIC OF THE SPHERES by Walt Sheldon. .s. . . . . .
. . . . SS Jul 50 113
MUSKETEERS IN PARIS, THE by William P.
McGivern. .nt . . . . FA Feb 44 92
MUTANTS, THE by Rog Phillips ps (Roger P.
Graham). .nt. . . . . .Amz Jul 46 40
MUTANT'S BROTHER, THE by Fritz Leiber, Jr. . . . .
. .s . . . . ASF Aug 43 53
MUTE QUESTION, THE by Forrest J. Ackerman . . . . .
. .ss. . . . . OW Sep 50 53
MUTEN by Duncan H. Munro ps (Eric Frank
Russell). .s . . . . .ASF Oct 48 126

Title. .Author. .Length . . . . Magazine. .Date. .Page No.

MUTINEERS, THE by Kurt von Rachen ps (L. Ron
Hubbard). .nt . . . . ASF Apr 41 127
MUTINEERS OF SPACE by Lloyd Arthur Eshbach. . . .
. .s . . . . DS Feb 39 69
MUTINY by Larry Offenbecker. .s . . . . PS Fal 45 29
MUTINY ABOARD THE "TERRA" by Ross
Rocklynne. .s . . . . PS Sum 41 80
MUTINY IN HELL by William A. Rossi. .s . . . .
. . . . .SSS Nov 40 92
MUTINY IN SPACE, THE by Gawain Edwards
(Pendray). .nt . . . . WS Sep 31 500
. .nt 2 pt . . . . CF Win 41 101
MUTINY IN SPACE by Jep Powell. .s . . . . Amz Sep 41 62
MUTINY IN THE VOID by Charles R. Tanner. .s . . . . .
. . . . PS Fal 43 45
MUTINY ON EUROPA by Edmond Hamilton. .nt. . . . .
. . . . TW Dec 36 64
MUTINY ON MERCURY by Clifford D. Simak. .s. . . . .
. . . . WS Mar 32 1166
MUTINY ON VENUS by A. Bertram Chandler. .nt . . . .
. . . . .PS Win 48 38
MY ASTRAL BODY by Anthony Hope. .s . . . .
. . . . .F&SF Win-Spr 50 89
MY BRIDE BELONGS TO THE AGES by Arthur J.
Burks. .s . . . . MSS Dec 39 80
MY BROTHER'S KEEPER by Alfred Coppel. .s . . . . . .
. . . . Amz Jun 50 36
MY LADY OF THE EMERALD by Wilfred Owen
Morley ps (Robert W. Lowndes). .s . . . .Ash Nov 41 60
MY LADY OF THE TUNNEL by Arthur J. Burks . . . . .
. .s . . . . ASF Nov 33 101
MY NAME IS LEGION by Lester del Rey. .s . . . .
. . . . ASF Jun 2 69
MY NAME IS MADNESS by Henry Gade. .nt. . . . .
. . . . .FA Nov 49 78
MY OBJECT ALL SUBLIME by Lyle Monroe ps (Robert
A. Heinlein). .s . . . . .Fut Feb 42 82
MY WORLD DIED TONIGHT by Richard Casey h ps . .
. .s . . . . FA May 48 160
MYE DAY by Martin Pearson ps (Donald A.
Wollheim). .s . . . . .Fut Apr 42 30
MYRIAD, THE by Harold S. Sykes. .s. . . . Amz Dec 37 16
MYSTERIES OF GEOLOGY
THE ENIGMA OF THE PACIFIC by L. Taylor
Hansen. .a . . . . Amz May 48 168
MYSTERIOUS CRATER, THE by Leroy Yerxa . . . . . .
. .s . . . . Amz Sep 45 110
MYSTERY FROM THE STARS by John Coleridge ps
(Earl Binder & Otto Binder). .s . . . . . . .Fut Nov 39 58
MYSTERY METAL, THE by Maurice James & T.
Howard James. .s. . . . . SW Mar 30 898
MYSTERY MOON by Edmond Hamilton. .nt. . . . . . .
. . . . Amz Jan 41 72
MYSTERY OF ELEMENT 117, THE by Milton K.
Smith. .nt . . . . Amz Dec 49 102

Title. .Author. .Length . . . . Magazine. .Date. .Page No.

MYSTERY OF MAGIC DRUGS, THE by Vincent H.
    Gaddis. .a. . . . . Amz Sep 49 147
MYSTERY OF PLANET DEEP, THE by George A.
    Dye. .s. . . . . WS Aug 33 102
MYSTERY OF PROFESSOR BROWN, THE by A. L.
    Hodges. .ss. . . . . Amz Aug 30 415
MYSTERY OF SHAFT 13, THE by Robert Moore
    Williams. .s. . . . . FA Jul 42 158
MYSTERY OF THE –/–, THE by W. Varick
    Nevins, III. .s . . . . WS Jun 35 41
MYSTERY OF THE AMAZING BATTERY by Donald
    Bern. .s . . . . Amz Mar 41 124
MYSTERY OF THE BLUE GOD by Harry Bates. .n . . .
    . . . . Amz Jan 42 54
MYSTERY OF THE BULAWAYO DIAMOND, THE by
    Arthur B. Reeve. .s . . . . SD Jan 30 8
MYSTERY OF THE CAT'S BACK, THE by G. L.
    Cleggett. .s. . . . . Amz Jul 49 88
MYSTERY OF THE COLLAPSING SKYSCRAPERS,
    THE by Harl Vincent (Schoepflin). .nt . . . .
    . . . . Amz Aug 39 74
MYSTERY OF THE CREEPING UNDERWEAR by
    Tarleton Fiske ps (Robert Bloch). .s . . . FA Oct 43 132
MYSTERY OF THE LOST RACE by E. K. Jarvis h ps . .
    . .nt . . . . FA Oct 42 8
MYSTERY OF THE MARTIAN PENDULUM by Thornton
    Ayre ps (John Russell Fearn) & A. R. Steber ps
    (Raymond A. Palmer). .s. . . . . Amz Oct 41 116
MYSTERY OF THE MIDGETS by E. K. Jarvis h ps. . . .
    . .s . . . . Amz Jul 48 60
MYSTERY OF THE MIND MACHINE by Don
    Wilcox. .nt. .s. . . . . Amz Aug 40 100
MYSTERY OF THE MUMMY by Duncan H. Farnsworth
    ps (David Wright O'Brien). .s . . . . . . Amz Sep 41 124
MYSTERY OF THE PHANTOM SHOT, THE by
    Amelia Reynolds Long. .s . . . . .AD Jul 30 600
MYSTERY OF THE WHITE RAIDER by Thornton
    Ayre ps (John Russell Fearn). .s . . . . . . FA Feb 40 58
MYSTERY ON BASE TEN by William P. McGivern. . . .
    . .s . . . . .Amz Jan 42 218
MYSTERY ON PLANETOID TEN by James
    Norman. .nt . . . . .Amz Jul 41 46
MYSTERY ON PLUTO by Ward Fleming. .s. . . . . . .
    . . . . FA Feb 50 126
MYSTERY WORLD by Eando Binder ps (Otto
    Binder). .s . . . . TW Apr 41 85

N

N DAY by Philip Latham. .s . . . . .ASF Jan 46 46
NAMELESS SOMETHING, THE by William Fitzgerald
    (Jenkins). .s . . . . TW Jun 47 66
NAMING OF NAMES, THE by Ray Bradbury. .s . . . . .
    . . . . TW Aug 49 137

NATURE OF THINGS, THE by Sir William Bragg. . . . .
    . .a . . . . .TW Aug 38 30
NATURE'S BULLETS by Jack West. .a. . . . .
    . . . . Amz Jun 42 126
NATURE'S "FLUORESCENT" LIGHTS by Robert
    William Conant. .a . . . . .FA May 42 222
NAVAL CONTROL by John Shamus O'Donnel . . . . . .
    . .s . . . . AQ Win 32 141
"NAZI, ARE YOU RESTING WELL?" by Leroy
    Yerxa. .s . . . . .FA Jul 43 176
NAZI DIAMOND by Richard O. Lewis. .s . . . .
    . . . . Amz Nov 42 204
NECESSITY by F. G. Rayer. .s . . . . .NW #5 49 74
NEEDLE by Hal Clement ps (Harry Clement
    Stubbs). .n 2 pt. . . . . .ASF May 49 7
NEEDLE POINTS TO DEATH, THE by Gerald Vance
    h ps. .s. . . . . .Amz Jan 44 176
NEGATIVE PROBLEM by Frances Yerxa. .s . . . .
    . . . . Amz Aug 47 58
NEGATIVE SPACE by Nat Schachner. .nt. . . . .
    . . . . ASF Apr 38 48
NEMESIS FROM LILLIPUT by Raymond Z. Gallun . . .
    . .ss. . . . . SS May 40 113
NEMESIS OF THE ASTROPEDE, THE by Stanton A.
    Coblentz. .s . . . . TW Fal 45 53
NEO-GEODUCK, THE by Margaret St. Clair. .s. . . . . .
    . . . . TW Aug 49 129
NERVELESS MAN, THE by Donald Wandrei. .s . . . . . .
    . . . . .ASF Jul 34 54
NERVES by Lester del Rey. .n . . . . ASF Sep 42 54
NEUTRAL VESSEL by Harl Vincent (Schoepflin) . . . .
    . .nt . . . . ASF Jan 40 9
NEVER-DYING LIGHT, THE by J. Lewis Burtt. .s . . . .
    . . . . Amz Aug 35 96
NEVER THE TWAIN SHALL MEET by Brett Sterling
    h ps (Edmond Hamilton). .s. . . . . . . TW Fal 46 60
NEVER TRUST A DEMON by Robert Bloch. .s . . . . . .
    . . . . Amz Apr 43 164
NEW ACCELERATOR, THE by H. G. Wells. .s . . . . . .
    . . . . Amz Apr 26 57
NEW ADAM, THE by Stanley G. Weinbaum. . . . .
    . .n 2 pt. . . . . Amz Feb 43 62
NEW BODIES FOR OLD by Jack Vance. .nt . . . .
    . . . . .TW Aug 50 46
NEW DAY ON AURORA by Stewart Fleming ps
    (Damon Knight). .s . . . . SSS May 43 98
NEW DIELECTRICS by E. L. Locke. .a. . . . .
    . . . . ASF Aug 48 72
NEW DIRECTIONS by Walter C. Davies ps (Cyril
    Kornbluth). .a. . . . . .Cos Mar 41 122
NEW EVIDENCE FOR ATLANTIS by Vincent H.
    Gaddis. .a. . . . . Amz Aug 46 151
NEW FACE–SAME HEEL by Samuel F. Rocca. .nt. . . .
    . . . . Amz Sep 48 40
NEW FOUNDATIONS by Wilmar H. Shiras. .nt . . . . . .
    . . . . .ASF Mar 50 5

Title. .Author. .Length . . . . Magazine. .Date. .Page No.

NEW FRONTIERS by Thomas Calvert McClary. .a . . . .
. . . . ASF Feb 37 89
NEW LIFE, THE by John Coleridge ps (Earl Binder &
Otto Binder). .s . . . . SF Mar 40 25
NEW LIVES FOR OLD by William Bade. .nt . . . .
. . . . ASF Feb 48 46
NEW MOON by Basil Wells. .s . . . . .Cos May 41 90
NEW NATURAL LAW, A by E. L. Locke. .a . . . .
. . . . ASF Nov 48 100
NEW ONE, THE by Fredric Brown. .s . . . . . UK Oct 42 86
NEW REALITY, THE by Charles L. Harness. .nt . . . . .
. . . . TW Dec 50 56
NEW STOMACHS FOR OLD by W. Alexander. .s . . . . .
. . . . Amz Feb 27 1039
NEW THEORY OF GEOLOGY, A by R. B. Hoag, ...
M.D. .a . . . . Amz Feb 48 140
NEW YORK FIGHTS THE TERMANITES by Bertrand L.
Shurtleff. .nt . . . . FA Feb 40 8
NEW WINGS by A. Bertram Chandler. .s . . ASF Apr 48 71
NEWS FROM OUR SUN by J. J. Coupling ps (John R.
Pierce). .a . . . . ASF Jun 47 76
NEWS OF THE MONTH fanews dept in OW from Nov 49
NEWSCAST by Harl Vincent (Schoepflin). .s . . . .
. . . . MSS Apr-May 39 119
NEXT FRIDAY MORNING by D. W. Meredith. .s . . . . .
. . . . ASF Feb 49 135
NEXT TIME I'LL GET YOU by Anton Reed. .s . . . . . .
. . .s. . . . . Amz Oct 42 94
N'GOC by Raymond Z. Gallun. .s . . . . . ASF May 35 145
NICKLE SAVED. . .", "A by Robert W. Krepps. .s . . . .
. . . . FA Mar 49 100
NICOLBEE'S NIGHTMARE by John York Cabot ps
(David Wright O'Brien). .s . . . . Amz Nov 41 62
NIEDBALSKI'S MUTANT by Spencer Lane h ps. .s. . . .
. . . . ASF May 38 129
NIGHT by Don A. Stuart ps (John W. Campbell, Jr.) . . .
. .nt . . . . ASF Oct 35 8
NIGHT BEFORE THE END OF THE WORLD, THE by
Murray Leinster ps (Will F. Jenkins). .s . . . .
. . . . FFM Aug 48 114
NIGHT HAS A THOUSAND EYES, THE by John &
Dorothy de Courcy. .s . . . . .PS Win 49 42
NIGHT OF GODS by Paul Edmonds ps (Henry
Kuttner). .nt. . . . . .Ash Dec 42 11
NIGHT THE WORLD ENDED, THE by Edmond
Hamilton. .s . . . . TW Sep 40 82
NIGHT WIRE, THE by H. F. Arnold. .s. . . . . AFR #9 12
NIGHTFALL by Isaac Asimov. .nt . . . . . . ASF Sep 41 9
NIGHTMARE, THE by Chan Davis. .s . . . . ASF May 46 7
NIGHTMARE ISLAND by Douglas Drew. .nt. . . . . . .
. . . . ASF Oct 36 98
NIGHTMARE ISLAND by E. Waldo Hunter ps
(Theodore Sturgeon). .nt . . . . UK Jun 41 132
9F19 by Arthur C. Parlett. .a . . . . ASF Apr 49 146
NINTH LIFE, THE by Jack Mann ps (E. Charles
Vivian). .n . . . . .AMF Apr 50 10

Title. .Author. .Length . . . . Magazine. .Date. .Page No.

NO CONNECTION by Isaac Asimov. .s . . . .
. . . . ASF Jun 48 72
NO ESCAPE FROM DESTINY by Arthur Leo Zagat . . .
. .s . . . . SS May 48 80
NO GRAVEN IMAGE by Cleve Cartmill. .nt . . . .
. . . . .UK Feb 43 79
NO GREATER LOVE by Henry Kuttner. .nt . . . .
. . . . UK Apr 43 105
NO GREATER WORLDS by Sam Merwin, Jr. .s. . . . .
. . . . TW Spr 45 85
NO HANDICAP ALLOWED by R. S. Richardson . . . . .
. .a . . . . ASF Jun 42 63
NO HEAD FOR MY BIER by Lester del Rey. .s . . . . . .
. . . . FA Sep 50 94
NO HELP WANTED by Alfred Bester. .s . . . TW Dec 39 89
NO HEROES WANTED by Robert Moore Williams . . . .
. .s . . . . .SS Sep 41 107
NO HIDING PLACE by Cleve Cartmill. .nt. . . . .
. . . . TW Jun 50 52
NO—MAN'S—LAND by John Buchan. .nt . . . .
. . . . .FFM Dec 49 82
NO MAN'S LAND IN SPACE by Leigh Brackett . . . . . .
. .nt . . . . .Amz Jul 41 70
NO—MAN'S—LAND OF TIME by Edmond Hamilton . .
. .s . . . . SF Apr 43 45
NO MAN'S WORLD by Henry Kuttner. .s . . . .
. . . . .TW Aug 40 42
NO MEDALS by Leigh Keith ps (H. L. Gold). .s . . . . . .
. . . . ASF Mar 35 45
NO MORE FRICTION by Dr. David H. Keller. .s. . . . . .
. . . . TW Jun 39 93
NO MORE TOMORROWS by David H. Keller, M.D. . .
. .s . . . . Amz Dec 32 804
NO NEWS TODAY by Cleve Cartmill. .s . . . .
. . . . UK Oct 41 59
NO PLACE TO GO by Edward J. Bellin h ps. .ss . . . . . .
. . . . .Cos May 41 64
NO STAR SHALL FALL by Wilfred Owen Morley ps
(Robert W. Lowndes). .ss . . . . .Fut Dec 41 60
NO TEETH FOR THE TIGER by Paul W. Fairman . . . .
. .s . . . . Amz Feb 50 82
NO TIME LIKE THE FUTURE by Forrest J.
Ackerman. .ss. . . . . MSS Nov 50 71
NO WINTER, NO SUMMER by Donald Laverty ps (James
Blish & Damon Knight). .s. . . . . TW Oct 48 140
NO WOMAN BORN by C. L. Moore. .nt . . . .
. . . . ASF Dec 44 134
NOBODY SAW THE SHIP by Murray Leinster ps (Will F.
Jenkins). .s. . . . . .Fut May-Jun 50 40
NOCTURNE by Wallace West. .s . . . . TW Apr 50 116
NOEKKEN OF NORWAY by Bob Olsen ps (Alfred John
Olsen, Jr.). .s . . . . Amz Nov 34 61
NOISE FROM OUTSIDE by Lorne MacLaughlan . . . . .
. .a . . . . ASF Apr 47 44
NOISE KILLER, THE by A. M. McNeill. .s . . . .
. . . . .Amz May 30 151

Title. .Author. .Length . . . . Magazine. .Date. .Page No.   Title. .Author. .Length . . . . Magazine. .Date. .Page No.

NOMAD by Wesley Long *ps (George O. Smith).* . . . . . .
. . .n 3 pt . . . . ASF Dec 44 7
NON-GRAVITATIONAL VORTEX, THE by A. Hyatt
Verrill. .nt . . . . Amz Jun 30 198
NONE BUT LUCIFER by H. L. Gold & L. Sprague de
Camp. .n . . . . UK Sep 39 9
NOON by Hudson Hastings *ps (Henry Kuttner & C. L.*
Moore). .s . . . . TW Aug 47 31
NOR MOON BY NIGHT by Peter Cartur. .ss . . . .
. . . . FFM Oct 50 116
NORDENHOLT'S MILLION by J. J. Connington . . . . .
. . .n . . . . FFM Dec 48 14
NORRIS TAPLEY'S SIXTH SENSE by Ed Earl Repp . .
. . .s . . . . FA Apr 40 78
NORTE AMERICANOS, YOU ARE DOOMED! by Alma
Hill. .s . . . . OW Mar 50 14
NORTH GOD'S TEMPLE by Henry J. Kostkos. .s . . . . .
. . . . Amz Aug 34 99
NORTH OF MATTO GROSSO by Bertrand L.
Shurtleff. .nt . . . . Amz Jul 32 310
NOSE FOR NEWS, A by Roby Wentz. .s . . . .
. . . . ASF Jun 42 56
NOT ACCORDING TO DANTE by Malcolm
Jameson. .s. . . . . UK Jun 41 59
NOT AS PLOTTED by Guy Archette *ps (Chester S.*
Geier). .s . . . . FA Mar 47 108
NOT FINAL by Isaac Asimov. .s . . . . ASF Oct 41 49
NOT ONLY DEAD MEN by A. E. van Vogt . . . .
. . .s . . . . ASF Nov 42 114
NOT QUITE ROCKETS. .a . . . . ASF Apr 44 99
NOT THE FIRST by A. E. van Vogt. .s . . . .
. . . . ASF Apr 41 94
NOT TO BE OPENED– by Roger Flint Young. .nt . . . .
. . . . .ASF Jan 50 33
NOT WITH A BANG by Damon Knight. .s. . . . .
. . . . .F&SF Win-Spr 50 123
NOT YET THE END by Frederic Brown. .ss. . . . .
. . . . CF Win 41 96
NOTHING by Martin Pearson *ps (Donald A.*
Wollheim). .s . . . . Ash Oct 42 56
NOTHING BUT GINGERBREAD LEFT by Henry
Kuttner. .s . . . . .ASF Jan 43 60
NOTHING HAPPENS ON THE MOON by Paul
Ernst. .s. . . . . ASF Feb 39 97
NOTHING HAPPENS TO LEFTY FEEP by Robert
Bloch. .s . . . . FA Feb 43 132
NOTHING IN THE RULES by L. Sprague de Camp. . . .
. . .nt . . . . .UK Jul 39 89
                                                      UK 48 36
NOTHING SIRIUS by Fredric Brown. .s . . . .
. . . . .CF Spr 44 106
NOTORIOUS C39, THE by Jack O. Bearden. .ss . . . . . .
. . . . Amz Nov 33 50
NOVA, THE by Edwin E. Sloat. .s . . . . . ASF Dec 39 86
NOVA IN MESSIER 33 by Chan Corbett *ps (Nathan*
Schachner). .nt . . . . ASF May 37 138

NOVA MIDPLANE by S. D. Gottesman *ps (Cyril*
Kornbluth & Frederik Pohl). .s. . . . . . .SSS Nov 40 102
NOVA SOLIS by E. V. Raymond *ps (Raymond Z*
Gallun). .s . . . . ASF Dec 35 34
NOVEL OF THE BLACK SEAL, THE by Arthur
Machen. .s . . . . FFM Jun 46 109
NOVEL OF THE WHITE POWDER, THE by Arthur
Machen. .s . . . . FFM Sep 44 111
NOW YOU SEE IT by Isaac Asimov. .n . . . .
. . . . ASF Jan 48 7
Nth DEGREE, THE by Mort Weisinger. .s . . . .
. . . . .TW Aug 36 61
Nth MAN, THE by Homer Eon Flint. .nt . . . .
. . . . AQ Spr 28 196
NUISANCE VALUE by Manly Wade Wellman . . . .
. . .n 2 pt . . . . ASF Dec 38 61
NULL F by Peter Worth *h ps.* .s . . . . . . FA Feb 50 116
NUMBER NINE by Cleve Cartmill. .s . . . . ASF Feb 50 98

O

OBEY THAT IMPULSE by George O. Smith. .a . . . . . .
. . . . .ASF Jul 47 84
OBSERVATORY, THE editorial dept of Amz
OBSERVER, THE by Robert Moore Williams. .s . . . . . .
. . . . FA Jan 45 80
OBSOLETE WEAPON, THE by L. Ron Hubbard . . . . .
. . .s . . . . ASF May 48 48
OCCUPATION: DEMIGOD by Nelson S. Bond. . . . . . .
. . .s . . . . UK Dec 41 60
OCEAN DEN OF MERCURY, THE by Miles Shelton
ps (Don Wilcox). .n . . . . Amz Jun 48 100
OCTOPUS CYCLE, THE by Irving Lester & Fletcher
Pratt. .s . . . . Amz May 28 110
OCTOPUS OF SPACE, THE by Alexander Blade *h ps* . .
. . .nt . . . . FA Oct 49 8
ODDS ON SERGEANT SHANE, THE by John York
Cabot *ps (David Wright O'Brien).* .s. . . . Amz Dec 41 98
ODYSSEY OF BATTLING BERT, THE by Stanton A.
Coblentz. .s . . . . Amz Dec 44 124
OF GODS AND GOATS by Richard S. Shaver. .nt . . . .
. . . . Amz Dec 47 58
OF JOVIAN BUILD by Oscar J. Friend. .s . . . .
. . . . TW Oct 38 63
OFF ON A COMET or HECTOR SERVADAC by Jules
Verne. .n 2 pt . . . . Amz Apr 26 4
OFF SEASON, THE by Ray Bradbury. .s. . . TW Dec 48 99
OFF THE BEAM by George O. Smith. .nt . . . .
. . . . ASF Feb 44 6
OGDEN'S STRANGE STORY by Edison Marshall. . . . .
. . .n . . . . FFM Dec 49 10
OGRE by Clifford D. Simak. .nt. . . . .
. . . . .ASF Jan 44 123
OIL by Don Wire. .s . . . . ASF Feb 39 137

Title. .Author. .Length . . . . Magazine. .Date. .Page No.

OKIE by James Blish. .nt . . . . ASF Apr 50 69
OLD COMPTON'S SECRET by Harl Vincent
(Schoepflin). .s . . . . ASF Feb 30 153
OLD DOC METHUSELAH by Rene Lafayette ps (L. Ron
Hubbard). .nt . . . . ASF Oct 47 6
OLD FAITHFUL by Raymond Z. Gallun. .nt . . . .
. . . . ASF Dec 34 106
OLD FIREBALL by Nat Schachner. .nt. . . ASF Jun 41 79
OLD MAN MARS by R. R. Winterbotham. .s . . . .
. . . . Fut Apr 42 59
OLD MAN MULLIGAN by P. Schuyler Miller. .nt . . . . .
. . . . ASF Dec 40 9
OLD MARTIAN PROVERB, AN by John M. Taylor . . .
. .s . . . . SF Jun 41 49
OLD NEPTUNIAN CUSTOM, AN by Scott Mariner
ps (Cyril Kornbluth & Frederik Pohl). .s . . . .
. . . . .SSS Aug 42 74
OLD ONES, THE by Betsy Curtis. .nt . . . .
. . . . Im Dec 50 98
OLD ONES, THE by Willy Ley. .a . . . . . ASF May 43 88
OLD ONES HEAR, THE by Malcolm Jameson. .s . . . . .
. . . . UK Jun 42 101
OLDER THAN METHUSELAH by Stanton A.
Coblentz. .s . . . . Amz May 35 67
OLE MOTHER METHUSELAH by Rene Lafayette ps
(L. Ron Hubbard). .nt . . . . .ASF Jan 50 80
OLIVER PERFORMS A MIRACLE by Leroy Yerxa . . .
. .s . . . . Amz Oct 42 216
OMEGA by Guy Archette ps (Chester S. Geier). . . . . .
. .nt .Amz Jan 50 108
OMEGA by Amelia Reynolds Long. .s . . . .
. . . . Amz Jul 32 370
                                                          AFR #10 116
OMEGA AND THE WOLF-GIRL by Lester del Rey. . . .
. .s . . . . OTWA Jul 50 30
OMEGA, THE MAN by Lowell Howard Morrow. .s . . . .
. . . . .Amz Jan 33 929
OMINOUS BEQUEST, THE by Warren Kastel ps. .s . . . .
. . . . FA Jun 48 140
ON A LIMB by Anthony Boucher ps (William
Anthony Parker White). .a . . . . UK Oct 41 92
ON ACCOUNT OF A WOMAN (Reprinted under the title
SHE SAID "TAKE ME IF YOU DARE") by Theodore
Roscoe. .nt. . . . . FanF May 50 3
ON BOARD THE MARTIAN LINER by Miles J.
Breuer, M.D. .s . . . . Amz Mar 31 1080
ON PAIN OF DEATH by Robert Moore Williams . . . .
. .nt . . . . ASF Jun 42 40
ON THE BACK OF A BEETLE by R. K. Dirk. .nt . . . . .
. . . . FA May 49 82
ON THE BRINK OF 2000 by Garrett Smith. .nt . . . . . .
. . . . FFM Jan 40 6
ON THE HOUSE by Benj. Miller ps (Noel Loomis) . . . .
. .s . . . . TW Apr 49 82
ON THE KNEES OF THE GODS by J. Allan Dunn . . . .
. .n 3 pt. . . . . UK Jan 40 132

ON THE MARTIAN WAY by Capt. H. G. Bishop,
U.S.A. . .s . . . . Amz Feb 27 1008
ON THE PLANET FRAGMENT by Neil R. Jones . . . . .
. .nt . . . . Amz Oct 37 97
ONCE AROUND THE MOON by Vic Phillips. .s . . . . .
. . . . ASF Jun 37 90
ONCE IN A BLUE MOON by Norman L. Knight. . . . .
. .nt . . . . .Fut Aug 42 10
ONCE IN A BLUE MOON by Harl Vincent
(Schoepflin). .s . . . . AQ Win 32 74
ONCE TO DIE by John & Dorothy de Courcy. .s . . . . .
. . . . FA Sep 47 126
ONCE UPON A PLANET by J. J. Allerton. .s. . . . .
. . . . Amz Dec 48 54
ONE AGAINST THE LEGION by Jack Williamson . . . .
. .n 3 pt. . . . . ASF Apr 39 43
ONE AGAINST THE STARS by Vaseleos Garson . . . . .
. .s . . . . PS Sum 44 104
ONE CAME BACK by George Whitley ps (A. Bertram
Chandler). .s. . . . . TW Fal 45 79
ONE-EYED MAN, THE by Philip St. John. .s . . . .
. . . . ASF May 45 48
ONE FOR THE ROBOT—TWO FOR THE SAME by Rog
Phillips ps (Roger P. Graham). .nt. . . . . .Im Oct 50 58
ONE HUNDRED GENERATIONS by Philip Jacques
Bartel ps. .s . . . . WS Sep 35 430
170 MILES A MINUTE by Ward Skeen. .s . . . .
. . . . Amz Jun 35 114
100th GENERATION, THE by Nat Schachner. .s . . . . .
. . . . ASF May 34 85
ONE LEG IS ENOUGH by Kris Neville. .s . . . .
. . . . .Amz Jul 50 166
ONE LEG TOO MANY by W. Alexander. .s . . . .
. . . . Amz Oct 29 612
ONE MAN'S HARP by Babette Rosmond. .s . . . .
. . . . UK Aug 43 120
                                                          UK 48 98
ONE MORE SPRING by Frances Yerxa. .s . . . .
. . . . Amz Sep 47 74
ONE OF OUR PLANETS IS MISSING! by Mack
Reynolds. .s . . . . Amz Nov 50 108
ONE OF THREE by Wesley Long ps (George O.
Smith). .n . . . . .SS Mar 48 13
ONE PREHISTORIC NIGHT by Philip Barshofsky
ps. .s. . . . . WS Nov 34 692
ONE THOUSAND MILES BELOW by Eando Binder
ps (Otto Binder). .nt . . . . PS Win 40 2
ONE WAS STUBBORN by Rene Lafayette ps (L. Ron
Hubbard). .s . . . . ASF Nov 40 82
ONE WAY. . . by Gilbert Grant. .s . . . . . FA Nov 50 108
ONE WAY STAR RIDE by Robert Moore Williams . . . .
. .s . . . . TW Oct 40 33
ONE-WAY TICKET TO NOWHERE by Leroy
Yerxa. .s . . . . Amz Dec 42 96
ONE-WAY TRIP by Anthony Boucher ps (William
Anthony Parker White). .nt . . . . ASF Aug 43 79

Title. .Author. .Length . . . . Magazine. .Date. .Page No.

ONE-WAY TUNNEL by David H. Keller. .s . . . .
. . . . .WS Jan 35 934
ONLY THING WE LEARN, THE by C. M. Kornbluth . .
. .s . . . . SS Jul 49 129
ONSLAUGHT FROM BELOW, THE by John Cotton ps
(John Russell Fearn). .s . . . . .Fut Nov 40 96
ONSLAUGHT FROM RIGEL, THE by Fletcher Pratt . .
. .n . . . . WQ Win 32 150
WSA 50 5
ONSLAUGHT FROM VENUS, THE by Frank Phillips
ps (Philip Francis Nowlan). .s . . . . SW Sep 29 326
ONSLAUGHT OF THE DRUID GIRLS by Ray
Cummings. .nt . . . . FA Jun 41 6
OOGIE FINDS LOVE by Berkeley Livingston. .s . . . . .
. . . . Amz Nov 48 114
OOMPH BEASTS, THE by Millard Verne Gordon ps
(Donald A. Wollheim). .s . . . . .Fut Dec 42 99
OONA & JIK series See MARGARET ST. CLAIR author
OPEN LETTER TO THE WORLD by Richard S.
Shaver. .a. . . . . Amz Jun 45 12
OPEN SECRET by Lewis Padgett ps (Henry Kuttner &
C. L. Moore). .s . . . . ASF Apr 43 33
OPENING DOORS by Wilmar H. Shiras. .nt . . . .
. . . . ASF Mar 49 9
OPERATION ASDEVLANT by Lt. Comdr. Warren
Guthrie, USNR. .a . . . . SS Jul 47 71
OPERATION DECOY by Walt Sheldon. .s . . . .
. . . . FA Jun 50 110
OPERATION SUCCESSFUL by Robert Arthur. .s . . . .
. . . . ASF Dec 41 86
OPERATION PUMICE by Raymond Z. Gallun. .s . . . .
. . . . TW Apr 49 37
OPPORTUNISTS, THE by E. A. Grosser. .s . . . .
. . . . .ASF Jan 41 116
OPPOSITES—REACT! by Will Stewart ps (Jack
Williamson). .n 2 pt . . . . ASF Jan 43 9
ORANGE GOD, THE by Walter Glamis ps (Nathan
Schachner). .s. . . . . ASF Oct 33 2
ORB OF PROBABILITY, THE by Nat Schachner . . . . .
. .nt . . . . .ASF Jun 35 110
ORBIT JUMPER, THE by Geo. C. Wallis. .s . . . .
. . . . ToW Win 38 100
ORBIT XXII–H by Robert Willey ps (Willy Ley) . . . . . .
. .nt . . . . ASF Sep 38 17
ORBITS, TAKE-OFFS AND LANDINGS by Willy
Ley. .a. . . . . ASF Aug 38 125
ORDEAL IN SPACE by Ralph Sloan. .s. . . . . PS Fal 49 53
ORDEAL OF LANCELOT BIGGS, THE by Nelson S.
Bond. .s. . . . . .Amz May 43 72
ORDERS by Malcolm Jameson. .s . . . . . ASF Dec 45 47
ORDERS FOR WILLY WESTON by William P.
McGivern. .s. . . . . .FA Jan 48 120
ORESTES REVOLTS by Eando Binder ps (Otto
Binder). .s . . . . ASF Oct 38 44
ORIDIN'S FORMULA by R. R. Winterbotham. .s . . . . .
. . . . .PS Mar 43 39

ORIGIN OF THOUGHT by Spencer Lane h ps. .s . . . . .
. . . . .ASF Jun 36 100
ORIGINAL SIN by S. Fowler Wright. .s. . . . .
. . . . AFR #13 68
ORMOLY OF ROONERION by Warner Van Lorne
ps. .nt . . . . .ASF JAn 38 6
ORPHAN OF ATLANS by William Lawrence
Hamling. .n . . . . .Amz Feb 47 8
OSA THE KILLER by Clifton B. Kruse. .s . . . .
. . . . .ASF Jan 35 91
OSCAR by Cleve Cartmill. .ss . . . . UK Feb 41 135
OSCAR AND THE TALKING TOTEMS by James
Norman. .nt . . . . FA Apr 42 130
OSCAR, DETECTIVE OF MARS by James Norman . . .
. .s . . . . FA Oct 40 58
OSCAR SAVES THE UNION by James Norman . . . . .
. .s . . . . FA Sep 41 52
OSMOTIC THEOREM, THE by Capt. S. P. Meek . . . . .
. .s . . . . WQ Win 30 234
OTHER, THE by Howard W. Graham, Ph.D. ps (Howard
Wandrei). .s . . . . ASF Dec 34 31
OTHER, THE by Robert W. Lowndes. .ss . . . .
. . . . Sti Apr 41 92
OTHER, THE by Sanford Vaid. .s . . . . . . SSS Jan 49 52
OTHER ABNER SMALL, THE by Clee Garson ps
(David Wright O'Brien). .s . . . . FA Mar 43 96
OTHER END OF THE TRAJECTORY, THE by Willy
Ley. .a. . . . . .ASF Jul 48 63
OTHER EYES WATCHING by Polton Cross ps (John
Russell Fearn). .n . . . . SS Spr 46 13
OTHER MAN'S BLOOD, THE by Ray Cummings. . . . .
. .nt . . . . .FFM Dec 40 56
OTHER SIDE OF ASTRONOMY, THEby R. S.
Richardson. .a. . . . . ASF Sep 39 85
OTHER SIDE OF THE MOON, THE by Edmond
Hamilton. .nt . . . . .AQ Fal 29 516
OTHER SPACE by Warner Van Lorne ps. .nt . . . . . .
. . . . .ASF May 37 8
OTHER TRACKS by William Sell. .s . . . . . ASF Oct 38 56
OTHER WING, THE by Algernon Blackwood. .s . . . . . .
. . . . AFR #8 74
OTHER WORLD, THE by Murray Leinster ps (Will F.
Jenkins). .n . . . . SS Nov 49 11
OTHER WORLD by Harl Vincent (Schoepflin). .s . . . . .
. . . . Ash Oct 40 78
OTHER WORLDS by Walton Blodgett. .nt . . . .
. . . . FA Jul 43 182
OUNCE OF PREVENTION by Philip Carter. .s. . . . . .
. . . . F&SF Sum 50 59
OUR DIRECTOR by John E. Harry. .s . . . .Ash Apr 41 47
OUR DIRECTOR MEETS TROUBLE by John E.
Harry. .s . . . . .Ash Dec 42 63
OUR ROBOT MAID by Bob Olsen ps (Alfred John
Olsen, Jr.). .ss . . . . .Fut Nov 40 72
OUR TURBULENT ATMOSPHERE by Willy Ley. . . . .
. .a 2 pt . . . . ASF Mar 50 124

Title. .Author. .Length . . . . Magazine. .Date. .Page No.

OUT AROUND RIGEL by Robert H. Wilson. .s . . . . ASF Dec 31 295
OUT OF NIGHT by Don A. Stuart ps (John W. Campbell, Jr.). .nt . . . . ASF Oct 37 10
OUT OF NOWHERE by E. A. Grosser. .s . . . . Fut Oct 41 94
OUT OF SMALLNESS by Ray Cummings. .s . . . . TW Jun 41 53
OUT OF THE DARK by Amabel Redman. .s . . . . FFM Oct 40 100
OUT OF THE DEPTHS by H. L. Gold. .s . . . . .TW Jul 40 44
OUT OF THE DESERT by L. Patrick Greene. .s . . . . FFM Oct 41 116
OUT OF THE DREADFUL DEPTHS by C. D. Willard. .s . . . . .ASF Jun 30 293
OUT OF THE JAR by Charles R. Tanner. .s . . . . .Sti Feb 41 101
OUT OF THE PAST by Lloyd Arthur Eshbach. .s . . . . ToW Aut 38 31
OUT OF THE SEA by Leigh Brackett. .s . . . . .Ash Jun 42 11
OUT OF THE SUB-UNIVERSE by R. F. Starzl. .s . . . . .AQ Sum 28 378
OUT OF THE SUN by L. A. Eshbach. .s . . . . . FB #4 52
OUT OF THE VOID by Leslie F. Stone ps (Mrs. Wm. Silberberg). .n 2 pt . . . . Amz Aug 29 440
OUT OF THE YEARS by Ivan Sandrof. .s . . . . TW Mar 41 102
"OUT OF THIS DUST. . ." by Charles Recour. .s . . . . FA Feb 49 36
OUT OF THIS WORLD by Henry Hasse. .s . . . . PS Sum 42 58
OUT OF TOMORROW by Vivian Shirley. .s. . . . . .OW Nov 50 132
OUTCAST, THE by E. F. Benson. .s . . . . FFM Aug 42 130
OUTCAST, THE by S. M. Tenneshaw h ps. .s . . . . Amz Jun 49 36
OUTCAST IN SPACE by Arthur G. Stangland. .s . . . . .WQ Sum 31 560
OUTCAST OF THE STARS by Ray Bradbury. .s . . . . .SSS Mar 50 41
OUTCASTS by Guy Wernham. .s . . . . . . ASF Nov 34 98
OUTCASTS FROM MARS by Arthur G. Stangland . . . . . .s . . . . WS Oct 32 406
OUTCASTS OF ETERNITY by Polton Cross ps (John Russell Fearn). .nt . . . . FA Sep 42 188
OUTCASTS OF SOLAR III, THE by Emmett McDowell. .nt . . . . .PS Spr 48 6
OUTLAW ECHO, THE by Clark South ps (Dwight V. Swain). .s . . . . FA Dec 42 162
OUTLAW OF MARS by Festus Pragnell. .nt . . . . .Amz Jan 42 142
OUTLAW OF SATURN by John Cotton ps (John Russell Fearn). .s . . . . SF Mar 39 94

Title. .Author. .Length . . . . Magazine. .Date. .Page No.

OUTLAW OF SPACE by Wallace Quitman ps (Raymond A. Palmer). .ss. . . . . Amz Aug 38 128
OUTLAW QUEEN OF VENUS by Wallace West. .nt . . . . FA Feb 44 8
OUTLAW WORLD by Edmond Hamilton. .n . . . . .SS Win 46 11
OUTLAWS OF CORPUS by Lee Francis h ps. .nt . . . . FA Dec 48 8
OUTLAWS OF THE MOON by Edmond Hamilton . . . . . .n . . . . .CF Spr 42 14
OUTLAWS OF THE SUN by Victor Rousseau (Emanuel). .nt . . . . .Mir Apr-May 31 78
OUTLAWS ON CALLISTO by Manly Wade Wellman . . . .nt . . . . ASF Apr 36 108
OUTLAWS ON VENUS by John E. Harry. .s . . . . SSS Jul 40 43
OUTPOST AT ALTARK, THE by Robert W. Lowndes. .ss. . . . . .SSS Nov 40 112
OUTPOST INFINITY by Raymond F. Jones. .nt . . . . SSS Jan 50 8
OUTPOST OF THE EONS by Dirk Wylie. .nt . . . . .Ash Apr 43 32
OUTPOST ON CERES, THE by L. A. Eshbach. .s . . . . Amz Oct 36 121
OUTPOST ON IO by Leigh Brackett. .s . . . . .PS Win 42 58
OUTPOST ON THE MOON, THE by Joslyn Maxwell. . . .n 2 pt. . . . . WS Dec 30 630
OUTSIDER, THE by H. P. Lovecraft. .s . . . . .FFM JUN 50 114
OUTSIDERS, THE by Duncan Farnsworth ps (David Wright O'Brien). .nt . . . . FA Feb 42 88
OVER THE BORDER by Eric Frank Russell. .a . . . . UK Sep 39 129
OVER THE RIVER by P. Schuyler Miller. .s . . . . UK Apr 41 96
OVER THE SPACE-WAVES by Stanton A. Coblentz. . . .ss. . . . . .SS Mar 41 111
OVER THE TOP by Lester del Rey. .s . . . . ASF Nov 49 41
OVERLORD OF EARTH by Lloyd Arthur Eshbach . . . .s . . . . MSS Nov 50 48
OVERLORD OF VENUS by Lt. William Lawrence Hamling. .s. . . . . Amz Sep 44 174
OVERSIGHT, THE by Miles J. Breuer. .s . . . . Com Dec 40 40
OVERTHROW by Cleve Cartmill. .nt . . . . .ASF Nov 42 9

P

P-PLUS by Peter Phillips. .nt . . . . ASF Aug 49 112
PACER by Raymond F. Jones. .s . . . . . . ASF May 43 71
PACIFICA by Nat Schachner. .nt . . . . . . .ASF Jul 36 74
PACIFIST OF HELL'S ISLAND by Robert Moore Williams. .nt . . . . Amz Jun 43 130

Title. .Author. .Length . . . . Magazine. .Date. .Page No.

PACKAGE OF POWER by David C. Cooke. .s . . . . . .
. . . . SFQ Sum 40 111
PAGANINI—MAN OR DEVIL? by Joseph J. Millard . . .
. .a . . . . FA Oct 40 130
PAIN MACHINE, THE by L. V. Heald. .s. . . . .
. . . . Fant Dec 46 70
PAINTED MIRROR, THE by Donald Wandrei. .s . . . .
. . . . AFR #9 121
PAINTED MURDER, THE by Eugene de Reszke . . . . .
. .s . . . . AD Aug 30 678
PAINTING OF THE PROPHET by David Wright
O'Brien. .s . . . . FA May 47 74
PALACE OF DARKNESS by Peter Dexter ps (Richard
S. Shaver). .nt. . . . . OW Sep 50 54
PALADINS OF THE SKY by Warwick Janus. .s . . . .
. . . . .AQ Fal 31 571
PALLAS REBELION by W. Malcolm White. .ss. . . . . .
. . . . OTWA Jul 50 70
PALOOKA FROM JUPITER by Nat Schachner . . . . . .
. .s . . . . ASF Feb 39 73
PALOS OF THE DOG STAR PACK by J. U.
Giesy. .n . . . . FFM Oct 41 6
PAMELA PAYS THE PIPER by Phyllis Lee Peterson. . .
. .s . . . . .F&SF Fal 50 60
PANDORA'S ICEBOX by Philip M. Morse. .a . . . .
. . . . .ASF Jun 39 120
PANDORA'S MILLIONS by George O. Smith. .nt . . . .
. . . . ASF Jun 45 7
PAPER PLANETS by Robert S. Richardson. .a . . . . . .
. . . . .ASF Sep 48 100
PARADISE by Clifford D. Simak. .nt . . . . ASF Jun 46 46
PARADISE AND IRON by Miles J. Breuer, M.D. . . . .
. .n . . . . .AQ Sum 30 292
PARADISE OF THE ICE WILDERNESS, THE by
Jul. Regis. .s . . . . Amz Oct 27 701
PARADISE STREET by Lawrence O'Donnell ps (C. L.
Moore). .nt. . . . . ASF Sep 50 63
PARADOX by Charles Cloukey. .s . . . . .AQ Sum 29 386
PARADOX + by Charles Cloukey. .s . . . . Amz Jul 30 312
PARADOX by Edwin James ps (James E. Gunn). . . . . .
. .s . . . . TW Oct 49 135
PARADOX LOST by Fredric Brown. .s. . . ASF Oct 43 83
PARADOXICAL EXCAPE by Isaac Asimov. .s . . . . . .
. . . . ASF Aug 45 79
PARALLEL IN TIME by Nelson S. Bond. .s. . . . . . .
. . . . TW Jun 40 72
PARASITE by Harl Vincent (Schoepflin). .nt . . . .
. . . . .Amz Jul 35 71
PARASITE PLANET by Neil R. Jones. .nt . . . .
. . . . .SSS Nov 49 104
PARASITE PLANET by Stanley G. Weinbaum. .nt . . . .
. . . . ASF Feb 35 50
PARDON MY IRON NERVES by Edmond Hamilton. . .
. .s . . . . SS Nov 50 78
PARDON MY MISTAKE by Fletcher Pratt. .ss . . . . . .
. . . . TW Dec 46 92

Title. .Author. .Length . . . . Magazine. .Date. .Page No.

PARIS GUN, THE by Willy Ley. .a . . . . . ASF Oct 42 50
PARKING, UNLIMITED by Noel Loomis. .s . . . .
. . . . .Fut May-Jun 50 70
PAROLE by Thomas Calvert McClary. .s . . . .
. . . . UK Jun 39 115
PARROTS OF VENUS by Walter Kubilius. .s . . . .
. . . . .SSS Nov 42 69
PASSAGE TO PLANET X by Henry Hasse. .s . . . . . .
. . . . .PS Win 45 70
PASSAGE TO SATURN by Jack Williamson. .s . . . . .
. . . . TW Jun 39 61
PASSAGE TO SHARANEE by Carol Grey ps (Robert
W. Lowndes). .s . . . . .Fut Apr 42 88
PASSEUR by Robert W. Chambers. .ss . . . .
. . . . FFM Apr 47 110
PASSING OF KU SUI by Anthony Gilmore ps (Harry
Bates & D. W. Hall). .nt . . . . ASF Nov 32 220
PASSING STAR, THE by Isaac R. Nathanson. .s . . . . . .
. . . . Amz Sep 30 506
PAST, PRESENT AND FUTURE by Nat Schachner . . .
. .nt . . . . ASF Sep 37 60
PATCH by William Shedenhelm. .s . . . . PS Fal 50 93
PATCHWORK QUILT series See DOROTHY QUICK
author
PATH, THE by Raymond Z. Gallun. .s . . . ASF Nov 36 38
PATH OF EMPIRE by Hugh Raymond ps (John
Michel). .s . . . . SFQ Sum 41 138
PATIENT, THE by E. M. Hull. .s . . . . . . UK Oct 43 121
PATRIOT NEVER DIES, A by Frank Patton h ps
(Raymond A. Palmer). .nt . . . . Amz Aug 43 12
PATRIOTISM PLUS by Ray Cummings. .s. . . . .
. . . . Fut Feb 43 91
PATROLMAN E–6 GETS HIS MAN by Benson
Herbert. .s . . . . Amz Dec 38 90
PATTERN FOR CONQUEST by George O. Smith. . . . .
. .n 3 pt . . . . ASF Mar 46 6
PATTERN FOR DESTINY by Chester Smith. .s . . . .
. . . . .Amz Jan 49 104
PAUL REVERE AND THE TIME MACHINE by A. W.
Bernal. .s . . . . Amz Mar 40 50
PAWN FOR A KING, A by Harry Jenkins, Jr. . .s . . . . .
. . . . Amz Feb 43 222
PAWNS OF CHAOS by Nelson S. Bond. .nt . . . .
. . . . TW Apr 43 15
PAYMENT IN FULL by Ray Bradbury. .ss . . . .
. . . . TW Feb 50 135
PE–RA, DAUGHTER OF THE SUN by Ralph Milne
Farley ps (Roger Sherman Hoar). .nt . . . .Amz Jul 39 44
PEA VINE MYSTERY, THE by A. L. Hodges. .ss . . . . .
. . . . Amz May 30 182
PEACE MISSION TO PLANETOID X by Dwight V.
Swain. .nt . . . . Amz Sep 42 150
PEACE WEAPONS by Abner J. Gelula. .s . . . .
. . . . Amz Jun 34 35
PEACEMAKER, THE by C. S. Forester. .n. . . . .
. . . . .FFM Feb 48 6

Title. .Author. .Length . . . . Magazine. .Date. .Page No.

PEACEMAKERS, THE by Mallory Kent ps (Robert W.
Lowndes). .ss . . . . .Fut Aug 42 98
PEARL-HANDLED POISON by Richard Casey h ps . . .
. .ss. . . . . FA Dec 43 68
PEBBLE IN THE SKY by Isaac Asimov. .n. . . . .
. . . . 2CSAB Win 50 2
PEBBLES OF DREAD by Gerald Evans. .s. . . . .
. . . . .TW Aug 40 51
PEGASUS by Henry Kuttner. .s. . . . .FFM May-Jun 40 78
PEGASUS PLAYS PRIORITIES by David Wright
O'Brien. .nt . . . . FA Dec 42 102
PELAGIC SPARK by Anthony Boucher ps (William
Anthony Parker White). .s. . . . . ASF Jun 43 32
PELLUCID HORROR, THE by B. F. Ruby. .s . . . .
. . . . Amz Aug 33 450
PELUCIDAR series See EDGAR RICE BURROUGHS
author
PENANCE CRUISE by David V. Reed ps (David
Vern). .nt. . . . . ASF Jul 42 46
PENAL WORLD by Thornton Ayre ps (John Russell
Fearn). .s. . . . . .ASF Oct 37 110
PENDULUM by Ray Bradbury & Henry Hasse. .s . . . . .
. . . . SSS Nov 41 102
PENT HOUSE, THE by David H. Keller, M. D. . .s . . . .
. . . . Amz Feb 32 989
PENTON & BLAKE series See John W. Campbell, Jr.
author
PENULTIMATE TRUMP, THE by R. C. W.
Ettinger. .s. . . . . .SS Mar 48 104
PEOPLE OF THE ARROW, THE by P. Schuyler
Miller. .s . . . . .Amz Jul 35 63
PEOPLE OF THE CRATER, THE by Andrew North . . .
. .nt . . . . FB #1 4
PEOPLE OF THE DEEP by Paul Hendred. .s . . . .
. . . . Fant #2 39 43
PEOPLE OF THE GOLDEN ATOM, THE by Ray
Cummings. .n. . . . . FN Sep 40 6
PEOPLE OF THE PIT, THE by A. Merritt. .s . . . .
. . . . Amz Mar 27 1130
                                        AA 27 98
                                   FN Jan 41 106
PEOPLE OF THE PYRAMIDS by P. F. Costello
h ps. .s. . . . . FA Dec 41 116
PEOPLE OF THE RUINS, THE by Edward Shanks . . . .
. .n . . . . FFM Jun 47 6
PEPPER POT PLANET by Duncan Farnsworth ps
(David Wright O'Brien). .s. . . . . Amz Jun 41 102
PERAMBULATING HOME, THE (HICK'S INVENTIONS
WITH A KICK). by Henry Hugh Simmons. .s . . . . . .
. . . . Amz Aug 28 450
PERCY THE PIRATE by Henry Kuttner. .s . . . .
. . . . .TW Sum 45 79
PERFECT COUNTERFEIT, THE by Captain S. P.
Meek. .s. . . . . .SD Jan 30 28
PERFECT CREATURE, THE by John Beynon
(Harris). .s . . . . ToW #1 37 116

Title. .Author. .Length . . . . Magazine. .Date. .Page No.

PERFECT HIDEOUT, THE by P. F. Costello h ps . . . . .
. .s . . . . FA Oct 41 104
PERFECT HUSBAND, THE by Dwight V. Swain . . . . .
. .s . . . . FA Jan 43 92
PERFECT IMITATION, THE by H. B. Hickey ps (Herb
Livingston). .s. . . . . Amz May 46 142
PERFECT INCINERATOR, THE by Arthur Lambert
(Widner) ps. .ss . . . . SFQ Win 42 139
PERFECT INVASION, THE by S. D. Gottesman ps
(Cyril Kornbluth). .s . . . . Sti Mar 42 4
PERFECT MACHINE, THE by A. Bertram
Chandler. .a . . . . .ASF Jan 45 107
PERFECT MURDER by H. L. Gold. .ss. . . . TW Mar 40 74
PERFECT PLANET, THE by Miles J. Breuer, M.D. . . .
. .s . . . . Amz May 32 136
PERFECT SERVANT by Walt Sheldon. .s . . SS Jul 48 115
PERFECT TRAP, THE by Miles Shelton ps (Don
Wilcox). .s . . . . Amz Apr 42 84
PERFECT WEAPON, THE by Poul Anderson. .s . . .
. . . . ASF Feb 50 46
PERFECT WORLD, THE by Benson Herbert . . . .
. .n 3 pt . . . . WS Oct 35 518
PERFECTIONIST PERDITION by John Wallace. .s. . . .
. . . . MSS Dec 39 96
PERFUME FOR A PRINCESS by Elroy Arno. .nt. . . . .
. . . . FA Dec 47 122
PERIL AMONG THE DRIVERS by Bob Olsen ps (Alfred
John Olsen, Jr.). .nt . . . . Amz Mar 34 36
PERIL FROM THE OUTLANDS by William Lawrence
Hamling. .s. . . . . Amz Jun 45 154
PERIL IN DRAGONIA by Mollie Claire. .nt. . . . .
. . . . FA Apr 49 114
PERIL OF THE BLUE WORLD by Robert Abernathy. .
. .s .PS Win 42 70
PERIL ON PHOEBUS by Nelson S. Bond. .s. . . . .
. . . . TW Fal 43 74
PERIL ORBIT by C. J. Wedlake. .s . . . . PS Sum 49 72
PERIOD PIECE by J. J. Coupling. .s . . . . . ASF Nov 48 71
PERISCOPE PREY by David Wright O'Brien. .s . . . . . .
. . . . Amz Apr 43 216
PERPETUAL MOTION MACHINES (FANTASTIC
INVENTIONS). .a . . . . .FA May 39 25
PERSECUTORS, THE by Cleve Cartmill. .nt . . . .
. . . . .SSS Feb 43 28
PERSEUS, SLAYER OF THE MEDUSA by Frank R.
Paul. .bacover . . . . FA Oct 42
PERSEUS HAD A HELMET by Richard Sale. .s . . . . .
. . . . .F&SF Fal 49 108
PERSIAN CARPET, THE by Dwight V. Swain. .n . . . .
. . . . Amz Feb 43 156
PERSON FROM PORLOCK, THE by Raymond F.
Jones. .nt. . . . . ASF Aug 47 96
PERSONALITY PLUS by Ray Cummings. .s . . . .
. . . . .Ash Oct 40 66
PERSONALS dept in OW from Nov 49
PERSONALS dept in Im from Oct 50

Title. .Author. .Length . . . . Magazine. .Date. .Page No.

PET NEBULA, THE by Alfred Bester. .s . . .Ash Feb 41 33
PETE CAN FIX IT by Raymond F. Jones. .nt . . . .
. . . . ASF Feb 47 64
PETER BACKS A PUNCH by C. A. Baldwin. .nt . . . . . .
. . . . .FA Jul 47 86
PETER FERENY'S DEATH CELL by William P.
McGivern. .s. . . . . FA Aug 41 124
PETER PETIGREW'S PRISONER by Nelson S. Bond . .
. .s .Amz Jul 42 76
PETTIGREW LIVES AGAIN by Don Tracy. .s . . . .
. . . . TW Aug 41 110
PHAETON (THE LEMURIAN DOCUMENTS No. 4) by
J. Lewis Burtt. .s. . . . . Amz Jun 32 222
PHAETON, SON OF APOLLO by Frank R. Paul. . . . .
. .bacover. . . . . FA Mar 43
PHAGOCYTES by A. H. Johnson. .s. . . Amz Feb 29 1018
PHALANXES OF ATLANS by F. V. W. Mason. . . . . .
. .n 2 pt. . . . . ASF Feb 31 228
PHALID'S FATE by Jack Vance. .s . . . . . TW Dec 46 74
PHANTOM ARMADA, THE by Stanton A.
Coblentz. .s . . . . FA May 42 192
PHANTOM CITY OF LUNA by P. F. Costello h ps . . . .
. .nt . . . . .Amz Jan 44 102
PHANTOM COMMANDO by Leroy Yerxa. .s. . . . . . .
. . . . FA Aug 43 142
PHANTOM DICTATOR, THE by Wallace West. . . . . .
. .s . . . . ASF Aug 35 123
PHANTOM ENEMY, THE by Morris J. Steele h ps
(Raymond A. Palmer). .s. . . . . Amz Feb 39 86
PHANTOM FROM NEPTUNE by Henry Andrew
Ackermann. .s. . . . . SSS Sep 40 121
PHANTOM FROM SPACE by John Russell Fearn. . . . .
. .s .SSS Mar 40 57
PHANTOM FROM THE FILM by Tarleton Fiske ps
(Robert Bloch). .s . . . . Amz Feb 43 208
PHANTOM HANDS, THE by Berkeley Livingston. . . . .
. .s . . . . Amz Feb 48 98
PHANTOM KILLER, THE by Morton Brotman . . . . . .
. .s . . . . AD Aug 30 724
PHANTOM MONSTERS by Joseph H. Kraus. .ss. . . . .
. . . . WS Apr 35 1305
PHANTOM OF GALON, THE by J. W. Ruff. .s. . . . . .
. . . . AW Dec 29 508
PHANTOM OF TERROR, THE by Ed Earl Repp. .s . . .
. . . . Amz Apr 33 60
PHANTOM OF THE FOREST by Lee Francis h ps . . . .
. .s . . . . Amz Nov 48 50
PHANTOM OF THE SEVEN STARS by Ray
Cummings. .nt . . . . .PS Win 40 74
PHANTOM OUT OF TIME by Nelson S. Bond. .nt . . . .
. . . . PS Fal 43 90
PHANTOM STAR by J. Harvey Haggard. .s . . . .
. . . . .ASF Oct 35 132
PHANTOM TELEVIEW, THE by Bob Olsen ps
(Alfred John Olsen, Jr.). .s . . . . SW Nov 29 486
SS Mar 40 92

PHANTOM TRANSPORT by Leroy Yerxa. .nt . . . . . .
. . . . Amz Feb 43 112
PHANTOMS OF REALITY by Ray Cummings. .nt . . . .
. . . . .ASF Jan 30 46
PHILOSOPHERS OF STONE by D. L. James. .s . . . . .
. . . . ASF Jun 38 62
PHILOSOPHY OF RELATIVE EXISTENCES, THE by
Frank R. Stockton. .s. . . . . .AFR #6 96
PHILTERED POWER by Malcolm Jameson. .s . . . . . .
. . . . UK Mar 40 63
PHOENIX NEST by John K. Aiken. .nt . . . . NW Spr 50 2
PHOENIX PLANET by James Blish. .nt . . . . Cos May 41 6
PHONY ATOMS by J. J. Coupling. .a . . . .
. . . . ASF May 46 105
PHONEY METEOR by John Beynon (Harris). .s . . . . .
. . . . Amz Mar 41 96
PHOTO CONTROL by Bernard Brown, B.Sc. . .s . . . .
. . . . Amz Aug 34 121
PHOTO FINISH by H. B. Hickey ps (Herb
Livingston). .s. . . . . FA Oct 47 118
PHRA THE PHOENICIAN by Edwin Lester Arnold. . . .
. .n .FFM Sep 45 8
PHYTIC EMPIRE, THE by Derald S. Walker. .s. . . . . .
. . . . Amz Jun 35 122
PI IN THE SKY by Fredric Brown. .s . . . . TW Win 45 46
PICTURE OF DEATH, THE by William P.
McGivern. .s. . . . . FA Nov 42 146
PIED PIPER by Lyle Monroe ps (Robert A.
Heinlein). .s . . . . .Ash Mar 42 54
PIED PIPER FIGHTS THE GESTAPO, THE by
Robert Bloch. .s . . . . FA Jun 42 108
PIED PIPER OF MARS by Frederic Arnold Kummer,
Jr. . .s. . . . . .PS Feb 42 80
PIED PIPER OF SPACE, THE by S. M. Tenneshaw
h ps. .s. . . . . Amz Jun 48 66
PIETY by Margaret St. Clair. .s . . . . TW Dec 47 85
PIEZOELECTRICITY by E. L. Locke. .a . . . .
. . . . ASF Apr 50 146
PIGEON SENSE by Raymond F. Jones. .a . . . .
. . . . ASF Mar 45 100
PIGGY BANK by Lewis Padgett ps (Henry Kuttner &
C. L. Moore). .nt . . . . ASF Dec 42 114
PIGMENTS IS PIGMENTS by Mortimer Weisinger. . . .
. .s . . . . WS Mar 35 1208
PILE OF TROUBLE by Henry Kuttner. .s . . . .
. . . . TW Apr 48 51
PILLAGE OF THE SPACE-MARINE by D. D.
Sharp. .s . . . . .CF Spr 43 78
PILLAR OF FIRE by Ray Bradbury. .nt . . . .
. . . . PS Sum 48 38
PILLARS OF DELIGHT by Stan Raycraft ps (Richard
S. Shaver). .nt . . . . Amz Dec 49 8
PILLOWS, THE by Margaret St. Clair. .s . . . .
. . . . TW Jun 50 133
PIN THE MEDALS ON POE by F. Anton Reeds. .s . . . .
. . . . .Ash Sep 41 61

Title. .Author. .Length . . . . Magazine. .Date. .Page No.

PINCH OF CULTURE, A by Bernard I. Kahn. .nt . . . . .
. . . . ASF Aug 50 78
PINEAL STIMULATOR, THE by I. M. Stephens &
Fletcher Pratt. .s . . . . Amz Nov 30 738
PING-TING by Charlton L. Edholm. .s . . . .
. . . . .ASF Oct 33 122
PINK HUMANS AREN'T REAL! by Edgar Polk. .s . . . .
. . . . FA Feb 49 84
PIONEER, THE by Arthur J. Burks. .s . . . .
. . . . Sti Jun 41 6
PIONEER—1957 by Henry Gade h ps (Raymond A.
Palmer). .s . . . . FA Nov 39 68
PIPELINE TO PLUTO by Murray Leinster ps (Will F.
Jenkins). .s . . . . ASF Aug 45 68
PIPER, THE by Ray Bradbury. .s . . . . TW Feb 43 89
PIPER'S SON, THE by Lewis Padgett ps (Henry
Kuttner & C. L. Moore). .nt . . . . ASF Feb 45 6
PIPES OF PAN, THE by Lester del Rey. .s . . . .
. . . . UK May 40 110
PIPING DEATH, THE by Robert Moore Williams . . . . .
. .s . . . . UK May 39 87
PIRACY PREFERRED by John W. Campbell, Jr.   . . . .
. .nt . . . . Amz Jun 30 228
PIRATE PLANET, THE by Charles Willard Diffin . . . . .
. .n 4 pt . . . . ASF Nov 30 168
PIRATES OF EROS by Frederic Arnold Kummer,
Jr. . .s . . . . Amz Nov 38 90
PIRATES OF SPACE by B. X. Barry. .nt . . . .
. . . . Amz Dec 31 798
PIRATES OF THE GORM by Nat Schachner. .s . . . . . .
. . . . ASF May 32 149
PIRATES OF THE TIME TRAIL by Ross
Rocklynne. .n . . . . SS Fal 43 15
PIT OF DEATH, THE by Don Wilcox. .s . . . .
. . . . Amz Jul 39 108
PIT OF DOOM, THE by David H. Keller. .s . Fut Feb 42 88
PITHECANTHROPUS ISLAND by I. R. Nathanson. . . .
. .s . . . . WQ Win 31 228
PITHECANTHROPUS REJECTUS by Manly W.
Wellman. .s . . . . .ASF Jan 38 68
PLACE IS FAMILIAR, THE by David Wright
O'Brien. .nt . . . . FA Feb 44 50
PLACE LIKE EDEN, A by H. B. Hickey ps (Herb
Livingston). .s . . . . FA Dec 48 116
PLACE OF MONSTERS, A by Thomas P. Byron. .s . . . .
. . . . FFM Mar 40 113
PLACET IS A CRASY PLACE by Fredric Brown . . . . .
. .s . . . . ASF May 46 118
PLAGIARIST by Peter Phillips. .s . . . . . . NW Sum 50 54
PLAGUE by Rene Lafayette ps (L. Ron Hubbard). . . . .
. .nt . . . . ASF Apr 49 6
PLAGUE by Murray Leinster ps (Will F. Jenkins) . . . . .
. .nt . . . . ASF Feb 44 52
PLAGUE FROM TOMORROW, THE by Frank
Belknap Long. .s . . . . Ash Sep 41 75

Title. .Author. .Length . . . . Magazine. .Date. .Page No.

PLAGUE OF THE LIVING DEAD, THE by A. Hyatt
Verrill. .s . . . . .Amz Apr 27 6
PLAID PTERODACTYL, THE by Geoff St. Reynard
ps (Robert W. Krepps). .s . . . . FA Mar 49 106
PLAN FOR A UNIVERSE by R. D. Swisher. .a . . . . . .
. . . . ASF Apr 46 120
PLANE COMPASS, THE by Harl Vincent
(Schoepflin). .s . . . . ASF Jun 35 42
PLANE PEOPLE by Wallace West. .nt . . . . ASF Nov 33 74
PLANET ALONE by Walter Kubilius. .s . . . .
. . . . .Fut Feb 43 49
PLANET CALLED AQUELLA, THE by Martin Pearson
ps (Donald A. Wollheim). .s . . . . .SSS Nov 42 115
(under title: AQUELLA by Donald A. Wollheim) . . .
. . . . .AFR #7 80
PLANET ENTITY, THE by E. M. Johnston & Clark
Ashton Smith. .s . . . . WQ Fal 31 110
PLANET FOR YOUR THOUGHTS, A by James Norman
. .s .PS Win 41 44
PLANET IN REVERSE by Henry Guth. .s . . . .
. . . . .PS Spr 48 59
PLANET JUGGLER, THE by J. George Frederick. . . . .
. .nt . . . . FFM Mar 40 42
PLANET LEAVE by Clifton B. Kruse. .s . . . .
. . . . .Cos Mar 41 77
PLANET MAKERS, THE by L. Ron Hubbard. .s . . . . .
. . . . TW Oct 49 123
PLANET OF BLACK TERROR by Ed Earl Repp . . . . .
. .nt . . . . Amz Jun 40 110
PLANET OF CHANGE, THE by Manly Wade
Wellman. .s . . . . TW Mar 40 56
PLANET OF CREATION by Chester S. Geier. .s . . . . . .
. . . . .PS Spr 47 52
PLANET OF DESPAIR, THE by R. F. Starzl. .s . . . . . .
. . . . .WS Jul 31 190
PLANET OF DOOMED MEN by Robert Moore
Williams. .nt . . . . .Amz Jan 42 100
PLANET OF DOUBT, THE by Stanley G. Weinbaum. . .
. .nt . . . . .ASF Oct 35 106
PLANET OF DREAD, THE by R. F. Starzl. .s . . . .
. . . . ASF Aug 3Q 147
PLANET OF ERRORS, THE by Milton Kaletsky . . . . .
. .ss . . . . Amz Dec 40 70
PLANET OF ETERNAL NIGHT by John W.
Campbell, Jr. . .nt . . . . TW Oct 39 95
PLANET OF GHOSTS by David V. Reed ps (David
Vern). .n . . . . Amz Mar 42 124
PLANET OF ILLUSION, THE by Millard V. Gordon
ps (Donald A. Wollheim). .ss . . . . Com Mar 41 119
PLANET OF LOST MEN by P. F. Costello h ps. .s . . . .
. . . . Amz Dec 41 110
PLANET OF LOVE, THE by Jep Powell. .s . . . .
. . . . Amz Mar 42 212
PLANET OF NO-RETURN by Wilbur S. Peacock . . . . .
. .s .PS Win 42 28

Title. .Author. .Length . . . . Magazine. .Date. .Page No.

PLANET OF PERPETUAL NIGHT, THE by John
    Edwards. .nt . . . . Amz Feb 37 15
PLANET OF SAND by Murray Leinster *ps (Will F.
    Jenkins)*. .nt . . . . FFM Feb 48 90
PLANET OF THE BLACK DUST by Jack Vance. .s . . . .
    . . . . SS Sum 46 70
PLANET OF THE DEAD by Rog Phillips *ps (Roger P.
    Graham)*. .nt . . . . FA Oct 49 36
PLANET OF THE DEAD, THE by Clark Ashton
    Smith. .s . . . . AFR #4 101
PLANET OF THE DOUBLE SUN, THE by Neil R.
    Jones. .s . . . . Amz Feb 32 1020
PLANET OF THE DUPLICATES by William Lawrence
    Hamling. .s . . . . Amz Dec 45 62
PLANET OF THE GODS by Robert Moore
    Williams. .nt . . . . Amz Dec 42 150
PLANET OF THE KNOB HEADS by Stanton A.
    Coblentz. .nt . . . . SF Dec 39 10
PLANET OF THE SMALL MEN by Murray Leinster
    ps (Will F. Jenkins). .nt . . . . TW Apr 50 11
PLANET OF YOUTH, THE by Stanton A.
    Coblentz. .s . . . . WS Oct 32 390
                                            ToW Win 38 4
PLANET PASSAGE by Martin Pearson *ps (Donald A.
    Wollheim)*. .ss . . . . Fut Oct 42 39
PLANET SMASHERS, THE by Ray Cummings. .nt . . . .
    . . . . OTWA Jul 50 6
PLANET THAT TIME FORGOT, THE by Donald A.
    Wollheim. .s . . . . PS Fal 40 70
PLANET WRECKER, THE by Coutts Brisbane. .s . . . . .
    . . . . ToW Win 39 39
PLANETOID OF DOOM, THE by Morrison
    Colladay. .s . . . . WS Dec 32 574
PLANETOID OF PERIL, THE by Paul Ernst. .s . . . . . .
    . . . . ASF Nov 31 151
PLANET'S AIR MASTER, THE by Edward E.
    Chappelow. .s . . . . AW Aug 29 160
PLANETS IN PERIL by Edmond Hamilton. .n . . . . . .
    . . . . .CF Fal 42 13
PLANT MAN, THE by Arthur G. Stangland. .nt . . . . .
    . . . . TW Spr 45 41
PLANTS, THE by Murray Leinster *ps (Will F.
    Jenkins)*. .s . . . . .ASF Jan 46 138
PLANTS MUST GROW by Frank Belknap Long . . . . . .
    . .s . . . . TW Oct 41 64
PLANTS MUST SLAY by Frank Belknap Long. . . . . . .
    . .s . . . . TW Apr 42 55
PLASTIC AIRSHIP OF EUROPA by James B.
    Settles. .bac . . . . Amz Sep 42
PLASTIC GENIE, THE by Arthur T. Harris . . . .
    . .s . . . . TW Apr 42 101
PLASTIC PIGSKIN DAZE by William Morrison
    ps (Joseph Samachson). .s . . . . TW Mar 41 83
PLATINUM by Owen Oliver. .s . . . . FN Sep 49 114
"PLATINUM PLANETS", THE by George B.
    Beattie. .s . . . . WS Aug 32 246

Title. .Author. .Length . . . . Magazine. .Date. .Page No.

PLATTNER STORY, THE by H. G. Wells. .s . . . .
    . . . . .Amz Jul 27 355
PLAYERS OF A, THE by A. E. van Vogt . . . .
    . .n 4 pt . . . . ASF Oct 48 7
PLEASURE AGE, THE by Joed Cahill. .s . . . .
    . . . . TW Feb 47 58
PLEASURE TROVE by P. Schuyler Miller. .nt . . . . . .
    . . . . ASF Aug 39 139
PLOT OF GOLD by Gerald Vance *h ps*. .s . . . .
    . . . . FA Nov 42 220
PLOTTERS, THE by Alexander Blade *h ps*. .s . . . .
    . . . . Amz Dec 48 30
PLUNGE OF THE KNUPFEN, THE by Leonard
    Grover. .s . . . . FFM Feb 40 116
PLURALITY OF WORLDS, THE by Willy Ley . . . .
    . .a . . . . ASF Feb 44 112
PLUTONIAN DRUG, THE by Clark Ashton Smith . . . .
    . .s . . . . Amz Sep 34 41
POBBY by Jane Rice. .nt . . . . UK Apr 42 110
POCKET UNIVERSES by Murray Leinster *ps (Will F.
    Jenkins)*. .s . . . . TW Fal 46 70
POETRY MACHINE, THE by H. Nearing, Jr. . .s . . . . .
    . . . . .F&SF Fal 50 53
POGO PLANET by Martin Pearson *ps (Donald A.
    Wollheim)*. .s . . . . Fut Oct 41 82
POINT OF VIEW, THE by Stanley G. Weinbaum. .s . . . .
    . . . . .WS Jan 36 806
                                            SS Spr 44 88
POISON REALM, THE by John Coleridge *ps (Earl
    Binder & Otto Binder)*. .s . . . . Fut Jul 40 83
POISONED AIR by Capt. S. P. Meek. .s . . . .
    . . . . ASF Mar 32 295
POKER FACE by Theodore Sturgeon. .s . . . .
    . . . . ASF Mar 41 75
POLAR DOOM by John Coleridge *ps (Earl Binder &
    Otto Binder)*. .s . . . . SFQ Sum 40 121
POLAR PRISON by Morris J. Steele *h ps (Raymond A.
    Palmer)*. .s . . . . Amz Dec 38 126
POLARIS AND THE GODDESS GLORIAN by Charles
    B. Stilson. .n . . . . FN Sep 50 10
POLARIS—OF THE SNOWS by Charles B. Stilson. . . . .
    . .n . . . . FFM Jul 42 6
POLICE CHECKMATE NEW MOVE OF SCIENTIFIC
    CRIMINALS by Ashur Van Dusen. .a . . .AD Jul 30 625
POLICE OPERATION by H. Beam Piper. .nt . . . .
    . . . . .ASF Jul 48 8
POLITICS by Murray Leinster *ps (Will F. Jenkins)*. . . . .
    . .s . . . . Amz Jun 32 268
POLLOCK AND THE PORROH MAN by H. G.
    Wells. .s . . . . Amz Feb 28 1072
PONAPE—THE REAL MOON POOL by Ben
    Nelson. .a . . . . .FN Jan 48 116
POOL OF DEATH, THE by Bob Olsen *ps (Alfred John
    Olsen, Jr.)*. .nt . . . . .Amz Jan 33 890
POOL OF INFINITY by W. Moore. .s . . . .
    . . . . .NW #5 49 93

Title. .Author. .Length . . . . Magazine. .Date. .Page No.

POOL OF LIFE, THE by P. Schuyler Miller. .nt . . . . . .
. . . . Amz Oct 34 12
POP GUN by Francis Wilson Powell. .s . . . Amz Aug 43 40
PORT OF MISSING PLANES, THE by Captain S. P.
Meek. .s. . . . . ASF Aug 31 255
PORTAL IN THE PICTURE, THE by Henry Kuttner. . .
. .s . . . . .SS Sep 49 9
PORTRAIT by Ray Cummings. .s. . . . . . UK Sep 39 121
PORTRAIT OF A VOICE by J. J. Coupling. .a . . . .
. . . . ASF Jul 46 101
PORTRAIT OF NARCISSUS by Raymond F. Jones . . .
. .s . . . . .OW May 50 56
POSI & NEGA series See JOSEPH WILLIAM SKIDMORE
author
POSITION LINE by A. Bertram Chandler. .s . . . .
. . . . .NW #4 49 73
POSITIVE INERTIA by Arthur Purcell. .s . . . .
. . . . ASF Oct 36 43
POSTERITY FUND, THE by Raymond Emery
Lawrence. .s. . . . . Amz May 29 162
POSTMAN OF OTFORD, THE by Lord Dunsany . . . . .
. .ss . . . . FFM Sep 44 108
POSTPAID TO PARADISE by Robert Arthur. .s. . . . . .
. . . . .F&SF Win-Spr 50 61
POSTWAR PLAN FOR MARS by R. S. Richardson. . . .
. .a . . . . .ASF Jan 44 101
POTTERS OF FIRSK, THE by Jack Vance. .s . . . .
. . . . ASF May 50 88
POWER, THE by Murray Leinster ps (Will F.
Jenkins). .s. . . . . ASF Sep 45 83
POWER by Hugh Raymond ps (John Michel). .s . . . . .
. . . . .Cos May 41 37
POWER by Harl Vincent (Schoepflin). .nt . . . .
. . . . .Amz Jan 32 872
POWER AND THE GLORY, THE by Charles W.
Diffin. .s . . . . ASF Jul 30 104
AFR #13 57
POWER AND THE GLORY, THE by Henry
Kuttner. .nt . . . . TW Dec 47 13
POWER AND THE PEOPLE, THE by Arthur R.
Tofte. .s. . . . . .Fut Nov 40 61
POWER FOR DARM by Basil Wells. .s . . . . . . FB #6 89
POWER FOR ZENOVIA by Willard E. Hawkins. .nt . . .
. . . . TW Jun 41 14
POWER PLANET, THE by Murray Leinster ps (Will F.
Jenkins). .nt. . . . . Amz Jun 31 199
AFR #1 7
POWER PLANT by Lee Gregor ps (Milton A.
Rothman). .s . . . . .SFQ Win 41–42 71
POWER PLANT by Harl Vincent (Schoepflin) . . . .
. .nt . . . . ASF Nov 39 129
POWER PLANTS OF TOMORROW
HARNESSING THE SUN'S RAYS by Willy Ley . . . .
. .a . . . . .ASF Jan 38 63
HARNESSING EARTH'S HEAT by Willy Ley . . . .
. .a . . . . ASF Feb 38 123

Title. .Author. .Length . . . . Magazine. .Date. .Page No.

PUTTING THE MOON ON THE JOB by Willy
Ley. .a. . . . . ASF Mar 38 108
POWER RAY, THE by Jack Barnette. .s . . . .
. . . . SD Mar 30 208
POWER SATELLITE, THE by R. F. Starzl. .s. . . . . . .
. . . . WS Jun 32 60
POWER SUPREME, THE by Geo C. Wallis. .s. . . . . . .
. . . . ToW Win 41 42
POWERFUL ONES, THE by Hugh Raymond ps (John
Michel). .s . . . . Fut Oct 42 31
POWERFUL PIPSQUEAK, THE by Ross
Rocklynne. .s . . . . Amz Sep 43 158
POWERS OF DARKNESS, THE by Dwight V.
Swain. .s . . . . .Amz Jul 42 58
PRANKSTERS, THE by Rog Phillips ps (Roger P.
Graham). .s . . . . Amz Feb 50 134
PRE-VISION by John Pierce, M.S. . .s . . ASF Mar 36 105
PRECOGNITION by Mack Reynolds. .s. . . . .
. . . . TW Jun 50 120
PREDICTION—PAST TENSE by R. S. Richardson . . . .
. .a .ASF Jun 45 100
PREFABRICATION by E. R. James. .s . . . Fant Apr 47 46
PRELUDE TO ARMAGEDDON by Cleve Cartmill . . . .
. .n .UK Apr 42 8
PRELUDE TO ENGINEERING by Willy Ley. .a . . . . . .
. . . . ASF Aug 41 110
PRENATAL PLAGIARISM, THE by Mortimer
Weisinger. .ss . . . . .WS Jan 35 932
PRESCIENCE by Nelson S. Bond. .s. . . . . . UK Oct 41 76
PRESENT FROM JOE, A by Eric Frank Russell. .s . . . .
. . . . ASF Feb 49 50
PRESENTING THE AUTHOR biog dept in Amz irregular
PRESIDENT'S DAUGHTER, THE by Anton
Kermac. .s . . . . FanF May 50 67
PRESSURE by Ross Rocklynne. .s. . . . . . ASF Jun 39 65
PREVIEW OF PERIL by A. Bertram Chandler. .s . . . .
. . . . PS Fal 48 67
PREY OF THE SPACE FALCON by Wilbur S.
Peacock. .nt . . . . PS Fal 43 2
PRICE OF ESCAPE, THE by Henry J. Kostkos. .s. . . .
. . . . .SF Jun 40 88
PRICE OF PEACE, THE by Mortimer Weisinger. .s . . . .
. . . . Amz Nov 33 115
PRIDE by Malcolm Jameson. .s . . . . ASF Sep 42 92
PRIEST OF QUICHE, A by Francis James. .s . . . .
. . . . .FN May 50 88
PRIESTESS OF PAKMARI by Albert de Pina. .s. . . . .
. . . . .TW Sum 44 64
PRIESTESS OF THE FLAME by Sewell Peaslee
Wright. .s. . . . . .ASF Jun 32 401
PRIESTESS OF THE FLOATING SKULL by Edwin
Benson. .n 2 pt . . . . Amz May 43 182
PRIESTESS OF THE MOON by Ray Cummings . . . . . .
. .nt . . . . Amz Dec 40 42
PRIESTESS OF THE SLEEPING DEATH by Neil R.
Jones. .s. . . . . Amz Apr 41 88

Title. .Author. .Length . . . . Magazine. .Date. .Page No.

PRIESTESS WHO REBELLED, THE by Nelson S.
Bond. .s. . . . . Amz Oct 39 88
PRIMA DONNA 1980 by Bernard Brown. .s. . . . .
. . . . Amz Oct 31 614
PRIMAL CITY, THE by Clark Ashton Smith .s . . . . . .
. . . . Com Dec 40 102
PRINCE DERU RETURNS by Harl Vincent
(Schoepflin). .nt . . . . Amz Dec 38 70
PRINCE OF LIARS, THE by L. Taylor Hansen. . . . . .
. .s . . . . Amz Oct 30 582
PRINCE OF MARS RETURNS, THE by Phil Nowlan . .
. .n 2 pt . . . . FA Feb 40 28
PRINCE OF PLUTO, A by Paul Dennis Lavond h ps
(Cyril Kornbluth & Frederik Pohl). .s . . . .
. . . . Fut Apr 41 85
PRINCE OF SPACE, THE by Jack Williamson . . . . . .
. .nt .Amz Jan 31 870
PRINCESS AND HER PIG, THE by Richard S.
Shaver. .s. . . . . FA Mar 47 158
PRINCESS OF ARELLI, THE by Aladra Septama. . . . .
. .nt .AQ Sum 30 402
PRINCESS OF CHAOS by Bryce Walton. .s . . . .
. . . . PS Spr 74 102
PRINCESS OF DETROIT, THE by Bob Tucker ps
(Arthur Wilson Tucker). .s. . . . . Fut Jun 42 42
PRINCESS OF PALLIS, A by Clifton B. Kruse . . . . . .
. .s . . . . ASF Oct 35 95
PRINCESS OF POWER by Frederic Arnold Kummer,
Jr. . .s. MSS May 40 72
PRINCESS OF THE SEA by Don Wilcox. .n. . . . .
. . . . FA Jan 47 8
PRISMS OF SPACE by Robert H. Leitfried. .s . . . . . .
. . . . ASF Nov 33 27
PRISON BRIGHT, PRISON DEEP by Frank Belknap
Long. .s. . . . . ASF Aug 50 108
PRISON IN SPACE by Henry Norton. .s . . . .
. . . . Amz Aug 43 58
PRISON OF TIME by Eando Binder ps (Otto
Binder). .n . . . . DS Apr-May 39 12
PRISON PLANET by Bob Tucker ps (Arthur Wilson
Tucker). .s. . . . . PS Fal 42 69
PRISON RATS by Gene Ellerman ps (Basil Wells) . . . . .
. .ss. . . . . FB #4 39
PRISONER IN THE SKULL, THE by Lewis Padgett
ps (Henry Kuttner & C. L. Moore). .nt . . . .
. . . . ASF Feb 49 100
PRISONER IN TIME by V. E. Thiessen. .s . . . .
. . . . FFM Apr 47 114
PRISONER OF MARS, THE by Edmond
Hamilton. .n. . . . . SS May 39 14
PRISONER OF THE BRAIN-MISTRESS by Bryce
Walton. .s. . . . . PS Sum 46 82
PRISONER OF TIME by Polton Cross ps (John
Russell Fearn). .nt . . . . SSS May 42 10
PRISONER'S BASE by Nelson S. Bond. .s. . . . .
. . . . .TW May 40 14

PRISONERS IN FLATLAND by Frank Belknap
Long. .s . . . . .SS Sep 41 89
PRISONERS ON THE ELECTRON by Robert H.
Leitfried. .s . . . . ASF Oct 30 75
PRIVATE BANK PUZZLE, THE by Edwin Balmer &
William B. MacHarg. .s . . . . .AD Jul 30 608
PRIVATE BROWN'S BLITZKRIEG by Frank
Johnson. .s. . . . . .TW Aug 42 99
PRIVATE ENTERPRISE by Edwin James ps (James
E. Gunn). .s . . . . ASF Jul 50 63
PRIVATE EYE by Lewis Padgett ps (Henry Kuttner &
C. L. Moore). .nt . . . . ASF Jan 49 7
PRIVATE—KEEP OUT! by Philip MacDonald. .s. . . . .
. . . . .F&SF Fal 49 32
PRIVATE PRUNE SPEAKING by Cpl. David Wright
O'Brien. .nt . . . . Amz Sep 44 62
PROBABILITY ZERO! dept of short-short tall tales
SOME CURIOUS EFFECTS OF TIME TRAVEL by
L. Sprague de Camp
PIG TRAP by Malcolm Jameson
TIME PUSSY by George E. Dale ps (Isaac Asimov) . .
. . . . ASF Apr 42 111
THE STRANGE CASE OF THE MISSING HERO by
Frank Holby
THAT MYSTERIOUS BOMB RAID by Bob Tucker
ps (A. W. Tucker)
ABOUT QUARRELS, ABOUT THE PAST by
John Pierce
THE QUERTY OF HROTHGAR by R. Creighton
Buck
EAT, DRINK AND BE WARY by Ray Bradbury
THE FLOATER by Selden G. Thomas
DE GUSTIBUS by Randall Hale. . . . . . ASF Jul 42 109
TIME MARCHES ON by Ted Carnell
THE IMAGE OF ANNIHILATION by Jack Speer
DESTINY AND UNCLE LOUIE by Joseph Gilbert
THE ANECDOTE OF THE NEGATIVE WUGUG by
L. Sprague de Camp. . . . . ASF Aug 42 99
AVENUE OF ESCAPE by Hal Clement ps (Harry
Clement Stubbs)
EUREKA! by Malcolm Jameson
THE SLEEP THAT SLAUGHTERED by Harry
Warner, Jr.
THE GREEN SPHERE by Dennis Tucker
A MATTER OF ECLIPSES by P. Schuyler Miller . . .
. . . . ASF Nov 42 126
TRUE FIDELITY by William M. Danner
THE HUMAN BOMB by Stanley Woolston
VALADUSIA by Jack Bivins
O'RYAN, THE INVINCIBLE by T. D.
Whitenack, Jr.
MY WORD by Frank J. Smythe
TAKE–OFF by L. M. Jensen. . . . . . . ASF Dec 42 104
BLUE ICE by Henry Kuttner
EFFICIENCY by Colin Keith ps (Malcolm Jameson)
NOISE IS BEAUTIFUL by Fox B. Holden

Title. .Author. .Length . . . . Magazine. .Date. .Page No.

Title. .Author. .Length . . . . Magazine. .Date. .Page No.

PROBABILITY ZERO! (continued)
THE ANECDOTE OF THE MOVABLE EARS by
L. Sprague de Camp . . . . ASF Feb 43 88
CORPUS DELICTI by Henry Kuttner
MIRACULOUS FLUID by Bob Tucker *ps (Arthur Wilson Tucker)*
DOWNFALL by Malcolm Jameson
CAMOUFLAGE by John K. Aiken
ULTIMATE OPPOSITION by Roscoe E. Wright
A SNITCH IN TIME by D. C. King
DOUBLE, DOUBLE, TOIL AND TROUBLE by
Nelson S. Bond . . . . ASF Apr 43 85
DER FUEHRER'S BASE by George O. Smith
YOU SAID IT by Charles Ben Davis
FINANCE by David Charles
Y = Sin X by Harold Wooster
UNIVERSAL SOLVENT by Clayton James MacBeth
AND WATCH THE FOUNTAINS by Ray
Bradbury . . . . ASF Sep 43 99
SOURDOUGH by George Holman
LIGHT TRAP by Jerry Shelton
PICTURE FROM TOKYO by H. O. Hoadley
VACUUMULATOR, THE by Malcolm Jameson
CASH ON THE DIMENSION by Ray Karden . . . . . .
. . . . ASF Jan 44 163
CONTAGION by George Holman
THE ABSENCE OF HEAT by Gordon Garrett
SECRET WEAPON by Robert Browning . . . .
. . . . ASF Jun 44 130
ICICLE BUILT FOR GROO by John H. Pomeroy
A MATTER OF RELATIVITY by P. Anderson
THE THIRTY-FIRST OF JUNE by Frank Holby
THE CASE OF THE INVINCIBLE PIRATE by Edward
Shulman . . . . ASF Sep 44 87
AGRICULTURAL GEOLOGY by George Holman
THAT'S A LOT OF HOT AIR by Francis William
Powell
APPLESAUCE by George W. Hall. . . . ASF Dec 44 128
PROBABLE MAN, THE by Alfred Bester. .nt . . . .
. . . . ASF Jul 41 75
PROBATE by Margaret St. Clair. .ss . . . . . TW Oct 47 80
PROBLEM IN ASTROGATION, A by Matt Lee *ps (Sam Merwin, Jr.)*. .ss. . . . . TW Apr 48 99
PROBLEM IN COMMUNICATION, A by Miles J. Breuer,
M.D. . .s .ASF Sep 30 293
PROBLEM IN DIATONICS, A by Nelson S. Bond. .s . . .
. . . . TW Aug 40 30
PROBLEM IN EIGHT DIMENSIONS. .a . . ASF Aug 44 99
PROBLEM IN ETHICS by Henry Kuttner. .s . . . .
. . . . SF Jul 43 58
PROBLEM IN LUMBERING by William Lawrence
Hamling. .s. . . . . FA Dec 45 140
PROBLEM IN MURDER by H. L. Gold. .nt . . . .
. . . . ASF Mar 39 119
PROBLEM IN SOLID by George O. Smith. .nt . . . . . .
. . . . ASF Oct 47 39

PROBLEM ON MARS by Duncan Farnsworth *ps (David Wright O'Brien)*. .s . . . . FA Aug 41 64
PROBLEMS OF SCIENCE
THE ENIGMA OF RIFTING by L. Taylor Hansen. . .
. .a . . . . Amz Mar 48 154
THE ENIGMA OF COMPRESSION by L. Taylor
Hansen. .a . . . . Amz Apr 48 161
PROBLEMS OF SPACE FLYING, THE by Capt.
Hermann Noordung, A.D., M.E. *(tr fr German by Francis M. Currier)*. .a. . . . . SW Jul 29 170
PROCESS by A. E. van Vogt. .s . . . . . . F&SF Dec 50 46
PROCESSION OF SUNS by R. R. Winterbotham . . . . .
. .s . . . . ASF May 38 63
PRODIGAL WEAPON by Vaseleos Garson. .s . . . .
. . . . PS Sum 45 30
PRODIGY by Theodore Sturgeon. .s . . . . . ASF Apr 49 71
PRODUCTION TEST by Raymond F. Jones. .s . . . .
. . . . ASF Oct 49 39
PROFESSOR CYCLONE by Alexander Blade *h ps* . . . .
. .nt . . . . FA Dec 43 72
PROFESSOR DIEL'S RAY by Frank J. Brueckel,
Jr. . .s . . . . SW Mar 30 926
PROFESSOR POWNALL'S OVERSIGHT by H. R.
Wakefield. .s . . . . F&SF Sum 50 111
PROFESSOR SPLITS, THE by J. Harvey Haggard. . . . .
. .s . . . . .Ash Feb 41 6
PROFESSOR THORNDYKE'S MISTAKE by Sgt. P. F.
Costello *h ps*. .s . . . . Amz Sep 44 82
PROFESSOR WAS A THIEF, THE by L. Ron
Hubbard. .nt . . . . ASF Feb 40 130
PROFESSOR'S HOBBY, THE by Robert Arthur. .s. . . .
. . . . UK Feb 41 140
PROGRESS REPORT by John H. Pomeroy. .a . . . .
. . . . ASF Sep 49 31
PROJECT by Jack Hess. .s . . . . Amz Oct 49 116
PROJECT by Lewis Padgett *ps (Henry Kuttner & C. L. Moore)*. .s . . . . ASF Apr 47 74
PROJECT SPACESHIP by A. E. van Vogt. .s . . . .
. . . . TW Aug 49 96
PROKTOLS OF NEPTUNE by Henry Hasse. .nt . . . . . .
. . . . PS Sum 41 104
PROMETHEUS by Arthur K. Barnes. .s . . . .
. . . . Amz Feb 37 58
PROMETHEUS *(THE LEMURIAN DOCUMENTS No. 6)*
by J. Lewis Burtt. .s . . . . Amz Sep 32 524
PROMETHEUS by Frank R. Paul. .bacover pic . . . . . .
. . . . FA Nov 42
PROMETHEUS' DAUGHTER by Alexander Blade *h ps* .
. .nt . . . . .Amz Nov 49 8
PROMETHEUS II by S. J. Byrne. .n . . . . . . Amz Feb 48 8
PROMINENCES by R. S. Richardson. .a . . . .
. . . . ASF Oct 45 99
PROMISED LAND by Lawrence O'Donnell *ps (C. L. Moore)*. .nt . . . . ASF Feb 50 137
PROMOTION TO SATELLITE by Ray Bradbury . . . . .
. .s . . . . TW Fal 43 68

Title. .Author. .Length . . . . Magazine. .Date. .Page No.

PROOF by Hal Clement *ps (Harry Clement Stubbs)*. . . .
. .s . . . . .ASF Jun 42 101
PROOF OF THE SHAVER MYSTERY, THE by The
Editor. .a . . . . .Amz May 48 7
PROOFS by Richard S. Shaver. .a . . . . . Amz Jun 47 136
PROP, THE by William Lawrence Hamling. .s . . . .
. . . . Amz Aug 47 44
PROPAGANDIST by Murray Leinster *ps (Will F.
Jenkins)*. .s . . . . ASF Aug 47 139
PROPHECIES OF GIZEH, THE by Joseph T.
Millard. .a . . . . Amz Apr 41 128
PROPHECY by Poul Anderson. .s . . . .
. . . . ASF May 49 52
PROPHECY OF DOOM by Ross Rocklynne. .s . . . .
. . . . Fut Jul 40 43
PROPHETIC VOICE, THE by Laurence Manning . . . . .
. .s . . . . WS Apr 35 1330
PROPHETS OF SCIENCE by Otis Adelbert Kline . . . . .
. .guest editorial . . . . .SS Jan 39 15
PROSPECTORS OF SPACE by Malcolm Jameson . . . . .
. .s . . . . TW Sep 40 43
PROTEUS ISLAND by Stanley G. Weinbaum. .nt . . . . .
. . . . ASF Aug 36 96
PROTOPLASMIC STATION by Paul Ernst. .nt . . . . . .
. . . . TW Feb 37 14
PROUD ROBOT, THE by Lewis Padgett *ps (Henry
Kuttner & C. L. Moore)*. .nt . . . . ASF Oct 43 95
PROWLER OF THE WASTELANDS by Harl
Vincent *(Schoepflin)*. .s . . . . ASF Apr 35 72
PROXIES ON VENUS by Nelson S. Bond. .s . . . .
. . . . .SF Jun 40 41
PROXIMA CENTAURI by Murray Leinster *ps (Will F.
F. Jenkins)*. .nt . . . . ASF Mar 35 10
PROXY PLANETEERS by Edmond Hamilton . . . .
. .s . . . . SS Jul 47 88
PRR–R–EET, THE by Eric Frank Russell. .s . . . .
. . . . ToW #1 37 76
PRUNING MAN, THE by Robert Moore
Williams. .s . . . . FA Oct 48 136
PS'S FEATURE FLASH biog dept of PS irregular
PSALMANAZAR, GEORGE *(FANTASTIC HOAXES)* by
Willy Ley. .a . . . . FA Apr 40 40
PSEUDOSCIENCE IN NAZILAND by Willy Ley. .a . . . .
. . . . ASF May 47 90
PSYCHE STEPS OUT by Gerald Vance *h ps*. .nt . . . . .
. . . . Amz May 50 138
PSYCHO POWER CONQUEST, THE by R. R.
Winterbotham. .s . . . . ASF Feb 36 140
PSYCHOLOGICAL REGULATOR, THE by Arthur
Cooke *ps (E. Balter, Cyril Kornbluth, Robert W.
Lowndes, John Michel & Donald A. Wollheim)* . . . . .
. .nt . . . . Com Mar 41 40
PSYCHOLOGICAL SOLUTION, THE by A. Hyatt
Verrill. .s . . . . .Amz Jan 28 946
PSYCHOLOGY OF ANGER, THE by Charles D.
Hornig. .a . . . . SF Aug 39 57

PSYCHOMORPH, THE by E. A. Grosser. .s . . . .
. . . . UK Feb 40 89
UK 48 112
PSYCHOPATHIC MARTIANS, THE by Allan Ingvald
Benson. .ss . . . . .SSS Aug 41 105
PSYCHOPHONIC NURSE, THE by David H. Keller,
M.D. . .s . . . . Amz Nov 28 710
PSYCH'S WAR by O. W. Hopkinson, Jr. . .nt . . . .
. . . . ASF Apr 47 63
PUFF-BALL MENACE, THE by John Beynon
(Harris). .s . . . . .ToW Sum 38 51
PULSATING PLANET, THE by John Broome. .nt . . . .
. . . . FA Sep 41 114
PUMPKIN EATER by Carlton Smith. .s . . . . PS Sum 46 36
PUNCHING PILLOWS by Cleve Cartmill. .s . . . .
. . . . ASF Jun 50 33
PUNISHMENT WITHOUT CRIME by Ray Bradbury . . .
. .s . . . . .OW Mar 50 6
PURCHASE OF THE NORTH POLE, THE by Jules
Verne. .n 2 pt . . . . Amz Sep 26 510
PURGE OF THE DEAF by A. R. Tofte & L. A.
Schmidt. .s . . . . Amz Dec 38 56
PURPLE BAT, THE by Richard Wilson. .s . . . .
. . . . TW Oct 41 108
PURPLE BRAIN, THE by Hal K. Wells. .s . . . .
. . . . ASF Dec 33 57
PURPLE CLOUD, THE by M. P. Shiel. .n . . . .
. . . . FFM Jun 49 10
PURPLE CONSPIRACY, THE by Stanton A.
Coblentz. .s . . . . FA Nov 39 26
PURPLE DANDELIONS by Millard Verne Gordon *ps
(Donald A. Wollheim)*. .ss . . . . .Cos Mar 41 105
PURPLE DEATH, THE by Jack Barnette. .s . . . .
. . . . Amz Jul 29 370
PURPLE DUSK, THE by Leslie Northern *h ps (Frank
Belknap Long)*. .s . . . . .TW Sum 45 68
PURPLE LIGHT, THE by E. Waldo Hunter *ps (Theodore
Sturgeon)*. .ss . . . . .ASF Jun 41 117
PURPLE MONSTERS, THE by Bob Olsen *ps (Alfred John
Olsen, Jr.)*. .s . . . . Amz Aug 32 458
PURPLE PLAGUE, THE by Russell Hays. .nt . . . .
. . . . Amz Feb 31 994
PURPLE SAPPHIRE, THE by John Taine *ps (Eric
Temple Bell)*. .n . . . . .FFM Aug 48 8
PURPOSE by Ray Bradbury. .s . . . . SS Jul 50 91
PURPOSE, THE by A. E. van Vogt. .nt . . . .
. . . . ASF May 45 139
PUSH FOR PUSHBUTTON WARFARE by Willy
Ley. .a . . . . ASF Sep 47 87
PUSH OF A FINGER, THE by Alfred Bester. .nt . . . . .
. . . . ASF May 42 108
PUTSCH by Vic Phillips & Scott Roberts. .s . . . .
. . . . ASF Mar 41 86
PUTTING THE MOON ON THE JOB *(POWER PLANTS
OF TOMORROW No. 3)* by Willy Ley. .a . . . .
. . . . ASF Mar 38 108

Title. .Author. .Length . . . . Magazine. .Date. .Page No.

PUZZLE DUEL, THE by Miles J. Breuer, M.D. . .s . . . .
. . . . AQ Win 28 133
PUZZLE OF PRIIPIIRII, THE by William Tenn ps (Philip
Klass). .s . . . . OTWA Jul 50 42
PUZZLES FROM EARTH'S PAST by Vincent H.
Gaddis. .a. . . . . Amz Aug 46 156
PYGMALION (THE LEMURIAN DOCUMENTS No. 1)
by J. Lewis Burtt. .s . . . . .Amz Jan 32 920
PYGMALION'S SPECTACLES by Stanley G.
Weinbaum. .s . . . . WS Jun 35 28
SS May 39 100
PYGMIES OF PHOBOS, THE by Ralph Robin. .s . . . . .
. . . . Amz Apr 36 116
PYGMY PLANET by Jack Williamson. .s . . . .
. . . . ASF Feb 32 151

Q

Q SHIP OF SPACE by Duncan Farnsworth ps (David
Wright O'Brien). .s . . . . .Amz Jan 42 206
Q. U. R. by H. H. Holmes ps (William Anthony Parker
White). .s . . . . ASF Mar 43 79
QRM—INTERPLANETARY by George O. Smith. .nt . . .
. . . . .ASF Oct 42 109
QUANDARY OF QUINTUS QUAGGLE, THE by William
P. McGivern. .s . . . . Amz Jun 41 88
QUARANTINE by George O. Smith. .s . . . .
. . . . TW Dec 47 48
QUARRY by Mallory Kent ps (Robert W. Lowndes) . . .
. .ss. Fut Dec 41 91
QUARTZ CITY ON MERCURY by Frank R. Paul. . . . .
. .bacover. . . . . Amz Sep 41
QUEEN OF THE BLACK COAST by Robert E.
Howard. .nt . . . . .AFR #8 3
QUEEN OF THE BLUE WORLD by Basil Wells. .s . . . .
. . . . .PS Win 41 22
QUEEN OF THE FLAMING DIAMOND by Leroy
Yerxa. .nt . . . . .Amz Jan 43 184
QUEEN OF THE ICE MEN by S. M. Tenneshaw h ps . . .
. .nt . . . . FA Nov 49 8
QUEEN OF THE LIVING PUPPETS by Don
Wilcox. .nt . . . . FA Oct 41 64
QUEEN OF THE MARTIAN CATACOMBS by Leigh
Brackett. .nt. . . . . PS Sum 49 4
QUEEN OF THE METAL MEN by Robert Bloch. .s . . .
. . . . FA Apr 40 62
QUEEN OF THE PANTHER WORLD by Berkeley
Livingston. .n . . . . .FA Jul 48 8
QUEEN OF THE SKIES by Eando Binder ps (Otto
Binder). .nt . . . . ASF Nov 37 76
QUEEN OF VENUS by John Russell Fearn. .n . . . . . .
. . . . MSS Nov 40 8
QUEEN OF ZAMBA, THE by L. Sprague de Camp . . . .
. .n 2 pt. . . . . ASF Aug 49 6

Title. .Author. .Length . . . . Magazine. .Date. .Page No.

QUEEN'S ASTROLOGER, THE by Murray Leinster
ps (Will F. Jenkins). .s . . . . TW Oct 49 83
QUEER STORY OF BROWNLOW'S NEWSPAPER, THE
by H. G. Wells. .s . . . . AFR #3 27
QUEST by F. G. Rayer. .s . . . . NW Sum 50 80
QUEST BEYOND THE STARS, THE by Edmond
Hamilton. .n . . . . CF Win 42 15
QUEST IN TIME, THE by Edmond Hamilton. .nt . . . . .
. . . . FA Jun 42 150
QUEST OF BRAIL by Richard S. Shaver. .n . . . .
. . . . .Amz Dec 45 8
QUEST OF THE STARHOPE by Leigh Brackett. .s . . . .
. . . . TW Apr 49 45
QUEST OF THIG by Basil Wells. .s . . . . . . .PS Fal 42 23
QUEST OF ZIPANTORIC by Robert Moore
Williams. .s . . . . DS Feb 39 88
QUEST ON IO by Robert Moore Williams. .s . . . .
. . . . PS Fal 40 33
QUEST ON PHOEBE by James R. Adams. .s . . . .
. . . . PS Sum 47 87
QUEST TO CENTAURUS by George O. Smith. .s . . . .
. . . . TW Apr 47 74
QUESTION IS ANSWERED, THE by Stewart Toland
(on story. ToC gives author as Stewart Todd). .s . . . .
. . . . UK Nov 39 133
QUESTION OF SALVAGE, A by Malcolm Jameson . . .
. .nt . . . . ASF Oct 39 69
QUEST'S END by Basil Wells. .s . . . . .PS Spr 44 65
QUICKSANDS OF YOUTHWARDNESS by Malcolm
Jameson. .n 3 pt . . . . .Ash Oct 40 6
QUICKSILVER, UNLIMITED by Harry Walton. .s . . . .
. . . . ASF Jul 37 116
QUIETUS by Ross Rocklynne. .s . . . . . . ASF Sep 40 86
QUIS CUSTODIET. . . .? by Margaret St. Clair. .s . . . . .
. . . . SS Jul 48 109
QUITE LOGICAL by Rog Phillips ps (Roger P.
Graham). .s . . . . TW Apr 49 68
QUIXOTE AND THE WINDMILL by Poul
Anderson. .s. . . . . ASF Nov 50 95

R

RA FOR THE RAJAH by John Victor Peterson. .s . . . .
. . . . ASF May 38 108
RA, THE INSCRUTABLE by R. DeWitt Miller. .a . . . . .
. . . . .ASF Oct 37 101
RABBIT AND THE RAT, THE by Robert Arthur . . . . .
. .s . . . . UK Jun 43 102
RACE AROUND THE MOON by Otis Adelbert Kline . .
. .nt .TW Aug 39 95
RACE THROUGH TIME, A by Donald Wandrei. .s . . . .
. . . . ASF Oct 33 18
RACE TO THE MOON, THE by Forrest J.
Ackerman. .a . . . . MSS Nov 50 60

Title. .Author. .Length . . . . Magazine. .Date. .Page No.

RACKETEER RAY, THE by Murray Leinster ps (Will F. Jenkins). .s. . . . . Amz Feb 32 1004
RACKETEERS IN THE SKY by Jack Williamson. .nt . . . . AMF Oct 50 100
RADAR: THE WAVES THAT "FEEL" by L. Jerome Stanton. .a. . . . . ASF Aug 46 100
RADIANT AVENGER by E. A. Grosser. .s . . . . Fut Apr 41 38
RADIANT ENEMIES, THE by R. F. Starzl. .s . . . . FFM Nov 39 118
RADIANT ROCK, THE by Frances M. Deegan. .s . . . . Amz Jun 45 100
RADIANT SHELL, THE by Paul Ernst. .s . . . . .ASF Jan 32 120
RADIATION IN UNIFORM by Herbert C. McKay . . . . .a . . . . ASF Apr 38 116
RADIATION OF THE CHINESE VEGETABLE, THE by C. Sterling Gleason. .s . . . . SW Dec 29 618
SS Win 45 80
RADIATION TRAP by Harry Walton. .s . . . Ash Sep 41 90
RADICALITE by Richard Rush Murray. .s. . . . . .Amz Jan 33 949
RADIO BEASTS, THE by Ralph Milne Farley ps (Roger Sherman Hoar). .n. . . . . FN Jan 41 6
RADIO DETECTIVE, THE by Lincoln S. Colby . . . . .s . . . . Amz May 31 125
RADIO GHOST, THE by Otis Adelbert Kline. .s . . . . Amz Sep 27 531
RADIO MAN, THE by Ralph Milne Farley ps (Roger Sherman Hoar). .n 3 pt. . . . . .FFM Dec 39 6
RADIO MAN RETURNS, THE by Ralph Milne Farley ps (Roger Sherman Hoar). .s . . . . Amz Jun 39 96
RADIO MATES by Benjamin Witwer. .s . . . . Amz Jul 27 368
RADIO MIND-RAY, THE by Stanton A. Coblentz . . . . . . .s . . . . .ASF Jul 34 90
RADIO PLANET, THE by Ralph Milne Farley ps (Roger Sherman Hoar). .n. . . . . .FFM Apr 42 6
RADIO ROBBERY, THE by Captain S. P. Meek . . . . .s . . . . Amz Feb 30 1046
AQ Fal 34 110
RADIO TELESCOPE, THE by Stanton A. Coblentz . . . . . .s . . . . Amz Jun 29 198
ToW Aut 40 44
RADIO TERROR, THE by Eugene Thebault (Tr fr French by Fletcher Pratt). .n 3 pt. . . . . . . WS Jun 33 6
RADIUM AIRSHIP OF SATURN by James B. Settles . . . .bacover. . . . . .Amz Jul 42
RADIUM-BUGS, THE by Helen Weinbaum. .s . . . . SSS Sep 40 102
RADIUM DOOM, THE by Milton R. Peril. .nt . . . . Amz Dec 37 90
RADIUM MASTER, THE by Jim Vanny. .s . . . . WS Aug 30 240
RADIUM POOL, THE by Ed Earl Repp. .n 2 pt . . . . SW Aug 29 218

RADIUM WORLD, THE by Frank K. Kelly. .s . . . . WS Feb 32 1058
RAID FROM MARS, THE by Miles J. Breuer, M.D. . . . . .s . . . . Amz Mar 39 8
RAID OF THE MERCURY, THE by A. H. Johnson. . . . . . .s . . . . Amz Jul 31 364
RAID ON THE TERMITES, THE by Paul Ernst. .nt . . . . .ASF Jun 32 354
RAIDERS FROM SPACE by Harold A. Lower. .ss. . . . . SW Mar 30 896
RAIDERS INVISIBLE by D. W. Hall. .s. . . . . ASF Nov 31 200
RAIDERS OF SATURN'S RINGS, THE by Raymond Z. Gallun. .s. . . . . PS Fal 41 70
RAIDERS OF THE AIR by Hubert Kelley & Fred T. Barton. .ss . . . . .FFM May–Jun 40 75
RAIDERS OF THE SECOND MOON by Gene Ellerman ps (Basil Wells). .s . . . . PS Sum 45 43
RAIDERS OF THE SOLAR FRONTIER by A. Bertram Chandler. .nt . . . . .OTWA Dec 50 4
RAIDERS OF THE UNIVERSES by Donald Wandrei . . . . .s . . . . ASF Sep 32 63
AFR #13 83
RAIDERS OUT OF SPACE by Robert Moore Williams. . . . .nt . . . . Amz Oct 40 10
RAIN CHECK by Lewis Padgett ps (Henry Kuttner & C. L. Moore). .s. . . . . .ASF Jul 46 47
RAIN OF FIRE by Ray Cummings. .s . . . . .Fut Aug 42 52
RAIN, RAIDS AND RAYS by Jep Powell. .s . . . . CF Sum 43 102
RAINBOW BRIDGE, THE by Herbert C. McKay. .a. ASF Feb 38 65
RAINBOW OF DEATH by Don Wilcox. .nt . . . . .FA Jan 42 110
RALPH 124C41+ by Hugo Gernsback. .n. . . . . AQ Win 29 4
RAMBLING THROUGH THE SOLAR SYSTEM by C. P. Mason. .a. . . . . TW Oct 38 44
RANDOM QUANTITY by Carl Jacobi. .s . . . . AFR #5 54
RANNIE, THE by Willard E. Hawkins. .nt . . . . .SSS May 41 106
RANSOM FOR TOLEDO, THE by Neil R. Jones . . . . . .nt . . . . .Com May 41 80
RAPE OF THE SOLAR SYSTEM, THE by Leslie F. Stone ps (Mrs. William Silberberg). .s. . . Amz Dec 34 12
RAT RACE by Dorothy & John de Courcy. .s . . . . .SS Sep 48 72
RAT RACE by George O. Smith. .s. . . . . ASF Aug 47 55
RAT RACKET, THE by David H. Keller, M.D. .s . . . . Amz Nov 31 698
RATS IN THE BELFRY by John York Cabot ps (David Wright O'Brien). .s. . . . . Amz Jan 43 84
RAY HOLMES, SCIENTIFIC DETECTIVE. .comic. . . . . .FA May 39 88
RAY OF ETERNITY, THE by Richard Tooker. .s . . . . .Amz Nov 38 8

Title. .Author. .Length. . . . . Magazine. .Date. .Page No.

RAY OF HYPNOSIS, THE by Milton Kaletsky. .ss . . . .
. . . . .Amz Jul 40 94
RAY OF MADNESS, THE by Captain S. P. Meek . . . . .
. .s . . . . ASF Apr 30 112
RAY THAT FAILED by Donald Bern. .s . . . FA Aug 40 84
RAYHOUSE IN SPACE by Duncan Farnsworth ps (David
Wright O'Brien). .s. . . . . Amz Dec 41 82
RAYS AND MEN by Miles J. Breuer, M.D. . .nt . . . . . .
. . . . .AQ Sum 29 360
RAYS FROM THE ASTEROID, THE by R. D.
Parkinson. .ss . . . . WS Nov 35 695
RAYS OF BLINDNESS by Will Garth h ps (Otto
Binder). .s . . . . TW Apr 38 106
RAYS OF DEATH by Tim Curry. .n 2 pt. . . . .
. . . . SD Apr 30 340
REACH FOR THE STARS by V. E. Thiessen. .s . . . . . .
. . . . .FanS Nov 50 71
READ IT AND WEEP by Peter Worth h ps. .s. . . . . . .
. . . . Amz Jun 50 124
READER, I HATE YOU! by Henry Kuttner. .s. . . . . . .
. . . . SSS May 43 48
READER SPEAKS, THE letter and ed dept in TW
READERS' ANALYSIS, THE dept in postwar Fant
READER'S COLUMN letter dept in AMF from Feb 50
READER'S FORUM, THE letter dept of Amz from Mar 50
READER'S PAGE letter dept of FA
READERS' REACTIONS letter dept of ToW
Nos. 2 thru 14
READERS' VIEWPOINT, THE letter dept of FFM
REAL McCOY, THE by Hugh Raymond ps (John
Michel). .s . . . . Fut Jun 42 84
REAL THRILL, THE by James Blish. .s . . . Cos Jul 41 67
REALITIES UNLIMITED by Emmett McDowell. .s. . . .
. . . . SS Jul 48 70
REAPING THE WHIRLWIND by Alfred I. Tooke. . . . .
. .s . . . . Amz Dec 30 850
REASON by Isaac Asimov. .s. . . . . ASF Apr 41 33
REBEL OF THE VALKYR by Alfred Coppel. .nt . . . . .
. . . . .PS Fal 50 4
REBEL SLUG, THE by Basil Wells. .ss . . . . Fut Apr 42 35
REBEL SOUL, THE by Austin Hall. .nt. . .FFM Aug 40 80
REBELLION by Don A. Stuart ps (John W. Campbell,
Jr.). .nt . . . . ASF Aug 35 64
REBELLION–5000 A.D. by Garth Bentley. .s . . . . . .
. . . . .WS Jul 31 224
REBELLION ON VENUS by Edward Morris & John
Bertin. .s . . . . .WQ Sum 32 494
REBELS, THE by E. R. James. .s . . . . . . .NW #4 49 59
REBELS, THE by Kurt von Rachen ps (L. Ron
Hubbard). .nt . . . . ASF Feb 42 49
REBELS OF THE MOON by Manley Wade Wellman &
Max Jergovic. .s. . . . . WQ Spr 32 354
REBIRTH by Thomas Calvert McClary. .n 2 pt . . . . . .
. . . . ASF Feb 34 10
REBIRTH OF MAN by Basil E. Wells. .s . . . .
. . . . .SSS Sep 40 94

REBIRTH OF TOMORROW by Hugh Raymond ps (John
Michel). .s . . . . Sti Apr 41 6
RECLAIMERS OF THE ICE by Stanton A. Coblentz. . .
. .n . . . . AQ Spr 30 148
RECOIL by George O. Smith. .nt . . . . ASF Nov 43 5
RECOMMENDED READING Book review dept of
F&SF from Win–Spr 50
RECRUITING STATION by A. E. van Vogt. .n . . . . . .
. . . . ASF Mar 42 8
RED ACE, THE by Eugen George Key. .s . . . .
. . . . AW Feb 30 692
RED APRIL, 1965 by Frank K. Kelly. .s . . . .
. . . . WS Mar 32 1154
RED DEATH, THE by David H. Keller, M.D. . .nt . . . .
. . . . Cos Jul 41 76
RED DEATH OF MARS, THE by Robert Moore
Williams. .nt . . . . .ASF Jul 40 130
RED DIMENSION, THE by Ed Earl Repp. .s . . . .
. . . . .SW Jan 30 696
SS Sum 45 66
RED DOOR, THE by Don Wilcox. .nt . . . . FA Nov 46 140
RED DUST, THE by Murray Leinster ps (Will F.
Jenkins). .nt . . . . .Amz Jan 27 878
ToW Win 39 6
FN May 49 58
RED FLAME OF VENUS by P. Schuyler Miller. .s . . . .
. . . . WS Sep 32 346
RED GEM OF MERCURY by Henry Kuttner. .s . . . . . .
. . . . .SSS Nov 41 109
RED GERM OF COURAGE, THE by R. F. Starzl . . . . .
. .s . . . . FFM Jan 40 65
RED HELL OF JUPITER, THE by Paul Ernst. .nt . . . . .
. . . . ASF Oct 31 70
RED HERITAGE by John Russell Fearn. .nt . . . .
. . . . .ASF Jan 38 76
RED LEGION, THE by Richard S. Shaver. .nt . . . .
. . . . Amz Jun 47 90
RED MAGICIAN, THE by John Russell Fearn. .nt . . . .
. . . . .Fant #1 38 58
RED MOON by Frank Belknap Long, Jr. . .s . . . .
. . . . TW Jun 40 56
RED MOON by Kenneth Sterling. .s . . . . . WS Nov 35 668
RED PERI, THE by Stanley G. Weinbaum. .nt . . . . . .
. . . . ASF Nov 35 10
RED PERIL, THE by Capt. S. P. Meek. .s . . . .
. . . . Amz Sep 29 486
RED PLAGUE, THE by P. Schuyler Miller. .s . . . .
. . . . .WS Jul 30 170
RED QUEEN'S RACE, THE by Isaac Asimov. .nt . . . . .
. . . . .ASF Jan 49 65
RED RAY, THE by Dan Fabers. .s . . . . . . AQ Spr 30 278
RED SHARDS ON CERES by Raymond Z. Gallun . . . .
. .s . . . . TW Dec 37 27
FSQ Spr 50 69
RED SLAG OF MARS by Laurence Schwartzman &
Jack Williamson. .s. . . . . WQ Spr 32 394

Title. .Author. .Length . . . . Magazine. .Date. .Page No.

RED SPHERES, THE by George C. Wallis. .s . . . . ToW Spr 41 46
RED SPOT OF JUPITER, THE by Dennis McDermott ps (P. Schuyler Miller). .s . . . . WS Jul 31 214
RED STORM ON JUPITER by Frank Belknap Long, Jr. .s. . . . . ASF May 36 32
RED SUN OF DANGER by Brett Sterling h ps (Edmond Hamilton). .n . . . . SS Spr 45 11
RED WITCH OF MERCURY by Emmett McDowell . . . . .nt . . . . PS Sum 45 2
REDEMPTION CAIRN by Stanley G. Weinbaum . . . . . . .nt . . . . ASF Mar 36 42
REDEVELOPMENT by Wesley Long ps (George O. Smith). .nt . . . . ASF Nov 44 136
REDMASK OF THE OUTLANDS by Nat Schachner . . . . .nt . . . . ASF Jan 34 2
REFERENT by Brett Sterling h ps (Ray Bradbury) . . . . . .s . . . . TW Oct 48 148
REFLECTION THAT LIVED, THE by Ross Rocklynne. .s . . . . FA Jun 40 42
REFORMATION OF JOSEPH REED, THE by Robert Moore Williams. .s . . . . FA Dec 41 68
REFRACTION AND LENSES by Gene Mitchell ps (H. Orlo Hoadley). .a . . . . ASF Aug 44 105
REFUGEE, THE by Jane Rice. .nt . . . . . UK Oct 43 111
                                         UK 48 30
REFUGEES, THE by Frank Belknap Long. .s . . . . UK Feb 42 92
REGENERATION by Ray Cummings. .s . . . TW Apr 42 90
REGENERATIVE WONDER by Winthrop W. Hawkins. .s. . . . . Amz Feb 34 58
REGGIE AND THE VAMPIRE by Gerald Vance h ps . . . . .s . . . . FA Sep 48 118
REGROWTH by J. W. Groves. .s . . . . SS Jan 50 133
REGULATIONS by Murray Leinster ps (Will F. Jenkins). .s. . . . . TW Aug 48 39
REGULATIONS PROVIDE by Raymond F. Jones . . . . . .s . . . . ASF Mar 50 39
REHEARSAL FOR DANGER by P. F. Costello h ps. .s. .Amz Jan 42 190
REIGN OF THE LONG TUSKS, THE by Stanton A. Coblentz. .s . . . . ASF Feb 37 29
REIGN OF THE RAY, THE by Irving Lester & Fletcher Pratt. .n 2 pt . . . . SW Jun 29 7
REIGN OF THE REPTILES, THE by A. Connell . . . . . . .s . . . . WS Aug 35 262
REIGN OF THE ROBOTS, THE by Edmond Hamilton. .s. . . . . WS Dec 31 848
REIGN OF THE STAR-DEATH, THE by A. Rowley Hilliard. .s . . . . WS Apr 32 1220
REIGN OF WIZARDRY, THE by Jack Williamson . . . . . .n 3 pt. . . . . UK Mar 40 9
REINCARNATE by Lester del Rey. .nt . . . . ASF Apr 40 100
REINMUTH RIDER, THE by John Victor Peterson. .s. . . . . TW Jun 38 31

REJUVENATION ASTEROID by William Lawrence Hamling. .s. . . . . Amz Jan 47 28
RELATIVITY TO THE RESCUE by J. Harvey Haggard. .nt . . . . Amz Apr 35 100
RELEASED ENTROPY by Jack Williamson. .n 2 pt . . . . ASF Aug 37 8
RELIC by Eric Frank Russell. .nt . . . . Fant Apr 47 5
RELICS FROM THE EARTH, THE by John Pierce . . . . . .ss . . . . SW Mar 30 894
RELUCTANT GENII, THE by P. F. Costello h ps . . . . . . .s . . . . FA Jul 50 130
RELUCTANT SHAMAN, THE by L. Sprague de Camp. .s . . . . TW Apr 47 90
REMARKABLE CASE OF DAVIDSON'S EYES, THE by H. G. Wells. .s. . . . . Amz Apr 27 21
REMARKABLE FLIRGLEFLIP, THE by William Tenn ps (Philip Klass). .s . . . . FA May 50 88
REMEMBER CASSANDRA by H. C. Goble. .a . . . . Amz Jun 48 164
REMEMBER ME, KAMA! by Walter Kubilius. .ss . . . . Ash Oct 42 31
REMEMBER TOMORROW by Henry Kuttner. .nt . . . . TW Jan 41 87
REMOTE CONTROL by Walter Kateley. .s . . . . Amz Apr 30 22
RENAISSANCE by Raymond F. Jones. .n 4 pt. . . . . .ASF Jul 44 6
RENDEZVOUS by John Berryman. .s. . . . ASF Aug 40 37
RENDEZVOUS IN SPACE by Guy Archette. .nt. . . . . Amz Jul 49 104
RENDEZVOUS IN THE VOID by Broox Sledge. .s . . . . .TW Feb 42 84
RENEGADE by J. Harvey Haggard. .ss . . . . TW Jun 37 88
RENEGADE, THE by Marion Henry. .s. . . . . .ASF Jul 43 87
RENEGADE FROM SATURN by Raymond Z. Gallun. .s. . . . . TW Mar 40 32
REPAIR JOB by Roy B. Frentz. .s . . . . . Amz Oct 50 46
REPETITION by A. E. van Vogt. .nt. . . . ASF Apr 40 51
REPRISAL by Thomas Richard Jones. .s . . . . Amz Oct 28 637
REQUIEM by Robert A. Heinlein. .s. . . . .ASF Jan 40 80
RESCUE BEACON by Craig Browning (on story) Rog Phillips (in ToC) ps (Roger P. Graham). .s . . . . .OW Nov 50 86
RESCUE FROM JUPITER, A by Gawain Edwards (Pendray). .n 2 pt . . . . SW Feb 30 774
RESCUE FROM VENUS by Ed Earl Repp. .n. . . . . SFQ Spr 41 4
RESCUE IN SPACE, A by Lowell Howard Morrow . . . . . .s . . . . WS Sep 30 346
RESCUE INTO THE PAST by Ralph Milne Farley ps (Roger Sherman Hoar). .s . . . . Amz Oct 40 34
RESCUE PARTY by Arthur C. Clarke. .nt . . . . ASF May 46 36
RESILENCE by Damon Knight. .ss . . . . . . Sti Feb 41 35

Title. .Author. .Length. . . . . Magazine. .Date. .Page No.

RESILENT PLANET by Warner Van Lorne *ps. .s* . . . . .
. . . . ASF Aug 38 48
RESISTANT RAY, THE by Francis Flagg *ps (George
Henry Weiss). .s.* . . . . Amz Jul 32 346
RESONANCE by Eric Frank Russell. .nt . . . .
. . . . ASF Jul 45 44
RESTITUTION by John Francis Kalland. .s . . . .
. . . . Amz Dec 35 118
RESURECTION FROM HELL by David Wright
O'Brien. .s . . . . FA Sep 42 172
RETREAT FROM UTOPIA, THE by Wallace West . . . .
. .s . . . . ASF Mar 34 143
RETREAT TO MARS, THE by Cecil B. White. .s . . . . .
. . . . Amz Aug 27 460
RETREAT TO THE STARS by Leigh Brackett. .s . . . . .
. . . . .Ash Nov 41 36
RETRIBUTION by Robert Baldwin. .ss. . . Amz Nov 33 78
RETURN FROM JUPITER, THE by Gawain Edwards
(Pendray). .n 2 pt . . . . WS Mar 31 1062
RETURN FROM M–15 by S. D. Gottesman *ps (Cyril
Kornbluth). .s.* . . . . Cos Mar 41 58
RETURN FROM ZERO by Ross Rocklynne. .s. . . . . .
. . . . .SSS Aug 42 130
RETURN OF A DEMON by Alexander Blade *h ps.* . . . .
. .s . . . . FA May 43 88
RETURN OF CAPTAIN FUTURE, THE by Edmond
Hamilton. .s . . . . SS Jan 50 94
RETURN OF CIRCE, THE by Nat Schachner. .n . . . . .
. . . . FA Aug 41 8
RETURN OF HAWK CARSE, THE by Anthony Gilmore
ps (Harry Bates). .n . . . . Amz Jul 42 158
RETURN OF JOAN OF ARC by David Wright
O'Brien. .s . . . . FA May 42 224
RETURN OF JONGOR, THE by Robert Moore
Williams. .n . . . . FA Apr 44 12
RETURN OF LAN-NING, THE by Guy Archette . . . . .
. .s . . . . FA Mar 49 40
RETURN OF LANCELOT BIGGS, THE by Nelson S.
Bond. .s. . . . . .Amz May 42 52
RETURN OF MAN, THE by Leo A. Schmidt. .s . . . . . .
. . . . Amz Feb 42 134
RETURN OF SATAN by Robert Moore Williams . . . . .
. .nt . . . . Amz Oct 39 28
RETURN OF SATHANAS, THE by Richard S. Shaver &
Bob McKenna. .n. . . . . .Amz Nov 46 8
RETURN OF SINBAD, THE by Chester S. Geier
. .n . . . . FA Jan 49 8
RETURN OF THARN, THE by Howard Browne. . . . . .
. .n 3 pt. . . . . Amz Oct 48 40
RETURN OF THE AIR MASTER, THE by Edward E.
Chappelow. .s. . . . . AW Mar 30 774
RETURN OF THE COSMIC GUN, THE by Morrison F.
Colladay. .s . . . . WS Oct 31 582
RETURN OFTHE GODS, THE by Robert M.
Coates. .s. . . . . F&SF Win–Spr 50 17

Title. .Author. .Length. . . . . Magazine. .Date. .Page No.

RETURN OF THE HUN, THE by William J.
Brittain. .s . . . . .FA Jul 42 74
RETURN OF THE ICE AGE, THE by Nathaniel
Nitkin. .s. . . . . .CF Spr 44 95
RETURN OF THE MARTIANS, THE by Cecil B.
White. .s . . . . Amz Apr 28 70
RETURN OF THE MURIANS, THE by Nat
Schachner. .nt. . . . . ASF Aug 36 60
RETURN OF THE PROWLER by Harl Vincent
(Schoepflin). .s . . . . ASF Nov 38 36
RETURN OF THE SPACEHAWK by Duncan Farnsworth
ps (David Wright O'Brien). .s . . . . . . Amz May 41 192
RETURN OF THE TRIPEDS, THE by Neil R.
Jones. .s. . . . . Amz May 32 120
RETURN OF THE WHISPERING GORILLA by David V.
Reed *ps (David Vern).* .n . . . . FA Feb 43 8
RETURN OF TYME, THE by A. Fedor & Henry
Hasse. .s. . . . . WS Aug 34 294
RETURN TO LILLIPUT by William Brengle *h ps (Howard
Browne).* .n . . . . .FA May 43 8
RETURN TO PELLUCIDAR, THE by Edgar Rice
Burroughs. .nt. . . . . Amz Feb 42 26
RETURN TO SUBTERRANIA, THE by Harl Vincent
(Schoepflin). .s . . . . SW Apr 30 992
RETURNED FROM HELL by Steve Fisher. .n . . . .
. . . . .UK May 39 9
REUNION ON GANYMEDE by Clifford D. Simak . . . .
. .s . . . . ASF Nov 38 66
REVENGE OF THE CHOSEN, THE by Thomas H.
Knight. .s. . . . . WQ Fal 30 128
REVENGE OF THE ROBOT by Otis Adelbert Kline . . .
. .s . . . . .TW Aug 36 68
REVENGE OF THE VERA by Henry Hasse. .s . . . .
. . . . PS Fal 43 81
REVERSE ATOMS by Henry Kuttner. .s . . . .
. . . . .TW Nov 40 40
REVERSE ENGLISH *(in ToC. HSILGNE ESREVER
on story)* by John S. Carrol *ps* . .s. . . . . TW Oct 48 125
REVERSE PHYLOGENY by A. R. Long. .s . . . .
. . . . ASF Jun 37 72
REVERSE UNIVERSE by Nat Schachner. .nt . . . .
. . . . ASF Jun 36 8
REVERSED MAN, THE by Arthur C. Clarke. .s . . . . . .
. . . . TW Jun 50 43
REVERSIBLE REVOLUTIONS, THE by Cecil
Corwin *ps (Cyril Kornbluth).* .s . . . . . . Cos Mar 41 107
REVERSION by M. C. Pease. .s . . . . ASF Dec 49 45
REVIEW COPY by H. H. Holmes *ps (William Anthony
Parker White).* .s . . . . .F&SF Fal 49 70
REVIEW OF FAN PUBLICATIONS dept in SS
*REVIEWS OF CURRENT SCIENCE FICTION BOOKS
dept in OW from May 50*
REVOLT by A. M. Phillips. .nt . . . . ASF Apr 39 89
REVOLT AGAINST LIFE by Frederic Arnold
Kummer, Jr. . .s . . . . TW Jan 40 12

Title. .Author. .Length . . . . Magazine. .Date. .Page No.

REVOLT IN PACIFICO by Anthony B. Ott. .s . . . . . .
. . . . .FA Jan 50 120
REVOLT IN THE ICE EMPIRE by Ray Cummings . . . .
. .nt . . . . PS Fal 40 101
REVOLT OF THE ANTS by Milton Kaletsky. .s . . . . .
. . . . Amz Apr 40 76
REVOLT OF THE ATOMS, THE by V. Orlovsky . . . .
. .s . . . . Amz Apr 29 6
REVOLT OF THE MACHINE MEN, THE by Charles R.
Tanner. .s . . . . .SSS Nov 43 32
REVOLT OF THE MACHINES, THE by Nat Schachner
& Arthur Zagat. .s . . . . ASF Jul 31 88
REVOLT OF THE PEDESTRIANS, THE by David H.
Keller, M.D. . .s . . . . Amz Feb 28 1048
REVOLT OF THE ROBOTS by Arthur R. Tofte. .s . . . .
. . . . .FA May 39 6
REVOLT OF THE SCIENTISTS by Nat Schachner . . . .
. .s . . . . WS Apr 33 806
2. THE GREAT OIL WAR. .s . . . . . . WS May 33 946
3. THE FINAL TRIUMPH. .s . . . . . . WS Jun 33 26
REVOLT OF THE STAR MEN, THE by Raymond
Gallun. .nt . . . . .WQ Win 32 222
REVOLT ON INFERNO by Victor Rousseau
(Emanuel). .nt . . . . .Mir Jun–Jul 31 195
REVOLT ON IO by Nelson Bond. .nt . . . .
. . . . PS Spr 41 106
REVOLT ON IO by Jack West. .nt . . . .
. . . . Amz Oct 40 106
REVOLT ON THE EARTH–STAR by Carl Selwyn . . . .
. .s . . . . PS Spr 40 71
REVOLT ON THE TENTH WORLD by Edmond
Hamilton. .nt . . . . Amz Nov 40 60
REVOLT ON VENUS by W. P. Cockroft. .s . . . .
. . . . .ToW #1 37 40
REVOLUTION OF 1950 by Stanley G. Weinbaum &
Ralph Milne Farley ps (Roger Sherman Hoar) . . . . . .
. .n 2 pt . . . . Amz Oct 38 106
REVOLUTION ON VENUS by Bradner Buckner . . . . .
. .nt . . . . Amz Apr 39 100
REVOLVING WORLD by Millard Verne Gordon ps
(Donald A. Wollheim). .ss . . . . .SF Sep 41 47
REWBARB'S REMARKABLE RADIO by William P.
McGivern. .s . . . . FA Dec 41 102
REX by Harl Vincent (Schoepflin). .s . . . .ASF Jun 34 143
RHYTHM by Charles Cloukey. .s . . . . . . Amz Apr 30 55
RHYTHM OF THE SPHERES by A. Merritt. .s . . . . . .
. . . . TW Oct 36 52
. . . . AFR #3 7
RHYTHM RIDES THE ROCKET by Bob Olsen ps (Alfred
John Olsen, Jr.). .s . . . . .SF Oct 40 28
RICE'S RAY by Harry Martin. .s . . . . . . .Amz Jan 28 958
RICHES FOR PLUTO by Stanton A. Coblentz. .s . . . . .
. . . . ASF Dec 34 98
RIDDLE OF TANYE, THE by W. P. Cockroft. .s . . . .
. . . . .Cos May 41 48

Title. .Author. .Length . . . . Magazine. .Date. .Page No.

RIDDLES OF SCIENCE. .pictorial feature
MT. EVEREST THE UNCONQUERABLE. . . . . . .
. . . . Amz Oct 38 83
HOW DID LIFE COME TO THE EARTH?. . . . . . .
. . . . Amz Nov 38 25
THE TITANS OF EASTER ISLAND . . . .
. . . . Amz Dec 38 37
THE CANALS OF MARS. . . . . Amz Jan 39 59
ANGKOR . . . . Amz Feb 39 73
WHAT IS GRAVITATION? . . . . Amz Mar 39 65
THE NATURE OF THOUGHT . . . . . . Amz Apr 39 53
THE MYSTERY OF ATLANTIS . . . . Amz May 39 33
THE LOST CONTINENT OF LEMURIA. . . . .
. . . . Amz Jun 39 95
THE MYSTERY OF THE MAYA. . . . .Amz Jul 39 107
THE SECRET OF THE STRATOSPHERE. . . . .
. . . . Amz Aug 39 27
THE MYSTERY OF EXPLODING STARS . . . . . .
. . . . Amz Sep 39 89
WHAT IS MATTER? . . . . Amz Oct 39 27
TIME. WHAT IS IT? . . . . Amz Nov 39 57
WHAT IS ENERGY? . . . . Amz Dec 39 79
LIGHT WITHOUT HEAT. . . . . Amz Jan 40 75
ORIGIN OF THE MOON . . . . Amz Feb 40 57
WHAT IS MOTION? . . . . Amz Mar 40 128
HOW LARGE IS THE UNIVERSE? . . . Amz Apr 40 49
WHAT KILLED THE DINOSAURS? . . . .
. . . . Amz May 40 87
MYSTERY OF THE ATEROIDS . . . . . Amz Jun 40 67
WHAT MAKES THE WIND BLOW? . . . .
. . . . .Amz Jul 40 73
MYSTERY OF THE SUNSPOTS . . . . . Amz Aug 40 99
IS THERE A DEATH RAY? . . . . Amz Sep 40 69
RIDOLPH, MAGNUS series See JACK VANCE author
RIFT IN INFINITY by Paul Ernst. .s . . . . .TW Aug 37 96
RIGHT EAR OF MALCHUS, THE by J. Allan
Dunn. .s . . . . UK Jun 39 67
RIKITS OF MARS, THE by Don Wilcox. .n . . . . . .
. . . . Amz Jan 48 80
RIM OF THE DEEP by Clifford D. Simak. .nt . . . . . .
. . . . ASF May 40 63
RING AROUND THE REDHEAD by John D.
MacDonald. .s . . . . SS Nov 48 98
RING AROUND THE SUN by Isaac Asimov. .s . . . . . .
. . . . .Fut Mar 40 89
RING BONANZA, THE by Otto Binder. .s . . . .
. . . . SS Jul 47 57
RING OF FAITH, THE by William P. McGivern. .s . . . .
. . . . FA Nov 48 122
RINGER FAMILY, THE by Guy Gifford. .Series of
single-panel cartoons in PS between 1942 and 1946.
RIOT AT SANDERAC, THE by Miles J. Breuer,
M.D. . .s . . . . Amz Dec 27 878
ROAD BEYOND, THE by Norman A. Daniels. .s . . . .
. . . . .UK Aug 41 81

Title. .Author. .Length . . . . Magazine. .Date. .Page No.

ROAD BLOCK by Robert Moore Williams. .s . . . .
. . . . .SS Nov 50 106
ROAD TO SPACE TRAVEL, THE by Willy Ley
Part I THE LAST TWELVE YEARS. .a . . . .
. . . . .SS Mar 49 68
Part II THE NEXT TWELVE YEARS. .a . . . .
. . . . SS May 49 116
STATION IN SPACE. .a . . . . SS Jul 49 73
MEDICINE AND SPACE TRAVEL. .a . . . .
. . . . .SS Sep 49 137
ROADS MUST ROLL, THE by Robert A. Heinlein . . . .
. .nt . . . . ASF Jun 40 9
ROADSIDE STRATEGY by Charlie Mills. .ss . . . .
. . . . .Amz Jul 34 130
ROADWAYS OF MARS by Harl Vincent. .s . . . .
. . . . Amz Dec 32 812
ROAMER OF THE STARS by Clyde Wilson. .s . . . . . .
. . . . TW Apr 38 66
ROAR OF THE ROCKET by Oscar J. Friend. .nt . . . . . .
. . . . TW Apr 40 91
ROARING BLOT, THE by Frank Belknap Long,
Jr. . .nt . . . . ASF Mar 36 12
ROARING TRUMPET, THE by L. Sprague de Camp
& Fletcher Pratt. .n . . . . .UK May 40 9
ROBINC by H. H. Holmes *ps (William Anthony Parker
White)*. .s . . . . ASF Sep 43 76
ROBOT A-1 by Oscar J. Friend. .s . . . . SS Jul 39 87
ROBOT AL 76 GOES ASTRAY by Isaac Asimov . . . . .
. .s . . . . Amz Feb 42 218
ROBOT ALIENS, THE by Eando Binder *ps (Earl
Binder & Otto Binder)*. .nt . . . . WS Feb 35 1032
                                              WSA 50 160
ROBOT AND THE LADY, THE by Manly Wade
Wellman. .ss . . . . TW Oct 38 110
ROBOT AND THE PEARLY GATES, THE by Peter
Worth *h ps*. .s . . . . Amz Jan 49 90
ROBOT BEASTS, THE by Otis Adelbert Kline . . . . . .
. .s . . . . TW Jan 41 68
ROBOT MASTER, THE by O. Beckwith. .s . . . .
. . . . AW Oct 29 360
ROBOT MEN OF BUBBLE CITY, THE by Rog
Phillips. .n . . . . .FA Jul 49 6
ROBOT NEMESIS by Edward Elmer Smith, Ph.D. . . . .
. .s . . . . TW Jun 39 72
                                              SS Jul 50 120
ROBOT PERIL, THE by Don Wilcox. .nt. . . FA Jan 40 6
ROBOT TECHNOCRAT, THE by Nat Schachner. .s . . .
. . . . WS Mar 33 742
ROBOT TERROR, THE by Melbourne Huff. .s. . . . . .
. . . . SD Mar 30 216
ROBOTCYCLE FOR TWO by Max Overton *ps (Don
Wilcox)*. .s . . . . Amz Sep 42 130
ROBOTS CAN'T LIE by Robert Leslie Bellem. .s . . . . .
. . . . .FA Jul 41 116
ROBOTS DON'T BLEED by J. W. Groves. .s . . . .
. . . . .NW Win 50 42

ROBOTS RETURN by Robert Moore Williams. .s . . . .
. . . . .ASF Sep 38 140
ROBUR THE CONQUEROR or THE CLIPPER OF THE
CLOUDS by Jules Verne. .n 2 pt . . . . Amz Dec 27 826
ROCKET ARTILLERY by Willy Ley. .a . . . .
. . . . ASF Apr 44 104
ROCKET COMES TO THE FRONT PAGE, THE. .a . . .
. . . . SW Dec 29 600
ROCKET FLIGHT by Leo Vernon. .a . . . .ASF Jan 38 106
ROCKET OF METAL MEN by Manly Wade
Wellman. .s . . . . .Ash Dec 40 26
ROCKET OF 1955, THE by Cecil Corwin. .ss . . . .
. . . . Sti Apr 41 53
ROCKET PANTS by Noel Loomis. .s . . . . . TW Spr 46 64
ROCKET RACE TO LUNA by Robert Moore
Williams. .s . . . . Amz Sep 39 112
ROCKET SKIN by Ray Bradbury. .s . . . . . . TW Spr 46 85
ROCKET SUMMER by Ray Bradbury. .s . . . .PS Spr 47 44
ROCKET TARGET NO. 2 by R. L. Farnsworth. .a . . . .
. . . . SS May 49 93
ROCKET TO LIMBO by Margaret St. Clair. .s . . . .
. . . . FA Nov 46 70
ROCKET WARSHIP by James B. Settles . . . .
. .bacover pic . . . . Amz May 44
ROCKETEERS HAVE SHAGGY EARS, THE by Keith
Bennett. .nt . . . . .PS Spr 50 2
ROCKETS OVER EUROPE by Robert Moore
Williams. .s . . . . Amz Feb 40 28
ROCKET'S RED GLARE, THE by Carter Sprague *ps
(Sam Merwin, Jr.)*. .a . . . . .SS Jun 43 100
ROCKET'S SWAN SONG by Vic Phillips. .s . . . .
. . . . .SFQ Spr 41 124
ROCKETSHIP X—M by Forrest J. Ackerman. .a . . . . . .
. . . . Im Oct 50 2
ROCKY GORDON'S BILLION DOLLAR TRAP by
Robert Moore Williams. .s . . . . Amz May 41 180
RODERICK'S STORY by E. F. Benson. .s . . . .
. . . . FFM Apr 46 116
ROGER BACON FORMULA, THE by Irvin Lester &
Fletcher Pratt. .s . . . . .Amz Jan 29 940
*ROGERS, BUCK series See PHILIP FRANCIS NOWLAN
author*
ROGUE SHIP by A. E. van Vogt. .nt . . . . . SSS Mar 50 10
ROMAN HOLIDAY by Kelvin Kent *ps (Arthur K. Barnes
& Henry Kuttner)*. .s . . . . .TW Aug 39 76
                                              SS Jan 50 80
ROMAN RESURECTION, A by Lee Meriwether. .s . . . .
. . . . .FFM Aug 42 115
ROMANCE ACROSS THE AGES by Willard E.
Hawkins. .s . . . . .TW Jul 40 54
ROMANCE OF POSI AND NEGA, THE by Joe W.
Skidmore. .s . . . . Amz Sep 32 512
ROMANCE OF THE ELEMENTS. .pictorial feature
ACTINIUM . . . . FA Jun 42 229
ALUMINUM . . . . .FA Jul 39 31
ANTIMONY. . . . . FA Sep 39 89

Title. .Author. .Length . . . . Magazine. .Date. .Page No.

ROMANCE OF THE ELEMENTS (continued)

ARGON . . . . FA Nov 39 41
ARSENIC . . . . FA Jan 40 57
BARIUM. . . . . .FA May 40 55
BERYLLIUM. . . . . FA Feb 40 47
BISMUTH . . . . FA Mar 40 83
BORON. . . . . FA Apr 40 17
BROMINE . . . . FA Oct 41 63
CADMIUM. . . . . FA Jun 40 69
CALCIUM . . . . FA Aug 40 83
CARBON. . . . . FA Oct 40 113
CERIUM . . . . FA Jan 41 97
CESIUM . . . . FA Mar 41 49
CHLORINE . . . . .FA May 41 59
CHROMIUM . . . . FA Jun 41 75
COBALT. . . . . .FA Jul 41 125
COLUMBIUM. . . . . FA Aug 41 123
COPPER . . . . FA Sep 41 87
FLUORINE . . . . FA Nov 41 43
GALLIUM. . . . . FA Dec 41 85
GERMANIUM . . . . FA Jan 42 69
GOLD. . . . . FA Feb 42 51
HAFNIUM by Rod Ruth . . . . FA May 47 89
HELIUM . . . . FA Mar 42 95
HYDROGEN . . . . FA Apr 42 129
INDIUM . . . . .FA Jul 42 169
IODINE. . . . . FA May 42 215
IRON by Rod Ruth & Gordon A. MacLean . . . .
. . . . FA Aug 42 78
LEAD. . . . . FA Sep 42 213
LITHIUM . . . . FA Jun 44 189
MAGNESIUM. . . . . FA Oct 42 147
MANGANESE . . . . FA Nov 42 105
MERCURY . . . . FA Dec 42 187
MOLYBDENUM. . . . . FA Jan 43 81
NEON. . . . . FA Jun 43 21
NICKEL . . . . FA Feb 43 147
NITROGEN. . . . . FA Mar 43 141
OXYGEN . . . . FA May 43 232
PALLADIUM. . . . . FA Oct 44 101
PHOSPHORUS . . . . FA Apr 43 69
PLATINUM . . . . .FA Jul 43 107
POTASSIUM by Rod Ruth & Gordon S. McLean . . .
. . . . FA Oct 43 192
RADIUM. . . . . FA Aug 43 38
RADON by Rod Ruth & Gordon MacLean. . . . . . .
. . . . FA Dec 47 80
SELENIUM by Gordon McLean & Rod Ruth . . . . . .
. . . . FA Apr 44 194
SILICON by Rod Ruth & G. A. McLean . . . .
. . . . .FA Jan 45 192
SILVER by Rod Ruth & Gordon McLean . . . .
. . . . FA Apr 45 114
SODIUM by Gordon McLean & Rod Ruth. . . . . . .
. . . . FA Dec 43 126

Title. .Author. .Length . . . . Magazine. .Date. .Page No.

SULPHUR by Gordon McLean & Rod Ruth. . . . . . .
. . . . FA Feb 44 176
TANTALUM by Rod Ruth & Gordon MacLean . . . .
. . . . FA Mar 47 157
TELLURIUM. . . . . FA Sep 46 79
THALLIUM. . . . . .FA Jul 45 123
TIN by Rod Ruth & Gordon McLean . . . .
. . . . FA Oct 45 174
TITANIUM . . . . FA Dec 45 83
TUNGSTEN by Rod Ruth & Gordon McLean. . . . . .
. . . . FA Feb 46 168
ROOM, THE by L. Ron Hubbard. .s . . . . . . UK Apr 42 93
ROOM FOR THE SUPER RACE by Walter Kateley. . . .
.nt . . . . Amz Aug 32 430
ROOM IN A HOUSE, A by August Derleth. .s . . . . . .
. . . . .F&SF Fal 50 44
ROOM WITH A VIEW, A by David Wright O'Brien . . . .
.nt . . . . Amz May 46 112
ROOUM by Oliver Onions. .s . . . . .F&SF Fal 49 95
ROPE FOR LUCIFER, A by Walt Sheldon. .s . . . . . .
. . . . F&SF Win–Spr 50 37
ROPE TRICK by Eando Binder ps (Otto Binder). .s . . . .
. . . . ASF Apr 39 73
ROTOHOUSE, THE by Margaret St. Clair. .s . . . .
. . . . TW Aug 48 119
ROUND ABOUT RIGEL by J. Harvey Haggard. .s . . . . .
. . . . .TW Aug 37 74
ROUND–THE–WORLD BOMBER, THE by Willy
Ley. .a . . . . .TW Aug 50 99
ROUT OF THE FIRE IMPS by Stanton A. Coblentz . . .
. .s . . . . MSS Nov 38 63
RUBBER FUTURE IS A SNAP, THE by A. A.
Preciado. .a . . . . TW Feb 43 100
RULE 18 by Clifford D. Simak. .nt . . . . . . ASF Jul 38 32
RULE OF MATH by Charles Stoddard h ps. .a . . . .
. . . . .TW Aug 42 82
RULE OF THE BEE by Manly Wade Wellman. .s . . . . . .
. . . . ASF Oct 37 51
RULE OF THUMB by Charles Stoddard h ps. .a . . . . . .
. . . . TW Dec 41 104
RULERS, THE by A. E. van Vogt. .s . . . . ASF Mar 44 27
RULL, THE by A. E. van Vogt. .nt . . . . .ASF May 48 7
RUNAROUND, THE by Craig Browning ps (Roger P.
Graham). .s . . . . FA Dec 49 108
RUNAROUND by Isaac Asimov. .s . . . . . . ASF Mar 42 94
RUNAWAY by Alfred Coppel, Jr. . .s . . . . . PS Spr 49 31
RUNAWAY CARGO by Nat Schachner. .s . . . .
. . . . ASF Oct 40 88
RUNAWAY SKYSCRAPER, THE by Murray Leinster
ps (Will F. Jenkins). .s . . . . Amz Jun 26 250
RUNNING OF THE ZAR, THE by Vaseleos Garson . . .
. .s . . . . .PS Win 47 67
RUSSIAN ZIEGFELD by William P. McGivern. .a . . . . .
. . . . Amz Aug 41 108
RUST by Joseph E. Kelleam. .s . . . . .ASF Oct 39 133

Title. .Author. .Length . . . . Magazine. .Date. .Page No.

S

S.O.S. APHRODITE! by Stanley Mullen. .s . . . .
. . . . PS Sum 49 45
S O S IN SPACE by Eando Binder ps (Otto Binder) . . . .
. .s .ASF Jan 37 68
SABOTAGE ON MARS by Maurice Duclos. .nt. . . . . .
. . . . .FA Jun 40 70
SABOTEUR OF SPACE by Robert Abernathy. .s . . . . .
. . . . PS Spr 44 48
SACK, THE by William Morrison ps (Joseph
Samachson). .s . . . . ASF Sep 50 46
SACRED CLOAK OF FEATHERS, THE (THE
LEMURIAN DOCUMENTS No. 5) by J. Lewis
Burtt. .s. . . . . Amz Jul 32 338
SACRED MARTIAN PIG, THE by Margaret St.
Clair. .nt . . . . SS Jul 49 78
SACRIFICE by John Hollis Mason. .s . . . . . Fut Feb 42 97
SAFARI TO THE LOST AGES by William P.
McGivern. .nt . . . . FA Jul 42 118
SAGA OF PELICAN WEST, THE by Eric Frank
Russell. .nt . . . . ASF Feb 37 12
SAGA OF POSI AND NEGA, A by Joseph Wm.
Skidmore. .s. . . . . Amz May 35 93
SAGES OF EROS, THE by John Frances Kalland . . . . .
. .s . . . . Amz Feb 32 992
SAILING SHIP OF VENUS by James B. Settles . . . . . .
. .bacover. . . . . .Amz Jan 43
SAILPLANES OF THE FUTURE by Timothy V.
Holley. .a. . . . . Amz Aug 41 128
SAINT MULLIGAN by Nelson S. Bond. .s . . . .
. . . . .FA May 43 74
SAKNARTH by Millard Verne Gordon ps (Donald A.
Wollheim). .ss. . . . . .SFQ Spr 42 118
SALAD CITIZENS, THE by Walt Sheldon. .s . . . .
. . . . TW Oct 50 133
SALVAGE by Cleve Cartmill. .s . . . . TW Aug 49 111
SALVAGE by Vic Phillips. .nt . . . . ASF Nov 40 9
SALVAGE IN SPACE by Jack Williamson. .s . . . .
. . . . ASF Mar 33 6
SALVAGE JOB by Leslie A. Crouch. .ss . . . Fut Dec 41 95
SALVAGE OF SPACE by Frederic Arnold Kummer,
Jr. .s. .Ash Apr 40 55
SAM GRAVES' GRAVITY NULLIFYER by George
Fredrick Stratton. .s. . . . . Amz Aug 29 465
SAMBO by William Fryer Harvey. .s . . . . .AFR #5 30
SAMMY CALLS A NOOBUS by Henry A. Norton. . . . .
. . .s . . . . .FA Jan 43 220
SANATORIS SHORT-CUT by Jack Vance. .s . . . .
. . . . SS Sep 48 113
SANCTUARY by H. H. Holmes ps (William Anthony
Parker White). .s . . . . ASF Jun 43 86
SANCTUARY by Charles Recour. .s . . . . . FA Jan 50 58
SAND by Colin Keith. .s . . . . ASF Nov 42 80

Title. .Author. .Length . . . . Magazine. .Date. .Page No.

SANDHOUND, THE by Ross Rocklynne. .s . . . .
. . . . PS May 43 38
SANDHOUND STRIKES, THE by Ross Rocklynne. . . .
. . .nt . . . . .PS Spr 45 2
SANDS OF TIME by P. Schuyler Miller. .nt . . . .
. . . . ASF Apr 37 116
SANITY by Fritz Leiber, Jr. . .s . . . . . . ASF Apr 44 160
SAPHROPHYTE MEN OF VENUS, THE by Nat
Schachner. .s . . . . ASF Oct 36 84
SAPPHIRE ENCHANTRESS, THE by Cleo Eldon ps
(Don Wilcox). .nt . . . . FA Dec 45 84
SARGASSO MONSTER, THE by Edsel Newton . . . . . .
. .s . . . . WS Apr 31 1252
SARGASSO OF SPACE, THE by Edmond
Hamilton. .s . . . . .ASF Sep 31 390
SARGASSO OF THE STARS by Frederick A. Kummer,
Jr. . .s . . . . PS Sum 41 46
SARKER'S JOKE BOX by Raymond Z. Gallun. .s . . . . .
. . . . Amz Mar 42 110
SATANIC CYSTS, THE by Paul Chadwick. .s . . . .
. . . . TW Aug 38 35
SATELLITE FIVE by Arthur K. Barnes. .nt . . . .
. . . . TW Oct 38 14
SATELLITE OF DOOM, THE by D. D. Sharp. .s . . . . .
. . . . .WS Jan 31 774
SATELLITE OF FEAR by Frederick Arnold Kummer,
Jr. . .s . . . . .PS Spr 41 96
SATELLITE OF PERIL by Frank Belknap Long. .s . . . .
. . . . TW Aug 42 88
SATELLITE SECRET by Kris Neville. .s . . . .
. . . . Amz Apr 50 166
SATELLITE SPACE SHIP STATION by James B.
Settles. .bacover pic. . . . . Amz May 46
SATELLITES OF DEATH by L. J. Johnson. .s . . . .
. . . . .ToW Sum 38 43
SATURN'S RINGMASTER by Raymond Z. Gallun. . . .
. .s . . . . TW Dec 36 80
SAUNDERS' STRANGE SECOND SIGHT by Clee
Garson ps (David Wright O'Brien). .s . . . .FA Jan 43 182
SAURIAN VALEDICTORY by Norman L. Knight . . . .
. .s . . . . .ASF Jan 39 33
SAVAGE GALAHAD by Bryce Walton. .s . . . .
. . . . .PS Win 46 77
SAXE MURDER CASE, THE by Eugene V.
Brewster. .s . . . . AD Aug 30 718
SCANDAL IN THE 4th DIMENSION by A. R.
Long. .s. ASF Feb 34 94
SCANNERS LIVE IN VAIN by Cordwainer Smith . . . .
. .n . . . . FB #6 32
SCAR–TISSUE by Henry S. Whitehead. .s . . . .
. . . . .Amz Jul 46 146
SCARAB, THE by Raymond Z. Gallun. .s . . . .
. . . . ASF Aug 36 80
SCARLET DREAM by C. L. Moore. .nt . . . . . .AFR #5 7
SCARLET PLAGUE, THE by Jack London. .nt . . . . . .
. . . . .FFM Feb 49 92

Title. .Author. .Length . . . . Magazine. .Date. .Page No.

SCARLET PLANET, THE by Don M. Lemon. .n. . . . . .
. . . . WQ Win 31 150
SCARLET ROLLERS, THE by Stanton A. Coblentz . . .
. .s . . . . FA Sep 42 48
SCARLET SWORDSMEN, THE by Don Wilcox . . . . . .
. .nt . . . . Amz Jun 45 120
SCHEDULE by Harry Walton. .s . . . . ASF Jun 45 54
SCHEUCHZER, JOHN JACOB (FANTASTIC HOAXES)
by Willy Ley. .a . . . . FA Oct 40 74
SCHIZOPHRENIC by Noel Loomis. .s. . . . .
. . . . TW Dec 48 58
SCHOOL FOR THE STARS by John D. MacDonald . . .
. .s . . . . .ASF Oct 48 100
SCIENCE AND DREAMS by Derwin Lesser ps (Charles
D. Hornig). .a . . . . .SF Oct 39 80
SCIENCE AND TRUTH by Derwin Lesser ps (Charles D.
Hornig). .a . . . . SF Aug 39 30
SCIENCE AND "TRUTH" (Pravda) by Willy Ley . . . . .
. .a . . . . ASF Dec 49 96
SCIENCE FANTASY FORUM dept in ToW from Aut 41
SCIENCE FICTION BOOK REVIEW dept in TW from
Aug 47
SCIENCE FICTION BOOKSHELF review dept in SS
from Jan 49
SCIENCE–FICTION QUIZ by Simpson H. Ritter . . . . .
. .dept . . . . SSS Jan 49 51
SCIENCE FICTIONEER, THE by Frederik Pohl dept in
SSS. Fan news dept in the early issues, it became a book
review dept with the post-war revival from Jan 49
SCIENCE FOR ART'S SAKE by J. J. Coupling ps (John R.
Pierce). .a. . . . . ASF Nov 50 83
SCIENCE FROM SYRACUSE by Polton Cross ps (John
Russell Fearn). .s. . . . . SF Mar 41 61
SCIENCE IS GOLDEN by Kelvin Kent ps (Arthur K.
Barnes & Henry Kuttner). .s . . . . TW Apr 40 80
SCIENCE ISLAND by Eando Binder ps (Otto Binder) . .
. .s . . . . SS Jan 39 112
SCIENCE OF SUCKERS, THE by Gerald Vance h ps. . .
. .a . . . . Amz Nov 41 55
SCIENCE OF TIME-TRAVEL, THE by Ray
Cummings. .a . . . . AMF Feb 50 114
SCIENCE OF WHITHERING, THE by L. Sprague de
Camp. .a 2 pt . . . . ASF Jul 40 108
SCIENCE, THE POLICE AND THE CRIMINAL
(SCIENTIFIC ACTUALITY) by Ashur Van A.
Sommers. .a . . . . SD Apr 30 336
SCIENTIFIC ACTUALITY
A MESSAGE FROM THE ULTRA-VIOLET by H.
Ashton-Wolfe. .a . . . . .SD Jan 30 46
TRUE ADVENTURES OF A SUPER-SCIENTIFIC
DETECTIVE by Joseph Gollcomb. .a . . . .
. . . . SD Feb 30 138
TEST-TUBE BLOODHOUNDS by H. H. Dunn . . . . .
. . . . .a . . . . SD Mar 30 232
SCIENCE, THE POLICE AND THE CRIMINAL by
Ashur Van A. Sommers. .a . . . . SD Apr 30 336

HUNTING VIPERS by Edmond Locard. .a . . . .
. . . . SD May 30 440
THE TELEGRAPHIC FINGER PRINT by Hector G.
Grey. .a . . . . AD Jun 30 549
ARRESTED BY RADIO by Hector Gavin Grey . . . .
. .a . . . . .AD Jul 30 591
TRACKED BY ULTRA-VIOLET by Hector Gavin
Grey. .a . . . . AD Aug 30 682
WHAT PRICE GLUES? by Herbert Mills. .a . . . .
. . . . AD Sep 30 812
THE MOST DANGEROUS FORGERIES by Edmond
Locard. .a . . . . AD Oct 30 898
SCIENTIFIC ADVENTURES OF MR. FOSDICK, THE
by Jacque Morgan
MR. FOSDICK INVENTS THE
SEIDLITZMOBILE. .s . . . . Amz Jun 26 238
FELINE LIGHT AND POWER COMPANY IS
ORGANIZED, THE. .s . . . . Amz Jul 26 319
AA 27 117
THE INTERNATIONAL ELECTRO GALVANIC
UNDERTAKING CORPORATION. .s . . . .
. . . . Amz Aug 26 417
SCIENTIFIC CRACKSMAN, THE by Arthur B.
Reeve. .s . . . . AD Aug 30 688
SCIENTIFIC GHOST, THE by Ed Earl Repp. .s . . . . . .
. . . . Amz Jan 39 72
SCIENTIFIC MILER OF BOWLER U by Ivan
Sandrof. .s . . . . FA Oct 40 104
SCIENTIFIC MYSTERIES dept with a short article & pic
THE FATE OF THE MAMMOTH by Joseph J.
Millard. . . . . Amz Oct 40 68
THE MYSTERY OF THE MOON by Joseph J.
Millard. . . . . Amz Nov 40 58
BOMB SIGHT OF THE GODS by Joseph J.
Millard. . . . . Amz Dec 40 98
HOW LONG WAS THE EARTH TO LIVE? by
Morrison Colladay . . . . Amz Jan 41 54
THE GREAT PYRAMID OF GIZEH by Joseph J.
Millard. . . . . Amz Feb 41 70
LIFE FROM ELECTRICITY by Jack West. . . . .
. . . . Amz Mar 41 44
EARTH'S AMAZING ATMOSPHERE by Joseph J.
Millard. . . . . Amz Apr 41 124
PLANTS THAT THINK by Joseph J. Millard . . . . . .
. . . . .Amz May 41 132
LIGHTNING by Joseph J. Millard . . . Amz Jun 41 132
SIZE by Joseph J. Millard . . . . .Amz Jul 41 132
ARE THERE STRANGE LIFE FORMS ON EARTH
UNKNOWN? by Joseph J. Millard. . . Amz Aug 41 124
GONDWANALAND by L. Taylor Hansen . . . .
. . . . Amz Sep 41 130
MYSTERY OF LIFE by Joseph J. Millard . . . .
. . . . Amz Oct 41 134
MATTO GROSSO by Joseph J. Millard . . . .
. . . . Amz Nov 41 112
VOTAN, THE CLEVER BUILDER by L. Taylor
Hansen . . . . Amz Dec 41 126

Title. .Author. .Length . . . . Magazine. .Date. .Page No.

SCIENTIFIC MYSTERIES (continued)
   THE SPIDER TOTEM by L. Taylor Hansen . . . .
. . . . .Amz Jan 42 230
   VANISHED CIVILIZATIONS by Joseph J.
   Millard. . . . . Amz Feb 42 228
   THE SEA SERPENT by Joseph J. Millard . . . .
. . . . Amz Mar 42 226
   THE LOST RACE OF ILLINOIS by Robert Moore
   Williams. . . . . Amz Apr 42 262
   LOST RACES OF AMERICA by Robert Moore
   Williams. . . . . Amz May 42 264
   (From Jun 42 to Dec 48, SCIENTIFIC MYSTERIES
   was taken over by L. TAYLOR HANSEN exclusively.
   See Author Index for full listing of titles in that period)
SCIENTIFIC ODDITIES by Lynn Standish *dept in* Amz &
  FA *from* 1948
SCIENTIFIC PIONEER, THE by Nelson S. Bond. .s . . .
. . . . Amz Mar 40 88
SCIENTIFIC PIONEER RETURNS, THE by Nelson S.
  Bond. .nt . . . . Amz Nov 40 88
SCIENTIFIC SPOOKS by Lloyd Norse. .s . . . .
. . . . TW Dec 42 56
SCIENTIFIC WIDOWHOOD, A by David H. Keller . . . .
. .s . . . . SD Feb 30 114
SCIENTIFILM CYCLE, THE by Forrest J.
  Ackerman. .a . . . . .OW Jul 50 153
SCIENTIST DISOWNED by Raymond Z. Gallun. .s. . . .
. . . . Amz Jun 42 102
SCIENTIST DIVIDES, A by Donald Wandrei. .s . . . . . .
. . . . ASF Sep 34 53
SCIENTIST OF THE AIR (LINCOLN ELLSWORTH) by
  Alexander Blade *h ps* .a . . . . Amz May 43 224
SCIENTIST RISES, A by D. W. Hall. .s . . . .
. . . . ASF Nov 32 165
SCIENTISTS REVOLT, THE by Edgar Rice
  Burroughs. .nt . . . . .FA Jul 39 6
SCISSORS, THE by William Wallrich. .s . . . .
. . . . .OW May 50 156
SCOURGE BELOW, THE by Sam Merwin, Jr. . .s. . . . .
. . . . TW Oct 39 46
SCOURGE OF A SINGLE CELL, THE by Bob Olsen
  ps (Alfred John Olsen). .s . . . . SF Mar 40 56
SCRAMBLED WORLD by Basil Wells. .s . . . .PS Spr 47 83
SCRAMBLER, THE by Harry Walton. .s . . . .
. . . . ASF Apr 41 70
SCREAMING SHAPES, THE by Franklin Gregory . . . .
. .nt . . . . Amz Aug 50 58
SCULPTORS OF LIFE by Wallace West. .s . . . .
. . . . ASF Dec 39 71
SEA KING'S ARMORED DIVISION, THE by L. Sprague
  de Camp. .a 2 pt . . . . ASF Aug 41 46
SEA KINGS OF MARS by Leigh Brackett. .n . . . .
. . . . TW Jun 49 9
SEA OF MYSTERY by Willy Ley. .a . . . . . ASF Jun 43 97
SEA PEOPLE, THE by Richard S. Shaver. .nt . . . .
. . . . .Amz Aug 46 8

Title. .Author. .Length . . . . Magazine. .Date. .Page No.

SEA TERROR, THE by Captain S. P. Meek. .s . . . .
. . . . ASF Dec 30 336
SEA THING, THE by A. E. van Vogt. .s . . . .
. . . . UK Jan 40 81
SEA THINGS, THE by Guy Arnold. .s . . . . SF Mar 39 82
SEAL MAIDEN, THE by Victor Rousseau
  (Emanuel). .s . . . . .AMF Feb 50 116
SEALED ROOM, THE by Henry Leverage. .s . . . .
. . . . AD Jun 30 541
SEARCH, THE by A. E. van Vogt. .nt . . . . .ASF Jan 43 44
SEARCH FOR IDEAS dept in ToW *from* Win 39 *thru*
  Spr 41
SEARCH FOR ZERO, THE by Willy Ley. .a 2 pt . . . . .
. . . . .ASF Oct 40 122
SEAT OF OBLIVION by Eric Frank Russell. .s. . . . . . .
. . . . ASF Nov 41 110
SEAWARD by Malcolm Jameson. .s . . . . . ASF Nov 38 82
SECOND APPROXIMATION by R. S. Richardson . . . .
. .a . . . . .ASF Sep 46 109
SECOND CATACLYSM, THE by Dow Elstar *ps (Raymond*
  Z. Gallun). .s . . . . ASF Mar 37 94
SECOND DELUGE, THE by Garrett P. Serviss . . . .
. .n 3 pt . . . . Amz Nov 26 676
. .n *(complete)* . . . . .AQ Win 33 2
. .n *(complete)* . . . . .FN Jul 48 6
SECOND MEETING by George Whitley *ps (A. Bertram*
  Chandler). .s. . . . . .F&SF Fal 50 84
SECOND MISSILE, THE by Ed Earl Repp. .s . . . .
. . . . Amz Dec 30 800
SECOND MOON, THE by R. R. Winterbotham. .s. . . . .
. . . . MSS Feb 39 105
SECOND NIGHT OF SUMMER by James H.
  Schmitz. .nt . . . . GSF Dec 50 4
SECOND SATELLITE, THE by Martin Pearson *ps (Donald*
  . .s . . . . ASF Aug 30 175
SECOND STELLITE, THE by Martin Pearson *ps (Donald*
  A. Wollheim). .s . . . . .Fut Feb 43 10
SECOND SHELL, THE by Jack Williamson. .s . . . . . .
. . . . .AW Nov 29 442
SECOND SOLUTION, THE by A. E. van Vogt. .s . . . .
. . . . ASF Oct 42 41
SECOND STAGE LENSMEN by E. E. Smith
  . .n 4 pt . . . . ASF Nov 41 9
SECOND SWARM, THE by J. Schlossel. .nt . . . .
. . . . AQ Spr 28 266
SECRET GIANT, THE by Willy Ley. .a . . . ASF Jul 45 101
SECRET KINGDOM, THE by Allen S. Kline & Otis
  Adelbert Kline. .n 3 pt . . . . Amz Oct 29 616
SECRET LEAGUE OF SIX by Don Wilcox. .s . . . .
. . . . .FA Aug 41 86
SECRET OF ANTON YORK, THE by Eando Binder
  ps (Otto Binder). .nt . . . . .TW Aug 40 89
SECRET OF ELENA'S TOMB, THE by Karl Tanzler Von
  Cosel. .n . . . . FA Sep 47 8
SECRET OF LORD FENNEL, THE by Frank G.
  Heiner. .s. . . . . Amz Nov 46 84

Title. .Author. .Length . . . . Magazine. .Date. .Page No.

SECRET OF LUCKY LOGAN, THE by Nelson S.
Bond. .s . . . . Amz Apr 42 96
SECRET OF PLANETOID 88, THE by Ed Earl
Repp. .n . . . . Amz Dec 41 10
SECRET OF SUTTER'S LAKE, THE by Don
Wilcox. .n . . . . Amz Jan 47 38
SECRET OF THE BURIED CITY by John Russell
Fearn. .nt . . . . Amz May 39 6
SECRET OF THE CANALI, THE by Clifton B.
Kruse. .s . . . . ASF Jul 38 20
SECRET OF THE COMET by Raymond Z. Gallun . . . .
. .s . . . . TW Jan 41 50
SECRET OF THE CRYPT by Oliver A. Saari . . . .
. .s . . . . .SSS Nov 40 82
SECRET OF THE CYCLOTRON by Jackson
Gregory, Jr. . .s . . . . TW Feb 40 32
SECRET OF THE EARTH STAR by Henry
Kuttner. .nt . . . . Amz Aug 42 110
SECRET OF THE GOLDEN JAGUAR by Robert Moore
Williams. .nt . . . . FA May 42 54
SECRET OF THE GROWING GOLD, THE by Bram
Stoker. .s . . . . FFM Aug 46 116
SECRET OF THE INVISIBLE GIRL, THE (Dr.
HACKENSAW'S SECRETS) by Clement
Fezandie. .s . . . . Amz Jul 26 376
SECRET OF THE LIGHTNING by H. H. Harmon ps
(Robert Moore Williams). .s . . . . FA Sep 49 100
SECRET OF THE LOST PLANET by David Wright
O'Brien. .nt . . . . Amz May 41 152
SECRET OF THE MICROCOSM, THE by F. Golub
(tr fr German by Francis M. Currier). .ss . . . .
. . . . .WS Jan 34 622
SECRET OF THE MOON TREASURE by Thornton
Ayre ps (John Russell Fearn). .nt . . . . . .Amz Jul 40 98
SECRET OF THE OBSERVATORY by Robert
Bloch. .s . . . . .Amz Aug 38 6
SECRET OF THE PYRAMID by Robert Moore
Williams. .nt . . . . .Amz Jul 39 8
SECRET OF THE RING, THE by Thornton Ayre ps
(John Russell Fearn). .nt . . . . Amz Nov 38 100
Amz Oct 42 64
SECRET OF THE ROBOT by Guy Archette (on story)
ps (Chester S. Geier, who is listed as author in the
ToC). .s . . . . Amz Apr 48 76
SECRET OF THE ROCKS, THE by Russell R.
Winterbotham. .s . . . . ASF Dec 37 105
SECRET OF THE SERPENT by Don Wilcox. .n . . . . . .
. . . . FA Jan 48 8
SECRET OF THE STONE DOLL by Don Wilcox . . . . .
. .nt . . . . FA Mar 41 106
SECRET OF THE SUN by Ray Cummings. .s . . . .
. . . . TW Aug 39 90
SECRET OF THE TOMB, THE by R. Crossley
Arnold. .nt . . . . WQ Fal 30 106
SECRET OF THE YELLOW CRYSTAL by Guy Archette
ps (Chester S. Geier). .nt . . . . Amz Apr 48 42

Title. .Author. .Length . . . . Magazine. .Date. .Page No.

SECRET OF THE YOMAR by Elroy Arno. .nt . . . .
. . . . .FA Jul 47 134
SECRET PEOPLE, THE by John Beynon (Harris) . . . . .
. .n . . . . .FFM Apr 50 10
SECRET PEOPLE, THE by James Blish & Damon
Knight. .s . . . . .Fut Nov 50 46
SECRET SENSE, THE by Isaac Asimov. .s . . . .
. . . . .Cos Mar 41 87
SECRET UNATTAINABLE by A. E. van Vogt . . . .
. .nt . . . . .ASF Jul 42 9
SECRET WEAPON by Alfred Coppel. .s . . . .
. . . . .ASF Jul 49 93
SECRET WEAPON by Joseph Farrell. .ss . . . .
. . . . SS Fal 43 114
SECRET WEAPON by Henry S. Lewis. .ss . . . .
. . . . .CF Fal 42 103
SECRET WEAPON by Terry Thor. .s . . . . FB #3 20
SECRETS OF THE FLYING SAUCERS TOLD AT LAST
by Major Vernon Piper. .nt . . . . .FanS Nov 50 4
SEE EARTH FIRST by Willy Ley. .guest ed . . . .
. . . . SS Jul 39 13
SEE YOU LATER by Henry Kuttner. .s . . . .
. . . . TW Jun 49 116
SEED OF EMPIRE by Guy Archette ps (Chester S.
Geier). .nt . . . . FA Aug 49 84
SEED OF THE ARCTIC ICE by H. G. Winter ps (Harry
Bates & Desmond Winter Hall). .s . . . . ASF Feb 32 202
SEED OF THE TOC-TOC BIRDS, THE by Francis Flagg
ps (George Henry Weiss). .s . . . . .ASF Jan 32 81
SEEDS FROM SPACE by John Russell Fearn. .nt . . . . .
. . . . .ToW #1 37 17
SEEDS FROM SPACE by Laurence Manning. .s . . . . .
. . . . WS Jun 35 9
SEEDS OF LIFE by John Taine ps (Eric Temple
Bell). .n . . . . .AQ Fal 31 434
SEEDS OF THE DUSK by Raymond Z. Gallun. .nt . . . .
. . . . ASF Jun 38 76
SEEING BLINDNESS, THE by J. Earle Wycoff. .s . . . .
. . . . .ASF Feb 36 33
SEEING EAR, THE by John Scott Campbell. .s . . . . . .
. . . . .TW Feb 37 82
SEEKER OF TOMORROW by Eric Frank Russell &
Leslie T. Johnson. .nt . . . . ASF Jul 37 124
SEEKERS, THE by Robert Moore Williams. .s . . . .
. . . . SS May 48 92
SEESAW, THE by A. E. van Vogt. .s . . . . . .ASF Jul 41 60
SEETEE SHOCK by Will Stewart ps (Jack
Williamson). .n 3 pt . . . . .ASF Feb 48 8
SEISMOGRAPH ADVENTURE, THE by Arthur B.
Reeve. .s . . . . SD Mar 30 200
SENSE OF DIRECTION. .a . . . . .ASF Jul 44 99
SENSE TWISTER, THE by W. Varick Nevins, III . . . . .
. .ss . . . . WS Aug 34 304
SENTIMENTAL MONSTER by Lee Francis h ps. .s . . . .
. . . . Amz Dec 46 136
SERAPION by Francis Stevens. .n . . . . . .FFM Jul 42 78

Title. .Author. .Length . . . . Magazine. .Date. .Page No.

SERENIS, WATER CITY OF CALLISTO by Frank R.
Paul. .bacover pic . . . . Amz Dec 41
SERGEANT SHANE GOES TO WAR by John York
Cabot ps (David Wright O'Brien). .s. . . Amz Jun 42 152
SERGEANT SHANE OF THE SPACE MARINES by John
York Cabot ps (David Wright O'Brien). .s. . . . .
. . . . Amz Oct 41 94
SERGEANT TERRY BULL'S TERRIBLE WEAPONS by
Willy Ley. .a. . . . . ASF Nov 41 76
SERPENT HAS FIVE FANGS, THE by Don Wilcox . . .
. .nt . . . . FA Dec 45 6
SERUM RUBBER MAN, THE by Ford Smith ps (Oscar J.
Friend). .s . . . . SS Sum 44 83
SERVICE FIRST by David H. Keller, M.D. . .s. . . . .
. . . . AQ Win 31 136
SERVOMECHANISMS by Lorne MacLaughlan. .a. . . . .
. . . . .ASF Jan 48 89
SET YOUR COURSE BY THE STARS by Eando Binder
ps (Otto Binder). .s . . . . ASF May 35 109
SEVEN AGES OF FAN, THE by Robert Bloch. .a. . . .
. . . . TW Jun 49 160
SEVEN CAME BACK by Clifford D. Simak. .s . . . .
. . . . Amz Oct 50 102
SEVEN COME A-LOVING by Craig Browning ps (Roger
P. Graham). .s. . . . . .OW Nov 49 72
SEVEN FOLLIES OF SCIENCE, THE by Willy Ley . . .
. .a . . . . .Amz Jan 43 228
SEVEN FOOTPRINTS TO SATAN by A. Merritt . . . . .
. .n . . . . FN Jan 49 8
SEVEN JEWELS OF CHAMAR, THE by Raymond F.
Jones. .nt. .PS Win 46 90
SEVEN PERILS TO QUINCHES by Joseph Wm.
Skidmore. .s . . . . Amz Feb 35 62
SEVEN SLEEPERS, THE by Arthur K. Barnes & Henry
Kuttner. .nt . . . . .TW May 40 93
SEVEN SUNSTROKES by Bob Olsen ps (Alfred John
Olsen, Jr.). .nt. . . . . Amz Apr 32 16
SEVEN TEMPORARY MOONS, THE by William
Fitzgerald (Jenkins). .s . . . . TW Feb 48 56
SEVENTH GENERATION, THE by Harl Vincent
(Schoepflin). .s . . . . AQ Win 29 54
SEX SERUM, THE by H. O. Dickinson. .s . . . .
. . . . WS Oct 35 588
SHACKLED STATUE, THE by Berkeley
Livingston. .s . . . . FA Jan 45 52
SHADES OF HENRY MORGAN by H. B. Hickey ps
(Herb Livingston). .nt. . . . . FA May 47 146
SHADES OF TOFFEE, THE by Charles F. Myers . . . . .
. .n . . . . FA Jun 50 8
SHADOW AND THE FLASH, THE by Jack
London. .s . . . . FFM Jun 48 102
SHADOW DWELLERS, THE by Frank Belknap
Long. .s. . . . . .TW Sum 45 52
SHADOW FOR SALE by Chester S. Geier. .s . . . .
. . . . FA Jun 48 112

Title. .Author. .Length . . . . Magazine. .Date. .Page No.

SHADOW GIRL, THE by Ray Cummings. .n . . . .
. . . . SFQ Spr 42 4
SHADOW–GODS, THE by Vaseleos Garson. .s . . . .
. . . . PS Sum 46 101
SHADOW GOLD by Ray Cummings. .nt . . . .
. . . . TW Oct 36 14
SHADOW–MAN by Eric Frank Russell. .ss . . . .
. . . . .Fant #1 38 49
SHADOW MEN, THE by A. E. van Vogt. .n . . . .
. . . . SS Jan 50 11
SHADOW OF LIFE by Clifford D. Simak. .nt . . . .
. . . . ASF Mar 43 50
SHADOW OF THE SPHINX by William Lawrence
Hamling. .n . . . . .FA Nov 46 8
SHADOW OF THE SPIDER by Lee Francis h ps
. .s . . . . Amz Mar 43 202
SHADOW OF THE VEIL, THE by Raymond Z.
Gallun. .s . . . . ASF Feb 39 109
SHADOW OF THE SAND by John D. MacDonald . . . . .
. .n . . . . TW Oct 50 11
SHADOW ON THE SPARK, THE by Edward S.
Sears. .s . . . . Amz Aug 27 498
SHADOW OUT OF TIME, THE by H. P. Lovecraft . . . .
. .n . . . . .ASF Jun 36 110
SHADOW OVER MARS by Leigh Brackett. .n . . . .
. . . . SS Fal 44 11
SHADOW OVER VENUS by Frank Belknap Long. . . . .
. .s . . . . .SS Mar 46 73
SHADOW PEOPLE, THE by Ray Cummings. .s . . . . . .
. . . . .Ash Mar 42 86
SHADOW WORLD by Ray Cummings. .s . . . .
. . . . TW Dec 39 80
SHADOW WORLD, THE by Sophie Wenzel Ellis. .s . . . .
. . . . Amz Dec 32 824
SHADOWLESS WORLD, THE by Oliver Saari. .s . . . . .
. . . . .Fut Aug 41 96
SHADOWS, THE by Henry S. Whitehead. .s . . . .
. . . . AFR #14 110
SHADOWS FROM HESPLON, THE by Lloyd Arthur
Eshbach. .nt . . . . SF Oct 40 8
SHADOWS OF EMPIRE by Lester del Rey. .s . . . .
. . . . Fut Jul–Aug 50 57
SHADOWS OF THE NIGHT by Neil R. Jones. .s . . . . . .
. . . . AD Oct 30 882
SHADRACH by Nelson S. Bond. .s . . . . PS Fal 41 106
"SHALL STAY THESE COURIERS" by Nelson S.
Bond. .s. .TW Nov 40 80
SHAMBLEAU by C. L. Moore. .nt . . . .
. . . . .AFR #7 3
SHAPE OF DESIRE, THE by Cleve Cartmill. .s . . . . . .
. . . . UK Jun 41 101
SHAPE OF SHIPS TO COME, THE by Arthur C.
Clarke, B.Sc. . .a . . . . .NW #4 49 40
SHAPE OF THINGS, THE by Ray Bradbury. .s . . . . . .
. . . . TW Feb 48 47

Title. .Author. .Length . . . . Magazine. .Date. .Page No.

Title. .Author. .Length . . . . Magazine. .Date. .Page No.

SHAPES, THE by R. DeWitt Miller. .s . . . . ASF Feb 36 60
SHARBEAU'S STARTLING STATUE by Clee Garson
  ps (David Wright O'Brien). .s . . . . FA Nov 42 166
SHAVER MYSTERY, THE by Richard S. Shaver (All-
  Shaver issue, summarizing the "Shaver Mystery") . . .
  . . . . Amz Jun 47
SHAVERIAN HYPOTHESIS, THE by Robert Paul
  Kidwell. .a . . . . .Amz Jan 48 150
SHAVERIAN SIDELIGHTS by Vincent H. Gaddis . . . .
  . .a . . . . .Amz Jan 49 130
SHAWN'S SWORD by Lee Gregor ps (Milton A.
  Rothman). .s . . . . .ASF Oct 39 111
SHAYLA'S GARDEN by Dwight V. Swain. .nt . . . . . .
  . . . . FA Nov 42 194
SHE by Rog Phillips ps (Roger P. Graham). .nt . . . . . .
  . . . . FA Apr 49 88
SHE SAID "TAKE ME IF YOU DARE" (ON ACCOUNT
  OF A WOMAN) by Theodore Roscoe. nt . . . .
  . . . . FanF May 50 3
SHE WALKED ALONE by John Russell Fearn. .s . . . . .
  . . . . .FA Jul 39 66
SHENADUN by John D. MacDonald. .s . . . . SS Sep 48 102
SHERIDAN BECOMES AMBASSADOR by Warren E.
  Sanders. .s . . . . .Amz Jul 32 356
SHERIFF OF THORIUM GULCH, THE by Miles J.
  Breuer. .nt . . . . Amz Aug 42 44
SHHHHH—DON'T MENTION IT! by Arthur McCann
  ps (John W. Campbell, Jr.). .a . . . . . . ASF Aug 40 104
SHIFTING SEAS by Stanley G. Weinbaum. .s . . . .
  . . . . Amz Apr 37 115
SHINING MAN, THE by Noel Gardner ps (Henry
  Kuttner). .nt . . . . .FA May 40 40
SHINING ONE, THE by Nat Schachner. .s . . . .
  . . . . ASF May 37 78
SHIP OF CALLISTO by James B. Settles. . . . .
  . .bacover pic . . . . Amz Mar 44
SHIP OF COLD DEATH by D. J. Foster. .s . . . .
  . . . . .Fut Nov 40 24
SHIP OF DARKNESS, THE by A. E. van Vogt. .s . . . . .
  . . . . FB #2 4
SHIP OF ISHTAR, THE by A. Merritt. .n . . . .
  . . . . FN Mar 48 8
SHIP OF JUPITER by James B. Settles . . . .
  . .bacover . . . . Amz Sep 43
SHIP OF SILENCE, THE by Albert Richard
  Wetjen. .s . . . . AFR #13 104
SHIP OF SILENT MEN, THE by Philip M.
  Fisher. .nt . . . . .FFM Feb 41 87
SHIP SAILS AT MIDNIGHT, THE by Fritz
  Leiber. .s . . . . FA Sep 50 54
SHIP THAT DIED, THE by John DeWitt Gilbert. . . . .
  . .s .FN Jan 41 118
SHIP THAT TURNED ASIDE, THE by G. Peyton
  Wertenbaker. .s . . . . Amz Mar 30 1130
SHIPS THAT COME BACK by Eando Binder ps (Otto
  Binder). .nt . . . . ASF Nov 35 54

SHIPWRECKED BOGEY MAN, THE by Lloyd
  Williams. .s . . . . OTWA Jul 50 83
SHOCK by Lewis Padgett ps (Henry Kuttner & C. L.
  Moore). .s . . . . ASF Mar 43 40
SHOES, THE by Robert Bloch. .s . . . . UK Feb 42 78
SHOOTING "DESTINATION MOON" by Robert A.
  Heinlein. .a . . . . .ASF Jul 50 6
SHORT–CIRCUITED PROBABILITY by Norman L.
  Knight. .s . . . . ASF Sep 41 61
SHORT-WAVE CASTLE by Calvin Peregoy ps (Thomas
  Calvert McClary). .s . . . . ASF Feb 34 47
SHORT-WAVE EXPERIMENT by Calvin Peregoy ps
  (Thomas Calvert McClary). .s . . . . ASF Feb 35 83
SHORT-WAVE MADNESS by Robert Castle ps (Edmond
  Hamilton). .s . . . . .SF Jun 39 57
SHORT-WAVE SUPERMAN, THE by Robert Leslie
  Bellem. .s . . . . Amz Nov 41 98
SHORTCUT, THE by Rog Phillips ps (Roger P.
  Graham). .s . . . . .Amz Jul 49 62
SHOT FROM THE SKY, THE by Benson Herbert . . . . .
  . .ss . . . . WS Feb 34 753
SHOT INTO INFINITY, THE by Otto Willi Gail (tr fr
  German by Francis Currier). .n . . . . WQ Fal 29 7
                                              SFQ Win 41 4
SHOT INTO SPACE by Isaac R. Nathanson. .s . . . .
  . . . . Amz Aug 34 111
SHOTTLE BOP by Theodore Sturgeon. .nt . . . .
  . . . . UK Feb 41 100
SHOULDN'T HAPPEN TO A DOG by Frances M.
  Deegan. .s . . . . FA Aug 50 126
SHROUD OF SECRECY, THE by Raymond F.
  Jones. .s . . . . TW Dec 49 64
SHROUD-SEWERS, THE by Berkeley Livingston . . . . .
  . .s . . . . FA Sep 47 160
SHUTTERED HOUSE, THE by August Derleth. .s . . . . .
  . . . . .AFR #1 45
SIDE STREET by Leroy Yerxa. .s . . . .
  . . . . Amz Nov 46 114
SIDEREAL TIME-BOMB, THE by Stanton A.
  Coblentz. .s . . . . .SS Win 44 100
SIDETRACK IN TIME by William P. McGivern. .s . . . . .
  . . . . .Amz Jul 41 90
SIDEWINDERS FROM SIRIUS by Fox B. Holden . . . .
  . . . . PS Nov 50 28
SIDEWISE IN TIME by Murray Leinster ps (Will F.
  Jenkins). .nt . . . . ASF Jun 34 10
SIDNEY, THE SCREWLOOSE ROBOT by William P.
  McGivern. .s . . . . FA Jun 41 116
SIGMA LYRA PASSES by Oliver E. Saari. .s . . . .
  . . . . SSS Jul 40 71
SIGN AND THE MESSAGE, THE by Ted Powell. .s . . .
  . . . . .SS Mar 50 105
SIGNAL POINT IN SPACE by Charles Recour. .s . . . . .
  . . . . FA Jun 49 102
SIGNAL RED by Henry Guth. .s . . . .
  . . . . PS Fal 49 69

Title. .Author. .Length . . . . Magazine. .Date. .Page No.

SIGNBOARD OF SPACE by Frederic Arnold Kummer,
Jr. . .s. TW Dec 39 12
SS May 50 80
SILENCE, THE by Ray Bradbury. .ss . . . . . SSS Jan 49 30
SILENCE, THE by Venard McLaughlin. .s . . . .
. . . . .Sti Jun 41 94
SILENCE IS—DEADLY by Bertrand L. Shurtleff . . . . .
. .nt . . . . ASF Apr 42 58
SILENT DESTROYER, THE by Hendrik Dahl Juve. . . .
. .s . . . . AW Aug 29 102
SILENT EDEN by Henry Kuttner. .s. . . . . .SS Mar 42 88
SILENT SCOURGE, THE by Morrison Colladay . . . . . .
. .s . . . . WS Dec 30 680
SILENT TREES, THE by Frank Owen. .s . . . . AFR #3 19
SILENT WORLD, THE by Guy Arnold. .s . . . .
. . . . SF Aug 39 102
SILICON EMPIRE, THE by Fritz Burg. .s . . . .
. . . . Amz Aug 33 456
SILLY SEASON, THE by C. M. Kornbluth. .s. . . . . . .
. . . . .F&SF Fal 50 3
SILVER COIL, THE by Thornton Ayre ps (John Russell
Fearn). .s. . . . . Amz Nov 42 214
SILVER DOME by Harl Vincent (Schoepflin). .s. . . . .
. . . . ASF Aug 30 192
SILVER KEY, THE by H. P. Lovecraft. .s . . . . AFR #3 44
SILVER MEDUSA, THE by Alexander Blade h ps. . . . .
. .s . . . . FA Feb 48 56
SILVER PLAGUE, THE by Albert de Pina. .nt . . . .
. . . . PS Spr 45 48
SILVER RAIDERS OF SIRIUS by P. F. Costello h ps . .
. .nt . . . . Amz Jul 43 164
SILVER SPHERE, THE by Royal W. Heckman. .s. . . .
. . . . ASF Nov 38 128
SIMPLE LIFE, THE by Ray Cummings. .s . . . .
. . . . SS May 48 61
SIMULTANEOUS WORLDS by Nat Schachner. . . . . . .
. .n 2 pt. . . . . ASF Oct 38 9
SIMWORTHY'S CIRCUS by Larry Shaw. .s . . . .
. . . . WB Dec 50 18
SINECURE 6 by Horace B. Fyfe. .s . . . . . .ASF Jan 47 55
SINGING MOONBEAMS, THE by Edward S.
Sears. .s. . . . . .AQ Sum 29 418
SINGING SKULLS, THE by Don Wilcox. .nt . . . .
. . . . FA Apr 45 66
SINGING WEAPON, THE by Bent Prout. .s . . . .
. . . . Amz May 27 180
SINISTER BARRIER by Eric Frank Russell. .n . . . . . .
. . . . UK Mar 39 9
GSFN #1
SIR MALLORY'S MAGNITUDE by S. D. Gottesman
ps (Cyril Kornbluth). .s. . . . . .SFQ Win 41–42 88
SIREN SATELLITE by Arthur K. Barnes. .s . . . .
. . . . TW Win 46 64
SIREN SONG by Lester Barclay. .nt . . . . . FA Feb 46 82
SIX-LEGGED GANGSTERS by Bob Olsen ps (Alfred
John Olsen, Jr.). .s. . . . . Amz Jun 35 98

Title. .Author. .Length . . . . Magazine. .Date. .Page No.

SIX-LEGGED SVENGALI by Mack Reynolds & Fredric
Brown. .s. . . . . .WB Dec 50 2
SIX TUESDAYS by Ross Rocklynne. .s. . . . . PS Fal 46 85
SIX WHO WERE MASKED by Henry J. Kostkos. . . . . .
. .s . . . . Amz Oct 36 70
SIXTH COLUMN by Anson MacDonald ps (Robert A.
Heinlein). .n 3 pt. . . . . ASF Jan 41 9
SIXTH GLACIER, THE by Marius. .n 2 pt. . . . .
. . . . .Amz Jan 29 900
SKELETON IN THE CLOSET, THE by Tarleton Fiske
ps (Robert Bloch). .s . . . . FA May 43 116
SKELETON MEN OF JUPITER by Edgar Rice
Burroughs. .nt. . . . . Amz Feb 43 8
SKEPTIC, THE by R. C. W. Ettinger. .s. . . . TW Feb 50 85
SKIDMORE'S STRANGE EXPERIMENT by David
Wright O'Brien. .s . . . . .Amz Jan 41 124
SKIN DEEP by Ford McCormack. .s . . . . . ASF Jul 50 78
SKIN-DEEP BEAUTY, THE by Dwight V. Swain . . . . .
. .s . . . . FA Jun 42 122
SKIN DUPE by William Morrison ps (Joseph
Samachson). .s . . . . TW Dec 49 98
SKIT-TREE PLANET by Murray Leinster ps (Will F.
Jenkins). .s. . . . . TW Apr 47 41
SKY COPS by Harl Vincent (Schoepflin) & Chas. Roy
Cox. .s. . . . . Amz Dec 31 818
SKY–GOING AIRCRAFT CARRIER, THE by Sam
Merwin, Jr. . .a. . . . . TW Aug 43 103
SKY IMP by Chester S. Geier. .s. . . . . FA Jun 43 10
SKY IS FALLING, THE by C. H. Liddell ps (Henry
Kuttner & C. L. Moore). .s . . . . PS Fal 50 42
SKY MANIAC, THE by Hendrik Dahl Juve. .s . . . . . .
. . . . AW Oct 29 294
SKY ROCK by Frank B. Long, Jr. . .s. . . . .
. . . . ASF Sep 35 59
SKY RULER, THE by Ed Earl Repp. .s. . . . .
. . . . .AW May 30 1014
SKY TERROR, THE by Ed Earl Repp. .s. . . . .
. . . . .SF Sep 41 31
SKY TEST by Dirk Wylie (& Frederik Pohl). .s. . . . . . .
. . . . .SSS Nov 42 50
SKY TRAP by Carl Jacobi. .s. . . . . SF Mar 40 69
SKY TRAP, THE by Frank Belknap Long. .s . . . .
. . . . .Com Jul 41 46
SKY WAS FULL OF SHIPS, THE by Theodore
Sturgeon. .s . . . . TW Jun 47 55
SKY WILL BE OURS, THE by Manly Wade
Wellman. .s. . . . . SSS Jan 49 94
SKY WOMAN, THE by Charles B. Stilson. .s . . . .
. . . . FFM Feb 40 33
SKYLARK series See EDWARD ELMER SMITH author
SKYLARK OF SPACE, THE by Edward Elmer Smith &
Lee Hawkins Garby. .n 3 pt. . . . . Amz Aug 28 390
SKYLARK OF VALERON, THE by Edward E. Smith,
Ph.D. . .n 7 pt . . . . ASF Aug 34 8
SKYLARK THREE by Edward Elmer Smith, Ph.D. . . .
. .n 3 pt. . . . . Amz Aug 30 388

Title. .Author. .Length . . . . Magazine. .Date. .Page No.

SKYLIGHT by Thomas Sheridan ps (Walter L.
    Gillings). .a. . . . . Fant Apr 47 70
SKYROVER by Leslie Northern h ps. .s . . . . SS Win 45 87
SLACKER'S PARADISE by Malcolm Jameson. .s . . . . .
    . . . . ASF Apr 41 82
SLAN by A. E. van Vogt. .n 4 pt . . . . ASF Sep 40 9
SLAVE OF ETERNITY by Roger Dee ps (Roger D.
    Aycock). .s. . . . . SSS May 50 84
SLAVE RAIDERS FROM MERCURY by Don
    Wilcox. .nt . . . . Amz Jun 40 6
SLAVE SHIP FROM SPACE, THE by A. R. Holmes
    ps (Harry Bates). .s . . . . ASF Jul 31 68
SLAVER, THE by L. Ron Hubbard. .s . . . ASF Jun 42 31
SLAVES OF MERCURY by Nat Schachner. .nt . . . . . .
    . . . . ASF Sep 32 78
SLAVES OF RHYTHM by Frederic Arnold Kummer,
    Jr. . .s. . . . . Amz Jan 40 98
SLAVES OF SLEEP by L. Ron Hubbard. .n. . . . .
    . . . . UK Jul 39 9
SLAVES OF THE CRYSTAL BRAIN by William Carter
    Sawtelle h ps. .n . . . . Amz May 50 8
SLAVES OF THE DUST by Sophie Wenzel Ellis. .s . . . .
    . . . . ASF Dec 30 295
SLAVES OF THE FISH MEN by Edgar Rice
    Burroughs. .nt. . . . . FA Mar 41 8
SLAVES OF THE LIFE RAY by Alfred Bester. .s . . . . .
    . . . . TW Feb 41 62
SLAVES OF THE LAMP by Arthur Leo Zagat . . . .
    . .n 2 pt. . . . . ASF Aug 46 7
SLAVES OF THE NINTH MOON by Ross
    Rocklynne. .s . . . . PS Mar 43 100
SLAVES OF THE UNKNOWN by Neil R. Jones. .s . . . .
    . . . . Ash Mar 42 10
SLAVES OF THE WORM by Richard S. Shaver. .n . . . .
    . . . . FA Feb 48 8
SLEDGE HAMMER. .a. . . . . ASF Oct 44 80
SLEEP OF AGES, THE by Stuart Martin. .s. . . . .
    . . . . FFM Dec 40 88
SLEEP SCOURGE by Henry J. Kostkos. .s. . . . .
    . . . . WS Dec 34 838
SLEEPER IS A REBEL, THE by Bryce Walton. .nt . . . .
    . . . . TW Feb 48 13
SLEEPERS, THE by John Wade Farrell ps (John D.
    MacDonald). .s . . . . SSS Nov 49 96
SLEEPERS OF MARS by John Beynon (Harris) . . . . .
    . .nt . . . . ToW #2 38 4
SLEEPING GODDESS, THE by Maurice Duclos . . . . .
    . .s . . . . FA May 39 44
SLEEPING WAR, THE by David H. Keller, M.D. . . . . .
    . .s . . . . WS Feb 31 980
SLEEPWALKER OF SANDWICH by Lee Prescott. . . . .
    . .s . . . . FA Nov 49 104
SLIM PEOPLE, THE by Wilfred Owen Morley ps (Robert
    W. Lowndes). .ss . . . . Fut Aug 42 91
SLUGLY BEAST, THE by Lord Dunsany. .s . . . .
    . . . . AFR #7 54

Title. .Author. .Length . . . . Magazine. .Date. .Page No.

SMALLER THAN YOU THINK by Kenneth Gray. . . . .
    . .s . . . . ASF Aug 48 32
SMALLEST GOD, THE by Lester del Rey. .nt . . . .
    . . . . ASF Jan 40 43
SMILE OF THE SPHINX, THE by William F.
    Temple. .s . . . . ToW Aut 38 42
                                                WB Dec 50 68
SMILING WIFE, THE by H. B. Hickey ps (Herb
    Livingston). .s. . . . . FA Nov 46 128
SMOKE GHOST by Fritz Leiber, Jr. . .s . . . .
    . . . . UK Oct 41 100
SMOKE RINGS by George McLociard. .ss . . . .
    . . . . Amz Feb 28 1103
SMOKING LAND, THE by George Challis ps (Frederick
    Faust). .n . . . . AMF Feb 50 8
SMOTHERED SEAS by Ralph Milne Farley ps (Roger
    Sherman Hoar) & Stanley G. Weinbaum. .nt . . . .
    . . . . ASF Jan 36 8
SMUGGLERS OF THE MOON by P. Schuyler
    Miller. .s . . . . SSS May 41 72
SNAKE MOTHER, THE by A. Merritt. .n . . . .
    . . . . FN Nov 40 6
SNAPDRAGON by Frank Belknap Long. .s . . . .
    . . . . TW Dec 41 93
SNARE FOR TOMORROW, A by Arthur J. Burks . . . .
    . .s . . . . TW Nov 40 110
SNULBUG by Anthony Boucher ps (William Anthony
    Parker White). .s . . . . UK Dec 41 78
SO SHALL YE REAP! by Rog Phillips. .n . . . .
    . . . . Amz Aug 47 8
SO YOU WANT TO BE A SPACE–FLIER? by Martin
    Pearson ps (Donald A. Wollheim). .a . . . Cos May 41 116
SOFTIE by Noel Loomis. .s . . . . TW Oct 48 133
SOFTLY SILKEN WALLET, THE by David Wright
    O'Brien. .s . . . . FA Jul 46 128
SOJARR OF TITAN by Manly Wade Wellman. .n . . . . .
    . . . . SS Mar 41 16
SOLANDER'S RADIO TOMB by Ellis Parker
    Butler. .s . . . . Amz Jun 27 268
SOLAR ASSIGNMENT by Mark Denholm. .s . . . .
    . . . . NW #1 46 23
SOLAR COMEDY, THE by James Blish. .s . . . .
    . . . . Fut Jun 42 52
SOLAR INVASION, THE by Manly Wade Wellman . . . .
    . .n . . . . SS Fal 46 13
SOLAR MAGNET, THE by Capt. S. P. Meek. .s . . . . . .
    . . . . ASF Oct 31 113
SOLAR MENACE, THE by S. K. Bernfeld. .s . . . .
    . . . . TW Aug 37 111
SOLAR PLEXUS by James Blish. .s . . . . . . Ash Sep 41 84
SOLAR SYSTEM, A STUDY OF THE by John W.
    Campbell, Jr.
    See STUDY OF THE SOLAR SYSTEM, A
SOLARITE by John W. Campbell, Jr. . .nt . . . .
    . . . . Amz Nov 30 706
SOLARIUS by Alcuin Dornisch. .ss . . . . Amz Dec 32 802

Title. .Author. .Length . . . . Magazine. .Date. .Page No.

SOLDIERS OF SPACE by Henry Kuttner. .s . . . .
. . . . .Ash Feb 43 87
SOLDIERS OF THE BLACK GOAT by Marian
O'Hearn. .n . . . . UK Jan 40 9
SOLOMON'S STONE by L. Sprague de Camp. .n . . . . .
. . . . UK Jun 42 8
SOLUTION UNSATISFACTORY by Anson MacDonald
ps (Robert A. Heinlein). .nt . . . . ASF May 41 56
SOMA RACKS, THE by Margaret St. Clair. .s . . . .
. . . . .SS Mar 47 65
SOME ARE NOT MEN by Dorothy & John de
Courcy. .nt. . . . . Amz Aug 46 102
SOME DAY WE'LL FIND YOU by Cleve Cartmill. . . . .
. .nt . . . . ASF Dec 42 38
SOME MINOR INVENTIONS (DR. HACKENSAW'S
SECRETS) by Clement Fezandie. .s . . Amz Jun 26 280
SOMERSET, THE SCIENTIFIC MONKEY by Donald
Bern. .s . . . . Amz Jan 42 44
SOMETHING FOR HERBERT by Frances M. Deegan . .
. .s . . . . Amz Sep 45 96
SOMETHING FROM BEYOND by Paul Dennis Lavond
ps (Robert W. Lowndes, Frederik Pohl & Dirk Wylie).
. .ss . . . . Fut Dec 41 100
SOMETHING FROM JUPITER by Dow Elstar ps
(Raymond Z. Gallun). .nt . . . . ASF Mar 38 6
SON IS BORN, A by A. E. van Vogt. .s . . . .
. . . . ASF May 46 61
SON OF A WITCH by Robert Bloch. .s . . . . FA Sep 42 32
SON OF DEATH, THE by Robert Moore Williams. . . . .
. .nt . . . . FA Aug 42 134
SON OF HIS FATHER by Frank Belknap Long. .s . . . .
. . . . .SS Jun 43 76
SON OF OLD FAITHFUL, THE by Raymond Z.
Gallun. .nt . . . . .ASF Jul 35 8
SON OF REDMASK, THE by Nat Schachner. .nt . . . . .
. . . . ASF Aug 35 100
SON OF SPACE by Francis H. Sibson. .s . . .Fant #1 38 86
SON OF THE STARS by Eando Binder. .s . . . .
. . . . FFM Feb 40 70
SON OF THE STARS by F. Orlin Tremaine. .s . . . . . .
. . . . SSS Apr 49 110
SON OF THE SUN. .bacover pic . . . . FA Nov 47
SON OF TWO WORLDS by Edmond Hamilton. . . . . .
. .n . . . . .TW Aug 41 14
SONG AT TWILIGHT by Robert Arthur. .nt . . . .
. . . . TW Jan 40 42
SONG FROM THE DARK STAR, THE by Richard
Tooker. .s . . . . .ASF Sep 36 125
SONG OF DEATH by Ed Earl Repp. .s . . . Amz Nov 38 26
SONG OF THE SHADOW DEATH by Robert Moore
Williams. .s . . . . TW Aug 38 106
SONGS OF THE SPACEWAYS conducted by Lilith
Lorraine poetry dept of FB from #3
SONS OF THE BEAR-GOD by Norvell W. Page. .n . . . .
. . . . .UK Nov 39 9

SONS OF THE DELUGE by Nelson S. Bond . . . .
. .n 2 pt . . . . Amz Jan 40 8
SONS OF THE PROPHET by Robert Moore
Williams. .nt . . . . FA Aug 49 54
SONS OF THE SERPENT by Wes Amherst ps (Richard S.
Shaver). .n . . . . OW Jan 50 6
SORCERER OF RHIANNON, THE by Leigh
Brackett. .nt . . . . ASF Feb 42 36
SORCERER'S APPRENTICE, THE by Colin Keith ps
(Malcolm Jameson). .s . . . . ASF Dec 41 56
SORCERER'S SHIP, THE by Hannes Bok. .n . . . .
. . . . UK Dec 42 9
SOUL EATERS, THE by William Conover. .nt . . . .
. . . . .PS Fal 44 2
SOUL MAKERS, THE by Robert Moore Williams . . . . .
. .s . . . . .SSS Nov 50 58
SOUL MASTER, THE by Will Smith & R. J.
Robbins. .s . . . . ASF Mar 30 350
SOUL SNATCHER, THE by Tom Curry. .s . . . .
. . . . ASF Apr 30 101
SOUL STEALERS, THE by Chester S. Geier. .nt . . . . .
. . . . Im Oct 50 6
SOUL TRAP, THE (Liberty or Death) by Charles B.
Stilson. .s . . . . .FN Jul 50 96
SOULLESS ENTITY, THE by Anthony Pelcher . . . . . .
. .s . . . . .WS Jan 31 844
SOULS ASPACE by Joe W. Skidmore. .ss . . . .
. . . . Amz Feb 33 1005
SOUND, THE by A. E. van Vogt. .nt . . . . ASF Feb 50 56
SOUND INVESTMENT, A by Rene Lafayette ps (L.
Ron Hubbard). .nt . . . . ASF Jun 49 36
SOUND OF BUGLES, THE by Robert Moore
Williams. .s . . . . .SS Mar 49 74
SOUP KING by Colin Keith ps (Malcolm Jameson) . . . .
. .s . . . . .ASF Jan 42 27
SOUTH POLAR BERYLLIUM, LIMITED by Peter Van
Dresser. .s . . . . Amz Aug 30 416
SOUTH TO PROPONTIS by Henry Andrew
Ackermann. .s. . . . . PS Fal 41 89
SPA OF THE STARS, THE by Jack Vance. .s . . . .
. . . . SS Jul 50 78
SPACE BAT by Carl Selwyn. .s . . . . .PS Win 46 48
SPACE-BEASTS, THE by Clifford D. Simak. .s . . . . . .
. . . . .Ash Apr 40 6
SPACE BEINGS, THE by Edmond Hamilton. .s . . . . . .
. . . . ToW Win 38 39
SPACE BENDER, THE by Edward L. Rementer. . . . . .
. .s . . . . Amz Dec 28 838
SPACE BLACKOUT by Sam Carson. .s . . . .
. . . . Com May 41 105
SPACE BLISTER by John D. Clark, Ph.D. . .s . . . .
. . . . ASF Aug 37 107
SPACE CAN by L. Ron Hubbard. .s . . . . . .ASF Jul 42 71
SPACE-CAN by Murray Leinster ps (Will F.
Jenkins). .s . . . . TW Jun 48 117

Title. .Author. .Length. . . . . Magazine. .Date. .Page No.

SPACE CHORE by Manly Wade Wellman. .s. . . . . . .
. . . . TW Aug 41 65
SPACE COFFIN, THE by A. Rowley Hilliard. .s. . . . . .
. . . . WS Aug 32 230
SPACE COMMAND by Robert Arthur. .s. . . . .
. . . . TW Win 44 97
SPACE DEVASTATOR by Julian S. Krupa . . . .
. .bacover pic . . . . Amz Jul 39
SPACE DOUBLE by Nat Schachner. .s . . . ASF May 40 83
SPACE-DWELLERS, THE by Raymond Gallun . . . . . .
. .s . . . . SW Nov 29 522
                                        SS Fal 43 106
SPACE EPISODE by Leslie Perri ps (Doris Wilson) . . . .
. .ss. . . . . Fut Dec 41 106
SPACE FIX by R. S. Richardson. .a 2 pt . . . .
. . . . .ASF Mar 43 68
SPACE FLAME, THE by Alexander M. Phillips. .s. . . .
. . . . PS Spr 40 84
SPACE-FLIGHT OF TERROR by Ray Cummings . . . .
. .nt . . . . .SF Jan 41 10
SPACE FLOTSAM by Raymond Z. Gallun. .s. . . . . . .
. . . . ASF Feb 34 59
SPACE GUARDS by Phil Nowlan. .nt . . . . .ASF May 40 9
SPACE HAS A SPECTRUM by R. S. Richardson. .a . . . .
. . . . ASF Mar 41 104
SPACE HERMIT, THE by E. Edsel Newton. .s . . . . . .
. . . . Amz Jul 29 326
SPACE HITCH-HIKER by Eando Binder. .s. . . . .
. . . . SSS May 42 64
SPACE-LANE OF NO-RETURN by George O.
Whittington. .s . . . . PS Sum 46 47
SPACE LENS, THE by Millard Verne Gordon ps
(Donald A. Wollheim). .s. . . . . WS Sep 35 452
                                        FSQ Fal 50 134
SPACE-LINER X87 by Ray Cummings. .nt . . . .
. . . . PS Sum 40 2
SPACE MARINES AND THE SLAVERS, THE by
Bob Olsen ps (Alfred John Olsen, Jr.). .nt . . . .
. . . . Amz Dec 36 61
SPACE MIRROR by Edmond Hamilton. .s. . . . .
. . . . .TW Aug 37 43
SPACE OASIS by Raymond Z. Gallun. .s. . . . .
. . . . PS Fal 42 30
SPACE PIRATE, THE by Eando Binder ps (Earl
Binder & Otto Binder). .s . . . . Amz Jun 38 108
SPACE RATING by John Berryman. .s . . . .
. . . . ASF Oct 39 55
SPACE RAYS by John W. Campbell, Jr. .s. . . . .
. . . . WS Dec 32 584
SPACE-ROCKET MURDERS by Edmond
Hamilton. .nt . . . . Amz Oct 32 582
SPACE ROVER, THE by Edwin K. Sloat. .s. . . . .
. . . . ASF Feb 32 222
SPACE SATAN by Arthur G. Stangland. .s. . . . .
. . . . .SF Jan 41 83

Title. .Author. .Length. . . . . Magazine. .Date. .Page No.

SPACE-SHIP AHOY! by Walter Gillings. .a . . . .
. . . . Fant Apr 47 38
SPACE-SHIP DERBY by Milton Kaletsky. .s . . . .
. . . . SFQ Sum 40 101
SPACE SHIP IN THE JUNGLE by James B.
Settles. .bacover . . . . .Amz Jul 48
SPACE SHIP 13 by Patrick S. Selby. .s . . . .
. . . . .NW #2 46 20
SPACE SHIPS AT ANKOR WAT? by James B.
Settles. .bacover . . . . Amz Apr 48
SPACE SHIPS IN ANTARCTICA by James B.
Settles. .bacover . . . . Amz Feb 48
SPACE SUIT, THE by L. Sprague de Camp. .a . . . .
. . . . ASF Mar 48 108
SPACE SIGNALS by A. B. L. Macfadyen. .s. . . . .
. . . . ASF Dec 37 82
SPACE STATION NO. 1 by Manly Wade Wellman. . . . .
. .s . . . . FFM Sep–Oct 39 27
SPACE-TIME-SIZE MACHINE, THE by Ray
Cummings. .s . . . . TW Oct 37 30
SPACE TRAP by Polton Cross ps (John Russell
Fearn). .s. . . . . .TW Fal 45 40
SPACE-TRAP AT BANYA TOR by W. J. Matthews . . .
. .s . . . . .PS Spr 48 68
SPACE VISITORS, THE by Edmond Hamilton. .s. . . . .
. . . . AW Mar 30 804
                                        SS Sep 39 110
SPACE WAR by Neil R. Jones. .nt . . . . .Amz Jul 35 9
SPACE WAR by Willy Ley. .a . . . . ASF Aug 39 72
SPACE-WAR STRATEGY by Malcolm Jameson. .a. . . .
. . . . .SSS Mar 41 94
SPACE WAR TACTICS by Malcolm Jameson. .a . . . . . .
. . . . ASF Nov 39 68
SPACE-WOLF by Ray Cummings. .s. . . . . PS Sum 41 95
SPACEHOUNDS OF IPC by Edward E. Smith,
Ph.D. .n 3 pt . . . . .Amz Jul 31 294
SPACEMAN, BEWARE! by Stanley Mullen. .s . . . .
. . . . SSS Jul 49 85
SPACEMAN'S SAVVY by Arthur G. Stangland. .s. . . . .
. . . . TW Apr 42 109
SPACEMATE by Walt Sheldon. .s . . . . . . .TW Aug 50 93
SPACESHIP FROM KORL by Frederic Arnold Kummer,
Jr. . .s . . . . .SSS Feb 42 58
SPACESHIP IN A FLASK by Clifford D. Simak. .s . . . .
. . . . .ASF Jul 41 45
SPACESHIP OF 2038 by Julian S. Krupa. . . . .
. .bacover pic . . . . Amz Dec 38
SPACESHIP SEEN OVER IDAHO by James B.
Settles. .bacover . . . . .Amz Jan 48
SPACESHIP TAKEOFF. .a . . . . ASF Apr 46 99
SPACESHIPS IN ANCIENT EGYPT by James B.
Settles. .bacover . . . . Amz May 48
SPACESHIPS LIMITED by Jackson Ross (First of a series
of articles appearing irregularly from:). . . . .
. . . . .Amz Jan 47 142

Title. .Author. .Length . . . . Magazine. .Date. .Page No.

SPACESHIP'S VIEW. .a . . . . ASF Dec 44 99
SPACEWARD by P. E. Cleator. .a. . . . . . .TW Aug 37 90
SPACEWRECK by Oscar A. Boch. .s. . . . . ASF Nov 39 79
SPACEWRECKED ON VENUS by Neil R. Jones. .s. . . .
. . . . WQ Win 32 260
SPARK, THE by Mack Reynolds. .ss. . . . . TW Dec 50 94
SPARK OF ALLAH, THE by Marian O'Hearn . . . .
. .n 3 pt. . . . . .UK Jul 40 129
SPAWN OF DARKNESS by Craig Browning ps (Roger
P. Graham). .s. . . . . FA May 50 106
SPAWN OF ETERNAL THOUGHT by Eando Binder
ps (Otto Binder). .n 2 pt. . . . . ASF Apr 36 66
SPAWN OF HELL by P. F. Costello h ps. .s . . . .
. . . . FA Feb 43 148
SPAWN OF INFINITUDE by Edward S. Pilsworth . . . .
. .s . . . . FN Sep 40 133
SPAWN OF JUPITER by Ed Earl Repp. .nt . . . .
. . . . Amz Mar 44 150
SPAWN OF THE COMET by H. Thompson Rich. . . . .
. .s . . . . ASF Nov 31 236
SPAWN OF THE FURTHER DARK by Frank Belknap
Long. .s. . . . . SS Spr 44 100
SPAWN OF THE GLACIER by Leroy Yerxa. .nt. . . . .
. . .s. . . . . FA Dec 43 152
SPAWN OF THE RAY by Maurice Duclos. .s . . . .
. . . . Amz Feb 38 55
SPAWN OF THE RED GIANTS by Frank Belknap
Long, Jr. . .nt. . . . . ASF May 37 110
SPAWN OF THE STARS by Charles Willard Diffin . . . .
. .s . . . . ASF Feb 30 166
SPAWN OF THE VENUS SEA by Harry Walton . . . . . .
. .s . . . . PS Fal 41 96
SPEAK OF THE DEVIL by Norman A. Daniels . . . . . .
. .n . . . . .SS Mar 43 15
SPEAK TO ME OF DEATH by Cornell Woolrich. . . . .
. .nt . . . . FanF May 50 91
SPECIAL AGENT TO VENUS by Thornton Ayre ps
(John Russell Fearn). .nt. . . . . FA Oct 40 78
SPECIAL DELIVERY by George O. Smith. .nt . . . . . .
. . . . ASF Mar 45 72
SPECIAL FLIGHT by John Berryman. .nt . . . .
. . . . ASF May 39 51
SPECIAL JOBBERY by H. B. Fyfe. .nt . . . ASF Sep 49 41
SPECIAL KNOWLEDGE by A. Bertram Chandler. . . . .
. .n . . . . ASF Feb 46 7
SPECIALIZATION by R. R. Winterbotham. .s . . . . . .
. . . . ASF Aug 37 31
SPECTATOR SPORT by John D. MacDonald. .ss . . . . .
. . . . TW Feb 50 81
SPECTER OF SHINTOISM, THE by Pete Bogg. . . . . .
. .a . . . . Amz Dec 44 189
SPECTRE SPIDERS, THE by W. James Wintle . . . . . .
. .s . . . . FFM Feb 47 114
SPECTRUM OF GENERATORS. .a . . . . .ASF Jan 45 99
SPEED WILL BE MY BRIDE by David H. Keller,
M.D. .s. . . . . Uc Apr 41 94

Title. .Author. .Length . . . . Magazine. .Date. .Page No.

SPHERE OF DEATH, THE by J. W. Groves. .s . . . . . .
. . . . Amz Oct 31 656
SPHERE OF SLEEP, THE by Chester S. Geier. .s . . . . .
. . . . Amz Dec 42 178
SPHERE OF THE NEVER–DEAD by Sam Carson. . . . .
. .s . . . . PS Sum 40 28
SPHERES by D. M. Edwards. .nt . . . . . . ASF Dec 40 44
SPHERES OF HELL by John Beynon Harris. .s . . . . . .
. . . . WS Oct 33 230
SPHINX, THE by Frank R. Paul. .bacover pic. . . . . . .
. . . . FA Oct 43
SPHINX, THE by Edgar Allan Poe. .s . . . .Amz Jul 26 357
SPHINX OF THE SPACEWAYS by Ed Earl Repp . . . .
. .nt . . . . SF Aug 39 10
SPIDER GOD OF AKKA, THE by Gardner Fox (text) &
John Guinta (pics). .comic . . . . . . .OTWA Dec 50 72
SPIDER MEN OF GHARR by Wilbur S. Peacock . . . . .
. .nt . . . . PS Sum 45 54
SPIDERS OF SATURN by V. E. Thiessen. .s . . . .
. . . . Amz Feb 50 94
SPIDERWEB. .a . . . . ASF May 46 99
SPIN, DEVIL! by John Wade Farrell ps (John D.
MacDonald). .s . . . . SSS Jan 50 81
SPIRIT OF EARTH, THE by Sydney J. Bounds. .s . . . .
. . . . .NW Win 50 74
SPIRIT OF EGYPT, THE by Leroy Yerxa. .ss. . . . .
. . . . Amz Aug 43 194
SPIRIT OF THE KEYS by Chester S. Geier. .s . . . .
. . . . FA Mar 48 56
SPIRIT OF THE SERPENT GOD by Chief
Sequoyah. .a. . . . . Amz Jun 48 158
SPIRIT OF TOFFEE, THE by Charles F. Myers. .nt. . . .
. . . . FA Nov 48 72
SPOILERS OF THE SPACEWAYS by Neil R. Jones . . .
. .s . . . . .PS Win 42 40
SPOKESMAN FOR TERRA by Hugh Raymond ps (John
Michel). .ss. . . . . .Sti Jun 41 29
SPONTANEOUS FROGNATION by Eric Frank
Russell. .a . . . . .UK Jul 40 83
SPOOK FOR YOURSELF by David Wright O'Brien. . . .
. .s . . . . FA Jan 42 70
SPOOR OF THE BAT by Arthur Leo Zagat. .nt . . . . .
. . . . .ASF Jul 34 62
SPORE DOOM, THE by Eando Binder ps (Earl Binder &
Otto Binder). .s. . . . . WS Feb 34 678
FSQ Fal 50 98
SPORE TRAPPERS by R. R. Winterbotham. .nt . . . . . .
. . . . .ASF May 37 62
SPORTS OF THE FUTURE by Leonard Gipson. .a . . . .
. . . . Amz Sep 40 128
SPOT OF LIFE, THE by Austin Hall. .n . . .FFM Feb 41 6
SPRING MACHINE, THE by Frederick A. Kummer,
Jr. . .s. . . . . Fut Jun 42 68
SPY SCARE by H. B. Fyfe. .s . . . . .ASF Sep 50 142
SQUADRON OF THE DAMNED by David Wright
O'Brien. .nt . . . . .Amz Jul 42 114

Title. .Author. .Length . . . . Magazine. .Date. .Page No.

SQUARE PEGS, THE by Ray Bradbury. .s. . . . .
. . . . TW Oct 48 101
SQUARES FROM SPACE, THE by P. F. Costello
h ps. .s. Amz Sep 50 78
SQUEEZE PLAY by Craig Browning *ps (Roger P.
Graham).* .s . . . . Amz Nov 47 50
SQUIRREL PEOPLE, THE by John C. Ross. .nt . . . . . .
. . . . Amz Sep 48 8
SRIBERDEGIBIT by Anthony Boucher *ps (William
Anthony Parker White).* .nt . . . . UK Jun 43 81
STABILITY by A. Bertram Chandler. .s. . . . .
. . . . ASF Jul 46 130
STALEMATE IN SPACE by Charles L. Harness. .s. . . . .
. . . . PS Sum 49 84
STALLION'S TRAPPINGS by Dean Collins. .ss . . . . . .
. . . . Amz Mar 33 1135
STAMP OF DOOM, THE by Jerry E. Cravey. .nt . . . . . .
. . . . AD Aug 30 694
STAR, THE by H. G. Wells. .s . . . . Amz Jun 26 242
STAR ARROW by Ray Cummings. .s . . . . TW Feb 43 58
STAR BASE X by Pvt. Robert Moore Williams. .nt . . . .
. . . . Amz Sep 44 8
STAR BEAST, THE by Poul Anderson. .nt . . . .
. . . . SSS Sep 50 10
STAR BEAST, THE by Damon Knight. .s . . . .
. . . . PS Spr 49 59
STAR–BROTHER by Stanley Mullen. .s . . SSS Sep 49 88
STAR COMRADES by Frank Belknap Long. .s. . . . . . .
. . . . SF Apr 43 95
STAR CRASH by Kent Casey. .s . . . . ASF Mar 39 95
STAR DUCKS, THE by Bill Brown. .s. . . F&SF Fal 50 121
STAR GUARDSMAN, THE by Albert de Pina. .nt . . . . .
. . . . .PS Win 43 86
STAR KINGS, THE by Edmond Hamilton. .n. . . . .
. . . . Amz Sep 47 8
STAR–MASTER, THE by Ray Cummings. .s . . . .
. . . . PS Sum 42 42
STAR MOUSE, THE by Fredric Brown. .s . . . .
. . . . .PS Spr 42 28
STAR OF BLUE by Milton Kaletsky. .s. . . . SF Mar 41 54
STAR OF DEAD LOVE, THE by Will H. Gray. .s . . . . .
. . . . Amz May 27 200
STAR OF DREAD, THE by Brett Sterling *ps (Edmond
Hamilton).* .n . . . . .CF Sum 43 13
STAR OF DREAMS, THE by Jack Williamson. .nt . . . .
. . . . Com Mar 41 18
STAR OF LIFE, THE by Edmond Hamilton. .n . . . . . .
. . . . SS Jan 47 13
STAR OF PANADUR by Albert de Pina & Henry
Hasse. .s. . . . . .PS Mar 43 65
STAR OF SATAN, THE by Henry Hasse. .s . . . .
. . . . PS Fal 41 50
STAR OF THE UNDEAD by Paul Dennis Lavond
h ps (Frederik Pohl & Dirk Wylie). .s. . . . . . FB #2 14
STAR OF TREASURE by Charles W. Harbaugh. .nt . . .
. . . . TW Spr 44 13

STAR PARADE, THE by Henry Kuttner. .nt . . . .
. . . . TW Dec 38 26
STAR PIRATE by Frederick Arnold Kummer, Jr. . . . .
. .s . . . . PS Sum 40 69
STAR ROVER, THE by Jack London. .n. . . . .
. . . . .FFM Feb 47 8
STAR SHEPHERD, THE by William Brengle *h ps
(Howard Browne).* .nt . . . . FA Aug 43 12
STAR SHIP by Poul Anderson. .s. . . . . PS Fal 50 66
STAR SHIP INVINCIBLE by Frank K. Kelly. .nt . . . . .
. . . . .ASF Jan 35 10
STAR SLAVER, THE by Carter Sprague *ps (Sam
Merwin, Jr.).* .s . . . . .FSQ Spr 50 76
STAR–STEALERS, THE by Edmond Hamilton. .nt. . . .
. . . . .AFR #6 65
STAR TAMER by Alfred Coppel. .s . . . . . .SSS Nov 50 48
STAR THAT WOULD NOT BEHAVE, THE by R. R.
Winterbotham. .s. . . . . ASF Aug 35 86
STAR TRAIL TO GLORY by Edmond Hamilton . . . . .
. .n .CF Spr 41 14
STARBUSTERS, THE by Alfred Coppel, Jr. . .s . . . . . .
. . . . PS Sum 49 60
STARDUST GODS by Dow Elstar *ps (Raymond Z.
Gallun)* & Robert S. McReady. .nt . . . .ASF Oct 37 122
STARKENDEN QUEST, THE by Gilbert Collins. . . . . .
. .n . . . . FFM Oct 49 10
STARS by David R. Daniels. .s. . . . . ASF May 35 37
STARS ALSO HAVE RINGS by R. S. Richardson. . . . .
. .a .ASF Jul 42 78
STARS ARE THE STYX, THE by Theodore
Sturgeon. .nt . . . . GSF Oct 50 72
STARS LOOK DOWN, THE by Lester del Rey. .nt . . . .
. . . . ASF Aug 40 9
STARS OVER SANTA CLAUS by William Morrison
ps (Joseph Samachson). .s. . . . . .SS Jan 50 71
STARSHIP FROM SIRIUS by Rog Phillips *ps (Roger P.
Graham).* .n . . . . Amz Aug 48 66
STARSTONE WORLD by Hannes Bok. .n . . . .
. . . . SFQ Sum 42 88
STARTING OVER, THE by Hodge Winsell. .s . . . . . .
. . . . OW Oct 50 70
STARTING POINT by Norman R. Goldsmith. .a. . . . . .
. . . . .ASF Jan 41 90
STARTING POINT by Raymond F. Jones. .s . . . .
. . . . ASF Feb 42 68
STARVATION by Fredric Brown. .ss . . . .ASF Sep 42 100
STARVATION IN SPACE by Earle H. Morris. .s. . . . . .
. . . . AQ Win 32 122
STATEMENT OF RANDOLPH CARTER, THE by
H. P. Lovecraft. .s . . . . .AFR #10 53
STATIC by Eando Binder. .s . . . . TW Dec 36 37
STATIC by Kent Casey. .s. . . . . ASF May 38 95
STATIC WAS LICKED TWENTY YEARS AGO by
H. C. Hefferlin. .a . . . . Amz Oct 46 166
STATION DEATH by Oscar J. Friend. .s . . . .
. . . . .SS Mar 40 106

Title. .Author. .Length . . . . Magazine. .Date. .Page No.

STATION X by G. McLeod Winsor. .n 3 pt . . . .
. . . . Amz Jul 26 292
STATIONS IN SPACE by Willy Ley. .a . . . .
. . . . Amz Feb 40 122
STATUS QUO by R. R. Winterbotham. .s . . . .
. . . . Fut Apr 41 97
STEAM GOD, THE by Walter Kateley. .s . . . .
. . . . Amz Oct 29 640
STEAM SHOVEL, THE by David H. Keller, M.D. . . . .
. .s . . . . Amz Sep 31 510
STEEL GIANTS OF CHAOS by James R. Adams . . . . .
. .s . . . . .PS Win 45 36
STELLAR EXODUS, THE by Oliver E. Saari . . . .
. .s . . . . ASF Feb 37 144
STELLAR LEGION, THE by Leigh Brackett. .s . . . . . .
. . . . .PS Win 40 95
STELLAR MISSILE, THE by Ed Earl Repp. .s . . . .
. . . . SW Nov 29 498
STELLAR SHOWBOAT by Malcolm Jameson. .s. . . . . .
. . . . PS Fal 42 78
STELLAR SNOWBALL by John Barrett. .s . . . .
. . . . .SS Mar 47 88
STELLAR VAMPIRES, THE by Frank Belknap
Long. .s . . . . SF Jul 43 79
STELLARITE by Richard Rush Murray. .s. . . . .
. . . . Amz Mar 33 1122
STENOGRAPHER'S HANDS by David H. Keller. .s. . . .
. . . . .AQ Fal 28 522
ToW #2 38 40
AFR #2 7
STENTON'S SHADOW by David Wright O'Brien. .s. . . .
. . . . FA Jun 43 56
STEP FARTHER OUT, A by Raymond Z. Gallun . . . . .
. .nt . . . . .SSS Mar 50 48
STEP INTO MY GARDEN by Frank Belknap Long. . . .
. .s . . . . UK Aug 42 98
STEPPING–STONE TO THE STARS by Willy Ley . . . .
. .a . . . . SSS May 43 92
STEPSON OF MARS by Ivar Towers h ps (Cyril
Kornbluth & Richard Wilson). .nt . . . . . Ash Apr 40 78
STEPSON OF SPACE by Raymond Z. Gallun. .s . . . . .
. . . . Ash Oct 40 36
STERILE PLANET by Nat Schachner. .nt . . . .
. . . . .ASF Jul 37 52
STERILE WORLD, THE by Warren E. Sanders. .s . . . . .
. . . . WQ Spr 32 408
STEVEDORE OF JUPITER, THE by Don Wilcox . . . .
. .s . . . . Amz Nov 41 70
STICK MEN, THE by J. M. Walsh. .s . . . .
. . . . Fant #3 39 21
STILL SMALL VOICE, THE by Clive B. G.
Jackson. .ss . . . . AFR #14 63
STILLWELL DEGRAVITOR, THE by Charles R.
Tanner. .s. . . . . Amz Feb 41 108
STITCH IN TIME, A by Frank Belknap Long, Jr. . . . .
. .s . . . . SSS Mar 40 108

Title. .Author. .Length . . . . Magazine. .Date. .Page No.

STOLEN BODY, THE by H. G. Wells. .s . . . .
. . . . .Amz Jan 28 998
STOLEN BRAINS by Captain S. P. Meek. .s. . . . .
. . . . ASF Oct 30 7
STOLEN CENTURIES by Otis Adelbert Kline. .s . . . . .
. . . . TW Jun 39 30
STOLEN CHRYSALIS, THE by J. Rogers Ullrich . . . .
. .s . . . . .Amz Jul 31 372
STOLEN DORMOUSE, THE by L. Sprague de
Camp. .n 2 pt . . . . ASF Apr 41 9
STOLEN ELEMENT, THE by Paul Ernst. .s . . . .
. . . . .ASF Sep 34 107
STOLEN MIND, THE by M. L. Staley. .s . . . .
. . . . .ASF Jan 30 75
STOLEN SPECTRUM, THE by Oscar J. Friend. .s . . . .
. . . . TW Sep 40 108
STONE AND A SPEAR, A by Raymond F. Jones . . . . .
. .nt . . . . GSF Dec 50 66
STONE CAT, THE by Miles J. Breuer, M.D. . .s . . . . . .
. . . . Amz Sep 27 553
STONE FROM THE GREEN STAR, THE by Jack
Williamson. .n 2 pt. . . . . . . Amz Oct 31 584
STONE FROM THE MOON, THE by Otto Willi
Gail. .n . . . . WQ Spr 30 294
STONE GODDESS OF YUNAN, THE by Lee Francis
h ps. .nt. . . . . Amz Aug 43 154
STONE MEN OF IGNOTA, THE by Victor Rousseau
(Emanuel). .s . . . . .Fut Aug 41 68
STONE SHIP, THE by William Hope Hodgson. .nt. . . . .
. . . . .AFR #9 87
STOP, THIEF! by Fox E. Holden. .ss . . . .
. . . . TW Win 45 63
STORED POWER by Arthur McCann ps (John W.
Campbell, Jr.). .a . . . . ASF Dec 38 151
STORIES OF THE STARS. .bacover pics
    CANUS MAJOR by Frank R. Paul . . . . . . Amz Feb 43
    LYRA by Frank R. Paul . . . . Amz Apr 43
    PROCYON by Frank R. Paul. . . . . Amz May 43
    THE GREAT NEBULA IN ORION by Frank R.
    Paul . . . . Amz Jun 43
    RIGEL by Frank R. Paul . . . . Amz Aug 43
    DEATH OF THE MOON by Robert Fuqua . . . .
    . . . . .Amz Jan 44
    BETELGEUSE IN ORION by Frank R. Paul . . . . . .
    . . . . Amz Sep 44
    SPICA by Frank R. Paul. . . . . Amz Mar 45
    GEMINI by Frank R. Paul. . . . . .FA Jul 45
    ANDROMEDA by Frank R. Paul . . . . FA Oct 45
    ALDEBARAN by Frank R. Paul . . . . FA Dec 45
    ALPHECCA by Frank R. Paul . . . . FA Feb 46
    MIZAR by Frank R. Paul . . . . .FA May 46
    ANTARES by Frank R. Paul. . . . . .FA Jul 46
    ALTAIR by Frank R. Paul . . . . Amz Aug 46
STORM, THE by A. E. van Vogt. .nt . . . . . ASF Oct 43 9
STORM BUSTER, THE by Ed Earl Repp. .s . . . .
. . . . AW Jan 30 614

Title. .Author. .Length . . . . Magazine. .Date. .Page No.

STORM CLOUD ON DEKA by Edward E. Smith,
Ph.D. . .nt . . . . Ash Jun 42 40
STORM IN SPACE by Ross Rocklynne. .s . . . .
. . . . TW Dec 42 90
STORM WARNING by Millard Verne Gordon ps
(Donald A. Wollheim). .s. . . . . Fut Oct 42 43
            by Donald A. Wollheim . . . . AFR #10 107
STORY BEHIND THE STORY, THE dept in TW
irregularly
STORY ESCAPES ME, THE by Leroy Yerxa. .s . . . . . .
. . . . FA Dec 45 148
STORY OF MODULATION, THE by C. Rudmore . . . .
. .a . . . . ASF Jul 47 86
STORY OF ROD CONTRELL, THE by Murray Leinster
ps (Will F. Jenkins). .s . . . . SS Jan 49 88
STORY OF ROGER BACON, THE by Norman
White. .a . . . . Amz Mar 43 220
STORY OF THE DAYS TO COME, A by H. G.
Wells. .n 2 pt . . . . Amz Apr 28 6
STORY OF THE LATE MR. ELVESHAM, THE by
H. G. Wells. .s . . . . Amz Jun 27 253
STORY OF THE STONE AGE, A by H. G. Wells . . . . .
. .nt . . . . Amz Nov 27 726
STOWAWAY by Nelson S. Bond. .s . . . . ASF Aug 39 101
STRAIN by L. Ron Hubbard. .s . . . . ASF Apr 42 72
STRANGE ADVENTURE OF VICTOR MacLIESH, THE
by Alexander Blade h ps. .nt . . . . Amz May 41 28
STRANGE ALLIANCE by Bryce Walton. .s . . . .
. . . . FB #1 22
STRANGE CASE OF JOHN KINGMAN, THE by Murray
Leinster ps (Will F. Jenkins). .s . . . . . . ASF May 48 34
STRANGE CASE OF LEMUEL JENKINS, THE by
Philip M. Fisher, Jr. . .nt . . . . AFR #2 27
STRANGE CITY by Warner Van Lorne. .nt . . . .
. . . . .ASF Jan 36 116
STRANGE CREATURE by Raymond Z. Gallun. .s . . . .
. . . . SF Aug 39 59
STRANGE DEATH OF RICHARD SEFTON, THE by
Carl Selwyn. .s . . . . Amz Jan 40 62
STRANGE DISAPPEARANCE OF GUY SYLVESTER by
Chester S. Geier & Taylor Victor Shaver. .s . . . .
. . . . Amz Mar 49 24
STRANGE EXODUS by Robert Abernathy. .s . . . .
. . . . PS Fal 50 85
STRANGE FLIGHT OF RICHARD CLAYTON, THE
by Robert Bloch. .s . . . . Amz Mar 39 78
STRANGE GATEWAY by E. Hoffman Price. .s . . . . . .
. . . . UK Apr 39 113
STRANGE LOVES OF BEATRICE JERVAN, THE (John
Ovington Returns) by Max Brand (Frederick
Faust). .s . . . . FanF May 50 36
STRANGE MENTAL PHENOMENA by Speyton
Henry. .a . . . . SF Mar 40 39
STRANGE MISSION OF ARTHUR PENDRAN, THE by
John X. Pollard h ps (Howard Browne). .n . . . .
. . . . FA Jun 44 10

STRANGE OCCURENCE IN CLERKENWELL by
Arthur Machen. .s . . . . FFM Feb 50 108
STRANGE PLAYFELLOW by Isaac Asimov. .s . . . . . .
. . . . .SSS Sep 40 67
STRANGE RETURN by Laurence Woods ps (Donald
A. Wollheim). .s . . . . Sti Feb 41 51
STRANGE TEA OF TING SUN FU, THE by Leroy
Yerxa. .nt . . . . Amz May 37 46
STRANGE VISION by Eando Binder ps (Otto
Binder). .s . . . . ASF May 37 46
STRANGE VISITORS by Charles D. Hornig. .a . . . . . .
. . . . .SF Oct 39 60
STRANGE VOYAGE OF DR. PENWING, THE by
Richard O. Lewis. .s . . . . Amz Mar 40 40
STRANGE VOYAGE OF HECTOR SQUINCH, THE
by David Wright O'Brien. .nt . . . . FA Aug 40 58
STRANGER CLUB series See LAURENCE MANNING
author
STRANGER FROM FOMALHAUT by Clifton B.
Kruse. .s . . . . .ASF Jan 36 106
STRANGER FROM SMALLNESS by Otis Adelbert
Kline. .nt . . . . SSS Aug 41 114
STRANGER FROM SPACE by Hannes Bok. .s . . . .
. . . . PS May 43 71
STRANGER FROM THE STARS by Frederick Arnold
Kummer, Jr. . .s . . . . .TW Mar 41 66
STRANGER THAN FICTION dept in pre-war Fant
STRANGERS ON THE HEIGHTS by Manly Wade
Wellman. .n . . . . SS Sum 44 11
STRANGEST BEDFELLOWS, THE by William Morrison
ps (Joseph Samachson). .s . . . . TW Jun 50 125
STRATOSPHERE AIRLINER OF 1988 by Julian S.
Krupa. .bacover pic . . . . Amz Nov 38
STRATOSPHERE TOWERS by Nat Schachner. .nt . . . .
. . . . ASF Aug 34 94
STREAMERS OF DEATH by Hendrik Dahl Juve. .s . . .
. . . . SW Feb 30 790
STREET THAT WASN'T THERE, THE by Clifford D.
Simak & Carl Jacobi. .s . . . . .Com Jul 41 18
                                    AFR #13 116
STRENGTH OF THE WEAK, THE by Miles J. Breuer,
M.D. . .s . . . . Amz Dec 33 33
STRESS FLUID by Arthur McCann ps (John W.
Campbell, Jr.). .a . . . . ASF Jun 37 45
STRICTLY FROM MARS by Robert Bloch. .nt . . . . . .
. . . . Amz Feb 48 106
STROHEIM by James Brooke. .s . . . . Amz Feb 36 55
STROKE by John L. Chapman. .ss . . . . . SFQ Sum 42 142
STROLLER, THE by Margaret St. Clair. .s . . . .
. . . . .TW Aug 47 79
STRONGER, THE by Frederic Arnold Kummer, Jr. . . .
. .s . . . . .DS Apr–May 39 94
STRUGGLE FOR NEPTUNE, THE by Hendrik Dahl
Juve. .s . . . . WQ Fal 30 94
STRUGGLE FOR PALLAS, THE by J. M. Walsh. .s. . . .
. . . . WQ Fal 31 126

Title. .Author. .Length . . . . Magazine. .Date. .Page No.

STRUGGLE FOR VENUS, THE by Wesley Arnold . . . .
. .s . . . . WS Dec 30 716
STUBBORN MEN, THE by Robert Moore Williams . . . .
. .ss. . . . . SS Nov 48 71
STUCK IN THE MUD by J. J. Coupling ps (John R.
Pierce). .a. . . . . ASF Nov 47 97
STUDY IN AMBER, A by Frank Owen. .s . . . AFR #5 100
STUDY OF THE SOLAR SYSTEM, A by John W.
Campbell, Jr.
  1. ACCURACY. .a . . . . ASF Jun 36 96
  2. TWO SCALES. .a . . . . ASF Jul 36 39
  3. MERCURY. .a . . . . ASF Aug 36 91
  4. THE VEILED PLANET *(Venus)*. .a . . . .
     . . . . ASF Sep 36 99
  5. THE DOUBLE WORLD *(Earth & Moon)*. .a . . . .
     .ASF Oct 36 125
  6. RED DEATH *(Mars)*. .a . . . . ASF Nov 36 43
  7. THE SINGLE CLUE *(Jupiter)*. .a . . . .
     . . . . ASF Dec 36 89
  8. COSMIC GOSSIP. .a . . . . .ASF Jan 37 122
  9. OTHER EYES WATCHING *(Jupiter)*. .a . . . . . .
     . . . . ASF Feb 37 34
  10. COSMIC CACTUS *(Jupiter's Satellites)* . . . . . .
     . .a . . . . ASF Mar 37 88
  11. BEYOND THE LIFE LINE *(Saturn)*. .a . . . .
     . . . . ASF Apr 37 81
  12. WEATHER REPORT *(Uranus)*. .a . . . .
     .ASF May 37 57
  13. COSMIC DISCOVERY. .a. . . . . . .ASF Jun 37 106
  14. INTERPLANETARY DIVIDENDS. .a. . . . . . .
     . . . . .ASF Jul 37 44
  15. SMALLPOX OF SPACE. .a. . . . . . ASF Aug 37 62
  16. BLUFF. .a. . . . . ASF Sep 37 90
  17. SLEET STORM. .a . . . . .ASF Oct 37 151
  18. ATOMIC GENERATOR. .a. . . . . . ASF Nov 37 69
STUPORMAN by Robert Bloch. .s . . . . FA Jun 43 22
STYGIAN TERROR, THE by Stanton A. Coblentz. . . .
. .s . . . . FA Nov 42 156
SUB–SATELLITE by Charles Cloukey. .s. . . . .
. . . . Amz Mar 28 1194
SUB–STANDARD SARDINES by Jack Vance. .s . . . . .
. . . . SS Jan 49 98
SUBCONSCIOUS by John Russell Fearn. .nt . . . . . .
. . . . Amz Aug 36 57
SUBCRUISER by Harry Walton. .s. . . . ASF May 41 109
SUBJUGATING THE EARTH by Walter Kateley . . . . .
. .nt . . . . Amz Jun 34 64
SUBLIME VIGIL, THE by Chester D. Cuthbert. .s. . . .
. . . . WS Feb 34 698
SUBMARINE OF NEPTUNE by James B. Settles . . . . .
. .bacover. . . . . Amz Mar 43
SUBMICROSCOPIC by Capt. S. P. Meek. .s . . . .
. . . . Amz Aug 31 390
SUBSTITUTE FOR WAR by D. D. Sharp. .s. . . . .
. . . . MSS Nov 40 90
SUBTERFUGE by Ray Bradbury. .s . . . . .Ash Apr 43 68

SUBTERRANEAN ADVENTURE, A by George Paul
Bauer. .n 3 pt . . . . WS Jun 30 6
SUBURBAN FRONTIERS by Roger Flint Young . . . . .
. .nt . . . . ASF Feb 50 77
SUBWAY NAMED MOBIUS, A by A. J. Deutsch . . . . .
. .s . . . . ASF Dec 50 72
SUCCUBUS by K. F. Ziska. .s . . . . ASF May 34 33
SUDDEN DEATH FROM SOUND by Ken Kober . . . . .
. .a . . . . .FA May 42 51
SUICIDE COMMAND by Stanley Mullen. .s . . . .
. . . . PS Sum 50 86
SUICIDE DURKEE'S LAST RIDE by Neil R. Jones . . .
. .s . . . . Amz Sep 32 534
SUICIDE ROCKET by Manly Wade Wellman. .s . . . . . .
. . . . Amz Mar 42 62
SUICIDE SHIP TO EARTH by Duncan Farnsworth
ps *(David Wright O'Brien)*. .s . . . . . . Amz Feb 42 176
SUICIDE SQUAD by Henry Kuttner. .s. . . . .
. . . . .TW Dec 39 42
SUICIDE SQUADRONS OF SPACE by David Wright
O'Brien. .nt . . . . .Amz Aug 40 6
SUITCASE AIRPLANES by E. D. Skinner. .s . . . .
. . . . .AW Nov 29 424
SUITOR BY PROXY, A by Harry Collier ps *(Harry
Walton)*. .s . . . . WS Apr 35 1308
SUMMER WEAR by L. Sprague de Camp. .s. . . . .
. . . . SS May 50 127
SUMMONS, THE by Don Evans. .s . . . . . . UK Jun 39 89
                                        UK 48 123
SUMMONS FROM MARS, A by John Russell Fearn . . .
. .s . . . . Amz Jun 38 82
SUN DOOM, THE by Stanton A. Coblentz. .s. . . . . . .
. . . . FA Jun 42 64
SUN ENGINE by Owen Fox Jerome ps *(Oscar J.
Friend)*. .s . . . . .TW Aug 43 98
SUN KING, THE by Gaston Derreaux. .s . . . .
. . . . Amz Apr 49 52
SUN MAKER, THE by Jack Williamson. .nt . . . .
. . . . TW Jun 40 95
SUN MAKERS, THE by Will McMorrow. .n . . . .
. . . . .FFM Dec 40 6
SUN POISONS, THE by John McCabe Moore. .a. . . . . .
. . . . Amz May 46 158
SUN–WORLD OF SOLDUS, THE by Nat Schachner . . .
. .nt .ASF Oct 38 106
SUNDAY IS THREE THOUSAND YEARS AWAY by
Raymond F. Jones. .nt . . . . TW Jun 50 11
SUNKEN CITIES by Douglas Newton. .nt . . . .
. . . . FFM May–Jun 40 6
SUNKEN EMPIRE, THE by H. Thompson Rich. .s . . . .
. . . . .ASF Jan 31 24
SUNKEN LAND, THE by Fritz Leiber, Jr. . .s . . . .
. . . . UK Feb 42 97
SUNKEN UNIVERSE by Arthur Merlyn ps *(James
Blish)*. .s . . . . SSS May 42 49
                                        SSS Nov 50 98

Title. .Author. .Length . . . . Magazine. .Date. .Page No.

SUNKEN WORLD, THE by Stanton A. Coblentz . . . . .
. .n . . . . .AQ Sum 28 292
AQ Fal 34 28
SUNLESS WORLD, THE by Neil R. Jones. .nt . . . . . .
. . . . Amz Dec 34 26
SUNLIGHT MASTER, THE by E. J. Van Name. .s . . . .
. . . . Amz Apr 35 31
SUNSPOT PURGE by Clifford D. Simak. .s . . . .
. . . . ASF Nov 40 49
SUNWARD by Stanton A. Coblentz. .s . . . . TW Apr 40 32
SUNWARD FLIGHT by Arthur Leo Zagat. .nt . . . .
. . . . .SSS Feb 43 82
SUPER-ATHLETE by Don Tracy. .s. . . . . TW Apr 42 66
SUPER-FAST EYES by Thomas Calvert McClary . . . . .
. .a . . . . .ASF Sep 37 122
SUPER-NEUTRON by Isaac Asimov. .s. . . . .
. . . . Ash Sep 41 36
SUPER-RADIO by Charles Cloukey. .s . . . .
. . . . Amz Jul 28 294
SUPER-SENSES by Maurice G. Hugi. .s . . . .
. . . . .ToW #2 (38) 74
SUPER TRAIN OF TOMORROW by James B.
Settles. .bacover . . . . Amz Dec 44
SUPER VELOCITOR, THE by S. C. Carpenter . . . . . .
. .s . . . . SW Dec 29 624
SS Mar 43 108
SUPER WHOST by Margaret St. Clair. .s . . . .
. . . . SS Jul 47 97
SUPERHUMAN by Geoffrey Armstrong ps (John
Russell Fearn). .s . . . . .ToW #1 37 4
by John Russell Fearn . . . . SS May 41 84
SUPERMAN, THE by Captain Meyer Friedenson . . . . .
. .ss . . . . Amz Mar 44 14
SUPERMAN, THE by A. H. Johnson. .s . . . .
. . . . Amz Aug 31 454
SUPERMAN OF DR. JUKES, THE by Francis Flagg
ps (George Henry Weiss). .s . . . . WS Nov 31 745
SS Fal 45 66
SUPERMEN, THE by David M. Speaker. .s . . . .
. . . . Amz Oct 33 592
SUPERMEN INCORPORATED by George
Grauman. .n . . . . Amz Jun 49 94
SUPERNAL NOTE, THE by Rog Phillips ps (Roger P.
Graham). .s . . . . Amz Jul 48 124
SUPERNOVA by P. E. Cleator. .s . . . . . . Fant Dec 46 40
SUPERPERFECT BRIDE, THE by Bob Olsen ps (Alfred
John Olsen, Jr.). .s . . . . .Amz Jul 29 300
SURGICAL ERROR, A by Walter Anton Coole,
M.D. . .s . . . . ASF Nov 37 106
SURVIVAL by Arthur J. Burks. .n . . . . MSS Aug 38 4
SURVIVAL by Henry Hasse. .s . . . . .OW Mar 50 24
SURVIVAL by Norman Lazenby. .s . . . . . Fant Apr 47 77
SURVIVAL by William P. McGivern. .s . . . . FA Jul 50 102
SURVIVAL by Basil Wells. .s. . . . . .PS Spr 46 30
SURVIVORS, THE by Bryce Walton. .s. . . . .
. . . . SSS Jul 49 104

Title. .Author. .Length . . . . Magazine. .Date. .Page No.

SURVIVORS FROM 9000 B.C. by Robert Moore
Williams. .n . . . . .Amz Jul 41 8
SURVIVORS IN SPACE by Charles Recour. .s . . . . . .
. . . . .FA May 49 130
SUSPENDED ANIMATION by Paul Maxwel . . . .
. .bacover pic . . . . .Amz Jan 40
SUTTON'S STRANGE VOYAGE by James Norman . . .
. .s . . . . Amz May 42 142
SWAMP GIRL OF VENUS by H. H. Harmon ps
(Robert Moore Williams). .s . . . . Amz Sep 49 44
SWAMP TRAIN by Harry Walton. .s. . . . . . UK Jan 40 71
SWAMPER by Jerry Shelton. .nt . . . . . . ASF Apr 46 62
SWEET MYSTERY OF LIFE by John Russell
Fearn. .s . . . . .NW #1 46 36
TW Feb 47 74
SWIFT PEOPLE, THE by Basil Wells. .s. . . . .
. . . . Fut Feb 43 100
SWIMMING LESSON by Raymond F. Jones. .nt . . . . . .
. . . . ASF Apr 43 9
SWING LOW by Elmer Perdue. .s . . . . . . .Sti Apr 41 119
SWING YOUR LADY by Kelvin Kent ps (Henry
Kuttner). .s . . . . TW Win 44 85
SWORD AND THE ATOPEN, THE by Taylor H.
Greenfield. .s . . . . .Amz Jan 30 904
SWORD AND THE POOL, THE by Berkeley
Livingston. .n . . . . FA May 46 120
SWORD OF AKALAH, THE by J. Leslie
Chamberlain. .s . . . . Amz Jun 36 123
SWORD OF FIRE by Emmett McDowell. .nt . . . .
. . . . .PS Win 49 70
SWORD OF JOHNNY DAMOKLES, THE by Hugh
Frazier Parker. .s . . . . .PS Mar 43 24
SWORD OF PEACE by Ward Moore. .nt . . . .
. . . . Amz Mar 50 124
SWORD OF THE SEVEN SUNS by Gardner F. Fox . . .
. .nt .PS Spr 47 58
SWORD OF TOMORROW by Henry Kuttner. .nt . . . . .
. . . . TW Fal 45 11
SWORDSMAN OF PIRA, THE by Charles Recour. . . . .
. .n . . . . Amz Mar 49 82
SWORDSMAN OF SARVON, THE by Charles
Cloukey. .n 3 pt . . . . Amz Aug 32 392
SWORDSMEN OF SATURN by Neil R. Jones. .n . . . . .
. . . . SF Oct 39 8
SWORDSMEN OF VARNIS by Clive Jackson. .ss . . . . .
. . . . OW Sep 50 38
SYMBIOTICA by Eric Frank Russell. .nt . . . .
. . . . .ASF Oct 43 128
SYMPHONY OF DEATH, THE by Raymond A.
Palmer. .s . . . . Amz Dec 35 92
SYNTHETIC by Charles Cloukey. .s . . . . Amz May 30 130
SYNTHETIC ENTITY, THE by Capt. S. P. Meek . . . . .
. .s . . . . .WS Jan 33 638
ToW Sum 40 72
SYNTHETIC HERO by Eric Fennel. .s . . . .
. . . . PS Fal 48 96

Title. .Author. .Length . . . . Magazine. .Date. .Page No.

SYNTHETIC MEN, THE by Ed Earl Repp. .s . . . .
. . . . WS Dec 30 698
SYNTHETIC MONSTER, THE by Francis Flagg ps
(George Henry Weiss). .s . . . . WS Mar 31 1152
SYNTHETIC WOMAN, THE by Jep Powell. .nt . . . . . .
. . . . Amz Sep 40 100

T

TAA THE TERRIBLE by Malcolm Jameson. .s . . . . . .
. . . . .Ash Dec 42 32
TABOO by Fritz Leiber, Jr. . .s . . . . ASF Feb 44 85
TAGGART'S TERRIBLE TURBAN by Don Wilcox . . .
. .n .FA Jan 45 122
*TAINE OF SAN FRANCISCO series See DAVID H.
KELLER, M.D. author*
TAINTED FLOOD, THE *(THE MENACE Part 3)* by David
H. Keller, M.D. . .s . . . . .AQ Sum 28 400
TAKE MY DRUM TO ENGLAND by Nelson S.
Bond. .s . . . . UK Aug 41 124
TAKE TWO QUIGGIES by Kris Neville. .nt . . . .
. . . . F&SF Dec 50 3
TALE OF THE ATOM, THE by Philip Dennis
Chamberlin. .s . . . . .Amz Jan 35 132
TALE OF THE LAST MAN, THE by Richard S.
Shaver. .s . . . . FA Jul 46 142
TALE OF THE RED DWARF WHO WRITES WITH HIS
TAIL, THE by the Red Dwarf Himself as told to
Richard S. Shaver. .nt. . . . . .FA May 47 8
TALES FROM TIBET by Vincent H. Gaddis. .a . . . . . .
. . . . Amz Feb 46 170
TALKING BRAIN, THE by M. H. Hasta. .s . . . .
. . . . Amz Aug 26 440
TALKING HILL, A by Battell Loomis. .a . . . .
. . . . ASF Apr 37 108
TALKING ON PULSES by C. Rudmore. .a . . . .
. . . . ASF Jul 49 105
TALL TALES by Mack Reynolds. .s . . . . . .SS Nov 50 130
TALU'S FAN by John York Cabot ps *(David Wright
O'Brien).* .nt. . . . . FA Nov 42 122
TAMING OF THE TYRANT by Leroy Yerxa. .nt . . . . .
. . . . FA Sep 46 128
TANGENTIAL SEMANTICIST, THE by Rog
Phillips. .s . . . . FA Aug 49 38
TANGLED PATHS by Raymond Z. Gallun. .s . . . . .
. . . . .TW Jul 40 84
TANI OF EKKIS by Aladra Septama. .nt . . . .
. . . . AQ Win 30 104
TANKS by Murray Leinster ps *(Will F. Jenkins)* . . . . . .
. .s . . . . .ASF Jan 30 100
TANKS UNDER THE SEA by Harl Vincent
(Schoepflin). .s . . . . .Amz Jan 31 896
TANNER OF KIEV, THE by Wallace West. .s . . . .
. . . . FA Oct 44 82

Title. .Author. .Length . . . . Magazine. .Date. .Page No.

TANTALUS DEATH, THE by Ross Rocklynne . . . . . .
. .s .PS Spr 40 61
TANYA'S NIGHT TO HOWL by Russell E. Nihlean. . . .
. .s . . . . FA Aug 48 148
TARGET by Peter Cartur. .s . . . . ASF Oct 47 60
TARNISHED UTOPIA by Malcolm Jameson. .n . . . . . .
. . . . .SS Mar 42 14
TARRANO THE CONQUEROR by Ray Cummings. . . .
. .n .SFQ Sum 41 4
TASK OF TAU by J. Harvey Haggard. .ss . . . .
. . . . PS Sum 48 103
TASK TO LAHRI by Ross Rocklynne. .s . . . .
. . . . PS Sum 42 2
TAVERN KNIGHT, THE by S. M. Tenneshaw *h ps* . . . .
. .s . . . . FA Jun 48 102
TAXI TO JUPITER by Don Wilcox. .s . . . .
. . . . Amz Aug 41 110
TEACHER FROM MARS, THE by Eando Binder *ps
(Otto Binder).* .s . . . . .TW Feb 41 52
TEARS FOR THE CROCODILE by Lee Francis
h ps. .s . . . . FA Dec 45 166
TECHNICAL ERROR by Arthur C. Clarke. .s . . . .
. . . . Fant Dec 46 58
TECHNICAL ERROR by Hal Clement *ps (Harry Clement
Stubbs).* .nt . . . . ASF Jan 44 7
TECHNICAL SLIP by John Beynon *(Harris).* .s . . . . . .
. . . . Im Dec 50 24
TELEGRAPH PLATEAU by Harl Vincent
(Schoepflin). .nt . . . . ASF Nov 33 115
TELEGRAPHIC FINGER PRINT, THE *(SCIENTIFIC
ACTUALITY)* by Hector G. Grey. .a . . . .
. . . . AD Jun 30 549
TELEPATHIC PICK–UP, THE by Samuel M. Sargent,
Jr. . .s . . . . Amz Dec 26 828
TELEPATHIC PIRACY by Raymond Z. Gallun. .s . . . .
. . . . ASF Mar 35 142
TELEPATHIC TOMB, THE by Frederic Arnold Kummer,
Jr. . .s . . . . .TW Feb 39 72
TELEPATHY IS NEWS by Paul Edmonds *ps (Henry
Kuttner).* .s . . . . .SF Jun 39 89
TELESCOPES vs. CAMERAS by H. A. Lower. .a . . . . .
. . . . .ASF Jan 39 96
TELEVISION ALIBI, THE *(CRIMES OF THE YEAR
2000)* by Ray Cummings. .s . . . . FFM Jun 42 129
TELEVISION HILL by George McLociard. .n 2 pt . . . .
. . . . Amz Feb 31 966
TEMPLE, THE by H. P. Lovecraft. .s . . . .
. . . . .AFR #8 89
TEMPLE OF DUST, THE by Eugene George Key . . . . .
. .s . . . . AD Sep 30 774
TEMPORARY WARP by Frank Belknap Long, Jr. . . . .
. .s . . . . ASF Aug 37 37
TEMPTRESS OF THE TIME FLOW by Gardner F.
Fox. .nt. . . . . MSS Nov 50 72
TEMPTRESS OF THE TOWER OF TORTURE AND
SIN by Robert E. Howard. .s . . . . .AFR #14 3

Title. .Author. .Length . . . . Magazine. .Date. .Page No.

TEN DAYS TO LIVE by C. J. Eustace. .s . . . .
. . . . .AQ Sum 28 418
TEN MILLION MILES SUNWARD by Geoffrey
Hewelcke. .nt . . . . Amz Mar 28 1126
10 SECONDS FROM NOWHERE by David Wright
O'Brien. .s . . . . .Amz Jul 41 96
TENANT ON THE 13TH FLOOR, THE by John York
Cabot ps (David Wright O'Brien). .s . . . .
. . . . FA Feb 42 124
TENTACLES FROM BELOW, THE by Anthony Gilmore
ps (Harry Bates & D. W. Hall). .nt . . . . ASF Feb 31 172
TENTH DEGREE, THE by Sam Merwin, Jr. . .s . . . . . .
. . . . TW Oct 50 104
TENTH WORLD, THE by John W. Campbell, Jr. . . . . .
. .s . . . . TW Dec 37 36
TEPONDICON by Carl Jacobi. .s . . . . .PS Win 46 40
TERMINAL IN SPACE by Willy Ley. .a . . . .
. . . . Fant #2 39 53
TERRIBLE MORNING, THE by Nick Boddie
Williams. .s. . . . . .NW #3 29
TERRIBLE SENSE, THE by Calvin Peregoy ps (Thomas
Calvert McClary). .s . . . . ASF Aug 38 99
TERRIBLE TENTACLES OF L–472, THE By Sewell
Peaslee Wright. .s. . . . . .ASF Sep 30 332
TERRIBLE THREE, THE by Tod Robbins. .n . . . .
. . . . FN Nov 48 8
TERROR, THE by Alfred Coppel. .s. . . . . .Fut Nov 50 62
TERROR FROM THE DEPTHS, THE by Sewell Peaslee
Wright. .s . . . . ASF Nov 31 222
TERROR FROM THE SEA, THE by Robert Arthur,
Jr. . .s. . . . . WS Dec 31 890
TERROR IN THE AIR, THE by Arthur B. Reeve . . . . .
. .s . . . . SD Apr 30 294
TERROR IN THE DUST by Paul S. Powers. .s . . . .
. . . . .TW Sum 44 55
TERROR IN UTOPIA by Paul Ernst. .s . . . .
. . . . TW Jun 38 106
TERROR OF AIR LEVEL SIX, THE by Harl Vincent
(Schoepflin). .nt . . . . .ASF Jul 30 62
TERROR OF THE MIST MAIDENS by A. Bertram
Chandler. .s . . . . OTWA Jul 50 88
TERROR OF THE STREETS, THE by George
McLociard. .s . . . . Amz Apr 29 18
TERROR ON THE TELEPHONE by Lee Francis
h ps. .s. . . . . Amz Sep 47 58
TERROR OUT OF SPACE by Leigh Brackett. .s . . . . . .
. . . . PS Sum 44 33
TERROR OUT OF SPACE by H. Haverstock Hill
. .n 4 pt . . . . Amz Feb 34 12
TERROR OUT OF THE PAST by Raymond Z.
Gallun. .nt . . . . Amz Mar 40 100
TERROR OUT OF TIME by Jack Williamson. .s . . . . . .
. . . . ASF Dec 33 116
TERRORS OF ARELLI by Aladra Septama. .nt . . . . . .
. . . . .AQ Fal 30 530

TERRORS OF ARYL, THE by R. F. Starzl. .s . . . .
. . . . WS Mar 31 1102
TERRORS OF THE UPPER AIR, THE by Frank
Orndorff. .s . . . . .AQ Win28 138
TERRORS UNSEEN by Harl Vincent (Schoepflin) . . . .
. .s . . . . ASF Mar 31 360
TEST FOR THE PEARL by Vaseleos Garson. .s . . . . . .
. . . . PS Fal 47 76
TEST OF AIRPLANE LIGHTNING HAZARDS, A by
Walter E. Burton. .a . . . . AW Mar 30 818
TEST OF THE GODS by Raymond F. Jones. .s . . . . . .
. . . . ASF Sep 41 85
TEST TUBE BLOODHOUNDS (SCIENTIFIC
ACTUALITY) by H. H. Dunn. .a . . . . . SD Mar 30 232
TEST TUBE GIRL, THE by Frank Patton h ps (Raymond
A. Palmer). .nt . . . . Amz Jan 42 8
TEST-TUBE MONSTER, THE by George E. Clark . . . .
. .s . . . . MSS May 40 55
TESTAMENT OF AKUBII by Norman L. Knight. .s . . .
. . . . ASF Jun 40 90
TETRAHEDRA OF SPACE by P. Schuyler Miller . . . . .
. .s . . . . WS Nov 31 728
                                            SS Sep 48 82
THAT DREADFUL NIGHT by John York Cabot ps
(David Wright O'Brien). .s . . . . FA Sep 42 162
THAT GUY, SATAN, SENDS ME! by George
Reese. .s . . . . .FA Jan 49 118
THAT LOW by Theodore Sturgeon. .s. . . FFM Oct 48 118
THAT MESS LAST YEAR by John D. MacDonald . . . .
. .s . . . . TW Oct 48 38
THAT MYTH ABOUT MAGIC by Guy Fauldes. .a . . . .
. . . . .Amz Jan 42 204
THAT ONLY A MOTHER by Judith Merril. .s . . . . . .
. . . . ASF Jun 48 88
THAT RECEDING BROW by Max Brand ps (Frederick
Faust). .nt . . . . FN Mar 50 96
THAT WE MAY RISE AGAIN by Charles Recour. . . . .
. .s .Amz Jul 48 94
THAT WORLDS MAY LIVE by Nelson S. Bond. .n . . . .
. . . . Amz Apr 43 8
THAT'S JUST LIKE A MARTIAN by Manly Wade
Wellman. .s. . . . . TW Fal 43 94
THEFT OF THE WASHINGTON MONUMENT by
Robert Arthur, Jr. . .s . . . . Amz Oct 33 507
"THERE AIN'T NO SUCH!" by L. Sprague de
Camp. .a 2 pt . . . . ASF Nov 39 92
THERE IS NO DEFENSE by Theodore Sturgeon . . . . .
. .nt . . . . ASF Feb 48 7
THERE SHALL BE DARKNESS by C. L. Moore . . . . .
. .nt . . . . ASF Feb 42 9
THERE SHALL BE NO DARKNESS by James
Blish. .nt . . . . TW Apr 50 72
THERE WAS NO PARADISE by Manly Wade
Wellman. .s. . . . . .TW Aug 40 14
THEY by Robert Heinlein. .s . . . . .UK Apr 41 84

Title. .Author. .Length . . . . Magazine. .Date. .Page No.

THEY BITE by Anthony Boucher ps (William Anthony
   Parker White). .s . . . . UK Aug 43 127
THEY BURIED HER BODY by Gordon Philip
   England. .s . . . . FA Feb 48 152
THEY CHANGED THE WORLD by Jack Binder. . . . . .
   . . . . .pictorial feature
   ALBERT EINSTEIN . . . . .SS Jan 39 98
   THE LIFE STORY OF MADAME CURIE WHO
      DISCOVERED RADIUM . . . . .SS Mar 39 94
   ROBERT A. MILLIKAN, DISCOVERER OF THE
      COSMIC RAY. . . . . SS May 39 98
   LEONARDO DA VINCI. . . . . SS Jul 39 94
   ALFRED BERNHARD NOBEL. . . . . . .SS Sep 39 88
   HEINRICH R. HERTZ. . . . . SS Nov 39 90
   BENJAMIN FRANKLIN . . . . SS Jan 40 106
   SIR ISAAC NEWTON . . . . .SS Mar 40 90
   THOMAS ALVA EDISON . . . . SS May 40 92
   LUTHER BURBANK. . . . . SS Jul 40 92
   GALILEO DE GALILEI. . . . . .SS Sep 40 88
   SIR WILLIAM PERKIN . . . . SS Nov 40 94
THEY FORGOT TO REMEMBER PEARL HARBOR
   by P. F. Costello h ps. .nt . . . . Amz Jun 42 54
THEY GAVE HIM A ROPE by H. B. Carleton h ps
   (Howard Browne). .nt . . . . FA Mar 43 74
THEY HAD RHYTHM! by Kent Casey. .s . . . .
   . . . . ASF Dec 38 141
THEY NEVER COME BACK by Fritz Leiber. .nt . . . . .
   . . . . .Fut Aug 41 10
THEY SCULP by Leslie Northern h ps (Frank Belknap
   Long). .s . . . . TW Win 45 76
"THEY WERE DEAD—" by Willy Ley. .a . . . .
   . . . . .ASF Jun 44 103
      (addenda to above). .a . . . . .ASF Jan 45 146
THEY WOULDN'T DARE by Samuel Mines. .s . . . . . .
   . . . . TW Dec 47 43
THEY'RE ALIVE ON MARS by Paul Lohrman
   h ps. .s. . . . . .Amz Jul 50 56
THIA OF THE DRYLANDS by Harl Vincent
   (Schoepflin). .s . . . . .Amz Jul 32 296
THICKER THAN WATER by Cleve Cartmill. .s . . . . . .
   . . . . TW Dec 49 123
THIEF IN TIME, A by Raymond A. Young. .ss . . . . . .
   . . . . .WS Jul 35 202
                                    FSQ Sum 50 146
THIEF OF MARS by Henry Hasse. .s . . . . . .PS Win 41 57
THIEF OF TIME, THE by Captain S. P. Meek. .s. . . . . .
   . . . . ASF Feb 30 259
THIEVES FROM ISOT, THE by Eando Binder ps (Earl
   Binder & Otto Binder). .nt . . . . WS Oct 34 521
THIEVES' HOUSE by Fritz Leiber, Jr. . .nt . . . .
   . . . . UK Feb 43 34
THIEVES OF TIME by Arthur J. Burks. .s . . . .
   . . . . TW Apr 48 60
THIN WOMAN by Richard S. Shaver. .s . . . . FA Mar 48 78
THING FROM ANTARES, THE by Myer Krulfeld . . . .
   . .s . . . . TW Feb 40 61

Title. .Author. .Length . . . . Magazine. .Date. .Page No.

THING FROM MARS, THE by Ray Cummings. .s . . . . .
   . . . . .TW Aug 38 78
THING FROM OUTSIDE, THE by George Allen
   England. .s . . . . Amz Apr 26 67
THING IN THE CELLAR, THE by David H. Keller . . . .
   . .s . . . . .AFR #6 42
THING IN THE ICE, THE by W. P. Cockroft. .s . . . . . .
   . . . . ToW Spr 39 37
THING IN THE POND, THE by Paul Ernst. .s . . . .
   . . . . ASF Jun 34 48
THING IN THE WOODS, THE by Fletcher Pratt &
   B. F. Ruby. .s . . . . Amz Feb 35 112
THING OF VENUS, THE by Wilbur Peacock. .s . . . . . .
   . . . . .PS Spr 42 66
THING ON OUTER SHOAL, THE by P. Schuyler
   Miller. .s . . . . ASF Sep 47 62
THING THAT KILLED, THE by Paul Chadwick. .s . . . .
   . . . . .TW May 40 72
THING THAT WALKED IN THE RAIN, THE by Otis
   Adelbert Kline. .s . . . . Amz Mar 31 1124
THING THAT WALKED ON THE WIND, THE by
   August Derleth. .s . . . . AFR #13 74
THINGS PASS BY by Murray Leinster ps (Will F.
   Jenkins). .nt. . . . . .TW Sum 45 11
THINKING CAP, THE by Sgt. William P. McGivern. . . .
   . .nt . . . . Amz Sep 44 38
THIRD BOLT, THE by Frances M. Deegan. .s. . . . . . .
   . . . . Amz Oct 47 24
THIRD FROM THE SUN by Richard Matheson. .s . . . .
   . . . . GSF Oct 50 61
THIRD LITTLE GREEN MAN, THE by Damon
   Knight. .s . . . . PS Sum 48 27
THIRD PERSON SINGULAR by Clemence Dane . . . . .
   . .nt . . . . FFM Oct 46 64
THIRD VIBRATOR, THE by John Beynon Harris. . . . .
   . .s . . . . WS May 33 938
                                    ToW Aut 38 94
THIRTEEN O'CLOCK by Cecil Corwin ps (Cyril
   Kornbluth). .s . . . . Sti Feb 41 70
THIRTEENTH MR. TUMPS, THE by Richard O.
   Lewis. .s . . . . Amz Feb 40 76
THIRTIETH CENTURY DUEL by Manly Wade
   Wellman. .s . . . . .Fut Apr 41 10
THIRTY AND ONE, THE by David H. Keller. .s . . . . . .
   . . . . MSS Nov 38 53
35TH MILLENNIUM, THE by Arthur G. Stangland. . . .
   . .s . . . . WS Aug 31 330
THIRTY SECOND OF MAY, THE by Paul Ernst . . . . .
   . .s . . . . ASF Apr 35 110
THIRTY SECONDS—THIRTY DAYS by Arthur C.
   Clarke. .s . . . . TW Dec 49 106
THIS AMAZING UNIVERSE by H. W. McCauley . . . . .
   . .bacover. . . . . Amz Jun 38
THIS ATOM, EARTH by Ray Cummings. .guest ed . . . .
   . . . . SS May 39 13
THIS ATOMIC AGE dept in post-war Fantasy all issues

Title. .Author. .Length . . . . Magazine. .Date. .Page No.

THIS IS HELL by Oscar J. Friend. .s. . . . .
. . . . TW Feb 42 108
THIS IS HOT! by Arthur C. Parlett, Jr. . .a . . . .
. . . . ASF Jul 50 94
THIS IS THE HOUSE by Lawrence O'Donnell ps (Henry
Kuttner). .s . . . . ASF Feb 46 80
"THIS MEANS WAR" by A. Bertram Chandler. .s. . . . .
. . . . ASF May 44 29
THIS SHIP KILLS by Frederick Engelhardt. .s . . . .
. . . . ASF Nov 39 107
THIS STAR SHALL BE FREE by Murray Leinster ps
(Will F. Jenkins). .s . . . . .SSS Nov 49 48
THIS TABLE RESERVED by Gilbert Grant. .s. . . . . .
. . . . Amz Sep 50 146
THIS TIME. . . by Rog Phillips ps (Roger P. Graham). . .
. .s . . . . OW Jan 50 60
THIS WAY OUT by Robert Moore Williams. .nt . . . . . .
. . . . Amz Sep 50 94
THIS WAY TO HEAVEN by Harold M. Sherman . . . . .
. .n . . . . FA Oct 48 8
THOMPSON'S TIME-TRAVELING THEORY by Sgt.
Mort Weisinger. .s . . . . Amz Mar 44 118
THOUGH DREAMERS DIE by Lester del Rey. .s . . . . .
. . . . ASF Feb 44 34
THOUGHT POPPIES GROW by Lester del Rey. .s. . . . .
. . . . UK Aug 42 115
THOUGHT by Fritz Leiber, Jr. . .s. . . . . . ASF Jul 44 84
THOUGHT-FEEDERS, THE by R. R. Winterbotham . .
. .s . . . . Fut Oct 41 72
THOUGHT IN TIME, A by Leroy Yerxa. .s . . . .
. . . . FA Feb 44 128
THOUGHT MACHINE, THE by Ray Cummings . . . . . .
. .s . . . . MSS Apr 41 48
THOUGHT MACHINE, THE by Ammianus
Macellinus. .s . . . . Amz Feb 27 1052
THOUGHT MATERIALIZER, THE by F. B. Long,
Jr. . .s. . . . . WQ Spr 30 414
THOUGHT MATERIALIZER, THE by Leo
Sonderegger. .s . . . . TW Mar 40 78
THOUGHT-MEN OF MERCURY, THE by R. R.
Winterbotham. .s. . . . . PS Fal 42 44
THOUGHT RECORDS OF LEMURIA by Richard S.
Shaver. .nt . . . . Amz Jun 45 16
THOUGHT ROBOT, THE by John York Cabot ps (David
Wright O'Brien). .s. . . . . FA Mar 41 78
THOUGHT WEB OF MINIPAR, THE by Chan Corbett
ps (Nathan Schachner). .s . . . . ASF Nov 36 112
THOUGHT-WOMAN, THE by Ray Cummings. .s . . . . .
. . . . SSS Jul 40 86
THOUGHT-WORLD MONSTERS, THE by Richard O.
Lewis. .s . . . . MSS Nov 40 67
THOUGHTS THAT KILL by John Russell Fearn. .s. . . .
. . . . .SF Oct 39 105
THOUSAND-AND-SECOND TALE OF
SCHEHERAZADE, THE by Edgar Allen Poe. .s . . . .
. . . . Amz May 28 126

THRALLS OF THE ENDLESS NIGHT by Leigh
Brackett. .s. . . . . PS Fal 43 54
THREAT OF THE ROBOT, THE by David H. Keller,
M.D. . .s . . . . SW Jun 29 63
THREE, THE by Burnham Eaton. .poem. . . . .
. . . . FFM Aug 49 116
THREE AGAINST THE STARS by Eric North ps
(Bernard Cronin). .n. . . . . .FN May 50 14
THREE BLIND MICE by Lewis Padgett ps (Henry
Kuttner & C. L. Moore). .nt . . . . ASF Jun 45 68
THREE ETERNALS, THE by Eando Binder ps (Otto
Binder). .nt . . . . .TW Dec 39 95
THREE EYED MAN, THE by Ray Cummings. .s. . . . .
. . . . AFR #14 30
THREE EYES IN THE DARK by Don Wilcox. .s . . . . .
. . . . .FA May 41 44
THREE FROM THE TEST TUBE by Raymond A.
Palmer. .s. . . . . WS Nov 36 674
THREE GO BACK by J. Leslie Mitchell. .n . . . .
. . . . .FFM Dec 43 8
THREE INFERNAL JOKES, THE by Lord
Dunsany. .s . . . . AFR #1 125
THREE LINES OF OLD FRENCH by A. Merritt . . . . .
. .s . . . . .FFM May–Jun 40 31
AMF Feb 50 102
THREE PLANETEERS, THE by Edmond Hamilton . . .
. .n .SS Jan 40 12
THREE PYLONS, THE by William F. Temple. .s. . . . . .
. . . . .NW #1 46 43
THREE SUNS, THE by Norman C. Pallant. .s. . . . . .
. . . . Fant Aug 47 56
THREE SUNS OF EV, THE by Edwin K. Sloat. .s . . . .
. . . . Amz May 33 152
3 TERRIBLE PEOPLE by John York Cabot ps (David
Wright O'Brien). .nt . . . . .FA Jul 41 90
THREE THOUSAND YEARS by Thomas Calvert
McClary. .n 3 pt . . . . ASF Apr 38 6
THREE WISE MEN by Lloyd Arthur Eshbach. .s . . . .
. . . . SS Nov 39 92
THREE WISE MEN OF SPACE by Donald Bern. .s . . . .
. . . . Amz Dec 40 102
THREE WORLDS TO CONQUER by D. D. Sharp. . . . .
. .s . . . . WQ Win 31 262
THRESHOLD by Henry Kuttner. .s . . . . . . UK Dec 40 92
THRILLS IN SCIENCE Dept in SS regularly from Jan 39
(first issue) thru Sum 45. by Mort Weisinger to end
of 1941, thereafter by Oscar J. Friend. Thumbnail
sketches of scientists.
THRONE OF VALHALLA, THE by Arthur T.
Harris. .s . . . . Amz Sep 41 92
THROUGH A DEAD MAN'S EYES by Geoff St. Reynard
ps (Robert W. Krepps). .s . . . . FA Oct 45 68
THROUGH EARTH'S CORE by John Russell Fearn . . .
. .s . . . . .ToW #2 38 86
THROUGH INVISIBLE BARRIERS by Edmond
Hamilton. .nt . . . . TW Oct 42 15

Title. .Author. .Length . . . . Magazine. .Date. .Page No.

THROUGH THE AIR TUNNEL by Harl Vincent
(Schoepflin). .s . . . . AW Oct 29 314
THROUGH THE ANDES by A. Hyatt Verrill . . . .
. .n 3 pt . . . . Amz Sep 34 49
THROUGH THE ASTEROIDS—TO HELL! by Leroy
Yerxa. .s . . . . PS Fal 46 71
THROUGH THE BLACKBOARD by Joel Townsley
Rogers. .nt . . . . TW Jun 43 13
THROUGH THE CRATER'S RIM by A. Hyatt
Verrill. .s . . . . Amz Dec 26 806
THROUGH THE DRAGON GLASS by A. Merritt . . . . .
. .s . . . . FN Sep 40 118
THROUGH THE EINSTEIN LINE by J. Harvey
Haggard. .s . . . . WS Nov 33 394
THROUGH THE METEORS by Lowell Howard
Morrow. .s . . . . AW Apr 30 870
THROUGH THE PURPLE CLOUD by Jack
Williamson. .s . . . . WS May 31 1398
                                          SS Nov 47 68
THROUGH THE TIME RADIO by Stanton A.
Coblentz. .s . . . . MSS Aug 38 83
THROUGH THE VEIL by Leslie F. Stone ps (Mrs.
William Silberberg). .s . . . . Amz May 30 174
THROUGH THE VIBRATIONS by P. Schuyler
Miller. .s . . . . Amz May 31 102
                                          AFR #9 18
THROW-BACK, THE by L. R. Sherman. .s . . . .
. . . . .FN Jul 49 98
THROWBACK by L. Sprague de Camp. .s . . . .
. . . . ASF Mar 49 48
THUNDER AND ROSES by Theodore Sturgeon . . . . . .
. .nt . . . . ASF Nov 47 76
THUNDER IN THE VOID by Henry Kuttner. .nt . . . . .
. . . . .Ash Oct 42 10
THUNDER OVER WASHINGTON by William P.
McGivern. .s . . . . FA Oct 41 48
THUNDER TO VENUS by Joseph J. Millard . . . .
. .nt . . . . TW Jun 42 11
THUNDER VOICE by Dow Elstar ps (Raymond Z.
Gallun). .s . . . . ASF Feb 38 142
THUNDERER, THE by A. H. Johnson. .s . . . .
. . . . AW Jan 30 634
THUNDERING PEACE by Kent Casey. .s . . . .
. . . . ASF Dec 39 35
THUNOR FLEES THE DEVILS by Russell Storm
ps (Robert Moore Williams). .s . . . . FA Feb 40 48
THURNLEY ABBEY by Perceval Landon. .s . . . .
. . . . .F&SF Fal 49 18
TICKETS TO PARADISE by D. L. James. .s . . . .
. . . . Com Dec 40 53
TIDAL MOON by Stanley G. Weinbaum & Helen
Weinbaum. .s . . . . TW Dec 38 78
TIDAL WAVES by Malcolm Jameson. .a . . . .
. . . . ASF Oct 43 30
TIDE PROJECTILE TRANSPORTATION CO., THE by
Will H. Gray. .s . . . . Amz Sep 27 544

Title. .Author. .Length . . . . Magazine. .Date. .Page No.

TIDES AND GRAVITY, THE by H. H. Hyers. .a . . . . . .
. . . . Amz Sep 49 142
TIDES OF TIME, THE by A. Bertram Chandler. .s . . . .
. . . . FA Jun 48 150
TIDES OF TIME, THE by Robert Moore Williams. . . . .
. .s . . . . TW Apr 40 12
TIGER DUST by Bassett Morgan. .s . . . . AFR #12 84
TIGER GIRL by Edgar Rice Burroughs. .nt . . . .
. . . . Amz Apr 42 48
TIGER HAS A SOUL, THE by Lester Barclay. .s . . . . . .
. . . . .FA Jul 45 70
TIGER RIDE by James Blish & Damon Knight. .s . . . . .
. . . . .ASF Oct 48 142
TIGER WOMAN OF SHADOW VALLEY by Berkeley
Livingston. .s . . . . Amz Oct 49 8
TIGHT PLACE by Murray Leinster ps (Will F.
Jenkins). .s . . . . ASF Jul 45 131
TILL DOOMSDAY (reprinted as "The Benevolent Ghost
and Captain Lowrie") by Richard Sale. .s . . . .
. . . . FanF May 50 71
TILLIE by Craig Browning ps (Roger P. Graham) . . . . .
. .s . . . . Amz Dec 38 42
TIME AND TIME AGAIN by H. Beam Piper. .s . . . . . .
. . . . ASF Apr 47 27
TIME ANNIHILATOR, THE by Edgar A. Manly &
Walter Thode. .s . . . . WS Nov 30 488
TIME AXIS, THE by Henry Kuttner. .n. . . . . SS Jan 49 13
TIME BENDER, THE by Oliver Saari. .s . . . .
. . . . ASF Aug 37 69
TIME CAPSULE, THE by Ralph Milne Farley ps (Roger
Sherman Hoar). .s . . . . .Ash Apr 41 26
TIME CAVE, THE by Walt Sheldon. .s . . . .
. . . . TW Apr 50 131
TIME CHEATERS, THE by Eando Binder ps (Otto
Binder). .nt . . . . TW Mar 40 14
TIME COLUMN by Malcolm Jameson. .n. . . . .
. . . . TW Dec 41 15
TIME CONQUEROR, THE by L. A. Eshbach. .s . . . . . .
. . . . .WS Jul 32 126
TIME CONTRACTOR, THE by Eando Binder ps (Otto
Binder). .s . . . . ASF Dec 37 143
TIME CONTROL, THE by Philip Jacques Bartel. .s . . . .
. . . . Amz Dec 36 51
TIME DECELERATOR, THE by A. Macfadyen, Jr.
. .s . . . . .ASF Jul 36 28
TIME DEFLECTOR, THE by Edward L. Rementer. . . . .
. .nt . . . . Amz Dec 29 806
TIME DREDGE by Robert Arthur. .s . . . . ASF Jun 42 81
TIME DRUG, THE by Charles F. Hall. .s . . . .
. . . . ToW Win 38 62
TIME ELIMINATOR, THE by Kaw. .s . . Amz Dec 26 802
TIME ENOUGH by Lewis Padgett ps (Henry Kuttner
& C. L. Moore). .s . . . . ASF Dec 46 124
TIME ENTITY, THE by Eando Binder ps (Otto
Binder). .s . . . . ASF Oct 36 73
TIME EXPOSURE by E. A. Grosser. .s . . . .Fut Aug 42 76

Title. .Author. .Length . . . . Magazine. .Date. .Page No.

TIME EXPRESS, THE by Nathan Schachner. .s . . . . . .
. . . . WS Dec 32 562
TIME FLIGHT, THE by Miles J. Breuer, M.D. . .s . . . . .
. . . . Amz Jun 31 274
TIME FOR A UNIVERSE by R. S. Richardson. .a . . . . .
. . . . ASF Nov 44 99
TIME FOR SALE by Ralph Milne Farley ps (Roger
Sherman Hoar). .s . . . . Amz Aug 38 32
TIME HAVEN by Howard W. Graham, Ph.D. . .s . . . . .
. . . . ASF Sep 34 42
TIME HEALS by Poul Anderson. .s . . . . . ASF Oct 49 58
TIME HOAXERS, THE by Paul Bolton. .s . . . .
. . . . Amz Aug 31 428
TIME IMPOSTOR, THE by Nat Schachner. .s . . . .
. . . . ASF Mar 34 128
TIME, INC. by John L. Chapman. .s . . . . . Cos May 41 69
TIME IS A COFFIN by Gilbert Mead. .s . . . .
. . . . Amz Sep 50 134
TIME JUMPERS, THE by Phil Nowlan. .s . . . .
. . . . Amz Feb 34 108
TIME LOCKER by Lewis Padgett ps (Henry Kuttner
& C. L. Moore). .s . . . . ASF Jan 43 100
TIME MACHINE, THE by H. G. Wells. .nt . . . .
. . . . Amz May 27 148
                                              FFM Aug 50 10
TIME MAKER, THE by R. R. Winterbotham. .s . . . . . .
. . . . Fut Aug 41 43
TIME MERCHANT, THE by Frederic Arnold Kummer,
Jr. . .s . . . . FA Jan 40 48
TIME MIRROR, THE by Clark South ps (Dwight V.
Swain). .nt . . . . Amz Dec 42 116
TIME OF MY LIFE by Gerald Vance h ps. .s . . . .
. . . . Amz Jun 50 148
TIME OF YOUR LIFE, THE by R. S. Richardson . . . . .
. .a . . . . ASF Nov 49 110
TIME ON MY HANDS by Mort Weisinger. .ss . . . .
. . . . TW Jun 38 104
TIME ON YOUR HANDS by John York Cabot ps
(David Wright O'Brien). .nt . . . . FA Apr 44 84
TIME OSCILLATOR, THE by Henry F. Kirkham . . . . .
. .s . . . . SW Dec 29 602
TIME OUT OF MIND by Chester S. Geier. .s . . . .
. . . . FA Nov 47 98
TIME PROJECTOR, THE by David Lasser & David H.
Keller, M.D. . .n 2 pt . . . . WS Jul 31 152
TIME QUARRY by Clifford D. Simak. .n 3 pt . . . .
. . . . GSF Oct 50 4
TIME RAY OF JANDRA, THE by Raymond A.
Palmer. .s . . . . WS Jun 30 46
TIME STREAM, THE by John Taine ps (Eric Temple
Bell). .n 3 pt . . . . WS Dec 31 824
TIME–TABLE FOR EARTH by C. P. Mason. .a . . . . . .
. . . . TW Aug 41 102
TIME TO DIE by Murray Leinster ps (Will F.
Jenkins). .s . . . . ASF Jan 47 141
TIME TO REGRET by Wilm Carver. .s . . . . TW Oct 42 71

TIME TO REST by John Beynon (Harris). .s . . . .
. . . . NW #5 49 82
TIME TOLLS FOR TORO by Robert Moore
Williams. .nt . . . . Amz Aug 50 124
TIME TRAGEDY, THE by Raymond A. Palmer . . . . . .
. .s . . . . WS Dec 34 822
TIME TRAP by Stanton A. Coblentz. .nt . . . .
. . . . Fant Aug 47 5
TIME TRAP by Charles Harness. .nt . . . .
. . . . ASF Aug 48 7
TIME TRAP, THE by Henry Kuttner. .n . . . .
. . . . MSS Nov 38 72
TIME TRAP by Frank Belknap Long. .s . . . .
. . . . PS Win 48 109
TIME–TRAVEL HAPPENS by A. M. Phillips. .a . . . . . .
. . . . UK Dec 39 112
TIME TWIN, THE by Lyle D. Gunn. .s . . . .
. . . . TW Aug 39 26
TIME TWISTER, THE by Francis Flagg ps (George
Henry Weiss) & Weaver Wright ps (Forrest J.
Ackerman). .s . . . . TW Oct 47 61
TIME VALVE, THE by Miles J. Breuer, M.D. . .s . . . . .
. . . . WS Jul 30 102
TIME WANTS A SKELETON by Ross Rocklynne . . . . .
. .nt . . . . ASF Jun 41 9
TIME WILL TELL by Emil Petaja. .s . . . .
. . . . Amz Jun 42 94
TIME–WISE GUY, THE by Ralph Milne Farley ps (Roger
Sherman Hoar). .s . . . . Amz May 40 6
TIME WOUNDS ALL HEELS by Robert Bloch. .s . . . . .
. . . . FA Apr 42 192
TIMELESS by Edsel Ford. .ss . . . . FB #5 19
TIMELESS MAN, THE by Frank Belknap Long. .s . . . .
. . . . SSS Nov 49 40
TIMELESS ONES, THE by Harry Walton. .s . . . .
. . . . SSS Jul 40 30
TIMELESS TOMORROW, THE by Manly Wade
Wellman. .s . . . . TW Dec 47 68
TIME'S MAUSOLEUM by Neil R. Jones. .s . . . .
. . . . Amz Dec 33 10
TIMID TIGER, THE by Eric Frank Russell. .s . . . . . .
. . . . ASF Feb 47 121
TINK FIGHTS THE GREMLINS by William P.
McGivern. .nt . . . . FA Oct 43 102
TINK TAKES A FLING by William P. McGivern . . . . . .
. .s . . . . FA Jun 42 136
TINK TAKES A HAND by William P. McGivern . . . . . .
. .s . . . . FA Oct 41 94
TINK TAKES COMMAND by William P. McGivern . . . .
. .s . . . . FA Aug 42 48
TIRELESS LEG, THE by P. F. Costello h ps. .s . . . . . .
. . . . FA Nov 42 176
TINY AND THE MONSTER by Theodore Sturgeon . . .
. .nt . . . . ASF May 47 50
TISSUE CULTURE KING, THE by Julian Huxley. . . . .
. .s . . . . Amz Aug 27 451

Title. .Author. .Length. . . . . Magazine. .Date. .Page No.

TITAN OF THE JUNGLE by Stanton A. Coblentz . . . .
. .nt . . . . .TW Sum 46 13
TITAN'S BATTLE by Heinrich Hauser. .n . . . .
. . . . Amz Mar 47 50
TITAN'S DAUGHTER by Richard S. Shaver. .n . . . . . .
. . . . Amz Sep 48 64
TO DUST RETURNETH by H. B. Hickey ps (Herb
Livingston). .nt . . . . FA Feb 48 70
TO DUST RETURNETH by Henry Kuttner. .s . . . .
. . . . CF Win 48 70
TO FIGHT ANOTHER DAY by Robert Moore
Williams. .s. . . . . ASF Jun 44 93
TO GIVE THEM WELCOME by Melva Rogers. .nt. . . .
. . . . OW Jan 50 84
TO FOLLOW KNOWLEDGE by Frank Belknap
Long. .s. . . . . ASF Dec 42 86
TO SCIENCE FICTION READERS ed dept of first WSA
TO SERVE MAN by Damon Knight. .s . . . GSF Nov 50 91
TO STILL THE DRUMS by Chan Davis. .s. . . . .
. . . . .ASF Oct 46 159
TO THE END OF TIME by Robert Moore Williams. . . .
. .s . . . . SSS Jul 50 108
TO THE MOON BY PROXY by J. Schlossel. .s. . . . . . .
. . . . Amz Oct 28 598
TO THE STARS by L. Ron Hubbard. .n 2 pt . . . .
. . . . ASF Feb 50 5
TO THE VICTORS by H. B. Hickey ps (Herb
Livingston). .s. . . . . FA Dec 50 70
TO WATCH BY NIGHT by Robert Moore Williams . . . .
. .n . . . . .FA Jul 46 8
TO WATCH THE WATCHERS by W. Macfarlane . . . . .
. .s . . . . ASF Jun 49 28
TO WHOM IT MAY CONCERN by Millicent
Holmberg. .s. . . . . Amz Jun 46 118
TODAY AND TOMORROW dept of Fut from
Jul–Aug 50
TODAY'S YESTERDAY by Rice Ray. .s. . . .WS Jan 34 608
TOFFEE HAUNTS A GHOST by Charles F. Myers . . . .
. .nt . . . . FA Nov 47 108
TOFFEE TAKES A TRIP by Charles F. Myers. .nt . . . .
. . . . .FA Jul 47 50
TOFFEE TURNS THE TRICK by Charles F. Myers. . . .
. .nt . . . . FA Feb 49 46
TOKA AND THE MAN BATS by J. W. Pelkie. .n . . . . .
. . . . FA Feb 46 108
TOKA FIGHTS THE BIG CATS by J. W. Pelkie . . . . . .
. .n . . . . FA Dec 47 8
TOMB FROM BEYOND, THE by Carl Jacobi. .s . . . . . .
. . . . WS Nov 33 354
TOMB OF THE SEVEN TAAJOS by Henry Hasse. . . . .
. .nt . . . . Amz Feb 50 106
TOMB OF TIME, THE by Robert Arthur. .s. . . . .
. . . . .TW Nov 40 16
TOMB OF TIME, THE by Richard Tooker. .nt . . . .
. . . . Amz Mar 33 1062

Title. .Author. .Length. . . . . Magazine. .Date. .Page No.

TOMBI SINK by J. Vale Downie. .s . . . . . .UK Aug 40 84
TOMMYKNOCKER, THE by Thomas Calvert
McClary. .n 2 pt . . . . UK Oct 40 129
TOMORROW by Robert Arthur. .s . . . . . . UK Jun 42 73
TOMORROW AND TOMORROW by Ray
Bradbury. .s . . . . FA May 47 102
TOMORROW AND TOMORROW by Lewis Padgett ps
(Henry Kuttner & C. L. Moore). .n 2 pt . . . .
. . . . ASF Jan 47 6
TOMORROW I DIE by Richard Casey h ps. .s. . . . . . .
. . . . FA Aug 48 154
TOMORROW'S CHILDREN by Poul Anderson &
F. N. Waldrop. .nt . . . . ASF Mar 47 56
TOMORROW'S HERO by Don Tracy. .s . . . .
. . . . .TW May 40 39
TOMORROW'S MAIL by Leslie Owen. .s. . . . .
. . . . FA Mar 43 204
TONE MACHINE, THE by Chester G. Osborne. . . . . . .
. .s . . . . WS May 34 1134
TONGUE CANNOT TELL, THE by Manly Wade
Wellman. .s. . . . . TW Oct 47 90
TONGUE OF THE DRAGON by Dale Hart. .s . . . .
. . . . FB #5 77
TOO EFFICIENT by Sydney J. Bounds. .s. . . . .
. . . . .NW #5 49 66
TOO MANY BOARDS by Harl Vincent
(Schoepflin). .s. . . . . Amz Apr 31 70
TOO MANY COOKS by Henry Kuttner. .s. . . . .
. . . . .TW Dec 42 80
TOO PERFECT by Wilbur S. Peacock. .s . . . .
. . . . .Fut Feb 43 60
TOOLS by Clifford D. Simak. .s. . . . . . . ASF Jul 42 118
TOOLS FOR BRAINS by Leo Vernon. .a . . . .
. . . . .ASF Jul 39 80
TOOLS OF THE TRADE by Raymond F. Jones. . . . . . .
. .nt . . . . ASF Nov 50 48
TOOTH, THE by Neil Moran. .s. . . . . . . ASF Apr 34 87
TOOTH OR CONSEQUENCES by Robert Bloch. . . . . .
. .s . . . . Amz May 50 118
TOP SECRET by David Grinnell. .ss . . . .
. . . . .F&SF Fal 50 31
TOPAZ GATE, THE by James Blish. .s . . . .
. . . . .Fut Aug 41 50
"TORPEDO" by Willy Ley. .a . . . . ASF Jul 44 113
TORPEDO TERROR, THE by Edsel Newton. .s . . . . . .
. . . . WS Sep 30 356
TOTAL RECALL by Larry Sternig. .s . . . . . .PS Fal 46 65
TOUCHING POINT, THE by Edward J. Bellin h ps (Henry
Kuttner). .s . . . . Sti Apr 41 96
TOUGH GUY by Arthur McCann ps (John W. Campbell,
Jr.). .a . . . . ASF Feb 40 101
TOUGH OLD MAN by L. Ron Hubbard. .s . . . .
. . . . .SS Nov 50 116
TOURISTS TO TERRA by Mack Reynolds. .s . . . . . .
. . . . Im Dec 50 36

Title. .Author. .Length. . . . . Magazine. .Date. .Page No.

TOWARD THE SUPERMAN by Richard Tooker. .a. . . .
. . . . ASF Mar 39 88
TOWER MYSTERY, THE by Ernest Zorbas. .s. . . . . . .
. . . . .AD Jul 30 582
TOWER OF BABBLE, THE by Robert Abernathy. . . . .
. .s . . . . Amz Jun 50 136
TOWER OF DARKNESS by A. Bertram Chandler. . . . .
. .s . . . . ASF Nov 46 78
TOWER OF EVIL, THE by Nat Schachner & Arthur L.
Zagat. .s. . . . . .WQ Sum 30 468
TOYMAKER, THE by Raymond F. Jones. .nt . . . . . .
. . . . ASF Sep 46 6
TOYS OF FATE by Tod Robbins. .s. . . . . FN Mar 49 102
TRACED BY A SCRATCH by H. H. Dunn. .a. . . . . . .
. . . . .AD Jul 30 599
TRACKED BY ULTRA–VIOLET (SCIENTIFIC
ACTUALITY) by Hector Gavin Grey. .a . . . .
. . . . AD Aug 30 692
TRACKS ACROSS THE DARKNESS by Robert
Arthur. .s. . . . . .Ash Mar 42 25
TRADE YOUR TROUBLE FOR A BUBBLE by James B.
Settles. .bacover pic. . . . . Amz Feb 46
TRADERS IN TREASURES by Epaminondas T. Snooks,
D.T.G. ps (C. P. Mason). .s . . . . WS May 34 1114
TRAFFIC by Bolling Branham. .s. . . . . TW Oct 50 59
TRAGEDY OF SPIDER ISLAND, THE by Capt. S. P.
Meek. .s. . . . . WS Sep 30 324
TRAGIC FATE OF THOSE WHO SOUGHT THE LOST
LEMON MINE (WEIRD TRAVEL TALES No.2) by
Bob Davis. .ss . . . . FFM Apr 40 64
TRAIL OF THE ASTROGAR by Henry Hasse. .nt . . . .
. . . . Amz Oct 47 42
TRAIL OF THE MAGIC SLIPPERS by John York Cabot
ps (David Wright O'Brien). .nt . . . . FA Mar 43 176
TRAIL'S END by John Broome. .s. . . . . . .SS Nov 41 109
TRAIL'S END by Walter Kubilius. .s. . . . . .Sti Jun 41 57
TRAIN THAT VANISHED, THE by R. R.
Winterbotham. .s. . . . . ASF Jul 36 118
TRAITOR, THE by Thomas S. Gardner. .ss . . . .
. . . . .SD Jun 39 103
TRAITOR, THE by Arthur T. Harris h ps. .s. . . . .
. . . . .FA Jul 42 98
TRAITOR, THE by James S. Hart. .s . . . .
. . . . .F&SF Fal 50 17
TRAITOR, THE by Kurt von Rachen ps (L. Ron
Hubbard). .s. . . . . .ASF Jan 41 74
TRAITOR TO WAR by John & Dorothy de Courcy. . . .
. .s . . . . Amz Aug 49 76
TRAMP, THE by L. Ron Hubbard. .n 3 pt. . . . .
. . . . ASF Sep 38 71
TRANS–GALACTIC TWINS, THE by George O.
Smith. .nt . . . . TW Jun 48 9
TRANS–PLUTONIAN TRAP by Ross Rocklynne . . . . .
. nt. . . . . .SSS Mar 40 80
TRANSIENCE by Arthur C. Clarke. .ss . . . . SS Jul 49 125

Title. .Author. .Length. . . . . Magazine. .Date. .Page No.

TRANSFER POINT by Anthony Boucher ps (William
Anthony Parker White). .s. . . . . GSF Nov 50 56
TRANSIENTS ONLY by Mary MacGregor ps (Malcolm
Jameson). .s . . . . UK Dec 42 71
TRANSITORY ISLAND by Richard Wilson. .s . . . .
. . . . Cos May 41 107
TRANSLATION OF JOHN FORSYTHE, THE by Edmund
W. Putnam. .s . . . . Amz Sep 30 518
TRANSMUTATION, 1939 by Jack Hatcher. .a . . . .
. . . . .ASF Jan 40 69
TRANSPARENT STUFF by Dorothy Quick. .s. . . . . . .
. . . . UK Jun 40 97
TRANSURANIC by Edmond Hamilton. .s . . . .
. . . . TW Feb 48 72
TRAP, THE by Frank Belknap Long. .s. . . ASF May 45 36
TRAP, THE by Henry S. Whitehead. .nt . . . .
. . . . AFR #6 102
TRAPPED BY TELEPATHY by Eando Binder ps (Otto
Binder). .s . . . . Amz Mar 39 100
TRAPPED IN ETERNITY by Ray Cummings. .s . . . . .
. . . . .TW Dec 36 29
TRAPPED IN THE DEPTHS by Capt. S. P. Meek. .s . . .
. . . . WS Jun 30 38
TRAPPED ON TITAN by David Wright O'Brien. .s . . . .
. . . . Amz Jun 40 68
TRAPPER, THE by Arthur J. Burks. .nt . . . .
. . . . .ASF Sep 38 118
TRAVELER'S TALE by George Whitley ps (A. Bertram
Chandler). .s. . . . . SS Jan 47 93
TREACHERY ON PLANETOID 41 by Floyd Gale . . . .
. .s . . . . Amz Jun 40 100
TREASURE, THE by William Morrison ps (Joseph
Samachson). .s . . . . CF Win 43 108
TREASURE ACCURSED! by Otis Adelbert Kline. . . . .
. .s . . . . .FanF May 50 121
TREASURE ASTEROID by Manly Wade Wellman . . . .
. .s . . . . ASF Sep 38 6
TREASURE DERELICT by Guy Archette ps (Chester S.
Geier). .s . . . . .Amz Jul 47 62
TREASURE OF PTAKUTH, THE by Leigh
Brackett. .s. . . . . ASF Apr 40 72
TREASURE OF THE GOLDEN GOD, THE by A. Hyatt
Verrill. .n 2 pt. . . . . .Amz Jan 33 870
TREASURE ON ASTEROID X, THE by Frederic Arnold
Kummer, Jr. . .s . . . . Amz Jan 39 60
TREASURE ON THUNDER MOON by Edmond
Hamilton. .n. . . . . Amz Apr 42 198
TREASURE TROVE IN TIME by David Wright
O'Brien. .s . . . . Amz Nov 40 44
TREASURES OF TANTALUS by Garret Smith . . . . . .
. .n 2 pt. . . . . Amz Oct 27 676
TREASURE OF TRITON by Charles A. Baker. .ss. . . . .
. . . . .PS Spr 41 52
TREE OF EVIL, THE by David H. Keller, M.D. . . . . .
. .s . . . . WS Sep 34 446

Title. .Author. .Length . . . . Magazine. .Date. .Page No.

TREE OF LIFE, THE by Paul Edmonds ps (Henry
    Kuttner). .s . . . . Ash Sep 41 44
TREE TERROR, THE by David H. Keller, M.D. . . . . .
    . .s . . . . Amz Oct 33 545
TREE'S A CROWD by Robert Bloch. .s . . . . .FA Jul 46 74
TRENDS by Isaac Asimov. .s . . . . ASF Jul 39 33
TREPIDATION by R. S. Richardson. .a . . . .
    . . . . ASF Apr 41 106
TRESPASS! by Poul Anderson & Gordon Dickson . . . .
    . .s .FSQ Spr 50 131
TRIAL BY TELEVISION by Fred Kennedy. .s . . . . . .
    . . . . Amz Dec 31 828
TRIAL OF ADAM LINK, THE by Eando Binder ps
    (Otto Binder). .s . . . . .Amz Jul 39 30
TRICK WITH A BRICK by Elroy Arno. .s . . . .
    . . . . FA Oct 43 182
TRICKY TONNAGE by Malcolm Jameson. .s . . . .
    . . . . ASF Dec 44 56
TRIGGER TIDE by Norman Menasco. .s . . . .
    . . . . ASF Oct 50 63
TRIN by Arthur J. Burks. .nt . . . . MSS Nov 50 6
TRIP ONE by Edward Grendon. .s . . . . . . ASF Jul 49 85
TRIP TO THE CENTER OF THE EARTH, A by
    Jules Verne. .n 3 pt . . . . Amz May 26 100
TRIPLANETARY by Edward E. Smith, Ph.D. . . . . . .
    . .n 4 pt . . . . Amz Jan 34 10
TRIPLE-GEARED by Stanton A. Coblentz. .s . . . . . .
    . . . . ASF Apr 35 41
TRIPLE RAY, THE by R. V. Happel. .s . . . .
    . . . . .AQ Fal 30 529
TRIUMPH OF CAPTAIN FUTURE, THE by Edmond
    Hamilton. .n . . . . .CF Fal 40 14
TRIUMPH OF THE PIG, THE by Berkeley
    Livingston. .s . . . . Amz Jul 48 112
TROG by Murray Leinster ps (Will F. Jenkins). .n . . . . .
    . . . . ASF Jun 44 7
TROGLODITES, THE by Fred M. Barclay. .nt . . . . . .
    . . . . Amz Sep 30 486
TROJAN BEAM, THE by John Beynon (Harris). .s . . . .
    . . . . .Fant #2 39 60
TROJAN FALL by Hal Clement ps (Harry Clement
    Stubbs). .s . . . . ASF Jun 44 57
TROJAN HORSE LAUGH by John D. MacDonald . . . .
    . .nt . . . . ASF Aug 49 73
TROPHY by Scott Morgan ps (Henry Kuttner). .s . . . . .
    . . . . TW Win 44 62
TROUBLE by George O. Smith. .nt . . . . . . ASF Jul 46 60
TROUBLE IN AVALON by Russell Storm ps (Robert
    Moore Williams). .s . . . . FA Jun 40 30
TROUBLE IN TIME by S. D. Gottesman ps (Cyril
    Kornbluth & Frederick Pohl). .s . . . . . . .Ash Dec 40 34
TROUBLE ON TANTALUS by P. Schuyler Miller. . . . .
    . .nt . . . . ASF Feb 41 48
TROUBLE ON TITAN by Arthur K. Barnes. .nt . . . . . .
    . . . . TW Feb 41 14

TROUBLE ON TITAN by Henry Kuttner. .s . . . .
    . . . . TW Feb 47 36
TROUBLE ON TRITON by Edmond Hamilton. .s . . . .
    . . . . SS Fal 45 75
TROUBLE ON TYCHO by Nelson S. Bond. .s . . . .
    . . . . .PS Mar 43 91
TROUBLE SHOOTER by Harl Vincent
    (Schoepflin). .s . . . . SSS Jul 40 54
TROUBLE TIMES TWO by George O. Smith. .nt . . . . .
    . . . . ASF Dec 45 125
TROUBLE WITH WATER by H. L. Gold. .s . . . .
    . . . . UK Mar 39 117
                                                UK 48 62
TROYANA by Capt. S. P. Meek. .n 3 pt . . . .
    . . . . Amz Feb 32 968
TRUANTS, THE by Leigh Brackett. .s . . . . . SS Jul 50 96
TRUE ADVENTURES OF A SUPER-SCIENTIFIC
    DETECTIVE (SCIENTIFIC ACTUALITY) by Joseph
    Gollomb. .a . . . . SD Feb 30 138
TRUE CONFESSION by F. Orlin Tremaine. .s . . . .
    . . . . TW Feb 40 74
TRUE, NO DOUBT! by John L. Blummer. .pic feat. . . . .
    . . . . .Ash Feb 40 87
TRUK ISLAND by Berkeley Livingston. .n . . . .
    . . . . Amz Dec 44 144
TRUMPET, THE by J. J. Allerton. .s . . . . FA May 50 124
TRUTH ABOUT CUSHGAR, THE by James H.
    Schmitz. .nt . . . . ASF Nov 50 6
TRUTH ABOUT PYECRAFT, THE by H. G. Wells . . . .
    . .s . . . . .AFR #1 92
TRUTH ABOUT THE PSYCHO-TECTOR, THE by
    Stanton A. Coblentz. .s . . . . ASF Oct 34 86
TRUTH ABOUT TIBET, THE by Millen Cooke. .a . . . .
    . . . . Amz Nov 46 159
TRUTH ABOUT TIBET, THE by Vincent H. Gaddis . . .
    . .a . . . . .Amz Jul 46 168
TRUTH GAS, THE by Edmond Hamilton. .s . . . .
    . . . . WS Feb 35 1060
TRUTH IS A PLAGUE by David Wright O'Brien. .s . . . .
    . . . . Amz Feb 40 58
TRUTHFUL LIAR, THE by John York Cabot ps (David
    Wright O'Brien). .s . . . . FA Oct 41 128
TRUTHFUL PENCIL, THE by Berkeley Livingston. . . . .
    . .s . . . . FA Jun 44 106
TRYST IN TIME by C. L. Moore. .nt . . . . ASF Dec 36 10
TUBBY series See RAY CUMMINGS author
TUBBY—ATOM SMASHER by Ray Cummings. .s . . . . .
    . . . . .TW Aug 43 86
TUBBY—MASTER OF THE ATOM by Ray
    Cummings. .s . . . . TW Fal 46 92
TUBBY—TIME TRAVELER by Ray Cummings. .s . . . . .
    . . . . TW Dec 42 47
TUBE TO NOWHERE by Henry Kuttner. .s . . . .
    . . . . TW Jun 41 63
TUBEMONKEY by Jerome Bixby. .s . . . . . .PS Win 49 29

Title. .Author. .Length . . . . Magazine. .Date. .Page No.

TUMITHAK IN SHAWM by Charles R. Tanner. .nt . . . .
. . . . Amz Jun 33 201
TUMITHAK OF THE CORRIDORS by Charles R.
Tanner. .nt. . . . . .Amz Jan 32 898
TUMITHAK OF THE TOWERS OF FIRE by Charles R.
Tanner. .nt. . . . . .SSS Nov 41 78
TURN ON THE MOON–MAKE IT HOTTER by R. S.
Richardson. .a. . . . . ASF Nov 43 101
TURNABOUT by H. S. W. Chibbett. .s . . . . FB #3 39
TURNABOUT by Will Garth h ps (Mort Weisinger) . . . .
. .ss. .SS Mar 39 117
TURNING POINT by Pendleton Banks. .s . . . .
. . . . ASF Mar 47 80
TURNOVER TIME by Noel Loomis. .s . . . .SS Mar 49 129
TWELVE EIGHTY–SEVEN by John Taine ps (Eric
Temple Bell). .n 5 pt . . . . .ASF May 35 8
TWELVE HOURS TO LIVE by Jack Williamson . . . . . .
. .s . . . . WS Aug 31 354
SS Mar 46 84
12,000 YEARS AGO by H. R. Hammond . . . .
. .bacover pic . . . . Amz May 40
TWENTIETH CENTURY HOMUNCULUS, A by David
H. Keller, M.D. . .s . . . . Amz Feb 30 1012
20TH CENTURY MEDUSA, A by R. F. Starzl. .s . . . .
. . . . WS Sep 31 476
TWENTY–FIFTH CENTURY SHERLOCK by Duncan
Farnsworth ps (David Wright O'Brien). .s . . . .
. . . . FA Mar 41 128
TWENTY–FIFTH HOUR, THE by Herbert Best. .n . . . .
. . . . .FFM Aug 46 10
TWENTY–FIRST CENTURY LIMITED, THE by Paul
Schlachta. .s . . . . Amz Dec 29 828
TWENTY–FIVE CENTURIES LATE by Philip J.
Bartel. .s . . . . WS Nov 34 704
TWENTY–FOOT MISS by Willy Ley. .a. . . GSF Dec 50 86
24 TERRIBLE HOURS by John York Cabot ps (David
Wright O'Brien). .s . . . . Amz May 42 250
TWENTY YEARS FROM TODAY by W. F. Collins. . . .
. .ss . . . . Amz Feb 31 1024
TWICE IN TIME by Manly Wade Wellman. .n . . . .
. . . . SSS May 40 14
TWICE TO DIE by Rog Phillips ps (Roger P.
Graham). .nt. . . . . FA Feb 48 92
TWILIGHT by Don A. Stuart ps (John W. Campbell,
Jr.). .s . . . . ASF Nov 34 44
TWILIGHT OF THE TENTH WORLD by Thornton Ayre
ps (John Russell Fearn). .nt . . . . .PS Win 40 104
TWILIGHT OF TOMORROW by Joseph Gilbert. .s . . . .
. . . . .Fut Aug 42 47
TWILIGHT PEOPLE, THE by Frank Edward
Arnold. .s. . . . . Com Jan 41 45
TWILIGHT PLANET by Polton Cross ps (John Russell
Fearn). .s . . . . .TW Sum 46 63
TWIN SATELLITE by Guy Archette ps (Chester S.
Geier). .s . . . . .FA Jul 49 70
TWIN WORLDS by Neil R. Jones. .nt . . . . Amz Apr 37 17

Title. .Author. .Length . . . . Magazine. .Date. .Page No.

TWIRL MY TURBINE, MAN ALIVE by Omar
Geer. .ss. . . . . Amz Mar 45 180
TWISTED DIMENSIONS by Daniel A. Alexander . . . . .
. .s . . . . TW Apr 42 81
TWISTED GIANT OF MARS by Festus Pragnell . . . . . .
. .nt . . . . Amz May 43 32
TWISTED HOUSE by Guy Archette ps (Chester S.
Geier). .s . . . . Amz Jun 49 54
TWO AGAINST NEPTUNE by Frank Belknap
Long. .s . . . . TW Jun 41 74
TWO AGAINST VENUS by Craig Browning ps (Roger P.
Graham). .nt. . . . . Amz Mar 50 144
TWO FOR A BARGAIN by Dorothy Quick. .s . . . .
. . . . UK Dec 40 104
240,000 MILES STRAIGHT UP by L. Ron
Hubbard. .s . . . . TW Dec 48 42
21931 by J. E. Keith. .s . . . . Amz Feb 36 119
TWO PERCENT INSPIRATION by Theodore
Sturgeon. .s . . . . ASF Oct 41 86
TWO SANE MEN by Oliver Saari. .s . . . . . ASF Jun 37 80
TWO SOUGHT ADVENTURE by Fritz Leiber, Jr. . . . .
. .nt . . . . .UK Aug 39 99
TWO THOUSAND MILES BELOW by Charles Willard
Diffin. .n 4 pt . . . . .ASF Jun 32 311
TWO–TIMING MAN by Thaedra Alden. .s . . . .
. . . . TW Jun 43 88
TWO–WAY TIME by Albert A. Gilmore. .s . . . .
. . . . .Fut Apr 42 46
TWO WORLDS FOR ONE by George O. Smith. .s . . . . .
. . . . Fut Jul-Aug 50 66
TWO WORLDS TO CONQUER by Elroy Arno. .nt . . . .
. . . . Amz Sep 45 130
TWO WORLDS TO SAVE by William Morrison ps (Joseph
Samachson). .n . . . . .SS Sep 42 13
TWONKY, THE by Lewis Padgett ps (Henry Kuttner &
C. L. Moore). .s . . . . ASF Sep 42 34
TYPEWRITER FROM THE FUTURE by Peter
Worth. .nt . . . . Amz Feb 50 44
TYPEWRITER IN THE SKY by L. Ron Hubbard . . . . .
. .n 2 pt. . . . . .UK Nov 40 9
TYRANNOSAURUS WAS NO KILLER by Willy
Ley. .a. . . . . ASF Apr 43 81
TYRANT OF MARS, THE by Frederic Arnold
Kummer, Jr. . .s . . . . TW Sep 40 12
TYRANT OF THE RED WORLD by Richard
Tooker. .s . . . . WS Aug 32 198
ToW Aut 40 6

U

U–TURN by Duncan H. Munro ps (Eric Frank
Russell). .s . . . . ASF Apr 50 133
ULTIMATE ADVENTURE, THE by L. Ron
Hubbard. .n . . . . .UK Apr 39 9

Title. .Author. .Length . . . . Magazine. .Date. .Page No.

ULTIMATE ANALYSIS, THE by John Russell
Fearn. .s . . . . TW Fal 44 89
ULTIMATE CATALIST, THE by John Taine ps (Eric
Temple Bell). .s. . . . . TW Jun 39 13
SS Nov 49 84
ULTIMATE EGOIST, THE by E. Hunter Waldo ps
(Theodore Sturgeon). .s . . . . UK Feb 41 57
ULTIMATE EXPERIMENT, THE by Thornton
DeKy. .ss . . . . Com Jul 41 120
ULTIMATE IMAGE, THE by P. Schuyler Miller . . . . . .
. .s . . . . Com Dec 40 23
ULTIMATE METAL, THE by Nat Schachner. .s . . . . . .
. . . . ASF Feb 35 90
ULTIMATE ONE, THE by John D. MacDonald. .ss . . . .
. . . . .SSS Mar 50 72
ULTIMATE PERIL, THE by Robert Abernathy. .n . . . .
. . . . Amz Mar 50 8
ULTIMATE PLANET, THE by Noel Loomis. .nt . . . . .
. . . . TW Apr 49 13
ULTIMATE QUEST, THE by Hal Annas. .s . . . .
. . . . Im Dec 50 60
ULTIMATE QUEST by John Holbrook ps (Jack
Vance). .s. SSS Sep 50 40
ULTIMATE SALIENT, THE by Nelson S. Bond . . . . . .
. .nt . . . . .PS Fal 40 2
ULTIMATE WISH, THE by E. M. Hull. .s . . . .
. . . . UK Feb 43 71
ULTIMATE WORLD, THE by Bryce Walton. .s . . . . . .
. . . . .PS Win 45 63
ULTIMATUM by Roger Dee ps (Roger D. Aycock) . . . .
. .s . . . . PS Spr 50 98
ULTIMATUM FROM MARS, AN by Ray
Cummings. .s . . . . ASF Aug 39 131
ULTRA-ELIXIR OF YOUTH, THE by A. Hyatt
Verrill. .s . . . . Amz Aug 27 476
ULTRA EVOLUTION by Polton Cross ps (John Russell
Fearn). .s. . . . . SS Jan 48 84
ULTRA-GAMMA WAVE, THE by D. E. Winstead,
M.D. . .s . . . . Amz May 34 43
UNAPPROACHABLE by George O. Smith. .a . . . .
. . . . ASF Apr 46 112
UNBROKEN CHAIN, THE by John Russell Fearn . . . .
. .s . . . . .SS Spr 46 90
UNCANNY POWER OF EDWIN COBALT by Noel
Gardner ps (Henry Kuttner). .ss . . . . . . FA Oct 40 98
UNCERTAINTY by John W. Campbell, Jr. . . . .
. .n 2 pt . . . . Amz Oct 36 14
UNCOMMON CASTAWAY by Nelson S. Bond. .s . . . . .
. . . . AFR #11 27
UNCOMMON SENSE by Hal Clement ps (Harry
Clement Stubbs). .s . . . . ASF Sep 45 47
UNDAMNED, THE by George O. Smith. .nt . . . .
. . . . .ASF Jan 47 72
UNDECIDED, THE by Eric Frank Russell. .nt . . . . . .
. . . . ASF Apr 49 44

UNDER ARCTIC ICE by Walter Kateley. .s . . . .
. . . . WS Jun 32 46
UNDER ARCTIC ICE by H. G. Winter ps (Harry Bates
& Desmond Winter Hall). .nt . . . . .ASF Jan 33 298
UNDER MARTIAN SANDS by Basil Wells. .s . . . .
. . . . .OTWA Dec 50 24
UNDER THE DYING SUN by Geo. C. Wallis. .s . . . . . .
. . . . .ToW Sum 40 62
UNDER THE KNIFE by H. G. Wells. .s . . . .
. . . . Amz Mar 27 1112
AA 27 120
UNDER THE NORTH POLE by Ed Earl Repp. .s . . . . .
. . . . .DS Apr-May 39 80
UNDER THE SAND SEAS by Oliver E. Saari. .s . . . . . .
. . . . SSS Jan 41 107
UNDER THE WHITE STAR by Edmond Hamilton . . . .
. .s . . . . SF Mar 39 6
UNDERGROUND CITY, THE by Bertrand L.
Shurtleff. .nt . . . . Amz Sep 39 38
UNDERGROUND WATERS by A. C. Webb, M.D. . . . .
. .s . . . . WQ Win 30 268
UNDERMOST by Manly Wade Wellman. .s . . . .
. . . . TW Spr 46 46
UNDERSEA EXPRESS, THE by J. Roaman. .s . . . .
. . . . Amz Dec 27 870
UNDERSEA GUARDIANS by Ray Bradbury. .s . . . . . .
. . . . Amz Dec 44 12
UNDERSEA PRISONER by Harl Vincent
(Schoepflin). .s . . . . Amz Feb 40 40
UNDERSEA SALVAGER by H. W. McCauley . . . .
. .bacover pic . . . . Amz Mar 39
UNDERSEA SNATCH by William Morrison ps (Joseph
Samachson). .s . . . . .CF Fal 41 107
UNDERSEA TUBE, THE by L. Taylor Hansen. .s . . . . .
. . . . Amz Nov 29 720
UNDERTONES OF DEATH by Frank Carter. .s . . . . . .
. . . . AD Sep 30 822
UNDESIRABLE ALIEN by David McCarthy. .s . . . . . .
. . . . .ASF Jan 50 24
UNDESIRED PRINCESS, THE by L. Sprague de
Camp. .n .UK Feb 42 7
UNDYING MONSTER, THE by Jessie Douglas
Kerruish. .n . . . . FFM Jun 46 12
UNDYING ONES, THE by Fredric Brown. .s . . . .
. . . . .SSS Sep 50 60
UNEXPECTED WEAPON, THE by Charles DeVet. . . . .
. .s . . . . Amz Sep 50 50
UNFINISHED BUSINESS by Enoch Sharp. .s . . . .
. . . . FA Aug 48 138
UNFINISHED CITY, THE by Martin Pearson ps (Donald
A. Wollheim). .ss. . . . . Sti Mar 42 60
UNFORSEEN, THE by Mark Champion. .s . . . .
. . . . ASF Nov 46 38
UNFORSEEN by Roger P. Graham. .s . . . .
. . . . .FA Jan 49 136

Title. .Author. .Length. . . . . Magazine. .Date. .Page No.

UNGUH MADE A FIRE by Ross Rocklynne. .s . . . . . .
. . . . ASF Apr 40 38
UNINVITED JEST, THE by Rog Phillips ps (Roger P.
Graham). .s . . . . Amz Sep 47 44
UNION IN GEHENNA by Nelson S. Bond. .nt . . . .
. . . . FA Oct 42 98
UNITE AND CONQUER by Theodore Sturgeon. . . . . .
. .nt . . . . ASF Oct 48 63
UNITED WE STAND by Mack Reynolds. .s . . . .
. . . . Amz May 50 164
UNIVERSAL MERRY-GO-ROUND by Roger Bird. . . .
. .s . . . . Amz Apr 33 76
UNIVERSE by Robert Heinlein. .nt . . . . . . ASF May 41 9
UNIVERSE IN DARKNESS by J. Harvey Haggard . . . .
. .s . . . . .Fut Nov 40 8
UNIVERSE OF BABEL by John Edwards. .s . . . .
. . . . ToW Win 38 33
UNIVERSE RANGER, THE by Stanton A.
Coblentz. .s . . . . FB #6 21
UNIVERSE WRECKERS, THE by Edmond
Hamilton. .n 3 pt. . . . . Amz May 30 102
UNIVERSES FOR LENSES by R. S. Richardson . . . . .
. .a . . . . ASF Sep 40 41
UNIVERSES TO ORDER by J. J. Coupling. .a . . . .
. . . . ASF Feb 44 102
UNKNOWN QUANTITY by Peter Phillips. .s . . . .
. . . . .NW #5 49 54
UNLOCKING THE PAST by David H. Keller, M.D. . . .
. .s . . . . Amz Sep 28 513
UNNATURAL FEUD, AN by Norman Douglas. .s. . . . .
. . . . FFM Apr 42 110
UNPLEASANT PROFESSION OF JONATHAN HOAG,
THE by John Riverside ps (Robert A. Heinlein) . . . .
. .n . . . . UK Oct 42 9
UNPREDICTABLE by Jack Williamson. .a 2 pt. . . . . .
. . . . ASF Feb 46 100
UNREMEMBERED, THE by Paul Lohrman h ps . . . . . .
. .s . . . . Amz May 50 170
UNSEEN BLUSHERS, THE by Alfred Bester. .s . . . . . .
. . . . Ash Jun 42 84
UNSEEN TOOLS by Leo Vernon. .a . . . . . ASF Jun 40 79
UNSPEAKABLE BETROTHAL, THE by Robert
Bloch. .s . . . . .AFR #9 75
UNSPEAKABLE McINCH, THE by Jack Vance. .s . . . .
. . . . .SS Nov 48 139
UNSUNG HERO by Ruth Washburn. .s . . . . TW Spr 44 73
UNTHINKABLE by Rog Phillips ps (Roger P.
Graham). .s . . . . Amz Apr 49 34
UNTHINKABLE by Francis Sibson. .n . . . FFM Dec 46 10
UNTHINKING CAP by John Pierce. .s . . . .
. . . . .ASF Jul 43 39
UNTHINKING DESTROYER, THE by Rog Phillips ps
(Roger P. Graham). .s . . . . Amz Dec 48 66
UNTO US A CHILD IS BORN by David H. Keller,
M.D. . .s . . . . Amz Jul 33 297

UNUSUAL CASE, THE by Walter Kubilius. .ss . . . .
. . . . Cos Jul 41 74
UNWELCOME TENANT by Roger Dee ps (Roger D.
Aycock). .ss . . . . PS Sum 50 96
UNWILLING HERO, THE by Rene LaFayette ps (L. Ron
Hubbard). .s . . . . SS Jul 49 98
UP AND ATOM by Ray Cummings. .s . . . . . .SS Sep 47 87
UP THERE by Martin Pearson ps (Donald A.
Wollheim). .ss . . . . .SFQ Sum 42 85
UPON THE DARK MOON by John L. Chapman. . . . . .
. .ss . . . . SF Dec 39 76
UPPER LEVEL ROAD, THE by Warner Van Lorne ps
(F. Orlin Tremaine). .s . . . . ASF Aug 35 41
UPWARD BOUND by Gerald Evans. .s . . . . TW Oct 40 82
URANIAN JUSTICE by Wilbur S. Peacock. .ss . . . .
. . . . .CF Fal 40 104
USURPERS, THE by Geoff St. Reynard ps (Robert W.
Krepps). .nt . . . . FA Jan 50 8
UTILITY by David Anderson. .nt . . . . . . ASF Jul 44 156
UTOPIA ISLAND by Otfrid von Hanstein (tr fr German by
Francis Currier). .n 2 pt . . . . WS May 31 1352

V

"V" FORCE, THE by Fred C. Smale. .s . . . .
. . . . FFM Jan 40 120
V IS FOR VENGEANCE by Duncan Farnsworth ps
(David Wright O'Brien). .s . . . . .FA Jan 42 102
V-2–ROCKET CARGO SHIP by Willy Ley. .a . . . . . .
. . . . ASF May 45 100
VACATION IN SHASTA by Rog Phillips ps (Roger P.
Graham). .nt . . . . FA Feb 46 26
VACANT WORLD by Dirk Wylie (w/Cyril Kornbluth &
Frederik Pohl). .s . . . . SSS Jan 41 46
VAGABONDS OF SPACE by Harl Vincent
(Schoepflin). .nt . . . . ASF Nov 30 244
VAGABONDS OF THE VOID by Peter Horn h ps (David
Vern). .nt. . . . . Amz Mar 40 66
VALIANT IS THE WORD by H. B. Hickey ps (Herb
Livingston). .s . . . . FA Oct 50 104
VALKYRIE FROM THE VOID by Basil Wells. .s . . . . .
. . . . PS Fal 48 102
VALLEY OF CREATION, THE by Edmond
Hamilton. .n. . . . . .SS Jul 48 9
VALLEY OF DELIRIUM by Richard Casey h ps. . . . . .
. .nt . . . . Amz Mar 45 150
VALLEY OF DOOM by Halliday Sutherland. .s . . . . . .
. . . . .Fant #2 39 31
VALLEY OF DREAMS, THE by Stanley G.
Weinbaum. .s . . . . WS Nov 34 676
SS May 40 94
VALLEY OF INVISIBLE MEN by Edmond
Hamilton. .nt . . . . Amz Mar 39 22

Title. .Author. .Length . . . . Magazine. .Date. .Page No.

VALLEY OF LOST SOULS by Eando Binder *ps (Otto Binder)*. .nt . . . . Amz Feb 39 52
VALLEY OF MADNESS, THE by Alexander Blade *h ps*. .s. . . . . Amz Jun 48 84
VALLEY OF PRETENDERS by Dennis Clive *ps (John Russell Fearn)*. .s. . . . . SF Mar 39 46
VALLEY OF SILENT MEN, THE by E. Charles Vivian. .n. .FFM Aug 49 8
VALLEY OF SIN by Douglas M. Dold. .n . . . . Mir Apr–May 31 10
VALLEY OF THE BLACK SUN by Leroy Yerxa. .s . . . . Amz Apr 43 124
VALLEY OF THE BLIND, THE by Abner J. Gelula. .s . . . . .AQ Spr–Sum 33 559
VALLEY OF THE CROEN by Lee Tarbell. .n . . . . Amz Apr 49 74
VALLEY OF THE FLAME by Keith Hammond *ps (Henry Kuttner & C. L. Moore)*. .n . . . . .SS Mar 46 13
VALLEY OF THE RUKH by Harl Vincent *(Schoepflin)*. .s . . . . Amz Feb 35 38
VALLEY OF TITANS, THE by L. A. Eshbach. .nt . . . . Amz Mar 31 1062
VAMPIRE FROM THE VOID by Eric Frank Russell. .s. Fant #2 39 79
VAMPIRE OF THE VOID by Neil R. Jones. .s . . . . PS Spr 41 38
VAMPIRE QUEEN by Thornton Ayre *ps (John Russell Fearn)*. .s. PS Fal 42 52
VAMPIRES OF SPACE by Sewell Peaslee Wright . . . . .s . . . . ASF Mar 32 402
VAMPIRES OF THE DESERT by A. Hyatt Verrill . . . . .s . . . . Amz Dec 29 774
VAMPIRES OF VENUS by Anthony Pelcher. .s . . . . ASF Apr 30 47
VAN MANDERPOOTS series See STANLEY G. WEINBAUM author
VANDALS FROM THE MOON by Marius. .s . . . . .Amz Jul 28 302
VANDALS OF THE STARS by A. T. Locke. .s. . . . . ASF Mar 30 390
VANDALS OF THE VOID by J. M. Walsh. .n . . . . .WQ Sum 31 438
VANDALS OF THE VOID by Robert Wilson. .nt . . . . PS Spr 45 84
VANDERDECKEN by Frederick Engelhardt. .s . . . . UK Dec 39 96
VANGUARD OF SCIENCE by Jack Williamson . . . . .guest ed .SS Sep 39 15
VANGUARD OF THE LOST by John D. MacDonald. .s. . . . . .FA May 50 60
VANGUARD TO NEPTUNE, THE by J. M. Walsh. .n . . . . WQ Spr 32 294
VANISHERS, THE by Arthur J. Burks. .nt . . . . .SSS May 50 104
VANISHING DIAMONDS, THE by Charles R. Tanner. .s. . . . . Amz Jun 38 72

VANISHING FLEET, THE by Hendrik Dahl Juve. . . . . .s .AW Feb 30 678
VANISHING GOLD by Capt. S. P. Meek. .s . . . . WS May 32 1320
VANISHING MAN, THE by Ralph Milne Farley *ps Roger Sherman Hoar)*. .s . . . . AD Aug 30 706
VANISHING MEN, THE by Ray Cummings. .s . . . . TW Sep 40 56
VANISHING METEORITES, THE by Willy Ley. .a . . . . .SSS Nov 42 119
VANISHING SPACEMAN, THE by Alexander Blade *h ps*. .s. . . . . .Amz Jul 47 94
VANISHING VENUSIANS, THE by Leigh Brackett . . . . . . .s . . . . .PS Spr 45 24
VANISHING WITNESS, THE by Ross Rocklynne. . . . . . . .s . . . . FA Jan 41 62
VANISHING YANKEE, THE by George O. Smith. . . . . . . .a . . . . ASF Mar 44 103
VAPOR DEATH, THE by Frank Belknap Long, Jr. . . . . . . .s . . . . ASF Oct 34 39
VAPOR INTELLIGENCE, THE by Jack Barnette . . . . .s . . . . .SW Jan 30 702
VAPORS OF DEATH by Edwin Balmer & William MacHarg. .s .AD Aug 30 712
VARIETIES OF CULTURE by Arthur J. Cox. .a . . . . ASF Dec 50 87
VASSALS OF THE LODE–STAR by Gardner F. Fox. .nt. . . . . .PS Sum 47 2
VASSALS OF THE MASTER WORLD by Eando Binder *ps (Otto Binder)*. .n . . . . .PS Fal 41 2
VAST BEYOND CONCEPT by Hal Remson. .s . . . . MSS Feb 39 120
VAULT OF THE BEAST by A. E. van Vogt. .nt . . . . ASF Aug 40 50
VAULTS OF YOH–VOMBIS, THE by Clark Ashton Smith. .s . . . . .AFR #1 101
VEIL OF ASTELLAR, THE by Leigh Brackett. .s . . . . TW Spr 44 50
VEILED ISLAND by Emmett McDowell. .nt . . . . .ASF Jan 46 63
VELOCITY OF ESCAPE, THE by Joe W. Skidmore . . . . . . .nt . . . . Amz Aug 34 55
VENDETTA ON VENUS by Kerry Lash. .s . . . . .SSS Aug 41 52
VENGEANCE FROM THE VOID by Frederic Arnold Kummer, Jr. .s . . . . Amz Mar 39 86
VENGEANCE IN HER BONES by Malcolm Jameson. .s. . . . . AFR #10 81
VENGEANCE OF A SCIENTIST, THE by Abner J. Gelula. .s . . . . WS Feb 34 708
VENGEANCE OF MARTIN BRAND, THE by G. H. Irwin *h ps (Raymond A. Palmer)*. .n 2 pt . . . . Amz Aug 42 10
VENGEANCE OF THE GOLDEN GOD by E. K. Jarvis *h ps*. .nt . . . . Amz Dec 50 6

Title. .Author. .Length . . . . .Magazine. .Date. .Page No.

VENGEANCE ON VENUS by P. F. Costello *h ps* . . . . .
. .s . . . . Amz Sep 42 116
VENGEANCE, UNLIMITED by Fredric Brown. .ss . . . .
. . . . SSS Jul 50 66
VENGEFUL PEARLS OF MADAME PODAIRE, THE by
Robert Arthur. .s. . . . . .FanS Nov 50 89
VENOMOUS GIRDLE, THE by Lester Barclay. .s . . . . .
. . . . Amz Feb 49 72
VENUS ADVENTURE, THE by John Beyon Harris. . . .
. .s . . . . WS May 32 1352
       by John Beynon *(Harris)*. .s . . . .ToW Sum 39 4
VENUS ENSLAVED by Manly Wade Wellman. .nt . . . .
. . . . PS Sum 42 90
*VENUS EQUILATERAL series See GEORGE O. SMITH
author*
VENUS EVIL, THE by Chester S. Geier. .s. . . . .
. . . . PS Sum 47 68
VENUS GERM, THE by R. F. Starzl & F. Pragnell . . . .
. .s . . . . WS Nov 32 487
VENUS HAS GREEN EYES by Carl Selwyn. .s. . . . . .
. . . . PS Fal 40 92
VENUS LIBERATED by Harl Vincent
(Schoepflin). .n. . . . . .AQ Sum 29 292
VENUS MINES, INCORPORATED by Nat Schachner
& Arthur L. Zagat. .s . . . . WS Aug 31 294
                                           SS Jan 47 72
VENUS OR EARTH? by Will McMorrow. .nt . . . .
. . . . .FFM Apr 41 72
VENUS SKY–TRAP by Ross Rocklynne. .s . . . .
. . . . TW Spr 45 48
VENUS STATION by Arthur Leo Zagat. .nt. . . . .
. . . . SF Apr 43 12
VENUS TROUBLE by John Wiley. .nt . . . . OW Oct 50 78
VENUS TROUBLE SHOOTER by John Wiley. .nt . . . .
. . . . .OW Nov 49 120
VENUSIAN, THE by Craig Browning *ps (Roger P.
Graham)*. .n . . . . Amz Aug 48 18
VENUSIAN INVADER by Larry Sternig. .s . . . .
. . . . .PS Win 45 90
VENUSIAN NIGHTMARE by Ford Smith *ps (Oscar
J. Friend)*. .s. . . . . TW Win 44 44
VENUSIAN QUARTZ by Oscar J. Friend. .s . . . .
. . . . CF Sum 43 112
VENUSIAN SLAVE SMUGGLERS by Jep Powell. . . . .
. .nt . . . . Amz Aug 42 176
VENUSIAN TRAGEDY by Max C. Sheridan. .s . . . . . .
. . . . SSS Sep 40 78
VERMIN OF THE SKY by R. S. Richardson. .a . . . . . .
. . . . ASF Jul 41 105
*VIA—series See GORDON A. GILES ps & EANDO
BINDER ps authors*
VIA ASTEROID by Gordon A. Giles *ps (Otto
Binder)*. .s . . . . TW Feb 38 29
VIA CATACOMBS by Gordon A. Giles *ps (Otto
Binder)*. .s . . . . TW Nov 40 66

Title. .Author. .Length . . . . .Magazine. .Date. .Page No.

VIA DEATH by Gordon A. Giles *ps (Otto Binder)*. . . . .
. .s .TW Aug 38 95
VIA ETHERLINE by Gordon A. Giles *ps (Otto
Binder)*. .s . . . . TW Oct 37 79
VIA INTELLIGENCE by Gordon A. Giles *ps (Otto
Binder)*. .s . . . . TW Dec 40 42
VIA JUPITER by Eando Binder *ps (Otto Binder)* . . . . .
. .nt . . . . TW Feb 42 44
VIA MERCURY by Gordon A. Giles *ps (Otto
Binder)*. .s . . . . TW Oct 40 67
VIA PYRAMID by Gordon A. Giles *ps (Otto
Binder)*. .s . . . . TW Jan 40 29
VIA SUN by Gordon A. Giles *ps (Otto Binder)*. .s . . . . .
. . . . TW Mar 40 45
VIA THE HEWITT RAY by M. F. Rupert. .s . . . .
. . . . WQ Spr 30 370
VIA THE TIME ACCELERATOR by Frank J. Bridge
ps (Francis J. Brueckel). .s . . . . .Amz Jan 31 912
VIA VENUS by Gordon A. Giles *ps (Otto Binder)*. . . . .
. .s . . . . TW Oct 39 33
VIAL OF IMMORTALITY by Craig Browning *ps (Roger P.
Graham)*. .nt. . . . . Amz Jan 50 82
VIBRATION, THE by Edwin K. Sloat. .s . . . .
. . . . Amz Dec 32 845
VIBRATION WASPS, THE by Frank Belknap Long. . . .
. .s . . . . Com Jan 41 82
VIBRATOR OF DEATH, THE by Harold F. Richards,
Ph.D. . .s . . . . AQ Spr 28 259
VIBRATORY by Warner Van Lorne *ps*. .s . . . .
. . . . ASF Mar 38 119
VICIOUS CIRCLE by Polton Cross *ps (John Russell
Fearn)*. .s . . . . .NW #2 46 26
                                           SS Sum 46 79
VICTIMS OF THE VORTEX by Clinton Ames. .nt . . . .
. . . . .Amz Jul 50 8
VICTORIOUS FAILURE by Bryce Walton. .s . . . .
. . . . TW Apr 47 66
VICTORY DRUMS by Ross Rocklynne. .s . . . .
. . . . .CF Spr 44 79
VICTORY FROM THE VOID by William P. McGivern
& David Wright O'Brien. .nt . . . . Amz Mar 43 158
VICTORY OF KLON, THE by Wilbur S. Peacock . . . . .
. .ss. PS Fal 41 46
VICTORY UNINTENTIONAL by Isaac Asimov. .s . . . .
. . . . .SSS Aug 42 86
VIEWPOINTS letter dept of post-war Fant Apr 47 &
Aug 47
VIGNETTES OF FAMOUS SCIENTISTS by Alexander
Blade *h ps Short biog sketches of scientists. Quite
regular in Amz from Jan 43 thru Aug 48 and in FA
from Dec 42 thru Jul 48*
VINTAGE SEASON by Lawrence O'Donnell *ps (C. L.
Moore)*. .nt. . . . . ASF Sep 46 54
VIRUS, THE by R. DeWitt Miller. .s . . . .
. . . . .ASF Jul 36 65

Title. .Author. .Length. . . . . Magazine. .Date. .Page No.

VISIBLE INVISIBLE MAN, THE by William P.
McGivern. .nt . . . . Amz Dec 40 74
VISIGRAPH, THE letter dept of PS
VISION OF THE HYDRA by Gordon A. Giles *ps (Otto
Binder).* .s . . . . .TW Aug 37 82
VISION OF VENUS, A by Otis Adelbert Kline. .s . . . . .
. . . . Amz Dec 33 97
VISIT TO SUARI, A by A. Hyatt Verrill. .s . . . .
. . . . .Amz Jul 30 292
VISIT TO VENUS, A by Festus Pragnell. .s . . . .
. . . . WS Aug 34 270
                                             FSQ Spr 50 106
VISITATION, THE by Cyril G. Wates. .s . . . .
. . . . Amz Jun 27 214
VISITING YOKEL by Cleve Cartmill. .s . . . .
. . . . TW Aug 43 107
VISITOR, THE by Ray Bradbury. .s . . . . . .SS Nov 48 131
VISITOR FROM THE TWENTIETH CENTURY, A by
Harold Donitz. .s . . . . Amz May 28 170
VISITOR TO EARTH by P. F. Costello. .s . . . .
. . . . Amz Feb 43 48
VISITORS FROM MLOCK, THE by Clark Ashton
Smith. .s . . . . WS May 33 962
VISITORS FROM THE VOID by Willy Ley. .a . . . .
. . . . ASF May 37 91
VITALITY FOR MURDER by Richard O. Lewis. .s. . . .
. . . . .FA Jul 42 110
VITAMINE Z by William Lemkin, Ph.D. . .s . . . .
. . . . Amz Feb 30 1056
VOCATION by George O. Smith. .s . . . . . ASF Apr 45 80
VOICE, THE by William P. McGivern. .s . . . .
. . . . Amz Oct 42 206
VOICE, THE by Ross Rocklynne. .s . . . . . . TW Oct 41 86
VOICE ACROSS THE YEARS, A by I. M. Stephens &
Fletcher Pratt. .n . . . . AQ Win 32 2
VOICE COMMANDS, THE by Dennis Clive *ps (John
Russell Fearn).* .s . . . . SF Jun 40 8
VOICE FROM A STAR by William P. McGivern. .s . . . .
. . . . Amz Oct 47 138
VOICE FROM BEYOND, A by John P. Lenahan. .s. . . .
. . . . FA Sep 46 88
VOICE FROM THE ETHER, A by L. A. Eshbach . . . . .
. .s . . . . Amz May 31 174
VOICE FROM THE INNER WORLD, THE by A. Hyatt
Verrill. .s . . . . .Amz Jul 27 328
VOICE FROM THE VOID by Harl Vincent
(Schoepflin). .s . . . . Amz Jun 42 244
VOICE FROM VENUS, THE by Don Wilcox. .nt . . . . .
. . . . Amz Sep 45 40
VOICE IN THE NIGHT, THE by William Hope
Hodgson. .s . . . . .AFR #1 57
VOICE IN THE VOID by Walter Kubilius. .s . . . .
. . . . .Ash Mar 42 77
VOICE IN THE VOID, THE by Clifford D. Simak. . . . .
. .s . . . . WQ Spr 32 382

Title. .Author. .Length. . . . . Magazine. .Date. .Page No.

VOICE OF ATLANTIS by Laurence Manning. .s . . . . .
. . . . .WS Jul 34 156
VOICE OF THE LOBSTER, THE by Henry
Kuttner. .nt . . . . TW Feb 50 114
VOICE OF THE VOID, THE by John W. Campbell,
Jr. . .s . . . . .AQ Sum 30 390
VOICE OUT OF SPACE, THE by Clifton B. Kruse . . . .
. .s . . . . .ASF Jan 38 34
VOLCANIC VALVE, THE by W. L. Alden. .s . . . .
. . . . F&SF Win–Spr 50 115
VOLCANO SLAVES OF MU by Frederic Arnold
Kummer, Jr. . .s . . . . FA Mar 40 54
VOLLUSWEN by Henry Kuttner. .s . . . . . . SF Apr 43 86
VON HULCKMAN'S PETS by George D. Lewis. .s . . . .
. . . . Amz Sep 49 120
VON KEMPELEN AND HIS DISCOVERY by Edgar Allan
Poe. .s . . . . Amz Jul 27 363
VORTEX BLASTER, THE by E. E. Smith, Ph.D.   . . . .
. .s . . . . .Com Jul 41 2
VORTEX BLASTER MAKES WAR, THE by E. E. Smith,
Ph.D. . .s . . . . Ash Oct 42 38
VOYAGE IN TIME, A by Warren F. Howard *ps (Frederik
Pohl).* .ss . . . . SSS Mar 41 110
VOYAGE INTO THE LIGHTNING by Robert Moore
Williams. .nt . . . . Amz Feb 42 98
VOYAGE OF SACRIFICE by Geo. C. Wallis. .s . . . . . .
. . . . ToW Spr 39 51
VOYAGE OF THE ASTEROID, THE by Laurence
Manning. .nt . . . . .WQ Sum 32 508
VOYAGE THAT LASTED 600 YEARS, THE by Don
Wilcox. .nt . . . . Amz Oct 40 82
VOYAGE 13 by Ray Cummings. .s . . . . . . .ASF Jul 38 6
VOYAGE TO KEMPTONIA, THE by E. M. Scott . . . . .
. .s . . . . Amz Oct 28 642
VOYAGE TO NOWHERE by Alfred Bester. .nt . . . . . .
. . . . .TW Jul 40 12
VULCAN, GOD OF HEAVY INDUSTRY by Frank R.
Paul. .bacover . . . . FA Aug 42
VULCAN: ICE KING by Malcolm Jameson. .a . . . .
. . . . ASF Nov 42 88
VULCAN'S WORKSHOP by Harl Vincent
(Schoepflin). .s . . . . .ASF Jun 32 293

W

W62 TO MERCURY by Clifton B. Kruse. .s . . . .
. . . . ASF Sep 35 30
W62'S LAST FLIGHT, THE by Clifton B. Kruse. . . . . .
. .s . . . . ASF May 36 115
"WA–AL, BUST MAH BRITCHES!" by J. J.
Pelletier. .s . . . . Amz Apr 48 30
WABBLER, THE by Murray Leinster *ps (Will F.
Jenkins).* .s . . . . ASF Oct 42 85

Title. .Author. .Length . . . . Magazine. .Date. .Page No.

WACKY WORLD by Edmond Hamilton. .s . . . .
. . . . Amz Mar 42 198
WADE, ARCOTT & MOREY series See JOHN W.
CAMPBELL, JR. author
WAKER DREAMS, THE by Richard Matheson. .s . . . . .
. . . . GSF Dec 50 93
WALDO by Anson MacDonald *ps (Robert A.*
Heinlein). .n . . . . ASF Aug 42 9
WALK IN THE DARK, A by Arthur C. Clarke. .s . . . . .
. . . . TW Aug 50 134
WALL, THE by Robert Arthur. .s. . . . . . . UK Dec 42 90
WALL, THE by Howard W. Graham, Ph.D. *ps (Howard*
Wandrei). .s . . . . ASF May 34 22
WALL OF DARKNESS, THE by Arthur C. Clarke. . . . .
. .s . . . . SSS Jul 49 66
WALL OF DARKNESS by Basil Wells. .s. . . . . . FB #4 26
WALL OF DEATH, THE by Victor Rousseau
(Emanuel). .s . . . . ASF Nov 30 151
WALL OF WATER, THE by Raymond Z. Gallun . . . . .
. .s . . . . SFQ Win 41 129
WALLS OF ACID by Henry Hasse. .s . . . . FB #1 32
WALTZ OF DEATH, THE by B. P. Maxon. . . . .
. .n 3 pt . . . . WS May 35 1416
WAND OF CREATION, THE by Stanton A.
Coblentz. .s . . . . Amz Aug 29 435
WAND OF CREATION, THE by Raymond Z.
Gallun. .s. . . . . ASF Sep 34 98
WANDERER OF INFINITY by Harl Vincent
(Schoepflin). .s . . . . ASF Mar 33 100
WANDERER OF LITTLE LAND by Eando Binder
ps (Otto Binder). .nt . . . . FA Jun 41 40
WANDERER OF THE VOID by Dr. Arch Carr . . . . . .
. .s . . . . TW Apr 37 64
WANDERER OF TIME by Polton Cross *ps (John*
Russell Fearn). .s. . . . . SS Sum 44 69
WANDERERS OF THE WOLF MOON by Nelson S.
Bond. .nt. . . . . PS Spr 44 72
WANDERERS OF TIME by John Beynon Harris. . . . .
. .s . . . . WS Mar 33 776
by John Beynon *(Harris)* . . . . ToW Win 41 6
WANDERING EGOS, THE by Emmett McDowell. . . . .
. .n . . . . Amz Apr 48 104
WANDERING SWORDSMEN, THE by William P.
McGivern. .s. . . . . FA Apr 48 148
WANDL, THE INVADER by Ray Cummings . . . .
. .n 4 pt . . . . ASF Feb 32 168
. .n *(complete)* . . . . SFQ Spr 43 4
WANTED: A TUBE by Lawrence Braymer. .a. . . . . . .
. . . . ASF Nov 45 101
WANTED–AN ENEMY by Fritz Leiber, Jr. . .s . . . . . .
. . . . ASF Feb 45 49
WANTED: 7 FEARLESS ENGINEERS by Warner Van
Lorne. .nt . . . . Amz Feb 39 8
WANTED: SUGGESTIONS by R. S. Richardson. . . . . .
. .a . . . . ASF Dec 40 103

Title. .Author. .Length . . . . Magazine. .Date. .Page No.

WAR AGAINST THE MOON, THE by Andre
Maurois. .s . . . . F&SF Sum 50 29
WAR CRIMINALS OF RENAULT ISLAND by C. A.
Baldwin. .nt . . . . Amz Dec 44 30
WAR GOD'S GAMBLE by Harry Walton. .s . . . .
. . . . SSS Feb 43 128
WAR–GODS OF THE VOID by Henry Kuttner. . . . . .
. .nt . . . . PS Fal 42 2
WAR LORD OF VENUS, THE by Frank J. Bridge *ps*
(Francis J. Brueckel). .n 3 pt . . . . WS Sep 30 294
WAR–LORDS OF THE MOON by Clinton Davies . . . . .
. .s . . . . PS Win 39 81
WAR–NYMPHS OF VENUS, THE by Ray
Cummings. .nt . . . . .PS Spr 41 2
WAR OF INTANGIBLES by Eric Fennel. .nt . . . .
. . . . .ASF Jun 48 118
WAR OF NERVES by A. E. van Vogt. .s . . . .
. . . . .OW May 50 36
WAR OF THE GIANT APES by Alexander Blade
h ps. .nt . . . . FA Apr 49 8
WAR OF THE GIANTS, THE by Fletcher Pratt. .s . . . .
. . . . WS May 31 1440
WAR OF THE GREAT ANTS, THE by Jim Vanny . . . .
. .s . . . . .WS Jul 30 140
WAR OF THE HUMAN CATS by Festus Pragnell . . . . .
. .s . . . . FA Aug 40 90
WAR OF THE MARSH–MEN by W. Malcolm
White. .ss . . . . .OTWA Dec 50 70
WAR OF THE PLANETS, THE by R. H. Romans . . . . .
. .n . . . . .WQ Sum 30 438
WAR OF THE PLANETS, THE by Harl Vincent
(Schoepflin). .s . . . . .Amz Jan 29 872
WAR OF THE SCIENTISTS by John Russell
Fearn. .nt. . . . . Amz Apr 40 50
WAR OF THE UNIVERSE, THE by Clinton
Constantinescue. .nt. . . . . .AQ Fal 31 534
WAR OF THE WEEDS, THE by Carl Jacobi. . . . .
. .s . . . . TW Feb 39 41
WAR OF THE WORLDS, THE by H. G. Wells . . . .
. .n 2 pt. . . . . Amz Aug 27 422
WAR ON VENUS by Edgar Rice Burroughs. .nt . . . . . .
. . . . FA Mar 42 8
WAR ROCKETS by Willy Ley. .a . . . . . . Amz May 40 126
WAR WITH JUPITER by W. Lawrence Hamling & Mark
Reinsberg. .s. . . . . .Amz May 39 74
WAR WORKER 17 by Frank Patton *h ps (Raymond A.*
Palmer). .s . . . . Amz Sep 43 72
WARBURTON'S INVENTION by Pvt. Russell Storm
ps (Robert Moore Williams). .nt . . . . . Amz Sep 44 154
WARDER AND THE WAMPUM, THE by Geoff St.
Reynard *ps (Robert W. Krepps). .s* . . . . FA Dec 47 164
WARLORD OF PEACE by Leroy Yerxa. .s . . . .
. . . . Amz Mar 47 32
WARLORDS OF MARS by Festus Pragnell. .s . . . .
. . . . Amz Jun 40 48

Title. .Author. .Length . . . . Magazine. .Date. .Page No.

WARM, DARK PLACES by H. L. Gold. .s . . . .
. . . . UK Oct 40 114
WARNING FROM LUNA by Charnock Walsby. .s. . . . .
. . . . ToW Spr 39 64
WARNING FROM THE PAST, THE by Robert Moore
Williams. .s. . . . . .TW Aug 39 34
WARNING TO THE CURIOUS, A by M. R. James . . . .
. .s . . . . AFR #4 112
WARRIOR-MAID OF MARS by Alfred Coppel. .nt. . . .
. . . . PS Sum 50 4
WARRIOR MAIDS OF LIBYA by Leroy Yerxa. .nt. . . .
. . . . FA Oct 43 148
WARRIOR OF THE DAWN by Howard Browne . . . . . .
. .n 2 pt. . . . . Amz Dec 42 8
WARRIOR OF TWO WORLDS by Manly Wade
Wellman. .nt. . . . . PS Sum 44 74
WARRIOR QUEEN OF LOLARTH by Ross
Rocklynne. .n. . . . . .Amz May 43 88
WARRIOR QUEENS OF MARS by Alexander Blade
h ps. .nt. . . . . FA Sep 50 6
WARRIOR RACE, THE by L. Sprague de Camp. .s . . . .
. . . . .ASF Oct 40 136
WARRIOR'S AGE by Peter Risk. .s . . . . . ASF Oct 42 32
WARRIORS OF ETERNITY by Carl Buchanan &
Dr. Arch Carr. .nt . . . . ASF Aug 34 74
WARRIORS OF MARS by Arthur Tofte. .nt . . . .
. . . . .Amz Aug 39 6
WARRIORS OF OTHER WORLDS. .bacover pics
URANUS by Malcolm Smith. . . . . FA Jun 43
VENUS by Malcolm Smith . . . . .FA Jul 43
CALLISTO by Malcolm Smith. . . . . FA Aug 43
MERCURY by Malcolm Smith. . . . . FA Dec 43
SATURN by Malcolm Smith . . . . FA Oct 44
WARRIORS OF SPACE by James P. Marshall. .s . . . . . .
. . . . SW Jun 29 39
WARRIORS OF ZANTOS by William Russell
Moore. .ss . . . . Amz Jun 33 233
WARSHIP OF MARS by James B. Settles . . . .
. .bacover pic . . . . .Amz Jul 43
WASHINGTON SLEPT HERE by Hugh Raymond
ps (John Michel). .s . . . . .Fut Aug 42 68
WATCH THAT WINDOW by L. Joe Fohn . . . .
. .s . . . . UK Sep 40 122
WATCHING EYES, THE by Robert Moore
Williams. .s. . . . . FA May 48 142
WATCH'S SOUL, THE by Jules Verne. .s . . . .
. . . . Amz Dec 33 111
WATER-BOUND WORLD by Harl Vincent
(Schoepflin). .s . . . . .AQ Spr-Sum 32 264
WATER FOR MARS by Ross Rocklynne. .nt . . . .
. . . . ASF Apr 37 10
WATER PIRATE by Leigh Brackett. .s . . . .
. . . . SSS Jan 41 35
WATER, WATER EVERYWHERE by Milton
Kaletsky. .a . . . . .Ash Apr 40 105

WATER, WATER EVERYWHERE by Jep Powell . . . . .
. .a . . . . FA Dec 41 136
WATER WORLD, THE by Oscar J. Friend. .n. . . . .
. . . . .SS May 41 14
WATERS OF DEATH by Eando Binder ps (Otto
Binder). .ss. . . . . TW Jan 40 84
WATERS OF WRATH by Arthur K. Barnes. .nt . . . . . .
. . . . TW Oct 40 14
WATERS UNDER THE EARTH, THE by James D.
Perry. .s. . . . . .SSS Feb 42 82
WATERSPOUT, THE by Eugene H. Scheftleman . . . . .
. .s . . . . WS Dec 34 828
WAVERIES, THE by Frederic Brown. .s . . . .
. . . . .ASF Jan 45 126
WAVES OF COMPULSION by Raymond Gallun. . . . . .
. .s . . . . WS Mar 32 1138
WAVES OF DEATH by Wesley Arnold. .s . . . .
. . . . WS Jun 30 58
WAY BACK, THE by Sam Moscowitz. .nt . . . .
. . . . Com Jan 41 60
WAY IN THE MIDDLE OF THE AIR by Ray
Bradbury. .s . . . . .OW Jul 50 142
WAY OF A DINOSAUR, THE by Harley S.
Aldinger. .ss . . . . Amz Apr 28 35
WAY OF ESCAPE by William F. Temple. .s . . . .
. . . . TW Jun 48 46
WAY OF THE EARTH, THE by David R. Daniels . . . . .
. .nt . . . . .ASF Oct 35 136
WAY OF THE GODS by Henry Kuttner. .nt. . . . .
. . . . TW Apr 47 11
WAY STATION by Herb Weiss. .s . . . . . . .UK Jul 39 109
WAYWARD WORLD by Gordon A. Giles ps (Otto
Binder). .s . . . . ASF Feb 38 106
"WE ALSO WALK DOGS." by Anson McDonald ps
(Robert A. Heinlein). .s . . . . .ASF Jul 41 126
WE ARE ONE by Eando Binder ps (Otto Binder) . . . . .
. .nt . . . . .Com May 41 34
WE CAN ROCKET TO THE MOON—NOW! by Arthur C.
Clarke. .a . . . . .ToW Sum 39 84
WE DANCE FOR THE DOM by Richard S. Shaver . . . .
. .nt . . . . Amz Jan 50 8
WE GUARD THE BLACK PLANET by Henry
Kuttner. .nt . . . . .SSS Nov 42 10
WE KILL PEOPLE by Lewis Padgett ps (Henry Kuttner &
C. L. Moore). .s. . . . . ASF Mar 46 82
WE OF THE SUN by Henry J. Kostkos. .s . . . .
. . . . Amz Feb 36 68
WE PRINT THE TRUTH by Anthony Boucher ps (William
Anthony Parker White). .n . . . . ASF Dec 43 125
WE, THE INVISIBLE by Frank Belknap Long, Jr. . . . .
. .s . . . . TW Feb 38 98
WE, THE OTHER PEOPLE by Bruce Manchester . . . . .
. .s . . . . MSS Apr 41 96
WEAKNESS OF RVOG, THE by James Blish & Damon
Knight. .s . . . . TW Feb 49 76

Title. .Author. .Length . . . . Magazine. .Date. .Page No.

WEAPON, THE by Raymond Z. Gallun. .s . . . . .
. . . . ASF May 36 79
WEAPON, THE by H. B. Ogden. .s . . . . .SSS May 42 115
WEAPON, THE by Robert Moore Williams. .s. . . . . . .
. . . . .Amz Jul 47 76
WEAPON FOR A WAC by Sgt. Morris J. Steele *h ps
(Raymond A. Palmer).* .s. . . . . Amz Sep 44 128
WEAPON FROM THE STARS by Rog Phillips *ps (Roger
P. Graham).* .nt . . . . Amz Oct 50 6
WEAPON MAKERS, THE by A. E. van Vogt. .n 3 pt . . .
. . . . ASF Feb 43 9
WEAPON OUT OF TIME by James Blish. .s . . . .
. . . . .SFQ Spr 41 135
WEAPON SHOP series See A. E. VAN VOGT author
WEAPON SHOP, THE by A. E. van Vogt. .nt . . . .
. . . . ASF Dec 42 9
WEAPON SHOPS OF ISHER, THE by A. E. van
Vogt. .n. . . . . TW Feb 49 11
WEAPON TOO DREADFUL TO USE, THE by Isaac
Asimov. .s . . . . Amz May 39 110
WEARIEST RIVER, THE by Wallace West. .nt . . . . . .
. . . . TW Aug 50 104
WEATHER ADJUDICATOR, THE by Stanton A.
Coblentz. .s . . . . MSS Feb 39 90
WEATHER MASTER, THE by Arthur Cave. .s . . . .
. . . . Amz Jul 35 124
WEB OF MOONS by Hannes Bok. .ss . . . . Fut Apr 42 86
*WEBSTER FAMILY series See CLIFFORD D. SIMAK
author*
WEDDING OF THE FORCES by Polton Cross *ps (John
Russell Fearn).* .s. . . . . .Fut Nov 40 86
WEDDING OF THE MOONS by Frederic Arnold
Kummer, Jr. .s . . . . .Ash Aug 40 73
WEDGE, THE by Isaac Asimov. .s . . . . . . ASF Oct 44 64
WEE BONNIE POUPON, THE by F. Anton Reeds. . . . .
. .s . . . . OW Mar 50 140
WEE MEN OF WEEHEN, THE by Lester Barclay. .s . . .
. . . . FA Aug 49 104
WEEP NO MORE, MY ROBOT by Chester S. Geier. . . .
. .s . . . . Amz Jun 45 54
WEIGHER OF SOULS, THE by Andre Maurois . . . . .
. .nt . . . . FFM Oct 50 86
WEIRD DOOM OF FLOYD SCRILCH, THE by Robert
Bloch. .s . . . . .FA Jul 42 86
WEIRD TRAVEL TALES by Bob Davis
    1. A CHAT WITH THE SKIPPER CONCERNING
        CLAIRVOYANCE. .ss . . . . FFM Jan 40 78
    2. TRAGIC FATE OF THOSE WHO SOUGHT THE
        LOST LEMON MINE. .ss . . . . . . FFM Apr 40 64
WEIRD WONDERS OF THE WAR by Vincent H.
Gaddis. .a. . . . . .Amz Jan 49 137
"WELL I'LL BE HEXED!" by Peter Phillips. .nt . . . . . .
. . . . FA Aug 50 90
WELL OF THE ANGELS by E. Hoffman Price. .s . . . . .
. . . . .UK May 40 91

Title. .Author. .Length . . . . Magazine. .Date. .Page No.

WELL–OILED MACHINE, THE by H. B. Fyfe. .s . . . . .
. . . . F&SF Dec 50 105
WELL–WISHER, THE by Bernie Kamins. .s . . . .
. . . . FA Oct 48 120
WENDIGO, THE by Algernon Blackwood. .nt . . . .
. . . . FFM Jun 44 90
WE'RE NOT ALL HUMAN by John W. Campbell,
Jr. .a. . . . . .ASF Sep 41 121
WERE–SNAKE, THE by Frank Belknap Long, Jr. . . . .
. .s .AFR #7 99
WEREWILE OF THE CRYSTAL CRYPT by Gardner F.
Fox. .s. . . . . PS Sum 48 106
WEREWOLVES OF WAR by D. W. Hall. .s . . . .
. . . . ASF Feb 31 153
WEST POINT OF TOMORROW by Arthur J. Burks. . . .
. .nt . . . . TW Sep 40 87
WEST POINT, 3000 A.D. by Manly Wade Wellman . . . .
. .n 2 pt . . . . Amz Nov 40 12
WEST WIND by Murray Leinster *ps (Will F.
Jenkins).* .nt . . . . ASF Mar 48 77
WET MAGIC by Henry Kuttner. .nt . . . . UK Feb 43 9
WHAT ARE POSITRONS? by R. D. Swisher, Ph.D. . . .
. .a . . . . ASF Aug 37 117
WHAT ARE THE GREAT DETECTIVE STORIES AND
WHY? by Arthur B. Reeve. .a . . . . SD Jan 30 6
WHAT DEAD MEN TELL by Theodore Sturgeon . . . . .
. .nt . . . . ASF Nov 49 122
WHAT DO YOU MEAN BY "UP"? by Malcolm
Jameson. .a . . . . .Ash Apr 41 44
WHAT DO YOU THINK? letter dept of FN from
    May 48
WHAT HAPPENED TO PROFESSOR STOCKLEY? by
E. M. Scott. .s . . . . Amz Dec 31 836
WHAT HATH ME? by Henry Kuttner. .nt . . . .
. . . . .PS Spr 46 50
WHAT MAD UNIVERSE? by Fredric Brown. .n . . . . . .
. . . . .SS Sep 48 11
*WHAT MAN CAN IMAGINE dept in Amz irregularly
from Feb 46*
WHAT PRICE CLUES (SCIENTIFIC ACTUALITY) by
Herbert Mills. .a . . . . AD Sep 30 812
"WHAT SO PROUDLY WE HAIL. . ." by Day Keene . .
. .s . . . . Im Dec 50 44
WHAT SORGHUM SAYS by Cecil Corwin *ps (Cyril
Kornbluth).* .s. . . . . .Cos May 41 101
WHAT THE SODIUM LINES REVEALED by L. Taylor
Hansen. .s . . . . AQ Win 29 120
WHAT WAS IT? by Fitz–James O'Brien. .s. . . . .
. . . . FFM Dec 49 106
WHAT YOU NEED by Lewis Padgett *ps (Henry Kuttner
& C. L. Moore).* .s . . . . .ASF Oct 45 133
WHATEVER by Mona Farnsworth. .s . . . . .UK May 39 97
WHAT'S IN A NAME? by Berkeley Livingston . . . . . .
. .s . . . . FA Feb 44 36
WHAT'S NEW? by E. E. Pelletier. .s . . . . . .FA Jul 45 110

Title. .Author. .Length . . . . Magazine. .Date. .Page No.

WHAT'S WRONG IN THE PATENT SYSTEM? by
    G. S. Curry. .a. . . . . ASF Oct 47 87
WHAT'S WRONG WITH ROCKETS? by Willy Ley . . . .
    . .a . . . . Amz Mar 40 39
WHEEL FROM SPACE, THE by E. K. Jarvis h ps . . . . .
    . .s . . . . FA Aug 49 118
WHEEL IS DEATH, THE by Roger Dee ps (Roger D.
    Aycock). .s. . . . . PS Fal 49 75
WHEEL OF TIME, THE by Robert Arthur. .s. . . . . . .
    . . . . SSS Mar 50 75
WHEELS OF IF, THE by L. Sprague de Camp. .n . . . . .
    . . . . UK Oct 40 9
WHEESHT! by Cleve Cartmill. .nt . . . . UK Jun 43 9
WHEEZERS, THE by William Morrison ps (Joseph
    Samachson). .s . . . . CF Sum 43 91
WHEN ANTEROS CAME by James Blish. .ss . . . .
    . . . . SFQ Win 41–42 143
WHEN ATLANTIS WAS by H. F. Arnold. .n 2 pt . . . . .
    . . . . Amz Oct 37 12
WHEN CAVERNS YAWNED by Captain S. P.
    Meek. .s . . . . ASF May 31 198
"WHEN DEAD FROGS KICK—" by John Davis
    Buddhue. .a . . . . ASF Nov 38 93
WHEN DESTINY DEALT by P. F. Costello h ps . . . . . .
    . .s . . . . FA Sep 42 214
WHEN FLESH DEFIES FIRE by Vincent H.
    Gaddis. .a. . . . . Amz May 46 160
WHEN FREEMEN SHALL STAND by Nelson S.
    Bond. .n . . . . FA Nov 42 8
WHEN HALF-WORLDS MEET by Hugh Raymond
    ps (John Michel). .s . . . . Cos Jul 41 21
WHEN INCA-LAND REVOLTED by Woods Peters. . . .
    . .s . . . . Amz Aug 30 458
WHEN IS WHEN? by Malcolm Jameson. .s. . . . .
    . . . . ASF Aug 43 143
WHEN IT WAS MOONLIGHT by Manly Wade
    Wellman. .s. . . . . UK Feb 40 124
WHEN KOHONNES SCREAMED by Gardner F.
    Fox. .s. PS Fal 48 43
WHEN METEORITES CRASH by Julian S. Krupa. . . . .
    . .bacover. . . . . Amz Jun 40
WHEN MOONS MET by Clyde F. Beck. .s . . . .
    . . . . WS Aug 30 236
WHEN NEW YORK VANISHED by Henry Kuttner. . . .
    . .n .SS Mar 40 14
WHEN OLD GODS WAKE by A. Merritt. .s . . . .
    . . . . AFR #7 94
WHEN PLANETS CLASHED by Manly Wade
    Wellman. .s. . . . . WQ Spr 31 400
    SS Mar 47 70
WHEN REPTILES RULED by Duane N. Carroll . . . . . .
    . .ss. . . . . .WS Jan 24 618
WHEN SHADOWS FALL by L. Ron Hubbard . . . .
    . .s . . . . SS Jul 48 83
WHEN SPACE BURST by Edmond Hamilton. .s . . . . . .
    . . . . TW Dec 37 90

Title. .Author. .Length . . . . Magazine. .Date. .Page No.

WHEN SPACE RIPPED OPEN by Ralph W.
    Wilkins. .s . . . . .AW Nov 29 412
WHEN THE ATOMS FAILED by John W.
    Campbell, Jr. .s. . . . . .Amz Jan 30 910
WHEN THE BOUGH BREAKS by Lewis Padgett ps
    (Henry Kuttner & C. L. Moore). .nt . . . ASF Nov 44 75
WHEN THE COMET RETURNED by Harl Vincent
    (Schoepflin). .nt . . . . Amz Apr 33 8
WHEN THE CYCLE MET by David H. Beaumont . . . . .
    . .s . . . . ASF Nov 35 71
WHEN THE DARKNESS CAME by William
    De Lisle. .nt . . . . Amz Sep 43 8
WHEN THE EARTH GREW COLD by Paul H.
    Lovering. .nt. . . . . .AQ Fal 29 556
WHEN THE EARTH LIVED by Henry Kuttner. .s. . . . .
    . . . . TW Oct 37 90
    SS Jul 48 92
WHEN THE EARTH SHOOK by Walter Kubilius . . . . .
    . .ss. Fut Oct 42 103
WHEN THE EARTH STOOD STILL by Arlyn H.
    Vance. .s . . . . Amz Dec 36 118
WHEN THE EARTH TILTED by J. M. Walsh. .s . . . . . .
    . . . . WS May 32 1342
    ToW Win 38 80
WHEN THE FUTURE DIES by Nat Schachner. .s . . . . .
    . . . . ASF Jun 39 29
WHEN THE GODS MAKE WAR by A. R. Steber ps
    (Raymond A. Palmer). .nt. . . . . .Amz Jul 40 6
WHEN THE HALF GODS GO by Amelia R. Long. . . . .
    . .s . . . . ASF Jul 39 111
WHEN THE ICE TERROR CAME by Jack West. .s . . . .
    . . . . Amz Apr 40 118
WHEN THE METEOR STRUCK by J. Lewis Burtt . . . .
    . .s . . . . Amz Jun 36 75
WHEN THE MOON BOUNCED by Frank Patton h ps
    (Richard A. Shaver). .nt . . . . .Amz May 49 58
WHEN THE MOON DIED by Don Wilcox . . . .
    . .nt . . . . Amz Sep 39 64
WHEN THE MOON MOONS by Webster Watson. .ss . . .
    . . . . Amz Nov 33 114
WHEN THE MOON RAN WILD by A. Hyatt
    Verrill. .n . . . . .AQ Win 31 90
WHEN THE MOON TURNED GREEN by Hal K.
    Wells. .s . . . . ASF May 31 241
WHEN THE MOUNTAIN CAME TO MIRIMAR by Charles
    W. Diffin. .s . . . . ASF Mar 31 297
WHEN THE ROCKETS COME by Robert Abernathy. . .
    . .s . . . . ASF Mar 45 158
WHEN THE SLEEPER WAKES by H. G. Wells. .n . . . . .
    . . . . AQ Win 28 55
WHEN THE SLEEPERS WOKE by Arthur Leo
    Zagat. .s. . . . . ASF Nov 32 171
WHEN THE SPIRIT MOVES ME by Lee Francis
    h ps. .s. . . . . .FA May 47 90
WHEN THE SUN DIES by Chan Corbett ps (Nathan
    Schachner). .s. . . . . ASF Mar 35 50

Title. .Author. .Length . . . . Magazine. .Date. .Page No.

WHEN THE SUN WENT OUT by Eando Binder ps (Otto
Binder). .s . . . . ASF Sep 37 38
WHEN THE TOP WOBBLED by Victor Endersby . . . . .
. .nt . . . . Amz Feb 36 78
WHEN THE UNIVERSE SHRANK by J. Lewis
Burtt. .n 2 pt . . . . Amz Oct 33 519
WHEN THE WORLD TOTTERED by Lester del
Rey. .n . . . . FA Dec 50 6
WHEN THE WORLD WENT MAD by Ronald M.
Sherin. .s .AQ Fal 28 554
WHEN TIME ROLLED BACK by Ed Earl Repp. .s . . . .
. . . . Com May 41 69
WHEN TIME STOOD STILL by Philip Jaques
Bartel. .s . . . . Amz Feb 35 123
WHEN TIME STOOD STILL by Chan Corbett ps (Nathan
Schachner). .s . . . . .ASF Jun 37 112
WHEN TIME STOOD STILL by Edwin K. Sloat. .s . . . .
. . . . .Amz Jul 39 76
WHEN TIME WENT MAD by Dirk Wylie & Frederic
Arnold Kummer, Jr. (& Frederik Pohl). .nt . . . .
. . . . TW Feb 50 11
WHEN TWO WORLDS MEET by Robert Moore
Williams. .nt . . . . Amz Apr 50 8
WHEN YOU THINK THAT. . .SMILE! by Dorothy Les
Tina. .s . . . . Fut Feb 43 55
WHENEVER THE SUN SHINES by Margaret St.
Clair. .s . . . . FA Oct 47 134
WHERE ANGELS FEAR by Manly Wade Wellman . . . .
. .s . . . . UK Mar 39 131
WHERE ETERNITY ENDS by Eando Binder ps (Otto
Binder). .nt . . . . .SF Jun 39 10
WHERE FOUR ROADS MET by G. St. John–Loe. . . . .
. .s . . . . .ASF Oct 33 133
WHERE GRAVITY ENDS by Robert H. Leitfred . . . . .
. .s . . . . AW Sep 29 214
WHERE IN THE WAREHOUSE by Bruce Dennis ps
(David Wright O'Brien). .s . . . .
. . . . FA Apr 43 50
WHERE IS ROGER DAVIS? by David V. Reed ps
(David Vern). .nt . . . . Amz May 39 34
WHERE NO FOOT WALKS by G. H. Irwin h ps
(Richard S. Shaver). .nt . . . . .OW Nov 49 42
WHERE TALL TOWERS GLEAM by Robert Moore
Williams. .s . . . . FA Aug 50 116
WHEREABOUTS OF MR. MOSES BAILEY, THE by
James B. Nevin. .s . . . . FFM Jun 41 117
WHIMPUS, THE by Tod Robbins. .nt . . . .
. . . . FFM Sep–Oct 39 37
WHIPS OF DOOM, THE by Helmar Lewis. .s . . . .
. . . . Amz Dec 44 132
WHIRLPOOL IN SPACE by Miles Shelton ps (Don
Wilcox). .s . . . . Amz Nov 39 58
WHISPER OF DEATH by Harl Vincent
(Schoepflin). .s . . . . Amz Nov 33 11
WHISPERERS, THE by Donald Wandrei. .s . . . .
. . . . ASF May 35 133

WHISPERING ETHER by Charles S. Wolfe. .s . . . .
. . . . Amz Jun 26 247
WHISPERING GORILLA, THE by Don Wilcox . . . . . .
. .nt . . . . .FA May 40 6
WHISPERING SATELLITE by Thornton Ayre ps
(John Russell Fearn). .s . . . . .ASF Jan 38 97
WHISPERING SPHERES, THE by R. R.
Winterbotham. .s . . . . .Com Jul 41 100
WHISTLING DEATH, THE by Abner J. Gelula. . . . . . .
. .nt . . . . Amz Jun 39 36
WHITE ADVENTURE by Warner Van Lorne . . . .
ps. .s . . . . ASF Apr 36 55
WHITE ARMY, THE by Dr. Daniel Dressler. .s . . . .
. . . . Amz Sep 29 528
WHITE BARRIER by Frank Belknap Long, Jr.
. .nt . . . . TW Apr 39 88
WHITE BROOD, THE by Hal K. Wells. .s . . . .
. . . . .TW Nov 40 52
WHITE CATASTROPHE by Arthur J. Burks. .s . . . . . .
. . . . TW Jun 49 100
WHITE CITY, THE by David H. Keller, M.D. . .s . . . . . .
. . . . .Amz May 35 11
WHITE COLLARS by David H. Keller, M.D. . .s. . . . . .
. . . . .AQ Sum 29 380
WHITE DWARF, THE by J. Lewis Burtt. .s . . . .
. . . . Amz May 34 91
WHITE DWARF STARS by John W. Abrams. .a . . . . . .
. . . . ASF Dec 47 83
WHITE GOD OF CHICHEN ITZA, THE by Gilbert
Mead. .nt. . . . . FA Nov 49 118
WHITE GOLD PIRATE, THE by Merlin Moore
Taylor. .s. . . . . Amz Apr 27 30
WHITE GORILLA, THE by Elmer Brown Mason. .s. . . .
. . . . FN Nov 49 114
WHITE INVADERS, THE by Ray Cummings. .nt . . . . .
. . . . ASF Dec 31 310
WHITE LAND OF VENUS by Frederic Arnold
Kummer, Jr. . .s . . . . .Ash Feb 40 26
WHITE LILY by John Taine ps (Eric Temple Bell) . . . .
. .n . . . . AQ Win 30 4
WHITE MOUSE by Thornton Ayre ps (John Russell
Fearn). .s. . . . . .NW #1 16 59
WHITE MUTINY by Malcolm Jameson. .s . . . .
. . . . ASF Oct 40 43
WHITE SLAVE, THE by Arthur B. Reeve. .s . . . .
. . . . .AD Jul 30 626
WHO GOES THERE? by Don A. Stuart ps (John W.
Campbell, Jr.). .nt . . . . ASF Aug 38 60
WHO GOES THERE? by Charles H. Davis. .s . . . .
. . . . .PS Spr 50 53
WHO IS CHARLES AVISON? by Edison Telsa
Marshall. .s. . . . . FFM Dec 39 110
WHO SUPS WITH THE DEVIL by S. M. Teenishaw
h ps. .s. . . . . FA Apr 48 54
WHO WANTS A GREEN BOTTLE? by Tod
Robbins. .s . . . . FN Nov 40 113

Title. .Author. .Length . . . . Magazine. .Date. .Page No.

WHO WANTS POWER? by Mona Farnsworth. .s . . . . . .
. . . . UK Mar 39 95
WHO WAS DILMO DENI? by Ross Rocklynne. .s . . . . .
. . . . ASF Nov 38 108
WHO WAS THOMAS MORROW? by Robert Moore
Williams. .s . . . . TW Apr 41 109
WHOM THE GODS LOVE by Lester del Rey. .s . . . . . .
. . . . ASF Jun 43 60
WHOM THE RAT BITES. .s . . . . Fant #3 39 33
WHO'S THAT KNOCKING AT MY DOOR? by S. M.
Tenneshaw h ps (Milton Lesser). .s . . . . Amz Nov 50 44
WHY ARE YOU WHAT YOU ARE ? by B. B.
Gibson. .a . . . . Amz Sep 42 225
WHY DO THEY DO IT? by L. Sprague de Camp. . . . . .
. .a . . . . .ASF Sep 50 121
WHY ROCKETS DON'T FLY by Peter Van Dresser. . . .
. .a . . . . ASF Oct 38 81
WHY SCIENCE FICTION? by John Taine ps (Eric
Temple Bell). .guest ed . . . . .SS Mar 39 15
WHY THE HEAVENS FELL by Epaminondas T.
Snooks, D.T.G. ps (C. P. Mason). .s . . . .
. . . . WS May 32 1374
WHY THE SKY IS BLUE by Ruppert Carlin. .ss . . . . . .
. . . . .Amz Jul 49 74
WICKED PEOPLE, THE by Ross Rocklynne. .s . . . . . .
. . . . .SSS Feb 42 96
WIDE–OPEN PLANET by L. Sprague de Camp. . . . . . .
. .nt . . . . .Fut Sep-Oct 50 8
WIDE–OPEN SHIP by Richard Wilson. .s . . . .
. . . . Fut Oct 42 88
WILBURY'S INCREDIBLE GADGET by Donald
Bern. .s . . . . FA Sep 41 104
WILD WULLIE, THE WASTER by Tod Robbins. . . . .
. .s . . . . FFM Sep 42 114
WILLFUL PUPPETS, THE by William P.
McGivern. .nt . . . . FA Feb 43 170
WILLIE by Frank Belknap Long. .s . . . .
. . . . .ASF Oct 43 118
WILLIE WINS A WAR by E. A. Grosser. .s . . . .
. . . . .SSS Aug 41 61
WILLOWS, THE by Algernon Blackwood. .nt . . . .
. . . . FFM Apr 46 90
WIND IN HER HAIR by Kris Neville. .s . . . .
. . . . .Im Oct 50 40
WINDOW TO THE FUTURE by Peter Worth. .s . . . . . .
. . . . Amz May 49 118
WINDOW TO THE PAST by Chester S. Geier. . . . . . .
. .s . . . . FA Aug 50 70
WINE OF THE DREAMERS by John D.
MacDonald. .n . . . . SS May 50 11
WINGED DEATH by O. L. Beckwith. .s . . . .
. . . . AD Sep 30 786
WINGED DOOM, THE by Kenneth Gilbert . . . .
. .s . . . . Amz Oct 27 668
WINGED MAN, THE by E. Mayne Hull. .n 2 pt . . . . . .
. . . . ASF May 44 37

WINGED MEN OR ORCON, THE by David R.
Sparks. .nt . . . . .ASF Jan 31 54
WINGED MENACE, THE by Packard Dow. .s . . . .
. . . . WQ Spr 31 416
WINGED TERROR by G. R. Malloch. .nt . . . .
. . . . .Fant #2 39 2
WINGS ACROSS THE COSMOS by Polton Cross ps
(John Russell Fearn). .s . . . . TW Jun 38 73
WINGS ACROSS TIME by Frank Edward Arnold . . . . .
. .nt . . . . SFQ Win 42 82
WINGS OF ICARUS by Ray Cummings. .n . . . .
. . . . .SS Jun 43 13
WINGS OF NIGHT, THE by Lester del Rey. .s . . . .
. . . . ASF Mar 42 46
WINGS OF THE LIGHTNING LAND by James MacCreigh
ps (Frederik Pohl). .nt . . . . .Ash Nov 41 11
WINGS OF THE STORM by Manly Wade Wellman . . . .
. .s . . . . ASF Mar 38 88
WINK VAN RIPPLE by Geoff St. Reynard ps (Robert W.
Krepps). .s . . . . FA Dec 45 128
WINKING LIGHTS OF MARS, THE by Gordon A. Giles
ps (Otto Binder). .s . . . . Amz Feb 41 120
WINTER AMID THE ICE, A or THE CRUISE OF THE
JEUNE-HARDIE by Jules Verne. .s . . . . AQ Win 33 74
WINTER ON THE PLANET by Warner Van Lorne
ps. .s . . . . ASF Apr 37 139
WISDOM OF AN ASS, THE by Silaki Ali Hassan. . . . . .
. .nt . . . . UK Feb 40 67
WISDOM OF THE DEAD by Ed Earl Repp. .s . . . .
. . . . SF Mar 41 75
WISDOM OF THE EAST, THE by L. Sprague de
Camp. .s . . . . .UK Aug 42 90
WISHER TAKE ALL by William F. Temple. .ss. . . . . .
. . . . OW Jul 50 20
WISHES WE MAKE, THE by E. M. Hull. .s . . . .
. . . . UK Jun 43 35
WITCH, THE by A. E. van Vogt. .s . . . .
. . . . UK Feb 43 118
WITCH–MAKERS, THE by Donald Wandrei. .s. . . . . . .
. . . . FFM Sep-Oct 39 100
WITCH OF BLACKFEN MOOR by Lee Francis. .nt. . . .
. . . . FA Dec 43 10
WITCH OF THE ANDES by Richard S. Shaver. .nt . . . .
. . . . FA Oct 47 8
WITCH SHALL BE BORN, A by Robert E.
Howard. .nt . . . . .AFR #10 3
WITCHES OF KARRES, THE by James H. Schmitz . . .
. .nt . . . . ASF Dec 49 7
WITCH'S DAUGHTER by Richard S. Shaver. .nt . . . . .
. . . . Amz Jun 47 62
WITH A BLUNT INSTRUMENT by Eric Frank
Russell. .s . . . . .UK Dec 41 97
WITH FLAMING SWORDS by Cleve Cartmill. .nt . . . . .
. . . . .ASF Sep 42 109
WITH FOLDED HANDS. . . by Jack Williamson . . . . . .
. .nt . . . . .ASF Jul 47 6

Title. .Author. .Length . . . . Magazine. .Date. .Page No.

Title. .Author. .Length . . . . Magazine. .Date. .Page No.

WITHIN THE PLANET by Wesley Arnold. .s . . . .
. . . . WQ Spr 30 360
WITHIN THE PYRAMID by R. DeWitt Miller. .s . . . . .
. . . . ASF Mar 37 41
WITHIN SIGHT OF HELL by Alcan Hirsch, Ph.D. . . . .
. .s . . . . Amz Dec 33 67
WITHOUT ROCKET FROM EARTH by H. L. Gold . . .
. .s . . . . TW Dec 41 110
WITNESSES OF THE PAST by Willy Ley. .a . . . .
. . . . .ASF Jun 38 136
WIVES IN DUPLICATE by Don Wilcox. .s. . . . .
. . . . Amz Aug 39 62
WIZARD OF BASEBALL, THE by Milton
Kaletsky. .s . . . . .FA May 40 68
WIZARD OF BLUE GAP, THE by Frances M.
Deegan. .s . . . . FA Dec 50 104
WIZARD OF LINN, THE by A. E. van Vogt. . . . .
. .n 3 pt . . . . ASF Apr 50 6
WOBBLIES IN THE MOON by Frank Belknap
Long. .s . . . . TW Jun 43 44
WOMAN FROM SPACE, THE by Richard Vaughan. . . .
. .s . . . . WQ Spr 32 364
WOMAN OF THE WOOD, THE by A. Merritt. .nt . . . . .
. . . . AFR #1 68
WOMAN OUT OF TIME by Frank Belknap Long . . . . .
. .s .Ash Aug 40 62
WOMAN WHO COULDN'T DIE, The by Arthur
Stringer. .n. . . . . FFM Oct 50 12
WOMAN'S ISLAND by Miles Shelton ps (Don
Wilcox). .s . . . . .Dec 45 46
WOMEN, THE by Ray Bradbury. .s . . . . FFM Oct 48 104
WOMEN WITH WINGS by Leslie F. Stone ps (Mrs.
William Silberberg). .s. . . . . .AW May 30 984
WOMEN'S WORLD by David C. Cooke. .s . . . .
. . . . SF Dec 39 78
WONDER ODDITIES dept in TW from Dec 49
WONDERFUL WINDOW, THE by Lord Dunsany . . . . .
. .ss. AFR #12 80
WONDERS OF THE ANCIENT WORLD. .bacover pics
BUILDING THE GREAT PYRAMID by James B.
Settles. .Amz Jun 46
THE COLOSSUS OF RHODES by James B.
Settles. Amz Jul 46
WONDERSMITH, THE by Fitz-James O'Brien. .nt . . . . .
. . . . F&SF Dec 50 52
WOODEN HAM, THE by Morris J. Steele h ps (Berkeley
Livingston). .s. . . . . FA Dec 43 62
WOODEN SHIPS OF THE AIR by Willy Ley. .a . . . . . .
. . . . .ASF Oct 44 104
WORD FROM THE VOID, THE by Mack Reynolds. . . .
. .ss . . . . SSS Sep 50 99
WORDS OF GURU, THE by Kenneth Falconer ps (Cyril
Kornbluth). .s. . . . . .Sti Jun 41 88
. . . . by C. M. Kornbluth. . . . . AFR #5 119
WORLD AFLAME, THE by Isaac R. Nathanson . . . . . .
. .nt . . . . Amz Jan 35 44

WORLD AT BAY by B. and Geo. C. Wallis. .n 2 pt . . . .
. . . . Amz Nov 28 678
WORLD ATAVISM by Edmond Hamilton. .s . . . .
. . . . Amz Aug 30 428
WORLD BEHIND THE MOON, THE by Paul Ernst. . . .
. .s . . . . ASF Apr 31 64
WORLD BENEATH ICE by Polton Cross ps (John
Russell Fearn). .nt. . . . . Amz Aug 39 28
WORLD BEYOND, THE by Guy Archette ps (Chester S.
Geier). .s . . . . Amz Dec 47 86
WORLD BEYOND, THE by Ray Cummings. .nt . . . . . .
. . . . .Amz Jul 42 90
WORLD BEYOND BELIEF by William P.
McGivern. .nt . . . . FA Aug 43 40
WORLD BEYOND THE SKY by Robert Moore
Williams. .n . . . . .SS Jan 43 15
WORLD FLIGHT by S. Gordon Gurwit. .s . . . .
. . . . Amz Jan 34 73
WORLD GONE MAD by Nat Schachner. .s . . . .
. . . . Amz Oct 35 122
WORLD IN A BOX, THE by Carl Jacobi. .s . . . .
. . . . TW Feb 37 103
WORLD IN BALANCE, THE by Millard Verne
Gordon. .s . . . . Fut Jun 42 76
WORLD IN SHADOW by John Brody. .nt . . . .
. . . . NW #4 49 3
WORLD IN THE ATOM, THE by Ed Earl Repp. .s . . . .
. . . . FA Jun 40 52
WORLD IN THE BALANCE, THE by J. P. Marshall
. .s . . . . FFM Nov 39 32
WORLD IN WILDERNESS, THE by Thornton Ayre
ps (John Russell Fearn). .nt . . . . .SF Jun 41 82
WORLD IS BORN, A by Leigh Brackett. .s . . . .
. . . . .Com Jul 41 56
WORLD IS DEAD, THE by Alexander Blade h ps . . . . .
. .nt . . . . Amz Aug 49 96
WORLD IS MINE, THE by Lewis Padgett ps (Henry
Kuttner & C. L. Moore). .nt. . . . . ASF Jun 43 9
WORLD–MOVER, THE by George O. Smith. .nt. . . . . .
. . . . .Fut Nov 50 8
WORLD OF Ā by A. E. van Vogt. .n 3 pt. . . . .
. . . . ASF Aug 45 7
WORLD OF ARLESIA by Margaret St. Clair. .s . . . . . .
. . . . F&SF Win–Spr 50 108
WORLD OF A HUNDRED MEN, THE by Walter
Kateley. .s . . . . SW Feb 30 818
WORLD OF HORROR by Clark Ashton Smith. .s . . . . .
. . . . ToW Aut 39 92
WORLD OF ILLUSION by John Coleridge ps (Earl
Binder & Otto Binder). .s . . . . .Fut Nov 40 40
WORLD OF INDEXED NUMBERS, A by Will
McMorrow. .nt . . . . .FFM May–Jun 40 87
WORLD OF LIVING DEAD by Wilm Carver. .s . . . . . .
. . . . TW Jun 43 108
WORLD OF MIRACLES, THE by David V. Reed ps
(David Vern). .s. . . . . Amz Oct 41 44

Title. .Author. .Length . . . . Magazine. .Date. .Page No.

WORLD OF MISTERS by Gene Ellerman *ps (Basil Wells)*. .s . . . . FB #6 103
WORLD OF MOCKERY by Sam Moskowitz. .s . . . . . .
. . . . PS Sum 41 74
WORLD OF NIGHTMARE FANTASIES, THE by Viktor Bolkhovitinov & Vassilij Zakhartchenko. .a . . . .
. . . . .ASF Jun 49 158
WORLD OF NO RETURN by Bryce Walton. .s . . . . . .
. . . . SSS Sep 49 56
WORLD OF PURPLE LIGHT by Warner Van Lorne *ps*. .nt . . . . ASF Dec 36 48
WORLD OF RELUCTANT VIRGINS, THE by Robert Moore Williams. .s . . . . Amz Nov 50 60
WORLD OF SINGING CRYSTALS, THE by Thos. S. Gardner.ss . . . . WS Mar 36 902
WORLD OF 61 CYGNI C, THE by R. S. Richardson. .a . . . . .ASF Jul 43 67
WORLD OF THE GIANT ANTS, THE by A. Hyatt Verrill. .n . . . . .AQ Fal 28 436
WORLD OF THE LIVING DEAD by Ed Earl Repp . . . .
. .n 2 pt . . . . Amz Nov 32 734
WORLD OF THE LOST, THE by Paul Lohrman *h ps (Richard S. Shaver)*. .n . . . . FA Mar 50 78
WORLD OF THE MIST by Laurence Manning . . . .
. .n 2 pt . . . . WS Sep 35 390
WORLD OF THE PAPER DOLLS by Don Wilcox . . . .
. .n . . . . FA Oct 43 22
WORLD OF THE PAPER SUN, THE by Clifford D. Simak. .s . . . . WS Dec 31 878
WORLD OF WULKINS, THE by Frank Belknap Long. .s . . . . TW Apr 48 102
WORLD ON A POGO STICK by F. Orlin Tremaine . . . .
. .a . . . . TW Dec 48 82
WORLD ON THE EDGE OF THE UNIVERSE, THE by Martin Pearson *ps (Donald A. Wollheim)*. .s . . . .
. . . . SFQ Sum 41 133
WORLD REBORN by Thornton Ayre *ps (John Russell Fearn)*. .nt . . . . .SSS Mar 40 6
WORLD REBORN by J. Harvey Haggard. .n . . . .
. . . . .Fut Nov 39 10
WORLD THAT DISSOLVED, THE by Polton Cross *ps (John Russell Fearn)*. .s . . . . Amz Feb 39 104
WORLD-THINKER, THE by Jack Vance. .s . . . .
. . . . .TW Sum 45 36
WORLD UNSEEN, A by Joseph William Skidmore . . . .
. .n 2 pt . . . . .WS Jan 36 774
WORLD UPSIDE DOWN by Ray Cummings. .s . . . . . .
. . . . TW Dec 40 83
WORLD WITH A THOUSAND MOONS, THE by Edmond Hamilton. .nt . . . . Amz Dec 42 64
WORLD WITHIN, THE by Nelson S. Bond. .s . . . .
. . . . SSS May 42 90
WORLD WITHIN, THE by Benson Herbert. .s . . . . . .
. . . . WS Aug 31 312

Title. .Author. .Length . . . . Magazine. .Date. .Page No.

WORLD WITHOUT, THE by Benson Herbert. .s . . . . . .
. . . . WS Feb 31 996
SS Sep 40 90
WORLD WITHOUT AIR by Henry Kuttner. .s . . . .
. . . . FA Aug 40 108
WORLD WITHOUT CHANCE by Polton Cross *ps (John Russell Fearn)*. .s . . . . .TW Feb 39 98
WORLD WITHOUT DARKNESS by Neil R. Jones . . . .
. .s . . . . .SSS Mar 50 100
WORLD WITHOUT DEATH by Polton Cross *ps (John Russell Fearn)*. .nt . . . . Amz Jun 39 6
WORLD WITHOUT MEN by Robert Moore Williams. .nt . . . . Amz Jun 50 60
WORLD WITHOUT NAME, THE by Edwin K. Sloat. .s . . . . WS Mar 31 1092
SS Jul 39 96
WORLD WITHOUT SEX by Robert Wentworth *ps (Edmond Hamilton)*. .s . . . . MSS May 40 41
WORLD WITHOUT WOMEN by Thornton Ayre *ps (John Russell Fearn)*. .nt . . . . Amz Apr 39 6
WORLD WRECKER, THE by Raymond Z. Gallun . . . .
. .s . . . . .ASF Jun 34 104
WORLDS ADRIFT by Stephen G. Hale. .nt . . . .
. . . . Amz May 32 158
WORLDS AT WAR by Ed Earl Repp. .s . . . .
. . . . .FA May 40 56
WORLDS DON'T CARE by Nat Schachner. .nt . . . . . .
. . . . ASF Apr 39 9
WORLD'S EIGHTH WONDER, THE by Eric Frank Russell. .s .ToW Sum 38 4
WORLD'S MOST FAMOUS ILLUSION, THE by Vincent H. Gaddis. .a . . . . FA Jun 48 158
WORLDS OF IF, THE by Stanley G. Weinbaum. .s . . . .
. . . . WS Aug 35 276
SS Mar 41 90
Fant Dec 46 46
WORLDS OF TOMORROW, THE by Manly Wade Wellman. .nt . . . . TW Oct 40 93
WORLD'S PHARAOH by Kelvin Kent *ps (Henry Kuttner)*. .s . . . . .TW Dec 39 57
WORLDS TO BARTER by John B. Harris. .s . . . .
. . . . WS May 31 1422
by John Beynon *(Harris)*. . . . ToW Spr 40 74
WORLDS TO COME by Brett Sterling *h ps (Joseph Samachson)*. .n . . . . .CF Spr 43 15
WORLDS WITHIN by John Russell Fearn. .nt . . . .
. . . . ASF Mar 37 12
WORLDS WITHIN WORLDS by Frederic Arnold Kummer, Jr. .nt . . . . .TW Mar 40 85
WORM, THE by David H. Keller, M.D. .s . . . .
. . . . Amz Mar 29 1099
WORMS TURN, THE by Oscar J. Friend. .s . . . .
. . . . SS Jul 40 109
WOW by William Seabrook. .s . . . . WB Dec 50 108

Title. .Author. .Length . . . . Magazine. .Date. .Page No.

WRATH OF AMEN–RA, THE by William Holloway . . .
. .s . . . . .FN Jan 49 102
WRATH OF THE PURPLE by Howard Melvin Fast . . . .
. .s . . . . Amz Oct 32 602
WRECK OF THE ASTEROID, THE by Laurence
Manning. .n 3 pt . . . . WS Dec 32 551
WRECKERS OF THE STAR PATROL by Malcolm
Jameson. .nt . . . . .SSS Aug 42 48

X

X–GAS, THE by Cyril Plunkett. .s . . . . . . AW Mar 30 812
X1–2–200 by Ray Cummings. .s. . . . . . . ASF Sep 38 59
X–RAY MURDER by Milton Kaletsky. .ss . . . .
. . . . Amz Sep 40 64
XANDLU by Jack Williamson. .n 3 pt . . . . WS Mar 34 806
XI EFFECT, THE by Philip Latham ps (Robert S.
Richardson). .s . . . . ASF Jan 50 6

Y

YANK AT VALHALLA, A by Edmond Hamilton. .n. . .
. . . . .SS Jan 41 14
YEAR FROM TONIGHT, A by Dorothy Quick. .s. . . . .
. . . . FA Jan 45 92
YEAR OF UNITING, THE by Hugh Raymond ps (John
Michel). .s . . . . SFQ Win 41–42 124
YEAR OF UNREASON, THE by J. Harvey
Haggard. .s . . . . TW Jun 38 84
YEAST MEN, THE by David H. Keller, M.D. . .s . . . . .
. . . . Amz Apr 28 26
                                         ToW Sum 39 70
                                         AFR #14 79
YEHUDI PRINCIPLE, THE by Fredric Brown. .s . . . . .
. . . . ASF May 44 68
YELLOW AIR PERIL, THE by Harl Vincent
(Schoepflin). .s . . . . AW Sep 29 198
YELLOW MEN OF MARS by Edgar Rice
Burroughs. .nt. . . . . Amz Aug 41 6
YELLOW MUD FOR COWARDS by P. F. Costello
h ps. .s . . . . Amz Sep 41 110
YELLOW SIGN, THE by Robert W. Chambers. .s . . . . .
. . . . FFM Sep 43 130
                                         AFR #2 81
YESTERDAY WAS MONDAY by Theodore
Sturgeon. .s . . . . UK Jun 41 112
                                         UK 48 54
YESTERDAY'S CLOCK by David Wright O'Brien . . . . .
. .nt . . . . FA Feb 43 106
YESTERDAY'S DOORS by Arthur J. Burks. .nt . . . . . .
. . . . TW Oct 48 65

Title. .Author. .Length . . . . Magazine. .Date. .Page No.

YESTERDAY'S FUTURAMA. .pictorial feature . . . . . .
. . . . .FFM May–Jun 40 114
YESTERDAY'S REVENGE by H. L. Nichols. .s . . . . . .
. . . . .Com Jan 41 114
YLLA by Ray Bradbury. .s . . . .
. . . . AFR #14 20
YOU ARE FORBIDDEN! by Jerry Sheldon. .s . . . . . .
. . . . TW Jun 47 89
YOU BET YOUR LIFE by Elroy Arno. .s . . . .
. . . . FA May 48 150
YOU CAN SAY THAT AGAIN by G. H. Irwin h ps . . . .
. .s . . . . FA Dec 43 112
"YOU CAN'T ESCAPE FROM MARS!" by E. K. Jarvis
h ps. .nt . . . . Amz Sep 50 6
YOU CAN'T KID LEFTY FEEP by Robert Bloch . . . . .
. .s . . . . FA Aug 43 148
YOU CAN'T SCARE ME! by Charles F. Myers. .nt . . . .
. . . . FA Mar 47 80
YOU CAN'T WIN by Malcolm Jameson. .s . . . .
. . . . ASF Nov 41 59
YOU MIGHT SAY VIRGINIA DARED by Dallas Ross
ps (Mack Reynolds). .s . . . . Amz Sep 50 70
YOU MUST FLEE AGAIN by Paul Spencer. .s . . . . . .
. . . . .FanS Nov 50 81
YOU ONLY LIVE TWICE by H. B. Hickey ps (Herb
Livingston). .s . . . . Amz Mar 50 112
YOU OUGHT TO BE DEAD by Robert Moore
Williams. .s . . . . .Amz Aug 41 86
YOU THOUGHT ME DEAD by William G. Bogart. . . . .
. .s . . . . UK Apr 39 63
YOU'LL SEE A PINK HOUSE by Wilm Carver. .s . . . . .
. . . . TW Win 45 85
YOUNG OLD MAN, THE by Earl L. Bell. .s . . . .
. . . . Amz Sep 29 504
YOUR NUMBER IS UP! by John W. Jakes. .s . . . .
. . . . Amz Dec 50 64
"YOUR ROPE IS WAITING!" by William Brengle
h ps. .s . . . . FA Aug 50 138
YOUR VIEWPOINT letter dept in AQ occasional
YOU'RE ALL ALONE by Fritz Leiber. .n . . . .
. . . . .FA Jul 50 8

Z

Z–DAY ON CENTAURI by Henry T. Simmons. .nt . . . .
. . . . PS Sum 48 4
ZAGRIBUD by John Russell Fearn. .n 3 pt . . . .
. . . . Amz Dec 37 58
ZARNAK by Max Plaisted. .comic
1. The Plunder Plague . . . . .TW Aug 36 65
2. The Metal World . . . . TW Oct 36 89
3. Madness on Mercury . . . . TW Dec 36 87
4. The Human Guinea Pig. . . . . TW Feb 37 63

Title. .Author. .Length . . . . Magazine. .Date. .Page No.

ZARNAK by Max Plaisted. .comic *(continued)*
  5. Etarre . . . . TW Apr 37 73
  6. The Supreme One, Master of Mercury . . . .
    . . . . TW Jun 37 101
  7. The Strange Deluge . . . . TW Aug 37 79
  8. Harnessed Elements . . . . TW Oct 37 87
ZEHRU OF XOLLAR by Hal K. Wells. .s . . . .
  . . . . ASF Feb 32 264
ZEOH–X by Ray Cummings. .s . . . . TW Apr 39 106
ZERO by Noel Loomis. .s . . . . .TW Sum 46 84
ZERO A.D. by Lee Francis *h ps*. .n . . . . . . FA Mar 48 90
ZERO AS A LIMIT by Robert Moore *(Williams)*. .s . . . .
  . . . . .ASF Jul 37 34
ZERO HOUR by Ray Bradbury. .s . . . . PS Fal 47 40
                                AFR #8 65
ZEUS, THE THUNDER GOD by Frank R. Paul . . . . . .
  . .bacover . . . . .FA Jul 42

Title. .Author. .Length . . . . Magazine. .Date. .Page No.

ZIGOR MEPHISTO'S COLLECTION OF MENTALIA by
  Richard S. Shaver. .nt . . . . Amz Jun 47 30
ZINA THE KILLER by Walter Livingston Martin . . . . .
  . .ss . . . . WQ Fal 31 108
ZONES OF SPACE by Max C. Sheridan. .s . . . .
  . . . . .TW Feb 38 38
ZORA OF THE ZOROMES by Neil R. Jones. .nt . . . . .
  . . . . Amz Mar 35 88
ZURK by Richard O. Lewis. .s . . . .
  . . . . .PS Win 41 92

NON-ALPHABETIC

!!! by X *ps (Donald A. Wollheim)*. .ss . . . . . Sti Apr 41 39

Checklist of Magazines Indexed

AIR WONDER STORIES *see WONDER STORIES*

AMAZING DETECTIVE TALES *see SCIENTIFIC DETECTIVE MONTHLY*

AMAZING STORIES

Date	Number	Page Size	No. of Pages	Cover Artist	
Apr 1926	V 1 N 1	8½x11	96	Frank R. Paul	
May 1926	2	"	"	"	"
Jun 1926	3	"	"	"	"
Jul 1926	4	"	"	"	"
Aug 1926	5	"	"	"	"
Sep 1926	6	"	"	"	"
Oct 1926	7	"	"	"	"
Nov 1926	8	"	"	"	"
Dec 1926	9	"	"	"	"
Jan 1927	10	"	"	"	"
Feb 1927	11	"	"	"	"
Mar 1927	12	"	"	"	"
Apr 1927	2 1	"	"	"	"
May 1927	2	"	"	"	"
Jun 1927	3	"	"	"	"
Jul 1927	4	"	"	"	"
Aug 1927	5	"	"	"	"
Sep 1927	6	"	"	"	"
Oct 1927	7	"	"	"	"
Nov 1927	8	"	"	"	"
Dec 1927	9	"	"	"	"
Jan 1928	10	"	"	"	"
Feb 1928	11	"	"	"	"
Mar 1928	12	"	"	"	"
Apr 1928	3 1	"	"	?	
May 1928	2	"	"	Frank R. Paul	
Jun 1928	3	"	"	"	"
Jul 1928	4	"	"	"	"
Aug 1928	5	"	"	"	"
Sep 1928	6	"	"	?	
Oct 1928	7	"	"	Frank R. Paul	
Nov 1928	8	"	"	"	"
Dec 1928	9	"	"	"	"
Jan 1929	10	"	"	"	"
Feb 1929	11	"	"	"	"
Mar 1929	12	"	"	"	"
Apr 1929	4 1	"	"	"	"
May 1929	2	"	"	"	"
Jun 1929	3	"	"	"	"
Jul 1929	4	"	"	Leo Morey	
Aug 1929	5	"	"	?	
Sep 1929	6	"	"	Frank R. Paul	

Date	Number	Page Size	No. of Pages	Cover Artist	
Oct 1929	V 4 N 7	8½x11	96	Leo Morey	
Nov 1929	8	"	"	"	"
Dec 1929	9	"	"	"	"
Jan 1930	10	"	"	"	"
Feb 1930	11	"	"	"	"
Mar 1930	12	"	"	"	"
Apr 1930	5 1	"	"	"	"
May 1930	2	"	"	"	"
Jun 1930	3	"	"	"	"
Jul 1930	4	"	"	"	"
Aug 1930	5	"	"	"	"
Sep 1930	6	"	"	"	"
Oct 1930	7	"	"	"	"
Nov 1930	8	"	"	"	"
Dec 1930	9	"	"	"	"
Jan 1931	10	"	"	"	"
Feb 1931	11	"	"	"	"
Mar 1931	12	"	"	"	"
Apr 1931	6 1	"	"	"	"
May 1931	2	"	"	"	"
Jun 1931	3	"	"	"	"
Jul 1931	4	"	"	"	"
Aug 1931	5	"	"	"	"
Sep 1931	6	"	"	"	"
Oct 1931	7	"	"	"	"
Nov 1931	8	"	"	"	"
Dec 1931	9	"	"	"	"
Jan 1932	10	"	"	"	"
Feb 1932	11	"	"	"	"
Mar 1932	12	"	"	"	"
Apr 1932	7 1	"	"	"	"
May 1932	2	"	"	"	"
Jun 1932	3	"	"	"	"
Jul 1932	4	"	"	"	"
Aug 1932	5	"	"	"	"
Sep 1932	6	"	"	"	"
Oct 1932	7	"	"	"	"
Nov 1932	8	"	"	"	"
Dec 1932	9	"	"	"	"
Jan 1933	10	"	" ?	"	"
Feb 1933	11	"	"	"	"
Mar 1933	12	"	"	"	"
Apr 1933	8 1	"	"	"	"
May 1933	2	"	"	"	"
Jun 1933	3	"	"	"	"
Jul 1933	4	"	"	"	"
Aug.–					
Sep 1933	5	"	"	Leo Morey	

Date	Number	Page Size	No. of Pages	Cover Artist
Oct 1933	V 8 N 6	7x10	144	Leo Morey
Nov 1933	7	"	"	" "
Dec 1933	8	"	"	" "
Jan 1934	9	"	"	" "
Feb 1934	10	"	"	" "
Mar 1934	11	"	"	" "
Apr 1934	12	"	"	" "
May 1934	9 1	"	"	" "
Jun 1934	2	"	"	" "
Jul 1934	3	"	"	" "
Aug 1934	4	"	"	" "
Sep 1934	5	"	"	" "
Oct 1934	6	"	"	" "
Nov 1934	7	"	"	" "
Dec 1934	8	"	"	" "
Jan 1935	9	"	"	" "
Feb 1935	10	"	"	" "
Mar 1935	11	"	"	" "
Apr 1935	10 1	"	"	" "
May 1935	2	"	"	" "
Jun 1935	3	"	"	" "
Jul 1935	4	"	"	" "
Aug 1935	5	"	"	" "
Oct 1935	6	"	"	" "
Dec 1935	7	"	"	" "
Feb 1936	8	"	"	" "
Apr 1936	9	"	"	" "
Jun 1936	10	"	"	" "
Aug 1936	11	"	"	" "
Oct 1936	12	"	"	" "
Dec 1936	13	"	"	" "
Feb 1937	11 1	"	"	" "
Apr 1937	2	"	"	" "
Jun 1937	3	"	"	" "
Aug 1937	4	"	"	" "
Oct 1937	5	"	"	" "
Dec 1937	6	"	"	" "
Feb 1938	12 1	"	"	" "
Apr 1938	2	"	"	" "
Jun 1938	3	"	"	(photo)
Aug 1938	4	"	"	" "
Oct 1938	5	"	"	Robert Fuqua
Nov 1938	6	"	"	" "
Dec 1938	7	"	"	" "
Jan 1939	13 1	"	"	" "
Feb 1939	2	"	"	" "
Mar 1939	3	"	"	" "
Apr 1939	4	"	"	" "
May 1939	5	"	"	" "
Jun 1939	6	"	"	William Juhre
July 1939	7	"	"	Robert Fuqua
Aug 1939	8	"	"	" "
Sep 1939	9	"	"	" "
Oct 1939	10	"	"	" "
Nov 1939	11	"	"	H. W. McCauley
Dec 1939	12	"	"	?

Date	Number	Page Size	No. of Pages	Cover Artist
Jan 1940	V14 N 1	7x10	144	Robert Fuqua
Feb 1940	2	"	"	C. L. Hartman
Mar 1940	3	"	"	H. W. McCauley
Apr 1940	4	"	"	H. R. Hammond
May 1940	5	"	"	C. L. Hartman
Jun 1940	6	"	"	Julian S. Krupa
Jul 1940	7	"	"	Robert Fuqua
Aug 1940	8	"	"	Julian S. Krupa & Leo Morey
Sep 1940	9	"	"	Robert Fuqua
Oct 1940	10	"	"	Leo Morey
Nov 1940	11	"	"	Robert Fuqua
Dec 1940	12	"	"	" "
Jan 1941	15 1	"	"	J. Allen St. John
Feb 1941	2	"	"	Leo Morey
Mar 1941	3	"	"	J. Allen St. John
Apr 1941	4	"	"	" "
May 1941	5	"	244	" "
Jun 1941	6	"	144	" "
Jul 1941	7	"	"	Stockton Mulford
Aug 1941	8	"	"	J. Allen St. John
Sep 1941	9	"	"	Robert Fuqua
Oct 1941	10	"	"	J. Allen St. John
Nov 1941	11	"	"	Robert Fuqua
Dec 1941	12	"	"	Rod Ruth
Jan 1942	16 1	"	244	Malcolm Smith
Feb 1942	2	"	"	L. Raymond Jones
Mar 1942	3	"	276	Robert Fuqua
Apr 1942	4	"	"	" "
May 1942	5	"	"	H. W. McCauley
Jun 1942	6	"	"	?
Jul 1942	7	"	"	J. Allen St. John
Aug 1942	8	"	244	H. W. McCaulley
Sep 1942	9	"	"	James D. Settles
Oct 1942	10	"	"	Malcolm Smith
Nov 1942	11	"	"	Robert Gibson Jones
Dec 1942	12	"	"	J. Allen St. John
Jan 1943	17 1	"	"	" "
Feb 1943	2	"	"	" "
Mar 1943	3	"	"	Robert Fuqua
Apr 1943	4	"	"	" "
May 1943	5	"	"	H. W. McCaulley
Jun 1943	6	"	212	Hadden
Jul 1943	7	"	"	H. W. McCaulley
Aug 1943	8	"	"	Robert Fuqua
Sep 1943	9	"	"	Robert Gibson Jones
Nov 1943	10	"	"	" "
Jan 1944	18 1	"	"	Robert Fuqua
Mar 1944	2	"	"	J. Allen St. John
May 1944	3	"	"	Malcolm Smith
Sep 1944	4	"	"	Julian S. Krupa
Dec 1944	5	"	"	James D. Settles
Mar 1945	19 1	"	"	Robert Gibson Jones

Date	Number	Page Size	No. of Pages	Cover Artist
Jun 1945	V13 N 2	7x10	212	Robert Gibson Jones
Sep 1945	3	"	180	" "
Dec 1945	4	"	"	" "
Feb 1946	20 1	"	"	Malcolm Smith
May 1946	2	"	"	Arnold Kohn
Jun 1946	3	"	"	" "
Jul 1946	4	"	"	Walter Parke
Aug 1946	5	"	"	H. W. McCaulley
Sep 1946	6	"	"	Robert Gibson Jones
Oct 1946	7	"	"	" "
Nov 1946	8	"	"	Arnold Kohn
Dec 1946	9	"	"	Bob Hilbreth
Jan 1947	21 1	"	"	McCaulley
Feb 1947	2	"	"	R. G. Jones
Mar 1947	3	"	"	Jones
Apr 1947	4	"	"	Krupa
May 1947	5	"	"	James Teason
Jun 1947	6	"	"	Jones
Jul 1947	7	"	"	Krupa
Aug 1947	8	"	"	Kohn
Sep 1947	9	"	"	Smith
Oct 1947	10	"	"	Jones
Nov 1947	11	"	"	Robert Gibson Jones
Dec 1947	12	"	"	Jones
Jan 1948	22 1	"	"	Ramon Naylor
Feb 1948	2	"	"	Smith
Mar 1948	3	"	"	Jones
Apr 1948	4	"	"	" "
May 1948	5	"	"	" "
Jun 1948	6	"	"	" "
Jul 1948	7	"	166	Kohn
Aug 1948	8	"	164	Jones
Sep 1948	9	"	156	" "
Oct 1948	10	"	"	Settles
Nov 1948	11	"	"	Jones
Dec 1948	12	"	"	McCaulley
Jan 1949	23 1	"	"	St. John
Feb 1949	2	"	"	Jones
Mar 1949	3	"	"	Edmond Swiatek
Apr 1949	4	"	"	Kohn
May 1949	5	"	"	McCaulley
Jun 1949	6	"	.148	Kohn
Jul 1949	7	"	"	Jones
Aug 1949	8	"	"	Kohn
Sep 1949	9	"	164	Richard Loehe
Oct 1949	10	"	"	McCaulley
Nov 1949	11	"	"	Kohn
Dec 1949	12	"	"	Jones
Jan 1950	24 1	"	"	Kohn
Feb 1950	2	"	"	Jones
Mar 1950	3	"	196	" "
Apr 1950	4	"	"	" "
May 1950	5	"	"	Kohn
Jun 1950	6	"	"	Robert Gibson Jones
Jul 1950	7	"	"	" "
Aug 1950	8	"	"	" "
Sep 1950	9	"	180	" "
Oct 1950	10	"	164	" "
Nov 1950	11	"	"	" "
Dec 1950	12	"	"	James D. Settles

AMAZING STORIES ANNUAL

Date	Number	Page Size	No. of Pages	Cover Artist
1927	V 1 N 1	8½x11	128	Frank R. Paul

AMAZING STORIES QUARTERLY

Date	Number	Page Size	No. of Pages	Cover Artist
Win 1928	V 1 N 1	8½x11	144	Paul
Spr 1928 Apr	2	"	"	" "
Sum 1928 Jul	3	"	"	" "
Fal 1928 Oct	4	"	"	" "
Win 1929 Jan	2 1	"	"	" "
Spr 1929 Apr	2	"	"	" "
Sum 1929 Jul	3	"	"	" "
Fal 1929 Oct	4	"	"	Wesso
Win 1930 Jan	3 1	"	"	?
Spr 1930 Apr	2	"	"	?
Sum 1930 Jul	3	"	"	Morey
Fal 1930 Oct	4	"	"	" "
Win 1930 Jan 1931	4 1	"	"	" "
Spr 1931 Apr	2	"	"	" "
Sum 1931 Jul	3	"	"	" "
Fall 1931 Oct	4	"	"	" "
Win 1932 Jan	5 1	"	"	" "
Spr-Sum 1932 Apr	2	"	"	" "
Fall-Win 1932 Sep	3	"	"	" "

Date	Number	Page Size	No. of Pages	Cover Artist
Spr-Sum 1933	V 6 N 4	8½x11	144	Morey
Win 1933	7 1	"	"	" "
Fal 1934	2	"	"	" "

ASTONISHING STORIES

Date	Number	Page Size	No. of Pages	Cover Artist
Feb 1940	V 1 N 1	7x9½	112	Binder
Apr 1940	2	"	"	" "
Jun 1940	3	"	"	Gabriel Mayorga
Aug 1940	4	"	"	?
Oct 1940	2 1	"	"	Gabriel Mayorga
Dec 1940	2	"	"	Bob Sherry
Feb 1941	3	"	"	Leo Morey
Apr 1941	4	"	"	? (R. C. S.)
Sep 1941	3 1	"	"	(R. S.)
Nov 1941	2	"	"	?
Mar 1942	3	"	"	Wesso
Jun 1942	4	"	"	Virgil Finlay
Oct 1942	4 1	"	"	Leo Morey
Dec 1942	2	"	"	Stephen Lawrence
Feb 1943	3	"	"	Milton Luros
Apr 1943	4	"	"	" "

ASTOUNDING STORIES

Date	Number	Page Size	No. of Pages	Cover Artist
Jan 1930	V 1 N 1	7x10	144	H. W. Wessolowski
Feb 1930	2	"	"	" "
Mar 1930	3	"	"	" "
Apr 1930	2 1	"	"	" "
May 1930	2	"	"	" "
Jun 1930	3	"	"	" "
Jul 1930	3 1	"	"	" "
Aug 1930	2	"	"	" "
Sep 1930	3	"	"	" "
Oct 1930	4 1	"	"	" "
Nov 1930	2	"	"	" "
Dec 1930	3	"	"	" "
Jan 1931	5 1	"	"	H. W. Wesso
Feb 1931	2	"	"	" "
Mar 1931	3	"	"	" "
Apr 1931	6 1	"	"	" "
May 1931	2	"	"	" "
Jun 1931	3	"	"	" "
Jul 1931	7 1	"	"	" "
Aug 1931	2	"	"	" "
Sep 1931	3	"	"	" "
Oct 1931	8 1	"	"	" "
Nov 1931	2	"	"	" "
Dec 1931	3	"	"	" "
Jan 1932	9 1	"	"	" "
Feb 1932	2	"	"	" "
Mar 1932	3	"	"	" "
Apr 1932	10 1	"	"	" "

Date	Number	Page Size	No. of Pages	Cover Artist
May 1932	V10 N 1	7x10	144	H. W. Wesso
Jun 1932	3	"	"	" "
Sep 1932	11 1	"	"	" "
Nov 1932	2	"	"	" "
Jan 1933	3	"	"	" "
Mar 1933	12 1	"	"	?
Oct 1933	2	"	"	?
Nov 1933	3	"	"	?
Dec 1933	4	"	"	?
Jan 1934	5	"	"	Howard V. Brown
Feb 1934	6	"	"	" "
Mar 1934	13 1	"	160	" "
Apr 1934	2	"	"	" "
May 1934	3	"	"	" "
Jun 1934	4	"	"	" "
Jul 1934	5	"	"	" "
Aug 1934	6	"	"	" "
Sep 1934	14 1	"	"	" "
Oct 1934	2	"	"	" "
Nov 1934	3	"	"	" "
Dec 1934	4	"	"	" "
Jan 1935	5	"	"	" "
Feb 1935	6	"	"	" "
Mar 1935	15 1	"	"	" "
Apr 1935	2	"	"	" "
May 1935	3	"	"	" "
Jun 1935	4	"	"	" "
Jul 1935	5	"	"	" "
Aug 1935	6	"	"	" "
Sep 1935	16 1	"	"	" "
Oct 1935	2	"	"	" "
Nov 1935	3	"	"	" "
Dec 1935	4	"	"	" "
Jan 1936	5	"	"	" "
Feb 1936	6	"	"	" "
Mar 1936	17 1	"	"	" "
Apr 1936	2	"	"	" "
May 1936	3	"	"	" "
Jun 1936	4	"	"	" "
Jul 1936	5	"	"	" "
Aug 1936	6	"	"	" "
Sep 1936	18 1	"	"	" "
Oct 1936	2	"	"	" "
Nov 1936	3	"	"	" "
Dec 1936	4	"	"	" "
Jan 1937	5	"	"	" "
Feb 1937	6	"	"	" "
Mar 1937	19 1	"	"	" "
Apr 1937	2	"	"	" "
May 1937	3	"	"	" "
Jun 1937	4	"	"	H. W. Wesso
Jul 1937	5	"	"	Howard V. Brown
Aug 1937	6	"	"	" "
Sep 1937	20 1	"	"	H. W. Wesso
Oct 1937	2	"	"	Howard V. Brown
Nov 1937	3	"	"	H. W. Wesso

Date	Number	Page Size	No. of Pages	Cover Artist
Dec 1937	V20 N 4	7x10	160	Howard V. Brown
Jan 1938	5	"	"	H. W. Wesso
Feb 1937	6	"	"	Howard V. Brown

Changed to:
ASTOUNDING SCIENCE FICTION

Date	Number	Page Size	No. of Pages	Cover Artist
Mar 1938	21 1	"	"	H. W. Wesso
Apr 1938	2	"	"	Howard V. Brown
May 1938	3	"	"	Schneeman
Jun 1938	4	"	"	H. W. Wesso
Jul 1938	5	"	"	H. W. Brown
Aug 1938	6	"	"	Wesso
Sep 1938	22 1	"	"	Thomson
Oct 1938	2	"	"	H. W. Brown
Nov 1938	3	"	"	" "
Dec 1938	4	"	"	Schneeman
Jan 1939	5	"	"	John Frew
Feb 1939	6	"	"	Rogers
Mar 1939	23 1	"	"	Graves Gladney
Apr 1939	2	"	"	Schneeman
May 1939	3	"	"	Carlson
Jun 1939	4	"	"	Graves Gladney
Jul 1939	5	"	"	" "
Aug 1939	6	"	"	Finlay
Sep 1939	24 1	"	"	Rogers
Oct 1939	2	"	"	" "
Nov 1939	3	"	"	" "
Dec 1939	4	"	"	Gilmore
Jan 1940	5	"	"	Schneeman
Feb 1940	6	"	"	Rogers
Mar 1940	25 1	"	"	Gilmore
Apr 1940	2	"	"	Rogers
May 1940	3	"	"	" "
Jun 1940	4	"	"	" "
Jul 1940	5	"	"	" "
Aug 1940	6	"	"	" "
Sep 1940	26 1	"	"	" "
Oct 1940	2	"	"	" "
Nov 1940	3	"	"	" "
Dec 1940	4	"	"	" "
Jan 1941	5	"	"	" "
Feb 1941	6	"	"	" "
Mar 1941	27 1	"	"	" "
Apr 1941	2	"	"	" "
May 1941	3	"	"	" "
Jun 1941	4	"	"	" "
Jul 1941	5	"	"	" "
Aug 1941	6	"	"	" "
Sep 1941	28 1	"	"	" "
Oct 1941	2	"	"	" "
Nov 1941	3	"	"	" "
Dec 1941	4	"	"	" "
Jan 1942	5	11½x8½	132	" "
Feb 1942	6	"	"	" "
Mar 1942	29 1	"	"	" "
Apr 1942	V29 N 2	11½x8½	132	Rogers
May 1942	3	"	"	" "
Jun 1942	4	"	"	" "
Jul 1942	5	"	"	" "
Aug 1942	6	"	"	" "
Sep 1942	30 1	"	"	William Timmins
Oct 1942	2	"	"	A. von Munchausen
Nov 1942	3	"	"	Modest Stein
Dec 1942	4	"	"	William Timmins
Jan 1943	5	"	"	" "
Feb 1943	6	"	"	" "
Mar 1943	31 1	"	"	" "
Apr 1943	2	"	"	" "
May 1943	3	7x9½	164	" "
Jun 1943	4	"	"	" "
Jul 1943	5	"	"	" "
Aug 1943	6	"	"	" "
Sep 1943	32 1	"	"	" "
Oct 1943	2	"	"	" "
Nov 1943	3	5½x8	180	" "
Dec 1943	4	"	"	" "
Jan 1944	5	"	"	" "
Feb 1944	6	"	"	" "
Mar 1944	33 1	"	"	" "
Apr 1944	2	"	"	" "
May 1944	3	"	"	" "
Jun 1944	4	"	"	" "
Jul 1944	5	"	"	Fred Haucke
Aug 1944	6	"	"	Timmins
Sep 1944	34 1	"	"	" "
Oct 1944	2	"	"	" "
Nov 1944	3	"	"	" "
Dec 1944	4	"	"	" "
Jan 1945	5	"	"	" "
Feb 1945	6	"	"	" "
Mar 1945	35 1	"	"	" "
Apr 1945	2	"	"	" "
May 1945	3	"	"	" "
Jun 1945	4	"	"	" "
Jul 1945	5	"	"	" "
Aug 1945	6	"	"	" "
Sep 1945	36 1	"	"	" "
Oct 1945	2	"	"	" "
Nov 1945	3	"	"	" "
Dec 1945	4	"	"	" "
Jan 1946	5	"	"	" "
Feb 1946	6	"	"	" "
Mar 1946	37 1	"	"	" "
Apr 1946	2	"	"	" "
May 1946	3	"	"	" "
Jun 1946	4	"	"	" "
Jul 1946	5	"	"	" "
Aug 1946	6	"	"	" "
Sep 1946	38 1	"	"	" "
Oct 1946	2	"	"	" "

Date	Number	Page Size	No. of Pages	Cover Artist
Nov 1946	V38 N 3	5½x8	180	Timmins
Dec 1946	4	"	"	Alejandro
Jan 1947	5	"	"	Timmins
Feb 1947	6	"	"	Sniffen
Mar 1947	39 1	"	160	Rogers
Apr 1947	2	"	"	Timmins
May 1947	3	"	"	Rogers
Jun 1947	4	"	"	Schneeman
Jul 1947	5	"	"	Timmins
Aug 1947	6	"	"	Rogers
Sep 1947	40 1	"	"	Alejandro
Oct 1947	2	"	"	Bonestell
Nov 1947	3	"	"	Rogers
Dec 1947	4	"	"	Alejandro
Jan 1948	5	"	"	Rogers
Feb 1948	6	"	"	Alejandro
Mar 1948	50 1	"	"	Rogers
Apr 1948	41 2	"	"	Bonestell
May 1948	3	"	"	Alejandro
Jun 1948	4	"	"	Timmins
Jul 1948	5	"	"	Bonestell
Aug 1948	6	"	"	Canedo
Sep 1948	42 1	"	"	Bonestell
Oct 1948	2	"	"	Rogers
Nov 1948	3	"	"	" "
Dec 1948	4	"	"	Orban
Jan 1949	5	"	"	Rogers
Feb 1949	6	"	"	" "
Mar 1949	43 1	"	"	Alejandro
Apr 1949	2	"	"	Santry
May 1949	3	"	"	Orban
Jun 1949	4	"	"	Bonestell
Jul 1949	5	"	"	Rogers
Aug 1949	6	"	"	" "
Sep 1949	44 1	"	"	Orban
Oct 1949	2	"	"	Alejandro
Nov 1949	3	"	"	Rogers
Dec 1949	4	"	"	Zboyan
Jan 1950	5	"	"	Bonestell
Feb 1950	6	"	"	Rogers
Mar 1950	45 1	"	"	" "
Apr 1950	2	"	"	" "
May 1950	3	"	"	Brush
Jun 1950	4	"	"	Miller
Jul 1950	5	"	"	"Destination Moon" photo
Aug 1950	6	"	"	Miller
Sep 1950	46 1	"	"	" "
Oct 1950	2	"	"	Cartier
Nov 1950	3	"	"	Pattee
Dec 1950	4	"	"	Timmins

AVON FANTASY READER

Date	Number	Page Size	No. of Pages	Cover Artist
N/d (1947)	N 1	5½x8	132	?
(1947)	2	"	"	?
(1947)	3	"	"	?
(1947)	4	"	"	?
(1947)	5	"	"	?
(1948)	6	"	126	?
(1948)	7	"	"	?
(1948)	8	"	"	?
(1949)	9	"	130	?
(1949)	10	"	128	?
(1949)	11	"	130	?
(1950)	12	"	"	?
(1950)	13	"	"	?
(1950)	14	"	"	?

CAPTAIN FUTURE

Date	Number	Page Size	No. of Pages	Cover Artist
Win 1940	V 1 N 1	7x10	132	Rosen
Spr 1940	2	"	"	?
Sum 1940	3	"	"	?
Fal 1940	2 1	"	"	Bergey
Win 1941	2	"	"	" "
Spr 1941	3	"	"	?
Sum 1941	3 1	"	"	Bergey
Fal 1941	2	"	"	?
Win 1942	3	"	"	?
Spr 1942	4 1	"	"	?
Sum 1942	2	"	"	?
Fal 1942	3	"	"	?
Win 1943	5 1	"	"	?
Spr 1943	2	"	"	?
Sum 1943	3	"	"	Earle K. Bergey
Win 1944	6 1	"	"	" "
Spr 1944	2	"	"	" "

COMET STORIES

Date	Number	Page Size	No. of Pages	Cover Artist
Dec 1940	V 1 N 1	7x10	128	Morey
Jan 1941	2	"	"	Frank Paul
Mar 1941	3	"	"	Leo Morey
May 1941	4	"	"	Frank R. Paul
Jul 1941	5	"	"	Leo Morey

COSMIC STORIES

Date	Number	Page Size	No. of Pages	Cover Artist
Mar 1941	V 1 N 1	7x10	132	Morey
May 1941	2	"	"	Hannes Bok
Jul 1941	3	"	116	Elliott Dold

Date	Number	Page Size	No. of Pages	Cover Artist

DYNAMIC SCIENCE STORIES

Date	Number	Page Size	No. of Pages	Cover Artist
Feb 1939	V 1 N 1	7x10	116	Frank R. Paul
Apr-May 1939	2	"	"	Norman Saunders

FAMOUS FANTASTIC MYSTERIES

Date	Number	Page Size	No. of Pages	Cover Artist
Sept-Oct 1939	V 1 N 1	7x10	128	No Cover Picture
Nov 1939	2	"	"	" "
Dec 1939	3	"	"	" "
Jan 1940	4	"	"	" "
Feb 1940	5	"	"	" "
Mar 1940	6	"	"	Virgil Finlay
Apr 1940	2 1	"	"	Frank R. Paul
May-June 1940	2	"	"	" "
Aug 1940	3	"	"	Virgil Finlay
Oct 1940	4	"	112	" "
Dec 1940	5	"	"	Frank R. Paul
Feb 1941	6	"	"	Virgil Finlay
Apr 1941	3 1	"	"	" "
Jun 1941	2	"	128	" "
Aug 1941	3	"	"	" "
Oct 1941	4	"	"	" "
Dec 1941	5	"	"	" "
Feb 1942	6	"	"	" "
Apr 1942	4 1	"	"	" "
Jun 1942	2	"	144	" "
Jul 1942	3	"	"	" "
Aug 1942	4	"	"	" "
Sep 1942	5	"	"	" "
Oct 1942	6	"	"	" "
Nov 1942	5 1	"	"	" "
Dec 1942	2	"	"	" "
Mar 1943	3	"	"	" "
Sep 1943	4	"	"	" "
Dec 1943	5	"	"	Lawrence
Mar 1944	6	"	"	" "
Jun 1944	6 1	"	132	" "
Sep 1944	2	"	"	" "
Dec 1944	3	"	"	" "
Mar 1945	4	"	"	" "
Jun 1945	5	"	"	" "
Sep 1945	6	"	"	" "
Dec 1945	7 1	"	"	" "
Feb 1946	2	"	"	" "
Apr 1946	3	"	"	" "
Jun 1946	4	"	"	" "
Aug 1946	5	"	"	" "
Oct 1946	8 1	"	"	" "
Dec 1946	2	"	"	Finlay
Feb 1947	3	"	"	" "
Apr 1947	4	"	"	Lawrence
Jun 1947	V 8 N 5	7x10	132	Finlay
Aug 1947	6	"	"	" "
Oct 1947	9 1	"	"	Lawrence
Dec 1947	2	"	"	Finlay
Feb 1948	3	"	"	" "
Apr 1948	4	"	"	Lawrence
Jun 1948	5	"	"	Finlay
Aug 1948	6	"	"	Lawrence
Oct 1948	10 1	"	"	" "
Dec 1948	2	"	"	" "
Feb 1949	3	"	"	" "
Apr 1949	4	"	"	" "
Jun 1949	5	"	"	" "
Aug 1949	6	"	"	" "
Oct 1949	11 1	"	"	" "
Dec 1949	2	"	"	" "
Feb 1950	3	"	"	" "
Apr 1950	4	"	"	" "
Jun 1950	5	"	"	Saunders
Aug 1950	6	"	"	" "
Oct 1950	12 1	"	"	De Soto

FANTASTIC ADVENTURES

Date	Number	Page Size	No. of Pages	Cover Artist
May 1939	V 1 N 1	8½x11¼	100	Robert Fuqua
Jul 1939	2	"	"	Leo Morey
Sep 1939	3	"	"	H. W. McCaulley
Nov 1939	4	"	"	Robert Fuqua
Jan 1940	2 1	"	"	H. W. McCaulley
Feb 1940	2	"	"	Robert Fuqua
Mar 1940	3	"	"	" "
Apr 1940	4	"	"	Frank R. Paul
May 1940	5	"	"	Stockton Mulford
Jun 1940	6	7x10	148	" "
Aug 1940	7	"	"	H. W. McCaulley
Oct 1940	8	"	"	J. Allen St. John
Jan 1941	3 1	"	"	H. W. McCaulley
Mar 1941	2	"	"	J. Allen St. John
May 1941	3	"	"	Robert Fuqua
Jun 1941	4	"	"	H. W. McCaulley
Jul 1941	5	"	"	J. Allen St. John & H. W. McCaulley
Aug 1941	6	"	"	Rod Ruth
Sep 1941	7	"	"	Robert Fuqua
Oct 1941	8	"	"	H. W. McCaulley
Nov 1941	9	"	"	J. Allen St. John
Dec 1941	10	"	"	Rod Ruth
Jan 1942	4 1	"	"	H. W. McCaulley
Feb 1942	2	"	"	Robert Fuqua & H. W. McCaulley
Mar 1942	3	"	"	J. Allen St. John
Apr 1942	4	"	244	Malcolm Smith
May 1942	5	"	"	" "
Jun 1942	6	"	"	" "
Jul 1942	7	"	"	J. Allen St. John

Date	Number	Page Size	No. of Pages	Cover Artist
Aug 1942	V 4 N 8	7x10	244	Robert Gibson Jones
Sep 1942	9	"	"	H. W. McCaulley
Oct 1942	10	"	"	J. Allen St. John
Nov 1942	11	"	"	H. W. McCaulley
Dec 1942	12	"	"	" "
Jan 1943	5 1	"	"	Robert Gibson Jones
Feb 1943	2	"	"	" "
Mar 1943	3	"	"	" "
Apr 1943	4	"	"	Malcolm Smith
May 1943	5	"	"	H. W. McCaulley
Jun 1943	6	"	212	" "
Jul 1943	7	"	"	Robert Gibson Jones
Aug 1943	8	"	"	" "
Oct 1943	9	"	"	" "
Dec 1943	10	"	"	" "
Feb 1944	6 1	"	"	Rod Ruth
Apr 1944	2	"	"	J. Allen St. John
Jun 1944	3	"	"	Robert Gibson Jones
Oct 1944	4	"	"	J. Allen St. John
Jan 1945	7 1	"	"	Robert Gibson Jones
Apr 1945	2	"	"	R. E. Epperley
Jul 1945	3	"	"	Arnold Kohn
Oct 1945	4	"	180	J. Allen St. John
Dec 1945	5	"	"	Paul Lehman
Feb 1946	8 1	"	"	Walter Parke
May 1946	2	"	"	H. W. McCaulley
Jul 1946	3	"	"	Arnold Kohn
Sep 1946	4	"	"	" "
Nov 1946	5	"	"	J. Allen St. John
Jan 1947	9 1	"	"	Robert Gibson Jones
Mar 1947	2	"	"	" "
May 1947	3	"	"	" "
Jul 1947	4	"	"	H. W. McCaulley
Sep 1947	5	"	178	Robert Gibson Jones
Oct 1947	6	"	180	" "
Nov 1947	7	"	"	" "
Dec 1947	8	"	"	" "
Jan 1948	10 1	"	"	" "
Feb 1948	2	"	"	" "
Mar 1948	3	"	"	" "
Apr 1948	4	"	"	" "
May 1948	5	"	"	" "
Jun 1948	6	"	"	" "
Jul 1948	7	"	164	Ramon Naylor
Aug 1948	8	"	"	Walter Haskell Jones
Sep 1948	9	"	156	Robert Gibson Jones
Oct 1948	10	"	"	" "

Date	Number	Page Size	No. of Pages	Cover Artist
Nov 1948	V10 N11	7x10	156	Arnold Kohn
Dec 1948	12	"	"	Malcolm Smith
Jan 1949	11 1	"	"	Robert Gibson Jones
Feb 1949	2	"	"	Arnold Kohn
Mar 1949	3	"	"	" "
Apr 1949	4	"	"	Edmond Swiatek
May 1949	5	"	"	Robert Gibson Jones
Jun 1940	6	"	148	James B. Settles
Jul 1949	7	"	"	" "
Aug 1949	8	"	"	Arnold Kohn
Sep 1949	9	"	164	Robert Gibson Jones
Oct 1949	10	"	"	Edmond Swiatek
Nov 1949	11	"	"	Robert Gibson Jones
Dec 1949	12	"	"	Edmond Swiatek
Jan 1950	12 1	"	"	Ramon Naylor
Feb 1950	2	"	"	Robert Gibson Jones
Mar 1950	3	"	"	" "
Apr 1950	4	"	"	" "
May 1950	5	"	"	H. J. Blumenfeld
Jun 1950	6	"	"	Robert Gibson Jones
Jul 1950	7	"	"	" "
Aug 1950	8	"	"	H. W. McCaulley
Sep 1950	9	"	148	Robert Gibson Jones
Oct 1950	10	"	132	" "
Nov 1950	11	"	"	" "
Dec 1950	12	"	"	" "

FANTASTIC NOVELS

Date	Number	Page Size	No. of Pages	Cover Artist
Jul 1940	1 1	7x10	144	Virgil Finlay
Sep 1940	2	"	"	Paul
Nov 1940	3	"	128	Virgil Finlay
Jan 1941	4	"	"	" "
Apr 1941	5	"	112	" "
Mar 1948	6	"	132	Lawrence
May 1948	2 1	"	"	" "
Jul 1948	2	"	"	" "
Sep 1948	3	"	"	" "
Nov 1948	4	"	"	Finlay
Jan 1949	5	"	"	Lawrence
Mar 1949	6	"	"	Finlay
May 1949	3 1	"	"	Lawrence
Jul 1949	2	"	"	" "
Sep 1949	3	"	"	" "
Nov 1949	4	"	"	Finlay
Jan 1950	5	"	"	Lawrence
Mar 1950	6	"	"	Saunders
May 1950	4 1	"	"	" "

Date	Number	Page Size	No. of Pages	Cover Artist
Jul 1950	V 4 N 2	7x10	132	Lawrence
Sep 1950	3	”	”	Saunders
Nov 1950	4	”	”	De Soto

FANTASTIC STORY QUARTERLY

Date	Number	Page Size	No. of Pages	Cover Artist
Spr 1950	V 1 N 1	7x10	164	Bergey
Sum 1950	2	”	”	Earle Bergey
Fal 1950	3	”	”	” ”

FANTASY (British)

Date	Number	Page Size	No. of Pages	Cover Artist
1938	N 1	7x10	128	S. R. Drigin
1939	2	”	”	” ”
1939	3	”	”	” ”
Dec 1946	V 1 N 1	5½x8½	96	” ”
Apr 1947	2	”	”	?
Aug 1947	3	”	”	?

FANTASY BOOK

Date	Number	Page Size	No. of Pages	Cover Artist
n/d (1947)	V 1 N 1	9x12	44	Milo
(1947)	2	”	”	Crozetti
(1948)	3	5½x8½	68	Loyd Crozetti (Roy Hunt)
(1948)	4	”	”	Neil Austin
(1949)	5	5¼x8	84	?
(1950)	6	5x7¼	116	Jack Gaughan

FANTASY FICTION

Date	Number	Page Size	No. of Pages	Cover Artist
May 1950	V 1 N 1	5¼x8	128	Bill Stone (photo)

change to FANTASY STORIES

Date	Number	Page Size	No. of Pages	Cover Artist
Nov 1950	1 2	”	”	” ”

FROM UNKNOWN WORLDS see UNKNOWN

FUTURE FICTION

Date	Number	Page Size	No. of Pages	Cover Artist
Nov 1939	V 1 N 1	7x10	114	J. W. Scott
Mar 1940	2	”	”	” ”
Jul 1940	3	”	”	” ”
Nov 1940	4	”	”	Paul
Apr 1941	5	”	”	” ”
Aug 1941	6	”	”	(John) Forte

Changed to:

FUTURE COMBINED WITH SCIENCE FICTION

Date	Number	Page Size	No. of Pages	Cover Artist
Oct 1941	2 1	”	”	Hannes Bok
Dec 1941	2	”	”	” ”
Feb 1942	3	”	”	” ”

Date	Number	Page Size	No. of Pages	Cover Artist
Apr 1942	V 2 N 4	7x10	114	John R. Forte, Jr.
Jun 1942	5	”	”	” ”
Aug 1942	6	”	”	” ”

Changed to:

FUTURE FANTASY AND SCIENCE FICTION

Date	Number	Page Size	No. of Pages	Cover Artist
Oct 1942	3 1	”	”	Hannes Bok
Dec 1942	2	”	”	Robert C. Sherry
Feb 1943	3	”	”	Milton Luros

Changed to:

FUTURE COMBINED WITH SCIENCE FICTION STORIES

Date	Number	Page Size	No. of Pages	Cover Artist
May–Jun 1950	1 1	7x10	100	Earle K. Bergey
Jul-Aug 1950	1 2	”	”	” ”
Sep-Oct 1950	3	”	”	Leo Morey
Nov 1950	4	”	”	Milton Luros

GALAXY SCIENCE FICTION

Date	Number	Page Size	No. of Pages	Cover Artist
Oct 1950	V 1 N 1	7½x5½	160	David Stone
Nov 1950	2	”	”	Don Sibley
Dec 1950	3	”	”	Don Hunter

GALAXY SCIENCE FICTION NOVELS

Date	Number	Page Size	No. of Pages	Cover Artist
1950	N 1	5½x7½	160	Dave Stone
1950	2	”	”	Calle

IMAGINATION

Date	Number	Page Size	No. of Pages	Cover Artist
Oct 1950	1 1	5½x8	164	Hannes Bok
Dec 1950	2	”	”	Harold McCauley

MAGAZINE OF FANTASY

Date	Number	Page Size	No. of Pages	Cover Artist
Fal 1949	1 1	5½x8	128	Photo by Bill Stone

Change to:

MAGAZINE OF FANTASY AND SCIENCE FICTION

Date	Number	Page Size	No. of Pages	Cover Artist
Win-Spr 1950	1 2	”	”	George Salter
Sum 1950	3	”	”	” ”
Fal 1950	4	”	”	” ”
Dec 1950	5	”	”	Chesley Bonestell

MARVEL SCIENCE STORIES

Date	Number	Page Size	No. of Pages	Cover Artist
Aug 1938	1 1	7x10	128	Norman Saunders
Nov 1938	2	”	”	Frank R. Paul

Date	Number	Page Size	No. of Pages	Cover Artist
Feb 1939	V 1 N 3	7x10	128	Wesso
Apr-May 1939	4	"	"	Norman Saunders
Aug 1939	5	"	114	Scott

Change to:
MARVEL TALES

Date	Number	Page Size	No. of Pages	Cover Artist
Dec 1939	1 6	"	"	?
May 1940	2 1	"	"	?

Change to:
MARVEL STORIES

Date	Number	Page Size	No. of Pages	Cover Artist
Nov 1940	2	"	"	Scott
Apr 1941	3	"	"	" "

Change to:
MARVEL SCIENCE STORIES

Date	Number	Page Size	No. of Pages	Cover Artist
Nov 1950	3 1	6½x9½	132	Norman Saunders

A. MERRITT FANTASY

Date	Number	Page Size	No. of Pages	Cover Artist
Dec 1949	1 1	7x9½	132	Lawrence
Feb 1950	2	"	"	Saunders
Apr 1950	3	"	"	" "
Jul 1950	4	"	"	" "
Oct 1950	2 1	"	"	" "

MIRACLE STORIES

Date	Number	Page Size	No. of Pages	Cover Artist
Apr-May 1931	1 1	7x10	144	Elliott Dold
Jun-Jul 1931	2	"	"	" "

NEW WORLDS (British)

Date	Number	Page Size	No. of Pages	Cover Artist
1946	1 1	7½x10	64	R. A. Wilkin
1946	2	"	"	Victor Caesari
n/d	3	"	"	Slack
1949	2 4	8½x5½	88	Dennis
1949	5	"	96	Clothier
Spr 1950	6	"	"	" "
Sum 1950	3 7	"	"	" "
Win 1950	8	"	"	" "

OTHER WORLDS

Date	Number	Page Size	No. of Pages	Cover Artist
Nov 1949	1 1	5½x8	160	Malcolm Smith
Jan 1950	2	"	"	" "
Mar 1950	3	"	"	" "
May 1950	4	"	"	" "
Jul 1950	2 1	"	"	" "
Sep 1950	2	"	"	" "
Oct 1950	3	"	"	Malcolm Smith & Arnold Kohn
Nov 1950	4	"	"	Hannes Bok

OUT OF THIS WORLD

OUT OF THIS WORLD ADVENTURES

Date	Number	Page Size	No. of Pages	Cover Artist
Jul 1950	1 1	7x9½	132	?
Dec 1950	2	"	"	?

PLANET STORIES

Date	Number	Page Size	No. of Pages	Cover Artist
Win 1939 Nov	1 1	7x10	128	A. Drake
Spr 1940 Feb	2	"	"	?
Sum 1940 May	3	"	"	A. Drake
Fal 1940 Aug	4	"	"	" "
Win 1940–1941 Nov 1940	5	"	"	" "
Spr 1941 Feb	6	"	"	" "
Sum 1941 May	7	"	"	Virgil Finlay
Fal 1941 Aug	8	"	"	Paul
Win 1941–1942 Nov 1941	9	"	"	Bok
Spr 1942 Feb	10	"	"	Leydenfrost
Sum 1942 May	11	"	"	Saunders
Fal 1942 Aug	12	"	"	Leydenfrost
Win 1942–1943 Nov 1942	2 1	"	"	Anderson
Mar 1943	2	"	"	Rozen
May 1943	3	"	"	" "
Fal 1943	4	"	"	" "
Win 1943	5	"	"	Gross
Spr 1944	6	"	"	Ingels
Sum 1944	2 7	"	"	Gross
Fal 1944	8	"	"	Parkhurst
Win 1944	9	"	"	" "
Spr 1945 Dec-Feb 1944–1945	10	"	"	" "

Date	Number	Page Size	No. of Pages	Cover Artist
Sum 1945 Mar-May	V 2 N11	7x10	128	Parkhurst
Fal 1945 Jun-Aug	12	"	"	" "
Win 1945 Sep-Nov	3 1	"	"	" "
Spr 1946 Mar-May	2	"	"	" "
Sum 1946 Mar-May	3	"	"	Martin
Fal 1946 Jun-Aug	4	"	"	" "
Win 1946 Sep-Nov	5	"	"	" "
Spr 1946–1947 Dec-Feb	6	"	"	Anderson
Sum 1947 Mar-May	7	"	"	?
Fal 1947 Jun-Aug	8	"	"	?
Win 1947 Sep-Nov	9	"	"	Anderson
Spr 1947–1948 Dec-Feb	10	"	"	?
Sum 1948	11	"	"	?
Fal 1948	12	"	"	Anderson
Win 1948	4 1	"	"	" "
Spr 1949	2	"	"	" "
Sum 1949	3	"	"	" "
Fal 1949	4	"	"	Anderson?
Win 1949	5	"	"	Anderson?
Spr 1950	6	"	"	Anderson?
Sum 1950	7	"	"	Anderson?
Fal 1950	8	"	"	Anderson?
Nov 1950	9	"	"	?

SCIENCE FICTION

Date	Number	Page Size	No. of Pages	Cover Artist
Mar 1939	1 1	7x10	132	Frank R. Paul
Jun 1939	2	"	"	" "
Aug 1939	3	"	"	" "
Oct 1939	4	"	"	" "
Dec 1939	5	"	"	" "
Mar 1940	6	"	116	" "
Jun 1940	2 1	"	"	" "
Oct 1940	2	"	"	" "
Jan 1941	3	"	"	" "
Mar 1941	4	"	"	" "
Jun 1941	5	"	"	" "
Sep 1941	6	"	"	" "

Combined with:
FUTURE FICTION

Changed back to:
SCIENCE FICTION STORIES

Date	Number	Page Size	No. of Pages	Cover Artist
Apr 1943	3 4	"	"	Milton Luros
Jul 1943	5	"	"	" "

SCIENCE FICTION QUARTERLY

Date	Number	Page Size	No. of Pages	Cover Artist
Sum 1940	1	6½x9½	148	Jack Binder
Win 1941	2	"	"	Paul
Spr 1941	3	"	"	" "
Sum 1941	4	"	"	" "
Win 1941–1942	5	"	"	?
Spr 1942	6	"	"	Hannes Bok
Sum 1942	7	"	"	John B. Mussachia
Fal 1942	8	"	"	Hannes Bok
Win 1942	9	"	"	Luros
Spr 1943	10	"	"	Milton Luros

SCIENCE WONDER QUARTERLY see WONDER STORIES QUARTERLY

SCIENCE WONDER STORIES see WONDER STORIES

SCIENTIFIC DETECTIVE MONTHLY

Date	Number	Page Size	No. of Pages	Cover Artist
Jan 1930	1 1	9x12	96	Jno. Ruger
Feb 1930	2	"	"	?
Mar 1930	3	"	"	Jno. Ruger
Apr 1930	4	"	"	Paul
May 1930	5	"	"	Jno. Ruger

Change to:
AMAZING DETECTIVE TALES

Date	Number	Page Size	No. of Pages	Cover Artist
Jun 1930	6	"	"	Jno. Ruger
Jul 1930	7	"	"	" "
Aug 1930	8	"	"	?
Sep 1930	9	"	"	Jno. Ruger
Oct 1930	10	"	"	?

STARTLING STORIES

Date	Number	Page Size	No. of Pages	Cover Artist
Jan 1939	1 1	7x10	132	?
Mar 1939	2	"	"	?
May 1939	3	"	"	H. V. Brown
Jul 1939	2 1	"	"	" "
Sep 1939	2	"	"	?
Nov 1939	3	"	"	?
Jan 1940	3 1	"	"	Brown?
Mar 1940	2	"	"	?
May 1940	3	"	"	H. V. Brown
Jul 1940	4 1	"	"	E. K. Bergey

Date	Number	Page Size	No. of Pages	Cover Artist
Sep 1940	V 4 N 2	7x10	132	E. K. Bergey
Nov 1940	3	”	”	” ”
Jan 1941	5 1	”	”	” ”
Mar 1941	2	”	”	” ”
May 1941	3	”	”	Rudolph Belarski
Jul 1941	6 1	”	”	” ”
Sep 1941	2	”	”	” ”
Nov 1941	3	”	”	” ”
Jan 1942	7 1	”	”	” ”
Mar 1942	2	”	”	Earle K. Bergey
May 1942	3	”	”	” ”
Jul 1942	8 1	”	”	” ”
Sep 1942	2	”	”	Rudolph Belarski
Nov 1942	3	”	”	Earle Bergey
Jan 1943	9 1	”	”	Rudolph Belarski
Mar 1943	2	”	”	Earle K. Bergey
Jun 1943	3	”	”	” ”
Fal 1943 Sep	10 1	”	”	” ”
Win 1944 Dec 1943	2	”	”	” ”
Spr 1944 Mar	3	”	”	” ”
Sum 1944 Jun	11 1	”	114	” ”
Fal 1944 Sep	2	”	”	” ”
Win 1945 Dec 1944	3	”	”	” ”
Spr 1945 Mar	12 1	”	”	” ”
Sum 1945 Jun	2	”	100	Earle Bergey
Fal 1945 Sep	3	”	”	” ”
Win 1946 Dec 1945	13 1	”	”	” ”
Mar 1946	2	”	116	” ”
Spr 1946 May 1946	3	”	”	” ”
Sum 1946 Jul	14 1	”	”	” ”
Fal 1946	2	”	”	” ”
Jan 1947	3	”	”	” ”
Mar 1947	15 1	”	”	Rudolph Belarski
May 1947	2	”	”	Earle Bergey
Jul 1947	3	”	”	” ”
Sep 1947	16 1	”	”	” ”
Nov 1947	2	”	”	” ”
Jan 1948	3	”	”	” ”
Mar 1948	17 1	”	148	” ”
May 1948	2	”	”	” ”
Jul 1948	3	”	”	” ”
Sep 1948	18 1	”	”	” ”
Nov 1948	2	”	180	” ”
Jan 1949	3	”	”	” ”

Date	Number	Page Size	No. of Pages	Cover Artist
Mar 1949	V19 N 1	7x10	164	Earle Bergey
May 1949	2	”	”	?
Jul 1949	3	”	”	Earle Bergey
Sep 1949	20 1	”	”	” ”
Nov 1949	2	”	”	? Bergey
Jan 1950	3	”	”	? ”
Mar 1950	21 1	”	”	? ”
May 1950	2	”	”	? ”
Jul 1950	3	”	”	Earle Bergey
Sep 1950	22 1	”	”	” ”
Nov 1950	2	”	”	” ”

STIRRING SCIENCE STORIES

Date	Number	Page Size	No. of Pages	Cover Artist
Feb 1941	1 1	7x10	132	Leo Morey
Apr 1941	2	”	”	Hannes Bok
Jun 1941	3	”	”	” ”
Mar 1942	2 1	8x10½	66	” ”

SUPER SCIENCE STORIES

Date	Number	Page Size	No. of Pages	Cover Artist
Mar 1940	1 1	7x10	128	?
May 1940	2	”	”	Gabriel H. Mayorga
Jul 1940	3	”	”	?
Sep 1940	4	”	”	?
Nov 1940	2 1	”	”	(Leo Morey) ?
Jan 1941	2	”	”	?

Change to:

SUPER SCIENCE NOVELS MAGAZINES

Date	Number	Page Size	No. of Pages	Cover Artist
Mar 1941	3	”	144	?
May 1941	4	”	”	?
Aug 1941	3 1	”	”	? (R. G.)

Change to:

SUPER SCIENCE STORIES

Date	Number	Page Size	No. of Pages	Cover Artist
Nov 1941	2	”	”	?
Feb 1942	3	”	”	?
May 1942	4	”	”	Virgil Finlay
Aug 1942	4 1	”	”	Hubert Rogers
Nov 1942	2	”	”	Stephen Lawrence
Feb 1943	3	”	”	Virgil Finlay
May 1943	4	”	132	” ”
Jan 1949	5 1	”	”	Lawrence
Apr 1949	2	”	”	” ”
Jul 1949	3	”	”	” ”
Sep 1949	4	”	”	” ”
Nov 1949	6 1	”	”	?
Jan 1950	2	”	”	Lawrence
Mar 1950	3	”	”	Saunders
May 1950	4	”	”	Lawrence
Jul 1950	7 1	”	”	” ”
Sep 1950	2	”	”	Van Dongen
Nov 1950	3	”	”	” ”

Date	Number		Page Size	No. of Pages	Cover Artist	

TALES OF WONDER *(British)*

Date	Number		Page Size	No. of Pages	Cover Artist	
n/d	n/#		7x9½	128	*"Nick"*	
n/d	N 2		”	”	”	”
Sum 1938	3		”	”	*W. J. Roberts*	
Aut 1938	4		”	”	”	”
Win 1938	5		”	”	”	”
Spr 1939	6		”	”	”	”
Sum 1939	7		”	”	*"Nick"*	
Aut 1939	8		”	”	”	”
Win 1939	9		”	96	*Caney*	
Spr 1940	10		”	”	*W. J. Roberts*	
Sum 1940	11		”	”	*Turner*	
Aut 1940	12		”	80	*W. J. Roberts*	
Win 1941	13		”	”	*J. Nicolson*	
Spr 1941	14		”	72	”	”
Aut 1941	15		”	”	”	”
Spr 1942	16		”	”	”	”

THRILLING WONDER STORIES *see WONDER STORIES*

TWO COMPLETE SCIENCE ADVENTURE NOVELS

Date	Number		Page Size	No. of Pages	Cover Artist
Win 1950	1	1	7x10	144	*Anderson*

UNCANNY STORIES

Date	Number		Page Size	No. of Pages	Cover Artist
Apr 1941	1	1	7x10	116	*?*

UNKNOWN

Date	Number		Page Size	No. of Pages	Cover Artist	
Mar 1939	1	1	7x9	164	*H. W. Scott*	
Apr 1939		2	”	”	*Graves Gladney*	
May 1939		3	”	”	*H. W. Scott*	
Jun 1939		4	”	”	”	”
Jul 1939		5	”	”	”	”
Aug 1939		6	”	”	*Graves Gladney*	
Sep 1939	2	1	”	”	*H. W. Scott*	
Oct 1939		2	”	”	*Modest Stein*	
Nov 1939		3	”	”	*Graves Gladney*	
Dec 1939		4	”	”	*Cartier*	
Jan 1940		5	”	”	*H. W. Scott*	
Feb 1940		6	”	”	*Ed. Cartier*	
Mar 1940	3	1	”	”	”	”
Apr 1940		2	”	”	”	”
May 1940		3	”	”	*M. Isip*	
Jun 1940		4	”	”	*Cartier*	
Jul 1940		5	”	”	*(cover pic discont)*	
Aug 1940		6	”	”		
Sep 1940	4	1	”	”		
Oct 1940		2	”	”		
Nov 1940		3	”	”		

Date	Number		Page Size	No. of Pages	Cover Artist	
Dec 1940	V 4 N 4		7x9	164	*(cover pic discont)*	
Feb 1941		5	”	”		
Apr 1941		6	”	”		
Jun 1941	5	1	”	”		
Aug 1941		2	”	”		

Change to:

UNKNOWN WORLDS

Date	Number		Page Size	No. of Pages	Cover Artist
Oct 1941		3	8½x11½	130	
Dec 1941		4	”	”	
Feb 1942		5	”	”	
Apr 1942		6	”	”	
Jun 1942	6	1	”	”	
Aug 1942		2	”	”	
Oct 1942		3	”	”	
Dec 1942		4	”	”	
Feb 1943		5	”	”	
Apr 1943		6	”	”	
Jun 1943	7	1	9½x7	164	
Aug 1943		2	”	”	
Oct 1943		3	”	”	

FROM UNKNOWN WORLDS

Date	Number	Page Size	No. of Pages	Cover Artist
1948	n/#	8½x11	130	*Ed. Cartier*

WONDER STORIES *(AIR WONDER, SCIENCE WONDER & THRILLING WONDER)*

SCIENCE WONDER STORIES

Date	Number		Page Size	No. of Pages	Cover Artist	
Jun 1929		1	8½x11½	96	*Paul*	
Jul 1929		2	”	”	”	”
Aug 1929		2	”	”	”	”
Sep 1929		4	”	”	”	”
Oct 192		5	”	”	”	”
Nov 1929		6	”	”	”	”
Dec 1929		7	”	”	”	”
Jan 1930		8	”	”	”	”
Feb 1930		9	”	”	”	”
Mar 1930		10	”	”	”	”
Apr 1930		11	”	”	”	”
May 1930		12	”	”	”	”

Combined with AIR WONDER TO MAKE
WONDER STORIES

AIR WONDER STORIES

Date	Number		Page Size	No. of Pages	Cover Artist	
Jul 1929	V 1 N 1		8½x11½	96	*Frank R. Paul*	
Aug 1929		2	”	”	”	”
Sep 1929		3	”	”	”	”
Oct 1929		4	”	”	”	”
Nov 1929		5	”	”	”	”
Dec 1929		6	”	”	”	”
Jan 1930		7	”	”	”	”
Feb 1930		8	”	”	”	”
Mar 1930		9	”	”	”	”
Apr 1930		10	”	”	”	”
May 1930		11	”	”	”	”

Combined with SCIENCE WONDER TO MAKE
WONDER STORIES

Date	Number	Page Size	No. of Pages	Cover Artist
Jun 1930	2 1	8½x11½	96	Paul
Jul 1930	2	"	"	" "
Aug 1930	3	"	"	" "
Sep 1930	4	"	"	" "
Oct 1930	5	"	"	" "
Nov 1930	6	7x10	144	" "
Dec 1930	7	"	"	" "
Jan 1931	8	"	"	" "
Feb 1931	9	"	"	" "
Mar 1931	10	"	"	" "
Apr 1931	11	"	"	" "
May 1931	12	"	"	" "
Jun 1931	3 1	"	"	" "
Jul 1931	2	"	"	" "
Aug 1931	3	"	"	" "
Sep 1931	4	"	"	" "
Oct 1931	5	"	"	" "
Nov 1931	6	8½x11½	96	" "
Dec 1931	7	"	"	" "
Jan 1932	8	"	"	" "
Feb 1932	9	"	"	" "
Mar 1932	10	"	"	" "
Apr 1932	11	"	"	" "
May 1932	12	"	"	" "
Jun 1932	4 1	"	"	" "
Jul 1932	2	"	"	" "
Aug 1932	3	"	"	" "
Sep 1932	4	"	"	" "
Oct 1932	5	"	"	" "
Nov 1932	6	"	"	(process)
Dec 1932	7	"	64	Paul
Jan 1933	8	"	"	" "
Feb 1933	9	"	"	" "
Mar 1933	10	"	"	" "
Apr 1933	11	"	96	" "
May 1933	12	"	"	" "
Jun 1933	5 1	"	"	" "
Aug 1933	2	"	"	" "
Oct 1933	3	"	"	" "
Nov 1933	4	7x10	128	" "
Dec 1933	5	"	"	" "
Jan 1934	6	"	"	" "
Feb 1934	7	"	"	" "
Mar 1934	8	"	"	" "
Apr 1934	9	"	"	" "
May 1934	10	"	"	" "
Jun 1934	6 1	"	"	" "
Jul 1934	2	"	"	" "
Aug 1934	3	"	"	" "
Sep 1934	4	"	"	" "
Oct 1934	5	"	"	" "
Nov 1934	6	"	"	" "
Dec 1934	7	"	"	" "
Jan 1935	8	"	"	" "

Date	Number	Page Size	No. of Pages	Cover Artist
Feb 1935	V 6 N 9	7x10	128	Paul
Mar 1935	10	"	"	" "
Apr 1935	11	"	"	" "
May 1935	12	"	"	" "
Jun 1935	7 1	"	"	" "
Jul 1935	2	"	"	" "
Aug 1935	3	"	"	" "
Sep 1935	4	"	"	" "
Oct 1935	5	"	"	" "
Nov-Dec 1935	6	"	"	" "
Jan-Feb 1936	7	"	"	" "
Mar-Apr 1936	8	"	"	" "

Change to:
THRILLING WONDER STORIES

Date	Number	Page Size	No. of Pages	Cover Artist
Aug 1936	8 1	7x10	128	Brown ?
Oct 1936	2	"	"	" "
Dec 1936	3	"	"	" "
Feb 1937	9 1	"	"	" "
Apr 1937	2	"	"	" "
Jun 1937	3	"	"	" "
Aug 1937	10 1	"	"	Wesso
Oct 1937	2	"	"	Brown ?
Dec 1937	3	"	"	" "
Feb 1938	11 1	"	"	?
Apr 1938	2	"	"	" "
Jun 1938	3	"	"	" "
Aug 1938	12 1	"	"	" "
Oct 1938	2	"	"	" "
Dec 1938	3	"	"	" "
Feb 1939	13 1	"	"	" "
Apr 1939	2	"	"	Brown
Jun 1939	3	"	"	Brown ?
Aug 1939	14 1	"	"	Brown
Oct 1939	2	"	132	Howard V. Brown
Dec 1939	3	"	"	" "
Jan 1940	15 1	"	"	" "
Feb 1940	2	"	"	" "
Mar 1940	3	"	"	" "
Apr 1940	16 1	"	"	" "
May 1940	2	"	"	" "
Jun 1940	3	"	"	" "
Jul 1940	17 1	"	"	" "
Aug 1940	2	"	"	" "
Sep 1940	3	"	"	E. K. Bergey
Oct 1940	18 1	"	"	" "
Nov 1940	2	"	"	" "
Dec 1940	3	"	"	" "
Jan 1941	19 1	"	"	Gabriel Mayorga
Feb 1941	2	"	"	Earl K. Bergey
Mar 1941	3	"	"	E. K. Bergey
Apr 1941	20 1	"	"	" "
Jun 1941	2	"	"	H. W. Wesso
Aug 1941	3	"	"	Rudolph Belarski

Date	Number	Page Size	No. of Pages	Cover Artist
Oct 1941	V21 N 1	7x10	132	Rudolph Belarski
Dec 1941	2	"	"	Earle K. Bergey
Feb 1942	3	"	"	Rudolph Belarski
Apr 1942	22 1	"	"	Earle K. Bergey
Jun 1942	2	"	"	" "
Aug 1942	3	"	"	Rudolph Belarski
Oct 1942	23 1	"	"	Earle Bergey
Dec 1942	2	"	"	Rudoph Belarski
Feb 1943	3	"	"	Earl Bergey
Apr 1943	24 1	"	"	Earle Bergey
Jun 1943	2	"	"	" "
Aug 1943	3	"	"	" "
Fal 1943 Nov	25 1	"	"	" "
Win 1944 Feb	2	"	"	Rudolph Belarski
Spr 1944 May	3	"	116	Earle K. Bergey
Sum 1944 Aug	26 1	"	"	Earl Bergey
Fal 1944 Nov	2	"	"	Rudolph Belarski
Win 1945 Feb	3	"	"	Earle Bergey
Spr 1945 May	27 1	"	"	" "
Sum 1945 Aug	2	"	98	" "
Fal 1945 Nov	3	"	"	" "
Win 1946 Feb	28 1	"	116	" "
Spr 1946 Apr	2	"	"	" "
Sum 1946 Jun	3	"	"	" "
Fal 1946 Oct	29 1	"	"	" "
Dec 1946	2	"	"	" "
Feb 1947	3	"	"	" "
Apr 1947	30 1	"	"	" "
Jun 1947	2	"	"	" "
Aug 1947	3	"	"	" "
Oct 1947	31 1	"	"	" "
Dec 1947	2	"	"	" "
Feb 1948	3	"	"	" "
Apr 1948	32 1	"	148	" "
Jun 1948	2	"	"	" "
Aug 1948	3	"	"	" "

Date	Number	Page Size	No. of Pages	Cover Artist
Oct 1948	V33 N 1	7x10	180	Earle Bergey
Dec 1948	2	"	"	" " "
Feb 1949	3	"	164	Earle Bergey
Apr 1949	34 1	"	"	" " "
Jun 1949	2	"	"	?
Aug 1949	3	"	"	?
Oct 1949	35 1	"	"	Earle Bergey
Dec 1949	2	"	"	?
Feb 1950	3	"	"	?
Apr 1950	36 1	"	"	?
Jun 1950	2	"	"	Earle Bergey
Aug 1950	3	"	"	" " "
Oct 1950	37 1	"	"	" " "
Dec 1950	2	"	"	" " "

WORLDS BEYOND

Date	Number	Page Size	No. of Pages	Cover Artist
Dec 1950	1 1	7½x5½	128	Paul Calle

WONDER STORIES QUARTERLY
(including Science Wonder Quarterly)

SCIENCE WONDER QUARTERLY

Date	Number	Page Size	No. of Pages	Cover Artist
Fal 1929	1 1	9x12	144	Paul
Win 1930	2	"	"	" "
Spr 1930	3	"	"	" "

Change to:
WONDER STORIES QUARTERLY

Date	Number	Page Size	No. of Pages	Cover Artist
Sum 190	4	"	"	" "
Fal 1930	2 1	"	"	" "
Win 1931	2	"	"	" "
Spr 1931	3	"	"	" "
Sum 1931	4	"	"	" "
Fal 1931	3 1	"	"	" "
Win 1932	2	"	"	" "
Spr 1932	3	"	"	" "
Sum 1932	4	"	"	" "
Fal 1932	4 1	"	"	" "
Win 1933	2	"	"	" "

WONDER STORY ANNUAL

Date	Number	Page Size	No. of Pages	Cover Artist
1950	1 1	7x10	196	?

Back Cover Pictures

AMAZING STORIES Back Covers

THIS AMAZING UNIVERSE by H. W. McCauley . . Jun 38
THE LIFE LINE. . . . . .Aug 38
FACES THROUGH THE AGES. . . . . Oct 38
STRATOSPHERE AIRLINER OF 1988 by Julian S.
    Krupa. . . . . .Nov 38
SPACESHIP OF 2038 by Julian S. Krupa. . . . . . .Dec 38
FUTURE ROCKET TRAIN by H. W. McCauley . . . Jan 39
FUTURE OCEAN LINER by Julian S. Krupa. . . . . Feb 39
UNDERSEA SALVAGER by H. W. McCauley . . . . Mar 39
FUTURE SKY FIGHTER by H. W. McCauley . . . . Apr 39
THE END OF THE WORLD by William Juhre . . . .May 39
FUTURE SPACE SUIT by Frank R. Paul. . . . . . . Jun 39
SPACE DEVASTATOR by Julian S. Krupa . . . . . . Jul 39
CITIES OF TOMORROW by Julian S. Krupa . . . . .Aug 39
ARCTIC RADIO FARMS by Julian S. Krupa . . . . Sep 39
ATOMIC POWER PLANT by Howard M. Duffin. . . Oct 39
INTERPLANETARY COMMUNICATION by Howard
    M. Duffin. . . . . .Nov 39
FUTURE WAR TANK by Stanley Ryter . . . . Dec 39
SUSPENDED ANIMATION by Paul Maxwell . . . . Jan 40
EVOLUTION GONE MAD by Howard M. Duffin . . . . .
    . . . . .Feb 40
THE EARTH'S CORE by H. R. Hammond. . . . . . Mar 40
COLONIZING THE OCEAN BOTTOM by Julian
    S. Krupa . . . . .Apr 40
12,000 YEARS AGO by H. R. Hammond . . . . . .May 40
WHEN METEORITES CRASH by Julian S. Krupa. . . .
    . . . . Jun 40
AS MARS SEES US by Frank R. Paul . . . . Jul 40
LIFE ON CALLISTO by Frank R. Paul . . . . .Aug 40
LIFE ON EUROPA by Frank R. Paul . . . . Sep 40
LIFE ON GANYMEDE by Frank R. Paul. . . . . . . Oct 40
LIFE ON TITAN by Frank R. Paul. . . . . .Nov 40
A CITY ON MARS by Frank R. Paul . . . . Dec 40
A CITY ON VENUS by Frank R. Paul. . . . . Jan 41
A CITY ON JUPITER by Frank R. Paul . . . . . . .Feb 41
A CITY ON NEPTUNE by Frank R. Paul. . . . . . .Mar 41
A CITY ON URANUS by Frank R. Paul . . . . . . .Apr 41
MARTIAN SPACESHIPS INVADE NEW YORK by
    Frank R. Paul. . . . . .May 41
A CITY ON PLUTO by Frank R. Paul. . . . . Jun 41
CRYSTALLIS, GLASS CITY OF IO by Frank R.
    Paul . . . . Jul 41
CRATER CITY ON SATURN by Frank R. Paul . . . . . .
    . . . . .Aug 41
QUARTZ CITY ON MERCURY by Frank R. Paul. . . . .
    . . . . Sep 41
CITY INSIDE THE MOON by Frank R. Paul . . . . Oct 41

FANTASTIC ADVENTURES Back Covers

THE MAN FROM MARS by Frank R. Paul . . . . .May 39

THE MAN FROM VENUS by Frank R. Paul . . . . . Jul 39

LIFE ON MERCURY by Frank R. Paul. . . . . Sep 39

LIFE ON SATURN by Frank R. Paul . . . . .Nov 39

LIFE ON JUPITER by Frank R. Paul . . . . Jan 40

LIFE ON PLUTO by Frank R. Paul . . . . .Feb 40
LIFE ON NEPTUNE by Frank R. Paul . . . . Mar 40

LIFE ON URANUS by Frank R. Paul . . . . .Apr 40
LIFE ON IO, MOON OF JUPITER by Frank R. Paul. . .
    . . . . .May 40

AMAZING STORIES Back Cover Pictures *(Continued)*

GOLDEN CITY ON TITAN by Frank R. Paul. . . . .Nov 41
SERENIS, WATER CITY OF CALLISTO by Frank R.
    Paul . . . . .Dec 41
GLASS CITY OF EUROPA by Frank R. Paul. . . . Jan 42
MAGNETIC CITY ON GANYMEDE by Frank R.
    Paul . . . . .Feb 42
AS MARS SEES US by Frank R. Paul. . . . . .Mar 42
CITY OF THE FUTURE by Frank R. Paul. . . . . . .Apr 42
AIRSHIP OF VENUS by James B. Settles . . . . . .May 42
ATOMIC AIRSHIP OF MARS by James B. Settles. . . . .
    . . . . .Jun 42
RADIUM AIRSHIP OF SATURN by James B.
    Settles. . . . . Jul 42
AIRCRAFT OF URANUS by James B. Settles . . . .Aug 42
PLASTIC AIRSHIP OF EUROPA by James B.
    Settles. . . . . Sep 42
FLYING WING OF PLUTO by James B. Settles . . . . . .
    . . . . .Oct 42
AIRSHIP OF IO by James B. Settles. . . . . .Nov 42
GLIDER OF GANYMEDE by James B. Settles. . . .Dec 42
SAILING SHIP OF VENUS by James B. Settles . . . . . .
    . . . . .Jan 43
STORIES OF THE STARS: CANUS MAJOR by
    Frank R. Paul. . . . . .Feb 43
SUBMARINE OF NEPTUNE by James B. Settles . . . . .
    . . . . .Mar 43
STORIES OF THE STARS: LYRA by Frank R. Paul. . .
    . . . . .Apr 43
STORIES OF THE STARS: PROCYON by Frank R.
    Paul . . . . .May 43
STORIES OF THE STARS: THE GREAT NEBULA IN
    ORION by Frank R. Paul . . . . Jun 43
WARSHIP OF MARS by James B. Settles . . . .
    . . . . Jul 43
STORIES OF THE STARS: RIGEL by Frank R.
    Paul . . . . .Aug 43
SHIP OF JUPITER by James B. Settles . . . . Sep 43
ETHER-POWER SHIP OF EUROPA by James B.
    Settles. . . . . .Nov 43
STORIES OF THE STARS: DEATH OF THE
    MOON by Robert Fuqua . . . . Jan 44
SHIP OF CALLISTO by James B. Settles. . . . . . . Mar 44
ROCKET WARSHIP by James B. Settles . . . .
    . . . . .May 44
STORIES OF THE STARS: BETELGEUSE IN ORION
    by Frank Paul. . . . . Sep 44
SUPER TRAIN OF TOMORROW by James B.
    Settles. . . . . .Dec 44
STORIES OF THE STARS: SPICA by Frank R.
    Paul . . . . .Mar 45
MICA SAILBOAT OF MERCURY by James R.
    Settles. . . . . .Jun 45
CABLE TRAIN OF TOMORROW by James B.
    Settles. . . . . .Sep 45

FANTASTIC ADVENTURES Back Cover Pictures
    (Continued)

ZEUS, THE THUNDER GOD by Frank R. Paul . . . Jul 42
VULCAN, GOD OF HEAVY INDUSTRY by Frank R.
    Paul . . . . .Aug 42
ATLAS, THE GOD OF STRENGTH by Frank R.
    Paul . . . . .Sep 42
PERSEUS, SLAYER OF THE MEDUSA by Frank R.
    Paul . . . . .Oct 42
PROMETHEUS by Frank R. Paul. . . . . .Nov 42
APOLLO by Frank R. Paul . . . . .Dec 42
MERCURY, GOD OF THE WINGED SANDALS by
    Frank R. Paul. . . . . Jan 43
ICARUS AND DAEDALUS, FIRST AVIATORS by
    Frank R. Paul. . . . . .Feb 43
PHAETON, SON OF APOLLO by Frank R. Paul. . . . . .
    . . . . .Mar 43
HERCULES, THE GOD OF STRENGTH by Frank R.
    Paul . . . . .Apr 43
THE CENTAUR, STEED OF THE GODS by J. Allen
    St. John. . . . . May 43
WARRIORS OF OTHER WORLDS: URANUS by Malcolm
    Smith . . . . Jun 43
WARRIORS OF OTHER WORLDS: VENUS by Malcolm
    Smith . . . . Jul 43
WARRIORS OF OTHER WORLDS: CALLISTO by
    Malcolm Smith . . . . .Aug 43
THE SPHINX by Frank R. Paul . . . . Oct 43
WARRIORS OF OTHER WORLDS: MERCURY by
    Malcolm Smith . . . . .Dec 43
APPOINTMENT WITH THE PAST by James B.
    Settles. . . . . .Feb 44
JASON by Frank R. Paul . . . . .Apr 44
BELLEROPHON AND THE CHIMERA by Frank R.
    Paul . . . . .Jun 44
WARRIORS OF OTHER WORLDS: SATURN by
    Malcolm Smith . . . . .Oct 44
KITE SHIP OF THE MOON by James B. Settles . . . . . .
    . . . . .Jan 45
JET-BOAT OF TOMORROW by James B. Settles . . . . .
    . . . . .Apr 45
STORIES OF THE STARS: GEMINI by Frank R.
    Paul . . . . Jul 45
STORIES OF THE STARS: ANDROMEDA by
    Frank R. Paul. . . . . .Oct 45

AMAZING STORIES Back Cover Pictures *(Continued)*

JET PROPELLED MONO TRAIN by James B.
Settles. . . . . .Dec 45
TRADE YOUR TROUBLES FOR A BUBBLE by
James B. Settles . . . . .Feb 46
SATELLITE SPACE SHIP STATION by James B.
Settles. . . . . .May 46
WONDERS OF THE ANCIENT WORLD: BUILDING
THE GREAT PYRAMID by James B. Settles . . . . . .
. . . . Jun 46
WONDERS OF THE ANCIENT WORLD: THE
COLOSSUS OF RHODES by James B. Settles . . . . .
. . . . Jul 46
STORIES OF THE STARS: ALTAIR by Frank R.
Paul . . . . .Aug 46
IMPOSSIBLE BUT TRUE: THE MYSTERY OF THE
BALL OF FIRE by James B. Settles . . . . .Nov 47
IMPOSSIBLE BUT TRUE: THE RAIN OF FISH. . . . . .
. . . . .Dec 47
SPACESHIP SEEN OVER IDAHO by James B.
Settles. . . . . Jan 48
SPACE SHIPS IN ANTARCTICA by James B.
Settles. . . . . .Feb 48
SPACE SHIPS AT ANGKOR WAT by James B.
Settles. . . . . .Apr 48
SPACESHIPS IN ANCIENT EGYPT by James B.
Settles. . . . . .May 48
SPACE SHIP IN THE JUNGLE by James B. Settles . . . .
. . . . Jul 48

FANTASTIC ADVENTURES Back Cover Pictures
(Continued)

STORIES OF THE STARS: ALDEBARAN by
Frank R. Paul. . . . . .Dec 45
STORIES OF THE STARS: ALPHECCA by Frank
R. Paul . . . . .Feb 46
STORIES OF THE STARS: MIZAR by Frank R.
Paul . . . . .May 46

STORIES OF THE STARS: ANTARES by Frank R.
Paul . . . . Jul 46

SON OF THE SUN . . . . .Nov 47
THE ARCHERS OF MONS by James B. Settles . . . . . .
. . . . .Dec 47
IMPOSSIBLE BUT TRUE: THE THING ON THE MOON
by Malcolm Smith. Jan 48
IMPOSSIBLE BUT TRUE: ALASKAN MIRAGE by
James B. Settles . . . . .Feb 48
IMPOSSIBLE BUT TRUE: THE BOMB OUT OF SPACE
by James B. Settles . . . . .Apr 48
IMPOSSIBLE BUT TRUE: THE INCREDIBLE WHEELS
by James B. Settles . . . . .May 48